# The Right of Access to Public Information

Hermann-Josef Blanke • Ricardo Perlingeiro
Editors

# The Right of Access to Public Information

## An International Comparative Legal Survey

Springer

*Editors*
Hermann-Josef Blanke
Faculty for Economics, Law
and Social Science
University of Erfurt
Erfurt, Germany

Ricardo Perlingeiro
School of Law
Fluminense Federal University
Niterói, Brazil

ISBN 978-3-662-55552-1 ISBN 978-3-662-55554-5 (eBook)
DOI 10.1007/978-3-662-55554-5

Library of Congress Control Number: 2017960414



Printed on acid-free paper

This Springer imprint is published by the registered company Springer-Verlag GmbH, DE part of Springer Nature.
The registered company address is: Heidelberger Platz 3, 14197 Berlin, Germany

*In memoriam*
Illaria Bachilo *(1926-2017)*
*Former Head of the Information Law*
*Department of the Institute of State and Law*
*of the Russian Academy of Sciences*

A popular Government, without popular information, or the means of acquiring it, is but a Prologue to a Farce or a Tragedy; or, perhaps both.
Knowledge will forever govern ignorance:
And a people who mean to be their own Governors
must arm themselves with the power which knowledge gives.

J. Madison to W.T. Barry *(1822), Writings 9:103-109*

"Publicity is justly commended as a remedy for social and industrial diseases.
Sunlight is said to be the best of disinfectants.. ."

L. D. Brandeis,
in: *Harper's Weekly (1913),*
"What Publicity Can Do"

Sunlight may well be a great disinfectant.
But as anyone who has ever waded through a swamp knows,
it has other effects as well.

L. Lessig
in: *New Republic (2009)*
"Against Transparency"

# Foreword

The editors of this book, with work contributed by authors from widely diverse countries in Latin America, the United States of America, Europe and Asia, have done a very praiseworthy job. That the subject matter—the right of access to public information—should also be so relevant and important for the operation of the democratic system shows the concern of the editors and authors of the book for an issue so critical to the proper operation of the political system and the revitalised development of democracy.

Why has there been so much continuing interest both within the political system and within what we might call the world of ordinary citizens in the right of access to information for so many decades now? There are various reasons, but the basic one is the crisis of the political system, closely linked to the existence of a deficit of democracy. Representative democracy and the traditional model of legitimacy are exhausted. So where does the origin of this crisis lie? The reasons are complex, but it is decisively influenced by the relationship between representatives and those who are represented, as well as the classic definition of representation, which means making present what in fact is absent. This requires representatives not to become completely divorced from public affairs or from the contents of the world of the lives of ordinary citizens. If they do, representation will lose its conceptual essence. Because of this, those represented must remain actively present in the course of the representation process. This concept of representation is a long way from that put forward by Sieyès in 1789, according to which once the representatives are chosen they act with complete freedom and are not linked to those they represent (representative mandate). However, in everyday life, they are imperatively linked (binding mandate) to the political party in whose lists they are elected.

Nowadays, citizens seek the capability of influencing representatives by various means (social forums, citizens' committees, demonstrations, etc.), which implies the need for civil society to be strengthened so it can control them. The other means of public participation is through direct democracy (participatory democracy, referendums, etc.) which, for example, is included in Article 23 of the Spanish

Constitution and in Article 11 of the European Union Treaty. This means the appearance of a second legislator which, in a legitimate way, relativises Parliament's monopoly. It does not mean replacing it, but rather complementing it in certain situations.

This way of making the political system work strengthens its democratic legitimacy but it also requires well-informed citizens with ways of participating actively in public life to act effectively. To achieve this, political publicity plays a fundamental role. This is understood as the establishment of conditions for communication between the State and citizens through which they can participate in State decision making via active public opinion. Spaces for public opinion are formed through citizens taking positions in the various forums, circles, associations, and so on, where they go with the problems they come across in private life in civil society. In this space they will seek to discuss them and deal with them to exercise an influence on political power. This space is that of civil society, consisting of a network of non-State and non-economic voluntary-based associations, which, although they are private, act in a public context. Opinion-forming associations are necessary for the existence and development of political publicity. Their antagonist is the apparatus of the secret services that have controlled and continue to control the communication practice of citizens in dictatorial and totalitarian countries.

This civil society needs to articulate its relations with the State, and fundamental rights play a vital role in this articulation. Rights such as association, freedom of expression, the freedom of the media and the right of access to public information are essential for the development of public communication. In this context, the political system can only remain sensitive to public influences and be linked, through the political parties and participatory democratic systems, with the sphere of public opinion and civil society.

The fact that the right of access to public information should be recognised as a fundamental right in the Constitutions of States and should also be taken up by international organisations will give greater legitimacy to the political authorities at a time like the present when they have lost a considerable part of their legitimacy. In addition, recognition of this right will allow citizens to take part in public affairs. In fact, the right facilitates access to the information the public authorities have; information which has connotations of general interest and it is not in the private and secret sphere. Recognition of the right of access to information on one hand facilitates access to the documents in the hands of the public authorities and, on the other, encourages active publicity. In other words, the same political authorities, and particularly the Government, pass on information without citizens having to ask for it.

As the principles of both publicity and secrecy play a role in the public sphere, the dichotomy between them must be resolved with the recognition of the rights of access to information and the protection of personal privacy as fundamental rights. However, in constitutional practice this does not happen, as States' Constitutions often place greater importance on the right to privacy and data protection than on the right of access to information, rather than weighing up the two and recognising them as having the same constitutional value; in other words as fundamental rights. This places the right of access to public information in a position of inferiority, halting both the development of a consolidated civil society standing firm against political power and effective citizen participation in public affairs.

The constitutional recognition of the right of access to public information is linked to what has been called in German public law the Administrative Right of Information. This is an administrative right conditioned and developed on the base of the information and knowledge society. This information and knowledge society has engendered a communication revolution that has required a new administrative model for communication. This is modernising the public authorities and has required a dogmatic review of administrative law. The new revolution, as important as the industrial revolution was in its time, has coincided with a far-reaching social and democratic crisis of the State and a loss of legitimacy for the public authorities. The Administrative Right of Information that establishes a new form of communication between citizens and the authorities is helping to achieve the implementation of greater transparency in these relationships and, to an extent, wiping out the democratic deficit through certain forms of participatory democracy (for example, in the spheres of environmental or town planning law).

It must be hoped that this book helps to achieve some reflection on the right of access to public information at global level because the fact that authors from several continents are taking part is likely to facilitate its dissemination. This could help to some extent in the debate on the inclusion of new routes for participation in the democratic system which so badly needs a boost in the current difficult times when it is not publicity that is winning the battle with secrecy but rather the manipulation of information.

University Jaume I
Castellón de la Plana, Spain

Council for Transparency, Access to
Public Information and Good
Government of the Valencian Region
Valencia, Spain

Ricardo Garcia Macho

March 2018

# Preface

This book is one outcome of the project "Estado de Derecho: Derecho Administrativo y Justicia Administrativa en América Latina", which was carried out at various universities throughout Germany and Latin America with sponsorship from and under the auspices of the German Academic Exchange Service (DAAD). Under the academic supervision of Professor Hermann-Josef Blanke, University of Erfurt (Germany), four Latin American universities have been cooperating in this project on "Rule of Law in Latin America": Andrés Bello Catholic University (Venezuela), Fluminense Federal University (Brazil), National Autonomous University of Mexico and the University of Buenos Aires (Argentina). For the purpose of the publication of the results of one of the subjects treated, i.e., the freedom of information legislation, the editors were able to recruit authors from all over the world. In November 2011, the Brazilian Law N° 12.527 on the Right of Access to Information had come into force. It has become a point of reference for nearly all contributions of this volume. The right of access to public information has become one of the big issues in constitutional and adminstrative law in many countries.

The editors present this volume in the run-up to the entry into force of the Council of Europe Convention on Access to Official Documents. This Convention will be the first binding international legal instrument on the regional level to recognise a general right of access to official documents held by public authorities.

The "Introduction", written by the editors, shall make it easier to understand the core elements of the right of access to public information by analysing certain aspects of transparency dealt with in the national reports. This piece shows that, in spite of all differences between the legal systems, transparency legislation has many patterns in common. While a comparative perspective will be taken, it is admittedly influenced by a German legal view.

The editors want to thank the assistants at the Chair for Public Law and Public International Law of the University of Erfurt, especially Sebastian Bunse, Franz Stockmann and Kristoffer Burck, for their efforts when controlling the formal standards of the manuscripts and preparing the Index of this book. The editors are grateful for all the advice and support which Prof. Keith Hendersen (American University College of Law) has engaged in Chap. 4. After years of efforts the authors can present this publication thanks to a close cooperation with the publisher Springer, especially with the Executive Editor Law, Dr. Brigitte Reschke.

Erfurt, Germany<br>Rio de Janeiro, Brazil<br>March 2018

Hermann-Josef Blanke<br>Ricardo Perlingeiro

# Contents

# List of Authors

- Dr. iur. *Pedro Aberastury*, Associate Professor of Administrative Law, Faculty of Law and Social Sciences, University of Buenos Aires, Argentina.
- *Alexandre Arruda*, Federal Judge of the Federal Regional Court of Rio de Janeiro of the 2nd Region (Rio de Janeiro), doctoral student at the Fluminense Federal University (Niterói, Rio de Janeiro) in the area of administrative justice, Brazil.
- Dr. iur *Illaria Bachilo* †, Professor of Administrative Law, Head of the Department of Information Law, Institute of State and Law of the Russian Academy of Science, Russia.
- Dr. iur. *Ana Paula de Barcellos*, postdoctorate of the University of Harvard, Professor of Constitutional Law, Faculty of Law, University of the State of Rio de Janeiro, Brazil.
- Dr. iur. *Hermann-Josef Blanke*, Professor of Public Law and International Public Law, University of Erfurt (Germany). His research areas are constitutional law, administrative law, administrative procedural law, law of the European Union and international public law. From 2009 to 2012 he was coordinator of the DAAD Project "Rule of Law: Administrative Law and Administrative Jurisdiction in Latin America". In 2017 he was accepted into the Order of *San Raimundo de Peñafort* ("Cruz de Honor") by the Kingdom of Spain.
- *Rosnell V. Carrasco Baptista*, Lawyer, Lecturer at the Catholic University Andrés Bello (UCAB), Caracas, Venezuela.
- Dr. iur. *Constance Chevallier-Govers*, Associate Professor of Law, CESICE – University of Grenoble, France.
- Dr. iur. *Ravindra Chingale* is practicing advocate at the Supreme Court of India. He is engineer turned lawyer and did his research in law and technology. He was consultant to the Department of Justice of the Ministry of Law and Justice on the National Mission for Justice Delivery and Legal Reforms. He was also a member of the subcommittee on Bilateral Investment Treaties of the Law Commission of India.
- *Ivonne Díaz*, Master of Law from the Autonomous National University of Mexico, Parliamentary Advisor at the Mexican Senate, participant in the DAAD Project "Rule of Law: Administrative Law and Administrative Jurisdiction in Latin America" (2009–2012).

- Dr. iur. *Diana-Urania Galetta*, Professor of Administrative Law, University of Milan, Italy.
- Dr. iur. *Ricardo García Macho*, Emeritus Professor of Public Law, University Jaume I, Castellón de la Plana, Spain, Chairman of the Council for Transparency, Access to Public Information and Good Government of the Valencian Region, Spain.
- Dr. iur. *Carla Huerta Ochoa*, Professor of Logic of Science, Normative Analysis, and Theory of Law, Institute of Legal Research, National Autonomous University of Mexico.
- *Jiang Ming'an*, Professor of Administrative Law, Law School of Peking, University of China, and director of the Center for Studies of Constitutional and Administrative Law of PKU. His research fields concern on administrative law and administrative litigation law of China.
- *Patricia Jonason*, LLD, Senior Lecturer, School of Social Sciences, Centre for Baltic and East European Studies, Södertörn University, Sweden.
- *Narufumi Kadomatsu*, LL.M., Professor of Administrative Law, Faculty of Law, Kobe University, Japan.
- *Milena Liani*, Lecturer in General Legal Theory, Writing of Legal Texts and Legal Research Methodology of the Catholic University Andrés Bello, Caracas, Venezuela.
- *Mariana Magalhães Avelar*, Bachelor of Law at Minas Gerais Federal University (UFMG), Master Student at Minas Gerais Federal University (UFMG), Finance Specialist at Fundação Dom Cabral (FDC) and Lawyer at Manesco, Ramires, Azevedo Marques Law Office, Brazil.
- *Álisson José Maia Melo*, LL.B., Federal University of Ceará (Brazil), LL.M.-Student, Regulation Analyst at the Regulatory Agency of Delegated Public Services of the State of Ceará (Arce).
- *Peter J. Messitte*, Senior United States District Judge of the District of Maryland and an Adjunct Professor of Comparative Law and Director of the Brazil-U.S. Legal and Judicial Studies Programme at American University Washington College of Law. For over 30 years he has been involved in Judicial Reform around the world—principally in Latin America and Brazil but as well in Turkey, Thailand and Yemen. He served formerly as a Member and currently serves as a Special Advisor to the International Judicial Relations Committee of the U.S. Judicial Conference. As a Member of the Council he chaired the Latin American and Caribbean Working Group. He also now serves as a Council Member of the American Bar Association's Rule of Law Initiative for Latin America. In 2008, in recognition of his work on judicial reform with the Brazilian Judiciary, he was made an Honorary Citizen of the City of San Paulo.
- Dr. *Luísa Neto*, Associated Professor, Faculty of Law, University of Porto, Portugal.
- Dr. iur. *Germana de Oliveira Moraes*, LL.M., Associate Professor, Federal University of Ceará, Federal Judge of the 5$^{th}$ Region in Ceará, Brazil, member of the National School of Training and Improvement of Magistrates Council (Enfam) and Director of Ceará's sectional core of the School of Federal Magistracy of the 5$^{th}$ Region, Brazil.

- Dr. iur. *Ricardo Perlingeiro*, Professor of Administrative Law, Fluminense Federal University (Niterói, Rio de Janeiro) and Federal Appellate Judge (*Desembargador Federal*) of the Federal Regional Court of the 2nd Region (Rio de Janeiro). He was the Brazilian Coordinator of the DAAD Project "Rule of Law: Administrative Law and Administrative Jurisdiction in Latin America" (2009–2012).
- Dr. iur. *Cristiana Maria Pinto e Silva Fortini*, Senior Professor of Administrative Law at Minas Gerais Federal University (UFMG), Visiting scholar at George Washington University (GWU) and Lawyer at Carvalho Pereira Pires Fortini Law Office, Brazil.
- Dr. iur. *Srikrishna Deva Rao*, Professor and vice chancellor of National Law University Odisha. He is a member of various committees of the Government of India. He has contributed in different research projects of access to justice, justice delivery and legal reforms by the Department of Justice, Ministry of Law and Justice of India. He has pioneered in initiating many clinical legal courses at the National Law Universities in Delhi and Odisha, India.
- *Joel Rheuben*, LL.M, solicitor, Associate in the antitrust, competition and trade group, based in the Brussels office of Freshfields Bruckhaus Deringer, United Kingdom.
- *Rogelio Robles*, LL.M. (UNAM), Lawyer, Civil servant of the Federal Jurisdiction, Mexico.
- Dr. iur. *Arno Scherzberg*, Professor of Public Law and Administrative Sciences, University of Erfurt (Germany). His fields of research are inter alia German General Administrative Law, German and European Freedom of Information Law, Environmental Law and Risk Law in areas of modern technology.
- Dr. iur. *Svenja Solka*, Legal advisor, German Federal Ministry for Economic Affairs and Energy, Department for European Policy (Berlin).
- *Daoming Tan*, Assistant Research Fellow in the Institute of Latin American Studies (ILAS), Chinese Academy of Social Sciences (CASS). He has expertise in Comparative Politics, Public Law and focuses on constitutionalism and rule of law in Latin America.
- *Robert G. Vaughn*, Ph.D., Emeritus Professor of Law at American University Washington College of Law in Washington, D.C. He has written several books, book chapters and articles on government information law and policy, including ones regarding freedom of information, privacy and whistleblower protection. He has been a visiting scholar or visiting professor at law schools in England, Australia and Japan. He has taught in foreign studies programs in Chile and Turkey. He has been a consultant for the Treasury and Civil Service Committee of the House of Commons, Office of Legal Cooperation of the Organization of American States and the World Bank.
- *Weibing Xiao*, Associate Professor at Shanghai University of Political Science and Law, Adjunct Researcher of Tasmania University Law School. His research interests include freedom of information and open government data.

# List of Abbreviations

| | |
|---|---|
| ACHR | American Convention on Human Rights |
| AL | Archives Law (China) |
| ALL | Administrative Litigation Law (China) |
| APA | German Federal Administrative Procedure Act |
| BVerfG | German Federal Constitutional Court (Bundesverfassungsgericht) |
| BVerfGE | Collection of the Decisions of the German Federal Constitutional Court (Entscheidungssammlung des Bundesverfassungsgerichts) |
| 1 BvR | First Section of the German Federal Constitutional Court |
| 2 BvR | Second Section of the German Federal Constitutional Court |
| BVerwG | Bundesverwaltungsgericht (German Federal Administrative Court) |
| BVerwGE | Collection of the Decisions of the German Federal Administrative Court (Entscheidungssammlung des Bundesverwaltungsgerichts) |
| C.A.A. | Cour Administrative d'Appel (France) |
| CADA | Commission d'Accès aux Documents Administratifs (France), Comissão de Acesso aos Documentos Administrativos (Portugal) |
| CAPIO | Central Appellate Public Information Officer (India) |
| CCP | Chinese Communist Party |
| C.E. | Council of State (Conseil d'Etat) |
| CETA | Comprehensive Economic and Trade Agreement between Canada and the EU |
| CFREU | Charter of Fundamental Rights of the European Union |
| CGU | Comptroller General of the Union (Brazil) |
| Chap. | Chapter |
| CI | ID card number (Brazil) |
| CIC | Central Information Commission (India) |
| CIS | Citizen Information Service (Brazil) |
| CMCS | Confidentiality Maintenance Commitment Statement (Brazil) |
| CNIL | Law on the Functioning of the *Commission Nationale Informatique et Libertés* |
| CNPD | National Data Protection Commission (Portugal) |

| | |
|---|---|
| Cons. Const. | Constitutional Council (Conseil Constitutionnel) |
| CPF | Cadastro de Pessoas Físicas (Natural Persons Register) (Brazil) |
| CPIO | Central Public Information Officer (India) |
| CPLA | Committee of Political and Legislative Affairs (China) |
| CPPSS | Center for Public Participation Studies and Supports (Peking University, China) |
| CRC | Regional Chambers of Audit (Chambres Régionales des Comptes) |
| CSJN | National Supreme Court of Justice (Corte Suprema de Justicia De La Nación—Argentina) |
| CSL | Civil Servant Law of the People's Republic of China |
| DCRA | Law on the Rights of the Citizens in their Relations with the Administrations (*Loi n° 2000-321 du 12 avril 2000 relative aux Droits des Citoyens dans leurs Relations avec les Administrations*) |
| DOF | Official Journal of the Mexican Federation (*Diario Oficial de la Federación*) |
| DÖV | Die Öffentliche Verwaltung |
| DPJ | Democratic Party of Japan |
| DVBl | Deutsches Verwaltungsblatt |
| ECHR | European Convention on Human Rights |
| ECJ | European Court of Justice |
| ECtHR | European Court of Human Rights |
| e-SIC | Electronic System source code of the Citizens Information Services (Brazil) |
| EU | European Union |
| FIA | German Federal Freedom of Information Act and the corresponding Acts of the German Länder (Informationsfreiheitsgesetz—IFG) |
| FOI | Freedom of Information |
| FOIA | U.S. Freedom of Information Act |
| FPA | Swedish Freedom of the Press Act |
| GDPR | General Data Protection Regulation (European Union) |
| GG | Basic Law of the Federal Republic of Germany (Grundgesetz) |
| I/A Court H.R. | Inter-American Court of Human Rights |
| IACHR | Inter-American Commission on Human Rights |
| IAHRS | Inter-American System for the Protection of Human Rights |
| IAJC | Inter-American Juridical Committee of the Organization of American States |
| IAP | Institute for the Monitoring of Advertising |
| ICCPR | International Covenant on Civil and Political Rights |
| ICDCI | Indexation Code of Document that contains Classified Information |
| ICT | Information Classification Term (Brazil) |
| IFG | German Federal Information Act and the corresponding Acts of the German Länder |
| INAI | National Institute of Transparency, Access to Information and Personal Data Protection (Mexico) |

| | |
|---|---|
| INSEE | Institut National de la Statistique et des Études Economiques |
| ITI | National Institute of Information Technology (Brazil) |
| JO | Justitieombudsman (Sweden) |
| LAI | Brazilian Law on Access to Information (Federal Law N° 12.527) |
| LFRASP | Federal Law on the Administrative Liability of Public Servants |
| LSSS | Chinese Law on Safeguarding State Secrets |
| NGO | Non-Governmental Organization |
| NPC | National People's Congress (China) |
| NPCSC | National People's Congress Standing Committee |
| NVwZ | Neue Zeitschrift für Verwaltungsrecht |
| OAS | Organization of American States |
| OBC | Other Backward Class (India) |
| OFPRA | Office Français de Protection des Réfugiés et des Apatrides |
| OGI | Open Government Information (China) |
| OIC | Internal Oversight Agencies |
| OSCE | Organization for Security and Co-operation in Europe |
| OVG | German Higher Administrative Court (Oberverwaltungsgericht) |
| PAISA | Swedish Public Access to Information and Secrecy Act |
| PAISO | Swedish Public Access to Information and Secrecy Ordinance |
| PCCDE | Permanent Commission for Classified Documents Evaluation (Brazil) |
| PIO | Public Information Officer (India) |
| PRADA | Persons Responsible for Access within Administrations (France) |
| PWC | PricewaterhouseCoopers |
| RAI | Right of Access to Information |
| RBI | Reserve Bank of India |
| REDLAD | Red Latinoamericana y del Caribe para la Democracia |
| RTI Act | Right to Information Act |
| SAPIO | State Appellate Public Information Officer (India) |
| SC/ST | Scheduled Caste/Scheduled Tribe (India) |
| SCC | Safety and Credentialing Core (Brazil) |
| SCC | Supreme Court Cases (Canada, India) |
| SCR | Supreme Court Records (India) |
| Sec. | Section (taken as meaning a distinct and numbered subdivision in legal codes, statutes etc.) |
| SECOM | State Secretary of the Chief Minister of Social Communication of the Presidency |
| Sect. | Section (taken as meaning sub-chapter) |
| SEK | Swedish Krona |
| SIC | Service of Integrated Information to the Citizens (Brazil) |
| SIGEN | General Auditing Office for Public Enterprises (Sindicatura General de Empresas Públicas—Argentina) |
| SPIO | State Public Information Officer (India) |
| TA | Decision of Administrative Court (Jugement du Tribunal Administratif) |

| | |
|---|---|
| TC | Decision of the Tribunal of Dispute Settlement (Arrêt du Tribunal des Conflits) |
| TEC | Treaty establishing the European Community |
| TEU | Treaty on European Union |
| TFEU | Treaty on the Functioning of the European Union |
| TTIP | Transatlantic Trade and Investment Partnership |
| UDHR | Universal Declaration of Human Rights |
| UN | United Nations |
| UNCAC | UN Convention Against Corruption |
| UNESCO | United Nations Educational, Scientific and Cultural Organization |
| UPN | Unique Protocol Number (Brazil) |
| U.S. | United States of America |
| VG | Administrative Court (Verwaltungsgericht) |
| WJP | World Justice Programme |
| WJP | World Justice Project |
| WTO | World Trade Organization |
| ZUM | Zeitschrift für Urheber- und Medienrecht |

# Chapter 1
# Essentials of the Right of Access to Public Information: An Introduction

**Hermann-Josef Blanke and Ricardo Perlingeiro**

## Contents



---

The author Hermann-Josef Blanke is responsible for Sects. 1, 2.1, 4.1.1, 4.1.2, 4.1.2.1, 4.1.2.2, 4.1.2.3, 4.1.3, 4.2, 4.2.1, 4.2.2, 4.3, 5, 5.1, 5.2, 5.3, 5.4, 6.1, 6.2.2, 6.5, 6.6, the author Ricardo Perlingeiro for Sects. 2, 4.1, 6.2, 6.2.1, 6.3, 6.4, 6.2.2, and 7 of the following chapter. Both authors are responsible for Sects. 2.2, 2.3, 3, 7.1, 7.2 and 8.

H.-J. Blanke (✉)
University of Erfurt, Erfurt, Germany
e-mail: LS_Staatsrecht@uni-erfurt.de

R. Perlingeiro
Fluminense Federal University and Estácio de Sá University, Rio de Janeiro, Brazil
e-mail: r.perlingeiro@terra.com.br



H.-J. Blanke, R. Perlingeiro (eds.), *The Right of Access to Public Information*,
DOI 10.1007/978-3-662-55554-5_1

## 1 History of Codification of the Right of Access to Information

The first freedom of information law was enacted in Sweden back in 1766 as the "Freedom of the Press and the Right of Access to Public Records Act" (*Tryckfrihetsförordningen*).[1] This code inspired by *Anders Chydenius* (1729–1803), an eminent philosopher of liberalism, abolished the censorship of all printed publications in the spirit of the Age of Enlightenment while at the same time establishing the legal principle of public access to official records ("transparency"—*offentlighetsprincipen*) as a binding requirement for public administration (Jonason, Chap. 5, Sect. 1). The legal formulation of the "public nature of official documents" in Chap. 2 of the Freedom of the Press Act (1999) still serves as a model, not least because of its rank among the basic constitutional principles of the Kingdom of Sweden.

Nevertheless, the global trend of freedom of access to state-held information was noticeably late in coming, triggered first by the U.S. "Freedom of Information Act" (FOIA), which was signed into law by President *Lyndon B. Johnson* in 1966. That Act was rooted in the 1960s movement for civil rights and democracy. It is based on the duty of all executive areas of government[2] to provide information to citizens, and impose any necessary exceptions to the general rule of transparency. Thanks to the FOIA, the U.S. Federal Government agencies practice a high degree of

[1] Ackermann & Sandoval-Ballestros 2006, p. 88.

[2] In European constitutional law the term "government" refers to the collegial body of the government which forms in accordance with the constitutional requirements the head of the executive branch (government in the institutional sense), or to one governmental branch as a whole, i.e., the executive branch (the national government agencies), in so far as it is entrusted with basic issues of the state (government in the sense of effective power to govern). In the American legal context, however, "government" means the legal system, i.e., an umbrella concept which refers to all three governmental branches, and the various political institutions of the state. This system provides a series of checks and balances because each branch is able to limit the power of the others. The U.S. executive branch consists of the President and the Vice-President, and government departments and agencies.

transparency, which is regarded as a key feature of good governance and an indicator of a genuinely democratic and pluralist society (Blanke, Chap. 3, Sect. 1.2). The right to access to official documents is considered essential to the self-determination of the people and to the exercise of fundamental human rights, while helping administrative agencies appear more legitimate and trustworthy in the public eye. A substantial number of auditing and investigative agencies are capable of functioning independently of political influence.[3] Such bodies are often spurred to action by the investigative work of journalists. U.S. Federal agencies regularly publish online information relevant to their terms of office to broaden public access. In an action widely praised by scholars and civil libertarians, Barack Obama ordered in 2009 that millions of government documents from the Cold War era be declassified, and instructed federal agencies to adopt a cooperative attitude toward public information requests.[4] However, the Obama administration came under criticism for its lack of openness towards the press and public and its determination to punish leaks by government officials (most famously in the case of *WikiLeaks*).[5]

As early as 1969, a groundbreaking precedent of the Supreme Court of Japan established the principle that *shiru kenri* (the "right to know") is protected by the Article 21.1 of the Japanese Constitution (guarantee of freedom of expression).[6] Then, in 1989 the Constitutional Court of South Korea ruled that the right to information (a "right to know") is a sine qua non for freedom of speech and of the press as guaranteed by Article 21 of the South Korean Constitution, and that sufficient access to the information held, collected, and processed by the government is essential to proper exercise of that right. Further, the Court stated that the public is entitled to demand disclosure of government-held information, and the government must comply with such requests. However, in accordance with this case-law, access to information can be reasonably restricted by balancing the direct interests of the person requesting information against the potential harm to the public interest.[7] In India, the Supreme Court has made several statements grounding the right to access to information in freedom of expression,[8] but it has also held that

[3]Freedom House, Report on the United States (Chapter: Political Rights and Civil Liberties), 2016 (Accessed on 20 October 2016).

[4]Obama 2009; see also Orszag 2009.

[5]Freedom House, Report regarding the U.S. (2014).

[6]Article 21.1 of the Japanese Constitution, as interpreted by the Japanese Supreme Court, also protects "the freedom to gather news for informational purposes"; see Japanese Supreme Court, *Kaneko v. Japan* (Judgment of 26 November 1969), 23 Keishu 1490; quoted also by Peled & Rabin 2011, p. 373); see Kadomatsu and Rheuben (in this volume), Chap. 12, Sect. 2.1.

[7]The Constitutional Court of Korea (2001). The first ten years of the Korean Constitutional Court, p. 132. Public Release. http://www.ccourt.go.kr/home/att_file/ebook/1255848884375.pdf.

[8]See Indian Supreme Court, *S. P. Gupta v. President of India and Ors.* (Judgment of 30 December 1981), 1981 Supp SCC 87; Indian Supreme Court, *Dinesh Trivedi, Union of India v. AS & Soacnioatthieorn for Democratic Reforms* (Judgment of 2 May 2002), 2002 INSC 244; and Indian Supreme Court, *People's Union of Civil Liberties (P.U.C.L.) & Anr v. Union of India and Anr* (Judgment of 13 March 2003), 2003 INSC 173.

the right to information flows from the right to life (Article 21 of the Indian Constitution).[9]

Even before the Inter-American Court of Human Rights (I/A Court H. R.) had to face the issue of a right of access to information under the American Convention on Human Rights (ACHR) in 2006, the African Commission on Human and Peoples' Rights had given a broad interpretation to Article 9.1 of the African Charter on Human and People's Rights,[10] concluding that its guarantee includes a "right of access to information".[11] For the same purpose, the I/A Court H. R. considers it evident that Article 13.1 of the American Convention on Human Rights[12] not only implies a fundamental right to seek and receive information, but also the positive obligation of the OAS States "to provide it, so that the individual may have access to such information or receive an answer that includes a justification when, for any reason permitted by the Convention, the State is allowed to restrict access to the information in a specific case".[13] Much more reticent is the European Court of Human Rights (ECtHR), which has not yet accepted that access to government information is a general right, but that it may exceptionally be granted to applicants having a special legal interest (Sect. 3).[14]

In 1979, the Parliamentary Assembly of the Council of Europe adopted the Recommendation No. 854 (1979) on "Access by the public to government records and freedom of information", whose principles were repeatedly refined by the

[9]Indian Supreme Court, *Reliance Petrochemicals Ltd., v. Proprietors of Indian Express Newspapers, Bombay Pvt. Ltd. and Others*, (Judgment of 23 September 1988), 1988 (004) SCC 0592 SC, para. 3: "Right to know is a basic right which citizens of a free country aspire in the broader horizon of the right to live in this age in our land under Article 21 of our Constitution." See also Rao and Chingale, Chap. 9, Sect. 3.

[10]Article 9.1 of the African Charter on Human and Peoples' Rights provides: "Every individual shall have the right to receive information."

[11]Cf. the "Declaration of Principles on Freedom of Expression in Africa", adopted by the African Commission in 2002, to supplement Article 9 of the African Charter which provides that "every individual shall have the right to receive information". While the Declaration has expanded on States Parties obligations under the African Charter, it does not specifically provide guidance on the form and content of the legislation to be enacted to give effect to these obligations at the domestic level. In adopting the "Model Law on Access to Information for Africa", the African Commission has therefore gone a step further than the Declaration, by providing detailed and practical content to the legislative obligations of Member States to the African Charter with respect to the right of access to information. This "Model Law" is available at: http://www.achpr.org/files/news/2013/04/d84/model_law.pdf.

[12]"Everyone has the right to freedom of thought and expression. This right includes freedom to seek, receive, and impart information and ideas of all kinds, regardless of frontiers, either orally, in writing, in print, in the form of art, or through any other medium of one's choice."

[13]I/A Court H. R., *Case of Claude-Reyes et al. v. Chile* (Judgment of 19 September 2006), Series C No. 151, para 58 (a)-(b) (regarding the Commission's arguments) and 77 (regarding the Court's findings).

[14]ECtHR, *Leander v. Sweden* (Judgment of 26 March 1987), Series A No. 116, para 74; ECtHR *Társasága Szabadságjogokért v. Hungary* (Judgment of 14 April 2009), No. 37374/05, para 35 to 39, with reference to ECtHR, *Chauvy and Others v. France* (Judgment of 29 June 2004), ECHR 2004-VI, No. 64915/01, para 66.

Committee of Ministers of the Council of Europe.[15] Then, in June 1998 the UN Convention on Access to Information, Public Participation in Decision-Making and Access to Justice in Environmental Matters was signed in Aarhus.[16] This Convention has implemented Principle 10 of the Rio Declaration on Environment and Development (1992)[17]: All citizens concerned by environmental issues should have access to the relevant government-held information, even if their statutory rights have not been violated.[18] Finally, in June 2009, the Convention on Access to Official Documents was opened for signature by the Parties to the Council of Europe.[19] Its preamble explains the reasons for implementing the Convention through appropriate national laws and other measures:

---

[15]See Declaration of the Committee of Ministers of the Council of Europe on the freedom of expression and information, adopted on 29 April 1982, as well as recommendations of the Committee of Ministers to Member States No. R (81) 19 on the access to information held by public authorities, No. R (91) 10 on the communication to third parties of personal data held by public bodies, No. R (97) 18 concerning the protection of personal data collected and processed for statistical purposes, No. R (2000) 13 on a European policy on access to archives and Rec (2002)2 on access to official documents.

[16]Cf. the Convention on Access to Information, Public Participation in Decision-Making and Access to Justice in Environmental Matters (25 June 1992).

[17]Principle 10 reads as follows: "Environmental issues are best handled with participation of all concerned citizens, at the relevant level. At the national level, each individual shall have appropriate access to information concerning the environment which is held by public authorities, including information on hazardous materials and activities in their communities, and the opportunity to participate in decision-making processes. States shall facilitate and encourage public awareness and participation by making information widely available. Effective access to judicial and administrative proceedings, including redress and remedy, shall be provided."

[18]Under the title "Objective" Article 1 of the Aarhus Convention lays down: "In order to contribute to the protection of the right of every person of present and future generations to live in an environment adequate to his or her health and well-being, each Party shall guarantee the rights of access to information, public participation in decision-making, and access to justice in environmental matters in accordance with the provisions of this Convention."

Recitals 8, 9 and 10 of the Convention read as follows: "Recognizing also that every person has the right to live in an environment adequate to his or her health and well-being, and the duty, both individually and in association with others, to protect and improve the environment for the benefit of present and future generations,

Considering that, to be able to assert this right and observe this duty, citizens must have access to information, be entitled to participate in decision-making and have access to justice in environmental matters, and acknowledging in this regard that citizens may need assistance in order to exercise their rights,

Recognizing that, in the field of the environment, improved access to information and public participation in decision-making enhance the quality and the implementation of decisions, contribute to public awareness of environmental issues, give the public the opportunity to express its concerns and enable public authorities to take due account of such concerns [. . .]."

[19]"This Convention enters into force on the first day of the month following the expiration of a period of three months after the date on which 10 member States of the Council of Europe have expressed their consent to be bound by the Convention" (Article 16.3 of the Council of Europe Convention on Access to Official Documents). It has been signed by five countries of the Council of Europe and ratified by nine as of 18 Sep. 2016, so it may be expected to enter into force soon.

[T]he exercise of a right to access to official documents:

- provides a source of information for the public;
- helps the public to form an opinion on the state of society and on public authorities;
- fosters the integrity, efficiency, effectiveness and accountability of public authorities, so helping affirm their legitimacy.

After its ratification this Convention will be the first binding international legal instrument to recognise a general right to access to official documents held by public authorities including natural or legal persons insofar as they exercise administrative authority.

## 2 The Development of the Right of Access to Information in Constitutional and Ordinary Legislation of the Nation State

In the past few decades, the access to information has become consecrated by many Constitutions as a self-standing fundamental right,[20] and even in those that do not expressly refer to such access we find traces of transparency or principles that depend on public disclosure, and constitutional court precedents suggest that transparency is a basic prerequisite for a constitutional state (legal state)[21] guided by the principles of democracy and rule of law. It should also be noted that in most cases legislators have defined the right to information as a fundamental right (Perlingeiro et al., Chap. 2, Sect 2; Blanke, Chap. 3, Sect 2).

[20]See for example in Europe: Albania (Article 23 Const. 1998), Austria (Article 20. 3 and 20.4 Const. 1920), Belgium (Article 32 Const. 1831), Bulgaria (Article 41 Const. 1991 as amended through 2007), Estonia (Article 44 Const. 1992), Finland (Sec. 12 Const. 1999), Greece (Article 5A Const. 2001), Hungary (Article VI.2 Const. 2011), Macedonia (Articles 16.2, 16.3 and 18 Const. 1991), Moldova (Article 34 Const. 1994), Spain (Article 20 Const. 1978); en Latin America: Bolívia (Articles 21.6 e 242.4 Const. 2008), Brasil (Articles 5 XXXIII, 37 § 3 II, e 216 § 2 Const. 1988), Costa Rica (Article 30 Const. 1949), Equador (Articles 18.2 e 91 Const. 2008), Guatemala (Article 30 Const. 1993), Mexico (Article 6A Constitution 1917 as amended in Feb. 2016), Nicarágua (Article 66 Const. 1987), Panamá (Articles 43 e 44 Const. 1972), Paraguai (Article 28 Const. 1992), Peru (Articles 2.4 and 5 Const. 1993), Dominican Republic (Article 49.1 Const. 2010) and Venezuela (Article 143 Const. 1999); in Asia: Afghanistan (Article 50 Const. 2003), Armenia (Article 23, 27, 33.2 and 83.5 Const. 2005), Azerbaijan (Article 50 I, II and III Const. 1995), Georgia (Articles 24 and 41 Const. 1995 as amended in 2006), India (Article 19.1 Const.), Kazakhstan (Articles 18, 20 and 31 Const. 1995 as amended in 1998), Maldives (Article 27, 28 and 29 Const. 2008); in Africa, Burkina Faso (Article 8 and 101 Const. 1991), Cape Verde (Article 29 and 48 Constitution 2010), Democratic Republic of Congo (Article 24 Const. 2006), Egypt (Article 31 and 68 Const. 2014), Eritrea (Article 19.3 Const. 1997), Ethiopia (Article 29 Const. 1994), Ghana (Article 21 Const. 1992), Guinea Bissau (Article 34 Const. 1996), Kenya (Article 35 Const. 2010), Malawi (Article 37 Const. 1994); and in Oceania, Fiji (Articles 17, 24 and 25 Const. 2013).

[21]See Sommermann 2010, p. 12, 19.

Legislative codification of the right to access to information has been a global tendency. There are currently about 130 special information access laws in effect that may be characterised as codes; yet the right of access to information does not necessary have to be regulated in a statutory system.[22] Most such laws were ratified in the 1990s and thereafter,[23] and about 50% of them reflect constitutional provision that expressly provide for information access as a fundamental right.[24] As established by the I/A Court H. R., the right to access to information has two different dimensions (individual and collective dimensions),[25] which it uses as a basis to confirm its universal nature and that everyone should be granted access to government-held information, even without a specific legal interest in such disclosure: to obtain access to information, it should suffice to invoke "citizen oversight".[26]

The right of access to official information is no longer consecrated only by the national laws of "western" nations, although the US-American "Freedom of Information Act" has had a big impact on the legal development of many countries in this regard (Bachilo, Chap. 10, Sect. 2.4). Especially in Latin America, the Brazilian Law N° 12.527/2011, the Mexican General Law on Transparency and Access to Public Information (2002/2015[27]) and most recently the Argentinian Law 22275/2016[28] exemplify the development of specific national forms of codification. For example, Article 2 of the above-cited Mexican law explicitly aims at democratisation (subsections 7 and 8) and reinforcement of judicial protection (subsection 4). African countries, such as Nigeria,[29] and albeit to a lesser extent, Indonesia and other Asian countries,[30] have now enacted their own national transparency laws. It may be legitimately asked, however, whether this abundant legislation has actually broadened the scope of the right of freedom of access to information as an enforceable right in reality (Sects. 6.5 and 6.6).

In fact, the right of access to information is mainly regulated by constitutions and international conventions, so that administrative and judicial authorities

[22]http://www.right2info.org/laws/constitutional-provisions-laws-and-regulations (Accessed on 29 October 2016).

[23]See Perlingeiro 2014, p. 2.414. Available at: http://dx.doi.org/10.2139/ssrn.2416760. See also http://www.rti-rating.org/country-data (Accessed on 29 October 2016).

[24]http://www.rti-rating.org/by-indicator?indicator=1 (Accessed on 29 October 2016).

[25]Inter-American Commission on Human Rights, *Case of Gomes Lund et al. (Guerrilha do Araguaia) v. Brasil* (Judgment of 24 November 2010), Available at: http://bit.ly/1KdWmN3 (Accessed on 14 March 2016).

[26]See Case Claude Reyes et al. v. Chile. § 157.

[27]Cf. "Ley General de Transparencia y Acceso a la Información Pública", *Diario Oficial* of the Mexican Federation of 4.5.2015.

[28]Cf. "Derecho de Acceso a la Información Pública", Boletín Oficial de la República Argentina, available at: https://www.boletinoficial.gob.ar/#!DetalleNorma/151503/null.

[29]http://www.right2info.org/laws/constitutional-provisions-laws-and-regulations#nigeria (Accessed on 29 October 2016).

[30]http://www.right2info.org/laws/constitutional-provisions-laws-and-regulations#indonesia (Accessed on 29 October 2016).

are confronted with the challenge of surmounting the obstacles created by infra-constitutional provisions restricting such access. This means that the constitutional courts, especially, but not only those with administrative jurisdiction, are particularly well-suited to enforce such rights. In that context, to compensate for the excessive number of vague concepts that permeate the laws of information, principles and general rules, when properly systematised and interpreted by the legislators, make a positive contribution by reducing the margin of appreciation of the authorities in teleological exegeses that give rise to controversy and uncertainty.[31]

## 2.1 Reasons for the Development of National Laws on Access to Information

The progressive codification of freedom of information can be mainly attributed to three factors: first, the end of the vast majority of military dictatorships and the breakdown of the former Eastern Bloc have led to a process of democratisation in these "de-liberated" countries. One result of this liberation is that citizens are interested to come to terms with past wrongs through critical confrontation with their recent history, and are interested in obtaining information about their own past. At the same time, they wish to "supervise" the political actors who previously used to withhold from the public information about "internal" issues of state and public administration so as to act at its own discretion.[32]

Simultaneously, at the international level, a broad interpretation of the classical right to information or, as in the Council of Europe, a codification of a special right to access to information has taken place. The global and regional covenants on human rights provide explicitly only for the right to freedom of expression, including the freedom to seek, receive and impart information and ideas of all kinds (e.g., Article 19.2 of the International Covenant on Civil and Political Rights—ICCPR, Article 10.1 of the European Convention for the Protection of Human Rights and Fundamental Freedoms (1950—ECHR), i.e., the right to communication which is limited to a mere defensive right ("Abwehrrecht"). Although Article 19 ICCPR does not oblige public authorities—in terms of a "positive right" of the citizen—to disclose available information, the guarantee under the convention may be assumed to serve as a motivating factor for the development of the right of access to information. The effects of such motivation are obvious in the interpretation of Article 9.1 of the African Charter on Human and People's Rights by the African Commission on Human and Peoples' Rights, and the interpretation of Article 13.1 ACHR by the I/A Court H. R. (Sect. 3). The preamble to the European Council Convention on Access to Official Documents (Sect. 1) explicitly mentions "Article 19 of the Universal Declaration of Human Rights" and to

[31] See Perlingeiro 2015.

[32] Ackerman & Sandoval-Ballesteros 2006, p. 86 et seq.

"Articles 6, 8 and 10 of the (European) Convention for the Protection of Human Rights and Fundamental Freedoms".

In a nutshell, the socio-economic change together with a restructuring of the economy in favor of the tertiary sector, the digital revolution, particularly the growing importance of the Internet (Sect. 2.2), and the global transformation into an Information society have speeded up the development of the right of access to information.

The right of access to information will take a few years to develop fully, as shown by the experience with the U.S. Freedom of Information Act. The highest costs have proven to be the hiring of additional civil servants, i.e., bureaucracy, to examine the individual requests.

## 2.2 *The Catalytic Role of the Internet for the Development of the Right of Access to Information*

The internet has now taken on a role of inestimable importance in protecting the right of access to information. The medium promises unprecedented dissemination of information, culture and knowledge, and is a vehicle for innovation, creation and wealth generation.[33]

The significance of the internet is inseparably intertwined with the significance of data for the societies of the twenty-first century. Digital data, in particular, as an important foundation for research and opinion-building, as well as basis for decision-making, has repeatedly been called the "fuel of the future" or "the new petroleum". In addition, it is necessary to consider Open Data's economic impact ("digital gold"), which the European Commission expects to attain the value of EUR 75.7 billion in Europe by 2020.[34] Countries can create an economically valuable basis for innovations and new business models—especially "start-ups"—by making their "data" available free of charge in machine-readable format.

Unlike traditional media, the internet enables individual users not only to be consumers of information but also to become involved as active participants and even interactive producers,[35] transforming the information society into an interactive society[36] ("social media"). The internet can also foster the rapid emergence of a knowledge-based economy through free access to public-sector research. Hence, the

---

[33]Cf. the Explanatory Memorandum regarding the French "Digital Republic Law"; available at http://www.republique-numerique.fr/pages/digital-republic-bill-rationale (Accessed on 29 October 2016).

[34]European Commission, Creating Value through Open Data: Study on the Impact of Re-use of Public Data Resources (Capgemini Consulting), 2015: "Between 2016 and 2020, the market size of Open Data is expected to increase by 36.9%, to a value of 75.7 bn EUR in 2020."

[35]Woods 2012, p. 141.

[36]Wiberg 2005, p. 1 et seqq.

main services should not be reserved for the elite. The notion of "net neutrality" refers to an indispensable prerequisite for safeguarding the right to information, including technical guarantees of that right.[37] Net neutrality means that all data sent over the internet should be treated the same and not depending on their contents to avoid practices such as unequal or discriminatory treatment or inconsistent pricing from one user to the next ("fairness online"). Equal rights for internet users, as well as universal access to the internet and its services, as a requisite for inclusion, career paths and social lives, therefore, have become main objectives of the French "Digital Republic Law".[38]

The development of new technologies through digital means to enable wide access to the information over the Internet brought a new dimension to the subject, requiring adequate legislation that urges the public authorities to use such means, as exemplified by the Brazilian Freedom of Information Act in Article 3, item III, which establishes procedures that are intended to safeguard "the fundamental right of access to information [. . .] and must be carried out in compliance with the basic principles of public administration and the following guidelines: [. . .] use of means of communication made available by information technology [. . .]" and in Article 8 para 2: "[. . .] the public entities and authorities shall use all the legitimate means and instruments at their disposal, with an obligation to publish information on official websites of the Internet, the global computer network". Similarly, Article 6.3 of the Mexican Constitution, as amended in this regard in 2013, reads as follows: "The State shall guarantee access to information and communication technology, access to the services of radio broadcast, telecommunications and broadband Internet. To that end, the State shall establish effective competition conditions for the provision of such services." Under the U.S. E-Government Act of 17 December 2002, government authorities are required to search for requested

[37]For the principle of net neutrality cf. Müller 2015, http://verfassungsblog.de/staatliche-gewaehrleistung-der-informationsfreiheit-zwischen-netneutrality-und-notneutrality/#.VjuK_isXvpY (Accessed on 20 October 2016); Wimmer 2013, p. 642 et seqq. (regarding the development in the U.S. cf. p. 644 et seq., regarding the development in Europe cf. p. 645); for the three main strands of the French Digital Republic bill (champion data and knowledge dissemination, protecting individuals in the digital society, and providing universal access to digital technology) see the Explanatory Memorandum, available at http://www.republique-numerique.fr/pages/digital-republic-bill-rationale (Accessed on 20 October 2016).

[38]Cf. the Law n° 2016-1321 of 7 October 2016 "pour une République numérique", JORF n° 0235 of 8 October 2016, text n° 1, available at https://www.legifrance.gouv.fr/affichTexte.do?cidTexte=JORFTEXT000033202746&fastPos=5&fastReqId=725542329&categorieLien=id&oldAction=rechTexte (Accessed on 25 November 2016), see especially Article 18 *quater* and Article 47.1 of the bill: Article 18 *quater* – "Les outils numériques et de l'internet étant d'usage banalisé, les langages et logiciels facilement accessibles et leurs utilisations en ligne valorisées par les administrations et les pouvoirs publics, leur bon usage est promu, notamment auprès des mineurs et jeunes majeurs en formation, en fonction de leur âge et de leur maturité, et tout au long de la vie, afin que les opportunités comme les risques inhérents à l'usage de ces technologies puissantes soient connus de tous." – Article 47.1 of this bill reads as follows: "Les services de communication au public en ligne des services de l'État, des collectivités territoriales et des établissements publics qui en dépendent ainsi que ceux des organismes délégataires d'une mission de service public doivent être accessibles aux personnes handicapées."

official information in its databases within a reasonable time and deliver it in the form requested by the requesting party. Moreover, the government must regard such information as subject to disclosure at all times and make optimal use of the new information technologies, and make information available to citizens even if they do not ask for it.[39] In December 2017, the U.S. Federal Communications Commission (FCC) suggested to revise the legal foundation for the agency's Open Internet regulations ("Restoring Internet Freedom"). According to that order, it should be allowed in the future that certain data can be preferred, delayed or even blocked.[40] This decision which is part of the U.S. administrative law can be considered as a rollback of the net neutrality. It will be granting broadband companies the power to potentially reshape Americans' online experiences.[41] Meanwhile, U.S. states are fighting against this rollback, also by filing numerous lawsuits.

The need for a proactive national information policy ("proactive disclosure" = transparency legislation in the strict sense) has recently been recognised by French, Italian and German legislatures.[42] In its legislative section, the French "Digital Republic Law" aims to extend the scope of the administrative documents that may already be made available, and which central and local government, and public and private legal entities having a public service mandate must voluntarily disseminate. This approach strives to cut down on the number of documents provided upon request by making them freely available on the Internet ("open government data").[43] The "Law Madia", also called "Italian FOIA",[44] designs now transparency as freedom of access to the data and documents held by public authorities guaranteed firstly, through a general public access to such data and documents (*accesso civico*); and, secondly, through the publication of documents, information and data (Galetta, Chap. 8, Sect. 4.1). Restrictions are nonetheless possible when they appear necessary "for the protection of legally relevant public and private interests" (Article 5.2 of the Italian Decree No. 33/2013 as amended by the Italian

[39]See Sanz Salla 2010, p. 230.

[40]The Rule by the Federal Communication Commission on 22 March 2018 is available at https://www.federalregister.gov/documents/2018/02/22/2018-03464/restoring-internet-freedom

[41]Kang 2017, p. A1.

[42]See the comparative legal analysis (France-Germany) published by Schnieders 2018, p. 177 et seqq., 180 et seqq.

[43]Cf. the Explanatory Memorandum of the drafted bill; available at http://www.republique-numerique.fr/pages/digital-republic-bill-rationale.

[44]Legislative Decree 25 May 2016, No. 97 on the review and simplification of the provisions on prevention of corruption, openness and transparency, amending Law of 6 November 2012, No. 190 and Legislative Decree of 14 March 14, 2013, No. 33, in accordance with Article 7 of Law of 7 August 2015, No. 124, on reorganisation public administrations, published in the Italian Official Gazette of 8 June 2016, No. 132.

Legislative Decree 97/2016 on transparency. The amendment of the E-Government Act adopted by German legislators in 2017[45] provides for the establishment of a broader legal basis for the active publishing of data held by federal authorities, which contain facts relating to circumstances outside these authorities, and mirrors internationally accepted open-data-principles as described, e.g., in the International Open-Data-Charta or in the G8 Open-Data-Charta[46] (Scherzberg and Solka, Chap. 7, Sect. 6). That Act reveals elements leading to a knowledge management in federal administrative authorities: One of the Act's purposes is to provide an opportunity for more public participation in administrative matters and to allow for an enhanced cooperation between citizens and the authorities. According to Sec. 12a.1 of this Act, federal authorities publish unprocessed data, which they collected to fulfill their public duties or which third parties collected on their behalf, via public networks. The publication is free of charge (Sec. 12a.7 sentence 1). The Act does not provide for an entitlement to publication of data (Sec. 12a.1 sentence 2). Sec. 12a.2 defines which data are subject to publication. This in particular includes data held by the federal authorities electronically or in collections such as tables and lists. Exemptions from publication are set out in Sec. 12a.3. According to Sec. 12a.3 point 1, data are not published especially in case of a legal impediment. This is the case, "if there is no right of access to the data or if there is only a restricted right of access, in particular pursuant to Sec. 3 to 5 of the FIA, or if a right of access exists only after the participation of third parties" (Sec. 12a.4). Sharp criticism has been levelled at this definition of the "legal impediment". According to the critics, this clause "opens the floodgates for more exceptions".[47] That criticism reveals issues characteristic of not only open-data laws but all transparency legislation. Both national legislators and the drafters of the Council of Europe Convention on Access to Official Documents are faced with the challenge of finding a proportionate balance between the broad scope of protection of the right of access to information, on the one hand, and the need to impose limits on such access to protect the right to privacy and the public interest, on the other. This tension is clearly set out in recital 6 of the ePrivacy Directive (2002/58/EC) of the European Union which harmonises the provisions of the Member States required to ensure an equivalent level of protection of fundamental rights and freedoms, and in particular the right to privacy, with respect to the processing of personal data in the electronic communication sector and to ensure the free movement of such data and of electronic communication equipment and services in the Union (Article 1): "The Internet is

[45]See Gesetz zur Förderung der elektronischen Verwaltung (5 July 2017 - E-Government Act), German Federal Law Gazette 2017 p. 2206.

[46]See the G8 Open Data Charter and Technical Annex (18.6.2013), available under https://www.gov.uk/government/publications/open-data-charter/g8-open-data-charter-and-technical-annex.

[47]Cf. Netzpolitik.Org: "[...] Open-Data-Gesetz wird Luftnummer", https://netzpolitik.org/2016/wir-veroeffentlichen-eckpunktepapier-open-data-gesetz-wird-luftnummer/ (Accessed on 14 December 2016).

overturning traditional market structures by providing a common, global infrastructure for the delivery of a wide range of electronic communications services. Publicly available electronic communications services over the Internet open new possibilities for users but also new risks for their personal data and privacy."[48]

## 2.3 *Objectives of the Right of Access to Information*

Constitutional and statutory freedom-of-information provisions do not conceive of such access as an end in and of itself but rather as a means of pursuing other objectives. The focus is on the functions of citizen oversight and participation, that is to say *options* that are made available not only to the citizen but to anyone who lawfully resides and/or maintains a community in the territory of a nation state or political community (such as the E.U. "compound of States"). The oversight function is supplementary to other national control mechanisms; with respect to the right of access to documents, it can also serve—at least preventively—the purpose of combatting illegality and corruption in state institutions, and more effectively than the "internal" control mechanisms of the national government agencies[49] (a rather sceptical view take Galetta, Chap. 8, Sect. 4.2; Blanke, Chap. 3, Sect. 1). Putting the scores of the "Perception of Corruption Index" 2016 in context the report of Transparency International comes to the conclusion that "higher-ranked countries tend to have higher degrees of press freedom, access to information about public expenditure, stronger standards of integrity for public officials, and independent judicial systems".[50] Oversight of the conduct of the public administrative authorities may also include government actions.[51] The participatory function of freedom of

[48]European Parliament and the Council, Directive 2002/58/EC of 12 July 2002 concerning the processing of personal data and the protection of privacy in the electronic communications sector, Official Journal L 201, 31 July 2002, P. 0037 – 0047. In particular, Article 5(1) of that Directive provides that the Member States must ensure, by means of their national legislation, the confidentiality of communications effected by means of a public communications network and publicly available electronic communications services, and the confidentiality of the related traffic data.

[49]This judgement is controversial. Cf. Puigpelat 2017, Sect. 4 who regards "a modern regulation on administrative transparency as a basic mechanism to try to restore the confidence of the Spanish citizens in their institutions"; according to Schoch 2016, Einleitung para 50 the threat of forced disclosure of records will trigger defense mechanisms. Instead, Schoch expects more effective detection of corruption through insiders in the public administrative authorities. That statement may apply to countries with an advanced administrative culture, such as Great Britain, France, Germany or the United States, but it is not unreservedly true of Latin American countries. The fight against corruption in Brazil shows that the population trusts the Judiciary alone to intervene effectively against corruption, which seems to have taken hold of the other branches of government like a cancer.

[50]Transparency International (2017), http://www.transparency.org/news/feature/corruption_perceptions_index_2016 (Accessed on 30 January 2017).

[51]Cf. Schoch 2016, Einleitung para 49.

information is considered to be closely related to the principle of democracy (Sect. 4.1). Along with elections and referendums, the right of access to information is considered to be one of the signs of a "living democracy" in a civil society (built upon the self-determination of the "citoyens"), promoting the common welfare in the areas as diverse as environmental and consumer protection or coming to terms with the past (e.g., "The Federal Commissioner for the Records of the State Security Service of the former German Democratic Republic").The transparency of public administration is only an intermediate objective.[52] It has been correctly pointed out that the laws of access to information promote the effective exercise of the individual's fundamental rights.[53] Transparency has even been referred to as a tool necessary to create the prerequisites for the protection of fundamental rights,[54] not only for the exercise of freedom of opinion but also basic economic rights (rights of ownership and occupational and entrepreneurial freedom).

The objectives of transparency laws depend on the specific addressees of such laws in each particular case (Blanke, Chap. 3, Sects. 2.2.2 and 3.2.2). Regarding administrative agencies, the objectives are to ensure optimal use of the available information under their control and to improve the efficiency of public administrative actions.[55] Administrative authorities are moving out of their previously indirect relationship with citizens into direct contact. As the administrative agencies grow more directly accountable to the people as a result of transparency laws, their accountability to Parliament is reduced accordingly. At the same time, the Parliament's accountability to the people is reduced in the same proportion (Sect. 4.1.1).[56]

With respect to the Judiciary and Legislative branch, the duty of disclosure mainly concerns the documents related to their administrative functions, such as public procurement contracts, use of public funding, etc. (Perlingeiro et al., Chap. 2, Sect. 3). The Brazilian law on access to government information makes it clear that access to information refers to administrative activities, of both the Legislative and Judicial branches.[57] In fact, the purpose of imposing duties of disclosure on the Judiciary and Legislature is not aimed at court judgments and statutes themselves, which have always been a prime example of public transparency. Incidentally, the recognition of the right of public access to parliamentary debates and court hearings (on legal issues) is founded in the possibility of public opinion influencing political decision-making as an inherent function of participatory democracy.[58] According to Mendel, "[t]here is no reason in principle why the legislative and judicial branches should not be covered, as long as the regime of exceptions protects legitimate secrecy interests, and experience in those countries that do cover all

[52] Cf. Rossi 2004, p. 325 et seq. (point 2).

[53] Kloepfer 2003, p. 221; Rossi 2004, p. 325 (points 4 and 5).

[54] Schoch 2016, Einleitung para 53; Rossi 2004, p. 112 et seqq.

[55] Cf. Rossi 2004, p. 325 et seq. (points 2, 6 and 7).

[56] Rossi 2004, p. 334 (points 52, 53 and 49).

[57] Article 1 Sole paragraph, item 1 of the Brazilian Law N°12.527/2011.

[58] Zippelius, R. Teoría general del Estado. 5a ed. Cidade do México: Porrúa 2009, p. 179–180.

three branches of government supports this view. Furthermore, limiting the scope of the law to certain branches of government runs contrary to the idea of access to information as a human right, which implies that the duty to provide such should be shared by all public bodies."[59]

Pursuant to the Model Inter-American Law on Access to Information (Model Inter-American Law)[60] issued by the Organization of American States' (OAS), the duty to inform includes "private organizations that receive substantial public benefits or funding (directly or indirectly), or that provide public services or perform public functions, but only regarding disclosure of the public benefits or funding received or the public services and functions performed".[61] Even more comprehensively, the Model Law for Africa establishes that every person has an enforceable right to access information from "(a) a public body or relevant private body; and (b) a private body, where the information may assist in the exercise or protection of any right".[62]

## 3 The Interpretative Role of the Regional Human Rights Commissions and of the Human Rights Courts

On the international level the right of access to *generally accessible information* (Blanke, Chap. 3, Sect. 2.1.1) is expressly formulated in the Universal Declaration of Human Rights (Article 19), in the International Covenant on Civil and Political Rights (Article 19.2), in the EU Charter of Fundamental Rights (Article 42), in the Council of Europe Convention on Access to Official Documents (Article 2), and the African Charter on Human and Peoples' Rights (Article 9.1).

The I/A Court H. R. has extensively interpreted the constituent elements of Article 13.1 ACHR: "This right (to freedom of thought and expression) includes freedom to seek, receive, and impart information and ideas of all kinds [. . .]". The Court's broad interpretation was inspired by the "Declaration on Freedom of Expression", ratified by the Inter-American Commission on Human Rights at its 108th regular session in October 2000.[63] This broad interpretation of a concept that was originally merely a right to have access to generally accessible information in

---

[59]Mendel 2008, p. 143.

[60]AG/RES. 2607 (XL-O/10).

[61]Article 3 of the Model Inter-American Law.

[62]Article 12.1 of the Model Law on Access to Information for Africa. The concept of "relevant private body" is defined in Article 1 of this Model Law and follows an approach similar to Article 3 of the Model Inter-American Law (totally or partially controlled or financed by public funds; carrying out a statutory or public function or a statutory or public service).

[63]Principle 4 of this Declaration states: "Access to information held by the State is a fundamental right of every individual. States have the obligation to guarantee the full exercise of this right. This principle allows only exceptional limitations which must be previously established by law in case of a real and imminent danger that threatens national security in democratic societies."

the sense of freedom of information is an attempt to incorporate the principal doctrines on that fundamental right, which constitutes one of the essential foundations of a pluralist, democratic society as set forth in different international instruments. However, this approach can also be considered a reaction by judicial institutions entrusted with "competence with respect to matters relating to the fulfillment of the commitments made by the States [p]arties" to the Convention (Article 33 ACHR), to the deficiencies in the legislative, governmental and administrative branches in the Member States of the Convention. Such a right of access to information (in the sense of access to "official documents") derived from a broad interpretation of regional human rights instruments should be regarded as a tool to strengthen the position of the citizen vis-à-vis the public authorities, even if such right has not been explicitly codified in the corresponding conventions.

The European Court of Human Rights has not (yet) interpreted Article 10.1 (2) of the ECHR[64] in such an extensive way. According to the case-law of that Court, the requester, without referring to a special legal interest, cannot invoke a comprehensive right to access to official documents on the grounds of Article 10.1 (2) ECHR[65] (Blanke, Chap. 3, Sect. 2.2.2).

In connection with the global development in this subject area,[66] the I/A Court H. R., in its 2006 Judgment in the Case of *Claude Reyes et al. v. Chile*, recognised the existence of a right of access to official information under Article 13.1 ACHR, according to which the freedom of thought and expression includes the "freedom to seek, receive, and impart information and ideas [. . .]".[67] With that decision, the I/A Court H. R. became the first international tribunal to recognise that the right of access to public information is a fundamental human right.[68]

The statutes and case-law of Latin American and African countries have been greatly influenced by two publications systematising the case-law of their respective regional human rights courts: the 2010 Inter-American Model Law and the 2013 Model Law on Access to Information for Africa drafted by the African Commission on Human and Peoples' Rights.[69] In 2008, the OAS Inter-American Juridical Committee (IAJC) promulgated ten principles of the right of access to official information derived from the precedents of the I/A Court H. R. to serve as a

---

[64]"Everyone has the right to freedom of expression. This right shall include freedom to hold opinions and to receive and impart information and ideas without interference by public authority and regardless of frontiers. This article shall not prevent States from requiring the licensing of broadcasting, television or cinema enterprises." (Article 10.1 (2) ECHR).

[65]See Barreto 2010, p. 276.

[66]See Mendel 2007, p. 6.

[67]I/A Court H. R., *Case of Claude-Reyes et al. v. Chile* (Judgment of 19 September 2006), Series C No. 151.

[68]Cf. Inter-American Commission on Human Rights 2015, p. 22; see also Article 4.1 of the Mexican General Law on Transparency and Access to Public Information (2015): "The human right of access to information includes requesting, investigating, disseminating, seeking and receiving information."

[69]See footnote 9.

benchmark, based on the theory of fundamental rights, on the level of the relationship between the Inter-American System of Human Rights and the statutes and case-law of the 18 Latin American States of Iberian origin subject to the American Convention (Perlingeiro et al., Chap. 2, Sect. 1).[70]

On the other hand, it should be noted that in the vast majority of cases, the regional human rights defense organisations developed a special human rights convention *in reaction to* the developments within the Member States (Council of Europe) or interpreted the guarantees under their conventions to include "the right to receive information" (Article 9.1 of the African Charter) or "the right to freedom of thought and expression" (Article 13.1 of the American Convention), making it possible to defend the right of access to information without a formal amendment to the convention. This tendency could be called the "bottom-up impact on conventions", meaning that the convention no longer unilaterally controls the Member States and institutions of the convention; rather there is a reciprocal relationship resulting from adaptation of the conventions to the legal developments in "its" Member States—and thus to their social needs—through extensive interpretation of the existing guarantees.

## 4 The Principles of Democracy, Rule of Law and the Welfare State as the Legal Framework for the Right of Access to Information

### *4.1 The Principle of Democracy as a Driving Objective*

The principle of democracy is repeatedly invoked in scholarly writings and case-law as the "pillar" of freedom of information, although it is occasionally criticised as "ideologically charged".[71] The I/A Court H. R. sees a close relationship between democracy and freedom of expression: "Freedom of expression is a cornerstone upon which the very existence of a democratic society rests. It is indispensable for the formation of public opinion. It is also a *conditio sine qua non* for the development of political parties, trade unions, scientific and cultural societies and, in general, those who wish to influence the public. It represents, in short, the means that enable the community, when exercising its options, to be sufficiently informed. Consequently, it can be said that a society that is not well informed is not a society

[70] Argentina, Bolívia, Brasil, Chile, Colômbia, Costa Rica, El Salvador, Equador, Guatemala, Honduras, México, Nicaragua, Panama, Paraguay, Peru, Dominican Republic, Uruguay and Venezuela.

[71] Cf. Rossi 2015, p. 48 et seqq., 57.

that is truly free".[72] Indeed, in a representative and participative democracy, it is easy to understand that the right to vote cannot be exercised fully without access to information and knowledge of the facts relevant to the political process of direct decision-making, as in a popular referendum or the choice of parliamentary representatives. Nevertheless, no individual right to claim to access to official information may be derived directly from the principle of democracy but must be grounded in a legal formulation under constitutional and/or statutory law.

### 4.1.1 Modification of the Principle of Democracy

In any case, resorting to the democratic principle derived from the Transatlantic constitutional tradition raises a whole series of questions regarding to the right of access to documents as "democracy" is an objective of the state that is open to multiple interpretations and often depends on the context. Transparency laws intended to achieve "democratisation" of government institutions and national authorities subject to such laws have a twofold effect. Firstly, "direct" representative democracy is replaced by an indirect relationship between "information citizens" and the state bodies subject to the resulting disclosure obligations. Secondly, in countries which guarantee freedom of information, the legitimation of state authority that arises from the People, which makes the state institutions guaranteeing freedom of information accountable to that People, is replaced by the larger circle of individuals entitled to receive information, i.e., the population residing in national territory (Blanke, Chap. 3, Sects. 2.2.1 and 3.2.1), without changing the concept of "People of the Nation" ("We the People [. . .]", 1788[73]) in the national constitution.[74]

In consequence, the state bodies subject to the transparency laws may be subject to oversight by individuals entitled to receive information (Sect. 2.3), but those state bodies (namely the public authorities) are accountable to only to such individuals as are entitled to information according to the constitutional definition of the "People of the Nation". It is true that the correlation between supervision and accountability is somewhat weakened as a result, but the "accountability" of the state institutions in the context of the right of access to information is still rather vaguely defined. At least, the penalties for a breach of obligations under the system of transparency laws tend to be connected with possession of the right of access to information rather than on belonging to a state that can be sued for damages for infringement of the

[72]Inter-American Commission on Human Rights, *Case of Ricardo Canese v. Paraguay* (Judgment of 31 August 2004), Série C N° 111, para 82.

Inter-American Commission on Human Rights, *Case of Herrera Ulloa v. Costa Rica* (Judgment of 2 July 2004), Série C N° 107, para 112.es.

Inter-American Commission on Human Rights. Parecer Consultivo OC-5/85 de 13 de novembro de 1985. Série A N° 5. Para 70.

[73]Cf. also Article 14 of the Brazilian Constitution: "The *sovereignty of the people* shall be exercised by universal suffrage and by the direct and secret voting" (emphasis added).

[74]Rossi 2004, p. 289 et seqq., 334 (points 52, 53).

obligations under the national right of access to information legislation (Huerta Ochoa, Chap. 19, Sect. 3).[75]

Questions are also raised by possible shifts in the rights of oversight in parliamentary systems of government as a result of the right of access to documents. In the parliamentary system of the Federal Republic of Germany, the *Informationsfreiheitsgesetz* (Federal Freedom of Information Act) acknowledges a "shift in accountability" for freedom of information only insofar as the branch of government in question (legislative, executive or judiciary) performs administrative tasks (Scherzberg and Solka, Chap. 7, Sect. 2.1). As a consequence of freedom of information, the Parliament has lost its role as the exclusive state body accountable to the People for the actions of the administrative authorities while at the same time maintaining its comprehensive powers of scrutiny and supervision over those same authorities. If the fundamental-rights bearers of freedom-of-information ("beneficiaries") frequently seek to enforce their rights, parliamentary supervision of the administrative authorities will involve increasing cooperation with the People. Such cooperation between the People and Parliament may be viewed as a positive feedback loop. Anyhow, because public-opinion-shaping in the media does not follow the same rules as parliamentary decision-making, the media coverage of the citizens' requests for government documents may end up changing the form and content of parliamentary supervision, *indirectly* weakening the degree of freedom inherent in the representative's mandate. Citizen oversight of state bodies *may* increase citizen participation in political decision-making, depending on the number and frequency of requests for access to official documents. As the role played by Parliament loses importance, so does the law, in the sense of parliamentary legislation. Citizen oversight and parliamentary control therefore influence one another (Sect. 4.2.2).

Naturally, such effects are intended from the outset by the drafters of transparency laws. Nevertheless, their consequences on a democratic constitutional state of the representative type should be clearly specified, especially as public participation in the form of oversight by certain individuals out of the total population cannot articulate all the interests of society equally and give them all the same degree of consideration. Even in the case of political decision-making, the power rooted in participative democracy is the power exercised by the People, not by an individual. Transparency laws cannot make up for the loss of importance of parliamentary legitimation, because such legislation has no legitimating effects but only contributes to activating fundamental rights.[76]

---

[75]Cf. for example the relevant provisions on sanctions of the Mexican "Ley General de Transparencia y Acceso a la Información Pública" (Articles 201–216), *Diario Oficial* of the Mexican Federation of 4.5.2016 and of the "Ley Federal de Transparencia y Acceso a la Información Pública" (Articles 174–206), *Diario Oficial* of the Mexican Federation of 9.5.2016.

[76]Rossi 2004, p. 297 et seqq., 335 (point 61).

### 4.1.2 The Institutionally Comprehensive Approach to the Right of Access to Information

Are there reasons to treat legislative or judicial bodies any differently than executive agencies with respect to disclosure obligations? One crucial argument against imposing uniform rules of disclosure on all three branches of government is that it would undermine the principle of separation of powers. For this reason, the U.S. legislation on access to information does not apply to the legislative or judicial branches of the U.S. government. However, as the Framers of the U.S. Constitution intended the branches of government to be co-equal and strong but not totally separate ("checks and balances"), the U.S. model of separation of governmental powers provides a set of formal and informal methods that the branches can use to provide information to one another, while anticipating conflicts that may arise when one branch refuses to disclose requested information to another. These conflicts are neither unexpected nor necessarily destructive. Although the U.S. branches of government generally cooperate to a considerable extent in sharing information and records, such conflicts still arise on occasion.[77]

In the relationship between the U.S. Congress and the executive branch, Congress hearings (confirmation hearings, legislative hearings, oversight hearings—the latter to monitor executive departments' and agencies' activities—and investigative hearings), as well as studies on current affairs, and (mandated) reports, for example, about specific issues (such as those addressed to the congressional Committees on Intelligence, e.g., on covered actions) or as periodic reports in the various policy areas, are the most important instruments for Congress oversight inquiry. This authority also includes congressional requests for confidential executive branch information. The courts have recognized that the general legislative interest gives Congress investigatory authority.[78]

If it is established that Congress has a legitimate legislative purpose for its oversight inquiry, the executive branch's interest in keeping the information confidential must be assessed. This subject is usually discussed in terms of "executive privilege". It is a necessary corollary of the executive function vested in the President by Article II of the U.S. Constitution. There are at least three generally-recognized components of executive privilege: state secrets, law enforcement, and deliberative process.[79]

[77]Ginsberg, W. & Greene, M. (2016), Access to Government Information in the United States: A Primer. Congressional Research Service, available at: http://www.fas.org/sgp/crs/secrecy/97-71.pdf.

[78]U.S. Supreme Court, McGrain v. Daugherty, 273 U.S. 135, 160 (1927).

[79]Barr (1989), p. 153 et seqq.; cf. also the survey in Fisher (2001).

#### 4.1.2.1 The Case-Law of the German Federal Constitutional Court on Parliamentary Requests for Information

The latest German Federal Constitutional Court case-law (in the leading Cases on "secret prisons",[80] and the "collection, storage and dissemination of information about Bundestag representatives by the German Federal Intelligence Agency"[81]) does not acknowledge rules allowing the branches of government to adopt certain procedures justifying denial of disclosure of information to the Bundestag. In the German legal system, in principle, the processes of internal governmental decision-making are subject to disclosure to the Bundestag, and any denials of such disclosure require extensive statements of the grounds and justifications.[82] In the Case of the "Investigation Committee of the German *Bundestag* on NSA activities", the German Constitutional Court acknowledged, however, valid reasons for withholding information from a subcommittee of the *Bundestag* based on the principle of separation of powers. Also in its Judgment of 13 June 2017 the Constitutional Court derived from the right to vote (Article 38.1, second sentence) in conjunction with the principle of people's sovereignty (Article 20.2, second sentence of the Basic Law) a right to ask questions and a right to information of the German Parliament, its political groups and the members of Parliament vis-à-vis the Federal Government to which corresponds, in principle, an obligation of the government to answer. This also applies to questions regarding the activity of intelligence services. But, in spite of Parliament's considerable interest in information in this area, the Federal Government can generally rely on a threat to the public welfare and to the basic rights of the persons acting under covert identity.[83]

These limitations of the general principle of disclosure in the relationship between the German Federal Government and the Bundestag seem to be based on similar grounds as the restrictions on disclosure between the branches of government in the U.S. model of separation of governmental powers. In the view of the German Constitutional Court, requests for information in parliamentary procedure do not have to be granted by the Federal Government as a general rule, if such information might allow an impact ("co-determination") of third parties on decisions for which the Federal Government is the sole competent authority. "That risk regularly occurs in the case of leaks of information about the preparation of governmental decisions before the final decision has been issued [. . .]. According to that principle, Parliament's powers of scrutiny are generally limited to governmental actions that have already been completed, without the power to interfere with ongoing negotiations and decision-making processes [. . .]. Even in the case of

[80]German Federal Constitutional Court (Bundesverfassungsgericht), 2 BvE 3/07 (Judgment of 17 June 2009), BVerfGE 124, 78.

[81]German Federal Constitutional Court (Bundesverfassungsgericht), 2 BvE 5/06 (Judgment of 1 July 2009). BVerfGE 124, 16.

[82]Cf. Leutheusser-Schnarrenberger 2015, p. 19 et seqq.; German Federal Constitutional Court (Bundesverfassungsgericht) 2 BvE 2/11 (Judgment of 7 November 2017) para 253.

[83]German Federal Constitutional Court (Bundesverfassungsgericht), 2 BvE 1/15 (Judgment of 13 June 2017), para 84 et seqq., 89 et seqq.

completed actions, the Federal Government does not always have the duty to disclose facts at the core of the Government's responsibilities which require secrecy."[84]

In the Court's opinion, an excessively broad parliamentary right to information, even if related to information about completed actions, would impair the Federal Government's ability to act independently as guaranteed by the separation of powers, especially because such premature parliamentary interference would prevent effective governmental decision-making.[85] In light of this judicial precedent, to prevent interference with the core of the Government's responsibilities through "co-determination by third parties", i.e., by members of Parliament or by the officials of the judicial branch, German constitutional law, too, must recognise the principle of separation of powers as an argument for the legislator to restrict the citizen's right of access to information to the administrative functions of public authorities. In any case, the different legal regimes governing the Parliament's powers of scrutiny on the one hand and, on the other, the freedom of information legislation, which establishes a civil right of access to public information, turn out to be intertwined in view of the constitutionally required limits and exemptions.[86]

The Constitutional Court, in its Judgment of 7 November 2017, has given contours to the principle of separation of powers that it deeems to be "the reason and the limitation of an information request of the German Parliament vis-à-vis Government".[87] According to this interpretation, the principle of separation of powers, especially in view of the German Federal Government's strong position and resulting in particular from Parliament's inability to intervene directly in the field of practical initiative and implementation of legislation, requires an interpretation of the Basic Law that parliamentary scrutiny can actually take effect. Without sharing in the Government's knowledge, Parliament cannot exercise its powers of scrutiny vis-à-vis the Government. Therefore, the parliamentary interest in information is particularly important as far as the detection of possible legal violations and similar irregularities within Government and administration is concerned. The responsibility of the Government vis-à-vis Parliament and people necessarily presupposes a core area of executive self-responsibility, which includes an area of initiative, consultation and action. Information which falls within that area is strictly be handled confidential by the executive branch of government. Against this backdrop, the powers of scrutiny of the Bundestag basically only cover completed actions; they do not contain the right to intervene in ongoing negotiations and decision-making preparations. Even in completed actions cases are possible in which the Government is not obliged to disclose secrets which fall

---

[84]German Federal Constitutional Court (Bundesverfassungsgericht), 2 BvE 2/15 (Judgment of 13 October 2016), para 117, 120 et seq., http://www.bundesverfassungsgericht.de/SharedDocs/Entscheidungen/DE/2016/10/es20161013_2bve000215.html (Accessed on 9 May 2017).

[85]German Federal Constitutional Court (Bundesverfassungsgericht), 2 BvE 2/15 (Judgment of 13 October 2016), para 121, http://www.bundesverfassungsgericht.de/SharedDocs/Entscheidungen/DE/2016/10/es20161013_2bve000215.html (Accessed on 9 May 2017).

[86]For more details Chap. 3, Sect. 3.2.2

[87]German Federal Constitutional Court (Bundesverfassungsgericht), 2 BvE 2/11 (Judgment of 7 November 2017) para 195 et seqq., 211 et seqq., 228

within the core area of executive self-responsibility. The limits of the parliamentary request for information can only be established in relation to completed actions, taking into account the particular circumstances.[88]

Accordingly, as an expression of the democratic responsibility of the Government vis-à-vis Parliament, parliamentary information requests can only be invoked in matters falling within the German Federal Government's sphere of responsibility. As explicitly decided in this Judgment, the responsibility of the Government in the context of democratic legitimacy covers also all the activities of private law enterprises which are entirely or predominantly owned by the Federal Government. Insofar, the responsibility of the Government is not limited to its rights of participation and control, which are granted in the legal statute of the state-owned enterprise.[89] Resuming partially its former rulings, the Court has derived from the principle of separation of powers the following legal specifications regarding the treatment of information requests of the members of the Bundestag:[90]

- Information regarding the preparation of government decisions which provide insight into the process of the formation of political objectives are the worthier of protection the closer they stand to the decision of the Government.[91]
- Furthermore, the parliamentarians' right to ask questions and the Government's obligation to answer can be limited by the obligation of the branches of government to respect the fundamental rights, according to Article 1.3 of the Basic Law.[92]
- If public authorities disclose trade or business secrets or require the disclosure of those secrets, the scope of protection of the freedom of vocational choice and the freedom of practicing an occupation (Article 12.1 Basic Law) is affected.[93] If a Government measure, which has an impact on competition, hinders a legal entity in its professional occupation, this restricts the right set up in Article 12.1 of the Basic Law.[94]
- The fundamental right to informational self-determination guarantees the authority of the individual to decide in principle independently when and within what limits real-world personal fact situations may be revealed. In particular, the right grants those who hold it protection against unlimited collection, storage, use or transmission of data relating to them which are individualized or can be individualized. For instance, this right is concerned when the Government provides information to Parliament about incomes of employees of a bank and if these persons are "ascertainable" or "identifiable".[95]

---

[88]German Federal Constitutional Court (Bundesverfassungsgericht), 2 BvE 2/11 (Judgment of 7 November 2017) para 229 et seqq.

[89]German Federal Constitutional Court (Bundesverfassungsgericht), 2 BvE 2/11 (Judgment of 7 November 2017) para 195 et seqq., 214, 216 et seqq.

[90]German Federal Constitutional Court (Bundesverfassungsgericht), 2 BvE 2/11 (Judgment of 7 November 2017) para 214 et seqq.

[91]German Federal Constitutional Court (Bundesverfassungsgericht), 2 BvE 2/11 (Judgment of 7 November 2017) para 232.

[92]German Federal Constitutional Court (Bundesverfassungsgericht), 2 BvE 2/11 (Judgment of 7 November 2017) para 233

[93]German Federal Constitutional Court (Bundesverfassungsgericht), 2 BvE 2/11 (Judgment of 7 November 2017) para 234.

[94]German Federal Constitutional Court (Bundesverfassungsgericht), 2 BvE 2/11 (Judgment of 7 November 2017) para 235.

[95]German Federal Constitutional Court (Bundesverfassungsgericht), 2 BvE 2/11 (Judgment of 7 November 2017) para 236.

- The Parliament's constitutional right to address questions to the Government and its right to information as well as the resulting obligation of the Government to provide the required information can be presumed as "a sufficient basis for an interference in fundamental rights caused by the provision of information". According to the case-law of the Constitutional Court, the attribution of competences in principle implies the right of the Government to inform the Parliament. There is no need for further regulation.[96] If, however, the legislator, by means of ordinary legislation, has outlined a way to solve the conflict between the parliamentary right to ask questions and the right of information of Parliament and its members on the one hand, and, on the other, the protection of fundamental rights of enterprises, its margin of assessment and discretion has to be taken into account when weighing the different interests. In the event that the legislator otherwise leaves the decision to the bodies that specifically implement or rule on the law, their acts of intervention have to be examined in accordance with the constitution if the underlying assumptions and rules of weighing, as well as the weighing of interests in the concrete case, have met the constitutional requirements. This also means that it has to be examined if these bodies have respected the margin of assessment which is thereby left to the decision-makers and if they have arrived at a "practical concordance" in the concrete conflict.[97]
- A further limit on the Bundestag's entitlement to information is set by the welfare of the Federation or a Land ("welfare of the state"), which could be put at risk if information requiring confidentiality became public.[98] The question of the constitutional limits to the parliamentary right to ask questions and to investigate, needs to be answered in light of its relevance within the overall structure of the Constitution. This also applies to the interpretation and application of the concept of endangerment of the welfare of the state. In a parliamentary government system as provided for in the Basic Law, the welfare of the state is not placed in the hands of the Federal Government alone, but in the hands of both the Bundestag and the Federal Government. Thus, as a rule, the Federal Government cannot invoke the welfare of the state vis-à-vis the Bundestag in cases in which both entities have taken effective measures against the disclosure of official secrets.[99]
- Finally, the parliamentary right to information is subject to reasonableness. All information that are at the Government's disposal or that can be obtained with reasonable effort, have to be disclosed. As to the parliamentary right to information regarding the political significance of issues from long ago and which fall within the sphere of responsibility of former Governments, the incumbent Federal Government has the duty to reconstruct the circumstances of a case within a reasonable extent.[100]
- The information available to the German Federal Government are not only limited to the totality of the existing documents but also include the personal, undocumented knowledge of the acting persons. The Government may, in the individual case, invoke the unreasonableness of a timely response due to a difficult accessibility or analysis of

[96]German Federal Constitutional Court (Bundesverfassungsgericht), 2 BvE 2/11 (Judgment of 7 November 2017) para 244.

[97]German Federal Constitutional Court (Bundesverfassungsgericht), 2 BvE 2/11 (Judgment of 7 November 2017) para 245.

[98]German Federal Constitutional Court (Bundesverfassungsgericht), 2 BvE 2/11 (Judgment of 7 November 2017) para 246.

[99]German Federal Constitutional Court (Bundesverfassungsgericht), 2 BvE 2/11 (Judgment of 7 November 2017) para 247.

[100]German Federal Constitutional Court (Bundesverfassungsgericht), 2 BvE 2/11 (Judgment of 7 November 2017) para 249.

sources. However, these circumstances do not justify a general restriction of its obligation to provide information to the Bundestag regarding documented issues.[101]

This recent jurisprudence is one of the several approaches which the Federal Constitutional Court has made within its case-law in order to strengthen Parliament's position vis-à-vis the Federal Government. It is a reaction to a development in the "system of government", which also as a result of globalization and Europeanization of originally national affairs has led to a preponderance of the executive branch and thus to a de-parliamentarization in its relationship with the legislators.[102] In a representative democracy, the right of Parliament to be informed by the executive branch is *at least* a necessary complementary institution of control, if the representatives in Parliaments shall be able to fulfill the principal task assigned to them in all (European) representative constitutions, that is to say to represent the entire people in political independence, thus without being bound by orders or instructions (Article 38.1 of the German Basic Law), and in so doing to decide in the public interest (Sect. 4.1.1). This parliamentary right, however, is not granted without limits either.

#### 4.1.2.2 Can Members of Parliament in Their Official Capacity Claim a Right of Access to Information?

In the context of the parliamentary request for information, the question arises whether, in addition to Parliament's powers of scrutiny and its right to be informed by government, parliamentarians or parliamentary groups can claim access on the basis of the right of access to information, which is held by or on behalf of the government. German case-law and German scholars have partly affirmed such right.[103] In this respect, it is assumed that the concept of government, spelt out in the German transparency legislation, also covers government activity.[104] Contrary to this view, it must be emphasised that the members of Parliament are only entitled to specific parliamentary control rights vis-à-vis the government. In contrast to the legislation in some German *Länder*, the German Federal legislation grants the right of access to the government-held files only to a parliamentary committee of inquiry and the Committee on Petitions. Even in that case it is not a right of the individual deputy.

The shift from an information, made available by the German Federal Government after receiving a parliamentary question, to the individual right of a deputy to

[101]German Federal Constitutional Court (Bundesverfassungsgericht), 2 BvE 2/11 (Judgment of 7 November 2017) para 250.

[102]Bauer 2005, p. 9; Sommermann 2005, p. 216 et seq., also sees parliamentary countermovements in some Member States of the EU; for the "increasingly compound and accumulated 'order' of executive power in contemporary Europe"; see also Curtin 2014, p. 206 et seqq.

[103]Schoch (2016), § 1 para 82 et seq.; similarly, with regard to parliamentary groups, the Higher Administrative Court of Munich, Judgment of 22 April 2017, 2 BV 15.799, NVwZ 2016, p. 1107; with a critical view Waldhoff, JuS 2017, p. 284 et seqq.

[104]German Federal Administrative Court, Judgment of 3 November 2011, *Access to information*, 7 C 3.11, BVerwGE 141, p. 122 et seqq.

access the files held by the Federal Government, marks a qualitative leap which requires explicit legal authorization.[105] This raises the question as to whether it can be constitutionally intended for the citizen or, alternatively, the deputy as a private individual, to have a more comprehensive right of access to information than the deputy by virtue of his political mandate. This is a largely unresolved issue which has not yet been discussed in the literature on German constitutional law.[106]

#### 4.1.2.3 Exercising the Right of Access to Information Against all Three Branches of Government

In the everyday reality of countries whose legal systems recognise a civil right of access to information exercisable against all three branches of government, the right of access to information held by the legislative and judicial branches and other non-administrative authorities mainly serves the purpose of granting citizens access to information that is "secondary", that is to say to factors influencing an action or decision taken by the relevant institutions (e.g., questions of whether the drafting of an amendment was influenced by corporate lobbying, or how budget allocations were used within a branch of government or agency or court or division of a court etc.). Such information generally concerns matters that may have a past or present impact on the action or decision by the institution from which the citizen is requesting the information but does not *directly* refer to the subject matter/core of the decision, which often is already public knowledge. This appears to differ from requests to administrative authorities, which frequently, but not without exception concern information about an upcoming or past decision affecting the citizens requesting the information, and thus having at least a potential direct impact on the individual's personal situation. It is even more difficult to determine empirically the underlying motive of a request submitted not only to "quasi-public" organisations (private entities exercising public functions) but also to merely private entities, which are required to respond to requests for access to information under the laws of South Africa, for example (Sect. 2.3 and Blanke, Chap. 3, Sect. 2.2.2). Regarding the coverage not only of public but also of private bodies, the right of access to information in the South African legislation is considered to be a vehicle to supplement market and political mechanisms and to achieve by this means public policy goals.[107]

A distinction, at least in degree, may be drawn in the exercise of the right to access to government-held information about an administrative act or decision, based on the potential impact that the administrative matter may have on the requesting party. It is certainly the case that many countries, especially mature democracies, have traditions of transparency concerning the conduct of legislative and judicial proceedings. In the case of judicial authorities, however, only trials and the delivery of judgments are

[105]Klein, in Maunz and Dürig (2014), Article 43 para 118; Schwanengel (2018), Teil C under "Die Kontrollinstrumente".

[106]Wissenschaftliche Dienste des Deutschen Bundestages, 2015, WD 3 - 3000 - 293/15.

[107]Klaaren, Currie & Smith 2000, p. 30.

required to be public but not the processes of selection, promotion or disciplining of judges. Another oft-criticised point is that the rules of judicial transparency have the sole aim of ensuring fair trials without taking wider considerations of the public interest into account. Similarly, the public may be allowed to attend their sessions and examine the minutes of legislative bodies, but the documents and reports on which national legislators base their decisions are not always available for inspection.

A study by the Argentinian Association for Civil Rights "on various good practices and experiences from different Latin American countries related to access to information and transparency of the State" comes to the conclusion that "the Judiciary – as a branch of government – should not only disseminate the information it generates in the course of its daily proceedings but also play a prominent role in effective enforcement of the right of access to such information. With that in mind, judges should respect the same standards in terms of access to information as the other branches of government. Although there has been some resistance or lack of interest on the part of judicial institutions in accepting said standards, there is a broad consensus that the same requirements apply to the courts as to the public administrative authorities, so that courts should be required to disclose information about their routine administrative work, as well as their adjudicative functions. The same is true with regards to transparency, since the Judiciary has to comply with the same requirements as other state bodies."[108] Argentinian legislators have also recognised that all three branches of government are subject to the obligation to comply with the information access rights under the Argentinian Law 27275/2016 (Article 7 points a to c).

### 4.1.3 A Culture of Transparency with No Alternative?

In terms of legal policy, the demands for access to the documents of all three branches of government focus on transparency as a requirement of publicness, democracy and an "effective" civil society. At first glance, there seems to be no room for secrecy in the contemporary ideal of democracy. Immanuel Kant already claimed that only pure reason must be capable of withstanding the test of free and open scrutiny. For Kant, a government's legality and legitimacy are inseparably bound with the principle of "publicness". He described the "transcendental formula of public law" as follows: "All actions affecting the right of other human beings are wrong if their maxim is not compatible with their being made public."[109] From this intellectual heritage of the Enlightenment era, publicness developed from a necessary criterion of proper governance to a leitmotif of political action, which can initially be achieved through the

---

[108] Álvaro Herrero & Gaspar López (2010), *Access to Information and Transparency in the Judiciary –A Guide to Good Practices from Latin America* (first published in Spanish in 2009), available at http://siteresources.worldbank.org/WBI/Resources/213798-1259011531325/6598384-1268250334206/Transparency_Judiciary.pdf (Accessed on 20 October 2016).

[109] Kant, I. (1795). *Zum ewigen Frieden. Ein philosophischer Entwurf.* Königsberg: F. Nikolovius (Ed.), translated in Reiss 1991, p. 126: "Alle auf das Recht anderer Menschen bezogenen Handlungen, deren Maxime sich nicht mit der Publizität verträgt, sind unrecht." Reiss, however, translates "Recht" with the plural form "rights".

technical process of making *public* (publication, publicising or publishing) and thus *transparent*. Yet, for centuries, the administrative authorities, as servants of the constitutional monarchy, remained bound by the principle of secrecy (*Arkantradition*). The call for publicness, transparency and "Open Data" is growing ever louder as a result of the growing possibilities offered by information technology ("WikiLeaks" and "whistleblowing"). The state is no longer allowed to withhold information on the grounds of confidentiality and secrecy (*disciplina arcani*) without providing special statements of justifications and reasons.[110] Although the secrecy of state actions was once the general rule and public disclosure was the exception, in the future public disclosure will become the rule and secrecy will be the exception[111]: "All the information in the possession or safekeeping or under the control of the authority subject to the law shall be accessible to all persons [. . .]"—according to the paradigmatic directive of the Argentinian legislators.[112] However, parliamentary and congressional committees and subcommittees are deliberating on bills requiring public access to decision-making (once in plenary) in processes which are (still) generally conducted behind closed doors, including the deliberations of judges in preparation for the final judgment, which are generally conducted *in camera*.[113]

Whether or not transparency will be good for democracy is still controversial. Certain transparency projects and open data websites are influenced by a vision of social controllability that is not without its opponents. In his polemical article "Against Transparency", Harvard Law Professor Lawrence Lessig advances arguments, including on ethical grounds, against the naïve expectation that Open Data und Open Governance will serve as a panacea while ignoring the indirect consequences of a "naked transparency movement": "[. . .] will the effect of these projects – at least on their own, unqualified or unrestrained by other considerations – really be for the good? Do we really want the world that they righteously envisage?"[114] Moreover, the participants in communication first need to learn to deal with new flows of communication.[115] The decision about what should be made transparent is a decision about what should be negotiated in the public arena. Decisions about transparency are about power, too.

### 4.2 The Right of Access to Information as a Vehicle for the Rule of Law

The guarantees of constitutional state governed by the rule of law (*Rechtsstaat*) run deeper than those of the principle of democracy. The subprinciples of the

[110]O'Regan 2000, p. 13 et seq.

[111]Cf. Leutheusser-Schnarrenberger 2015, p. 25.

[112]Article 1, principle 2 ("Transparency and maximum dissemination") of the Argentinian Law 27275/2016 on the "Right of Access to Public Information".

[113]Schulzki Haddouti 2012, p. 187 et seqq.

[114]Lessig 2009.

[115]Schulzki Haddouti 2012, p. 198 et seq.

constitutional state may be viewed as guidelines for the objectives of the codification and designing of the right of access to information. Such objectives include, in particular, protection of the citizen and imposing legal boundaries and limits on the state's exercise of power. Subjection of all of the state's actions to the rule of law is a key component of the principle of the constitutional state. The legislature is, therefore, bound by the "constitutional order" (Article 20.3 of the German Basic Law) and all decisions that are deemed essential according to the Constitutional Court's "theory of materiality" (*Wesentlichkeitstheorie*) are reserved for Parliament.[116] According to that theory, material decisions must be laid down by the legislature rather than decided by the executive. It is held to be "essential" (material) whenever it affects a fundamental right and, therefore, needs a parliamentary decision in form of a formal law which conveys the legitimation to limit the scope of a fundamental right.

### 4.2.1 Distinguishing Procedural Rights to Information from the Right of Access to Information

The administrative authorities are empowered to make decisions in certain cases within the limits of the legality principle, if and only if no essential decision by Parliament is required. The administrative authorities are therefore subject to principles of the primacy of the law and the principle of legality, which together form the principle of administrative legality.[117] Hence, the administrative authorities are required to respect and implement the laws governing administrative proceedings, including provisions on the individual's right of access to information, because such proceedings result in government decisions affecting individual citizens and, for this reason, require a legal framework guaranteeing a fair and objective procedure. The administrative authorities are bound to respect all fundamental rights, including the obligations assumed by the state through ratification of a human rights convention.

Not least of all, administrative proceedings have an independent function of judicial protection and must, therefore, allow citizens to defend their individual rights against a potentially detrimental administrative decision (Sect. 6.6). Individuals whose fundamental rights are at issue must be given an opportunity to assert their substantive rights and claims in the administrative proceedings, especially in the case of large, complex proceedings. The principle of the constitutional state governed by the rule of law guarantees the protection of individual rights, which necessarily includes the right to a fair hearing.[118] The right to a fair hearing is therefore a right of participation guaranteed by both the principle of the rule of

[116]In its "Kalkar I" Judgment, the German Federal Constitutional Court, BVerfGE (Fed. Const. Ct. Judgments) 49, 89 (Judgment of 8 August 1978)) expressed the notion that in the German system of separation of powers fundamental and essential decisions must be taken by the legislators.

[117]Cf. also regarding the following Kugelmann 2001, p. 35 et seqq.

[118]German Federal Administrative Court (Bundesverwaltungsgericht), BVerwGE 74, 109 (Judgment of 21.03.1986) p. 112.

law and democratic theory, but only the latter aims at conveyance of legitimacy (Sect. 4.1.1).[119]

Another consequence of the principle of the rule of law is the right to inspect documents for the purpose of legal defense.[120] The right to information assists citizens in asserting their substantive legal positions in the administrative proceeding. The objective may also consist in expanding one's knowledge of the facts, however, especially in the case of rights to substantive information.[121] Beyond the administrative proceeding, rights to information are important to allow citizens to protect themselves from abuse by the administrative authorities. Especially relevant in such cases are the constitutionally guaranteed individual rights of access to information (Galetta, Chap. 8, Sect. 3.1).

With respect to the public administrative authorities, the principle of the rule of law, therefore, creates a normative basis for rights of access to information, due process of law and citizen participation, The scope of such rights depends on whether an individual is entitled to access information in a personal capacity and, if so, in what form. It is the principle of the rule of law, not the principle of democracy, that requires citizens to have at least certain minimum legal guarantees to obtain access to relevant records in the realm of the administrative authorities in course of an administrative proceeding.[122] According to the case-law on Sections 13.2,[123] 28[124] and 29[125] of the German Federal Administrative Procedure Act (APA) such is

---

[119]Cf. for this distinction Schmidt-Aßmann 1991, p. 329 et seqq.

[120]Kallenhoff in Stelkens et al. (2018), Article 28 para 2.

[121]Kugelmann 2001, p. 37.

[122]Sobota 1997, p. 503.

[123]Sec. 13.2 of the Federal Administrative Procedure Act reads as follows: "The authority may ex officio or upon request involve as participants those whose legal interests may be affected by the result of proceedings. Where such result has a legal effect for a third party, the latter may upon request be involved in the proceedings as a participant. If the authority is aware of such third parties, it shall inform them that proceedings have commenced."

[124]Sec. 28 of the Federal Administrative Procedure Act reads as follows: "(1) Before an administrative act affecting the rights of a participant may be executed, the latter must be given the opportunity of commenting on the facts relevant to the decision.

(2) This hearing may be omitted when not required by the circumstances of an individual case and in particular when:

1. an immediate decision appears necessary in the public interest or because of the risk involved in delay;

2. the hearing would jeopardise the observance of a time limit vital to the decision;

3. the intent is not to diverge, to his disadvantage, from the actual statements made by a participant in an application or statement;

4. the authority wishes to issue a general order or similar administrative acts in considerable numbers or administrative acts using automatic equipment;

5. measures of administrative enforcement are to be taken.

(3) A hearing shall not be granted when this is grossly against the public interest."

[125]Sec. 29 of the Federal Administrative Procedure Act reads as follows: "(1) The authority shall allow participants to inspect the documents connected with the proceedings where knowledge of their contents is necessary in order to assert or defend their legal interests. Until administrative

the case only to the extent that such rights are necessary for the individual's judicial protection.[126] In a nutshell, the right of access to information and the right to inspect documents (e.g., Sec. 29 APA) differ in that the participant of an administrative procedure is entitled to inspect the documents which refer to the procedure. In contrast, the right to access to information is granted in a general way to all citizens who can request such access without a particular reason (especially, outside of the context of an administrative procedure), but always on their own initiative.

### 4.2.2 Modifications of the Constitutional System

A constitutional state governed by the rule of law is characterised by a government that is predictable, overseeable and respects the division of powers, and those qualities seem to be strengthened by general freedom of access to information. Upon closer analysis, however, indirect consequences have been noted that may lead to weakening certain aspects of that general rule, too. Modifications of the democratic system (Sect. 4.1.1) may have repercussions on the constitutional system. With the weakening of Parliament, the importance and controllability of parliamentary legislation are reduced because the administrative authorities are no longer exclusively accountable to Parliament, but at the same time placed in a direct relationship with the people. Moreover, individuals (persons of the general population) may assert rights of access to information in pursuit of a variety of individual interests that sometimes oppose or conflict with another. For example, an administrative authority's behaviour in dealing with freedom of information may be monitored and analysed from the perspectives of efficiency, of compliance with the principle of inclusion, or of equal treatment of the disabled.

Non-disclosure of records to the general public may also be understood as a means of protecting impartiality and maintaining non-partisan distance and efficiency.[127] This is not meant as an argument against the accessibility of records, but rather to illustrate the result of a general right of access to official information from the perspective of the rule of law. An administrative authority that is accountable not

proceedings have been concluded, the foregoing sentence shall not apply to draft decisions and work directly connected with their preparation. Where participants are represented as provided under Sections 17 and 18, only the representatives shall be entitled to inspect documents.

(2) The authority shall not be obliged to allow the inspection of documents where this would interfere with the orderly performance of the authority's tasks, where knowledge of the contents of the documents would be to the disadvantage of the country as a whole or of one of the *Länder*, or where proceedings must be kept secret by law or by their very nature, i.e., in the rightful interests of participants or of third parties.

(3) Inspection of documents shall take place in the offices of the record-keeping authority. In individual cases, documents may also be inspected at the offices of another authority or of the diplomatic or consular representatives of the Federal Republic of Germany abroad. The authority keeping the records may make further exceptions."

[126]Cf. for ex. Kugelmann 2001, p. 37 with numerous references in footnote 39.

[127]Masing 2003, p. 385.

only to Parliament but also to the people as a result of transparency laws might use the resulting lines of communication with the people to reach a decision favorable to the authority's own interests without violating the statutory limits. Yet there is always a risk that the administrative authorities will pursue specific interests to the detriment of the general public interest expressed in the relevant statutes. The constitutional obligation for the executive powers to respect law and justice (Article 20.3 of the German Basic Law;[128] Article 37, first sentence—main clause—of the Brazilian Constitution[129]) is not completely suspended as a result, but it may be comparatively weakened by transparency laws in an indirect manner in the long run (not by a single administrative proceeding or decision). This indirect impact, which is non-negligible in case of frequent exercise of the right to access to official records, must be considered, in particular, for the *standard* that the administrative authorities develop and apply when exercising the margin of appreciation (discretion) granted to them by the legislators. Nor should this indirect influence be overlooked in cases in which legislators intended to ensure not only the legality but also the appropriateness of administrative actions: if private interests are allowed to achieve supremacy as a result of transparency laws, the legal decision-making procedures may be gradually eroded, exposing the administrative authorities to excessive political influence.[130]

## 4.3 Do Constitutional Guarantees of Social Welfare Encourage Freedom of Information?

The constitutional guarantees of a welfare state do not establish any principle according to which government actions should generally be made public or legislators have a duty to ensure freedom of access to information. With respect to the right of access to information, the guarantees of a welfare state might be interpreted to impose duties to advise, enlighten and providing information on the administrative authorities in certain situations, however. No resulting obligations are imposed on national authorities to ensure general freedom of information.[131] Nevertheless, the general policy of participating in the reduction of social inequalities requires

[128] Article 20.3 of the German Basic Law reads as follows: "The legislature shall be bound by the constitutional order, the executive and the judiciary by law and justice."

[129] Article 37 (1) in Chap. VII (Public Administration) of the Brazilian Constitution reads as follows: "The governmental entities and entities owned by the Government in any of the powers of the Union, the States, the Federal District and the Municipalities shall obey the principles of lawfulness, impersonality, morality, publicity, and efficiency [. . .]", and also the following.

[130] Rossi, 2004, p. 304 et seqq., 335 (point 58).

[131] Regarding the legal situation in Germany (Article 20.1 Basic Law: "The Federal Republic of Germany is a democratic and social federal state.") cf. Schoch 2016, Einleitung para 84. No different conclusions can be drawn from the Brazilian Constitution (Articles 193 et seqq., especially Article 194: "Social welfare comprises an integrated whole of actions initiated by the Government and by society, with the purpose of ensuring the rights to health, social security and assistance.").

national authorities to consider social equality in their actions and decisions so as to create the necessary social conditions for all those who reside lawfully on the national territory to effectively exercise their rights to liberty.[132] A right of access to relevant information, on the other hand, is an individual right but not a prerequisite for the exercise of freedom.[133] The right to political participation in democracy is situated between the "rights to liberty" (Article 5, item 33 of the Brazilian Constitution) and the "citizen's rights" (Article 42 of the Charter of Fundamental Rights of the European Union-CFREU) and may therefore be said to have a fundamental status that grants the citizen a right to state performance (*status positivus*) beyond the status of a welfare state (Blanke, Chap. 3, Sect. 2.1).

## 5 Limitations of the Right of Access to Information in Bipolar and Tripolar Legal Relationships

Before publicly disclosing official information, it is always important to ask whether any important concerns of public welfare or private interests would be adversely affected. An analysis of the national transparency laws is, therefore, highly dependent on the interaction between the scope of the freedom of information and the limitations (exemptions) imposed on its exercise. Such colliding duties, values and interests are found not only in national constitutions (e.g., Article 21 of the Brazilian Constitution: maintaining relations with foreign states; ensuring national defence) but also in international conventions and the supranational legal system of the European Union (e.g., Article 8 of the CFREU: protection of personal data). Such duties of the state in collision with freedom of information and rights to liberty lead to intrinsic limits on the right of access to information because they are decisive in determining *how* the relevant statutes will take shape (Neto, Chap. 9, Sect. 2).

The colliding interests arising from duties assigned to the state by the constitution and third parties' freedom rights include national interests in secrecy and confidentiality, as well as various rights of natural or juridical persons under private law (e.g., protection of personal data, intellectual property and of business or trade secrets). On this subject, the Model Inter-American Law (Article 44) states that "Public Authorities may not refuse to indicate whether or not it holds a record or refuse to disclose that record [. . .] unless the potential harm to the interest protected by the relevant exception outweighs the general public interest in disclosure." It is also worth mentioning that countries have the option of adopting laws that impose "limits on the limits" on the general duty of public disclosure, e.g., by prohibiting the state from invoking national defence to justify non-disclosure in cases of genocide, war crimes

[132] Cf. also Article 170 and Articles 193 et seqq. of the Brazilian Constitution: "social well-being and justice".

[133] Cf. Kugelmann (2001), p. 38 et seq.

or human rights violations[134] (Perlingeiro et al., Chap. 2, Sect. 5.2.2). Independently from such statutory limits, the principle of proportionality applied by the administrative authorities under the control of the courts constantly limits not only the limits that may be imposed by law on the right to access to information but also the application of those limits by the state institutions.

If an individual who is generally entitled to access official records asks a public authority for information about a third party within the state's sphere of influence, then the legal relationship of disclosure becomes tripolar. In such cases, any public authority subject to the transparency laws must also give due consideration to the third party's right to protect personal data ("privacy"), which may outweigh the applicant's right to information to such an extent as to limit or entirely preclude disclosure. In such a tripolar relationship involving the rights of third parties, i.e., when an individual asks a public authority for access to a third party's personal data, legislators have substantially less leeway in drafting statutes than in purely bipolar "Citizen vs. State" relationships. In such situations, the state must respect the fundamental rights of the third party, as well, and comply with the corresponding constitutional principles: unlike general public interests, the individual's fundamental rights are largely inviolable and any statute deemed to restrict such rights unnecessarily may be repealed as unconstitutional.[135] As mentioned above, a third party's interest in non-disclosure may often be derived from the defensive function of (other) fundamental rights, namely the right to protection of personal data and freedom of enterprise ("entrepreneurial freedom") justifying the confidentiality of business or trade secrets (Blanke, Chap. 3, Sect. 3.4.4). When measured according to the constitutional principle of proportionality, the (constitutionally anchored) primacy of the interest in information access[136] is reduced to a mere quantity to be weighed against the rights of the third party (unless, of course, the latter consents to disclosure of the information in question[137]).

The application of the exemptions to the right of access to information illustrates the importance of an access. Hence, even under legislation which creates a practical presumption that government documents and records should be accessible to the public unless an exemption applies, it is difficult to sustain the view point that it is secrecy and not access that must be justified. This difficulty arises because the application of the exemptions focuses on their interpretation. Moreover, the exemptions themselves contain positions inconsistent with openness. Comparative analysis

[134]See e.g., Article 45 of the Model Inter-American Law, and most recently Article 8.2 of the Argentinian Law 27275/2016.

[135]Cf. Rossi 2004, p. 327 (points 12 and 13), p. 329 (point 20).

[136]Cf. Article 6.4 subparagraph (A), item 1, sentence 2, of the Mexican Constitution: "En la interpretación de este derecho deberá prevalecer el principio de máxima publicidad." [The principle of maximum disclosure shall prevail when interpreting this right.].

[137]Cf., e.g., Article 5.1 (1) of the German Freedom of Information Law: "Access to personal data may only be granted where the applicant's interest in obtaining the information outweighs the third party's interests warranting exclusion of access to the information or where the third party has provided his or her consent."

also addresses the various articulations of the same value of transparency and may lead to different judgments regarding the exemption and access. The judicial decisions interpreting the exemptions determine the scope and effectiveness of access laws (Vaughn and Messitte, Chap. 4, Sects. 6.2 and 6 regarding the U.S. FOIA).

Among the public authorities, case-law plays an important role in the implementation of claims for information access (Sect. 6.2.6). In some countries, courts are requiring ever greater justifications and statements of reasons from public authorities that wish to withhold requested information.[138] Yet, when weighing of the conflicting interests, the judges' interpretations must abide by the standards imposed by the legislators based on their own weighing of those interests. Critical voices are already complaining that the definitions of the exemptions in many laws, which often require laborious administrative processing, "are so extensive that they lose sight of the principle that they were initially intended to implement, namely that government-held information should accessible to the public."[139]

## *5.1 Laws Protecting State Secrecy*

As the Canadian Supreme Court has put it, "many government functions [...] require privacy. To extend a right of free expression to such venues might well undermine democracy and efficient governance."[140] Freedom of Access Acts all over the world contain provisions that deny public access to documents and records whose disclosure might be detrimental to public interests. The historic function of a particular institution may assist in determining the bounds of institutional confidentiality. Government agencies label certain documents as "classified" if their disclosure might jeopardise the effective performance of their mission,[141] especially documents concerning national defence, foreign policy and international relations; international negotiations are still considered confidential, also under Article 3.3 point (a) of the German Freedom of Information Act (*Informationsfreiheitsgesetz*). To mention only a few of the key areas of state secrecy and confidentiality, national laws often restrict access to information about broadly defined public interests such as the prevention, investigation and prosecution of criminal activities, government inspection, control and supervisory activities, and the economic, monetary and

---

[138] Regarding the German courts, especially the precedents of the Federal Constitutional Court and Federal Administrative Court, as well as the European Court of Justice in Luxemburg, see: Leutheusser-Schnarrenberger 2015, p. 24.

[139] Cf. Schaar 2015 p. 31 regarding Sec. 5 of the German FIA.

[140] Canadian Supreme Court, *Montréal (City) v. 2952-1366 Québec Inc.* (Judgment of 03 November 2005), [2005] 3 S.C.R. 141, 2005 SCC 62, para 76; cf. Guttman (2010), p. 199 et seqq. (219 et seq.).

[141] Canadian Supreme Court, *Ontario (Public Safety and Security) v. Criminal Lawyers' Association* (Judgment of 17 June 2010), 2010 SCC 23, [2010] 1 S.C.R. 815 2010 SCC 23, [2010] 1 S.C.R. 815, para 40.

exchange rate policies of the state.[142] According to the Model Inter-American Law, disclosure of official information should not be denied on the grounds of public interests unless "allowing access would create a clear, probable and specific risk of substantial harm, [which should be further defined by law], to the following public interests: public safety; national security; the future provision of free and open advice within and among public authorities; effective formulation or development of policy; international or intergovernamental relations; law enforcement, prevention, investigation and prosecution of crime; the ability of the state to manage the economy; legitimate financial interests of the public authority; tests and audits, and testing and auditing procedures."[143] Disclosure may also be denied if "allowing access would constitute an actionable breach of confidence in communication, including legally privileged information".[144]

"Judicial secrecy", according to which public access is required only for court judgments and hearings, may be considered a "instrumental" limit on information access, which should not be confused with limits based on public or private interests. In other words, its purpose is not to protect an interest per se, but rather safeguards other interest protected by such restriction (Moraes and Melo, Chap. 17, Sect. 2.3).

## 5.2 *Laws Protecting Other Public Interests in Non-Disclosure*

In the case of information about matters such as national security and defence strategies, laws governing state interests in secrecy and confidentiality need not provide for the weighing of conflicting interests based on the principle of proportionality because they regulate a purely bipolar relationship between a citizen requesting information and the administrative authority that grants or denies the request. In such relationships, the national legislators enjoy a certain degree of leeway in drafting the law and are only subject to the requirement of avoiding regulatory gaps or insufficiencies, i.e., the absence or insufficiency of legal protection of public interests to such an extent as to jeopardise the constitutional order.[145]

The amount of leeway enjoyed by the legislators depends to a decisive extent on whether the right of access to information is merely anchored in a statute or, on the contrary, is a fundamental right guaranteed by the national constitution or by an international convention. In the latter case, there may be a general presumption that the right of access may be restricted only under exceptional circumstances in which it is necessary to weigh two opposing constitutionally guaranteed interests to

[142] Cf. in this regard Article 3 of the Council of Europe Convention on Access to Official Documents.

[143] Article 41 item (b) of the Model Inter-American Law.

[144] Article 41 item (c) of the Model Inter-American Law.

[145] Cf. Rossi 2004, p. 327 et seq. (point 15).

establish a practical balance between them. In contrast, in the case of only statute-based information access rights, national legislators, enjoy significantly greater leeway to stipulate either absolute or merely relative exemptions from the disclosure obligations, at their discretion.

Relative exemptions give administrative authorities the option of granting or denying requests for information access in matters of public interest on a case-by-case basis, subject to strict compliance with the limits of their authority. Such relative exemptions always leave the door open to abusive withholding of information, thereby infringing the citizen's right to information. To limit the margin of appreciation of the information officer, the framers of the Model Inter-American Law (Article 44) and the Model Law for Africa have set out the principal rule on "Public Interest Override": "Notwithstanding any of the exemptions in this Part, an information holder may only refuse a requester access to information if the harm to the interest protected under the relevant exemption that would result from the release of the information demonstrably outweighs the public interest in the release of the information" (Article 25 of the Model Law for Africa).

The Argentinian legislators, too, anticipated the danger that the citizen's right of access to information could be undermined by a conflict with the public interest in secrecy and confidentiality. The statement of guiding principles for the interpretation of Law 27275/2016[146] therefore includes a rule of interpretation on the "limited scope of the exemptions": "The limits on the right of access to official information shall be exceptional, established in advanced by the stipulations of the present Law, and formulated in clear and precise terms, and the entity receiving the request shall bear the burden of proof of the validity of any restriction on information access."[147] To safeguard the essence of the right of access to information, the exemptions should also be applied and interpreted in accordance with the rule of interpretation "*in dubio pro petitor*", as a supplement to the principle of the "presumption of the publicness of all state-held information",[148] which guides the interpretation and implementation of this law on the "Right of Access to Official Information" (*Derecho de Acceso a la Información Pública*). Pursuant to this rule which accords with the Article 8 of the Model Inter-American Law, the provisions on the right of access to information should always be interpreted "in case of doubt, in such a way as to maximize the effectiveness and scope of the right to information".[149] The Model Law for Africa contains a similar rule of interpretation.[150] The principle that the *digital citizen's* requests for access to information should be treated according to international conventions will now be applied in the legal system of Argentina, which has not expressly codified the right

[146]Available at https://www.boletinoficial.gob.ar/#!DetalleNorma/151503/null.

[147]Article 1, principle 12 of the Argentinian Law 27275/2016 in accordance with Article 54 of the Model Inter-American Law.

[148]Article 1, principle 1 of the Argentinian Law 27275/2016.

[149]Article 1, principle 13 of the Argentinian Law 27275/2016.

[150]Pursuant to Article 5 of the Model Law for Africa "[. . .] any reasonable interpretation that favours the presumption of a right to access information must be preferred to any adverse or restrictive interpretation."

of access to information in its Constitution, but has set forth this guarantee in statutory law (Perlingeiro et al., Chap. 2, Sect. 3; Aberastury et al., Chap. 18, Sect. 1).[151]

## *5.3 The Protection of Private Interests as a Legal Objective of the Twenty-First Century*

The right of access to information and the right to protection of personal data are opposing positions,[152] because one person's right of access to information may conflict with another's right to protection of personal data (e.g., under Sec. 5 of the German FIA, Article 16.1 TFEU or Article 8 CFREU). The constitutional or statutory rights of access to information are generally opposed to individual (fundamental) rights in the form of claims to data protection. Further evidence of this dichotomy may be found in U.S. legislation in the interplay between the 1966 FOIA (5 U.S.C. §552) and the 1974 Privacy Act (5 U.S.C. §552a) and in the relationship in the Brazilian Constitution between the fundamental right to the protection of personal data under Article 5, items 10[153] and 72,[154] and the at least potentially conflicting right of access to information under Article 5, item 33.[155] In such cases, the transparency laws restrict access to information (Article 23 of the Brazilian Law N° 12.527; Article 3 of the German FIA; Sec. 552 (1)(F)(b) (1)–(7) of the U.S. FOIA).[156] According to the

---

[151]Already in 2014, the Supreme Court of Argentina affirmed that the "obligation to guarantee access to information by constitutional norms is incumbent on the State" and that the Constitution "establishes that the right to access official information is a necessary condition in order to organize a democratic republic"; to provide effective guarantees for the right to information, it was doubtless necessary for "the State to enact an urgent law ensuring compliance with the principle of reasonableness and the applicable international principles on the subject, with exhaustive provisions regulating the manner in which the public authorities are required to satisfy that right"; see National Supreme Court of Justice, Argentina (Corte Suprema de Justicia de La Nación Argentina), CIPPEC c/ EN – M° Desarrollo Social – dto. 1172/03 s/amparo, Ley 16.986, Fallos C. 830. XLVI, 2014 (Judgment of 26 March 2014) para 32.

[152]Regarding the "Right to Privacy" see for the first time Warren & Brandeis 1890.

[153]"[...} the privacy, private life, honour and image of persons are inviolable, and the right to compensation for property or moral damages resulting from their violation is ensured" (Article 5, item 10 of the Brazilian Constitution).

[154]"[...} habeas data shall be granted: a. to assure knowledge of personal information about the petitioner contained in records or data banks of government agencies or entities of a public character; b. to correct data whenever the petitioner prefers not to do so through confidential judicial or administrative proceedings" (Article 5, item 72 of the Brazilian Constitution).

[155]"[...} all persons have the right to receive, from the public agencies, information of private interest to such persons, or of collective or general interest,..." (Article 5, item 33 of the Brazilian Constitution).

[156]At this point, there is no need to examine the mainly theoretical issue of whether the right to freedom of information does not already exist, i.e., whether the "substantive area of protection" is not available at all, or whether the question does not arise until the stage of justification (within the analysis, whether the interference with this guaranteed right can be justified).

Model Inter-American Law, public authorities may deny access to information only if allowing such access would harm the following private interests: the right to privacy, including life, limb or safety; legitimate commercial and economic interests, or patents, copyrights and trade secrets.[157]

Many countries prohibit access to legally protected documents concerning a third party's personal information on the grounds of privacy, including private correspondence, commercial and economic interests such as intellectual property rights, copyrights and trade secrets of an individual or legal entity (Perlingeiro et al., Chap. 2, Sects. 6.3.1–6.3.4; Blanke, Chap. 3, Sects. 3.4.3 and 3.4.4; Vaughn and Messitte, Chap. 4, Sect. 6).[158] Also in light of the EU Regulation 2016/679 of 27 April 2016 on the protection of natural persons with regard to the processing of personal data and on the free movement of such data a broad definition of the concept of personal data is appropriate: "[. . .] 'personal data' means any information relating to an identified or identifiable natural person ('data subject'): an identifiable person is one who can be identified, directly or indirectly, in particular by reference to an identifier such as a name, an identification number, location data, online identifier or to one or more factors specific to the physical, physiological, genetic, mental, economic, cultural or social identity of that natural person."[159]

Faced with worldwide recognition of the "right of access to information", the need of citizens for protection of their personal data is particularly apparent in light of use of the new technologies by public administrative authorities in their citizen information services, especially when an applicant requests disclosure of the personal data of third parties. In fact, personal data which have become public knowledge should not be considered *res nullius* even if the disclosure was required by law or made with the data subject's consent, because citizens should have the right to restrict access on such information again later on, or to limit access to a certain period or to specific situations. Moreover, events that occur after the enactment of a law may make such subsequent restrictions necessary. The need for such standards of protection can also be inferred from the case-law of the German Federal Constitutional Court, which has stressed that "the dangers to the rights of personality that accompany the right to informational self-determination [. . .arise from] the manifold possibilities of the State and, in some cases, of private actors [. . .] to collect, process and exploit personal data. Such information may be used to generate further information, especially by means of electronic data processing, making it possible to discover the data subject's constitutionally protected confidential information through a process of deduction and be accompanied by infringements of the data subject's freedom of action."[160]

---

[157]Article 41 item (a) of the Model Inter-American Law.

[158]Cf., e.g., second paragraph of Article 5 bis of the Italian Law 33/2013 as amended by the Law Madia.

[159]See regarding this definition of "personal data" Article 4 No. 1 of the General Personal Data Regulation of the EU.

[160]German Federal Constitutional Court (Bundesverfassungsgericht), 1 BvR 370/07 and 1 BvR 595/07 (Judgment of 27 February 2008), para 198 et seq.

This may be formulated in the principle that public access to official documents must be brought into balance with the citizen's right to protection of his personal data. The scope of the right of access to information is regularly determined by the right to protection of personal data, which may already be derived from the guarantee of the right to the protection of personal data under the Charter of Fundamental Rights of the European Union. According to Article 8.2 (1) CFREU, "data must be processed fairly for specified purposes and on the basis of the consent of the person concerned or some other legitimate basis laid down by law", which is rightly considered to be a "mechanism of limiting the flow of data and information".[161] In terms of legal theory, the processing and disclosure of a third party's personal data to the applicant constitutes an infringement of a fundamental right that must be justified by an underlying statute in compliance with the principle of proportionality (Article 52.1 CFREU).[162]

Members of the international blogger community deem it necessary to rethink and redefine the legal protection of the private sphere in light of the radical digital revolution that is transforming every aspect of our lives. This should make it possible to completely overcome the "standard notion of data protection from the industrial era" as an "obsolete and unrealistic concept of the 1970s".[163] The EU Commission, however, in the explanatory memorandum of its proposal for a European General Data Protection Regulation, stated that "a more comprehensive and coherent policy on the fundamental right to personal data protection" needs to be developed in EU legislation. Citing the case-law of the European Court of Justice (ECJ),[164] the Commission pointed out that "the right to the protection of personal data is not an absolute right, but must be considered in relation to its function in society."[165] As a result, the "social function" of the protection of personal data, all other things being equal, should also be applied as the standard when drafting the statutory exemptions to which the right of access to information is subject.

### 5.4 *Balancing the Competing Interests as a Task of the Legislators*

In the German legal system, the "right to informational self-determination" was developed through the case-law of the Federal Constitutional Court on the occasion

---

[161]Britz 2009, p. 10.

[162]Schoch 2016, Article 5 para 16.

[163]Such as the freelance journalist and blogger *Mario Sixtus;* similarly, *Mariana Weisband* of Piratenpartei Deutschland.

[164]Joined Cases 92/09 and 93/09 *Volker and Markus Schecke and Eifert* (ECJ 9 November 2010) para 48; see also Case 131/12 *Google Spain SL, Google Inc. v Agencia Española de Protección de Datos (AEPD) and Mario Costeja González* (ECJ 13 May 2014) para 80.

[165]European Commission (2012), *Datenschutz-Grundverordnung*, KOM (2012) 11, p. 2, 6.

of the national collection of demographic data ("census"). The Court held that "individual self-determination [. . .] – even under the conditions of modern information processing technologies – presupposes that individuals have the freedom to decide which actions should be carried out or omitted, and must also be given an opportunity to behave in accordance with that decision. An individual who lacks a sufficiently certain understanding of what items of his personal information are known in certain circles of his social environment, and who is incapable of estimating the knowledge of his potential communication partners, may be significantly restricted in terms of his freedom to make plans and decisions on the basis of personal self-determination. The right to informational self-determination is incompatible with a social order (and a corresponding legal system) in which citizens can no longer know who knows what about them when, and on what occasion."[166]

When weighing the opposing interests involved in access to personal data, the fundamental right of self-determination weighs in on the side of the right to privacy: "The right to informational self-determination goes beyond protection of the private sphere. In principle, it empowers individuals to determine the degree of disclosure and use of their personal data [. . .]. It supports and extends the constitutional protection of freedom of action and privacy, by guaranteeing its protection already when the right of personality could come into threat. Such a situation of endangerment may already begin prior to specific threats of identifiable legal interests, especially when personal information can be used and lined in a way that is neither transparent nor controllable for the data subject. The scope of protection of the right to informational self-determination is not limited to information which is sensitive by nature and, therefore, already protected by the constitution. The same right extends to personal data that, although containing low information content *per se*, may result in a significant infringement of the constitutional rights to privacy and freedom of action, depending on the purpose of access and the possible ways in which such data may be processed and linked."[167]

With this fundamental right to informational self-determination, the German Federal Constitutional Court has formulated an extended concept of data protection that goes beyond protection of the private sphere.[168] Transparency of data processing is a condition precedent for fulfilment of the right to informational self-determination. With that in mind, German data protection law gives the data subject a right to access to his or her *own* personal data in storage.[169] Yet beyond the

---

[166]German Federal Constitutional Court (Bundesverfassungsgericht), BVerfGE (Fed. Const. Ct. Judgments) 65, 1 (Judgment of 15 December 1983), p. 41 et seq. – well-established case-law. Wieland 2000, p. 91; on the right to data protection as an element of the right to informational self-determination in Germany, cf. Deutlmoser & Filip 2015, para 6.

[167]German Federal Constitutional Court (Bundesverfassungsgericht), 1 BvR 370/07 and 1 BvR 595/07 (Judgment of 27 February 2008), para 198 et seq., with a reference to the German Federal Constitutional Court, 1 BvR 1550/03 (Judgment of 13 June 2007), NJW 2007, p. 2464 (2466).

[168]Cf. Schaar 2015, p. 29.

[169]Cf. especially Sections 6.1, 19 and 34 of the German Federal Data Protection Act (Bundesdatenschutzgesetz).

individual collection and processing of personal data, the private and public data controllers must provide applicants with certain information about the data processing operations upon demand. Even before collecting personal data, the data controllers are required to inform the data subject about the circumstances providing the legal justification for data collection and processing, and the details of those operations.[170] Only if the data subject knows who is collecting his personal data and why can he determine who should know what about him, i.e., exercise his right to informational self-determination. From that perspective, data protection and the freedom of information are mutually complementary objectives rather than diametrically opposed. Moreover, in such cases, both data protection and the right of access to government-held information constitute a limitation of state power, especially with respect to government actions.[171] In the requested access to information, the collision with the protection of personal data is often created by the subject matter.

The conflict between the right of access to information and the right to protection of personal data is clarified paradigmatically based on point (e) under Article 7 of Directive 95/46/EC,[172] which expressly authorises the processing of personal data, including by the public authorities, if such processing "is necessary for the performance of a task carried out in the public interest or in the exercise of official authority." According to point (f) of Article 7 of Directive 95/46/EC[173] public administrative authorities are authorised to process personal data when "necessary for the purposes of [other public [. . .] legitimate interests [. . .], except where such interests are overridden by the interests for fundamental rights and freedoms of the data subject". Once Directive 95/46/EC has been superseded by the General Data Protection Regulation ("GDPR") of the European Union (2016/679) with effect from 25 May 2018, the "lawfulness" of the processing of personal data will be determined according to Article 6 GDPR. In the absence of any other of the legitimate grounds listed under Article 6.1 GDPR (which imposes a ban on processing of personal data while reserving the right to grant a permit or license: *Verbot mit Erlaubnisvorbehalt*)—such as "consent [of] . . . the data subject" (point a), "compliance with a legal obligation to which the controller is subject" (point c) or "in order to protect the vital interests of the data subject or another natural person" (point d)—point (e) of Article 6.1 GDPR allows public authorities to process personal data when handling a claim for access to information if such processing "is necessary for the performance of a task carried out in the public interest or in the exercise of official authority vested in the controller". However, in

[170]Cf. especially Sec. 4 g para 2, 2a of the German Federal Data Protection Act.

[171]Cf. Schaar 2015, p. 29 et seq.

[172]See Directive 95/46/EC of the European Parliament and of the Council of 24 October 1995 on the protection of individuals with regard to the processing of personal data and on the free movement of such data, *Official Journal L 281, 23/11/1995, p. 31 et seqq.*

[173]Article 7 point (f) of the Directive 95/46/EC reads as follows: "Member States shall provide that personal data may be processed only if: [. . .] processing is necessary for the purposes of the legitimate interests pursued by the controller or by the third party or parties to whom the data are disclosed, except where such interests are overridden by the interests for fundamental rights and freedoms of the data subject which require protection under Article 1 (1)."

the future, public authorities will no longer be able to invoke the need for personal data processing "for the purposes of the legitimate interests pursued by the controller or by a third party" (Article 6.1 (2) GDPR[174]).

The General Data Protection Regulation does not provide for a right to access to information. While Article 85 GDPR obliges the legislators of "the Member States to reconcile the right to the protection of personal data pursuant to this Regulation with the right to freedom of expression and information" (Articles 11 and 13 CFREU), Article 86 GDPR enables especially a public authority to disclose "personal data in official documents [. . .] in order to reconcile public access to official documents with the right to the protection of personal data".[175] All public authorities or public or private bodies vested with public authority and acting in accordance with Union or Member State law are allowed to disclose these data. In the areas of freedom of information and access to information Articles 85 and 86 GDPR include "opening clauses" which leave room for national legislation by the Member States or even require such national laws (Article 85 GDPR) or for more specific EU provisions or statutory provisions by the Member States (Article 86 GDPR).[176] The necessary balance between the conflicting interests in the right of access versus the protection of personal data has been described by the drafters of the General Data Protection Regulation as follows in recital 154: "This Regulation allows the principle of public access to official documents to be taken into account when applying this Regulation. Public access to official documents may be considered to be in the public interest. Personal data in documents held by a public authority or a public body should be able to be publicly disclosed by that authority or body if the disclosure is provided for by Union or Member State law to which the public authority or public body is subject. Such laws should reconcile public access to official documents and the re-use of public sector information with the right to the protection of personal data and may therefore provide for the necessary reconciliation with the right to the protection of personal data pursuant to this Regulation."

---

[174]Regarding the conditions of a legitimate processing, Article 6.1 (2) GDPR reads as follows: "Point (f) of the first subparagraph shall not apply to processing carried out by public authorities in the performance of their tasks." Point (f) of Article 6.1 GDRP states: "Processing shall be lawful only if and to the extent that at least one of the following applies: [. . .] processing is necessary for the purposes of the legitimate interests pursued by the controller or by a third party, except where such interests are overridden by the interests or fundamental rights and freedoms of the data subject which require protection of personal data, in particular where the data subject is a child."

[175]Article 86 of the General Data Protection Regulation reads as follows: "Personal data in official documents held by a public authority or a public body or a private body for the performance of a task carried out in the public interest may be disclosed by the authority or body in accordance with Union or Member State law to which the public authority or body is subject in order to reconcile public access to official documents with the right to the protection of personal data pursuant to this Regulation."

[176]Albrecht & Jotzo 2017, p. 133 et seq.; Kühling & Martini 2016, p. 285 et seqq. and 295 et seqq.; Pauly in Paal & Pauly 2017, Article 86 para 2; Schulz & Heilmann in Gierschmann et al. 2018, Article 85 para 7; Schulz & Heilmann in Gierschmann et al. 2018, Article 86 para 5 et seqq.

That recital is reformulated in broad terms in Article 86 GDPR. This provision does not stipulate how the Member States have to reconcile the personal data protection and the right of access to information. As a result, a variety of solutions is to be expected in the legislation of the Member States when third parties seek access to personal data filed in official documents.[177] Pursuant to Article 86 GDPR the Member States may decide how to alleviate the conflict between the interests of the public in access to information and the protection of personal data, in particular to what extent they give priority to which of the positions worthy of protection.[178]

In the wake of the EU General Data Protection Regulation, the French Digital Republic Act (Sect. 2.2) especially[179]

- seeks to enhance the rights of individuals by introducing under the Data Protection Act a general right allowing them to decide and to control the uses that are made of their personal data. For example, the Digital Republic Act explicitly requires controllers to grant individuals the right to exercise their rights electronically whenever their data is collected electronically;
- requires data controllers to inform their data subjects about the period during which the personal data will be stored, or if that is not possible, the criteria used to determine that period. Furthermore, all providers of online communication services to the public must inform their users specifically about the right to decide how their personal data will be processed following their death, including the right to provide their last instructions regarding the processing of their data;
- creates an innovative new right for individuals to decide how their personal data may be processed after their death. Before dying, any individual may give general or specific instructions regarding the storage, erasure or disclosure of his/her personal data. On the one hand, general instructions apply to all data that is collected and processed about an individual;
- introduces a new obligation for telecom operators and providers of electronic communication services to the public who offer online communication services (for example, providers of online messaging services) to maintain the secrecy of correspondence, including the content of the message, the sender and recipient's identity and, where applicable, the subject line and attachments of the message. The automatic processing of emails or other type of digital communications for purposes of advertisement, statistics or the enhancement of services is forbidden unless the data subject has given his/her express consent to such processing at least one year before the processing. Moreover, there must be a specific consent for each type of processing;
- introduces a new section under the Consumers Code, which grants consumers a right to the recovery and portability of their personal data. This new provision requires all providers of online communication services to the public to enable consumers to recover, free of charge, all data that they have stored online, including data files, all data stored and accessible from the user's online account, and other types of data that are associated with the user's online account and that can be easily re-used and exploited by another data controller;

[177] Pauly in Paal & Pauly 2017, Article 86 para 2; Hoidn 2017, p. 273.

[178] See Kühling & Martini et al. 2016, p. 296.

[179] See Proust & Goossens, 2016, http://privacylawblog.fieldfisher.com/2016/france-adopts-digital-republic-law/.

- introduces specific obligations for online platform providers. They are defined as businesses that offer to customers an online communication service to the public that 1) enables the ranking or referencing by means of a computer algorithm of content, goods or services that are offered or displayed online by third parties (e.g., search engines), or 2) allows parties to get in contact with one another to sell goods, offer a service, or exchange or share content, goods or services (e.g., online auction or shopping websites).

# 6 The Specific Manifestations of the Right of Access to Information in National Administrative Law and Case-Law

## *6.1 The Normative Form of the Scope of Protection and its Limits*

Public access to a source of information lying within the state's sphere of responsibility is determined by legal guidelines. It is primarily up to the legislators to give a concrete constitutional and/or statutory definition of the accessibility to information on public actions and procedures. Legislators regulate the extent of disclosure of the source of information by specifying the limits of the rights of freedom of information. In general, such sources are available to everyone, as opposed to the previous legal situation in which official information was not available, in principle, to any individual outside a certain specific set of persons, whether in the form of examination of records or official dissemination of information or processing of information in any other way. In particular, the legal definitions of the exceptions are based on the principle of legality, which limits the generality of freedom of access to information while at the same time defining the scope of opposing third-party rights to protection of personal data. To regulate such limits, a formal parliamentary law is needed (Sects. 4.2 and 4.2.1).

## *6.2 The Patterns of Legislation on the Right of Access to Information*

A general information access law should pursue the following objectives: adapting the administrative authorities to an extensive notion of the principle of legality, reaffirming the institutional role of the legislators in a state governed by democratic rule of law; restricting the broad freedom of action of the administrative authorities in favor of legal certainty; mobilisation of society in pursuit of the implementation of the right to information, leading to strengthening of the corresponding institutional guarantees and procedures, and the gradual increase in their credibility.

In this context, it should be noted that the national information access laws have similar structures, such as the inclusion of undeterminate legal concepts (requiring authentic interpretation) and a statement of the basic principles and general rules subdivided into at least two levels: a first level providing legal definitions of the specific undeterminate legal concepts related to the basic principles, and the substantive and procedural rights and duties. On the second level, regarding the substantive rights and duties, it has been common to specify the following: the scope of the duties of performance of the state; the duties of proactive disclosure, including the protection of the state's interests and of the rights of third parties that may be affected by such disclosure; the exceptions to the general duty to provide access to information (Moraes and Melo, Chap. 17, Sect. 2); and the various criminal, civil measures and sanctions for a breach of such duties (Huerta Ochoa, Chap. 19, Sect. 1.1). As far as procedural rights are concerned, information access laws have pointed out the following: the institutional guarantees, such as the organisation of the competent administrative authorities to decide on the request for information, the procedural requirements and the extrajudicial and judicial dispute-resolution proceedings in matters of information access (Aberastury et al., Chap. 18, Sect. 3).[180]

### 6.2.1 The Scope of the Right to Access

The Model Inter-American Law provides an extensive definition of the entities subject to duties to provide access to information: "This Law applies to all public authorities, including the executive, legislative and judicial branches at all levels of government, constitutional and statutory authorities, non-state bodies which are owned or controlled by government, and private organisations which operate with substantial public funds or benefits (directly or indirectly) or which perform public functions and services insofar as it applies to those funds or to the public services or functions they undertake. All of these bodies are required to make information available pursuant to the provisions of this Law".[181]

According to the statement of grounds of that Model Law, "[t]hat right of access to information applies broadly to all information in possession of public authorities, including all information which is held or recorded in any format or medium [. . .]." The Inter-American Judicial Committee of the Organization of American States defines the scope as follows: "The right to access applies to all significant information, defined broadly to include everything which is held or recorded in any format or medium."[182]

[180] See Perlingeiro 2015, p. 119–128.

[181] Article 3 of the Model Inter-American Law.

[182] Inter-American Juridical Committee of the OAS, Principles on the right of access to information (CJI/RES.147 – LXXIII-O/08), point 3.

Regarding the duty of proactive disclosure, the Model Inter-American Law details the procedures and information to be disseminated and the public policies, including the following stipulation: "No one shall be subject to any prejudice because of the application of a policy that has not been disclosed".[183] To the same effect, the Model Law for Africa spells out: "Where a public body or relevant private body has failed to timely publish information (as enshrined in the list about information determined for proactive disclosure pursuant to Article 7), a member of the public who was not aware of that information may not be subjected to any prejudice if he or she could lawfully have avoided that prejudice had they been aware of the information."[184]

### 6.2.2 Case-by-Case Weighing of Interests as an Administrative Task

In each specific case, it is incumbent on the authority that is responsible for granting access to the requested information according to the national laws to weigh the interests in disclosure versus the interest in secrecy, in compliance with any applicable statutory and constitutional guidelines concerning state secrecy. The administrative authorities therefore play a salient role as the principal holder of public information. Depending on the circumstances, the administrative authorities will decide whether the request for information involves a bipolar or tripolar relationship (Sect. 5). If a bipolar relationship is involved, the authority subject to the transparency laws is required to weigh the relevant interests in full compliance with the relevant legislation. When deciding within a tripolar relationship of information, however, the administrative authority's legal obligation to respect the data subject's constitutionally guaranteed rights to protection of personal information is superimposed on the authority's obligation to comply with the relevant transparency laws.[185]

In legal systems that classify the right of access to information as a fundamental constitutional and/or human right, the applicant's interest in receiving information must be given particular emphasis in the weighing process. When weighing the applicant's right to access against public or private interests in secrecy/confidentiality, particular importance is attached to the objective pursued by the requested access to information. Nevertheless, the applicant is not required to disclose that objective ("unconditional and unreserved right"). From the legislator's standpoint, the administrative authorities called upon to weigh the interests must therefore focus not on the applicant's specific individual interests but rather, in principle, on the interest in access in the abstract. Using this special weighing method in the administration of freedom-of-information cases entails a risk of infringing the legally protected interests of third parties, especially the right to protection of

---

[183] Articles 9–14 of the Model Inter-American Law.

[184] Article 9 of the Model Law for Africa.

[185] Rossi 2004, p. 329 (point 20).

personal data.[186] The resulting relative weakening of the fundamental right to protection of personal data has aroused criticism.[187] Opposing critics blame the complexity of numerous statutory exceptions responsible for undermining the principle that government-held information should be generally accessible to the public.[188] Although the balance between general rules and exceptions formulated in transparency laws tends to favor free access, it is clearly recognisable that the interest in disclosure is consistently considered to be outweighed or even overridden by the private data subject's specific interest in confidentiality whenever the private interest is clearly defined by law and its meaning is made clear to the authority applying the law, not least of all through the relevant case-law (Sect. 5).[189] The legal rules on freedom-of-information interpretation (Sect. 5.2), especially the relationship between rule and exception, remain unharmed. Where *special legislation* provides for a right of access to information and if the protection of confidentiality is subordinated to the prevailing interest in the information, it has to be considered to what extent the granting of the information also promotes the ratio legis beyond the individual case.[190]

### 6.3 Some Guidelines of the Procedure Ensuring Access to Information

The administrative procedure for accessing information has to be established by law. A general information access law is expected to implement clear, fair, non-discriminatory and simple rules for the handling of requests for information. Such rules should include clear and reasonable deadlines, within which the authorities shall decide, in a reasoned manner, whether there is a right to access to the information, whether the authority to which the request for access has put forward is authorised to provide said information, and if not, it must indicate the proper authority or agency. It should provide for assistance to the information applicants, and access free of charge or at most for a price no higher than the cost copying and/or sending the information. The rules should require the authorities to state the specific reasons for any denial of access within a reasonable time.[191]

---

186 Rossi 2004, p. 329 (points 21, 22).

187 Rossi 2004, p. 331 et seq. (point 34).

188 Cf. Schaar 2015, p. 31 et seq.

189 Rossi 2004, p. 329 et seq. (point 23).

190 Fehling (2017), p. 82.

191 Inter-American Juridical Committee of the OAS, Principles on the right of access to information (CJI/RES.147 – LXXIII-O/08), point 5; see also the Report 2009 of the Office of the Special Rapporteur for Freedom of Expressionof the Inter-American Commission on Human Rights (OAS), points 5.18 and 5.19.

### 6.4 The Competent Authorities to Implement the Right of Access to Information

There has been a tendency to create independent extrajudicial bodies to rule on claims for access to information[192]; but there are also countries without a single government-wide access to information body like South Africa, whose Promotion of Access to Information Act of 2000 has installed only an "information officer of a public body". The Model Law for Africa, however, provides an independent and impartial oversight mechanism (Articles 45 et seqq., 53 et seqq.), which is responsible for "all work necessary for the promotion, monitoring and protection of the right to access information in all sectors of society" (Articles 58 et seqq.). In Latin America, there are five examples of supervisory bodies which tend to favor effective independence guaranteed by legally established prerogatives: *Consejo de Transparencia* (Council of Transparency) in Chile[193]; *Instituto de Acceso a la Información Pública* (Institution of Public Information Access) in El Salvador[194]; *Instituto de Comisários* (Institution of Commissioners) in Honduras[195]; the *Organismos Garantes* (Oversight Agencies) in Mexico[196]; and, as a consequence of the latest developments in Argentina, the *Agencia de Acceso a la Información Pública* (Agency of Access to Public Information) "as a self-governing entity that will operate with functional autonomy in the sphere of the national Executive Branch".[197]

Independent supervisory bodies can be found in other parts of the world, as well, but there are not many with similar characteristics: e.g., France's "Commission d'accès aux documents administratifs" (CADA—Chevallier-Govers, Chap. 6, Sect. 5), Portugal's homonymous "Commission of Access to Public Documents" (CADA—Neto, Chap. 9, Sect. 5.1.1), Serbia's "Commissioner", Slovenia's "Commissioner for Access to Public Information", Spain's "Independent and Specialized Authority to Guarantee the Right of Access to Information" (*Consejo de Transparencia y Buen Gobierno*) on state level and in the Autonomous Communities, Liberia's "Independent Information Commissioner", India's "Central Information Commission", Antigua and Barbuda's "Information Commissioner",

[192] On the subject of the lack of independent bodies as a cause of difficulties in developing a culture of transparency in Peru, see Burt & Cagley 2013.

[193] Articles 31–44 of the Law on Access to Public Information of Chile.

[194] Articles 51–60 of the Law on Access to Public Information of El Salvador.

[195] Articles 8–11 of the Law on Transparency and Access to Public Information of Honduras.

[196] Articles 8.3 and 8.4, 30, 37–42 of the Law on Transparency and Access to Public Information of Mexico.

[197] Articles 19–29 of the Law 22275/216 of Argentina. As a federal institution within the Agency of Access to Public Information the *Consejo Federal para la Transparencia*(Federal Council for Transparency) was established "as a permanent interjurisdictional body for purposes of technical cooperation and harmonization of policies of transparency and access to official information" (Article 29 of Law 22275/216 of Argentina).

Macedonia's "Commission for Protection of the Right to Free Access to Information of Public Character", and Azerbaidjan's "Authorized Agency".[198]

Generally speaking, they are autonomous bodies, with independent legal personality and a specific budget allocation. The members of such bodies hold a term of office, are appointed and removed from office according to specific rules, with the participation of the Legislative and Executive branches and, in certain cases, the Judiciary.

The scarcity of supervisory bodies endowed with prerogatives to act independently is understandable in the judicial systems of countries with civil law traditions (in which independence is a prominent attribute of a court), considered incompatible with the quasi-judicial administrative bodies, leading to close judicial review, typical of the administrative law associated with common law.[199] This situation is gradually changing, however, as shown by the provisions of Article 6 of the Directive 2003/4/EC on public access to environmental information, which indicates that EU Member States are granting their citizens the right to appeal to independent and impartial authorities both in and out of court.[200] The Council of Europe Convention on Access to Official Documents, however, leaves it up to the Contracting States to grant an "applicant, whose request for an official document has been denied, expressly or impliedly, whether in part or in full [...] access to a review procedure *before a court or another independent and impartial body* established by law."[201]

## 6.5 Procedural Requirements of Administrative Law

The Inter-American Court of Human Rights has noted that the right to seek and receive information is substantiated during the administrative phase through a procedure carried out by the corresponding authority. Therefore, any response to a request for access to information must be duly reasoned and legally justified. The separate opinion of Judge Sergio García Ramírez points out that the obligation of its being reasoned and legally justified according to the principle of legality is a procedural guarantee which is not exclusive to court proceedings, but it also

[198] Articles 32–35 of the Law on Free Access to Information of Public Importance of Servia. Articles 28–30 of the Access to Public Information Act of Slovenia. Chap. 5 of the Freedom of Information Act of Liberia 2010. Articles 12–14 of the Indian Act 22/2005. Articles 35–40 of the Freedom of Information Act of Antigua and Barbuda 2004. Articles 30–35 of the Law on Free Access to Information of Public Character of Macedonia. Article 44 of the Law of the Republic of Azerbaijan on Right to Obtain Information.

[199] See Perlingeiro 2016; see also Asimow 2015.

[200] Article 6 of Directive 2003/4/EC of the European Parliament and of the Council of 28 January 2003 on public access to environmental information and repealing Council Directive 90/313/EEC, of 28 January 2003.

[201] Article 8 of the Council of Europe Convention on Access to Official Documents (emphasis added).

constitutes an obligation for administrative authorities[202] (Huerta Ochoa, Chap. 19, Sect. 1). Specific legally protected interests such as the right of access to information require procedures to become a reality. These procedural rights are essential for protection of the citizen's rights to information. From the perspective of such procedural issues, as well, the *supreme importance of the principle of the constitutional state* is apparent to put the right to access to information into practice. In public law, the principle of the constitutional state also creates a duty of the administrative authorities, according to the principle of good faith (*bona fides*) "[to guarantee] the effective exercise of [the right to] information access, i.e., to interpret [the respective transparency laws] in such a way as to ensure that the purposes pursued by the information access law are accomplished and that the law is applied to the letter, providing the applicants with the necessary means of assistance, promoting a culture of transparency and acting with diligence, professionalism and institutional loyalty".[203]

It is of particular significance that also in the process of implementation of transparency laws—as of all national laws and international conventions—the fundamental rights *as a whole* have an impact on the administrative procedure. It is a deeply anchored principle, especially in German constitutional and administrative legal theory, that the laws of administrative procedure must enshrine fundamental rights. This is particularly true of the right to human dignity, the right to protection of life, limb and health, and the rule of equality, but every fundamental right must be respected in administrative procedure according to the case-law of the German Constitutional Court.[204] Fundamental rights exercise a particularly strong influence on the form of administrative proceedings ruling on cases involving the right of access to information. This is especially true of legal systems in which the right to demand disclosure of government-held information sources is anchored in the list of fundamental rights of the national constitution (e.g., Sweden or Spain). Yet the same impact is noticeable in any legal order in which the right of access to information has been classified as an immediately applicable fundamental right, even in cases where the constitutional reality of it had to be set forth in statutory law (e.g., Brazil) or recognised in ordinary (non constitutional) transparency legislation (e.g., Argentina) according to the standards of international human rights conventions ("convencionalidad", i.e., through adherence to the conventions), or in which—according to an opinion held by a minority[205]—freedom-of-information rights are derived from a complementary relationship between the fundamental

[202]Judgment and Separate Opinion of Judge Sergio García Ramírez regarding the Judgment delivered by the Inter-American Court of Human Rights, *Claude Reyes et al. v. Chile* (Judgment of 19 September 2006), available at http://www.corteidh.or.cr/docs/casos/articulos/seriec_151_ing.pdf (Accessed on 26 October 2016).

[203]Cf. Article 1, principle 15 of the Argentinian Law 27275/2016 on the "Right of Access to Public Information".

[204]German Federal Constitutional Court (Bundesverfassungsgericht), 1 BvR 385/90 (Judgment of 27 October 1999), EuGRZ 2000, p. 167 (172).

[205]Cf. Schoch 2016, Einleitung para 54, 283 et seqq., 287 et seq.

freedom to gather information from *generally accessible* sources (e.g., the right of every person "to inform himself without hindrance from generally accessible information" under Article 5.1 of the German Basic Law) in conjunction with Sec. 1.1 of the German Federal Freedom of Information Act (Blanke, Chap. 3, Sect. 2.1.1). Such an implementation of the right to access in accordance with the corresponding rights of a national constitution or an international convention is required by the established rules of interpretation ("administrative law as 'concretised' constitutional law"[206]). In its essence the right guaranteed by the constitution or international convention entitles citizens to information access procedure which complies with the principle of efficiency. Yet the fundamental rights only mark the minimum required standard of administrative guarantees; legislators have considerable leeway to draft laws imposing higher standards.[207]

Procedural laws can be designed in such a way as to prevent the violations of fundamental rights by public authorities. Moreover, the existing rules of procedure should be applied in compliance with constitutional law, in the sense of providing "protection of fundamental rights through administrative procedural due process" ("Grundrechtsschutz durch Verfahren").[208] In conjunction with the principle of democracy (Sects. 4.1 and 4.1.1), the duty to protect fundamental rights through guarantees of administrative procedural due process and resulting case-law require the addressees of requests for information access, namely the public administrative authorities, to interpret the laws regulating access to the requested information in a manner "favorable to information and communication",[209] an approach which exemplifies the general principle of interpretation in compliance with the constitution and/or convention (Sect. 5.2). Such an approach is especially important whenever it is impossible to scrutinise the administrative authority's decision on a request for access to information according to the standard of fundamental rights because the fundamental right in question does not specify any criteria enabling administrative revision or judicial review of the decision. A violation of a rule of procedure even constitutes a *direct violation* of a fundamental right if the provision in question was enacted to implement a fundamental right to protect (*grundrechtliche Schutzpflicht*)[210]

---

[206]See Werner, DÖV 1959, p. 527.

[207]Schulte 1995, p. 117.

[208]German Federal Constitutional Court (Bundesverfassungsgericht), 1 BvR 385/77 (Judgment of 20 December 1979), BVerfGE (Fed. Const. Ct. Judgments) 53, 30 (73).

[209]Cf. Kugelmann 2001, p. 48, 53 et seq.; Sec. 29 German Administrative Procedure Act and Sec. 25 of the Tenth Code of Social Law regarding the "exchange of information in administrative proceedings"; he is apparently referring primarily to legal norms outside of the transparency legislation, such as Sec. 29 of the German Administrative Procedure Act and Sec. 25 of the German Tenth Code of Social Law. Nevertheless, his line of argument is also applicable to transparency legislation.

[210]Cf., e.g., Article 6.3 of the Mexican Constitution 1917 as amended in this regard in 2013: "The State shall guarantee access to information and communication technology, access to the services of radio broadcast, telecommunications and broadband Internet. To that end, the State shall establish effective competition conditions for the provision of such services."

or a fundamental right to performance (*grundrechtliches Leistungsrecht*).[211] This is true of all rules of procedure enacted by national legislators to implement constitutionally guaranteed rights of access to information.[212]

Although the procedural prerequisites for the aforementioned procedural rights, especially the rights to a fair hearing and procedural due process, depend on the nature of the specific proceeding, they are implemented against a backdrop of decisions for or against granting information based on constitutional law. The independent legal character of the transparency legislation is revealed in the legal consequences of violating such rights. If a decision regarding the existence and scope of a right to access to information is found to be unlawful, it has to be withdrawn or annulled, whether in administrative authority's internal appeal proceedings or in a (subsequent) judicial proceeding (action for performance). The unlawful proceeding ruling on a request for access to information influences the decision on the merits.

## 6.6 *Substantial Requirements Regarding the Judicial Protection*

The right to effective judicial protection has become, in several parts of the world, the point of crystallisation of a general discourse about the rule of law. The prerequisites for such protection are the subjection of the public powers to the law, the effectiveness of the principle of division of powers, especially the guarantee of independent courts, and the recognition of an increasing subjectivisation (*Subjektivierung*) of the individual's position vis-à-vis the state under procedural and substantive law.[213] The right to effective judicial protection (e.g., Article 19.4 of the Basic Law) has become a constitutional guarantee of enforceability of the right of access to all relevant documents in judicial proceedings.[214] Yet such enforceability is anchored, from a strictly normative perspective, not only in the right to effective judicial protection, but in every constitutionally guaranteed fundamental right of relevance to the access to the file. Consequently, public authorities are subject to an obligation to provide justifications for any denial of a request to access to information.[215] The guarantee of effective judicial protection

[211] German Federal Constitutional Court (Bundesverfassungsgericht), 1 BvR 385/77 (Judgment of 20 December 1979), BVerfGE (Fed. Const. Ct. Judgments) 53, 30 (65 f.).

[212] E.g., Article 19, Article 65.1 of the Brazilian Decree N° 7.724; Article 68 of the Mexican Decree passed into law in the *Ley General de Transparencia y Acceso a la Información Pública*.

[213] See Perlingeiro & Sommermann 2014, p. 1.

[214] See Kugelmann 2001, p. 40 et seqq.

[215] See Article 54 of the Model Inter-American Law in conjunction with Chap. 2 on "Exceptions from Disclosure", point B of the "Commentary and Guide for Implementation" for this Model Law: "With respect to the invocation of private interests as grounds for denial of the right of access to information before a jurisdictional body or an information review committee, the organs of the

under German constitutional law unfolds "advance effects" already within the administrative proceedings.[216] It ensures that the proceeding can neither prevent judicial protection nor make it unreasonably difficult.[217] Essentially, it is a question of the right to a fair trial (Article 6.1 ECHR, Articles 8.1 and 25.1 ACHR) which legislators are required to implement by designing administrative proceedings with appropriate guarantees of due process. In the German legal system, the right to a fair hearing in administrative proceedings is expressly anchored in Article 28.1 of the Administrative Procedure Act (*Verwaltungsverfahrensgesetz*) but is also implied, from the perspective of constitutional law, by the principle of the constitutional democratic state under Article 20 of the German Basic Law and the protection of human dignity under Article 1.1 of the German Basic Law, which prohibits making a person into a mere object of actions of the state. Finally, the right to a fair hearing is a corollary of the need for administrative proceedings to protect any significant fundamental rights involved.[218] The right to a fair hearing can also be derived from Article 6.1 of the ECHR or Articles 8.1 and 25 of the ACHR.[219] Significant fundamental rights beyond the right to effective judicial protection can justify special and *additional* requirements for judicial proceedings.[220]

Thus, a mere declaratory judgment confirming the existence of a substantive right, without a judicial order to enforce that right, is incompatible with the guarantees of a fair trial under Articles 6.1 of the ECHR or Articles 8.1 and 25 of the ACHR (Aberastury et al., Chap. 18, Sect. 3 and Huerta Ochoa, Chap. 19, Sect. 1). The same can be said of the special guarantees of the International Covenant on Civil and Political Rights (Article 14), the Charter of Fundamental Rights of the European Union (Article 47), the African Charter on Human and Peoples' Rights (Article 7), and the Asian Charter of Fundamental Rights (Article 15.4).

The right of access to information is no exception to this trend, although the intensity of judicial review will depend on the effectiveness of the procedural guarantees provided the extrajudicial proceeding. In other words, judicial review will be less intense, if the information access request in question was decided on

---

Inter-American system have determined in their interpretation of Article 13 of the American Convention on Human Rights that the burden is on the state to justify a denial of access to information, not on the requester or the party to whom the information pertains."

[216] German Federal Constitutional Court (Bundesverfassungsgericht), 2 BvR 23/65 (Judgment of 14 December 1969), BVerfGE (Fed. Const. Ct. Judgments) 27, 297 (305); and 1 BvR 385/77 (Judgment of 20 December 1979), BVerfGE 53, 30 (60).

[217] German Federal Constitutional Court (Bundesverfassungsgericht), 2 BvR 375, 53/60 and 18/65 (Judgment of 6 June 1967), BVerfGE 22, 49 (81); 2 BvR 1187/80 (Judgment of 8 July 1982), BVerfGE 61, 82 (110); and 2 BvF 2, 3, 4/83 and 2/84 (Judgment of 24 April 1985), BVerfGE 69, 1 (49).

[218] German Federal Constitutional Court (Bundesverfassungsgericht), 2 BvR 827/79 (Judgment of 15 April 1980), BVerfGE 54, 86 (91). See Ramsauer, in Kopp & Ramsauer (2016), Article 28, para 3.

[219] See for Article 6 of the ECHR Kallenhoff, in Stelkens et al. (2018), Article 28 para 2.

[220] German Federal Constitutional Court (Bundesverfassungsgericht), 1 BvR 385/90 (Judgment of 27 October 1999), EuGRZ 2000, p. 167 (172).

previously by an independent and impartial administrative authority which has adopted guarantees of procedural due process. Thus, when a claim for access is examined by administrative authorities in a fair hearing, an appeal of the decision in court will tend to be limited to "closed judicial review", which is generally restricted to scrutinizing the reasonableness of the authority's decision (Perlingeiro et al., Chap. 2, Sect. 6.5).

In light of the autonomy of the EU legal order, the European Court of Justice is repeatedly required to weigh the importance of the right of access to documents against the fundamental right to respect for private life and the related protection of personal data.[221] With regard to access to the documents of the institutions of the European Union, the Luxembourg Court of Justice in the Case *Bavarian Lager*[222] has outlined the dichotomy ("different objectives") between a regulation "which is designed to ensure the greatest possible transparency of the decision-making process of the public authorities and the information on which they base their decisions", i.e., "the exercise of the right of access to documents" aiming also at "good administrative practices" on the one hand, and, on the other, a regulation "which is designed to ensure the protection of the freedoms and fundamental rights of individuals, particularly their private life, in the handling of personal data". The weighing of the opposing interests by the EU Court of Justice has not always proven favorable to the applicant in each case, however.[223] The Court has begun to establish case-law favorable to freedom of information, however, by adopting a "general presumption" of the validity of requests for information access, which in effect reverses the burden of proof between the applicant and authority by requiring the authority which denies such a request to prove that the criteria are met for exceptional non-disclosure and restrictions.[224] With this precedent, the ECJ has developed an interpretation *contra legem* in competition law. The reversed burden of proof of the validity of an "exception" is increasingly common in transparency legislation. In keeping with Article 54.1 of the Model Inter-American Law, the Argentinian legislators recognise the reversal of the burden of proof as one of the principles in the Argentinian Law 27275/2016 "Derecho de Acceso a la

[221]For this need see, e.g., Case 28/08 P, *European Commission v. Bavarian Lager* (ECJ 29 June 2010) para 78, and Case 365/12 P, *European Commission v. EnBW Energie Baden-Württemberg AG* (ECJ 27 February 2014) para 63.

[222]Case 28/08 P *European Commission v. Bavarian Lager* (ECJ 29 June 2010) para 49. A beer importer requested the minutes of a meeting among the Commission, the British government and the beer brewers association CBMC. The occasion of that meeting was a complaint that the beer importer in question, Bavarian Lager, which wanted to import German beer into Great Britain in bottles, had difficulties because of various rules favoring trade in draft beer, which Bavarian Lager considered to violate Article 34 TFEU (formerly Article 28 TEC).

[223]Case 28/08 P, *European Commission v. Bavarian Lager* (ECJ 29 June 2010) para 78 et seq. As a result, the ECJ has approved the position of the Commission, and declared to be lawful "to reject the application for access to the full minutes of the meeting of 11 October 1996"; see Steinbeis 2010.

[224]Case 365/12 P, *European Commission v. EnBW Energie Baden-Württemberg AG* (ECJ 27 February 2014), para 64 et seqq.

Información Pública": When invoking an exception, "the entity receiving the request shall bear the burden of proof of the validity of any restriction on information access"[225] (Sect. 5.2).

The European Court of Justice has consistently ruled that any exceptions to the general protection of personal data and any restrictions on that fundamental right must be limited to "what is absolutely necessary".[226] In its Judgment in the *Max Schrems* Case, the ECJ argued as follows: "In particular, legislation permitting the public authorities to have access on a generalised basis to the content of electronic communications must be regarded as compromising the essence of the fundamental right to respect for private life, as guaranteed by Article 7 of the Charter" ("Respect for private and family life").[227] Thus, the Court found the intrusion in question to threaten the very *essence* of the protection of personal data.

## 7 Exercise of the Right and Sanctions for its Violation

It is worth thinking about the extent to which the effectiveness of information access laws is connected with the chances of success of citizens with claims that are derived from access to information of general interest. Is the legal system adequately structured to achieve the objectives of the "rights" of access to information with respect to its social dimensions? What in fact are those objectives? One extremely important concern is to check for honest conduct on the part of the public authorities and—at least preventively—to combat illegality, especially corruption, in government institutions and national or supranational authorities. Yet in practice, the question of the lawfulness of the public authorities' decisions regarding the exercise of the right of access to information tends to be pushed into the background.[228] What is the good of granting general access to information (without requiring the applicant to have a direct interest in the subject matter), if citizens are not provided with a tool enabling direct proposals of (judicial and extrajudicial) corrective and punitive measures for corrupt and criminal practices? In fact, the state is considered to have a monopoly on the power to prosecute and punish criminals. Such being the case, would access to information (about questions of general interest) enable citizens to push (lawfully constituted) regulatory authorities to act in a certain way? If so, would the disclosure of such information be exploitable by the press to that purpose and lead to the shaping of public opinion? Freedom of access to information is an intermediate objective designed to

[225] Article 1, principle 12 of the Argentinian Law 27275/2016 on the "Right of Access to Public Information".

[226] Joined Cases 293/12 and C-594/12, *Digital Rights Ireland et al.* (ECJ 8 April 2014) para 52; Case 362/14, *Schrems v. Data Protection Commissioner* (ECJ 6 October 2015) para 92.

[227] Case 362/14, *Schrems v. Data Protection Commissioner* (ECJ 6 October 2015) para 94. Article 7 CFREU provides: "Everyone has the right to respect for his or her private and family life, home and communications."

[228] See Rossi 2015, p. 56, regarding the German Freedom of Information Act.

make government authorities transparent, yet experience has shown that legislators are unable to control the extent and underlying intention of the applicants in asserting their claims for information.[229] Expecting more than "hard facts" from information access laws, for instance a more workable and democratic political community bringing the state closer to the citizen, could result in feelings of frustration.

## 7.1 *Exercise*

In fact, the exercise of the right of access to information has been extensive. Between July and September 2015, 25,852 requests for information access were filed with Brazilian federal administrative authorities.[230] In the USA, 22,555 requests for information in fiscal year 2015,[231] and 35,550 requests in Australia in the same year.[232] The citizens of different European countries seem to use their freedom of access to information in very different ways. In the UK, for example, between July and September 2015, monitored central government bodies received 11,990 non-routine Freedom of Information (FOI) requests.[233]

In Germany, which only recognises the right of access to information against public authorities that perform duties of public administration, experience has shown the extent of exercise of this freedom to be rather "reserved"[234] or "moderate"[235] or even "ridiculously low".[236] In the portfolios of the Federal Ministries, the requests for access to information under the German Freedom of Information Act totaled 3280 in 2011, 6077 in 2012 and 4736 in 2013. Out of the 4736 requests in 2013, the Federal Ministry of Finance accounted for 1390, the Ministry of Economics 662 and the Ministry of Labor 507. Out of the total number of requests, 786 were denied by the authority in question. That amounts to an overall rejection rate of 16.6%, calculated from the above-average rates of 24% at the Federal Ministry of Labor and 20.1% at the Federal Finance Ministry, and the extremely low rates of 7.4% at the Federal Ministry of Justice and 0% Federal Ministry for Development.[237]

---

[229] Rossi 2004, p. 326 (point 6); Rossi 2015, p. 49 et seq.

[230] See http://www.acessoainformacao.gov.br/assuntos/relatorios-dados/relatorios-estatisticos/relatorios-estatisticos (Accessed on 29 October 2016).

[231] http://www.foia.gov/data.html?foia/Services/DataRequest.jsp?agencyName=NARA&requestYear=2015 (Accessed on 29 October 2016).

[232] See https://data.gov.au/dataset/freedom-of-information-statistics/resource/e835719d-856c-4e9f-a858-aa772c56dcbf (Accessed on 29 October 2016).

[233] See https://www.gov.uk/government/uploads/system/uploads/attachment_data/file/486494/freedom-of-information-statistics-jul-sep-2015.pdf (Accessed on 29 October 2016).

[234] Schoch 2016, Einleitung para 401.

[235] Rossi 2015, p. 47.

[236] Tillack 2015, p. 81.

[237] Cf. the statistics of the German Federal Ministry of the Interior.

On the level of the European Union (with a current population of over 504 million citizens in 2012), the three bodies of the Parliament, Council and Commission together received about 8000 requests to process in 2012 pursuant to the European Transparency Regulation,[238] of which the Commission—as the guardian of the European Treaties—received by far the greatest share, i.e., 66%. Approximately 7% of the requests were granted, but the percentage of requests which are favorably received is not the sole measure of the effectiveness of freedom-of-information rights; from the perspective of general compliance with the law, it is also necessary to consider the extent to which the statutory exceptions and limitations of the general duties of disclosure are respected.[239] Nevertheless, the only available empirical data are often limited to a single aspect of the right to information—the requests submitted—and are therefore insufficient to achieve a conclusive analysis of the effectiveness of information access laws.

The right of access to information is used primarily for private or professional interests of the applicant rather than by ideally purely altruistic organisations or individuals. Yet this is not an abuse of the right granted. The legislator assumes that the granting of information in these cases also serves the public interest in transparency, at least indirectly.[240] There seems to be a lack of empirical studies on the development of national transparency laws which are comprehensive, i.e. not limited to a specific law; instead, often only statute-specific individual studies and assessments are available.[241] For an assessment of the effectiveness of transparency laws, the *quality* of the information made available by a public authority should be considered a factor carrying at least as much weight as the number of requests for access to documents.

## 7.2 Sanctions

Sanctions in the area of access of information are related to liability or responsibility issues, but have not been addressed by international jurisprudence as the

[238]Regulation (EC) No. 1049/2001 of 3rd December 2001 regarding public access to European Parliament, Council and Commission documents. This Regulation is applicable for all requests concerning the access to documents and registers of the Union which are filed by EU citizens and others when EU institutions are (exceptionally) implementing Union law.

[239]Cf. Rossi 2015, p. 47. This finding provides further confirmation of the author's well-grounded general skepticism towards the exaggerated expectations placed in transparency legislation and their "ideological excess " (p. 48).

[240]Fehling 2017, p. 82 with further references in footnote 30.

[241]This finding put forward by Rossi in 2015, p. 45, which applies to the patchwork situation in German transparency legislation (Scherzberg and Solka, Chap. 7, Sects. 1 and 2) can be said to apply, with a grain of salt, on the level of international level and comparative law, despite the fact that the laws of many countries (especially outside the EU) are far more uniform thematically and in terms of the competent authorities.

imposition of penalties corresponds to national authorities under the terms established in the laws in force. Nevertheless, the non-existence of a special law or specific regulation on the imposition of penalties (as in Germany) or liability concerning access to information does not justify inaction or pose an impediment for the state to protect this right. Hence, it falls to national states to guarantee this right, not only by providing the means to give access to information, but mainly by establishing the liability of public officials and sanctions in the event of non-compliance (as pursuant to Article 32 of the Brazilian Law N° 12.527). The need to regulate on liability is an issue which both the Inter-American Court of Human Rights and the European Court of Human Rights hold as important (Huerta Ochoa, Chap. 19, Sect. 1).

To improve the efficiency of the administrative authorities in charge of providing official information, information access laws all around the world commonly but not without exception empower the state to impose two different types of punitive measures: disciplinary administrative measures for general obstruction of access to information in violation of the law; and criminal prevention, investigation and prosecution for tampering with or destroying documents which have been subject to a request for information including the safeguarding against and the prevention of threats to public security and the free movement of such data.[242] Those criminal penalties may also allow for the deprivation of the profits obtained through infringements of the relevant laws.[243] Equivalent sanctions including administrative fines should be imposed for any infringement of the applicable statutory rules, in addition to appropriate measures imposed by the supervisory or judicial authority pursuant to those laws.[244] Such penalties shall be effective, proportionate and dissuasive.[245] The imposition of penalties including administrative fines should be subject to appropriate procedural safeguards in accordance with fundamental rights, including effective judicial protection and due process.[246]

---

[242]See Articles 66 and 67 of the Model Inter-American Law. Pursuant to Article 88.1 of the Model Law for Africa "[a] person who with intent to deny a right of access to information (a) destroys, damages or alters information; (b) conceals information; (c) falsifies information or makes a false record; d) obstructs the performance by an information holder of a duty under this Act; (e) interferes or obstructs the work of the oversight mechanism; or (f) directs, proposes, counsels or causes any person in any manner to do any of the above, commits a criminal offence and *is liable to a fine or imprisonment or both.*" According to Article 88.2 of this Model Law "*a financial penalty* [...] may be imposed each day until the request is received or determined", for example (point d), "[w]here a person, without reasonable cause [...] has given incorrect, incomplete or misleading information" (emphasis added). Regarding the constitutional foundations for the sanctions applicable to violations of transparency laws in Brazil and Mexico; cf. Huerta Ochoa, Chap. 19, Sects. 3 and 4; cf. also recitals 19, and 73 of the General Data Protection Regulation of the EU (GDPR).

[243]Cf. recital 149 GDPR.

[244]Cf. recital 148 GDPR.

[245]Cf. Article 84.1 (2) GDPR.

[246]Cf. recital 148 GDPR.

It can be said that because the competent authority has the power to impose penalties to ensure compliance with the provisions on access to information, it is essential that the nature of such penalties, criminal or administrative, is determined by law, whether in general terms through provisions of administrative or criminal liability or specifically in special laws on information. However, this is not enough, as can be noticed in what has been explained regarding the case of Mexico, since the current situation has not reached the expected results after so many reforms. The lack of certainty in terms of the applicability of the provisions on access to information leads to legal uncertainty (Huerta Ochoa, Chap. 19, Sect. 4).

The highest priority should be given to raising the awareness of the principle of transparency among all the civil servants of the authorities required to disclose official information.[247] From another angle, the laws of certain countries (such as India, South Africa and Uganda) protect civil servants against lawsuits for disclosure provided that they acted in good faith in the performance of their lawful duties (or what they believed to be such).[248] According to Tobel, "the protection of whistleblowers constitutes an important safety valve which can help promote the disclosure of essential information of public interest".[249] This view deserves to be endorsed if the whistleblower acts in good faith. In April 2018, the European Commission has submitted a proposal for a Directive on the protection of persons reporting on breaches of Union law which aims at fully exploiting the potential of whistleblower protection with a view to strengthening enforcement. It sets out a balanced set of common minimum standards providing robust protection against retaliation for whistleblowers reporting on breaches in specific policy areas where (1) there is a need to strengthen enforcement; (2) underreporting by whistleblowers is a key factor affecting enforcement; and (3) breaches may result in serious harm to the public interest.[250]

## 8 Efficiency of the Right of Access to Information

The Global Right to Information Rating (RTI) has established a global ranking of the general laws on information access based on 61 criteria, divided into seven different categories, namely: Right of Access, Scope, Requesting Procedures, Exceptions and Refusals, Appeals, Sanctions and Protections, and Promotional Measures. According to its current state (2017/18), the ten highest ranking legal frameworks are, for the most part surprisingly, those of Mexico, Serbia, Sri Lanka, Slovenia, India, Albania, Croatia, Liberia, El Salvador, and Sierra Leone. The ten lowest rankings are actually assigned for various reasons to Austria, Liechtenstein, Philippines, Tajikistan, Iran, Jordan, Germany, Taiwan, Uzbekistan and Belgium. Out of a total of 111 laws on access to information, France is ranked 88th, Spain 80th, Portugal 79th, China 77th, Japan 73rd, Switzerland 70th, Australia 58th, the

[247]This view is also shared by Schoch 2016, Einleitung para 404 et seq.

[248]Mendel 2008, p. 152.

[249]Mendel 2008, p. 153.

[250]European Commission, COM(2018) 218 final of 23.4.2018, p. 2 et seq.

U.S. 57th, Argentina 48th, Russia 36th, United Kingdom 35th, Sweden 33th, Brazil 22nd, and South Africa 21st.[251]

Nevertheless, it is important to note that the RTI Rating is limited to measuring the legal framework, and does not measure quality of implementation.[252] In some cases, countries with relatively weak laws may nonetheless be very open, due to positive implementation efforts, while even relatively strong laws cannot ensure openness if they are not implemented properly. Regardless of these outlying cases, over time a strong legal framework on access to information can contribute to advancing openness and help those using it to defend and promote this right.[253] The Spanish Law 9/2013 on transparency, access to public information and good governance[254] has thus been praised as an "authentic paradigm shift" in the field of transparency legislation.[255]

In fact, an analysis is needed that recognises the fundamental distinction between the quality of transparency legislation and the quality of implementation of such laws, which, in the eagerness to promise the best of all possible words, are often applied and interpreted without considering traditional legal concepts. Constant monitoring of the use of information access laws is of fundamental importance to ensure their effectiveness, but that does not suffice without a change of attitude on the subject.[256]

Moreover, it is the role of the legislator to indicate the necessary means of shaping reality in the direction indicated by the law (Barcellos, Chap. 15, Sect. 1), in such a way as to implement policies designed to foster a culture of information access, and capable of overcoming the obstacles resulting from a lack of human, technical and financial resources (Fortini and Avelar, Chap. 16, Sect. 5).

In fact, according to Snell, the key lesson to be learned by countries that wish to boost the effectiveness of their transparency legislation is not to ignore or underestimate the importance of the political and administrative culture,[257] since the first years following the enactment of a law are critical for building citizens' confidence in their ability to obtain information from the authorities, which must be constantly subject to pressure by the supervisory administrative entities or court.[258] Terril's affirmation that information access laws operate on three levels—political, bureaucratic and legal—and that they can become dysfunctional if the authorities,

---

[251]http://www.rti-rating.org/country-data. Accessed on 31 December 2017.

[252]http://www.rti-rating.org/methodology. Accessed on 29 October 2016. This explains why, despite the good placement of South Africa in the RTI ranking, the *Shadow Report* (2016) has come to the result that 46% of requests submitted to the South African government were refused – i.e. no information was provided. 58% of these refusals were deemed refusals – i.e. the requests were ignored. The *Shadow Report* is available at http://www.r2k.org.za/wp-content/uploads/CER-Shadow-Report-2016-Final.pdf (Accessed on 1st January 2018).

[253]It is also important to note that, while openness extends to factors beyond the legal framework for RTI, a strong legal framework is an important pre-requisite to full implementation of the right analysed in this publication.

[254]Boletín Oficial del Estado/Official Gazette of 10 December 2013, p. 97922.

[255]Puigpelat 2017, especially Sects. 1, 4.1. and 5.

[256]See Galetta 2016.

[257]Snell 2007, p. 14.

[258]Rabin & Oeled 2005.

especially the administrators, are incapable of appreciating those three levels, is still as applicable as ever.[259] It must not be overlooked that the additional transparency generated by transparency legislation can strengthen the confidence in the governmental decision-making processes, which can boost the efficiency of the internal administrative treatment of information. It is even viewed as "exemplary" when the legislators impose a duty of active disclosure on a variety of information from public registers.[260] This step towards a proactive governmental information policy has now been taken also in Europe by several legislators, such as in France ("Digital Republic Bill"[261]) and in Germany ("Open Data Law"[262]) or in Spain ("Proactive disclosure"[263]), in addition of the reactive transparency legislation through a proactive duty of disclosure on national or regional governments (Sect. 2.2). It is of fundamental importance for a culture of information, including in the sense of learning to deal with flows of communication (Sect. 4.1.3), to be established simultaneously with the creation of information access laws and their implementation in accordance with the rule of law, that is to say in compliance with the fundamental right to privacy.

## References

Ackermann, J. M., & Sandoval-Ballesteros, I. E. (2006). The global explosion of freedom of information laws. *Administrative Law Review, 58*, 85–130.

Albrecht, J. P., & Jotzo, F. (2017). *Das neue Datenschutzrecht der EU. Grundlagen, Gesetzgebungsverfahren, Synopse*. Baden-Baden, Germany: Nomos.

Asimow, M. (2015). Five models of administrative adjudication. *Forthcoming American Journal of Comparative Law, 63*. Available at http://ssrn.com/abstract=2502210.

Barr, W. P. (1989). Congressional requests for confidential executive branch information. Memorandum opinion for the General Counsel's Consultative Group. In Office of Legal Counsel, FBI Authority to Seize Suspects Abroad (Hearing). Retrieved December 28, 2017, from https://www.justice.gov/file/24236/download

Barreto, I. C. (2010). *A Convenção Europeia dos direitos do homem anotada*. Coimbra, Portugal: Coimbra Editora.

Bauer, H. (2005). Demokratie in Europa – Einführende Problemskizze. In H. Bauer, P.M. Huber, & K.-P. Sommermann (Eds.), *Demokratie in Europa* (p. 1–20). Tübingen, Germany: Mohr Siebeck.

[259]Terrill 2007, p. 37.

[260]See the Law on transparency ("Transparenzgesetz") which the Free and Hanseatic City of Hamburg has adopted in 2012; see Hamburger Gesetz- und Verordnungsblatt of 6.7.2012, p. 271; regarding the above evaluations cf. Schaar 2015, p. 30, 33, regarding the German Freedom of Information Act; an evaluation of the Hamburg Transparency Law can be found in the contribution of Herr et al. (2018), p. 168 et seqq.

[261]Loi n°2016-1321 *pour une République numérique*.

[262]See Gesetz zur Förderung der elektronischen Verwaltung (5 July 2017 - E-Government Act), German Federal Law Gazette 2017 p. 2206.

[263]See Article 3 and Chap. II of the Spanish Law 9/2013 on transparency, access to public information and good governance; cf. Mir Puigpelat 2017, Sect. 4.2.

Britz, G. (2009). Europäisierung des grundrechtlichen Datenschutzes? *Europäische Grundrechte-Zeitschrift (EuGRZ), 36*, 1–11.

Burt, J.-M., & Cagley, C. (2013). Access to information, access to justice: The challenges to accountability in Peru. *SUR International Journal on Human Rights, No. 10*.

Curtin, D. (2014). Challenging executive dominance in European democracy. In C. Joerges & C. Glinski (Eds.), *The European crisis and the transformation of transnational governance. Authoritarian managerialism versus democratic governance* (pp. 203–226). Oxford, England: Hart.

Deutlmoser, R., & Filip, A. (2015). In T. Hoeren et al. (Eds.), *Handbuch Multimedia-Recht* (Part 16.6). München, Germany: C.H. Beck.

Deutscher Bundestag – Wissenschaftliche Dienste (Research Services of the German Bundestag), 2015: *Das Akteneinsichtsrecht als Auskunftsrecht des einzelnen Abgeordneten*, Report No. WD 3 – 3000 – 293/15.

Fehling, M. (2017). Freier Informationszugang zwischen öffentlichen und privaten Interessen. *Deutsches Verwaltungsblatt (DVBl), 132*, 79–88.

Fisher, L. (2001). Congressional access to executive branch information: Legislative tools. The Library of Congress. Washington, U.S. Retrieved December 28, 2017, from https://fas.org/sgp/crs/secrecy/RL30966.pdf

Galetta, D. (2016). *Accesso civico e trasparenza della Pubblica Amministrazione alla luce delle (previste) modifiche alle disposizioni del Decreto Legislativo n. 33/2013*. Federalism.it.

Gierschmann, S., Schlender, K., Strentzel, R., & Veil, W. (2018). *Kommentar Datenschutzgrundverordnung*. Köln, Germany: Bundesanzeiger Verlag GmbH.

Guttman, D. (2010). Criminal Lawyers' Assn. v. Ontario: A limited right to government information under Section 2(b) of the charter. *The Supreme Court Law Review: Osgoode's Annual Constitutional Cases Conference*, No. 51, 199 et seqq.

Herr, M., Müller, C. E., Engewald, B., & Ziekow, J. (2018). Transparenzgesetzgebung in Deutschland in der Bewährung - Erfahrungen einer Gesetzesevaluation. *Die Öffentliche Verwaltung (DÖV), 71*, 165–175.

Hoidn, D. (2017). Informationsfreiheit. In A. Roßnagel (Ed.), *Europäische Datenschutz-Grundverordnung. Vorrang des Unionsrechts – Anwendbarkeit des nationalen Rechts* (pp. 269–276). Baden-Baden, Germany: Nomos.

Inter-American Commission on Human Rights (2015). *Acceso a la información, violencia contra las mujeres y la administración de justicia en las Américas*. Costa Rica: OEA. Retrieved March 14, 2016, from http://bit.ly/1OrOPIQ

Kang, C. (2017). F.C.C. reverses rules requiring net neutrality. The New York Times, 15.12.2017 (p. A1). Retrieved December 25, 2017, from https://www.nytimes.com/2017/12/14/technology/net-neutrality-repeal-vote.html

Klein, H. D. (2014). Artikel 43. In T. Maunz & G. Dürig (Eds.), *Grundgesetz Kommentar* (Loseleaf, 80. Suppl. 2017). München, Germany: C. H. Beck.

Klaaren, J., Currie, I., & Smith, A. (2000). Analysing foreign access to information legislation from a South African Viewpoint. In Konrad Adenauer Foundation (Ed.), *The constitutional right of access to information* (pp. 29–40). Retrieved February 9, 2017, from http://www.kas.de/wf/doc/kas_4936-1522-2-30.pdf?040625152235

Kloepfer, M. (2003). Informationszugangsfreiheit und Datenschutz: Zwei Säulen des Rechts der Informationsgesellschaft. *Die Öffentliche Verwaltung (DÖV), 56*, 221–231.

Kopp, F. O., & Ramsauer, U. (2016). *Verwaltungsverfahrensgesetz. Kommentar*. München, Germany: C.H. Beck.

Kugelmann, D. (2001). *Die informatorische Rechtsstellung des Bürgers*. Tübingen, Germany: Mohr Siebeck.

Kühling, J., Martini, M. et al. (2016). *Die DSGVO und das nationale Recht*. Münster, Germany: Monsenstein und Vannerdat.

Lessig, L. (2009, October 9). Against transparency. The perils of openness in government. *New Republic*. Retrieved October 29, 2016, from https://newrepublic.com/article/70097/against-transparency

Leutheusser-Schnarrenberger, S. (2015). Ein paradigmatischer Wandel vom Amtsgeheimnis zum gläsernen Staat? In H. H. von Arnim (Ed.), *Transparenz contra Geheimhaltung in Staat, Verwaltung und Wirtschaft* (pp. 13–26). Berlin, Germany: Duncker & Humblot.

Masing, J. (2003). Transparente Verwaltung – Konturen eines Informationsverwaltungsrechts. *Veröffentlichungen der Vereinigung der Deutschen Staatsrechtslehrer, 63*, 377–441.

Mendel, T. (2007). Access to information. In E. Villanueva (Ed.), *Derecho de la información* (pp. 3–12). México City: UNAM.

Mendel, T. (2008). *Freedom of information: A comparative legal survey*. Paris: UNESCO. Retrieved October 30, 2016, from http://portal.unesco.org/ci/en/files/26159/12054862803freedom_information_en.pdf/freedom_information_en.pdf

Mir Puigpelat, O. (2017). Access to public information in Spanish Transparency Law: The chronicle of a paradigm shift. *Revista catalana de dret públic (RCDP), 55*, p. 1–18.

O'Regan, K. (2000). Democracy and access to information in the South African Constitution: Some reflections. Analysing foreign access to information legislation from a South African viewpoint. In Konrad Adenauer Foundation (Ed.), *The constitutional right of access to information* (pp. 29–40). Retrieved February 13, 2017, from http://www.kas.de/wf/doc/kas_4936-1522-2-30.pdf?040625152235

Obama, B. (2009). *Memorandum on Transparency and Open Government*. Issued on 21 January 2009.

Orszag, P. R. (2009). *Memorandum for the Heads of Executive Departments and Agencies on Open Government*. Issued on 8 December 2009.

Paal, B. P., & Pauly, D. A. (2017). *Datenschutz-Grundverordnung. Kommentar*. München, Germany: C.H. Beck.

Peled, R., & Rabin, Y. (2011). The constitutional right to information. *Columbia Human Rights Law Review, 42*, 357–401.

Perlingeiro, R. (2014). *Information access laws in the world: Compilation of national laws, legislative bills and model codes on the right of access to the official Information*. Niterói, Brazil: Eduff. Retrieved October 29, 2016, from http://dx.doi.org/10.2139/ssrn.2416760

Perlingeiro, R. (2015). The codification of the right of access to information in Latin America. *Páginas A&B: Arquivos e Bibliotecas*. 3ª Série, n. 3, 119–128. Retrieved October 29, 2016, from http://ssrn.com/abstract=2441585

Perlingeiro, R. (2016). A historical perspective on administrative jurisdiction in Latin America. Continental European Tradition *vs*. US Influence. *British Journal of American Legal Studies – BJALS, 5*(1), 241–289. Retrieved October 29, 2016, from http://ssrn.com/abstract=2592418

Perlingeiro, R., & Sommermann, K.-P. (2014). *Euro-American model code of administrative jurisdiction: English, French, German, Italian, Portuguese and Spanish Versions*. Niterói, Brazil: Editora da UFF. Retrieved October 29, 2016, from http://ssrn.com/abstract=2441582

Proust, O., & Goossens, G. (2016). *France adopts Digital Republic Law*. Retrieved December 14, 2016, from http://privacylawblog.fieldfisher.com/2016/france-adopts-digital-republic-law/

Rabin, Y., & Oeled, R. (2005). Between FOI law culture: The Israeli experience. *Open Government: A Journal on Freedom of Information, 1*, 1–30. Retrieved September 23, 2016, from http://papers.ssrn.com/sol3/papers.cfm?abstract_id=777244

Rossi, M. (2004). *Informationszugangsfreiheit und Verfassungsrecht. Zu den Wechselwirkungen zwischen Freedom-of-information laws und der Verfassungsordnung in Deutschland*. Berlin, Germany: Duncker & Humblot.

Rossi, M. (2015). Informationsfreiheit – Anspruch und Wirklichkeit. In H. H. von Arnim (Ed.), *Transparenz contra Geheimhaltung in Staat, Verwaltung und Wirtschaft* (pp. 43–58). Berlin, Germany: Duncker & Humblot.

Sanz Salla, C. O. (2010). El derecho a la información administrativa en la era digital: una aproximación al derecho norteamericano. In R. García Macho (Ed.), *Derecho administrativo de la información y administración transparente* (pp. 203–230). Madrid, Spain: Marcial Pons.

Schaar, P. (2015). Zwischen Öffentlichkeit und Datenschutz. In H. H. von Arnim (Ed.), *Transparenz contra Geheimhaltung in Staat, Verwaltung und Wirtschaft* (pp. 27–34). Berlin, Germany: Duncker & Humblot.

Schnieders, R. (2018). Die neue Open-(Government)-Data-Gesetzgebung in Frankreich und in Deutschland. *Die Öffentliche Verwaltung (DÖV), 71*, 175–185.

Schmidt-Aßmann, E. (1991). Verwaltungslegitimation als Rechtsbegriff. *Archiv des öffentlichen Rechts, 116*, 329–390.

Schoch, F. (2016). *IFG. Informationsfreiheitsgesetz. Kommentar*. München, Germany: C.H. Beck.

Schulte, M. (1995). *Schlichtes Verwaltungshandeln. Verfassungs- und verwaltungsrechtsdogmatische Strukturüberlegungen am Beispiel des Umweltrechts*. Tübingen, Germany: Mohr Siebeck.

Schulzki Haddouti, C. (2012). Wikileaks und das Ideal der Öffentlichkeit. In U. Herb (Ed.), *Open Initiative; Offenheit in der digitalen Welt und Wissenschaft* (p. 185 et seqq). Saarland, Germany: University Press.

Schwanengel, W. (2018). Das Parlament im Gefüge der Staatsorganisation. Ein Studien- und Handbuch. LIT-Verlag: Münster, Germany (forthcoming).

Snell, R. (2007). Freedom of information analysis. In E. Villanueva (Ed.), *Derecho de la Information* (pp. 13–52). Mexico City, Mexico: UNAM.

Sobota, K. (1997). *Das Prinzip Rechtsstaat. Verfassungs- und verwaltungsrechtliche Aspekte*. Tübingen, Germany: Mohr Siebeck.

Sommermann, K.-P. (2005). Demokratiekonzepte im Vergleich. In H. Bauer, P. M. Huber, & K.-P. Sommermann (Eds.), *Demokratie in Europa* (pp. 191–221). Tübingen, Germany: Mohr Siebeck.

Sommermann, K.-P. (2010). La exigencia de una Administración transparente en la perspectiva de los principios de democracia y del Estado de Derecho. In R. García Macho (Ed.), *Derecho administrativo de la información y administración transparente* (pp. 12–19). Madrid, Spain: Marcial Pons.

Steinbeis, M. (2010). EuGH zieht Informationsfreiheit in der EU die Zähne. Verfassungsblog. Retrieved October 29, 2016, from http://verfassungsblog.de/eugh-zieht-informationsfreiheit-der-eu-die-zhne/#.VeYRuUbz8oM

Stelkens, P., Bonk, H. J., & Sachs, M. (2018). *Verwaltungsverfahrensgesetz. Kommentar*. München, Germany: C.H. Beck.

Terrill, G. (2007). Democratising secrecy? The characteristics and context of freedom of information legislation. Apud Rick Snell, Freedom of information analysis. In E. Villanueva (Ed.), *Derecho de la Information* (pp. 13–52). Mexico City, Mexico: UNAM.

Tillack, H.-M. (2015). Wer nutzt die Informationsfreiheit? In H. H. von Arnim (Ed.), *Transparenz contra Geheimhaltung in Staat, Verwaltung und Wirtschaft* (pp. 81–92). Berlin, Germany: Duncker & Humblot.

U.S. Supreme Court, McGrain v. Daugherty, 273 U.S. 135, 160 (1927). Retrieved December 28, 2017, from https://supreme.justia.com/cases/federal/us/273/135/case.html

Waldhoff, C. (2017). VGH München, 22.04.2016 - 5 BV 15.799: Staatsorganisationsrecht und Verwaltungsrecht: Landtagsfraktion als Inhaberin eines Informationsanspruchs. *Juristische Schulung (JuS), 57*, 284–286.

Warren, S., & Brandeis, L. D. (1890). The right to privacy. *Harvard Law Review, 4*(193). Retrieved October 29, 2016, from http://groups.csail.mit.edu/mac/classes/6.805/articles/privacy/Privacy_brand_warr2.html

Werner, F. (1959). Verwaltungsrecht als konkretisiertes Verfassungsrecht. *Deutsches Verwaltungsblatt, 64*, 527–533.

Wiberg, M. (2005). The emerging interaction society. In M. Wiberg (Ed.), *The interaction society: Practice, theories and supportive technologies* (pp. 1–25). Hershey, PA: Information Science Publishing.

Wieland, J. (2000). Freedeom of information. In C. Engel & K. H. Keller (Eds.), *Governance of global networks in the light of differing local values* (pp. 83–104). Baden-Baden, Germany: Nomos.

Wimmer, N. (2013). Netzneutralität – Eine Bestandsaufahme. *Zeitschrift für Urheber- und Medienrecht (ZUM), 57*, 641–652.

Woods, L. (2012). User generated content: Freedom of expression and the role of the media in a digital age. In M. Amos, J. Harrison, & L. Woods (Eds.), *Freedom of expression and the media* (pp. 141 et seqq.). Leiden, the Netherlands/Boston: Martinus Nijhoff.

# List of Cases

## *Canadian Supreme Court*

Canadian Supreme Court 03.11.2005, *Montréal (City) v. 2952-1366 Québec Inc.*, 3 S.C.R. 141, 2005 SCC 62.

Canadian Supreme Court, 17.06.2010, *Ontario (Public Safety and Security) v. Criminal Lawyers' Association*, SCC 23, 2010 1 S.C.R. 815.

## *European Court of Human Rights*

European Court of Human Rights 26.03.1987, *Leander v. Sweden*, Series A No. 116, Appl. No. 9248/81.

European Court of Human Rights 29.06.2004, *Chauvy and Others v. France*, ECHR 2004 VI, Appl. No. 64915/01.

European Court of Human Rights 14.04.2009, *Társaság a Szabadságjogokért v. Hungary*, Appl. No. 37374/05.

## *European Court of Justice*

European Court of Justice 29.06.2010, *European Commission v. Bavarian Lager Co. Ltd.*, C-28/08 P, ECLI:EU:C:2010:378.

European Court of Justice 09.11.2010, *Schecke and Eifert*, C-93/09 and C-92/09, ECLI:EU:C:2010:662.

European Court of Justice 27.02.2014, *European Commission v. EnBW Energie Baden-Württemberg AG*, C-365/12 P, ECLI:EU:C:2014:112.

European Court of Justice 08.04.2014, *Digital Rights Ireland Ltd.*, C-293/12 and C-594/12, ECLI:EU:C:2014:238.

European Court of Justice 13.05.2014, *Google Spain SL, Google Inc. v. Agencia Española de Protección de Datos (AEPD)*, C-131/12, ECLI:EU:C:2014:317.

European Court of Justice 06.10.2015, *Schrems v. Data Protection Commissioner*, C-362/14, ECLI:EU:C:2015:650.

## *German Federal Constitutional Court*

German Federal Constitutional Court 06.06.1967, *Administrative Sanctions by Fiscal Authorities*, 2 BvR 375, 53/60 and 18/65 (BVerfGE 22, p. 49).

German Federal Constitutional Court 14.12.1969, *Effectivity of Restorative Justice*, 2 BvR 23/65 (BVerfGE 27, p. 297).

German Federal Constitutional Court 08.08.1978, *Kalkar I*, 2 BvL 8/77 (BVerfGE 49, p. 89).

German Federal Constitutional Court 20.12.1979, *Mülheim-Kärlich*, 1 BvR 385/77 (BVerfGE 53, p. 30).

German Federal Constitutional Court 15.04.1980, *Violation of the Right to be Heard*, 2 BvR 827/79 (BVerfGE 54, p. 86).
German Federal Constitutional Court 08.07.1982, *Sasbach*, 2 BvR 1187/80 (BVerfGE 61, p. 82).
German Federal Constitutional Court 15.12.1983, *Census of Population*, 1 BvR 209 and others (BVerfGE 65, p. 1).
German Federal Constitutional Court 24.04.1985, *Conscientious Objection II*, 2 BvF 2, 3, 4/83 and 2/84 (BVerfGE 69, p. 1).
German Federal Constitutional Court 27.10.1999, *Right to Inspect Records*, 1 BvR 385/90 (EuGRZ 2000, p. 167).
German Federal Constitutional Court 13.06.2007, *Access to Account Master Data*, 1 BvR 1550/03 and others (NJW 2007, p. 2464).
German Federal Constitutional Court 27.02.2008, *Fundamental Rights Protection against Infiltration of IT-Systems*, 1 BvR 370/07 and 1 BvR 595/07 (BVerfGE 120, p. 274).
German Federal Constitutional Court 17.06.2009, *Parliamentary Inquiry Committee, Federal Intelligence Service*, 2 BvE 3/07 (BVerfGE 124, p. 78).
German Federal Constitutional Court 01.07.2009, *Surveillance of Members of the Bundestag*, 2 BvE 5/06 (BVerfGE 124, p. 16).
German Federal Constitutional Court 13.10.2016, *Parliamentary Inquiry Committee, NSA Selector List*, 2 BvE 2/15.
German Federal Constitutional Court 13.06.2017, *Answering two brief requests of information about the knowledge of the German intelligence services regarding the assassination attempt on the Munich Oktoberfest in 1980*, 2 BvE 1/15.
German Federal Constitutional Court 07.11.2017, *Request of information by members of the German Parliament about the attack on the Munich Oktoberfest in 1980*, 2 BvE 2/11.

## *German Federal Constitutional Court 07.11.2017,* Request of information by members of the German Parliament about the attack on the Munich Oktoberfest in 1980*, 2 BvE 2/11.German Federal Administrative Court*

German Federal Administrative Court 21.03.1986, *Expropriation*, 4 C 48.82 (BVerwGE 74, p. 109).
German Federal Administrative Court 03.11.2011, *Access to information*, 7 C 3.11 (BVerwGE 141, p. 122).

## *Higher Administrative Court of Munich*

Higher Administrative Court of Munich 22.04.2017, *Right of Access to Information of a Parliamentary Group*, 2 BV 15.799 (NVwZ 2016, p. 1107).

## Indian Supreme Court

Indian Supreme Court 30.12.1981, *S.P. Gupta v. President of India and Orthers*, (1981) Supp. SCC 87.

Indian Supreme Court 23.09.1988, *Reliance Petrochemicals Ltd., v. Proprietors of Indian Express Newspapers, Bombay Pvt. Ltd. and others*, 004 SCC 0592 SC.

Indian Supreme Court 02.05.2002, *Dinesh Trivedi, Union of India v. AS & Soacnioatthieorn for Democratic Reforms*, 2002 INSC 244.

Indian Supreme Court 13.03.2003, *People's Union of Civil Liberties (P.U.C.L.) & Another v. Union of India & Another*, INSC 173.

## Inter-American Court of Human Rights

Inter-American Court of Human Rights 19.09.2006, *Claude Reyes, et al. v. Chile*, Series C No. 151.

## Inter-American Commission on Human Rights

Inter-American Commission on Human Rights 02.07.2004, *Herrera Ulloa v. Costa Rica*, Série C N° 107.

Inter-American Commission on Human Rights 31.08.2004, *Ricardo Canese v. Paraguay*, Série C N° 111.

Inter-American Commission on Human Rights 13.11.1985, Advisory Opinion OC-5/85, Série A N° 5.

Inter-American Court of Human Rights 24.11.2010, *Case of Gomes Lund, et al. (Guerrilha do Araguaia) v. Brazil*, Retrieved April 14, 2016 from http://www.corteidh.or.cr/docs/casos/articulos/seriec_219_ing.pdf.

## Japanese Supreme Court

Japanese Supreme Court 26.11.1969, Kaneko v. Japan, 23 Keishu 1490. Retrieved October 4, 2017, from www.right2info.org/cases/r2i-kaneko-v.-japan-201chakata-station-film-case201d

U.S. Supreme Court, McGrain v. Daugherty, 273 U.S. 135, 160 (1927). Retrieved December 28, 2017, from https://supreme.justia.com/cases/federal/us/273/135/case.html

# Part I
# Fundamental Issues on Access to Information

# Chapter 2
# Principles of the Right of Access to Official Information in Latin America

**Ricardo Perlingeiro, Milena Liani, and Ivonne Díaz**

## Contents



---

I wish to express my gratitude for the legal research performed by Alexandre Arruda, Flavia Martins Affonso and Lívia Pitelli Zamarian, Doctoral Candidates at the Law School of Federal Fluminense University, and Graziela De Caro, who has completed her final year of studies at that same Law School at the end of 2017.

R. Perlingeiro (✉)
Fluminense Federal University Law School/Estácio de Sá University, Rio de Janeiro, Brazil
e-mail: r.perlingeiro@terra.com.br

M. Liani
Andrés Bello Catholic University, Caracas, Venezuela

I. Díaz
National Autonomous University of Mexico, Mexico City, Mexico

 
H.-J. Blanke, R. Perlingeiro (eds.), *The Right of Access to Public Information*,
DOI 10.1007/978-3-662-55554-5_2

## 1 Introduction

In connection with the global developments in the subject area,[1] the Inter-American Court of Human Rights (I/A Court H.R.), in its 2006 Judgment *Claude Reyes et al. v. Chile*, recognized the right to access (seek and receive) official information anchored in Article 13.1 *Freedom of Thought and Expression* of the American Convention on Human Rights (ACHR).[2] With that Judgment, the I/A Court H.R. became the first international court to recognize that the right to access official information is a fundamental human right.[3]

Significant changes subsequently occurred in the Latin American scene. In 2008, the Inter-American Juridical Committee (IAJC) of the Organization of American States (OAS) approved the following principles of the right of access to information:

> a) In principle, all information is accessible; b) Access to information applies to all public bodies, including private bodies operating with public funds; c) The right of access to information applies to all information; d) Public bodies should disseminate information about their functions and activities; e) Clear, fair, non-discriminatory and simple rules should be established regarding requests for information; f) Any exceptions to the right of access should be established by statute; g) The burden of proof in justifying any denial of access to information lies with the body from which the information was requested; h) Individuals should have the right to appeal against any refusal or obstruction to provide access to information; i) Anyone who willfully denies or obstructs access to information in breach of the rules should be subject to sanction; j) Measures should be taken to promote, to implement and to enforce the right to access to information.[4]

In 2010, a Model Inter-American Law on Access to Official information and Implementation Guide, approved by the OAS General Assembly, incorporated the precepts established by the Inter-American Court of Human Rights in the Case of *Claude Reyes et al. v. Chile* (2006), as well as the above-stated Inter-American Juridical Committee's principles of information access.[5]

Against that backdrop, this comparative study will examine—in light of the theory of fundamental rights—the 10 IAJC principles enumerated above and try to determine the degree to which they have influenced the laws and judicial precedents of the 18 Latin American countries of Iberian origin under the jurisdiction of the

[1]Mendel 2007, p. 6.

[2]Inter-American Court of Human Rights, *Case of Claude Reyes et al. v. Chile* (Judgment of 19 September 2006).

[3]Inter-American Commission on Human Rights 2015, p. 22.

[4]Inter-American Juridical Committee 2008; See also Mendel 2009, p. 13.

[5]Organization of American States 2010, Model Inter-American Law on Access to Information.

Inter-American Court of Human Rights (Argentina, Bolivia, Brazil, Chile, Colombia, Costa Rica, El Salvador, Ecuador, Guatemala, Honduras, Mexico, Nicaragua, Panama, Paraguay, Peru, Dominican Republic, Uruguay and, until 2013, Venezuela[6]). This will involve pointing out the positive and negative aspects of the national legal systems of Latin America with respect to the right to access information.

Our analysis of the aforementioned principles will follow a logical sequence based on the theory of fundamental rights.

## 2 Information Access as a Tool of Democracy

> Information is the oxygen of democracy. If people do not know what is happening in their society, if the actions of those who rule them are hidden, then they cannot take a meaningful part in the affairs of that society. But information is not just a necessity for people – it is an essential part of good government. Bad government needs secrecy to survive. It allows inefficiency, wastefulness and corruption to thrive. As Amartya Sen, the Nobel Prize-winning economist has observed, there has not been a substantial famine in a country with a democratic form of government and a relatively free press. Information allows people to scrutinise the actions of a government and is the basis for proper, informed debate of those actions.[7]

The OAS General Assembly has adapted several resolutions according to which public information access is an indispensable prerequisite to allow a democracy to run smoothly, with optimal transparency and proper public management, and to ensure that the population can exercise its constitutional rights in a representative and participative system with ample freedom of expression and free access to information.[8]

The Inter-American Court considers that there is a close relationship between democracy and freedom of expression: "[. . .] freedom of expression is a cornerstone of the very existence of democratic society. It is indispensable for the formation of public opinion. It is also a *conditio sine qua non* to ensure that political parties, syndicates, scientific and cultural societies and, in general, whoever wishes to influence the collective body, can develop fully. Finally, it is a prerequisite to ensure that the community will be sufficiently well informed when it comes to making choices. A society that is not well informed may therefore be said not to be fully alive".[9]

---

[6]With the State of Venezuela's denunciation of the American Convention on Human Rights on 10 September 2013, the I/A Court H.R. has jurisdiction over only such human rights violations in Venezuela as occurred before that date (Inter-American Commission on Human Rights 2013, IACHR Deeply Concerned over Result of Venezuela's Denunciation of the American Convention).

[7]Mendel 1999, p. 1.

[8]Resolution AG/RES. 1932 (XXXIII-O/03) held on June 10, 2003 on *Access to Public Information: Strengthening Democracy*; Resolution AG/RES. 2057 (XXXIV-O/04) held on June 8, 2004 on *Access to Public Information: Strengthening Democracy*; Resolution AG/RES. 2121 (XXXV-O/05) held on June 7, 2005 on *Access to Public Information: Strengthening Democracy*; and AG/RES. 2252 (XXXVI-O/06) held on June 6, 2006 on *Access to Public Information: Strengthening Democracy.*

[9]Inter-American Court of Human Rights, *Case of Ricardo Canese v. Paraguay,* (Judgment of 31 August de 2004), para 82; Inter-American Court of Human Rights *Case of Herrera Ulloa*

In fact, (in a representative and participatory democracy), it is easy to see that full exercise of the right to vote is contingent on access to information and knowledge of facts relevant to the political process of direct decision-making (as in a popular referendum) or choice of parliamentary representatives.

According to the dicta of the Inter-American Court, the right to information has two dimensions (individual and collective)[10] that can be used to assert its universal nature, so that every citizen is entitled to access State-held information, even without a specific interest in the relevant information: the concept of *social supervision of the State* suffices to justify such information access.[11]

Indeed, "the supplying of information to an individual allows such information to circulate in society and become known, accessed and evaluated".[12]

Yet, when relying on democracy as the basis of the universality of the right to information (about any official subject), it is necessary to bear in mind that the system cannot be changed directly through the mere circulation of information, which do no more than help shape public opinion and encourage the supervisory bodies to take action.[13]

It would be unwise to raise false hopes among citizens that they have the authority to review the legality of administrative acts outside the sphere of their personal interests: the citizen, acting alone, cannot directly use the information thus acquired to change the administrative authorities or governmental policy but can only report such information to the supervisory authorities so that they can take appropriate measures. Moreover, even in a case of political decision-making, the power that is supported in a participatory democracy is the power exercised by the people, (not by an individual).

## 3 Right to Information as a Fundamental Human Right

The right to information is a right shared by everyone, both citizens and non-citizens; it is a human right originating in the freedom of thought and expression. It is therefore a right that precedes the State rather than being

*v. Costa Rica,* (Judgment of 2 July 2004), para 112; Inter-American Court of Human Rights, *Compulsory membership in an Association prescribed by law for the practice of journalism (Article 13 and Article 29 American Convention on Human Rights).* Advisory Opinion OC-5/85 of November, 13 1985, Série A No. 5, para 70.

[10]Inter-American Court of Human Rights, *Case of Gomes Lund et al. (Guerrilha do Araguaia) v. Brazil* (Judgment of 24 November 2010).

[11]Inter-American Court of Human Rights, *Case of Claude Reyes et al. v. Chile* (Judgment of 19 September 2006), para 157.

[12]Inter-American Court of Human Rights, *Case of Claude Reyes et al. v. Chile* (Judgment of 19 September 2006), para 77.

[13]Inter-American Court of Human Rights, *Case of Claude Reyes et al. v. Chile* (Judgment of 19 September 2006), para 89.

merely granted by it. It is a right that can only be limited by a specific statute.[14]

The OAS Inter-American Juridical Committee stipulates as follows:

> Access to information is a fundamental human right which establishes that everyone can access information from public bodies, subject only to a limited regime of exceptions in keeping with a democratic society and proportionate to the interest that justifies them. States should ensure full respect for the right to access to information through adopting appropriate legislation and putting in place the necessary implementation measures.[15]

Regarding the individual dimension of the right to access information,

> [...] the international human rights systems have made it abundantly clear that access to information facilitates the exercise of other human rights; in other words, information is often indispensable to allow individuals to exercise other rights.[16]

Access to information has been established as an autonomous fundamental right in the Constitutions of Bolivia,[17] Brazil,[18] Costa Rica,[19] Ecuador,[20] Guatemala,[21] Mexico,[22] Nicaragua,[23] Panama,[24] Paraguay,[25] Peru,[26] Dominican Republic[27] and Venezuela.[28]

---

[14]Regarding the concept of fundamental rights, human rights and positive natural law, see Pieroth & Schlink 2012, p. 12–13.

[15]Inter-American Juridical Committee 2008, resolution item 1.

[16]Inter-American Commission on Human Rights 2015, p. 22.

[17]Article 21.6 and Article 242.4 of the Bolivian Constitution (Nueva Constituición Política del Estado de 2008).

[18]Article 5, item 33, Article 37 para 3, item 2, and Article 216 para 2 of the Brazilian Constitution (Constituição da República Federativa do Brasil de 1988).

[19]Article 30 of the Costa Rican Constitution (Constitucion Politica de la República de Costa Rica de 1949).

[20]Article 18.2 and Article 91 of the Ecuadorian Constitution (Constituición Política del Ecuador de 2008).

[21]Article 30 of the Guatemalan Constitution (Constitución Política de la República de Guatemala de 1993).

[22]Article 6.2. and 6.4 sub-paragraph (A), item 1 of the Mexican Constitution (Constitución Política de los Estados Unidos Mexicanos de 1917).

[23]Article 66 of the Nicaraguan Constitution (Constitución Política de la República de Nicaragua de 1987).

[24]Article 43 and Article 44 of the Panamanian Constitution (Constitución Política de la República de Panamá de 1972).

[25]Article 28 of the Paraguayan Constitution (Constitución Nacional de la República del Paraguay de1992).

[26]Article 2.4 and Article 5 of the Peruvian Constitution (Constitución Política del Peru de 1993).

[27]Article 49.1 of the Constitution of the Dominican Republic (Constitución Política de la República Dominicana de 2010).

[28]Article 143 of the Venezuelan Constitution (Constitución de la República Bolivariana de Venezuela de 1999).

In certain Latin American countries, the right to information is missing from the constitution but has been defined by the legislators as a fundamental right, as in the cases of Colombia,[29] El Salvador,[30] Guatemala[31] and Uruguay.[32] In Honduras, although the right to access official information is not expressly defined by law as a fundamental right, violations of that right may be tried in a special judicial action known as *amparo,* which is reserved for the protection of constitutional rights.[33]

Indeed, generally speaking, countries whose constitutions do not expressly mention the right to information (Chile, Colombia, El Salvador, Guatemala, Honduras, Uruguay and, above all, Argentina[34]), frequently show signs of transparency or principles requiring public disclosure, and the case-law of their constitutional courts ensures transparency as one of the basic prerequisites for a democratic constitutional state.[35]

In 2014, the Supreme Court of Argentina affirmed that the "obligation to guarantee access to information by constitutional norms is incumbent on the State" and that the Constitution "establishes that the right to access official information is a necessary condition in order to organize a democratic republic"; to provide effective guarantees for the right to information, it was doubtless necessary for "the State to enact an urgent law ensuring compliance with the principle of reasonableness and the applicable international principles on the subject, with exhaustive provisions regulating the manner in which the public authorities are required to satisfy that right".[36]

Similarly, in 2007, the Constitutional Court of Chile ruled that the right to official information is supported by their constitution, "because the right to access information held by bodies of the State is part of the freedom of expression [...]

---

[29]Article 4 (1) of the Law No. 1.712 on Access to Information of 6 March 2014(Ley de Transparencia y del Derecho de Acceso a la Información Pública Nacional).

[30]Whereas clause I of the Decree No. 534 of 3 March 2011 on Access to Information (Ley de Acceso a la Información Pública).

[31]Article 46 of the Decree No. 57 of 22 October 2008 on Access to Information (Ley de Acceso a la Información Pública).

[32]Article 2 of the Law No. 18.381 of 17 October 2008 on Access to Information (Ley de Acceso a la Información Pública).

[33]Article 26 of the Legislative Decree No. 170 of 30 December 2006 on Access to Information (Ley de Transparencia y Acceso a la Información Pública).

[34]In Argentina, the Federal Executive Branch had promulgated a Decree that regulates the *right* to access information held by Federal Public Administrative Authorities (Decree No. 1172 of 3 December 2003 on Access to Information (Reglamento Argentino de Acceso a la Información Pública del Poder Ejecutivo Nacional)). This Decree was replaced in 2016 by the Law 22275/2016 on "Derecho de Acceso a la Información".

[35]Sommermann 2010, p. 12, 19. See also Perlingeiro 2015, p. 129.

[36]National Supreme Court of Justice, Argentina (Corte Suprema de Justicia de La Nación Argentina), CIPPEC c/ EN – M° Desarrollo Social – dto. 1172/03 s/amparo, Ley 16.986, Fallos C. 830. XLVI, 2014 (Judgment of 26 March 2014) para 32. See now the Argentinian Law 22275 on the "Right of Access to Public Information" (*Derecho de Acceso a la Información Pública*) of 2016.

anchored in Article 19.12 of that fundamental charter", and because "Article 8 of the Chilean Constitution [. . .] includes the principles of honesty, public disclosure and transparency applicable to the conduct of bodies of the State".[37]

The Constitutional Section of the Supreme Court of Honduras, too, has recognized the right to access official information as a fundamental right, not based on that country's constitution but under international treaties. This may be observed in the following passage of the Court's Judgment addressing the restrictions on the right to access information regulated by the Law on Transparency and Access to Official Information:

> [. . .] the refusal by the Information Officer of the PRAF (family allowance program) to supply the information demanded by the IAI (information access institution) has no legal basis and consequently violates the aforementioned fundamental rights.

The Court concludes as follows:

> We can say that the refusal (by the PRAF Information Officer) to obey the decision issued by the IAI violates the petitioner's right to access official information and therefore violates the guarantees under Article 19 of the Universal Declaration of Human Rights and Article 13 of the American Convention on Human Rights, so that the amparo (appeal) lodged by the petitioner should be allowed.[38]

That same Constitutional Section even recognized that the exercise of the right to access information strengthens the Rule of Law and the democratic process.[39]

The judicial precedents in Uruguay, as well, stress the fact that the right to information is a fundamental right,

> [. . .] it is a basic right inherent in the human personality [. . .], and the right to access official information is a corollary of it. [. . .] The right to access official information is one of the third-generation rights, since it is both an individual right and a collective right of any society; it is associated with the transparency of public administration and the need to investigate, analyze and inform public opinion of the content of public documents [. . .].[40]

The Colombia Constitutional Court has established that the right to information "is a right that expresses the natural human tendency to gain knowledge. [. . .] The subject of that right is universal: *any person – without discrimination* – and object of that right is true and impartial information, as enshrined in Article 20 of the National Constitution".[41] The Court further ruled that:

---

[37]Constitutional Court of Chile (Tribunal Constitucional de Chile), Rol. 634-2006 (Judgment of 9 August 2007).

[38]Constitutional Section of the Supreme Court of Justice of Honduras (Sala de lo Constitucional de la Corte Suprema de Justicia de Honduras), Recurso de Amparo Administrativo 715 (Judgment of 8 June 2011).

[39]Constitutional Section of the Supreme Court of Justice of Honduras, Recurso de Amparo Administrativo 0296-15 (Judgment of 8 April 2015).

[40]Honorable Court of the Second Panel of the City of Mercedes, Uruguay (Juzgado Letrado de Segundo Turno de Mercedes de Uruguay), Sentencia 48 (Judgment of 11 September 2009).

[41]Constitutional Court of the Republic of Colombia (Corte Constitucional de la República de Colombia), Sentencia C-488/93 (Judgment of 28 October 1993).

> [...] An exceptional duty is implied by the principles of solidarity (Article 1 of the Constitution) and of the efficacy of principles, rights and duties (Article 2 of the Constitution), in cases in which information access is a prerequisite for an individual's free and independent existence, denying such access directly violates a fundamental right, and the legal remedies are inadequate to prevent such a violation. [...] The fundamental right to vital information held by any person in the exceptional circumstances described above is anchored in Articles 1, 2 and 49 of the Constitution [...].[42]

The Supreme Court of Costa Rica has expressed the following interpretation:

> [...] the right to information is considered an indispensable legal guarantee allowing citizens to participate, to a greater or lesser degree, in public affairs; from that point of view, it is both a public and a personal right. Moreover, the right to information is high-priority right, since it guarantees a constitutional interest: the formation and existence of free public opinion; a guarantee that takes on particular importance since, as necessary prerequisite for the exercise of other rights inherent in the functioning of a democratic system, it becomes, in turn, one of the pillars of a free and democratic society.[43]

In Venezuela, the Constitutional Section of the Supreme Court, in a 2010 Judgment whose contents were declared binding *erga omnes* recognized that Article 143 of the Constitution expressly established the "extremely novel right of citizens to request information and be informed in a timely and truthful manner about questions of public interest". Initially, there had been no such recognition in the precedents of the Constitutional Court, which pointed out in an administrative procedure,

> Article 143 grants citizens another right to information which must be respected by the public administrative authorities to ensure that the citizens under its administration are aware of the state of proceedings in which they have a direct interest, as well as the decisions adopted.[44]

Although, in the above-cited 2010 Judgment, the Court recognized it as an autonomous right, it denied the petitioners' claim on the grounds that the exercise of the right to access official information is conditional on another constitutional principle, i.e., it is "legitimated by the principle of transparency of public administration, which is one of the values expressly enshrined in Article 141 of the Constitution [...]".[45]

---

[42] Constitutional Court of the Republic of Colombia, Sentencia T-443 (Judgment of 12 October 1994). Also see: Constitutional Court of the Republic of Colombia, Sentencia T-960-01 (Judgment of 6 September 2001) and Sentencia T-275/05 (Judgment of 17 March 2005).

[43] Constitutional Section of the Supreme Court of Justice of Costa Rica (Sala Constitucional de la Corte Suprema de Justicia de Costa Rica), Exp: 08-003718-0007-CO. Res. 2008-013658 (Judgment of 5 September 2008).

[44] Constitutional Section of the Supreme Court of Justice of the Bolivarian Republic of Venezuela (Sala Constitucional del Tribunal Supremo de Justicia de la República Bolivariana de Venezuela), *Case Red de Veedores de la Universidad Católica Andrés Bello v. Consejo Nacional Electoral*, Sentencia 1050 (Judgment of 23 August 2000).

[45] Constitutional Section of the Supreme Court of Justice of the Bolivarian Republic of Venezuela, *Case Asociación Civil Espacio Público v. La Contraloría General de la República Bolivariana de Venezuela,* Sentencia 745(Judgment of 15 July 2010).

The Constitutional Court of Guatemala ruled on the various charges of unconstitutionality leveled against the Law on Access to Official Information (*Ley de Acceso a la Información Pública*). The Court decided, in keeping with the established international principles, that "all acts of public administrative authorities are public" and that citizens "as the bearers of national sovereignty, have a right to access such information". Consequently, to exercise that right,

> the citizen need only express a legitimate desire to know about the organization, functioning and decision-making processes of the governmental apparatus designed to ensure the welfare of himself and his peers; the configuration of the citizen's interest in the relevant subject should be considered in that light rather than according to the strict procedural definition of the term.[46]

In El Salvador, "the right to access official information is derived from an interpretation of the first part of Article 6 of the National Constitution".[47] Moreover, the case-law of the constitutional court has repeatedly recognized the fundamental nature of the right to access information (public and private). The following Judgment provides a summary of the terms of such recognition:

> According to the Judgment of 5 Dec. 2012, No. 13-2012, (Regulations of the Law on Access to Official Information Case), the right to access information is undeniably a fundamental right implied by the right to freedom of expression (Article 6 of the Constitution), which presupposes the right to investigate or seek and receive information of any nature, whether public or private, provided that such information is of public interest (Judgment of 24 Sep. 2010, Ref. No. 91-2007, "Freedom of Expression" Case); and by the democratic principle of the Rule of Law (Article 85 of the Constitution), according to which it is the duty of the public powers to guarantee transparency and public disclosure in public administrative actions, and to render accounts on the use of public resources and funds (Judgment of 25 Aug. 2010, Ref. No. 1-2010, *Transfers between Public Administrative Authorities* Case).[48]

The Supreme Court of El Salvador emphasized the importance of recognizing the fundamentality of the right to information:

> the fundamental nature of the right of access to information helps reinforce transparent and effective democracies, facilitates accountability and generates constant, robust and well-informed public debate. From that perspective, access to information allows citizens to play an active role in the government by forming individual and collective opinions based on public themes, facilitating more responsible political participation with improved orientation and deliberations; this allows citizens to question, investigate and consider whether the civil servant is contributing to proper performance of the public functions. Citizen control on this level forces government bodies to conduct their activities transparently, especially

[46]Constitutional Court of Guatemala (Corte de Constitucionalidad de Guatemala), Expedientes 1373-2009, 1412-2009, 1413-2009 (Judgment of 30 November 2010), "Whereas clause" No. IV.

[47]Constitutional Section of the Supreme Court of Justice of El Salvador (Sala de Ló Constitucional de la Corte Suprema de Justicia de El Salvador), Expediente 155-2013 (Judgment of 25 July 2014).

[48]Constitutional Section of the Supreme Court of Justice of El Salvador, Expediente 94-2014 (Judgment of 8 April 2014).

with respect to their recruitment procedures for civil servants – in this case, civil servants of the Judiciary.[49]

# 4 Responsibilities for Implementing the Right of Access to Information

All branches of government (Executive, Legislative and Judicial) are required to protect fundamental rights. The fundamental right to information is also enforceable against private entities and individuals exercising public functions in the domain of public law, as well as private entities and individuals which, in the domain of private law, act on behalf of the public administrative authorities,[50] according to the principle that *administrative law does not allow taking refuge in private law*[51] so that "authorities cannot exempt themselves from public-law obligations by placing their actions on the level of private law".[52]

According to O. Mayer, for the purposes of classifying a legal relationship of an administrative entity, the fact that a public administrative authority participates in the *private market economy* in pursuit of the public interest is irrelevant. Even in the case of an essentially private activity outside the sphere of administrative law (i.e., an activity in pursuit of *profit together with public interests*,[53] the administrative authority remains subject to the obligation to disclose information whenever *public funds* are involved, as is currently the case in Brazil, with Petróleo Brasileiro S.A. (Petrobrás) or in Venezuela, with Petróleos de Venezuela, S.A.

The IAJC has pointed out the following:

> The right of access to information applies to all public bodies, including the executive, legislative and judicial branches at all levels of government, constitutional and statutory bodies, bodies which are owned or controlled by government, and organizations which operate with public funds or which perform public functions.[54]

According to the Model Inter-American Law, the duty to inform applies to:

> All public authorities, including the executive, legislative and judicial branches at all levels of government, constitutional and statutory authorities, non-state bodies which are owned or controlled by government, and private organizations which operate with substantial public funds or benefits (directly or indirectly) or which perform public functions and services insofar as it applies to those funds or to the public services or functions they

[49]Constitutional Section of the Supreme Court of Justice of El Salvador, Expediente 94-2014 (Judgment of 8 April 2014) para 44.

[50]Pieroth & Schlink 2012, p. 45–46.

[51]Fleiner 1928 apud Wolf et al. 2006, p. 315. Regarding the flight to private law and the real motives for administrative decentralization in German law, see Forsthoff 1958, p. 664–665.

[52]Wolff et al. 2006, p. 315. See also Coutinho 2011, p. 107–139.

[53]Mayer 1982, p. 188. Regarding the theory of attribution (theory of imputation, theory of exorbitant law) formulated by Hans Wolff, see Wolff et al. 2006, p. 267–286.

[54]Inter-American Juridical Committee 2008, resolution item 2.

undertake. All of these bodies are required to make information available pursuant to the provisions of this Law[...] (Article 3 of the Model Inter-American Law on Access to Information).

Along the same lines, the Mexican Constitution asserts:

all information held by any authority, entity, organization or agency of the Executive, Legislative and Judicial Branches, autonomous organizations, political parties, trust funds and public funds, as well as any other individual or legal entity or association that receives and uses public resources or performs acts of authority on the federal, state or municipal level, is public [...] (Article 6.4 subparagraph (A), item 1 of the Mexican Constitution)

This general scope of applicability covering all public spheres is found in the information access laws of Brazil,[55] Chile,[56] Colombia,[57] El Salvador,[58] Ecuador,[59] Guatemala,[60] Honduras,[61] Mexico,[62] Nicaragua,[63] Paraguay,[64] Peru,[65] Dominican Republic[66] and Uruguay.[67] In Argentina, which had until 2016 no (parliamentary) statute governing information access,[68] the Executive, Legislative and Judicial Branches all had regulations requiring the disclosure of information.[69]

---

[55]Article 1 and Article 2 of the Law N° 12.527 of 18 November 2011 on Access to Information (Lei que regula o acesso a informações).

[56]Article 2 §3, Transitional Provisions, Articles 8 and Article 9 of the Law No. 20.285 of 11 July 2008 on Access to Information (Ley sobre acceso a la información pública).

[57]Article 5 (a) of the Law No. 1.712.

[58]Article 7 and Article 8 of the Decree No. 534.

[59]Article 1 and Article 3 of the Law No. 24 of 18 May 2004 on Access to Information (Ley Orgánica de Transparencia y Acceso a la Información Pública).

[60]Article 2 and Article 6 of the Decree No. 57/2008 on Access to Information (Ley de Acceso a la Información Pública).

[61]Article 3.4 of the Legislative Decree No. 170.

[62]Article 1 Sole paragraph and Article 6 of the Law of 4 May 2015 on Access to Information (Ley General de Transparencia y Acceso a la Información Pública).

[63]Article 4 (c) and (d) of the Law No. 621 of 22 June 2007 on Access to Information (Ley de Acceso a la Información Pública).

[64]Article 1 and Article 2 of the Law No. 5.282 of 19 September 2014 on Access to Information (Ley de Libre acceso ciudadano a la información pública y transparencia gubernamental).

[65]Article 1 of the Peruvian Law No. 27.806 of 3 August 2003 on Access to Information (Ley de transparencia y acceso a la información pública).

[66]Article 1 of the Law No. 200 of 28 July 2004 on Access to Information (Ley General de Libre Acceso a la Información Pública).

[67]Article 1 of the Law No. 18.381.

[68]See now the Argentinian Law 22275 on the "Right of Access to Public Information" (*Derecho de Acceso a la Información Pública*) of 2016.

[69]The Argentinian Decree on Access to Public Information held by the National Executive of Argentina mentioned in its Article 10 that "the public entities must publish basic information in order to guide the public in the exercise of its right to information access" (Decree No. 1172/2003). The Decrees of the Senate of the Republic and of the Chamber of Deputies, respectively, provided for the publication of information about legislative activity (Article 104 Sole paragraph) of the Argentine Law [Decree of the National Senatorial Chamber]; and Articles 45 and 110 of the

However, the official comments on Article 4 of the Model Inter-American Law contain the following statement:

> While the model law does not contain a provision whereby private information that is required for the exercise or protection of international recognized human rights would be brought under the scope of the law, some states, including South Africa have adopted this approach.[70]

In fact, the Model Law on Access to Information for Africa shows that one of the objectives is to give effect to the right of access to information as guaranteed by the African Charter on Human and Peoples' Rights, to any information held by a *private body* that may assist in the exercise or protection of *any right*.[71]

## 5 Scope of Protection of the Right of Access to Information

The right to information is a fundamental right whose scope of protection is delimited by the relevant legal system, i.e., whether or not a document is considered *official information* depends on the laws of each country.[72] This being the case, the right to information is shaped by the legislators. The delimitation of the scope of protection is formulated in law, but this does not necessarily imply intervention by the State in the private sphere because the legislators are not granted such broad powers that they can manipulate the right to information or circumvent the normal understanding of the access to information.[73]

According to the statement of grounds of the Model Inter-American Law, "the right to access information is applicable to all information held by public bodies, broadly defined to include everything which is held or recorded in any format or medium [. . .]".

The national legislation of all the Latin-American countries studied contains a similar rule with a broad definition of the information and documents subject to

Argentine Resolution 2019 of 26 December 1996 [Decree of the National Chamber of Deputies]). The Judicial Branch was also imposed the obligation to publish, *ex officio*, the full list of penalties the records of public contracting and bidding procedures or, the annual budget of the Court and its monthly enforcement reports, and the six-monthly statistics (Supreme Court of Justice of the National, Resolution 1/2004. Case File 315/2004 – General Adm.).

[70]Official comments on Article 4 of the Model Inter-American Law on Access to Information.

[71]Article 3 (a) § 2 and Article 12.1 (b) of the Model Law on Access to Information for Africa.

[72]"The sphere of protection is the sphere of interests protected by a fundamental right; protected rights, according to the relevant definition, means legal positions, statuses or acts in the respective subject areas of a right to defense" (Borowski 1998, p. 184 apud Silva 2011, p. 72). For Alexy, the sphere of protection is, along with "intervention", the element that constitutes the factual support for a fundamental right (Alexy 1994, p. 273 et seq.).

[73]See Pieroth & Schlink 2012, p. 56–57, 145. The delimitation of the sphere of protection must not be confused with intervention in the sphere of protection (regarding the inherent limits, see Silva 2011, p. 130).

disclosure: Brazil,[74] Chile,[75] Colombia,[76] El Salvador,[77] Ecuador,[78] Guatemala,[79] Honduras,[80] Mexico,[81] Nicaragua,[82] Panama,[83] Paraguay,[84] Peru,[85] the Dominican Republic[86] and Uruguay.[87]

For the Inter-American Juridical Committee, "the right to access information applies to all *significant* information, broadly defined to include everything which is held or recorded in any format or medium".[88] Nevertheless, a value judgment, and thus a margin of uncertainty, is involved in interpreting the terms *relevant*, *proportional* or *significant*, as prerequisites for the exercise of the right to information.

According to the interpretation of the Venezuelan Supreme Court, the claimant bears the burden of proof to demonstrate that requested information serves specific purposes and is proportional to the use that will be made of it.[89]

In Chile, access to information is to be denied in the following case:

> Requests that are general in nature, concern a great number of administrative acts or their history, or cannot be satisfied without unduly distracting civil servants from proper performance of their routine tasks.[90]

In the Dominican Republic, access is not granted to "outlines or drafts that are not final documents and therefore do not form part of an administrative procedure".[91]

Finally, in Uruguay,

> [. . .] nor does the law allow petitioners to require organizations to perform evaluations or analyses of the information that they hold, except for such evaluation and analyses as they are required to produce by virtue of their institutional duties. The production of information

---

[74] Article 7 of the Law N° 12.527.

[75] Article 5 of the Law No. 20.285.

[76] Article 2 of the Law No. 1.712.

[77] Article 6 (c) of the Decree No. 534.

[78] Article 1 of the Law No. 24.

[79] Article 2 of the Decree No. 57.

[80] Article 3.5 of the Legislative Decree No. 170.

[81] Article 3, item 6 and 7 of the Mexican General Law on Transparency and Access to Information.

[82] Article 4 (k) of the Law 621 of 22 June 2007 on Access to Information.

[83] Article 1.4 of the Law No. 6 of 22 January 2002 on Access to Information (Ley de Acceso a la Información).

[84] Article 2.2 of the Law No. 5.282.

[85] Article 1 of the Law No. 27.806.

[86] Article 2 of the Law No. 200.

[87] Article 2 of the Law No. 18.381.

[88] Principles on the right of access to information, resolution item 3 (emphasis added).

[89] Constitutional Section of the Supreme Court of Justice of the Bolivarian Republic of Venezuela, *Case Asociación Civil Espacio Público v. La Contraloría General de la República Bolivariana de Venezuela,* Sentencia 745 (Judgment of 15 July 2010).

[90] Article 21.1 (c) of the Law No. 20.285.

[91] Article 2 Sole paragraph of the Law No. 200.

> shall not be considered to include the collection or compilation of information that is distributed throughout the various areas of the [administrative] body, for the purpose of supplying information to the petitioner.[92]

# 6 Duty to Protect Against Threats to Other Fundamental Rights That May Arise from Access to Information

With respect to the functions of fundamental rights, States have a duty to protect individuals against danger, especially by intervening in cases of conflicting fundamental rights, and a duty to interpret and enforce the law in harmony with such fundamental rights.[93] The uncontrolled exercise of fundamental rights would lead to conflicts among the various types of rights and rights-holders. State intervention is therefore necessary to impose limits (in general) and restrictions (in specific cases).

This is important to bear in mind for a proper understanding of the exceptions to the right to access information: the conflict sometimes involves [an interest in] public disclosure *versus* [an interest in] secrecy directly connected with another fundamental right, which the law associates with *private interest* (right to privacy, commercial interests); at other times, the conflict is between (the interest in) public disclosure *versus* (the interest in) secrecy indirectly related to the State's duty to protect other fundamental rights, which the law considers to be matters of *public interest* (such as security, health or foreign relations).

## 6.1 *Principle of Legality in the Legal Doctrine of Fundamental Rights*

According to Caballero, "the connection with the law is the traditional criterion of administrative legitimacy in a democratic State. The term *positive connection* to the Public Administration requires that each administrative action be previously authorized or programmed by the law".[94]

In this context, it is necessary to understand the dual implications in the administrative law of the principle of legality: the principle of supremacy of law (in the sense of a statute or act of Parliament) over other forms as norms, and the principle that only the law may set limits to fundamental rights (*Grundsatz des*

[92] Article 14 of the Law No. 18.381.

[93] Pieroth & Schlink 2012, p. 29, 27.

[94] Caballero 2010, p. 94.

*Vorbehalts des Gesetzes*—interferences in the freedom of citizens need to be covered by a law that was adopted by parliament in accordance with the Constitution).[95]

It is generally agreed that the administrative authorities in a well-established State under the rule of law should act according to the hierarchy of fundamental rights. The principle that the public authorities must act in accordance with pre-established laws, is connected with the idea that statutory law, in the strict sense of the term, has a threefold foundation: the powers and duties of the public authorities must: (a) respect the constitutional rights and liberties of the citizens; (b) be derived from effective democratic deliberations by society.[96]

Consequently, the limits on fundamental rights depend on a law that is *qualified*, adopted through the legislative process (formal statute), and is proportional.

According to B. Pieroth and B. Schlink, certain fundamental rights may be limited by simple laws, without requiring a statement of grounds; in such cases, legislators have a broad margin of discretion in evaluating the danger to other fundamental rights; other fundamental rights may be limited by laws that require a statement of grounds (principle of qualified legality) and legislators should have a narrower margin of discretion; finally, there are fundamental rights that cannot be limited by law, in which case legislators can do no more than reinforce the limits on the scope of the spheres of protection of fundamental rights.[97]

These days, the State has violated the principle of legality by its general delegation to administrative authorities of the power to intervene in cases of conflicting fundamental rights by promulgating their own regulatory provisions.[98] The administrative decisions and rules that give rise to such interventions must be directly related to the law that authorized such interference.[99]

Against this backdrop, it is the duty of the legislator to regulate the essential nature of the intervention; in other words, the content, purpose and extent of the authorization to intervene must be specified in a statute. If the statute is too vague, then, in practice, the administrative authorities will be in charge of deciding whether the prerequisites are met for intervention with fundamental rights, which, according to the German Federal Constitutional Court, should be prohibited by the

[95]Perlingeiro 2015, p. 130.

[96]Perlingeiro 2015, p. 130.

[97]Pieroth & Schlink 2012, p. 73.

[98]Stern 1980, §37 I 4.

[99]Pieroth & Schlink 2012, p. 73.

*theory of essentiality*.[100] Nevertheless, such vagueness can be observed in most laws on the right to information.[101]

The requirement of a *proportional* law for interference with fundamental rights is closely related to the idea that certain fundamental rights may be limited through *qualified* laws.[102] According to the principle of proportionality, it is necessary to examine whether a law of intervention is appropriate, necessary and proportional in the strict sense of protecting other fundamental rights. In the case of access to information, it is necessary to evaluate whether a law authorizing interference with the right to information should give priority to the right to privacy (private interest) or to the right to security (public interest) and whether such interference is the only possible and appropriate means (of resolving the conflict).

For a law to be considered *appropriate*, it does not necessarily have to achieve the objective but it should at least make it easier to do so[103]; *necessary* means that the State cannot create any other solution for the same purpose; *proportional*, in the strict sense, means *properly weighed*, balanced, reasonable or tolerable.[104]

Such weighing, based on *proportionality stricto sensu*, in compliance with most German Federal Constitutional Court precedents, amounts to weighing public and private interests in a specific case (without strict adherence to the text of the constitution). Weighing interests in isolation from the text of the Constitution creates a risk of excessive subjectivity and lack of control. The Constitutional Court therefore tends to resort to proportionality only when strictly necessary.[105]

Fundamental rights that are not subject to the principle of legality—because such is the intention of the Constitution—may conflict with other fundamental rights, since, by the nature of things, the risk of potential conflicts between such rights does not disappear.[106] An analogous situation results when laws protecting fundamental rights subject to the principle of legality are not enacted or, although

[100] German Federal Constitutional Court (Bundesverfassungsgericht), 2 BvR 883/73, 2 BvR 379/74, 2 BvR 497/74, 2 BvR 526/74 (Judgment of 28 October 1975). Regarding the theory of essentiality: "According to this theory, the legislators themselves are obligated to make all the essential decisions in fundamental areas of law, especially when it comes to exercising fundamental rights, to the extent that such the State is entitled to regulate the exercise if such regulatory rights, i.e., it is not permissible for legislators to delegate such essential decisions to the Public Administrative Authorities. The principle that each administrative action be previously authorized by the law has therefore been intensified by moving towards a *principle of pre-established laws adopted by parliament* (Pieroth & Schlink 2012, p. 64). See also Wolff et al. 2006, p. 441–442. "The extended role of the legality principle (that each administrative action be previously authorized or programmed by the law) is based on its dimension of fundamental rights; as a result, it is not constituted but rather specified by the theory of essentiality" (Maurer 2012, p. 118).

[101] Perlingeiro 2015, p. 137–140.

[102] Pieroth & Schlink 2012, p. 66

[103] Pieroth & Schlink 2012, p. 68.

[104] Stern 1994, p. 782. Regarding the concepts of appropriateness, necessity and proportionality in the strict sense of the terms, see Galetta 1998, p. 14–21.

[105] Pieroth & Schlink 2012, p. 69–70.

[106] Pieroth & Schlink 2012, p. 75.

enacted, are too generic or vague (without meeting the requirements of the theory of essentiality).[107]

In certain cases, there is merely an appearance of compliance with the principle of legality: e.g., a statute that makes a general reference to *public safety* as a justification for exceptional limitation of the duty to inform amounts to the same thing as a failure by legislators to define the prerequisites for imposing such limitations.[108] Such rules undoubtedly address issues that are difficult for legislators to handle on the abstract level,[109] but more detailed provisions are necessary,[110] as the objective of the principle of legality is to prevent the public authorities from an infinite range of interpretations at their disposal.[111]

The fact remains that conflicts occur and need to be resolved by the administrative authorities and courts; such solutions should be subject to prerequisites as strict as those imposed on the legislator to *limit* a fundamental right. As a result, the most suitable technique for conflicts of fundamental rights is systematic interpretation, carefully delimiting the sphere of protection of the fundamental rights.[112]

## 6.2 *Principle of Legality in Latin America*

For the Inter-American Juridical Committee, "exceptions to the right to access information shall be clear, limited and established by law"[113] based on the *principle of legality* under Article 30 of the American Convention on Human Rights:

> The restrictions that, pursuant to this Convention, may be placed on the enjoyment or exercise of the rights or freedoms recognized herein may not be applied except in

---

[107]For a contrary example, see Pieroth & Schlink 2012, p. 45–46 and p. 77.

[108]Perlingeiro 2015, p. 138. Regarding the criticisms of the *vague* nature of the right to information in the Dominican Republic, see Skoufias et al. 2014, p. 23–27. See also Caballero 2010, p. 94.

[109]Regarding the difficulty of abstract interpretation of poorly defined legal concepts, see Maurer 2012, p. 141. On concepts and terms in information law, see Bachilo 2015, p. 207–222. Regarding the notorious difficulty of defining *privacy*, see Bradley & Ewing 2007, p. 513.

[110]Regarding the possibility of using *definitions* to reduce the poorly defined nature of the laws, including general clauses, see Guastini 2011, p. 56. Regarding abstract interpretation and authentic interpretation, see Messineo 2011, p. 81–90. Regarding general clauses, poorly defined legal concepts, abstract interpretation and legal definitions, see Wolff et al. 2006, p. 448–450.

[111]Constitutional Court of the Republic of Colombia, Sentencia C-491/07, Expediente D-6583 (Judgment of 27 June 2007).

[112]Pieroth & Schlink 2012, p. 76–77. Pieroth and Schlink reject a model of fundamental rights based on broad factual support (Silva 2011, p. 160). According to Virgílio Afonso da Silva, the technique of weighing has been associated with legal uncertainty (Silva 2011, p. 148) and broad factual support of fundamental rights related to judicial inflation (Silva 2011, p. 150). Regarding the legality principle (that each administrative action be previously authorized or programmed by the law and complementary judicial acts, see Casal 2010, p. 142, 145, 158.

[113]Principles on the right of access to information, resolution item 6.

accordance with laws enacted *for reasons of general interest and in accordance with the purpose for which such restrictions have been established.*

According to Inter-American Court precedents, to prevent the arbitrary exercise of discretion by the public authorities, it is necessary to apply the principle of legality to exceptions to the right to information,[114] with the proviso that *laws*, as used in Article 30, means *parliamentary statutes* as opposed to regulations and decrees of the public administrative authorities.[115]

In El Salvador, the Supreme Court did not hesitate to point out that the *principle of legality* is applicable to any limits that can be imposed on the right to access information, because, like any fundamental right, the restrictions must be formally provided for by law:

> [...] a restriction on the exercise of this right, as such, *must be discussed and approved by the representatives of those who will be affected by it,* in proceedings that are explicitly public and transparent. The requirement of a formal statute helps increase legal certainty in the exercise of that right and respect for the State's powers to restrict it, so as to prevent public authorities from creating arbitrary obstacles to information access through decisions distinct from the decisions made by Legislature.[116]

According to the Official Commentaries on Article 41 of the Model Inter-American Law, the principle of legality includes "the definitions produced by mean of both legislation and judicial precedents, from which a definition of the exceptions would be derived".[117] According to the Constitution of Panama, any administrative decision that imposes exceptions on the right to access information must be anchored *in law*,[118] and the Constitution of Ecuador states that "there shall be no limitation of the right to information except in the cases expressly established *by law*."[119]

Following the same guidelines as Commentaries on the Model Law, according to which "the expression *public order* should be rejected as extremely vague and likely to give rise to abuses in its application",[120] the Colombian Constitutional Court rejects:

> [...] *vague or generic norms* that could end up becoming a sort of *general permission for the authorities to impose the veil of secrecy on any information that they deem fit, at their discretion.* To prevent this and violations of the general principle of public disclosure, the law should clearly and precisely define the type of information that may be held secret, the conditions under which such secrecy may be imposed on citizens, the authorities

[114]Inter-American Court of Human Rights, *Case of Claude Reyes et al. v. Chile* (Judgment of 19 September 2006) para 89.

[115]Inter-American Court of Human Rights, *The Word "laws" of the American Convention on Human Rights*. (Advisory Opinion OC-6/86 of 9 May 1986) para 26–29.

[116]Constitutional Section of the Supreme Court of Justice of El Salvador, Expediente 13-2012 (Judgment of 5 December 2012).

[117]Commentaries on Article 41 of the Model Inter-American Law on Access to Information.

[118]Article 43 of the Panamanian Constitution.

[119]Article 18.2 of the Ecuadorian Constitution.

[120]Commentaries on Article 41 of the Model Inter-American Law on Access to Information.

empowered to impose it and the systems of supervising actions that are kept secret for that reason.[121]

However, according to the I/A Court H.R.,

> [...] the degree of precision required of domestic legislation depends significantly on the subject-matter. The precise definition [taxativeness] of a civil norm may be different from that required by the principle of legality in criminal matters, given the nature of the conflicts that the first is designed to solve. It cannot be required that the civil norm, contrary to what usually happens with criminal law, which provides extremely precise factual circumstances that may arise; this prevents the civil norm from resolving countless conflicts that arise permanently and that are impossible to forecast for the legislator. The Court finds that the law must be formulated with sufficient precision to enable people to regulate their conduct so as to be able to predict with a degree that is reasonable under the circumstances, the consequences that a given action may entail. As has been noted, while the certainty of the law is highly desirable, it may bring with it excessive rigidity. On the other hand, the law must be able to remain in force despite changing circumstances. Consequently, many laws are formulated in terms, that to a greater or lesser extent, are vague and whose interpretation and application are questions of practice.[122]

It is also the understanding of the Inter-American Court that any limitations imposed by law should pursue an objective of the Convention (Article 13.2) and that any such interference must be justified by a need to ensure "respect of the rights or reputation of others" or "the protection of national security, public order or public health or morals".[123] Thus, in the words of the Court:

> The limitations imposed must be necessary in a democratic society and oriented to satisfy an imperative public interest. This implies that from all the possible alternatives there must be elected those measures that restrict or interfere in the most minimal possible manner with the effective exercise of the right to seek and receive information.[124]

Exceptions to the right to information based on proportionality are explicitly enshrined in the national legislation of Latin America, e.g., in Colombia,[125] Guatemala,[126] Mexico,[127] Nicaragua[128] and the Dominican

[121] Constitutional Court of the Republic of Colombia, Sentencia C-491/07, Expediente D-6583 (Judgment of 27 June 2007) Legal Basis 11.

[122] Inter-American Court of Human Rights, Case of *Fontevecchia y D'Amic v. Argentina* (Judgment of 29 November 2011) para 89 and 90.

[123] Inter-American Court of Human Rights, *Case of Claude Reyes et al. v. Chile* (Judgment of 19 September 2006) para 90.

[124] Inter-American Court of Human Rights, *Case of Claude Reyes et al. v. Chile* (Judgment of 19 September 2006) para 89–91; *Case of Gomes Lund et al. (Guerrilha do Araguaia) v. Brazil* (Judgment of 24 November 2010) para 229; *Case of Palamara Iribarne v. Chile* (Judgment of 22 November 2005) para 85; *Case of Ricardo Canese v. Paraguay* (Judgment of 31 August 2004) para 96; *Case of Herrera Ulloa v. Costa Rica* (Judgment of 2 July 2004) para 121 and 123.

[125] Article 3 (introductory paragraph) and Article 4, sentence 3 of the Law No. 1.712.

[126] Article 26.3 of the Decree No. 57.

[127] Article 11, Article 104, item 3, and Article 149 of the Mexican General Law on Transparency and Access to Information.

[128] Article 3.7 (c) of the Law No. 621 of 22 June 2007 on Access to Information.

Republic.[129] The case-law of the Constitutional Court of Peru,[130] the Supreme Court of Mexico,[131] the Supreme Court of Justice of Venezuela[132] and the Supreme Court of Argentina, which adhere to the principle of reasonableness, are moving in the same direction.[133]

## 6.3 *Limits on the Right of Access to Information*

### 6.3.1 Limitations on the Right to Information to Protect Private Interests and Interests of the State

The Model Inter-American Law establishes exceptions to the right to access information in cases in which such access would harm private interests or interests of the State.

In the list of private interests, it enumerates: (a) the right to privacy, including privacy related to life, health or safety; (b) business interests and legitimate economic interests; and (c) patents, copyrights and trade secrets.[134]

As far as interests of the State are concerned, after making the limits on information access conditional on a clear, probable and specific risk of significant damage, which must be defined in detail by statute, the Model Law lists the following public interests justifying exceptions to disclosure:

> a) public safety; b) national security; c) the future provision of free and frank advice within and among public authorities; d) effective formulation or development of policy; e) international and intergovernmental relations; f) law enforcement, prevention, investigation and prosecution of crime; g) the ability of the State to manage the economy; h) legitimate financial interests of a public authority; i) tests and audits, and testing and auditing procedures[135]; and j) if allowing access would violate confidential communications, including legal information that should be considered privileged.[136]

---

[129] Article 20.2 of the Law No. 200.

[130] Constitutional Tribunal of Peru (Tribunal Constitucional de Perú), STC No. 1797-2002-HD/TC (Judgment of 29 January 2003).

[131] Harmonized Regulations of the National Supreme Court of Justice and the Federal Judicial Council for the application of the Federal Law on Transparency and Access to Government-held Information, and the judicial interpretation of both instruments in the relevant precedents. Mexico, p. 115 (Suprema Corte de Justicia La Nación de Mexico 2014).

[132] Constitutional Section of the Supreme Court of Justice of the Bolivarian Republic of Venezuela, *Case Asociación Civil Espacio Público v.la Contraloría General de la República Bolivariana de Venezuela*, Sentencia 745 (Judgment of 15 July 2010).

[133] National Supreme Court of Justice, Argentina, CIPPEC c/ EN – M° Desarrollo Social – dto. 1172/03 s/amparo, lei 16.986, Fallos, C. 830. XLVI, 2014(Judgment of 26 March 2014), para 23.

[134] Article 41 (a) of the Model Inter-American Law on Access to Information.

[135] Article 41 (b) of the Model Inter-American Law on Access to Information.

[136] Article 41 (c) of the Model Inter-American Law on Access to Information.

Following a similar logic, between private interests and interests of the State, many national laws of Latin America provide for exceptions to the right to information access, such as those of Brazil,[137] Chile,[138] Colombia,[139] El Salvador,[140] Ecuador,[141] Guatemala,[142] Honduras,[143] Mexico,[144] Nicaragua,[145] Panama,[146] Peru,[147] Dominican Republic[148] and Uruguay.[149]

The exceptions defined by such laws are sometimes excessively generic and succinct however. Article 22 of Paraguayan Law No. 5.282, for example, merely states that "secret official information consists of any information that is characterized or defined as such in the manner expressed by law".

### 6.3.2 Right to Privacy

Article 11 of the Inter-American Human Rights Convention acknowledges that everyone has a right to privacy and prohibits any arbitrary or abusive interference in private life in the sphere of the family, home, and correspondence.

According to the I/A Court H.R.,

> [...] the scope of privacy is characterized as being free and immune to invasions or abusive or arbitrary attacks by third parties or public authority and may include, among other dimensions, the freedom to make decisions related to various areas of a person's life, a peaceful personal space, the option of reserving certain aspects of private life, and control of the dissemination of personal information to the public.
>
> In addition, Article 11.2 of the first American Convention protects the individual against arbitrary interference or possible abuse of the State. Nevertheless, it does not mean that the State meets its treaty obligations by merely refraining from such interference. Furthermore, Article 11.3 of the Convention imposes on States the duty to provide the protection of the law against those interferences. Consequently, the State has an obligation to guarantee the right to privacy through positive actions, which may involve, in some cases, the adoption of measures to ensure that private life is protected against interference by public authorities as well as by individuals or private institutions, including the media.

---

[137] Articles 23–26 of the Law N° 12.527.

[138] Article 21 of the Law No. 20.285.

[139] Article 18 and Article 19 of the Law No. 1.712.

[140] Article 19 and Article 24 of the Decree No. 534.

[141] Article 17 and Article 18 of the Law No. 24.

[142] Articles 21–23 of the Decree No. 57.

[143] Article 16 and Article 17 of the Legislative Decree No. 170.

[144] Article 113 and Article 116 of the Mexican General Law on Transparency and Access to Information.

[145] Article 15 of the Law No. 621 of 22 June 2007 on Access to Information.

[146] Article 14 and Article 15 of the Law No. 6.

[147] Article 15, Article 15-A and Article 15-B of the Law No. 27.806.

[148] Article 17 and Article 18 of the Law No. 200.

[149] Article 8–10 of the Law No. 18.381.

> In this context, the Court must find a balance between private life and freedom of expression that, not being absolute, are two fundamental rights guaranteed by the American Convention and of great importance in a democratic society. The Court recalls that every fundamental right is to be exercised with regard for other fundamental rights. This is a process of harmonization in which the State has a key role in trying to determine responsibilities and impose sanctions as may be necessary to achieve such purpose. The need to protect the rights that may be affected due to an abuse of freedom of expression requires the proper observance of the limits established in this regard by the Convention itself.[150]

In this context, for the above-mentioned reasons the Court denied information requests concerning a civil servant's home address,[151] and personal contact information of police and military authorities.[152]

### 6.3.3 Salaries of Civil Servants

Questions of the right to privacy *versus* the right to access information have been debated in Latin American courts in relation to the proactive disclosure of civil servants' salaries, as recommended in the Model Inter-American Law[153] and the laws of Honduras,[154] El Salvador,[155] Nicaragua[156] and Mexico.[157]

The National Supreme Court of Argentina has ruled as follows:

> The requested information alone, separately from any sensitive personal data whose disclosure is prohibited, cannot be denied on the grounds of a need to protect the privacy of the beneficiaries, since such a denial would be contrary to the public interest forming the basic motive for the request for information which, it is worth repeating, does not seem to be aimed at satisfying curiosity about the private life of the recipients but rather at ensuring effective supervision of the manner in which civil servants implement a social policy.[158]

In harmony with that Argentine ruling, the Brazilian Supreme Court considers that: "the compensation paid for parliamentary activities is public in nature, since there are no reasons of security or privacy that generally justify classifying it as secret".[159] Along the same lines of interpretation, the Constitutional Court of Peru decided that the expenses of the ex-President of the Republic and his entourage

[150] Inter-American Court of Human Rights, *Case* of *Fontevecchia y D'Amic v. Argentina* (Judgment of 29 November 2011) para 48–50.

[151] Federal Regional Court of the 2nd Region (Tribunal Regional Federal da 2ª Região), APELRE 201151030006267 (Judgment of 4 July 2012).

[152] Constitutional Tribunal of Peru, EXP. No. 05173-2011-PHD/TC (Judgment of 11 May 2012).

[153] Article 12 (b) of the Model Inter-American Law on Access to Information.

[154] Article 13.7 of the Legislative Decree No. 170.

[155] Article 10.7 of the Decree No. 534.

[156] Article 20 (c) of the Law No. 621 of 22 June 2007 on Access to Information.

[157] Article 70, item 8 of the Mexican General Law on Transparency and Access to Information.

[158] National Supreme Court of Justice, *Case CIPPEC* (Judgment of 26 March 2014) para 27.

[159] Federal Supreme Court of Brazil (Supremo Tribunal Federal), Mandado de Segurança 28.178 (Judgment of 4 March 2015).

should be made public, on the grounds that the right to access information is a collective right.[160] (In Brazil, however,) the question of *online publication of civil servants* salaries (active transparency) *versus* the right to privacy", is still pending decision by the Federal Supreme Court.[161]

Rather than limiting access to information about civil servants, the Supreme Court of Paraguay has decided that the pay sheets showing their salaries should be considered public information accessible to any citizen.[162]

The Transparency Committee of the Mexican Supreme Court has affirmed that:

> [...] civil servants' salaries should be made public even if there is a risk of affecting their personal lives or safety. According to the Article 13 IV of the Federal Law on Transparency and Access to Governmental Public Information [2002], information should be classified as confidential if it is in administrative files whose distribution would jeopardize any person's life, safety or health. Nevertheless, according to Article 7 of that same law, the periodic or extraordinary compensation of civil servants should not be classified as confidential: all income earned by public servants for the performance of their duties should be publicly disclosed, because such income constitutes government spending funded by the taxpayers.[163]

In Venezuela, in contrast, the Supreme Court considers that the salaries of civil servants should:

> [...] be indicated as a general total under the budget headings included each year in the Draft Budget Act, specifying the amounts allocated to each public administrative entity or body for the salaries of its personnel or in the jobs and salaries plan.[164]

That way, "it is impossible to tell which salary corresponds to which civil servant" because "such information belongs to the private sphere of each individual". And in the case at hand, in which the petitioner requested information about the base salary and other compensation of the personnel of the *Comptroller General of the Republic,* including its top management, the Supreme Court denied the request on the grounds that the petitioner had failed to demonstrate "how the requested information would be useful for citizen participation in the interest of transparency in public administration", so that "the magnitude of the requested

---

[160]Constitutional Tribunal of Peru, EXP. No. 05173-2011-PHD/TC (Judgment of 29 January 2003).

[161]Federal Supreme Court of Brazil ((Supremo Tribunal Federal), Recurso Extraordinário com Agravo 652.777 (Judgment of 23 April 2015).

[162]Paraguayan Supreme Court of Justice (Corte Suprema de Justicia Paraguaya), Acuerdo y sentencia 1.306 (Judgment of 15 October 2013).

[163]Opinions issued by the Personal Data Protection and Information Access Committee [Comité de Acceso a la Información y de Protección de Datos Personale]. Opinion 01/2003 (p. 1) Mexico: Personal Data Protection and Information Access Committee of the National Supreme Court of Justice (Comité de Acceso a la Información y Protección de datos Personales de la Suprema Corte de Justicia de la Nación) (Suprema Corte de Justicia de La Nación de Mexico 2003).

[164]Constitutional Section of the Supreme Court of Justice of the Bolivarian Republic of Venezuela, *Case Asociación Civil Espacio Público v. La Contraloría General de la República Bolivariana de Venezuela*, Sentencia 745 (Judgment of 15 July 2010).

information does not seem proportional to the interest in transparency of fiscal administration or even to the specific actions for which the requested information would be used".[165]

### 6.3.4 Commercial Interests and Trade Secrets

On the question of commercial interests justifying exceptions to the right to access information, in the case of state-financed businesses, the Brazilian Federal Supreme Court has stated that:

> The common maxim that secrecy is the 'soul of business' does not apply to cases like that one at hand, particularly since any party who signs a contract with a public authority cannot have secrets, especially when disclosure is necessary to make sure that public funds are being used legitimately. Public contracting cannot be carried out in 'secret hiding places concealed by a legal framework' capable of preventing social supervision of the use of public funds.[166]

There is one example of a case in which the Court, in the absence of an applicable statute, instead of weighing the conflicting interests and intervening reduced the scope of protection of the commercial interests (limit on the limits), on the grounds that the access to information cannot be denied when the commercial interests involve public authorities. Moreover, the precedent in question recognized that the involvement of public funds, even in matters of private law, imposes an obligation on the State to disclose information.[167] Along the same lines, the laws of Honduras require transparency in any commercial and contractual relationship that is related to the State.[168]

Contrary to the idea that the State has a duty to disclose information about its legal relationships under private-law, Brazilian law protects the confidentiality of the intellectual property created by a State enterprise or by any private individual or entity that maintains a relationship with the public authorities.[169] In the Dominican Republic, the protection of industrial secrets and commercial interests involving the public authorities is preserved whenever there is a possibility that disclosure might cause financial losses.[170]

---

[165]Constitutional Section of the Supreme Court of Justice of the Bolivarian Republic of Venezuela, *Case Asociación Civil Espacio Público v. La Contraloría General de la República Bolivariana de Venezuela*, Sentencia 745 (Judgment of 15 July 2010).

[166]Federal Supreme Court of Brazil (Supremo Tribunal Federal), Mandado de Segurança 33.340 (Judgment of 26 May 2015).

[167]See item 3 of this Chapter.

[168]Article 7 of the Legislative Decree No. 170.

[169]Article 22 of Brazilian Law N° 12.527.

[170]Article 17 (i) of Law of Dominican Republic No. 200.

### 6.3.5 National Security

As an example of secrecy obligations imposed for the sake of national defense, the Supreme Court of Chile held that the obligation extends to information about purchases of weapons, including the associated budget forecasts, in particular, so as to prevent public disclosure of the characteristics of the weapons purchased and thereby safeguard an effective military strategy.[171]

In the Case of *Palamara Iribarne v. Chile*, however, the Inter-American Court of Human Rights held that national security was not violated by a book based on "open sources" that was written by a civil servant hired as a contractor by the Chilean Navy.[172]

### 6.3.6 Effective Preparation or Implementation of Public Policies

According to the doctrine of K.-P. Sommermann, the objective of transparency between public administrative authorities and individuals in planning and scheduling is to compensate for the relatively undemocratic nature of administrative procedure as compared to the legislative process, and to make up for the problems encountered in judicial review of administrative decisions involving broad margins of discretion, by virtue of the fact that transparency itself constitutes a form of supervision.[173]

Incidentally, the Brazilian Federal Supreme Court is currently trying an appeal against a court judgment that denied access to municipal policy information and documents on the grounds that it would create undue interference and violate the principle of separation of powers.[174]

### 6.3.7 International Relations

In 2012, in a case in which an NGO asked the Ministry of Foreign Affairs for information about the procedure leading to ratification of the Optional Protocol to the International Covenant on Economic, Social and Cultural Rights, the Venezuelan Supreme Court held that was no *obligation to respond* because, according to the Constitution:

---

[171] Supreme Court of Chile (Corte Suprema), Recurso de Queja Rol No. 24.118-2014, *Case CDE (Fuerza Aérea de Chile) v. CPLT* (Judgment of 30 December 2014).

[172] Inter-American Court of Human Rights, *Case of Palamara Iribarne v. Chile* (Judgment of 22 November 2005).

[173] Sommermann 2010, p. 52.

[174] Federal Supreme Court of Brazil, Repercussão Geral no Recurso Extraordinário 865.401 (Judgment of 14 August 2015).

> [. . .] both the [choice of the] occasion on which a Law ratifying an international treaty or convention should be enacted and the final ratification or adherence fall within the discretionary powers of the President of the Republic, according to international practices and the convenience of the Republic.[175]

The Supreme Court of Chile, in its decision on Article 21.4 of Law 20.285 (on Access to Official Information), regarding the limitation of public access or disclosure (particularly on the subject of international relations) that affect the national interest, stated as follows:

> Although it is true that the expression *national interest* has not been formally defined, it is equally true that the rules of interpretation in our legal system lead to the conclusion that, despite its vagueness and complexity, in substance it forms part of a general standard intended to protect an important part of the common welfare of the political society composed of all the nation's inhabitants or to satisfy the national community's specific needs, objectives and demands which, in connection with the sphere of diplomatic relations and the defense of its basic international aspirations, must be attended to, evaluated, and resolved by the appropriate state bodies under the central direction of the President of the Republic, to whom, as Chief of State, the constituency has entrusted the management of the country's interests in such matters.[176]

To help us understand how *international relations* are used to maintain the secrecy of certain information, it is worthwhile quoting the Chilean Appellate Court's interpretation:

> the standard to be applied in cases of *national interest* involving international relations, such as the present case is claimed to be, demands the required degree of prudence, knowing that any slip-up in such matters may have serious international repercussions for our country. That is why diplomatic memoranda are considered confidential by their very nature, as they generally are in most cases, since the international community and countries who exchange them as a method of official communication understand that aspect. The same is true of any past events whose disclosure would threaten or jeopardize the readiness to communicate among the parties to an international treaty or change the positions of the States or create tensions or difficulties in their relations.[177]

### 6.3.8 Law Enforcement, Prevention, Investigation and Prosecution of Crime

Brazilian case-law used to favor secrecy in matters of law enforcement and criminal investigations, including when such information is requested by the suspects

---

[175] Constitutional Section of the Supreme Court of Justice of the Bolivarian Republic of Venezuela, *Case Programa Venezolano de Educación-Acción en Derechos Humanos (PROVEA) v. Ministro del Poder Popular para Relaciones Exteriore,* Sentencia 249 (Judgment of 20 March 2012).

[176] Supreme Court of Chile, *Case Ministerio Relaciones Exteriores v. CPLT,* Recurso de Queja Rol No. 13.510-2013 (Judgment of 13 January 2014).

[177] Appeal Court of Santiago de Chile (Corte de Apelaciones de Santiago), *Case Ministerio de Relaciones Exteriores v. CPLT*, Reclamo de Ilegalidad Rol No. 4680-2012 (Judgment of 13 November 2013).

themselves in relation to questions by the accused, not only to ensure effective action by the State (proportionality) but also because the accused will be able to exercise his right to defense in due form after the formal indictment.[178]

Recently, however, in Binding Precedent No. 14, the Brazilian Federal Supreme Court granted the suspect's attorney the right to access the case file of the investigation even before the indictment, so long as the evidence in question was already complete, excluding investigatory reports and measures that were still in progress and thus undocumented in the case file.[179]

According to Chilean case-law, even if there is no risk to the effectiveness of the investigatory administrative proceedings, public disclosure of an inquiry is inadmissible if it would damage the image and reputation of the suspects, although it is allowed to request and supply information of a general nature, or merely marginal or tangential to the substantive aspects of the matter under investigation.[180] Nevertheless, that position might be contrary to the collective objectives of access to information: the circulation of information as an instrument facilitating the formation of public opinion and, indirectly, the citizens' supervision of the public authorities, including the authority in charge of preparing the indictment (in Brazil, the *Ministério Público*).

## 6.4 Limits on the Limits on the Right of Access to Information

Although legislative privileges allow law-makers to interfere with fundamental rights, their powers to impose such restrictions are not completely discretionary: there are the *limits on the limits* that may impose, the most significant of which is expressed by the principle of proportionality.[181]

*Limits on limits* are considered an integral part of the fundamental rights.[182] As any such limit must be formulated in a pre-existing statute, it might also be expected

[178]Superior Court of Justice of Brazil (Superior Tribunal de Justiça), Mandado de Segurança 19.243 (Judgment of 16 November 2012); Federal Regional Court of the 2nd Region, APELRE 200451010135240 (Judgment of 23 March 2013); Federal Regional Court of the 5th Region (Tribunal Regional Federal da 5ª Região), Mandado de Segurança 00162626320114050000 (Judgment of 12 July 2012); Federal Regional Court of the 3rd Region (Tribunal Regional Federal da 3ª Região), REOMS 00034351520134036108 (Judgment of 28 May 2015).

[179]Federal Supreme Court of Brazil, Rcl 16436 AgR (Judgment of 29 May 2014).

[180]Appeal Court of Santiago de Chile, *Case I.M. La Reina v. CPLT*, Reclamo de Ilegalidad Rol No. 2335-2010 (Judgment of 1 December 2010).

[181]Pieroth & Schlink 2012, p. 66–67.

[182]Pieroth & Schlink 2012, p. 66. Canotilho associates the limits on the limits with the need for a law of intervention to guarantee protection of the constitutional imperatives (Canotilho 1997, p. 411 et seqs.).

that any exception to the limit would require a pre-existing statute, but it is not always so in practice.

The Inter-American System for the Protection of Human Rights proposes nine different categories of limits on the limits on the right to information: three of them are common to all the exceptions; the other six are specific to certain limits.

The *generic limits on limits* applicable to all exceptions are: (a) overriding public interest; (b) serious human rights violations; and (c) secret information that is declassified after a certain period defined by a statute of limitations.[183]

Regarding the specific limits on limits, the Model Inter-American Law defines three situations that override the right to privacy: (a) the individual has consented to disclosure; (b) the individual in question has been dead in excess of 20 years; and (c) matters related to the functions of public officials that are clearly subject to disclosure.[184]

Moreover, the Model Inter-American Law mentions two cases in which secrecy on the grounds of interests of the State is not applicable, thereby favoring disclosure[185]: (a) information about the actual elaboration or development of public policies must be disclosed if the public policies in question have already been approved[186]; and (b) the secrecy of information concerning administrative procedures for the purposes of audits, public funding and public policy marking does not extend to the facts, technical information and statistics contained therein.[187]

### 6.4.1 Predominant Public Interest

According to the Canadian Supreme Court, "it follows that, in order to apply this criterion properly, it is necessary to weigh the pros and cons of disclosure, including the public interest in disclosure".[188] The administrative margin of discretion

[183]Article 43 of the Model Inter-American Law on Access to Information.

[184]Article 41 (a) para 1 and 2 of the Model Inter-American Law on Access to Information.

[185]Article 41 (b) para 1 and 2 of the Model Inter-American Law on Access to Information.

[186]In Chile, the disclosure of published proceedings is permitted (Article 21.1 (b) of the Law No. 20.285), and the same is true in the Dominican Republic (Article 17 (h) of the Law No. 200), Peru (Article 15 B.4 of the Law No. 27.806) and Nicaragua (Article 15 of the Law No. 621).

[187]In Brazil, there is no equivalent limit on the protection of State secrecy, but only on the protection of privacy, insofar as it is the presumed that the individual consents to the disclosure of information to that is necessary for the purposes of "statistics and scientific research of obvious general or public interest, provided for by law, provided that the information in question is rendered anonymous" (Article 31 para 3, item 2 of the Law N° 12.527). The same is true in El Salvador (Article 34 point (a) of the Decree No. 2.534) and in Guatemala (Article 32.1 of the Decree No. 57). In contrast, to protect State secrecy, scientific research findings are kept secret in Brazil whenever necessary for the "security of the society and the State" (Article 7 para 1 of the Law N° 12.527). A similar provision exists in the Dominican Republic (Article 17 of the Law No. 200).

[188]Supreme Court of Canada, *Case of Baker v. Canada [Minister of Citizenship and Immigration]*, 2 S.C.R. 817 (Judgment of 7 September 1999) para 53, 56, 65; Kazmierski 2013, p. 61, 67, 70.

concerning the limits on limits on information access should mainly be guided by the search for the predominant public interest based on the criterion of reasonableness.[189]

Not infrequently administrative authorities and judges are called upon to use the technique of weighing according to the principle of proportionality in the strict sense of the term, i.e., to determine whether the harm to the interest (in secrecy) protected by the relevant exception outweighs the general public interest (in disclosure) in a specific case.[190]

That same Article 44 of the Model Inter-American Law further provides that "no public authority may refuse to indicate whether or not it holds a record, or refuse to disclose that record [. . .] unless the harm to the interest protected by the relevant exception outweighs the general public interest in disclosure".

According to the laws of El Salvador, information must not be held secret unless it is demonstrated that the potential harm that would be caused by releasing information outweighs the public interest in disclosure.[191] Similar formulations are found in the laws of Guatemala[192] and Mexico.[193] In Brazil, on the subject of the limits on the right to privacy, the law speaks of "protection of the general and predominant public interest".[194]

As in the Model Inter-American Law and above-cited national statutes, proportionality in the *limits on limits* on the right to access information takes on the form of proportionality *stricto sensu* and is mainly addressed to the public authorities and, in the final analysis, to judicial review based on weighing in the absence of a statute covering the "essential aspects" of the colliding interests. In that respect, determining the importance and degree of achievement of the purpose of the law are factors inherent in the technique of weighing, in proportionality *stricto sensu*, and is related to the *probability of occurrence of harm* to the legal interest that is to be prevented.[195]

In this context, the situation is similar to the category of fundamental rights that cannot be limited even by statutes. The situation is also similar to fundamental rights for which the Constitution allows exceptions by statute (a law of

---

[189]Regarding the search for the predominant public interest in the exercise of the public authority's margin of discretion, see Perfetti 2013, p. 309–400. Also see Piñar Mañas 2010, p. 100. The technique of weighing is used to find a solution in case of conflicting public interests (Wolff et al. 2006, p. 427).

[190]Article 44 of the Model Inter-American Law on Access to Information.

[191]Article 21 point (c) of the Decree No. 534.

[192]Article 26.3 of the Decree No. 57.

[193]Article 101, item 3, Article 104, item 2, and Article 149, item 3 of the Mexican General Law on Transparency and Access to Information. Article 149, item 3, defines *proportionality in the strict sense of the term* as *"[t]he balance between prejudice and benefits in favor of the public interest,* so that the decisión made should represent a benefit that outweighs the prejudice caused to the population".

[194]Article 31 para 3, item 5 of the Law N°12.527.

[195]Casal 2010, p. 254. Ver Stern 1994, p. 836.

intervention), the required statute has not been enacted yet (inaction by the legislators) or, although enacted, is too vague, which is equivalent to an absence of law. In such cases, the legislator (or interpreter of the law) therefore needs to resolve the conflict between secrecy and transparency, preferably through delimitation of the scope of those two conflicting rights, in accordance with the relevant German case-law[196]; the technique of weighing typical of proportionality *stricto sensu* should be applied only if the technique of delimitation would obviously lead to an unfair result.[197]

### 6.4.2 Serious Human Rights Violations

In the search for the predominant public interest, legislators may opt for serious violations of human rights or fundamental rights as a limit on the limits on the right to information.

According to the Inter-American Court, the veil of secrecy should be lifted whenever there are *serious violations* of human rights, which is formulated in Article 45 of the Model Inter-American Law: "The exceptions in Article 41 do not apply in cases of serious violations of human rights or crimes against humanity".

As a result, according to the I/A Court H.R.,

> It is not, therefore, a matter of denying that the Government must continue to safeguard official secrets, but of stating that in such a *paramount issue* its actions must be subject to control by other branches of the State or by a body that ensures respect for the principle of the division or powers[...].[198]

Thus, what is incompatible with the Rule of Law and effective judicial protection "is not that there are secrets, but rather that these secrets are outside legal control, that is to say, that the authority has areas in which it is not responsible because they are not juridically regulated and are therefore outside any control system".[199] The I/A Court H.R. has stated that:

> It is essential that, in order to guarantee the right to information, the public powers act in good faith and diligently carry out the necessary actions to assure the effectiveness of this right, particularly when it deals with the right to the truth of what occurred in cases of gross

[196]Regarding the German Federal Constitutional Court's understanding of the possibility of the State defining and delimiting the right to access to State-held information, without constituting *intervention*, see Pieroth & Schlink 2012, p. 145.

[197]The lack of a law limiting a fundamental right is recalled by Konrad Hesse, as in the case of two conflicting principles, which creates a situation in which the judge's decision should be based on weighing. See Hesse 1999, para 347 et seq.

[198]Inter-American Court of Human Rights, *Case of Myrna Mack Chang v. Guatemala* (Judgment of 25 November 2003) para 181.

[199]Inter-American Court of Human Rights, *Case of Myrna Mack Chang v. Guatemala* (Judgment of 25 November 2003) para 180–182.

violations of human rights such as those of enforced disappearances and the extrajudicial execution in this case.[200]

The Mexican Supreme Court of Justice has set a limit on the *limits* (exceptions) to the right to the investigator's right to information in criminal proceedings: "The defense of confidentiality cannot be invoked if the preliminary investigation is intended to reveal acts constituting serious human rights violations or crimes against humanity".[201] In such cases, the right to information outweighs "the interests that seek to limit it, so that it is generally enforceable despite any exceptional limitations established by law".[202]

The laws of El Salvador[203] and Mexico[204] adopt the same line of reasoning, i.e., that any and all exceptions to the right to access information are inapplicable in cases of *serious violations of fundamental human rights* and crimes against humanity.

In that respect, the Constitutional Court of Colombia ordered the National Police to supply two citizens with information about the patrols assigned to a certain zone, the jobs done and the team who performed them. The purpose of the request for information was to investigate the kidnapping and death of an individual who was passing through the same zone at the relevant time. The Court held that the right to access information is an essential tool to satisfy the right to know the truth about the victims of arbitrary wrongdoings and human rights violations, and to safeguard society's right to an accurate historical record".[205]

It should be noted, however, that a number of laws have been vague on this subject, making generic references to violations of fundamental human

[200] Inter-American Court of Human Rights, *Case of Gomes Lund et al. (Guerrilha do Araguaia) v. Brazil* (Judgment of 24 November 2010) para 211.

[201] Mexican National Supreme Court of Justice (Suprema Corte de Justicia de la Nación de Mexico), Amparo en Revisión 168/2011 (Judgment of 30 November 2011), "Whereas clause" No. III.

[202] Mexican National Supreme Court of Justice, Amparo en Revisión 168/2011 (Judgment of 30 November 2011), "Whereas clause" No. I.

[203] Article 19 Sole paragraph of the Decree No. 534: "Confidentiality cannot be invoked in cases of investigation of serious violations of fundamental rights or of crimes of international importance". Nevertheless, according to Article 34 point (d), secrecy may be lifted by "court order".

[204] See Article 5.1 and Article 115, item 1 of the Mexican General Law on Transparency and Access to Information. Article 5.1 stipulates as follows: "It may not be classified as confidential any information that is related to serious human rights violations or crimes against humanity, in accordance with national law or international treaties to which the Mexican State is a party." Article 115, item 1 of that law mentions "[...]The privileged character may not be invoked when [. . .] it relates to serious human rights violations or crimes against humanity." Article 115, item 2 of the Mexican General Law on Transparency and Access to Information states as follows: "[...] related to acts of corruption according to the applicable laws". However, Article 120, item 3 of that law stipulates that any Mexican law limiting the right to privacy may be overridden by court order, which is a very general statement.

[205] Constitutional Court of the Republic of Colombia, Sentencia T-511/10 (Judgment of 18 June 2010).

rights,[206] instead of simply *serious* violations, which, in practice, might lead to uncertainty in applying the rule. Such vague references may be found, for example, in the laws of Brazil,[207] Colombia,[208] Ecuador,[209] Guatemala,[210] Peru,[211] Dominican Republic[212] and Uruguay.[213]

### 6.4.3 Provisional Nature of the Limits to Protect Interests of State

The provisional nature [of confidentiality] established by the *Historic Disclosure* Article of the Model Inter-American Law[214] is based on proportionality. A parallel concept is found in the Mexican Constitution, which stipulates that the secrecy imposed on official information for reasons of public interest and national security must be subject to a *time limit, to be specified by law.*[215]

[206]See the final part of subsection 3 of the official commentaries on Article 4 of the Model Inter-American Law on Access to Information. Also see the Article 3 point (a) (ii) and Article 12.1 (b) of the Model Law on Access to Information for Africa.

[207]Article 21 of the Law N° 12.527: "Access shall not be denied to such information as is necessary for the protection of fundamental rights by the courts or administrative authorities. Sole paragraph: No restriction on access shall be imposed on information or documents concerning conduct involving human rights violations committed by government agents or by order of public authorities." Brazilian law, too, specifies that the right to privacy must not be invoked [by the citizens] in cases of "compliance with a court order" and "defense of human rights" (Article 31 para 3, item 3 and 4 of the Law N° 12.527), and whenever such secrecy is intended to interfere with the investigation of "irregularities in which the holder of information is involved, as well as actions related to jeopardize the retrieval of highly relevant historical facts" (Article 31 para 4 of the Law N° 12.527).

[208]Article 21.2 of the Law No. 1.712: "[...] in cases of human rights violations or crimes against humanity [. . .]".

[209]Article 6.2 of the Law No. 24: "Confidentiality shall not be invoked in cases of investigations conducted by the competent public authorities concerning violations of the rights of persons established by the Mexican Constitution, or in declarations, pacts, conventions, international instruments or the domestic legal system".

[210]Article 24 of the Decree No. 57: "[...] in cases of human rights violations or crimes against humanity [. . .]." Article 29 and Article 32.3 of the Decree No. 57 allow for the disclosure of information declared secret or confidential provided that it is requested by a court of law.

[211]Article 15-C para 7 of the Law No. 27.806: "[...] the violation of human rights or of the Geneva Convention of 1949 [. . .]."

[212]Article 20.2 of the Law No. 200: "[...] justified violation of fundamental rights".

[213]Article 12 of the Law No. 18.381: "[...] violations of human rights, i.e., relevant to investigating, preventing or avoiding the violation thereof [. . .]."

[214]The Model Inter-American Law on Access to Information, in the Article 43 defines a period of 12 years, which may be extended by a further 12-year period.

[215]Article 6.4 subparagraph (A), item 1 of the Mexican Constitution.

Similar policies are reflected by the national laws of Brazil,[216] Chile,[217] Colombia,[218] El Salvador,[219] Guatemala,[220] Honduras,[221] Mexico,[222] Nicaragua,[223] Panamá,[224] Peru,[225] Dominican Republic[226] and Uruguay.[227]

### 6.4.4 Data Subject's Prior Consent

As seen in Sect. 6.4 above, when the right to information collides with the right to privacy, the Model Inter-American Law refuses to protect the data subject's privacy if he consents to disclosure of the information in question.[228] The same principle has been adopted by the laws of Mexico,[229] Colombia,[230] Guatemala[231] and the Dominican Republic.[232] In Brazil, the data subject is presumed to have given his prior consent by law in certain cases[233] including when the information is necessary for the medical treatment of the data subject himself.[234]

Concerning this presumption of consent, the Colombian Constitutional Court has recognized that [immediate] family members of a deceased data subject may access his confidential [medical] information, which could [otherwise] not be disclosed without the data subject's prior consent, provided that the confidentiality is maintained within the family circle. In the opinion of the Colombian Court, family members clearly have the right to consult the clinical records of their

[216] Article 23, Article 24 and Articles 27 to 30 of the Law N° 12.527. Time limits are divided into three levels by Brazilian law: top secret information: 25 years; secret: 15 years; restricted: 5 years (Article 24 para 1 of the Law N° 12.527).

[217] Article 22 of the Law No. 20.285.

[218] Article 22 of the Law No. 1.712.

[219] Article 20 of the Decree No. 534.

[220] Article 27 and Article 28 of the Decree No. 57.

[221] Article 19 of the Legislative Decree No. 170.

[222] Article 101.1, item 2, Article 101.2 and 101.3 of the Mexican General Law on Transparency and Access to Information.

[223] Article 17 of the Law No. 621 of 22 June 2007 on Access to Information.

[224] Article 14.9 § 2 of the Law No. 6.

[225] Article 15.3 of the Law No. 27.806.

[226] Article 21 of the Law No. 200.

[227] Article 11 of the Law No. 18.381.

[228] Article 41 lit. (a) para 1 of the first part of the Model Inter-American Law on Access to Information.

[229] Article 120.1 of the Mexican General Law on Transparency and Access to Information.

[230] Article 18 Sole paragraph of the Law No. 1.712.

[231] Article 22 Sole paragraph and Sec. 31 of the Decree No. 57.

[232] Article 19 of the Law No. 200.

[233] Article 31 para 1, item 1 of the Law N° 12.527.

[234] Article 31 para 3, item 1 of the Law N° 12.527.

deceased or seriously ill relative so long as there is a *fundamental legal interest* in requesting such information.[235]

According to the Model Inter-American Law, there is no reason to protect privacy if "it was clear when the information was provided that it was part of a class of information that was subject to disclosure".[236] A similar provision is found in the laws of Colombia[237] as well as Mexico,[238] a country that authorizes disclosure [of otherwise confidential information] if "it must be made public to protect third-party interests or for reasons of national security and public health"[239] or if it must be disclosed to protect the rights of third parties, provided that the public authority substantiates its claim.[240]

Moreover, Article 41 point (a) No. 2 of the Model Law denies the right to privacy of a data subject who "has been dead in excess of 20 years", a rule unparalleled in other Latin American countries except Brazil, whose laws permit the disclosure of personal information if a period of one hundred (100) years has elapsed since the date on which the relevant document was written.[241]

### 6.4.5 Information Inherent in the Duties Exercised by Public Officials

To cite another example from the Model Inter-American Law, the protection of privacy does not apply to matters related to the functions of public officials.[242]

In this respect, in its report on the Case *of Fontevecchia y D'Amic v. Argentina* (before the I/A Court H.R.), the Inter-American Committee pointed out that:

> [. . .] the importance of protection of private life regarding it as one of the most important achievements of democratic regimes. It developed the various areas of protection of private life, noting that although the American Convention recognizes this right to every person, its level of protection decreases as with the importance that a person's activities and functions may have for a debate of general interest in a democratic society. It noted that to resolve the conflict between the right to a private life of a public official and the right to freedom of expression, in the first place, it is necessary to verify whether or not there really was damage to the right allegedly affected. This damage is not present in those cases in which the information disseminated is already in the public domain or if the person gave tacit or explicit permission to publish this information, since in these cases there is no legitimate expectation of privacy. Second, any claim for alleged violation of privacy should compel the judge to consider the information allegedly disclosed in the context in which it occurred. Third, the decisive factor in resolving this conflict is the public relevance of the

---

[235]Constitutional Court of the Republic of Colombia, Sentencia T-837/08 (Judgment of 26 August 2006).

[236]Article 41 point (a) para 1 of the Model Inter-American Law on Access to Information.

[237]Article 18 Sole paragraph of the Law No. 1.712.

[238]Article 120.1, subparagraphs 1 and 2 of the Mexican General Law on Access to Information.

[239]Article 120.1 subparagraph 4 of the Mexican General Law on Access to Information.

[240]Article 120.2 of the Mexican General Law on Access to Information.

[241]Article 31 para 1, item 1 of the Law N° 12.527.

[242]Article 41 point (a) No. 2 first part of the Model Inter-American Law on Access to Information.

information. *In this regard, relevant information is public when: a) in any way, despite having a component that involves private life, it is information that has to do with the functions that person carries out, b) it refers to the noncompliance of citizen's legal obligation, c) it is important information regarding trust in an official; and d) it refers to the competence and capabilities of an official to perform his or her duties.*[243]

According to the I/A Court of HR,

> [. . .] in a democratic society political and public personalities are more exposed to scrutiny and the criticism of the public. This different threshold of protection is due to the fact that they have voluntarily exposed themselves to a stricter scrutiny. Their activities go beyond the private sphere to enter the realm of public debate. This threshold is not only based on the nature of the individual but also on the public interest inherent in the actions performed.[244]

Along the same lines, the Santiago Court of Appeals, while recognizing that the privacy of public officials, as public officeholders, are not entitled to the same stringent protection of privacy as ordinary citizens,[245] nevertheless posits that the e-mail of civil servants may be disclosed *only* if there is no other means of obtaining the information transmitted.[246]

## 7 Guarantees of Protection of the Right to Information

The guarantees protecting fundamental rights may include[247]: (a) interpretation according to the Constitution; (b) recognition of personal rights (rights to protection: the right to petition; the right to a fair hearing (in court or before a quasi-judicial body); (c) institutional guarantees (qualified, independent and impartial public authorities); (d) public policies that require administrative authorities to disclose information *ex officio* and impose penalties on those who obstruct the exercise of fundamental rights.

---

[243] Inter-American Court of Human Rights, *Case of Fontevecchia y D'Amic v. Argentina* (Judgment of 29 November 2011) para 17.

[244] See Inter-American Court of Human Rights *Case of Herrera Ulloa v. Costa Rica* (Judgment of 2 July 2004) paras 128 and 129, and *Case of Tristán Donoso v. Panamá* (Judgment of 27 January 2009) para 115.

[245] Appeal Court of Santiago de Chile, *Case Medina Rodrigo v. CPLT*, Reclamo de Ilegalidad Rol No. 1002-2010 (Judgment of 3 April 2012).

[246] Appeal Court of Santiago de Chile, *Case SEGPRES v. CPLT,* Reclamo de Ilegalidad Rol No. 2496-2012 (Judgment of 17 December 2012).

[247] Pieroth & Schlink 2012, p. 54, 27.

## 7.1 Principle of Maximum Disclosure

The Inter-American Commission on Human Rights has made the following observation:

> [...] to be guaranteed, State administration must be governed by the principles of maximum disclosure – pursuant to which transparency and access to information must be the general rule, subject to limited exceptions – and good faith. In view of these principles and of the provisions of Article 13.2 of the American Convention, the right of access to information may only be limited in compliance, that such limitations be of an exceptional nature, established by law, have a legitimate purpose, and be necessary and proportional.[248]

In the definition of its scope and purpose, the Model Inter-American Law affirms that "the right of access to information [in possession, custody or control of any public authority] is based on the principle of maximum disclosure" and, in Article 8, that "everyone tasked with interpreting this Law, or any other legislation or regulatory instrument that may affect the right to information, must adopt any reasonable interpretation of the provision that best gives effect to the right to information."

The Inter-American Court therefore believes that, in a democratic society, it is indispensable for the State to be guided by the principle of maximum disclosure, which establishes the presumption that all official information is accessible and subject to a limited set of exceptions.[249]

Thus, in the Inter-American system for the protection of human rights, the principle of maximum disclosure involves the presumption that all official information should be available to the public and that presumption must be considered when interpreting laws. The Model Law further stipulates that limits on the right to access official information must respect the principles of legality (i.e., be anchored in a pre-existing statute) and proportionality.

According to the Mexican Constitution, "when interpreting this right (to access official information), the principle of maximum disclosure must prevail".[250] Explicit references to the principle of maximum disclosure are found in the laws of El Salvador,[251] Chile,[252] Colombia,[253] Guatemala,[254] and Mexico itself.[255]

---

[248] Inter-American Commission on Human Rights 2015, p. 10.

[249] Inter-American Court of Human Rights, *Case of Claude Reyes et al. v. Chile* (Judgment of 19 September 2006) para 92. See also Inter-American Commission on Human Rights 2012, p. 13–15. The same interpretation is shared by Tobel, who considers that "the principle of maximal disclosure establishes the presumption that all government-held information should be subject to disclosure and that presumption may be overridden in only very few situations" (Mendel 1999, p. 2–11).

[250] Article 6.4 subparagraph (A), item 1 of the Mexican Constitution.

[251] Article 4 lit. (a) para 5 of the Decree No. 534.

[252] Article 11 para (d) of the Law No. 20.285.

[253] Article 2 of the Law No. 1.712.

[254] Art 3.1 (8) of the Decree No. 57.

[255] Article 7 and Article 8, item 6 of the Mexican General Law on Transparency and Access to Information.

In 2005, the Constitutional Section of the Costa Rican Supreme Court cited the principle of maximum disclosure in support of its Judgment:

> In a democratic state governed by the rule of law and social justice, each and every one of the public administrative bodies and authorities must be subject to the implied constitutional principles of transparency and public disclosure, the rule by which every administrative function or act should be guided [. . .].[256]

In 2007, a court of the Dominican Republic emphasized the saliency of that principle in one of its decisions:

> It needs to be made clear that democratic states must be governed by the principles of public disclosure and transparency when dealing with the public, so as to allow individuals to exercise democratic control, which is what legitimates the actions of those who handle public affairs.[257]

## 7.2 *Right of Access to Information as a Universal Right*

The universal nature of the right to information is emphasized in the Model Inter-American Law on Access to Information,[258] which enables citizens to request such information anonymously and/or without providing any justifications, in keeping with the Inter-American Court's opinion that "that the social control sought through access to State-held information and the nature of the information requested are sufficient motives for responding to the request for information, without requiring the applicant to prove a specific interest or a direct involvement".[259]

The same principle is echoed in the Constitutions of Peru ("every person has the right to request necessary information without stating the cause")[260] and Mexico ("every person, without being required to demonstrate any specific interest or justifications for his use [of the requested information]"),[261] as well as the laws of

[256]Constitutional Section of the Supreme Court of Justice of Costa Rica (Sala Constitucional de la Corte Suprema de Justicia de Costa Rica), Recurso de Amparo, Expediente 04-012878-CO, Res. 2005-03673 (Judgment of 6 April 2005), "Whereas clause" No. III – I. See also Inter-American Commission on Human Rights 2012, p. 62.

[257]Administrative and Tax Dispute Court of the Dominican Republic (Tribunal Contencioso Tributario y Administrativo de República Dominicana). Expediente 30-07-00078, Sentencia 024 (Judgment of 27 April 2007).

[258]Article 5 point (d) and Article 5 point (e) of the Model Inter-American Law on Access to Information.

[259]Inter-American Court of Human Rights, *Case of Claude Reyes et al. v. Chile* (Judgment of 19 September 2006) para 157.

[260]Article 2.5 of the Peruvian Constitution.

[261]Article 6.4 subparagraph (A), item 3 of the Mexican Constitution.

Brazil,[262] Colombia,[263] El Salvador,[264] Guatemala,[265] Mexico,[266] Nicaragua,[267] Panama,[268] Paraguay,[269] Peru[270] and Uruguay.[271]

The Colombian Constitucional Court has confirmed the universality of the right to official information, defining its beneficiaries, scope and contents as follows:

> The right to access official information is exercisable by any person without having to demonstrate any particular qualifications or interests justifying his right to request and receive such information in accordance with the rules established by the Constitution and the [applicable] draft law. This provision is subject to the constitutional parameters of the right to petition, to information, and to free access to official documents, as well as the principles of public office established by Articles 20, 23, 74 and 209 of our Constitution.[272]

The Supreme Court of Panama ruled that the Ministry of Agriculture had unduly obstructed access to information by requiring the applicant to demonstrate a particular interest:

> [since the requested information was] neither confidential nor classified as restricted, the applicant had every right to make such a request, so that the public authority should have supplied copies without requiring proof of a legitimate interest.[273]

The opposite position has been adopted in Venezuela, where the Constitutional Court has limited the scope of the right by holding that it was unlawful to submit a request for information anonymously and/or without a statement of reasons, because it is contrary to the requirements for the exercise of that right as established by its case-law:

> With binding effect from the date of publication of his Judgment, in the absence of an express statute, in order to safeguard the limits of exercise of the fundamental right to information, it shall be necessary: a) for the applicant for information to expressly state the reasons or purposes for which the information is requested; and b) for the extent of the requested information to be proportional to the intended utilization and purpose of the requested information [. . .].[274]

---

[262]Article 3 para 2 and Article 10 para 3 of the Law N°12.527.

[263]Article 25 Sole paragraph of the Law No. 1.712.

[264]Article 2 of the Decree No. 534.

[265]Article 41 Sole paragraph of the Decree No. 57.

[266]Article 16 of the Mexican General Law on Transparency and Access to Information.

[267]Article 28 Sole paragraph of the Law No. 621 of 22 June 2007 on Access to Information.

[268]Article 2.1 of the Law No. 6.

[269]Article 4 of the Law No. 5.282.

[270]Article 7 of the Law No. 27.806.

[271]Article 3 of the Law No. 18.381.

[272]Constitutional Court of the Republic of Colombia, Sentencia C-274/13(Judgment of 9 May 2013).

[273]Supreme Court of Justice of Panama (Corte Suprema de Justicia de Panamá), Accíon de Habeas Data, Expediente 1068-10 (Judgment of 27 December 2011).

[274]Constitutional Section of the Supreme Court of Justice of the Bolivarian Republic of Venezuela, *Case Asociación Civil Espacio Público v. La Contraloría General de la República Bolivariana de Venezuela,* Sentencia 745 (Judgment of 15 July 2010).

## 7.3 *Right to Petition (and the Right to a Reasoned Decision)*

### 7.3.1 Administrative Requests

According to the principle in question:

> Clear, fair, non-discriminatory and simple rules should be put in place regarding the processing of requests for information. These should include clear and reasonable timelines, provision for assistance to be given to those requesting information, free or low-cost access, and does not exceed the cost of copying and sending the information, and a requirement that where access is refused reasons, including specific grounds for the refusal, be provided in a timely fashion.[275]

In the words of the Model Inter-American Law, public authorities must honor the citizen's right of access to official information without discrimination and free of charge or at a cost limited to the cost of reproduction.[276]

The Model Law outlines the ideal procedure for requesting information in Articles 20 through 40, which may be summarized as follows:

The request, which may be made by any means (Article 20), must be registered and assigned a tracking number given to the requester, along with the contact information of the Information Officer assigned to the request (Article 21). No fee may be charged for making such requests (Article 22), which must be registered in the order in which they are received and handled in a fair and non-discriminatory manner (Article 23). Each request must contain the requester's contact information, a description of the desired information (Article 24.1) and an indication of the preferred form of delivery, failing which the information will be provided in the most efficient and cost-effective manner for the public authority (Article 24.2). The authority must interpret the scope and nature of the request in a reasonable manner and, in case of doubt, contact the requester to clarify the request (Article 25). If the receiving authority reasonably determines that it is not the proper authority to handle the request, it must forward it to the proper authority as soon as possible (Article 26). Interested third parties must be promptly informed of the request (Article 27). The requester must be charged no more than the actual cost of the copies of the document or information (Article 28). The authorities must facilitate access to the original documents (Article 29). The contact details of the Information Officer in charge of implementing the law in question must be published on the authority's website (Article 30). The Information Officer must also receive individual complaints concerning violations of the law in question (Article 31). The authority must search for the relevant documents as soon as it receives the request (Article 32). The [body responsible for archives] must develop, in coordination with the Information Commission, a records management system which will be binding on all public authorities (Article 33), make reasonable efforts to collect any

---

[275] Inter-American Juridical Committee 2008, resolution item 5.

[276] Article 5 point (f) and point (g) of Chapter I of the Model Inter-American Law on Access to Information.

information that it is unable to locate (Article 34), respond to the request within 20 days (Article 35) unless it was routed by one public authority to another, in which case the latter must respond within 10 days of receipt (Article 36). Under no circumstances may a third party notification excuse the public authority from complying with the time limits (Article 37). If the public authority believes that the costs will exceed a certain level or that it may take longer than 20 working days to respond, the authority must inform the requester and give him or her a change to narrow the scope of the request (Article 38). Public authorities must provide access in the requested form, unless doing so would damage the record, breach a copyright or be impractical because of the need to redact some information in the requested document (Article 39), and the public authority must supply a statement of reasons for any refusal of request for information (Article 40).

Similar provisions may be found in the laws of Brazil,[277] Chile,[278] Colombia,[279] El Salvador,[280] Ecuador,[281] Guatemala,[282] Honduras,[283] Mexico,[284] Nicaragua,[285] Panama,[286] Paraguay,[287] Peru,[288] the Dominican Republic[289] and Uruguay.[290]

### 7.3.2 Duty to Indicate and Prove Compliance with the Requirements for the Imposition of Limits

According to the Inter-American Court, the burden of proof is on the State to demonstrate that its general duty of maximum disclosure of information does not apply in a certain case because the requested information is subject to one of the exceptions defined by law.[291]

In the Case of *Gomes Lund et al. v. Brazil (Guerrilha do Araguaya)*, the Inter-American Court ruled that the State "must establish the reason for denying the provision of said information, demonstrating that it has adopted all the measures

[277] Articles 10–14 of the Law N°12.527.

[278] Articles 12–20 of the Law No. 20.285.

[279] Article 25 and Article 26 of the Law No. 1.712.

[280] Articles 61–75 of the Decree 534.

[281] Articles 19–21 of the Law No. 24.

[282] Articles 16–18 and Articles 38–45 of the Decree No. 57.

[283] Articles 20–22 of the Legislative Decree No. 170.

[284] Articles 121–141 of the Mexican General Law on Transparency and Access to Information.

[285] Articles 26–34 of the Law No. 621 of 22 June 2007 on Access to Information.

[286] Articles 4–7 of the Law No. 6.

[287] Articles 12–20 of the Law No. 5.282.

[288] Article 12, Article 13 and Article 17 of the Law No. 27.806.

[289] Articles 7–16 of the Law No. 200.

[290] Articles 13–18 of the Law No. 18.381.

[291] Inter-American Court of Human Rights, *Case of Claude Reyes et al. v. Chile* (Judgment of 19 September 2006) para 93, 159.

under its power to prove that, in effect, the information sought did not exist [. . .]".[292]

The principle developed by the Inter-American Juridical Committee that "the burden of proof to justify any refusal of a request for information must be borne by the body from which the information was requested"[293] has been adopted by the Model Inter-American Law:

> The burden of proof shall lie with the public authority to establish that the information requested is subject to one of the exceptions contained in Article 41. In particular, the public authority must establish: a) that the exception is legitimate and strictly necessary in a democratic society based on the standards and jurisprudence of the Inter-American system; b) that disclosure would cause substantial harm to an interest protected by this Law; and c) that the likelihood and gravity of that harm outweighs the public interest in disclosure of the information.[294]

That same principle has been enshrined in the laws of Nicaragua,[295] Guatemala,[296] Colombia,[297] Mexico,[298] Panama[299] and Uruguay.[300] In the words of the Panamanian Supreme Court:

> Government entities that refuse to disclose information because they consider it confidential or classified as restricted must provide a statement of grounds for their decision, indicating the reasons underlying the refusal and the specific laws on which it is based.[301]

Similar arguments have been expressed by the Chilean Constitutional Court:

> in general, all documents are public unless their disclosure would compromise human rights, national security or proper operation of the [public] service, but civil servants must not refuse such information arbitrarily. Any public official who denies such information must provide a statement of reasons for his refusal and, if disputed by the requester, a fast and simple proceeding should be provided so that the dispute may be resolved by a judge.[302]

The Canadian Supreme Court, too, is of the opinion that any refusal to disclose information must be accompanied by a statement of reasons and evidence of the causes that led to the refusal:

---

[292] Inter-American Court of Human Rights, *Case of Gomes Lund et al. (Guerrilha do Araguaia) v. Brazil.* (Judgment of 24 November 2010) para 211.

[293] Inter-American Juridical Committee 2008, resolution item 7.

[294] Article 53 of the Model Inter-American Law on Access to Information.

[295] Article 3.7 and Article 16 of the Law No. 621 of 22 June 2007 on Access to Information.

[296] Article 26 of the Decree No. 57.

[297] Article 28 of the Law No. 1.712.

[298] Article 20 and Article 105 Sole paragraph of the Mexican General Law on Transparency and Access to Information.

[299] Article 16 of the Law No. 6.

[300] Article 18 of the Law No. 18.381.

[301] Supreme Court of Justice of Panama (Corte Suprema de Justicia de Panamá), Expediente 748-11 (Judgment of 5 June 2012).

[302] Constitutional Court of Chile (Tribunal Constitucional de Chile), Rol 634-2006 (Judgment of 9 August 2007).

> It follows that to properly exercise this discretion, the head [of the relevant public body] must weigh the considerations for and against disclosure, including the public interest in disclosure.[303]

Incidentally, in the US Supreme Court ruling on the "Pentagon Papers" Case, the Court affirmed that if the government wishes to prevent the publication of certain information in the interest of the State, it must provide justifications for the imposition of such a restraint,[304] and supply proper proof that the classified documents might do real harm to the national interest.[305]

### 7.3.3 Effects of Administrative Omissions

According to the laws of Chile,[306] El Salvador,[307] Ecuador,[308] Paraguay[309] and the Dominican Republic,[310] a public authority's failure to respond to a request for information is deemed equivalent to an express refusal, based on the principle that such procedures must be completed within the applicable time limits, as established by the Model Code of Administrative Procedures—Judicial and Extrajudicial—for Ibero-America.[311]

The Inter-American Court goes even further, arguing that such an administrative omission may give rise to a positive remedy,[312] namely the court's recognition that the authority is under an obligation to disclose the information in question.[313]

---

[303]U.S. Supreme Court, *Case Baker v. Canada [Minister of Citizenship and Immigration*] (Judgment of 9 July 1999), 2 S.C.R. 817.

[304]U.S. Supreme Court, *New York Times Co. v. United States,* 403 US 713(Judgment of 30 June 1971). See also Beltrán de Felipe & González García 2006, p. 381. Opinion of Justice Brennan.

[305]Beltrán de Felipe & González García 2006, p. 384–385. Concurring opinion of Justices White and Stew Article.

[306]Article 24 (introductory paragraph) of the Law No. 20.285.

[307]Article 75 of the Decree No. 534.

[308]Article 21 of the Law No. 24.

[309]Article 20 of the Law No. 5.282.

[310]Article 10 of the Law No. 200.

[311]Article 8.3 of the Model Code of Administrative Procedures – Judicial and Extrajudicial – for Ibero-America: "unless provided otherwise, in the administrative procedures initiated by individuals, the failure to take measures or issue a decision within established time limit shall result in dismissal of the procedure, making it possible to file an administrative appeal or to resort to courts of law" Grinover, Perlingeiro et al. 2014, p. 107–120.

[312]On the idea that an administrative omission is not merely *negative* (passive) but may also be considered a *positive* (active) refusal to disclose the requested information, see Saddy 2013, including observations on comparative law. See also Achem 2014, p. 147–175.

[313]Inter-American Court of Human Rights, *Case of Claude Reyes et al. v. Chile* (Judgment of 19 September 2006) para 158.

Similar principles have been adopted by the laws of Guatemala,[314] Nicaragua,[315] and Uruguay[316] and in the administrative case-law in Mexico.[317]

In Uruguay, for example, courts have held that if a government agency fails to disclose requested information within a certain time limit without providing justifications for its refusal, then its omission is transformed from "negative" (passive) to "positive" (active) silence, within the meaning of Article 18 of Law No. 18.381, and therefore constitutes an action against which "the applicant may request injunctive relief". The Court's interpretation of the above-cited article on "Positive Administrative Silence" implies that, contrary to the constitutional provisions governing ordinary petitions, the authority's failure to notify the applicant of express decisions may be considered equivalent to a grant of the request, rather than as a denial.[318] The court concluded that "the legal system favors the right to information in cases in which the public authority fails to announce its decision within the applicable time limits", by analogy to the rule of procedural law according to which an allegation is deemed to be admitted if no objection is made by the adverse party.[319]

In any case, this *principle of maximum disclosure* advocated by the Inter-American Court and enshrined in certain national laws, must be made compatible with any limitations imposed when needed to preserve secrecy in the public interest. As a result, the court's recognition of a duty to disclosure information in cases of unreasonable delay by the authorities is based on a relative, rather than an absolute presumption of the admissibility of the applicant's arguments.

## *7.4 Independent and Impartial Authorities: Non-judicial and Judicial*

The *Information Commission* established by the Model Inter-American Law is an institution of fundamental importance, although it has been adopted by only a minority of the OAS Member States. The Commission is described as independent body with full legal personality, in charge of promoting effective access to official

---

[314] Article 44 of the Decree No. 57.

[315] Article 35 of the Law No. 621 of 22 June 2007 on Access to Information.

[316] Article 18 of the Law No. 18.381.

[317] Federal Institute of Access to Government-Held Information of the Mexican United States (Instituto Federal de Acceso a la Información Pública dos Estados Unidos Mexicanos), Ref. No. 279/09, Decision of 25 March 2009.

[318] Court of Appeals of the Third Civil Panel of Uruguay (Tribunal de Apelaciones en lo Civil Tercer Turno de Uruguay), *Bachetta Grezzi, Víctor c/ Ministerio de Industria, Energía y Minería. Acción de Acceso a la Información Pública (Article 22 Ley 18381)* IUE 2-050654/2014 (Judgment of 10 November 2014).

[319] Court of Appeals of the Third Civil Panel of Uruguay, *Bachetta Grezzi, Víctor c/ Ministerio de Industria, Energía y Minería.* IUE 2-050654/2014 (Judgment of 10 November 2014).

information, with the powers to enforce compliance and to settle disputes through (extrajudicial) mediation between parties in an appeal from a refusal to disclose information.[320]

The Mexican Constitution calls for similar institutions: "The mechanisms to access information and expedite review procedures shall be established. These procedures must be formalized before specialized and impartial autonomous agencies established by this Constitution."[321]

In 1999, the creation of such bodies was also proposed by Toby Mendel's in his *Right to Know: Principles of Freedom of Information*:

> In all cases, the law should provide for an individual right of appeal to an independent administrative body from a refusal by a public body to disclose information. This may be either an existing body, such as an Ombudsman or Human Rights Commission, or one specially established for this purpose.[322]

Although quite a new concept worldwide, the trend has been to create such independent extrajudicial bodies which, *without prejudice to* judicial appeals, are considered of key importance for the right to information access.[323]

Along with the Inter-American system for the protection of human rights, it is worth mentioning the African Commission on Human and People' Rights' *Model Law on Access to Information for Africa* of 2013, which calls for the creation of independent authorities to conduct appeals in matters of information access.[324] Further examples of independent extrajudicial bodies for review of information access decisions may be found in countries as diverse as Serbia[325]; Slovenia[326]; Liberia[327]; India[328]; Antigua and Barbuda[329]; Macedonia[330]; and Azerbaidjan[331].

[320]Articles 54–63 of the Model Inter-American Law on Access to Information.

[321]Article 6.4 subparagraph (A), item 4 of the Mexican Constitution.

[322]Mendel 1999, p. 7.

[323]Mendel 2007, p. 9. See also Snell 2007, p. 29.

[324]African Commission on Human and People' Rights, 2013, Article 53 of the Model Law on Access to Information for Africa.

[325]The Commissioner under Articles 32 to 35 of the Law on Access to Information (Law on Free Access to Information of Public Importance).

[326]The Commissioner for Access to Public Information under Articles 28 to 30 of the Law on Access to Information (Access to public information Act).

[327]Independent Information Commissioner, Cap. 5 of the Law on Access to Information (The freedom of information act of 2010).

[328]The Central Information Commission, Articles 12 to 14 of the Law on Access to Information (Act No. 22/2005).

[329]The Information Commissioner, Articles 35 to 40 of the Antigua and Barbuda Law on Access to Information (The Freedom of Information act of 2004).

[330]Commission for Protection of the Right to Free Access to Information of Public Character, Article 30 to 35 of the Law on Access to Information (Law on free access to information of public character).

[331]Authorized Agency, Article 44 of the Law on Access to Information (Law of the Republic of Azerbaijan on right to obtain information).

Only four Latin-American countries have adopted bodies of review endowed with sufficient legally established prerogatives to adjudicate independently without having to fear negative repercussions from other authorities: Chile[332]; El Salvador[333]; Honduras[334]; and Mexico.[335] The general reluctance in Latin America to create such bodies[336] is only to be expected in light of the legal culture inherited from Continental Europe, according to which only which the court of last resort should be endowed with independence. As Latin-American administrative law is rooted in that European model, it tends to be incompatible with the US system of highly specialized *quasi-judicial administrative bodies*, which leads to deferential *closed judicial review* of administrative decisions.[337]

Incidentally, it should not be forgotten that common law, countries like the USA, Australia and Canada have been the pioneers in right to information access, with over 30 years of experience.[338]

In contemporary Europe, the principles of *access to justice* set out in Article 6 of Directive 2003/4/EC are particularly worth highlighting:

> 1. Members States shall ensure that any applicant [. . .] has access to a procedure in which the acts or omissions of the public authority concerned can be reconsidered by that or another public authority or *reviewed administratively by an independent and impartial body established by law*. [. . .] 2. In addition to the review procedure referred to in paragraph 1, Member States shall *ensure that an applicant has access to a review procedure* before a *court of law or another independent and impartial body* established by law, in which the acts or omissions of the public authority concerned can be reviewed and whose decisions may become final.[. . .].[339]

## 7.5 *Rights of Non-judicial and Judicial Appeal*

The Inter-American Juridical Committee has expressed the following opinion on the appeal of administrative decisions:

> Individuals should have the right to appeal against any refusal or obstruction to provide access to information to an administrative jurisdiction. There should also be a right to bring

---

[332]*Conselho de Transparência*, Articles 31 to 44 of the Law No. 20.285.

[333]*Instituto de Acesso à Informação Pública*, Articles 51 to 60 of the Decree No. 534.

[334]*Instituto de Comissários*, Articles 8 to 11 of the Legislative Decree No. 170.

[335]The Guarantor Agencies, Article 8, items 3 and 4, Articles 30 and 37 to 42 of the Mexican General Law on Transparency and Access to Information.

[336]Regarding the absence of such independent bodies as a cause of difficulties in developing a culture of transparency in Peru, see Burt & Cagley 2013, p. 88–89.

[337]See in general Perlingeiro 2016; see also Asimow 2015, p. 9–11.

[338]Snell 2007, p. 14.

[339]Article 6 of the Directive 2003/4/EC of the European Parliament and Council, of 28 January 2003, on public access to environmental information, repealing Council Directive 90/313/EEC.

an appeal to the courts on the full merits of the case against the decisions of this administrative body.[340]

The Model Inter-American Law provides three different means of protecting a citizen's right to information: (a) internal appeal or *request for reconsideration* addressed to the administrative authority that denied the request for information, as an optional step prior to the other means of challenging the decision; (b) an external appeal to a entity other than the authority that denied the request, as a prerequisite for judicial review; (c) judicial review.[341] Similar provisions may be found in the national information access laws of Latin-American countries with respect to the internal and external appeals mentioned in items (a) and (b) above. Laws providing for the review of administrative decisions through extrajudicial proceedings within the originating authority (internal review) or in an external entity (external review) have been adopted by Brazil,[342] Chile,[343] Colombia,[344] El Salvador,[345] Ecuador,[346] Guatemala,[347] Honduras,[348] Mexico,[349] Nicaragua,[350] Paraguay,[351] Peru,[352] Dominican Republic[353] and Uruguay.[354]

With a minor variation however: Latin American legislators are reluctant to impose such an external appeal as a prerequisite for judicial review for fear that doing so might fully deprive citizens of their rights of information access. This is so because in Latin America, with its European traditions of *civil law*, as mentioned above, the extrajudicial bodies lack sufficient independence to review administrative decisions fairly and objectively. Moreover, extrajudicial administrative proceedings are often no more than *an attempt to draw water from a dry well*,[355] creating an unjustifiable delay in access to the court for protection of the right to information. In the majority of Latin-American countries, administrative decisions

[340]Inter-American Juridical Committee 2008, resolution item 8.

[341]Articles 46–52 of the Model Inter-American Law on Access to Information.

[342]Articles 15–20 of the Law N° 12.527.

[343]Articles 24–30 of the Law No. 20.285.

[344]Article 27 of the Law No. 1.712.

[345]Articles 82–102 of the Decree No. 534.

[346]Article 22 of the Law No. 24.

[347]Article 35 and Articles 52 to 60 of the Decree No. 57.

[348]Article 26 of the Legislative Decree No. 170.

[349]Articles 142–188 of the Mexican General Law on Transparency and Access to Information.

[350]Articles 35–39 of the Law No. 621 of 22 June 2007 on Access to Information.

[351]Article 21 and Articles 23 to 27 of the Law No. 5.282.

[352]Article 11 point (g) of the Law No. 27.806.

[353]Articles 26–29 of the Law No. 200.

[354]Articles 22–30 of the Law No. 18.381.

[355]Cassagne points out the precedent-setting decision by the Constitutional Section of the Costa Rican Supreme Court in the Fonseca Ledesma case, in which a prior administrative appeal is considered equivalent to an attempt to "draw water from a dry well" as higher courts are reluctant to overturn the lower-court judgments (Cassagne 2012, p. 75).

are reviewed by courts of general jurisdiction. Only Colombia, Guatemala, the Dominican Republic and Uruguay dedicate a separate branch of the justice system to administrative law cases, although almost all of the countries have specific laws of judicial procedure applicable on a subsidiary basis to the judicial review of administrative decisions denying requests for information. The only exception is Brazil, Code of Civil Procedure is applied to all proceedings.[356]

## 7.6 Proactive Disclosure

In the opinion of the Inter-American Juridical Committee

> Public bodies should disseminate information about their functions and activities – including, but not limited to, their policies, opportunities for consultation, activities which affect members of the public, their budget, and subsidies, benefits and contracts – on a routine and proactive basis, even in the absence of a specific request, and in a manner which ensures that the information is accessible and understandable.[357]

To a similar extent, a duty of proactive disclosure has been established by the laws of Brazil,[358] Chile,[359] Colombia,[360] El Salvador,[361] Ecuador,[362] Guatemala,[363] Honduras,[364] Mexico,[365] Nicaragua,[366] Panama,[367] Paraguay,[368] Peru,[369] the Dominican Republic[370] and Uruguay.[371]

In Chapter II of the Model Inter-American Law, Articles 9 through 14 specify which information is to be proactively disclosed by the authorities and the procedure to be used. Such disclosures include the qualifications and salaries of senior officials,[372] and public policy documents, with the admonition that "no one shall be

[356] Brazilian Law No. 13.105 of 16 March 2015 (Code of Civil Procedure) (Código de Processo Civil do Brasil).

[357] Principles on the right of access to information, resolution item 4.

[358] Article 8 of the Law N° 12.527.

[359] Article 7 of the Law No. 20.285.

[360] Article 11 of the Law No. 1.712.

[361] Articles 10 to 18 of the Decree No. 534.

[362] Article 7 of the Law No. 24.

[363] Articles 10 to 14 of the Decree No. 57.

[364] Article 13 of the Legislative Decree No. 170.

[365] Articles 70–80 of the Mexican General Law on Transparency and Access to Information.

[366] Articles 20–25 of the Law No. 621 of 22 June 2007 on Access to Information.

[367] Article 9 of the Law No. 6.

[368] Articles 8–11 of the Law No. 5.282.

[369] Article 5 and Article 6 of the Law No. 27.806.

[370] Article 3 and Article 4 of the Law No. 200.

[371] Article 5 of the Law No. 18.381.

[372] Article 12 point (b) of the Model Inter-American Law on Access to Information.

subject to any prejudice because of the application of a policy that is not disclosed" as required hereunder".[373]

## 7.7 *Penalties for Obstructing the Right of Access to Information*

The principle according to which *Anyone who willfully denies or obstructs access to information in breach of the rules should be subject to sanction*[374] is established in the Model Inter-American Law, which refers to administrative and criminal sanctions, because it is considered a crime to modify or destroy documents that have been subject to a request for information, and the following are considered administrative offenses: (a) obstruct access to any record contrary to [the provisions of the Model Law]; (b) obstruct the performance by a public authority of a duty [under the Model Law]; (c) interfere with the work of the Information Commission; (d) fail to comply with provisions of the Model Law; (e) fail to create a record either in breach of applicable regulations and policies or with the intent to impede access to information; and (f) destroy records without authorization.[375]

Similarly, the Mexican Constitution warns that "Failure to comply with these dispositions in regard to the access to public information shall be penalized according to the law."[376]

Countries whose laws have adopted such administrative penalties include Brazil,[377] El Salvador,[378] Ecuador,[379] Guatemala,[380] Mexico,[381] Nicaragua,[382] Paraguay[383] and Uruguay[384]; criminal penalties have been adopted by Colombia,[385] Guatemala,[386] Honduras,[387] Panama,[388] Peru[389] and the Dominican Republic.[390]

373 Article 13.1 and 13.2 of the Model Inter-American Law on Access to Information.

374 Inter-American Juridical Committee 2008, Resolution item 9

375 Articles 64–66 of the Model Inter-American Law on Access to Information.

376 Article 6.4 subparagraph (A), item 7 of the Mexican Constitution.

377 Articles 32–34 of the Law N° 12.527.

378 Articles 77–80 of the Decree No. 534.

379 Article 23 of the Law No. 24.

380 Articles 61–63 of the Decree No. 57.

381 Articles 206–217 of the Mexican General Law on Access to Information.

382 Articles 47–49 of the Law No. 621 of 22 June 2007 on Access to Information.

383 Article 28 of the Law No. 5.282.

384 Article 31 of the Law No. 18.381.

385 Article 29 of the Law No. 1.712.

386 Articles 64–67 of the Decree No. 57.

387 Articles 27–28 of the Legislative Decree No. 170.

388 Articles 22–23 of the Law No. 6.

389 Article 4 of the Law No. 27.806.

390 Article 30 of the Law No. 200.

The general laws of Panama also provide for the civil liability of a public official who harms the interest parties in this respect.[391]

From another perspective, Toby Mendel argues that:

> [. . .] officials should be protected from sanctions where they have, reasonably and in good faith, disclosed information pursuant to a freedom of information request, even if it subsequently transpires that the information is not subject to disclosure. Otherwise, the culture of secrecy which envelopes many governing bodies will be maintained as officials may be excessively cautious about requests for information, to avoid any personal risk.[392]

One of the principles established by the author is that *Individuals who release information on wrongdoing – whistleblowers – must be protected.*[393]

## 7.8 Public Policies Related to Information Access

Legislators and authorities enjoy a certain range of policy-making discretion with respect to the implementation of the right to information but are not permitted to modify the law's substantive protection of that fundamental right.

According to the Inter-American Juridical Committee:

> Measures should be taken to promote, to implement and to enforce the right to access to information including creating and maintaining public archives in a serious and professional manner, training public officials, implementing public awareness-raising programmes, improving systems of information management, and reporting by public bodies on the measures they have taken to implement the right of access, including in relation to their processing of requests for information.[394]

The Model Inter-American Law stipulates that legislators must monitor the application of the law of information access and amend it whenever necessary, and even requires the Ministry of Education to "ensure that core education modules on the right to information are provided to students in each year of primary and secondary education", and the implementing authorities to provide "appropriate training for their officials on the application of this Law".[395]

In sum, OAS countries must adapt their laws to meet the requirements of the right to information, to promote a culture of information access,[396] and to adopt suitable implementing measures for information access.

---

[391] Article 21 of the Law No. 6.

[392] Mendel 1999, p. 2–11.

[393] Mendel 1999, p. 2–11.

[394] Inter-American Juridical Committee 2008, resolution item 10.

[395] Articles 67–70 of the Model Inter-American Law on Access to Information.

[396] In the Dominican Republic, community organizations played an outstanding role in promoting a culture of access to information (Skoufias et al. 2014, p. 23–27. See Banisar 2005 para 93).

On the subject of specific implementing measures, according to the Special Rappporteur for Freedom of Expression of the Inter-American Commission on Human Rights[397]:

> First, the State has a duty to design a plan that allows for the real and effective satisfaction of the right of access to information within a reasonable time period. This obligation implies a duty to budget the necessary funds to meet, progressively, the demand that the right of access to information will generate. Second, the State must adopt laws, policies, and practices to preserve and administer information adequately. The Offices of the Special Rapporteurs for Freedom of Expression of the UN, OAS, and the OSCE declared in their Joint Statement in 2004 that '[p]ublic authorities should be required to meet minimum record management standards' and '[s]ystems should be put in place to promote higher standards over time.'[398] Third, States must adopt a systematic policy for training public officials who will work in satisfying the right of access to information in all of its facets, as well as 'training [of] public entities, authorities and agents responsible for responding to requests for access to State-held information on the laws and regulations governing this right.' This obligation also means the training of public officials on the laws and policies on the creation and maintenance of information archives that the State is obligated to safeguard, administer, and produce or gather. In this sense, the Inter-American Court has referred to the States' obligation to 'train [...] public entities, authorities and agents responsible for responding to requests for access to State-held information on the laws and regulations governing this right'.[399]

Similarly, the Inter-American Court held that the failure to train public officials properly in responding to the information access requests constitutes a violation of the right of access to State-held information, and that such training must cover the parameters established in the Convention concerning restrictions to access to such information. OAS Countries are therefore required to provide such training, within a reasonable time, to public entities, authorities and agents responsible for responding to requests.[400]

It must be borne in mind that:

> Proper training is essential to successful adoption of FOI. The countries that have most successfully implemented their laws generally have adopted a comprehensive approach, ensuring that everyone in the government has at least a basic understanding of the law and its necessity. Different levels of staff receive training based on their needs, ranging from intensive and comprehensive to general awareness. As noted by the Scottish Executive 'FOI implementation should not come as a surprise to staff and managers in any organization'.[401]

[397]Inter-American Commission on Human Rights 2012, p. 14.

[398]International mechanisms to promote freedom of expression. Joint Declaration of the Special Rapporteur of the United Nations (UN) on the Freedom of Opinion and Expression, the Representative for the Freedom of Means of Communication of the Organization for Security and Cooperation in Europe (OSCE), and of the Special Rapporteur of the Organization of American States (OAS) for the Freedom of Expression.

[399]Inter-American Court of Human Rights, *Case of Claude Reyes et al. v. Chile* (Judgment of 19 September 2006) para 165.

[400]Inter-American Court of Human Rights, *Case of Claude Reyes et al. v. Chile* (Judgment of 19 September 2006) para 164 and 165.

[401]Banisar 2005, para 91.

The laws of Brazil,[402] Colombia,[403] El Salvador,[404] Ecuador,[405] Guatemala,[406] Honduras,[407] Mexico,[408] Nicaragua[409] and Panama[410] provide for the promotion and implementation of access to information. Nevertheless, although the Mexican General Law mentions *professionalism* as the guiding principle of the institutions defending transparency and information access,[411] none of them expressly establishes an obligation of advanced legal training for civil servants.

## 8 Closing Considerations

The classification of the right to information as a fundamental human right, as declared by the OAS Inter-American Juridical Committee, in keeping with the precedents of the Inter-American Court of Human Rights, has become well established in Latin-American legal systems of Iberian origin and is a key consideration for legislators, authorities and national judges in implementing the other principles recommended by the OAS.

As a result, the debate centers on the national constitution whenever the statutes and case-law in OAS countries deviate on a certain point from any of the guiding precepts of the Model Inter-American Law on Access to Information. Yet there are two issues related to the State's duty to guarantee protection of the right to information that would be more easily resolved in the political arena than in the constitutional courts.

First of all, the decision-making administrative authorities in Latin America do not have the necessary legal training to make correct decisions in cases involving two conflicting rights that must be weighed against one another in light of the supremacy of fundamental laws. Nor do they have the skills of legal interpretation necessary to fill in the legislative gaps or contradict the existing laws and regulations on the right to information, which are generally characterized by vague terminology and concepts. Consequently, they lack credibility among the general public and other authorities.

The second issue is that the administrative authorities in charge of hearing appeals against decisions denying access to information are not endowed with the

[402] Article 40 and Article 41 of the Law N° 12.527.

[403] Articles 30–32 of the Law No. 1.712.

[404] Articles 45–47 Decree No. 534/2011.

[405] Article 8 of the Law No. 24/2004.

[406] Article 50 and Article 51 of the Decree No. 57/2008.

[407] Article 5, Article 6, Article 30 and Article 31 of the Legislative Decree No. 170.

[408] Articles 53–55 of the Mexican General Law on Transparency and Access to Information.

[409] Articles 43–46 of the Law No. 621 of 22 June 2007 on Access to Information.

[410] Article 26 of the Law No. 6.

[411] Article 8, item 8 of the Mexican General Law on Access to Information.

prerogatives of independence that would allow them to challenge such decisions with impunity. The proposal of the Model Inter-American Law, which has been adopted by only four OAS countries (Chile, El Salvador, Honduras and Mexico), contains traces of *quasi-judicial authorities* and *closed judicial review* typical of administrative adjudication in *common-law* countries, which are difficult to assimilate in Latin America countries with *civil law* traditions.

Thus, to ensure that information access performs its function of democratic supervision of the political powers effectively, which is of vital importance in the political and economic context of contemporary Latin America, it is not enough to ensure that the national laws are compatible with the OAS principles and I/A Court H.R. case-law on the rights and duties of information access. It is imperative to revise the institutional guarantees of the right to information yet again to ensure that the initial decisions reflect the proper level of legal qualifications among the primary administrative authorities and that the secondary administrative authorities responsible for hearing appeals have sufficient independence to examine such decisions fairly and objectively, especially when it comes to evaluating vague principles defining permissible exceptions to the general fundamental right of access to official information.

## References

Achem, D. W. (2014). Processos administrativos reivindicatórios de direitos sociais: dever de decidir em prazo razoável vs. silêncio administrativo. *Revista de Direito Administrativo & Constitucional, 14*(56), 147–175.

Africa Commission on Human and People' Rights. (2013). Model law on access to information for Africa. Retrieved January 28, 2016, from http://bit.ly/1xKH0qm

Alexy, R. (1994). *Theorie der Grundrechte*. Baden-Baden, Germany: Suhrkamp.

Asimow, M. (2015). Five models of administrative adjudication. *Forthcoming American Journal of Comparative Law*, 63, 3–31. Retrieved February 13, 2016, from http://bit.ly/1yp8y4i

Bachilo, I. L. (2015). Sobre os termos e definições no direito da informação. *Revista de Investigações Constitucionais*, 2(3), 207–222. Retrieved February 13, 2016, from http://bit.ly/1WJiMut

Banisar, D. (2005). Effective open government: Improving public access to government information (*OECD Working Paper*). Organisation for Economic Co-operation and Development, Paris. Retrieved May 4, 2016, from http://ssrn.com/abstract=2069870

Beltrán de Felipe, M., & González García, J. V. (2006). *Las sentencias básicas del Tribunal Supremo de los Estados Unidos de América*. Madrid, Spain: Centro de Estudos Políticos y Constitucionales.

Borowski, M. (1998). *Grundrechte als Prinzipien*. Baden-Baden, Germany: Nomos.

Bradley, A. W., & Ewing, K. D. (2007). *Constitutional and administrative law*. London: Pearson.

Burt, J.-M., & Cagley, C. (2013). Access to information, access to justice: The challenges to accountability in Peru. *SUR International Journal on Human Rights, 10*(18), 74–95.

Caballero, F. V. (2010). The legitimacy of the administration in Spain. In M. Ruffert (Ed.), *Legitimacy in European administrative law: Reform and reconstruction* (pp. 82–114). Amsterdam: Europa Law Publishing.

Canotilho, J. J. G. (1997). *Direito constitucional e teoria da Constituição*. Coimbra, Portugal: Almedina.

Casal, H. J. M. (2010). *Los derechos fundamentales y sus restriccion es*. Caracas, Venezuela: Legis.

Cassagne, J. (2012). El procedimiento administrativo y el aceso a la justicia. In P. Aberastury et al. (Eds.), *Tendencias actuales del procedimiento administrativo en Latinoamérica y Europa* (pp. 53–74). Buenos Aires, Argentina: Universidad Buenos Aires.

Coutinho, J. (2011). A geometria variável do direito administrativo. *Revista da Faculdade de Direito da Universidade do Porto, 8*, 107–139.

Fleiner, F. (1928). *Institutionen des deutschen Verwaltungsrechts*. Tübingen, Germany: J. C. B. Mohr.

Forsthoff, E. (1958). *Tratado de derecho administrativo*. Madrid, Spain: Instituto de Estudios Politicos.

Galetta, D.-U. (1998). *Principio di proporzionalità e sindicato giurisdizionale nel diritto amministrativo*. Milano: Giuffrè.

Grinover, A. P., & Perlingeiro, R. et al. (2014). Código Modelo de Procesos Administrativos – Judicial y Extrajudicial – para Iberoamérica. In V. Moraes (Ed.), *Seminário Demandas Repetitivas na Justiça Federal* (pp. 107–120). Brasília, Brazil: Conselho da Justiça Federal. Retrieved March 15, 2016, from http://ssrn.com/abstract=2250852

Guastini, R. (2011). Interpretare e argomentare. In F. Messineo et al. (Ed.), *Trattato di Diritto Civile e Commerciale* (pp. XIV–454). Milano: Giuffrè.

Hesse, K. (1999). *Grundzüge des Verfassungsrechts der Bundesrepublik Deutschland*. Heidelberg, Germany: C.F. Müller.

Inter-American Commission on Human Rights. (2012). *The Inter-American legal framework regarding the right to access to information*. Costa Rica: Office of the Special Rapporteur for Freedom of Expression Inter-American Commission on Human Rights. Retrieved May 4, 2016, from http://bit.ly/1W9aoVa

Inter-American Commission on Human Rights. (2015). *Access to information, violence against women, and the administration of justice in the Americas*. Costa Rica: Organization of American States. OAS/Ser.L/V/II.154. Retrieved May 4, 2016, from http://bit.ly/1U6trM9

Inter-American Juridical Committee. (2008). *Principles on the right of access to information*. CJI/RES. 147 (LXXIII-O/08). Retrieved May 4, 2016, from http://bit.ly/1nSf3fu

Kazmierski, V. (2013). Lights, judges, access: How active judicial review of discretionary decisions protects access to government information. *Alberta Law Review*, 51(1), 49-76. Retrieved February 13, 2016, from http://bit.ly/1YN2Xk9

Maurer, H. (2012). *Derecho administrativo alemán*. Mexico: UNAM. Retrieved February 13, 2016, from http://biblio.juridicas.unam.mx/libros/libro.htm?l=3143

Mayer, O. (1982). *Derecho administrativo alemán*. Buenos Aires, Argentina: Depalma. Translated from the French version by Horacio H. Heredia et al.: Mayer, O (1904). *Le droit administratif allemand*. Paris: Brière.

Mendel, T. (1999). *The public's right to know*. Principles on freedom of information legislation. London: ARTICLE 19. Retrieved February 13, 2016, from http://bit.ly/1lYHR4n

Mendel, T. (2007). Access to information: The existing state of affairs around the world. In E. Villanueva (Ed.), *Derecho de la información* (pp. 3–12). Mexico: UNAM.

Mendel, T. (2009). *El derecho a la Información en América Latina – Comparación Jurídica*. Ecuador: UNESCO. Retrieved January 2, 2016, from http://bit.ly/1MVf6BA

Organization of American States (2010). Model Inter-American Law on Access to Information. AG/RES. 2607 (XL-010).

Organization of American States. (2004). *International mechanisms for promoting freedom of expression*. Costa Rica: OAS Special Rapporteur on Freedom of Expression. Retrieved February 13, 2016, from http://bit.ly/1U6vZY3

Perfetti, L. R. (2013). Discrezionalità amministrativa, clausole generali e ordine giuridico della società. *Diritto amministrativo, 21*, 309–400.

Perlingeiro, R. (2015). The codification of the right of access to information in Latin America. *Páginas A&B*, 3(3), 129–146. Retrieved May 4, 2016, from http://bit.ly/1nTZTG9

Perlingeiro, R. (2016). A historical perspective on administrative jurisdiction in Latin America: Continental European Tradition vs. US Influence. *British Journal of American Legal Studies, 5* (1). Retrieved May 6, 2016, from http://ssrn.com/abstract=2592418

Pieroth, B., & Schlink, B. (2012). *Grundrechte Staatsrecht II*. Heidelberg, Germany: C.F. Müller.

Piñar Mañas, J. L. (2010). Transparencia y protección de datos: las claves de un equilibrio necesario. In R. García Macho (Ed.), *Derecho administrativo de la información y administración transparente* (pp. 81–102). Madrid, Spain: Marcial Pons.

Saddy, A. (2013). *Silêncio administrativo no direito brasileiro*. Rio de Janeiro, Brazil: Forense.

Silva, V. A. (2011). *Direitos fundamentais*. São Paulo, Brail: Malheiros.

Skoufias, E., Narita, R., & Narayan, A. (2014). Does access to information empower the poor? Evidence from the Dominican Republic (*World Bank Policy Research Working Paper,* 6895). Retrieved March 14, 2016, from http://ssrn.com/abstract=2445212

Snell, R. (2007). Using comparative studies to improve freedom of information analysis. Insights from Australia, Canada and New Zealad. In E. Villanueva (Ed.), *Derecho de la información* (pp. 13-52). Mexico: UNAM. Retrieved May 10, May, 2016 http://bit.ly/1YJAA6o

Sommermann, K.-P. (2010). La exigencia de una Administración transparente en la perspectiva de los principios de democracia y del Estado de Derecho. In R. García Macho (Ed.), *Derecho administrativo de la información y administración transparente* (pp. 11–27). Madrid, Spain: Marcial Pons.

Stern, K. (1980). *Das Staatsrecht der Bundesrepublik Deutschland. Band II: Staatsorgane, Staatsfunktionen, Finanz- und Haushaltsverfassung, Notstandsverfassung*. München, Germany: C.H. Beck.

Stern, K. (1994). *Das Staatsrecht der Bundesrepublik Deutschland. Band III/2: Allgemeine Lehren der Grundrechte*. München, Germany: C.H. Beck.

Suprema Corte de Justicia de La Nación de Mexico. (2003). *Criterios emitidos por el Comité de Acceso a la Información y de Protección de Datos Personale (*Opinions issued by the Personal Data Protection and Information Access Committee). Criterio 01/2003 (Opinion 01/2003). Mexico: Comité de Acceso a la Información y Protección de datos Personales de la Suprema Corte de Justicia de la Nación (Personal Data Protection and Information Access Committee of the National Supreme Court of Justice). Retrieved February 14, 2016, from http://bit.ly/1V2bcXN

Suprema Corte de Justicia La Nación de Mexico. (2014). *Reglamento Concordado de la Suprema Corte de Justicia la Nación e del Consejo de la Judicatura Federal para la aplicación de la Ley Federal Transparencia y Aceso a la Información Pública Gubernamental, y la interpretación jurisprudencial de ambos instrumentos*. México: Suprema Corte de Justicia de la Nación, Coordinación de Compilación y Sistematización de Tesis, 2014. Retrieved February 14, 2016, from http://bit.ly/1Xq7f0x

Wolff, H. J., Bachof, O., & Stober, R. (2006). *Direito Administrativo*. Lisboa, Portugal: Fundação Calouste Gulbenkian.

## List of Cases

### *Administrative and Tax Dispute Court of the Dominican Republic*

Administrative and Tax Dispute Court of the Dominican Republic (Tribunal Contencioso Tributario y Administrativo de República Dominicana) 27.04.2007, Expediente 30-07-00078, Sentencia 024. http://bit.ly/1R1DpwO (Accessed on 13 February 2016).

### *Appeal Court of Santiago de Chile (Corte de Apelaciones de Santiago)*

Appeal Court of Santiago de Chile 3.04.2012, *Case Medina Rodrigo v. CPLT*, Reclamo de Ilegalidad Rol n° 1002-2010. http://bit.ly/1RCY5Zh (Accessed on 29 May 2016).
Appeal Court of Santiago de Chile 13.11.2013, *Case Ministerio de Relaciones Exteriores v. CPLT*, Reclamo de Ilegalidad Rol N° 4680-2012. http://bit.ly/1ffL0by (Accessed on 23 June 2016).
Appeal Court of Santiago de Chile 1.12.2010, *Case I.M. La Reina v. CPLT*, Reclamo de Ilegalidad Rol n° 2335-2010. http://bit.ly/1RCY5Zh (Accessed on 29 May 2016).
Appeal Court of Santiago de Chile 17.12.2012, *Case SEGPRES v. CPLT*, Reclamo de Ilegalidad Rol n° 2496-2012. http://bit.ly/1RCY5Zh (Accessed on 29 May 2016).

### *Brazilian Federal Regional Court of the 2nd, 3rd and 5th Region*

Brazilian Federal Regional Court of the 2nd Region (Tribunal Regional Federal da 2ª Região) 23.3.2013, APELRE 200451010135240. http://bit.ly/1Y3vsft (Accessed on 5 May 2016).
Brazilian Federal Regional Court of the 2nd Region (Tribunal Regional Federal da 2ª Região) 4.7.2012, APELRE 201151030006267. http://bit.ly/1TKEE2Z (Accessed on 5 May 2016).
Brazilian Federal Regional Court of the 3rd Region (Tribunal Regional Federal da 3ª Região) 28.5.2015, REOMS 00034351520134036108. http://bit.ly/28UEwSj (Accessed on 5 May 2016).
Brazilian Federal Regional Court of the 5th Region (Tribunal Regional Federal da 5ª Região) 12.7.2012, Mandado de Segurança 00162626320114050000. http://bit.ly/2c0OMcw (Accessed on 5 May 2016).

### *Constitutional Court of Chile*

Constitutional Court of Chile (Tribunal Constitucional de Chile) 9.8.2007, Rol 634-2006. http://bit.ly/1oxfXy9 (Accessed on 12 February 2016).

## *Constitutional Court of Guatemala*

Constitutional Court of Guatemala (Corte de Constitucionalidad de Guatemala) 30.11.2010, Expedientes 1373-2009, 1412-2009, 1413-2009.

## *Constitutional Court of the Republic of Colombia (Corte Constitucional de la República de Colombia)*

Constitutional Court of the Republic of Colombia 27.6.2007, Sentencia C-491/07. Câmara Plena. http://bit.ly/1Kh5UHt (Accessed on 13 February 2016).
Constitutional Court of the Republic of Colombia 9.5.2013, Sentencia C-274/13. http://bit.ly/1eSJx6c (Accessed on 12 February 2016).
Constitutional Court of the Republic of Colombia 28.10.1993, Sentencia C-488/93. http://bit.ly/209Duq2 (Accessed on 12 February 2016).
Constitutional Court of the Republic of Colombia 18.6.2010, Sentencia T-511/10. http://bit.ly/24i2B6T (Accessed on 12 February 2016).
Constitutional Court of the Republic of Colombia 26.8.2006, Sentencia T-837/08. http://bit.ly/281FGBc (Accessed on 12 February 2016).
Constitutional Court of the Republic of Colombia 17.3.2005, Sentencia T-275/05. http://bit.ly/1TIuAM2 (Accessed on 17 February 2016).
Constitutional Court of the Republic of Colombia 12.10.1994, Sentencia T-443/94. http://bit.ly/1OAnykv (Accessed on 26 February 2016).
Constitutional Court of the Republic of Colombia 6.9.2001, Sentencia T-960/01. http://bit.ly/1IWITo6 (Accessed on 17 February 2016).

## *Constitutional Section of the Supreme Court of Justice of Costa Rica*

Constitutional Section of the Supreme Court of Justice of Costa Rica (Sala Constitucional de la Corte Suprema de Justicia de Costa Rica) 05.09.2008, Exp: 08-003718-0007-CO. Res. 2008-013658.

## *Constitutional Section of the Supreme Court of Justice of El Salvador (Sala de Ló Constitucional de la Corte Suprema de Justicia de El Salvador)*

Constitutional Section of the Supreme Court of Justice of El Salvador 5.12.2012, Expediente 13-2012. http://bit.ly/1QkDDNt (Accessed on 20 February 2016).
Constitutional Section of the Supreme Court of Justice of El Salvador 25.7.2014, Expediente 155-2013. http://bit.ly/1OAorcN (Accessed on 20 February 2016).
Constitutional Section of the Supreme Court of Justice of El Salvador 8.4.2014, Expediente 94-2014. http://bit.ly/1R7bw42 (Accessed on 20 February 2016).

## *Constitutional Section of the Supreme Court of Justice of Honduras (Sala de lo Constitucional de la Corte Suprema de Justicia de Honduras)*

Constitutional Section of the Supreme Court of Justice of Honduras 8.4.2015, Recurso de Amparo Administrativo 0296-15. http://bit.ly/28YD3pQ (Accessed on 17 February 2016).

Constitutional Section of the Supreme Court of Justice of Honduras 8.6.2011, Recurso de Amparo Administrativo 715. http://bit.ly/1OAmX2o (Accessed on 17 February 2016).

## *Constitutional Section of the Supreme Court of Justice of the Bolivarian Republic of Venezuela (Sala Constitucional del Tribunal Supremo de Justicia de la República Bolivariana de Venezuela)*

Constitutional Section of the Supreme Court of Justice of the Bolivarian Republic of Venezuela 20.3.2012, *Case Programa Venezolano de Educación-Acción en Derechos Humanos (PROVEA) v. Ministro del Poder Popular para Relaciones Exteriore,* Sentencia 249. http://bit.ly/209E0UY (Accessed on 13 February 2016).

Constitutional Section of the Supreme Court of Justice of the Bolivarian Republic of Venezuela 23.8.2000, *Case Red de Veedores de la Universidad Católica Andrés Bello v. Consejo Nacional Electoral,* Sentencia 1050. http://bit.ly/1myfcn8 (Accessed on 13 February 2016).

Constitutional Section of the Supreme Court of Justice of the Bolivarian Republic of Venezuela 15.7.2010, *Case Asociación Civil Espacio Público v. La Contraloría General de la República Bolivariana de Venezuela,* Sentencia 745. http://bit.ly/1Qdppgr (Accessed on 26 February 2016).

## *Constitutional Tribunal of Peru (Tribunal Constitucional de Perú)*

Constitutional Tribunal of Peru 29.1.2003, STC n° 1797-2002-HD/TC. http://bit.ly/1myQ1Rp (Accessed on 13 February 2016).

Constitutional Tribunal of Peru 11.5.2012, EXP. n° 05173-2011-PHD/TC. http://bit.ly/1sJ8b6c (Accessed on 1 June 2016).

## *Court of Appeals of the Third Civil Panel of Uruguay*

Court of Appeals of the Third Civil Panel of Uruguay (Tribunal de Apelaciones en lo Civil Tercer Turno de Uruguay) 10.11.2014, *Bachetta Grezzi, Víctor c/ Ministerio de Industria, Energía y Minería. Acción de Acceso a la Información Pública (Article 22 Ley 18381),* IUE 2-050654/2014. http://bit.ly/1oMQbGG (Accessed on 14 March 2016).

## Federal Supreme Court of Brazil (Supremo Tribunal Federal)

Federal Supreme Court of Brazil 4.3.2015, Mandado de Segurança 28.178. http://bit.ly/209DW7H (Accessed on 13 February 2016).
Federal Supreme Court of Brazil 26.5.2015, Mandado de Segurança 33.340. http://bit.ly/1Pv8o1y (Accessed on 13 February 2016).
Federal Supreme Court of Brazil 29.5.2014, Rcl 16436 AgR. http://bit.ly/1Z7mGey (Accessed on 29 May 2016).
Federal Supreme Court of Brazil 29.6.2015, Recurso Extraordinário com Agravo 652.777.. http://bit.ly/1R1BN6l (Accessed on 13 February 2016).
Federal Supreme Court of Brazil 14.8.2015, Repercussão Geral no Recurso Extraordinário 865.401. http://bit.ly/1Qwa3Xj (Accessed on 14 February 2016).

## German Federal Constitutional Court

German Federal Constitutional Court (Bundesverfassungsgericht) 28.10.1975, 2 BvR 883/73, 2 BvR 379/74, 2 BvR 497/74, 2 BvR 526/74. http://bit.ly/1PgId0J (Accessed on 5 May 2016).

## Honorable Court of the Second Panel of the City of Mercedes, Uruguary

Honorable Court of the Second Panel of the City of Mercedes, Uruguary (Juzgado Letrado de Segundo Turno de Mercedes de Uruguay) 11.9.2009, Sentencia 48. http://bit.ly/1Ll1Wsc (Accessed on 12 February 2016).

## Inter-American Court of Human Rights

Inter-American Court of Human Rights (1986) 9.5.1986, *The Word "laws" of the American Convention on Human Rights*. Advisory Opinion OC-6/86. http://bit.ly/1WLG8QM (Accessed on 14 February 2016).
Inter-American Court of Human Rights 19.9.2006, *Case of Claude Reyes et al. v. Chile*. http://bit.ly/1EJmcBE (Accessed on 2 January 2016).
Inter-American Court of Human Rights 29.11.2011, *Case of Fontevecchia y D'Amic v. Argentina*. http://bit.ly/1sVK6tL (Accessed on 29 May 2016).
Inter-American Court of Human Rights 24.11.2010, *Case of Gomes Lund et al. (Guerrilha do Araguaia) v. Brazil*. http://bit.ly/1KdWmN3 (Accessed on 14 March 2016).
Inter-American Court of Human Rights 2.7.2004, *Case of Herrera Ulloa v. Costa Rica*. http://bit.ly/20ggnpx (Accessed on 2 January 2016).
Inter-American Court of Human Rights 25.11.2003, *Case of Myrna Mack Chang v. Guatemala*. http://bit.ly/1rZs0X0 (Accessed on 13 February 2016).
Inter-American Court of Human Rights 22.11.2005, *Case of Palamara Iribarne v. Chile*. http://bit.ly/28SZU9z (Accessed on 23 June 2016).

Inter-American Court of Human Rights 31.8.2004, *Case of Ricardo Canese v. Paraguai*. http://bit.ly/1qzigkW (Accessed on 2 January 2016).
Inter-American Court of Human Rights 27.1.2009, *Case of Tristán Donoso v. Panamá*. http://bit.ly/1Us13Ev(Accessed on 1 June 2016).

## Paraguayan Supreme Court of Justice

Paraguayan Supreme Court of Justice (Corte Suprema de Justicia Paraguaia) 15.10.2013, Acuerdo y sentencia 1.306. http://bit.ly/1vNsNH0 (Accessed on 13 February 2016).

## Superior Court of Justice of Brazil

Superior Court of Justice of Brazil (Superior Tribunal de Justiça) 16.11.2012, Mandado de Segurança 19.243. http://bit.ly/2922LMw (Accessed on 13 February 2016).

## National Supreme Court of Justice, Argentina (Corte Suprema de Justicia de La Nación)

National Supreme Court of Justice 26.3.2014, *Case CIPPEC,* CIPPEC c/ EN – M° Desarrollo Social – dto. 1172/03 s/amparo, Lei 16.986. Fallos, C. 830. XLVI, 2014. http://bit.ly/1Uu9e23 (Accessed on 11 February 2016).
National Supreme Court of Justice, Argentina 11.2.2004, Acordada 1/2004. Exp. 315/2004 – Adm. Gral. http://bit.ly/1Tf6pmZ (Accessed on 13 February 2016).

## Supreme Court of Canada

Supreme Court of Canada 7.9.1999, *Case of Baker v. Canada [Minister of Citizenship and Immigration*], 2 S.C.R. 817. http://bit.ly/1WtapTZ (Accessed on 13 February 2016).

## Supreme Court of Chile

Supreme Court of Chile (Corte Suprema) 13.1.2014, *Case Ministerio Relaciones Exteriores v CPLT,* Recurso de Queja Rol n° 13.510-2013. http://bit.ly/1RCY5Zh (Accessed on 29 May 2016).
Supreme Court of Chile (Corte Suprema) 30.12.2014, Recurso de Queja Rol n° 24.118-2014, *Case CDE (Fuerza Aérea de Chile) v. CPLT*. http://bit.ly/1RCY5Zh (Accessed on 29 May 2016).

## *Supreme Court of Costa Rica*

Supreme Court of Costa Rica (Corte Suprema de Justicia de Costa Rica), Recurso de Amparo 6.4.2005, Expediente 04-012878-CO, Res. 2005-03673.

## *National Supreme Court of Justice (Mexico)*

Mexican National Supreme Court of Justice (Suprema Corte de Justicia de la Nación de Mexico) 30.11.2011, Amparo en Revisión 168/2011. http://bit.ly/1KNwk3w (Accessed on 13 February 2016).

## *Supreme Court of Justice of Panama*

Supreme Court of Justice of Panama 27.12.2011, Expediente 1068-10. http://bit.ly/28Y9OrF (Accessed on 15 March 2016).

Supreme Court of Justice of Panama 5.6.2012, Expediente 748-11. http://bd.organojudicial.gob.pa/registro.html (Accessed on 21 March 2016).

## *U.S. Supreme Court*

U.S. Supreme Court 30.6.1971, *New York Times Co. v. United States,* 403 US 713. http://bit.ly/1KhjP08 (Accessed on 13 February 2016).

# Chapter 3
# Scope and Aim of a General Regulation on Access to Public Information

**Hermann-Josef Blanke**

## Contents



The author wishes to thank his research fellow Isabelle Oberthür, junior lawyer at the higher regional court of Cologne, for her assistance with the redaction of this article.

H.-J. Blanke (✉)
Faculty for Economics, Law and Social Sciences, University of Erfurt, Erfurt, Germany
e-mail: LS_Staatsrecht@uni-erfurt.de



H.-J. Blanke, R. Perlingeiro (eds.), *The Right of Access to Public Information*,
DOI 10.1007/978-3-662-55554-5_3

# 1 The Right of Access to Information in the Societal and Legal Context

Since October 2015, hundreds of thousands of demonstrators have gathered in protest rallies "for fair world trade". The protests were aimed at the free trade agreement between the EU and Canada (CETA), as well as a planned but de facto failed parallel agreement with the U.S. (TTIP).[1] In the demonstrations, many citizens are not only concerned about a reduction in consumer protection, but they have also been afraid of the so-called "arbitration proceedings", and the "partially privatized" special jurisdiction in international trade. The negotiation processes for the treaties have been criticized, especially for their lack of transparency. The call for international treaties to be negotiated in a transparent manner makes it clear that foreign policy is bound not only to the principle of the rule of law in the run-up to the ratification procedure of an international treaty. Rather, according to the opinion of broad population strata, especially in German-speaking countries, it should be subject to a wide understanding of democracy. However, pursuant to the rules of international conventions and national transparency legislation, the "democratic right of access to information" is limited in case of "international relations".[2]

In Brazil, on the other hand, the demonstrations ("Lava Jato") against the government relating to alleged corruption in the context first of the scandal surrounding the state-owned oil company Petrobras, and than on the occasion of the Case *Odebrecht*, have reached an extent that—especially in combination with the introduction of a hard austerity policy—has become a threat to the country's internal peace.[3] At the end of December 2016, the U.S. Department of Justice informed that Odebrecht S.A., a global construction conglomerate based in Brazil, and Braskem S.A. (Braskem), a Brazilian petrochemical company, had pleaded guilty to having paid nearly 800 million dollars of bribes between 2001 and 2016. The bribe flowed in ten Latin American and two African countries; the highest sum paid in Brazil itself was almost 350 million dollars.[4]

[1]Cf. the press release at http://ttip-demo.de/presse/pressemitteilungen/ (Accessed on 30 December 2016).

[2]Cf. Article 3.1 point (a) of the Council of Europe Convention, which enumerates in this article the "possible limitations to access to official documents"; Article 3.3 point (a) of the German Freedom of Information Act [FIA]; regarding some Latin-American countries see Perlingeiro et al. (in this volume), Chap. 2, Sect. 6.3.7.

[3]An illustrative example of the fight against "corrupção sistêmica" in Brazil is juiz federal de primeira instância Sergio Moro.

[4]See https://www.justice.gov/opa/pr/odebrecht-and-braskem-plead-guilty-and-agree-pay-least-35-billion-global-penalties-resolve (Accessed on 10 May 2017).

In the fight against corruption, transparency and freedom of information are increasingly important.[5] The Worldwide Governance Indicators show a significant diminishment of the "Control of Corruption" indicator in 2014 with regard to Brazil which means a fall from in the ranking also far behind the average of other Latin American and Caribbean countries. However, at the same time Brazil's "Rule of Law" indicator has increased.[6] With regard to the accessibility to information, Brazil was ranked 38th among 102 countries and 4th among 19 countries of the region within the World Justice Project Open Government Index 2015.[7] It is necessary to question whether the right of access to official documents, which is committed in Brazil to all branches of government,[8] is an effective instrument for combating corruption. Transparency International in the "Perception of Corruption Index 2016" perceives the level of access to information about public expenditure as one of the criteria, which provides insight into the position of higher-ranking countries in the Corruption Perception Index.[9]

## 1.1 *Freedom of Information and Right of Access to Information*

On the one hand, freedom of information is a fundamental prerequisite for the exercise of other fundamental rights of communication, particularly in the form of freedom of expression and freedom of the press. Thus, freedom of expression can only be regarded as guaranteed if the citizen is able to form his own opinion based on freely accessible information originating from different sources and not from state-controlled media, and thus from "provided" "information", when forming an opinion.[10] An integral part of these fundamental rights of communication, the freedom to obtain information from generally accessible sources plays a prominent

[5]See Article 10 point (c) of the UN Convention against corruption, Res. 58/4, Sarkis, 2012, http://www.right2info.org/recent/access-to-public-information-in-brazil-what-will-change-with-law-no.-12.527-2011 (Accessed on 29 March 2017). However, after long debates and votes in the Brazilian Congress there is not much left of the "Dez medidas contra corrupção" ("Ten measures against corruption"); see http://politica.estadao.com.br/blogs/fausto-macedo/congresso-destruiu-as-10-medidas-contra-corrupcao-diz-procurador-da-lava-jato/.

[6]See http://info.worldbank.org/governance/wgi/index.aspx#reports (Accessed on 29 March 2017).

[7]Within the World Justice Project (WJP) Open Government Index 2015 the question was: "How would you rate the accessibility of information published by the government?"; see http://data.worldjusticeproject.org/opengov/#/groups/BRA (Accessed on 29 March 2017).

[8]See Perlingeiro (in this volume), Chap. 2, Sect. 4.

[9]Transparency International 2017, http://www.transparency.org/news/feature/corruption_perceptions_index_2016. Accessed on 30 January 2017.

[10]This relationship can be found also in the ECHR: Article 10.1 ECHR perceives the freedom to receive information as part of the freedom of expression. On the relationship between freedom of information and freedom of expression, see Dörr, in Merten & Papier (2011), vol. 4, § 103, Rn. 7.

role in a democracy based on the rule of law. The presupposition of democracy and the rule of law is, on the other hand, the transparency of state action, i.e., (the possibility of) knowing who is involved in state decisions—above all legislative acts, the executive or the judiciary—and evaluating whether they meet constitutional and legal requirements.[11]

It should be noted that, beyond the relevance of transparency legislation for these regulatory principles, which determine the relationship between citizens (also in the sense of cooperation) or between citizens and society or state, the right of access to information plays a significant and varied role in professional (e.g., the scientists search for data) or personal life (e.g., the search of patients for a suitable public hospital).

The right of access to information exceeds the scope of the fundamental right of freedom of information, even though the Inter-American Court of Human Rights (I/A Court H. R.) has derived it from the defensive right of freedom to information (Sect. 2.2.1). There shall be a right of access to information, even though the document or record is not generally accessible. It differs from the right of inspection of documents, which is standardized in national administrative procedural law[12] and under which access to a document is granted to a participant in an administrative procedure. In contrast, the access to information as a general right is requested by the applicant without a particular motivation (especially, outside of the context of an administrative procedure), but always on his own initiative.[13]

Ensuring the right of access to official documents also pursues objectives that are guided by the principles of democracy and the rule of law.[14] With regard to information in the area of administration, the citizen strives to exercise his or her right of access to information, to control the lawfulness and efficiency of the administration that is beyond his own involvement, and at the same time to enter into a dialogue with the administration, whereby the decision-making tool is expanded.[15] Such advantages, however, cannot hide the detrimental effects, which this right may cause to the representative democracy. That form of government necessarily includes conveyance of legitimacy from the legislative bodies to the administration and its control by the Parliament.[16]

[11]Ackermann & Sandoval-Ballestros 2006, p. 92.

[12]Cf., e.g., Sec. 29.1 of the German Federal Administrative Procedure Act reads as follows: "The authority shall allow participants to inspect the documents connected with the proceedings where knowledge of their contents is necessary in order to assert or defend their legal interests. Until administrative proceedings have been concluded, the foregoing sentence shall not apply to draft decisions and work directly connected with their preparation. Where participants are represented as provided under Sections 17 and 18, only the representatives shall be entitled to inspect documents [. . .]."

[13]See Blanke and Perlingeiro (in this volume), Chap. 1, Sect. 4.2.1.

[14]See Blanke and Perlingeiro (in this volume), Chap 1, Sects. 4.1 and 4.2.

[15]Stern, in Stern (2006), § 108 II 4 e (p. 1418); Kugelmann 2001, p. 373.

[16]See Blanke and Perlingeiro (in this volume), Chap. 1, Sect. 4.1.1, 4.1.2 and 4.1.2.1.

## 1.2 Development and Aims of the Transparency Legislation and Conflicting Interests

The first transparency legislation was adopted in Sweden as early as 1766 as "Freedom of the Press Act" (*Tryckfrihetsförordningen*).[17] It is one of the four fundamental laws, which form the Swedish constitution, and as such, it sets an example even today. However, the "triumph" of the freedom of information did not take place until much later. Many western legal systems arose from the American Freedom of Information Act (FOIA), which was signed into law by President *L.B. Johnson* in 1966. It has its roots in the civil rights and democracy movement of the 1960s and is the most obvious example of the U.S. history of open and transparent government. This Act obliges all administrative authorities to provide information to citizens and imposes any necessary limitations. In an exemplary manner, it standardizes the objective of administrative control to protect citizens from government interference with their fundamental rights. Limitations regarding the interests of third parties have been namely regulated in the U.S. "Privacy Act" (1974).

The importance of the freedom of access to information as an aspect of transparency and a condition for the rule of law and democracy is now also becoming apparent in international treaties at a regional level. On the regional level the Council of Europe's Convention on Access to Official Documents will be the first binding international legal instrument to recognize a general right of access to official documents held by public authorities. The Convention sets forth the minimum standards to be applied in the processing of requests for access to official documents (forms of and charges for access to official documents), review procedure and complementary measures, and it has the flexibility required to allow national laws to build on this foundation and provide even greater access to official documents. In the European Union, Article 15.3 TFEU, in conjunction with Article 42 CFREU, guarantees transparency, and openness to any natural or legal person when demanding access to the documents of the institutions, bodies and agencies of the Union. It is a right to free and unimpeded access to the information administrated by the Union. As a regulatory objective, Article 15.1 TFEU calls for the promotion of good governance and ensuring the participation of civil society.[18] With this arrangement, Article 15.1 TFEU concurs directly with the democratic principles enshrined in Articles 10 and 11 TEU,[19] which under Article 10.3 TEU and Article 11 TEU in particular highlight the participation of the citizens. However, unlike Article 15.3 TFEU, Article 15.1 TFEU does not confer a subjective public right of access (Sect. 2.2.3).

The question of democratic control of the administration by the citizens is also based on the laws on access to information of the federal government and twelve of

[17] Ackermann & Sandoval-Ballestros 2006, p. 88; Jonason (in this volume), Chap. 5, Sect. 1.2.

[18] Article 15.1 TFEU provides: "In order to promote good governance and ensure the participation of civil society, the Union institutions, bodies, offices and agencies shall conduct their work as openly as possible."

[19] Schäfer, in Dauses (2015), A.II., Appendix, para. 448.

the sixteen German *Länder,* which have enacted laws in this area.[20] As stated in the explanatory memorandum, the German Federal Freedom of Information Act (FIA) of 2005[21] aims to make the Federal Government's administrative action more transparent and, on the other hand, to strengthen citizens' rights of participation.[22] Transparency of public authorities is a key feature of good governance—with the key elements of impartiality and incorruptibility of the officials, equal and non-discriminatory treatment of the citizens, compliance with due diligence, accountability, a thrifty administration, efficiency and effectiveness[23]—and an indicator of whether or not a society is genuinely democratic and pluralist. Also in the Brazilian Law N° 12.527 of 2011 the U.S. understanding is conceived as "freedom from the state";[24] but this Law has a broader range of addressees who are obliged to implement the right. This is linked to the expectation that transparency will be created by this act, and thus, will be able to control the office holders, politicians and administration, not least to prevent and reveal the ubiquitous corruption (Sect. 1).

The UN Convention against Corruption (UNCAC) makes it clear that state legislatures should also standardize the freedom of access to information as a means of combating corruption. According to Article 10 of this Convention, each Contracting Party is to take measures to combat corruption to make public administration more transparent. As an example of such measures, Article 10 point (a) of the Convention proposes "regulations allowing members of the general public to obtain, where appropriate, information on the organization, functioning and decision-making processes of its public administration".[25] To enhance "the transparency of and to promote the contribution of the public to decision-making processes", this Convention requires States to ensure "that the public has effective access to information" (Article 13.1 points (a) and (b) UNCAC).

Thus, depending on the political and social situation of a state, different legal objectives arise in the national legal order with regard to the legal expression of the right of information access. While the European Union as a whole and Germany in particular are concerned primarily with the participation of the citizens and with the

[20]Until now four German *Länder* have not adopted freedom of information legislation or transparency legislation (in the sense of "proactive disclosure"). For more details see Herr et al. 2018, p. 167 et seq.

[21]BGBl. 2005 I p. 2722 amended by the law of 7 August 2013, BGBl. I S. 2722.

[22]BT-Drucksache 15/4493 p. 1.

[23]See Article 26 within the Title II on "Good Governance" of the Spanish Law 9/2013 on transparency, access to public information and good governance.

[24]See Vaughn and Messitte (in this volume), Chap. 4, Sect. 2.

[25]Article 10 point (a) UNCAC provides: "[. . .] Such measures may include, inter alia a) allowing members of the general public to obtain, where appropriate, information on the organization, functioning and decision-making processes of its public administration and, with due regard for the protection of privacy and personal data, on decisions and legal acts that concern members of the public;[. . .]."

control of the administration, and the USA with the protection of freedom, the *controle social* (social control) is a major concern of the Brazilian legislature.[26]

Access to information, on the other hand, means that public authorities or private bodies carrying out governmental tasks pass on personal data or information that may affect important public interests, such as national security or the functioning of state institutions. In these cases, the transparency laws restrict access to information (Article 23 of the Brazilian Law N° 12.527; Sec. 3 of the German FIA; Sec. (b) No. 1-9 of the U.S.-FOIA).[27] Secrecy of information, such as the defence strategies and national security, is a legitimate interest of the respective legal entity affected, which needs to be balanced with conflicting interests in access to official documents pursuant to the principle of proportionality. Such a weighing of interests is the responsibility of the legislators, because constitutional or statutory exceptions (exemptions) to the right of access always provide an incentive to deprive citizens of information and thereby erode freedom of information. On the other hand, the confidentiality of personal data (as protected, e.g., in Sec. 5 of the German FIA, Article 16.1 TFEU or Article 8 CFREU) with a strong tendency to collide with the right of access, is usually also constitutionally or statutorily guaranteed as a subjective (fundamental) right.[28]

Unlike other legal orders, especially the U.S., the "right to informational self-determination"[29] has special weight in Germany.[30] In case of a collision between the right of access to information and the protection of personal data, also the Court of Justice of the European Union (ECJ) has outweighed or even overridden the right of access by the interest to protect personal data.[31] It is therefore well-settled case-law of the ECJ that exceptions to the protection of personal data and restrictions of that fundamental right must be "absolutely necessary".[32] Based on Article 7 CFREU ("respect for private and family life"), the ECJ has stated in its decision *Max Schrems*: "In particular, legislation permitting the public authorities to have access on a generalized basis to the content of electronic communications (on a casual and generalized basis without any objective justification based on considerations of national security or the prevention of crime) must be regarded as compromising the *essence* of the fundamental right to respect for private life, as

[26]See Barcellos (in this volume), Chap. 15, Sect. 2.1.

[27]This is without regard to the question whether there is no right of access to information (outside the scope of application) or whether this constitutes a justification to limit the right of access.

[28]On data protection as part of the informational self-determination in Germany, see Deutlmoser & Filip, in Hoeren et al. (2015), Teil 16.6, Rn. 6.

[29]German Federal Constitutional Court (Bundesverfassungsgericht), 1 BvR 209, 269, 362, 420, 440, 484/83 (Judgment of 15 December 1983), BVerfGE 65, 1 (41 et seq.) – well-settled case-law.

[30]Wieland 2000, p. 91.

[31]Case 28/08, *European Commission v. Bavarian Lager* (ECJ 29 June 2010) para 49 et 55 et seqq.

[32]Joined Cases 293/12 and C-594/12, *Digital Rights Ireland Ltd* (ECJ 8 April 2014) para 52; Case 362/14, *Schrems v Data Protection Commissioner*(ECJ 6 October 2015) para 92.

guaranteed by Article 7 of the Charter."[33] As a result, the analysis of national freedom to information legislation is highly influenced by the interrelation between the scope of the freedom of information and its limitations—in particular, the protection of national secret interests and personal data of private third parties. Evidence for this is provided by the interplay between the FOIA and the Privacy Act in the U.S. legislation, but also by the relationship between the fundamental right to privacy (Article 5, item 10 of the Brazilian Constitution[34]) and the colliding right of access to information (Article 5, item 33[35]).

## 2 Constitutional Key Features of the Freedom of Information and of the Right of Access to Information

### 2.1 *The Position of the Right of Access to Information According to the Doctrine of Georg Jellinek*

As the scope of the freedom of information in its (original) meaning as a basic right to seek and receive information is to protect the citizen from state interference when accessing "generally accessible sources" (Article 5.1 (1) second clause of the German Basic Law; Article 5, item XIV, Article 220, first sentence and Article 220 para 1 of the Brazilian Constitution), it is a defensive right (*status negativus; status of negative freedom; Abwehrrecht*) according to the doctrine of G. Jellinek on the legal status of man in his relationship with the state (*Statuslehre*).[36] According to this model the law has indeed only an instrumental function to safeguard freedom.[37] Freedom of information is traditionally not one of the "democratic fundamental rights". Rather, it is about pre-shaping the political will of the people in the social sphere, which, according to the German understanding, must be distinguished from the legally structured participation of the citizen in the exercise of public power.[38] Because of the interpretation by the institutions of regional human rights protection in America and Africa, the guarantees of freedom of

[33]Case 362/14, *Schrems v Data Protection Commissioner*(ECJ 6 October 2015) para 94. Article 7 CFREU provides: "Everyone has the right to respect for his or her private and family life, home and communications."

[34]Article 5, item 10 of the Brazilian Constitution reads as follows: "[. . .] the privacy, private life, honour and image of persons are inviolable, and the right to compensation for property or moral damages resulting from their violation is ensured [. . .]."

[35]Article 5, item 33 of the Brazilian Constitution reads as follows: "[. . .] all persons have the right to receive, from the public agencies, information of private interest to such persons, or of collective or general interest [...]."

[36]Jellinek 1905, p. 86 f.

[37]Cf. Kirste 2014, p. 39.

[38]See German Federal Constitutional Court (Bundesverfassungsgericht), 2 BvF 3, 6/58 (Judgment of 30 July 1958), BVerfGE 8, 104 (115); Höfling 1994, p. 505 et seqq.

information as set forth in Article 13.1 of the American Convention on Human Rights ("Pact of San José") and Article 9 of the African Charter on Human and People's Rights (Banjul Charter) have now developed into fundamental rights to performance (*Leistungsrechte*). In the case-law of these courts, the right of access to information as a right of performance was derived from the "freedom of information" (Sects. 2.2.1 and 2.2.2). This right to performance resembles the quality and scope of social rights. The task of the state to ensure the realization of the civil rights and liberties is largely acknowledged today. A big part of his tasks relevant to this area comes from the obligation of every state to protect against threats to the right to life, health, and other basic human rights. This obligation has become a major focus amongst state tasks in recent years.

To what extent there is a duty of the state to promote the actual exercise of the rights and freedoms by means of performance has never been clarified in the German constitutional doctrine. In any case, the public task to underpin the effectiveness of basic rights cannot be to achieve complete equality in the possibilities of the "exercise of, fundamental human rights and freedoms".[39] The construction of such a "fundamental right to a state providing services" ("*Grundrecht im Leistungsstaat*"),[40] presented to us as a result of the extensive interpretation of the guarantees of the freedom of information in the Pact of San José and the Banjul Charter, must be seen in the light of the developments in numerous national constitutions of the American and African continents. A right of access to information had already been explicitly recognized here in the national "Magna Carta" of several States in terms of a special basic right. The Brazilian constitution and the South African constitution are prominent examples.

It is acknowledged that the right of access to information provides a right to performance as part of the *status positivus*.[41] Whether at the constitutional level or by statutory law, the right of access to information gives the individual an enforceable subjective right to claim a performance from public authorities, i.e., the access to documents within a procedure. Therefore, it is a question of a positive obligation of public (or quasi-public) bodies and institutions.[42] R. Alexy, in view of such legal positions within the analysis of the system of fundamental rights, speaks of a right to a "factual positive performance" (*Recht auf eine "faktische positive Leistung"*), characterized by the fact that in principle it could be provided also by private parties.[43] However, according to the decisions of the majority of legislatures, access to official documents can be only granted by public authorities.

[39]Cf. Rüfner 2006, para 48 who refers to Schmitt Glaeser, DÖV 1980, p. 6.

[40]Cf. the title of the contributions by Martens 1972 and Häberle 1972 on the occasion of the conference of the Association of German Public Law Professors in 1971.

[41]Stern, in Stern (2006) § 108 II 4 e; see also Jarass 2016, Article 42 para 2; a different view holds Lukaßen 2010, p. 47: no right to performance.

[42]Frenz 2009, Kap. 3 Rn. 331.

[43]Alexy 1986, p. 179 et seqq.

## 2.2 *The Human Rights Dimension of the Right to Social Communication and Freedom of Access to Information*

In light of the increasing codification of transparency laws or—under the designation of the U.S. legislation—"freedom-to-information legislation", it seems appropriate to examine the national legal systems, and how they further this right as a fundamental right in the constitution or whether they designate it as a simple statutory guarantee.[44] A distinction must be made between freedom of information as an integral part of the freedom of communication and the right of access to information. Notably, the distinction must be drawn, in particular—but not exclusively—between freedom of expression and freedom of the press on one hand, and freedom of access to information as a right of access by the citizen to documents which are within the sphere of the state, on the other hand (Sect. 1.1).[45] It is only against the backdrop of this distinction that it is clear that the extension of the guarantees in Article 13.1 of the Pact of San José and of the Banjul Charter is a result of the extensive interpretation of the freedom of thought, opinion and information, which is understood as a uniform fundamental right by these institutions of regional human rights protection.

### 2.2.1 Freedom of Information as an Element of Freedom of Communication

In the context of the right to social communication, Article 19 of the Universal Declaration of Human Rights (1948)[46] already guarantees freedom of expression and, as an integral part of this guarantee, the right to seek, receive, and distribute information and ideas through media of any kind regardless of borders. Further, as part of the freedom of expression, Article 19.2 of the International Covenant on Civil and Political Rights (ICCPR) guarantees the right to obtain, receive, and distribute information and ideas of any kind orally, in writing, in print, through works of art, or other means of one's own choosing, and thus is clearly in the formulation of the general principles of the Declaration of Human Rights. General Comment 16 of the Human Rights Committee has pointed out that the right to respect for privacy, family, home or correspondence, and protection of honor and reputation (Article 17 ICCPR), i.e., a right which differs regarding its scope from the guarantee enshrined in Article 19.2 ICCPR, means that: "Every individual should also be able to ascertain which public authorities or private individuals or

[44]See on this Birkinshaw 2006.

[45]Inaccurately so, this fundamental distinction is blurred in the contribution by the Free World Centre, Article 19, A Healthy knowledge. Right to information and the right to health, p. 10 et seqq.; https://www.article19.org/data/files/medialibrary/3452/12-09-12-POLICY-right-to-health-WEB.pdf (Accessed on 29 March 2017).

[46]Res. 217 A (III) of the General Assembly of 10 December 1948.

bodies control or may control their files. If such files contain incorrect personal data or have been collected or processed contrary to the provisions of the law, every individual should have the right to request rectification or elimination."[47]

To this date (February 2018), the International Covenant on Civil and Political Rights of 1966 has been ratified by 169 countries. The right to freedom of information is also regularly reflected in regional human rights law as an element of freedom of expression: Article 10.1 ECHR, as well as Article 13.1 ACHR, and Article 23 of the Asian Human Rights Declaration[48] guarantee the right to obtain and distribute information. In the Banjul Charter, the right to receive information and the right to freedom of expression are standardized in Article 9.[49] Even before, the I/A Court H.R. has adopted a broad interpretation of this right, the African Commission on Human and Peoples' Rights had interpreted this right in the sense of a "right of access to information", so that, in accordance with these two regional human rights systems, the defensive right of freedom of communication was reinterpreted as a right to performance (Sect. 2.1).[50]

This extensive interpretation of freedom, originally conceived as a right to communication, strives to incorporate the principal doctrines as set forth in different international instruments, but can also be considered as a reaction of the responsible institutions of regional human rights protection to the deficiencies with respect to the rule of law in the legislative, executive and judicial branches of the States Parties to the Convention. The distillation of a right of access to information in the jurisprudence of the I/A Court H.R. based on Article 13.1 of the Pact of San José and Article 9 of the Banjul Charter is evidence of the method of *effet utile*, which is a recognized method of interpretation of international treaties (Article 31.1 of the Vienna Convention on the Law of Treaties). This broad interpretation of the right to information is also a consequence which the judges and eventually the national legislatures have drawn from the violent Latin American dictatorships of the 1970s and 1980s, and from the continued atrocities in some African states, to establish a new culture of transparency. As is well known, the so-called "state order" was based on the structures of commands, which were not disputable, and unconditional obedience, even in the execution of violations of human rights.

A right of access to information, derived from the regional human rights conventions of Africa and America, is intended to strengthen the position of the

[47]General Comment of the United Nations of 4 August 1988, CCPR/C/GC/16; also see communication No. 726/1996, Zheludkov v. Ukraine, Views adopted on 29 October 2002.

[48]Article 23 of the Asian Human Rights Declaration reads as follows: "Every person has the right to freedom of opinion and expression, including freedom to hold opinions without interference and to seek, receive and impart information, whether orally, in writing or through any other medium of that person's choice."

[49]Article 9 of the Banjul Charter reads as follows: "1. Every individual shall have the right to receive information.

2. Every individual shall have the right to express and disseminate his opinions within the law."

[50]Cf. the "Declaration of Principles on Freedom of Expression in Africa", adopted by the African Commission in 2002, to supplement Article 9 of the Banjul Charter.

citizen vis-à-vis the public authorities, even without prior explicit codification of this right in the conventions. In the past, the African Commission on Human and Peoples' Rights scrutinized the state of freedom of the media and access to information in Africa, citing specific examples that include The Gambia. The presidential elections in Nicaragua in November 2016 have spurred non-governmental organizations to call into question the lawfulness of the election. In this context, the Nicaraguan government has been accused of human rights violations, in particular of the right of access to public information.[51]

Also Article 11.1 CFREU states that "the right to freedom of expression (includes) the freedom to [. . .] receive and impart information and ideas without interference by public authority and regardless of frontiers." However, this guarantee is characterized by the fact that it conceives the freedom of information as a media-related right, i.e., a defensive right, which protects the citizen from such interventions by the state, that restrict the use of the media for expression and as a source for obtaining information.

The right to inform oneself without hindrance from generally accessible sources is not one of the classical liberties, whose origins are found in the times of the Reformation and the Enlightenment. The *Declaration des droits de l'homme et du citoyen* (1789) guarantees freedom of expression and freedom of communication, but does not specifically address freedom of information, which must be regarded as a prerequisite for freedom of opinion and freedom of the press. Hitherto, a number of veteran democracies have not incorporated the right to freedom of information in the national constitutions; for example, in the French Constitution or the Constitution of the United States, there is no mention of a fundamental right to freedom of information.[52] In other national constitutions, freedom of information has been codified, for example, in the Swedish "Fundamental Law on Freedom and Expression",[53] in the German Basic Law,[54] in Article 6.1 (3) of the Mexican Constitution

[51]See the information of the Permanent Secretary of the Red Latinoamericana y del Caribe para la Democracia (REDLAD) of 30 January 2017.

[52]According to Peled & Rabin 2011, p. 370, the reason is that the freedom of information is a comparably modern right; see Vaughn and Messitte (in this volume), Chap. 4, Sect. 2.2; see also Chevallier-Govers (in this volume), Chap. 6, Sect. 2.3.8.

[53]Cf. especially Article 1 first and second para of the Fundamental Law on Freedom and Expression of Sweden: "Every Swedish citizen is guaranteed the right under this Fundamental Law, vis-à-vis the public institutions, publicly to express his or her thoughts, opinions and sentiments, and in general to communicate information on any subject whatsoever on sound radio, television and certain similar transmissions, through public playback of material from a database, and in films, video recordings, sound recordings, and other technical recordings. The purpose of freedom of expression under this Fundamental Law is to secure the free exchange of opinion, free and comprehensive information, and freedom of artistic creation. No restriction of this freedom shall be permitted other than such as follows from this Fundamental Law."

[54]Article 5.1 of the German Basic law reads as follows: "Every person shall have the right freely to express and disseminate his opinions in speech, writing and pictures, and to inform himself without hindrance from generally accessible sources."

as a result of the "Reforma Política" (1977),[55] later also in the "New Democracies" of East-Central Europe, as in Article 29.4 of the Russian Constitution[56] and Sec. 45 of the Estonian Constitution.[57] The Brazilian Constitution of 1988 also ensures the freedom of information in Article 5, item 14 in the context of the catalogue of classical freedom rights as a defensive right. According to Article 5 para 1 of the Brazilian Constitution, it is one of the freedoms that is "immediately applicable," and therefore does not require a statutory implementation. Article 220 of the Brazilian Constitution also guarantees this freedom as an unconditionally granted fundamental right, with the result that only restrictions inherent in the Constitution in terms of conflicting fundamental rights or other constitutional values can limit the freedom of information as a right of social communication.

The freedom of information initially protects the right to seek and to receive information; the active acquisition of information, including research on the Internet, is, therefore, guaranteed by this right. In addition, the processing and storage of information is within the scope of its guarantee. Finally, in the sense of digitizing the information, the freedom not to be confronted with information ("negative freedom") is also protected under this right.[58] In a *strictly communication-related context*, a right of access to information which is not generally accessible, cannot be found in the constitutional guarantees of the freedom of information without interpreting this right in an extensive way (Sect. 2.2.2). An example of a restrictive codification and interpretation can be found in Article 5.1 (1) second clause of the German Basic Law, which gives every person the right "to inform himself without hindrance from generally accessible sources". While in principle, the fundamental rights of communication are characterized by a "thematic universality" (-*Ch. Degenhardt*), the freedom of information does not entitle to access to (unpublished) official documents according to the jurisprudence of the German Federal Constitutional Court.

The freedom of information is not a right to access to documents to be provided by an administrative authority, and certainly not to information free of charge. As the European Convention on Human Rights,[59] the Basic Law restricts the freedom

[55]Cf. the Decree published in the Mexican Federal Official Gazette (DOF) of 6 December 1977: "[. . .] The right to information shall be guaranteed by the State."

[56]Article 29.4 of the Russian Constitution reads as follows: "Everyone shall have the right freely to seek, receive, transmit, produce and disseminate information by any legal means. The list of types of information which constitute State secrets shall be determined by federal law."

[57]Sec. 45 of the Estonian Constitution reads as follows: "Everyone has the right to freely disseminate ideas, opinions, beliefs and other information by word, print, picture or other means. This right may be restricted by law to protect public order, morals, and the rights and freedoms, health, honour and good name of others [...]"; cf. Kofmel 1993, p. 141.

[58]Dörr, in Merten & Papier (2011), vol. 4, § 103 para 57 et seq., 63.

[59]While this does not flow from the wording of the ECHR, it results from the case-law of the European Court of Human Rights; Cf. ECtHR, *Leander v. Sweden* (Judgment of 26 March 1987), Nr. 9248/81, para 74, cited in Hudoc, Khurshid; ECtHR, *Mustafa and Tarzibachi v. Sweden* (Judgment of 16 December 2008), Nr. 23883/06, para 34.

of information by protecting only the gathering of information from "generally accessible" sources. A source is generally accessible if it is suitable and destined to convey information to the general public, that is, to an indeterminable group of people.[60] It is the holder of the information, i.e., the institution that manages the information, who determines if the information is generally accessible. State regulations on access to official information are not qualified as intrusion, but rather as a form to set up the constitutional right to freedom of information in statutory law.[61] Non-public sources include, in particular, the files administered by authorities or other government bodies (including the legislative bodies and the judiciary) as part of the fulfillment of their tasks.[62] However, the problem is that, ultimately, statutory regulation can define what is "generally accessible", thus shortening the scope of protection and undermining the limitations of Article 5.2 of the German Basic Law.[63] The right to information under the German Federal Freedom of Information Act does not render the federal government's documents and records a "generally accessible source".

In the purely *defensive dimension* of constitutional rights to information, the state cannot prevent individuals from gathering information, but there is no obligation to set up or maintain sources of or to provide certain information.[64] The exercise of the freedom of information is therefore mainly to gather information from the different media. Only in exceptional cases, namely when access to a generally accessible source is prevented by the state, there is, according to decisions of the German Federal Constitutional Court, a right of access in the sense of the *status positivus*, as otherwise it would be an unlawful intrusion in the right of access to information.[65]

Parts of the literature, however, express the controversial view that, as constitutional provisions on the right of access to information are lacking, statutory regulation can serve the same function as the constitutional right to freedom of information as an element of the fundamental rights of communication. From this view, the right of access to documents and the right to receive information—in

[60]German Federal Constitutional Court (Bundesverfassungsgericht), 1 BvR 46/65 (Judgment of 3 October 1969), BVerfGE 27, 71 (83 f.); and 1 BvR 1687/92 (Judgment of 9 February 1994), BVerfGE 90, 27 (32) – well-settled case-law; Fechner 2016, Article 5 para 106 with further references.

[61]Jarass & Pieroth 2016, Article 5 para 24.

[62]Stern, in Stern (2006), § 108 II 4 a β (p. 1408).

[63]Dörr, in Merten & Papier (2011), vol. 4, § 103 para 30.

[64]This is the prevailing view in German case-law and literature: cf. German Federal Constitutional Court (Bundesverfassungsgericht), 1 BvR 2623/95 and 1 BvR 622/99 (24 January 2001) para 58; Dörr, in Merten & Papier (2011), vol. 4, § 103 para 77; Fechner 2016, Article 5 para 114.

[65]German Federal Constitutional Court (Bundesverfassungsgericht), 1 BvR 2623/95 and 1 BvR 622/99 (Judgment of 24 January 2001), BVerfGE 103, 44, (60) para 58; Dörr, in Merten & Papier (2011), vol. 4, § 103 para 77.

the German legal order—are then covered by the criterion of the generally accessible sources pursuant to Article 5.1 (1) of the German Basic Law.[66] Some scholars refer to the freedom of information in Article 5.1 (1) of the German Basic Law, partly in conjunction with a "general principle of publicity"[67] or the principle of democracy[68] and/or other constitutional principles in conjunction with statutory law[69] to assume an objective duty of the state with regard to "a public information policy to provide citizens with timely and complete information" ("Informationsvorsorge").[70] However, as the advocates of such a mandate for state action to implement a public information policy have to concede, it does not result directly from the constitution how the state must fulfill this obligation; rather the legislature has considerable powers to shape and establish the objective legal directives of the fundamental freedom to seek information.[71]

### 2.2.2 The Right of Access to Information

The legal guarantees which give the citizen, or other individuals, the right of access to documents in the public or even the private sphere (transparency legislation) are meant to be distinguished from the guarantees of the right to communicate. However, the I/A Court H.R. in a broad interpretation deduced from Article 13.1 ACHR[72] not only a basic right to seek and receive information, but also includes the positive obligation of a state "to allow its citizens access to information under its

[66] Jarass & Pieroth 2016, Article 5 para 24; According to Lukaßen 2010, p. 43, 47, Article 5.1 (1), second clause of the Basic Law contains the constitutional right of access, from which the author deduces an objective duty of the state for a public information policy to provide citizens with timely and complete information.

[67] For the principle of publicity see German Federal Constitutional Court (Bundesverfassungsgericht), 1 BvR 2623/95 (Judgment of 24 January 2001), BVerfGE 103, 44, (63); German Federal Constitutional Court (Bundesverfassungsgericht), 2 BvE 14/83 and 4/84 (Judgment of 14 January 1986), BVerfGE 70, 324 (358).

[68] Jarass & Pieroth 2016, Article 20 para 20, Article 5 para 21.

[69] Angelov 2000, p. 68 et seqq.; see also Scherzberg 2000, p. 336 et seqq.

[70] Trute 1998, p. 250; Schoch 2016, Introduction para 81; Bethge, in Sachs (2018), Article 5 para 58; A different view holds Stern, in Stern (2006) § 108 II 4 e (p. 1418), who correctly points out that Article 5.1 of the Basic Law is a right of defense (status negativus), which cannot be turned into a positive right (status positivus) by means of ordinary legislation; Laubinger Fachbuch journal 1/2014, p. 10, correctly notes that it would not make much sense, if the statutory legislator could amend the scope of a constitutional provision and define the term "publically accessible sources" in an authentic way; a critical view holds also Rossi 2004, p. 83 et seqq.

[71] Schoch 2016, Introduction para 81; Rossi 2004, p. 92.

[72] Article 13.1 of the ACHR reads as follows: "Everyone has the right to freedom of thought and expression. This right includes freedom to seek, receive, and impart information and ideas of all kinds, regardless of frontiers, either orally, in writing, in print, in the form of art, or through any other medium of one's choice."

control with the exceptions permitted under the strict regime of restrictions established in the Convention".[73] The constituent legal elements of this right, i.e., "the freedom to seek, receive, and impart information and ideas of all kinds [. . .]" are interpreted broadly in this case-law. The I/A Court H.R. found the template for this extensive interpretation in the "Declaration on Freedom of Expression" which had been approved by the Inter-American Commission on Human Rights at its 108th regular sessions in October 2000[74] (Sect. 2.2.1). The African Commission on Human and Peoples' Rights has also opted for a broad interpretation of the freedom of expression, and derived in the "Declaration of Principles of Freedom of Expression in Africa", from the basic right of Article 9.1 of the Banjul Charter, the "right of access to information."[75]

In contrast, the European Convention for the Protection of Human Rights and Fundamental Freedoms (1950) has not been interpreted in such an extensive way (Blanke and Perlingeiro, Chap. 1, Sect. 3). Although it contains guarantees which are to be respected within the framework of the freedom of access to information (Article 6 ECHR: fair trial) or even restricts the freedom (Article 10 ECHR: right to privacy), the freedom of information in Article 10 ECHR is only guaranteed as a defensive

[73] I/A Court H. R., *Case of Claude-Reyes et al. v. Chile* (Judgment of 19 September 2006), Series C No. 151 para 58 points (a) and (b) and para 76–78.

[74] Principle 4 of this Declaration states: "Access to information held by the state is a fundamental right of every individual. States have the obligation to guarantee the full exercise of this right. This principle allows only exceptional limitations that must be previously established by law in case of a real and imminent danger that threatens national security in democratic societies."

[75] See the Declaration of Principles on Freedom of Expression in Africa as adopted by the African Commission on Human and Peoples' Rights at the 32nd Session, 17–23 October 2002 – Principle IV on "Freedom of Information":

1. Public bodies hold information not for themselves but as custodians of the public good and everyone has a right to access this information, subject only to clearly defined rules established by law.
2. The right to information shall be guaranteed by law in accordance with the following principles:
   - everyone has the right to access information held by public bodies;
   - everyone has the right to access information held by private bodies which is necessary for the exercise or protection of any right;
   - any refusal to disclose information shall be subject to appeal to an independent body and/or the courts;
   - public bodies shall be required, even in the absence of a request, actively to publish important information of significant public interest;
   - no one shall be subject to any sanction for releasing in good faith information on wrongdoing, or that which would disclose a serious threat to health, safety or the environment save where the imposition of sanctions serves a legitimate interest and is necessary in a democratic society; and
   - secrecy laws shall be amended as necessary to comply with freedom of information principles.
3. Everyone has the right to access and update or otherwise correct their personal information, whether it is held by public or by private bodies.

("negative") right in a communication-based context with the freedom of expression (Sect. 2.2.1).[76] In the specific context of access to information, the European Court of Human Rights[77] has held that the right to receive information basically prohibits a Government from preventing a person from receiving information that others wished or were willing to impart.[78] Furthermore, it has held that the right to receive information cannot be construed as imposing on a state positive obligations to collect and disseminate information of its own motion.[79] However, in the Case *Társasága Szabadságjogokért*–which concerned a request for access to information by a non-governmental organisation for the purposes of contributing to public debate–the Court noted that it had recently advanced towards a broader interpretation of the notion of the "freedom to receive information" and thereby towards the recognition of a right of access to information. Furthermore it drew a parallel to its case-law concerning the freedom of the press, stating that the most careful scrutiny was called for when authorities enjoying an information monopoly interfered with the exercise of the function of a social watchdog.[80] Only a part of the literature regards the Case *Társasága Szabadságjogokért* as a new approach of the ECtHR, which might indicate that the right of access to information can be anchored in the fundamental right of Article 10.1 ECHR.[81] Against this background, the Council of Europe's Convention on Access to Official Documents (2009) was drafted as a special regime to guarantee the right of access to information. After its ratification by ten Member States of the Council of Europe it will be the first binding international legal instrument to recognize a general right of access to official documents held by public authorities.

Even according to the wording of various guarantees of the national constitutions, the freedom of access to information is directly linked to freedom of expression. Thus, Article 1 of Chapter 2 of the Swedish Freedom of the Press Act states the right of access "in order to promote the free exchange of opinion and the availability of comprehensive information." Other constitutional texts highlight at least the systematic context between freedom of expression and information on one hand and freedom of access to information on the other.[82] The *rationale* of freedom

[76]Prevailing opinion: cf., e.g., Grabenwarter 2014, Article 10.

[77]The following summary of its relevant case-law is taken from ECtHR, Österreichische Vereinigung zur Erhaltung, Stärkung und Schaffung eines wirtschaftlich gesunden land- und forstwirtschaftlichen Grundbesitzes v. Austria (Judgment of 28 November 2013) Appl. No. 39534/07, para 41.

[78]See ECtHR, Leander v. Sweden (Judgment of 26 March 1987), Series A No. 116, p ara 74.

[79]See ECtHR, Guerra and Others (Judgment of 19 February 1998), Reports of Judgments and Decisions 1998-I, para 53.

[80]ECtHR, *Társasága Szabadságjogokért* v. Hungary (Judgment of 14 April 2009), No. 37374/05, para 35 et seq., with reference to Chauvy and Others v. France (Judgment of 29 June 2004), ECHR 2004-VI, No. 64915/01, para § 66.

[81]Schiedermair, in Pabel & Schmahl (2013) , Article 10 para 62, a ssumes such a shift in the caselaw of the ECtHR; Grote & Wenzel in Dörr & Grote (2013), para 50; see also Hins & Voorhoof, EuConst 2007, p. 114 et seqq.

[82]Cf., e.g., Article 6.1 and 6.2 of the Mexican Constitution; Article 40 and 41 of the Constitution of Uganda.

to access to information as the driving force of freedom of expression is therefore obvious. According to the decision of the German Constitutional Court in the leading Case *Lüth*, "the basic right of freedom of expression as the most immediate aspect of the human personality in society, is one of the most precious rights of man ('un des droits les plus precieux de l'homme', according to Article 11 of the Declaration of the Rights of Man and of the Citizen of 1789). It is essential for a free and democratic state, because it facilitates continuous intellectual controversy, 'the conflict of opinions' which is a free democratic system's primary element. In a certain way it is the basis of freedom itself, 'the matrix, the indispensable condition of nearly every other form of freedom' (Cardozo)."[83]

However, in the constitutions of the European states, the right of access to information is not found in the freedom of information as a basic "communicative" guarantee. This is demonstrated by the fact that, with the exception of Luxembourg, the right of access to official information meanwhile is explicitly protected by special provisions (*leges speciales*) of the EU Member States. In 21 of these countries, this guarantee has a constitutional rank. Worldwide at least 53, and arguably 59 states guarantee a right of access to "information" or to "documents" at the constitutional level, or else impose an obligation on the government to make information available to the public.[84]

In particular, Sweden, (Article 1 of Chapter 2 of the Freedom of the Press Act[85]), as well as many of the "New Democracies" in East-Central Europe[86] (e.g., Poland,[87] Moldova,[88] Czech Republic[89]), and countries such as Egypt,[90]

[83]German Federal Constitutional Court (Bundesverfassungsgericht), *Lüth*, 1 BvR 400/51 (Judgment of 15 January 1958), BVerfGE 7, 198 para 33.

[84]Cf. Open Society, Right 2 Info http://www.right2info.org/constitutional-protections (Accessed on 23 February 2016).

[85]Article 1 of Chapter 2 of the Freedom of the Press Act states that "Every Swedish citizen shall be entitled to have free access to official documents, in order to encourage the free exchange of opinion and the availability of comprehensive information [. . .] Any restriction of the right of access to official documents shall be scrupulously specified in a provision of a special act of law, or, if deemed more appropriate in a particular case, in another act of law to which the special act refers. With authority in such a provision, the Government may however issue more detailed provisions for its application in an ordinance."; See Jonason (in this volume), Chap. 5, Sect. 1.

[86]Peled & Rabin 2011, p. 370.

[87]Cf. Article 61 of the Constitution of Poland.

[88]Article 34 of the Constitution of Moldova.

[89]Article 17.5 of the Constitution of the Czech Republic: "State bodies and territorial self-governing bodies [. . .] with respect to their activities"; Article 35.2 of the Constitution of the Czech Republic regarding "the state of the environment and natural resources".

[90]Article 68 of the Egyptian Constitution: "Information, data, statistics and official documents are the property of the People and the disclosure thereof from their various sources is a right guaranteed by the State for all citizens. The State is committed to provide and make them available to citizens in a transparent manner. The Law shall regulate the rules for obtaining them and terms for their availability and confidentiality; the rules for their deposit and storage; and the rules for and filing complaints against the refusal to provide them. The Law shall also impose penalties for withholding information or deliberately providing wrong information."

South Africa,[91] Uganda,[92] New Zealand,[93] Indonesia[94] or Mexico[95] have set forth, in their constitutions, the documents held by state authorities and sometimes also certain information in the hands of individuals, to be publicly accessible and implemented the right of access in different ways. Among them, as the oldest historical guarantee, Article 1 of Chapter 2 of the Swedish Freedom of the Press Act ("On the public nature of official documents") stands out because here, the conditions and general principles of this guarantee are defined at the constitutional level. Even this constitutional law, however, refers to statutory regulation to implement the rules governing restrictions of the right of access to official documents.[96] On the whole, national constitutional guarantees have, however, seldom been conceived as a directly applicable fundamental right to claim the right of access to documents as most of them are subject to the requirement of a parliamentary decision in the form of a formal law (Sect. 2.2.3).

In the Brazilian constitution, the right of access to information is codified in different contexts. Here the right of access to information, which is in the sphere of the state and agencies with a quasi-governmental area of responsibility, is laid down as a directly applicable fundamental right within the Fundamental Rights and Guarantees Catalog (Article 5, items 14 and 33—see Sect. 2.2). In the context of the constitutional requirements for the public administration, this duty is subsequently defined in Article 37 para 3, item 2 of the Brazilian Constitution. Finally, freedom of access to documents relating to the preservation of the cultural heritage of Brazil is guaranteed (Article 216 main clause in conjunction with para 2 of the

---

[91] Article 32 of the Constitution of South Africa: "1. Everyone has the right of access to

a. any information held by the state; and

b. any information that is held by another person and that is required for the exercise or protection of any rights.

2. National legislation must be enacted to give effect to this right, and may provide for reasonable measures to alleviate the administrative and financial burden on the state."

[92] Article 41 of the Constitution of Uganda sets forth: "(1) Every citizen has a right of access to information in the possession of the State or any other organ or agency of the State except where the release of the information is likely to prejudice the security or sovereignty of the State or interfere with the right to the privacy of any other person.(2) Parliament shall make laws prescribing the classes of information referred to in clause (1) of this article and the procedure for obtaining access."

[93] Cf. the Official Information Act 1982, which is part of the Constitution Act 1986 of New Zealand.

[94] Cf. Article 28F of the Constitution of the Republic of Indonesia.

[95] Article 6.4 subparagraph (A), item 1 of the Mexican Constitution (1917) as last amended in this regard in 2016.

[96] Cf. Article 2.2 of Chapter 2 of the Swedish Freedom of the Press Act. The Mexican constitution is another example where the "principles and basis (*principios y bases*) of the right of access to information is laid down at constitutional level (Article 6.4 subparagraph (A), especially items 1 to 5 and 7 of the Mexican Constitution) and the implementation of this right shall be governed by statutory provisions. However, in this legal order as well the balancing of colliding rights (in particular the protection of personal data of third parties) needs to be regulated by law (Article 6.4 subparagraph (A), item 1, second sentence, and item 2 of the Mexican Constitution).

Brazilian Constitution[97]). This latter regulation is particularly special because of Brazil's foundation history and its responsibility to the indigenous population. To make governmental action more transparent and to strengthen the acceptance of official decisions, access to information laws are intended to provide the requester with first-hand insight into documents of public or quasi-public authorities ("official information"[98]). Under the influence of the Banjul Charter, national constitutional legislators on the African continent in a horizontal relationship sometimes also grant this right to the citizen vis-à-vis another natural person or legal body of private law (legal or "juristic" private body),[99] if it is information about the requester ("records of private bodies"). That right is limited by the necessity that the information ("record") "is required for the exercise or protection of any rights".[100] This reveals a more contemporary rationale for access to information laws that focus on information held by the private sector and on using access laws to supplement market and political mechanisms to achieve public policy goals.[101]

While pursuing the same aim of giving access to public information, the U.S. American and the German legislatures have opted for a different regulatory technique. Here, the freedom of information is not protected in the constitution as a subjective right, as is the case of Brazil, but only in statutory regulation. Therefore, the transparency laws of the German Federation and eleven (out of sixteen) German federal states are not an implementation of the right of access to information, but instead are constitutive. From the principle of democracy (participation of citizens in the exercise of political power), the democratic requirement of "publicity", as well as from the rule of law (control of the legality of administrative action), i.e., objectives of the German Basic Law (Article 20.1), arises the obligation of the

[97]Article 216 para 2 of the Brazilian Constitution states that "It is the responsibility of public administration, as provided by law, to maintain governmental documents and take measures to make them available for consultation by those that need to do so."

[98]Cf. for example Article 2.1 of the Official Information Act 1982 of New Zealand; Article 6.4 subparagraph (A), item 1 of the Mexican Constitution: "All information in custody of any authority, entity or organ of the Executive, Legislative and Judicial Powers, autonomous organisms, political parties, public funds or any person or group, such as unions, entitled with public funds or that can exercise authority at the federal, state or municipal level is public."; Article 41.1 of the Constitution of Uganda: "information in the possession of the State or any other organ or agency of the State".

[99]See the definition of "private body" in Article 1 of the South African Promotion of Access to Information Act 2 of 2000; see also the Spanish Law 9/2013, which imposes obligations under the Spanish transparency legislation, inter alia, on natural and legal persons who provide public services or exercise administrative powers (Article 4) and—in the area of "proactive disclosure"—on private organisations ("entitades privadas"), which receive during the period of one year public grants or subsidies of a given amount (Article 3 point b).

[100]Article 32.1 point (b) of the Constitution of South Africa in conjunction with Articles 50 to 73 of the Promotion of Access to Information Act 2, in accordance with the Declaration of Principles on Freedom of Expression in Africa as adopted by the African Commission on Human and Peoples' Rights at the 32nd Session, 17–23 October 2002.

[101]Klaaren et al. 2000, p. 30.

German legislators to enact transparency legislation.[102] These laws underpin the idea of an uninterrupted "chain of legitimation" (*Legitimationskette*), which is traced back to the will of the people, i.e., the requirement that "all state authority is derived from the people" (Article 20.2 of the Basic Law) and political decisions must be taken by democratically legitimized institutions. The chain of legitimation, ranging from the people through the parliament to the government and administration up to the actual office holder, must not be interrupted.[103] To produce this chain in a substantive manner and to secure it permanently in the complex decision-making processes, there is a need that the citizens can seek information also beyond the generally accessible sources (such as radio, television, internet, newspapers, etc.). The legislators have however a margin of appreciation for the achievement of these objectives, also regarding the conception of the statutory transparency legislation.

### 2.2.3 The Need of Constitutional Transparency Guarantees for Statutory Implementation

As is often the case, the written constitutional law as a framework does not in itself suffice as a vehicle for the control of parliamentary democracy[104] or for the protection of the rule of law (legality of the administration). In particular, it is not

[102]Angelov 2000, p. 68 et seqq., in the run-up to the adoption of the German Freedom of Information Act (2005), has affirmed, in addition to the objective state obligation of ensuring for a functioning publicness, a subjective right of access to public information and based this subjective right in a broad interpretation – in addition to the (objective) democratic publicity requirement – on the right to information (Article 5.1 (1) second clause of the German Basic Law) in conjunction with the right to vote (Article 38 of the German Basic Law). To this end, in his opinion an obligation of the legislators should correspond to adopting an "implementing law", i.e., a freedom-to-information law. Scherzberg 2000, p. 336 et seqq., prescribes the decision on access to public information sources of the objective dimension of fundamental rights [...]. This objective function of protection and benefit of the fundamental right is, however, in his opinion limited to guaranteeing a minimum standard of real freedom on a regular basis and includes a "prohibition of insufficient actions" of the legislators. At the same time, Scherzberg derives from the right to information (Article 5.1 (1) second clause of the Basic Law) a subjective right of access to administrative information. For him this is justified by the fact that this basic right is "aimed at the defense against violations of the objective basic norm". The ruling German doctrine has not followed these approaches which aim to establish the right of access to information as a subjective right laid down in Article 5.1 (1) of the Basic Law.

[103]Böckenförde 2004, esp. para 11–25; Grzeszick, in Maunz & Dürig (2010), Article 20 II GG, para 61; Sommermann, 2005, p. 191, 203 et seqq., proves that the doctrine of derivation is not the prevailing model in the constitutional law of the Member States of the Union. With a critical view Nettesheim 2005, p. 143, 178, who rejects this model as "chain-of-legitimation fetishism" and who, not without irony, refers to Luhmann 2000, when speaking of the inept idea of the people as a sort of overarching entity in which the miracle of the fusion of the individual wills to common will can happen.

[104]Cf. already Council of Europe, Recommendation 854 (1979) on the "Access by the public to government records and freedom of information", Considerations 1 and 2.

able to strike a balance between the right of access to information and conflicting rights and interests, especially with the interests of official secrecy or confidentiality and the interests of private third parties in the protection of their personal data. The extent to which the right of access to information is effective is only apparent when it is exercised in practice. This practice of public administration, or, as for example in the case of Brazilian legislation, of all three branches of government (public authorities and judicial institutions), and especially of all "quasi-governmental organizations, public foundations or public enterprises", can, as a rule, only be achieved by (implementing) statutory regulations. It explains why the framers of the constitution have opted for regulatory technique which has subjected the fundamental right of access to information to a legal reservation regarding the details of this right ("reservation of the regulation of the details"—to say it in the terms of the German Basic Law´s theory); this applies, for example, also to the guarantees of the South African, Estonian and Egyptian Constitution. Such reservations are not part of the system of limitations of fundamental rights in the proper meaning of this term and, in particular, do not provide a sound basis for the restrictions of fundamental rights.[105]

In this respect, the relationship between Article 15.3 of the TFEU as part of the primary law of the EU, and its implementation in the Regulation (EC) No. 1049/2001 ("Transparency Regulation")[106] as part of the secondary legislation is particularly revealing. This Regulation sets out the principle of free access to all documents held by three institutions of the European Union: Parliament, Council and Commission. According to Article 52.2 CFREU, the fundamental right of access to the documents (Article 42 CFREU) is exercised under the conditions and limits set out in Article 15 TFEU. The fundamental right of Article 42 CFREU, in turn, is to be viewed as a *lex specialis* with respect to the freedom of information under Article 11.1 CFREU in relation to the right of access to information. Article 15.3 second subparagraph of the TFEU provides that "general principles and limits on grounds of public or private interest governing this right of access to documents shall be determined by the European Parliament and the Council, by means of regulations, acting in accordance with the ordinary legislative procedure." Thus, the provision is not directly applicable but instead requires the legislative institutions to exercise their legislative discretion.[107] For comparative analysis of the national constitutional codifications of the right to inform oneself and to gain access to information, it is of interest to point out that not only the conditions and the restrictions, but also the *definition of the general principles* for exercising this legal guarantee result from the implementation of Article 15.3 TFEU within the

[105]Cf. Sachs, in Stern (1994), § 80 III 5 c. (p. 421 et seq.).

[106]Regulation (EC) No 1049/2001 of the European Parliament and of the Council of 30 May 2001 regarding public access to European Parliament, Council and Commission documents, O.J.L.145/43 (2001).

[107]This argumentation is based on Case T-191/99, *Petrie a.o. v. Commission* (Court of First Instance of the European Communities 11 December 2001), para 35.

Regulation (EC) No. 1049/2001. This is particularly true in the light of the fact that the right of access to documents can enter into a conflict with other, no less legitimate legal interests, such as official or private secrecy interests (Article 16, Article 339 TFEU), but in particular the right of each person to protection of personal data. The necessary balancing of these interests can only be carried out at the level of secondary legislation, which defines the determining principles and conditions.[108] This need for a legal structure on the level of secondary EU legislation does not alter the legal character of Article 15.3 TFEU, which includes features similar to a fundamental right.

In the Brazilian Constitution, on the other hand, the right of access to information is explicitly enshrined as an "immediately applicable" freedom within the meaning of Article 5 para 1 and, as is also the case in Article 1 of Chapter 2 of the Swedish Freedom of the Press Act or Article 6.2 of the Mexican Constitution, as a freedom which seems to give the individual a right of access to information that can be directly deduced from the Constitution. Article 5, item 33 of the Brazilian Constitution is, therefore, a constitutionally guaranteed right of access to information. This does not change the fact that Article 5, item 33 of the Brazilian Constitution requires the time-limit within which the Brazilian public agencies shall provide the requested information to be "established by law".[109] Article 37 para 3, item 2 of the Brazilian Constitution must also be interpreted as a rule which merely delegates the regulation of the procedure regarding the exercise of the right of access vis-à-vis the Brazilian public administration to the statutory legislator (i.e., a reservation of a regulation regarding the details), but not as a provision which places the freedom of access to information in the Brazilian legal order under the proviso of the law. Brazilian legal practice such as that which prevailed before the entry into force of the Brazilian "Implementing Act" (Brazilian Law N° 12.527) contrasts with this constitutional-normative finding. Unless special legislation on the access to certain information was relevant, the freedom of access to information held by the public authorities could only be enforced by judicial means.[110] The relevant Brazilian case-law makes it clear that such a right was only enforceable insofar as it concerned the core content of the fundamental right of access to information under Article 5, item 33 of the Brazilian Constitution. It is not, however, from a constitutional, but from a factual, empirical point of view, that Brazilian Law N° 12.527, has made effective and applicable for the citizens the fundamental right of access to information in the legal practice.

[108]Schöbener, in Stern & Sachs (2016), Article 42 para 5.

[109]Article 37 para 3 of the Brazilian Constitution reads as follows: "The law shall regulate the forms of participation of users in governmental entities and in entities owned by the Government, especially as regards [...} II – the access of users to administrative records and to information about Government initiatives, with due regard for Article 5, items X and XXXIII [...]."

[110]Cf. Brazilian Law N° 11.111/2005, with regard to the a necessary information about the security of the society and the States; Law N° 10.650/2003, regarding the right of access to information on the protection of the environment; Law N° 9.784/99, on the access to information in administrative proceedings; Law N°. 8.159/91, regarding national politics on public and private archives.

## 2.3 *Beneficiaries and Addressees of the Constitutional Right of Access to Information*

### 2.3.1 Beneficiaries of the Right of Access to Information

In many constitutions the personal scope of protection of the right of access to information is broadly defined, and—in line with the wording of the constitutional guarantees—often irrespective of nationality or residence in the state whose authorities are requested to give access to information. The Brazilian Constitution grants the freedom of access to information according to Article 5, item 33 to "all persons"; the same applies, for example, to Article 6.2 of the Mexican Constitution ("every person"). In light of these guarantees, the right of access to information is a universal human right. The broad formulation of the fundamental right of access to information in some legal systems corresponds to the principles developed at regional level by the Inter-American Commission on Human Rights,[111] the African Model Law,[112] and the Council of Europe's Convention on Access to Information.[113] A wide personal scope of protection is foreseen also, for example, by Article 44.4 of the Estonian Constitution ("citizens of foreign states and stateless persons"), which, however, is subject to a regulation by statutory law ("unless otherwise provided by law") regarding the legal position of these groups when exercising this right.[114] Less extensive is the personal scope of protection pursuant to Article 15.3 TFEU in conjunction with Article 42 CFREU: The supranational European Union provides for access to information to "any citizen of the Union, and any natural or legal person residing or having its registered office in a Member State", thus making access conditional at least on the residence or the registration of the requester within the Union.

Other constitutions are, in contrast, similar to the tradition of the Swedish Freedom of the Press Act, which in Article 1.1 of Chapter 2 has developed the right to information as a pure civil right: "Every Swedish citizen is entitled to have access to official documents [...]." This is the case, for example, in the Egyptian

[111]Cf. the "Principles on the Right of Access to Information" as framed by the Inter-American Juridical Committee of the Organization of American States, Resolution 147 of the 73rd regular period of sessions, 7 August 2008, Principle 1: "[...] Access to information is a fundamental human right which establishes that *everyone* can access information from public bodies [...}" (my emphasis).

[112]Cf. Article 12.1 of the African Model Law. This "Model Law" is available at: http://www.achpr.org/files/news/2013/04/d84/model_law.pdf

[113]Cf. Article 2.1 of the Council of Europe Convention: "Each Party shall guarantee the right of everyone {...]".

[114]See, however, the broad formulation of the "Purpose" in Article 1 of the Estonian Public Information Act (2000/2001): "The purpose of this Act is to ensure that the public and *every person* has the opportunity to access information intended for public use, based on the principles of a democratic and social rule of law and an open society, and to create opportunities for the public to monitor the performance of public duties." (my emphasis).

Constitution (Article 68, first and second sentence: "guaranteed to all citizens"; "The state shall provide and make them available to citizens") and the Ugandan Constitution (Article 41.1: "Every citizen"). A fourth category of constitutional provisions on the fundamental-rights bearers of the freedom of information can be identified according to the category of information. Thus, certain categories of information are accessible to "every person"; however, only citizens or permanent residents or persons resident in the country for a certain period of time, as well as the bodies of private law (body corporates, legal persons) who at least are registered in the country, are entitled to access to "any category of official information" (Sections 20 to 23 of the Official Information Act 1982 of New Zealand). At the same time, this means that the right of access to information can also be exercised by legal persons of private law, if either—as is the case in Sec. 8 of the South African Constitution– the national constitution provides for the horizontal application of the fundamental rights to legal persons to the extent required by the nature of the rights and the nature of those legal ("juristic") persons or the statutory law sets forth the active legitimization/capacity to request information in favor of private legal persons (e.g., Article 4 of the Argentinian Law 27275/2016 on the Right of Access to Public Information).

### 2.3.2 Addressees of the Right of Access to Information

In many legal orders the right of access to information generates obligations to all public authorities, i.e., the executive, legislative and judicial branches at all levels of government, including the territorial self-governing bodies.[115] With regard to at least a part of the quasi-governmental bodies, it seems to be a widespread manor of codification, especially within the statutory law,[116] to include into the definition of "public authorities" or "public bodies" also natural or legal persons insofar as they perform public functions or operate with public funds, according to national law.[117]

[115]E.g., Article 44.2 of the Estonian Constitution: "All state agencies, local governments, and their officials have a duty to provide information about their activities [. . .]."

[116]E.g., see Article 1 (Definitions) of the South African Promotion of Access to Information Act 2 of 2000 regarding the meaning of "public body":

(a) any department of state or administration in the national or provincial sphere of government or any municipality in the local sphere of government; or
(b) any other functionary or institution when-
  (i) exercising a power or performing a duty in terms of the Constitution or a provincial constitution; or
  (ii) exercising a public power or performing a public function in terms of any legislation.

[117]Cf. for example Article 1.2 point (a) ii) No. 3 of the Council of Europe Convention on Access to Official Documents, which leaves inter alia this extension of the definition of "public authorities" to the discretion of the Parties at the time of signature or when depositing its instrument of

With this background, this right can be binding also for those entities that carry out public functions, provide public services, or manage public funds in the name of the public authorities. Regarding the latter group, the transparency legislation of some countries obligates them to turn over information exclusively on the handling of public funds, the provision of services in their care, and the performance of public functions.

In so far as there are no final constitutional requirements, it is up to the statutory prerogative of the legislature to determine whether the citizen is entitled to access to information (1) only vis-à-vis a part of the public authorities, namely the federal administrative agencies (e.g., U.S.[118]), or (2) vis-à-vis public authorities which perform tasks of public administration (as in Germany, for example[119]) or (3)—as in Brazil, where the statutory legislation exceeds the list of authorities which are compelled to uphold the right of Article 5, item 33 of the Brazilian Constitution ("public agencies")—vis-à-vis not only all public entities integrated in the direct administration of executive, legislative (including Court of Accounts) and judicial powers, and of the Public Prosecutor's Office, but also with regards to enterprises and legal persons insofar as they perform public functions or operate with public funds,[120] including the quasi-governmental organizations, or (4)—more extensively, as in South Africa—also with respect to natural and legal persons who do not perform public functions.

This right of access to private information of an individual, however, concerns in some legislations only a narrow circle of information in the hands of the individuals or legal persons of private law (Sect. 2.2.2). Nevertheless, it is important to keep in mind that the existing or emerging international instruments, whether it be within the framework of the interpretation of Article 13.1 of the American Convention on Human Rights and Article 9 of the Banjul Charter or the Council of Europe's Convention on Access to Official Documents (Article 2.1 in conjunction with Article 1.2 point a), which is pending for ratification, have a wide understanding

ratification etc. See also the "Principles on the Right of Access to Information" of the Inter-American Juridical Committee, Resolution 147 of the 73rd regular period of sessions which states in principle 2: "The right of access to information applies to all public bodies, including the executive, legislative and judicial branches at all levels of government, constitutional and statutory bodies, bodies which are owned or controlled by government, and organizations which operate with public funds or which perform public functions." Cf. also Article 37 para 3 of the Brazilian Constitution: "[. . .] governmental entities and in entities owned by the Government [. . .]"; Article 2.1 and 2.1 point (A) of the Official Information Act 1982 of New Zealand: "State enterprises" or "State-Owned Enterprises"; also the Spanish Law 9/2013 imposes obligations unter the Spanish transparency legislation on natural and legal persons who provide public services or exercise administrative powers (Article 4) and—in the area of "proactive disclosure"—on political parties, trade unions and business organisations as well as on private organisations, which receive during the period of one year public grants or subsidies of a given amount (Article 3).

[118]Cf. Article 552 point (a) of the U.S. FOIA: "*Each agency* shall make available to the public information as follows [. . .]" (my emphasis).

[119]Article 1 of the German FIA.

[120]Article 1 Sole paragraph, items 1 and 2 of the Brazilian Law N° 12.527.

of those public bodies that are obliged by the right of access to information (public authorities or quasi-public authorities).[121]

## 2.4 *Further Elements of the Objective Scope of the Constitutional Right of Access to Information*

In addition to the core content of the constitutional guarantees, which recognize a right of access to official documents held by (quasi-)public authorities (Sect. 2.3.2) directly deducible from the Constitution or under a reservation of a regulation regarding the details, the following criteria can be found in a comparative way as constituent elements of the scope of the right of access to information:

1. The right of access to information is to be understood as the widest possible distribution of official documents: "In principle, all information is accessible."[122] Principle 4 of the Declaration of Principles on Freedom of Expression in Africa, therefore sets the conditions as follows: "Public bodies hold information not for themselves but as custodians of the public good and everyone has a right to access this information, subject only to clearly defined rules established by law."[123] This idea is also expressed in a concept which is, in fact, more a constitutional promise than state practice, in Article 68 (1) of the Egyptian Constitution: "[...] official documents are the property of the People [...]" In addition, the I/A Court H. R. has emphasized in its case-law that this principle "establishes the presumption that all information is accessible, subject to a limited system of exceptions."[124] Consequently, Article 6.4 subparagraph (A), item I of the Mexican Constitution, as well as Article 1 (Principle 14) of the Argentinian Law 22275/2016 on the Right of Access to Public Information set forth: "The principle of maximum disclosure shall prevail when interpreting this right." The term "official document" therefore must be defined broadly. As the Council of Europe's Convention on Access to Official Documents sets forth, the concept of "official documents" means all information recorded in any form, drawn up or received and held by public authorities.[125] This definition is the

[121]See, e.g., the Spanish Law 9/2013 that imposes the same obligations under the transparancy legislation on both public authorities (Article 2) on the one hand and on the other hand natural and legal persons who provide public services or exercise administrative powers (Article 4).

[122]See the "Principles on the Right of Access to Information" of the Inter-American Juridical Committee, Resolution 147 of the 73rd regular period of sessions, Principle 1; see also Article 1, second principle and Article 3 of the Argentinian Law 27275/2016, which was adopted in accordance with this set of principles laid down by the Inter-American Juridical Committee.

[123]Cf. African Commission on Human and Peoples' Rights, 32nd Session, 17–23 October 2002.

[124]See I/A Court H. R., *Case of Claude-Reyes et al. v. Chile* (Judgment of 19 September 2006), Series C No. 151 para 92; I/A Court H. R., *Case of Gomes Lund et al. v. Brazil (Guerrilha do Araguaia)* (Judgment of 24 November 2010), Series C No. 219, para 230.

[125]Cf. Article 1.2 point (b) of the Council of Europe Convention on Access to Official Documents.

basis for national legislation also in non-European countries.[126] Correspondingly, there is a broad understanding of the concept of "information," as the comprehensive definition of the African Model Law shows: "[. . .]information includes any original or copy of documentary material irrespective of its physical characteristics, such as records, correspondence, fact, opinion, advice, memorandum, data, statistic, book, drawing, plan, map, diagram, photograph, audio or visual record, and any other tangible or intangible material, regardless of the form or medium in which it is held, in the possession or under the control of the information holder to whom a request has been made under this Act."[127] A limited regime of exceptions (Sect. 2.5) corresponds to this broad claim.

2. The right of access to official information exists without the requester having to present a legal interest. For example, the Council of Europe Convention states in Article 4.1: "A requester for an official document shall not be obliged to give reasons for having access to the official document." This already results from the labeling of the right of access to information as a "human right;"[128] if the individual invokes a human right, he does not have to justify his claim. In some national constitutions and statutory laws it is expressly stated that the individual can request public information "without the necessity to argue interest or justification".[129]
3. States must satisfy the claim to access to information without discrimination on any ground.[130] Therefore, all people should be afforded equal opportunities to seek information by any means of communication without any discrimination on the grounds of race, color, sex, language, religion, political or other opinions, national or social origin, economic status, birth or any other social condition.[131] To ensure such treatment it needs clear, fair, non-discriminatory, and simple rules, which should be put in place regarding the processing of requests for

---

[126] Cf. Article 3 point (b) of the Argentinian Law 27275/2016: "[. . .] every record which has been generated which is controlled or held in custody by the obliged subjects listed in Article 7° of the present law, regardless of its form, method of storage, origin, date of creation or official character"; see also the detailed enumeration of Article 3.7 of the Mexican General Law on transparency and access to public information.

[127] Cf. Article 1 of the African Model Law: "information".

[128] "Principles on the Right of Access to Information" as framed by the Inter-American Juridical Committee of the Organization of American States, Resolution 147 of the 73rd regular period of sessions., 7 August 2008, Principle 1.

[129] Cf. Article 6.4 subparagraph (A), item 3 of the Mexican Constitution; see also Article 4 of the Argentinian Law 27275/2016: "[. . .] Every natural or legal person, public or private, has the right to request and receive public information. It is not allowed to require the applicant to state to motivation for the request, to attest a subjective right or legitimate interest, or to be assisted by a legal adviser."

[130] Article 2.1 of the Council of Europe Convention on Access to Official Documents.

[131] Principle 2 of the Inter-American Declaration of Principles on Freedom of Expression.

information.[132] Constitutional provisions reserving the right of access to information to nationals must be described as discriminatory with regard to the human rights nature of the guarantee. The requirement that the requester must have residence in the country,[133] on the other hand, can be regarded as objectively justified to ensure that the number of inquiries can still be met by the public authorities (Sect. 2.3.1). The criterion of presence on the territory of the state is based on the assumption that a certain factual effect on the requester is provided by the action of the public authorities, which requires the granting of the right of access to information. For these reasons, a more limited circle of official information, to which nationals of other countries are granted access under a national constitution,[134] also appears justifiable.

4. Access to the information must be free of charge for the requester, or at most a small fee, which does not exceed the cost of copying and sending the information (Sect. 4.1).[135] The requested information must be accessible in electronic formats, which enable their processing by means of electronic media and thus allow their re-use or their re-distribution by third parties.[136]

## 2.5 *Restrictions on the Fundamental and Human Right of Access to Information*

The right of access to information is not an absolute right, but it is subject to limitations ("exemptions" or "restrictions"). For this reason, also the framers of the Brazilian Constitution have constitutionally limited this right regarding the "information whose secrecy is essential to the security of society and of the State" (Article 5, item 33 of the Brazilian Constitution: "except for [. . .]"). These exemptions are spelt out by the Law N° 12.527 (Chap. IV on "Restrictions on Access to Information") and complemented by additional regulations on "Personal Information" (Article 31 et seqq. of the Law N° 12.527) in accordance with the guarantee of "personal intimacy, private life, honour and reputation" (Article 5, item 10 of the Brazilian Constitution). Besides Government secrecy and trade secret exemptions on the grounds of private lives and personal data are the most common enshrined in

[132]Cf. the "Principles on the Right of Access to Information" as framed by the Inter-American Juridical Committee of the Organization of American States, Resolution 147 of the 73rd regular period of sessions 7 August 2008, Principle 5.

[133]Cf., e.g., Article 21 to 23 Official Information Act 1982 of New Zealand.

[134]Cf., e.g., Article 44.4 of the Estonian Constitution.

[135]Inter-American Juridical Committee 2008, Principles on the right of access to information, resolution item 5.

[136]Cf. Article 6.4 subparagraph (A), item 5 of the Mexican Constitution; Article 3. 6 point (h) of the Mexican General Law on transparency and access to public information.

national constitutions.[137] The U.S. American framework on the Freedom of Information, a pure statutory and not a constitutional regulation, is characterized by a regime of exemptions.[138]

However, these limitations must comply strictly with the requirements derived from the national constitution and, if applicable, from the provisions of the regional human rights instruments on access to information.[139] In principle, the limitations are of an exceptional nature. Moreover, by virtue of the principle that only a parliamentary decision in the form of a formal law may set limits to fundamental rights ("proviso" of formal legislation) limitations of the right of access must be legally enshrined (e.g.: "except information for which its disclosure is prohibited by law"[140]). Article 3.1 of the Council of Europe's Convention on Access to Official Documents requires that "limitations shall be set down precisely in law".[141] With regard to the European Convention on Human Rights, it is acknowledged that "a general exclusion of certain legal entities as 'legislative authorities' is not possible." In addition to parliament, therefore, the executive and the judiciary, as well as intermediary powers (in particular, autonomous bodies under public law) may, in principle, enact laws as understood by the provisions of the Convention.[142] However, restrictions on human rights and fundamental freedoms as guaranteed by the Convention can only be legally enacted by the national Parliaments by virtue of its direct legitimacy by the people. The primacy of parliamentary decision-making powers within the framework of the division of powers, prescribed by the understanding of democracy, is safeguarded especially if the "reservation of statutory regulation" for restrictions of the right of access is interpreted as a reservation of a parliamentary act.[143] These requirements, which are derived from the European Convention on Human Rights, are also applicable to the Council of Europe Convention on Access to Official Documents. The latter Convention must be interpreted in the light of the ECHR. In the legal area of the American Convention on Human Rights, the understanding of "law" within the meaning of the Model

[137]Cf. Article 6.4 subparagraph (A), item 1, second sentence, and item 2 of the Mexican Constitution; Article 41.1 of the Constitution of Uganda; Article 9.2 of the Official Information Act 1982 of New Zealand; cf. also Articles 24, 26, 27, and 40 to 43 of the British Freedom of Information Act 2000.

[138]See Vaughn and Messitte (in this volume), Chap. 4, Sect. 6.

[139]Cf. for these constitutional or legal precautions: I/A Court H. R. 2012, p. 4 et seqq., 15 et seqq.

[140]See Article 44.2 of the Estonian Constitution.

[141]See also Principle 6 of the "Principles on the Right of Access to Information" as framed by the Inter-American Juridical Committee of the Organization of American States, Resolution 147 of the 73rd regular period of sessions, 7 August 2008. Cf. also Sachs, in Stern 1994 § 80 IV 3 c (p. 448) regarding this type of reservation in the German Basic Law.

[142]Cf. Weiß 1996, p. 70 et seqq., 153.

[143]Cf. Hesse 1999, para 508 et seq., 314; Weiß 1996, 73 et seq.

Inter-American Law seems to differ inasmuch as also the "jurisprudence", i.e., the case-law, meets the requirement of "law".[144]

Often this reservation is conceived in a specific ("qualified") manner (e.g.: "except for information whose secrecy is essential to the security of society and of the State"[145]). For reasons of constitutionality all exceptions (exemptions) need to be based on a legitimate aim, and can be applied only in accordance with the principle of proportionality, i.e., if necessary and proportional for pursuing that aim. Article 3.1 of the Council of Europe Convention has expressed these criteria of the substantive legality of limitations in a formula, which is also based on numerous guarantees of the European Convention on Human Rights: Limitations to access to official documents must be "necessary in a democratic society and be proportionate to the aim of protecting" a defined list of public or private interests. This formula is also formative for the limitations to freedoms protected under the Inter-American system.[146] These requirements are met when the "limitation", i.e., the "exception" is at least capable of promoting the aim of the intervention, also if it is the least onerous to the individual among several equally suitable means. Finally, the intensity of the infringement must not be disproportionate to the purpose pursued by the legislature. Within the context of the necessary balancing of conflicting interests—in the sense of the German doctrine of "practical concordance"—the limitation on the right to access to information for reasons based on the "necessity" of an interference with this right "in a democratic society",[147] serves to integrate this national human right, guaranteed constitutionally or statutorily, into the regional system of human rights protection.The notion of necessity implies that the interference corresponds to a pressing social need and, in particular, that it is proportionate to the legitimate aim pursued.[148]

However, in assessing the necessity of interferences with the right to access, the European Court of Human Rights emphasizes that by virtue of the principle of democracy the Member States have a margin of appreciation, which is subject to

---

[144]Regarding the exceptions to disclosure in Article 41 point (b) of the Model Inter-American Law – "Allowing access would create a clear, probable and specific risk of substantial harm, [which should be further defined by law] to the following public interests [. . .]" – the framers of this Model Law have held in a comment on Article 41 point (b) that "'further defined by law' should be understood to include both legislation and/or jurisprudence, from which the definition of the exceptions shall emanate."

[145]See Article 5, item 33 of the Brazilian Constitution.

[146]See Article 54.1 point (a) ("Burden of Proof") of the Model Inter-American Law; I/A Court H. R., *Case of Claude-Reyes et al. v. Chile* (Judgment of 19 September 2006), Series C No. 151 para 85.

[147]Cf. Article 3 Council of Europe Convention on Access to Official Documents; "Principles on the Right of Access to Information" as framed by the Inter-American Juridical Committee of the Organization of American States, Resolution 147 of the 73rd regular period of sessions., 7 August 2008, Principle 1: "Access to information is a fundamental human right [. . .] subject only to a limited regime of exceptions in keeping with a democratic society [. . .]."

[148]Cf., e.g., ECtHR, *Leander v. Sweden* (Judgment of 26 March 1987), Series A No. 116, para 58– well-settled case-law.

only limited judicial review when judging on the objects of protection referred to in the European Convention on Human Rights and the scope of the corresponding exceptions.[149] Such margin of appreciation seems, however, much more limited in the transparency legislation of the American and African states. This is caused by the rule on "Public Interest Override",[150] which is recognized in the regional Model Laws and which requires a higher level of justification of exceptions compared to the similar Article 3.2 of the Council of Europe Convention on Access to Official Documents.[151]

In the words of the Special Rapporteur for Freedom of Expression (IACHR), an exception must pass a three-part test: (1) it must relate to legitimate aims that justify it; (2) it must be demonstrated that the disclosure of the information effectively threatens to cause substantial harm to this legitimate aim; and, (3) it must be demonstrated that the harm to the objective is greater than the public's interest in having the information.[152] All three criteria have to be scrutinized in the light of the underlying "principle of maximum disclosure"[153] or rather the "presumption of a right of access information".[154]

Article 3 of the Council of Europe's Convention on Access to Official Documents recognizes the following (enumerative) legitimate aims:

(a) national security, defence and international relations;
(b) public safety;
(c) the prevention, investigation and prosecution of criminal activities;
(d) disciplinary investigations;
(e) inspection, control and supervision by public authorities;
(f) privacy and other legitimate private interests;
(g) commercial and other economic interests;
(h) the economic, monetary and exchange rate policies of the State;
(i) the equality of parties in court proceedings and the effective administration of justice;
(j) environment; or

[149]Cf. ECtHR, *Leander v. Sweden* (Judgment of 26 March 1987), Series A No. 116, para 59; ECtHR, *Österreichische Vereinigung zur Erhaltung, Stärkung und Schaffung eines wirtschaftlich gesunden land- und forstwirtschaftlichen Grundbesitzes v. Austria* (Judgment of 28 November 2013) Appl. No. 39534/07, para 40 et seqq.–well-settled case-law; Weiß 1996, p. 126 et seqq., 155 et seq. regarding the "necessary in a democratic society test" pursuant to the ECtHR.

[150]Cf. Article 44 of the Model Inter-American Law; Article 25 of the African Model Law.

[151]"Access to information contained in an official document may be refused if its disclosure would or would be likely to harm any of the interests mentioned in paragraph 1, unless there is an overriding public interest in disclosure."

[152]Catalina Botero, Report of the Office of the Special Rapporteur for Freedom of Information, OEA/Ser.L/V/II.134 Doc. 5, approved by the Inter-American Commission on Human Rights on 25th of February 2009.

[153]Cf. Article 2 of the Model Inter-American Law.

[154]Article 5 of the African Model Law.

(k) the deliberations within or between public authorities concerning the examination of a matter

Similar limitations on the right of access to information are provided in the Model Inter-American Law (Articles 41 et seqq.)[155] and in the African Model Law (Articles 24 et seqq.). The relevant parameters for a proportional application of the exemptions can be found in the values of pluralism, openness and transparency; hence, limitations have to satisfy a compelling public interest. Primarily, they must consider that access to information is the rule and secrecy the exception.

The presumption in support of "public accessibility" of information, including the accessibility of documents by everyone, and the rule of interpretation that "in case of doubt, in such a way as to maximize the effectiveness and scope of the right to information" ("in dubio pro petitor")[156] are part of numerous Model Laws, as well as on their basis of the national transparency legislation. It has the greatest impact with regard to the interpretation and application of the exceptions to the right of access to information. Therefore, exceptions "must be interpreted restrictively insofar as they limit a fundamental right."[157] Hence, domestic legislation must spell out that confidential documents remain under this status only as long as their publication could effectively compromise the collective or general interest of a state or political community. This means that these documents must be published after a reasonable period of time.

The burden of proof in justifying any denial of access to information lies with the body from which the information was requested.[158] The application of the exemptions in individual cases must be subject to an effective judicial protection of the petitioners whose request has been rejected for reasons of an exemption.[159]

[155]See Perlingeiro (in this volume), Chap. 2, Sect. 6.3.1.

[156]Article 1, principle 13 of the Argentinian Law 27275/2016 on the "Right of Access to Public Information".

[157]Cf. Constitutional Court of Peru, Case No. 2579-2003-hd/TC, 6 April 2004.

[158]Cf. I/A Court H. R., *Case of Claude-Reyes et al. v. Chile* (Judgment of 19 September 2006), Series C No. 151 para 93; I/A Court H. R., *Case of Gomes Lund et al. v. Brazil (Guerrilha do Araguaia)*, (Judgment of 24 November 2010), Series C No. 219, para 230; "Principles on the Right of Access to Information" as framed by the Inter-American Juridical Committee of the Organization of American States, Resolution 147 of the 73rd regular period of sessions., 7 August 2008, Principle 7.

[159]For the Latin American case-law regarding restrictions on the right of access to information see Inter-American Commission on Human Rights 2012, The Inter-American Legal Framework regarding the Right to Access to Information, p. 107 et seqq., 110 et seqq.; for the U.S. case-law see Vaughn and Messitte (in this volume), Chap. 4, Sect. 6.3.

# 3 Type and Scope of a Statutory Right of Access to Information

## *3.1 Transparency Legislation as a Statutory Implementation of Constitutional and Human Rights Guarantees*

### 3.1.1 Legal and Federal Fragmentation of the Transparency Legislation in Germany

Transparency legislation is not simply an implementation of a constitutional right. This becomes evident in the fact that in some states there is no fundamental rights guarantee to access to information at all.[160] Even if public regulations on the right of access to information are adopted only within the framework of statutory transparency legislation, they must be consistent with the requirements of the national constitution.

The powers of the legislature to design the transparency legislation is evident in the German legal system in view of the large number of legal regimes which guarantee a right of access to information in favor of the citizen. There can be no talk of consistent transparency legislation. In Germany, this is represented in the juxtaposition of the Federal Access to Information Law (2011), the Federal Environmental Protection Law (2009) (with its impacts by European Union law and also by public international law), and the Federal Consumer Information Act (2006). There are also a number of sectoral laws, such as the Archival Law and the Press Law. Moreover, in the Federal Republic of Germany both the Federation and the *Länder* have adopted laws on environmental protection and freedom of information. Additionally, the *Länder* have enacted press laws. A prime example of this fragmentation is the German legislation on trade and business secrets (Sect. 3.4.4). In some transparency laws or sectoral laws of the Federation and of the *Länder* which set forth provisions on the right of access these secrets are absolutely protected, i.e., they are not conceived for balancing with the interests of access, whereas other provisions on trade and business secrets are open for a relativization through the legal recognition of access interests of others.[161]

The German transparency legislation is also inconsistent in that, within the same law, e.g., the Federal Freedom of Information Act, certain confidentiality interests are more protected than others. The protection of personal data is under the reservation of a graduated weighing of the conflicting interests (Sect. 3.4.3), while the protection of trade and business secrets and copyright are protected in an absolute manner in this law. This inconsistent assessment by the German legislature is most likely not because of the protection of these legal assets under

[160]For the German constitutional order, see Sect. 2.2.1 in fine.

[161]Fehling 2017, p. 81 et seq., 84 et seq.

different fundamental rights—right to informational self-determination on one hand and freedom of profession and right to property on the other.[162]

In view of this objective fragmentation and inconsistency, as well as federal diversification, the German legal system does not provide "the one" solution to resolve the conflict between informational and confidentiality interests (Sect. 3.4).[163] In the German legal order, the highest standards of freedom with regard to "transparency-friendliness" are the regulations of the Federal Environmental Protection Act.[164]

### 3.1.2 Harmonization, Consistency and Requester-Friendly Shaping of the Transparency Legislation in the Federal Legal Systems of Latin America

With regard to its contents the Brazilian, Mexican, or Argentinian legal order in the area of transparency legislation is much more consistent. The framers of the Model Inter-American Law, have deliberately commented on this requirement of consistency regarding the "exceptions" of the basic right of access to information as follows: "To this effect, the Law ... establishes that this law [scil.: the national transparency law] prevails over any other law, in cases of inconsistency (Article 4 [of the Model Inter-American Law]) [...]."[165] The transparency laws of these countries correspond to this demanded consistency to a large extent by having codified the right of access in a manner which encompasses all legal areas, as well as all federal state levels.

The Brazilian Constitution refers several times to the need of a statutory implementation of the constitutional right of access to information. Article 5, item 33 states that "all persons have the right [...] to receive information [...] which shall be provided in the period *established by law*." Even more clearly, such a right is found in Article 37 para 3, item 2 of the Brazilian Constitution of 1988, which provides that "the law shall regulate the forms of participation of users in governmental entities and in entities owned by the Government, especially as regards [...] the access of users to administrative records and to information about Government initiatives, with due regard for Article 5, items X and XXXIII." From these provisions we infer that the framers of the constitution have not only subjected the specific form of the conditions and restrictions, but also and precisely the setting of the general principles of the guarantee to access to public information to a statutory implementation. At the same time, in doing so, they have established a

[162]Fehling 2017, p. 81.

[163]Fehling 2017, p. 81 et seq.

[164]Fehling 2017, p. 86.

[165]Cf. the "Comment" on Article 41 point (b) of the Model Inter-American Law. Article 4 of this Model Law sets forth: "To the extent of any inconsistency, this Law shall prevail over any other statute."

duty of the statutory legislator to adopt such regulations applicable to all legal areas. Without the statutory act, as laid down in the General Brazilian Law N° 12.527, the right of access to information enshrined in Article 5, item 33 would remain a *lex imperfecta*, despite its constitutional "direct applicability". This statutory implementation of the constitutional right was therefore a necessary condition for the effective exercise of the right of access to information. Another effect is that the differences in conditions of access to information which could be found between the regulations in different areas of the Brazilian legislation[166] have been leveled out under that General Brazilan Law.

The legal situation in Mexico is similar. Here the legislature, as an act of implementation of Article 6.2 of the Mexican Constitution, adopted a General Law on Transparency and Access to Public Information[167] addressed to all federal levels nationwide,[168] as well as a corresponding Federal Law on Transparency and Access to Public Information addressed to the Mexican Federation.[169] The General Law gives the individual states a framework within which they must develop the transparency legislation under their jurisdiction. The Argentinian legislators address the national regulations on the right of access to public information as laid down in Law 22275/2016—without any constitutional guarantee of this right—only to the institutions at the national level (in particular the national administration and all branches of government—Article 7), while clearly expressing its harmonizing regulatory approach for all state levels. Thus, they declare all other national legal acts which include provisions on "the right of access to official documents" applicable only for a transitional period (one year after the publication of Argentine Law 22275 pursuant to Article 38, second sentence). At the same time, they call on the Provinces and the Autonomous City of Buenos Aires to "adhere to the provisions of Law 22275" (Article 32) to achieve uniform rules in the area of the transparency legislation, which cover all levels of government.

Furthemore, the distinction of the German transparency legislation between absolutely protected secrecy interests and those which are subject to a graduated weighing of the conflicting interests compromises in the latter case, which leaves a margin of appreciation to the public authorities, the predictability of their decisions

[166]Cf. Brazilian Law N° 11.111/2005, with regard to the a necessary information about the security of the society and the States; Law N° 10.650/2003, regarding the right of access to information on the protection of the environment; Law N° 9.784/99, on the access to information in administrative proceedings; Law N°. 8.159/91, regarding national politics on public and private archives.

[167]According to Article 1 of the Federal Law on Transparency, it shall apply "en el ámbito federal", i.e under the jurisdiction of the Federation inluding the three branches of government and all their public authorities, agencies etc., and the private sector as far as it receives or spends public funds.

[168]Published in the Law Gazette of the Federation (DOF) of 4 May 2015.

[169]Article 1 of the Federal Law on Transparency (Law Gazette of the Federation (DOF) of 9 March 2016, most recently amended in 2017 and published in DOF of 27 January 2017) states regarding the scope of application of this law: "at the federal level" ("en el ámbito federal"), i.e under the jurisdiction of the Federation inluding the three branches of government and all their public authorities, agencies etc. and also the private sector as far as it receives or spends public funds.

on access to official documents. However, similar to the U.S. FOIA, this differentiation protects, above all, the confidentiality interests of third (private) parties. This interest is only outweighed or even overridden, when circumstances allow the access of the requester to such confidential information (as exceptions to the law), after setting out the reasons and the evidence for the need of such an access. Even in case of an absolute legal protection of confidential information, according to a view which is growing among German scholars, no legitimate interest in the secrecy of legal infringements should be recognized.[170]

Regarding the definition of "exceptions", the transparency legislation of Latin American states is generally more consistent with regard to the principle of free access. The decisive difference in this respect is that the right of the individual to access to information is recognized in legal terms as a principle and thus a rule, and eventually also carried through in the system of exceptions. This rule of free access is only broken in case of the exceptions of "confidentiality", i.e., for reasons of secrecy or confidentiality laid down by law for all legal areas. They are based in the Mexican and Brazilian legal systems on the principle that access of third parties to confidential information, in particular personal data, can only be granted with the consent of the affected person.

The requirement of consent shall be waived, in particular, in cases where (1) the information is available in public registers or sources which are publicly accessible, (2) the information due to legal provisions is public or (3) pursuant to a judicial order the information is to be made public, or (4) if reasons of public security or public health are present or (5) for the protection of the rights of third parties the information has to be published. The essential pillars contributing to a requester-friendly transparency legislation are the right of access to all official documents which contain private information on third parties as a rule, the need of substantial and detailed justification of a "public interest override" (Sect. 2.5), handful exceptions stipulated under the sign of "confidentiality," as well as the removal of these exceptions, what acknowledges the public interest in access to the information (and thus not the confidentiality of the requested information), and thereby restores the rule of free access.[171] The determining factor of this legislation is the maxim of the widest possible distribution (*máxima divulgación*) and the motto "in dubio pro petitor" (in case of doubts in favor of the requester). The Argentinian legislators, who explicitly enshrined these principles in Article 1 of the Law on the Right of Access to Public Information, have opted for an even more requester-friendly regulation, by listing certain secrecy interests in an enumerated manner.[172] Such

[170]Fehling 2017, p. 84 et seq. with fn. 71. Rightly so, *Fehling* raises the question if the violation has to be determined before by another institution or as a preliminary question by the institution providing the information.

[171]Cf. Article 120.1 and 2 of the Mexican General Law on Transparency and Access to Information; Article 31 of the Brazilian Law N° 12.527.

[172]Article 1 principles 2 and 13 in conjunction with Article 8.1 points (a) – (m) of the Argentinian Law 27275/2016; only in cases of grave breaches of human rights, genocide, war crimes or crimes against humanity these "exceptions" shall not be applicable pursuant to Article 8.2 of this Law.

an enumerative and standardized regulation about grounds of secrecy, which encompasses all areas of public information management, with the consequence of an exemption from access to the protected information, abides the rule of law principle which includes clarity and predictability of the decisions of public authorities.

## 3.2 *Legitimacy and Subjects Obliged to Provide Information*

### 3.2.1 The Right to Claim Access to Information

As is the case with constitutional access to information rights, it is common to the statutory transparency legislation that the group of entitled persons is expansive. In accordance with the U.S.-American model, Sec. 1.1 (1) of the German FIA grants "everyone" the right to get access to official information from public authorities.[173] This also corresponds to Article 2.1 of the Council of Europe's Convention on Access to Official Documents ("everyone"). Irrespective of their citizenship or nationality and regardless of their place of abode, natural persons as well as legal persons[174] fall under the scope of the entitled persons; requests can also be made by foreigners.[175] The right to apply is also independent of a residence in Germany.[176]

Article 10 of the Brazilian Law N° 12.527 entitles "any interested party" to present a request. Likewise, "any request of records" is allowed according to Sec. (a) subsec. 3.A. of the U.S. FOIA. In line with the idea of codifying a wide range of active legitimacy, many national transparency laws, including U.S. FOIA, the Brazilian Law N° 12.527, the Argentinian Law 22275/2016, the German FOI Act, and also Article 4 of the Council of Europe's Convention state that a requester for an official document shall not be obliged to give reasons for having access to the official document.[177] This is in line with the concern of national legislators and Parties of the Convention (Council of Europe) to codify a broad scope of personal protection of the right of access to information, even if this right is not constitutionally guaranteed.

### 3.2.2 Subjects Obliged to Provide Information

On the other hand, the circle of institutions obliged by the German FIA to give access to official information is limited. In Germany, the branches of government

[173]See also Sec. 24.1 of the New Zealand Official Information Act.

[174]Kugelmann 2005, p. 3610; Rossi 2006, § 1 para 7.

[175]Schmitz & Jastrow 2005, p. 987.

[176]Rossi 2006, § 1 para 9.

[177]Cf. regarding Germany Schmitz & Jastrow 2005, p. 986.

(legislative, executive and judiciary) are obliged by the FIA only in so far as they perform tasks of public administration. These institutions include the Federal administrative authorities (Sec 1.1 (1) of the German FIA) and other federal bodies and facilities, provided they perform such public administrative tasks (Sec. 1.1, second sentence of the German FIA in conjunction with Sec. 1.4 of the German Federal Administrative Procedure Act).[178] The same applies to natural and legal persons, in so far as an authority avails itself of these persons to fulfill tasks subject to public law (Sec. 1.1, third sentence of the German FIA).[179] Hence, the reference to tasks of public administration creates the obligation to give access to information (Scherzberg and Solka, Chap. 7, Sect. 2.1).

The link to the performance of administrative tasks is irrespective of the fact that the authority requested by the applicant, such as the German Bundestag, is, in principle, part of the legislative branch. The scope of the German FIA (Sec. 1) therefore refers solely to the performance of an administrative function. In this context, the concept of administration is to be defined as functionally and therefore negatively, by means of a distinction from other state functions.[180] Thus, the Federal Administrative Court (*Bundesverwaltungsgericht*) ruled that the German Bundestag was obliged to provide information on the mandate-based support of the members of parliament in connection within the work of the Research Services of the German Federal Parliament (*Wissenschaftliche Dienste*).[181] The "information processing and knowledge generation" of the Research Services of parliament should be defined as such a performance of an administrative task.[182] On the other hand, the German Bundestag is not obliged to give access to information not only in its legislative capacity and in the exercise of budgetary powers but also comprehensively in the sphere of other parliamentary matters; in addition to its right to "create" (elect) other constitutional organs (such as the chancellor, the

[178]Cf. German Federal Administrative Court (Bundesverwaltungsgericht), 7 C 20/12, E 151 (Judgment of 27 November 2014), 1 para 17, with regard to the administration of the German parliament (Bundestag).

[179]Vgl. dazu Article 4 of the South African Promotion of Information Act 2 of 2000.

[180]German Federal Administrative Court (Bundesverwaltungsgericht), 7 C 1/14 (Judgment of 25 June 2015), NJW 2015, 3258, para 13a.

[181]German Federal Administrative Court (Bundesverwaltungsgericht), 7 C 1/14 (Judgment of 25 June 2015), NJW 2015, 3258, first guiding principle, regarding the opinion of the German Parliament's Research Services drafted in the case of the plagiarism accusations concerning the doctoral thesis of the former Federal Minister of Defence Karl-Theodor Freiherr zu Guttenberg; see, to that effect, also the decision of the Mainz Administrative Court, 4 K 147/17.MZ (Judgment of 29 November 2017), regarding the opinion of the Rhineland-Palatinate state Parliament's Research Services on the respective regional regulations on live streamed broadcasting about the municipal Council and committee meetings. A legal analysis of that case is available at https://www.lto.de/recht/nachrichten/n/vg-mainz-4k14717mz-transparenzgesetz-auch-fuer-gutachten-wissenschaftlicher-dienst-landtag-auftrag-fraktionen/

[182]German Federal Administrative Court (Bundesverwaltungsgericht), 7 C 1/14 (Judgment of 25 June 2015), NJW 2015, 3258, para 18.

federal president etc.) and to represent the German people, this includes, in particular, its parliamentary function of the control vis-à-vis the Federal Government.[183]

Further, the U.S. FOIA focuses on the executive as a provider of access to information, but by referring to the "agency", so that not only the federal administrative branch in the narrow sense is the addressee of this Act. Instead, "any executive department, military department, government corporation, government controlled corporation, or any other entity in the executive branch of the government, or any independent regulatory agency", and thus also other parts of the federal government are among the institutions, which are obliged to comply with an information request.[184]

The Mexican General Law on Transparency and Access to Public Information (2015[185]), or the Brazilian Law N° 12.527 go even further: According to Article 1 Sole paragraph of the Brazilian Law, this law is applicable to "public entities integrated in the direct administration of Executive, Legislative (including Court of Accounts) and the Judicial powers, and of the Public Prosecutor's Office". Unlike the German Freedom of Information Act (that is addressed to all branches of government which perform *administrative* tasks) and the U.S. FOIA (which obliges "each agency [to] make available to the public information") all three branches of government in *all their official activities* are responsible to fulfill the obligations set out by the Brazilian Law. Even quasi-governmental organizations, public foundations, public enterprises, mixed capital corporations and remaining entities directly or indirectly controlled by the Union, States, Federal District and Municipalities are addressed by Article 1 Sole paragraph, item 2 of Law N° 12.527. In 2016, the Argentinian legislators followed this conception of the Model Inter-American Law and declared all three branches of government, as well as an enumerative list of quasi-governmental organizations, as "sujetos obligados a brindar información pública" (subjects obliged to give access to public information).

The number of "addressees" is, thus, significantly more comprehensive in the Latin American national transparency legislation than, for example, in the U.S. FOIA or the German Freedom of Information Act.[186] There are many reasons for that wide range of subjects which are compelled to uphold the right of access to information. This is certainly an expression of the attempt for achieving "democratization" of the Latin American societies.[187] A main objective of the Latin American transparency legislation is also combating corruption, which can be identified in all three branches of government because of the interaction between inequality and corruption. This causal relation is a noticeable fact regarding the

[183]German Federal Administrative Court (Bundesverwaltungsgericht), 7 C 1/14 (Judgment of 25 June 2015), NJW 2015, 3258, para 16.

[184]See Vaughn and Messitte (in this volume), Chap. 4, Sect. 2.2.

[185]Cf. Article 23 of the Mexican General Law on Transparency and Access to Public Information, published in the DOF of 4 May 2015.

[186]See Blanke and Perlingeiro (in this volume), Chap. 1, Sect. 4.1.2, especially subsection 4.1.2.3.

[187]See Blanke and Perlingeiro (in this volume), Chap. 1, Sects. 2.1 and 4.1.

Latin American countries (Blanke and Perlingeiro, Sect 1, 1.2). In the Corruption Perception Index 2016, Argentina ranked 95th, Brazil 79th.[188] This institutionally comprehensive approach concerning the addressees of the transparency legislation must be aware of the potential conflicts with the principle of the separation of powers, especially regarding the dividing line between the legislative and the executive branch.[189]

### 3.3 *Objective Scope of the Statutory Right of Access to Information*

Just as the Council of Europe's Convention speaks of a right of access to "official documents", Sec. 1.1 (1) of the German FIA also conveys a right of access to "official information". The Mexican legislators have specified the definition of "information" by the need "of public interest".[190] Except for drafts and notes, the nature of the medium containing the information is irrelevant in the German legal order.[191] The legal term "official documents" must be interpreted in a broad sense (Sect. 2.3). They are found not only in official files or data in the narrower sense, but in all records relating to the service of public authorities. The German Federal Chancellor's calendar of events was also counted.[192]

Usually, the right of access refers solely to information held by public authorities or quasi-governmental institutions.[193] Hence, there is no obligation on the part of the state to acquire and organize the requested information.[194] Given that,

---

[188]Cf. Transparency International 2017, http://www.transparency.org/news/feature/corruption_perceptions_index_2016 (Accessed on 30 January 2017).

[189]Blanke and Perlingeiro (in this volume), Chap. 1, Sect. 4.1.2 and subsections.

[190]Cf. Article 3.12 of the Mexican General Law on Transparency and Access to Public Information: "Information of public interest: It refers to information that is relevant or beneficial to society and is not simply of individual interest, the disclosure of which is useful for the public to understand the activities carried out by the obligated subjects."

[191]Kugelmann 2005, p. 3610; Sec 2.1 of the German FIA; Chap. 1 of the South African Promotion of Access to Information Act 2 of 2000 on the definition of "record"; Article 2.7 of the Mexican General Law on Transparency and Access to Public Information.

[192]So Berlin-Brandenburg Higher Administrative Court (OVG Berlin-Brandenburg), OVG 12 B 27/11 (Judgment of 20 December 2011), NVwZ 2012, p. 1196 (1197, 1198 et seq.) with regard to Sec. 1.1 of the German FIA; with a different view regarding the agenda of the Governing Mayor of Berlin as it is not a "record" in the sense of Sec. 3 of the FIA of Berlin see Berlin-Brandenburg Higher Administrative Court (OVG Berlin-Brandenburg), OVG 7 B 9/05 (Judgment of 14 December 2006), para 12 et seqq.

[193]Schmitz & Jastrow 2005, p. 988; Schoch 2016, § 1 para 36 et seqq.; cf. also Article 6 of the Mexican General Law on Transparency and Access to Public Information: "access of any person to the information in the possession of any entity"; Article 4 of the South African Promotion of Access to Information Act 2 of 2000: "[...] a record in the possession or under control [...] is regarded as being a record of that public body or private body, respectively."

[194]Kloepfer & von Lewinski 2005, p. 1280.

according to the German Freedom of Information Act, the required information must be related to the administrative activities of public authorities, information which the authorities received incidentally on private matters is not covered by their information obligation.[195]

Nevertheless, with the duty to make "records"[196] available, the move away from the confidentiality of files to the publicness and accessibility of files and documents took place. As a precursor to the actual disclosure of the information, the transparency legislation provides that the obligated parties must publish publicly accessible registers about the information available to them,[197] or provide information or support as to how information can be obtained at all.[198] To satisfy a request for information, the requester's application is primarily relevant: According to Sec. A. of the FOIA, the information is to be provided "in any form or format requested". According to the German legislation, the access to documents can be provided in the form of a written, verbal or electronic disclosure (Sec. 7.3 (1) of the German FIA), or, as a catch-all provision, in a "different way" (Sec. 1.2 of the German FIA). In this respect, the type of providing the information should, in principle, also conform to the request.

There is no obligation of the public authorities to recover or replace, for example, missing information[199] (which, without implying the intention to do so, also means that inconvenient information can be lost without great consequences) nor are the authorities obliged to check the correctness of the information (Sec. 7.3 of the German FIA). In such cases, at most claims for damages can result under the strict conditions of Sec. 839.1 German Civil Code[200] in conjunction with Article 34 of the German Basic Law[201] (state liability in case of breach of official duty). In contrast, the rule of Brazilian Law N° 12.527 states in this respect that the public authorities, with regard to requested information, are obliged to guarantee "its availability, authenticity and integrity" (Article 6, item 2). This corresponds to the right of the requester to obtain "primary, complete, authentic and updated

[195] Schmitz & Jastrow 2005, p. 988.

[196] Thus Sec. (a) subsec. 3.A. of the U.S. FOIA and Chap. 1 of the South African Promotion of Access to Information Act 2 of 2000 refer to "records".

[197] Sec. 1.1 of the German FIA; Article 9 of the Brazilian Law N° 12.527.

[198] Sec. (a). 1. of the U.S. FOIA; Article 7, item 1 of the Brazilian Law N° 12.527; Articles 10 and 14 of the South African Promotion of Access to Information Act 2 of 2000.

[199] Schoch 2016, § 1 para 36, 43 et seqq.

[200] Sec. 839.1 German Civil Code read as follows: "If an official intentionally or negligently breaches the official duty incumbent upon him in relation to a third party, then he must compensate the third party for damage arising from this. If the official is only responsible because of negligence, then he may only be held liable if the injured person is not able to obtain compensation in another way [...]."

[201] Article 34 of the German Basic Law reads as follows: "If any person, in the exercise of a public office entrusted to him, violates his official duty to a third party, liability shall rest principally with the state or public body that employs him. In the event of intentional wrongdoing or gross negligence, the right of recourse against the individual officer shall be preserved. The ordinary courts shall not be closed to claims for compensation or indemnity."

information". Providing obsolete information therefore constitutes a breach of the Brazilian transparency legislation, irrespective of the fact if it is the authority's fault or not.

## *3.4 Reasons for Exclusion and Grounds for Refusal*

The abandonment of the principle of secrecy (*Arkantradition*) in the German administration must, or should, translate the specific grounds for the refusal to access to information mainly in a restrictive interpretation. Although the provision of the information should be the rule and the refusal of the requested information the exception, the national legislators have nevertheless created numerous provisions that allow the public authorities not to issue the requested information. The legal "exemptions" and "exceptions" correspond regularly to the limits of constitutionally (Sect. 2.5) or statutorily (Sect. 3.4.1) enshrined rights of access to information. In addition, restrictions of the right of access to information, which is only guaranteed by statutory law, require a parliamentary law (Sect. 2.5) in accordance with the insofar undifferentiating case-law of the I/A Court H. R. and the Council of Europe's Convention on Access to Official Documents (2009).[202] The addressee of this right must substantiate and provide evidence for any refusal to access to requested information as to why the requester should be excluded from access, whether for public or private reason.[203]

### 3.4.1 General Limits of the Statutory Right of Access to Information

When there are restrictions on transparency legislation, German law distinguishes three constellations: first, the cases of legal "protection of special public interests", in which case a corresponding right to information is excluded by the legislators (Sec. 3 German FIA). However, the obligation to respect official secrecy does not constitute a protected official secret. A second category consists of those cases in which, in principle, there is a right of access to information, but it cannot (fully) be met owing to the rights of third parties (Sec. 5 German FIA). The protection of personal data is one of the most important objects of protection, which is enshrined in statutory law; in some legal orders in which the right of access to information is constitutionally guaranteed, the limits of the right of access to information results

[202]Cf. I/A Court H. R., *Case of Claude-Reyes et al. v. Chile* (Judgment of 19 September 2006), Series C No. 151 para 89: "In relation to the requirements with which a restriction in this regard should comply, first, they must have been established by law to ensure that they are not at the discretion of public authorities."

[203]German Federal Administrative Court (Bundesverwaltungsgericht), 7 C 18/12 (Judgment of 27 November 2014), NVwZ 2015, 823 para 19; Case 506/08, *Sweden v. My Travel and Commission* (ECJ 21 July 2011) para 19.

especially from a balancing between these constitutional values. A third category of restrictions concerns the protection of intellectual property, as well as trade and business secrets.

### 3.4.2 Protection of Public Interests

Sec. 3 of the German FIA stipulates that a right of access to information does not exist if access to the information sought can jeopardize a legal interest which falls within the scope of "public interests". For example, the right does not exist if the publication of the information can have detrimental effects on international relations (Sec. 3 No. 1 point (a)), in the case of deliberations of an authority beyond the process of (preparing) a legislation[204] (Sec. 3 No. 4), as well as the access concerns internal or external security interests[205] (Sec. 3 No. 1 point (c)), or the monitoring or supervisory tasks of the financial, competition and regulatory authorities (Sec. 3 No. 1 point (d)) or public security (Sec. 3 No. 2). The burden of proof for the existence of such exclusionary grounds shall rest on the authority that is in possession of the information.[206]

A legal comparison shows that the transparency laws of other countries recognize the same or similar "exceptions" and "exemptions".[207] This is also a consequence of the harmonizing effect that the American and African "Model Laws", as well as the Council of Europe's Convention (which has not yet entered into force), have developed with regard to possible limitations to access to official documents (Sect. 2.5). Pursuant to Article 23 of the Brazilian Law N° 12. 157 restrictions on access to information are provided, for example, if a dissemination or unrestricted access to this information could "jeopardize national defence, sovereignty, or the integrity of the national territory" (Article 23.1), or "damage or jeopardize negotiations or the Country's international relations, or even secret information provided by other states or international organisations" (Article 23.2). However, a right to claim access to information is not categorically excluded in these cases, as is the case in the German legislation of Sec. 3 of the FIA, especially because according to this German law the access can be excluded for the very possibility of detrimental effects. A balancing between the interest in information on the one hand and on the other hand the seriousness of detrimental effects does not occur at this point.

---

[204] Cf. German Federal Administrative Court (Bundesverwaltungsgericht), 7 B 14.11 (Judgment of 18 July 2011), NVwZ 2011, 1072 para 5.

[205] Münster Higher Administrative Court (OVG Münster), A 8 475/10 (Judgment of 2 November 2010), para 83 et seqq. (juris).

[206] Schmitz & Jastrow 2005, p. 991.

[207] Cf., e.g., Article 15 points (a) to (i) of the Peruan Law No. 27806; Articles 100 et seqq., 113 et seqq. and 116 et seqq. ("Classified information") of the Mexican General Law on Transparency and Access to Public Information; Article 8 of the Argentinian Law 27275/2016; Article 33 of the South African Promotion of Access to Information Act 2 of 2000.

The principle of a right to maximum access is also laid down in Brazilian legislation by Article 21 of Brazilian Law N° 12.527, which states under the title "Restrictions on Access to Information" in a prominent position that "access to information required for the judicial and administrative protection of fundamental rights may not be denied". Even if one of the restrictions of Article 23 of the Brazilian Law applies with regard to information whose "content and indispensability" is relevant to the "safety of society or the State", Article 24 para 1 of that Law sets time limits, which exclude in a differentiated way those information from access which are, for example, with regard to those classified as "top secret" up to 25 years. The particular weight which the Brazilian legislators, with point 7 of "Principles on the Right of Access to Information"[208] ("Exceptions to the right of access should be established by law, be clear and narrow") in mind, ascribes to the right of access in balancing it with conflicting interests, can be explained only partly by the circumstance that the Brazilian legal system has codified a constitutional right of access to information, which by Law N° 12.527 is "only" implemented. As a result, the essence of this constitutional guarantee must not be infringed.

A comparison with Argentinian Law 27275/2016 shows, however, that this statutory law, which does not serve to implement a constitutional right, also includes a "presumption of the publicness of all state-held information".[209] In principle, "all the information in the possession or safekeeping or under the control of the authority subject to the law shall be accessible to all persons [. . .]".[210] This result demonstrates the influence of the interpretation of Article 13.1 ACHR by the I/A Court H. R. (Sects. 2.2.1 and 2.2.2). This jurisprudence has had a lasting impact on the Parties to the American Convention on Human Rights and is an element within the reciprocal relationship raised in the Introduction to this volume (Sect. 3) with reference to the relationship between Member States and institutions of the Convention (*Convencionalidad*).[211]

The application of the exemptions of the U.S. FOIA illustrates the importance of an access-focused law. Even under a law like the FOIA, which grants "any person" access and creates a practical presumption that government documents and records, are public unless there is an exemption, it is difficult to sustain the viewpoint that it is secrecy and not access that must be justified. This difficulty arises because the application of the exemptions focuses on their meaning.[212] As R. G. Vaughn and P. J. Messitte have pointed out in this volume (Chap. 4, Sect. 6.2), it is easier to

---

[208] Inter-American Juridical Committee of the OAS 2008, Principles on the right of access to information, CJI/RES. 147 (LXXIII-O/08).

[209] Article 1, principle 1 of the Argentinian Law 27275/2016 on the "Right of Access to Public Information".

[210] Article 1, principle 2 ("Transparency and maximum dissemination") of the Argentinian Law 27275/2016 on the "Right of Access to Public Information"; with regard to a narrow interpretation of the exceptions which restrict the right of access to information see also Article 15 of the Peruan Law No. 27806; see also Blanke and Pelingeiro (in this volume), Chap. 1, Sect. 5.2.

[211] See Blanke and Perlingeiro (in this volume), Chap. 1, Sect. 3.

[212] See Vaughn and Messitte (in this volume), Chap. 4, Sects. 6 and 7.

articulate in this context the values in secrecy than consider the value of access. Moreover, the exemptions themselves contain positions inconsistent with openness. The deliberative process privilege illustrates this paradox of the exemptions. This common-law principle (Exemption Five within the FOIA legal framework) incorporates the importance of secrecy in bureaucratic decision making—the need for candid exchange of opinions and the reduction of "emotional" or "political" responses to rational choices. The result is that the internal processes of the executive branch of a government are immune from normal disclosure or discovery in civil litigations.[213]

Comparative analysis permits to see how various articulations of the same value may lead to different judgments regarding the exemption and access. Examination of the exemptions to the U.S. FOIA identity issues likely to arise in the application of exemptions that might otherwise be more difficult to foresee. Such analysis also suggests that access laws require a particularly careful analysis of the institutional framework and traditions in which they will be applied.[214]

A general clause, which excludes notoriously trouble-making or obviously unfounded requests for information which aim to hinder the performance of an administrative procedure, is generally not included in the German transparency legislation. When the Ministry of Education of the Land of North Rhine-Westfalia was confronted in the year 2015 with the application of a 17-year-old pupil, who had previously demanded access to the questions of his upcoming high school examination,[215] the authority dismissed this application with reference to Sec. 6 point (c) FIA of the Land of North Rhine-Westfalia[216] in conjunction with Sec. 29.1, second sentence of the Administrative Procedure Act.[217] Pursuant to Sec. 6 point (c) of that FIA an application can be dismissed, if the communication of the information would have severe detrimental effects for the course of a pending administrative procedure, administrative offence proceedings, or disciplinary proceedings, or for the success of an impending administrative measure.[218] This rule, which is somewhat exceptional in international comparison, was actually issued to protect the process of undisturbed administrative decision-making in a current administrative procedure, and thus to ensure the integrity and efficiency of the

[213] Cf. on this subject U.S. Department of Justice, Policy Guidance: When to Assert the Deliberative Privilege Under FOIA Exemption Five. Available at: https://www.justice.gov/oip/blog/foia-update-policy-guidance-when-assert-deliberative-privilege-under-foia-exemption-five

[214] See Vaughn and Messitte (in this volume), Chap. 4, Sect. 6.2.

[215] http://www.spiegel.de/lebenundlernen/schule/abitur-aufgaben-vorab-schueler-aus-muenster-scheitert-mit-anfrage-a-1027885.html (Accessed on 8 February 2017).

[216] This law essentially has the same scope and content as the German (Federal) FIA.

[217] Sec. 29.1 of the German Federal APA reads as follows: "The authority shall allow participants to inspect the documents connected with the proceedings where knowledge of their contents is necessary in order to assert or defend their legal interests. Until administrative proceedings have been concluded, the foregoing sentence shall not apply to draft decisions and work directly connected with their preparation [. . .]."

[218] See the analogue provision in Sec. 4.1 of the German FIA.

public administration.[219] This protection has time limits and ends no later than the conclusion of the proceedings.[220] A similar approach was made by the Court of Justice of the European Union regarding the EU Transparency Regulation 1049/ 2001.[221]

### 3.4.3 Protection of Personal Data

There is a special kind of tension between the right of access to information on the one hand, and the protection of personal data on the other. German lawmakers—like the legislators of other countries—have not opted one-sidedly for the protection of data, even if "the protection against the unlimited storage, use and transfer" of the personal data of a person "is included in the general right to protection of personality, enshrined in Article 2.1 in conjunction with Article 1.1 [human dignity] of the German Basic Law".[222] According to the view of the German Federal Constitutional Court, restrictions on the right to self-determination of information are to be accepted only in the "overriding general interest" and only if they are based on a constitutional legal basis.[223] The German Freedom of Information Act transposes such "public interests" into law and thus provides the legal basis for restrictions of the general right to protection of personality as part of the constitutional order. This assessment is in line with the legislators' view who emphasizes in the grounds of the German FIA that the fundamental right to self-determination is not unlimited, but that restrictions must be accepted if they are imposed on the individual in an overriding general interest and do not interfere in the "last inviolable sphere of private life", which is absolutely beyond the influence of public authority.[224] Therefore, in the event of a conflict, i.e., if the third party does not agree, a weighing up and balancing of the interests must be carried out. According to the wording of Sec. 5.1 (1) of the German FIA, access to personal data may only be granted if, in a specific case, the requester's (private) interest in the information sought overrides the legitimate interests of the third party.[225] This interest can be further strengthened by the general public's interest in information and transparency.[226] The weight of the private interest can range from mere curiosity for

---

[219]Schmitz & Jastrow 2005, p. 985; Schoch 2016, § 4 Rn. 4 et seq.

[220]German Federal Administrative Court (Bundesverwaltungsgericht), 7 C3.11 141, 122 (Judgment of 3 November 2011), para 28.

[221]Cf. Case 506/08, *Sweden v. My Travel and Commission* (ECJ 21 July 2011), para 77 et seqq.

[222]German Federal Constitutional Court (Bundesverfassungsgericht), 1 BvR 209, 269, 362, 420, 440, 484/83 (Judgment of 15 December 1983), BVerfGE 65, 1, first guiding principle.

[223]German Federal Constitutional Court (Bundesverfassungsgericht), 1 BvR 209, 269, 362, 420, 440, 484/83 (Judgment of 15 December 1983), BVerfGE 65, 1, second guiding principle.

[224]BT-Drucksache No. 15/4493, p. 13.

[225]Schoch 2016, § 5 para 38.

[226]Schoch 2016, § 5 para 41 et seq.

information that is of little relevance in transparency legislation, to a relevant legal interest (for example, the preparation of actions for damages). The individual interest of a person affected by the official document is particularly important for access to information.[227]

The German administrative court of Neustadt an der Weinstraße denied such an overriding interest of the requester in a case in which the list of all extension numbers of all the agents and intermediaries of an employment office were requested based on the freedom-of-information law.[228] These lists were classified by the court as "personal data".[229] As the requester did not receive any benefits from the office, and moreover this particular employment office was not in charge for him, the court did not recognize any particular public interest in the required information, especially, as the hurdles to the employees of this agency in an immediate on-site contacting were not particularly highly rated.[230]

It is the requester who must justify his "interest in obtaining the information" (Sec. 5.1 of the German FIA). This requirement is not problematic if the third party, who is concerned by the request, agrees to the disclosure of its data (Sec. 5.1, second sentence FIA). Even if the interest in data protection overrides, this does not necessarily mean that the request for access to the requested information must be dismissed. Instead of dismissing the request entirely, it is also possible that the competent authority removes parts of the document containing private data or blackens them, or instead of an inspection of records only provides the information for the requester.[231]

The principle that the interest of the requester in the information should be fulfilled to the greatest extent is laid down in Sec. (b) subsect. 9 of the U.S. FOIA in such a manner, that "the amount of information deleted [. . .] shall be indicated on the released portion of the record". The Brazilian Law N° 12.157 recognizes the balancing of the conflicting positions by the legislators when it comes to disseminating and accessing (of third parties) to "personal information relating to intimacy (and) private life". This is because, in addition to an "express consent of the person to whom the information refers" (Article 31 para 1, item 2 of the Brazilian Law N° 12.157), that information is only accessible "through an authorization obtained by means of legal provision". However, consent is dispensable in the exceptional cases referred to in Article 31 para 3 of that law. These exceptions refer to information in which (1) medical prevention and diagnosis are necessary, (2) the carrying out of statistical or scientific research is of noticeable public or general interest, (3) to

227 Schoch 2016, § 5 Rn. 42.

228 Neustadt Administrative Court (VG Neustadt), 4 466/14.NW (Judgment of 4 September 2014), juris.

229 Neustadt Administrative Court (VG Neustadt), 4 466/14.NW (Judgment of 4 September 2014), juris, second guiding principle.

230 Neustadt Administrative Court (VG Neustadt), 4 466/14.NW (Judgment of 4 September 2014), juris, para 52 et seqq.

231 Schoch 2016, § 5 para 53.

comply with a judicial decision, (4) for the defense of human rights or (5) the protection of an overriding general public interest is at stake. Restrictions of the right of access to information related to the protection of private life, honor and public image of third parties may not be required with the purpose of jeopardizing the determination of irregularities in which the holder of information is involved, as well as actions related to jeopardize the retrieval of highly relevant historical facts (Article 31 para 4 of the Brazilian Law N° 12.157).

However, under certain circumstances, the protection of personal data may be guaranteed only by granting access to such data—that is, if it concerns the data of the requester himself: only if it is possible to know who is in the possession of an information and who is able to correct or delete such information, an effective protection of personal data is given.[232] The provision of Article 31 para 1, item I of the Brazilian Law complies with this principle.[233]

### 3.4.4 Protection of Trade and Business Secrets

Sec. (b) subsect. 9 of the U.S. FOIA addresses confidential business and financial information acquired by the government and thus protects as the fourth exemption in U.S. law regarding the freedom to information primarily—but not exclusively—the governmental interest in obtaining such information from businesses and corporations (Vaughn and Messitte, Chap. 4, Sect. 6.2.4). In contrast, other transparency laws aim to protect private interests in the sphere of trade and business (e.g., Sec. 6, second sentence of the German FIA). The German legislature—as well as many other national legislators[234]—has, in contrast to Sec. 9.1 of the German Environmental Information Act, conferred an absolute protection of the confidentiality of the trade and business information.[235] It follows that a balancing of conflicting interests of third parties is excluded in this respect. According to German jurisprudence, public enterprises should also be able to rely on such trade and business secrets, given that such protection shall not fall short because of the missing legal capacity of public enterprises to refer to fundamental rights.[236] With regard to private parties, German case-law even tends to significantly extend the scope of protection of trade and business secrets

[232]Case 362/14, *Schrems v Data Protection Commissioner* (ECJ 6 October 2015) para 95.

[233]This provision reads as follows: "The personal information, referred to in this article, relating to intimacy, private life, honour and image [...] shall have access to it restricted, regardless of the secrecy classification and for a maximum period of 100 (one hundred) years from the date of its production, to legally authorized public agents *and the persons it refers to [...]*" (my emphasis).

[234]Cf. Article 116.3 of the Mexican General Law on Transparency and Access to Information; Article 8 point (c) of the Argentinian Law 27275/2016; Articles 36, 64.1 and Article 68 of the South African Promotion of Access to Information Act 2 of 2000.

[235]Pursuant to Article 3 point (g) of the Council of Europe Convention "commercial and other economic interests" constitute only a "limit" to the right of access to official documents.

[236]Cf. for example Koblenz Higher Administrative Court (OVG Koblenz), 10 A10172/14 (Judgment of 12 March 2015), GewArch 2016, p. 29 (30).

beyond the company's know-how. It shall cover all the information from which conclusions can be drawn—even if only indirectly—on competitive circumstances, such as production processes or production capacity.[237] The Higher administrative court of Berlin-Brandenburg has mastered the challenge to narrow the interpretation of the category of trade and business secrets in a decision on the request for information on Hermes guarantees for the export of surveillance technologies. As far as it concerns mere information, which are conclusions from other (protected) information, the case-law imposes far higher requirements on the requested enterprise to back up the denial of access. In that situation it must give evidence about a *legitimate economic interest* to justify the secrecy.[238]

Invoking trade and business secrets is to be expected in particular when the legislature has given special weight to the interest in the freedom of information and transparency, for example to limit or even to rule out a legally doubtful accommodating attitude of public authorities to defend entrepreneurial interests. According to the legal concept behind the "violation of a statutory prohibition" (Sec. 134 of the German Civil Code), voidness of contractual secrecy clauses should always be assumed if they exceed the level of protecting of trade or business secrets that is mandatory under (constitutional or statutory) law.[239]

### 3.4.5 Restrictions of Access to Information as an Expression of the Legislators' Margin of Appreciation

In addition to specific national interests or the protection of conflicting fundamental rights, there are other reasons that a request for access to information may not be successful. According to Sec. 9.3 of the German FIA, for example, the application may be refused if the requester already possesses the requested information or can reasonably obtain it from generally accessible sources. As with the restrictions of the right of access to information, the statutory legislator also has a margin of appreciation when it comes to the procedure or the decision on who is obliged to publish the information. However, to the extent that the right of access to information is guaranteed in regional human rights instruments in a manner that is binding on the informational aspects of national law (in most cases, the regional human rights instruments are only subject to minimum standards) or insofar as the right of access to information is enshrined in national constitutional law, the margin of appreciation is limited. In comparison to the regional standards of protection of the right of access, this analysis has highlighted that the margin of appreciation of the Parties to the Council of Europe's Convention on "Access to Official Documents", regarding the standardization of "exceptions", is wider than that of those legislators who follow the Model Inter-American or the African Model Law (Sect. 2.5).

[237]Cf. for example German Federal Administrative Court (Bundesverwaltungsgericht), 7 C 2.09, E 135 (Judgment of 24 September 2009), 43 para 56.

[238]Berlin-Brandenburg Higher Administrative Court (OVG Berlin-Brandenburg), OVG 12 N 88.14 (Judgment of 18 March 2016), para 11 et seqq.

[239]Fehling 2017, p. 84.

A restriction of the right of access to information must not violate the essence of a constitutional or human right which guarantees freedom of information (Article 19 para 2 of the Basic Law, Article 52.1 CFREU).[240] In other words, "the essence of the fundamental right" is the threshold, the minimum protection which all three branches of government, the statutory legislator, the public administration and the judicial power, have to respect whenever the first branch adopts transparency laws, the second branch implements such laws or the third branch rules on the lawfulness of both measures. According to general transparency legislation, the interest in information should be particularly important when it is necessary to identify potentially serious grievances.[241] On the other hand, however, the interests of secrecy and confidentiality must first be weighed by the legislators in an abstract and general manner, and by the requested public (or private) authority in a particular case.

# 4 Procedures and Legal Protection

Especially the implementation of the provisions on the exemptions and exceptions from the right of access to registers and documents, e.g., with regard to the protection of commercial secrets, in particular when absolute limits are concerned, call for a judicial protection which corresponds to their substantive legal scope.[242] This is also because the access to the files in the process pre-empts the substantive right to claim access. However, an effectively enforceable right of access to information exists only if the procedure for the enforcement of that right is set out in a way that it does not require any special expertise for its enforcement and is made possible from a purely factual point of view by a timely processing of requests without further hurdles.

## *4.1 Procedure*

The request for access to the documents may be submitted in accordance with Article 10 of the Brazilian Law N° 12.527 "by any legitimate means"; the U.S. FOIA or the German FIA does not provide any formal requirements for this application. According to the Spanish Law 9/2013 on transparency, access to public information and good governance an application will be processed once the data is available on the identity of the requester, the information requested, a contact address for communications purposes, and the form (in writing, verbally or electronically) that is preferred to access the requested information (Article 17.2).

[240] Cf. Weiß 1996, p. 137 et seqq., regarding the ECHR standard.

[241] So Lüneburg Higher Administrative Court (OVG Lüneburg), 2 LB 69/15 (Judgment of 24 March 2016), para 11.

[242] Cf. Schoch 2016, p. 85 et seqq.; Fehling 2017, p. 80.

The levying of charges shall be determined pursuant to Article 12 of the Brazilian Law N° 12.527 or similiar provisions in other transparency laws such as Article 22.4 of the Spanish Law 9/2013. Only if actual costs are incurred for the production of copies or the transposition of the document or register into a format different from the original, an appropriate refund may be required. The collection of fees is also included in Sec. (a) subsec. 4.1 (i) of the U.S. FOIA, but only pertaining to the actual costs for the processing of the request. Such a close linkage of the fees in relation to the expenses of the requested authority is not provided in Sec. 10.1 of the German FIA. According to Sec. (a) subsec. 4.A of the U.S. FOIA[243] and Sec. 10.2 of the German FIA, however, it is clear that the fees are to be calculated in such a way that an information can be accessed effectively.

Another significant aspect of effective enforcement is the temporal component: Sec. (a) subsec. 6.A. (i). of the FOIA states that within a period of 20 days (excluding weekends and public holidays) it shall be decided whether the application is accepted. Article 11 of the Brazilian Law N° 12.527 also provides for a period of 20 days, whereas in the Spanish regulation this period is restricted to 10 days only (Article 22.1 of Law 9/2013). Sec. 7.5 of the German FIA establishes that the requester is to be informed immediately, but no later than within one month. Hence, the obligation to reply to the request quickly is a legal requirement. However, as far as the disclosure of the required information might affect the interests or rights of third parties, national legislation stipulates that the period to file an (administrative) appeal has elapsed (Article 22. 2 of Spanish Law 9/2013). According to the 2012 evaluation report published on the German FIA, the one-month deadline has been exceeded in about one third of the cases.[244]

## 4.2 Legal Protection

In case a request for access is declined, the principle of effective legal protection (Article 19.4 of the German Basic Law) requires that the negative decision can be subject to an independent (judicial) review. Sec. 9.4 (1) of the German FIA and Articles 23 et seq. of Spanish Law 9/2013 provide for the possibility of objection proceedings in the event of an unfavorable administrative decision, and ultimately an enforcement action to the competent administrative court. The U.S. FOIA also provides for complaints before the competent district courts, which must now fully re-evaluate the application (Sec. (a) subsec. 9.4.(B)). By contrast, the Brazilian Law N° 12.527 in accordance with Article 15 of the Decree N° 7.724/2012 provides an appeal which has to be addressed "within ten days of being informed of the decision [...] to the authority hierarchically above the one that registered the disputed

[243]"Such fees shall be limited to reasonable standard charges for document search and duplication and provide for recovery of only the direct costs of such search and duplication."

[244]Ziekow et al. 2012, p. 14.

decision". In case of a request to an entity or institution of the Federal Executive, the appeal may be addressed to the Office of the Comptroller General under certain conditions (Article 16 of the Decree N° 7.724/2012). If this request is also unsuccessful, the applicant may ultimately submit the case to the Joint Commission of Information Reassessment, pursuant to Article 35 of the Law N° 12.527. However, this does not mean that proper legal action in the sense of an independent judicial review can be taken. This is a lacuna in the Brazilian transparency legislation, which is incompatible with the principle of effective and "complete" judicial protection.

## 5 Concluding Results

Many references were made in this article to the German Freedom of Information Act in order to explain the scope and aim of a general regulation on access to public information. This served also to compare it with the main principles and provisions for regulating legal relationships between public authorities and citizens in the field of transparency from the viewpoint of foreign legal systems. Unsurprisingly, and as highlighted in various chapters of this book,[245] the "strength" of the right of access to (public) information depends to a large extent on the exemptions which aim to protect colliding interests or rights (allegedly or as a matter of fact) of a request for information. Likewise, the interpretation of these exemptions by the executive and the judicial branch is a crucial factor, which determines the enforceability of the right of public access to documents.

The German Act is based on a difficult compromise, which aims at "confidence-building measures" in the relationship between the public authorities and the citizens. At the same time, the German legislator intended to avoid "a resistance of the administration" against the transparency legislation. Critics point to the numerous exemptions from the principle of free access to information as the sore point of this law. Already on the occasion of the debate on the draft bill in 2005, the "exceeding number of exemptions" has been regarded as "a casuality list for the freedom of information" (M. Kloepfer). In the eyes of the critics, the legislator did not take the principle to heart which they had invoked in the summary of the grounds for and content of the draft bill: "As much access to information as possible, as little protection of secrets as necessary". Rather, it seems to the critics that the legislators have reversed this principle. They hold that, with these restrictions, any official refusal to grant access to information can be arbitrarily justified.[246] Others argue that in the subsequent implementation of that law the public authorities have too often rejected requests with reference to trade secrets or other

[245] See to that effect, in particular, Chap. 1; Sect. 5; Chap. 2, Sect. 6.3; Chap. 4, Sect. 6; Chap. 9, Sect. 2; Chap. 16, Sect. 4; Chap. 17.

[246] Cf., regarding this criticism, Sietmann 2005.

exemptions (P. Schaar). Such criticism highlights the function of the principle of "public interest override"[247] as well as the interpretation method "in dubio pro petitor",[248] and, as condition for and a result of these approaches, the importance of an access-focused law.[249] These rules have not been defined in the German legal framework governing the access to public information.

In 2005, the German Federal Government still considered the bill an entry into the freedom of information rather than a definitive solution in the area of transparency legislation. It was intended as a "law on a trial basis" (sunset legislation). Meanwhile, it has been a cornerstone within the German transparency legislation for nearly 20 years. However, it performs poorly in the international RTI rating.[250] The moderate use made of this right in Germany[251] may be due to the fact that the general public is not aware of this piece of legislation. But an evaluation of the Hamburg Transparency Act revealed that the introduction of a proactive information policy has led to far-reaching changes regarding the public administration, the enterprises acting for public authorities and the citizens. The advantages of such disclosure clearly outweigh the disadvantages.[252]

## References

Ackermann, J. M., & Sandoval-Ballestros, I. E. (2006). The global explosion of freedom of information laws. *Administrative Law Review (ALR)*, *58*, 85.

Alexy, R. (1986). *Theorie der Grundrechte*. Berlin, Germany: Suhrkamp.

Angelov, J. (2000). *Grundlagen und Grenzen eines staatsbürgerlichen Informationszugangsanspruchs*. Frankfurt, Germany: Peter Lang.

Bethge, H. (2018). Artikel 5. In M. Sachs (Ed.), *Grundgesetz Kommentar*. München, Germany: C.H. Beck.

Birkinshaw, P. (2006). Freedom of information and openness: Fundamental human rights? *Administrative Law Review (ALR)*, *58*(1), 177.

Böckenförde, E.-W. (2004). § 24, Demokratie als Verfassungsprinzip. In J. Isensee & P. Kirchhof (Eds.), *Handbuch des Staatsrechts der Bundesrepublik Deutschland* (vol. II, 3rd ed.). Heidelberg, Germany: Müller.

Deutlmoser, R., & Filip, A. (2015). Part 16.6. In T. Hoeren, U. Sieber, & B. Holznagel (Eds.), *Handbuch Multimedia Recht. Loose leaf.* München, Germany: C.H. Beck.

Dörr, D. (2011). Informationsfreiheit. In D. Merten & H.-J. Papier (Eds.), *Handbuch der Grundrechte* (Vol. 4, § 103, p. 965). Karlsruhe, Germany: C.F. Müller.

Fechner, F. (2016). *Medienrecht*. Stuttgart, Germany: utb.

Fehling, M. (2017). Freier Informationszugang zwischen öffentlichen und privaten Interessen. *Deutsches Verwaltungsblatt (DVBl)*, *132*, 79.

---

[247] See Article 44 of the Inter-American Law; Article 25 of the African Model Law.

[248] See Article 1, principle 13 of the Argentinean Law 27275/2016 on the "Right of Access to Public Information".

[249] Chap. 4, Sects. 6.1 and 6.2.

[250] See Chap. 1, Sect. 8.

[251] Cf. Chap. 1, Sect. 7.1.

[252] Herr et al. (2018), p. 175.

Frenz, W. (2009). *Handbuch Europarecht. Vol. 4: Europäische Grundrechte*. Heidelberg, Germany: Springer.

Grabenwarter, C. (2014). *European convention on human rights: Commentary*. München, Germany: C.H. Beck.

Grote, R., & Wenzel, N. (2013). Die Meinungsfreiheit. In O. Dörr, R. Grote, & T. Marauhn (Eds.), *EMRK/GG Konkordanz-Kommentar. Band 1*. Tübingen, Germany: Mohr Siebeck.

Grzeszick, B. (2010). Article 20. In T. Maunz & G. Dürig (Eds), *Grundgesetz. Kommentar. Loose leaf*. München, Germany: C.H. Beck.

Häberle, P. (1972). Grundrechte im Leistungsstaat. In Grundrechte im Leistungsstaat. Die Dogmatik des Verwaltungsrechts vor den Gegenwartsaufgaben der Verwaltung. In *Veröffentlichungen der Vereinigung der Deutschen Staatsrechtslehrer (VVDStRL), 30* (p. 43), Berlin, Germany: De Gruyter.

Herr, M., Müller, C. E., Engewald, B., & Ziekow, J. (2018). Transparenzgesetzgebung in Deutschland in der Bewährung: Erfahrungen einer Gesetzesevaluation. *Die Öffentliche Verwaltung (DÖV), 71*, 165–175.

Hesse, K. (1999). *Grundzüge des Verfassungsrechts der Bundesrepublik Deutschland*. (reprint of the 20th edn.). Heidelberg, Germany: C.F. Müller Verlag, Hüthig.

Hins, V., & Voorhoof, D. (2007). Access to state-held information as a fundamental right under the European convention on human rights. *European constitutional law review, 3*, 114.

Höfling, W. (1994). Demokratische Grundrechte. *Der Staat, 33*, 493.

Jarass, H. D. (2016). *Charta der Grundrechte der EU. Kommentar*. München, Germany: C.H. Beck.

Jarass, H. D., & Pieroth, B. (2016). *Grundgesetz für die Bundesrepublik Deutschland – Kommentar*. München, Germany: C.H. Beck.

Jellinek, G. (1905/reprint 2011), *System der subjektiven öffentlichen Rechte*. Frankfurt, Germany: Mohr Siebeck.

Kirste, S. (2014). Philosophical foundations of the principle of the legal state (Rechtsstaat) and the rule of law. In J. R. Silkenat, J. E. Hickey (Jr), & P. D. Barenboim (Eds.), *The legal doctrine of the rule of law and the legal state (Rechtsstaat)* (p. 29). Heidelberg, Germany: Springer.

Klaaren, J., Currie, I., & Smith, A. (2000). Analysing foreign access to information legislation from a South African viewpoint. In Konrad Adenauer Foundation (Ed.), *The constitutional right of access to information* (pp. 29–40). Retrieved February 9, 2017, from http://www.kas.de/wf/doc/kas_4936-1522-2-30.pdf?040625152235

Kloepfer, M., & von Lewinski, K. (2005). Das Informationsfreiheitsgesetz des Bundes. *Deutsches Verwaltungsblatt (DVBl)*, 1277.

Kofmel, S. (1993). Legal developments in the Baltic: The new constitution of the Republic of Estonia of June 28, 1992. *Zeitschrift für öffentliches Recht und Völkerrecht (ZaöRV)*, 135.

Kugelmann, D. (2001). *Die informatorische Rechtsstellung des Bürgers*. Tübingen, Germany: Mohr Siebeck.

Kugelmann, D. (2005). Das Informationsfreiheitsgesetz des Bundes. *Neue Juristische Wochenschrift (NJW)*, 3609.

Luhmann, N. (2000). *Die Politik der Gesellschaft*. Frankfurt/Main, Germany: Suhrkamp.

Lukaßen, D. (2010). *Die Fallpraxis der Informationsbeauftragten und ihr Beitrag zur Entwicklung des Informationsfreiheitsrechts*. Berlin, Germany: Duncker & Humblot.

Martens, W. (1972). Grundrechte im Leistungsstaat. In Grundrechte im Leistungsstaat. Die Dogmatik des Verwaltungsrechts vor den Gegenwartsaufgaben der Verwaltung. *Veröffentlichungen der Vereinigung der Deutschen Staatsrechtslehrer (VVDStRL), 30* (p. 7), Berlin, Germany: De Gruyter.

Nettesheim, M. (2005). Demokratisierung der Europäischen Union und Europäisierung der Demokratietheorie – Wechselwirkungen bei der Herausbildung eines europäischen Demokratieprinzips. In H. Bauer, P. M. Huber, & K.-P. Sommermann (Eds.). *Demokratie in Europa* (pp. 143–190). Tübingen, Germany: Mohr Siebeck.

Peled, R., & Rabin, Y. (2011). The constitutional Right to information. *Columbia Human Rights Law Review, 42*, 357.

Rossi, M. (2004). *Informationszugangsfreiheit und Verfassungsrecht. Zu den Wechselwirkungen zwischen Informationsfreiheitsgrenzen und der Verfassungsordnung in Deutschland.* Berlin, Germany: Duncker & Humblot.

Rossi, M. (2006). *Informationsfreiheitsgesetz. Handkommentar.* Baden-Baden, Germany: Nomos.

Rüfner, W. (2006). Leistungsrechte. In D. Merten & H.-J. Papier (Eds.), *Handbuch der Grundrechte in Deutschland und Europa. Vol. II:Grundrechte in Deutschland: Allgemeine Lehren I (§ 40, p. 679).* Heidelberg, Germany: C.F. Müller.

Sachs, M. (1994). Die Gesetzesvorbehalte. In K. Stern (Ed.), *Das Staatsrecht der Bundesrepublik Deutschland, Vol. III/2 (§ 80, p. 369).* München, Germany: C.H. Beck.

Sarkis, M. (2012). *Access to public information in Brazil: What will change with Law N° 12.527/ 2011?.* right2info.org. Retrieved February 9, 2017, from http://www.right2info.org/recent/ access-to-public-information-in-brazil-what-will-change-with-law-no.-12.527-2011

Schäfer, P. (2015). A.II. Anhang, Vertrag von Lissabon. In M. Dauses (Ed.), *Handbuch des EU-Wirtschaftsrechts (para 440–516), 38. Loose leaf.* München, Germany: C.H. Beck.

Scherzberg, A. (2000). *Die Öffentlichkeit der Verwaltung.* Baden-Baden, Germany: Nomos.

Schiedermair, S. (2013). Artikel 10. In K. Pabel & S. Schmahl, (Eds.). *Internationaler Kommentar zur Europäischen Menschenrechtskonvention.* Vol. 2 (Lose-leaf, 15. Suppl. 2013). Köln, Germany: Heymann.

Schmitt Glaeser, W. (1980). Planung und Grundrechte. *Die Öffentliche Verwaltung (DÖV)*, 1.

Schmitz, H., & Jastrow, S.-D. (2005). Das Informationsfreiheitsgesetz des Bundes. *Neue Zeitschrift für Verwaltungsrecht (NVwZ)*, 984.

Schoch, F. (2016). *Informationsfreiheitsgesetz. Kommentar.* München, Germany: C.H. Beck.

Sietmann, R. (2005). Informationsfreiheitsgesetz in der Kritik. Available at: https://www.heise.de/ newsticker/meldung/Informationsfreiheitsgesetz-in-der-Kritik-144367.html

Sommermann, K.-P. (2005). Demokratiekonzepte im Vergleich. In H. Bauer, P. M. Huber, & K.-P. Sommermann (Eds.), *Demokratie in Europa* (pp. 191–221). Tübingen, Germany: Mohr Siebeck.

Stern, K. (1994). *Das Staatsrecht der Bundesrepublik Deutschland. Allgemeine Lehren der Grundrechte (Vol. III/2).* München, Germany: C.H. Beck.

Stern, K. (2006). *Das Staatsrecht der Bundesrepublik Deutschland. Die einzelnen Grundrechte (Vol. IV/1).* München, Germany: C.H. Beck.

Stern, K., & Sachs, M. (Eds.). (2016). *Europäische Grundrechte-Charta (GRCh). Kommentar.* München, Germany: C.H. Beck.

Trute, H.-H. (1998). Öffentlich-rechtliche Rahmenbedingungen einer Informationsordnung. *In Veröffentlichungen der Vereinigung der Deutschen Staatsrechtslehrer (VVDStRL), 57*, 216. (Berlin: De Gruyter).

Weiß, R. (1996). *Das Gesetz im Sinne der Europäischen Menschenrechtskonvention.* Berlin, Germany: Duncker & Humblot.

Wieland, J. (2000). Freedom of information. In C. Engel & K. H. Keller (Eds.), *Governance of global networks in the light of differing local values* (p. 91). Baden-Baden, Germany: Nomos.

Ziekow, J., Debus, A. G., & Musch, E. (2012). *Evaluation des Gesetzes zur Regelung des Zugangs zu Informationen des Bundes – Informationsfreiheitsgesetz des Bundes (IFG).* Berlin, Germany: Deutscher Bundestag, Innenausschuss.

## List of Cases

### *German Federal Constitutional Court* (Bundesverfassungsgericht)

German Federal Constitutional Court 15.1.1958, *Lüth-Entscheidung*, 1 BvR 400/51BVerfGE 7, 198.

German Federal Constitutional Court 30.7.1958, 2 BvF 3, 6/58 (BVerfGE 8, 104).
German Federal Constitutional Court 03.10.1969, 1 BvR 46/65, (BVerfGE 27, 71).
German Federal Constitutional Court 15.12.1983, 1 BvR 209, 269, 362, 420, 440, 484/83, (BVerfGE 65, 1).
German Federal Constitutional Court 14.1.1986, 2 BvE 14/83 und 4/84 (BVerfGE 70, 324).
German Federal Constitutional Court, 1 BvR 1687/92 9.2.1994 (BVerfGE 90, 27).
German Federal Constitutional Court 24.1.2001, 1 BvR 2623/95 and 1 BvR 622/99 (BVerfGE 103, 44).
German Federal Constitutional Court 13.10.2016, 2 BvE 2/15. (http://www.bundesverfassungsgericht.de/SharedDocs/Entscheidungen/DE/2016/10/es20161013_2bve000215.html) (Accessed on 9 May 2017).

## *German Federal Administrative Court (Bundesverwaltungsgericht)*

German Federal Administrative Court 3.11.2011, 7 C 3.11 141, 122. (http://www.bverwg.de/entscheidungen/entscheidung.php?lang=de&ent=031111U7C3.11.0) (Accessed on 9 May 2017).
German Federal Administrative Court 18.7.2011, 7 B 14.11. (http://www.bverwg.de/entscheidungen/entscheidung.php?lang=de&ent=180711B7B14.11.0) (Accessed on 9 May 2017).
German Federal Administrative Court 27.11.2014, 7 C 18/12. (http://www.bverwg.de/entscheidungen/entscheidung.php?lang=de&ent=271114U7C18.12.0) (Accessed on 9 May 2017).
German Federal Administrative Court 27.11.2014, 7 C 20/12. (http://www.bverwg.de/entscheidungen/entscheidung.php?lang=de&ent=271114U7C20.12.0) (Accessed on 9 May 2017).
German Federal Administrative Court, 7 C 1/14 25.6.2015. (http://www.bverwg.de/entscheidungen/entscheidung.php?lang=de&ent=250615U7C1.14.0) (Accessed on 9 May 2017).

## *Administrative Courts of the German Länder*

Berlin-Brandenburg Higher Administrative Court (OVG Berlin-Brandenburg) 14.12.2006, OVG 7 B 9/05. (http://www.judicialis.de/Oberverwaltungsgericht-Berlin-Brandenburg_OVG-7-B-9-05_Urteil_14.12.2006.html) (Accessed on 9 May 2017).
Berlin-Brandenburg Higher Administrative Court (OVG Berlin-Brandenburg) 20.3.2012, OVG 12 B 27/11. (https://openjur.de/u/404100.html) (Accessed on 9 May 2017).
Berlin-Brandenburg Higher Administrative Court (OVG Berlin-Brandenburg) 18.3.2016, OVG 12 N 88.14. (https://www.juris.de/jportal/?quelle=jlink&docid=MWRE160001166&psml=jurisw.psml&max=true) (Accessed on 9 May 2017).
Koblenz Higher Administrative Court (OVG Koblenz) 12.3.2015, 10 A 11044/14. (http://www.landesrecht.rlp.de/jportal/portal/t/7qe/page/bsrlpprod.psml?pid=Dokumentanzeige&showdoccase=1&doc.id=MWRE150001040&doc.part=L) (Accessed on 9 May 2017).
Lüneburg Higher Administrative Court (OVG Lüneburg) 24.3.2016, 2 I.B 69/15. (http://www.rechtsprechung.niedersachsen.de/jportal/?quelle=jlink&docid=MWRE160001084&psml=bsndprod.psml&max=true) (Accessed on 9 May 2017).

Mainz Administrative Court (VG Mainz) 29.11.2017, 4 K 147/17.MZ.
Münster Higher Administrative Court (OVG Münster) 2.11.2010, A 8 475/10. (http://www.justiz.nrw.de/nrwe/ovgs/ovg_nrw/j2010/8_A_475_10urteil20101102.html) (Accessed on 9 May 2017).
Neustadt Administrative Court (VG Neustadt) 4.9.2014, 4 466/14.NW. (http://www.landesrecht.rlp.de/jportal/portal/t/7qe/page/bsrlpprod.psml?pid=Dokumentanzeige&showdoccase=1&doc.id=MWRE140002488&doc.part=L) (Accessed on 9 May 2017).

## *European Court of Justice*

ECJ 29.06.2010, C-28/08, *European Commission v. Bavarian Lager, Co. Ltd.,* ECLI:EU:C:2010:378.
ECJ 21.07.2011, C-506/08, *Sweden v. MyTravel Group and Commission*, ECLI:EU:C:2011:496.
ECJ 08.04.2014, C-293/12 and C-594/12, *Digital Rights Ireland*, ECLI:EU:C:2014:238.
ECJ 06.10.2015, C-362/14, *Schrems v Data Protection Commissioner*, ECLI:EU:C:2015:650.
The Court (of First Instance of the European Union) 11.12.2001, T-191/99, *Petrie a.o. v. Commission*, http://curia.europa.eu/juris/showPdf.jsf?text=&docid=46940&pageIndex=0&doclang=EN&mode=lst&dir=&occ=first&part=1&cid=125880 (Accessed 1 May 2017).

## *European Court of Human Rights*

European Court of Human Rights 26.03.1987, *Leander v. Sweden*, No. 9248/81.
European Court of Human Rights 19.02.1998, Guerra and Others v. Italy, Reports of Judgments and Decisions 1998-I.
European Court of Human Rights 29.06.2004, Chauvy and Others v. France, ECHR 2004-VI, No. 64915/01.
European Court of Human Rights 16.12.2008, *Mustafa and Tarzibachi v. Sweden*, No. 23883/06.
European Court of Human Rights 14.04.2009, Társasága Szabadságjogokért v. Hungary, No. 37374/05.
European Court of Human Rights 28.11.2013a, *Österreichische Vereinigung zur Erhaltung, Stärkung und Schaffung eines wirtschaftlich gesunden land-und forstwirt schaftlichen Grundbesitzes v. Austria*, No. 39534/07.
European Court of Human Rights 28.11.2013b, *Österreichische Vereinigung zur Erhaltung, Stärkung und Schaffung eines wirtschaftlich gesunden land- und forstwirt schaftlichen Grundbesitzes v. Austria*, No. 39534/07.

## *Inter-American Court of Human Rights*

I/A Court H. R. 19.09.2006, *Case of Claude Reyes et al. v. Chile*, Series C No. 151.
I/A Court H. R. 24.11.2010, *Case of Gomes Lund et al. v. Brazil (Guerrilha do Araguaia)*, Series C No. 219.

# Part II
# The Access to Public Information in the United States of America, Europe and Asia

# Chapter 4
# Access to Information Under the Federal Freedom of Information Act in the United States

**Robert G. Vaughn and Peter J. Messitte**

## Contents



R.G. Vaughn (✉)
American University, Washington, DC, USA
e-mail: vaughn@wcl.american.edu

P.J. Messitte
United States District Court, Greenbelt, MD, USA



H.-J. Blanke, R. Perlingeiro (eds.), *The Right of Access to Public Information*,
DOI 10.1007/978-3-662-55554-5_4

# 1 Introduction

The federal Freedom of Information Act in the United States is one of the oldest in the world. In Sects. 2–5, United States District Court Judge *Peter J. Messitte* describes the history of the law and sets out its structure. Although a portion of the law requires that Government make public administrative rules and regulations, this chapter focuses on the process by which persons make requests for information. In this context, that process and the review of rejections of requests emphasize the importance of judicial review of these rejections by Government officials. For this reason, this chapter does not consider obligations imposed in the last two decades that place affirmative obligations on the government to disseminate information.

Most Government rejections of requests rely on one of the exemptions to the law that permit withholding. In Sects. 6 and 7, Professor *Robert G. Vaughn* examines the exemptions to the FOIA. Most litigation under law considers the meaning of these exemptions. Because of FOIA's age, many judicial decisions interpret the exemptions and Congress has amended one or more of the exemptions several times. This history with the exemptions suggests the issues may arise in the application of similar exemptions under the Brazilian Access Law.

# 2 History of the Freedom of Information Act (FOIA)

## 2.1 *Enactment and History of the Law*

The United States adopted its Freedom of Information Act (FOIA) in 1966 to provide citizens and non-citizens alike broader access to information held by the Federal Government (see 5 U.S.C. § 552). This Act represented a vast improvement over prior law, that Congress had come to believe kept too much governmental information secret and placed too heavy a burden on individuals and entities seeking access to information compiled and kept by the Government. In short, it supplemented a regime more characterized by the withholding instead of the disclosure of information.

Despite the proclaimed purpose of the FOIA to give the public greater access to Government-held information and subsequent congressional legislation intended to increase public access, some executive withholding of information took place during the Administration of President George Bush, especially with respect to media access to information pertaining to the War in Afghanistan.

With the advent of the Barack Obama administration, however, according to the President himself almost immediately upon taking office, "FOIA [...] is the most prominent expression of a profound national commitment to ensuring an open Government."[1]

Despite some criticism of the Obama Administration's FOIA policies, mostly regarding the slow responsiveness of certain federal agencies to requests, public access to governmental information in the U.S. is currently both wide and deep.

## 2.2 *Contemporary Application*

The fundamental rationale of the law, of course, continues to guide. Transparency in Government lies at the core of democratic Government. As Supreme Court Justice Louis Dembitz Brandeis, one of America's preeminent jurors, once observed, "If the broad light of day could be let in upon men's actions, it would purify them as the sun disinfects."

Another significant and distinguishing aspect of American FOI law follows from the federal system in the United States. In addition to federal FOI law, the fifty individual states have adopted many FOI laws. The discussion of U.S. law in the present chapter, however, will focus on the federal FOIA, not only the most important American law on the subject, but clearly the paradigm that most state laws follow. Bear in mind, however, that federal FOIA does not apply to state governments.

Indeed, the federal FOIA has limited application in other important respects with FOI law in other countries. In the U.S., for example, the FOIA applies only to federal administrative agencies, i.e., most agencies of the Executive Branch of the Government, including the military. It does not apply to the Judicial Branch (although public access to judicial hearings and court records is generally available unless sealed). Nor does the Act apply to the Legislative Branch or to Presidential papers or parts of the Office of the President that exist exclusively to advise and assist him. To be sure, notwithstanding the inapplicability of FOIA to them, these Branches of Government still make a great deal of information accessible to the public both in paper form and electronically. However, there is no law in place that presumes public accessibility to information of the Judiciary and Congress as it does with administrative agencies. Still, the bulk of sought-after information is located within the administrative agencies. Because administrative agencies

[1]See the Presidential Memorandum "For Heads of Departments and Agencies – Transparency and Open Government" from 21.01.2009 (First Day in Office), weblink: https://obamawhitehouse.archives.gov/the-press-office/2015/11/16/memorandum-transparency-and-open-government (Accessed on 14 February 2017).

possess most governmental records, requesters go to where the records are located (bringing to mind the famous reply of bank robber Willie Sutton who, when asked why he robbed banks, said "Because that's where the money is.").

In the United States, the First Amendment to the United States Constitution does not provide a right to acquire information held by federal or state governments. Thus, access to government information is a statutory and not a constitutional right.

## 3 Information Available Under FOIA

The administrative agencies invariably caution the information seeker. In many cases, they point out, it may be unnecessary to make a formal FOIA request because the sought-after information may already be available from the agency. Thus, certain matters may be required to be published, including descriptions of the agency's organization and its functions; its rules and procedures; its substantive rules of general applicability; its statements of general policy and rules; its regulations of general rule applicability; and other of its administrative interpretations. Moreover, certain records must be produced upon request, including, for example, applications for employment; audits of public offices; billing statements for use of public facilities and equipment; and collective bargaining agreements, among other documents. The Act does not apply to elected public officials in their individual capacities, private companies, private citizens, and nearly all government contractors.

## 4 Requests for Information

### *4.1 Procedures*

Requests cannot be made to a central agency because no single agency applies the law or controls the requested information. As to how one goes about requesting information under FOIA, it should be understood that there is no single FOIA agency that applies the law. Each agency covered by the Act applies the law on its own, although they obviously apply the same statute, essentially the same regulations and the same case-law. For example, the Department of Homeland Security, a typical agency subject to FOIA, has its own FOIA officer, its own internal set of regulations and procedures, and its own procedures for internal appeals, provisions which, as indicated, tend to replicate those of other federal administrative agencies. In addition, Homeland Security, like almost every administrative agency covered by the Act, has its own website pertaining to FOIA, although there are a few generic websites such as <FOIA.gov> that serve as portals to the FOIA practices and procedures of multiple governmental agencies. Non-governmental organizations, including academic institutions, maintain websites that provide guidance on how to proceed under the FOIA.

Although requests for information must be made to the individual agency concerned, the nature of requests is similar. No special forms are required. All that is needed is a letter directed to the head of the agency maintaining the documents, describing the desired information with as much precision as possible. The requester should also describe himself or itself as a representative of the media or as representing an educational or scientific organization, or as an individual seeking information for non-commercial purposes. Although any person may make a request, certain categories of requesters can receive waiver or reduction of fees.

## 4.2 Access Fees

Fees vary depending on who is seeking the information. Generally, agencies impose an hourly charge to search for the requested documents and a modest charge per duplicated page. If the number of pages sought is apt to be numerous, the requester may ask to cap the fees at a certain amount. Educational and non-commercial scientific institutions, as well as news media, pay no charge for a search and receive the first 100 pages of documents for free, then pay the modest per page rate for duplication costs. All other requesters receive up to 2 h of search costs and the first 100 pages free. In fact, filing fees may be waived entirely if the requester can show that the information sought is in the public interest because it is likely to contribute to public understanding of the activities of Government and not in the commercial interest of the requester. Agencies, however, are not obliged to answer questions, analyze requests, do research, or create records for the requester.

## 4.3 Deadlines for Government Response

Upon receipt of the request, as a matter of practice, the agency must promptly advise the requester that the request has been received and will be processed. Afterwards, within 20 business days of receipt or as extended, the agency is expected to provide the requested information or explain why it is not doing so. Although one might believe that a 20-day turnaround time for providing the information is unrealistically short, a constant criticism is that, even with reasonable extensions, some agencies continue to be inordinately slow in responding. The counterpoint, of course, is that hundreds of thousands of FOIA requests are received by the federal administrative agencies annually, some of which can be quite complex. Meanwhile, the backlog of requests continues to grow.

# 5 Treatment of Rejected Requests

Some FOIA requests will be rejected in whole or part, either at the outset or over the course of the agency search. In such cases, agencies will promptly advise requesters of the rejection. Obviously, a request that seeks to obtain clearly exempted information, e.g., information pertaining to national security matters, will be rejected out of hand. The reasons for rejecting other requests may be more debatable.

In a well-publicized Case, *U.S. Department of Justice v. Landano*, 508 U.S. 165 (1993), information was sought under FOIA with regard to the identity of certain informants of the Federal Bureau of Investigation. While one might suppose that such a request would automatically be rejected, the United States Supreme Court held that there might indeed be circumstances where such information would have to be provided. Although any such determination would have to be made on a case-by-case basis, where the agency would be required to demonstrate that under the circumstances, the information had originally been provided with an expectation of confidentiality.

## 5.1 *Agency Appeals*

Various levels of appeal with respect to rejected requests are available within the agencies themselves. Typically, if the agency has acted arbitrarily in withholding information, even in denying a fee waiver, or where it has been inordinately slow in processing a request, a letter of appeal may be filed with the agency and the agency will then consider whether disciplinary action is warranted. The law provides that a response to an appeal should be given within 20 days although, again, reasonable extensions are not uncommon. In addition to internal appeals, a disappointed requester has the option of contacting the Office of Government Information Services of the National Archives and Records Administration to seek mediation with respect to the request.

## 5.2 *Judicial Review*

Eventually, there may come a point where the agency, after the internal agency appeal has been decided, declines to provide the requested information and the requester wishes to pursue the matter further.

### 5.2.1 Scope of Review

The FOIA establishes a right to judicial review of any disputed FOIA decision. So long as administrative remedies have been exhausted, a de novo action will lie in the United States District Court for the District of Columbia (the seat of virtually all Government agencies) or in the United States District Court where the applicant resides, has its principal place of business or where the documents are held. The District Court, either on the papers or supplemented by an oral evidentiary hearing if appropriate, will render its decision, applying the relevant statutes, regulations and case-law (especially decisions of the U.S. Supreme Court or of the regional Federal Appeals Court in which the District Court is located).

FOIA does not authorize the District Court to award money damages for the wrongful non-disclosure of requested information. The court may not only order disclosure of the information withheld (or reverse the denial of a waiver of fees, etc.) but may also frame its order to enjoin future violations of the FOIA or any inappropriate conduct by the agency likely to recur in the future. A federal District Court may also hold a responsible governmental employee guilty of contempt of court, if the employee willfully fails to comply with the court's order, which could include a fine and/or imprisonment.

### 5.2.2 Attorney Fees

FOIA also authorizes a district court to award a requester who is represented by an attorney (but not requesters representing themselves) reasonable attorney's fees and costs. The FOIA represents an express statutory exception to the general rule in the U.S. that a prevailing party is not entitled to attorney's fees (although a prevailing party is generally entitled to certain litigation costs).

Final review of a disputed claim, while entirely discretionary pursuant to its writ of certiorari authority (and in all candor highly unlikely), lies with the U.S. Supreme Court. Decisions of the Supreme Court, indeed of all the Federal Courts in FOIA as in all matters, are easily accessible over the Internet where the more prominent cases are discussed and dissected by any number of commentators.

## 6 Exemptions to Access under the Freedom of Information Act

A significant percentage of federal court decisions regarding the federal Freedom of Information Act interpret and apply the exemptions to it. These exemptions describe the circumstances in which federal agencies may refuse to release documents requested under the law. All access laws contain limitations on access. The character of the exemptions illustrates the types of public and private interests that justify secrecy. These judicial decisions interpreting the exemptions determine the scope and effectiveness of access laws.

This section explores the justifications for secrecy and examines the difficulties of implementing these justifications without undermining the principle of access that is embodied in freedom of information and right-to-know statutes. This examination describes general aspects of the exemptions, discusses some of the issues that have arisen in their application, and analyzes various approaches to interpretation of them. The section does not present a primer on these specific exemptions but describes the difficulties that accompany attempts to limit the principles of public access to information generated or held by government.

Given these purposes, this discussion relies upon selected judicial opinions, often of the United States Supreme Court. References are general rather than specific. A reader interested in a more comprehensive collection of the history and application of these exemptions can access the website of the Collaboration of Government Secrecy[2]; that website contains one of the most complete and helpful online resources. It also contains audio and video records of dozens of professional and academic conferences addressing many of the issues surrounding these exemptions. The United States Supreme Court decisions referenced here can be found here, as well as the Executive Orders, Department of Justice memoranda, and other government documents that direct or guide agencies in the application of the exemptions.

The last part of this essay applies lessons regarding the application of the exemptions to the federal Freedom of Information Act in the United States to the exemptions contained in the Brazilian law. These lessons include possible interpretations of the exemptions, the risks posed to access by the possible scope of the exemptions, and concerns about the interpretation of them.

## 6.1 *Introduction to the Exemptions and the Importance of Judicial Review*

An examination of the exemptions requires some background of the nature of public access granted under the federal Freedom of Information Act in the United States. The FOIA modified an access provision contained in the 1946 Administrative Procedure Act. An Information access provision was first included in this 1946 landmark law that created modern administrative law in the United States,[3] and in this sense, freedom of information is part of the administration of agencies.

---

[2]Collaboration on government secrecy, website: https://www.wcl.american.edu/lawandgov/cgs/ (Accessed on 14 February 2017).

[3]Administrative Procedure Act § 3, 60 Stat. 238, 1946. The website on the Freedom of Information act Contains current sources within government regarding the FOIA. www.foia.gov (Accessed on 14 February 2017).

That provision gave agencies great discretion in deciding whether to release requested records. Agencies balanced the reasons for which a person requesting records sought them against an agency's need for secrecy. Not surprisingly, agencies overwhelmingly found that this balance supported secrecy. As a result, that 1946 access provision failed to provide access except in the most unusual circumstances. In response, the 1966 Freedom of Information Act permitted "any person" access.[4] Any person could request documents and records. No reason was required for a request. The FOIA created the presumption that government documents or records were public. If an agency withheld requested documents, it had to rely on one of the exemptions created in the law. Congress also, through the requirement that an agency segregate and release non-exemption portions of a document, sought to limit the ability of an agency to withhold an entire document or group of documents when exempt portions could be separated from non-exempt ones.

Generally, the exemptions permitted but did not require an agency to withhold documents and records.[5] An agency had discretion not to claim an applicable exemption in a particular case. At least two of the exemptions, however, have been seen as requiring withholding if they apply. These are the (b)(1) exemption for documents and records in fact properly classified in the interests of national defense and foreign policy and the (b)(6) exemption applicable to documents and records the release of which would constitute a clearly unwarranted invasion of personal privacy.[6] The (b)(3) exemption incorporates a number of other statutes that direct government agencies to withhold information or that establish criteria for withholding. To the extent that statutes that come under this exemption require withholding, they may also limit the discretion of agencies to release information falling under them.

The 1966 FOIA relied upon judicial enforcement of the mandate for access. The abandonment of a number of doctrines for judicial review of administrative action illustrates this reliance and the importance given to judicial enforcement. For example, under the FOIA, judicial review did not rest on the agency record and the normal deference given to administrative decisions did not, as a matter of law, apply. Actions seeking a judicial order for the release of requested documents are *de novo* through entirely new proceedings.[7] The agency's findings of facts are not the basis for the decision and a court is free to make its own judgments regarding the meaning and application of the law. The agency has the burden of persuading the court that an exemption applies.

---

[4]5 U.S.C. § 552.

[5]In U.S. Supreme Court, *Chrysler Corporation v. Brown*, 441 U.S. 281 (Judgment of 18 April 1979), the Supreme Court held that FOIA was a disclosure statute and did not create mandatory bars to disclosure.

[6]In these instances, classification orders and the Privacy Act, respectively, bar release and limit the discretion of agencies to release documents that fall under one of the exemptions.

[7]5 U.S.C. § 552(a)(4)(b).

Just as the FOIA abandoned doctrines empowering agency discretion, the courts likewise refused to apply judicial principles that could have given courts additional discretion. In common law systems, the orders of courts to individuals or to organizations, including government agencies, to perform a particular action or to refrain from doing so were considered powers within a court's discretion. Under this doctrine even if a person might be entitled to such an order, a court could decline to issue a directive to act because of ameliorating circumstances. Early the courts determined that under the provisions of the FOIA they did not have this traditional judicial power.[8] The structure and history of the FOIA demonstrate the importance of the exemptions and explain why the meaning of these exemptions quickly became the focus of litigation regarding the FOIA. This emphasis on the interpretation of the exemptions increases the value of the U.S. experience in the consideration of exemptions in other countries. This increased value comes from the extensive analysis of the language and purpose of the exemptions. This analysis suggests issues and problems that become more apparent in the subsequent application rather than in the initial articulation of the grounds for secrecy.

The exemptions incorporate congressional judgments regarding the public and private interests that justify secrecy for government documents and records. The original nine exemptions to the law, although many have been subsequently amended, capture these judgments[9]—judgments that can be compared with those made in other countries in other contexts.

It is not surprising that many of these public and private interests are similarly described while others seem more parochial or idiosyncratic. The two exemptions already noted seem more generally applicable in other countries, including Brazil, the (b)(1) exemption for classified documents (Brazilian Law N° 12.527, Chap. IV, Sections II and III) and the (b)(6) exemption for documents the release of which would invade personal privacy (Brazil Law N° 12.527 Chap. IV, Section V). The (b)(3) exemption addresses a requirement that any FOIA law describe how other statutory provisions addressing the withholding of government documents will be integrated into a more general access law.

Other similar exemptions that affect the activities and operations of government also seem more generic. The (b)(2) exemption concerns internal government personnel documents and records; the (b)(4) addresses confidential business and financial information acquired by the government; the (b)(5) exemption seeks to protect the government deliberative process by attempting to describe a deliberative process privilege and related litigation privileges that likewise seek to shield certain

[8]This power of federal judges reflects the historical distinctions in English law between courts of law and courts of equity. Court of equity granted relief such as injunctions and established standards for the provision of this discretionary relief.

[9]The website of the Collaboration on Government Secrecy contains history of the exemptions. Another important resource containing a description of judicial decisions addressing the exemptions is the United States Department of Justice, Freedom of Information Guide and Privacy Act Overview (2009). An online version is at https://www.justice.gov/oip/department-justice-freedom-information-act-reference-guide (Accessed on 14 February 2017).

types of deliberations; the (b)(7) exemption applies to certain types of law enforcement records if the release of those records will lead, or are reasonably likely to lead, to certain types of harms.

On the other hand, the (b)(8) exemption dealing with access to documents of certain financial regulatory agencies and the (b)(9) exemption applying to documents regarding access to government documents containing geological and geophysical information and data and maps concerning wells seem more specialized. The most striking is the (b)(9) exemption concerning oil wells. This exemption principally applied to a single industry. At the time of the enactment of the FOIA, many of the most powerful figures in Congress and the President were from significant oil producing states.

## 6.2 Survey of Issues Surrounding the Exemptions

Those who drafted the exemptions faced a number of challenges. Similar challenges confront the articulation of exemptions in FOIA laws in other countries. First, exemptions require some consensus on what values justify restrictions on the principle of access. Too many exemptions or too broad ones undermine the principle of access. This task thus requires more than articulating these values.

The scope and character of the exemptions depends on the commitment to access. In considering exemptions must we justify access in light of the other values in secrecy or must the other values in secrecy be strong enough to limit access? The difference may seem subtle but it represents the most important question to be resolved. It alters the burden of proof as to whether a specific exemption is required at all. It also influences how the exemption will seek to describe the value of secrecy in terms of the operation of the law.

Second, the exemptions require foresight into the problems likely to arise in their application. This foresight includes some sensitivity to the risks of bureaucratic resistance and to the attitudes of relevant institutions charged with interpretation of the exemptions.

Comparative analysis of the exemptions under the U.S. federal Freedom of Information Act aids in meeting both of these challenges. The application of the exemptions in the federal FOIA illustrates the importance of an access-focused law. Even under a law like the FOIA, that adopts "any person" access and that creates a practical presumption that government documents and records are public absent the application of an exemption, it is difficult to sustain the viewpoint that it is secrecy and not access that must be justified. This difficulty arises because the application of the exemptions focuses on their meaning. In this context, it is easier to articulate the values in secrecy than consider the value of access. Moreover, the exemptions themselves contain positions inconsistent with openness. The deliberative process privilege illustrates this paradox of the exemptions. The deliberative process privilege incorporates the importance of secrecy in bureaucratic decision-making, the need for candid exchange of opinions and the reduction of "emotional" or "political" responses to rational choices.

Comparative analysis also addresses the second challenge. It permits us to see how various articulations of the same value may lead to different judgments regarding the exemption and access. Examination of the exemptions to the U.S. FOIA identity issues likely to arise in the application of exemptions that might otherwise be more difficult to foresee. Such analysis also suggests that access laws require a particularly careful analysis of the institutional framework and traditions in which they will be applied.

To an extent the distinction between the drafting and application of the laws cannot be separated. However, this part examines the values underlying the exemptions and the issues that have arisen in their application. Another aspect of the application of these exemptions lies in the approaches to interpretation. The difference between the U.S. legal system and others does not prevent conclusions being drawn from U.S. approaches to interpretation regarding related issues in other legal systems. In particular, the role of administrative interpretation seems applicable in both common and civil law countries.

### 6.2.1 Protection of Classified Information

The first exemption exemplifies an exemption based on the values of national security. However, that description of the underlying value is broader than the exemption. The difference between a broad characterization of the underlying value and the language describing the exemption illustrates how that description incorporates the underlying value but gives it legal effect in light of the value of access and the risks of bureaucratic exploitation of justifications for withholding.

The issues identified with the (b)(1) exemption reflect an articulation of the underlying value but in light of the prevailing importance of access. The exemption originally applied to documents authorized to be classified under criteria provided in an executive order of the President to be kept secret in the interests of national defense or foreign affairs. Instead of adopting a broad national security exemption that gave agencies considerable discretion to determine what documents related to national security, the exemption protected only documents that had been classified under an appropriate executive order. Each administration usually modifies criteria for classifying and declassifying documents, as well as establishing procedures and lines of authority for the application of these criteria. These procedures, lines of authority and criteria respond in part to fears of abuse by individual agencies. These classification orders expand the discretion of the executive branch but bind individual agencies to government-wide standards.

In 1974, Congress amended the exemption in light of a decision of the United States Supreme Court in *Environmental Protection Agency v. Mink*.[10] That decision

[10]U.S. Supreme Court, *EPA v. Mink*, 410 U.S. 73 (Judgment of 22 January 1973).

held that the courts must accept the executive decision to classify a document. In 1974, Congress amended the exemption to require that the document "in fact" must "be properly classified" enabling the courts to evaluate the application of classification criteria.[11]

This amendment was consistent with the way in which Congress had earlier characterized the exemption. It also may have responded to evidence of widespread abuses of civil liberties and violations of legal restraints involving the activities of the Central Intelligence Agency and the Federal Bureau of Investigation, evidence disclosed in part through investigations of abuse by the Nixon Administration triggered by the Watergate scandal. A detailed description and sweeping condemnation of these practices followed in 1975 in a report by the United States Senate Select Committee to Study Governmental Operations with Respect to Intelligence Activities.[12] Appeals to national security were effective in hiding misconduct, fraud and abuses of civil liberties.

The power of the underlying value of "national security" explains subsequent interpretation and application of the exemption. Courts rarely do more than review secretly affidavits submitted by agencies to support the classification of the documents. The requirement that documents be in fact properly classified seems to have made little difference in the interpretation of the exemption. Great deference is given to agency decisions in applying the classification criteria.

Developments after the terrorist attacks on September 11, 2001 demonstrate that this broad value of national security has migrated to other exemptions allowing some courts to give executive agencies the broad deference applied to classified documents when agencies claim exemptions that do not involve classified documents. For example, the United States Court of Appeals for the District of Columbia Circuit applied the same deference to law enforcement documents alleged by the agency to involve national security when those documents were not classified.[13] As a result, the Department of Justice did not have to disclose the names of persons that it had arrested in a nationwide "roundup" of suspected terrorists. The underlying value of national security became untethered from the Congressional application of that value in the (b)(1) exemption. In the same period agencies developed a number "internal" standards, such as "for official use only" unconnected with classification.[14]

---

[11]The Conference Committee Report regarding the 1974 amendments of the (b)(1) exemption states that the language, "in fact properly classified pursuant to an executive order" was added to emphasize that judicial review of classifications under the exemption would be *de novo*, see House of Representatives Report No. 1380, 93rd Congress, 2nd Session (1974).

[12]This Report is commonly referred to as the "Church Committee Report" after its chairperson Senator Frank Church. Senate Report No. 94-755 (1976).

[13]U.S. Court of Appeals for the District of Columbia Circuit, *Center of National Security Studies v. U.S. Department of Justice*, 331 F.3d 918 (Judgment of 17 June 2003).

[14]An academic conference sponsored in April 2011 by the Collaboration on Government Secrecy, "Protection of Homeland Security Information," is available on the CGS website.

### 6.2.2 Protection of Internal Personnel Rules and Practices

The House of Representative and the Senate appear to have taken different views of the values underlying this exemption.[15] One view was that the exemption was designed to protect minor and trivial matters of internal administration. In light of this value, the exemption would be a narrow one that would not apply when the documents addressed more substantial matters in which the public might have an interest. This view is also consistent with the proposition that it is secrecy not access that must be justified and that doubts about the scope of the exemption protecting secrecy should be read against this background.

The other view of the underlying value was the protection of agency enforcement of the law. For example, investigative manuals and guides that direct the activities of agency inspectors, investigators and prosecutors contain criteria which if known to potential lawbreakers could allow them to avoid detection or prosecution. This broader articulation of the underlying value of the exemption led to a number of decisions (the most important being *Crooker v. ATF* in the United States Court of Appeals for the District of Columbia Circuit) that applied the second exemption in those circumstances even if some segment of the public would be interested in the documents.[16] This interpretation of the exemption based on this articulation of its underlying value came to be called "high-2" representing a higher value given to the exemption.

In a recent decision, *Milner v. Department of the Navy*,[17] the Supreme Court rejected an "anti-circumvention" purpose for the exemption because the language of the exemption did not sufficiently incorporate this underlying value. Eight of the nine justices believed that the language of the exemption was insufficient to cover these manuals and guides. Thus, interpretation of the second exemption contrasts with the acceptance of a broader conception of the underlying value of national security in the first exemption.

The first challenge now returns to Congress. Congress must now decide whether the importance of preventing circumvention of administrative and criminal standards justifies claims of secrecy in a statute designed to guarantee public access to government documents and records.

[15]Davis (1970), § 3A.

[16]U.S. Court of Appeals for the District of Columbia Circuit, *Crooker v. ATF*, 789 F.2d 64 (Judgment of 29 April 1986).

[17]U.S. Supreme Court, *Milner v. Department of the Navy*, 131 S.Ct. 1259 (Judgment of 7 March 2011).

### 6.2.3 Reconciliation of FOIA Access and Other Laws Authorizing Secrecy

The third exemption seeks to relate the exemptions of the FOIA with other statutes that agencies might use to justify secrecy. This reconciliation is important, particularly with those laws that preceded the FOIA, because those articulations of secrecy may have been enacted when the value of access evidenced in the FOIA had not yet been recognized. Thus, these earlier secrecy provisions may have been more easily enacted. Even subsequently enacted laws may not have considered the implications for the FOIA. The context of these subsequently enacted laws may also have focused on protecting the values at stake in areas that do not seem to require the same justification if they had been seen as exemptions to an access law.

Therefore, freedom of information and other access laws should address how previously enacted statutes that gave government agencies authority to withhold information should be treated under a statute applicable to all government agencies. Legislatures may be disinclined to identify all such laws claimed by agencies. Legislatures may also not want to examine and evaluate each of the statutes to enact legislation that renders an individual judgment on the validity of each one. Both of these legislative tasks could be daunting ones and in the context of intense legislative activity surrounding enactment of access laws unlikely to be considered a high priority. In the enactment of such a law, a legislature confronts many important and contentious decisions regarding the articulation of exemptions that government agencies may generally assert to deny requests of agency documents and records. Access laws around the world illustrate the character of these overarching exemptions, including classified information, agency decision making and business records held by the government, personal privacy, and law enforcement information.

Perhaps these considerations explain the approach taken in the 1966 Freedom of Information Act in the United States. In that landmark federal law, Congress chose to incorporate both past and future enactments that allowed specific agencies to withhold information otherwise available under the Freedom of Information Act. Rather than evaluate each law, Congress established general criteria that could be applied by agencies and by the courts to determine which of these statutory provisions could be treated as exempting information under the FOIA. A specific exemption to the FOIA incorporated these criteria, an exemption usually referred to by its statutory subsection as the "(b)(3) exemption" or as "exemption three." As a result, statutory provisions that fell under the exemption are referred to as "(b)(3) statutes" or "exemption 3 statutes."

The 1966 language of the exemption suggests that Congress may have sought to limit the exemption to those laws in which Congress made an explicit judgment about withholding. At that time, the exemption applied to agency records "specifically exempted from disclosure by statute." The history of the FOIA supports this view. Crucial aspects of that law, including access to government records by any person and a presumption of availability of government documents and records, responded to abuse by agencies of an earlier access provision that enabled agencies to judge independently the interests of the requester in access against the interests of the agency in secrecy.

If Congress intended exemption three to limit agency discretion, the language of the statute did not accomplish this purpose. In 1975, the United States Supreme Court concluded that exemption 3 applied to a statute that permitted the Federal Aviation Administration "to withhold information, public disclosure of which in the [FAA's] judgment would adversely affect the interests of the objecting party and is not required to be disclosed in the interests of the public."[18] This decision permitted application of the exemption because of an agency's balancing of the interests in secrecy and access. As a result of the decision, many statutes, preceding the enactment of the FOIA, that permitted agency discretion would now be treated as exemptions to the FOIA and arguably inconsistent with its fundamental policy of open government.

In 1976, Congress amended exemption three to respond to the Supreme Court's interpretation of it. The limited legislative history of the amendment indicates that Congress sought to reduce administrative discretion and to ensure that policy decisions regarding secrecy be made by Congress and not by the executive branch.[19] The language of the exemption also suggests that Congress sought to limit the number of statutes falling under the exemption. If this is an accurate reading of it, this history demonstrates that Congress sought to apply the exemption only when it can be reasonably argued that Congress made a legislative decision in favor of secrecy. The history of the FOIA supports this view.

The current language of the (b)(3) exemption reflects this background. That language states that a statute qualifies as an exemption three statute only if "(i) it requires that the matters be withheld from the public in such a manner to leave no discretion on the issues or (ii) establishes particular criteria for withholding or refers to particular types of matters to be withheld." Although the amendment barred from exemption three the types of statutes like the FAA provision granting immense discretion to agency officials, it left decisions regarding many other statutes to agencies and to the courts.

In the application of this language, courts must resolve a number of questions. The clearest cases are ones in which the statute at issue explicitly directs withholding. Here the courts can turn to and rely on the plain meaning of the statutory language. In other circumstances, the courts must consider other rules of interpretation and identify the structure of analysis of a law. In administrative law in the United States, the courts normally grant deference to an agency's interpretation of statutes that it administers. With the FOIA an individual agency has a self-interest in the interpretation of provisions which arguably regulate and restrain the agency's ability to keep secret its documents and records.

[18]U.S. Supreme Court, *FAA Administrator v. Robertson*, 422 U.S. 255 (Judgment of 24 June 1975).

[19]House of Representatives Report No. 94-880, 1976.

The authoritative website of the Collaboration on Government Secrecy cautions that some statutes that are often considered to fall under the (b)(3) exemption do not do so under any reasonable interpretation of the exemption.[20] For example, the Trade Secrets Act provides for criminal penalties to government employees who disclose trade secrets but this aspect of the law does not qualify the Trade Secrets Act as an exemption three statute. Likewise, other laws that address "operational records" of some national security agencies are not exemption three statutes because they remove these files from the FOIA as a threshold matter. Overall, the Collaboration of Government Secrecy concludes that agencies claim many more, close to twice as many, statutes as falling under exemption three than legitimately do.

Agencies have every incentive to characterize statutes as exemption three ones. The importance of access and the proposition that secrecy requires justification suggests possible legislative responses. One is a systematic examination of all agency statutes that would meet criteria similar to those now contained in an exemption similar to the federal exemption three in the United States. This undertaking regarding previously enacted statutes should have been undertaken at the time of the enactment of an access law. First, at that time, the importance of the justification of secrecy is a central consideration of an access law. Second, the time of the enactment of an access law is an appropriate time to consider not only general standards but also specific statutes under those standards. The immensity of this task could be transferred to the executive by requiring agencies to list any statutes that they believe meet the general criteria for the exemption. An agency that believes it administers such a statute has superior ability to identify and justify its inclusion. If it does not do so, the law could prohibit it from relying on the statute to withhold requested documents or records or create a strong presumption that it is prohibited from doing so.

As to subsequently enacted statutes, one approach recently undertaken by the United States Congress in recent amendments to the FOIA requires the identification of any pending legislation that would fall under exemption three. This identification at least alerts committees considering that legislation of the need for the justification for such secrecy in light of the values of access and informs other members of Congress of the potential risks to public access.

### 6.2.4 Protection of the Ability of the Government to Obtain Trade Secrets and Commercial or Financial Information That Is Privileged and Confidential

The fourth exemption protects the governmental interest in obtaining such information from businesses and corporations. The government relies on such

[20] See the website of the Collaboration on Government Secrecy, https://www.wcl.american.edu/lawandgov/cgs/ (Accessed on 14 February 2017).

information for a variety of purposes. Most government regulation of health, safety, and economic interests relies on information from regulated parties. A variety of other government activities establishing policy in a wide range of fields requires information held by private companies and associations. Sometimes, however, the exemption is described as protecting the interests of private business in their trade secrets and other types of privileged and confidential information. This exemption, like the first, can be described as implementing a broader value than the articulation of the exemption supports. More cogently, the underlying value protected is a governmental one but one that invites characterization as a private one.

The exemption of certain information obtained by the government from private parties protects its ability to acquire information crucial to accomplishment of public purposes. Protection appears most important to information that is voluntarily provided to government agencies. Protection, however, may also facilitate the acquisition of information that the government can demand of businesses. For example, without protection, business not only would be unwilling to submit information voluntarily but also more willing to resist government efforts to acquire required information. This resistance could increase the costs of administration, reduce the amount of information obtained, and delay its acquisition.

As with the interpretation of other exemptions, clarity as to the narrow value in secrecy that has been justified in the exemption affects the application of the exemption. The more that the underlying value is connected with the importance of confidentiality to the protection of private business interests, the more broadly the exemption is likely to be applied. Differences as to whether both mandatory and voluntary disclosures fall under the exemption can be resolved simply by different characterizations of the government interest protected. The view, however, that protection of business is an underlying value supports a broader reading of the scope of the exemption. Likewise, the characterization of the underlying value justifying the exemption influences the likely interpretation of other terms in the exemption including trade secrets, the type of harm required, and when commercial or financial information is privileged or confidential.

If the underlying value is seen as a governmental one it is much easier to see that a government agency has discretion to release information even if falls under the exemption. Such an interpretation of the exemption has generated attempts to emphasize private interests underlying the exemption. Indications of attempts to emphasize these private interests are "reverse FOIA" suits by submitters of information seeking judicial orders to prevent agencies from releasing information that companies believe is confidential. In addition, President Reagan in Executive Order 12,600[21] established procedures that agencies must follow to permit submitters to object to the release of information that falls under the exemption.

[21]Executive Order 12,600, 1987.

### 6.2.5 Protection of Government Decision Making

The fifth exemption uniquely challenges access to government documents and records. This exemption articulates values that question the broad access provided by the federal FOIA. The fifth exemption protects bureaucratic decision making from public view. Its justifications emphasize the importance of secrecy in deliberations, the risk of premature disclosures of government actions and confidentiality. These values describe a model of bureaucratic accountability and practice inconsistent with the importance attached to public access contained in right to know laws.

The deliberative process privilege and related litigation privileges rest on a particular view of how a public bureaucracy should function and how the discretion of agency officials is regulated.[22] The deliberative process privilege protects advice and debate regarding agency standards and practices. Like Executive Privilege applicable to subordinates' advice to the President, the deliberative process privilege ensures that agency decision makers will receive candid and comprehensive opinions from other agency employees, such as subordinates and agency policy makers. The protection of such candid advice improves the quality of agency decisions and exposes weaknesses in agency analysis. Such protection encourages expression of politically unpalatable or unpopular positions relevant to proposed agency decisions.

Moreover, the deliberative process privilege reduces the damage from premature disclosure of preliminary decisions. Such likelihood of premature disclosure can limit the scope of persons from whom advice is sought and the character of the deliberations. Such premature disclosures can reduce options considered and endanger the implementation of any policy finally adopted; it may foreclose the definition of alternatives.

These reasons supporting the protection rely on a vision of agency decision making and accountability. That vision links the exercises of agency discretion to rational decisions relying on the experience and expertise of agency personnel.[23] That process of rational decision-making suspects politics in administration and sees the intrusion of politics in the formulation of policy as skewing rational and expert consideration. Likewise, the process of rational decision-making rejects democratic participation in agency decisions as impractical and public commentary on policies still under consideration as destructive of administrative efficiency.

These suspicions of administrative officials support secrecy, a secrecy rejected by right to know laws. Proponents of politics and democratic participation as means of administrative accountability and as part of appropriate agency decision making fear that rational decision making and expertise are other ways of describing agency

---

[22]A discussion of the relationship between these views of the bureaucracy and the deliberative process privilege, in particular, and of federal information policy can be found in Vaughn 1994, p. 467 et seqq.

[23]Vaughn 1994, p. 470–472.

bias.[24] Rather, public knowledge and participation expose bias and bureaucratic self-interest. The importance of public access also reflects a belief that rational decision making resting on expertise often serves only as a rationale for secret political manipulation of the administrative process.

The provisions of the federal Sunshine in Government Act that require the heads of multi-headed federal agency to conduct their deliberations in public is an exception that illustrates the power attached to the protection of the secrecy of administrative deliberations.[25] Under this law, the meetings of these government commissions must be public. It illustrates the power of the secrecy of administration because of the number of provisions of the law that permit closed meetings to protect sensitive areas, such as personnel decisions, and to prevent premature disclosure of decisions that could undermine the policies being adopted. The Sunshine in Government Act, moreover, does not address the deliberations of the staff of these multi-headed boards and commissions.

Public access to preliminary deliberations addresses objections to secrecy and argues that such access can improve agency decisions and provide greater democratic accountability. For example, public knowledge of proposed agency decisions and the debate surrounding them by those with much valuable information about the effects of the decision are crucial to public response. With access to this information public response is more likely to come at a time when it may influence the final agency decision, a decision that might in light of such scrutiny be seen as an unwise exercise of agency discretion.

Articulation of the exemption attempts to contain the arguments for secrecy found in the exemption. For example, interpretation of the language of the exemption seeks to confine the deliberations covered by it to discussions regarding proposed and preliminary policies, not final agency decisions. In one of the first cases in which it discussed the exemption, the United States Supreme Court limited the exemption to inter-agency or intra-agency memoranda and letters.[26] The Court emphasized that the documents must be used in the decision-making process of an agency. In addition, the Court concluded that the public would in any event be entitled to such documents if a private party could obtain them in litigation with the agency. Thus, the exemption incorporates some litigation privileges available to the government in litigation.

Other opinions of the Court also seek to contain the exemption in light of the breadth of the justifications supporting it.[27] The documents must be part of decision-making process used by the agency. The exemption does not apply to summaries or tables of factual information and does not apply to documents that were prepared after a final decision was made. Because much turns on these

[24]Frug 1984, p. 1276, 1326–1328.

[25]See generally, Berg et al. 2005, describing the agencies to which the Act applies.

[26]U.S. Supreme Court, *EPA v. Mink*, 410 U.S. 73 (Judgment of 22 January 1973).

[27]U.S. Supreme Court, *NLRB v. Sears, Roebuck and Company*, 421 U.S. 132 (Judgment of 28 April 1975).

distinctions, the difference between facts and deliberation and between pre-and post-decisional documents are likely to be a common source of contention. In drawing these distinctions courts may look to the specific circumstance but they are also likely to return to the justifications for the exemption. These limitations on application of the exemption likely encourage agencies to structure decision-making to expand the scope of the exemption. For example, the agency may seek to intertwine fact and opinion in documents created by it. Certainly, an agency may simply limit the number of documents created and used in decision-making.

When attorneys are involved in agency decision making, the attorney-client privilege and work product protection apply. Limitations on the scope of these privileges are important because of the number of government attorneys involved in agency decision making and because of the incentives created by these protections to involve attorneys in this process.

The scope of work-product protection could be broader in a freedom of information case that in other litigation.[28] In litigation, the party seeking a document to which work-product protection arguably applies may still obtain factual information with a showing of substantial need and the inability to obtain the equivalent information without undue hardship is satisfied. In FOIA cases, the requirement of any person access means that this showing may be more difficult to make. Indeed the showing itself may be inconsistent with any person access. In these instances, some courts have been inclined to treat work product protection more generically, an inclination that may broaden the protection.

Exemption five represents one of the strongest arguments for bureaucratic secrecy. These justifications for secrecy are contained in a right to know law and in conflict with it. In this way, the values supporting this exemption uniquely challenge the values attached to access. Other exemptions identify areas where justifications for secrecy are sufficient to limit access. On the other hand, the fifth exemption more generally questions the reasons for access.

### 6.2.6 Protection of "Clearly Unwarranted Invasions of Personal Privacy"

The sixth exemption applies to the protection of "personnel, medical or other files" and the courts have seen this language as an articulation of a protection for information regarding the personal privacy of those individuals. Personnel files contain a wealth of personal information that persons would not want disclosed without their permission; medical files contain the types of personal information that should not be public simply because the government possess them. Values protected included ones regarding embarrassment or personal interests in sheltering information from public disclosure. A similar provision protecting personal privacy

[28]See Federal Rules Civil Procedure 26(b)(6).

can be found in the law enforcement exemption a portion of which addresses the release of files involving an "unwarranted invasion of personal privacy."[29]

Some experts have argued that the sixth exemption describes information the release of which is prohibited. If so, agencies would not have the discretion, usually applicable to the exemptions, to release the documents even though the exemption applied. The mandatory character of the exemption arises not from the FOIA but from the relationship of the FOIA with the Federal Privacy Act. Thus, if the sixth exemption applies, the Privacy Act prohibits the release of the information.

The sixth exemption incorporates a balancing test not expressly included in most of the exemption. This test arose because the exemption does not allow the withholding of any information regarding personal privacy. The exemption applies only if the release of the documents would "constitute a clearly unwarranted invasion of personal privacy." Thus, the exemption requires that the interests in personal privacy must be balanced against the interests served by disclosure. This balance tips strongly in favor of disclosures of the requested documents because the disclosure affecting personal privacy must be "clearly unwarranted." Under this approach to balancing, requesters may still obtain documents invading personal privacy as long as the reasons for disclosures are sufficient that the interest in personal privacy do not clearly outweigh them. Arguably, even if the interests in person privacy outweigh the interests supporting the disclosure, the exemption may not apply. For the exemption to apply, the balance must be substantially favoring the interests in personal privacy.

The outcome of this balancing approach to the application of the sixth exemption depends heavily upon how the interests in personal privacy and the interests in disclosure are described. Descriptions that broaden the meaning of personal privacy and ones that narrow the interests in access can dramatically expand the scope of the exemption. The Supreme Court recently rejected one attempt to expand the meaning of personal privacy.

In a description of the meaning of personal privacy at the time of its enactment, one distinguished administrative law scholar asserted that personal privacy referred to the privacy interests of an individual.[30] One attempt to broaden the character of personal privacy protected by the exemption was to assert that corporations and "other artificial entities" are entitled to the protection of privacy under the sixth exemption, an assertion approved by a United States Circuit Court of Appeals. These assertions regarding the meaning of personal privacy applied to a portion of the law enforcement exemption but directly affected the more general personal privacy protection contained in exemption six.

In 2011, the Supreme Court held in *FCC v. American Telephone and Telegraph*[31] that personal privacy protection did not apply to corporations and other

---

[29] 5 U.S.C. § 552(b)(7)(C). A discussion, infra, considers the law enforcement exemption.

[30] Davis 1967, p. 761 et seqq.

[31] U.S. Supreme Court, *Federal Communications Commission, et al. v. AT&T Inc., et al.*, 131 S. Ct. 1177 (Judgment of 1 March 2011).

artificial entities. The Court unanimously held that based on ordinary usage of the word "personal", as well as the context in which the term applied limited privacy protections to individuals. The Court applied this limitation of the character of information protected by the law enforcement exemption to the sixth exemption. In ruling against *AT&T*, Chief Justice Roberts added cogently, "We trust that AT&T will not take [our opinion] personally."

The description of the character of the interest in disclosure also affects the scope of the exemption. One approach to the description of such interests in disclosure focuses on the reasons that the requester seeks the information and balances the interests of the requester against the interests in personal privacy. This way of describing the interests in disclosure is unappealing for two reasons. First, the FOIA relies on access by any person and focusing on the interests of the individual requester is inconsistent with access by any person. The exemption could apply toward one requester and not another based on their reasons for seeking the information. Second, this approach fails because once one person possesses the documents and records, that person can widely share them with others, including with persons who as requesters would have had insufficient interest in the documents to obtain them. These objections suggest that those interests balanced in favor of disclosure must be more general ones. As a result the Supreme Court has held that the purposes of access under the FOIA that must be balanced against the interests in personal privacy. The Court advocated "categorical balancing" in which broad interests supporting and opposing access were balanced rather than an analysis of the interests of the person seeking the documents.

In the 1989 decision that adopted the balancing of the public purpose of the FOIA with the interests in personal privacy, *United States Department of Justice v. Reporters Committee for Freedom of the Press*,[32] the Supreme Court broadened the scope of the exemption and converted the exemption into an important one for government secrecy. The Court accomplished this transition by increasing the scope of personal privacy and limiting the public purpose of the FOIA. First, the Court broadened the concept of personal privacy to protect information contained in public documents but that was as a practical matter difficult to obtain and obscure until the information was collected in one place by the government. The example before the Court concerned rap sheets that contained information on the criminal record of an organized crime figure with alleged ties to defense contracts and a corrupt member of Congress. The Court held that a legitimate privacy interest in the information contained in these rap sheets was not diminished because the individual pieces of information could be found in public records.

The Court also concluded that only the "core purpose" of the FOIA could be balanced against the interest in personal privacy in determining whether the exemption applied. The Court defined that core purpose as opening agency action to public scrutiny. Despite alleged connections of organized crime with the

[32]U.S. Supreme Court, *U.S. Department of Justice v. Reporters Committee for Freedom of the Press*, 489 U.S. 749 (Judgment of 22 March 1989).

Department of Defense and a member of Congress, the Court believed that the rap sheet of the organized crime boss contained nothing about these connections excluding the request from the core purpose of the FOIA. The combination of "practical obscurity," "categorical balancing" and "core purpose" clearly tipped the balance in favor of the application of the exemption.

The decision failed to recognize that FOIA treated government documents and records as a public asset. Government documents and records permitted an understanding of issues such as racially based redlining of African American communities by banks in granting mortgages, health and safety risks posed by a variety of products and activities, and information about ties between government and private actors. Thus, access was important to health and safety, civil rights enforcement and anti-corruption efforts. Access allowed victimized groups to respond to systematic discrimination. Access allowed citizens to evaluate the risks of products and services and to judge the character and quality of government regulation. Access allowed the public to know with whom the government was dealing. Such documents identified persons who served as government officials often exercising immense discretion, and identified those who were affected by government action or inaction.

Subsequent decisions of the Supreme Court strengthened the weight granted to personal privacy while weakening the ability of requesters to establish that core purpose of the FOIA. These subsequent decisions have expanded further the scope of the exemption.

In *National Archives and Records Administration v. Favish*,[33] the Court denied access to photographs showing the location of the body of a senior Presidential advisor at the site of his assumed suicide. The Court broadly defined personal privacy and imposed a requirement that made more difficult use of the core purpose of the FOIA. The right to privacy according to Court involved more than the right to control information about one's self but in this case included the interests of close relatives to the aide's death-scene images. The court constructed this view of personal privacy not from the history of the FOIA but from an application of common law views of privacy and the historical legal treatment of corpses and burial. The Court incorporated this societal history rather than the value of access on which the FOIA rests by assuming "Congress legislated against this background [.]".

On the other side of the balance, the Court refused to assume that the information sought would support the core value of access, the discovery of government misconduct. In this regard, the person seeking the documents carries the burden of demonstrating the request implicates the core purpose. If the public interest is the discovery of some form of misconduct, the requester "must produce evidence that would warrant a belief by a reasonable person that the alleged government

[33]U.S. Supreme Court, *National Archives and Records Administration v. Favish*, 541 U.S. 157 (Judgment of 30 March 2004).

impropriety might have occurred."[34] Perhaps it is unfair so to assert because in this instance, the requester had conducted some investigation, but the Court's standard for invoking the core purpose seems perilously close to denying access to investigate wrongdoing because a requester has no evidence of wrongdoing.

The Court also expanded the scope of the exemption by permitting consideration of derivative uses of the documents and records in evaluating the privacy interests balanced under the exemption while denying consideration of the derivative uses of the documents in evaluating the public purposes to be balanced. In *United States Department of State v. Ray*,[35] Haitians seeking political asylum in the United States sought the names of Haitians who had been returned to Haiti. The public interest claimed by the requesters was that the names could be used to investigate the treatment of Haitian refugees who had been returned to Haiti. The Court rejected this articulation stating that there is "nothing in the record to suggest that a second series of interviews with the already-interviewed returnees would produce" any new relevant information.[36] Thus, the public interest had to be based only on what was contained in those government files not on what additional information those files might be used to acquire.

On the other hand, the Court relied on a derivative effect of the disclosure of the names that would strengthen the privacy interests of those returned Haitians. These derivative effects included the risks of retaliation caused by renewed interest in them and that a pledge of confidentiality increased the weight given to the privacy interest. Justice Scalia objected to this approach and asserted that "derivative uses, whether to establish a public interest or to establish an invasion of privacy, is impermissible."[37]

In constructing the public interest to be weighed against the interest in privacy, the Court limited the public interest to the core purpose of the FOIA, excluding other statutorily articulated interests. In *U. S. Department of Defense v. Federal Labor Relations Authority*,[38] a federal labor union requested the names and home addresses of employees in work units represented by the union. Under the relevant labor relations statute the names and addresses would have been disclosed. In addition, the invasion of privacy was small. Almost any interest in access would have been sufficient to prevent application of the exemption. The Court, however, held that only the core purpose of the FOIA can be balanced against the privacy interest and the policies and purposes contained in the labor relations statute could

---

[34]U.S. Supreme Court, *National Archives and Records Administration v. Favish*, 541 U.S. 174 (Judgment of 30 March 2004).

[35]U.S. Supreme Court, *U.S. Department of State v. Ray*, 502 U.S. 164 (Judgment of 16 December 1991).

[36]U.S. Supreme Court, *U.S. Department of State v. Ray*, 502 U.S. 178 et seq. (Judgment of 16 December 1991).

[37]U.S. Supreme Court, *U.S. Department of State v. Ray*, 502 U.S. 180 (Judgment of 16 December 1991).

[38]U.S. Supreme Court, *U.S. Department of Defense, et al. v. Federal Labor Relations Authority, et al.*, 510 U.S. 487 (Judgment of 23 February 1994).

not be considered. Because there was no public interest to be balanced against the violation of privacy, the sixth exemption applied.

The application of the sixth exemption demonstrates how neither the purposes nor language of exemption necessarily predict the ultimate scope of an exemption. Subsequent parts of this discussion explore in more detail the effects of varying interpretative approaches employed by the courts and by executive agencies.

### 6.2.7 Records and Information Compiled for Law Enforcement Purposes to the Extent That Production of the Records or Information Would or Could Reasonably Be Expected to Result in Certain Types of Harms

Exemption seven although referred to as the law enforcement exemption, in the original FOIA applied only to investigatory records. Amendments in 1986 to exemption seven broadened the scope of the exemption in a number of ways.[39] Many of these expansions can arguably be seen to respond to the difficulty of drawing many of the distinctions required by the exemption as first written. The broadening of the exemption also reflects a judgment that the values and interests supporting the exemption justified greater secrecy than originally permitted.

The law enforcement exemption encompasses information and records of administrative and civil law enforcement agencies, as well as agencies enforcing the criminal law. The exemption covers a variety of agencies and records. To an extent, the defined harms reflect the breadth of the circumstances to which the exemption applies.

These articulated harms reflect the character of risks posed by access to administrative and criminal law enforcement records. Protection from these harms catalogue the interests justifying secrecy. The harms include: interference with enforcement, risks to fair adjudication for the accused, unwarranted invasions of personal privacy, disclosure of the identities of confidential sources for criminal law enforcement agencies; circumvention of the law through revelation of techniques and procedures, for law enforcement investigations or prosecutions and guidelines for them and risks to the life or physical safety of any individual.

The law enforcement exemption also challenges the concept of "any person" access. It is true that once any person obtains law enforcement records other persons including the target of an investigation can obtain the information but the risks of access are much higher if the target is the person seeking the documents. With this exemption, courts have struggled with the extent to which the identity and thus the motives of the requester should be considered in evaluating the risks to the protected interests described in the harms. In these circumstances, some courts believe that the risks of intimidation of witnesses, the identities of confidential sources, the uncovering of secret investigative techniques and the dangers to law

[39]Freedom of Information Reform Act of 1986, Pub. L. No. 97-570 §1802.

enforcement personnel are greater than when the requester is not a neutral. For one reason, the target of an investigation may possess much information that enables the requester to draw conclusions not apparent on the face of the documents. The identified interests also include interests of the accused and of other persons covered in these records whose release would constitute an unwarranted invasion of personal privacy. The range of interests suggests that application of the exemption will be complicated and controversial.

The history of the exemption illustrates the difficulties of resolving the many issues that arise in the application of a complex and controversial provision. Amendments to FOIA in 1974 narrowed the exemption by rejecting several broad judicial interpretations of it. For example, the amendments rejected a "blanket" exemption that exempted all records in an investigative file.

Amendments in 1986 significantly broadened the exemption. One of the changes applied the exemption beyond investigative files and encompassed not only records but also information. After the amendments, the exemption covered all law enforcement records and information compiled for law enforcement purposes. Arguably, the amendments exempted from disclosure information, as well as records, thus protecting information so compiled and that contained in records so compiled. These two changes may have addressed the difficulty of distinguishing investigative and other records and the difficulty of characterizing the process by which a physical record was created when the focus should be on the information contained in the record. That these difficulties led to an expansion of the exemption speaks to the importance that Congress attached to justifications for the secrecy of this information.

The elimination of the requirement that the records be investigative ones included many records that concerned "routine" activities of a law enforcement unit but were still records compiled for law enforcement purposes. Law enforcement purposes may include background investigations of government personnel and investigations of these personnel that address unlawful activity by federal employees. Issues arise with agencies that combine both civil or criminal law enforcement authority with other responsibilities. In these instances, an agency may need to demonstrate that the records were involved in the enforcement of a statute or regulation. The broadened scope of the exemption may apply to records that are not related an agency's law enforcement responsibilities.

The amendments in 1986 also eased the burden on the government to show that access to the law enforcement records implicate the harms specified in the exemption. Previously, the language of the exemption required that access "would" interfere with one of the described interests. After the amendments, for several of the interests, the agency need only show that access "could reasonably be expected" to interfere with them. Among these are interference with enforcement proceedings, that access could reasonably be expected to constitute an unwarranted invasion of personal privacy, to identify a confidential source, to endanger the life or physical safety of an individual.

The articulation of the law enforcement exemption describes the justifications for secrecy in a way not found in many of the other exemptions. With the seventh exemption, the detail of the requirements for withholding may have encouraged expansion of the exemption. The seventh exemption represents an instance where Congressional action, as much as interpretation, acted to broaden the scope of the exemption.

### 6.2.8 Certain Records of Financial Institutions and Oil Well Information

The eighth and ninth exemptions illustrate the type of specific, sometimes narrowly stated exemptions that focus less on broad values justifying secrecy than on identification of less inclusive categories of records that may be kept secret. In this regard, these exemptions suggest an approach often found in state freedom of information laws, some of which often contain dozens of exemptions that define more narrowly the categories of records that may or must be withheld. These exemptions may be narrow in their scope, in the sense that they address limited categories of records, but they may be broadened in application to these records.

Exemption eight seeks to ensure the integrity of financial institutions by permitting the withholding of matters contained in "examination, operation, or conditions reports" of an agency "responsible for the regulation or supervision of financial institutions." Because the exemption applies to reports prepared "by and on behalf of, or for the use of" an agency regulating financial institutions, it may cover many records not directly created by such an agency. Among the institutions covered are the Federal Reserve Board, the Comptroller of the Currency and the Federal Home Loan Bank Board.

Exemption nine appears in part to be a specific application of more general justifications underlying exemption five regarding business information submitted to the government. Some of the geological and geophysical information supplied to federal energy agencies contained information that companies considered confidential business data.

The exemptions contained in the federal Freedom of Information Act in the United States exemplify the types of exemptions that may be found in such access laws. These exemptions also illustrate the difficulties of constructing exemptions that implement the justifications for secrecy without weakening the commitment to access. That commitment to access requires that exemptions represent those instances where these justifications of secrecy are sufficient but limited. The exemptions in the FOIA show several strategies for doing so. Because a freedom of information law will be imposed on law and practice that has accepted secrecy, it is no easy task to contain the exemptions and maintain the proposition that it is secrecy not access that must be justified. The exemptions to the federal FOIA offer examples of both success and failure in that undertaking. Both the successes and failures stress the need to consider not only the areas for exemption but also the strategies for limiting the expansion of exemptions.

With some exceptions, expansion of the exemptions under the FOIA results from interpretation and application rather than changes in legislative judgments regarding the scope of the exemptions. Instead, many amendments to the exemptions seek to alter interpretations that gave inappropriate scope to them. Such legislative response is less effective than the consideration of devices that can be employed at the time of the enactment of an access law. The following section explores techniques and approaches to interpretation of the exemptions used by the Supreme Court and by the executive branch.

### *6.3 Approaches to Interpretation of the Exemptions*

The FOIA places enforcement of the FOIA with the courts and gives them authority to determine the meaning of language chosen by Congress to recognize interests justifying secrecy. The courts, however, examine a limited number of disputes. The structure of the federal courts in the United States ensures conflicting decisions among district courts and among the several circuit courts of appeal that review those decisions.

In the United States, courts rely on judicial precedent in interpreting statutes. Some scholars argue that once the meaning of the language is decided by an appellate court that interpretation should not be altered by the court absent rejection of the interpretation by the Supreme Court.[40] In a recent opinion in the Supreme Court's interpretation of exemption two, Justice Breyer dissented to the Court's interpretation because a consistent course of interpretation by other federal courts and administrative agencies had given the exemption "a clear meaning that this Court should hesitate to change."[41] According to this view, the Supreme Court does not have the discretion to alter its precedent interpreting statute (or perhaps the long standing precedent of lower federal courts) as it does with either its precedent regarding the meaning of the constitution or of common-law, judge-made rules. The Court's position that the exemptions are "explicitly exclusive" magnifies the importance of judicial interpretation of the exemptions.

Although the United States Supreme is the final authority in interpretation of the exemptions, the Supreme Court resolves a small percentage of disputes. These interpretations by the Supreme Court control the meaning of the exemptions absent legislative action. This portion of this discussion examines different approaches to the interpretation of exemptions and explores the implications of these approaches for the scope of the exemptions.

Administrative agencies interpret the exemptions in each of the hundreds of thousands requests for documents and record made annually to government agencies. These interpretations have a significant effect on the scope of the exemptions and the ability of the FOIA to compel access to government documents and records.

---

[40]See generally, Levi 1948.

[41]U.S. Supreme Court, *Milner v. Department of the Navy*, 131 S.Ct. 1259 (Judgment of 7 March 2011).

With the executive directives that establish standards for administration but do establish standards enforceable by third parties, the President and the Attorney of the United States influence how the exemptions are interpreted in practice. This portion of the discussion also examines the memoranda of five attorneys general directing agency discretion in the application of the exemptions.

This portion of the discussion ends with a brief examination of ways of addressing interpretation of the exemptions. It suggests techniques that a legislative body, Congress, can use to influence interpretation and to ensure that secrecy not access must be justified.

### 6.3.1 Approaches to Interpretation of the Exemptions by the United States Supreme Court

The Supreme Court's approach to interpretation influences the scope of the exemptions and therefore the availability of government documents and records. The previous review of the issues regarding the exemptions exemplifies how interpretation of some of the exemptions has reduced access.

The Supreme Court uses different rules of interpretation in determining the scope and meaning of the exemptions. The Court applies some rules applicable to most statutes including the FOIA. These rules of general application include: (1) that statutory language should be given its "plain meaning" (2) that interpretation of the statutes should seek to define clear rules that can be easily followed (3) that interpretation requires "a balancing" of the interests supporting the exemptions. In the case of the FOIA, the balance is between the values protected by the exemptions with the purpose(s) for the access provided by that law.

The Court's most important rule of interpretation applying specifically to the exemptions requires that the exemptions "be narrowly construed." This rule seeks to ensure that interpretation will not expand the scope of the exemptions and thus narrow access under the FOIA. The Court has often invoked the rule but experience shows that its invocation alone may fail to circumscribe the scope of the exemptions.

A common approach to statutory interpretation relies on giving words in the statute their "plain meaning." Advocates of the rule argue that it focuses attention on the language chosen by Congress and enacted into law. It is that language on which those using or subject to the law will rely in deciding its meaning. The rule discourages the use of legislative history in deciphering the meaning of the statute unless the plain meaning would lead to absurd results. In response, opponents of the rule argue that often the meaning of the language of the rule is not "plain" without examination of the legislative history, a legislative history that may describe a different possible meaning of the language. The rule does not necessarily exclude reliance on the "purpose" of the law but that purpose must be construed by a court from the language of the statute.

The Supreme Court's decision in *Tax Analysts v. Department of Justice*[42] illustrates the application of the plain meaning rule of interpretation. In this case, a company that published tax materials and guides requested that the Department of Justice provide copies of district courts' resolution of disputes regarding the federal tax laws. The DOJ obtained these documents in the course of representing the United States. Although the requester could itself obtain these documents from the courts, it argued that it could not do so as efficiently as the DOJ. The Department denied the requests and argued that the documents were not "agency records improperly withheld." The documents were records of the district courts and could be obtained from them. The Supreme Court parsed the language of the FOIA allowing courts to order the disclosure of "agency records" "improperly withheld." The Court relied on its previous interpretation of these terms and held that the meaning of the terms required disclosure. A dissenting opinion urged the Court to consider more than the meaning of the language. The dissent believed that the Court's interpretation "cannot be one within the intent of Congress when the FOIA was enacted."[43] The material was available elsewhere and the documents added "nothing whatsoever to public knowledge of government operations."

A preference for interpretation that creates "bright-line rules" rests on assumptions that such rules are more easily understood and applied, give greater predictability to the law, and reduce the role of discretion in the application of the laws. These benefits of bright-line rules advance the rule of law. Similar arguments are made for clear rules of interpretation. Clear interpretative rules make the law easier to apply, increase predictability and reduce discretion in determining the outcome of a dispute. That discretion regarding the meaning of the exemptions simply may involve choosing among competing and perhaps inconsistent rules of interpretation. Such clear rules of interpretation also alert Congress how the statutory language will be interpreted. Such knowledge by Congress allows it to legislate with an understanding of how statutes will be interpreted.[44]

Conflicts as to whether the law enforcement exemption seven applies to exclude access to broad categories of documents reflect debate regarding the use of bright-line rules. In *Reporters Committee*,[45] the Supreme Court concluded that all "rap sheets" (compilations of arrests, charges, and convictions from multiple sources) were exempt from disclosure because they fell under the portion of the law enforcement exemption regarding the protection of personal privacy. In *United*

---

[42]U.S. Supreme Court, *Tax Analysts v. Department of Justice*, 429 U.S. 136 (Judgment of 23 June 1989).

[43]U.S. Supreme Court, *Tax Analysts v. Department of Justice*, 429 U.S. 136, 156 (Judgment of 23 June 1989).

[44]U.S. Supreme Court, *John Doe v. John Doe Corp.*, 493 U.S. 146, 164 (Judgment of 11 December 1989).

[45]U.S. Supreme Court, *U.S. Department of Justice v. Reporters Committee for Freedom of the Press*, 489 U.S. 749 (Judgment of 22 March 1989).

*States v. Landano*,[46] the Court declined to give "generic" protection to all records the release of which would identify confidential informants. Although it permitted the "inference" that paid informants expected that their cooperation would be kept secret, it recommended "a more particularized approach" in other instances involving confidential sources.

In other instances, conclusions regarding the application of the exemption might vary because of differences in the circumstances leading to the cooperation of the source. Such circumstances might include the nature of the crime and the relationship of the source to that crime. In *Reporters Committee*, Justice Blackmun attacked the use of a bright-line rule by emphasizing the importance of the facts of the individual case.[47] He believed that a bright-line rule regarding the rap sheets might not apply to a rap sheet that disclosed a Congressional candidate's "conviction for tax fraud five years before." A single contrary example can weaken the support for interpretation that seeks to create such rules.

The "workable balance" used by the Supreme Court in interpreting the exemptions is not necessarily inconsistent with the establishment of bright-line rules because a workable balance of the values underlying the exemptions with access provided under the law could recommend the creation of a bright-line rule. The "workable balance" technique, however, competes with the rule that the exemptions should be narrowly construed.

*John Doe v. John Doe Agency*[48] contains the articulation of the "workable balance" approach. In *John Doe*, the Supreme Court considered the threshold requirement for application of the exemptions that the requester sought "records or information compiled for law enforcement purposes." The Defense Contract Audit Authority created the records as part of its accounting inquiry and not for law enforcement purposes. Eight years later, the contractor requested these documents from the audit agency; 2 days after the request the agency transferred the records to the Federal Bureau of Investigation that used these records for law enforcement purposes.

In interpreting the language, "compiled for law enforcement purposes" the Court used a "workable balance" approach to define the relative language. This balancing considered that disclosure was the "dominant objective of the Act." The Court, however, stated that "the statutory exemptions are intended to have meaningful reach and application." The Court derived the term, "workable balance," from language in a Congressional report that in drafting the exemptions Congress intended to create a workable balance between access and the need for secrecy. The Court created a balancing test between the values and interests covered by the

[46]U.S. Supreme Court, *Department of Justice v. Landano*, 508 U.S. 165 (Judgment of 24 May 1993).

[47]U.S. Supreme Court, *U.S. Department of Justice v. Reporters Committee for Freedom of the Press*, 489 U.S. 749, 780-81 (Judgment of 22 March 1989; Blackmum, dissenting).

[48]U.S. Supreme Court, *John Doe v. John Doe Corp.*, 493 U.S. 146 (Judgment of 11 December 1989).

exemptions and access required by the Act. In defining the value of access, the Court emphasized that the value of that access were the needs of an informed citizenry to control corruption and make government accountable.

In doing so, the Court focused not on the plain meaning of "compiled" but on a balancing of interests. The Court described its balancing approach as firmly grounded in Supreme Court precedent and as "a practical approach when it has been confronted with an issue of interpretation of the Act, it has endeavored to apply a workable balance between the interests of the public in access to information and the needs of the Government to prevent certain kinds of information from disclosure. The Court looks to the reasons for the exemption from disclosure in determining whether the Government has properly invoked a particular exemption."[49]

Congress's view that its construction of the language of the exemption creates a workable balance does not authorize the Court to engage in its own balancing in deciding how to interpret the language chosen by Congress. Indeed, recognition of such balancing by Congress should counsel narrow construction by the courts of the language chosen by Congress to represent the balance that it has made.

The problems described earlier regarding the exemptions illustrates why the Court's balancing approach leads to expansion of the exemptions. First, this approach invites courts to articulate the values supporting each exemption and permits an expansive view of these values, a view much broader than the language chosen. Second, a balancing test, as it was applied in *Reporters Committee* creates incentives to define narrowly the interests justifying access. The Court's articulation of a "core purpose" of the FOIA disregards other justifications of access and suggests that access like the exemptions must be justified.

The "clearinghouse function" whereby the FOIA provides taxpayers access to valuable information generated or acquired by the government at the expense of taxpayers illustrates another important basis for access. This information is relevant to understanding the risks posed by many government and private activities and provides information for the efficient functioning of markets in information important to consumer choice. Congressional materials describing the purpose of the 1974 Amendments to the FOIA contain statements by a principal architect of the amendments supporting such a clearinghouse function.[50]

---

[49]U.S. Supreme Court, *John Doe v. John Doe Corp.*, 493 U.S. 157 (Judgment of 11 December 1989).

[50]"The processes of government touch every aspect of our lives, every day. From the food we eat to the cars we drive, to the air we breathe, Federal agencies constantly monitor, regulate and control. . . . The Freedom of Information Act guarantees citizen access to a vast storehouse of information." Freedom of Information Act and Amendments of 1974 (P.L. 93-502). Source Book: Legislative History, Text and Other Documents, Committee on Government Operations, U.S. House of Representatives, Committee on the Judiciary States Senate, 94. Congress (P.L. 93-502), 1st Session 284-85 (Chapter VI: House and Senate Debates on Freedom of Information Act Amendments of 1974) (comments of Senator Edward Kennedy).

Third, the focus on the values underlying the exemptions will over time give those values inordinate weight. "Any person" access and the presumption of the availability of government documents and records is a commitment to access that need not be repeatedly justified. This structure of the Act ensures that in disputes about the scope of the exemptions the focus on the values underlying the exemptions will tend to obscure the values supporting access. These "access values" are likely to be relied on but not articulated with the same specificity as the more discrete values supporting each of the exemptions. This approach thus can lead to practices of interpretation that are perilously close to requiring the justification of access rather than secrecy.

Thus, the "workable balance" approach sharply contrasts with the rule of interpretation that the exemptions be narrowly construed. This second rule of interpretation specifically seeks to limit the scope of the exemptions and to resist the incentives for their expansion through interpretation. Justice Anton Scalia's dissent in *John Doe v. John Doe* agency emphasizes the challenge that "workable balance" poses to the canon of narrow interpretation of the exemptions. Justice Scalia, certainly no supporter of the FOIA,[51] argued: "Narrow construction of an exemption means, if anything, construing ambiguous language in the exemption in such a fashion that the exemption does not apply."[52] Under the canon of narrow construction, if there are several permissible meanings of the language of the exemption, the courts must adopt that meaning which gives the least scope to the exemption. Justice Scalia asserted that such a clear rule of interpretation would make it "inescapably clear to Congress what changes need to be made."[53] The rule also arises from the proposition that it is secrecy not access that must be justified.

In a recent Supreme Court decision restricting the scope of exemption two, Justice Kagan relied on the canon of narrow construction of the exemption, an approach to interpretation that "stands on especially firm footing with respect to Exemption 2."[54] In this context, she contrasts a narrow construction of the exemption with interpretation of the access provision of the Administrative Procedure Act antecedent to the enactment of the FOIA. In the antecedent provision, the interpre tation of vague language converted the access provision to a withholding statute.

The variety of interpretative approaches employed by the Supreme Court illustrates the difficulties of interpretation and the inconsistencies among interpretative approaches. Choices among the approaches cannot avoid the need for interpretation of the exemptions. To the extent the choice of an interpretative approach does much to determine the outcome; it increases the ability of judges to indulge their values

[51]Scalia (1982). Scalia stated, "The Freedom of Information Act is the Taj Mahal of the Doctrine of Unanticipated Consequences, the Sistine Chapel of Cost-Benefit Analysis ignored."

[52]U.S. Supreme Court, *John Doe v. John Doe Corp.*, 493 U.S. 146, 161 (Judgment of 11 December 1989; Scalia, dissenting).

[53]U.S. Supreme Court, *John Doe v. John Doe Corp.*, 493 U.S. 164 (Judgment of 11 December 1989, 1989).

[54]U.S. Supreme Court, *Milner v. Department of the Navy*, 131 S. Ct. 1259 (Judgment of 7 March 2011).

supporting the exemptions not by articulation and defense of them but by selection of an approach to interpretation. Rules of interpretation should reduce rather than increase the ability of judges to substitute their views of the values of the exemptions for the choices made by Congress.

This risk is greater in interpretation of the FOIA because the Department of Justice devotes its resources to the defense of suits against agencies who withhold documents. The credibility and expertise of the Department may influence judges to accept the permissible meaning of language that expands rather than limits the exemptions. Perhaps no set of rules can ensure that a commitment to access controls the interpretation of any right-to-know law.

The lack of a constitutional basis for access to information increases the risks to access posed by approaches to statutory interpretation of the exemptions. First, absence of a constitutional norm regarding access frees courts to expand the values supporting the exemptions; a constitutional norm articulates powerful justifications for access against which all exemptions must be measured.

Second, approaches to interpretation of statues likely vary from interpretation of a constitution. For example, a court exercises power in interpreting a statutory provision because a statute is unclear. As described in this section, the interpretative approaches of the United States Supreme Court permit the Court to prefer secrecy over access. Thus, expansive interpretation of the exemptions are more likely and these interpretations are more likely to be lasting ones.

On the other hand, the Court has greater responsibility to evaluate and apply a constitutional norm, a responsibility uniquely within its purview and one not subject to statutory rejection. Thus, a subsequent Court could conclude that the constitutional norm was previously too narrowly applied. The importance of the constitutional norm may explain why advocates for access to government documents and records are tempted to describe the FOIA as a statute supporting the First Amendment rights contained in the Constitution.

Advocates for the connection of the FOIA with the First Amendment can assert the importance of access to information as vindicating these constitutional rights. How is the right to speak against governmental policies and practices meaningful without information regarding them? The contours of the First Amendment developed in the twentieth century failed to provide a firm foundation for citizen access to information held by the government. Thus, the FOIA buttresses First Amendment rights.

The issues that arise with judicial interpretation suggest that Congress may wish to play a role not only in framing the language of the exemptions but also in directing interpretative approaches to be followed in the interpretation of the exemptions. The discussion of the Supreme Court's interpretation of exemptions illuminates the importance of the interpretation of the exemptions by executive agencies.

### 6.3.2 Approaches to Interpretation of the Exemptions Contained in the Memoranda of U.S. Attorneys General

Several sources influence agencies' interpretation of the exemptions. The practices and standards of agencies regarding the meaning of the exemptions may vary; in large departments, units and divisions within them may approach interpretations in different ways. This variance suggests that agencies themselves may not uniformly apply the exemptions. In addition, the Department of Justice's Freedom of Information Guide discusses federal court decisions that affect the meaning of the exemptions. The Department's Office of Information Policy provides more specific guidance to agencies regarding the scope of the exemptions.

The memoranda of five attorneys general addressing agency application of the exemptions span nearly 36 years.[55] These memoranda describe the policies of several administrations regarding the character and scope of the exemptions. These memoranda demand attention from agencies because they articulate the criteria that the Department will use in deciding whether to defend suits against agencies for denial of requests for information.

These memoranda influence application of the exemptions in several ways. First, the memoranda address how agencies should exercise their discretion to release records even though one or more of the exemptions would permit withholding. With the notable exception of the first exemption regarding classified information and the sixth exemption regarding personal privacy, the exemptions permit agencies to release exempt documents and records.

Second, the memoranda suggest approaches to interpretation of the exemptions. Although the memoranda do not articulate specific rules of interpretation, they do suggest standards by which the Department will evaluate legal support for an agency's interpretation of the exemptions. In this way, the memoranda also influence how agencies interpret the scope of the exemptions.

Third, each of the memoranda conveys an attitude toward the exemptions and toward the importance of access. The language and tone of them often express clearly an administration's attitude toward withholding. This attitude influences agencies' interpretation of the exemptions. This attitude may also magnify or reduce the specific statements regarding the exercise of agency discretion in releasing exempt documents. For example, one of the memoranda appears to elevate the status of exemption five regarding the protection of internal agency decision making to that given to exemptions one and six.

A brief review of the memoranda demonstrates their potential scope and influence. This review also shows that administrations differ significantly in the

---

[55]Griffin Bell, Attorney General's Letter, May 7, 1977; William French Smith, Attorney General's Memo on FOIA, May 4, 1981; Janet Reno, Attorney General Reno's FOIA Memorandum, October 4, 1993; John Ashcroft, Memorandum for Heads of All Federal Departments and Agencies, October 12, 2001; William Holder, Memorandum for Heads of Executive Departments and Agencies, March 19, 2009. These memoranda maybe found on the website of the Collaboration on Government Secrecy: http://www.wcl.american.edu/lawandgov/CGS.

importance attached to the exemptions and to the justifications for secrecy. In this regard, the memoranda of attorneys general appointed by Republican presidents vary from those of attorneys general appointed by Democratic presidents.

#### 6.3.2.1 Discretion to Disclose

Regarding the exercise of agency discretion in releasing exempt records, Attorney Griffin Bell, appointed by Jimmy Carter, announced that the Department of Justice "will defend Freedom of Information suits only when the disclosure is *demonstrably harmful*" (emphasis added). Attorney General Bell, however, described four factors that the Department would consider in defending an agency's denial of a request. One of these factors asks whether there is "a *sufficient prospect* of actual harm to legitimate public or private interests" if the requested documents were released (emphasis added). Perhaps these two statements regarding discretion to release documents consider varying aspects of the same standard. The requirement to show "demonstrable harm" addresses the character of the harm; that is, one that is significant enough. The second factor, "a likely prospect of harm" addresses the likelihood of the harm; that is whether the demonstrable harm is a likely prospect if the document is released. These statements describe the burden that agency must meet when it exercises its discretion to deny a requested documents. Such a burden supports the proposition that it is secrecy and not access that must be justified.

In response, Attorney General William French Smith, appointed by Ronald Reagan, issued a memorandum that superseded that of Griffin Bell. French described that the policy of the Department was "to defend all suits challenging an agency's decision to deny a request." The only exception to this policy of support for an agency's decision to withhold was when the denial "lacks a substantial legal basis" or the defense could create "an unwarranted risk of adverse impact" on another agency's ability to withhold records. Both the exceptions address the strength of the defense. Unless a defense was not credible, the Department of Justice would defend it. In effect, the statement supports broad agency discretion in withholding. Unlike the Bell's memorandum, French's places no burden on an agency to justify withholding if a credible argument can be made that an exemption applies.

In contrast, the memorandum of Attorney General Janet Reno, appointed by Bill Clinton, rescinded the guidelines contained in Smith's memorandum. Janet Reno "strongly encourage[d] your FOIA officers to make 'discretionary disclosures' whenever possible [.]" Reno called attention to the "number of FOIA exemptions" under which discretionary releases are possible. She also stated that her strong encouragement of discretionary release applied "especially when only a government interest would be affected." She stated that "the policy of the Department of Justice [is] to defend the assertion of an FOIA exemption *only* in those cases where the agency *reasonably foresees* that the disclosure *would* be harmful to an interest protected by that exemption" (emphasis added).

The memorandum of Attorney General John Ashcroft, appointed by George W. Bush, is the most supportive of discretionary withholding of exempt documents. In the memorandum, Ashcroft emphasized a position taken by Attorney General Smith. Ashcroft told agencies, "*You can rest assured* that the Department of Justice will defend your decisions unless they lack a sound legal basis or present an unwarranted risk of adverse impact on the ability of other agencies to protect other important records" (emphasis added). Like French, Ashcroft supported broad discretion to withhold exempt documents. Ashcroft described the "fundamental values" the administration was committed to protect to include ones beyond national security and personal privacy (prohibited from release by exemptions one and six) to other values protected by exemptions that did not require mandatory withholding. The additional values included "the effectiveness of law enforcement agencies and protecting sensitive business information" (references to exemptions seven and four). In striking contrast to Janet Reno's memorandum, Ashcroft's memorandum included "fully functional and efficient government" to "ensure candid and complete agency deliberations without fear that they will be made public" and litigation privileges available to the government (references to exemption five). The addition of these values encouraged an application of the memorandum to impose a burden on agencies to justify *disclosures* of information exempt under exemptions four, five and seven.

The most current memorandum issued by Attorney General Eric Holder, appointed by President Barack Obama, recalls language used by Janet Reno. Attorney General Holder stated: "An agency should not withhold information simply because it may do so legally." "I strongly encourage agencies to make discretionary disclosure of information." The Department will defend a denial "*only*" if the agency "*reasonably foresees* that the disclosure *would* harm an interest protected by one the exemptions" or "disclosure is prohibited by law" (emphasis added).

#### 6.3.2.2 Approaches to Interpretation

Although these memoranda focus on the exercise of agency discretion regarding disclosure of exempt records, they also indicate how the agency should interpret the exemptions. More narrow reading of the exemptions increases disclosure as a matter of right rather than as an exercise of agency discretion; both the scope of the exemptions and the discretion to release exempt documents work together either to increase or decrease secrecy. The comments regarding the scope of the exemptions are more indications than declarations but nonetheless clear.

In his memorandum, Attorney General Bell lists as one of the factors in determining if the Department will defend a denial is whether "the agency's denial seems to have a *substantial* legal basis." "Substantial" has more than one meaning but common ones include: considerable, large, firm, strong, stout, real, true and not illusive. These meanings suggest an approach to interpretation that gives considerable weight to access rather than to the justifications for secrecy. It suggests an approach to interpretation that shares much with the judicial canon that the exemptions should be narrowly construed.

Attorney General Reno's memorandum asserts a similar standard in asserting that "a substantial legal basis" alone is not enough for the Department to defend an agency's denial of a request. Likewise, Attorney General Holder's memorandum adopts the same legal standard, "substantial legal basis", regarding agency interpretation of the exemptions.

Although he takes a different view regarding the exercise of discretion to disclose, Attorney General French's memorandum similarly describes the Department's decision to defend must rest on "a substantial legal basis" for the agency's denial and thus its interpretation of the applicable exemption. Attorney General Ashcroft articulates this same standard. Despite striking differences in the assessments of access and secrecy, all of the five memoranda articulate this same standard.

#### 6.3.2.3 Attitudes Toward Secrecy and Access

The tone and language of the memoranda, however, may influence the application of the standard for interpretation and the exercise of agency discretion in disclosure. The discussion of the treatment of discretion to disclose provided the strongest sense of the relative values of access and secrecy. Griffin Bell emphasizes "the spirit, appearance and reality of open government." Janet Reno speaks of "a presumption of disclosure," asserts that the "American public's understanding of the workings of its government is a cornerstone of democracy." Erik Holder declares "In the face of doubt, openness prevails" and, quoting President Obama, states: "The Government should not keep information confidential merely because public officials might be embarrassed by disclosure, because errors and failures might be revealed, or because of speculative or abstract fears." William French Smith makes supportive statements that "disclosure is the foremost goal in administrating the Act" and that agencies "should ensure that nondisclosure will not serve to conceal or otherwise facilitate fraud, waste, or other wrongdoing by government employees."

In contrast, much of John Ashcroft's memorandum addresses the importance of secrecy. He declares that the Department of Justice and George W. Bush's Administration "are equally committed to protecting other fundamental values" that "I encourage your agency to carefully consider the protection of all such values and interests when making disclosure determinations under the FOIA." He urges that any discretionary decision regarding disclosure "should be made only after full and deliberate consideration of institutional, commercial, and personal privacy interests". This language suggests that at best the justifications for access underlying the FOIA and the justifications for secrecy are to be treated equally but in the admonitions regarding the importance of the interests underlying the exemptions and of an examination of them, it suggests that it is access not secrecy that is to be justified.

The crucial role of interpretation and discretion in determining the scope of the exemptions directs attention to the source of articulation of these important buttresses for access under a public access law. The Department Justice represents the United States in litigation and this role can influence its view of the appropriate rule of interpretation.

Some states within the United States use independent or neutral advisory bodies to mediate disputes and to provide guidance regarding the interpretation of the law.[56] One example is the State of New York Committee on Open Government which is empowered to give advisory opinions regarding the meaning of the law. Some New York courts have given deference to these opinions when interpreting the law in litigation. Some Information Commissioners in other countries also provide guidance regarding the meaning and application of access laws.

Amendments to the Freedom Information Act in 2007 authorized the creation of the Office of Government Information Services located in the National Archives and Record Administration.[57] The Office (OGIS) was considered an information ombudsman that would not only work to resolve disputes between agencies and requesters but also recommend changes to the FOIA, and aid improvements in agency practices and procedures. In addition, OGIS could provide guidance regarding the FOIA. OGIS might give advice regarding the interpretation of the FOIA.

At a minimum OGIS provides a vehicle available to Congress to ensure an access-biased and consistent policy toward agency interpretation of the FOIA. If OGIS exercised such a role, courts might defer to its interpretations of the exemptions in circumstances where they might be unwilling to do so regarding interpretation of the Department of Justice as an advocate for agencies.

## 7 Implications of the U.S. Experience for Exemptions Contained in the Brazilian Access Law

The discussion thus far counsels caution in applying the experiences with the exemptions in the U.S. FOIA to the exemptions in the Brazilian law. Several potential differences between the U.S. and Brazilian laws cannot be captured simply by a comparison of their language. For example, principles of interpretation of statutes may vary. Such variance seems likely given the distinctions between civil and common law approaches. The legal traditions of the country play crucial roles in the application of legislation.

Few countries have the tradition of legal realism that dominates U.S. legal education and practice. Legal realism emphasized how the practical application of law rather than its formal articulation determined its meaning. Legal realism

[56] Vaughn 1984, p. 185 et seqq., describing administrative schemes in Connecticut and New York.

[57] A thorough examination of the Office of Government information Services can be found at http://www.c-span.org/programAUW (Accessed on 16 March 2011).

asserted several propositions regarding law that scholars and jurists in some countries may find unfamiliar, objectionable, and even offensive to accepted propositions about law. The views of legal realism can be captured for our purposes in a few brief statements: Law is not a set of rules but the standards that are followed in practice; Law is judged by its effect and not by its content; a study of law focuses on the behavior of judicial and regulatory officials; evaluation of law appeals to public policy or policy science; a study of law requires the integration of the social sciences.[58]

The institutional frameworks in which the law will be interpreted and applied may vary between the two countries. For example, a government, such as that in the United States that rests on the separation of power between the executive, legislative and judicial branches may differ from one that lacks such stark distinctions. These differences may be significant when the executive plays a greater role in law making than is permitted in the United States.

An observer of U.S. practice not well versed in Brazilian law and government will find it difficult to judge whether the issues identified with the application of the exemptions in the U.S. apply in the Brazilian context. The combination of these factors recommends humility in making suggestions. The most important contribution may be a summary of insights and cautions suggested by the experience in the United States.

The following propositions reflect the experience previously described in some detail. These propositions may be considered as a list of items to consider in the construction of exemptions to a public access or freedom of information law.

### 7.1 Freedom of Information Laws Pose Challenges to Common Approaches to Statutory Interpretation

Freedom of information laws and other transparency laws are unlike most statutes defining the rights and obligations of administrative agencies. Freedom of information laws apply to the entire executive branch and can thus be considered a regulation of government administration. They pursue goals of accountability, rule of law, prevention of corruption and improvement of government regulation of such areas as public health and safety.

Although access provisions are sometimes tailored to specific agencies, freedom of information laws of broad application are first interpreted by those agencies subject to the requirements of such laws. The deference sometimes given to administrative interpretation of relevant statutes should not apply to these laws of government-wide scope. To defer to these interpretations is analogous to allowing regulated parties to determine the meaning of the laws that restrict and guide their activities.

---

[58] See generally, White 2003, p. 63–113 (describing the intellectual foundations of legal realism).

## 7.2 Freedom of Information Laws Should Give Attention to Rules of Interpretation Regarding Them

Civil codes ordinarily contain rules to guide interpretation of the provisions of these codes. The U.S. experience suggests why the interpretation of the exemptions calls for the articulation of special rules of interpretation. Perhaps the best example of such rules in the U.S. is that of narrow construction of the exemptions. In a law that presumes access with limited exceptions, such as the law in the U.S. and in Brazil, [Brazilian Law N° 12.527, Article 3, item 1] other rules of interpretation are fraught with risk. Perhaps the best example of such rules in the U.S. is the "balancing approach" that interprets the exemptions by balancing the interest protected by the exemption against the value of access.

## 7.3 Exemptions to Freedom of Information Laws Must Be Clearly Expressed

Ambiguity or inconsistencies in the articulation of the exemptions invites and encourages interpretations that broaden their meaning. Many obstacles to clear expression face the drafters of such laws. Among these are the broad scope of the exemptions, the application of the exemptions in many different circumstances, conflicts in goals of an exemption, and the inability to predict those circumstances and to recognize in advance the uncertainties created by these circumstances. The exemption incorporating other prohibitions against disclosure in the U.S. law illustrates both the need of clear expression and the difficulties of providing it.

## 7.4 Exemptions Must Anticipate the Context in Which They Will Be Interpreted and Applied

Different institutions will interpret and apply the exemptions. The language of exemptions should anticipate how these institutions will approach the exemptions in different ways. The language must also reflect an understanding of the relationship between different sources of interpretation and the implication of these relationships for the language chosen to express the exemptions. In the United States, for example, the Department of Justice serves both as an interpreter of the laws and as the legal representative of agencies charged with improper withholding of requested documents.

### 7.5 *Some Exemptions Will Address Subject Areas That Especially Challenge Access to Information*

The nature of these areas may well vary from country to country but the exemptions in United States concerning the protection of the agency deliberative process, the protection of personal privacy and classified documents implicating national security exemplify areas that may pose challenges in many countries. The U.S. experience demonstrates the difficulties of limiting the expansion of these exemptions.

### 7.6 *Exemptions Require the Continued Interest and Involvement of Legislative Bodies*

The propositions articulated above show that an effective freedom of information law is never complete. Attention must be paid to the restating of exemptions when they are deemed to have been too broadly applied. The U.S. Congress has revised several of the exemptions. In some instances, a legislature may conclude that an exemption is too narrowly stated, a judgment reflected in 1986 amendments to the law enforcement exemption of the federal FOIA.

### 7.7 *Exemptions May Play Different Roles in Different Schemes of Access to Government Information*

In freedom of information provisions that do not adopt "any person" access, exemptions will play a different role because the right of access itself is limited. Freedom of information laws, such as the U.S. and Brazilian ones, that impose an affirmative obligation on government agencies to disseminate information may also alter the role of exemptions. A broad definition of that affirmative obligation permits specific legislative judgments about the documents and records that become available without request. It also may reduce the opportunity to claim the exemptions and thus reduce their importance.

## References

Berg, R., Klitzman, S., & Edeles, G. (Eds.). (2005). *An interpretive guide to the government in Sunshine Act*. Chicago: ABA Publishing.
Davis, K. C. (1967). *University of Chicago Law Review, 34*, p. 761 et seqq.
Davis, K. C. (1970). *Administrative Law* (1970 Supp.). New York: Aspen Publishing.

Frug, G. (1984). The ideology of bureaucracy in American Law. *Harvard Law Review, 97*, p. 1126 et seqq.
Levi, E. (1948). *Introduction to legal reasoning*. Chicago: University of Chicago Press.
Scalia, A. (1982). *The Freedom of Information Act has no clothes*. Regulation 5 Mar./Apr. 1982.
Vaughn, R. G. (1984). Administrative alternatives and the Federal Freedom of Information Act. *Ohio State Law Review, 45*, p. 185 et seqq.
Vaughn, R. G. (1994). Federal Information Law and Policy. In D. Rosenbloom & R. Schwartz (Eds.), *Handbook of regulation and administrative law* (p. 467 et seqq.). New York: CRC Press.
White, G. E. (2003). *Tort Law in America: An intellectual History*. New York: Oxford University Press.

## List of Cases

United States Supreme Court 22.01.1973, *Environmental Protection Agency v. Mink*, 410 U.S. 73
United States Supreme Court 28.04.1975, *National Labor Relations Board v. Sears, Roebuck and Company*, 421 U.S. 132
United States Supreme Court 24.06.1975, *Federal Aviation Administration v. Robertson*, 422 U.S. 255
United States Supreme Court 18.04.1979, *Chrysler Corporation v. Brown*, 441 U.S. 281
United States Court of Appeals for the District of Columbia Circuit 29.04.1986, *Crooker v. Bureau of Alcohol, Tobacco & Firearms*, 789 F.2d 64
United States Supreme Court 22.03.1989, *U.S. Department of Justice v. Reporters Committee for Freedom of the Press*, 489 U.S. 749
United States Supreme Court 23.06.1989, *Tax Analysts v. Department of Justice*, 429 U.S. 136
United States Supreme Court 11.12.1989, *John Doe v. John Doe Corporation*, 493 U.S. 146
United States Supreme Court 16.12.1991, *U.S. Department of State v. Ray, et al.*, 502 U.S. 164
United States Supreme Court 24.05.1993, *Department of Justice v. Landano*, 508 U.S. 165
United States Supreme Court 23.02.1994, *U.S. Department of Defense, et al. v. Federal Labor Relations Authority, et al.*, 510 U.S. 487
United States Court of Appeals for the District of Columbia Circuit 17.06.2003, *Center for National Security Studies v. U.S. Department of Justice*, 331 F.3d 918
United States Supreme Court 01.03.2011, *Federal Communications Commission, et al. v. American Telephone and Telegraph Inc., et al.*, 131 S. Ct. 1177
United States Supreme Court 07.03.2011, *Milner v. Department of the Navy*, 131 S.Ct. 1259
United States Supreme Court 30.03.2004, *National Archives and Records Administration v. Favish*, 541 U.S. 157

# Chapter 5
# The Swedish Legal Framework on the Right of Access to Official Documents

**Patricia Jonason**

## Contents



P. Jonason (✉)
Södertörn University, Huddinge, Stockholm, Sweden
e-mail: patricia.jonason@sh.se

 
H.-J. Blanke, R. Perlingeiro (eds.), *The Right of Access to Public Information*,
DOI 10.1007/978-3-662-55554-5_5

The Swedish legal framework on the right of access to information—or more precisely the legal framework on the right of access to official documents—is not only distinctive because it is the worlds' oldest, since its first adoption dates back to 1766.[1] It is also distinguished by virtue of its legislative technique, as the right of access to official documents is partly regulated at the constitutional level as opposed to being solely mentioned and guaranteed in general terms in the constitution, as it is common in national legal systems.[2]

The following presentation of the Swedish legal framework on the right of access to official documents will be divided in six sections. The first, introductory section, provides a general picture of the right of access to information in Sweden, whereas the succeeding sections respectively deals with the scope of the right of access to official documents (Sect. 2), the limitations of the right (Sect. 3), the procedure of access to official documents (Sect. 4), the relationship between freedom of access and the rules of access in accordance with the legislation on administrative procedure (Sect. 5), and the compliance mechanisms to strengthen the application of the right of access to official documents (Sect. 6).

## 1 Generalities About the Right of Access to Information in Sweden

After examining the rationales of the right of access to official documents (Sect. 1.1) we will present shortly the pieces of legislation of relevance for the exercise of this right (Sect. 1.2).

### *1.1 The Rationales of the Right of Access to Official Documents*

The right of access to official documents is in Sweden fundamentally seen as a tool to achieve a transparent exercise of the state's powers. In conjunction with the right of access to court hearings and the right of access to meetings of decision-making assemblies, as well as together with the principle of freedom of communication for public officers,[3] it forms the so-called *Offentlighetsprincip*. This principle, which means that citizens have the right to an unimpeded view of activities pursued by public authorities,[4] is approximately translated in English as *Principle of Public*

[1]The right of access to official documents was included in the first Freedom of the Press Act enacted on December 2nd 1766. On the sources and history of the right of access of information in Sweden, see for instance Pöysti 2010.

[2]As for example in the Brazilian context. See the Constitution of Brazil, Article 5, item XIV.

[3]This legal institute, called "meddelarfrihet", constitutes a sort of whistle-blower right. It allows civil servants – and other- to communicate, for publishing purposes, information that normally should be to be kept secret, without being penalised.

[4]Sefastsson 2003, p. 11.

*Access*[5] or *Principle of Publicity*.[6] It is "above all [. . .] a general idea, an ideology",[7] whose most preeminent component,[8] often assimilated to the principle itself,[9] is the right of access to official documents.

The main rationales attributed to the principle of access to information are, besides that it strengthens the control of the administration by the citizens, that it facilitates a free democratic exchange of views and contributes to the improvement of the efficiency of the administration.

## 1.2 Short Presentation of the Swedish Legal Framework on the Right of Access to Information

The right of access to official documents is enshrined primarily in the second Chapter of the Freedom of the Press Act (1949:105) supplemented by the Public Access to Information and Secrecy Act (2009:400).

The *Freedom of the Press Act* (hereinafter referred to as FPA), which forms together with three other fundamental laws[10] the Constitution of Sweden, dedicates its second Chapter to the right of access to official documents. Under the heading *On the public nature of official documents*, this chapter regulates different aspects of the access to information regime: it poses the definition of the term *official document*, lays down the general rules on when documents may be kept secret and sets out the procedure of getting access to official documents.[11]

---

[5]See for instance *Public Access to Information and Secrecy Act – Information concerning public access to information and secrecy legislation* (2009), Ministry of Justice.

[6]See for instance Elder 1973. However, it constitutes one of those legal institutes that are so peculiar and interwoven with a certain legal and societal context that all attempt to find an adequate translation in another language are futile.

[7]Hans-Gunnar Axberger, who was a Parliamentary Ombudsman between 2008 and 2013, made this comment regarding the right of access to official documents. However, the remark may apply on the principle of access in its entirety. See Lecture held on May the 3rd 2011 in Brussels at a conference arranged by the Council of Europe. *Redogörelse 2011/12:JO1 Justitieombudsmännens ämbetsberättelse*.

[8]Bohlin 2012, p. 19.

[9]It is interesting to note that the Principle of Public Access is frequently assimilated with the sole right of access to information. Indeed, when asked to define the principle of public access, citizens relate often exclusively to the right of access to official documents, forgetting the other components of the principle.

[10]Those fundamental laws are the Instrument of Government, the Act of Succession and the Fundamental Law on Freedom of Expression.

[11]The Instrument of Government itself mentions the right to receive information in its catalogue of fundamental rights. Chapter 2, Article 1 guarantees that all citizens have the right of (2) freedom of information: that is, the freedom to procure and receive information and otherwise acquaint oneself with the utterances of others.

Adopted in 1949, the Freedom of the Press Act has been amended several times since its enactment. The most consequential reform concerning the second Chapter took place in 1976 and aimed to adapt the legal framework—and not least the definition of the "documents" covered by the Act—to keep pace with developments in technology, which resulted in the passage from a paper-based administration to a digitised administration.

The *Public Access to Information and Secrecy Act* (hereinafter referred to as PAISA) from 2009,[12] which is a voluminous act of legislative status containing more than 400 provisions, supplements the FPA. It contains among other provisions on public authorities' handling of official documents such as general measures for facilitating the searching of official documents and provisions on registration and secrecy marking of official documents. Furthermore, it includes provisions on disclosure of official documents and information, as well as provisions on appeal. The major party of the Act is, however, constituted of provisions, both general and specific, regulating secrecy.

Beside those two major pieces of legislation, one can also mention the Public Access to Information and Secrecy Ordinance (2009:641), the Fees Ordinance (1992:191), and the Municipal Act (1986:223). The Public Access to Information and Secrecy Ordinance (hereinafter referred to as PAISO), enacted by the Government, contains provisions supplementing the PAISA, while the Fees Ordinance and the Municipal Act regulate respectively the fees to be levied when copies of documents are provided by state agencies or by the regional or local governments.

## 2 The Scope of the Right of Access

Both Swedish citizens[13] and foreign nationals[14] are entitled by the Freedom of the Press Act to have free access to *official documents*. Before considering in more depth what is meant by the concept of 'official' document, which delimits the scope *ratione materiae* of the right of access enshrined at the constitutional level (Sect. 2.4), we aim firstly to establish the kind of access the Swedish legislation on access to information provides for in terms of the obligations incumbent on the public authorities (Sect. 2.1); secondly, to discuss the issue of the right of access to information extracted from an official document (Sect. 2.2); and, thirdly, to address the question of whether the right of access to official documents encompasses the right of citizens to require from the administration to produce documents on demand (Sect. 2.3).

[12]It replaces the Secrecy Act from 1980, which in turn had replaced a Secrecy Act from 1937.

[13]Chap. 2, Sec. 1 FPA.

[14]Chap. 2, Sec. 14 (5) FPA, which provides for this possibility also states that the foreign citizens right of access may be restrained by means of an act of Parliament (Riksdag).

## 2.1 A Reactive Right of Access to Information

The Freedom of the Press Act only regulates the right of access to official documents upon request, which, seen from the Government perspective, constitutes the *passive* or *reactive* aspect of the right of access. Proactive disclosure, which represents the *active* aspect of the right of access and consists of obligations for the public authorities to disseminate information without the need for a specific request, is on the contrary not directly covered by the genuine freedom of information legal framework. Nevertheless, inclined to openness and transparency, several Swedish public authorities are used to disclosing information of their own accord, using especially their websites for that purpose.[15] Additionally, in the context of e-government policies, there is an encouragement to disclose information proactively, especially for improving the conditions for the re-use of public sector information.[16]

## 2.2 Access to Information Extracted from a Document

The right of access laid down at the constitutional level concerns *documents*. However, the Access to Information and Secrecy Act states the obligation for public authorities to, upon request from an individual, disclose *information* from an official document (Chap. 6, Sec. 4 of PAISA). The provisions on the right to get information orally are less protective than the right of access enshrined in the FPA. There is no explicit requirement to deal with the request promptly as is the case for the right of access to official documents. Furthermore, there is no right of appeal attached to this type of right of access.[17] Nevertheless, the rules laid down in Chap. 6, Sec. 4 of PAISA "have to be considered being an important complement to the right to view of activities pursued by public authorities set out in the Freedom of the Press Act" as the Parliamentary Ombudsman put it, underlying that it is important that the administration applies these rules correctly.[18]

[15]This habit, particularly present in regional and local governments, may be problematic from a legal standpoint when personal information is disclosed on the Internet, leading to breaches of the data protection legislation. The Data inspection Board, the authority in charge of monitoring the Data Protection legislation, has published a checklist to be used by regional and local authorities to avoid that kind of infringements. See http://www.datainspektionen.se/lagar-och-regler/personuppgiftslagen/e-forvaltning/webbpublicering-av-protokoll-och-diarier/.

[16]See *Vidareutnyttjande av offentlig information – En vägledning för myndigheter* (2013), e-delegation.

[17]See for example the Parliamentary Ombudsman's decision of 9 December 2010 in case No. 6673-2009.

[18]See JO 1990/91, p. 382, quoted in the Parliamentary Ombudsman's decision of 9 December 2010 in case No. 6673-2009.

## 2.3 Access to "Potential Documents"

The point of departure in Swedish law is that the right of access to official documents applies to documents that already exist in the shape they are requested and that public authorities have no duty to produce a "new" document using information contained in existing documents.[19] The legislator, inclined to take into consideration the possibilities offered by information technology for improving the right of access, has, however, extended the right of access to "potential documents", i.e., compilation of electronic data that the administration is able to produce with the means of data that is kept by the administration.[20]

Nevertheless, access to potential documents cannot be unlimited. The obligation of the administration to carry on a compilation of data prevails, according to Chap. 2, Sec. 3.2 FPA, so long the public authority can produce the document "using routine means".[21] The wording of the Freedom of the Press Act, which corresponds to an enshrinement of the principle of accessibility (*tillgänglighetsprincipen*)[22] for determining the scope of the obligation incumbent on the administration to produce new documents, is simultaneously consistent with the principle of equivalence (*likställighetsprincipen*), according to which the public should have access to documents, including recordings, to the same extent as the administration itself.[23]

## 2.4 The Scope Ratione Materiae of the Right of Access to Information: The Concept of Official Document

The FPA provides for the right of access to documents that are official *(allmänna handlingar)*.[24] A document is considered an official document when it is a

---

[19]Bohlin 2012, p. 54.

[20]See for instance Seipel 1988.

[21]This provision indeed states that "a compilation of information taken from material recorded for automatic data processing is [. . .] regarded as being held by the authority only if the authority can make it available using routine means".

[22]According to the principle of accessibility, which emerged in the 1970s, each collection of information linked together in a coherent manner and made comprehensible with routine means, constitutes a document in the sense of the Freedom of the Press Act (see Magnusson Sjöberg 1992, p. 410). This theory is opposed to the one of fixation (*fixeringsprincipen*) according to which the public should be entitled to have access to potential documents, which have been envisaged in advance *inter alia* by means of a list of key words allowing to produce those documents (see Ryden 1986, p. 40).

[23]The technological development providing the administration with possibilities to produce new constellations of data consequently enlarges the number of documents public authorities can have access to. The principle of accessibility enables the public to have equal access to this augmented amount of documents.

[24]A discussion on the terminology used by the FPA and specifically on the adjective *"allmän"* is conducted in Blanc-Gonnet Jonason P. 2001.

*document* that is held by a public authority and when the document can be deemed to have been received or drawn up by such an authority. The determination of the scope of application *ratione materiae* of the right of access to official documents presupposes therefore to define what the concepts of document (Sect. 2.4.1) and public authority (Sect. 2.4.2), as well as the expressions held (Sect. 2.4.3), received and drawn up (Sect. 2.4.4) by an authority mean.

### 2.4.1 The Concept of Document

The Swedish law adopts a neutral technical approach for defining the concept of document.[25] Indeed, according to Chap. 2, Sec. 3 FPA a "[d]ocument is understood to mean any written or pictorial matter or recording which may be read, listened to, or otherwise comprehended only using technical aids". Such a definition allows for new technological formats, such as cookies[26] or text messages. However, to be classed as a document, the information has to be fixed to a form of media—such as a paper sheet, a tape, etc.—so that the content can be kept and examined many times.[27] Consequently, a telephone call is not a document in itself but becomes a document if the call is transcribed on paper or is recorded.[28] Indeed, as the Swedish Supreme Administrative Court pointed out, there is a document when there is "a form for storing and keeping information".[29]

### 2.4.2 The Concept of Public Authority

A document has to be deemed as held by a public authority to be considered official and, therefore, potentially subject to the right of access to official documents. The concept of public authority as it is employed in the Freedom of the Press Act and in the Public Access to Information and Secrecy Act is so to say an "autonomous concept" within the Swedish legal order. Indeed, for the purpose of the application of the legislation on the right of access, the concept has been extended, by analogy, for comprising public entities that do not fall into the traditional meaning given to the term in Swedish law. It covers also, to a certain extent, publicly owned entities and private entities.

[25]In the same manner as the Brazilian law (Article 4, item 2 of the Brazilian Law N° 12.5272011).

[26]See Administrative Supreme Court (Regeringsrättens), RÅ 1999 ref. 18, cases n° 3148-1998 and 5556-1998 (Judgment of 19 April 1999).

[27]Strömberg & Lundell 2009, p. 15.

[28]Strömberg & Lundell 2009, p. 15.

[29]See Administrative Supreme Court (Regeringsrättens), RÅ 1971:15, quoted by Bohlin 2012, p. 42.

When it concerns the public sector *stricto sensu*, beside the authorities[30] defined as public authorities according to the Instrument of Government—i.e., the Government, the courts, as well as the central and municipal governments—the Parliament (the Riksdag) and the local government assemblies (county council and municipal assemblies) are also deemed to be public authorities. Those entities are indeed expressly equated to public authorities by the FPA (Chap. 2, Sec. 5) and by the PAISA (Chap. 2, Sec. 2).[31]

In a similar manner, entities related to the public sector but outside the public sector *stricto sensu* are equated with public authorities. Indeed, the PAISA (Chap. 2, Sec. 3) extends, in a general manner, the application of the second Chapter of the FPA (and the application of the PAISA itself) to limited companies, partnerships, for-profit associations and companies and foundations where a municipality or a county council exercises legal powers of control. The criteria for appreciating, if a municipality or a county council exercises the decisive legal influence, are precisely defined in the PAISA (Chap. 2, Sec. 3).

The constitutional and legislative rules governing the right of access to official documents apply additionally to several bodies belonging to the private sector, when it comes to certain of their activities as specified in the Appendix of the PAISA (which Chap. 2, Sec. 4 FPA refers to). The extension of the scope of the right of access to official documents to private bodies is justified by the fact that the listed entities, in these specific cases, either exercise public power[32] and/or deal with public resources.[33]

### 2.4.3 A Document Held by a Public Authority

The qualify criteria of 'official'—which is the condition for being covered by the right of access—presupposes that the document is being considered held by a public authority. The criteria for determining whether a document is *held* or not by a public authority differ depending on the format of the document. For conventional documents—i.e., documents that do not need the use of technical aids to be comprehended—the physical place of the storage is in principle decisive for

[30]In the precedent Swedish Freedom of the Press Acts, the legislative technique employed consisted of an enumeration of the public authorities liable to apply the legal framework on the right of access to official documents. See Bohlin 2012, p. 58.

[31]The Royal family is anyhow not covered by the legislation on the right of access to official documents.

[32]For instance, Posten AB, which is a joint stock company dealing with postal services, is subject to the provisions on the right of access to official documents when it concerns the arrangement for the conduct of elections and referendums, including the postal voting, which Posten AB takes care of.

[33]For example, the Stockholm School of Economics is liable to apply the legislation on the right of access when it concerns documents related to the allocation of public resources to research students.

determining if the document is deemed to be held by a public authority. However, it is not necessary for the document in question to be physically in the possession of the public authority when the request is made.[34] It is enough that the document should have been in the possession of the authority but is temporarily in the hands of a civil servant or with someone else from whom the public authority can easily demand the document back.[35]

The criteria for determination are different when it concerns the documents that the FPA calls "recordings". The Swedish legislator has indeed considered their technical specificities. Those documents are deemed to be held by a public authority under the condition that they are "available to the authority using technical aids, which the authority itself employs, for communication in such form that [they] may be read, listened to, or otherwise comprehended". In other words, the possession presupposes that the public authority disposes *de facto* of the possibility to transfer the recording into reading format or other format for being comprehended.[36] Although the criteria of storage are related to the accessibility of the information itself, the physical storage of the medium is often decisive for determining where the recording is stored.[37] However, when it concerns automated data processing, the record may be deemed accessible to an authority—and held by it—not only when the data is stored in the computers of the public authority but also when the authority can access it by means of a terminal connection. As mentioned earlier, compilations are, however, regarded as held by the authority only if the authority can extract them using routine means (Chap. 2, Sec. 3.2 FPA). If the request concerns compilation of personal data for automatic data processing, the technical possibility to access the data is nevertheless not a sufficient condition for considering the recording held by a public authority. In that case it is also required that the authority has the legal competence to transfer the recording into a comprehensible format.[38] Indeed, according to Chap. 2, Sec. 3.3 FPA, "A compilation of information taken from material recorded for automatic data processing is not [...] regarded as being held by the authority if the compilation contains personal information and the authority is not authorized in law, or under a statutory instrument, to make the compilation available". This provision has a protective purpose and aims to prevent the situation where members of the public access compilations of personal data that the public authority is legally impeached to produce for considerations related to the protection of privacy.

The qualification "official" does not imply that the content of the document has to be related to "public affairs". Therefore, an official document may concern all kinds of issues. However, the letters and messages that are addressed to the public servants at the authority are only considered to be official documents "if they refer

[34]Strömberg & Lundell 2009, p. 16.

[35]Strömberg & Lundell 2009, p. 16.

[36]Bohlin 2012, p. 53.

[37]Bohlin 2012, p. 53.

[38]Bohlin 2012, p. 56.

to a case or other matter falling within the authority's purview, and if it is not intended for the addressee solely in his capacity as incumbent of another position" (Chap 2, Sect. 4 FPA). Other documents are exempted from the qualification of "official documents": the documents held by a public authority as part of a technical processing or technical storage (Chap. 2, Sec. 6.3 FPA), the documents intended solely for the purpose of forwarding a communication (Chap. 2, Sec. 11.1 FPA), the documents intended solely for the purpose of publication in a periodical (Chap. 2, Sec. 11.1 FPA) and the documents forming part of a library or deposited by a private person in a public archive (Chap. 2, Sec. 11.1 FPA).

### 2.4.4 A Document Received or Drawn up by a Public Authority

The qualification of official presupposes additionally that the document held by a public authority has been received or drawn up by the authority. As for the concept of "held", the criteria for ascertaining whether documents are considered to be received by a public authority is contingent on the format of the documents. The general rule[39] concerning conventional documents is that those documents are deemed to have been received by a public authority when they have arrived at the authority or are in the hands of a competent official (Chap. 2, Sec. 6 FPA). "Competent official" refers to the person in charge of receiving the documents (the registrar) and the official in charge of the case the document is related to.[40] The document is also considered as received if the civil servant has received it at his/her private home address[41] or to his/her personal e-mail account.[42] The same rules might apply regarding SMS messages.[43] Regarding the documents consisting of recordings, the rule is that they are deemed "received" when they have been made comprehensible by another (Chap. 2, Sec. 6 FPA). The word "another" meaning an external person (*utomstående*), such as another public authority or a data company.[44]

The term "drawn up" used by the FPA relates to the fact that the documents in question have been produced by the authority itself, but also suggests that the documents are considered to be official documents when they "exist in their definitive form".[45] Before reaching this final stage, the documents are considered as internal working material and are not covered by the right of access to information. The moment when a document can be considered to be drawn up varies between different kinds of documents. Chap. 2, Sec. 7 FPA lays down the general

[39]There are special rules concerning competition and tender documents.

[40]Strömberg & Lundell 2009, p. 24.

[41]See for example the case JO 1989/90 mentioned by Bohlin 2012, p. 69.

[42]Bohlin 2012, p. 69.

[43]Bohlin 2012, p. 69.

[44]Bohlin 2012, p. 70.

[45]Bohlin 2012, p. 80.

rules aiming to apply to the majority of documents. According to the first general rule, a document is deemed received when an authority sends it out. For documents that are not subject to dispatching, Chap. 2, Sec. 7 FPA provides for two cases. In the first case, the document is deemed to have been drawn up when the matter to which it relates has been finally settled by the authority. In the second case, when the document does not pertain to a specific matter, it is deemed to be drawn up when it has been finally checked and approved by the authority or has otherwise received its final form.

The FPA provides also for special rules concerning specific categories of documents, for instance for documents that are kept on an on-going basis (such as diaries and journals) and for judgments (Chap. 2, Sec. 7.2 FPA).

It has to be said that the classification of "official document" is not related to the registration of the document, which means that the documents do not need to be registered by the authorities to constitute official documents.[46]

A document fulfilling the above mentioned requirements—i.e., *held* by a *public authority* and *received* or *drawn up* by such an authority—is deemed as an official document covered by the right of access. However, such a document is only accessible when it is *public*, which means when the document is not encompassed by specific secrecy provisions. Indeed, the right of access may be submitted to limitations.

## 3 The Limitations of the Right of Access to Official Documents

After presenting the general rules setting out limitations to the right of access (Sect. 3.1) we aim to focus more in depth on two kinds of limitations: the limitations aimed to protect public interests (Sect. 3.2) and the limitations intended for protecting personal information (Sect. 3.3). This section will end with a brief comparison between the Swedish and the Brazilian methods for restricting access to information (Sect. 3.4).

### *3.1 General Features Concerning the Limitations of the Right of Access*

The general principle guiding the Swedish regime on access to official documents is openness. Therefore, the possibilities to restrict the right of access to official documents are strictly circumscribed. This stringent approach is firstly because of the legal technique employed to set out limitations (Sect. 3.1.1), and secondly

[46]Bohlin 2012, p. 69.

due to the obligation incumbent on civil servants to systematically conduct a secrecy review in the concrete case when secrecy provisions may apply (Sect. 3.1.2).

### 3.1.1 The Legal Framework Setting Out Limitations to the Right of Access

The system for limiting the right of access to information in Sweden consists of a two-level mechanism: At the first level, the Freedom of the Press Act provides in an exhaustive manner for the interests that may be protected by restricting the right of access (Chap. 2, Sec. 2). Those interests are:

1. the security of the Realm or its relations with another state or an international organisation;
2. the central fiscal, monetary or currency policy of the Realm;
3. the inspection, control or other supervisory activities of a public authority;
4. the interest of preventing or prosecuting crime;
5. the economic interest of the public institutions;
6. the protection of the personal or economic circumstances of private subjects;
7. the preservation of animal or plant species.

At the *second level*, and according to the FPA, the limitations of the right of access have to be "scrupulously specified in a provision of a special act of law, or, if this is deemed more appropriate in a particular case, in another act of law to which the special act refers" (Chap. 2, Sec. 2.2). The *Riksdag* (Parliament) has the exclusive right to decide on the secrecy provisions. However, it may entitle the Government in the above-mentioned special Act to issue supplementary rules for the application of the special Act.

The adverb "scrupulously" (*noga*) used by the fundamental law signifies that the provisions providing for restrictions on the right of access must in a clear manner state the conditions for applying secrecy, suppressing the discretionary power of the public servants to decide when the documents may be kept secret. Indeed, if the content of a certain document cannot be related to a secrecy provision, then the document has to be disclosed on request. The term "scrupulously" refers furthermore to the requirement that the rules on secrecy must be easily accessible.[47]

The "special act of law" in which the limitations of the right of access to information have been laid down according to the requirement of the FPA is the Public Access to Information and Secrecy Act (2009:400). Several Acts of law to which the special Act refers have also been adopted, as for instance the Act on the Schengen Information System (2000:344).[48] The Government has been entitled to enact certain kind of provisions such as exemptions from the registration requirement for documents that are kept in large numbers (Chap. 5, Sec. 3 PAISA). Those

[47] Bohlin 2012, p. 190–191.

[48] The PAISA refers to this Act in Chap. 9, Sec. 2.

Government regulations setting additional provisions are laid down in the Public Access to Information and Secrecy Ordinance (2009:641).

The secrecy provisions determine with great precision the kind of information, the sort of handling and the category of activities/public authorities that are subject to secrecy. The provisions are grouped under seven headings. Part I contains introductory provisions about the issues regulated in the Act; Part II contains provisions on authorities' handling of official documents; Part III gathers general provisions about secrecy; Part IV contains secrecy provisions aiming to protect public interests; Part V encompasses secrecy provisions that protect information about the personal or financial circumstances of the individuals; Part VI contains special provisions on secrecy at particular bodies (inter alia the *Riksdag*, the Government, the Parliamentary Ombudsmen and the courts); and, lastly, Part VII contains provisions on the duty of confidentiality. It is interesting to note that the Swedish legislation contains provisions concerning specifically the issue of secrecy between public authorities (such as for example Chap. 6, Sec. 5; Chap. 7, Sec. 2 and 3, Chap. 8, Sec. 2 PAISA).

The system adopted by the Swedish legislator, which uses both the constitutional instrument (the FPA) and a legislative Act (the PAISA) for setting out the limitations of the right of access, differs from the Brazilian one where the provisions limiting the right of access to information are laid down at law level only.

### 3.1.2 Application of the Secrecy Provisions

Having regard to the two levels—constitutional and legislative—of the secrecy framework, the public officers shall only refuse to disclose a document when they can point out a specific provision of the PAISA. Those secrecy provisions with their detailed precision leave no margin of manoeuvre for the official when it concerns the scope of application of the provisions. However, the official detained a certain margin of appreciation regarding how to interpret in each specific case the "requirement of damage" set out in the provisions.[49] Indeed, except for the few provisions that do not lay down any special condition for the applicability of secrecy and which provide for so called "absolute secrecy",[50] the secrecy provisions contain the requirement that certain special conditions, formulated as "requirement of harm", have to be met for public officers to be able to refuse to disclose information. This requirement signifies that secrecy applies when assessing that some stated *risk of harm* arises if the information contained in the document is disclosed. Harm may, depending on the specific case, refer to economic harm (*skada*), or privacy infringements (*men*).[51] The requirements are classified in two categories: the straight

[49]Blanc-Gonnet Jonason 2001, p. 70.

[50]This is the case, for example, concerning information given in the context of municipal family counselling (Chap. 26, Sec. 3 PAISA).

[51]Bohlin 2012, p. 203–204.

requirement of harm and the reversed requirement of harm. The straight requirement of harm assumes disclosure to be the main rule. Secrecy applies in this case only if it can be deemed that a stated risk will occur. Such a straight requirement applies for example in the activities of the Competition Authority regarding supervision and investigation when it concerns information on business secrets[52] (Chap. 30, Sec. 1 PAISA). The reversed requirement of harm assumes to the contrary that secrecy is the main rule, unless it is manifestly evident that the information may be disclosed without causing the harm stated in the relevant secrecy provision. This is for instance the case concerning information concerning a private party's personal circumstances held by social services (Chap. 26, Sec. 1 PAISA).

Secrecy is, as in Brazilian law, limited in time. Several provisions of the PAISA contain rules regarding the longest period secrecy may be applied. The time period varies between 2 and 70 years[53] depending on the category of information concerned, as the risk attached to the disclosure of the information is not the same for all the categories. However, those periods have to be considered as maximum time and not as standards.[54]

In the case that a document contains information that can be assumed to be subject to secrecy according to PAISA, the main rule is that the authority *may (får)* mark this by a special note—a "secrecy mark". The law specifies that the note has to be made directly on the document (Chap. 5, Sec. 5 PAISA). Concerning electronic documents, the note is entered into the document or in the data system where the document is handled (Chap. 5, Sec. 5 PAISA). The note shall provide information about the relevant secrecy provision, the date when the note was made and identify the authority which has made the note.

In any case, secrecy is applied independently of the marking procedure and a secrecy mark is only to be considered to operate as a "warning signal" and does not release the official from the duty to carry out a secrecy review for each request.

In practice, when the conditions for secrecy are fulfilled, the limitations affecting the right of access consist in the public officers' refusal to disclose the entire document requested or in the refusal to disclose some parts of a document. The limitation may also take the form of a reservation pronounced by the public authority, which means that the document required is disclosed but the public authority limits the requester's right to re-communicate or use the information. A reservation can consist, for instance, of a prohibition against the requester using the information for purposes other than research.[55]

---

[52] "A private party's business or operational circumstances, inventions and research results" as the law states.

[53] In some cases the possibility exists to introduce longer periods (see the next section of this chapter titled Secrecy and the protection for public interests).

[54] Bohlin 2012, p. 209.

[55] The requester may be held criminally liable if he/she does not respect the reservation (Chap. 20, Sec. 3 of the Penal Code).

An illustrative example of the requirements posed by PAISA and their interpretation by the courts is provided by a famed case related to a request to get access to the so-called Scientology Bible.[56] The Scientology Bible had been sent to and received by several Swedish authorities, and was therefore considered an official document subject to requests of access. Some of the authorities accepted to disclose the requested document, leading to the protest of the American authorities, which argued that Sweden was infringing its obligations regarding copyright protection under the Bern Convention and the TRIPs agreement.[57] The Swedish Government, one of the public authorities to which the request was made, decided to deny access to the Scientology Bible based on Chapter 2, Sec. 1 of the then-applicable 1980 Secrecy Act. The Act stated secrecy for information "which concerns Sweden's relation to another country or concerns another state, international organisation, public authority, citizen or moral person from another state or stateless if it can be deemed that it will disturb Sweden's international relations or, in another manner, will harm the country if the information is disclosed".

The requester of the Bible, following the steps of the appeal procedure, first brought an action to an administrative court of appeal, and then, after the court refused to grant the claim, lodged an appeal at the Administrative Supreme Court. When examining if the harms requirement for applying secrecy was fulfilled, the Court, referring to preparatory works and former case-law, stated that it must be the concrete content of the information, or in some cases the nature or connecting factors to international relations or other international activities, that cause that the disclosure of the information may harm the country. This condition was not fulfilled. As the Court expressed it, "[in the present case] it is not the circumstance that the content of the requested document be known or that information of this sort be disclosed that can be deemed to generate the disturbance, but the application in Sweden of a legal framework which gives priority to the principle of publicity before copyright." The Government could therefore not refuse to give access to the Scientology Bible.[58]

## 3.2 Secrecy and the Protection of Public Interests

Secrecy provisions for the protection of public interests are gathered in Part IV of the PAISA, constituting Chapters 15 to 20, which encompasses about 50 provisions. The secrecy provisions cover the security of the Realm or its relations with another state or an international organisation; the central fiscal, monetary or currency policy of the Realm; inspection, control or other supervisory activities of a public

[56]Administrative Supreme Court (Regeringsrättens), RÅ 1998 ref 42 (Judgment of 17 June 1998).

[57]Trade Related Aspects of Intellectual Property Rights.

[58]A secrecy provision that protect copyright under certain conditions was introduced to the 1980 Secrecy Act two years after this court decision. It is now to be found in PAISA.

authority; economic interest of the public institutions; the interest of preventing or prosecuting crime; the economic interest of the public institutions and the preservation of animal or plant species.[59]

The interests protected by the Swedish legislation are thus similar as the ones guaranteed by Brazilian law, although some differences exist. Indeed, the Swedish legislation refers to the preservation of animal or plant species, which the Brazilian law does not mention. On the contrary, the Swedish law does not lay down as interests which may be taken into consideration for limiting the right of access, the life, safety or health of the population, nor the scientific or technological research and development projects, as does the Brazilian Law (Article 23.3, respectively Article 23, item 6 Brazilian Law N°12.527 2011). Additionally the specific protection set out in the Brazilian law through the mechanism of classification provided for information that might jeopardise the safety of the highest political officials (the President and Vice-President of the Republic) and their family members (Article 24 para 2 Brazilian Law N°12.527 2011) has no counterpart in the Swedish legal framework.

Some specific secret marking rules apply concerning documents that are of great importance to national security. In this particular case the marking is compulsory and the note shall indicate which authority is empowered to determine whether the document may be released (Chap. 5, Sec. 5 PAISA). The secrecy period varies depending on the type of information concerned. It is, for example, 20 years when secrecy is aimed to protect public subjects' financial circumstances and 40 years when it concerns the international relations of the Realm or defence issues. The Government is entitled to decide that the secrecy period shall be longer for defence secrets, when "particular reasons" exist. The secrecy period has on that basis been extended to 150 years when it concerns, *inter alia*, certain defence buildings (*fasta försvarsanläggningar*) (Sec. 4 PAISA).

### 3.3 Secrecy and the Protection of Personal Information

Before going deeper on this issue we aim to shortly present how the Swedish legislator perceives and regulates the relationship between the legislation on the

[59]In a case brought before the European Court of Human Rights, the plaintiff Mr. Leander, who had been refused employment by a Maritime Museum located on a naval base after information on him had appeared in a register of the Swedish Security Service, complained that he should have been provided with the information in question and that Sweden had infringed his freedom to receive information under Article 10 of the European Convention. Nevertheless the Strasbourg Court states that "the right to freedom to receive information basically prohibits a Government from restricting a person from receiving information that others wish or may be willing to impart to him. Article 10 does not, in circumstances such as those of the present case, confer on the individual a right of access to a register containing information on his personal position, nor does it embody an obligation on the Government to impart such information to the individual." European Court of Human Rights, *Leander v. Sweden* (Judgment of 26 March 1987), Nr. 9248/81.

right of access to information and the legislation on data protection. This question, which has been especially highlighted at the time of the drafting of the European Data Protection Directive 95/46/EC,[60] is at stake again because of the adoption of the European Data Protection Regulation 2016/679.[61] At the time the *Data protection Directive* was drafted the Swedish authorities were feared that the transposition of the European text would impair the generous right of access to information as laid down in the Freedom of the Press Act. For this reason, they pushed for the introduction of a recital 72 in the Preamble of the Directive. Recital 72 states that "[. . .] this Directive allows the principle of public access to official documents to be taken into account when implementing the principles set out in this Directive." The Swedish transposition Act, the Personal Data Act (1998:204), has in turn been provided with a provision (Sec. 8)[62] according to which "The provisions of this Act are not applied to the extent that they would limit an authority's obligation under Chapter 2 of the Freedom of the Press Act to provide personal data". The EU Regulation, which supersedes the EU Directive, will not impact this regime. In fact, as the Swedish Government notes in the terms of reference it established to guide the special investigator appointed for proposing adaptations and complements of the legislation in place, "the Data protection regulation contains provisions providing a clear margin for the national legislation to regulate the relationship between on one side the protection for personal data and, on the other side [. . .] the publicity principle".[63] The Government, which refers to Article 80a of the Regulation when it concerns the question of the compatibility of the legislation on the right of access to information and the protection of personal data, underlines further that "it is even clearer as it is in the Data Protection Directive that the European Data Protection legislation does not impinge the field of the Freedom of the Press Act [. . .]."[64] Consequently, "it is not a part to the mandate of the special investigator to consider nor propose constitutional amendments".[65]

Access to personal information is—like access to other kinds of information—only restricted if the PAISA provides for secrecy in the circumstances of the specific case and the public officer in charge of the requested document considers, after having carried on a "secrecy review", that the information cannot be disclosed. This system is profoundly different to the Brazilian regime where sensitive personal information "relating to intimacy, private life, honor and image" (Article 31.1) benefit from a special protection. Indeed, access to this kind of personal information

---

[60]Directive 95/46/EC of the European Parliament and of the Council of 24 October 1995 on the protection of individuals with regard to the processing of personal data and on the free movement of such data.

[61]Regulation (EU) 2016/679 of the European Parliament and of the Council of 27 April 2016 on the protection of natural persons with regard to the processing of personal data and on the free movement of such data.

[62]Under the heading "Relationship to the principle of public access to official documents".

[63]Kommittedirektiv Dataskyddsförordningen Dir. 2016:15, p. 21.

[64]Kommittedirektiv Dataskyddsförordningen Dir. 2016:15, p. 22.

[65]Kommittedirektiv Dataskyddsförordningen Dir. 2016:15, p. 22. See also SOU 2017:39, p. 21.

is restricted for a 100-year period, regardless of the secrecy classification. Additionally, during this period, only the authorised public agents and the individuals the information refers to may access the information, unless the dissemination or access is permitted by a legal provision or the consent of the person the information refers to (Art 31.1 (1) and (2)).

Other secrecy grounds, as those contained or referred to in the PAISA, are not accepted by the courts. This has been established in a case from 2006[66] concerning the refusal of the National Audit Office (riksrevision) to disclose personality tests carried out as part of an employment procedure, invoking that the disclosure would violate Article 8 of the European Convention on Human Rights. Recognising that the Convention had been incorporated into the Swedish legal order in 1995, reminding of the Constitutional rules limiting access to information,[67] and noting that the Secrecy Act makes no mention of the European Convention, the Administrative Supreme Court didn't acknowledge the grounds of refusal put forward by the public authority.[68]

In addition to the detailed secrecy provisions for the protection of personal or financial circumstances for the private subjects laid down in Part VI of the PAISA (encompassing Chapters 21 to 40 with more than 250 provisions) there is also a provision that considers specifically the conflict that may occur between access to information legislation and data protection legislation. Indeed, Chapter 21, Sect. 7 PAISA states that secrecy applies on personal information if it can be deemed that disclosure can lead to a violation of the Data Protection Act.

In 2015, the Supreme Court applied this provision in a case regarding the request of a digital copy of a court's register (dagboksblad) for the period 2010–2012.[69] The Court stated that the assessment of the conditions for secrecy posed by Chap. 21, Sec. 7 PAISA that the disclosure would lead to the processing of personal data in a manner that violates the Data Protection Act has to be made with regard to the intended use the requester will make of the information, and not with regard to the disclosure itself. As the requested court's register contained data about criminal offences, their processing was prohibited for the requester, who was not a public authority (Article 8(5) DPA). One of the questions to clarify was then if the plaintiff could claim the exception contained in the Data Protection Act, which states that the Act does not apply "in the course of a purely personal or household activity" (Article 3(2) DPA). The Swedish Court, making *inter alia* reference to the

[66]Administrative Supreme Court (Regeringsrättens), RÅ 2006, ref 87 (Judgment of 27 November 2006).

[67]See Sect. 3.1.1.

[68]Interesting to notice is that in only discussing Article 8 of the European Convention as a national legal ground (the Convention, incorporated in the Swedish legal order has law status) the court ignores the international side of this provision and the arguments put forward by the National Audit Office for invoking it and the reference this public authority made to the case-law of the European Court of Human Rights (Z. v. Finland, 25 February 1997).

[69]NJA 2015 p. 624.

European Case *Ryneš*,[70] in which the exception is narrowly interpreted, dismissed the plaintiff of his appeal.

The legislator has granted the person concerned by the personal information rights that may be said to be related to a kind of right to self-determination. Indeed, in principle, secrecy aimed to protect individuals does not apply in relation to the person the personal information pertains to (Chap. 12, Sec. 1 PAISA). However, PAISA provides for the possibility to make exemptions to this rule. For example, information concerning health held by the Health Care sector may be subject to secrecy in relation to the patient himself/herself if, with regard to the purpose of the care/treatment, it is of special importance that the information is not disclosed to the patient (Chap. 25, Sec. 6 PAISA). Other rights granted to the person the information pertains to are the right to waive secrecy partially or completely (Chap. 12, Sec. 2 PAISA) in relation to another private party or to an authority (Chap. 10, Sec. 1 PAISA) and the right to require that the authority makes a reservation when secret information is disclosed with his/her consent to another private party (Chap. 12, Sec. 2 PAISA).

The secrecy period applicable for the protection of personal circumstances of private subjects is usually 50 or 70 years. The period is shorter, often 20 years, when the non-disclosure rule is intended to protect private subjects' financial circumstances. Unlike many countries, if not all, whose point of departure is a high level of protection for privacy and where therefore access to personal information is strongly restricted, the conditions for accessing personal information are rather liberal and generous in Sweden.[71]

### 3.4 Brief Comparison Between the Swedish and the Brazilian Methods for Restricting Access to Information

The way of thinking about the limitations to the right of access to information and the applied legal techniques differ significantly between the Swedish and the Brazilian regimes.

The focus of the Brazilian Law is on classification, which leads to the restriction of access. The Brazilian legislator lists, in a broad manner, in Law N°12.527/2011, the interests to be taken into consideration for deciding about classification (Sect. II) while the concrete decisions to classify are taken by the authorities determined by the same law (Article 27). The focus of the Swedish legislation lies for its part on the secrecy provisions. The Swedish legislator has, as mentioned above, by means of the secrecy provisions laid down in a comprehensive piece of legislation, the

[70] Case 212/13, *František Ryneš* (ECJ 11 December 2014) para 28.

[71] As Sand put it, "there is good access to personal information", in *PSI in Sweden: from infringement to enforcement?* European Public Sector Information Platform Topic Report No. 9, 2010, p. 14.

PAISA, determined in a detailed manner the situations where access to information may be refused. If classification occurs, it has no binding effect but serves the sole purpose[72] of acting as a "warning signal." If a secrecy provision may apply, civil servants are always obliged to carry on a secrecy review to assess if the conditions laid down in the secrecy provisions are fulfilled.

The proportionality principle to be applied according to the Brazilian Law N°12.527/2011 (Art 24 para 5) for classifying information at a determined security classification has no equivalent in the Swedish legal framework. Indeed, according to the letter of the PAISA, the application of secrecy and therefore the restriction of the right of access depend on the fulfilment or not of the requirement of harm. The mechanisms laid down in Article 21 of the Brazilian Law prohibiting the denial of access to information required for the judicial and administrative protection of fundamental rights, and prohibiting restricted access for information or documents related to the commission of violations of human rights by public bodies, also have no counterpart in the Swedish legislation, except when it concerns environmental information. Indeed, according to PAISA Chapter 10, Article 5 "secrecy does not apply if it can be deemed that the information is of such significant importance from an environmental standpoint that the interest of making the information public has precedence over the interest secrecy is meant to protect".[73]

In other words, while the highest responsibility for restricting access in Brazilian law seems to rest on the authorities making the decision of classification, in Swedish law it can instead be described as lying primarily on the legislator, who decides precisely the cases where secrecy may apply, and in concrete cases on the civil servants in charge of the secrecy review.

## 4 The Procedure of Access to Official Documents

The Swedish legislation contains rules directly related to the procedure of access itself (Sect. 4.2). It also contains accessory rules intended to improve the exercise of the right of access to official documents (Sect. 4.1).

[72]With the exception of matters of national security. See Sect. 3.2.

[73]This provision has been introduced in the Swedish legal system to transpose the European Directive 2003/4/EC on environmental information.

## *4.1 Accessory Rules Improving the Exercise of the Right of Access*

Beside the rules related to the registration of documents (Sect. 4.1.1), the Swedish legislation contains rules aiming at facilitating searches for official documents (Sect. 4.1.2).

### 4.1.1 Registration of Official Documents

Public authorities are required, according to Chap. 5 PAISA, to register official documents as soon as they have received them or drawn them up (Sec. 1). The register shall contain information about the date the official documents have been received or drawn up, the registration number of the document, information about the sender or addressee of the document, if appropriate, and a short description of the content of the document (Sec. 2). Some categories of official documents are exempted from the registration requirement: documents that are obviously of little importance to the authorities' activities (such as press cuttings and advertising material), documents that are not covered by secrecy provisions[74] and are kept in a manner such that it can be ascertained without difficulty whether they have been received or drawn up by the authority, and recordings for automated data processing already registered by the authority which has made the recording available for the authority. Additionally, the Access to Information and Secrecy Ordinance exempts from the registration requirement documents that are kept in large numbers (Sec. 2[75]).

### 4.1.2 Rules Aiming at Facilitating the Searching for Official Documents

Beside the registration of the documents, which is, at least for conventional documents, a *sine qua non* condition for their retrieval, the PAISA provides in Chapter 4 for two kinds of general measures to facilitate searching for the documents: rules concerning the handling of official documents and rules concerning the description of official documents. The first set of rules (Chap. 4, Sec. 1) is related to the obligations of the public authorities to consider the principle of public access to information when they deal with official documents. The authorities have, *inter alia*, to ensure that official documents can be disclosed with the expedition required by the FPA and that official documents can be separated from other documents. They are also required to ensure that automated data processing of information is arranged in a manner that considers the interest the individuals may have in making

[74]This means, *en contrario*, that all official documents covered by secrecy must be registered.

[75]Examples are documents concerning jobseekers held by the Swedish Public Employment Service and patient journals held by hospitals.

use of technical means at the authority to access documents. Public authorities are secondly required (Chap. 4, Sec. 2 PAISA) to draw up a description providing information of, inter alia, the authority's organisation and activities, the technical means the individual may make use of, who is in charge to give information about official documents and which secrecy provisions are commonly applicable for the kind of information contained in the official documents held by the authority.

Some of the above-mentioned measures are more particularly an illustration of the concept of the so-called «good structure of access» (*god offentlighetsstruktur*), i.e., an automatised infrastructure which is appropriate for the exercise of the right of access to official documents.[76] This notion, which corresponds to the will to adapt the information technology systems of the public authorities to meet the needs of the right of access, instead of allowing the technical, financial and administrative conditions deciding the kind of IT infrastructure to be in place, has been embedded in the Swedish law since the late 1980s.

## 4.2 The Rules on the Procedure of Access

A person wishing to access a document disposes of two possibilities: the possibility to access the document *in situ*, free of charge, and the possibility to obtain a transcript or copy of the document for a fee.

The right to read or copy, photograph or record the requested document by the public authority holding the document is provided in Chap. 2, Sec. 2 of the Freedom of the Press Act. According to that provision, the document shall be made available "on request forthwith, or as soon as possible", which means that the document should be released in direct connection to the request. The delay has sometimes to be extended, for instance when a secrecy review is needed.[77] However, unnecessary delays are not allowed.[78] If the document is partially subject to secrecy, the public authority has to disclose the parts of the document that are not secret in transcript or by a copy (Chap. 2, Sec. 12 (1)).

The applicant is also entitled to obtain a transcript or a copy of the document for a fee (Chap. 2, Sec. 13 FPA). The size of the fees that may be levied is regulated by the Fees Ordinance when copies of documents are provided by national authorities and by the Municipal Act when copies of documents are requested from regional or local governments. According to the Fees Ordinance, applying to national authorities, the first nine pages are free-of-charge but a charge of SEK 50[79] and of SEK 2 per copy is levied from the tenth page. The Fees Ordinance sets also out with

[76]Magnusson Sjöberg 1992, p. 411.

[77]See for example, the Parliamentary Ombudsman's decision of 23 November 2007 in Case No. 5628-2006.

[78]Bohlin 2012, p. 131.

[79]This corresponds to about 5 Euros or 7 US dollars.

precision the amount of the fees regarding videotape and sound recording. When it concerns fees for electronic information, the ordinance entitles the public authority to decide the amount of the fee to be levied, in the frame of full cost recovery principle.[80] According to the Municipal Act, applying on regional and municipal authorities, those authorities shall follow the self-cost principle, which mean that if fees are levied they may not exceed the cost of the services provided.[81]

Independently of the authorities where the request to access to official documents is made, the applicant is not entirely free to choose the format for the disclosure as a public authority "is under no obligation to release material recorded for automatic data processing in any form other than a printout except insofar as prescribed by law" (Chap. 2, Sec. 13 FPA).[82] The Freedom of the Press Act specifies that requests for transcripts of copies "shall be dealt with promptly", which has to be interpreted in a similar manner as the time conditions required for the requests *in situ*.[83] One or some waiting days are sometimes inevitable; nonetheless, "each delay has to be motivated".[84]

To ensure compliance with the obligation of promptness the Swedish law lays down minimal requirements in terms of open hours. Indeed, according to the Administrative Procedure Act, Sect. 5 (3), "An authority shall remain open for at least two hours on each normal working day, Monday-Friday, to be able [...] to receive request for the production of official documents that are kept by the authority".[85]

The request to access official documents is handled in the first instance by the civil servant responsible for the care of the document (i.e., the registrar or the public officer dealing with the matter the document is related to). In the case of doubt, and when this procedure will not delay determination of the matter, the public officer should refer the matter to the authority, which means a more senior official or the authority board.

There are no specific formalities for requesting access to documents. The requests can be made orally, by mail, email etc. Several public authorities furnish, on their website, an electronic form to be fulfilled, form which generally is not reserved for making access to information requests but is to be used for all kind of questions posed to the public authorities.

The applicant is not required to describe the requested document in detail. Nevertheless, he/she shall be able to provide the necessary information so that the

[80]Sec. 4 in combination to Sec. 5. See also DS 2009/10:75, p. 161.

[81]In practice, the charges are determined based on schedules set by municipal councils.

[82]This rule aims to inhibit, or at least to complicate, the copying of recordings in a way that would cause infringements of privacy. See Bohlin 2012, p 154.

[83]Bohlin 2012, p. 145.

[84]The Parliamentary Ombudsman's decision of 27 March 2013 in Case No. 4506-2012. In the present case the Government's Office had been criticised by the Ombudsman for having granted access to information after three days although there was no reason for such a long delay.

[85]This rule does not apply if such day is Midsummer Eve, Christmas Eve or New Year's Eve.

public authority does not need to make deeper examinations. The underlying principle/rule for the release of official documents is that the request shall be handled regardless the identity of the applicant.[86] Therefore, a person who requests access to a document is entitled to request document without any need to disclose his/her name nor the purpose of the request.[87] The protection of anonymity applies not only in relation to the public authority in charge of granting access but also in relation to third party.[88]

## 5 The Relationship Between Freedom of Access and the Rules of Access to Official Documents in Accordance with the Legislation on Administrative Procedure

When the information subject to the request consists of information collected for the investigation of the matter concerning parties to an administrative procedure before a court or another authority, the rules on access to official documents laid down in FPA and PAISA are supplemented by rules set out respectively in the Administrative Courts Procedure Act and in the Administrative Procedure Act. The general rules on access to official documents do not constitute for the parties a sufficient guarantee to be able to safeguard their interests in a satisfactory fashion.[89] Thus, both administrative acts lay down a specific right of access (*partsinsyn*), namely, the right to "have access to the material that has been brought into the matter/case".[90] This right is going beyond the general right of access as it covers documents that are not considered as official documents because they have not obtained their final form. Furthermore, this specific right of access is wider than the

[86]Bohlin 2012, p. 161.

[87]This rule is stated in Chap. 2, Sect. 14 (3) FPA: "No public authority is permitted to inquire into a person's identity on account of a request to examine an official document, or inquire into the purpose of his request, except insofar as such inquiry is necessary to enable the authority to judge whether there is any obstacle to release of the document".

[88]For example, the Parliamentary Ombudsman has criticised a university which, to be able to send the requested document (a certificate of study) promptly, asked the person the certificate pertained to but who was not the requester, if he knew the postal address of the requester. Parliamentary Ombudsman's decision of 11 April 2011 in Case No. 2932-2010.

[89]Bohlin 2012, p. 250.

[90]See Sec. 16 of the Administrative Procedure Act and Sec. 43 of the Administrative Courts Procedure Act. As specified in Sect. 16 of the Administrative Procedure Act, this specific right of access applies only when it is question of exercise of public authority. The right of disclosure, which has to be claimed by the party to be triggered is supplemented by the *principle of communication,* set out in both administrative acts (Sect. 17 and Sect. 18 respectively) which encompasses the authority's obligation to inform the parties about any material that has been added to their dossier and the right of the party to state his/her views before the authority takes a decision.

right provided by the FPA and the PAISA as the main rule states that secrecy does not impede a party in a matter before a court or in a case of accessing a document or other material related to the current matter or the case (Chap. 10, Sec. 3 PAISA).

The rule of the non applicability of secrecy has however some limitations: According to Chap. 10, Sect. 3 PAISA, the document or other material may not be disclosed, with regard to a general or individual interest, if it is of utmost importance that the information covered by the secrecy should not be released. To keep the essence of the right of disclosure, as it is crucial for the party, the decision of the authority is only taken on grounds known to him/her,[91] the legislator, balancing the secrecy interest on the one hand and the necessity of the rights of the defence on the other hand, sets out the duty for the public authority to, in another manner, inform the party about the content of the material. This duty is in turn surrounded by conditions: the duty applies so long it is needed for the party to exercise his/her right and if this can occur without causing serious damages to the interests the secrecy is intended to protect.

The refusal to deliver information applies for example when the danger exists that a whistle-blower from the social work sector, the health sector, or the police, runs the risk of being subject to acts of violence or other serious harms if information about their name is disclosed to another party.[92] However, the secrecy provisions can never impede a part in a case or matter to have access to the judgment or decision in the case or the matter (Chap. 10, Sec. 3 PAISA).

It has to be noticed that the constitutional requirement that the release of the document has to be dealt with *promptly* does not apply when the party of a matter makes the request for access based on the Acts on administrative procedure.[93]

## 6 The Compliance Mechanisms

Beside the right of the citizens to have the decision taken by a civil servant be examined by the authority where the document is kept and the right to lodge an appeal (Sect. 6.1), as well as the right to make complaints before the Parliamentary ombudsman (Sect. 6.2), the sanctions susceptible to be applied to civil servants (Sect. 6.3) may be included amongst the mechanisms contributing to the authorities compliance with the legislation on the right of access to official documents.

---

[91] Hellners & Malmquist 2007, p. 170.

[92] Bohlin 2012, p. 253.

[93] The general rules of obligation of service and on the handling of matters are applicable instead, see Bohlin 2012, p. 131.

## 6.1 Right of Appeal

Prior to the judicial review, the applicant disposes of the right to require that the authority examines the decision taken by the civil servant (Chap. 6, Sec. 3 PAISA). Three kinds of decisions of public authorities in the field of access to information are subject to judicial review according to PAISA: the decision to refuse partially or entirely the disclosure of a document, the decision to disclose document with reservation, and the decision to not meet thc applicants demand to make use of the technical means used by the public authority to access data processing (Chap. 6, Sec. 7 PAISA).[94] The main rule is that the appeal is to be addressed to an administrative court of appeal and ultimately to the Supreme Administrative Court. When a public authority is the appellant, the appeal has to be addressed to the Government (Chap. 6, Sec. 8 PAISA). Decisions taken by the Parliament, the Government and the supreme courts cannot be subject to appeal (Chap. 6, Sec. 7 PAISA).

A decision of a public authority to give access to an official document cannot be appealed.[95] The European Court of Human Rights has not considered this as a breach of Article 6.1 of the European Convention on Human rights, as argued by the applicant, in the case *Anne-Marie Andersson v. Sweden*.[96] The applicant complained about not having been entitled to challenge before a court a decision concerning the communication of a psychiatrist's statement pertaining to her to the Social Council but the ECtHR stated that "a 'right' to prevent communication of such data could not, on arguable grounds be said to be recognised under national law", which made Article 6.1 of the European Convention inapplicable. Article 6.1 had, therefore, not been violated according to the Court.[97]

According to the Swedish administrative rules, there is a need to have a decision from a public authority to make an appeal. The PAISA considers this rule and states (Chap. 6, Sec. 3) that the applicant must be advised that there is a need for a written decision to be able to appeal against the decision.

## 6.2 Complaints to the Parliamentary Ombudsmen

Besides lodging an appeal before the administrative courts, the applicants have the possibility to submit a complaint to the Parliamentary Ombudsmen (*Justitieombudsmannen*—JO), whose task is to supervise the application of the

[94] Additionally, the decisions regarding the imposition of fees according to Ordinance of fees may be challenged before the Tax Agency.

[95] See Strömberg & Lundell 2009, p. 77.

[96] European Court of Human Rights, *Anne-Marie Andersson v. Sweden*. Application No. 72/1996/691/883 (Judgment of 27 August 1997).

[97] Para 36 and 37.

law by public authorities and their staff. The Ombudsmen deal primarily with issues of procedural nature, such as, in right of access to information matters, questions concerning the delay in granting access or concerning the requirement to register official document.[98] They can pronounce critical advisory comments, and guiding statements, which are not legally binding but which have, however, persuasive force and are generally followed. The ombudsmen are also empowered to initiate a disciplinary proceeding against a civil servant for misdemeanours. Furthermore, they can act as special prosecutors in cases of misuse of office. This competence is rarely used in practice.[99]

The Parliamentary Ombudsmen deals with about 5000 complaints per year, with around 300 related to freedom of expression and the right of access to documents.[100]

## 6.3 *Sanctions and Liability*

Two kinds of situations may be of relevance when it concerns penal sanctions that may be applied to civil servants in the context of the application of the right of access to official documents: offences against secrecy (Sect. 6.3.1) and misuse of office because of a breach of the rules on access to information (Sect. 6.3.2).

### 6.3.1 Breach of Confidentiality Obligation

Civil servants who release information covered by secrecy may be sentenced for breach of the confidentiality obligation (14 Chap., Sec. 2). The Public Access to Information and secrecy Act does not provide for the penalties itself but refers to the provisions imposing penalties for breach of professional secrecy contained in the Penal Code (Chap. 20, Sec. 3). The penalty consists of a fine—which is the sole sanction to be imposed in case of carelessness—or imprisonment for at most one year. Petty cases are, however, not subject to penalty. The cases of breaches of secrecy provisions handled by the courts are rare.[101]

---

[98]Sefastsson 2003, p. 134.

[99]One of the cases when an Ombudsman brought criminal proceedings against a civil servant for violation of the legislation on access to official documents concerns a researcher who refused to grant access to data collected in the context of a research project although injunctions to that effect had been made to him by administrative courts. See further under footnote 103.

[100]Between July the 1st 2011 and June the 30th 2012, the Parliamentary Ombudsmen dealt with 326 complaints concerning freedom of expression and the right of access to documents ("*offentlighet och sekretess*") and issued admonitions to public authorities in 100 cases. *Justitieombudsmännens ämbetsberättelse, Redogörelse 2012/13:JO1.*

[101]Sefastsson 2003, p. 137.

### 6.3.2 Misuse of Office

Civil servants who do not apply the legislation on the right of access to information correctly may be sentenced to the general crime of misuse of office pursuant to Chap. 20, Sec. 1 of the Penal Code.[102] The penalty consists of a fine or imprisonment for at most two years. However, "If, having regard to the perpetrator's official powers or the nature of his office considered in relation to his exercise of public power in other respects or having regard to other circumstances, the act may be regarded as petty, punishment shall not be imposed". Cases in which civil servants are prosecuted for misuse of office concerning the legislation on access to information are exceptional. One of those cases concerned an academic researcher, responsible for a research project on hyperactivity and attention deficit disorders in children, who was prosecuted and convicted for having refused to execute two judgments from the administrative courts granting two other researchers access to research material.[103]

## 7 Concluding Remarks

To summarise the specificities of the Swedish right of access to information regime, three features are prominent, besides the long history of the legal framework and the distinctiveness of regulating the right of access partly in a legal instrument with constitutional rank. Those specific features are the short delay required from the public authorities to grant access to the requested documents, the extensive possibility, in principle, for anyone to access personal information and the design of the secrecy framework which leaves, so to speak, little or no discretionary power to the civil servants applying the legislation on the right of access to official documents. Together these features make the Swedish legislation on the right of access to official documents a generous one. Undeniably, this legislation encounters some difficulties in its application[104] and is subject to new implementation and

[102]On the contrary, in the case for offences against secrecy, the PAISA does not make any reference to the crime of misuse of office.

[103]The Professor Gillberg who then lodged an application with the Strasbourg Court of Human Rights, complaining *inter alia* that his criminal conviction violated his rights under Article 10 on Freedom of expression was however told by the Court that Article 10 did not contain a "negative" right to freedom of expression in the form of the right not to give information. European Court of Human Rights, *Gillberg v. Sweden*. Application No. 41723/06 (Judgment of 3 April 2012), para. 94.

[104]Examples of incorrect application of the legislation on the right of access are shown both at the lower level of the administrative hierarchy and at the higher sphere of the Swedish Government. An alarming illustration of the latter is given by a case where four journalists had, independently of each other, brought complaints against the Government Offices for the long delays applied for granting access, and where the Ombudsman concluded that the Government Offices had seriously neglected the expedition requirements set out in the Freedom of the Press Act. The Ombudsman

application challenges caused by developments in technology[105] and to the phenomenon of Europeanisation and globalisation.[106] Nevertheless, the right of access to official documents may be considered as a fundamental pillar of the Swedish administrative and political system, and infusing Swedish society as a whole.

## References

Blanc-Gonnet Jonason, P. (2001). Protection de la vie privée et transparence à l'épreuve de l'informatique, droit francais, droit suédois et directive 95/46/CE du Parlement européen et du Conseil du 24 octobre 1995. University of Paris XII.

Bohlin, A. (2012). *Offentlighetsprincipen*. Mölnlycke, Sweden: Norstedts Juridik.

Elder, N. C. M. (1973). *Regionalism and the publicity principle in Sweden* (Research Papers: Regionalism and the Publicity Principle in Sweden No. 3). Commission on the Constitution, H.M. Stationery Office, pp. 25–31.

Flinn, A., & Jones, H. (Eds.). (2009). *Freedom of Information: Open access, empty archives?* London: Routledge.

Hellners, T., & Malmquist, B. (2007). *Förvaltningslagen med kommentarer*. Stockholm: Norstedts juridik.

Magnusson Sjöberg, C. (1992). *Rättsautomation*. Stockholm: Nordstedts juridik.

Östberg, K., & Eriksson, F. (2009). The problematic Freedom of Information Principle: The Swedish experience. In A. Flinn & H. Jones (Eds.), *Freedom of Information: Open access, empty archives?* (p. 119). London: Routledge.

---

strongly expressed his concern that the failure to respect the principle of access by the Government Offices themselves could incite other public authorities to do the same, which could, in the end, constitute a threat against the principle of access. See the Parliamentary Ombudsman's decision of 27 March 2013 in Cases No. 639-2012, 463-2012 and 2732-2012. The failures to apply the law correctly do not only occur at the disclosure phase but also earlier on. Some deplore what has been called the "syndrome of empty archives", which refers to the fact that when "faced with the possibility that potentially controversial decisions could be released immediately into the public domain, politicians and civil servants might simply avoid committing themselves on paper, leading to an 'oral' culture of policy-making that renders government unaccountable, not only in the short term, but also potentially damaging the historical record", Flinn & Jones 2009, p. 5. See also Östberg & Eriksson 2009.

[105]The last decades, commissions of inquiry have succeeded one another and proposed reforms to adapt the set of rules on the right of access to documents for better taking into consideration the opportunities offered in that matter by the technical development, see for instance SOU 1997:39 Integritet, Offentlighet, informationsteknik and SOU 2010:4 Allmänna handlingar i elektronisk form - offentlighet och integritet.

[106]At the European institutional level for instance, the rather secretive tradition of the civil servants originating from countries with a less liberal access to information legislation than Sweden has certainly an influence on their Swedish counterparts. The enactment of European legislation may also have an impact on the Swedish approach on the right of access to information. For instance, the transposition of the Directive 2003/98/EC on the re-use of public sector information into Swedish law has constituted a challenge, conceptually speaking for the Swedish legislator and the civil servants.

Pöysti, T. (2010). Scandinavian idea of informational fairness in law – Encounters of Scandinavian and European Freedom of Information and Copyright Law. *Stockholm Institute for Scandinavian Law*, 1957–2010.

Ryden, N. (1986). *Företagsintegriteten i datasamhället*. Stockholm: SAF:s förlag.

Sefastsson, T. (2003). *Offentlighetsprincipen i praktiken*. Värnamo, Sweden: Bokförlaget Arena.

Seipel, P. (1988). ADB-upptagningars offentlighet, Rapport till Data- och Offentlighetskommittén. *IRI-rapport*, 1988:1, p. 11.

Strömberg, H., & Lundell, B. (2009). *Handlingsoffentlighet och sekretess*. Lund, Sweden: Studentlitteratur AB.

# List of Cases

## *Court of Justice of the European Union*

European Court of Justice 11.12.2014, *František Ryneš v Úřad pro ochranu osobních údajů*, Case C-212/13.

## *European Court of Human Rights*

European Court of Human Rights 26.03.1987, *Leander v. Sweden*, Application No. 9248/81.

European Court of Human Rights 25.02.1997, Z. v. Finland, 25 February 1997, Application No. 22009/93.

European Court of Human Rights 27.08.1997, *Anne-Marie Andersson v. Sweden*, Application No. 72/1996/691/883.

European Court of Human Rights 03.04.2012, *Gillbert v. Sweden*, Application No. 41723/06.

## *Swedish Courts*

Regeringsrätten (Swedish Administrative Supreme Court), RÅ 1971:15.

Regeringsrätten 19.04.1999, cases n° 3148-1998 and 5556-1998, RÅ 1999 ref. 18.

Regeringsrätten 17.06.1998, case n° 7357-97, RÅ 1998 ref. 42.

Regeringsrätten 27.11.2006, case n° 7516-05, RÅ 2006 ref. 87.

Högsta domstolen (Swedish Supreme Court) 13.07.2015, case n° Ö2345-15, NJA 2015 p. 624.

# Chapter 6
# Right of Access to Public Documents in France

**Constance Chevallier-Govers**

## Contents



"Freedom of information is a fundamental human right and [. . .] the touchstone of all freedoms to which the United Nations is consecrated".[1] Its practical application underpins two distinctive principles of a democratic republican system of

With contribution of Tetiana Ratushna, researh assistant and PhD student in International Law at the University Grenoble Alpes.

[1]General Assembly resolution 59 (1), *Calling of an International Conference on Freedom of information,* (14 December 1946), 65th Plenary Meeting.

C. Chevallier-Govers (✉)
Univ. Grenoble Alpes, CESICE, F-38000 Grenoble, France
e-mail: constance.chevallier-govers@univ-grenoble-alpes.fr

 
H.-J. Blanke, R. Perlingeiro (eds.), *The Right of Access to Public Information*,
DOI 10.1007/978-3-662-55554-5_6

government: the publicity of acts and the transparency of public administration. In this context, information is a tool of democratic control over State institutions, intimately linked to the concept of participatory democracy and the respect for fundamental rights.

# 1 Historical and Legal Context of the 17 July 1978 Act

Sweden was the first State to introduce a system of access to administrative documents as early as 1766. In France, the idea that the action taken by the administration should be known to the public is not new, and Article 15 of the 1789 Declaration of rights provided that "society has the right to request account to any public official of his administration".[2]

## *1.1 Adoption of the 17 July 1978 Act*

At the end of the nineteenth century, several laws provided measures to ensure public knowledge of administrative decisions. The claim of right of access to administrative documents dates back to the 1960s and was developed for three reasons: the public, which has become better educated has "the right to know"; the administration, criticized for its taste of secrecy, has an interest to improve its image by opening its records; and access to information held by the administration is a way to make public opinion support collective projects. One can note the contemporaneity with the concurrent development of "CNIL" (*Commission Nationale Informatique et Libertés*) law[3] and the Act Archives.[4]

The 1978 Act has been modified several times.[5] The most important modification was the one, which culminated with the adoption of the 6 June 2005 Ordinance

---

[2]Scoffoni 1992.

[3]Law No. 78-17 of 6 January 1978.

[4]Law No. 79-18 of 3 January 1979.

[5]All the modifications to the 1978 Law:

- *Law No.79-587 of 11 July 1979*
- *Decree No.81-860 of 15 September 1981*
- *Law No.82-599 of 13 July 1982*
- *Decree No.85-34 of 9 January 1985*
- *Law no 87-588 of 30 July 1987 Article 1 JORF 31 July 1987*
- *Decree No.88-465 of 28 April 1988*
- *Law No.2000-321 of 12 April 2000*
- *Law No.2002-303 of 4 March 2002*
- *Law No.2002-1487 of 20 December 2002*
- *Ordonnance No.2005-650 du 6 juin 2005*
- *Order No.2006-346 of 23 March 2006*

relating to freedom of access to administrative documents and the re-use of public information.[6] This ordinance, taken based on the law of 9 December 2004 on simplification of the law, modified the legal framework on access to administrative documents. These changes aim to harmonize the provisions of the July 17, 1978 Act with national and European case-law by extending the general access right to certain domains governed by special law; and by improving opportunities of access to documents through partial access and even electronic access.[7]

The ordinance also transposes the European Directive 2003/98/EC of 17 November 2003 by establishing a legal regime providing the re-use of public information. This regime, which applies to information held or developed by public or private persons with a mission of administrative public service, concerns the re-use of this information for commercial or non-commercial purposes. This scheme imposes minimum requirements concerning the preservation and traceability of information. The use of licenses is binding only when the administration subordinates the re-use of its information to the payment of a fee. Public authorities are required to make known the main held reusable information and conditions of its re-use.

Finally, the ordinance recognizes the status of an independent administrative authority to the *Commission d'accès aux documents administratifs* (CADA). Its powers are extended, and particularly in advisory proceedings. It now has the power to impose fines, when the rules of re-use of public information are disregarded. Additionally, its system of composition has been supplemented and clarified, as it is now seized of the regime organizing the re-use of public information.[8]

The Law No. 2008-696 of 15 July 2008 on archives empowered the Government to amend the Heritage Code and the 17 July 1978 Act. From this authorization, Ordinance No. 2009-483 of 29 April 2009 makes several changes in legislation.[9] First, it continues the alignment between the scopes of the two main regimes:

- *Law No.2006-686 of 13 June 2006*
- *Law No.2008-696 of 15 July 2008*
- *Law No.2008-1091 of 28 October 2008*
- *Order No.2008-1161 of 13 November 2008*
- *Law No.2009-323 of 25 March 2009*
- *Order No.2009-483 of 29 April 2009*
- *Law No.2009-526 of 12 May 2009*
- *Order No.2009-536 of 14 May 2009*
- *Decree No.2009-1393 of 11 November 2009*
- *Order No.2010-462 of 6 May 2010*
- *Law No.2011-334 of 29 March 2011*
- *Law No.2011-525 of 17 May 2011*
- *Law No. 2015-1779 of 28 December 2015.*

[6]Order No. 2005-650 of 6 June 2005, JORF of 07/06/2005.

[7]Lallet 2014.

[8]The Ordinance has been implemented by the Decree on freedom of access to administrative documents and the re-use of public information of, JORF of 31/05/2005, p. 1–8.

[9]Ordinance No. 2009-483 of 29 April 2009, JORF of 30 April 2009.

namely administrative documents and the public record to better articulate the access of common law regimes and special ones, expanding the powers of the CADA to rule on the application of certain special regimes. The ordinance also provides that the most favorable regime to the plaintiff is systematically applied. Chapter II on the re-use of the public information was also modified by the Law No 2015-1779 of 28 December 2015 on free access and modalities of the re-use of information in the public sector, the object of which was to transpose the directive 2013/37/EU of the European Parliament and the Council of 26 June 2013 modifying the directive 2003/98/CE concerning the re-use of the information of the public sector.

The latest change, which allowed bringing together the legal provisions on the right to access, is the codification process of the 1978 Act. The Code of Relations between Public and Administration, which is in force since 1 January 2016, includes the provisions of Chapter I of the Act of 1978, of the Decree No. 2005-1755 of 30 December 2005 and of the Decree No. 2008-1281 of 8 December 2008. The book III of the Code of Relations between Public and Administration corresponds to access to administrative documents. The Chapter II of the Act of 1978 is not yet the subject to codification and it is still in force.[10]

## *1.2 Constitutional Basis*

The Preamble of the 1958 Constitution states that "The French people solemnly proclaim their attachment to the Rights of Man and the principles of national sovereignty as defined by the Declaration of 1789, confirmed and complemented by the Preamble to the Constitution of 1946, and to the rights and duties as defined in the Charter for the Environment of 2004". According to its decision of 16 July 1971 on "Freedom of association", the Constitutional Council acknowledged unambiguously that the Declaration of the Rights of Man and the Citizen of 26 August 1789 and the Preamble to the 1946 Constitution, to which the Preamble to the 1958 Constitution refers, form part of the reference rules of constitutional law, and may therefore be invoked during the constitutional review procedure.[11]

In a landmark decision, the Constitutional Council even stated that accessibility and comprehensibility of the law is an objective of constitutional value. Indeed, equality in front of the law expressed by Article 6 of the Declaration of Rights of Man and the citizen and the guarantee of the rights required by its Article 16 cannot be effective if citizens do not have sufficient knowledge of the law as applicable to them.[12] The principle of equality in front of the law in the broad sense cannot be implemented without easy access to the legal rule.

[10]Ordinance No. 2015-1341 of 23 October 2015, JORF 25 October 2015.

[11]Constitutional Council (Conseil constitutionnel), Dec. 71/44 DC (Decision of 16 July 1971).

[12]Constitutional Council, Dec. 99-421 DC (Decision of 16 December 1999).

## 1.3 International Treaties

The right of access to public information is established in the International Covenant on Civil and Political Rights (ICCPR). Indeed, Article 19 ICCPR foresees that the right to freedom of expression includes freedom to seek, to receive and to impart information. Article 10 of the European Convention of Human Rights (ECHR) is not as explicit but the European Court of Human Rights (ECtHR, the Court) has, on several occasions, recognized "the right of the public to be properly informed" and "the right to receive information".[13] It is only recently that the ECtHR derived from Article 10 a right to have access to public or administrative documents. In the cases of *Leander v. Sweden* (1987),[14] *Gaskin v. United Kingdom* (1989)[15] and *Sîrbu v. Moldova* (2004), the ECtHR indeed recognized "that the public has a right to receive information as a corollary of the specific function of journalists, which is to impart information and ideas on matters of public interest". The Court was of the opinion that the freedom to receive information basically prohibits a government from restricting a person from receiving information that others wish or may be willing to impart to that person. However, it was decided in these cases that the freedom to receive information as guaranteed by Article 10 could not be construed as imposing on a State a positive obligation to disseminate information or to disclose information to the public.

For the first time in 2006, the ECtHR applied Article 10 of the Convention in the case *Sdruženi Jihočeské Matky v. Czech Republic* where the request for access to administrative documents was refused by the authorities.[16] The case concerns a refusal to grant an ecological NGO access to documents and plans regarding a nuclear power station in Temelin, Czech Republic. Although the Court is of the opinion that there has not been a breach of Article 10, it explicitly recognized that the refusal by the Czech authorities is to be considered as an interference with the right to receive information as guaranteed by Article 10 of the Convention. Hence, the refusal must meet the conditions set out in Article 10.2. In this case, the Court refers to its traditional case-law, emphasizing that the freedom to receive information "aims largely at forbidding a State to prevent a person from receiving information which others would like to have or can consent to provide". The Court is also of the opinion that it is difficult to derive from Article 10 a general right to have access to administrative documents. The ECtHR, however, recognizes that the

[13]Article 10 ECHR: "Everyone has the right to freedom of expression. This right shall include freedom to hold opinions and to receive and impart information and ideas without interference by public authority and regardless of frontiers".

[14]Europeam Court of Human Rights, *Leander v. Sweden*, Application No. 9248/81 (Judgment of 26 March 1987).

[15]European Court of Human Rights, *Sîrbu, et al. v. Moldova*, Applications No. 73562/01 a.o. (Judgment of 15 June 2004).

[16]European Court of Human Rights, *Sdruženi Jihočeské Matky v. Czech Republic*, Application No. 19101/03 (Judgment of 10 July 2006).

refusal to grant access to administrative documents, in this case relating to a nuclear power station, is to be considered as interference to the applicant's right to receive information. Because the Czech authorities have reasoned in a pertinent and sufficient manner the refusal to grant access to the requested documents, the Court was of the opinion that there had been no breach of Article 10.2 of the Convention in this case. The refusal was justified in the interest of protecting the rights of others (industrial secrecy), national security (risk of terrorist attacks) and public health. The Court also emphasized that the request to have access to essentially technical information about the nuclear power station did not reflect a matter of public interest. For these reasons, it was obvious that there had not been an infringement of Article 10 of the Convention, thus, the Court declared the application inadmissible.

The ruling in the case of *Sdruženi Jihočeské Matky* is nonetheless important as it contains an explicit and undeniable recognition of the application of Article 10 in cases of a rejection of a request for access to public or administrative documents. The right of access to administrative documents is not an absolute one and can indeed be restricted under the conditions of Article 10.2, which imply that such a rejection must be prescribed by law, have a legitimate aim, and must be necessary in a democratic society. The Court's decision of 10 July 2006 gives additional support and opens new perspectives for citizens, journalists and NGOs to access administrative documents in matters of public interest.

The Council of Europe's Convention on Access to Official Documents adopted by the Committee of Ministers on 27 November 2008 is the first treaty to establish a comprehensive right of access to official documents. In this, the convention fills a gap that existed at the international and European level, as international recognition of the right of access to official documents was previously limited in terms of both scope and effectiveness. Guaranteed by a system of non-contentious controls, the convention establishes a right of comprehensive access, along the lines of a fundamental subjective right. It introduces binding provisions creating a minimum European standard for right of access, and has some optional provisions allowing those Member States that wish to extend the protection.[17]

The Charter of Fundamental Rights of the European Union, annexed to the European Union's treaties by the Treaty of Lisbon, contains an Article 41.1, which recognizes the right to good administration in the following terms (lit. b): "Every person has the right to have his or her affairs handled impartially, fairly and within a reasonable time by the institutions, bodies, offices and agencies of the Union". Amongst the rights enumerated in this Article is "the right of every person to have access to his or her file, while respecting the legitimate interests of confidentiality and of professional and business secrecy".

[17]Edel 2011, p. 59.

## 2 The Scope of the Right of Access

According to French Law, the right of access applies to all documents, whatever the form and support, produced by the administrative authorities, but also to documents they receive from private individuals. The Code applies to all public authorities and private bodies with a public service mission. Anyone can access his/her medical or tax records, written correspondence, deliberations, public inquiries, local authority budgets, building permit records, procuring, and an analysis report on the environment.[18]

To preserve the serenity of the administration action and limit the constraints imposed on it by the right of access, the Act does not impose the disclosure of documents that are: unfinished, preparatory or publicly disseminated. Authorities are also not required to meet any requests that are clearly abusive by their volume or frequency and formulated in the intent to obstruct the work of the services.

### *2.1 The Concept of Administrative Document*

Article L. 300-1 of the Code of Relations between Public and Administration (Article 1 of the Act of 17 July 1978) gives a very broad definition of an administrative document: any documents originating from or received by the State, territorial authorities, or from public or private-law organizations managing a public service, as part of their public service mission, regardless of their date, repository, format or medium. Such documents include files, reports, studies, records, minutes, statistics, orders, instructions, ministerial circulars, memoranda or replies, correspondence, recommendations, forecasts, and decisions.

On the other hand, not administrative documents records of the courts, including administrative and financial courts, are those that are related to the function of judge; judicial documents; documents of civil status; private documents; and the documents of parliamentary assemblies. The Code and the Act of 17 July 1978 is intended to only govern access to documents held by the administrative authorities, designed as those that fall under the Executive branch. Therefore, records under the control of the legislature and the judiciary are excluded from its scope. The CADA considers moreover that it is incompetent to rule on their communicable nature.

#### 2.1.1 The Absence of a Formal Requirement

Article L. 300-2 of the Code of Relations between Public and Administration (Article 1 of the Act of July 17, 1978, as amended by the order of 6 June 2005), considers that "documents include files, reports, studies, records, minutes, statistics, orders, instructions, ministerial circulars, memoranda or replies, correspondence,

[18]CADA 2008, 2012 and Conseil d'Etat 1997.

recommendations, forecasts and decisions". The 2005 and 2009 Ordinances amended the wording of Article 1 of the Act by mentioning that these documents are considered as administrative "regardless of their date, repository, format or medium".

It follows from this broad definition that the form of the document requested does not matter. The definition given by the Act imposes no condition of material form, as these are all writings, video and sound recordings or automated information to be disclosed. This list given by the law is not exhaustive: the CADA has thus considered that the disclosure character of a file should be extended to all kinds of parts that constitute it, such as invoices, quotations, contracts, financial, budgetary and accounting documents,[19] registers and investigative reports.[20] However, the existence of a document implies an embodiment. Information that is not recorded nor reproduced, oral submissions, drafts or informal annotations, do not deserve the appellation of "documents".[21] However, the mere fact that a document was not typed shall not preclude its qualification as a "document".

The CADA held that an administrative report may take the form of a personal correspondence and that a manuscript notebook kept by the Secretary of municipal Council meetings was an administrative document complementary to the official minutes of a sitting, and not an unfinished version of the latter. The Council of State (*Conseil d'Etat*) ruled that an exchange of letters between two Ministers may constitute an administrative document.[22]

### 2.1.2 Documents Produced or Received by Administrative Authorities

The term of administrative authority covers the administrations of the State, local authorities and their establishments. Central Government and decentralized State services are administrative authorities and as such within the scope of application of the Act of 17 July 1978. Independent administrative authorities are also subject to the Act, such as the Supervisory Commission of insure, mutual societies and institutions of foresight, *Conseil supérieur de l'audiovisuel*, *Autorité des marchés financiers*, *Commission bancaire*, CNIL, as well as the CADA itself. However, in contrast to the services of the Presidency, the President of the Republic himself is not subject to the Act of 17 July 1978, as Article 67 of the Constitution provides that "he cannot, during his tenure and to any court or French administrative authority, be required to testify whether subject to an action, an action information, instruction or prosecution".

[19]Council of State, *Office public HLM de Paris*, Case No. 83476 (Judgment of 16 June 1989); Council of State, *Association Comité tous frères*, 9/10 SSR, Case No. 188431 (Judgment of 27 November 2000).

[20]Administrative Court Toulouse, *Dumeaux* (Judgment of 16 February 1987).

[21]Administrative Court Versailles, *Union locale CGT Chesnay* (Judgment of 31 January 1980).

[22]Council of State, *Association SOS Défense et Bertin*, Case No. 39196 (Judgment of 21 July 1989).

All public, national and local institutions and whatever their administrative, industrial, commercial, scientific or cultural character are subject to the disclosure obligation resulting from the Act of 17 July 1978 only for documents pertaining to their public service mission; for examples are administrative authorities educational institutions, OFPRA (*Office Français de Protection des Réfugiés et des Apatrides*), national museums, public hospitals, "welfare offices and communal social action centres, tourist offices, river basin organizations, consular bodies, public development institutions.

### 2.1.3 Documents Held by Private Organizations with a Public Service Mission

Legal persons governed by private law are not systematically excluded from the field of application of the Code and 17 July 1978 Act. When they perform an action in the framework of a public service mission, the documents they produce or receive are likely to be of administrative nature. To determine if a private organization is in charge of a public service mission, the rules provided by the *Conseil d'Etat* in its decision of 22 February 2007 apply as follows.[23] Has the legislator given, explicitly or implicitly (*travaux préparatoires*), an appreciation on the qualification of the body? If it has excluded the qualification of body with a public service mission, it is not subject to the Act of 17 July 1978 (such was the case in the matter before the *Conseil d'Etat* of support through labor centres). Conversely, if the law or its preparatory works qualify the activity of "public service mission", documents held in this context by the organization are subject to Act 1978. If the legislature has not taken position or that there is an ambiguity, the question is whether the body has prerogatives of public power that it exercises in the aim of general interest and under the control of the State. If this is the case, activity in respect of which it has such prerogatives must be classified as public service mission. In the negative, there is a place to appreciate if "having regard to the general interest of its activity, conditions of its creation, organization or conditions of its operation, the obligations imposed on him as well as the measures taken to verify that the assigned objectives are met", the administration heard to entrust to this organization a public service mission. For examples, bar associations are private organizations in charge of a public service mission according to the CADA, but also the Banque de France.[24] Conversely, Air France and the Banque Postale are considered as organizations associated to public activities, but are not recognized as administrative authorities.[25]

---

[23]Council of State, *Association du personnel relevant des établissements pour inadaptés*, Case No. 264541 (Judgment of 22 February 2007).

[24]French National Olympic Committee – Council of State, *Comité national olympique et sportif français*, Case No. 280069 (Judgment of 10 January 2007).

[25]Banque postale (Avis No. 20073859 of 11 October 2007).

### 2.1.4 The Link with the Mission of Public Service

A document is administrative only if it maintains a sufficiently direct link with the mission of public service of the administrative authority that produced or received it. Article L. 300-2 of the Code of Relations between Public and Administration (the Ordinance of 6 June 2005 amended Article 1 of the 1978 Act) specifying that are only considered to be administrative documents the documents produced or received "as part of the public service mission". The CADA is therefore not competent to take position on the communicable nature of documents insusceptible to be part of the public service mission and which are of a purely private nature. Mere transmission to an administrative authority does not, in general, give a document an administrative nature.

Considering their scope, documents held by State administrations are, generally, considered as being within a public service mission. It is the same for local authorities, which set by their deliberations cases falling within their jurisdiction. By way of exception, however, some documents held by these authorities are, because of their nature, excluded from the scope of the Code and the Act of July 17, 1978. This is the case for documents concerning companies that the Labour Inspectorate collects outside any legal obligation as documents relating to the terms of a collective agreement[26]; or agreement on the reduction of working time. This is also the case for documents that relate to the management by a public community of its private domain unless they are appended to a deliberation of the deliberative body (which gives them an administrative character and makes them discoverable). These documents retain a private nature and are not subject to the right of access provided by the Code and the Act of 17 July 1978.[27] This is the case, for example, of the management of electoral premises, of the management of the booking of a "*salle des fêtes*", deeds, acts under private deed, as a testament and notarial deed regarding a bequest to a municipality, a title establishing a right of way, a certificate of an emphyteutic lease.

In some cases, documents that, taken in isolation, may be private in nature in application of the rules mentioned above are granted to be of an administrative nature. This is the case of private documents inserted in an administrative file and on which the administration is based or is likely to take a decision. These documents generally acquire an administrative "coloring" under the principle of unity of the file.[28] This is the case, for example, of documents filed by an employer to obtain an authorization for dismissal.

[26]Council of State, *Federation de la mutualité agricole d' Île-de-France*, Case No. 68502 (Judgment of 8 July 1988).

[27]Council of State (Section), Case No. 43468 (Judgment of 26 July 1985).

[28]Council of State, *Ministre de l'urbanisme c / Durand* 3, Case No. 65457 (Judgment of 3 June 1987).

### 2.1.5 Documents Unrelated to the Public Service Missions

The records of private law agents employed by a public institution or a private law body, including the employment contract that binds them to their employer, are not administrative documents. This is the case of social security local fund agents.[29] Documents relating to the contractual relationship between industrial and commercial public services with their customers-clients, including invoices and statements of consumption.

Documents dealing exclusively with the operation of the statutory bodies of private bodies in charge of a public service mission are not administrative; for instance, the internal documents of the French Federation of Taekwondo and its associated disciplines.

Procurements are not administrative documents passed by public in industrial or commercial establishments or semi-public companies based on Ordinance of 6 June 2005 and have no link with the public service missions of these institutions. This is also the case for documents relating to a dispute between a professional order and legal advice.[30]

#### 2.1.5.1 Acts of Parliamentary Assemblies

Initially, only documents relating to the exercise of the legislative function or control functions of the Chambers and those not detachable were excluded from the right to communication, for example the investigation report of a parliamentary Committee.[31] According to Article L. 311-5 of the Code (Act of 17 July 1978 was amended by the Act of 12 April 2000) the following documents are excluded from the scope of application: the acts of parliamentary assemblies, including actions relating to the organization and the functioning of the services of the assemblies. The CADA is declared incompetent for the annual rating of an officer of the National Assembly or the copy of the result of an administrative investigation; a copy of letters sent by the President of the National Assembly or the Senate and all documents relating to a procurement by the Assembly.

The CADA is regularly seized by sectarian movements. In a decision of 3 July 2006, *Ministre d'Etat, Ministre de l'Intérieur et de l'aménagement du territoire c. Fédération chrétienne des témoins de Jehovah*, the *Conseil d'Etat* ruled that documents drawn up or held by the intelligence services do not, solely because of their transmission to the investigation commission of the National Assembly for the preparation of the report, acquire the character of "acts of parliamentary assemblies" within the meaning of Article L. 300-2 of the Code (Article 1 of the Act of

---

[29]Council of State, *Vinçot*, Case No. 44883 (Judgment of 24 January 1986).

[30]Council of State, *Ordre des avocats de Pontoise,* Case No. 57285 (Judgment of 6 June 1986).

[31]Nantes Administrative Court of Appeals (Cour administrative d'appel Nantes), *Association "L'arbre au milieu"*, Case No. 00NT01259 (Judgment of 30 June 2003).

17 July 1978). As a result, it is only if it appears from the documents in the file that these documents were collected only for the work of the parliamentary commission that they can be regarded as "acts of parliamentary assemblies" and that the CADA is incompetent.

The Ordinance of 29 April 2009 clarifies that those that are excluded from the scope of application of the Code and the Act of 17 July 1978 are the "acts and documents produced or received by the parliamentary assemblies". This precision does not change the state of the law. In particular, a document produced by an administrative authority, for its own needs, and transmitted then to the Assemblies remains subject to the Code and can be obtained from the administrative authorities who hold it (but not the assemblies). The communication of acts and documents produced or received by the parliamentary assemblies is governed by the provisions of the Ordinance of 17 November 1958 No. 58-1100 on the functioning of the parliamentary assemblies and the CADA is not competent to interpret it.

#### 2.1.5.2 Judicial Documents

The CADA and the administrative judge place in this category documents produced by a judge or at the request of a judge, as well as documents produced by an administrative authority for a judge.[32]

The CADA, seized of a request for an opinion concerning such documents, declared itself incompetent. It is in particular the case for judgments, orders, decisions or rulings by the courts of the judiciary or of the administrative order; statements of legal aid application files; documents and materials prepared for the needs and during judicial proceedings leading to a judicial decision such as the decisions of the public prosecutor. This is also the case concerning working documents from the services of the judicial bodies for the members of the courts and contributing to the statement of affairs or to the formation of judgments[33] and the conclusions of the *Commissaire du Gouvernement* (public rapporteur) before the administrative court. The ECtHR considers that the fact that the conclusions of the *Commissaire du Gouvernement* are not communicated to Parties does not constitute a violation of the right to a fair trial.[34]

The CADA does not exclusively consider the nature of the institution to which the document is requested and has issued a favorable opinion on the communication of the entire file relating to an application for a certificate of nationality held by the services of a court. In general, documents produced or received by a court in administrative activities and non-judicial proceedings, are administrative documents.

[32]Council of State, Case No. 30590, *Association SOS Défense* (Judgment of 27 July 1984).

[33]Council of State, Case No. 45736, *Association SOS Defense* (Judgment of 9 March 1983) and Council of State, Case No.95139, *Mme P* (Judgment of 28 April 1993).

[34]European Court of Human Rights, *Kress v. France*, Appeal No. 39594/98 (Judgment of 7 June 2001).

However, among those documents, the Council of State introduced a distinction for documents that relate to the functions of a judge. It estimated that the monthly table of assessors, determining the composition of the Court during a period, could not be regarded as an administrative document.[35]

In addition, certain documents held by the courts under their jurisdictional activity are administrative documents for which the CADA is competent. For instance, documents produced by administrative authorities and which, on a dispute, were transmitted to the judge: this transmission does not give them a judicial character. However, these documents may not be releasable if their disclosure could affect the conduct of proceedings before the courts.

To finish, records under the control of the judicial authority cannot be considered as administrative documents. This category includes documents that fit in a procedure involving the judicial authority, independently of the commitment of legal proceedings, for instance: minutes and documents noting criminal offenses.[36]

## 2.2 Communicable Documents

The right of access is exercised if three conditions are met: it is a document of an administrative nature that the administration has actually in his possession. Another condition for the exercise of this right is that the document should be formally completed, which excludes for example draft or study underway. Similarly, to enable the administration to decide calmly, preparatory documents to a decision are not communicable as long as the decision has not intervened. Article 311-2 (4) of the Code does not require the administration to communicate documents which are subject of a public broadcast that anyone can get on its own.

Article L. 311-5 of the Code (Article 6.1 of the 17 July 1978 Act) provides that certain documents are not, by nature, communicable: opinions of the administrative sections of the Council of State, documents of the financial courts (Court of audit and regional audit chambers), as well as certification and audits of health facilities. Documents relating to named individuals shall not be disclosed to interested parties or their agents. Similarly, third parties cannot access information covered by industrial and commercial secrecy. To preserve the confidentiality of such information, the administration may disclose a record by obscuring certain passages.

[35]Council of State, *M. Bertin*, Case No. 303168 (Judgment of 7 May 2010).

[36]A snapshot of a speeding: Administrative Court Bordeaux (Tribunal administrative), *Mr. A.* (Judgment of 2 May 2007).

### 2.2.1 The Existence of the Document

The document must exist in a physical state or can be obtained by automated processing in common use. The Code and the 17 July 1978 Act do not have for object or effect to compel the administration to develop a document to respond to a request. Communication can therefore be refused for documents in preparation, through treatment, research, synthesis, analysis.[37] As the law on the rights of the citizens in their relations with Governments (DCRA) of 12 April 2000, Article L. 300-2 of the Code (Article 1 of the 17 July 1978 Act) imposes communication when the document does not exist at the state level but can be obtained by automated processing in common use. In the version in force from April 2000 the Law states: "*Ces documents peuvent revetir la forme d'écrits, d'enregistrements sonores ou visuels, de documents existant sur support informatique ou pouvant etre obtenus par un traitement automatomatisé d'usage courant*". In the version of the Code of Relations between Public and Administration: "*Sont considérés comme documents administratifs, au sens des titres Ier, III et IV du présent livre, quels que soient leur date, leur lieu de conservation, leur forme et leur support, les documents produits ou reçus, dans le cadre de leur mission de service public, par l'Etat, les collectivités territoriales ainsi que par les autres personnes de droit public ou les personnes de droit privé chargées d'une telle mission. Constituent de tels documents notamment les dossiers, rapports, études, comptes rendus, procès-verbaux, statistiques, instructions, circulaires, notes et réponses ministérielles, correspondances, avis, prévisions et décisions.*"

The condition of existence leads to the non-communicability of documents that do not exist in the form indicated by the request and documents whose existence is not established. Doomed to fail are requests for information such as the request that a citizen makes so that the administration shall communicate the name of the doctor who provided information on his account[38] or the name of a person having settled invoices in water on behalf of the condominium.[39] This is also the case concerning request for motivation, such as the request for disclosure of the reason justifying the repeal of a clearance for access to the reserved areas of aerodromes or the request that a certificate be established or that a decision be taken: in these cases, CADA recalls that the Act does not "allow the obtaining of a document or a title following a decision of refusal on the part of the administration".

The right of access to administrative documents applies only in respect to the records administrative authorities have in their possession under Article L. 311-1 of the Code (under the first paragraph of Article 2 of Act of 17 July 1978). The applicant must therefore take care to address the right administration. A request must in principle be brought before the administrative department or public body

---

[37]Council of State, *Association SOS Défense*, Case No. 43501 (Judgment of 9 March 1983).

[38]Council of State, *Thorel*, Case No. 46591 (Judgment of 16 January 1985).

[39]Council of State, *Compagnie générale des eaux*, Case No. 66573 (Judgment of 30 September 1987).

that owns the documents, either as it is the author, or that it has been the recipient of. An administration that holds the document does not have to solicit the agreement of its author or any other person. A single document can therefore be requested from several administrative authorities, so that the applicant may have the choice of the authority he seeks. For example, when the requested document is a letter, the applicant may, at his choice, solicit the parts either from the issuing authority, or from the recipient of the written correspondence, in the event where the latter would be also subject to the provisions of the Act. Accounting documents of a subsidized association may be required either to this association, if it is charged with a mission of public service or the public administration that pays this grant.

When an administration does not hold the requested document, it is not, however, subtracted from any obligation. It has in fact, under Article L. 311-2 of the Code (Article 2.4 of the 17 July 1978 Act), introduced by the Ordinance of 29 April 2009, to transmit the request wrongly submitted to it to the administrative authority that may be able to satisfy this request, and to notify the applicant. When the CADA has already pronounced on the communicability of the document in question, the administration is required to join the opinion of the Committee to the transmission document. The implicit denial of access comes at the end of a period of 1 month from the initial referral.

This obligation of transmission disappears in two cases: when no administrative authority can be identified and when the application is manifestly unfounded, particularly when the document requested is not of an administrative nature.

### 2.2.2 The Document Should Be Formally Completed

Article L. 311-2 of the Code (Article 2 of the Act of 17 July 1978) provides that "the right to communication applies to completed documents only". When an administrative document passes through successive forms in a complex development process or involves several departments, it is not clear at which point it becomes a discoverable administrative document. A document is incomplete when it is only an intermediate step in the development of a final document and when its provisional content does not properly reflect the intention of its author. A partial, non-operable document is therefore regarded as unfinished. On the other hand, the mere fact that a document is likely to be the subject to amendments in the future (for example, a study that could subsequently be amended by reason of new investigations) or that it is vitiated by an error is not reason enough to make it an unfinished document.

### 2.2.3 The Document Should No Longer Be in a Preparatory Stage

Article L.311-2 of the Code (Article 2 of the 1978 Act) states that the right to communication does "not apply to documents that are instrumental in an administrative decision until the latter has been taken". Documents preparing a simple policy, and not a true administrative decision, cannot be of preparatory nature. The CADA distinguishes preparatory documents as those that lead to a decision by the administration or government, and which become communicable once this decision is taken and the documents covered by the exception relating to the secrecy of the deliberations of the government which would be communicated at the end of the 60 years deadline according to Article L. 213-3 e) of the Heritage Code.

For the CADA, the communication of preparatory documents occurs after the decision that they were preparing has been made. This is especially the case when early information would paralyze administrative action. A document loses also any preparatory character when the administration has clearly waived taking a decision based on this document (e.g., an expert's report, which preparatory to a mission of arbitration of the Prefet, becomes discoverable from the day where the Prefet waives this mission).[40] There do exist however, communicable documents, which are necessary for the preparation of the budget such as those relating to State subsidies. In addition, the provisions of the Environment Code resulting from the Law No. 2005-1319 of 26 October 2005 (Article L. 124-4 and seqq.) exclude the notion of "preparatory document" information concerning the environment: this information must be delivered immediately, once it is completed, even if it is preparing a future decision. Finally, the preparatory documents in the complex procedure of preparation of town planning documents deserve a particular development because of abundance of jurisprudence that frames this regime.

### 2.2.4 Documents Which Are Subject to a Public Release

Governments are not required to disclose records subject to public dissemination under the Article L. 311-2 of the Code (para. 2 of Article 2 of the July 17, 1978 Act as amended by the Act of 12 April 2000), which has replaced this word by that of "publication", which had a narrower field of definition.[41]

To characterize "public dissemination", the CADA considers the accessibility of the document in terms of geographical, technical or price conditions. When these conditions are met, and to avoid the administration having to respond to claims based solely on the search for economies of effort or the price of photocopies, the CADA shall consider inadmissible any application for a document which is the subject of such a publication. It considers that there has been a public release in case of publication in the Official Journal of the European Union, in the Official Journal of the French Republic, in the Gazette of a Ministry, and in the compendium of administrative acts. The CADA also checks the reality of the issuance of the requested document by considering any difficulties of access to such collection.

[40] Administrative Court Versailles, *SA Montenay* (Judgment of 11 July 1985).

[41] "Le droit à communication ne s'exerce plus lorsque les documents font l'objet d'une diffusion publique."

Until the beginning of the 2000s, the CADA considered that, given the limited number of people who had access to the Internet and the insufficient rate of public facilities in this area, the release of a report on the website of a Department was not a public release. This position has changed and the CADA now considers that easily accessible documents on the Internet, at the time when it has to deal with the request for disclosure, are subject to public dissemination. The CADA considers the practical accessibility of the document. Nonetheless, the creation of a document on an "intranet" accessible only by a password cannot be considered as a public release. In this case, the CADA may indicate the web address where the document can be viewed or downloaded. The publication of documents on the intranet of a Department is not comparable to a public release. In the case where the document is no longer available online, the CADA will dismiss the objection based on public release and examine the application under the other provisions of the law. It considers that provision on the Internet during a limited period of time is not sufficient to consider that the document was subject to a public release.

The CADA considers that a publication by an editor constitutes a public release: for example, a report of the Court of Auditors; a doctoral thesis or a university thesis. The CADA checks the actual existence of this publication. The fact that a decree provides that an annual report is subject to a "special publication" is not sufficient, as it is not apparent from the record that the report has been published.

The "public dissemination" exception will play an increased role in the future as the administration becomes subject to publication requirements laid down in texts or decides spontaneously to widely disseminate the documents at its disposal.

### 2.2.5 Non-Communicable Documents by Nature

This relates to documents that, before the 29 April 2009 Ordinance, were purely and simply excluded from the scope of application of the 17 July 1978 Act. The CADA declared itself incompetent to hear applications for the communication of such documents. Included in this classification are administrative documents but those of which Article L. 311-5 of the Code (1° of Article 6-I of the Act) prohibits their communication. From the outset, the 17 July 1978 Act explicitly rejected its application to the opinions of the Council of State's administrative sections.[42] However, the administration may decide to spontaneously communicate these opinions.[43] Claim statement documents made to the mediator of the Republic are also not releasable. The CADA however considered that this rule applies only to the mediator of the Republic and that a document held by the Ombudsman of a Department or any other administrative authority is discoverable (the Ombudsman of the Ministry of the Economy or the Ombudsman of the City of Paris).

[42] Council of State, *Association SOS Défense*, Case No. 45736 (Judgment of 9 March 1983).

[43] Council of State, *Louard*, Case No. 222672 (Judgment of 27 October 2000).

With regard to the Court of Auditors, Article 25 of the Law No. 88-13 of 5 January 1988 brought an end to the communicable nature of the investigative measures, communications and reports adopted in the exercise of its control powers. The 12 April 2000 Act introduced in Article 1 of the 17 July 1978 Act a reference to Article L. 140-10 of the Code of the Financial Courts, to broaden the inapplicability of the right of communication to the audit reports and opinions of the regional or departmental review committees of the accounts of the social security agencies. With regard to the regional account Chambers (*Chambre Régionale des Comptes*—CRC), the Act of 12 April 2000 subtracted from the category of administrative documents the ones referenced in Sec. L. 241-6 of the Code of the Financial Courts, namely proposals, reports and instruction of regional chambers of accounts.[44]

The documents "prepared in the performance of a service contract performed for one or several specific persons" are not releasable by nature, under Article L. 311-5 of the Code. They are the documents "established by Governments for the benefit of outsiders on command" (wording in French). In other words, the Code excludes from its scope of application, documents made by an administrative authority to be sold: this is the case, for example, of market analyzes, some studies of INSEE, *Mété o France* or other public institutions such as the *Office national d'études et de recherches aérospatiales*.

### 2.2.6 Releasable Documents to Stakeholders Only

In some cases, the right to communication is reserved for those "interested". This is the case for documents "passing remarks or value judgment on a natural person, referred to by his/her name or easily identifiable" and documents "showing the behavior of a person, the disclosure of which could harm the latter" under Article L. 311-6 of the Code (Article 6.2 of the 17 July 1978 Act). The Act of 12 April 2000 abolished the terms of "nominative document" using strictly the definition developed by the CADA. It is also the case for documents whose delivery would be harmful to privacy, to the secrecy of personal files, to medical secrecy or to trade and manufacturing secrets according to Article L. 311-6 of the Code (Article 6.2 of the Act of 17 July 1978). If these documents are also covered by another exception as to right of access, one of the secrets listed in the paragraph 1 of the same Article, the communication even to the interested person is not possible (a document whose disclosure would be injurious to the security of the State while it relates to the situation of the applicant).

The concept of an "interested person" has been clarified in other legal situations. In some cases, the law designates clearly the interested person, for instance: medical secrecy is not opposable to the persons listed in Article R. 1111-1 of the

[44]Administrative Court of Appeals Bordeaux, *Soule*, Case No. 00BX00267 (Judgment of 27 April 2004).

Code of Public Health. In other cases, the document has been adopted considering this person: an employee who requests access to his/her personal file, a taxpayer who wishes to consult his/her tax record, parents of a student wishing to access their child's school records. The person is also interested when he/she is the author of the document or the person whose behavior is described by this document and the disclosure of which might be harm to him/her: thus, the person submitting a complaint to the administration has the right to obtain copy from any administrative authority holding it. On the other hand, the person against whom the complaint has been submitted does not have the quality of interested person. Thus, a record of admission in psychiatric facility at the request of a third party is in principle accessible only to the latter (subject to the provisions of Article l. 1111-7 of the Code of Public Health regarding medical information). A person is classified as well interested when the object of the document, its content or its function affects this person personally and directly. It can also be the case when the disclosure is requested by the successors or family members in case of a person's death. Regarding medical confidentiality, communication to the family members is governed by the provisions of Article l 1110-4 of the Code of Public Health. When documents relate to the secret of the privacy of a deceased person, their successors or even relatives can receive the communication if this person had not objected during his/her lifetime and they can support their request with a legitimate reason, which should be assessed on a case by case basis and with regard to the nature of the document and the interest of the deceased and the applicant.

Disabled persons are not regarded as interested persons. The only people to be qualified for this role are their legal representatives. When the interested person is a minor, holders of parental authority can exercise the right of access in its name without any consent required.

Third parties, defined as persons not having the quality of interested person, will not be communicated the documents that relate to other people, except in three cases. These can be communicated when they have a person's express mandate. By way of exception, a lawyer may, on behalf of his clients, request documents concerning them, without having to justify a written mandate, unless there is a serious doubt on the reality of this representation. There is also the example of when third parties request a document "whose submissions are set up against him/her." Indeed, under the provisions of Article 311-3 of the Code (Article 3 of the 17 July 1978): "[. . .] every person has the right to know the information contained in an administrative document whose submissions are set up against him/her [...]." These provisions, which are based on the general principle of the rights of defense, are intended to enable a person to effectively challenge the meaning of a document the administration uses to take a decision in its regard, even though this document would be preparatory to a decision or would be covered in all or part by one of the secrets of Article L. 311-6 of the Code (Article 6.2 of the 17 July 1978 Act). The CADA strictly appreciates the notion of documents "whose submissions are set up against him/her." There are documents which the administration deems appropriate in content and on which it relies directly and decisively to take a decision against this person. This is the case of the expert report of the insurer to a public entity on which it relied to deny a request for compensation.

From these provisions, the applicant communication may include indications covered by one of the secrets of Article L. 311-6 of the Code (Article 6.2 of the 17 July 1978 Act), including the secret of the privacy of third parties, in the only measure where this disclosure is strictly necessary for the defense of his rights, in particular to effectively challenge the measure which is the subject. This is the case, for example, of the report prepared by the social services, which includes elements relating to the privacy of persons other than the beneficiary, but whose communication is necessary to establish the absence of marital life.

Upon the expiration of a certain period, documents covered by the secrets provided for in Article L. 311-6 of the Code (Article 6.2 of the 7 July 1978 Act) become freely discoverable based on the legislation on archives. Thus, documents relating to privacy are communicable until the expiration of a period of 50 years from the date of the deed under 3° of Article L. 213 I-2 of the Heritage Code.

### 2.2.7 The Secrets of Natural Persons

Article L. 311-6 of the Code (Article 6.2 of the 17 July 1978 Act) reserves to interested persons the communication of documents concerning private life or covered by medical secrecy. Also considered concerned documents are "passing remarks or value judgment on a natural person, referred to by his/her name or easily identifiable; or showing the behavior of a person, the disclosure of which could harm the latter". These exceptions apply only to natural persons. Thus, in no case may the administration refuse to disclose a document on the grounds that it would be an assessment of a legal person, as a company.

#### 2.2.7.1 The Protection of Privacy

Article 9 of the Civil Code provides that "everyone has right to respect of his private life". Article L. 311-6 of the Code (Article 6.2 of the 17 July 1978 Act) translated this requirement by stating that only individuals have the right to access to documents "whose delivery would be harmful to privacy, to the secrecy of personal files, to medical secrecy or to trade and manufacturing secret". This formula, resulting in the Archives Act of 15 July 2008 has a strictly identical content to the expression "secret of private life and personal folders" which was previously included in this Article and that the CADA sometimes continues to use.

The CADA and the administrative judge have over time gradually circumscribed the definition of the field of privacy. Thus covered by this exception is the following information: civil status, date of birth and age, place of birth, marital status and, more generally, the family status of a person, or even the identity of his godfather and godmother in the context of the "Republican sponsorship", personal contact information, (including mailing addresses, e-mail addresses and telephone numbers, as well as the list of numbers called from a telephone and the place of accommodation of a hosted person).

By way of exception, protection of privacy is not enforceable with respect to orders granting or denying a building permit or other authorization of town planning, as well as all parts of the file relating to it (application, plans, reports and studies). In addition, certain financial information relating to privacy can be communicated if they relate to public funds. This is the case, for example, of remuneration from public funds to an employee of the public service. On the other hand, the name and family name of a person are not, by themselves, part of the protected elements in respect of private life.[45] It follows that a "nominative document", which no longer appears in the 17 July 1978 Act, is not excluded from this solely because of the scope of the right of access: it is only if it is also covered by the secrecy of private life and that the person to whom the information relates is identifiable. The fact that a person is deceased does not have an effect, by itself, to lift the secrecy of his life private but can give the beneficiaries or even relatives access to certain documents. Thus communicable are the Decree of appointment of an official, the list of agents of a commune,[46] list of teachers by institution, an organizational chart of the services of a municipality or the decisions of appointment and promotion of officials.

There is not a general right to access to one's personal origins as a mother who decided to give away her child at birth can refuse to reveal her identity. The ECtHR confirmed this position in a case *Odièvre v. France* of 13 February 2003 where it considered that there was no violation of Article 8 in this case where France refused to reveal the secret of the birth origin.[47]

#### 2.2.7.2 How to Protect Privacy?

When the administration has before it a request for disclosure of documents containing the names of persons, accompanied by elements covered by the secrecy of private life, it must decide either to transmit the document through the concealment of the particulars covered by secrecy of privacy; or to do so merely by anonymizing the document; or to refuse purely and simply disclose the communication.

Only the administrative authority is able to choose between these three forms, depending on the context of the application and risks of overlap. If the second option is likely to be of interest in the context of requests for statistical purposes, the first is preferred in cases where shadowing does not deprive the provision of interest and where no overlap is possible. However, the administration is entitled to refuse to disclose lists containing only elements covered by the secrecy of private life, for example: a list of recipients of social assistance or minimum income students a list of children using school transport; a list of disabled staff employed by a municipality; the register of a crematorium.

[45]Council of State, *Mme D*, Case No. 90237 (Judgment of 30 March 1990).

[46]Council of State, *Commune de Louviers*, Case No. 112904 (Judgment of 10 April 1991).

[47]Bonnet 2004, p. 405 et seqq.

### 2.2.8 The Principle of Medical Secret

Medical information may be communicated only to a person to whom they are related and to interested persons. Third parties have no access to these documents, except with the consent of the patient. This secret is one of the "basic rights" of the person according to Article l 1110-4 of the Code of Public Health. It protects "health information" within the meaning of Article l. 1111-7 of the same Code.

Article l. 1111-7 of the Code of Public Health gives anyone access to "all information about his/her health held by professionals and health care facilities, which are formalised and contributed to the development and monitoring of diagnosis and treatment of preventive action, or have been the subject of exchanges between health professionals". These include the "medical record" opened in case of hospitalization, containing the information and documents listed in Article R. 1112-2 of the same Code. These can be results of review of radiographs, minutes of consultation, protocols and therapeutic requirements implemented.

These documents do not have to be completely formalized and they can be handwritten. Documents established by a health care professional and not by a doctor such as hospitalization orders, social or psychological reviews, and investigative reports are not "medical", unless they are attached to a medical record. However, informal but completed notes contained in a medical file and having contributed to the establishment of the diagnosis fall within this framework, even though the quality of healthcare of their author is not proven.

### 2.2.9 Documents Involving a Person

This concept covers documents containing an appreciation or value judgments on a natural person, referred to by his/her name or being easily identifiable; or showing the behavior of a person, the disclosure of which could harm the latter. These documents are only communicated to stakeholders under Article L. 311-6 of the Code (Article 6.2 of the 17 July 1978 Act). This notion must be differentiated from the secrecy of private life. Thus, the list of owners of a vehicle is considered to be a document covered by the secrecy of private life, while the list of persons who were the subject of a suspension of driving license is a document involving the persons because it reveals behavior in conditions that may harm them. However, it has the same consequences as the secret of private life.

### 2.2.10 Industrial and Commercial Secrecy

The application of this exception is probably the most difficult because it requires a detailed analysis of the context and the consequences of the communication in a competitive environment. This secret is of common application because the assumptions in which information relevant to competition are provided to the administrative authority are numerous: request approval or authorization, in fields as varied as the permissions for the placing on the market, commercial town planning, Sunday opening; application for grants or assistance; procurement and public service delegations.

Commercial and industrial secrecy applies to any moral person who has its activity, in whole or in part, in a competitive environment. It may also be of a private company and association (including not-profit) or a public institution. However, it is necessarily interpreted more extensively with regard to bodies exercising exclusively a competitive activity. This secret can only come into play if disclosure of the document is likely to harm the agency concerned, which presupposes that it is always in activity or that it has been resumed. It has three dimensions: trade secrets, the secret of economic and financial information and the secret of financial strategies.

### 2.2.11 The Case of the Procurement or Public Service Delegations

Documents relating to public procurement and public service delegations are subject to complex rules that the CADA has gradually reported. In principle, these documents are administrative in nature. Records of consultation do not have preparatory character; they are therefore communicable to any person before even the signing of the contract. Other documents, in particular those that relate to submitted tenders, lose their preparatory character once the market or the delegation have signed them, even if the contract might be cancelled or terminated subsequent to its signature. All these documents must be communicated to any person who so requests, including companies whose candidacy has been ruled out, and the administration cannot waive this obligation by merely indicating the reasons for its rejection. This communication must, however, be carried out accordingly to respect commercial and industrial secrecy.

## *2.3 The Secrets Protected*

The communication of documents must be refused when this process may undermine the exercise of the sovereign activities of the State and that of the general interest. Thus the following documents are not communicable: the deliberations of the Government, national defense secrets, those that are used for foreign policy, currency and public credit documents, those that are used for the security of the State, public safety or persons, those used in the act of carrying out administrative proceedings, and those documents which concern tax and customs offenses.

Article L. 311-5 of the Code (Article 6.2 No. 2 of the 17 July 1978 Act) which lists specific secrets protected by law, concludes the enumeration by a general reference to secrets protected by law. There is no comprehensive census of the texts thus covered, but the CADA has, so far, used some of them: especially those relating to international conventions and national laws that protect confidentiality.

### 2.3.1 The Secrecy of the Proceedings of the Government and Proper Authorities Coming Under Executive Power

The formula thus adopted by the legislator has led to the development of a certain margin of uncertainty. Indeed, if the term "proceedings of the Government" clearly covers constitutional activities of collegial bodies such as the Council of Ministers, councils and interdepartmental committees, and the decisions taken by the Prime Minister and Ministers, the reference "to the responsible authorities within the Executive power" is vaguer. It excludes the deliberations of those bodies responsible within local communities. To delimit the scope of the exception, the CADA uses three criteria: the status of the deliberating body, the content and the purpose of the document and the scope of decision-making.

Concerning the first criteria, these documents are those covered by the secrecy of deliberations and records on which the Council of Ministers deliberated, documents retracing governmental deliberations, whether letters exchanged between Ministers or members of the cabinet and the leading officials of the Ministry, reports of a meeting in which representatives of the Government discussed a draft, and minutes of interdepartmental meetings.

There are additionally some documents that are exempt from disclosure according to the second criteria. These documents are those that foster governmental consideration processes before the latter takes a decision. For example: cantonal cutting proposals addressed to the Minister of the Interior and decentralization by the prefect of the Haute-Loire for the cantonal elections, or results of the monthly survey on the morale of the French by the service and information dissemination of the Prime Minister. This criterion is also applied to archives of a political nature. The CADA handed down a negative opinion on decision concerning applications for documents relating to the policy of France in Iraq from 1981 to 1983.

Finally, the existence of discretion (pure opportunity) argues that some documents may be non-communicable (for example, records for the award of decorations).

### 2.3.2 The Secret of National Defense: Defence and Foreign Policy

#### 2.3.2.1 The Secret of National Defence

A secret of national defence is defined by Article 413-9 of the Criminal Code. Those documents deemed a secret of national defence are: information, processes, documents, computer data or files affecting national defence, which were the subject of a classification in the conditions laid down by Decree No. 98-608 of 17 July 1998.[48]

Article L. 311-5 of the Code (Article 6.1 of the 17 July 1978 Act) precludes the communication of classified documents. The latter can be obtained only in the following three cases: if the competent authority decides to declassify the document, at the end of the period of 50 years foreseen in 3 ° of Article L. 213 I-2 of the Heritage Code; before the expiry of that period, by way of derogation granted by Article L. 213-3 of the Heritage Code.

In addition, archives classified by NATO can be declassified only by the organization and are releasable only with its agreement according to the Agreement on the security of the information between the Parties to the North Atlantic Treaty, ratified and published by Decree No. 2001-480 of 5 June 2001, which is inspired by the so-called principle of "control by the entity of origin".

#### 2.3.2.2 The Conduct of Foreign Policy

The CADA considers the contents of the requested document, as well as its form (a diplomatic telegram, even considered as "restricted" does not escape, for this reason alone, the right of access), and the context of the access request. They are in particular documents used as a basis for international negotiations, depicting such negotiations or which mention the position of France (for example: the decision of the mixed Monegasque commission on a tax rebate; archives that can have an impact on the ongoing negotiations in the WTO); and exchanges of letters with another State who wanted to keep them secret and that a French administration may not disclose without impacting the conduct of foreign policy. On the other hand, not covered by this exception is the communication to a foreigner of the dossier on which consular services have refused him a long stay visa.[49]

### 2.3.3 The State Security and Public Safety

The attachment of a document to an activity of public security does not make it non-discoverable. Its disclosure has to violate public safety, including the possibility of endangering persons.

Generally, the CADA is in favor of a partial disclosure of civil security documents (for example: communicability of the special intervention plan of the Creys-Malville nuclear power plant without the operational schedule), or other documents related to the security of the State (record of detention of a person, with the

[48]Council of State, *Association Reporters sans Frontières*, Case No. 260926 (Judgment of 25 May 2005).

[49]Council of State, *El Fourti*, Case No. 195072 (Judgment of 31 March 1999).

exception of some reports of police and their annexes). The CADA understands the risk of disturbing public order depending on the circumstances and the local situation at the date of the application, and in light of two main criteria when disclosure could undermine the protection of persons or property; and when it could interfere with the maintenance of order and public security.

It can leave it to the holder of the document authority to assess the reality of the risk of infringement of public order when it receives a request. It may request the concealment of the names of those who have worked in the public service. Discoverable are the minutes of the police or gendarmerie, cards, notes or records held by the General Intelligence, plans, protection or relief plans, instructions for the maintenance of security, whenever the authority concerned does not establish that their communication would be likely to impact security (minutes of police may not be reportable especially when they are part of proceedings brought before the courts), the organizational structure of a detention centre; instructions, circulars and guides developed by the Ministry of the Interior for the use of breath analyzers; a circular on speed controls; the opening or receipt of mutation of a flow of beverages. Some documents can only be communicated to affected persons for instance the police or gendarmerie reports following a dispute between two persons or on neighborhood disturbances.

The CADA has given an unfavorable opinion in some cases considering that there was a risk of interference with public safety. The CADA estimated that the documents describing precisely some sensitive locations and including security measures implemented should not be disclosed such as excerpts from reports of intervention by firefighters describing the safety devices (type, localization) implemented preemptively, and certain documents relating to nuclear installations under Article 3.3 of Decree No. 63-1 228 of 11 December 1968 concerning plants. It considered that the communication of documents describing precisely the modalities of completion of service or revealing the methods implemented by the administration could be prejudicial to the security such as decisions determining the modalities of completion of the night services in a penitentiary. The CADA has also issued opinions refusing the communication of records contained in individual folders: such as a police report from which has been issued an order of placement; emails from third parties and indicating the hazardous behavior of a person having been the subject of a detention and requesting disclosure of his or her file of hospitalization.

### 2.3.4 Currency and Public Credit

This exception prohibits the release of documents that might encourage speculation or complicate the actions of the public authorities. This does not exclude from the scope of the communicable documents from monetary authorities such as the Bank of France or the Treasury. Its scope is strictly limited to those cases in which the disclosure of the document would promote speculative movements or weaken the monetary policy. This is the reason why the CADA found, for example, this exception was raised wrongly to withhold the approval of Exchange issued by the Bank of France to a banking establishment. On the other hand, documents relating to policy investment and investment pension reserve funds are protected by this exception, given the amounts placed in the financial markets and the risk of financial speculation.

### 2.3.5 The Conduct of Proceedings Before the Courts or the Preliminary Operations

A document may not be in itself of a legal nature, but its communication might undermine the conduct of jurisdictional or pre-litigation procedures: in this case, the CADA, although competent, shall issue an opinion unfavorable to its communication. The mere fact that a procedure is engaged in the courts, or that it is about to be, is not enough to justify a denial of access. The communication is excluded if it is likely to complicate the conduct of preliminary operations, such as an investigation, or the judge's office or to unduly delay the judgment. Noting that this exception was provided in Article 311-5, and not 311-6 of the Code (Article 6.1 of 17 July Act) which protects private interests, the CADA thus considered that the possible breakdown of equality between the parties is not a criterion that should be considered. The CADA found that the following documents should be communicated: the copy of the social services' report on the circumstances in which a person contracted a legionellosis while the person concerned initiated litigation against the establishment suspected of being the cause of intoxication. When the legal proceeding in question is a recourse for excess of power before the administrative judge, the CADA stressed that the "objective character of litigation of excess of power" leads to exclude the exception.

### 2.3.6 The Research of Tax and Customs Offenses

Para 2 lit. g) of Article L. 311-5 of the Code (Article 6.1 of the 17 July 1978 Act) states, "Shall not be handed over any other administrative documents whose consultation or delivery would be harmful to actions, by the proper services, to detect tax and customs offences". The concept of offense not only applies to criminal offenses but also to all cases of breach of the law, resulting for example in a tax adjustment. Any taxpayer is entitled to the communication of his/her tax case, except parts or references that might impair looking for tax offenses; his/her personal record held by the cadastral services; documents from which were determined the taxation of property tax bases. In case of a fiscal control, the opinion of accounting audit and letters exchanged as part of the audit are also communicable.

Communication may however be refused if it may prejudice looking for offenses. The CADA makes application of this exception in five cases: when the communication indicates the sources of the tax administration; when the communication would reveal the criteria implemented by the administration to trigger a control[50]; when the communication would reveal some methods implemented by the tax administration, for instance the instructions given by the Directorate General of customs to its agents in accordance with a Decree of 11 December 1981[51]; when the communication would reveal the results of some research of offense; and when the documents were obtained from a foreign administration as part of a request for administrative assistance.

### 2.3.7 International Conventions

Some international conventions protect confidentiality of information. For instance, Article 15 of the Convention n° 81 of International Labour Organisation stipulates that labor inspectors shall treat as absolutely confidential the source of any complaint reporting an offense to legal provisions. However, the communication to the interested party to the investigative report does not affect the obligation of secrecy to which officials of the Labour Inspectorate is required.[52] Another example is Article 27 of the Convention of 9 September 1974 between France and Singapore for the avoidance of double taxation and prevention of fiscal evasion with respect to taxes on income.

### 2.3.8 Legal Regime of Access to Information

Article 15 of the Declaration of the Rights of Man and of the Citizen incorporated in the French Constitution says expressly: "*The society has the right of requesting account from any public agent of its administration*". In this light of the right to access to information is nothing else but the right to receive this information. Its constitutional core is clear. However, there is always a place for constitutional interpretation, as it seems impossible to enumerate the specific behavior of individuals in the exercise of this right in one single act.

Diversity of behaviors and practices gives rise to interpretation in the sense of general freedom, such as "what is not prohibited is allowed" and in the sense of priority between private and public interests in society. The first approach *in dubio pro liberate*, which refers to "general freedom right"[53] as the United States for example reflects on the right to express, to think, to know, to speak and also to support and to ensure the entire constitutional order, though it is never specific and impose certain ambiguity.

---

[50]Council of State, *Ministre du budget c /Durand*, Case No. 65457 (Judgment of 12 October 1992).

[51]Council of State, *Mesmin*, Case No. 50234 (Judgment of 16 November 1984).

[52]Council of State, *Ministre du travail, de l'emploi et de la formation professionnelle c /Thomé*, Case No. 107566 (Judgment of 21 September 1990).

[53]Schultz 2010, http://ir.polytechnic.edu.na/handle/10628/89 (Accessed on 14 February 2017).

There is no such expressed provision in the French Constitution, which consolidates this general freedom rule. Moreover, the Constitution does not contain general limitation clause of fundamental rights. The main tendency is to regulate the more specific extent possible of the wide range between public and private interests by the means of sub-constitutional laws. The main example of such law is the recent Code of Relationships between the Administration and Public. As the fundamental right to access to information can be limited (if to trace this right up to Article 19 of the UDHR, Article 10 of the ECHR and especially Article 19 of the ICCPR, which was meant to elaborate the Universal Declaration) the conditions should be as follows: must be necessary, provided by law, for respect of the rights or reputations of others and for the protection of national security or public order (*ordre public*), or of public health or morals. It brings us to conclusion that "general freedom" concept and division between public and private interests both are right. However, the latter is much more expressed. Thus, specific exceptions to the right of access are necessary to protect certain scope of interests and secrets. These exceptions are found in regulation of non-communicable documents, secrets of national persons, industrial and commercial secrets, secrets in relation to exercise of sovereign activities of the State.

### 2.3.9 Comparative Perspective on the Right to Access

In the comparative perspective, the limits of the right to access differ from one State to another. For instance, in Germany or in the United Kingdom there are different reasons for non-communication of the documents. No country discloses the documents to protect its national security, safety, foreign affairs policy, financial or economical affairs, in relation to private life, industrial and commercial secrets. Under the regime in the United States, in Germany, in Italy, as well as in France, the documents are not communicable on preparation stage until the issue in question is decided.[54]

The Brazilian Law N° 12.527/2011 on the right to access to information has been passed to regulate Article 5, item 33, Article 37 para 3, item 2 and Article 216 para 2 of the Brazilian Constitution. Article 5, item 33 of the Constitution guarantees "*the right to receive, from the public agencies, information of private interest to such persons, or of collective or general interest, which shall be provided within the period established by law, subject to liability, except for the information whose secrecy is essential to the security of society and of the State*".

The scope of the right to access to information under Brazilian Law on access to information guarantees the right to access public documents of three power branches: "*Public entities integrated in the direct administration of Executive, Legislative (including Court of Accounts) and the Judicial powers, and of the*

[54]La liberté d'accès en Europe et dans le monde. http://www.cada.fr/la-liberte-d-acces-en-europe-et-dans-le-monde,6084.html (Accessed on 14 February 2017).

*Public Prosecutor's Office*", whereas French right to access to information excludes the communication of records of courts, including financial and administrative courts. The documents of parliamentary assemblies are also excluded. Under French Code of Relationships between the Administration and Public, only the executive branch falls in the scope of the communication of administrative documents. The secrecy of the document under the Brazilian Law N° 12.527 must be ensured to protect national sovereignty, integrity of national territory (Article 23, item 1), life and safety or health of the population (Article 23, item 3), strategic operations or plans of the Armed Forces (Article 23, item 5) etc. The Brazilian Law much reflects on the rate of secrecy of the document and the procedure of its classification, according to which the documents may be top-secret and not for disclosure during 25 years, 15 years for secret and 5 years for restricted documents under Article 24 para 1.

The close equivalent of CADA was regulated by Article 35 of the Brazilian Law N° 12.527, but this authority (Joint Committee on Information Reassessment) in contrast to CADA is responsible for treatment and classification of secret information. The authority, which is not expressly defined and is responsible for protection of the right to access, is the entire state: "It is the duty of the state to control the access and dissemination of secret information produced by its entities and institutions, guaranteeing its protection" under Article 25 of the Brazilian Law.

## 3 The Exercise of the Right of Access

### *3.1 The Modalities of Communication*

Everyone has the right to request, without distinction of nationality or justification of interest to act, the communication of an administrative document not involving a person. It is important to clearly identify the document concerned and to formulate a clear written request to the administration that holds the document. The communication arrangements are at the choice of the applicant (free on-site consultation, copy paper or electronic media). The photocopying fees may be charged to the applicant but must not exceed the costs of returns.[55] According to Article L. 231-1 of the Code, the administration has 2 months to respond to request; otherwise, the silence is viewed as a positive answer. This term is applicable to the list of procedures published on "legifrance". If it is a medical record less than 5 years old, the administration has 8 days to respond and 2 months if it is older than 5 years. Past these deadlines, the CADA can be seized. The investigation of claims by the CADA is fast, as the law imposes a period of 1 month for the respective body to react. Once notice has been given, the authority that holds the documents must inform the CADA of the follow-up given to the opinion. To facilitate the

[55]The maximum fee is € 0.18 per page, 1.83 the floppy and € 2.75 the CD-ROM.

application of the law and the processing of applications, the CADA has correspondents in major public institutions. Despite the effectiveness of the appeal to the CADA, in the case of persistence of refusal, the administrative jurisdiction can be seized.

The requested documents must be easily identifiable. It is imperative to identify accurately documents whose communication is desired. Under Article L. 311-2 of the Code (Article 2 of the 17 July 1978 Act), the administration is never required to respond to requests that, by their generality and vagueness, do not identify correctly the requested documents. In addition, the Act does not require the administration to respond to requests for information—except in a case of 'environmental information'.

Article 17 of the 17 July 1978 Act provides that "The public services that elaborate or hold public information shall give users access to a directory of the main documents in which such information is presented". According to Article 36 of Decree of 30 December 2005, this directory, which must be brought online when the administrative authority has a website, must specify, for each of the identified documents, its exact title, its purpose, the date of its creation, re-use conditions and, where appropriate, the date and purpose of its updates. The development of these directories, which is still ongoing within administrations, will ultimately facilitate the tracking of documents by the plaintiffs.

For applicants to receive access to documents, the document should not only exist, but also be easily identifiable by the administration without being forced to carry out searches. To do this, the claim must be sufficiently precise: the application should not be too broad, documents must be specifically listed, which is not the case when the applicant is seeking, without further qualification, communication of a letter that the administration has addressed. The CADA accepts, however, that the formulation of the applicant may contain some errors of a secondary nature or adopt general terminology, as long as the document is easily identifiable by the authority.

### 3.1.1 Principle of the Free Choice to Mode of Access

This principle is the notion that the plaintiff has the choice of the forms in which the communication occurs. Article L. 311-9 of the Code (Article 4 of the July 17, 1978 Act, amended by the Ordinance of June 6, 2005) provides three modes of access to administrative documents:

- Free consultation documents on-site, the applicant may be accompanied by a third person;
- Their reproduction at the expense of the person seeking them, which then can be sent by mail, to a residence, or to an address indicated by the applicant. The request may be only on a simple copy and not the original, which may merely be consulted. There is no requirement for Governments to issue certified copies; and

- Sending by e-mail free of charge, when the document is available in electronic format: the applicant can be notified of system and software used by the administration and the latter is required to provide an identical copy, both from the point of view of the support and format, or one which is likely to have the same content and format at the end of the transfer.

This principle of free choice of the mode of access has certain conditions intended to reconcile the right of access with the proper functioning of the public service. Primarily, the applicant cannot require the administrative authority that it communicates the requested document in form that is inconsistent with the material means at its disposal. The right of access is therefore exercised within the limits of the technical possibilities of the administration. In particular, the administration does not have the obligation to digitize documents available only in paper form to send them electronically. Secondly, the state of conservation of the documents may justify a restriction on the terms of access. This is the case when their reproduction may cause damage. When the consultation is also a risk, it may be delayed so that documents are restored or transferred to another medium. Thirdly, in case of application on a large volume of documents, the authority may invite the applicant to consult them on the spot to copy only parts that he/she wants. To this end, the administrative authority can develop a regulation on consultation specifying the modalities of this consultation, provided they do not deprive citizens of their right of access. Thus, opening a morning a week for a small town may be sufficient. In addition, the consultation of documents must in principle take place on the premises of the service that ensures conservation,[56] and the administration is not required to transfer these documents on the premises of another service for the purposes of this consultation.[57] The administration should endeavor to meet the deadline of 1 month allotted to meet demand, unless the volume of the requested documents makes it impossible. Fourthly, the administration is not required to comply with the request of a person for photography of documents, on consultation on the spot, except if it is the only way or the easiest way to get the communication. Such is the case, for example, where the state of documents does not allow their manipulation or reproduction[58] or when the document itself does not lend itself easily to a reproduction, because of its size or its nature, (for example, a model). Finally, no provision requires nor prohibits the administration to use a support provided by the applicant.

The CADA has declared itself incompetent to rule on the merits of the refusal by the administration at the request of a person who wishes to record its comments on a document. Refusal to such a request is therefore likely to be challenged directly before administrative justice of 9 September 2004.

---

[56]Council of State (Assembly), *Mirlit*, Case No. 144042 (Judgment of 14 February 1996).

[57]Council of State, *Lalande*, Case No. 197018 (Judgment of 26 October 1988).

[58]Council of State (Assembly), *Ministre de la santé c /Tête*, Case No. 45172 (Judgment 8 April 1987).

Contrary to the January 6, 1978 Act relating to data processing, files and freedoms, Article L. 311-3 of the Code (Article 3 of the 17 July 1978 Act) does not give the citizen the right to erase, rectify or correct the contents of the administrative document. The administration may, however, accept such a request but outside of any legal obligation.[59] Article L. 311-3 of the Code (Article 3 of the 17 July 1978 Act) entitles any person, to whom the findings of an administrative document are opposed, to record its observations on these conclusions in the annex to the document concerned. This "right of reply" or "annotation", may be exercised by adding at the end of the documents the remarks made by the applicant or by the addition of a piece (for example, for a medical certificate).

### 3.1.2 Detailed Rules for Concealment

The administration cannot refuse the disclosure of a document on the sole ground that it would include a statement covered by one of the secrets protected by law. Article L. 311-7 of the Code (Article 6-III of the 17 July 1978 Act), as resulting from the 6 June 2005 Ordinance, provides that: "When the requested document includes information that may not be handed over under this article, but that may be concealed or severed from it, the document shall be handed over to the requesting person once that information has been concealed or severed".

Partial disclosure is subject to two conditions[60]: the document must be divisible, such is the case of a detachable notebook, a registered Appendix, but also documents where the references to obscure are not numerous. Concealment should not distort the meaning of the document or deprive the interest of communication. Thus, a document containing huge number of entries covered by a secret, and which concealment would be particularly difficult for the administration, should be regarded as non-discoverable.

### 3.1.3 Abusive Requests

Article L 311-5 of the Code (Article 2 of the 17 July 1978 Act) expressly provides that "the administration is not required to respond to abusive requests, in particular by their number, their repetitive or systematic nature". The CADA considers this good administration rule applies to all communications, even when the legislature has not specifically provided it or that it exhaustively enumerated the legal grounds for refusal (for instance, information relating to the environment).

A request is abusive when it is clearly intends to disrupt the functioning of the public service. For the request to be declared as such by the CADA, the administration should first assert it in writing. If this condition is met, the CADA mobilizes

[59]Council of State, *Murlidhar*, Case No. 13132 (Judgment of 6 February 1980).

[60]Council of State, *David*, Case No. 110211 (Judgment of 4 January, 1995).

the following indices beam: the number of applications and the volume of documents requested; the repetitive nature and the use of systematic applications, including on the same subject; the will to interfere with the administration or in another definition, the physical impossibility of a body to process applications; the possibility that the applicant has already had to access the document; the existence of a tense situation or even multiple litigation between the applicant and the authority; and the refusal of the applicant to pay the costs which had been requested on the occasion of previous communications. Requests from associations or unions are traditionally subject to a more flexible review, given the nature of these bodies and their object.

Undueness is appreciated request by request, and not according to the applicant. The latter cannot be denied, in general, his/her right of access. In no case the administration may use the concept of unreasonable demands to "quota" the annual number of requests from the same person.

### 3.1.4 In Which Situation Is There a Refusal to Disclose?

The communication refusal by the administration can be either explicit or tacit. If explicit, it must be motivated, under Article 25 of the 17 July 1978 Act. The regime of the tacit refusal is regulated by Article R. 311-12 and Article R. 311-13 of the Code, according to which the administration has 1 month to respond. In case of silence, the response is considered negative. There is a delay of 2 months for the administration to answer according to Article L. 231-1 of the Code. Article D. 231-2 of the Code states that the silence means positive answer in relation to the list of procedures that are published on the site of "legifrance.gouv.fr". In case of a tacit refusal, the denial of access results from "the silence kept for more than a month by the competent authority seized of a request for disclosure of documents" Article R. 311-13 of the Code (para 1 of Article 17 of Decree No. 2005-1755 of 30 December 2005). These implied decisions are exempt from the motivation obligation according to Article L. 232-4 of the Code (Article 5 of the Act of 11 July 1979), unless otherwise provided for in a text.[61]

The CADA can only be seized because of a denial of access, which can be a disagreement as to the modalities of communication. A referral formed before the expiry of the period of 1 month allowed for the administration to answer is therefore inadmissible. In the event of an unsatisfactory communication to the applicant without denial, the CADA requires the applicant to wait for the expiry of the period of 1 month from its application.

[61]Council of State, *Ministre de l'emploi c /Farida Dall*, Case No. 204761 (Judgment of 14 December 2001).

## 3.2 Appeal to the CADA in Case of Refusal

A request for an opinion on a refusal to disclose does not require particular formalism. Deadlines should however be respected and the CADA has to be provided the necessary information for opening a file including a proof of a request of communication to the administration.

### 3.2.1 Time and Mode of Referral to the CADA

Article L. 342-1 of the Code (3rd paragraph of Article 20 of the 17 July 1978 Act) provides that appeal to the CADA is a mandatory prerequisite for any contentious procedures. The fact that the administration has consulted the CADA before it refuses to disclose information, does not exempt the applicant to make this referral prior to its contentious action.[62] In principle, the CADA must be informed within the time limit of 2 months from the notification of the refusal or the intervention of the tacit refusal according to Article R. 343-1 of the Code (2nd paragraph of Article 17 of Decree No. 2005-1755 of 30 December 2005). However, the CADA rejects an application for foreclosure only when, because of the delay and/or a change in the circumstances of law or fact, the very existence of denial of access does appear more certain at the time of the appeal.

Requests may be addressed to the CADA on plain paper, by simple letter, fax or electronically. Under the terms of Article R. 343-1 of the Code (Article 17 of the Decree of December 30, 2005), these requests shall contain legibly a specific purpose, with a detailed list of the documents requested, the name and surname of the applicant, as well as his/her postal address. In appropriate cases electronic addresses may be given. If it is the situation that an application for a copy has remained without answer for over a month, this must be mentioned, and additionally when refusal of a demand has been incurred this must be stated. If it is appropriate, the legislative or regulatory provisions on which these demands are based must be indicated.

The application may relate only to denial of access itself. The CADA is certainly not competent to pronounce on the legality of an administrative or administrative practice or to give a person an "interpretation of the Code". Only administrative authorities may refer to the CADA requests for advice. Moreover, it is not competent to disclose the requested records.

### 3.2.2 Procedure

To begin the procedure, the CADA acknowledges receipt of the request and immediately contacts the authority specified by the applicant as the author of a

[62]Council of State, *SARL Villerupt auto école*, Case No. 89251 (Judgment of 21 septembre 1990).

refusal to disclose. This takes place so that documents in question and the grounds for the refusal can be transmitted to the applicant. The procedure then requires the challenged authority to respond within the time limit prescribed by the Chairman of the CADA, to communicate all the necessary documents and information. Each case is then registered by the general secretariat in its computerized management database, and is given to one of the rapporteurs according to his/hers specialty and is recorded in the role of the next meeting. In the context of the statement, the rapporteur may have to make contact, including by telephone, with the administration. CADA members and the rapporteurs designated by the Chairman may conduct any investigation necessary for the accomplishment of their mission on-site.

The investigation closes at the time of the opening of the official meeting of the CADA. Any correspondence received after this meeting is not considered. The CADA meets twice a month at the Council of State in plenary session under the authority of its president. Administrations involved may, at the request of the president, be brought to participate in the work of the CADA in an advisory capacity for the most delicate files. CADA meetings are not public. After deliberation, the applicant is notified of the decision and a simple letter with the meaning of the notice and the motivation to the appropriate administration.

The CADA has a period of 1 month to notify its opinion to the competent authority and to the applicant under Article R. 343-3 of the Code (Article 19 of the Decree of December 30, 2005). This period of 1 month is taken from the day of registration of the application. However, if the CADA is not able to deliver its opinion within the time limit of 1 month, this has no bearing on the legality of the decision of refusal to disclose.[63]

### 3.2.3 Scope and Suites of CADA's Opinions

The opinions of the CADA are not binding. They do not constitute administrative decisions and are therefore not subject to recourse for an excess of power,[64] not more than letters sent to the applicant by the CADA secretariat to support his/her appeal.[65]

The administrative authority has 1 month from the receipt of the opinion of CADA to tell the CADA the answer it intends to give to the request. The silence of the authority for more than 2 months from the CADA registration of the request is a confirmation of refusal under Article R. 343-4 and R. 343-5 of the Code (Article 19 of the Decree of December 30, 2005). No provision requires the administration to inform the applicant of its final position. In the case of persistence of a denial of access, the applicant can challenge this decision before the administrative judge.

[63]Council of State, *Association SOS Défense*, Case No. 45736 (Judgment of 9 March 1983).

[64]Council of State, *Epoux Deplace*, Case No. 34773 (Judgment of 27 April 1983).

[65]Council of State, *Holland*, Case No. 28097 (Judgment of 25 May 1983).

### 3.2.4 Persons Responsible for Access Within Administrations (PRADA)

Article L. 330-1 of the Code (Article 24 of the Act of July 17, 1978) provides for the designation of those responsible for access to administrative documents and the re-use of public information issues. The bases of the network of those responsible are clarified by the provisions of Article R. 330-2, R. 330-3, R.330-4 (title IV (Article 42–44) of the Decree No. 2005-1755 of 30 December 2005) on the freedom of access to administrative documents and the re-use of public information, as well as Article L. 124-3 and R. 124-2 of the Code of the environment. The Decree specified that the person responsible for this mission is to receive requests and possible claims, to ensure their training, liaison between administrations and the CADA, and that it can be also charged to prepare an annual report on access to administrative documents and license for the re-use of public information requests.

The network of those responsible to respond to the requests of access concerns most entities that hold or develop administrative documents, such as defined in Article L. 300-2 of the Code (Article 1 of the 1978 Act) (Ministers and prefects, the Chairmen of the regional and general councils, the mayors of the municipalities with more than 10,000 inhabitants and the presidents of public institutions of inter-communal cooperation over 10,000 inhabitants, the directors of national and local public institutions that employ at least 200 agents, and the obligation extends to persons of public law and private law persons entrusted with the operation of a public service that employ at least 200 officers).

Article R. 330-2 and R.330-3 of the Code (Articles 42 and 43 of Decree No. 2005-1755 of 30 December 2005) do not impose a strict formalization of the appointment of the person in charge. However, it must result in an act of designation of an official that includes the name, first names, profession and professional address. The description of the appointed person is then brought to the attention of the public under the most appropriate terms, such as in an advertisement placed on the website of the administration.

The first objective is to allow a person who wishes to access a document or re-use public information to be able to apply to a competent person who will facilitate the processing of his/her request. One must however specify that in most jurisdictions, the organization of administrative documents communication depends on the services concerned by the requests. The "responsible person" is therefore often considered as the referent that is kept informed of the difficulties encountered in the access to administrative documents and the re-use of public information. The second objective is to ensure that the different levels of government have some legal expertise to facilitate the full implementation of the Act and become more aware of the obligations arising for them according to access and reuse rights. The person in charge, depending on the mission entrusted to him, will advise his/her administration on the instruction of specific files or carry this out itself, but also suggest organizational improvements to facilitate access to documents. For re-use, this role can, in jurisdictions that are not familiar with such requests, prove more important even by contributing to the development of the register provided for by Article 17 of 1978 Act. The third objective is to improve the transmission of the information between the administrative authorities and the CADA for the dissemination of case-law on access and to make the processing of requests more efficient and faster for opinions and advice.

## 3.3 *The Contentious*

### 3.3.1 The Competent Court and the Remedies

The administrative jurisdiction must hear and solve disputes concerning the implementation by the administration of the Code,[66] as well as conduct all special arrangements. These disputes must be brought in first instance before the Administrative Court. However, the Council of State will be competent if the refusal comes from a collegiate body with national jurisdiction. The judgment of the administrative court cannot be subject to an appeal before the administrative Court of appeal (3rd Article 222-13 and R. 811-1 of the Code of administrative justice). It can thus only be challenged before the Council of State, through the appeal in cassation.

In principle, the recourse before the administrative judge is admissible only if the CADA has been previously seized. However, the process of referral to the administrative tribunal might intervene before the CADA has delivered its opinion, provided it is made during the proceeding before the delivery of the judgment.[67] By way of derogation, when the CADA is not competent to interpret a text on which a claim is based, the applicant does not have to seize it and can apply directly to the administrative judge, in the conditions of ordinary law. The rule of the prior request before the CADA may present difficulties in its implementation, particularly in the event of incomplete communication. The application, presented before an administrative tribunal against the refusal of "missing parts" communication is inadmissible failing new referral to the CADA.[68] However, when the incomplete communication focuses on specific and identified documents, a new referral to the CADA is not required.[69]

It is worth noting that when the judge ordered as an interim emergency measure the disclosure of administrative documents in application of Article L. 521-3 of the

[66]Tribunal of dispute settlement (Tribunal des conflits), *Vinçot et Leborgne c /Caisse MSA du Finistère*, Cases No. 02324, 02325 (Decision of 2 July 1984).

[67]Council of State, *Humbrecht*, Case No. 62332 (Judgment of 12 February 1988).

[68]Council of State, Audebert, Case No. 551194 (Judgment of 20 February 1985); Council of State, *Parkinson*, Cases No. 41589, 41699 (Judgment of 6 May 1985).

[69]Council of State, *Commune de Gravelotte c /Bauchat*, Case No. 144921 (Judgment of 28 January 1998).

Code of administrative justice, communication does not fall within the scope of the 1978 Act and the applicant is not required to apply first to the CADA.[70]

The rejected applicant may attack the decision of refusal within the time limit of 2 months from the day when the CADA had first recorded its request for an opinion. The starting point of the time limit is set to avoid any delaying tactic on the part of the administration. The CADA be seized 1 month after the initial request with the administration, therefore, at the end of a period of 3 months from their application the citizen will be able to refer to the administrative judge the implied refusal to his/her request for disclosure.

### 3.3.2 The Control and the Powers of the Administrative Judge

The judge has important investigation powers. He may "require competent authorities the production of all necessary documents" to settle the dispute, including "documents" which the refusal to disclose is the object of the dispute.[71] In such cases, the document does not have to be communicated to the applicant.[72]

The administrative judge appreciates the lawfulness of the refusal decision and therefore, indirectly, the merits of the opinion of CADA. This is the reason why close coordination is established between the CADA and the administrative judge. However, unlike the administration and the CADA, the administrative judge is not required to automatically consider the legality of the refusal to disclose in light of all of the special arrangements provided for in Article L. 340-1, L.342-1 and L. 342-1 of the Code (20 and 21 of the 17 July 1978 Act). The applicant is therefore required to explicitly refer to these special arrangements.

A decision of nonsuit is pronounced when the document is communicated or published officially after the beginning of proceeding.[73]

## 4 Specific Communication Plans

Pursuant to Article L. 342-2 of the Code (Article 21 of the 17 July 1978 Act), the CADA is competent to interpret the specific communication arrangements provided for in the texts listed in this Article. These schemes often establish more liberal access which articulates however with the provisions of the general regime of the Code and the Act of 17 July 1978. Nonetheless, other provisions establishing a

---

[70]Council of State, *Société Baggerbedrijf de Boer*, Case No. 239466 (Judgment of 29 April 2002).

[71]Council of State, *Banque de France c /Huberschwiller*, Case No. 95310 (Judgment of 23 December 1988).

[72]Council of State, Kevin, Case No. 231661 (Judgment of 14 March 2003).

[73]Council of State (Section), *MINEFI c /SA Dumons, Leb. et CE, idem, MINEFI c /Société Chanel*, Case No. 62282 (17 January 1986).

system of special access exclude the application of this law and the jurisdiction of CADA. This incompetence does not mean that the administration may exempt applications to such regimes. It only means that the challenge of communication denials by the administrative authority based on these provisions may not result in referral to the CADA, but must be brought directly before the administrative tribunal that is territorially competent.

When a particular regime is likely to apply to an application, the authority examines its articulation with the Code and 17 July 1978 Act. Indeed, the latter can continue to apply notwithstanding the existence of specific rules. There are a few general rules to determine if the application should be examined under the Code or under only those of special arrangements. If the particular plan is established exclusively by a text of regulatory value (without legislative basis), or even by a simple circular, it cannot preclude the application of the Code. If the text establishing the special scheme is statutory, then the principle according to which special laws derogate from the provisions of the acts of general scope. The principle being the freedom of access to documents, the legislative provisions, which establish an access regime less favorable than the Code, shall be interpreted in a restrictive manner. A special regime prevents the Code and the 17 July Act to apply if it governs communication of a given document. Legislative provisions which deal with certain documents, or even which govern the publication arrangements do not prevent the Code and the Act of 1978 to apply. In addition, when the special scheme is intended to take effect only for a specified period, the Code and the Act of 1978 once again become applicable until the expiry of this period. Finally, some special arrangements are applicable only to persons designated by them. In this situation, the Code and the 1978 Act should be applied when the request comes from someone else. Schematically, one can distinguish plans that apply excluding the Code and the 1978 Act, and those that apply successively in time with this Act.

## 5 The *Commission d'accès aux documents administratifs* (CADA)

The Commission on access to Administrative Documents (CADA) is an independent and consultative administrative authority responsible for ensuring freedom of access to administrative documents. Its composition guarantees its independence. Its role is primarily to deliver opinions on the refusal by the administration to requests of individuals, companies or associations. Its seizure is mandatory before any contentious issues. It advises governments on the communicable nature of documents and can be accessed by the Government or propose amendments on legislative or regulatory texts. It informs the public on the right of access to documents. Over the past 5 years the CADA has reviewed about 5000 applications, for which it has given an opinion or for which the Council has given an opinion, which are widely followed by the administrative authorities, the applicant often receiving a positive response to his/her claim.

## 5.1 The Role of CADA

The CADA was founded in 1978 to ensure the correct application of the right of access. It is an organization whose aim is to help private citizens, as well as the authorities, and is the first point of contact in the request for information. Any person who is denied access to an administrative document, or gets no response within a period of 1 month, may seize CADA so that it can give an opinion on the communicable nature of this document. He/she can also apply for appeal when he/she receives a negative decision for the re-use of public information.

Any administrative authority may make use of the CADA to be illuminated on the communicable nature of an administrative document or archive or on the possibility and conditions of re-use of public information. Through its opinions and advice, which are widely followed by the administration, it ensures the transparency of administrative actions and makes known its interpretation of the applicable texts. This organization gives proposals to the Government for the necessary modifications to improve the exercise of the right of access and of the re-use of public information; it can also impose penalties against those who recycle public information in violation of the requirements of the Act.

## 5.2 Composition

The 6 June 2005 Ordinance gave the status of independent administrative authority to the CADA, whose independence is guaranteed by its composition. Since the effectivity of this ordinance, the composition of the CADA is contained in the Code (Article 341-1). It is chaired by a Councilor of State and includes, in addition, ten members: a magistrate of the Court of cassation and a magistrate of the Court of Auditors, a Deputy and a Senator, a local official, a University Professor, a qualified citizen, a member of the CNIL, and three citizens in various fields (archives, competition and price, and public dissemination of information).

There are two forms of deliberation: the plenary panel (for general cases) with a quorum rising to six members. The Government Commissioner may give oral representations (Article R. 341-6 of the Code). It can also deliberate in a small group (for sanctions in the case of re-use of public information). The quorum is made up of three members, which must not be in a situation of conflict of interest with regard to the case in question. The functioning rules have been adapted to consider the repressive nature of the procedure (Article R. 343-6—R. 343-12 of the Code). Decisions are made with a vote—the majority of the members present decides on the outcome.

To ensure that CADA is functioning effectively, the president calls on rapporteurs whose activity is coordinated by a rapporteur-general and a deputy general rapporteur. A Commissioner of the Government, appointed by the Prime Minister sits with the Board and attends its deliberations. For the accomplishment of its mission, the CADA relies finally on a general secretariat whose officers (currently 13) are placed at its disposal by the services of the Prime Minister.

## 5.3 Activities

The CADA has at its disposal means of action to fulfill its mission defined in Article 340-1 of the Code, which is to "ensure respect for freedom of access to administrative documents and archives as well as the application of Chapter II relating to the re-use of public information". It issues opinions "when it is seized by a person who is opposed to a denial of access to an administrative document [...], a refusal of consultation of archives documents [...], or an adverse decision on re-use of public information". The CADA advises the authorities referred to in Article L.300-2 of the Code (Article 1 of 17 July 1978 Act) "on all matters relating to the application of chapters I, II and IV of title I of this book and title I of book II of the Heritage Code" (Article 27 of the Decree of December 30, 1995) under Article R. 342-4 of the Code. It proposes all modifications to the texts that it considers useful (Article R. 342-5 of the Code). It draws up an annual report. The Code ordinance gave the CADA also a power of sanction concerning the re-use of documents by the public. Indeed according to Article 18 of the 1978 Act, any person re-using public information in violation of this Act shall be punished with a fine imposed by the CADA.

For the year 2012, the CADA has been seized of 4749 requests out of which 65.2% from natural persons, and 34.8% by legal persons. The communications were mainly concerning town planning (16.8%), public service (15.1%) and social affairs (13.8%). The CADA supported the communication in 45.3% of the cases and refused it only in 10.4% of them (the rest of the requests declared non-admissible). A request is treated in an average of 39 days. It is noteworthy that only 4% of the instructed files were requests for advice from public administrations.

The mechanism of protection set up in French law is original but also effective to limit the number of judicial review cases. The case-law of the Commission achieves a subtle balance between transparency and secrecy within a general legal framework. Its interpretations, which are particularly favorable to citizens, do not leave the judge and the legislator indifferent.[74]

[74]Laluque 2003.

# 6 The Principle of Freedom of Re-use

Originally, Article 10 of 17 July 1978 Act foresaw that the right of access excludes the right for the beneficiaries or third parties to reuse data for commercial use. The Ordinance of 6 June 2005 affirms the general principle of freedom of the re-use of public information, for commercial purposes or not. It implements the EC Directive 2003/98/EC, which includes measures to guarantee the effectiveness of this principle, but also to ensure free competition in its exercise. As a corollary, obligations are imposed on the administration but also on private operators.

## 6.1 *Obligations for the Administration and Private Operators*

The main three types of obligations facing the administration are to facilitate access to information, to organize the freedom of its reuse, and to respect free competition. For information developed or held by a public body to be reused, the most important thing is that potential customers are aware of its existence. In this regard, new Article 17 the Act 17 July 1978 provides that "The public services that elaborate or hold public information shall give users access to a directory of the main documents in which such information is presented". The re-use of public information is subject to the condition that this information should not be altered, its meaning not be transformed, and the sources and the date of the last update of this information be mentioned.

If the administration considers that the production of the directory entails a cost or if it wishes to obtain a remuneration of its intellectual property rights, it may require payment of a fee to issue a license. The license shall set out the conditions of re-use of the public information. Non-compliance with the terms of the license, or the distortion of public information, is subject to penalties imposed by the CADA on a complaint from the administration.

## 6.2 *Control and Sanctions*

As in all other sectors related to the communication of administrative documents, the CADA has jurisdiction in disputes over the re-use of public information: the commission gives an opinion when notified by an individual denied access to an administrative document. However, it is only in this area that the CADA has the power to sanction certain illegal behaviors by imposing fines. Three behaviors are targeted: the alteration or denaturation of public reused information or the re-use of documents without mentioning sources, the ignorance of the reuse conditions under a license issued for this purpose, the breach of the obligation of obtaining a license. The amount of the fine imposed depends on whether public information has been re-used for commercial purposes or non-commercial purposes. In the first case, the amount of the fine is proportionate to the seriousness of the offense committed and the profits derived from the breach. For a first violation, the amount of the fine may not exceed 150,000 euros "if the repeated breach takes places within the five years from the date the sanction previously imposed becomes final, it may not exceed EUR 300,000 or, in the case of a company, 5% of turnover excluding taxes within the limit of 300,000 euros". In the second case, the maximum amount of the fine is equal to that provided for contraventions of the 5th class (up to EUR 1500 and 3000 in case of recidivism). The CADA may, instead of or in addition to the fine, ban the offender of the reuse of public information for a maximum period of 2 years. This time may be extended to 5 years for a second offense within 5 years of the first infringement. The board may also order the publication of the sanction at the offender's expenses.

## References

Bonnet. (2004). L'accouchement sous X et la Cour européenne des droits de l'homme (à propos de l'arrêt Odièvre v. France du 13 février 2003). *Revue trimestrielle des droits de l'homme, 58*, 405–421.

CADA. (2008). *Documents administratifs- Droit d'accès et réutilisation*. Paris: La Documentation française.

CADA. (2012). *Rapport d'activité 2012*. Retrieved February 14, 2017, from http://www.cada.fr

Conseil d'Etat. (1997). *Pour une meilleure transparence de l'administration- Etude sur l'harmonisation des textes et l'amélioration des droits du citoyen en matière d'accès aux données publiques*. Paris: La Documentation française.

Edel, F. (2011). La Convention du Conseil de l'Europe sur l'accès aux documents publics: premier traité consacrant un droit général d'accès aux documents administratifs. *Revue Française d'Administration Publique*, 137–138.

Lallet, A. (2014). *Documents administratifs: accès et réutilisation*, Répertoire Dalloz de contentieux administratif.

Laluque, L. (2003). *La Commission d'accès aux documents administatifs: contribution à l'étude de la transparence administative* (PhD Thesis). University Orleans.

Schultz, S. (2010). *In dubio pro libertate – the General Freedom Right* (GFR). Retrieved February 14, 2017, from http://ir.polytechnic.edu.na/handle/10628/89

Scoffoni, G. (1992). *Droit à l'information administrative aux Etats-Unis-Du modèle américain au système français de transparence*. Paris: Economica.

## *List of Cases*

## *European Court of Human Rights*

European Court of Human Rights 26.03.1987, *Leander v. Sweden*, Application No. 9248/81

European Court of Human Rights 07.07.1989, *Gaskin v. the United Kingdom*, Application No. 10454/83

European Court of Human Rights 07.06.2001, *Kress v. France*, Application No. 39594/98

European Court of Human Rights, 15.06.2004, *Sîrbu and Others v. Moldova*, Applications No. 73562/01, 73565/01, 73712/01, 73744/01, 73972/01 and 73973/01
European Court of Human Rights 10.07.2006, *Sdruženi Jihočeské Matky v. Czech Republic*, Application No. 19101/03

## *French Courts*

## *Conseil Constitutionnel (Constitutional Council)*

Constitutional Council 16.07.1971, Decision 71/44 DC, JORF of 18 July 1971, p. 7114
Constitutional Council 16.12.1999, Decision 99-421 DC, JORF of 22 December 1999, p. 19041

### Council of State (Conseil d'Etat)

Council of State 06.02.1980, *Murlidhar*, Case No. 13132, Leb.
Council of State 09.03.1983, *Association SOS Défense I*, Case No. 45736, Leb., p. 728
Council of State 27.04.1983, *Epoux Deplace*, Case No. 34773
Council of State 25.05.1983, *Holland,* Case No. 28097
Council of State 27.07.1984, *Association SOS Défense II*, Case No. 30590, Leb.
Council of State 16.11.1984, *Mesmin*, Case No. 50234
Council of State 16.01.1985, *Thorel*, Case No. 46591, Leb., p. 635
Council of State 20.02.1985, *Audebert*, Case No. 551194, Leb., p. 51
Council of State (Section) 26.07.1985, *A.*, Case No. 43468, Leb., p. 243
Council of State (Section) 17.01.1986, *MINEFI c/SA Dumons*, Case No. 62282, Leb.
Council of State 24.01.1986, Vinçot, Case No. 44883, Leb. p. 536
Council of State, 06.06.1986, *Ordre des avocats de Pontoise*, Case No. 57285, Leb., p. 159
Council of State (Assembly) 08.04.1987, *Ministre de la santé c/Tête*, Case No. 45172, Leb., p. 144
Council of State, 03.06.1987, *Ministre de l'urbanisme c/Durand*, Case No. 65457, Leb., p. 190
Council of State 30.09.1987, *Compagnie générale des eaux*, Case No. 66573, Leb.
Council of State 12.02.1988, *Humbrecht*, Case No. 62332, Leb., p. 798
Council of State 08.07.1988, *Federation de la mutualité agricole d' Île-de-France*, Case No. 68502, Leb.
Council of State 26.10.1988, *Lalande*, Case No. 197018, Leb.
Council of State 23.12.1988, *Banque de France c/Huberschwiller*, Case No. 95310, Leb., p. 688
Council of State 16.06.1989, *Office public HLM de Paris*, Case No. 83476, Leb. 1989
Council of State 21.07.1989, *Association SOS Défense et Bertin*, Case No. 39196, Leb.
Council of State 30.03.1990, *Mme D*, Case No. 90237, Leb.
Council of State 12.09.1990, *Ministre du travail, de l'emploi et de la formation professionnelle c/Thomé*, Case No. 107566, Leb.
Council of State 21.09.1990, *SARL Villerupt auto école*, Case No. 89251
Council of State 31.03.1991, *El Fourti*, Case No. 195072, Leb.
Council of State 10.04.1991, *Commune de Louviers*, Case No. 112904, Leb.
Council of State 12.10.1992, *Ministre du budget c/Durand*, Case No. 65457, Leb., p. 781
Council of State 28.04.1993, *Mme P*, Case No. 95139, Leb.
Council of State 04.01.1995, *David*, Case No. 110211, Leb.
Council of State (Assembly) 14.02.1996, *Mirlit*, Case No. 144042, Leb.
Council of State 28.01.1998, *Commune de Gravelotte c/Bauchat*, Case No. 144921

Council of State 27.10.2000, *Louard*, Case No. 222672, Leb.
Council of State 27.11.2000, *Association Comité tous frères*, Case No. 188431, Leb. 2000
Council of State 14.12.2001, *Ministre de l'emploi c/Farida Dall*, Case No. 204761, Leb., p. 643
Council of State 29.04.2002, *Société Baggerbedrijf de Boer*, Case No. 239466
Council of State 14.03.2003, *Kevin*, Case No. 231661, Leb.
Council of State 25.05.2005, *Association Reporters sans Frontières*, Case No. 260926, Leb.
Council of State 22.02.2007, *Association du personnel relevant des établissements pour inadaptés*, Case No. 264541, Leb.
Council of State 10.01.2007, *Comité national olympique et sportif français*, Case No. 280069, Leb.
Council of State 07.08.2008, *Ministre d'Etat, Ministre de l'Intérieur et de l'aménagement du territoire c/Fédération chrétienne des témoins de Jehovah*, Case No. 310220, Leb.
Council of State 07.05.2010, *M. Bertin*, Case No. 303168, Leb.

## Administrative Courts of Appeal (Cours administratives d'appel)

Administrative Courts of Appeal Nantes 30.07.2003, *Association "L'arbre au milieu"*, Case No. 00NT01259, Leb.
Administrative Courts of Appeal Bordeaux 27.04.2004, *Soule*, Case No. 00BX00267, Leb.

## Administrative Courts (Tribunaux administratifs)

Administrative Court Versailles 11.07.1985, *SA Montenay*.
Administrative Court Versailles 31.01.1980, *Union locale CGT Chesnay*.
Administrative Court Toulouse 16.02.1987, *Dumeaux*.
Administrative Court Bordeaux 02.05.2007, *Mr. A*.

## Tribunal of Dispute Settlement (Tribunal des conflits)

Tribunal of Dispute Settlement 02.07.1984, *Vinçot et Leborgne c/Caisse MSA du Finistère*, Cases No. 02324 and No. 02325

## List of the Websites of All National Courts

Constitutional Council (Conseil constitutionnel). http://www.conseil-constitutionnel.fr/
Conseil d'Etat (Council of State). http://www.conseil-etat.fr/
Cour administrative d'appel de Bordeaux (Administrative Court of Appeal of the City of Bordeaux). http://bordeaux.cour-administrative-appel.fr/
Cour administrative d'appel de Nantes (Administrative Court of Appeal of the City of Nantes). http://nantes.cour-administrative-appel.fr/
Tribunal administratif de Bordeaux (Administrative Court of Bordeaux). http://bordeaux.tribunal-administratif.fr/
Tribunal administratif de Toulouse (Administrative Court of Toulouse). http://toulouse.tribunal-administratif.fr/
Tribunal administratif de Versailles (Administrative Court of Versailles). http://versailles.tribunal-administratif.fr/
Tribunal des conflits (Tribunal of dispute settlement). http://www.tribunal-conflits.fr

# Chapter 7
# Access to Information in German Law in Comparison to Brazilian Law N° 12.527/2011

**Arno Scherzberg and Svenja Solka**

**Contents**



## 1 Introduction

Because of the authoritarian so-called "Arkanprinzip" (principle of secrecy), predominant since the times of absolutism, free access to information held by the state has been established in Germany only in recent times and not even to its full extent. The Federal Freedom of Information Act (FIA) took effect in 2006, following forerunners in the constitution of the federal state of Brandenburg and several


A. Scherzberg (✉)
University of Erfurt, Erfurt, Germany
e-mail: arno.scherzberg@uni-erfurt.de

S. Solka
German Federal Ministry of Economics and Energy, Berlin, Germany


 
H.-J. Blanke, R. Perlingeiro (eds.), *The Right of Access to Public Information*,
DOI 10.1007/978-3-662-55554-5_7

sub-constitutional provisions as e.g., in the Federal Environmental Information Act (EIA). Today, in addition to the Federal law, FIAs exist in 12 of the 16 German *Länder* (federal states). Four of them (Berlin, Brandenburg, North Rhine-Westphalia and Schleswig-Holstein) were already in force before the federal law has passed the national legislative bodies. Thus on the federal level and in most of the German *Länder* unconditional access to information held by the state marks the rule, while its limitation is an exception that needs to be justified. Bavaria, Lower Saxony, Saxony and Hesse, however, to this day do not have a FIA. Thus in these states access to information is still at the discretion of the competent authority. Whether this is compatible with the constitution has been often disputed. The prevailing opinion denies that freedom of access to information held by the state is a direct implication of the principle of democracy and of the fundamental right of freedom of information.[1] In our opinion, this is not justified.[2]

Today, compared to Germany, many other countries and supranational institutions provide a higher level of freedom of access, e.g., Article 11 and Article 42 of the Charta of Fundamental Rights of the European Union and Chapter 2, Article 1 of The Freedom of the Press Act Sweden.[3] However, even in Germany the further development of freedom of information has recently become an issue again. In 2012 Hamburg's Transparency Act was passed according to which access to the state's data collections no longer depends on a citizen's application, but shall additionally be provided ex officio. Authorities are obliged to actively enter information into an information register. The law provides for an extensive list of information that needs to be published. Following Hamburg's example, several other German states have begun the debate about passing Transparency Acts, which would exceed the existing Freedom of Information Acts in a similar way.[4] At present, an open-data act is being prepared on the federal level. Thus, a new chapter in the struggle for more state transparency has been opened.[5]

## 2 The Scope of the Right of Access

Besides the procedural rules that give parties a right of access to information with regard to ongoing administrative proceedings, various laws in Germany provide for general rights of access to information. Which provisions are applicable depends on

[1]Schoch 2016, Introduction para 68, 83.

[2]Scherzberg, in Fluck et al. (2003), Die verfassungsrechtlichen Grundlagen des Informationszugangs (The Constitutional Basis of Access to Information), para 19, 104.

[3]English version: http://www.riksdagen.se/en/Documents-and-laws/ (Accessed on 25 February 2017). The Freedom of the Press Act is one of four fundamental laws which form the Swedish constitution, see Jahn 2009, p. 107.

[4]See Chap. 6 regarding the Transparency Act of Rhineland-Palatinate, which entered into force on January 1st 2016.

[5]For more information about a recent draft of an Open Data Act on the federal level see Chap. 6.

the type of information sought and, because of Germany's federal structure, on the addressee (federation or federal state) of the request of information.

- Sec. 3.1 sentence 1 EIA provides for a right of access to environmental information from federal authorities (Sec. 1.2 and 2.1 EIA) without the applicant having to set forth a legal interest. Access to information is granted on application (Sec. 4.1 EIA). Along with the Federal EIA all German *Länder* provide for corresponding rules on access to environmental information from federal state authorities (partly referring to the federal law).
- Sec. 2.1 sentence 1 of the Consumer Information Act (CIA) provides the right of access to certain information. It refers to products as defined in the Food and Feed Code and to so-called consumer products. The applicant can inter alia gain information on data concerning any risks a product may pose to consumer health and safety, as well as data on its identification, origin, use, manufacture and treatment. Access to information is granted on application (Sec. 4.1 CIA).
- In a general clause Sec. 1.1 FIA grants the general right of access to official information. In 12 of the 16 German *Länder* equivalent FIAs exist (see 1).

## 2.1 Beneficiaries and Addressees of the Right of Access[6]

According to Sec. 1.1 sentence 1 FIA everybody has a right of access to official information. This includes natural and private legal persons.[7] Natural persons are entitled to require access regardless of their nationality.[8] Likewise, domestic and foreign private legal persons are among the group of beneficiaries.[9] They need to have a legal personality; however, partial legal capacity is sufficient.[10] In some of the laws of the German *Länder* the group of beneficiaries is defined more precisely as "every private natural and legal person" (Sec. 1.2 sentence 1 FIA Mecklenburg-Vorpommern, Sec. 3 sentence 1 Access to Information Act Schleswig-Holstein, similar also Sec. 3.1 sentences 1, 2 FIA Berlin). In North Rhine-Westphalia only natural persons are entitled (Sec. 4.1 FIA North Rhine-Westphalia).

Article 10 of the Brazilian Law N° 12.527/2011 stipulates that any interested party may submit a request to access information. Using the term "any interested party" leaves the scope of the group of beneficiaries unclear. However, on 16 May 2012, Decree N° 7.724/2012 entered into force, which addresses organs and entities of the Federal Executive Branch (see Article 1, 2, 5 of Decree N° 7.724/2012). Article 11 of the Decree stipulates that a request may be formulated by any natural

[6]The following remarks refer to the Federal FIA. When the FIA differs considerably from the EIA, the CIA or the provisions at the federal states level, this will be noted.

[7]Rossi 2006, Sec. 1 para 7.

[8]Explanatory memorandum, Parliamentary Document 15/4493, p. 7.

[9]Rossi 2006, Sec. 1 para 12.

[10]Schoch 2016, Sec. 1 para 61, 71; disagreeing: Jastrow & Schlatmann 2006, Sec. 1 para 10.

or juridical person. Thus, the group of beneficiaries is equivalent to those in the German Federal FIA and the majority of the laws of the *Länder*.

According to Sec. 1.1 sentences 1 and 2 FIA, the claim can be directed towards the federal authorities or other federal bodies and facilities, as far as they perform administrative tasks. This clarifies that also the German parliament, the Federal Constitutional Court, federal courts, and the German Central Bank are also obliged to grant access, as far as they perform administrative tasks. Conversely, there is no requirement to grant access when parliamentary affairs (inter alia legislation and scrutiny of elections) or jurisdiction are concerned.[11] Furthermore, private natural and legal persons can be obliged to grant access as well, as far as an authority has involved them in performing its public services (Sec. 1.1 sentence 3). This widening of the scope of addressees is meant to set up access to information in the most comprehensive way possible.[12] However, the application has to be submitted to the authority having engaged the private person (Sec. 7.1 sentence 2). The respective authority (and not the private person) is thus addressee of the right of access.[13]

Provisions at the level of the *Länder* address public bodies of the state, the municipalities, the associations of local authorities, public legal persons under the state's supervision, and private natural or legal persons performing public service tasks.[14]

The Brazilian Law N° 12.527/2011 obliges the Union, as well as the States, Federal Districts and Municipalities (Article 1) to grant access. Addressees of the right of access are public bodies integrated in one of the three branches of government (Article 1 Sole paragraph 1), as well as municipal authorities, public foundations, public companies, public-private entities and other bodies directly or indirectly controlled by the Union, States, Federal District and Municipalities (Article 1 Sole paragraph 2). Article 2 and 5 of Decree N° 7.724/2012 refer to all organs and entities of the Federal Executive Branch. Comparing Brazilian and German Law we see that the same bodies are obliged to grant access, however, in Germany this arises not from a single law but from a number of laws.

## 2.2 Accessible Information

The FIA grants access to official information that is defined as any recording serving official purposes, regardless of the manner of its storage (Sec. 2 No. 1 sentence 1). Drafts and notes that are not meant to become an integral part of a case file are not included (Sec. 2 No. 1 sentence 2). The usage of the term "recording" emphasizes that the relevant information may be embodied in any

[11] Explanatory memorandum, Parliamentary Document 15/4493, p. 7, 8.

[12] Explanatory memorandum, Parliamentary Document 15/4493, p. 8.

[13] Schmitz & Jastrow 2005, p. 988.

[14] See, e.g., Sec. 2.1 and 2.4 FIA North Rhine-Westphalia; Sec. 2.1 and 2.2 FIA Thuringia.

form, thus ideas and thoughts of the employees do not qualify as official information according to Sec. 1.1.[15] The right of access only concerns information already held by the authority and entails no obligation to secure new relevant information.[16] Therefore, no new research is required; however, authorities have to ascertain whether private natural or legal persons involved in administrative tasks are in possession of the information sought.

According to Article 4, item 1 of the Brazilian Law N° 12.527/2011 access has to be granted to data that may be used to produce and convey knowledge, contained in any medium, form or format. Article 3.1 of Decree N° 7.724/2012 contains a similar definition. In this respect, the Brazilian provisions are restrictive, as the data's possible usage for producing and conveying knowledge has to be proven, whereas the German FIA grants access without this requirement.

Article 7 of the Brazilian Law N° 12.527/2011 contains further guidelines regarding accessible information and the scope of the right of access. The applicant inter alia has the right to obtain primary, complete, authentic and updated information (Article 7, item 4). There is no such obligation in German law. According to Article 7, item 3 of the Brazilian Law N° 12.527/2011 the applicant's access includes information produced or held by a natural person or a private institution if the information results from any (ceased or still existing) bond with an authority. German law includes access to information held by private persons only insofar as they take part in the authorities' performance of public services as mentioned above.

## 2.3 *Prerequisites of Claims*

Sec. 1 FIA grants an unconditional right of access.[17] Thus, the applicant is required neither to outline any legitimate interest in the information sought nor to point out any purpose why he/she applies for access. In contrast other administrative provisions partly require the applicant to set forth a legal interest (e.g., Sec. 29.1 of the Administrative Procedure Act, APA) or a specific interest (e.g., Sec. 6.3 of the Crafts Code).[18] However, if a third person's rights can be affected, the applicant is obliged to disclose his/her motives and interests, as Sec. 7.1 sentence 3 FIA demands him/her to give reasons for his/her request in these cases.[19]

Article 10 para 3 of the Brazilian Law N° 12.527/2011 expressly stipulates that the motives for requesting access do not have to be disclosed if the information being requested is of the public interest. This leaves the question open whether the applicant's motives then need to be shared in all other cases. However, as the law's

[15]Rossi 2006, Sec. 2 para 6, 8.

[16]Kloepfer & von Lewinski 2005, p. 1280; Leopold 2006, p. 594.

[17]Explanatory memorandum, Parliamentary Document 15/4493, p. 7.

[18]Rossi 2006, Sec. 1 para 29, 30.

[19]Schoch 2016, Sec. 1 para 22.

wording does not positively indicate any such obligation and it also does not find any grounds in the rules regarding the application's content, it can be assumed that Article 10 para 3 merely is a clarifying provision. This interpretation is supported by the wording of Article 14 of Decree N° 7.724/2012 that prohibits imposing any requirements regarding the motives of the request of access. Accordingly, the Brazilian law does not provide for an obligation to reveal the motives for access and thus in general complies with the German provisions. However, one has to keep in mind the exception of Sec. 7.1 sentence 3 FIA, which forces the applicant to disclose his/her interests, as mentioned above.

## 2.4 Mode of Access

The authorities can either disclose information themselves, which means that they report on the information's content orally, electronically or in writing (see Sec. 7.3 sentence 1 FIA),[20] allow access to the files by the applicant, or make information available in any other suitable way (Sec. 1.2 sentence 1 FIA). The applicant has the right to apply for one of these options (see Sec. 1.2 sentence 2 FIA). If he/she does so, the authority can only opt for another mode of access in exceptional circumstances (in particular in cases of significantly higher administrative costs, Sec. 1.2 sentences 2 and 3 FIA). As further examples of exceptions, the explanatory memorandum mentions mass procedures in which a large group of people files uniform applications, and cases in which the need for protection of personal data calls for a particular mode of access.[21] If the applicant does not exercise his/her right of option, it is up to the authority's discretion to choose the mode of access.[22] It is also admissible to combine different modes of access.[23]

Access to the files usually takes place by the applicant inspecting the official documents. The applicant is allowed to take notes and can obtain copies and printouts (Sec. 7.4 sentence 1 FIA). If it is not possible to give access by disclosing information or inspection of files, because of matters of fact or because the applicant disagrees with these modes, access is to be given in another suitable way, for example in acoustic form or by presenting video recordings.[24]

In principle, the Brazilian law does not prescribe a certain mode for granting access (Article 10 of the Brazilian Law N° 12.527/2011: "by any legitimate means"). The same applies to Decree N°7.724/2012. However, Article 11 para 5 of the Brazilian Law N° 12.527/2011 stipulates an exception according to which access to digital information shall be granted electronically if the applicant agrees.

[20] Schoch 2016, Sec. 1 para 255.

[21] Explanatory memorandum, Parliamentary Document 15/4493, p. 8.

[22] Rossi 2006, Sec. 1 para 81.

[23] Rossi 2006, Sec. 1 para 82, 95.

[24] Rossi 2006, Sec. 1 para 92.

If granting access requires the handling of a large number of documents or if moving the documents might interfere with their proper processing, the applicant shall be informed about date, place and manner of consulting the information, reproducing or obtaining a certified copy of said information (Article 15 para 2 of the Decree N° 7.724/2012). A similar rule is stipulated by Article 15 para 3 of the Decree N° 7.724/2012 for cases of possible endangering of information's or document's integrity. In case the information is already accessible to the public Article 11.6 of the Brazilian Law N° 12.527/2011 and Article 17 of the Decree N° 7.724/2012 stipulate that the applicant shall be informed in writing about the location and possible ways of access. The public body then is not obliged to grant individual access unless the applicant does not have the necessary means for access at his/her disposal. Finally, Article 13 of the Brazilian Law N° 12.527/2011 specifies that in cases of information contained in documents that could possibly be damaged, a copy shall be made available for the applicant, as well as a certificate attesting its correspondence with the original.

## 2.5 *Applicability of Concurring Provisions Stipulating a Right of Access*

According to Sec. 1 FIA priority must be given to other provisions granting a right of access to official information (Sec. 1.3 FIA). According to the majority of academics this refers to all provisions more specific than Sec. 1,[25] regardless of whether they grant more or less extensive entitlements[26] or exclude the right of access by reason of an exemption clause being applicable.[27] Likewise, it is irrelevant whether the provision in question was enacted before or after the FIA.[28] Examples for more specific provisions are Sec. 3.1 sentence 1 EIA regarding environmental information and Sec. 2.1 sentence 1 CIA regarding so-called consumer information.[29] The precedence of specific rules does not apply with regard to Sec. 29 APA and Sec. 25 Tenth Code of Social Law, thus both may be applicable simultaneously with Sec. 1 FIA.[30] One may argue that during administrative proceedings only the parties of the proceedings may claim a right of access as granted in Sec. 29 APA in case of a legal interest while the FIA is only applicable outside of administrative proceedings.[31] However, this opinion has no grounds in the wording of Sec. 1.3 FIA.[32] Therefore, during administrative proceedings both Sec. 29 APA

[25]Scheel, in Berger et al. (2006), Sec. 1 para 114; Sellmann & Augsberg 2006, p. 2295.

[26]Explanatory memorandum, Parliamentary Document 15/4493, p. 8.

[27]Schoch 2016, Sec. 1 para 298; Matthes 2006, p. 70.

[28]Schoch 2016, Sec. 1 para 287.

[29]Schoch 2016, Sec. 1 para 306, 308.

[30]Rossi 2006, Sec. 1 para 116.

[31]Kugelmann 2005, p. 3611.

[32]Schoch 2016, Sec. 1 para 383.

and Sec. 1 FIA are applicable,[33] and the parties of administrative proceedings can choose which regulation they base their claim on for access to the files.[34]

## 3 Limitations to the Right of Access

While access to information marks the rule, its refusal shall be the exception.[35] Limitations to the right of access are stipulated by Sections 3 to 6 FIA. They enable the refusal of access to protect special public interests (Sec. 3), the authorities' decision-making process (Sec. 4), personal data (Sec. 5), as well as intellectual property and trade and business secrets (Sec. 6). In the following paragraphs the protection of public interests and personal data shall be examined more in detail.

### *3.1 Protection of Special Public Interests*

Sec. 3 FIA contains 15 mostly multi-part exemption clauses, which are to be interpreted restrictively.[36] Applications may not be rejected because of other public interests not protected by Sec. 3 FIA (prohibition of analogy).[37] However, as the explanatory memorandum points out, the federal government may—without reference to any explicit exemption clause—invoke the unwritten exemption of the so-called "core area of executive responsibility". This exemption derives directly from the constitution.[38] The term "core area" refers to certain core activities of the government, a sphere of initiative, intra-governmental consultations and activities not being subject to investigation such as the government's decision-making process regarding the preparation of decisions by the cabinet to which access is denied even to parliamentary committees of inquiry.[39] However, the opinion expressed in the memorandum is to be rejected. Instead, Sec. 3 No. 3 point (b) FIA represents the required legal basis for these cases.[40]

---

[33]Leopold 2006, p. 594; Burholt 2006, p. 2202; Matthes 2006, p. 70.

[34]Schoch 2016, Sec. 1 para 383; Burholt 2006, p. 2202.

[35]Berger, in Berger et al. (2006), before Sec. 1 para 7.

[36]Explanatory memorandum, Parliamentary Document 15/4493 p. 9.

[37]Schoch 2016, before Sections 3 to 6 para 18.

[38]Explanatory memorandum, Parliamentary Document 15/4493, p. 12 regarding Sec. 4; in case of a gap in protection the Federal Administrative Court wants to revert to such an unwritten exemption clause, see German Federal Administrative Court (Bundesverwaltungsgericht), 7 C 3.11 (Judgment of 3 November 2011) para 31.

[39]German Federal Constitutional Court (Bundesverfassungsgericht), 2 BvE 3/07 (Judgment of 17 June 2009) para 122.

[40]Scherzberg & Solka, in Fluck et al. (2012), Sec. 3 FIA para 58.

For cases in which an exemption according to Sec. 3 FIA applies, it is discussed controversially whether the exclusion of access is mandatory[41] or the granting of access still lies under the discretion of the respective authority.[42] The latter approach is supported by the wording of Sec. 3 FIA according to which the applicant cannot assert a claim of access in the case of protected public interests being affected. Yet, a voluntary granting of access is not expressly excluded.[43]

In Sec. 3 FIA five areas of public interests are protected: internal and external security of the state and its international relations, proper functioning of government and administration in general and the effective exercise of certain control and supervisory responsibilities, the proper functioning of the courts, certain economic interests of the Federation, and finally interests of secrecy and confidentiality already protected elsewhere within the legal system.[44] The different clauses of Sec. 3 FIA do not form a consistent overall concept. Some clauses protect a certain interest (No. 1 point (a)–(c), No. 2, No. 3, No. 6), others a whole range of responsibilities (No. 1 point (d), (e), (g)). In clause No. 5 the authorship of the relevant information and in clause No. 7 the mode of the information's gathering are significant for the exclusion of access. No. 8 stipulates a general field exemption for intelligence services.[45]

Most of the clauses are formulated very broadly and vaguely (e.g., Sec. 3 No. 1 point (a), No. 2 FIA); therefore, the required restrictive interpretation is difficult to realize. For some of the clauses no practical scope of application can be easily identified, making them in effect superfluous (see Sec. 3 No. 4 second alternative, No. 5, No. 6 second alternative FIA). Sec. 3 No. 6 second alternative FIA protects economic interests of social insurances that include information protected as trade and business secrets by Sec. 6 sentence 2 FIA. Next to that, hardly any scope of application will remain for Sec. 3 No. 6 second alternative FIA.[46] Several clauses are overlapping. E.g., Sec. 3 No. 1 point (a) FIA protects international relations while the object of protection of Sec. 3 No. 3 point (a) FIA is the necessary confidentiality of international negotiations. Likewise, Sec. 3 No. 1 point (c) FIA protects matters of internal and external security while Sec. 3 No. 2 FIA concerns public safety. The contradictions arising from these overlaps and the difficulties in application are even strengthened by the fact that the relevant clauses contain different standards of protection: No. 1 requires the possibility of adverse effects to its objects of protection, No. 2 the possibility of their endangerment, No. 3 their impairment, and No. 6 the potential of their impairment.[47] The application of Sec. 3 FIA is made even more difficult when the purpose of some of the overlapping

[41] Schoch 2009, p. 2991; Kugelmann 2007, Sec. 3 p. 50.

[42] Kloepfer 2006, p. 25; Scherzberg & Solka, in Fluck et al. (2012), Sec. 3 FIA para 61.

[43] Scherzberg & Solka, in Fluck et al. (2012), Sec. 3 FIA para 60.

[44] Scherzberg & Solka, in Fluck et al. (2012), Sec. 3 FIA para 64.

[45] Scherzberg & Solka, in Fluck et al. (2012), Sec. 3 FIA para 68.

[46] Scherzberg & Solka, in Fluck et al. (2012), Sec. 3 FIA para 67, 151.

[47] Scherzberg & Solka, in Fluck et al. (2012), Sec. 3 FIA para 67, 68; Sitsen 2009, p. 157.

clauses is taken into consideration. In some cases, although the respective degree of impairment is formulated differently, the purpose of the provisions demands the same quality of impairment. E.g., Sec. 3 No. 1 point (a) FIA requires possible adverse effects on international relations for which a serious, considerable and noticeable impairment is necessary. Hence, a noticeable impediment of pursuing external policy objectives is necessary. This is particularly the case when a serious disruption of the relationship to other states or an impairment of Germany's reputation abroad is to be suspected.[48] Thus the concrete possibility of impairment is sufficient, for which the authorities have to provide a comprehensible prognosis based on facts.[49] No. 1 point (a) overlaps with No. 3 point (a) which requires an impairment of the confidentiality necessary in international negotiations. At first sight, this exemption is only applicable in case of an actual impairment.[50] However, if the protective purpose is considered, a considerable and noticeable impairment must be considered as sufficient as well[51]; this also has to be set forth by a comprehensible prognosis based on facts.[52] Otherwise, if only an actual impairment would lead to the exclusion of access, the exemption clause would be practically ineffective.[53] Another example are the competition authorities that are protected by various overlapping clauses.[54] In consequence, their protection is equivalent to that of a field exemption—an instrument that the legislator only intended to use for intelligence services (No. 8).

Another inconsistency of the concept of Sec. 3 FIA is that it does not only protect public interests, but also partially private interests: No. 1 point (g) second alternative refers to a person's right to a fair process and thus protects their private interests in the proceedings. No. 4 denies the right of access when the information in question is subject to professional secrecy. No. 7 primarily aims at protecting the informant by keeping his or her anonymity.[55]

In summary, the precept of rule and exception is only formally respected in Sections 1 and 3 FIA; in substance, however, the catalogue of exemption clauses in Sec. 3 FIA is so broad that the rule of access to information is disregarded.[56]

All federal state laws provide for exemption clauses to protect public interests as well, even if they often are less encompassing than Sec. 3 FIA. Some of the

---

[48] Scherzberg & Solka, in Fluck et al. (2012), Sec. 3 FIA para 74, 79.

[49] Schmitz & Jastrow 2005, p. 991; Rossi 2006, Sec. 3 para 9. The Federal Administrative Court's opinion that authorities have a margin of discretion regarding international relations (German Federal Administrative Court (Bundesverwaltungsgericht), 7 C 22/08 (Judgment of 29 October 2009) para 15) is to be rejected.

[50] Kugelmann 2005, p. 3611.

[51] Scherzberg & Solka, in Fluck et al. (2012), Sec. 3 FIA para 128.

[52] Schoch 2016, Sec. 3 para 186.

[53] Scherzberg & Solka, in Fluck et al. (2012), Sec. 3 FIA para 128.

[54] Burholt 2006, p. 2203 et seqq.: Sec. 3 No. 1 points (d), (g), No. 3 points (a) and (b), No. 4 and No. 7.

[55] Scherzberg & Solka, in Fluck et al. (2012), Sec. 3 FIA para 66.

[56] Scherzberg & Solka, in Fluck et al. (2012), Sec. 3 FIA para 164.

provisions also mention private interests. The right of access is, for example, denied to protect confidentially collected or transmitted information if the third party's interest in confidential treatment persists (Sec. 3 No. 7 FIA Bremen, Sec. 3.1 No. 7 Act on Access to Information Saxony-Anhalt, Sec. 7.2 No. 2 point (a) FIA Thuringia, Sec. 1 FIA Saarland refers to Sec. 3 No. 7 of the Federal FIA). Furthermore, several laws provide for field exemptions for their State Office for the Protection of the Constitution (Sec. 3 No. 8 FIA Bremen, Sec. 5 No. 3 Transparency Act Hamburg, Sec. 2 FIA Saarland, Sec. 3.1 No. 8 Act on Access to Information Saxony-Anhalt). Brandenburg and Schleswig-Holstein do not completely exclude access but rather stipulate in relation to certain protected public interests that, if the public interest in the information's disclosure prevails, access may be granted (Sec. 4.2 Law on the Access to Files and Information Brandenburg, Sec. 9.1 Access to Information Act Schleswig-Holstein).

The Brazilian Law N°12.527/2011 provides for restrictions to the right of access to protect public interests as well, though not as extensively as the German FIA. Mainly, Article 7 para 1 of the Brazilian Law N°12.527/2011 (and Article 6, item 2 of the Decree N°7.724/2012 regarding information to which federal level authorities are obliged to grant access) states that information regarding research projects and scientific or technological developments whose secrecy is indispensable to the safety of society and the State is not subject to the right of access. Thus, from the start the provisions enumerate which type of information is not accessible. Article 7 para 1 of the Brazilian Law N° 12.527/2011 corresponds with Article 23 et seqq. of the Brazilian Law N°12.527/2011 according to which information has to be kept confidential for safety reasons. Reasons for excluding unrestricted access to information are inter alia: the endangering of national defence and sovereignty or of the integrity of national territory, damage or endangering of international relations or negotiations, the need for protection of secrets of foreign states or international organizations, the endangering of public health and safety, and of the country's financial and economic stability. The following rules define the different levels of secrecy along with their associated periods (Article 24 of the Brazilian Law N°12.527/2011) and detailed rules on competences and procedures regarding the classification of documents as secret (see as well Article 25 et seqq. of the Decree N°7.724/2012). There are three levels of secrecy—top-secret, secret, and reserved—with different periods for restricting access—25 years for top-secret, 15 years for secret, and 5 years for reserved documents (Article 24 para 1 of the Brazilian Law N°12.527/2011). The law does not provide for more detailed definitions of the levels of secrecy. According to Article 24.2 of the Brazilian Law N°12.527/2011 information is automatically classified as secret if the safety of the president, the vice president or their families is endangered. The classification is valid until the end of their term of office.

The FIA does not recognize any exclusion of information regarding elected representatives or single persons. However, the FIA also provides for an exclusion of access to protect confidential information. According to Sec. 3 No. 4 FIA, access is excluded inter alia in case of an obligation of confidentiality owing to a legal provision or the General Administrative Regulation for the Protection of Classified

Information. No. 4 does not stipulate itself when information needs to be kept secret. It rather draws on special federal laws such as the Law on the Protection of the Federal Constitution and the Act on the Federal Intelligence Service. Therefore, information that has to be kept secret according to a special federal law cannot be accessed based on Sec. 1 FIA either. An extension of confidentiality in a special law automatically leads to an extension of the exception clause of Sec. 3 No. 4 FIA as well. The clause frequently has been subject to criticism because of its broadness and regulatory structure. It is pointed out inter alia that the decision on confidentiality is left to other regulations independently of the FIA's objectives, which is questionable in terms of dynamic references.[57] Sec. 4 Security Clearance Check Act and Sec. 3 General Administrative Regulation for the Protection of Classified Information define the four levels of secrecy—top-secret, secret, confidential, and restricted. According to Sec. 8 General Administrative Regulation for the Protection of Classified Information, the processing authority decides on the necessity to keep information secret, as well as the level of secrecy. Hence, authorities indirectly decide themselves on access to the respective documents what is constitutionally problematic. Therefore, according to the German Federal Administrative Court, Sec. 3 No. 4 FIA is not applicable on the basis of a formal classification as secret only. It rather needs to be examined as well whether the classification is materially correct.[58]

Article 21 of the Brazilian Law N° 12.527/2011 strengthens the right of access by stipulating that access to information required for the protection of fundamental rights—probably mostly through judicial or administrative actions—may not be denied. According to Article 21 Sole paragraph access to the relevant documents may also not be restricted if the violation of human rights by public authorities or by their order is at stake. Both can be classified as reverse exceptions.

## 3.2 Protection of Personal Data

According to Sec. 5.1 sentence 1 FIA, access to personal data may only be granted as far as the applicant's interest in the information outweighs the third person's legitimate interest in keeping his personal data secret or as far as the third person has given his/her consent. Thus, in case of personal data being affected, access to information is prohibited in principle while its admissibility is an exception.[59]

This provision is in accordance with Regulation (EU) 2016/679 on the protection of natural persons with regard to the processing of personal data and on the free movement of such data (General Data Protection Regulation, GDPR) which standardizes the protection of personal data within the European Union as of 25 May

[57] Scherzberg & Solka, in Fluck et al. (2012), Sec. 3 FIA para 133 et seqq.

[58] Scherzberg & Solka, in Fluck et al. (2012), Sec. 3 FIA para 136.

[59] Explanatory memorandum, Parliamentary Document 15/4493, p. 13.

2018.[60] The relation between freedom of access to information and data protection is in particular addressed in recital 154 and Articles 6.2, 6.3 and 86 GDPR. These provisions show that the GDPR largely leaves the regulation of the relation between data protection and access to information to the member states' legal systems. According to Article 88 GDPR, this also applies, as far as personal data of employees are concerned. Member states should, as is stated in recital 154, "reconcile public access to official documents and the re-use of public sector information with the right to the protection of personal data and [...] provide for the necessary reconciliation with the right to the protection of personal data pursuant to this Regulation". However, granting access according to the FIA needs to comply with the requirements of Article 6.3 GDPR and thus national law defining the conditions of access to personal data must provide for the weighing of interests in access and in data protection. The GDPR does not stipulate any further conditions. Especially Article 6.4 GDPR, which stipulates that the purposes for which personal data have been collected shall be considered, is not applicable according to the purpose and intention of the above-mentioned provisions.

As the FIA does not provide for a definition of "personal data" itself, the definition of Sec. 3.1 Federal Data Protection Act is used according to which personal data means specific data about personal or objective affairs of a specified or specifiable natural person.[61] Specific data refers to information regarding a single natural person or being likely to relate to this person.[62] Personal affairs, e.g., are a person's name, address, and date of birth. Objective affairs inter alia include criminal offenses.[63]

If the respective *third person has consented*, access is granted without the need to consider the balance of interests.[64] The consent needs to be given in advance, a subsequent approval is not sufficient.[65] The consent has to be based on a free decision of the person concerned, which requires that the decision's purpose and consequences were pointed out to him/her.[66] If the consent is limited, these limits have to be respected in the access granted.[67] All state level laws include the possibility of

[60]The provisions of the GDPR are directly applicable in the EU member states. However, it partly leaves room for national legislation, especially via various so-called "opening clauses". To this end the Federal Government passed a draft act to adjust the Federal Data Protection Act to the GDPR on 1 February 2017. Core of the draft act is the revision of the Federal Data Protection Act, but at the same time it implements EU-Directive No. 2016/680 into German law. The German version of the draft act can be found here http://www.bmi.bund.de/SharedDocs/Downloads/DE/Gesetzestexte/Entwuerfe/entwurf-datenschutz-grundverordnung.pdf?__blob=publicationFile (Accessed on 25 February 2017).

[61]Schoch 2016, Sec. 5 para 22. Article 4.1 GDPR defines "personal data" as any information relating to an identified or identifiable natural person.

[62]Jastrow & Schlatmann 2006, Sec. 5 para 6.

[63]Schoch 2016, Sec. 5 para 23.

[64]Schoch 2016, Sec. 5 para 33.

[65]Fetzer, in Fluck et al. (2005), Sec. 5 FIA para 41; Schoch 2016, Sec. 5 para 34.

[66]Schoch 2016, Sec. 5 para 35.

[67]Schoch 2016, Sec. 5 para 53.

the third person's consent. Sec. 5.3 FIA North Rhine-Westphalia stipulates that the consent is to be considered as refused if it is not given within 1 month. Sec. 6.4 sentence 2 FIA Thuringia stipulates the same regarding specially protected data.

Without consent, the authorities have to weigh *the interest in disclosing the information and the interest in its confidentiality*. When regarding the applicant's interests, the purpose of access is relevant.[68] A possible public's interest in revealing the respective information is to be considered, as well as transparency also serves the public.[69] The opposing interest in confidentiality has to qualify as relevant for protection to be granted which fails if personal data can already be obtained through generally accessible sources.[70] The data's qualification for protection depends on the type of data so that the more the inviolable personal sphere is affected the greater is the level of protection. Furthermore, it depends on the context of their use and the possible consequences of their release (e.g., a threatening stigmatization).[71]

When the opposing interests are evaluated, the specific circumstances of each case have to be considered.[72] If the interest in confidentiality prevails, access to information is to be rejected, and vice versa, if the interest of the applicant is predominant, access has to be granted.[73] Academics have criticized the necessity of weighing the opposing interests, especially as Sec. 5 FIA does not provide clear criteria for it.[74]

Most laws at the state level also order the weighing of the opposing interests.[75] However, instead of referring to the applicant's interest in information Sec. 10 of the Access to Information Act Schleswig-Holstein points out that access may be granted if the *public* interest in disclosure prevails.

Several state laws also allow the information's disclosure if it is authorized by specific legal provisions.[76]

Sec. 5.1 sentence 2 FIA stipulates stricter requirements for specific types of personal data as described in Sec. 3.9 of the Federal Data Protection Act, i.e. information about a person's racial or ethnic origins, political opinions, religious or philosophical beliefs, trade union membership and health or sex life. In this case, access to information is only permitted with the third person's explicit consent. This consent has to clearly include the above-mentioned issues.[77]

---

[68] Schoch 2016, Sec. 5 para 40.

[69] Explanatory memorandum, Parliamentary Document 15/4493, p. 13.

[70] Schoch 2016, Sec. 5 para 44.

[71] Fetzer, in Fluck et al. (2005), Sec. 5 FIA para 35; Schoch 2016, Sec. 5 para 45.

[72] Schoch 2016, Sec. 5 para 46.

[73] Schoch 2016, Sec. 5 para 52.

[74] Masing 2004, p. 402 et seq.; according to Schoch 2016, Sec. 5 para 2, 29 criticism is too strict, as Sec. 5.2, 5.3, and 5.4 contain criterions for weighing the opposing interests.

[75] See, e.g., Sec. 6.1 FIA Berlin; Sec. 9.1 No. 5 FIA Thuringia.

[76] See, e.g., Sec. 7 No. 2 FIA Mecklenburg-Vorpommern; Sec. 9.1 point (b) FIA North Rhine-Westphalia.

[77] Fetzer, in Fluck et al. 2005, Sec. 5 FIA para 43.

Sec. 5.2 FIA determines in its first alternative that the interest in confidentiality is predominant in case of information being connected to the third person's service, official public-law relationship or mandate. This clause constitutes an absolute exclusion of access.[78] With the term "service", it refers to employment relationships between a third person and the federal state, which includes civil servants, public employees, judges and soldiers. The term "official public-law relationship" refers to legal relationships between a third person and the federal state marked by a special bond of loyalty. An example would be the relationship between the federal state and the members of the federal government.[79] The term "mandate" was added to the law's text during the legislative procedure and pertains to parliamentary mandates. Although the exercise of a mandate cannot be classified as an administrative activity and, therefore, does not fall within the scope of application of the FIA, the integration of this clause was justified by stating that it allows for the protection of documents of the German *Bundestag*'s administration concerning its representatives and staff, provided that their activities are subject to the FIA.[80]

The second alternative of Sec. 5.2 FIA—stating that the interest in confidentiality is of priority when information is subject to professional or official secrecy—has significant overlaps with Sec. 3 No. 4 FIA (see 3.1). Many academics consider the scope of both regulations to be identical, thus Sec. 5.2 FIA would be superfluous.[81] However, Sec. 5 FIA is applicable only with respect to personal data; therefore, Sec. 5.2 FIA must be considered a lex specialis.[82]

Personal data encompasses inter alia name, title, academic degree, indications of professional and functional status, office address and telephone numbers. However, because of the close link between this personal data and a person's business life there is less need for legal protection. The FIA is governed instead by the intention to make the authorities' activities transparent and controllable.[83] Thus, as a rule, the applicant's interest in information prevails if personal data of experts and consultants once active in administrative proceedings is to be disclosed (Sec. 5.3 FIA). This rule can be refuted in individual cases resulting in access being denied.[84] According to the explanatory memorandum this would be the case for example if the participation in the proceedings itself needs to be kept secret. For that, it is decisive whether the person concerned might experience noticeable disadvantages in case of the data's disclosure.[85] Academics emphasize the importance of this

[78]Schoch 2016, Sec. 5 para 67.

[79]Schoch 2016, Sec. 5 para 70.

[80]Resolution recommendation & report of the internal affairs committee, Parliamentary Document 15/5606 p. 6.

[81]Rossi 2006, Sec. 5 para 16; Mecklenburg & Pöppelmann 2007, Sec. 5 para 23.

[82]Likewise Berger, in Berger et al. (2006), Sec. 5 para 19.

[83]Rossi 2006, Sec. 5 para 17.

[84]Rossi 2006, Sec. 5 para 31.

[85]Explanatory memorandum, Parliamentary Document 15/4493, p. 13, 14.

exemption: if experts needed to fear personal or economic disadvantage, finding experts for proceedings would become most difficult.[86]

If the above-mentioned personal data refers to public employees, access to information is not excluded unless another exemption clause is applicable (Sec. 5.4 FIA).

Article 31 para 1, item 1 of the Brazilian Law N°12.527/2011 prescribes that access to personal information shall in principle be restricted to legally authorized public agents and the persons the information pertains to for a maximum time period of 100 years. According to Article 31 para 1, item 2 access is possible if it is permitted by a legal provision or the person concerned expressly gives his/her consent. At this point, a weighing of opposing interests is not established. In this regard, Article 31 of the Brazilian Law N°12.527/2011 seems to be stricter than the respective German law. However, according to Article 31.3 of the Brazilian Law N°12.527/2011 personal information can be released for specific purposes, inter alia if the information is required for the protection of superior public and general interests. Using the term "superior" indicates that the Brazilian law as well provides for a possibility of weighing the opposing interests, even though in a more restrictive way than the FIA requires, as Article 31 para 3 of the Brazilian Law N°12.527/2011 only mentions superior *public and general* interests. Article 31 para 4 of that Law denominates further constellations in which the release of personal information is possible, inter alia in relation to the retrieval of highly relevant historical facts. Article 55 et seqq. of the Decree N°7.724/2012 contain provisions on access to personal information that largely correspond to the provisions of Brazilian Law N°12.527/2011. Article 59 of the Decree N°7.724/2012 stipulates requirements for access if requested to recover highly relevant historical facts. Article 60, 61 of the Decree N°7.724/2012 contain procedural rules, especially if access to personal information is requested by third parties. Overall, the Brazilian provisions regarding personal information appear to be access-friendlier than those of the German FIA.

## 4 Procedure and Costs

### *4.1 Procedure*

The procedure is governed by the German APA unless the FIA provides for specific rules.[87] Procedural requirements are particularly regulated by Sec. 7 FIA. Sec. 7.1 FIA implies that access to information can only be granted by application.[88] Sec. 4.1 EIA and Sec. 4.1 CIA expressly stipulates the necessity of an application. The

[86]Rossi 2006, Sec. 5 para 31.

[87]Steinbach & Hochheim 2006, p. 522.

[88]Schoch 2016, Sec. 7 para 11.

same applies to several state laws (Sec. 10.1 sentence 1 FIA Mecklenburg-Vorpommern, Sec. 5.1 sentence 1 FIA North Rhine-Westphalia, Sec. 4.1 Access to Information Act Schleswig-Holstein). Likewise, Article 10 of the Brazilian Law N°12.527/2011 prescribes that access to information is only granted by application.

The FIA does not prescribe a certain form for applications.[89] However, the explanatory memorandum points out that authorities may demand a written application and further clarifications. This may be needed to prove the applicant's identity or to inform third persons concerned about it who only then may be able to decide whether to consent to access.[90] The Brazilian Law N°12.527/2011 does not stipulate anything regarding the application's form either. Article 11 para 1, item 1 of Decree N°7.724/2012 seems to differ in that it demands the use of a standard form made available in electronic format and hardcopy. However, according to Article 11 para 3 of Decree N° 7.724/2012 institutions and entities are entitled to receive requests by other legitimate means as well. The provision mentions requests by telephone, e-mail or postal correspondence as examples. However, those other legitimate means need to meet the requirements of Article 12 of the Decree N°7.724/2012 (see below). Article 10 of the Brazilian Law N°12.527/2011 contains rules on the application's content, even though it is not formulated as a binding provision. The application should reveal the applicant's identity and describe precisely what information is requested. Article 12 of Decree N°7.724/2012 stipulates in addition that the request shall contain the number of the applicant's current identity document and his/her postal or e-mail address for receiving communications or the requested information. In German law, the necessity to determine the applicant's identity can only be derived from the explanatory memorandum, as mentioned above.

The decision about granting access is made by the authority that holds the requested information (Sec. 7.1 sentence 1 FIA) respectively by the authority whose vicarious agent holds the information concerned (Sec. 7.1 sentence 2 FIA). An authority, however, is only entitled to grant access to the information it itself collected. If information was received by third persons or other authorities, the authority must obtain the right to grant access by law or by agreement.[91] Sec. 7 FIA does not provide for any rules for cases in which the application is submitted to an incompetent authority. According to Sec. 25 APA, authorities are then obliged to make this known to the applicant.[92] Other laws on access to information stipulate an obligation to forward the application to the competent authority and to inform the applicant hereof (Sec. 13.1 sentence 4 FIA Berlin, Sec. 6.1 sentence 6 Law on the Access to Files and Information Brandenburg; only in case the competent authority

[89]Explanatory memorandum, Parliamentary Document 15/4493, p. 14; Leopold 2006, p. 599.

[90]Explanatory memorandum, Parliamentary Document 15/4493, p. 14; Matthes 2006, p. 50.

[91]Explanatory memorandum, Parliamentary Document 15/4493, p. 14.

[92]Explanatory memorandum, Parliamentary Document 15/4493, p. 14; whether the incompetent authority is authorized to forward the application to the competent authority, is discussed controversially; see Schoch 2016, Sec. 7 para 55.

is known to the contacted authority: Sec. 4.3 EIA and Sec. 4.3 Access to Information Act Schleswig-Holstein) or to notify the applicant about the competent authority (Sec. 10.3 sentence 2 FIA Mecklenburg-Vorpommern).

According to Article 11 para 1, item 3 of the Brazilian Law N°12.527/2011 and Article 15 para 1, item 4 of Decree N° 7.724/2012 the applicant has either to be informed about the competent authority or the contacted authority needs to forward the application to the respective body if it is known to them. Otherwise, the notification that it does not possess the requested information is sufficient (see Article 11 para 1, item 3 of the Brazilian Law, Article 15 para 1, item 3 of Decree N°7.724/2012).

In principle, the application does not need to be justified because of the fact that the applicant does not need a legitimate interest for his/her application.[93] As an exception, the application has to be justified if information about third persons as defined in Sec. 5.1 and 5.2 or Sec. 6 is concerned (Sec. 7.1 sentence 3 FIA). This enables the authority to weigh the opposing interests properly. Furthermore, the third person can thereby be informed about the applicant's identity and interests.[94] In these cases, the applicant has de facto to disclose his/her interest in access to information to realize his/her claim.[95] The Brazilian provisions do not establish the obligation to reveal the motives for access at all (see 2.3).

If uniform applications are submitted by more than 50 persons (mass procedure), Sections 17 to 19 APA are applicable (see Sec. 7.1 sentence 4 FIA). According to Sec. 17.1 sentence 1 APA, applications are uniform if they are signed by more than 50 persons or are presented in the form of duplicated and identical texts. The applicants have to name a representative with his/her name, profession, and address (Sec. 17.1 sentence 1 APA). Otherwise, the authority may disregard the applications (Sec. 17.2 APA). A second type of mass procedure is mentioned in Sec. 18.1 APA for cases of applications signed by more than 50 persons having the same interest. As an applicant does not have to disclose his/her motives, the term "having the same interest" needs to be read in this context as "referring to the same pieces of information".[96] According to Sec. 18.1 APA, the authorities may require the appointment of a joint representative where otherwise the regular execution of administrative proceedings would be impaired. If the applicants do not comply with this requirement within the time period set, the authority may ex officio appoint a joint representative.

Sec. 7.2 FIA clarifies that access to information may be granted partially if the right of access only exists to a portion of the information requested. In this case, access has to be granted to the extent to which confidential information is not revealed and the administrative effort would not be disproportionate. Information is confidential if one of the exemption clauses (Sections 3 to 6 FIA) is applicable.[97] If

[93]Kloepfer & von Lewinski 2005, p. 1285.

[94]Schoch 2016, Sec. 7 para 29.

[95]Schoch 2016, Sec. 1 para 22.

[96]Rossi 2006, Sec. 7 para 24.

[97]Schoch 2016, Sec. 7 para 88, 90.

a third person's interests are concerned and said person's consent is missing, access to information may only be granted if the applicant agrees to the removal or blackening of the respective parts (Sec. 7.2 sentence 2 FIA). According to the explanatory memorandum, access needs to be denied if the information was distorted by separation or blackening of its confidential parts.[98] This opinion, however, has no correspondence in the law's wording and thus should be rejected.[99] Article 7 para 2 of the Brazilian Law N° 12.527/2011 as well states the possibility of a partial access to information with the secret portion hidden.

The FIA does not stipulate any explicit period for granting access to information. Access has to be granted without delay (Sec. 7.5 sentence 1). Sec. 7.5 sentence 2 supplements this by stating that access shall occur within 1 month. As the FIA does not provide for a definition of "without delay", one can consult Sec. 121.1 sentence 1 of the Civil Code according to which this means "without undue delay".[100] The period commences when the competent authority receives the application.[101] The period of 1 month is not applicable if a third person is involved because the procedure as provided in Sec. 8 FIA has to be completed first (see Sec. 7.5 sentence 3 FIA).[102] Article 11 of the Brazilian Law N°12.527/2011 and Article 15 of Decree N° 7.724/2012 state that access has to be granted immediately. If no immediate access is possible, Article 11 para 1 of the Brazilian Law and Article 15 para 1 of the Decree stipulate the further proceedings that have to be fulfilled within 20 days. This period can be exceeded in exceptional cases for another 10 days (Article 11 para 2 of the Brazilian Law, Article 16 of the Decree).

If a third person's interests are affected by the application, he/she is to be given the opportunity to comment in writing within 1 month if there are indications that he/she may have a legitimate interest in the denial of access to information (Sec. 8.1 FIA). The term "affected interests" relates to interests protected by Sections 5 and 6 FIA.[103] A concrete possibility of his/her interests being affected is sufficient.[104] If the applicant agrees with the third person's data being omitted, the third person does not need to be involved. According to the explanatory memorandum, his/her involvement is also unnecessary if this person is evidently not able to express his or her will in due time or if it is recognizable that he/she would presumably give his/her consent.[105] This assumption is worthy of criticism—even if the third person is difficult to reach, he/she might still have a legitimate interest in denying access;

---

[98]Explanatory memorandum, Parliamentary Document 15/4493, p. 15.

[99]Schoch 2016, Sec. 7 para 120.

[100]Kloepfer & von Lewinski 2005, p. 1285.

[101]Berger, in Berger et al. (2006), Sec. 7 para 7, 22.

[102]Schoch 2016, Sec. 7 para 170.

[103]This results from the enumeration in the explanatory memorandum, Parliamentary Document 15/4493, p. 15 ("personal data, intellectual property, trade or business secrets"); Schoch 2016, Sec. 8 para 26.

[104]Berger, in Berger et al. (2006), Sec. 8 para 3.

[105]Explanatory memorandum, Parliamentary Document 15/4493, p. 15.

thus, e.g., an extension of time would be preferable.[106] At what time the third person needs to become involved is not regulated by law. With regard to Sec. 7.5 sentence 1 FIA, he/she has to be involved without delay upon receiving the application.[107] Whether and in what form he/she actually uses the opportunity to comment, is up to him/her.[108] The authority's notification to the third person needs to be submitted in writing (Sec. 8.1 FIA). Most state laws are similar to Sec. 8 FIA. However, the provisions in Hamburg and North Rhine-Westphalia differ as they only point out that persons concerned need to have the opportunity to comment if access to information could infringe on his/her interests worthy of protection, without stipulating further procedural rules (Sec. 4.5 sentence 2 Transparency Act Hamburg, Sec. 9.2 sentence 2 FIA North Rhine-Westphalia).

If access to information is granted, the FIA does not provide for any rules on how the respective decision should appear. However, in case of a third person being involved the decision on the application needs to be submitted in writing (Sec. 8.2 sentence 1 FIA) and communicated to the third person as well. According to Sec. 8.2 sentence 2 FIA access to information is not permitted until the decision becomes final towards the third person or the authority ordered its immediate enforcement and two weeks have passed since the order's announcement. A decision becomes final when it can no longer be contested by legal remedies.[109]

Sec. 9 FIA regulates the denial of access. The denial has to be announced within 1 month (Sec. 9.1 in conjunction with Sec. 7.5 sentence 2). However, in case of a third person's involvement he/she first has to be given the opportunity to comment within 1 month (Sec. 8.1 FIA, as mentioned above).[110] It is also to be considered a rejection of the application if the applicant made a choice regarding the type of access (Sec. 1.2 sentence 2 FIA) and the authority does not agree to grant access in this manner.[111] The FIA does not provide any rule about decisions rejecting access neither does it state an explicit obligation to give reasons for the decision. However, the vast majority of academics derive such an obligation from Sec. 39 APA.[112] It is controversial whether the applicant has to be heard before his/her request is rejected. The FIA does not include any rule on the applicant's hearing. Consequently, one would have to refer to Sec. 28 APA according to which a party needs to be heard prior to the enactment of an administrative act infringing the party's rights. However, according to the prevailing opinion a hearing is not necessary if the infringement is based on the rejection of a requested beneficial treatment.[113] Thus

[106]Critical as well: Schoch 2016, Sec. 8 para 55 et seq.: The explanatory memorandum is not confirmed by the wording of the provision.

[107]Schoch 2016, Sec. 8 para 37.

[108]Schoch 2016, Sec. 8 para 44, 46.

[109]Ziekow & Debus, in Fluck et al. (2007), Sec. 8 FIA para 33.

[110]Schoch 2016, Sec. 9 para 18 et seq.

[111]Schoch 2016, Sec. 9 para 8.

[112]Leopold 2006, p. 599; Matthes 2006, p. 55;Jastrow & Schlatmann 2006, Sec. 9 para 11.

[113]Schoch 2016, Sec. 9 para 12; German Federal Administrative Court (Bundesverwaltungsgericht), 3 C 46/81 (Judgment of 14 October 1982) para 35.

for applications under the FIA a rejection of access does not require a prior hearing. Along with the denial, the authority according to Sec. 9.2 FIA has to inform the applicant if and when access to this information may be possible, wholly or partly, at a later point in time. Otherwise, the applicant has to be informed that access is denied permanently.[114] There are no formal rules about this notification.[115]

If access is rejected, Article 14 of the Brazilian Law N°12.527/2011 stipulates the applicant's right to obtain the decision's full content. Although the provision's wording ("It is the right of the applicant to obtain [...]") might imply that it lies with the applicant to ask for a justification of the decision, the law's systematic interpretation suggests that authorities are obliged to justify their decisions, as a rejection of access which is not properly justified results in disciplinary measures for the responsible person (Article 7 para 4, Article 32 of the Brazilian Law N° 12.527/2011).

According to Article 11 para 1, item 2 of that Law, authorities shall indicate the factual or legal reasons of the refusal within 20 days. Article 19 of Decree N°7.724/2012 contains more detailed rules on decisions denying access. Decisions have to include the denial's reasons, information on the right of appeal and the right to request the information's declassification. The decision is sent to the applicant "within the time limit for response", i.e. in principle immediately, respectively within 20 days (Article 15 of Decree N°7.724/2012). In total, the Brazilian provisions on decisions denying access are more detailed than the German ones and in principle provide for a shorter processing time.

Sec. 9.3 FIA stipulates in addition to the above-mentioned limitations to the right of access (Sections 3 to 6) two further constellations in which the authorities can reject applications. This is the case when the applicant already has the information requested at his/her disposal or can obtain the relevant information from generally accessible sources in a reasonable manner. The term "generally accessible sources" is also used in Article 5.1 (1) second clause of the German constitution (right to freedom of expression). Against this background, it is to be interpreted according to the considerations made in the context of Article 5.[116] Therefore, "source" means every possible medium of information, and "generally accessible" means that it has to be technically suitable and designated to provide the public, an indeterminate group of persons, with information.[117] This includes the internet.[118] However, a general reference to searching the internet is not sufficient. If searching is not possible without difficulties, the authority needs to give appropriate guidance owing to its obligation to give advice (Sec. 25 APA).[119] With regard to the

[114]Schoch 2016, Sec. 9 para 37.

[115]Ziekow & Debus, in Fluck et al. (2007), Sec. 9 FIA para 21.

[116]Schoch 2016, Sec. 9 para 47.

[117]German Federal Constitutional Court (Bundesverfassungsgericht), 1 BvR 2623/95, 1 BvR 622/99 (Judgment of 24 January 2001) para 56; Schoch 2016, Sec. 9 para 47.

[118]Explanatory memorandum, Parliamentary Document 15/4493, p. 16.

[119]Schoch 2016, Sec. 9 para 48.

reasonableness of obtaining information from generally accessible sources, the explanatory memorandum states that the applicant's individual circumstances have to be considered which includes, e.g., disabilities, technical equipment, and the place of residence.[120] Furthermore, education and the applicant's financial situation can be considered.[121]

Article 17 of the Brazilian Decree N°7.724/2012 provides for similar rules stipulating that the authority in principle is released from its obligation to grant access directly. It has rather to give advice about where and how the applicant him-/herself can find the information sought for. However, authorities are not released from their obligation to grant access if the applicant declares that he/she does not possess the necessary means for obtaining the information by him-/herself.

Finally, the explanatory memorandum clarifies that abusive applications have neither to be accepted nor to be processed. This can be derived from general principles of administrative law.[122] Sec. 8.2 No. 1 EIA and Sec. 4.4 sentence 1 CIA provide for respective provisions according to which abusive applications have to be rejected.

Article 13 of the Brazilian Decree N° 7.724/2012 stipulates that very general, disproportionate or unreasonable requests, or requests requiring additional work of analysis, interpretation or data consolidation shall not be processed. In this respect the Brazilian regulation is more specific than the German one.

## 4.2 Costs

According to Sec. 10.1 FIA, fees and expenditures are charged for individually attributable services based on the FIA unless the authority gives simple information. While considering administrative effort, fees are to be measured in a way that access to information can be used effectively.[123] Next to simple information (which in particular includes verbal information without any research effort) decisions rejecting access are free of charge.[124] The same is applicable when the request to access is withdrawn.[125] The amount of fees and expenditures can be derived from the Ordinance on Fees Payable under the FIA.[126] According to the ordinance fees up to a maximum of 500 € are possible. Sec. 2 of the ordinance stipulates that fees

[120]Explanatory memorandum, Parliamentary Document 15/4493, p. 16.

[121]Ziekow & Debus, in Fluck et al. (2007), Sec. 9 FIA para 32.

[122]Explanatory memorandum, Parliamentary Document 15/4493, p. 16.

[123]Explanatory memorandum, Parliamentary Document 15/4493, p. 16.

[124]Explanatory memorandum, Parliamentary Document 15/4493, p. 16; Sellmann & Augsberg 2006, p. 2297.

[125]Kloepfer & von Lewinski 2005, p. 1286; Matthes 2006, p. 59.

[126]German Federal Law Gazette I (BGBl. I) 2006, p. 6.

can be reduced by up to 50% or not charged at all for reasons of equity or public interest.

According to Article 12 of the Brazilian Law N°12.527/2011 and Article 4 of Decree N°7.724/2012 access to information in principle is free of charge. Only in case of the information's reproduction, the applicant has to reimburse the costs for service and material. Although the relevant rules in the German FIA are formulated reversely (principle of levying of charges and an exception when granting simple information), both regulations might lead to the same results in practice. Article 12 Sole paragraph of the Brazilian Law N°12.527/2011 and Article 4 Sole paragraph of Decree N°7.724/2012 provide for an exemption from the obligation to bear the costs on economic grounds when otherwise the applicant's and/or his/her family's livelihood would be endangered. The corresponding German provision is formulated in a more general way ("for reasons of equity") and in addition refers to the public interest as a reason for an exemption. Overall, the German law is more broadly formulated and therefore might offer more possibilities for exemptions.

## 5 Judicial Protection

### *5.1 The Applicant's Legal Remedies*

According to Sec. 9.4 FIA, the applicant may file an objection or an enforcement action if access to information was denied. The predominant opinion among academics is that the reference to the enforcement action is only of declaratory nature. All other forms of actions may be appropriate as well.[127] There is controversy over whether access can be granted as a measure of interim relief. The majority of academics points out that this kind of judicial protection would preempt the decision in the principle proceedings and could not be reversed later. Therefore, interim measures may only be considered in exceptional cases of unreasonable and irreparable harm for the applicant and a high probability for access to information to be granted in the main proceedings.[128]

Furthermore, it is problematic whether files the applicant requires access to have to be submitted to the court. According to Sec. 99.1 of the Administrative Procedure Code (APC) authorities shall be obliged to submit certificates or files, to transmit electronic documents and provide information. This obligation solely regards files relevant to the proceedings pending before the respective court.[129] Parties to the proceedings then can claim access to the court records and those files submitted to the court (Sec. 100.1 APC). In this way, the applicant would be able to obtain the

[127]Schoch 2016, Sec. 9 para 67; Sellmann & Augsberg 2006, p. 2300 et seq.

[128]Mecklenburg & Pöppelmann 2007, Sec. 9 para 25; Ziekow & Debus, in Fluck et al. (2007), Sec. 9 FIA para 51; disagreeing: Schoch 2016, Sec. 9 para 108, 111.

[129]Lang, in Sodan & Ziekow (1999), Administrative Procedure Code, Sec. 99 para 20.

sought information. On the other hand, the court needs to have the opportunity to examine the lawfulness of the authority's decision. To this purpose the knowledge of the files' content is necessary. Therefore, some scholars advocate the application of the so-called In-camera-proceedings.[130] In these proceedings, the respective files are submitted to the court which decides on the necessity for confidentiality (Sec. 99.2 sentences 1 and 2 APC). When they are deemed confidential, the files are not made available to the proceedings' parties (see Sec. 99.2 sentence 9 APC). In contrast other scholars assume that only the circumstances that led to the denial of access have to be made plausible and not the respective files/information themselves. Accordingly, the reasons for denial are subject to judicial review.[131] Therefore, the respective authority has to create a separate file regarding the denial of the application for access that can then be submitted to the court.[132] This assumption, however, is highly questionable. Without knowledge of the information itself, it will, in most cases, not be possible to assess whether the denial of access was legitimate or not.

Article 15 of the Brazilian Law N° 12.527/2011 provides for the admissibility of an appeal if access to information was rejected. The appeal has to be filed within 10 days after receipt of the decision denying access and has to be addressed to the next highest authority (Article 15 Single paragraph) which must decide on the appeal within 5 days. In its regulatory structure the appeal is similar to the objection in German administrative law. In German law, the period for filing an objection is 1 month from the date of notification of the decision (Sec. 74 APC); however, there is no specific period for the decision on the objection. The appellant is instead entitled to file an action without awaiting a decision on the objection if the administration has not decided upon it within 3 months (action for failure to act, Sec. 75 APC). It is notable that Brazilian Law provides for a clearly shorter period to launch an appeal and the appeal also has to be decided upon much quicker. This is preferable as it accelerates the proceedings.

Article 18 of the Brazilian Law N° 12.527/2011 authorizes the enactment of specific procedural rules regarding the decision on appeals. In Germany the rules of the APA on administrative proceedings are applicable as mentioned above. Article 16 of that Law provides for a limited scope of action if access has been rejected by an authority of the Federal Government. Firstly, the applicant has to launch an appeal to at least one higher authority which shall decide within 5 days (Article 16 para 1). If the appeal was rejected, the applicant can in certain cases contact the Office of the Comptroller General, which decides within 5 days. If this decision also rejects access, Article 16 para 3 provides for the right of appeal to the Joint Commission of Information Reassessment. Article 21 and 23 of Decree N°7.724/2012 contain comparable rules providing for a three-stage possibility to appeal. In addition, the applicant may submit a complaint within 10 days to the monitoring authority if his/her application remains

[130]Kugelmann 2005, p. 3613.

[131]Steinbach & Hochheim 2006, p. 523; Schmitz & Jastrow 2005, p. 991.

[132]Schmitz & Jastrow 2005, p. 990.

unanswered after 30 days (Article 22 of Decree N°7.724/2012). In Germany Sec. 9.4 sentence 2 FIA also provides for the right to appeal if the decision denying access derives from a supreme federal authority. A rule regarding applications which have not been answered is missing in the German FIA. So far, the Brazilian regulation is broader than the German one because of the three-stage possibility to appeal. Article 17 of the Brazilian Law N°12.527/2011 concerns requests to declassify secret information and provides for a two-stage possibility to appeal in case the request is rejected. In contrast to Article 15 and 16 of the Brazilian Law there are no periods prescribed regarding the decision about the appeal. However, Article 18 of the Brazilian Law allows for the enactment of specific procedural rules. If access to information of public interest is denied, Article 19 para 2 of the Brazilian Law prescribes certain reporting obligations for the bodies of the Judiciary and the Public Prosecutor's Office to the National Council of Justice and the National Council of the Public Prosecutor's Office.

In addition to Sec. 9.4 FIA, Sec. 12.1 FIA offers the possibility to contact the Federal Commissioner for Data Protection and Freedom of Information[133] if an appellant considers his/her right of access infringed upon. Thus the Federal Commissioner, formerly only responsible for Data Protection, is now also acting as Commissioner for Freedom of Information. According to the explanatory memorandum the reason for this extension of competences is that experiences abroad and at the German state level showed that a Commissioner could balance freedom of information and data protection in an appropriate and citizen friendly way. An applicant can contact the Federal Commissioner and file an objection, respectively an action, at the same time.[134] The Federal Commissioner is not competent to trace possible infringements of the right of access ex officio.[135]

According to Sec. 12.1 FIA, "everybody" has the right to contact the Federal Commissioner. "Everybody" includes the applicant and third persons.[136] No certain form or time period is required. However, contacting the Federal Commissioner must be directly related to an application to access or an authority's decision upon thereof. Solely abstract questions of law may not be submitted to the Federal Commissioner.[137] Contacting the Federal Commissioner is free of charge.[138] If the Commissioner comes to the conclusion that the applicant's concern is justified, he/she will advise the competent authority to remedy the situation. This action, however, has no legal consequences. Thus, the Commissioner can only rely on his/her authority and the power of his/her arguments.[139] The Brazilian Law N°12.527/2011and Decree N°7.724/2012 include no comparable rules.

---

[133]For further information on the Federal Commissioner see http://www.bfdi.bund.de/DE/Home/home_node.html (Accessed on 25 February 2017).

[134]Explanatory memorandum, Parliamentary Document 15/4493, p. 17.

[135]Rossi 2006, Sec. 12 para 4.

[136]Explanatory memorandum, Parliamentary Document 15/4493, p. 17.

[137]Schoch 2016, Sec. 12 para 32.

[138]Roth, in Berger et al. (2006), Sec. 12 para 17.

[139]Schoch 2016, Sec. 12 para 41, 44.

### 5.2 *The Third Person's Legal Remedies*

According to Sec. 8.2 sentence 3 FIA, Sec. 9.4 FIA is applicable by analogy to the third person's judicial protection. He/she has the right to contest the decision granting access to information.[140] The Brazilian Law N°12.527/2011 and Decree N°7.724/2012 do not include a comparable regulation.

## 6 Active Information Policy

Sec. 11 FIA stipulates several publication requirements for the authorities. According to Sec. 11.1 authorities shall maintain registers that indicate available collections of information and their intended use. The regulation uses the term "shall" by which it states an obligation that is binding except in atypical constellations.[141] Sec. 11.1 refers to registers containing all information present at the relevant authority. As they have to contain all information present at the relevant time, they need to be updated continually.[142] The maintaining of the registers both facilitates the filing of an application and the finding of the information sought by authorities.[143] Sec. 11 does not set guidelines on how registers have to be maintained. This is up to the authority's discretion, which also encompasses the decision on how detailed the registers shall be. The register may be made available for example via internet or in a printed form.[144]

Sec. 11.2 stipulates that organization plans and filing plans have to be made publicly available. According to the explanatory memorandum organization plans contain information, e.g., about structure of and competences within an authority while filing plans provide for an overview of the relevant authority's scope of duties. This does not include the names, business telephone numbers and the field of responsibility of each employee. The rational of this exemption is to assure the personal safety of the employees, the maintaining of their working capacity and the orderly performance of their duties.[145]

Concerning the publication of organization and filing plans the exemption clauses of the FIA (Sections 3 to 6) have to be applied. Therefore, information, which may not be made available upon application, cannot be made publicly accessible based on Sec. 11.2 FIA either.[146] As there is no right of access to

[140]Schoch 2016, Sec. 9 para 64.

[141]Rossi 2006, Sec. 11 para 22.

[142]Schoch 2016, Sec. 11 para 24.

[143]Berger, in Berger et al. (2006), Sec. 11 para 6.

[144]Schoch 2016, Sec. 11 para 21.

[145]Explanatory memorandum, Parliamentary Document 15/4493, p. 16.

[146]Rossi 2006, Sec. 11 para 28.

information held by intelligence services (Sec. 3 No. 8 FIA), accordingly, these services have no publication obligations.[147]

According to Sec. 11.3 FIA registers and plans mentioned in Sec. 11.1 and 11.2, as well as any other information which is assumed to be of interest to the citizens,[148] shall be made publicly available in electronic form. The explanatory memorandum calls Sec. 11.3 an internet clause, thus authorities shall use the internet for publication. This serves the purpose of administrative simplification, and individual processing of applications is reduced.[149] However, because of the usage of the term "shall", authorities are entitled to choose other forms of publication in case of atypical constellations.[150] It is up to the authority to decide what information is deemed appropriate for electronic publication.[151] Although it is not stipulated expressly by Sec. 11.3, publication is obligatory only if no exemption clause of Sections 3 to 6 applies. Otherwise, information that is not accessible upon individual application would have to be made public in electronic form.[152]

There are efforts to extend the authorities' active publication duties. On 25 January 2017 the Federal Government passed a draft act to implement the open-data principle on the federal level. The establishment of a broader legal basis for the active publishing of data held by the federal authorities was part of the governing parties' coalition agreement and mirrors internationally accepted open-data-principles as described, e.g., in the International Open-Data-Charta or in the Open-Data-Charta of the (former) G8 states. One of the act's purposes is to provide an opportunity for more public participation in administrative matters and to allow for an enhanced cooperation between citizens and the authorities.[153] The Act, which came into force in July 2017,[154] amends the E-Government-Act by inserting inter alia a new Sec. 12a. According to Sec. 12a.1 federal authorities publish unprocessed data, which they collected to fulfill their public duties or which third parties collected on their behalf, via public networks. The publication is free of charge (Sec. 12a.7 sentence 1). The Act does not provide for an entitlement to publication of data (Sec. 12a.1 sentence 2). Sentence 12a.2 defines which data are subject to publication. This in particular includes data held by the federal authorities electronically or in collections such as tables and lists. According to the explanatory memorandum applications, notes, administration records, reports and e-mails stored in the authority's e-mail-system are not included, i.e. are not subject to

[147]Schoch 2016, Sec. 11 para 45.

[148]See Explanatory memorandum, Parliamentary Document 15/4493, p. 16.

[149]Explanatory memorandum, Parliamentary Document 15/4493, p. 16.

[150]Rossi 2006, Sec. 11 para 32.

[151]Schoch 2016, Sec. 11 para 51.

[152]Schoch 2016, Sec. 11 para 58, 59.

[153]See draft act, p. 1: https://www.bmi.bund.de/SharedDocs/Downloads/DE/Gesetzestexte/Entwuerfe/entwurf-open-data-gesetz.pdf?__blob¼publicationFile (Accessed on 25 February 2017)

[154]See Gesetz zur Förderung der elektronischen Verwaltung (5 July 2017), German Federal Law Gazette 2017, p. 2206.

publication.[155] Sec. 12a.2 stipulates inter alia that only unprocessed data are published (Sec. 12a.2 No. 3). Exemptions from publication are set out in Sec. 12a.3. According to Sec. 12a.3 No. 1 data are not published, in particular, in case of a legal impediment. This, e.g., is the case, when one of the exemptions of Sections 3 to 5 FIA is applicable or when there are reasons to assume that trade and business secrets could be disclosed (see Sec. 12a.4 No. 1 and 5). Thus the amount of data subject to publication is restricted and the draft is not likely to make Germany a pioneer in establishing open data as the government proclaims.[156]

Several state laws contain provisions regarding active publication duties of the authorities as well. Some of them are largely identical with the federal level's regulation, respectively refer to Sec. 11 FIA (Sec. 11 FIA Saxony-Anhalt, Sec. 1 FIA Saarland). According to the Access to Information Act of Schleswig-Holstein, however, the obligation to actively provide information refers only to information concerning the environment (Sections 8 and 11). In Bremen, North Rhine-Westphalia and Thuringia the provisions are broader. According to the respective laws plans on the allocation of duties have to be made publicly available as well (Sec. 11.2 FIA Bremen, Sec. 12 FIA North Rhine-Westphalia, Sec. 11.1 FIA Thuringia). Furthermore, in Thuringia administrative provisions of general interest shall also be published, and Sec. 11 includes the authorization to issue ordinances regulating further details concerning the operation and use of the information register. In Bremen administrative provisions (without a restriction to those of general interest) and other appropriate information shall be made electronically available to the public as well (Sec. 11.4). Sec. 11.6 contains the obligation to establish a central electronic information register. Details are regulated by ordinance (Sec. 11.8).

Hamburg's Transparency Act contains the most far-reaching provisions on active publication by the authorities (Sec. 3). They are obliged to actively enter information into the information register (Sec. 2.8). Sec. 3.1 contains an extensive list of information to be published. This includes inter alia plans on the allocation of duties, administrative provisions, the essential content of issued building permits, and the essential data on companies the City of Hamburg is a shareholder of, including the annual remunerations on the management level. The list of Sec. 3.1 is not conclusive.[157] According to Sec. 3.2 authorities shall publish all further comparative information of public interest. Sections 4 to 7, 9 and 17 contain several restrictions to the obligation of publication, inter alia to protect personal data (Sec. 4), public interests (Sec. 6) and trade and business secrets (Sec. 7). Furthermore, certain authorities are completely exempt from publication as, e.g., courts, prosecution and law enforcement authorities, Hamburg's Court of Audit and the State Office for the Protection of the Constitution (Sec. 5). As far as publication is required, authorities shall make appropriate organizational arrangements to be able to separate restricted from unrestricted information without disproportionate effort (Sec. 8, so-called separation rule). The information in the register has to be published electronically in full

[155]Explanatory memorandum, p. 8.

[156]See Coalition Agreement, p. 153.

[157]Jauch 2013, p. 19.

text for at least 10 years (Sec. 10.1). Access to the register is free of charge and is granted inter alia via internet (Sec. 10.4). The technical requirements for the implementation of the law and thus also for the information register have to be established within 2 years after the law has entered into force (Sec. 18.2 sentence 1).

Rhineland-Palatinate adopted a Transparency Act as well which entered into force on 1 January 2016. According to Sec. 2.1 the state establishes and operates an electronic platform (transparency platform) to provide information. Sec. 7.1 contains an extensive list of information to be published. This includes inter alia plans on the allocation of duties, administrative provisions, the essential contents of contracts of general public interest with a value of more than 20.000 € and donations exceeding 1000 €. Sections 14 to 17 contain several restrictions to the obligation of publication, inter alia because of conflicting public interests (Sec. 14) and to protect personal data and trade and business secrets (Sec. 16). Information in the transparency platform has to be kept available for 10 years, environmental information in principle permanently (Sec. 4.5).

Among other German states,[158] Thuringia is also planning to adopt a Transparency Act. In the coalition agreement from November 2014,[159] the governing parties expressed their intention to follow the example of Hamburg and extend the existing FIA to a Transparency Act, provide for the proactive publication of information by the administration and strengthen the supervisory rights of the Thuringian Commissioner for Data Protection and Freedom of Information.[160]

According to Article 6 para 1 of the Brazilian Law N°12.527/2011 public bodies and authorities are inter alia obliged to guarantee broad access to the information and its dissemination. This obligation is restated in Article 8 of the Brazilian Law concerning information of collective or general interest. Article 8 para 1 of the Brazilian Law lists the minimal requirements for the dissemination. In contrast to the German FIA this list also includes records of any relocation or transfer of financial resources and of expenditures. Article 8 para 2 of the Brazilian Law makes dissemination of the information in the internet mandatory. Article 8 para 3 contains

[158]For further information see, e.g., https://transparenzgesetz-nds.de/, http://www.nrw-blickt-durch.de/home/ (Accessed on 25 February 2017).

[159]Coalition Agreement (2014), Thüringen gemeinsam voranbringen – demokratisch, sozial, ökologisch. Koalitionsvertrag zwischen den Parteien DIE LINKE, SPD, BÜNDNIS 90/DIE GRÜNEN für die 6. Wahlperiode des Thüringer Landtags, http://gruene-thueringen.de/sites/gruene-thueringen.de/files/r2g-koalitionsvertrag-final.pdf, para. 11.4, p. 78 (Accessed on 25 February 2017).

[160]For further information on the status of the legislative procedure see the Thuringian government's statement to the first progress report of the Commissioner for Data Protection and Freedom of Information: http://www.parldok.thueringen.de/ParlDok/dokument/55226/stellungnahme-der-landesregierung-zum-1-t%C3%A4tigkeitsbericht-zur-informationsfreiheit-des-th%C3%BCringer-landesbeauftragten-f%C3%BCr-den-datenschutz-und.pdf and http://www.parldok.thueringen.de/ParlDok/dokument/54510/1-t%C3%A4tigkeitsbericht-des-th%C3%BCringer-landesbeauftragten-f%C3%BCr-den-datenschutz-und-die-informationsfreiheit-gem%C3%A4%C3%9F-%C2%A7-12-abs-5-th%C3%BCringer-informationsfreiheitsgesetz.pdf (Accessed on 25 February 2017).

detailed guidelines for the webpages' design and states, inter alia, that the latest information needs to be published (Article 8 para 3, item 4 of the Brazilian Law). Article 8 para 4 of the Brazilian Law stipulates an exception from this obligation for municipalities with a population of up to 10,000 inhabitants. However, they shall maintain real-time mandatory dissemination of information regarding budget and financial execution. Article 7 and 8 of Decree N°7.724/2012, titled "active transparency", provide for comparable provisions as they, e.g., also contain a list of information that shall be disclosed and requirements for the website's content. In summary, the Brazilian regulation is broader than Sec. 11 FIA, particularly because of its internet publication clause. The FIA partially uses the term "shall", thus leaving the possibility of denial of the publication of information in atypical constellations.

## 7 Conclusion

The Brazilian Law N°12.527/2011 addresses authorities both on the federal and state level whereas German regulations differentiate between addressees on the federal level and on the level of the *Länder* and between types of information. In this respect, regulations on access to information constitute a complex and broad field of law in Germany.

In Brazilian law, the authorities' obligations to actively publish information are further reaching than those stipulated in the FIA. In Germany, however, there have been increased efforts to introduce more extensive rules on active information policy, as illustrated by the Transparency Act of Hamburg.

The German and the Brazilian regulations contain provisions stipulating the possibility to refuse access to information to protect special public interests and personal data. In Germany the respective provision of the federal FIA regarding the protection of special public interests is extensive and contains 15 mostly multi-part exemption clauses. Since most of the clauses are formulated very broadly and vaguely, a restrictive interpretation is required - but at the same time difficult to realize. It may therefore be questioned whether the precept of rule and exception can indeed be respected when applying the FIA. In Brazilian law the list of exemptions is less extensive. However, the Brazilian exemption concerning secret information deserves particular attention. It is disputed whether the respective rules keep the disclosure of information at the state's discretion and thus allow for the excessive use of the exemption. However, if the intention of free access is to be preserved, discretion must be reduced to a minimum.

In regards to personal data, according to the German federal FIA in principle access may only be granted upon consent or as far as the applicant's interest in the information outweighs the third person's legitimate interest in keeping his personal data secret. With regard to the interest in disclosing information, one not only has to consider a possible interest of the public in disclosure, but also the *applicant's* interest, especially his/her purpose of access. The Brazilian law as well provides for a possibility of weighing the opposing interests, when it stipulates that personal information can be released for specific purposes, inter alia if the information is required for the protection of *superior* public and general interests. However, the Brazilian regulations are more restrictive in this respect as only superior *public and general* interests are mentioned. Apart from that Brazilian law allows access if the person concerned expressly gives his/her consent or if it is permitted by a legal provision. Having in mind all the other constellations in which Brazilian Law N°12.527/2011 allows the release of personal information, the Brazilian provisions regarding personal information appear, on the whole, to be more access-friendly than those of the German FIA.

In the area of judicial protection, the German FIA rules are broader as they also grant judicial protection to concerned third persons and furthermore allow for an informal appeal to the Federal Commissioner for Data Protection and Freedom of Information. Concerning the proceedings, Brazilian law is preferable as the respective periods are clearly shorter and lead to an acceleration of the proceedings.

## References

Berger, S., Roth, J., & Scheel, C. (2006). *Informationsfreiheitsgesetz. Kommentar*. Köln, Germany: Carl Heymanns.

Burholt, C. (2006). Die Auswirkungen des Informationsfreiheitsgesetzes auf das Akteneinsichtsrecht in Kartell- und Fusionskontrollverfahren. *Betriebsberater (BB)*, 2201–2207.

Coalition Agreement Thuringia. (2014). Thüringen gemeinsam voranbringen – demokratisch, sozial, ökologisch. Koalitionsvertrag zwischen den Parteien DIE LINKE, SPD, BÜNDNIS 90/DIE GRÜNEN für die 6. Wahlperiode des Thüringer Landtags. http://gruene-thueringen.de/sites/gruene-thueringen.de/files/r2g-koalitionsvertrag-final.pdf

Fluck, J., Fischer, K., & Fetzer, T. (Eds.). (2003). *Informationsfreiheitsrecht mit Umweltinformations-, Verbraucherinformations-und Informationsweiterverwendungsrecht, IFG/UIG/VIG/IWG, Kommentar, Band 1*. Heidelberg, Germany: Hüthig Jehle Rehm.

Jahn, D. (2009). Das politische System Schwedens. In W. Ismayr (Ed.), *Die politischen Systeme Westeuropas* (pp. 107–149). Wiesbaden, Germany: VS, Verlag für Sozialwissenschaften.

Jastrow, S.-D., & Schlatmann, A. (2006). *Informationsfreiheitsgesetz. Kommentar*. Heidelberg, Germany: R. v. Decker.

Jauch, O. (2013). Das Hamburgische Transparenzgesetz (HmbTG) – Ein Paradigmenwechsel in der Informationsfreiheit. *Deutsches Verwaltungsblatt (DVBl.)*, 16–24.

Kloepfer, M. (2006). Grundprobleme der Gesetzgebung zur Informationszugangsfreiheit. *Kommunikation und Recht (K&R)*, 19–27.

Kloepfer, M., & von Lewinski, K. (2005). Das Informationsfreiheitsgesetz des Bundes (IFG). *Deutsches Verwaltungsblatt (DVBl.)*, 1277–1288.

Kugelmann, D. (2005). Das Informationsfreiheitsgesetz des Bundes. *Neue Juristische Wochenschrift (NJW)*, 3609–3613.

Kugelmann, D. (2007). *Informationsfreiheitsgesetz. Kommentar*. Wiesbaden, Germany: Kommunal- und Schul-Verlag Wiesbaden.

Leopold, A. (2006). Die Kartellbehörden im Angesicht der Informationsfreiheit. *Wirtschaft und Wettbewerb (WuW)*, 592–601.

Masing, J. (2004). Transparente Verwaltung: Konturen eines Informationsverwaltungsrechts. *Veröffentlichungen der Vereinigung der DeutschenStaatsrechtslehrer (VVDStRL)*, Band 63, 344–468.
Matthes, R. (2006). *Das Informationsfreiheitsgesetz. Eine praktische Erläuterung*. Berlin: Lexxion Verl.-Ges.
Mecklenburg, W., & Pöppelmann, B. H. (2007). *Informationsfreiheitsgesetz: Gesetzestexte, Kommentierungen, Fallbeispiele, Erläuterungen*. Berlin: Dt. Journalisten-Verband.
Rossi, M. (2006). *Informationsfreiheitsgesetz. Handkommentar*. Baden-Baden, Germany: Nomos.
Schmitz, H., & Jastrow, S.-D. (2005). Das Informationsfreiheitsgesetz des Bundes. *Neue Zeitschrift für Verwaltungsrecht (NVwZ)*, 984–995.
Schoch, F. (2009). Aktuelle Fragen des Informationsfreiheitsrechts. *Neue Juristische Wochenschrift (NJW)*, 2987–2994.
Schoch, F. (2016). *Informationsfreiheitsgesetz. Kommentar* (2nd ed.). München, Germany: C. H. Beck.
Sellmann, C., & Augsberg, S. (2006). Chancen und Risiken des Bundesinformationsfreiheitsgesetzes – Eine "Gebrauchsanleitung" für (private) Unternehmen. *Wertpapier-Mitteilungen (WM)*, 2293–2301.
Sitsen, M. (2009). *Das Informationsfreiheitsgesetz des Bundes. Rechtsprobleme im Zusammenhang mit dem Anspruch auf Informationszugang nach dem IFG*. Hamburg, Germany: Kovač.
Sodan, H., & Ziekow, J. (1999). *Kommentar zur Verwaltungsgerichtsordnung, Band II*. Baden-Baden, Germany: Nomos.
Steinbach, R., & Hochheim, D. (2006). Das Informationsfreiheitsgesetz des Bundes unter besonderer Berücksichtigung der Auswirkungen im Organisationsbereich des Sozialrechts. *Neue Zeitschrift für Sozialrecht (NZS)*, 517–525.

## List of Cases

### *German Federal Administrative Court*

Bundesverwaltungsgericht 14.10.1982, 3 C 46/81, BVerwGE 66, 184.

### *German Federal Constitutional Court*

Bundesverfassungsgericht 24.01.2001, 1 BvR 2623/95, 1 BvR 622/99, BVerfGE 103, 44.
Bundesverfassungsgericht 17.06.2009, 2 BvE 3/07, BVerfGE 124, 78.
Bundesverwaltungsgericht 29.10.2009, 7 C 22/08, NVwZ 2010, 321.
Bundesverwaltungsgericht 03.11.2011, 7 C 3.11, DVBl 2012, 176.

# Chapter 8
# Access to Administrative Documents and to Public Sector Information in Italy

**Diana-Urania Galetta**

## Contents



---

This paper is part of the publications related to project PRIN 2012 (2012SAM3KM) on Codification of EU Administrative Procedures. All translations from Italian contained in this paper are mine, unless otherwise indicated. Last update: December 2016.

D.-U. Galetta (✉)
University of Milan, Milan, Italy
e-mail: diana.galetta@unimi.it



H.-J. Blanke, R. Perlingeiro (eds.), *The Right of Access to Public Information*,
DOI 10.1007/978-3-662-55554-5_8

## 1 Introduction

Law No. 241 of 1990 on administrative procedure (Italian APA) established general rules on the right of access to administrative documents for the first time in the Italian legal system,[1] which partly reproduced rules defined in sectorial legislations.

Law No. 241/90 was the first concrete and organic attempt by the Italian legislator to implement the principles provided in the first paragraph of Article 97 of the Constitution, according to which public bodies are organized in such a way as to ensure good administration and impartiality.

Nevertheless, 15 years later, with Law No. 15/2005,[2] the Italian Parliament re-wrote almost the entire Chapter V of Law No. 241/90 on access to administrative documents and made some steps back, insofar as access to administrative documents is concerned.

At the same time, in 2006 a Legislative Decree (No. 36/2006)[3] was adopted to transpose Directive 2003/98/EC[4] on the re-use of public sector information.

Although the aim of this Directive was only to establish a minimum set of rules governing the re-use (for private or commercial purposes) of existing documents held by public bodies of the Member States, and although the Directive aimed at building on the existing access regimes in the Member States, without changing the national rules on access to documents,[5] it did represent a starting point for the adoption of open data policies in many Member States, including Italy. In fact, while it merely aimed at providing a minimal harmonization and did not pose any obligation to allow re-use of documents, *de facto* it encouraged a broader availability of public sector information with the idea that such an extended availability would represent some sort of added value also for the public body itself, by promoting transparency and accountability.[6]

Following this Open Data Policy trend, in 2009 and in 2013 the Italian Government adopted two legislative decrees bearing the paradigmatic headings: "Optimization of productivity of public work and efficiency and transparency of the public

[1]Law No. 241 of 11 August 1990 setting new rules concerning administrative procedure and the right of access to documents, published in the Official Gazette of 18 August 1990, No. 192.

[2]Law No. 15 of 11 February 2005 that introduces Amendments to Law No. 241 of 7 August 1990, relating to general rules on administrative action, published in the Official Gazette of 21 February 2005, No. 42.

[3]Legislative Decree No. 36 of 24 January 2006, published in the Official Gazette of 14 February 2006.

[4]Directive 2003/98/EC of the European Parliament and Council of 17 November 2003 on the re-use of public sector information, at http://www.eurlex.eu. Directive 2003/98/EC was recently amended by Directive 2013/37/EU of the European Parliament and Council of 26 June 2013, at http://www.eurlex.eu.

[5]Directive 2003/98/EC quoted above, recital No. 9.

[6]See now Directive 2003/98/EC as amended by Directive 2013/37/EU quoted above, recital No. 4.

administration" (Legislative Decree No. 150/2009[7]) and "Reorganization of the rules concerning the obligations of publicity, transparency and dissemination of information by public authorities" (Legislative Decree No. 33/2013[8]).

## 2 The Right of Access to Administrative Documents in Italian Law No. 241/90 on Administrative Procedure

### 2.1 *Origin and Nature of the Right of Access*

The general discipline on the right of access to administrative documents, which in Italy was defined for the first time under Chapter V of Law No. 241/1990 setting new rules concerning administrative procedure and the right of access to documents,[9] is the result of a long and complex development process.

The Report of the Constituent Assembly, which was submitted to the Investigation Commission set up by order of the Prime Minister on 11 October 1944, already pointed out that a general law on the public administration was required to regulate, amongst other things, the possibility for citizens to view and obtain copies of administrative documents to "counter the bad habit prevailing in the public administration to hinder such knowledge."[10] However, the scheme of the aforementioned general law designed by the *Forti* Commission did not receive the expected support, as was the case with the following bills presented in 1954 and in 1955, and the bills in Parliament submitted during the same period and later re-submitted in 1963.[11]

After several failed attempts made in the previous decades, at the beginning of the 1980s increasingly pressing requests were made to issue a whole series of general rules governing the administrative procedure, reflecting what had recently happened in Germany with the introduction of the *Verwaltunsgverfahrensgesetz* in 1976. As a result, a new commission chaired by Professor Mario Nigro[12] was appointed, which concluded its work in 1984. The commission prepared two different law drafts: one on the administrative procedure and one on the right of access to administrative documents. The documents in point were then unified and,

---

[7]Legislative Decree No. 150 of 27 October 2009, published in the Official Gazette of 31 October 2009, No. 254.

[8]Legislative Decree No. 33 of 14 March 2013, published in the Official Gazette of 5 March 2013, No. 80.

[9]Quoted above, note No. 1.

[10]Quoted in Cuocolo 1995, p. 527.

[11]See Pastori 1986, p. 49 et seq.; Selleri 1989, p. 359 et seq.

[12]Leading exponent of the Italian legal theory on administrative law for many decades. For information visit http://www.treccani.it/enciclopedia/mario-nigro_%28Enciclopedia_Italiana%29/ (Accessed on 10 June 2014).

together, were formalized into Law No. 241/90 under the heading "New rules concerning administrative procedure and the right of access to documents".

As will be described below (Sect. 2.3, along with subsequent sections), under Law No. 15/2005 Chapter V of Law No. 241/90 on access to administrative documents was later re-written, almost entirely.

Before Law No. 241/90 was passed, the right of access to administrative documents had already been established—specifically as from the beginning of the 1980s—by several sectorial legislations.[13] However, the Italian legal theory had long identified sound constitutional grounds on which a general right of access to the public administration documents could be based. Such grounds included, primarily, the principles of democracy, protection of personal rights, and equality set under Articles 1, 2, and 3 of the Constitution; secondly, the general guarantee of those freedoms that provide a democratic connotation to the citizen/authority relationship, most notably the freedom of information, which is guaranteed under Article 21 of the Constitution, but more than that, by the entire Italian Constitution.[14] This right to information is, in turn, also a result of the provisions of Articles 97 and 98 of the Constitution.[15] Further constitutional grounds supporting access to administrative documents are also found in Articles 24 and 113 of the Constitution due to the broader guarantee that the right of access to administrative documents provides to the judicial protection of the rights and interests set forth therein.[16]

After Law No. 241/90 was passed, the legal theory agreed that, with the provisions on the right of access set forth under Article 22 of Law No. 241/90, the principle of secrecy in administrative activities had finally been overturned in favor of the opposite principle of transparency.[17] Indeed, in its original version, Article 22 of Law No. 241/90 explicitly provided that "[i]n order to ensure transparency in the administrative activities and to facilitate impartiality thereof, anyone who may be interested therein for the protection of legally relevant situations is granted the right to access administrative documents pursuant to the formalities established under this law." However, in the years following the introduction of the abovementioned legislation, a restrictive interpretation approach began to widespread commonly in court rulings,[18] aimed at equating the interest to gaining access to administrative documents to the so-called interest to bring a legal action. The consequence of this was that the applicant was required to provide evidence of a

[13]For a general overview of the previous sectorial legislation on this topic: Sandulli, M.A., 2000, para 3.

[14]See Selleri 1984, p. 24.

[15]Morbidelli 2005, *passim*.

[16]Sandulli, M.A., 2000, para 2.

[17]See Sandulli, A., 1998, p. 535, who underlines the overcoming of the idea of secrecy as a subjective predicate (a document is secret just because it is of the public administration), for a transition to a concept of secrecy as an objective requirement of the document, rather related to the substance of the information contained therein.

[18]Italian Council of State, IV, 10 June 1996, No. 1024; VI, 7 December 1993, No. 966; VI, 19 July 1994, No. 1243; IV, 26 November 1993, No. 1036. See also Gallo & Foà 2000, p. 6 et seq.

*direct, concrete, and actual* interest to access administrative documents as is required, in the Italian system of administrative judicial protection, of anyone who wants to bring a legal action.[19]

Later on, the new legislation introduced in 2005[20] radically changed the provision of Article 22 of Law No. 241/90 and adopted this restrictive interpretation established in court rulings. This meant that, on that occasion, transparency was expunged from the right of access[21] and included in Article 1 of Law No. 241/90, i.e. among the general principles governing administrative action.[22] In essence, as from 2005, pursuant to the general rules established under Article 22, the exercise of the right of access was explicitly limited to "private parties, including stakeholders representing public or widespread interests, who have a direct, concrete, and actual interest corresponding to a legally protected situation that is linked to the document to which access is requested."[23]

As a complement to such restrictive provision, Article 24.3 of Law No. 241/90 (also introduced with the new provisions of Law No. 15/2005) explicitly provides that "no requests of access made with the intention of generally monitoring the work of public administrative bodies shall be accepted."

As to the nature of the right to access, while in the European Union Law the nature of such access is that of a proper right to citizenship,[24] in the Italian legal system the nature of such access is still debated, both in court rulings and in the legal theory.

While some authors, referring to the literal meaning (right of access) and to other elements (e.g., exclusive jurisdiction of the administrative court), consider it a subjective right,[25] others, focusing on different elements (judicial protection entrusted to the administrative court, request subject to the discretionary approval of the administration), speak of a mere legitimate interest.[26] Therefore of an individual subjective legal position that undoubtedly is less protected and largely ancillary to the protection of public interest.[27] Incidentally, this understanding of

---

[19]Villata 1989a, p. 3.

[20]Quoted above, note No. 2.

[21]See Carloni 2009, *passim*. See *infra*, Sect. 3.1.

[22]Pursuant to Article 1 of Law No. 241/90, in the version amended in 2005, "Administrative activities shall pursue the objectives established by the law and shall be governed by the criteria of economy of action, effectiveness, impartiality, publicity and transparency, in accordance with the formalities laid down both in this law and in the other provisions governing individual procedures, as well as by the principles established in the legal order of the European Community."

[23]Article 22.1 point (b) of Law No. 241/90.

[24]Court of First Instance, 17 June 1998, in Case T-174/95, Svenska Journalistförbunde v. Council, in ECR, 1998, p. II-2289 et seq.

[25]See Figorilli 1995, p. 598 et seq.; Perini 1996, p. 109 et seq.

[26]See Paleologo 1991, p. 12; Morbidelli 1998, p. 1310 et seq.; Mazzarolli 1998, p. 58 et seq.

[27]According to the Italian legal theory on administrative law, a "legitimate interest" is an individual interest that is closely connected to a public interest and protected by the law only

the right of access as a mere legitimate interest is also supported in the rulings of the Italian Council of State.[28]

## 2.2 *Ownership and Formalities for Exercising the Right of Access*

As anticipated in the previous section, the right of access is now granted—pursuant to Article 22 c. 1 point (b) of Law No. 241/90—only to the stakeholders, who are understood to be "all private parties, including stakeholders representing public or widespread interests, who have a direct, concrete, and actual interest corresponding to a legally protected situation that is linked to the document to which access is requested." As was discussed above, the new provision seems more restrictive than the original one established under Article 22, but it fully reflects not only the position that has gradually gained consensus in the court rulings, but also a typical tradition of the Italian administrative system that, starting from the unification of Italy, has always been based on the principle of confidentiality of information,[29] which was a binding duty of civil servants who were obliged to keep the strictest confidentiality on all information that they became aware of in the performance of their working tasks, as a result of an authoritative and all but transparent model of public administration.[30]

However, the provisions of Article 22 in its currently applicable version do not prevent the possibility to introduce a broader right of access in special sectorial legislations. This is the case, for instance, of Legislative Decree No. 195/2005[31] on the environment, which makes environmental information available to anyone who applies for it, with no need to state or qualify his or her interest. Another example is

---

through the legal protection of the latter. For an introduction to Italian Public Law, see Ferrari 2008.

[28]Italian Council of State, V, 2 December 1998, No. 1725 confirmed by a later decision of the plenary session of 24 June 1999, No.16.

[29]Pursuant to Sec. 15 of the Consolidated Law on civil servants approved by Presidential Decree No. 3 of 10 January 1957: "Employees must keep full confidentiality on their civil service. They shall not disclose information regarding administrative measures or operations, whether ongoing or completed, or information that has come to their knowledge by virtue of their duties, to persons who are not entitled to it, except in the situations and in the ways provided for by the rules governing the right of access. Within their individual fields of competence, employees who are responsible for an office shall issue copies and excerpts from official instruments and documents only in those cases that are not prohibited by the internal rules of the office."

[30]Arena 1984, *passim*.

[31]Legislative Decree No. 195 of 19 August 2005, "Implementation of Directive 2003/4/EC on public access to environmental information," published in the Official Gazette of 23 September 2005, No. 222.

offered by the consolidated law on local government agencies,[32] where Article 10, in addition to granting citizens the right to access information to documents and proceedings that directly involve them, recognizes the right to access "the information held by the administration in general."[33] However, the prevailing interpretation of this legislation in the court rulings is extremely restrictive as, in this case too, it requires evidence of a specific interest in the document in point.[34]

As to the formalities for exercising the right of access, pursuant to Article 22 c. 1 point (a) of Law No. 241/90, the right of access is understood to be "the right of interested parties to view and to take copies of administrative documents."

Pursuant to the provisions of Presidential Decree No. 184/2006,[35] access may be both informal, "upon request, including a verbal request" (Article 5), and formal, "[s]hould it not be possible to immediately fulfil the request informally, or should there be doubts on the title of the applicant, his/her identity or power of representation, or on the actual interest based on the supplied information or documents, on the accessibility to the document or on the existence of other interested parties" (Article 6).

In both cases, the request of access must be duly motivated to show the qualified interest that is now necessarily required for the right of access to be granted.

In the case of informal access, "the request is examined immediately, is subject to no formalities, and is deemed to be approved by the act of indicating the publication containing the relevant information, or showing the relevant document, or making copies, or any other suitable act."[36] Conversely, in the case of formal access, "the access procedure must be concluded within a term of 30 days."[37] Within 10 days, the administration may suspend the term should it be necessary to supplement the documentation that turned out irregular or incomplete.[38]

The act, whereby a formal request of access is approved, is an administrative decision proper and in all respects. Such administrative act "always comes with the indication of the office and the branch to which reference can be made, as well as with an appropriate period of time of no less than 15 days in which the relevant documents can be viewed or copies thereof can be obtained."[39] The documents must be viewed at the office indicated in the request approval administrative decision, during the working hours, before the staff in charge, if necessary.[40]

---

[32]Legislative Decree No. 267 of 18 August 2000, "Consolidated law on local government," published in the Official Gazette of 28 September 2000, No. 227.

[33]Back in the pre-Republican time, citizens were entitled to view and obtain copies of all the resolutions taken by municipalities and provinces under Article 62 of the consolidated provincial and municipal laws. See Sandulli, M.A., 2000, para 1.

[34]For general reference, see Italian Council of State V, No. 1412 of 18 March 2004, at http://www.giustizia-amministrativa.it.

[35]Presidential Decree No. 184 of 12 April 2006, "New regulations on access."

[36]Article 5.3 of Presidential Decree No. 184/2006.

[37]Article 6.4 of Presidential Decree No. 184/2006.

[38]Article 6.5 of Presidential Decree No. 184/2006.

[39]Article 7.1 of Presidential Decree No. 184/2006.

[40]Article 7 of Presidential Decree No. 184/2006.

Finally, pursuant to the provisions of Article 25 of Law No. 241/90, "[t]he right of access shall be exercised by viewing and taking copies of the relevant administrative documents, in the ways and subject to the limitations established under this law. Document viewing is subject to no charge. Without prejudice to the provisions currently in force on stamp duties, as well as (re)search and survey rights, the issuance of a copy shall be subject only to payment of the copying costs incurred into." Therefore, no document can be taken away or altered in any manner. In addition to asking for copies of such documents subject to payment of the relevant copying costs, the person in point will only be allowed to take notes and transcribe the viewed documents in full or part thereof.

## 2.3 *Subject and Scope of the Right of Access*

Pursuant to the provisions of Article 22 point (d), as amended by Law No. 15/2005, "administrative documents include [. . .] every graphic, photographic or filmed, or electromagnetic or any other kind of representation of the contents of documents, including internal documents or those not relating to a specific procedure, that are held by a public administrative body and concern activities of public interest, regardless of whether the substantive law governing them is public or private law."

In addition to confirming that access is granted also with reference to a pending administrative procedure and, hence, the right can be exercised also on documents that are still internal to the administration (the so-called "access during the course of the procedure"), the aforementioned provision now points out that the right is also granted on documents that do not relate to a specific administrative procedure (the so-called informative access or "access outside of the course of the procedure.")[41] This confirms that the scope of the right of access is broader than that of the administrative procedure.[42]

As to the scope of the right of access, Article 23 of Law No. 241/90 points out that the right of access may be exercised *vis à vis* administrative bodies, autonomous and special corporations, public bodies, and private parties operating public services. The right of access *vis à vis* independent regulatory and supervisory authorities shall be exercised within the framework of their respective regulations, in accordance with the provisions of Article 24 of Law No. 241/90.

In this regard, it should also be pointed out that, while access is granted to all documents when it comes to public administrative bodies, including those governed by the private law,[43] when it comes to private parties, access to their documents is granted only limited to those that are of public interest and all other activities that may be instrumental thereto. In this respect, the courts ruled that, for example, the

[41]See also Sandulli, M.A., 2000, para 4 and 5.

[42]Falcon 2008, *passim*.

[43]Italian Council of State, plenary section, Decision of 22 April 1999, No. 4, Giornale di Diritto amministrativo, 1999, p. 946.

documents relating to staff enrolment for "Ente Poste s.p.a." could be accessed because they are instrumental to managing a service of public interest.[44]

The same remarks apply to economic public bodies.

## 2.4 Restrictions to the Right of Access

Pursuant to Article 25.3, of Law No. 241/90, "Access may be denied, postponed, or restricted in the cases and to the extent established under Article 24. The reasons for such denial, postponement or restriction must be stated."

Article 24 then lists a number of cases in which access to documents is excluded, namely: (a) documents under State secret; (b) tax proceedings, which remain governed by specific rules applicable to them; (c) those activities of the public administration that are aimed at issuing regulatory, general administrative, planning, and programming documents, which remain governed by specific rules applicable to their finalization; (d) selection procedures, in relation to administrative documents containing psycho-aptitude information on third parties.

Article 24.5 further specifies that documents containing information connected to the interests referred to in paragraph 1 of the same Article "shall be deemed secret solely within the limited scope of such connection" and that "to such end, if applicable, the public administrative authorities shall also establish, for each category of documents, the timeframe during which the right of access shall not be granted." However, paragraph 6 of the same Article provides that the Government may establish, via a regulation, other cases in which administrative documents shall not be accessible to protect one of the interests set forth therein (national security and defence, international relations, monetary and currency policies, protection of the public order, documents relating to the private life or confidentiality of third parties, etc.).

However, access is only denied as a last resort, namely, "Access to administrative documents cannot be denied in cases in which it suffices to resort to the power of deferment."[45]

## 2.5 Right of Access and Privacy Protection

The most delicate issue regarding accessibility of documents is undoubtedly the relationship between the right of access and privacy protection. This issue was firstly solved via the interpretations given in the legal theory and court rulings,[46] and later was formally regulated by the novel provisions of Law No. 15/2005.

[44]Italian Council of State, VI, Decision of 5 March 2002, No. 1303, at http://www.giust.amm.it.

[45]Article 24.4.

[46]For further details, see Sandulli, M.A, 2000, para 8.

In this specific regard, the new paragraph 7 of Article 24 states that whereas, on the one hand, access has to be guaranteed to those administrative documents whose knowledge is necessary to protect or defend legal interests (see indent 1), on the other hand (see indent 2) "[i]n the case of documents containing sensitive or judicial data, access shall be permitted to the extent that it is strictly indispensable and within the terms established under Article 60 of Legislative Decree No. 196 of 30 June 2003, in the case of data that might reveal information on health conditions and sexual life."

However, the court rulings seem to take a wavering position on the issue of the actual balance between access and privacy. In fact, extremely difficult and delicate comparative evaluations need to be made, which require "an accurate assessment to be made on a case by case basis as to the legal situations that are to be taken into consideration from time to time."[47] In light thereof, the solution seems to lie in the "limitation" of access referred to in Article 25.3 (in addition to the cases of denial and deferment). Such limitation—as the court rulings point out—may well consist in using, if necessary, "the wording "omissis/omitted" to replace the information that fall under the protection of the right to privacy.[48]

## 2.6 *Protection of the Right of Access*

Pursuant to Article 25.4, also amended by Law No. 15/2005, "Upon expiry of a thirty-day term as from the date of the request without any successful result, such request shall be deemed rejected." This is namely a case of the so-called "silence-denial."

When faced with a decision to explicitly or implicitly deny access or with the postponement thereof, two options can be pursued in accordance with Article 25.4: one is to appeal to the Italian Administrative Tribunal (*Tribunale amministrativo regionale*—TAR), which decides following a special "ruling in chambers" within 30 days as from the expiry of the term established for lodging an appeal and after hearing the defense counsels, if thus requested by the parties. The decision of the Administrative Tribunal is not temporary or preparatory to any other judgment. Indeed, it settles the dispute and can be appealed, within 30 days as from the date of notification, to the Council of State, which will decide on the appeal following the same procedure and within the same timeframe as the Administrative Tribunal.

The second alternative option offered by Article 25.5, is to appeal to the Ombudsman with competence in that territorial jurisdiction if the matter is related to official documents of local, provincial, or regional administrations, or to the Commission for Access—referred to in Article 27—if the case concerns official documents of the central and de-centralized state administrative bodies. In both

[47] Italian Council of State, V, 28 September 2007, No. 4999.

[48] Italian Council of State, V, 28 September 2007 quoted.

cases, the appeal will consist in asking for a reversal of the decision concerning access to documents taken by the administration responsible for granting access.

Should the thirty-day term for the decision on the appeal expire without any decision being taken, the appeal shall be deemed rejected (Article 24.4).

Conversely, should the Ombudsman or the Commission for Access deem the denial or the postponement of access to documents unlawful, "they shall inform the applicant and notify the authority responsible for granting access thereof." Should the latter "fail to issue an act confirming and stating the reasons for its decision within thirty days as from receipt of the notification by the Ombudsman or the Commission, access shall be granted."

Special rules apply, however, if access is denied or postponed for reasons concerning personal data referring to third parties. In such case, the Commission for Access shall decide upon prior consultation with the Data Protection Supervisor, which shall issue its opinion within 10 days as from the request and which opinion shall be deemed to have been given, should such period expires unsuccessfully.

According to Article 25.5, as amended in 2010, disputes concerning access to administrative documents are now ruled by the new administrative process code.[49]

As the decision of the administrative judge is concerned, it shall order the production of the requested documents, within a period not exceeding, usually, thirty days (dictating, where necessary, also the relevant procedures), provided that the applicable conditions are fulfilled.[50]

## 3 Transparency and Access: Between National Law and European Union Law

### *3.1 Lack of Connections Between the Right of Access Pursuant to Law No. 241/90 and Transparency, and Discrepancies with European Union Law*

European Union law recognizes a fundamental connection between transparency, good governance, and right of access to public documents. The existence of such connection emerges quite clearly from several speeches that already the first European Ombudsman, Mr. Jacob Söderman, delivered specifically on these issues.[51]

These concepts are also dealt with in the Treaty of Rome as last amended by the Treaty of Lisbon, which entered into force on 1 December 2009. In fact, Article

---

[49]See Legislative Decree No. 104 of 2 July 2010, published in the Official Gazette of 7 July 2010, especially Art. 116.

[50]Article 116.4 of Legislative Decree No. 194/2010.

[51]Galetta 2006, *passim*.

15.1 of the Treaty on the Functioning of the European Union (TFEU), provides that "In order to promote good governance and ensure the participation of civil society, the Union institutions, bodies, offices, and agencies shall conduct their work as openly as possible." Then, paragraph 3 reiterates the provisions of old Article 255 TEC, according to which "Any citizen of the Union, and any natural or legal person residing or having its registered office in a Member State, shall have a right of access to documents of the Union institutions, bodies, offices, and agencies, whatever their medium [. . .]."[52]

In this respect, till the adoption of the recent FOIA Decree (see Sect. 4), there was a clear discrepancy between the approach chosen by the Italian legislator and the approach adopted by the European Union. As the Italian APA restricted access to all acts and documents—including the internal records—by means of which the administrative function is carried out, and while the latter is being carried out, only to those persons who have a legitimate title thereto and have an interest therein for the protection of their title.[53] Therefore, in the Italian legal system the right of access to document provided for by Italian APA (to be clearly distinguished from the new "public access"—*accesso civico*—provided for by the Italian FOIA—see Sect. 4) is basically understood as a form of guarantee given specifically to those subjects, with the specific purpose of putting them, through a more comprehensive representation of the factual and legal situation that they have a more direct interest in, in a position to best exercise the rights—of participation and/or objection—that the legal system grants to them for the protection of their title, thus only indirectly enhancing—also and mainly through their involvement in the administrative procedure—the impartiality of the administrative action. The goal of transparency in the administrative action, while stated in general terms in Article 22.2 of Law 241/90,[54] is thus guaranteed only in special circumstances and with extremely weak effects on administrative impartiality.

In fact, after the 2005 reform, the only element reflecting the principle of transparency to be still found in the context of Law No. 241/90, did not relate to the right of access to documents of the administration, but to the much more limited duty to publish "directives, programmes, instructions, circulars and every act that, in general, poses requirements for the organisation, functions, goals, and procedures of a public administrative authority, or which establishes the interpretation of legal rules, or provides for their implementation."[55]

---

[52]See also Ziller 2014, *passim*.

[53]See above, Sect. 2.1.

[54]According to Article 22.2, introduced by law No. 69/2009, "In light of its important goals of public interest, access to administrative documents shall constitute a general principle governing administrative activity with the aim of fostering participation and of guaranteeing its impartiality and transparency."

[55]Such was the wording of Article 26.1 of Law No. 241/90, now repealed by Legislative Decree No. 33/2013.

### 3.2 *Transparency as an "Open Data Policy": From Legislative Decree No. 150/2009 to Legislative Decree No. 33/2013*

After the first approach in 2006,[56] with a legislation adopted to transpose Directive 2003/98/EC[57] on the re-use of public sector information, the first concretization of the principle of transparency was represented by the rules contained in the so-called Brunetta Decree No. 150/2009,[58] "Implementation of Law No. 15 of 4 March 2009 on the optimization of the productivity of public work and the efficiency and transparency of public administration,"[59] whose objectives include "transparency of the public administrations also as a guarantee of lawfulness" (Article 2.2).

Article 11 of the Brunetta Decree points out that "transparency has to be understood as *full accessibility*, including by publishing information on the institutional websites of the public administration." This provision generates a qualified legal position for every citizen who is now entitled to obtain public information, which, unlike the provisions that apply to the right of access to administrative documents,[60] is patently aimed "at fostering widespread forms of monitoring so as to make sure that the principles of efficiency and impartiality are complied with" (Article 11.1).

As far as the pursued goals are concerned, transparency—as regulated by the legislator in 2009—can be considered to be aimed at two main goals, i.e., the efficiency of the public administration, which is pursued through the transparency of the performance of the administration and of public services, and prevention of corruption, which is pursued through the transparency of the procedure and of the organization.[61]

---

[56]Legislative Decree No. 36 of 24 January 2006, published in the Official Gazette of 14 February 2006.

[57]Directive 2003/98/EC of the European Parliament and Council of 17 November 2003 on the re-use of public sector information, at http://www.eurlex.eu. Directive 2003/98/EC was recently amended by Directive 2013/37/EU of the European Parliament and Council of 26 June 2013, at http://www.eurlex.eu.

[58]Renato Brunetta was Minister for Public Administration and Innovation from 2008 until 2011, during the fourth Berlusconi's Government.

[59]Legislative Decree No. 150 of 27 October 2009, quoted above, note No. 7.

[60]See above par. 2.1, where a reference is made to Article 24.3, according to which "no request of access made with the intention of generally monitoring the work of public administrative bodies shall be accepted." On this specific point see Patroni Griffi 2013, para 2.

[61]In accordance with the provisions of Article 9 of the United Nations Convention against corruption, stating that "taking into account the need to combat corruption, each State Party shall, in accordance with the fundamental principles of its domestic law, take such measures as may be necessary to enhance transparency in its public administration, including with regard to its organization, functioning and decision-making processes, where appropriate". https://www.unodc.org/documents/treaties/UNCAC/Publications/Convention/08-50026_E.pdf (Accessed on 10 June 2014).

The second goal is actually the focus of the subsequent Legislative Decree No. 33/2013, whose specific aim—pursuant to law No. 190/2012—is to prevent and eradicate illegality in the Public Administration.

More specifically—according to the first version of this Decree (amended by the Italian FOIA—see Sect. 4) public administration authorities were obliged to comply with the transparency requirements set forth in Decree No. 33/2013 (and applicable to all of their activities) mainly by using the "institutional website" of each administration.

Indeed, any user may access such website to look for information regarding the activity and the organization of the public bodies without having to go through an authentication process or be identified in any manner. The aforementioned information must be published on the home page of the institutional websites in the section on "Transparent Administration" and the Decree forbids the setting up of any filter and/or other technical device "aimed at preventing web-based search engines from indexing and searching this section".

Specific limitations to transparency were defined from the very beginning, with a view to guaranteeing some balance between the transparency obligation and the need to protect privacy. Indeed, full accessibility is excluded for sensitive and legal data.[62] On the other hand, exceptions to transparency are admitted also in cases of public grants allotted to specific categories of beneficiaries because of their critical personal conditions—including economic, family and health-related situations—as disclosing such information would imply a severe, patent, and unjustified violation of personal or even sensitive data.[63]

### 3.3 *Implementation of Transparency Rules: The Transparency Officer, Sanctions, and Public Access (accesso civico)*

Pursuant to the explicit provisions of Legislative Decree No. 33/2013, public administrations shall have to guarantee the quality of the information published on the institutional websites in compliance with the duty of disclosure established by the law, ensuring that such information is intact, currently updated, comprehensive, timely, user-friendly, easily understandable, easy to access, true to the original documents held by the administration, and indicating its origin and re-usability.[64]

[62]Referred to in Article 4.1, points (d) and (e) of Legislative Decree No. 196 of 30 June 2003. See also Article 4 of Legislative Decree No. 33/2013 in its original version (now Article 7-bis).

[63]Article 26.4 of Legislative Decree No. 33/2013, which has remained unchanged.

[64]Articles 6 et seq. of Legislative Decree No. 33/2013.

The transparency officer is the key subject, which was instituted *ex novo* under Decree No. 33/2013, in charge of monitoring that the public administrations comply with the applicable provisions.[65] The duties of this subject include the obligation to update the 3-year plan for the prevention of corruption[66]—which also provides specific monitoring measures on the fulfillment of transparency duties and further measures and initiatives aimed at promoting transparency—and to report any failure or delay in complying with the disclosure duties to the policy-making body, the Independent Assessment Body (*Organismo indipendente di valutazione*—OIV), the National Anti-Corruption Authority, and, in the most severe cases, the disciplinary office.

In this regard, Sec. VI of Legislative Decree No. 33/2013, which governs the supervision of the implementation of provisions and sanctions, is particularly important. Indeed, the Italian legislator was stricter here than it was in the past as it introduced sanctions in case of failure to comply with the applicable rules, which provide for disciplinary, management, and administrative responsibilities, as well as the application of administrative sanctions, publication of the relevant measures, and cancellation of resources previously allocated to agencies or bodies.[67]

The applicable sanctions apply both to the transparency officer, with reference to his/her specific duties, and to the managers of the Public administration and political bodies that are required to supply data to finalize the publication. In addition to the sanctions that are applicable to individual subjects, there are sanctions that are applicable to the relevant administrative decision, thus making it ineffective.[68]

A remarkably peculiar sanction is that of the so-called public access (*accesso civico*), which was established already under the original Article 5 of the Decree and which has undergone substantial changes through the Italian FOIA (see *infra* Sect. 4). This provision explicitly stated, from the very beginning, that "the obligation established under the legislation in force for the public administration to publish documents, information, or data implies the right for anyone to request such documents, information or data in case of failure to publish them."[69]

[65]See Article 43 of Legislative Decree No. 33/2013.

[66]The "Three-Year Programme for transparency and integrity" in the original version of Articles 46 et seq. of Legislative Decree No. 33/2013.

[67]See Articles 46 et seq. of Legislative Decree No. 33/2013, in the 2016 modified version.

[68]See Article 15.2; Article 26.3; Article 39.3 of Legislative Decree No. 33/2013.

[69]Article 5.1 of Legislative Decree No. 33/2013.

# 4 The Latest Stage of the Italian Journey Towards Transparency. "Law Madia" and the Italian FOIA: Designing the New "Public Access Era" in Italy?

## *4.1 Transparency as Freedom of Access to the Data and Documents Held by Public Authorities*

With an important Law of August 2015 (No. 124/2015) the President of the Council Renzi, together with Minister for Public Administration Madia, have launched a general reform of Italian Public Administration.[70]

Law No. 124/2015 (the so called "Law Madia"), which was widely glorified in the press as a revolutionary law, contains also an important provision concerning the topic of access to administrative documents and to public sector information.

According to its Article 7, "without prejudice to the obligations of publication", freedom of information through the right of access to data and documents held by public authorities, also by electronic means, shall be granted "to anyone, regardless of ownership of a legally protected situation", except in cases of secrecy or prohibition of disclosure provided for by law and in the limits for the protection of public and private interests. The aim shall be to "promote widespread forms of control over the pursuit of official duties and the use of public resources".[71]

The provision of Article 7 certainly deserves a positive comment, because, as I already underlined in a previous papers of mine,[72] the current limitation contained in Article 22.1 point (b) of Law No. 241 of 1990 on administrative procedure, of the right of access to administrative documents *only* to private parties having a "direct, concrete and existing interest corresponding to a legally protected situation that is linked to the document to which access is requested"[73] widely disappoints those who—like myself—believe that it is more consistent with the very meaning of the right of access to administrative documents to provide for a right of access connected to the need for informational-social control of the administrative action, regardless of the participation in a specific administrative procedure, or of the link with the adoption of an administrative decision in which the person is individually involved.[74] Further, in this respect, the "journey towards transparency" outlined in

---

[70] Law of 7 August 2015, No. 124, published in the Official Gazette of 8 August 2015 and entered into force on 28 August 2015.

[71] So Article 7.1, point (h).

[72] See Galetta 2014a, p. 231 et seq.

[73] This limitation was introduced – first by way of interpretation of the existing provisions and then by the Italian legislator itself – to avoid organizational problems to the public administration. Moreover, therefore, in the name of a further and different goal, i.e., better efficiency and speed of the administrative action, which is also identified as a guiding principle in Article 1 of Law No. 241/90 (quoted above, note No. 22).

[74] See Pastori 1986, p. 147 et seq.; D'Auria 1990, p. 111 et seq.; Alberti 1992, p. 122; Pubusa 1993, p. 134 et seq.; Romano Tassone 1995, p. 318 et seq.

Legislative Decree No. 150/2009 and in the original version of Decree No. 33/2013 was certainly not matching the desired change.

To implement the provision of Article 7 of "Law Madia",[75] a Legislative Decree on transparency, dated 25 May 2016, n. 97, has recently been passed (hereafter the Italian FOIA).[76]

A part from the unchanged first paragraph of Article 5,[77] Legislative Decree No. 97/2016 operates a radical modification of the provisions of Decree No. 33/2013 concerning public access (*accesso civico*). While, in fact, in the original provisions of Article 5 of the Decree No. 33/2013 public access was limited only to those documents, information, or data which the public administration are obliged to publish and was meant (and designed), therefore, as a mere sanction in relation to the infringement of this 'obligation to publish', the Italian FOIA operates here a true revolution.

The new Article 5.2 of the Decree states that "In order to promote widespread forms of control on the pursuit of the institutional functions and on the use of public resources and to promote public participation in public debate, everyone has the right to access data and documents held by the public administrations, additional to those which are subject to publication in accordance with this Decree". Public access to data and documents held by the public administrations is therefore to become the default rule. Restrictions are nonetheless possible when they appear necessary "for the protection of legally relevant public and private interests" (new Article 5.2, last paragraph—see Sect. 4.2).

It is a real 'paradigm shift': as the Italian FOIA designs now transparency as *freedom of access to the data and documents held by public authorities* guaranteed, firstly, through a general public access to such data and documents (*accesso civico*); and, (only) secondly, through the publication of documents, information and data.

Public access (*accesso civico*) to data and documents held by public authorities is therefore to become the main instrument to achieve transparency and is not to remain relegated, as it was till now, in the role of a mere exception to the general rule stated in Article 22 of Law No. 241/90. A rule which clearly designs access to documents as a peculiar right granted only to the stakeholders and with the sole

---

[75]With Decision No. 251/2016 of November 25, 2016 (ECLI:IT:COST:2016:251) the Italian Constitutional Court has recently declared part of "Law Madia" unconstitutional. Consequently, it has deprived of legal basis some of the legislative decrees adopted on its basis. This Decision does not affect, however, the FOIA Decree.

[76]Legislative Decree 25 May 2016, No. 97, Review and simplification of the provisions on prevention of corruption, openness and transparency, amending Law of 6 November 2012, No. 190 and Legislative Decree of 14 March 14, 2013, No. 33, in accordance with Article 7 of Law of 7 August 2015, No. 124, on reorganization public administrations, published in the Official Gazette of 8 June 2016, No. 132.

[77]Public access to documents, information, or data for which Legislative Decree No. 33/2013 provides a disclosure obligation and just in case of failure to publish them. See *supra*, at the end of Sect. 3.3.

purpose of ensuring the defense of a subjective legal position which could be adversely affected by the decision of a public authority.

The Italian FOIA states on the contrary that, in addition to the 'classical' right of access for stakeholders, provided for in Law No 241/90 (and which remains totally unchanged),[78] according to its provisions a general public access (*accesso civico*) to data and documents held by public authorities shall be granted for the future. Indeed, according to Article 6 of the Italian FOIA an applicant which requests public access does not need to possess a so called "qualified interest" and does not need to give any reason for his or her request. The application may be transmitted electronically and the release of information or documents in electronic or printed form is free, except for the reimbursement of the cost actually incurred and documented by the administration for the reproduction of material supports.

## 4.2 Restrictions to Public Access and the Role of the Anti-Corruption Authority

This new, extended right to public access provided for by the Italian FOIA is, anyhow, by no means designed as an unlimited right. On the contrary, it is surrounded by a vast number of possible restrictions, aimed at protecting a wide number of public and private interests.

Alongside the 'classical' access restrictions, aimed at protecting public interests such as the ones relating to public safety and public order, national security, defence and military matters, international relations, policy, financial and economic stability of the State, investigations on crimes and their prosecution, inspections, there is also a rather long list of other possible restrictions concerning the protection of private interests. This includes the protection of personal data, secrecy of correspondence, as well as economic and business interests of a natural or legal person, including intellectual property, copyright and corporate secrets.[79]

It is a rather long list, including many different restrictions to public access which can concretely lead to access denial, to postponement of access or to limiting access only to certain parts of the requested documents. Even if they aim at protecting the core of legitimate public and private interests, they are too broadly defined[80] and certainly need further concretization.[81]

In fact, in the absence of further concretization by the national legislator, it remains a discretionary decision of each single public administration to identify the actual content of such potentially unlimited restrictions to public access; or it will

[78] See to this regard Galetta 2016a, para 10, p. 15 et seq.

[79] See Article 6 of the Italian FOIA.

[80] Galetta 2016b, p. 9 et seq.

[81] Cf. Opinion of the Italian Council of State n. 515/2016, at: http://giustizia-amministrativa.it, p. 85 et seq. (Consultative Section for Normative Acts, 18 February 2016, No. 515).

be up to the administrative courts to finally decide: if concrete restrictions to public access are challenged by their addressee.[82]

To address the above mentioned problem the FOIA legislator has in the end chosen to involve to the National Anti-Corruption Authority (hereafter ANAC) in the matter. Accordingly, Article 5-bis of the Decree No. 33/2013 has been integrated with a sixth and last paragraph, according to which it will be up to the ANAC (in agreement with the Authority for the protection of personal data and after consultation with the Joint Conference of State, cities' and local governments) to adopt guidelines (*linee guida*)[83] containing 'operational indications' for the purpose of defining the exclusions and limitations to civic access.

Doubts arise about the appropriateness of entrusting also this competence to an Independent Agency such as ANAC, whose aim and nature is that of working as an 'anticorruption watchdog'. In fact, the choice made by the Italian legislator to this regard is based on the questionable assumption, that it is possible to identify a clear and unambiguous link between public access, transparency and combating corruption.

## 5 Conclusions

The adoption of an 'Italian FOIA' has been a manifesto commitment of the *Renzi* Government since its inception. On the day of its definitive approval the Minister for Simplification and Public Administration, *Marianna Madia*, gloriously stated as follows: "We have kept that promise. With the Decree implementing the public administration reform, finally approved, Italy has adopted a *Freedom of Information Act*. Citizens have now the right to know data and documents held by the public administration, even without possessing a direct interest".[84]

These are, in the opinion expressed by Minister *Madia*, the central points of the Italian FOIA:

1. requesting a document will be free of charge;
2. an administration that refuses to issue a document will have to give clear reasons for its refusal;

[82]Up to now the most delicate issue regarding accessibility of documents has concerned the relationship between the right of access and privacy protection and the Italian administrative courts that took a rather wavering position on the issue of the actual balance between access and privacy. See, e.g., Italian Council of State, V, 28 September 2007, No. 4999.

[83]There is at present a great debate in Italian academic literature – involving also the Council of State in its advisory role – regarding the legal nature of guidelines adopted by an Independent Agency such as the National Anti-Corruption Authority. See to this regard the opinion delivered by the Italian Council of State on the scheme of the Public Contracts Code (opinion of 1 April 2016, No. 855, at: http://www.giustizia-amministrativa.it (Accessed on 14 February 2017).

[84]See at: http://www.funzionepubblica.gov.it/articolo/riforma-della-pa/16-05-2016/foia-e-trasparenza-ora-e-legge (Accessed on 14 February 2017).

3. the citizen who has been refused by an administration to release information will be able to contact the transparency and anticorruption officer (*responsabile della prevenzione della corruzione e della trasparenza*) or the ombudsman and, in any case, to appeal to the competent Regional Administrative Tribunal (TAR).

An important criticism addressed by early commentators to the Italian FOIA concerns the choice made by the Italian legislator to move away from the idea of transparency understood as an "Open Data Policy" (with a pro-active-disclosure-of-information approach) to embrace the public access model (the transparency-on-request approach). Thus, while confirming the obligation of public administrations to publish a certain amount of documents and data on their institutional websites,[85] the Italian legislator opts, with the FOIA Decree, for transparency understood as free-access-on-request to data and documents held by public administrations.

Nonetheless, this was in my opinion a good choice: as it allows, on one hand, to avoid the risk of generating "opacity for confusion" rather than transparency[86]; and, on the other hand, it minimizes the risk of neglecting data protection, thus assuring also full compliance with the provisions of the new EU General Data Protection Regulation.[87]

To this regard, a real risk of detachment of the Italian Open Data Policy from the principles of protection of personal data was, on the contrary, clearly underlined by the Italian Data Protection Supervisor—at the time when this was still in its draft form—in its opinion released on the first version of Legislative Decree No. 33/2013.[88]

In fact, while transparency of the Public Administration is certainly an important issue for modern democracies, it still cannot be understood as a value in itself and its consistency with other founding values, such as privacy and data protection, has to be guaranteed at all times.[89] Furthermore, if the ultimate reason for national transparency policies is to ensure accountability of Public Administration, the extent to which transparency, understood as a mere Open Data Policy, can actually deliver on its revolutionary potential has also to be called into question.[90]

Hence, to conclude, the new direction in which the 'Italian journey' towards transparency has recently moved towards is likely to be the right one. From a very restrictive regime of access to administrative documents (the one designed by Law No. 241/90, which is however still applicable for those documents and data which are excluded from public access)—lately accompanied by a rather demagogical

[85]To this regard, the Italian FOIA introduces also a rationalization, by reducing excessive burdensome obligations to publish. See Galetta 2016c, p. 17.

[86]See Carloni 2009, p. 806.

[87]Regulation (EU) 2016/679 of the European Parliament and of the Council of 27 April 2016 on the protection of natural persons with regard to the processing of personal data and on the free movement of such data (and repealing Directive 95/46/EC).

[88]Opinion of the Italian DPS No. 49 of 7 February 2013, doc web. No. 2243168.

[89]See further Galetta and Ibler 2015, p. 17 et seq.

[90]See also Galetta 2014b, p. 6.

obligation imposed on public administrations to disclose a set of information in the context of so-called open data policies[91]—Italy has namely moved forth to the hoped-for[92] public access to data and documents held by public administrations: which, in my opinion, is the most correct way to implement the principle of transparency.

More so because, to do it the other way round—i.e., by obliging public administrations to publish an increasingly large amount of incomprehensible and, in themselves, meaningless documents and data—has in fact very little to do with making information not only downloadable to citizens, but also useable and meaningful.[93]

## References

Agrifoglio, S. (1990). La trasparenza dell'azione amministrativa e il principio del contradditorio: tra procedimento e processo. *Diritto Processuale Amministrativo, 1*, 46–67.

Alberti, M. (1992). L'accesso ai documenti amministrativi. In M. Alberti et al. (Eds.), *Lezioni sul procedimento amministrativo* (pp. 126–146). Torino, Italy: Giappichelli.

Allegretti, U. (1984). Pubblica amministrazione ed ordinamento democratico. *Il Foro Italiano, 1984*(7–8), 205–220.

Arena, G. (1984). *Il segreto amministrativo. Profili storici e sistematici*. Padova, Italy: CEDAM.

Arena, G. (1991). *L'accesso ai documenti amministrativi*. Bologna, Italy: Il Mulino.

Arena, G. (1995). Trasparenza. *Enciclopedia giuridica Treccani*, update vol. IV (pp. 1–13). Roma: Treccani.

Arena, G. (1996). Trasparenza amministrativa e democrazia. In G. Berti & G. De Martin (Eds.), *Gli istituti della democrazia amministrativa* (pp. 13–27). Milano: Giuffrè.

Arena, G. (2008). Le diverse finalità della trasparenza amministrativa. In F. Merloni (Ed.), *La trasparenza amministrativa* (pp. 29–44). Milano: Giuffré.

Barile, P. (1987). Democrazia e segreto. *Quadernicostituzionali, 1*, 29–50.

Bonomo, A. (2012). *Informazione e pubbliche amministrazioni. Dall'accesso ai documenti alla disponibilità delle informazioni*. Bari, Italy: Cacucci Editore.

Bottino, G. (2014). Il nuovo articolo 97 della Costituzione. *Rivista Trimestrale di Diritto Pubblico, 3*, 691–719.

Brancasi, A. (2012). L'introduzione del principio del c.d. pareggio di bilancio: un esempio di revisione affrettata della Costituzione. *Quaderni costituzionali, 1*, 108–111.

Buttarelli, G. (1997). *Banche dati e tutela della riservatezza. La Privacy nella Società dell'Informazione*. Milano: Giuffré.

Butti, G., & Butti, L. (1991). Il "diritto di accesso" alle informazioni ambientali disponibili presso la pubblica amministrazione. *Rivista giuridica dell'ambiente, 3*, 461–468.

Canaparo, P. (2014). La via italiana alla trasparenza pubblica: Il diritto di informazione indifferenziato e il ruolo proattivo delle pubbliche amministrazioni. *Federalismi.it, 4*, 1–60.

Caringella, F., Garofoli, R., & Sempreviva, M. T. (2007). *L'accesso ai documenti amministrativi*. Milano: Giuffré.

[91]On this point, see specifically Patroni Griffi 2013, para 2.

[92]See Galetta 2014b, p. 234.

[93]See Canaparo 2014, para 10.; Napolitano 2005; Galetta 2016c.

Carloni, E. (2009). La "casa di vetro" e le riforme. Modelli e paradossi della trasparenza amministrativa. *Diritto pubblico, 3*, 779–812.

Carloni, E. (2012). La trasparenza (totale) delle pubbliche amministrazioni come servizio. *Munus, 1*, 179–198.

Carullo, A. (1998). *La trasparenza nelle amministrazioni locali. Per una nuova legge comunale e provinciale*. Bologna, Italy: Il Mulino.

Chieppa, R. (1994). La trasparenza come regola della pubblica amministrazione. *Diritto dell'Economia, 3*, 613–625.

Clarich, M. (1996). Diritto d'accesso e tutela della riservatezza: regole sostanziali e tutela processuale. *Diritto processuale amministrativo, 3*, 430–458.

Cocco, G. F. (1980). *I segreti di informazione e di sicurezza nell'ordinamento italiano*. Padova, Italy: CEDAM.

Cuocolo, F. (1995). Commento all'articolo 22. In V. Italia & M. Bassani (Eds.), *Procedimento amministrativo e diritto di accesso ai documenti (Legge 7 agosto 1990, n. 241 e regolamenti di attuazione)* (2nd ed., pp. 527–545). Giuffré: Milano.

D'Auria, G. (1990). Trasparenze e segreti nell'Amministrazione italiana. *Politica del diritto, 1*, 93–121.

De Cesaris, A. (1991). Informazione ambientale e accesso ai documenti amministrativi. *Rivista trimestrale di diritto pubblico, 3*, 851–861.

Ferrari, G. F. (2008). *Italian Public Law*. Milano: Giuffré.

Figorilli, F. (1995). Il contraddittorio nel giudizio speciale sul diritto di accesso. *Diritto processuale amministrativo, 3*, 584–607.

Galetta, D.-U. (2006). Transparency and administrative governance in European Law. In M. P. Chiti (Ed.), *General principles of administrative action* (pp. 153–181). Bologna, Italy: Bononia University Press.

Galetta, D.-U. (2012). La Ley Italiana 241/90 de Procedimiento Administrativo. In P. Aberastury & H.-J. Blanke (a cura di), *Tendencias actuales del procedimiento administrativo en Latino América y Europa* (pp. 231–268). Editorial Universitaria de Buenos Aires (EUDEBA), Buenos Aires eFundación Konrad Adenauer, Oficina México, México

Galetta, D.-U. (2014a). Alcuni recenti sviluppi del diritto amministrativo italiano (fra riforme costituzionali e sviluppi della società civile). *Giustizia amministrativa*, XI(June), 1–6 (http://www.giustamm.it).

Galetta, D.-U. (2014b). Transparency and access to public sector information in Italy: A proper revolution? *Italian Journal of Public Law, 6*, 212–240.

Galetta, D.-U. (2016a). Accesso civico e trasparenza della Pubblica Amministrazione alla luce delle (previste) modifiche alle disposizioni del Decreto Legislativo n. 33/2013. *Federalismi.it, 5*, 2–19.

Galetta, D.-U. (2016b). La trasparenza, per un nuovo rapporto tra cittadino e Pubblica Amministrazione: un'analisi storico-evolutiva in una prospettiva di diritto comparato ed europeo. *Rivista italiana di diritto pubblico comunitario*, 5.

Galetta, D.-U. (2016c). The Italian Freedom of Information Act 2016 (why transparency-on-request is a better solution). *Italian Journal of Public Law*, 8, 268–290 (http://www.ijpl.eu/assets/files/pdf/2016_volume_2/IJPL_volume2_2016.pdf).

Galetta, D.-U., & Ibler, M. (2015). Decisioni amministrative "multipolari" e problematiche connesse: la libertà di informazione e il diritto alla riservatezza in una prospettiva di diritto comparato (Italia-Germania). *Federalismi.it, 9*, 1–29.

Gallo, C. E., & Foà, S. (2000). Accesso agli atti amministrativi. *Digesto delle discipline pubblicistiche*, update 2000 (1 – 27). Torino, Italy: UTET.

Guglielmi, G. J., & Zoller, E. (Eds.). (2014). *Démocratie, transparence et gouvernance citoyenne*. Paris: Editions Panthéon-Assas.

Leonardi, R. (2012). Il diritto di accesso ai documenti amministrativi: a proposito dei soggetti attivi per un'azione amministrativa trasparente, ma non troppo. *Il Foro amministrativo T.A.R, 6*, 2155–2182.

Losano, M. G. (2008). Trasparenza o privacy? Due recenti polemiche italiane. *Diritto dell'Informazione e dell'Informatica, 4–5*, 471–486.

Manganaro F. (2012). L'evoluzione del principio di trasparenza. In *Scritti in memoria di Roberto Marrama*. Editoriale Scientifica: Napoli.

Marrama, R. (1989). La pubblica amministrazione tra trasparenza e riservatezza nell'organizzazione e nel procedimento amministrativo. *Diritto processuale amministrativo, 3*, 416–452.

Massera, A. (2011). I criteri di economicità, efficacia ed efficienza. In M. A. Sandulli (Ed.), *Codice dell'azione amministrativa* (pp. 22–82). Milano: Giuffré.

Mazzarolli, L. (1998). *L'accesso ai documenti amministrativi. Profili sostanziali*. Padova, Italy: CEDAM.

Merloni, F. (2008). Trasparenzadelleistituzionieprincipiodemocratico. In F. Merloni & G. Arena (Eds.), *Latrasparenza amministrativa*. Giuffré: Milano.

Merloni, F. (2013). La trasparenza come strumento di lotta alla corruzione tra legge n. 190 del 2012 e d. lgs. n. 33 del 2013. In B. Ponti (Ed.), *La Trasparenza amministrativa dopo il d.lgs. 14 marzo 2013, n.33*. Rimini, Italy: Maggioli.

Merloni, F., & Arena, G. (2008). *La trasparenza amministrativa*. Milano: Giuffré.

Merloni, F., Arena, G., et al. (Eds.). (2008). *La trasparenza amministrativa*. Milano: Giuffré.

Morbidelli, G. (2005). Il procedimento amministrativo. In L. Mazzarolli et al. (Eds.), *Diritto amministrativo* (Vol. I). Monduzzi: Bologna, Italy.

Napolitano, G. (2005). L'attività informativa della pubblica amministrazione: 'less is better'. In F. Manganaro & A. Romano Tassone (Eds.), *I nuovi diritti di cittadinanza: il diritto d'informazione*. Giappichelli: Torino, Italy.

Nigro, M. (1989). Il procedimento amministrativo fra inerzia legislativa e trasformazioni dell'amministrazione (a proposito di un recente disegno di legge). *Diritto processuale amministrativo, 1*, 5–24.

Occhiena, M. (1998). Diritto di accesso, atti di diritto privato e tutela della riservatezza dopo la legge sulla privacy (il diritto di accesso e la riforma dell'organizzazione della p.a.) *Diritto processuale amministrativo, 2*, 377–418.

Occhiena, M. (2006). I poteri della Commissione per l'accesso ai documenti amministrativi: in particolare, la funzione giustiziale ex L. n. 241/1990 e D.P.R. n. 184/2006. *Giustizia amministrativa, 6*, 1242–1252.

Occhiena, M. (2008). Necessaria riforma del diritto di accesso: diffusione e accesso telematico alle informazioni amministrative. *Il diritto dell'economia, 1*, 177–207.

Occhiena, M. (2012). I principi di pubblicità e trasparenza. In M. Renna & F. Saitta (Eds.), *Studi sui principi del diritto amministrativo* (pp. 141–148). Milano: Giuffré.

Pastori, G. (1986). Il diritto d'accesso ai documenti amministrativi in Italia. *Amministrare, 1*, 147–170.

Patrito, P., & Pavoni, F. (2012). La disciplina del riutilizzo dei dati pubblici dal punto di vista del diritto amministrativo: prime riflessioni. *Il Diritto dell'Informazione*, 87–109.

Patroni Griffi, F. (1992). Un contributo alla trasparenza dell'azione amministrativa: partecipazione procedimentale e accesso agli atti (legge 7 agosto 1990, n. 241). *Diritto processuale amministrativo, 1*, 56–72.

Patroni Griffi, F. (2013). La trasparenza della pubblica amministrazione tra accessibilità totale e riservatezza. *Federalismi.it, 8*, 1–12 (http://www.federalismi.it).

Perini, A. (1996). L'autonomia del diritto di accesso in giudizio. *Diritto processuale amministrativo, 1*, 107–120.

Perini, A. (1997). Il diritto di accesso e la tutela della riservatezza nelle amministrazioni locali. *Rivista Amministrativa della Repubblica Italiana, 12*, 1147–1163.

Pignataro, S. (2012). *Il principio costituzionale del "buon andamento" e la riforma della pubblica amministrazione*. Bari, Italy: Cacucci.

Ponti, B. (2008). *Il regime dei dati pubblici. Esperienza europee e ordinamento nazionale*. Rimini, Italy: Maggioli.

Ponti, B. (2011). Open data and transparency: A paradigm shift. *Informatica e Diritto, 1–2*, 305–320.

Ponti, B. (2013). *La trasparenza amministrativa dopo il d.lgs.14 marzo 2013, n. 33*. Rimini, Italy: Maggioli.

Pubusa, A. (1993). *L'attività amministrativa in trasformazione. Studi sulla l. 7 agosto 1990, n. 241*. Torino, Italy: Giappichelli.

Puliatti, P. (1997). Primi avvisi giurisprudenziali sul diritto di accesso ai documenti amministrativi. *I Tribunali amministrativi regionali, 12*, 497–501.

Raines, J. (2012–2013). The Digital Accountability and Transparency Act of 2011 (DATA): Using open data principles to revamp spending transparency legislation. *New York Law School Law Review, 57*, 313–360.

Ricciardi, M. (1993). Appunti sul segreto di Stato e principio di trasparenza. *Politica del diritto, 1*, 35–50.

Romano Tassone, A. (1995). A chi serve il diritto di accesso. Riflessioni su legittimazione e modalità di esercizio del diritto di accesso nella legge n. 241 del 1990. *Diritto amministrativo*, 317–340.

Romeo, G. (1999). Accesso ai documenti e riservatezza: rovescio e diritto di una medesima realtà. *Il Foro amministrativo*, *9*(III), 435–444.

Salvatore, P. (1996). Trasparenza, dovere di comunicazione e tutela del segreto e della riservatezza. *Il Consiglio di Stato, 11*(2), 2019–2025.

Sandulli, A. (1998). La riduzione dei limiti all'accesso ai documenti amministrativi. *Giornaledidiritto amministrativo*, 529–537.

Sandulli, M. A. (2000). Accesso alle notizie e ai documenti amministrativi. *Enciclopedia del Diritto*, update vol. IV (pp. 1–30). Milano: Giuffré.

Santoro, P. (1992). Diritto di accesso partecipativo e diritto di accesso conoscitivo: posizioni soggettive ed effettività. *Il Foro amministrativo, 7–8*, 1799–1806.

Savino, M. (2013). *Lanuovadisciplina dellatrasparenzaamministrativa. Giornaledidirittoamministrativo, 8/9*, 795–805.

Scognamiglio, A. (1996). Il diritto di accesso nella disciplina della l. 7 agosto 1990 n. 241 e il problema della legittimazione. *Rivista trimestrale di diritto pubblico, 1*, 93–114.

Scognamiglio, A. (2005). Diritto di accesso e banche dati pubbliche. *Il Foro Amministrativo–Consiglio di Stato, 2*, 493–502.

Selleri, B. (1984). *Il diritto di accesso agli atti del procedimento amministrativo*. Napoli, Italy: Jovene.

Selleri, B. (1989). Il diritto di accesso agli atti amministrativi tra tensione alla riforma e fedeltà alle strutture del sistema positivo. In *In La disciplina generale del procedimento amministrativo (Atti del XXXII Convegno di studi di scienza dell'amministrazione, Varenna-Villa Monastero, 18-20 settembre 1986)*. Milano: Giuffré.

Sorace, D. (2012). *Diritto delle amministrazioni pubbliche. Una introduzione*. Bologna, Italy: Il Mulino.

Spasiano, M. R. (2011). I principi di pubblicità, trasparenza e imparzialità. In M. A. Sandulli (Ed.), *Codice dell'azione amministrativa* (pp. 83–95). Milano: Giuffré.

Spasiano, M. R., Corletto, D., Gola, M., Galetta, D. U., et al. (Eds.). (2012). *La Pubblica Amministrazione e il suo diritto*. Bologna, Italy: Monduzzi Editoriale.

Truini, P. (1993). Diritto all'informazione e riservatezza. *Rivista Amministrativa della Repubblica Italiana, 6–7*, 799–803.

Villata, R. (1987). La trasparenza dell'azione amministrativa. *Diritto Processuale Amministrativo, 4*, 528–557.

Villata, R. (1989a). *Interesse ad agire (Diritto processuale civile). Enciclopedia giuridica Treccani* (Vol. XVII). Roma: Treccani.

Villata, R. (1989b). La trasparenza dell'azione amministrativa. In *In La disciplina generale del procedimento amministrativo (Atti del XXXII Convegno di studi di scienza dell'amministrazione, Varenna-Villa Monastero, 18-20 settembre 1986)*. Milano: Giuffré.

Villata, R. (1992). Riflessioni in tema di partecipazione al procedimento e legittimazione processuale. *Diritto Processuale Amministrativo, 2*, 171–205.

Virga, G. (1998). *La partecipazione al procedimento amministrativo*. Milano: Giuffré.

Volpe, F. (1991). Trasparenza e partecipazione nell'ordinamento delle autonomie locali. *I Tribunali amministrativi regionali, 5-6*, 253–265.

Ziller, J. (2014). Origines et retombées du principe de transparence du droit de l'Union européenne.

Zito, A. (1996). *Le pretese partecipative del privato nel procedimento amministrativo*. Milano: Giuffré.

## *List of Cases*

Court of First Instance 17.06.1998, Case T-174/95, *Svenska Journalistförbunde v. Council.*
Italian Constitutional Court 25.112016, No. 251.
Italian Council of State 26.11.1993, IV, No. 1036.
Italian Council of State 07.12.1993, VI, No. 966.
Italian Council of State 19.07.1994, VI, No. 1243.
Italian Council of State 10.06.1996, IV, No. 1024.
Italian Council of State 02.12.1998, V, No. 1725.
Italian Council of State 22.04.1999, plenary section, No. 4.
Italian Council of State 24.06.1999, plenary section, No. 16.
Italian Council of State 05.03.2002, VI, No. 1303.
Italian Council of State 18.03.2004, V, No. 1412.
Italian Council of State 28.09.2007, V, No. 4999.
Italian Council of State 18.02.2016, Consultative Section for Normative Acts, No. 515.

# Chapter 9
# Right of Access to Public Information: The Portuguese Case

Luísa Neto

## Contents



## 1 The Scope of the Right of Access to Public Documents

It is known that a Democratic State of Law requires the end of the invisible way of power, and proposes that government acts should take place *au grand jour*, in a transparent[1] environment. In fact, many identify the disclosure of public information and a right to *truth* as conditions for an active citizenship. Therefore, in the

[1]Brin 1998.


L. Neto (✉)
University of Porto, Porto, Portugal
e-mail: lneto@direito.up.pt







H.-J. Blanke, R. Perlingeiro (eds.), *The Right of Access to Public Information*,
DOI 10.1007/978-3-662-55554-5_9

Portuguese democratic legal system, regulation of public access to official ('administrative') information—and also of data protection—is treated by the Constitution of the Portuguese Republic (1976: CPR)[2] and also in several legislative acts. First, Article 37 CPR ensures the right to inform, to be informed and to seek sources of information.[3] Likewise, Article 20.2 CPR ensures the right to legal information and other specific constitutional provisions relate to information in what regards, for instance, information due to consumers.

We shall not detain ourselves in this general framework,[4] but we will aim to focus on the *specific right of access to public* ('administrative') *documents*.[5] In fact, the Portuguese Constitution provides the principle of open government,[6] enshrined in Article 268 of this fundamental law. Article 268.1 and 2 CPR establishes the individual's right of information and access to databases or registries of public entities, in the following way:

1. Citizens have the right to be informed by the Administration, whenever they so request, as to the progress of the procedures and cases in which they are directly interested, together with the right to be made aware of the definitive decisions that are taken in relation to them.
2. Without prejudice to the law governing matters concerning internal and external security, criminal investigation and personal privacy, citizens also have the right of access to administrative files and records.

However, the Portuguese Constitution also expressly protects individual's right of privacy in its Article 26.1 and 2. Other articles inserted in the Constitution complement this general provision, namely Article 35 CPR applicable to computer databases: "All citizens have the right to be informed of any data referring to them and used in computer databases [...]" (paragraph 1) and, "unless expressly authorised by law, prevent its use by third parties" (paragraph 2).[7]

---

[2]An English version of the Constitution of the Portuguese Republic (CPR) and of the main legislation hereby quoted may be found at the site of the Portuguese Parliament, Assembly of the Republic (www.parlamento.pt) or at the sites of CADA and CNPD (www.cada.pt and www.cnpd.pt) (Accessed on 14 February 2017).

[3]Cunha 2006, p. 623–651.

[4]For further developments, AA VV 1999 and 2001, Almeida 2004, Ascensão 2001.

[5]This subject was already brought to our study: Neto et al. 2002, p. 187–200.

More recently, these matters have also been addressed to in Neto 2012b, p. 41–55 and also Neto 2012c, p. 7–16.

[6]This principle is developed by the Article 62 of the Code of Administrative Procedure of 1991 and has specific remedies relief since at least 1985. This principle is also known as "open archive". In what concerns the fullfillment of this goal, see Ribeiro 2003 and Ribeiro 2005, p. 83–100.

[7]After the constitutional revision of 1997, there is also a reference made in Article 26 to the protection of genetic information, also addressed by Law No. 12/2005 of 26 January 2005 and by Law No. 5/2008 of 12 February 2008, that created a genetic database.

### 1.1 The Former Law No. 65/93 of 26 August 1993 (as Amended by Law No. 8/95 of 29 March 1995 and Law No. 94/99 of 16 July 1999)

In 1993, giving account of the guidelines provided by the Constitution, Portuguese primary legislation (Law No. 65/93) stipulated that citizens may accede to public ('administrative')[8] documents according to the principles of publicity, transparency, equality, justice and impartiality (Article 1). These principles were not defined in this law because they are commonly seen as basic principles that guide the activity of the Public Administration: that is an imposition of the Constitution, and of the Administrative Procedure Code of 1991, and all the way a necessary consequence of the concept of a State of Law.

The access to the documents should be free[9] as far as public documents ('administrative documents') were concerned. In case of nominative documents, only the individual concerned could accede to them. However, derogations could apply to third parties under the 'direct and personal interest' criteria, in case an authorisation was granted by the individual or if the document could be used without compromising the privacy of the individual.

Access could be refused to protect industrial or intellectual property rights (Article 10). The request should be presented in a written form containing a description of the essential features of the document and identification of the applicant (name, address and signature).[10] Within a period of 10 days, the public entity should reach a decision and, if the case, mention dates, local and procedure to accede to the document. In case of refusal, the legal or factual reasoning of its decision should also be conveyed to the applicant.[11]

### 1.2 Further Regulation (Law No. 46/2007 of 24 August 2007) and the Law Now Enforced: Law No. 26/2016 of 22 August 2016

The Law No. 46/2007 of 24 August 2007 came to regulate the access to and the re-use of administrative documents,[12] revoking Law No. 65/93 of 26 August 1993 and

[8]The concept 'document' was then defined in Article 3 of Law No. 65/93: "Documents enacted or used by governmental bodies with administrative functions, public institutes and public associations, council bodies and other entities defined by law". Furthermore, Article 4 distinguished between two types of documents: a) Administrative documents (documents issued or used by public entities) and b) Nominative documents (documents containing personal data).

[9]The law now enforced refers to fees due by those who require information, as we will point out in Sect. 3.1.

[10]See Article 13 of Law No. 65/93.

[11]See Article 15 of Law No. 65/93.

[12]On the specific matter of the re-use of public information, Ascensão 2004, p. 65–82.

transposing into Portuguese law Directive No. 2003/98/EC of the European Parliament and of the Council of 17 November 2003, on the re-use of public sector information.

However, this Law was already repealed by Law No.26/2016 of 22 August 2016, which entered into force on 1 October 2016. This Law (L2016) regulates in a single piece of legislation matters relating to the access to administrative documents and to environmental information drawn by Directive 2012/37/UE, of the European Parliament and Council, of 26 June 2013 and is the Law now enforced in Portugal.

The principle of open administration/government constitutionally placed, as told, in Article 268.1 and 2 CPR, is restated in Article 2 of L2016: "[A]ccess to and the re-use of administrative documents shall be ensured in accordance with the principles of equality, proportionality, justice, impartiality and cooperation with citizens." Considering those principles, however, Article 7 of L2016 remembers that this law shall govern access to nominative documents,[13] particularly when they include health-related data,[14] by the person to whom the information refers, by a third party authorised by the person to whom the information refers, or by anyone who demonstrates a direct, personal and legitimate interest. In what matters to specific public interest, Article 1.4 point (c) of L2016 states that "access to documents kept by notaries public or in official registries, to civil and criminal identification documents, and to documents deposited in historical archives shall be governed by specific legislation."

Articles 3 and 4 of L2016 define 'administrative document' as any information medium in written, visual, aural, electronic or other material form, which is in the possession, or is held on behalf, of:

1. Bodies which belong to the State[15] and the autonomous regions and form part of the Public Administration;
2. Other bodies which belong to the State and the autonomous regions, to the extent to which they perform materially administrative functions;
3. Bodies which belong to public institutes and public associations and foundations;
4. Bodies which belong to state-owned companies;
5. Bodies which belong to local authorities and to their associations and federations;
6. Bodies which belong to regional, metropolitan, inter-municipal and municipal companies;
7. Other bodies that engage in administrative functions or exercise public authority.
8. Moreover, the provisions of Law L2016 shall also apply to documents held or drawn up by anybody—even companies or private law associations or

[13]In L2016, the definition of "nominative documents" now covers administrative documents containing "personal data" as defined by the legal regime of personal data protection.

[14]Law No. 12/2005 of 26 January 2005 already mentioned.

[15]However, L2016 states clearly in Article 3.2 that shall not be deemed 'administrative documents' those drawn up from administrative activities, particularly those concerning meetings of the Council of Ministers and Secretaries of State, and the preparation thereof.

foundations—which possesses legal personality and has been created to fulfill needs of general interest that do not possess an industrial or commercial nature in a specific manner, and to which any of the following circumstances applies:

(a) The majority of the funding for the body's activities is provided by any of the public entities that fall within the scope of the Act;
(b) The body's management is subject to a control by any of the public entities previously referred to;
(c) More than half the members of the body's management or supervisory boards are appointed by any of the public entities previously referred to.

## 2 The Limitations of this Right Enshrined in the National Law, in Particular the Protection of Public Interest and Personal Data

The restrictions—that in some way derive from the constitutional text—are stated in Article 6 of L2016, hereafter summed up:

1. Documents that contain information, knowledge of which is deemed capable of endangering or damaging the internal and external security of the State, shall be subject to prohibited access or access with authorisation, for such time as is strictly necessary, by means of their classification as such in accordance with specific legislation.
2. Access to documents concerning the confidentiality of legal proceedings shall be governed by specific legislation.[16]
3. Access to administrative documents which are preparatory to a decision or which are included in incomplete files may be delayed until the decision in question is taken, the file is archived, or one year has passed since they were drawn up.
4. Access to inquiries and investigations shall occur after the period for any disciplinary proceedings has passed.
5. Third parties shall only possess the right of access to nominative documents if they are in possession of written authorisation from the person to whom the data refers, or if they demonstrate a direct, personal and legitimate interest which is sufficiently important under the principle of proportionality.
6. Third parties shall only possess the right of access to administrative documents which contain commercial or industrial secrets or the internal life of a company, if they are in possession of written authorisation from the company in question, or if they demonstrate a direct, personal and legitimate interest which is sufficiently important under the principle of proportionality.

Other restrictions may derive from the breach of copyright or industrial property rights (Article 8)[17] or misuse of nominative documents communicated to third

[16]This issue is set by the Criminal Procedure Code.

[17]Pereira 2001.

parties.[18] Let us point out that there is some confusion of the doctrine under the notions of the 'right to privacy[19]' (Article 26 CPR) and the 'right to protection of personal data' or 'data self-determination' (Article 35 CPR).[20] It seems however clear that they should be seen as complementary and not overlapping.[21]

## 2.1 The Concerns of Public Interest: The State Security

Organic Law No. 2/2014 of 6 August 2014 (amended by Organic Law No. 1/2015 of 8 January 2015), regulates the issue of *State Secret*. In Article 1.2 of the regime approved ensures the principles of exceptionality, subsidiarity, necessity, proportionality, timeliness, equality, justice and fairness.

Article 2 of this Law considers, covered by state secret, those documents and information whose knowledge by unauthorised persons is likely to endanger or cause damage to national independence, unity and integrity of the state and its internal and external security. These risks and damages are evaluated on a case to case basis in light of their particular circumstances and would not result automatically from the nature of the matters addressed.

However, the law also provides general criteria of secret classification to documents concerning the following matters:

(a) that are transmitted, in confidence, by foreign states or international organisations;
(b) concerning strategy to be adopted by the country under present or future negotiations with other States or international organisations;
(c) to prevent and ensure the operability and safety of personnel, equipment, material and facilities of the Armed Forces and the forces and security services;
(d) the procedures relating to security in transmission of data and information with other States or international organisations;
(e) those whose disclosure may facilitate the commission of crimes against the security of the State;
(f) the commercial, industrial, scientific, technical or financial interest in the preparation of the military defence of the State.

[18]On the other hand, "nominative document" are now defined as administrative documents that contain an assessment or value judgment, or information covered by the reservation on the intimacy of private life, about an identified or identifiable natural person. Furthermore, L2016 demands that the third party interest is constitutionally protected.

[19]Pinto 1993.

[20]Moniz 1997, p. 231–300.

[21]We list some general references on this topic in what concerns portuguese legal system: Casimiro 2000, Castro 2005, Farinho 2006. In what concerns the liability for internet providers, Fachana 2012. In what concerns liability for the possible misuse of information, Matos 2011 and Monteiro 1989.

The classification as a state secret is the responsibility of the President, the President of the Assembly of the Republic and the Prime Minister. Furthermore, because of urgency,[22] the classification can also be determined by:

(a) The Chief of General Staff of the Armed Forces;
(b) The directors of the Information System of the Republic.[23]

The Law also sets the process for declassification. Both classification and declassification must be soundly motivated. It is also important to stress that classification as State secret of the document, process, or file does not determine restrictions on access to parts not classified, except to the extent strictly necessary to show that the protection due to parts classified.

The enforcement of this law is verified by the Portuguese parliament and by the Commission for the Supervision of the Secret State, who must ensure compliance with the provisions of this Act. Moreover, and with much public discussion, Organic Law n. 4/2017 of 25 August 2017, regulates the special procedure for access to telecommunication and Internet data by the information officers of the Security Intelligence Service and the Strategic Defence Information Service.

## 2.2 *First Portuguese Dispositions About the Right of Privacy and Computer Use: Law No. 10/91, of 29 April 1991*

The first approach of the Portuguese legislator to the topics of personal data protection had been enacted during the early nineties—mainly regarding informatics—and resulted from Law No. 10/91 of 29 April 1991. Let us point out that this legislative act is prior to the approval and publication of Directive No. 95/46/EC of 24 October 1995,[24] all the way central to the analysis of this topic. Consequently,

---

[22]However, in this latter case, this temporary classification must be ratified within ten days, as determined by Article 3 of Organic Law No. 2/2014.

[23]The Portuguese Republic Intelligence System is grounded on Law No. 9/2007 of 19 February 2007 that establishes nowadays the framework regulation for the Secretary-General of the Portuguese Republic System, for the Defence Strategic Intelligence Service (SIED) and for the Security Intelligence Service (SIS).

[24]The agreement between the Council, European Parliament and European Commission of EU reached on 15 December 2015 a major step in the adoption process of the EU General Data Protection Regulation (GDPR), that get together Regulation (EU) 2016/679 of the European Parliament and of the Council of 27 April 2016 on the protection of natural persons with regard to the processing of personal data and on the free movement of such data, thus repealing Directive 95/46/EC (General Data Protection Regulation) and Directive (EU) 2016/680 of the European Parliament and of the Council of 27 April 2016 on the protection of natural persons with regard to the processing of personal data by competent authorities for the prevention, investigation, detection or prosecution of criminal offences or the execution of criminal penalties, and on the free movement of such data, and repealing Council Framework Decision 2008/977/JHA. Those two set of rules were published on the 4th of May on the EU Official Journal. While the Regulation will enter into force on 24 May 2016, it shall apply from 25 May 2018, according to Article 94.1 of the Regulation. The Directive enters into force on 5 May 2016 and EU Member States have to

and notwithstanding the extensive legislative coverage undertaken—almost *avant la lettre*, *id est*, before being obligated to undertake the protection given by this Directive of 1995—the Directive has been, for a long time, only partially implemented in the Portuguese legal system. Nevertheless, the constitutional protection—of Article 35 CPR, already mentioned—made the difference and surmounted the difficulties and the lacks of the ordinary legislation. Thus, it was clear that the Portuguese legislator was well aware of the international tendencies[25] and concerns, essential to the historical comprehension of the Portuguese legal evolution.

The concept of 'personal data' was defined in Article 2 point (a) of Law No. 10/91 as any type of information relating to an individual identified in accordance with the principle of proportionality. Put simply, the individual identification should not involve unnecessary or excessive costs. 'Public data' related then to personal information included in public documents excepting confidential information such as address, job description or incapacities mentioned in the birth certificate.

Other definitions were presented in this Article such as 'database', 'computer database', 'representative', all of them in consonance with the definitions provided in Article 2 of the Directive of 1995. However, at 1998 time, Portuguese legislation did not cover important definitions such as 'consent' or 'third parties' (*stricto* and *lato sensu*). Accordingly, legislation necessarily would have to be updated to include all the definitions inserted in the Directive of 1995.

Individual's access rights were generally mentioned in Chapter VI (Articles 27 to 32) of Law 10/91. Accordingly, all citizens when identified could access to data relating to them, without restrictions, unless the Official Secrets or Justice Acts apply. Regarding this context, Portuguese law was written in a very general way, which enabled full reception of the provisions of the Directive (see Article 12 of the Directive of 1995). However, the right to prevent disclosure of personal data (Articles 14 and 15 of the Directive of 1995) was not implemented in the Portuguese legal system of 1991.

---

transpose it into their national law by 6 May 2018. Perhaps the most significant change from the current Data Protection Directive is that the GDPR will be directly applicable in all EU Member States, without the necessity of national implementing laws, thereby mitigating the current fragmentation of national data protection laws.

[25]These guidelines were established by the Council of Europe Convention for the Protection of Individuals against the Automatic Handling of Personal Data (1981) or the OECD Guidelines on the Protection of Privacy and Transborder Flows of Personal Data (1981). In accordance with this latter Convention, the general principle was that sensitive data could be processed automatically as long as the domestic law provided appropriate safeguards which were no more than the translation of so-called principles of fairness and lawfulness, purpose, quality and that are shed in the right to be informed about the purpose, the right of access to data, the right to correct or delete, and the right of opposition as the safeguard clause.

## 2.3 *The Second Step in Protection of Personal Data: The Law No. 67/98 of 26 October 1998 (Now Enforced) and Future Developments*

It took the Portuguese legislator 3 years to give legislative account of the Directive 95/46/EC of the European Parliament and of the Council of 24 October 1995 (on the protection of individuals with regard to the processing of personal data and on the free movement of such data) that nowadays inspires the guidelines of the system being object of enforcement in the European Union. In fact, only in 1998, 3 years after the adoption of the Directive, did the ordinary Portuguese law really take account of all of its provisions, mainly in connection with data protection and with legalisation of several databases of Portuguese public administration and implementation of administrative measures required by the Directive of 1995. Nevertheless, and as we already explained, the system granted in most aspects, sufficient protection to the individuals, not only because of Law No. 10/91, but also because of the constitutional dispositions, that already had taken account of the main aspects focused by the Directive and of its concerns.

The Law No. 67/98 of 26 October 1998 (L1998) matched perfectly the referred Directive of 1995, thus revoking Law No. 10/91 and Law No. 28/94 of 29 August 1994 (that had introduced some modifications). It is also applicable to video surveillance and other forms of capture, processing and dissemination of sound and images allowing persons to be identified, provided the controller is domiciled or based in Portugal or makes use of a computer or data communication network access provider established on Portuguese territory.

Unlike what we said about Law No. 10/91, Article 3 of L1998 matched all the definitions proposed by Article 2 of the Directive of 1995. The law goes even further, referring to the interconnection of data (point 1.), that is then developed in Article 9 of the Law.

However, the GDPR and Regulation 2016/679 amend some of the key concepts of EU data protection law currently contained in the Data Protection Directive and introduce new concepts:

1. The concept of 'personal data' is broadened, adding to the definition examples of identifiers such as location data or online identifiers (Article 4.1 of the Regulation)
2. Pseudonymisation, pseudonymous data and encrypted data (Article 4.5 and Recital 25 of the Regulation)
3. Genetic and biometric data (Article 4.13 and 14 of the Regulation). The processing on a large scale of special categories of data, including genetic and biometric data, may trigger some specific obligations such as the requirement to conduct a data protection impact assessment (Article 35).

In what concerns the scope of L1998, it would "apply to the processing of personal data wholly or partly by automatic means, and to the processing other than by automatic means of personal data which form part of manual filing systems or which are intended to form part of manual filing systems." Furthermore, this Act shall apply to the processing of personal data carried out:

(a) in the context of the activities of an establishment of the controller on Portuguese territory;
(b) outside national territory, but in a place where Portuguese law applies by virtue of international public law;
(c) by a controller who is not established on European Union territory and who for purposes of processing personal data makes use of equipment, automated or otherwise, situated on Portuguese territory, unless such equipment is used only for purposes of transit through the territory of the European Union.

However, the GDPR of 2016 will have extraterritorial effect by extending its scope of application to non-EU controllers or processors, where the processing activities are related to: (a) the offering of goods or services to individuals located in the EU; or (b) the monitoring of their behavior (Article 3). Non-EU companies will also be subject to the Regulation if they target EU residents by profiling, or proposing products or services.

L1998 should not apply to the processing of personal data carried out by a natural person in the course of a purely personal or household activity. Moreover, and in what concerns public interest, L1998 "shall apply to the processing of personal data regarding public safety, national defence and State security, without prejudice to special rules in instruments of international law to which Portugal is bound and specific laws pertinent to the respective sectors."

Also in what concerns 'quality of data', Article 5 of L1998 matches the dispositions of Articles 5 and 6 of the Directive of 1995 and of Articles 5 and 6 of the Regulation 2016/679. Thus, personal data must be:

(a) processed lawfully and with respect for the principle of good faith;
(b) collected for specified, explicit and legitimate purposes and not further processed in a way incompatible with those purposes;
(c) adequate, relevant and not excessive in relation to the purposes for which they are collected and/or further processed;
(d) accurate and, where necessary, kept up to date; adequate measures must be taken to ensure that data which are inaccurate or incomplete, having regard to the purposes for which they were collected or for which they are further processed, are erased or rectified;
(e) kept in a form that permits identification of their subjects for no longer than is necessary for the purposes for which they were collected or for which they are further processed.

Also in what regards legitimacy of treatment, there is a perfect coincidence between Article 6 of the Law and Article 7 of the Directive of 1995 and Articles 6 and 7 of Regulation 2016/679. However, let us remind here that under Regulation 2016/679, companies must consider privacy risk—data protection by design and by default—throughout the process of designing a new product or service.

Unlike Law No. 10/91, and following Article 35.3 CPR, L1998 also gives special attention to 'sensible data'[26]—personal data revealing philosophical or political beliefs, political party or trade union membership, religion, privacy and racial or ethnic origin, and the processing of data concerning health or sex life, including genetic data, shall be prohibited—treated in Article 7 in the same way they are referred to in Article 8 of the Directive of 1995 and Article 9 of Regulation 2016/679.

The collection of these sensitive data (no matter now their support) and their automated treatment is prohibited in absolute terms by the Constitution either by the common law or, in relative terms, when referring to "ethnic origin, criminal convictions, suspected of illegal activities, health status and financial position." However, that prohibition is largely distorted by admitting exceptions.

In fact, exceptions related to research or statistics are justified, as well as the cases of consent or data treatment "when carried out by public services, under the law, with guarantees of non-discrimination."

L1998 has special dispositions about suspicion of illegal activities, criminal offences and administrative offences in its Article 8, and about interconnection of personal data, in its Article 9.

Also unlike Law No. 10/91, L1998 makes a direct and long reference in its Article 10 to a right to information (Articles 10 and 11 of the Directive and Articles 13 and 14 of the Regulation 2016/679), and to a right of access in its Article 11 (Article 12 of the Directive and Article 15 of Regulation 2016/679). Even more significant is the prevision of a right of opposition and need of consent in Article 12 of the L1998, thus matching the Article 14 of the Directive and Art 21 of Regulation 2016/679, and putting an end to the lack of express regulation in Law 10/91. However, the Regulation 2016/679 also provides a purpose limitation principle (Article 18) making it mandatory that the controller must ascertain whether the processing for another purpose is compatible with the purpose of the data collection.

Also, in what concerns new rights put forward by GDPR, there is the prevision of a new right to data portability on its Article 20—favouring interoperable systems and making it mandatory that the organisations ensure that data subjects can easily transfer their data files from one service provider to another—and also of a right to erasure and to be forgotten—the right to require a controller to delete data files relating to them if there are no legitimate grounds for retaining it within Arts. 17 to 19 of the Regulation 2016/679, affirmed by the European Court of Justice in its 2014 *Costeja* decision ("right to be forgotten").[27]

Matters concerning security and confidentiality are treated in Articles 14 to 17 of the Law just matching the rules expressed in Articles 16 and 17 of the Directive and Articles 32 to 34 of Regulation 2016/679.

---

[26]Or "sensitive data".

[27]Court of Justice of the European Union, *Costeja,* C-131/12 (Judgment of 13 May 2014). For further discussion within the articulation with the portuguese legal system, Raimundo 2012.

Further, the transference of personal data to other countries, inside and outside the European Union, is now regulated in Articles 18 to 20 of L1998, just in the way pointed out by the Articles 25 and 26 of the Directive of 1995 and Articles 44 to 50 of Regulation 2016/679.

Under the GDPR of 2016 (Arts. 4/7 and 8 and Arts. 24 to 31 of Regulation 2016/679), the appointment of a data protection officer is mandatory for controllers and processors when the core data processing activities involve monitoring of individuals on a large scale or encompass sensitive data, including criminal convictions and offences.

Notifications must be made to the *Comissão Nacional de Protecção de Dados* (National Data Protection Commission—CNPD)[28] before carrying out any wholly or partly automatic processing operation or set of such operations intended to serve a single purpose or several related purposes.[29]

On the other hand, CNPD's authorisation, which must be published in the official journal (*Diário da República)*, is required for:

(a) the processing of "sensible data";
(b) the processing of personal data relating to credit and the solvency of the data subjects;
(c) the interconnection of personal data;
(d) the use of personal data for purposes not giving rise to their collection.

Applications for opinions, authorisation and notifications submitted to the CNPD shall include the following information[30]:

(a) the name and address of the controller and of his representative, if any;
(b) the purposes of the processing;
(c) a description of the category or categories of data subjects and of the data or categories of personal data relating to them;
(d) the recipients or categories of recipients to whom the data might be disclosed and in what circumstances;
(e) the body entrusted with processing the information, if it is not the controller himself;
(f) any combinations of personal data processing;
(g) the length of time for keeping personal data;
(h) the form and circumstances in which the data subjects may be informed of or may correct the personal data relating to them;
(i) proposed transfers of data to third countries;
(j) a general description enabling a preliminary assessment to be made of the adequacy of the measures taken to assure security and confidentiality of processing.

---

[28]This is the Portuguese supervisory body in what concerns personal data that we will refer to in Sect. 5.1.2. However, the 2016 Regulation sets a "*one-stop shop and cooperation procedure*".

[29]Article 27 of L1998.

[30]Article 29 of L1998.

Besides the public registry of these decisions, the processing referred to in the previous number may be authorised by legal ruling. Furthermore, Article 32 of the L1998 now points out the codes of conduct, not predicted in Law No. 10/91, in consonance with Article 27 of the Directive of 1995.

## 3 Contents of the Right of Access to Public ('Administrative') Documents

According to Article 5 of L2016, everyone shall possess the right of access to administrative documents without the need to state any interest, to include the rights of consultation, reproduction, and information as to the administrative documents' existence and content. Furthermore, the model of the respective application must now be made available on the entities' websites. If the requests are not sufficiently precise, the requested entity shall, within 5 days from the receipt of the request, invite the applicant to remedy the deficiency within the deadline set out for that purpose.

### *3.1 Exercise of the Right of Access to (and of the Re-use of) Administrative Documents*

In what concerns this issue, L2016 states that the authorisation by the entity holding the documents is not required when those documents are made available on the Internet unless indicated otherwise or when it is clear to any recipient that copyright or related rights protect the document.

If that is not the case, the body to which an application for access to an administrative document is made shall, within 10 days:

(a) Communicate the date, place and means on, in and by which the consultation, if one is requested, is to take place;
(b) Issue the requested reproduction or certificate;
(c) Communicate in writing the reasons for any total or partial denial of access to the desired document, together with a description of the guarantees applicable to administrative and litigious appeals against the decision in question;
(d) Inform the applicant that it does not possess the document and, if it knows what body does hold it, send the application to that body with a copy to the applicant;
(e) Expound any doubts which it has about the decision it has to make to CADA so that the latter may issue a formal opinion thereon.[31]

[31]Articles 12, 13 and 15 of L2016.

However, the Public Administration shall not be obliged to satisfy applications whose repetitive and systematic nature or the number of documents they entail reveal a manifestly improper nature. Likewise, in exceptional cases, if the volume or complexity of the information so warrant, the period of 10 days may be extended to a maximum of 2 months, whereupon the applicant shall be informed of the fact and of the grounds therefore within a maximum of 10 working days.[32]

L2016 also states upon reproduction costs: the reproduction shall take the form of a single copy, which shall be subject to payment by whoever requests it of a fixed fee, which shall be equal to the sum of the proportional costs of the use of machines and tools and of the materials used and the service provided, but shall not exceed the average amount for the equivalent service practiced by the market.

With due regard to the provisions of the previous paragraph and after consulting the Commission on Access to Administrative Documents ("CADA"), the Government of the Republic, the Governments of the Autonomous Regions, and the national associations of local authorities shall set the fees to be charged for reproductions and certificates of administrative documents.

Bodies which possess an autonomous power to tax shall not set fees that exceed the various amounts set in accordance with the previous paragraph by more than 100%, and shall abide by those amounts until such time as they publish their own tables of fees.[33]

According to Article 13 of L2016, access to administrative documents shall occur by one of the following means, at the applicant's option:

(a) Consultation, which shall take place in the departments or services that hold the documents in question and shall be free of charge;
(b) Reproduction by photocopying or any technical, particularly visual, aural or electronic, means;
(c) The issue of a certificate.

On the other hand, the re-use of documents applies to documents held or drawn up by the bodies within the scope of L2016 (Sect. 1.2) and allow other purposes than the public service purpose for which they were produced (Articles 19 to 27 of L2016).

## 3.2 *Right to Complaint*

The refusal of access—lack of response or denial—may cause *a complaint* to the Commission of Access to Administrative Documents, to which we will refer to (Sect. 5.1.1).

[32] Articles 12, 13 and 15 of L2016.

[33] Articles 12, 13 and 15 of L2016.

## 4 Access to Public Documents and Administrative Procedure

The Portuguese legal system contains other legal instruments that interact with public access to official information and data protection.

In fact, special mention shall be made to the following secondary legislation: Decree of Law 442/91 and 6/96 (Administrative Procedure Code—APC) and the Procedure Code in Administrative Courts (Law No. 15/2002 of 22 February 2002, last time amended by Decree of Law No. 214-G/2015 of 2 October 2015). Article 62 of the Administrative Procedure Code grants the right to accede to documents relating to administrative proceedings. However, exceptions apply to nominative documents with personal data, classified documents or documents disclosing industrial or intellectual property secrets.

If we cross the L2016 with the Portuguese Administrative Procedure Code, we come to the awareness that the access to public documents shall be requested in writing in the form of an application that shall contain such elements as are essential to the identification of the documents in question, together with the applicant's name, address and signature. If an application is not sufficiently precise, within 5 days the body to which it was made shall inform the applicant of the shortcoming and invite him to make it good within a period to be set for that purpose. Furthermore, acting in the person of their members of staff, the bodies and entities referred to by Article 4 of L2016 shall assist the public in identifying the documents they want, particularly by informing them of the way in which their archives and registers are organised and used.[34]

In what concerns Law No. 15/2002 of 22 February (Procedure Code in Administrative Courts), the relevant provisions are Articles 104 to 108 that regulate a special proceeding of judicial intimation to obtain a certain information or document from the Administration.

## 5 The Judicial and Administrative Protection of Freedom of Access to Information

Let us start by pointing out that even the Constitutional Portuguese court is well aware of these matters, namely because of the implication with some fundamental rights previously identified. For a quick reference, we can point out some decisions in which the Constitutional Court in several rulings ("Acórdãos") has discussed those topics.[35] Thus:

---

[34]Articles 10 and 12.5 of L2016.

[35]All decisions of the Portuguese Constitutional Court (*Tribunal Constitucional*) are available at http://www.tribunalconstitucional.pt/ (Accessed on 14 February 2017).

- *Acórdão* 182/89, about the concept of 'personal data';
- *Acórdão* 176/92 and *Acórdão* 394/93, about restriction of the right of access because of the right to privacy regarding nominative documents;
- *Acórdão* 514/94, about the publicity of the income of politicians;
- *Acórdão* 278/95, about the secrecy of bank accounts;
- *Acórdão* 355/97, about the protection of private life *versus* informatics, and
- *Acórdão* 254/99 discussing the limits to the right to information as a matter of conflicts of rights.
- *Acórdão* do TC n°s 213/2008 e 486/2009, about digital proof[36]

Furthermore, and as we have already mentioned in Sect. 4, Portuguese Procedure Code in Administrative Court regulates a special proceeding of judicial intimation to obtain a certain information or document from the Administration.[37]

## 5.1 *Decisions of the Main Supervisory Bodies*[38]

Each of the two laws that we have been mainly talking about till now—L2016 and L1998—picture two supervisory bodies, one supervising the access to public documents, the *Comissão de Acesso aos Documentos Administrativos* (CADA), and one regarding personal data, the *Comissão Nacional de Protecção de Dados* (CNPD).

[36]Neto 2011, p. 315–343.

[37]The decisions and rulings *("Acórdãos")* on this subject are available at www.dgsi.pt: Administrative Supreme Court (Supremo Tribunal Adminsitrativo), Process 0896/07 (Judgment of 17 January 2008); Administrative Supreme Court, Process 0848/08 (Judgment of 7 January 2009); Administrative Supreme Court, Process 0838/08 (Judgment of 18 February 2009); Administrative Supreme Court, Process 0998/08 (Judgment of 25 February 2009); Administrative Supreme Court, Process 0288/09 (Judgment of 20 May 2009); Administrative Supreme Court, Process 0453/09 (Judgment of 30 September 2009); Administrative Supreme Court, Process 01110/09 (Judgment of 20 January 2010); Administrative Supreme Court, Process 0169/10 (Judgment of 12 May 2010); Administrative Supreme Court, Process 0668/11 (Judgment of 24 January 2011); Administrative Supreme Court, Process 0671/11 (Judgment of 7 December 2011); Administrative Supreme Court, Process 0758/11 (Judgment of 31 August 2011); Administrative Central Court – North, Process 511/11.2BECBR (Judgment of 4 November 2011); Administrative Central Court – South (Tribunal Central Administrativo Sul), Process 08214/11 (Judgment of 12 January 2012); Administrative Central Court – North, Process 354/12.6BEPRT (Judgment of 13 July 2012); Administrative Central Court – North (Tribunal Central Administrativo Norte), Process 01721/12.0BEPRT (Judgment of 25 January 2013).

[38]We have also mentioned in Sect. 2.1. the framework regulation for the Secretary-General of the Portuguese Republic System, for the Defence Strategic Intelligence Service and for the Security Intelligence Service.

### 5.1.1 The Commission of Access to Public Documents (CADA)

CADA[39] is an independent administrative body, which shall operate under the aegis of the Assembly of the Republic and shall be responsible for making its best efforts to ensure compliance with the provisions of L2016 and is composed by the following members:

(a) One Justice of the Supreme Administrative Court, who shall be appointed by the Supreme Council of Administrative and Fiscal Courts and shall chair the Commission;
(b) Two Members of the Assembly of the Republic, to be appointed by the latter, one upon a proposal from the parliamentary group of the largest political party which supports the Government, and one upon a proposal from the largest opposition party;
(c) A Professor of Law, to be appointed by the President of the Assembly of the Republic;
(d) Two prominent persons, to be appointed by the Government;
(e) One prominent person appointed by the Governments of each of the autonomous regions;
(f) One prominent person, to be appointed by the National Association of Portuguese Municipalities;
(g) A lawyer, to be appointed by the Lawyers' Order;
(h) One member, to be appointed by the National Data Protection Commission from among its own members.

Members of CADA shall be under the following duties:

(a) To be unbiased, rigorous and independent in the performance of their functions;
(b) To actively and assiduously take part in CADA's work.

CADA shall be responsible for[40]:

(a) Drawing up its own internal regulations, which shall be published in Series II of the *Diário da República*;
(b) Considering complaints which are submitted to;
(c) At the request of the bodies and entities referred to by Article 4 of L2016, issuing a formal opinion on access to administrative documents;
(d) At the request of a body to which an application has been made or of an interested party, issuing a formal opinion on the communication of documents between departments, services and bodies belonging to the Public Administration, unless there is a foreseeable risk that data will be linked to other data, in which case the question shall be put to the National Data Protection Commission (CNPD);

---

[39]For further information, and consultation of decisions, please see www.cada.pt (Accessed on 14 February 2017).

[40]Article 30 of L2016.

(e) Pronouncing on the document registration and classification system;
(f) At the request of the Assembly of the Republic, the Government, or other bodies and entities issuing a formal opinion on the drawing up and implementation of complementary legislation;
(g) Drawing up an annual report on the implementation of the L2016 and on its own activities, to be sent to the Assembly of the Republic for publication and consideration and to the Prime Minister;
(h) Helping to clarify and publicise the different means of access to administrative documents, within the overall framework of the principle of open administration.
(i) Imposing fines in proceedings involving administrative offences.

Every director, member of staff and agent of the bodies and entities referred to by Article 4 of L2016 shall be under a duty to cooperate with CADA, failing which they may be held responsible in disciplinary or other terms, as provided by law.

According to Article 16.2 of L2016, a complaint made to CADA "shall interrupt the time period for judicial submission of a request for a court order to provide information, consult files, or issue certificates, and shall be made within the said time period, to which the provisions governing the submission to a court of procedural items shall apply mutatis mutandis."

CADA shall have 40 days in which to draw up the applicable situation assessment report and send it with its due conclusions to all the interested parties. Let us point out, however, that "an interested party may impugn either the decision or the absence of decision referred to by the previous paragraph before the administrative courts" (Article 16.6).

Articles 38 to 42 of L2016 state also upon *administrative offences* punishable by CADA with a fine (re-use of public sector documents without the authorisation of the competent body or re-use of public sector documents without having paid the amount set,[41] re-use of public sector documents without complying with the conditions governing re-use laid down by L2016[42]). Negligence and attempts shall always be punished. Differently from Law No. 46/2007, L2016 also defines a criminal offence as: "one, who with intent to unduly access nominative data falsely declares or attests before a body or entity referred to in Article 4.1 to hold a direct, personal, legitimate and constitutionally protected interest, justifying access to required information or documents is punishable by imprisonment of up to one year or by a fine".

---

[41]In those cases, the fines are

a) In the case of a natural person, a minimum of € 300.00 € and a maximum of € 3,500.00 €;
b) In the case of a corporate body, a minimum of € 2,500.00 € and a maximum of € 25,000.00 €.

[42]In that case, the fines are:

a) In the case of a natural person, a minimum of € 150.00 € and a maximum of € 1,750.00 €;
b) In the case of a corporate body, a minimum of € 1,250.00 € and a maximum of € 12,500.00 €.

A judicial impugnation of a final decision made by CADA shall take the form of a claim, which shall be submitted within 10 days of notification of the decision. In the event of such an impugnation, CADA may modify or revoke its decision, whereupon it shall notify the impugner of its new final decision. In the event that it maintains its existing decision, within 10 days CADA shall forward the claim to the Public Prosecutors' Office at the Lisbon Administrative and Fiscal Court (Articles 36 and 37 of L2016).

### 5.1.2 The National Data Protection Commission (CNPD)

According to Article 22 of L1998, the CNPD[43] is "the national authority endowed with the power to supervise and monitor compliance with the laws and regulations in the area of personal data protection, with strict respect for human rights and the fundamental freedoms and guarantees enshrined in the Constitution and the law and must be consulted on any legal provisions and on legal instruments in preparation in Community or international institutions relating to the processing of personal data."

This National Data Protection Commission is an independent body with powers of authority that operates within the *Assembleia da República*. The CNPD may be requested to exercise its powers by a data protection supervisory authority of another Member State of the European Union or the Council of Europe. Furthermore, the CNPD shall cooperate with the data protection supervisory authorities of other States in disseminating national law and regulations in the area of personal data protection and in the defence and exercise of the rights of individuals residing abroad.

CNPD is composed[44] of seven members of recognised integrity and merit, the chairperson and two members being elected by the *Assembleia de República* by means of the d'Hondt highest average rule. The remaining members shall be:

(a) two magistrates with over 10 years experience, one being a legal magistrate appointed by the *Conselho Superior da Magistratura*, and the other a Public Prosecution Service magistrate appointed by the *Conselho Superior do Ministé rio Público*;
(b) two individuals of recognised competence appointed by the Government.

The members of the CNPD shall have a 5-year mandate, which shall cease when the newly appointed members take office.

The CNPD is authorised to engage in legal proceedings where the provisions in this Act have been violated and must report to the Public Prosecution Service any criminal offences it becomes aware of in exercising and arising out of its functions, and shall take the necessary and urgent precautionary measures to provide the

---

[43]For further information and consultation of the public registry of decisions, please go to www.cnpd.pt.

[44]Article 25 of L1998.

evidence.[45] Furthermore, the CNPD is represented at law by the Public Prosecution Service and is exempt from costs in the proceedings in which it is involved.

The Portuguese legal system concerns liability for an unlawful processing operation or of any other act incompatible with legal provisions in the area of personal data protection is entitled to receive compensation from the controller for the damage suffered.[46] Furthermore, the general system of administrative offences, adapted according to the following Articles, is subsidiarily applicable to the offences provided for in this section.[47]

L1998 also states upon compliance with duty omitted and omission or inadequate compliance with obligations—ensuring fines to bodies which negligently fail to comply with the obligation to notify the CNPD of the processing of personal data referred, provide false information or comply with the obligation to notify without observing the requirements of Article 29 of L1998 or, having been notified by the CNPD, continue to allow access to open data transmission networks to controllers who fail to comply with the provisions of this Act.

Fines are imposed by the chairperson of the CNPD, subject to prior deliberation by the Commission.[48] Furthermore, if the same fact is simultaneously a crime and an administrative offence the agent shall always be punished by virtue of the crime. In fact, Articles 43 to 47 of L1998 establish criminal typification—"non-compliance with obligations relating to data protection, undue access, invalidation or destruction of personal data, qualified non-compliance and violation of the duty of secrecy"—and any attempt to commit the crimes provided for in the above provisions shall always be liable to punishment. The fact that L1998 expressly typificates some cases of criminal offences in this field—Articles 43 to 50 of L1998—is of great importance, because it shows the relevance given to the individuals rights and to the social goods here in presence.

To pursue legal obligations, public and private bodies shall cooperate with the CNPD by providing it with all the information requested in carrying out its responsibilities. Likewise, CNPD or its members and the staff delegated thereby have the right of access to the computer systems supporting the data processing and the documentation referred to in the previous number, within the scope of its duties and responsibilities.

Without prejudice to the right to submit a complaint to the CNPD, according to the law any individual may have recourse to administrative and legal means to guarantee compliance with legal provisions in the area of personal data protection.[49]

---

[45] Articles 22 and 23 of L1998.

[46] Article 34 of L1998.

[47] Article 35 of L1998.

[48] Regulation 2016/679 sets a new type of violation of personal data (Article 4 No. 12) and harmonises data protection enforcement in the EU. It will introduce two levels of fines: (1) up to € 10 million or 2% of the undertaking's global annual turnover, whichever is higher, for certain infringements; and (2) up to € 20 million or 4% of the undertaking's global annual turnover, whichever is higher, for more severe infringements.

[49] Article 33 of L1998.

## 6 Conclusions

We can say that today the relevant issues moved the discussion about "what is outside the scope of protection of the right of information" to the need to protect against the new means of infringement, moreover in a digital context.[50] Hence, the growing importance of attention to the new computer crimes, the discussion about the so-called localisation data enabled by the use of mobile phones, the need to broaden the concept of inviolability of correspondence to cover electronic communications, the controversy on biometric methods, the discussion of surveillance cameras, the recommendations of the Council of Europe on specific categories of personal data such as medical databases,[51] scientific data and statistics, or data used for "direct marketing".[52]

We may conclude that under Regulation 2016/679, a privacy impact assessment will become a mandatory prerequisite before processing personal data for operations that are likely to present higher privacy risks for the rights and freedoms of individuals.

---

[50]Please consider Fachana 2012, Gonçalves 2003 and Neto 2010 and 2012a for further developments.

[51]In Portugal, the Law No. 12/2005 of 26 January 2005 defines the concept of health information and genetic information. In this sense, health information covers all kinds of information directly or indirectly linked to health, present or future, of a person, whether you are alive or have died, and your medical history and family, taking special care with issues concerning ownership, storage and access to health information (Article 3) and the treatment of health information (Article 4).

Incidentally, it should be noted that the genetic information that does not have immediate implications for the health status cannot be included in the clinical process – Article 6 of the same Law – and should in general be protected by legislative and administrative measures to protect strengthened in terms of access, security and confidentiality.

Even more crucial, the design and construction of a genetic database can be considered or understood in different and opposing perspectives, both as to the type of material collected either on the purpose of use, or as storage conditions. In fact, it can only be thought of as a means of criminal investigation or civil identification.

The Portuguese solution was molded in Law No. 5/2008, of 12 February 2008, which regulate the genetic database has long been claimed in terms mixed: mandatory in the case of criminal identification, optional in the case of civil identification.

[52]Hence, the growing importance of the institutional guarantee poured in the topics covered by the most relevant guidelines of the National Commission for Data Protection – operating under the Law No. 42/2004, of August 18, and charged even the organisation of public record:

- Treatment of personal data in the context of clinical trials of medicinal products for human use (2007);
- Treatment of personal data in the context of scientific research studies in the field of health (2007);
- Access to health data holders deceased (2006);
- Data processing for video surveillance (2004);
- Treatment of biometrics for access control and attendance (2004);
- Privacy in the workplace: the control of the electronic mail, access the Internet and phone calls workers (2002);
- Access to health data by third parties (2001).

In fact, those issues nowadays[53] raise awareness of the limits that derive from the gigantic hypothesised data identification or possibility of data identification spoken in number 3 of Article 35 of the Portuguese Constitution, in connection with the principle of human dignity, which is all the way the cornerstone of the legal system.

## References

AA VV. *Direito da Sociedade de Informação*, Volumes I (1999) e II (2001). Coimbra, Portugal: Coimbra Editora.

Ascensão, J. d. O. (2001). *Estudos sobre Direito da Internet e da Sociedade de Informação*. Coimbra, Portugal: Almedina.

Ascensão, J. d. O. (2004). A reutilização de documentos do sector público. In: Associação Portuguesa do Direito Intelectual. *Direito da Sociedade da Informação* (Vol. V, p. 65 et seqq.). Coimbra, Portugal: Coimbra Editora.

Brin, D. (1998). *The transparent society*. New York: Addison Wesley.

Casimiro, S. d. V. (2000). *A responsabilidade civil pelo conteúdo da informação transmitida pela internet*. Coimbra, Portugal: Almedina.

Castro, C. S. (2005). *Direito da Informática, Privacidade e Dados Pessoais*. Coimbra, Portugal: Almedina.

CNPD. (2004). *Privacidade e Comércio Electrónico, Actas do Colóquio na Assembleia da República, 28 de Novembro de 2000*. Lisboa, Portugal: CNPD.

Cunha, P. F. (2006). Sociedade da Informação e Estado de Direito Democrático, Direito à Informação ou deveres de protecção informativa do Estado. *Revista da FDUP*, Edição comemorativa dos dez anos da FDUP: Coimbra, Portugal: Coimbra Editora, p. 623 et seqq.

Almeida, R. R. (2004). *Sociedade Bit: da Sociedade da Informação à Sociedade do Conhecimento*. Lisboa, Portugal: Quid Juris.

Fachana, J. (2012). *A responsabilidade civil pelos conteúdos ilícitos colocados e difundidos na Internet*. Coimbra, Portugal: Almedina.

[53]Let us remember that L1998 has also been complemented by the Law No. 69/98, of 28 October 1998, that regulates the treatment of personal data and the protection of privacy regarding telecommunications, thus matching the Directive No. 97/66/EC of the European Parliament and of the Council, of 15 December 1997. It gives special emphasis to the questions of security and confidentiality that have to be considered in an era of new technological possibilities. Furthermore, the connections are obvious with the legal framework for electronic commerce approved by Decree-Law No. 7/2004, of 7 January 2009 and amended in 2012) and with the scope or Law No. 46/2012, of 29 August 2012, implementing Directive No. 2009/136/EC on the amending Directive No. 2002/58/EC of the European Parliament and of the Council of 12 July 2002, concerning the processing of personal data and the protection of privacy in the sector electronic communications, proceeding to the first amendment of the Law No. 41/2004, of 18 August 2004, and the second amendment Decree-Law No. 7/2004. On these matters, CNPD (2004). Further, the Decree-Law 122/2000 matches the Directive No. 96/9/EC of the European Parliament and of the Council, of 11 March, regarding the legal protection of databases. This text gives special attention to the matters of multispacial situations and of intellectual and industrial property, in a way that in a certain manner follows Decree-Law 16/93, regulating the management, conservation and access to archives. Personal data was already protected here in Article 17, which prevented disclosure of documents containing personal information of judicial, criminal or health nature. Further limitations would apply to preserve personal security and privacy.

Farinho, D. S. (2006). *Intimidade da vida privada e media no ciberespaço*. Coimbra, Portugal: Almedina.

Gonçalves, M. E. (2003). *Direito da Informação. Novos direitos e modos de regulação na sociedade da informação*. Coimbra, Portugal: Almedina.

Matos, F. M. C. A. (2011). *Responsabilidade Civil por Ofensa ao Crédito ou ao Bom Nome*. Coimbra, Portugal: Almedina.

Moniz, H. I. G. (1997). Notas sobre a Protecção de Dados Pessoais perante a Informática. *Revista Portuguesa de Ciência Criminal*, Ano 7, No. 2, 231 et seqq.

Monteiro, J. S. (1989). *Responsabilidade por Conselhos, Recomendações ou Informações*. Coimbra, Portugal: Almedina.

Neto, L. (2010). *Novos direitos ou novos objectos para o Direito*. Porto, Portugal: Editorial UP.

Neto, L. (2011). Acórdãos do TC n°s 213/2008 e 486/2009: a prova numa sociedade transparente. *Revista da FDUP*, VIII, 315 et seqq.

Neto, L. (Ed.). (2012a). A informação jurídica na era digital, 24 e 25 de Fevereiro de 2011. Porto, Portugal: Afrontamento, CETAC Media.

Neto, L. (2012b). Ciência da Informação e Direito: um novo paradigma de reconstrução do papel do Estado no contexto da sociedade global de informação. In *A informação jurídica na era digital*, 24 e 25 de Fevereiro de 2011 (p. 41 et seqq.). Porto, Portugal: Afrontamento e CETAC Media.

Neto, L. (2012c). Limitações normativas ao acesso à informação. In S. R. Gomes et al. (Eds.), *Incursões interdisciplinares: Direito e Ciência da Informação* (p. 7 et seqq.). Rio de Janeiro, Brazil: Beco do Azougue e Pensamento brasileiro.

Neto, L., Feyo, D., & de Amorim, J. P. (2002). Study on data protection and public access to official information. In G. Teixeira (Ed.), *O comércio electrónico – Estudos Jurídico-Económicos* (p. 187 et seqq.) Coimbra, Portugal: Almedina.

Pereira, A. L. D. (2001). *Informática, direito de autor e propriedade tecnodigital*, BFDUC. Studia Iuridica, 55. Coimbra, Portugal: Coimbra Editora.

Pinto, P. M. (1993). *O Direito à Reserva sobre a Intimidade da Vida Privada, BFDUC* (Vol. LXIX). Coimbra, Portugal: Coimbra Editora.

Raimundo, J. (2012). *Uma nova frente da protecção de dados pessoais: a (im)possibilidade de assegurar um eventual direito ao esquecimento*. Dissertação do Mestrado em Direito (Ciências Jurídico-Políticas). Porto, Portugal: FDUP.

Ribeiro, F. (2005). Organizar e representar informação: apenas um meio para viabilizar o acesso? *Revista da Faculdade de Letras. Ciências e Técnicas do Património*, Porto, 4, 2005, 83 et seqq.

Ribeiro, F. (2003). *O Acesso à informação nos arquivos*. Lisboa, Portugal: Fundação Calouste Gulbenkian; Fundação para a Ciência e a Tecnologia, Ministério da Ciência e do Ensino Superior.

## List of Cases

Judicial decisions may be found. at www.dgsi.ptand in what regards data protection, a sum up can be found at https://www.cnpd.pt/bin/legis/juris/jurisprudencia.htm. The judgments of the Consitututional Court can be found at http://www.tribunalconstitucional.pt/tc/acordaos/ (Accessed on 14 February 2017).

## European Court of Justice

European Court of Justice 13.05.2014, C-131/12, *Costeja*. ECLI:EU:C:2014:317.

## Portuguese Constitutional Court (Tribunal Conctitutional)

Constitutional Court 02.03.1989, Judgment 182/89, Process 298/87.
Constitutional Court 16.06.1993, Judgment 394/93, Process 188/92.
Constitutional Court 22.09.1994, Judgment 514/94, Process 69/DPR.
Constitutional Court 07.05.1996, Judgment 176/92, Process 214/90.
Constitutional Court 31.05.1995, Judgment 278/95, Process 510/91.
Constitutional Court 07.05.1997, Judgment 355/97, Process 182/97.
Constitutional Court 04.05.1999, Judgment 254/99, Process 456/97.
Constitutional Court 02.04.2008, Judgment 213/08, Process 671/07.
Constitutional Court 28.09.2009, Judgment 486/09, Process 4/09.

## Administrative Courts

Administrative Supreme Court 17.01.2008, Process 0896/07.
Administrative Supreme Court 07.01.2009, Process 0848/08.
Administrative Supreme Court 18.02.2009, Process 0838/08.
Administrative Supreme Court 25.02.2009, Process 0998/08.
Administrative Supreme Court 20.05.2009, Process 0288/09.
Administrative Supreme Court 30.09.2009, Process 0453/09.
Administrative Supreme Court 20.02.2010, Process 01110/09.
Administrative Supreme Court 12.05.2010, Process 0169/10.
Administrative Supreme Court 24.01.2011, Process 0668/11.
Administrative Supreme Court 31.08.2011, Process 0758/11.
Administrative Central Court–North (Tribunal Central Administrativo Norte) 04.11.2011, Process 511/11.2BECBR.
Administrative Supreme Court 07.12.2011, Process 0671/11.
Administrative Central Court–South (Tribunal Central Administrativo Sul) 12.01.2012, Process 08214/11.
Administrative Central Court–North 13.07.2012, Process 354/12.6BEPRT.
Administrative Central Court–North 25.01.2013, Process 01721/12.0BEPRT.

# Chapter 10
# Right to Information and Access to Information in the Russian Federation

**Illaria Bachilo**

## Contents



---

Illaria Bachilo was deceased at the time of publication.

The author thanks Anton Antopolsky, Candidate of Law, Senior Researcher at the Department of Information Law, Institute of State and Law of the Russian Academy of Science, and Ekaterina Andryushchenko, Candidate of Law, LL.M. in Legal Informatics, LL.M. in Legal Linguistics, for their assistance.

I. Bachilo (✉)
Institute of State and Law of the Russian Academy of Sciences, Moscow, Russia
e-mail: antopolsky@yandex.ru



H.-J. Blanke, R. Perlingeiro (eds.), *The Right of Access to Public Information*,
DOI 10.1007/978-3-662-55554-5_10

## 1 Access to Information in Russian Information Law

The current research paper has been written on the initiative of Professor Ricardo Perlingeiro within the framework of the scientific cooperation agreement between the Institute of State and Law of the Russian Academy of Sciences and the Fluminense Federal University (Brazil). The purpose of this publication is to make a comparative analysis of the Russian and Brazilian law on access to information.

Information law is a complex and developing branch of Russian law. It is now included in the Russian legal system along with the existing thirty branches of law. Information law as a branch of law emerged in Russia in the 1970s–1990s. It was included into universities' curriculums and MA/PhD training programs in the beginning of the twenty-first century. As a branch of law, information law is expressed in four forms:

- doctrine;
- legislation and law enforcement practice (the main part);
- an academic discipline;
- sense of justice and legal culture.[1]

This article shows the history of the institution of access to information, as well as the legislative history of two Russian Laws on Information, adopted in 1995 and 2006, and examines the following topics: the structure of information legislation; the place of the institution of access to information in the architecture of information rights; the history of this institution; the relationship between access to information and problems of transparency and openness; and the concept of "access to information" as searching for and obtaining information.[2]

The basis of all laws on information is the Constitution of the Russian Federation of 1993. Article 18 of the Constitution states that "the rights and freedoms of man and citizen shall be directly operative. They determine the essence, meaning and implementation of laws, the activities of the legislative and executive authorities, local self-government and shall be ensured by the administration of justice." This norm is further specified in Article 29 of the Constitution and in its several other provisions, which will be pointed out in this work. The main idea is that the Russian state secures realization of human rights in the process of information society development.

---

[1]Bachilo 2012a, p. 50–51.

[2]Bachilo 2013.

## 1.1 The Structure of Russian Information Law

The structure of the branch of information law (legislation) includes the following super institutions (sub-branches):

1. information resources and their legal regime;
2. the right to information;
3. information security.

Legal institutions form within these super institutions.

Matters regarding information resources and their legal regime (documentation, categories of access, determining property rights and intellectual property rights to the information, protection) are manifested through the institutions of open information (open data) and restricted information, and the institution of state secrets. The institution of classified information is comprised of sub-institutions of the rules regulating relations concerning the use of personal data, trade secrets, professional confidential information, official and state secrets.

The variety of information resources and information systems is a fact that is due to the flood of information. The different ressources and systems are used to support information dissemination (mass media, Internet sites etc.), the activities of various bodies and authorities, public and private services, and interpersonal communication and relationships.[3] No public institution, state authority, or social actor can exist and operate without information.

## 1.2 The Institution of Access to Information

Issues of *access to information,* as a part of the super institution of the right to information, form their own separate institution of legal regulation. Great attention is given to them in the process of legal regulation of the infrastructure of the information society.

One significant institution of Russian information law is the legal regime of information resources. The term "information resource" means a document or a set of documents, or other data carrier. The legal regime of information resources is a term currently used in the Russian doctrine of information law. It includes rules for documenting information, access regimes for information, property rights to information, and forms of information security.

There are different types of information resources regimes in Russian legislation and in the doctrine of information law:

- personal data;
- privacy information (personal secrets);
- know-how (trade secrets);
- professional confidential (privileged) information;

[3]Bachilo 2012b.

- state secrets;
- official (governmental service) secrets;
- information in governmental and municipal information systems;
- scientific and cultural knowledge;
- mass media content and Internet content.

## 1.3 History of Legislation on Openness and Access to Information

The right to information in the USSR and modern Russia includes "access" as the most important form of this right's exercise. The theme of access to information was made actual, academically and in practice, with the introduction of two draft legislative acts, one of which (introduced to Parliament in 1987) concerned the issue of *glasnost*, which means transparency and openness of information. The history of two versions of these drafts is described in detail by Y.M. Baturin.[4] A few proposed laws in 1996 and 1999 were also dedicated to the right to information. The first version of the Right to Information Law was elaborated together with the Federal law "On Information, Informatization, and Information Security" (Russian Federal Law No. 24-FZ of February 20, 1995; hereinafter—the Law on Information (1995), the year is written in parentheses to distinguish this law from the second Law on Information adopted in 2006).

The Law on Information (1995) was the first significant law in the Russian Federation dealing with the regulation of information processes and relations. This law touched upon the right to information in general, but lacked detailed regulation. It was based on the Constitution of the Russian Federation of 1993, as well as the Universal Declaration of Human Rights of 1948 and the International Covenant on Civil and Political Rights of 1966 (effective 1976). Some foreign laws were also considered, including a number of European conventions and US laws (Freedom of Information Act, Government in the Sunshine Act) and many more.

Chapter 3 of the Law on Information (1995), "The Use of Information Resources", set forth that "Users – citizens, state authorities, local authorities, organizations, and non-governmental organizations – have an equal right to *access* to state information resources, and shall not be obliged to give their reason for seeking to obtain the requested information to the owner of these resources. An exception is "information of limited access" (Article 12.1 of the Law on Information, 1995). In this law, *access to state information resources* was regarded as the basis for civic oversight.[5] The owner or possessor of the information resource has to establish the procedure for obtaining the information, in compliance with the law and other formal requirements. Lists of information and information services, as well as the conditions and procedures for obtaining the information, had to be

[4] See Baturin 2009, p. 4–115.

[5] Bachilo 2003.

provided free of charge. The law also specified the procedure for citizens and organizations to obtain information on themselves, i.e., the right to know who has used the information and for what purposes. The Law on Information (1995) also guarantees that the information would be provided, and obliged the Government of the Russian Federation to issue lists of information services that can be obtained free of charge or for a fee that does not exceed expenses for the services. The law stated that *refusal to provide information can be appealed to a court*. Thus, the term "access" was employed in federal law for the first time. The scope of this law will be analyzed more thoroughly later in this article.

It is important to point out that the general provisions of the Law on Information (1995) were initially elaborated in a separate Federal Law, "On the Right to Information", the reason being that the Law on Information (1995) dealt with three issues simultaneously: (1) information resources and their legal status, (2) informatization and access to information, and (3) information security. Legal norms regarding rights to information resources need to be elaborated in detail.

The first proposed law on the right to information was prepared in 1996. Its description and full text can be found in publications related to the subject.[6] The issue of access to information in this proposed legislation requires a closer look. The term "access" was used simultaneously with the terms "search" and "acquisition". This approach was taken from the Constitution, in which the issue of access was specified as "search and acquisition". The proposed law stated that the main methods of access to information were: "obtaining official information from mass media and government legal information systems; obtaining information on the activities of government bodies and local authorities; request; subscription; other methods of obtaining information determined in a contract or by law; via personal computers; by purchasing information products; and other forms of civil law interactions relating to information access" (Article 7). The proposed law contained articles on procedures for requesting information, on the grounds and procedures for refusal to grant information, and on procedures for accessing the information resources of archives and libraries.

This proposed law also covered issues of access to information besides those in the Constitution of the Russian Federation. It distinguished information access rights of different entities: it delineated the rights of a natural person (human and civil rights) and rights of a legal entity (private entities and state and municipal bodies).

The main point of this proposed law was that the issue of access to information (search and acquisition) was considered part of the system of implementation of civil rights. This was done in compliance with the Constitution of the Russian Federation. Clause 4 of Article 29 sets a general legal rule. It states: *"Everyone shall have the right to freely search for, receive, transmit, produce, and distribute information in any legal manner. The list of data comprising state secrets shall be determined by a federal law"* (Article 29.4 of the Constitution of the Russian Federation). Clause 5 of the abovementioned Article says "*The freedom of mass communication shall be guaranteed. Censorship shall be banned.*"

[6]Bachilo 2009b.

The proposed law on the right to information in its constitutional sense was discussed at scientific conferences along with the first results of the implementation of the Law on Information (1995). A detailed discussion of the issue was held at two international conferences in Moscow in 1996 and 1998.[7] The discussion was led by law professors from other countries, experts of the Council of Europe, and the authors of the proposed law "On the Right to Information". The concept of the law and its elaboration in the text of the proposed law received a positive response from the experts, including the experts of the Council of Europe.

The proposed law "On the Right to Information" was discussed in the State Duma (the lower Chamber of the Parliament of the Russian Federation) at a wider conference, although it was not included in legislative plans. Some years later, in 1999, a similar draft law was officially presented to the State Duma. However, its passing was postponed for a number of reasons after the first reading. In practice, issues of access to information were decided based on the Law on Information (1995).

The development of legislation in the information sphere considers the objective processes in the field of information and communication technologies and a global information space forming. The Federal Target Program "Electronic Russia" acted in Russia since 2002 for 2010. In 7 February 2008, the President of the Russian Federation approved the "Strategy of information society development". The goals of the Strategy include: the strengthening of state guarantees of the constitutional human rights in the information society; equal opportunities for access to information, countering the use of information and communication technologies (IT) to damage Russia's national interests.

## 2 The State of Russian Legislation on Access to Information

### 2.1 *Reform of Legislation on Access to Information*

Since the Federal Law "On Information, Informatization, and Information Security" was passed in 1995, rights to information were exercised based on this law.[8] However, the law was repealed and replaced in 2006 with a new federal law with a different name and a different approach to information regulation. That new Law, "On Information, Information Technology, and Information Security" (Russian Federal Law No. 149-FZ of 27 July 2006; hereinafter, the Law on Information, (2006), concentrated more on technological issues rather than informatization. This significantly affected the regulation of interactions between users of information and information holders. The scope of the rules devoted to access to information is broader in the new law.

[7] See Sergienko 2013.

[8] Bogdanovskaya 2009.

This law defines information as knowledge (messages, data) in any form of representation (Article 2.1 No. 1 of the Law on Information, 2006). The scope of the law was defined as having its focus on exercise of the right to search for, receive, transmit, produce, and distribute information (Article 1.1 of the Law on Information, 2006). The term "access to information" is defined as "the ability to receive and use information" (Article 2.1 No. 6 of the Law on Information, 2006). Another concept which is used in this law is "provision of information", defined as "actions aimed at specific group of persons receiving information or giving information to a specified group of persons" (Article 2.1 No. 8 of the Law on Information, 2006). The law asserted that only federal law (Article 3 No. 2 of the Law on Information, 2006) can impose limitations on access to information.

Based on the adopted requirements for the legal regime surrounding information, the Law on Information (2006) provided different starting points. Thus, Article 5 of the Law on Information (2006), entitled "Information as the Subject of Legal Relations", states that information is divided into two categories of access: publicly accessible information and information, access to which is limited by a federal law (limited access information). Instead of rules on ownership of information resources, this law introduced the term "possessor of information" (not of specific information resources), and stated that information can be the subject of public, civil, and other legal interactions (Article 5 of the Law on Information, 2006).

## 2.2 The Issue of Access to Information

Article 8.1 of the Law on Information (2006), entitled "The Right to Access to Information", states that citizens (natural persons) and organizations (legal persons) have the right to search for and receive any information in any form and from any sources, if they comply with the requirements set by this federal law and other federal laws. Oftentimes, the word "any" is used without the caveat that there are indeed limits set by law. Thus, users and officials sometimes assume that they are allowed to provide/obtain any information. This might well cause conflicts and even breaches of law. However, the law clearly states that limitations to access are set by federal laws to protect fundamental principles of the constitutional system, morality, health, and the rights and lawful interests of other people, as well as for ensuring defence of the country and security of the state. Limited access information includes state, trade, and professional secrets (third parties may gain access with a court order). The procedure for gaining access to the personal data of individuals is set by the Federal Law "On Personal Data" of 27 July 2006 No. 152-FZ.

The most difficult problem concerns information related to official (governmental service) secrets. The term "official secret" is mentioned in the law, but no specific legislation yet exists for this category of information. The Decision of the Government of the Russian Federation of 1994 No. 1233 on procedures for federal governmental agencies' use of limited access governmental service information is applied to matters regarding official secrets. The law prohibits requesting information on the private life of a citizen (natural person) or information that comprises personal or family secrets, or obtaining this sort of information without the individual's prior consent, unless otherwise prescribed in federal law. These provisions can be found in a separate Federal Law, "On Personal Data".

## 2.3 When Restriction of Access Is Prohibited and When Communication Is Banned

There is another important aspect of the issue of access related to information to which access cannot be restricted. Such information includes: regulatory legal acts concerning the rights and freedoms of persons and citizens and acts defining the legal status of organizations and governmental and municipal bodies; information on the state of the environment; information on activities of the government and municipal authorities; and information concerning the use of budget funds, with the exception of information related to state secrets. Other information to which access cannot be restricted includes information from open archives and libraries and from museums and information systems meant for the public. Other categories of information with unrestricted access may also be specified in federal laws.[9]

For a better understanding of the rights to access information, it is important to consider such provisions of the law as the rule on provision of access to information on the activities of public authorities in Russian or in a language of a republic (component state) within the Russian Federation. A person seeking information is not obliged to give reasons for his/her request.

An important precondition for access is related to provision of information free of charge. This includes information on the activities of state and municipal authorities that is put onto the Internet, information related to the rights and duties of a citizen imposed by the legislation of Russian Federation, and other information defined by the law. This information can be accessed free of charge if not otherwise stated in any relevant federal law.[10]

So called "open data" are actively integrated into the system of open information. The problem of open data and open government is especially important now. The Federal Law №149 has recently been amended by adding a new Article 15.1. It prescribes to create a unified register of the domain names, website references and network addresses identifying websites containing information, distribution of which is forbidden in the Russian Federation.[11] Article 15.2 establishes the procedure for limiting access to information, distribution of which violates copyright and

[9]Article 8.4 of the Russian Federal Law No. 149-FZ. See also Bachilo 2010a.

[10]Article 7 of the Russian Federal Law No. 149-FZ.

[11]Article 15.1 of the Russian Federal Law No. 149-FZ.

(or) related rights, as well as the procedure for limiting access to the Internet sites that have repeatedly and illegitimately published information protected by copyright and (or) related rights, or information how to get such protected materials on the Internet (Article 15.6).[12]

In addition, the law restricts access to information distributed in violation of the law including the law on personal data. The problem of dissemination and use of harmful information, especially on the Internet, becomes increasingly important. Article 13.5 of the Russian Constitution declares that "the creation and activities of public associations whose aims and actions are aimed at a forced change of the fundamental principles of the constitutional system and at violating the integrity of the Russian Federation, at undermining its security, at setting up armed units, and at instigating social, racial, national and religious strife shall be prohibited." Article 19.2 of the Constitution declares equality of all people before the law and court and guarantees "the equality of rights and freedoms of man and citizen regardless of sex, race, nationality, language, origin, property and official status, place of residence, religion, convictions, membership of public associations, and also of other circumstances". These provisions are important not only for establishing the legal regime of information, but also for strengthening information security. Consequently, the system of information security requires additional regulations on information security of man, society and the state.

## 2.4 Federal Law on "Providing Access to Information on the Activities of State and Municipal Bodies"

The duty of state authorities to provide individuals with information is actively elaborated in the legislation of the Russian Federation. The Federal Law "On Providing Access to Information on the Activities of State and Municipal Bodies" (No. 8-FZ of 9 February 2009—hereinafter, the Law on Access to Information) has been passed. It was not the first law related to this matter. The Federal Law "On Coverage of the Activities of State Authorities in State-Run Mass Media" had been effective since 1995, as had the Federal Law "On Procedures for Publication and Entry into Force of Federal Constitutional Laws, Federal Laws, and Acts of the Federal Assembly" since 1994, and the Federal Law "On Mandatory Copies of Documents" since 1995.

In connection with the adoption of the Law on Information (2006), it is worth pointing out that many western legal systems arose from the American Freedom of Information Act, which is based on the duty of government to provide information to citizens and impose any necessary limitations. To a certain extent, the Russian law resembles this model, but it is broader in scope. It contains some extra articles and is more specific in providing detailed regulation of exercise by citizens and

[12]Article 15.2 and 15.6 of the Russian Federal Law No. 149-FZ.

organizations of their right to access information, as determined by the Constitution of the Russian Federation and the Law on Information (2006).

Below are the most important points of the Russian Law on Access to Information:

1. It contains a definition of information on the activities of state and municipal bodies, phrased as "information (including documented information) that was produced by state authorities, their territorial bodies, municipal authorities, and organizations dependent on state and municipal authorities, within the limits of their powers, or information which was received by the abovementioned authorities. Information on the activities of governmental and municipal bodies also includes laws and other legal regulations; information on municipal bodies includes municipal legal regulations that state the structure, powers, procedures for the establishing of, and activities of the abovementioned bodies and organizations, as well as other information relating to their activities" (Article 1.1 of the Law on Access to Information). Besides this, a party accessing the information is defined. The term "user" embraces citizens (natural persons), legal entities, social organizations, and state and local authorities who are seeking information in compliance with the law.
2. The definition of the scope of law also includes limitations. The Law on Access to Information is not applicable to (1) provision of access to personal data that is processed by state and municipal authorities; (2) citizens' petitions seeking not information, but the solution to a problem; (3) procedures for provision of information by one state or municipal authority to another, associated with the authorities' performance of their functions (Article 2.5 of the Law on Access to Information). The term "access" is not defined as such; however, provision is made for regulation of a user's rights, and the main requirements for providing access are set forth (principles, procedures for providing information that can be accessed online, accuracy requirements, terms and procedures for granting information, the right to remove pieces of limited access information, creation of technical facilities for access, and accounting for expenses connected with providing access when planning budgets).
3. The law contains a separate chapter dedicated to how information is provided to users, with details regarding disclosure (publication) of information on the activities of state and municipal (local) authorities in accordance with mass media legislation. The article includes a detailed list of types and forms of information that can be obtained online from authorities' web pages (Articles 13 and 14 of the Law on Access to Information). This part of the law also contains regulations on attendance of sessions of collegiate state and municipal bodies in compliance with relevant regulations, and on creating public access points.
4. The Law on Access to Information specifies the request form and procedures for processing a request received from a user for specific public state authorities, as well as grounds for refusal to grant the information. In accordance with Article 20 of the Law on Access to Information:

Information on state and municipal bodies' activities is not provided in the following cases: (1) the desired information on the activities of governmental and municipal bodies is not clear from the request; (2) the request does not contain a mailing address, e-mail address, or fax number to reply to the query, or a contact phone number; (3) the requested information is not related to the activities of the body to whom the request was sent; (4) access to the requested information is limited; (5) the requested information has already been given to the user; (6) the request raises questions regarding a legal evaluation of acts passed by a state or a municipal authority, asks that an analysis of the activities of the state authority, its territorial body, a municipal authority, or organizations dependent on state authorities and municipal authorities be conducted, or asks that some other type of analysis not related directly to the protection of the right of the user be conducted. A state authority or municipal authority has the right not to provide information on its activities if this information can be found in mass media resources or online (Article 20 of the Law on Access to Information)

The grounds excluding the possibility of providing information on the activities of the courts are specified in the Federal Law "On Providing Access to Information on Courts' Activities in the Russian Federation".

It also contains regulations on granting information free of charge (orally or online), information involving a user's rights, and other information specified by the authority itself (Article 21 of the Law on Access to Information). There is a charge for the provision of information if provided in a large volume exceeding free of charge services, if copied from original documentation, or for a repeated request, unless the information originally contained errors. The prices are set by the Government of the Russian Federation (Article 22 of the Law on Access to Information).

5. The Law on Access to Information sets consequences for violation of the procedures for access. The right to access information is protected by the provision that decisions and actions of authorities that violate the right to access information may be appealed to a higher body or to the court. The grounds for appeal are as follows: illegal refusal to grant access, untimely provision of access, and the response not corresponding to the request. All damages inflicted on the user are recovered in compliance with civil law (Article 23 of the Law on Access to Information).

Complying with these established procedures of information acquisition is the responsibility of the heads of state authorities (Article 24 of the Law on Access to Information). The activities of state authorities and municipal authorities are in turn monitored by the prosecutor's office of the Russian Federation, in compliance with the Federal Law "On the Public Prosecution Office of the Russian Federation".

Officials and employees who violate the right to access to information are subject to administrative, disciplinary, civil, and criminal liability, in compliance with the legislation of the Russian Federation (Article 25 of the Law on Access to Information).

The Code of Administrative Offences (Russian Federal Law No. 195-FZ of 30 December 2001) contains articles on liability for refusal to provide requested information that must be provided in accordance with federal law. These articles also apply if the information provided is misrepresented or not provided in due time

(Article 5.39 of the Administrative Code). Two new articles were added to the Code of Administrative Offences in 2010. They set forth liability for violation of the right to access information on the activities of state and municipal authorities and its publication on the Internet. The offender may be fined from 3000 to 5000 RUB (Article 13.27 of the Administrative Code). The second new Article (13.28 of the Administrative Code) concerns violation of the procedures for provision of limited access information, the second part of which deals with liability for improperly charging for the provision of information on the activities of state and local authorities, as well as with violations connected to charging procedures if they exist. Penalties here also range from 3000 to 5000 RUB.

The Criminal Code of the Russian Federation (Russian Federal Law No. 63-FZ of 13 June 1996) contains an article on liability for refusal to provide information (Article 140 of the Criminal Code). It prescribes penalties that a body will be subject to if it refuses to provide requested documents and files directly related to civil rights and freedoms if such information is deliberately misrepresented or is not provided in full and has violated the rights and legitimate interests of an individual. In these cases, the penalty is either a 2000 RUB fine or 18 months of wages or other earnings, or deprivation of the right to hold specific posts or engage in certain activities for 2–5 years.

## 2.5 *Access to Information on the Activities of Courts*

The Federal Law “On Providing Access to Information on the Activities of Courts in the Russian Federation” (No. 262-FZ of 22 December 2008) was passed before the Federal Law “On Providing Access to Information on the Activities of State and Municipal Bodies”. The scope of this federal law concerns the provision of access to information on the activities of the courts. The provisions of the law are applied in compliance with the legislation of the Russian Federation; in addition, legislation of the constituent entities of the Russian Federation also applies in relation to information on the constitutional courts and magistrates of the respective constituent entity. The law covers relations associated with provision of information on the activities of the courts to media in areas that are not regulated by the Law on Media. The law introduces a list of legal regulations to deal with relations associated with the provision of information on the activities of the courts, and specifies in which cases this law is not applicable. According to Article 2 No. 262-FZ, it does not apply to (1) procedures for constitutional, civil, administrative, or criminal court proceedings; arbitration proceedings; or the work of the Judges’ Qualification Board; (2) procedures for executing court acts; (3) access to personal data processed by the courts, the Justice Department, or bodies of the judicial community; or (4) the procedures of information interoperability for courts, the Justice Department, or bodies of the judicial community (Article 2.3 262-FZ). It also provides a list of limited access information. The *main principles* of provision of information are as follows: (1) openness and availability of information; (2) accuracy;

(3) freedom of search, access, exchange, and distribution of information on the activities of the courts by any legal means; (4) observance of privacy rights and rights to private and family secrecy; (5) protection of honor and dignity; (6) the right of an organization to protect its business reputation; (7) observance of the rights and legal interests of participants in judicial proceedings when information on the proceedings is disclosed; (8) and non-interference and non-obstruction of justice policies (Article 4 No. 262-FZ).

The law establishes the rights of users of information as follows: (1) the right to receive credible information on the activities of the courts, (2) the right to obtain information whose availability is not limited without stating the reasons for such, (3) the right to appeal actions of officials that violate the right to access information on the activities of the courts or the procedures of information acquisition, (4) the right to claim compensation for violation of the right to access information on the activities of the courts (Article 8 262-FZ).

The main requirements for provision of access to information on the activities of the courts' include: (a) that the information provided on the activities of the courts be accurate, (b) that the information be provided within the established timeframe, (c) the removal of limited access information from information provided on courts, (d) that the technical conditions necessary to exercise the right to access information on the activities of the courts be provided and that public information systems be established, and (e) that the expenses associated with provision of access to information on the activities of the courts be considered when planning government funding for the courts, the Justice Department, and the subdivisions of the Justice Department (Article 11 No. 262-FZ).

Including the regulatory policies and requirements for the provision of access and users' rights into one law has allowed for the creation of a single information network for the federal courts of general jurisdiction and magistrates in the Russian Federation. This is reinforced by the fact that this law includes use of the Internet as one means of communication with the users.[13] The transparency of public authorities and local self-government bodies is guaranteed by the laws discussed above. All official public information must be available through the websites of each body, its subdivisions and through national portals.

## 2.6 A New Step in Access Development: Federal Law "On Organizing the Provision of State and Municipal Services"

The Federal Law "On Organizing the Provision of State and Municipal Services" No. 210-FZ of 27 July 2010 was passed after much debate, and has already proved

[13]The named Law was amended in this regard and online information was added; the law is now effective as amended on 20 June 2010 No. 123-FZ, of 18 July 2011 No. 240-FZ.

crucial in its practical importance. With respect to accessing information, it marks a new step in the development of this institution. All preceding laws and sublegislative regulatory acts associated with them shed light on the question of *where* and *what kind of* information is available on information resources. Most importantly, this law focuses on *the purpose* of the desired information and the means by which a practical result in the field of the human and civil rights can be obtained on its basis. This is the main objective of this law. It connects a person's entire social existence with information technologies and the active use of information resources.

A platform for the interaction of the personal data of every user with information resources of state and municipal authorities was created. Consequently, there is now a more sophisticated mechanism for accessing and using information, created to resolve issues important to the individual. A functional system of interaction with the public is then formed on this basis, in compliance with the needs of individuals (i.e., users of information and communication system resources) and the population of the region and country at large, using a single methodological and legal system. Russian Federation Government resolution of 24 October 2011, "On the federal governmental information system 'Universal Portal for Governmental and Municipal Services'" is a case in point. Multifunctional centres were established to provide governmental e-services at "one stop shop" principle.[14] The adoption of new methods of working with information (supervision of access to information by various entities to achieve specific goals set by an individual) seriously affects the work of the state bodies. A notable observation was made by Professor A.V. Sosnin (Ukrainian Academy of Science) regarding the reaction of the public to the Ukrainian Law "On Access to Public Information" in May 2011. He draws attention to the insufficient objectivity and declarative character of rules on "access" as such, and notes the law's weakness with respect to meeting the current needs of citizens, and most importantly its insufficient influence on how public authorities work.[15] The adoption of a law on the provision of governmental and municipal services caused changes in a number of other federal laws and legislation of the constituent entities of the Russian Federation. The first application of this law revealed the need for more specifics into the law on services.

## 2.7 *Issues Regarding Personal Data in the Information Access Structure*

Another aspect of the problem of access to information is dealt with in the Federal Law "On Personal Data" (Russian Federal Law No. 152-FZ of 27 July 2006). This act was passed in 2006, and came into force on 26 January 2007. Its main purpose is

[14]Bachilo 2015; Talapina 2009; Talapina 2015.

[15]See Sosnin 2012, p. 122–134.

not to provide access to information but to protect human rights and freedoms with regard to the processing of personal data, including the protection of privacy and personal and family secrets. In terms of access, this act elaborates relations between owners of personal data and operators, authorities in the sphere of civil rights protection, with oversight and supervisory authorities, and with courts if necessary.

The law defines personal data as any information relating to an identified or identifiable individual, and includes last name, first name, year and place of birth, address, marital status, property status, education, occupation, etc. Personal data includes publicly available data that does not require any special permission from the owner of the data to collect or disseminate.

However, the general principles and rules in this law establish the data owner's right to know who is collecting this data and for what purpose, who is using them, and the procedure for making such a request. For these purposes, the law grants the personal data owner the right:

1. to make a request;
2. to give and to revoke consent to the processing of the data;
3. to stop the operator from processing the data;
4. to make a complaint to the competent authority and to the court. (Articles 14, 15, 18, 20, 21 No. 152-FZ)

The Law also provides for cases in which personal data can be processed without informing its owner. These are set forth in Article 22, and include certain aspects of contractual and labor relations, the use of publicly available data, indication of only the name and surname of a person, and processing data in public automated information systems established for state security and public order.

There are some problems in the area of personal data protection. Personal data leakages occur relatively often. Personal data systems frequently appear on the black market. There are no clear criteria to distinguish personal data from information on the private life of an individual or from personal secrets. Family secrets are currently more of an open topic than a closed one.

Anti-corruption rules make an exception for information concerning, among other things, the assets of public officials.

The area of access to personal data is the most difficult area when it comes to legal practices. Protection of the honor and dignity of an individual falls under civil law (Article 152 of the Civil Code of the Russian Federation, No. 51-FZ of 30 November 1994), but one means of doing harm to honor and dignity is by misuse of personal data, which is the responsibility of information law, while another is media activity, regulated by civil and public law, including information law. Anonymity in the Internet environment on the one hand and crime on the other exacerbates the problem of access and use of personal information, and often are associated with problems within law enforcement agencies, especially in terms of search and investigation.[16]

[16]Jarova 2009.

A number of laws were amended in 2013 in accordance with the European Convention for the Protection of Individuals with regard to Automatic Processing of Personal Data and the Federal law on personal data (Russian Federal Law No. 99-FZ of 27 April 2013): now there is the regulation of personal data databases of nongovernment pension foundations and civil registries, personal data of orphans, recipients of social aid, state attorneys' and government personnel's personal data, etc.

## *2.8 Classified Information*

In the Russian Federation, there is the Federal Law of 2004 "On Commercial Secrets" (Russian Federal Law No. 98-FZ of 29 July 2004, amended in 2014), which also covers know-how. It establishes what types of information will be deemed commercial secret, the list of information prohibited to be classified as commercial secret, and the legal regime of the information and protection measures.[17]

There are quite a few professional secrets in Russia (the term "secret" is usually used, not "privilege"). They are stipulated by the laws on the related activities. For example, the Law "On the Advocacy and the Bar in the Russian Federation" (Russian Federal Law No. 63-FZ of 31 May 2002) guarantees the attorney secret; the Law "On the Fundamentals of Citizens' Health Protection in the Russian Federation" (Russian Federal Law No. 323-FZ of 21 November 2011) regulates the medical secrets etc.

The Federal Law "On Banks and Banking Activities" (Russian Federal Law No. 395-I of 2 December 1990) contains Article 26 on banking secrecy. Moreover, there is the Federal Law "On Credit Histories" (Russian Federal Law No. 218-FZ of 30 December 2004), which aims to safeguard borrowers interests. It is generally accepted that commercial information within the competence of public authorities retains its regime and requires an appropriate way of handling it.

The problem of insider information in public authorities and local self-government institutions remains in the state of uncertainty. There is no federal law on administrative procedures in Russia. Records management systems (and use of information technologies in them) of specific institutions or their associations is governed by inner regulations.[18]

The Law "On State Secrets" (Russian Federal Law No. 5485-1 of 21 July 1993) establishes the procedure of classifying information as a state secret, regulates the protection of these information, including questions of admission and access to it, and its declassification.

[17]See Antopolsky 2009.

[18]Sheveleva 2012.

## 2.9 *Organizational and Control Activity in the Sphere of Access to Information*

The Ministry of Telecom and Mass Communications of the Russian Federation is a federal executive body which determines state policy and implements legal norms in the following spheres:

information technologies (including the use of information technologies to form and access to state information resources);
mass communications and media, including electronic media, digital television, broadcasting and new technologies in these areas;
development of the Internet;
personal data protection;
state property management and provision of public services in the field of information technologies;
development and implementation of state policy on protection of children from information harmful to their health and (or) development.

To perform its duties, Ministry of Telecom and Mass Communications also deals with applications from private persons: it organizes personal reception of citizens, receives oral and written applications and answers to them within the prescribed period; it protects information classified as a state secret competence secret in the sphere of their competence, and conducts the control and coordination of subordinate federal services, federal agencies and organizations activities in the named field.

The Ministry of Telecom and Mass Communications has in its subordination the Federal Service for Supervision of Communications, Information Technologies, and Mass Media (*Roskomnadzor*) that ensures compliance with personal data protection law and controls submission of legal deposit copies of prescribed documents. *Roskomnadzor* is in charge of protection of children from information harmful to their health and (or) development: it controls that educational and scientific organizations comply with the legal rules, it examines what information materials are used in educational process and what information is accessible from educational and scientific organizations via Internet. *Roskomnadzor* also keeps mass media registers and issues permissions to distribute foreign print media in Russia. *Roskomnadzor* performs its functions directly and through its territorial divisions, as well as in cooperation with other governmental bodies, local self-government bodies, social and other organizations.

In Russia, since 2012 the system "Open Government" has been implemented. The Standard of Federal Executive Authorities Openness was developed and approved in 2014. The main functions of named system include the monitoring of how the requirements of the Standard are complied with by Russian authorities. The internet-portal "Open Government"[19] is working currently. The Openness Rating of Russian ministries and agencies is published there. How useful the institute of Open Government in such meaning will be to mass communication time will tell. A separate line of transparency providing is so called Open Data. Rating of Open Data publishing activity at the federal, regional and municipal levels one can see in the Open Data Bulletin.[20]

The Analytical Center for the Government of the Russian Federation held a summit on the use of open data and open government in 2015. The summit was devoted to organization of providing access to packaged information on the open data portal.

## 3 Problems in Court Practice

Every law about access to information contains provisions on liability. The Law on Information (2006) and Law on Access to Information contain rules regarding various types of liability for breaking the law. One of the first information laws, the Federal Law "On Mass Media" (Russian Federal Law No. 2124-1 of 27 December 1991), guaranteed the rights of journalists by establishing liability for breach of the law.

Note that the legal guarantees of access to information include judicial procedures protecting the interests of citizens and the responsibility of the offender. This is provided in the Code of Administrative Offenses rules related to the violations of the access to information. On sanctions for administrative and criminal offenses mentioned above.

There are three main types of court cases regarding the exercise of the right to information:

1. conflicts and disputes on non-provision of information to a person who has a right to such information;
2. breaches of information security rules by those responsible for information security;
3. unlawful access to information of limited access.

Legislation deals mostly with limited access information, which is why court practice is mostly on limited access information as well. Information rights violations in social segments of the Internet are also growing in number because of open information and open source software. File sharing services do not have mechanisms for control or prevention of unlawful dissemination of information.

[19]http://open.gov.ru (Accessed on 14 February 2017).

[20]http://ac.gov.ru/files/publication/a/7116.pdf (Accessed on 14 February 2017).

One example of the first type of court case is the case[21] involving the Freedom of Information Foundation (St. Petersburg). Its lawyers compelled, through court, a number of federal government agencies to create Internet sites, as governmental agencies themselves do not seem to be in a hurry to create official sites and put information on them. This activity required a citizens' initiative. These were individual court claims, filed by natural persons. Some cases went to court, and had the effect that, while only 54 of 84 federal government agencies had sites in 2004, by 2006 only 5 federal government agencies did not have sites. This type of mobilization was used later to enhance the quality of said sites.

This example shows that an individual's initiative often requires support from civil society. Currently, there is not much court practice in the area of access to information. A frequent problem is that authorities refuse to provide some document that contains personal data. However, sometimes an applicant needs only general information, not personal data. Courts do not consider in such cases the possibility that the document could be issued to an applicant with the personal data removed.

The Institute of State and Law conducts research on the topic of information conflicts.[22]

Legislation on the right to information is developed simultaneously with the legislation on criminal and administrative responsibility for offenses and crimes in the information sphere. The Criminal Code of the Russian Federation (Federal Law No. 63-FZ of 13 June 1996) contains a norm establishing responsibility for "Illegal refusal by an official to submit documents and materials, collected in the statutory order and directly affecting the rights and freedoms of an individual, or the submission of incomplete or deliberately falsified information to an individual, if these deeds have caused harm to the rights and legally-protected interests of individuals" (Article 140 of the Criminal Code) and quite a few other crimes in information sphere: invasion of personal privacy (Article 137 of the Criminal Code), violation of the secrecy of correspondence, telephone conversations, postal, telegraphic and other messages (Article 137 of the Criminal Code), swindling in the sphere of computer information (Article 159.6 of the Criminal Code), the illegal receipt and disclosure of information classified as a commercial, tax or banking secret (Article 183 of the Criminal Code), high treason (Article 275 of the Criminal Code), espionage (Article 276 of the Criminal Code), disclosure of a state secret (Article 283 of the Criminal Code), illegal receipt of information classified as a state secret (Article 283.1 of the Criminal Code), loss of documents containing state secrets (Article 284 of the Criminal Code). Chapter 28 devoted to computer crimes should be especially noted. Those articles criminalize illegal access to computer information (Article 272 of the Criminal Code); creation, distribution and use of

[21]Dzerzhinsky district Court of St. Petersburg decision of 18 October 2005 in Case No 2-1133/2005.

[22]Bachilo 2009a.

malicious computer programs (Article 273 of the Criminal Code), etc. The Criminal Code establishes liability for impeding the lawful professional activities of journalists, for committing acts of violence against journalists.

Administrative responsibility for offenses in the field of information law is determined by the Code of Administrative Offences of the Russian Federation (Federal Law No. 195-FZ of 30 December 2001). In the context of this work, the most notable is Article 5.39 of the Administrative Code on liability for unlawful refusal to provide the requested information, delay or providing false information. The Code also establishes liability for the violation of the requirements for the providing access to information about public authorities and local self-government bodies, for not posting this information on the Internet and for the illegal charging for providing this information (Article 13.27 and Article 13.28 of the Administrative Code).

Statistics and analytical information on the law enforcement practice and about judicial authorities is still scarce. The study of the transparency and openness of anti-corruption executive authorities reveals the following. The norms on access to information are incorporated in 62 regulations of the federal executive authorities. However, only 46% of them contain information on anti-corruption measures and their monitoring. In one of federal subjects of Russia, which has 30 official sites of municipal areas and urban districts, 71 violation reports were received by the local government authorities and 6 applications were sent to the court. The claims were related to inactivity of the administration of local districts and demanded to post information on the Internet sites. The courts also keep statistics of offenses specified by Article 13.27 of the Administrative Code. However, we have to admit that the judicial statistics on the information rights violations has not yet received adequate attention.

Analysis of ECHR cases shows that the applications from Russian citizens mostly concern civil law problems. Russian applications to the ECtHR often concern access to information only indirectly or partly.

## 4 A Comparison Between Russian and Brazilian Legislation on Access to Information

Below I compare the basic laws on information in both countries. These laws are the Russian Federal Law "On Providing Access to Information on the Activities of Governmental and Municipal Bodies" of 9 February 2009 No. 8-FZ and the Brazilian General Law on Access to Information 12.527/2011.

The table reflects the structures of both laws.

| Federal Law "On Providing Access to Information on the Activities of State and Municipal Bodies" | General Law on Access to Information 12.527/2011 | Notes |
|---|---|---|
| ***Chapter 1. General Provisions***<br>– definitions,<br>– scope of application,<br>– general principles,<br>– rights of those requesting information,<br>– forms of information provision,<br>– limited access | ***Chapter 1. General Provisions***<br>– purposes of the law,<br>– scope of application,<br>– definitions,<br>– general principles,<br>– general guarantees | The Brazilian Law provides a broad listing of activities related to data processing: a set of actions concerning the production, receipt, classification, use, access, reproduction, transport, conveyance, distribution, archiving, storage, elimination, evaluation, allocation, or control of information. |
| ***Chapter 2. Organization of Access to Information.***<br>– duties of state and municipal bodies<br>– official sites of state and municipal bodies,<br>– requirements regarding disseminated information | ***Chapter 2. Access to Information and its Dissemination***<br>– duties of public bodies and authorities,<br>– what information is subject to rules on the right to obtain data,<br>– dissemination of information without a request,<br>– official sites of public organizations and authorities | |
| ***Chapter 3. Provision of Information***<br>– through mass media,<br>– on official sites of governmental and municipal bodies,<br>– by providing access to sessions of collegiate governmental and municipal bodies,<br>– on bulletin boards in governmental and municipal offices,<br>– in libraries and archives,<br>– by answering requests for information | ***Chapter 3. Procedure for Accessing Information***<br>– The request must identify the applicant.<br>– Immediate access to the information must be provided. If this is impossible, the body or authority that receives the request must provide the information or refuse to do so within 20 days.<br>– Information stored in digital format must be provided in that format.<br>– The appeals procedure | The term for provision of information in the Russian Federation is 30 days (can be prolonged by an additional 10 days). |
| | ***Chapter 4. Restrictions on Access to Information***<br>Sec. 1. General provisions | These issues are regulated in Russia by the Federal Law "On State Secrets". |
| | Sec. 2. Classification of information as to the level of secrecy and timeframe for classification<br>Sec. 3. Protection and control of secret information<br>Sec. 4. Classification, reclassification, and declassification<br>Sec. 5. Personal information | The Russian Federation has a separate Federal Law dealing with this—"On Personal Data". |

(continued)

| Federal Law "On Providing Access to Information on the Activities of State and Municipal Bodies" | General Law on Access to Information 12.527/2011 | Notes |
|---|---|---|
| ***Chapter 4. Liability for Breach of the Rules for Access to Information***<br>General, reference rules:<br>– Actions and decisions of governmental and municipal bodies can be appealed to a higher body or to a court.<br>– Bodies or officials found guilty are subject to civil, disciplinary, administrative, or criminal liability.<br>General attorney survey the implementation of the Law by governmental and municipal bodies. | ***Chapter 5. Liability***<br>Penalties for public or military agents, natural persons or private institutions, public organizations or authorities. | Specific rules regarding liability and punishment in Russia are contained in the Criminal Code of the Russian Federation and the Code of Administrative Offences of the Russian Federation. |

A comparison between these two laws shows the following:

1. The scopes of these acts do overlap, but differ, because in Russia state secrets, trade secrets, and personal data are regulated by separate laws. Some issues are covered by other Russian laws, such as the Law on Information and the Federal Law "On Rendering State and Municipal Services". This is also the reason why the Brazilian law contains more chapters and articles: there are 33 articles in the Brazilian law and 25 articles in the Russian law.
2. One distinctive and positive feature of the Brazilian law is the emphasis on procedures that public authorities and other governmental information keepers must follow when providing access to information. Russian law does not focus as much on these procedures. This is evident, for example, on the websites of governmental bodies. Russian law contains lists of the information that are published on these sites. Brazilian law not only lists information to be placed on the sites, but also requirements to the format of the information: the type of files, search capabilities, etc. (Article 8 of Law No. 8-FZ). Put simply, it prescribes not only what should be on the site, but how it should be done.
3. What is the most important when comparing these two laws is the similarity of the basic elements of access to information: the scope of obliged and empowered persons; the presumption that the right to access information is a fundamental right; and transparency, accessibility, adequacy, and the protection of privacy, honor, and business reputation.
4. Both laws are based on certain principles, but the lists of these principles do not fully coincide. It is important to note that both laws limit the freedom of searching for information—it may only be done legally.

This work does not aim to compare all the rules on access to information on the activities of public authorities. It is more important to show that the legal practices in different countries produce the same approaches to providing access to information for everybody, and that this allows us to set up a platform for the realization of all human and civil rights.

Getting information is just the first step in exercising one's rights. It is the passive stage of using information resources. The active stage begins when services are received from governmental and municipal bodies and courts. It may be that this is the reason there are not many court cases on access to information. The use of information and the application of knowledge has become the central element in every social sphere (education, healthcare, housing, freedom of movement, employment, and overcoming hunger and social inequality). The modernization of all mechanisms of governance based on IT will be the way that we move from a service-based and paternalistic state to a social and democratic state.

Accessibility to information is important for governmental and municipal bodies themselves as well. It mobilizes their work, makes governance processes more ordered and better organized, and stimulates employees to acquire IT skills.

## 5 Forms of Digital Access to Various Sources of Information

This aspect is a separate but also important issue. It is related to the architecture of network-based methods and forms of distribution, as well as free access to various sources of information. On the one hand, uncontrolled publication of any information source asserts the right of a citizen to freely access any content of their choice. On the other hand, it creates conditions that complicate people's ability to orient themselves in a space not conducive to organization and management, with due consideration for a person's safety and the development of civic institutions.

Although Russian legislation guarantees free access and use of information "by any legal means", this is in relation only to the jurisdiction of the Russian Federation. The provision can, however, be adopted at regional levels of international cooperation.

However, such an approach cannot resolve all issues mirroring the ethical and legal conscience of society. There are a number of factors that depend on the orientation of politics in different countries regarding such concepts as "power", "dominance", "monopoly" and "uni- and multi-polarity" with respect to interaction between different countries at the global scale. Today we are going through a stage of merging cultures and civilizations. Access to information both complicates and hastens this process, reflecting the trends of conservatism, liberalism, and progressive thinking. Access is a double-edged sword, and it requires great attention to ensure the safety of people, society, and its many institutions, including the system of state authorities.

### 5.1 *Access to Information as Aid to Dilution of Legal Nihilism and a Step Forward in the Modernization of the Legal System: The Legal Status of Information Distributors*

Many researchers point out that in modern Russia there are already over 2000 regulatory enactments dealing with the issues of public information resources and public access to information. The consolidation, harmonization, and integration of these sources of law require special attention.

Certain activities are carried out in this regard. These include the introduction of *official electronic publication of regulations*. Other key changes include the elaboration of problems with the use of information systems and databases of regulatory acts at the level of the Ministry of Justice of the Russian Federation, monitoring of legislation and enforcement practices in the whole state; working towards social engagement in the discussion on draft laws and other legal enactments via a system of "e-management" (of the Government and the Civic Chamber of the Russian Federation) via the web pages and portals of civic government authorities, the work of non-governmental organizations, etc.

Activities concerning right to information and access to information are regulated not only by the Strategy of Information Society Development and the laws mentioned above. In the present conditions, new types of threats to information security demand attention. In response to them, the Strategy of National Security of the Russian Federation was entered into force on 31 December 2015. The Strategy has both political and legal significance; it emphasizes that the system of national security includes, along with military defence, information security of state, society and individuals.

### 5.2 *The Readiness of the Public to Adopt Information and Communication Technology Strategies*

Access to any form of communication is unlimited in Russia. More than 70% of the population use Internet resources at their discretion, and nearly every Russian citizen has a mobile phone. However, it takes time to bridge the gap between the extensive growth of users of IT products and the intensity and effectiveness of their use. The main hindrances to this process are: the level of the legal culture and of the civic understanding of the connections between personal and civil interests, the wide gap between the socio-economic conditions of different groups of the population, and the decreasing standards of education in areas such as the humanities, etc.

## 5.3 *Transforming the Methods and Forms of State and Municipal Authorities' Activities by Acquiring Information and Communication Technologies*

In this paragraph, it is important to point out the delayed transition from the "e-government" program whereby attention was drawn to technological issues and their assessment using market mechanisms, to issues and programs of "e-administration", which affect all structures and management processes of the government. This requires that we change the indicators of the transition to the use of IT in administration.

Specialists point out the delay in the development of a legal and information culture in the public service community at every level. Freedom of access to information, in the general sense of the term, has also affected government and municipal sector officials. The lack of thorough organization of official information, and officials' involvement with state secrets and confidential and inside information, as well as their attitude towards having these resources be "open", causes some officials in the government sector to violate the law. The situation is also complicated by the lack of procedural mechanisms for detection of violations in the sphere of information security in public management.

## 5.4 *Access to Information and Its Use: An Indicator of Civic Health*

Scientifically, this issue is described in detail in my textbooks and in publications of the Department of Information Law of the Institute of State and Law of the Russian Academy of Sciences.[23] In this publication, it is important to highlight the most important trends for the development of an information society as civic, welfare, democratic, and legal:

1. the search for a balance between official information sources (e.g., web portals, web pages, web cameras, Internet-media) and free file exchange servers;
2. access to legal information as a factor contributing to the dilution of legal nihilism and regulation of the legal system;
3. the readiness of individuals and citizens as responsible participants in the Internet information environment;
4. the information legal status of the government;
5. clarification of legislation on social, state and individual information security is needed to answer new trends on international and national levels;
6. model legislation on the right to information and access to information are being developed by international organizations (unions, associations). For example, the Model Law of the CIS Interparliamentary Assembly (IPA CIS), "On information, informatization and information security".

---

[23]Bachilo 2001; Bachilo 2012a; Bachilo 2010b; Bachilo 2009c; Bachilo 2012c.

## References

Antopolsky, A. A. (2009). Right to information in public law and private law. *Works of the Institute of State and Law of the Russian Academy of Sciences, 5*, 118–134.

Bachilo, I. L. (2001). *Information law. An introduction to applied informatics.* Moscow: Jurinformcentr.

Bachilo, I. L. (Ed.). (2003). *Information resources of Russian Federation: Legal problems.* Moscow: Nauka.

Bachilo, I. L. (Ed.). (2009a). *Conflicts in the sphere of information: Legal aspects.* Moscow: Institute of State and Law.

Bachilo, I. L. (Ed.). (2009b). *Information law. Actual problems of theory and practice.* Moscow: Urait.

Bachilo, I. L. (2009c). On the right to information. In M. A. Fedotov (Ed.), *"Glasnost" as a subject of legal regulation. Proceedings of the intellectual property* (pp. 116–150). Moscow: Higher School of Economics.

Bachilo, I. L. (Ed.). (2010a). *Conditions for citizens' and organizations' rights realization.* Moscow: Institute of State and Law.

Bachilo, I. L. (Ed.). (2010b). *Information society and welfare state.* Moscow: Institute of State and Law.

Bachilo, I. L. (2012a). *Information law. Textbook for universities.* Moscow: Urait.

Bachilo, I. L. (2012b). Law and legislation: Infocommunication aspect. *Information Law, 30*(3), 3–15.

Bachilo, I. L. (2012c). *State and law of XXI century, real and virtual.* Moscow: Urcompany.

Bachilo, I. L. (2013). On causes and motives of breaches of law in the sphere of race, ethnic, national and religious relations. *State and Law, 3*, 33–43.

Bachilo I. L. (2015). Reading Kissinger: Information society, Internet as a factors of global order forming. *Eurasian Law Journal, 7*, 232–235 (review of Kissinger, H. (2014). *World Order.* New York: Penguin Random House).

Baturin, Y. (2009). Glasnost' attempt: The history of one legislative failure. In M. A. Fedotov (Ed.), *"Glasnost" as a subject of legal regulation. Proceedings of the intellectual property* (pp. 4–115). Moscow: Higher School of Economics.

Bogdanovskaya, I. Y. (Ed.). (2009). *Right to access to information: Access to open information.* Moscow: Higher School of Economics.

Jarova, A. K. (2009). Problems of persons anonymity on the Internet. *Works of the Institute of State and Law of the Russian Academy of Sciences, 5*, 135–158.

Sergienko, L. A. (2013). *The history of development of information law in USSR and Russian Federation 1960–2000.* Moscow: Urcompany.

Sheveleva, N. A. (Ed.). (2012). *Right to access to information: Opportunities and limitations in the information environment. Materials of international scientific-practical conference.* Saint Petersburg, Russia: B.N. Yeltsin President Library.

Sosnin, A. V. (2012). On access to information and information security. In I. L. Bachilo (Ed.), *Evolution of state and legal institutions in developing an information society: Collection of papers* (pp. 122–134). Moscow: Urcompany.

Talapina, E. V. (2009). Principles of access to economic information. *Works of the Institute of State and Law of the Russian Academy of Sciences, 5*, 64–77.

Talapina, E. V. (2015). *Public administration in the information society. Legal aspect.* Moscow: Jurisprudence.

# Chapter 11
# Access to Information: A National Report About India

**Srikrishna Deva Rao and Ravindra Chingale**

## Contents



The Authors acknowledge the research inputs from Kanchan, Shrey Patnaik, Anushka Sachdev and Jesselina Rana, Fifth Year Students of B.A. LL.B. (Hons.) of National Law University Delhi.

S.D. Rao
National Law University Odisha, Cuttack, India

R. Chingale (✉)
Supreme Court of India, New Delhi, India
e-mail: advchingale@gmail.com



H.-J. Blanke, R. Perlingeiro (eds.), *The Right of Access to Public Information*,
DOI 10.1007/978-3-662-55554-5_11

# 1 Introduction

Access to information and communication encompass the core principles of democratic governance like participation, transparency and accountability. These principles are necessary for efficient and quick functioning of good governance. Democracy requires that the citizen of the country should be informed about the actual working and happenings of the Governance. This information is having vital importance to curb corruption and to hold government and their instrumentalities accountable to the governed.

The government of India enacted the Right to Information Act (RTI Act) in 2005 to provide for setting out the practical regime of right to information for citizens and to secure access to information under the control of public authorities to promote transparency and accountability in the working of every public authority. The Act also constituted a body of Central Information Commission and State Information Commissions for effective implementation of the Act and to inquire complaints of denial of the information, and to solve the dispute arising while functioning of the Act. The RTI Act 2005 opens pathways to governmental policies and decisions to ensure that these are consistent with the principles of public interest, probity and justice. It is also an instrument to usher in participative governance and help citizens to influence policy formulation and program implementation by securing the legally enforceable right to know.

Part III of the Indian Constitution deals with Fundamental Rights. The Right to freedom of speech and expression inter alia contributes vastly supporting the Right to Information. For healthy growth of democratic society, transparency, accountability and openness carry high importance. The Indian Supreme Court stated that a government that functions in secrecy not only acts against democratic decency, but also buries itself with its own burial.[1] The preamble of the RTI Act 2005 also categorically mentions that the democracy requires an informed citizenry and transparency of information which are vital to its functioning and also to contain corruption and to hold Governments and their instrumentalities accountable to the governed.[2] Thus, seeking and obtaining information are part of that human right and it is an ultimate sign of participatory democracy. Rabindranath Tagore, one of the great Nobel laureates in the nineteenth century expressed the importance of freedom of information. He said, "Where the mind is without fear and the head is held high; Where knowledge is free [...]; Where the mind is led forward by thee into ever-widening thought and action – Into that heaven of freedom, my Father, let my country awake."[3]

---

[1]Justice Krishna Iyer in Supreme Court, *Maneka Gandhi v. Union of India*, (1978) AIR SC 59 (Judgment of 25 January 1978) emphasized on the transparency in the Government as it is generally said that power corrupts and absolute power corrupts absolutely.

[2]Preamble of the RTI Act 2005 available at http://righttoinformation.gov.in/rti-act.pdf (Accessed on 15 February 2017).

[3]Verse xxxv from Gitanjli by Rabindranath Tagore.

The Constitution of India, under Article 19, recognizes access to information and right to know as a basic fundamental right of a citizen. Therefore, exercising the right to know is the essential first step in strengthening citizen leadership and in democratizing governance. Citizen participation if the crux of any democratic governance and thus, if they are kept apart from the access to information, they are not only deprived of information relevant to their own lives and livelihood, but also denied the possibility of acting as citizens.

The Right to Information Act grants every citizen the right to seek information from every public authority about the various tasks and activities performed by them. The Act mainly focuses on maximum disclosure and minimum exceptions by providing an appellate mechanism for adjudication and review of functioning of public authorities, as well as penal provisions to check and contain intentional and willful non-disclosure of information.

In this paper, the Right to Information Act in India is compared with the Access to Information enacted in Brazil. Both the acts are enacted with an aim of achieving transparency, accountability and good governance in the system. This contribution focuses on the scope of the right to access by analyzing the aspect and provisions in Indian and Brazilian statutes. The paper also throws light on the issue of secrecy provisions for providing information in terms of protection of public interests and personal data, procedure and judicial decisions.

## 2 Scope of Access to Information

The scope and extent of coverage of access to information legislation is fundamental to its efficacy. Legislations that have limited the scope of their coverage have been regarded as deficient[4] and not conducive of transparency and accountability. The scope, laying down the coverage and applicability of such legislations, is inherently fundamental to their very ideals. In a sensitive issue as access to information, its scope can normatively be described as its essence.

India recognized the need for legislations regarding access to information in the past few decades. The Freedom of Information Act was passed by the Central Government in December 2002.[5] However, it was widely criticized by the civil society for its limited scope and the breadth of its exemptions. The overall efficiency, applicability and citizen friendliness of the Act was questioned because of its greater protection of confidential machinery owing to its extremely myopic scope.

These criticisms regarding the scope of the Act, amongst other factors, lead to the passing of the RTI Act, which sought to expand its scope for increasing its accessibility and efficiency.[6] The Act was hailed as groundbreaking for its

[4]Commonwealth Human Rights Initiative 2004.

[5]Naib 2011.

[6]Naib 2011.

increased focus on enhancing the scope of the earlier legislation, consequently enhancing the efficacy of the Act.[7]

To undertake an effective comparative analysis of the Indian law on access to information, a two-tiered approach would suffice. First, analysis has to be undertaken regarding the legislations themselves, expounding on the core principles of law provided. Second, it is imperative to compare the application of the law as decreed by the judicial systems of the respective countries, along with their usage in actual practice.

## 3 Comparative Perspectives on Access to Information Legislation

As Brazilian laws are responsible for the regulation of the constitutional provisions regarding the right to access of information provided in Articles 5, 37 and 216, their scope, perceptibly, seems broad. Article 5 establishes the constitutional right of access to information, as Article 5.14 states "[. . .] access to information is assured to everyone, protecting the confidentiality of sources when necessary for professional activity".[8] The other aforementioned articles further substantiate this guarantee.

While considering the Constitution of India, though right of access to information has not been guaranteed, it has been interpreted to implicitly contain this right.[9] Further, it is also recognized that this right can be enforced in a court of law.[10] A broader meaning of the terminology of the right of freedom of speech and expression ensures the right to access to information to its citizens.

The overarching term 'scope of access to information' can be broken down into several fundamental units for a broader understanding of the concept. Questions regarding this would include the scope of the extension of this right to people (including the grounds for requesting the access), the scope of the applicability of this right on governmental (or other) machinery. Further, the type of access is also discussed, concerning requirements that need to be fulfilled before a request can be made. Instead, an independent unit is devoted for them.

[7]Naib 2011.

[8]Article 5, item 14 of the Constitution of the Federative Republic of Brazil (1988).

[9]Naib 2011.

[10]Naib 2011.

## 3.1 The Scope of the Right

Article 3 of the Brazilian Law N°12.527/2011 lays down the scope of the type, including qualitative aspects, of access to information law.[11] The objective provided in Article 5, "[...] duty of the state to guarantee the right to access information, which will be conceded by means of objective and speedy procedures, in a transparent and clear manner, and in easily understandable language",[12] is enhanced by the guidelines provided in Article 3. This article lays down certain guidelines that are expected to identify and enhance such qualitative aspects, these guidelines being "observance of a general rule of publicity with secrecy being an exception; dissemination of information of public interest, independent of requests; use of communication means made feasible by information technology; promotion of the development of a culture of transparency in public administration; and development of social control of public administration."[13] This right is constitutionally extended to the citizens of Brazil.

Further articles articulate the elaboration of this right. Article 7 of the Brazilian Law establishes the right to obtain guidance regarding the process,[14] documental records that may be uncompiled in public archives,[15] information regarding activities of organizations,[16] including their policies,[17] organizations and services and information regarding administration of public assets, among others.[18]

In India, the RTI Act regulates the right of access to information. Sec. 3 of the Act specifies that all citizens have the right to information.[19] These citizens have a right of access to information. The right to information is defined as "[...] the right to information accessible under this Act which is held by or under the control of any public authority and includes the right to inspection of work, documents, records; taking notes, extracts or certified copies of documents or records; taking certified samples of material; obtaining information in the form of diskettes, floppies, tapes, video cassettes or in any other electronic mode or through printouts where such information is stored in a computer or in any other device."[20] Further, the concept of 'records' is elaborated as "[...] any document, manuscript and file; any microfilm, microfiche and facsimile copy of a document; any reproduction of image or images embodied in such microfilm (whether enlarged or not); and any other material produced by a computer or any other device."[21]

[11] Article 3 of the Law N° 12.527/2011.

[12] Article 5 of the Law N° 12.527/2011.

[13] Article 3 of the Law N° 12.527/2011.

[14] Article 7 para 1 of the Law N° 12.527/2011.

[15] Article 7 para 2 of the Law N° 12.527/2011.

[16] Article 7 para 4 of the Law N° 12.527/2011.

[17] Article 7 para 5 of the Law N° 12.527/2011.

[18] Article 7 para 6 of the Law N° 12.527/2011.

[19] Sec. 3 RTI Act.

[20] Sec. 2 point (j) RTI Act.

[21] Sec. 2 point (i) RTI Act.

### 3.2 The Scope of the Applicability of the Right

Article 1 of the Brazilian Law N°12.527/2011, along with subsequent provisions, lays down the scope of the applicability of the right of access to information. According to Article 1, the law is applicable to "[...] Public entities integrated in the direct administration of Executive, Legislative (including Court of Accounts) and the Judicial powers, and of the Public Prosecutor's Office"[22] and "[...] Quasi-governmental organizations, public foundations, public enterprises, mixed capital corporations and remaining entities directly or indirectly controlled by the Union, States, Federal District and Municipalities".[23]

Article 2 of the Brazilian Law expands upon the scope of the law by enhancing its applicability to "[...] non-profit public entities that receive public resources, to undertake actions of public interest, directly from the budget or by means of social aid, management contract, partnership agreement, conventions, adjustments or other similar instruments".[24]

The Decree N° 7.724/2012 improves on the provisions of the 2011 Law to streamline the scope of the right of access to information. Chapter II of the Decree concerns this scope.

Article 5 of the Decree establishes that "[...] All government entities of direct administration, quasi- governmental organizations, mixed capital corporations, public or semi-public companies and other entities controlled directly or indirectly by the Federal Government are subject to the provisions of this Decree."[25]

Meanwhile, Sec. 4 of the RTI Act contains provisions regarding the obligations of public authorities. Public authorities are defined as "[...] any authority or body or institution of self-government established or constituted by or under the constitution, by any other law made by Parliament, by any other law made by State Legislature, by notification issued or order made by the appropriate Government, and includes anybody owned, controlled or substantially financed and non-Government organisation substantially financed, directly or indirectly by funds provided by the appropriate Government."[26]

### 3.3 Type of the Access

According to the formulation of the 2012 Brazilian Law, the form detailing the access to information request must contain "the applicant's name; the number of [the applicant's] current identity document; a clear and precise specification of the

[22] Article 1 para of the Law N° 12.527/2011.

[23] Article 1 para 2 of the Law N° 12.527/2011.

[24] Article 2 of the Law N° 12.527/2011.

[25] Article 5 of Decree No. 7.724/2012.

[26] Sec. 2 point (h) RTI Act.

requested information; and the applicant's postal or e-mail address for receipt of communications or of the requested information."[27]

In India, here is no prescribed format of application for seeking information. The application can be made on plain paper. The applicant should mention the address where the information is required to be sent.

## 3.4 Exemption for Providing Information

India considers the Right to Information as a basic human right. Though Article 19.1 point (a) of the Constitution of India recognizes the Right to Information as a part of the basic fundamental right of freedom of speech and expression, the second part of the Article 19 of the Constitution provides reasonable restrictions for using the right.[28] Some exemptions do not allow public authorities to disclose the information. The statues like the Official Secrets Act 1923 and the Indian Evidence Act 1872 contain certain provisions which immune the public authorities from disclosing information.

Sec. 8.1 and Sec. 9 of the RTI Act enumerate the types of information that is exempt from disclosure. The information related to affect sovereignty and integrity of India, information affecting to security, strategic, scientific or economic interest of the State, information forbidden by the order of court of law, information causing breach of privilege of parliament, information including commercial confidence, trade secrets, intellectual properties, information received in confidence of government, information available to a person in his fiduciary relationship, information relating to personal information which has no relationship with public activity or interest are the various kinds of information which are exempted.

According to the Brazilian Law, the information relating to security of society and of the state has been considered as secret information. Chapter V speaks about the information classified under security classification. In addition, the information in which secrecy is required by law can also be considered as secret information. This act classifies information under the level and period of secrecy. The information affecting to national defense, sovereignty, integrity of national territory, relating to nation's negotiations to internal relation, information jeopardizing safety or health of the population and strategic operations or plans of armed forces, scientific or technological research and development projects etc. The act classifies the security of the information as per the public's interest in knowing the information, and to apply the least restrictive criteria possible.

[27] Article 12 of Decree No. 7.724/2012.

[28] Article 19.2 of the Constitution of India states that 'the State can impose reasonable restrictions on it'.

Further, the information has also been classified into top secret, secret and restricted information. Information relating to President, Vice President and their spouses, children, are also considered under restricted category.

In the case of *Reserve Bank of India v. Jayantilal N. Mistry*, information sought from Reserve Bank of India and other banks were rejected because of economic interest, commercial confidence, fiduciary relationship and public interest. Reserve Bank of India took stand that the information sought was exempted under Sec. 8.1 points (a), (d) and (e) of the RTI Act. It was also contended that the provisions of the RTI Act could not override the confidentiality conferred on Reserve Bank of India. Supreme Court of India upholding the decision given by Central Information Commission stated that, "The ideal of 'Government of People' makes it necessary that people have access to information on matters of public concern. The free flow of information about the affairs of Government paves way for debate in public policy and fosters accountability in Government. It creates a condition for 'Open Government' which is the foundation of democracy."[29] Thus, the Supreme Court of India asked RBI to provide the information.

## 3.5 *Judicial Protection and Practice*

The legislative basis of the right of access to information notwithstanding, another key concern arises regarding first, the implementation aspect of the Act and second, the evolution and inception of principles governing the aforementioned regulation, principles not covered in the ambit of the legislative provisions. This practice has been supplemented by judicial decisions that seek to add another practical dimension to the pre-existing legislative basis.

Article 8 of the Brazilian Law highlights the duty of public entities regarding the dissemination of information, irrespective of enquiries pertaining to the same.[30] This 'active transparency model' focuses on the dissemination of "record of the responsibilities and structure, addresses and telephones of the respective units and schedules of office hours; records of any relocation or transfer of financial resources; records of expenses; information regarding a bidding process, including the respective notices and results, and all the contracts signed; general data for monitoring programmes, actions, projects and works undertaken by entities and institutions; and answers to society's most frequently asked questions."[31]

This model has to be regulated by several procedural conditions, also provided in Article 8 of the Brazilian Law. These concern the following requirements: "contain a content research tool that allows access to information in an objective, transparent

[29]Supreme Court of India, *Reserve Bank of India v. Jayantilal N. Mistry*, (2016) 3 SCC 525 (Judgment of 16 December 2015).

[30]Article 8 of the Law N° 12.527/2011.

[31]Article 8 of the Law N° 12.527/2011.

and clear manner, and in easily understandable language; allow for the recording of reports in several electronic formats, including open non-proprietary, such as spreadsheets and text to facilitate analysis of information; allow for external systems automated access in open, structured formats and that are machine legible; detailed dissemination of the formats used to structure information; guarantee the authenticity and integrity of the accessible information; keep the accessible information up to date; designate the location and instructions that allow an interested party to communicate, electronically or by telephone, with the entity or institution that maintains the site."[32]

This was further enhanced by the 2012 Decree, which specifies the meeting of the following requirements: "contain an information access request form; contain a content search tool that enables access to information objectively, transparently, clearly and in easily understandable language; make it possible to record reports in various electronic formats, including open and non-proprietary formats, such as spreadsheets and text, so as to facilitate the analysis of information; enable automated access by external systems in open, structured, machine- readable formats; provide detailed disclosure of the formats used for information structuring; ensure the authenticity and integrity of the accessible information; instruct the applicant on how to communicate with the institution by e-mail or telephone; and ensure that the contents are accessible to persons with disabilities."[33]

In India, Sec. 4 of the RTI mandates several obligations to be performed by public authorities, including publishing "the particulars of its organisation, functions and duties; the powers and duties of its officers and employees; procedure followed in the decision making process, including channels of supervision and accountability; the norms set by it for the discharge of its functions; the rules, regulations, instructions, manuals and records, held by it or under its control or used by its employees for discharging its functions; a statement of the categories of documents that are held by it or under its control; the particulars of any arrangement that exists for consultation with, or representation by, the members of the public in relation to the formulation of its policy or implementation thereof; Sec. 4.1 point (b) (viii) a statement of the boards, councils, committees and other bodies consisting of two or more persons constituted as its part or for the purpose of its advice, and as to whether meetings of those boards; councils, committees and other bodies are open to the public, or the minutes of such meetings are accessible for public; a directory of its officers and employees; the monthly remuneration received by each of its officers and employees, including the system of compensation as provided in its regulations; the budget allocated to each of its agency, indicating the particulars of all plans, proposed expenditures and reports on disbursements made; the manner of execution of subsidy programmes, including the amounts allocated and the details of beneficiaries of such programmes; particulars of recipients of concessions, permits or authorisations granted by it; details in respect of the

[32] Article 8 of the Law N° 12.527/2011.

[33] Article 8 of Decree N° 7.724/2012.

information, available to or held by it, reduced in an electronic form; the particulars of facilities available to citizens for obtaining information, including the working hours of a library or reading room, if maintained for public use; the names, designations and other particulars of the Public Information Officers; such other information as may be prescribed."[34]

## 3.6 Relationship Between RTI Act and Rules of Access to Public Documents

There is not per se an administrative procedural law in India. However, in India administrative law has been evolved through various legislations and judgments by the Supreme Court and various High Courts. Indian Constitution also provides basic fundamental rights to every citizen to enshrine inter alia natural justice and access to information. The Supreme Court of India well recognized that the right to information has been included within the right to freedom of speech and expression as guaranteed in Article 19.1 point (a) of the Indian Constitution.[35] Transparency is an utmost important part of the good governance. It not only increases participation of the people in the governance but also provides legitimacy to the State. Principal of natural justice requires greater transparency in governance as it derecognizes various privileges which promotes secrecy in the administration.

The Indian Official Secrets Act was enacted in the time of British regime in the year 1923. It was passed to restrict the use and dissemination of government information. Wade called this act as "a hasty piece of catch all legislation which made a criminal offence of all unauthorised disclosure of information from official sources regardless of the question whether the public interest really demand secrecy".[36] Similarly, there was restriction to disclose information under the Atomic Energy Act 1962. The debate over the right to information as a fundamental right got legal backing after the passing of the RTI Act. The Act itself provides procedure for the access of public documents.

In recent case of *Kerala Public Service Commission and Another v. State Information Commission and Another*,[37] the Supreme Court of India discussed about the nature of fiduciary relationship and disclosure of information. In this case the Apex Court of India held that the information seeker has a right to get the information about his answer sheets and details of the interview marks as it is not the information that can be kept by public authority under the fiduciary relationship. However, the

[34]Sec. 4 RTI Act.

[35]The Supreme Court of India in Case *Bennett Coleman v. India*, (1972) 2 SCC 788 (Judgment of 30 October 1972) for the first time recognized the right to information as a fundamental right.

[36]Wade & Forsyth 2010, p 63. The same statement is reiterated by Sathe 2004, p. 646.

[37]Supreme Court of India, *Kerala Public Service Commission and Another v. State Information Commission and Another*, (2016) 3 SCC 417 (Judgment of 4 February 2016).

information relating to details of the examiner cannot be provided as it comes under the purview of fiduciary relationship between public authority and examiner. After the landmark decision *Justice K.S. Puttaswamy (Retd.) & Another v Union of India and Others*, Writ Petition (Civil) No. 494 of 2012 (decided on August, 24, 2017), wherein the Supreme Court of India held that individual privact is a fundamental right, it has become very interesting to see the effect of the right to privacy on the right to information.

## 4 Challenges Faced by RTI and the Future Possibility in the Brazilian Law

The Right to Information Act has been quite successful since the time of its inception; however, there are still great milestones to cover. Like any other law, the RTI also has a few drawbacks, which could be a future possibility in the Brazilian Law as well. The researcher would be listing the drawbacks seen over the course of time of the RTI Act in India and comparing with the future possibility with the Brazilian Law. The following points can be mainly considered as challenges faced in the effective implementation of the RTI Act. Considering the recency of the Brazilian Law, it is important to look into these challenges for proper enforcement of that Brazilian Law.

### *4.1 Low Public Awareness*

One of the key drawbacks, which need to be dealt with by the government, is the fact that the RTI is still a vague concept or even unknown to some in the country. As of Sec. 26 of the RTI Act, it is the government's responsibility to ensure financial support or making sure resources are given to that section of the society to ensure that the Act is in the awareness of all the citizens.[38]

A survey conducted by PricewaterhouseCoopers (PWC) in five states of India, namely Andhra Pradesh, Assam, Maharashtra, Orissa and Uttar Pradesh in the year 2009, has shown that the level of awareness not only differs among states but also among gender and caste. Women accounted to having less knowledge and awareness of the RTI than men have, and the difference varied from 9% to 20%; however, the average awareness among women was 12% as opposed to 26% among men.[39] The awareness level among general caste people was higher in comparison to those

[38]Khan & Premji 2012, http://journalofdevelopment.wordpress.com/2012/10/12/a-policy-critique-of-right-to-information-act (Accessed on 23 September 2014).

[39]PricewaterhouseCoopers 2009, http://righttoinformation.gov.in/rticorner/studybypwc/key_issues.pdf (Accessed on 23 September 2014).

who belonged to the ST/SC caste, 27% and 14% respectively. It was also noted that those who belonged to an urban surrounding had a higher level of awareness as compared to those from rural areas.[40]

To assume the same problems for Brazil in this scenario might be a challenge because of the difference in situation and ratio in the two countries, for example in India the sex ratio of men is much higher in comparison to that of the women, however it is the opposite in Brazil. In India, there are 107 males for every 100 females, however in Brazil there are 97 males for every 100 females.[41] Consequently, if a situation is to arise where the Brazilian Law may face problems of awareness levels it might be contradictory to the statistics of India because of the difference in sex ratio in the countries.

One of the other major factors, which would also have a contradictory result in case of Brazil as opposed to India in terms of awareness of the law, could be the literacy rate in each country. In India, the fact that most people are unaware about the RTI Act could be a direct result of the low literacy rate. According to the census of 2013, the literacy rate in India is 74.04%, however in Brazil it is 90%.[42] However, a similar fact, which would make the possibility of awareness in Brazil a similar fashion to that of India, could be the caste structure present there. In India, through the statistics, it was seen that the general caste had a higher percentage of awareness as compared to the other backward classes (OBC) and the Scheduled caste/Scheduled tribe (SC/ST) committee. Similarly even in Brazil there seems to be an imaginary caste system, consisting of the Whites, Afro-Brazilians, Mulato, OBC and the Indigenous people. Such a caste system even if imaginary would exist in the mind of people thus having an impact on the varied level of awareness among them.

One of the other notable issues that must be looked into is the fact that the awareness of the Act is not only low, but the quality of the information that the citizens have is not of an adequate level. Put simply, the quality of the information found among the public seems to be of a very low and unacceptable level. The survey conducted by PWC would further explain this concept. The survey involved asking those people who claimed to be aware of the RTI provisions and mandates, trick questions or trap questions to properly test their knowledge. The most startling result was that the awareness level of Sec. 18 RTI was 48% among the citizens who were not happy with the response from the Public Information Officer (PIO). Out of these 48% people only 20% of the people used it from 48% who knew about it.[43]

Similarly, in Brazil, the problem of awareness might come as an issue among the public, however, this problem is directly related to the working capacity of the

[40] PricewaterhouseCoopers 2009.

[41] United Nations Department of Economic and Social Affairs/Population Division (2013), https://www.unfpa.org/gender/docs/Sex_Ratio_by_Country_in_2013.pdf (Accessed on 23 September 2014).

[42] Statistics provided by UNICEF Brazil http://www.unicef.org/infobycountry/brazil_statistics.html (Accessed on 23 September 2014).

[43] PricewaterhouseCoopers 2009.

government and their efforts to maximize their roles for quality high-level awareness to be available to the citizens of their country.

### 4.2 Constraints Faced in Filing Applications

The RTI presently contains of three such provisions, which directly or impliedly hold importance in helping out the citizens of India to file complaints to gain knowledge on the inquiries that they possess. Sec. 6 of the RTI Act deals with the procedure to be followed for obtaining information. As per Article 6.1 of the RTI Act, the request can be made in writing or through electronic means in English or Hindi or in the official language of the area in which the application is being made. It is also prescribed in the section that if any request cannot be made in writing the Central Public Information Officer (CPIO) or State Public Information Officer (SPIO) will render all reasonable assistance to the person making the request orally to reduce the same in writing.

Further, Sec. 26 of the RTI Act talks about publishing of user manuals for proper guidance of citizens to help them with drafting and submitting of application. However, the five states that have been surveyed by the PWC showed that in none of the five states (Assam, Maharashtra, Uttar Pradesh, Orissa and Andhra Pradesh) there is an availability of the guidelines to help citizens.[44] The Act clearly mentions that it is the duty of the government at the point of time to publish these guidelines in all states through the Nodal department. Consequently, the government's laxity in publishing these guidelines has acted as a great step back for the Act and thus making it difficult for laypersons to actually submit and file an application of inquiry. The fact that this problem, which is rooted in the mechanics of the government itself, is further supported by the fact that the survey showed that 52% of the citizens had requested for a guideline manual to seek more knowledge to file an application.[45]

Such a problem in Brazil would not be easy to presume, as it would depend on the type of government, the various initiatives taken by the government in handling issues related to grass root level implementation and proper guidance to the citizens.

### 4.3 Poor Quality of Information Provided

One of the other drawbacks, which has led to the set back of the RTI Act, is the fact that the information provided to those who file applications of inquiry are not of a

[44]PricewaterhouseCoopers 2009.

[45]PricewaterhouseCoopers 2009.

satisfactory level. As the Act suggests it is the right of every citizen to be fully aware and more importantly rightly aware of any grievance on any issues that they face. This is further supported by the survey wherein 70% of the citizens are unsatisfied with the quality of information provided to them. Among the OBC/ST/SC community, the rate is higher to an 86% and the states which have the highest level of dissatisfaction are Andhra Pradesh (91%) and Uttar Pradesh (96%). Further, the survey was conducted on the quality of the information based on two different grounds, i.e., incomplete information provided and irrelevant information provided; again, Andhra Pradesh had an alarming rate of 98% and 82% respectively.[46]

The main reasons for low quality of information provided to the application as per the survey are:

1. The record management practices within the public authority
2. The transparency in the process
3. The training provided to the concerned PIO
4. Drafting of the RTI application itself

For an act like the RTI to be successful in all spheres requires constant work on side of the government in its implementation in the correct manner and making sure the authorities who are directly working with the citizens are competent enough to avoid failure or unnecessary hassles. The role of the information commission assumes importance in maintaining a process to continuously identify the public authorities that do not posses an infrastructure for compliance to the RTI Act and making them comply with the provision of this Act as per Sec. 19.8 point (a).[47] Again, such a problem could only be avoided through effective and strong government working throughout the implementation of the Act and thus for Brazil it would entirely depend upon the type of government that is at the center.

However, the problems that have arisen through the act do not only reach to the demanding section of the society, even the supply side that is the ones who are trying to implement the act are facing problems.

## 5 Comparison of Procedure of Indian and Brazilian Right to Information

Under the RTI Act, every public authority, within 100 days of the enactment of the Act, has to designate as many officers as the Central Public Information Officers or State Public Information Officers in all administrative units or offices under it as may be necessary to provide information to persons requesting for the information under this Act.[48] In *R. K. Jain v. CESTAT*[49] it was held that no

[46]PricewaterhouseCoopers 2009.

[47]PricewaterhouseCoopers 2009.

[48]Sec. 5 RTI Act.

[49]Central Information Commission, *R. K. Jain v. CESTAT*, CIC/SS/A/2011/001982 (Decision of 18 December 2012).

specific order was required to appoint deemed CPIO. As soon as CPIO seeks assistance of any officer, who is holder of information, under Sec. 5.4 of the RTI Act, he is treated as deemed CPIO under Sec. 5.5 of the RTI Act for that purpose. Thus, a person who is holder of information and whose assistance is sought is deemed CPIO. Under the Brazilian legislation all the institutions and entities have to create a citizen information service (CIS) with the objective of providing the public with support and guidance for information access; providing information about the processing of documents in the units; and receiving and registering information access requests. It is the responsibility of the CIS to receive access requests, to register them in a specific electronic system and issue a reference number, which shall contain the date of submission of the request and to forward the received and registered requests to the unit in charge of supplying the information, where appropriate.[50] This CIS has to be established in a specified physical unit that is accessible and open to the public. The local units that do not have a CIS have to offer a service of receipt and registration of information access requests. If they do not possess the required information, the request shall be routed to the CIS of the central institution, which will give the applicant the reference number and date of receipt of the request, which shall mark the commencement of the time limit for response.[51]

In *R. K. Jain v. Department of Legal Affairs*,[52] the power of Sections 6 and 7 of the RTI Act was dealt with. The appeal was filed to challenge order because CAPIO had provided wrong information and if CAPIO was authorized to respond to application made under Sec. 6.1 of the Act. It was held that the Act does not authorize CAPIO/SAPIO to respond to RTI applications. This duty is specifically entrusted upon CPIO/SPIO under Section 7.1 of the Act. Therefore, CPIO(s) and CAPIO (s) of public authority were advised to act as per law. Therefore, CAPIO was not authorized to respond to application made under Sec. 6.1 of the Act. According to Articles 10 and 11 para 5 and 6 of the Brazilian Law N° 12.527 the request to obtain information can be made by legitimate means, such as by telephone, e-mail or postal correspondence. This request will be made available in both electronic format and hardcopy on the website and in the CIS of the institutions and entities.

As per Sec. 6.2 of the RTI Act, the applicant requesting information shall not be asked about the reason for such request and the authorities shall seek no personal details except contact details. In *Re Manoj Kumar Saini*,[53] it was held that in a dowry case that invariably have the component of 'Criminal Breach of Trust' relating to misappropriation of property, the applicant has a right to know the details of property reflected in ITRs, which is allegedly misappropriated. Mandate

[50] Article 9 of the Law N° 12.527/2011.

[51] Article 10 of the Law N° 12.527/2011.

[52] Central Information Commission, *R. K. Jain v. Department of Legal Affairs*, CIC/SS/C/2013/000308 (Decision of 21 October 2013).

[53] Central Information Commission, *Manoj Kumar Saini v. The Chief Commissioner, Income Tax*, CIC/Ls/A/2010/001044-Ds (Decision of 24 March 2011).

of disclosure of personal information is stricter because it appends the word 'larger' to 'public interest'. Mere public interest would not be sufficient to get the required information such as ITRs of an assessed, unless the applicant can prove that a 'larger public interest' demands such disclosure. Similarly, Article 14 of the Brazilian Law prohibits keeping the motives for request of information as a requirement while seeking information under the Act.

As per Sec. 6.3 of the RTI Act, if the information requested for pertains to a public authority other than to the one who the request is made to or is more closely related to another public authority the public authority to which such application is made shall transfer the application or such part of it as may be appropriate to that other public authority in maximum of 5 days and inform the applicant immediately about such transfer. In *R.K. Jain v. Department of Legal Affairs,*[54] the application under RTI was filed to Solicitor General of India but responded by Department of Legal Affairs. The issue was that whether appellant's application was rightly transferred to Department of Legal Affairs. It was held because there was no CPIO designated in office of Solicitor General of India and Respondents look after administrative function of Solicitor General of India. The department of Legal Affairs and Officer of Solicitor General of India was in the same footing. In *R.K. Jainv. CPIO, Cabinet Secretariat*[55] the CPIO in the Cabinet Secretariat did not transfer the RTI application within 5 days of receiving it as per the provisions of Sec. 6.3 of the RTI Act. Consequently, the appellant received the information much beyond the stipulated period of 30 days. Further, it was held that the appellate authority was wrong in not giving an opportunity of hearing to the appellant when he had asked for it specifically.

There is no such provision of transfer of information under Brazilian legislation. As per Chapter III and IV dealing with active and passive transparency every institution and entity is required to make available basic information regarding the working etc. of the institution on the website (the particulars of which are prescribed under Articles 7 and 8 of the legislation). Also every institution and entity is required to set up Citizen Information Service with the objective of providing the public with support and guidance for information access; providing information about the processing of documents in the units; and receiving and registering information access requests. The responsibilities of CIS are prescribed under Article 9 of the legislation and the information regarding location of CIS is provided in Article 10 of the Brazilian Law.

Under the Brazilian legislation, the information access request has to have the applicant's name; the number of [the applicant's] current identity document; a clear and precise specification of the requested information and the applicant's postal or

---

[54]Central Information Commission, *R. K. Jain v. Department of Legal Affairs*, CIC/SS/C/2013/000308 (Decision of 21 October 2013).

[55]Central Information Commission, *R.K. Jain v. CPIO, Cabinet Secretariat*, CIC/SM/A/2012/000776 (Decision of 11 December 2012).

e-mail address for receipt of communications or of the requested information.[56] There are no such prescribed requisites for the content of the request under RTI.

As per Sec. 7.1 of the RTI Act, the CPIO or SPIO shall provide the required information as soon as possible and in any case within 30 days of the receipt of the request. The authority can also reject the request if it falls under Sections 8 and 9 of the Act within 30 days of the receipt of the request. If the information requested for concerns the life or liberty of a person, the same shall be provided within 48 h of the receipt of the request. If the information is not furnished within 30 days time limit, the authority is deemed to have rejected the request. Under the Brazilian Law, the access is to be granted immediately after date of submission of the request to the CIS. An initial period of 20 days is given for responding to the request, which can be extended by 10 days subject to sending the applicant a statement of justification before the expiration of the initial 20-day time limit.[57]

Under the Indian Act if a request has been rejected the CPIO or SPIO shall communicate to the person making the request the reasons for such rejection; the period within which an appeal against such rejection may be preferred; and the particulars of the appellate authority.[58] In the Brazilian legislation, if the information access request is denied the applicant is sent, within the time limit for response a communication containing the reasons for denying access and the underlying legal basis; the possibility of appeal, to which authority appeal shall be made, and within what time limit; and the possibility of presenting a request to declassify the information, where applicable, with an indication of the classifying authority that will evaluate the request.[59]

In certain cases where a decision is taken to provide the information on payment of any further fee representing the cost of providing the information, (e.g.: when the requested information is to be provided in printed or electronic format[60]) intimation will be sent to the person making the request with the details of further fees representing the cost of providing the information as determined by him, together with the calculations made to arrive at the amount in accordance with fee prescribed.[61] The intimation will request him to deposit that fees and the period intervening between the dispatch of the said intimation and payment of fees shall be excluded in calculating the period of 30 days. No fees shall be charged from a person below the poverty line[62] and the person will be provided the information free of charge if the authorities fail to prescribe to the tie limit.[63] According to Article 18 of the Brazilian Law when supplying the information involves the reproduction of documents,

[56]Article 12 of the Law N° 12.527/2011.

[57]Article 15 of the Law N° 12.527/2011.

[58]Sec. 7.8 RTI Act.

[59]Article 19 of the Law N° 12.527/2011.

[60]Sec. 7.5 RTI Act.

[61]Sec. 7.3 RTI Act.

[62]Sec. 7.5 RTI Act

[63]Sec. 7.6 RTI Act.

the institution, within the time limit for response to the request, shall provide the applicant with the Federal Payment Form [*Guia de Recolhimento da Unión* (GRU)] or an equivalent document to pay for the costs of the services and materials used.

There is a special provision in cases where disabled request for information under both RTI Act and Brazilian Law. Special assistance is to be provided by CPIO and SPIO under the Indian Law[64] and under Article 8.3 (8) of the Brazilian Law the websites of the institutions and entities, in accordance with the regulation of the Ministry of Planning, Budgeting and Management meet to ensure that the contents are accessible to persons with disabilities.

In the Indian Act, when a CPIO or SPIO intends to disclose any information or record that pertains to a third party and has been treated as confidential by that third party, the SPIO or CPIO has to give a written notice to such third party within 5 days of the request and of the fact that the CPIO or SPIO, as the case may be, intends to disclose the information or record and invite the third party to make a submission in writing or orally, regarding whether the information should be disclosed, and such submission of the third party shall be kept in view while taking a decision about disclosure of information.[65] In the case of trade or commercial secrets protected by law, disclosure may be allowed if the public interest in disclosure outweighs in importance any possible harm or injury to the interests of such third party.[66] The third party shall, within 10 days from the date of receipt of such notice, be given the opportunity to make representation against the proposed disclosure. While under the Brazilian Law, access to personal information by third parties is conditioned upon signing a declaration of assumption of responsibility concerns the obligations to be assumed by the applicant, which shall regulate the purpose and intended use underlying the third party's authorization. Thus, the utilization of personal information by third parties is restricted to the purpose and intended use underlying the access authorization, and any other manner of use is prohibited, and any person who obtains access to the personal information of third parties shall be held responsible, in the manner prescribed by Law, for the misuse of said information.[67]

Under the Indian Act, if a person does not receive a decision within the time specified or is aggrieved by a decision of the CPIO or SPIO he/she may, 30 days from the expiry of such period or from the receipt of such a decision, prefer an appeal to such officer who is senior in rank to the CPIO or SPIO as the case may be.[68] Such officer may admit the appeal after the expiry of the period of 30 days if he or she is satisfied that the appellant was prevented by sufficient cause from filing

[64] Sec. 7.4 RTI Act.

[65] Sec. 11 RTI Act.

[66] Sec. 11 RTI Act.

[67] Articles 33 and 34 para 2 of the Law N° 12.527/2011.

[68] Sec. 19 RTI Act.

the appeal in time. A second appeal against the decision shall lie within 90 days from the date on which the decision should have been made or was actually received, with the Central Information Commission or the State Information Commission.[69]

In the Brazilian legislation, if the access to information is denied or the reasons for denial of access are not supplied, the applicant may submit an appeal within 10 days after the date of notice of the decision to the authority hierarchically superior to the authority that made the decision, which shall evaluate the appeal within 5 days after the submission of the appeal.[70] If this appeal is denied, the applicant may submit another appeal within 10 days after notice of the decision to the institution's or highest authority, which shall express its opinion within 5 days after receipt of the appeal. The time limit for submitting a complaint shall commence 30 days after the submission of the request.[71] In case of denial of the appeal or dismissal of the complaint, the applicant may submit an appeal within 10 days after notice of the decision to the Federal Comptroller-General's Office, which shall express its opinion within 5 days after receipt of the appeal. If the appeal is denied, the Federal Comptroller-General's Office shall set a time limit for the institution to comply with the decision.[72] If the appeal is denied by the Federal Comptroller-General's Office, the applicant may submit an appeal, within 10 days after notice of the decision, to the Joint Committee of Information Re-evaluation.[73]

## 6 Judicial Protection

The present part of our article will deal with the perspective of the Indian Judiciary over the conflict between the right to know and the need of secrecy in some areas. There are some issues on which information cannot be disclosed because of the sensitive nature of that area. In those cases, a balance has to be struck between the two competing interests—the citizens' right to know and the State's right to protect the information.

This part includes both pre-RTI and post-RTI cases. The Indian Judiciary has always strived towards more transparency and accountability in the society. The response of the Indian Judiciary to the present applications under the RTI Act has a very strong basis in the way the Supreme Court protected the Right to Information when the RTI Act was not there.

[69]Sec. 19 RTI Act.

[70]Article 21 of the Law N° 12.527/2011.

[71]Article 22 of the Law N° 12.527/2011.

[72]Article 23 of the Law N° 12.527/2011.

[73]Article 24 of the Law N° 12.527/2011.

## 6.1 National Security, Public Interest and Other Heads Under Section 8.1 point (a) of the RTI Act

### 6.1.1 Dinesh Trivedi v. Union of India[74]

In the present case, the member of Rajya Sabha, Dinesh Trivedi, alleged that the report of Vohra Committee tabled in the Parliament is not an authenticated one because of the difference in the number of pages as tabled in the Parliament and as stated by one of the member of the Central Government. He also alleged that there was mismatch between the numbers of paragraphs. He also demanded that the reports of various intelligence services, which formed the basis of this report, should also be made public.

The Vohra Committee was appointed under the chairmanship of N.N. Vohra, which would study all the information regarding the Mafia groups and their activities and accordingly suggest the future course of action. Several agencies like CBI, IB, RAW and other submitted their own reports for providing the information. The report was authored by N.N. Vohra and signed by him alone.

During this time, murder of a young activist was committed and it was believed that it was the act of mafia group and one politician was also involved in it. Therefore, the attention was focused on to the Vohra Committee Report. Then, Dinesh Trivedi asked that as a matter of fundamental right to information, the Supreme Court should direct the government to make public not only the correct and authentic report, but also the reports of various agencies that form the foundation of this report. He argued that the right to information is already recognized as part of the fundamental right of freedom of speech in Article 19 of the Indian Constitution.

The court held that right to information is the right of citizens and the disclosure of information should be the norm and secrecy should be exception. The citizens have every right to know about the decision that the elected representatives of this country are going to make so that the decisions are taken for the welfare of the individuals. However, this right is not absolute. Some secrets are ought to be kept secrets for national and public security. The right to information, though it is a fundamental right, it has some reasonable restrictions.

The court ruled that the various agencies submitted their own reports after being assured of the confidentiality. That is the reason N.N. Vohra himself authored and signed the report. The information that the report is going to be tabled in the Parliament might have affected their decisions. The report tabled in the Parliament is correct, genuine, and unabridged. Because it has already been tabled in the Parliament, it is now a public document. However, the various reports cannot be made public because they did not form the annexure of this reports and the Vohra Committee Report is summary of the backhand material. Moreover, disclosure of the

[74]Supreme Court of India, *Dinesh Trivedi and Others v. Union of India and Others,* (1997) 4 SCC 306 (Judgment of 20 March 1997).

information is not in the interest of public, national security etc. For these reasons, the Supreme Court refused to direct the government to make the backhand material public.

### 6.1.2 People's Union for Civil Liberties and Another v. Union of India and Others[75]

The appellants in this case sought the information regarding the purported safety violations and defects in all the nuclear power stations of the country. The respondents, on the other hand, claimed that as per Sec. 18.1 of Atomic Energy Act, 1962,[76] this information is classified as 'secrets' therefore, cannot be disclosed. They argued that if this information is disclosed then it might cause a great injury to the interests of State and the national security.

The Supreme Court held that the sought information was sensitive in nature. This information cannot be made public because there are high possibilities that it may fall into wrong hands and may pose danger to the security of India. The court held that there are restrictions on the right to information and the sought information in this case comes under the restrictions.

## *6.2 Cabinet Papers Including Deliberations of Council of Ministers, Secretaries and Other Officers*

### 6.2.1 Union of India v. Central Information Commission[77]

The Judgment in this case came through a bunch of petitions. The Delhi High Court interpreted various terms included in Sec. 8 of the Act, which lists out the exceptions.

---

[75]Supreme Court of India, *People's Union of Liberty and Another v. Union of India and Others*, (2004) 2 SCC 476 (Judgment of 3 March 2003).

[76]Sec. 18 of the Atomic Energy Act (1962): "Restriction on disclosure of information– (1) The Central Govt. may by order restrict the disclosure of information, whether contained in a document, drawing, photograph, plan, model, or in any other form whatsoever, which relates to, represents or illustrates–

(a) an existing or proposed plant used or proposed to be used for the purpose of producing, developing or using the atomic energy, or

(b) the purpose or method of operation of any such existing or proposed plant, or

(c) any process operated or proposed to be operated in any such existing or proposed plant."

[77]High Court of Delhi, *Union of India Thr. Director and Others v. Central Information Commission and Another* (Decision of 30 November 2009), available at http://www.cic.gov.in/sites/default/files/court%20orders/UOI%28MOP-and-Ors%29-Vs-CIC.pdf (Accessed on 15 February 2017).

The court first interpreted the term "fiduciary". Sec. 8.1 point (e)[78] protects that information which is available to that person on the account of him being in a fiduciary relationship. Such information cannot be divulged unless the larger public interest warrants the disclosure. Whenever information is given based on trust and confidence, the public interest is served when that information is not divulged. Not betraying that confidence and trust is the public interest. In cases, where it is possible to give information without disclosing the identity of that person, the information should be disclosed for the larger public interest. The principle of severability should also be applied if applicable. It means that if the information sought can be divided into parts, the one which would need disclosure of the identity of the person, thus making compromise with the trust and confidence, such information should not be disclosed. However, if, on the other hand, the other part of the information sought is such that it can be disclosed without disclosing the identity of that person, then that part of information should be disclosed.

The court then interpreted Sec. 8.1 point (i)[79] of the Act which protects the Cabinet Papers, deliberations of Council of Ministers, Secretaries etc. The proviso stipulates that once the matter is over, the decisions of the Council of Ministers and the material which forms the basis of that material will be made public unless they come under the exceptions. Therefore, it means that Cabinet papers including deliberations of the Council of Ministers, secretaries and other officers shall not be disclosed. Once the matter is over and complete, they can be disclosed provided that they do not come under any of the exemptions. The Cabinet papers do include Council Ministers papers as Council of Ministers is a big body and the Cabinet is a small body within it. These papers are protected not because of their contents but because of the class to which they belong. The papers included under Article 74.2 of Indian Constitution[80] are protected by virtue of the class to which they belong.

The court held that disclosure of the information such as related to the working of the government is highly desirable, but every government needs some sort of secrecy. It is needed so that the Ministers can give advice freely and wrong public opinion is not made on those points. It is the duty of the courts to balance the two competing interests: the larger public interest and the interest of the government to keep some things secret for the security and other reasons. When some things are kept secret for the security and other reasons, the larger interest of the public is

[78]Sec. 8.1 point (e) RTI Act: "Exemption from disclosure of information – information available to a person in his fiduciary relationship, unless the competent authority is satisfied that the larger public interest warrants the disclosure of such information."

[79]Sec. 8.1 point (i) RTI Act: "Exemption from disclosure of information– cabinet papers including records of deliberations of the Council of Ministers, Secretaries and other officers: Provided that the decisions of Council of Ministers, the reasons thereof, and the material on the basis of which the decisions were taken shall be made public after the decision has been taken, and the matter is complete, or over: Provided further that those matters which come under the exemptions specified in this section shall not be disclosed."

[80]Article 74.2 of the Constitution of India (1950): "The question whether any, and if so what, advice was tendered by Ministers to the President shall not be inquired into in any court."

protected. However, the exceptions should be interpreted strictly to widen the scope of the Act to disclose increasing information.

### 6.2.2 Union of India v. Chief Information Commissioner and Others[81]

The plaintiff, Shri C. Ramesh, who is one of the respondents, sought copies of all correspondence through letters between the former president, Shri K.R. Narayan, and former Prime Minister, Shri Atal Bihari Vajpayee, between 28 February 2002 and 15 March 2002, related to the Gujarat Riots of 2002.

The PIO refused the information stating that such correspondence is protected under Article 74.2 of the Indian Constitution and Sec. 8.1 point (a)[82] of the RTI Act. The respondent filed an appeal, which was dismissed. Subsequently, he filed appeal in the Central Information Commission (CIC). The CIC ordered the production of those letters before itself to examine whether the disclosure of those letters would harm or serve public interest.

The petitioner challenged the decision of CIC. The petitioner argued that these letters form part of the advice tendered to the President, therefore are saved by the virtue of the class to which they belong under Article 74.2 of the Indian Constitution. The petitioner argued that freedom of speech and expression under Indian Constitution is not an absolute right and it is subject to the reasonable restrictions such as public health, decency etc. The Plaintiff, here respondent no. 2, argued that CIC has full authority to call over such documents and peruse them to decide that whether disclosure should be made or not. He also argued that sought information is not the advice tendered to the President but the material on which such advice was formed.

The Supreme Court held that the word "advice" under Article 74.2 of the Constitution is not a single piece of communication or opinion but refers to collaboration of many discussions and to and from correspondences between the president and the Prime Minister or the Council of Ministers. Thus, the correspondence that is sought by respondent no. 2 is not the material on which the advice was formed, but it is the intrinsic part of the advice given by the Council of Ministers to the President. The argument of the respondent no. 2 was that correspondence may not contain advice, but the material is an assumption and the CIC is not the appropriate authority to call over production of such documents to decide. The powers of CIC cannot be equated with the powers of the judges of the High Courts and the Supreme Court.

[81]High Court of Delhi, *Union Of India v. Central Information Commission and Another* (Decision of 11 July 2012), available at https://indiankanoon.org/doc/151302580/ (Accessed on 15 February 2017).

[82]Section 8.1 point (a) RTI Act: "Exemption from disclosure of information–information, disclosure of which would prejudicially affect the sovereignty and integrity of India, the security, strategic, scientific or economic interests of the State, relation with foreign State or lead to incitement of an offence."

The court clarified the reasoning of *S.P. Gupta case*, which was related to the interpretation of these articles, and held that it is settled law and was clearly provided in *State of U.P. v. Raj Narain* that there has to be classes of documents and some classes may require secrecy in the larger interest of public good. The documents under these classes are accorded immunity, not because of the content but the class to which they belong. Such documents will include cabinet minutes, minutes of discussions between the heads of Departments, high level inter departmental communications and dispatches from ambassador abroad.

Therefore, the Supreme Court refused the disclosure of such letters because they formed part of the advice rendered by the Council of Ministers to the President, thus immune by virtue of Article 74.2 of the Indian Constitution.

## 6.3 *Third Party Information or Information by Virtue of Being in Fiduciary Relationship*

### 6.3.1 PIO/Joint Secretary to Chief Commissioner of Land Administration, Nampally, Hyderabad and Others v. A.P. Information Commission[83]

The case before the High Court had its origin in the civil suit between the two parties relating to the property dispute. One party asked for the copy of Muntakhab under the RTI Act. Muntakhab is a document in which the names of people with number of fields who own them are written. The PIO refused the copy stating that Muntakhab is of personal nature and as the party's name does not figure in the list either as the holder or as successor, he cannot provide the information. The matter finally came up to the High Court. The issue to be decided that whether the Muntakhab can be given only to the legal heir of that holder and therefore, thus private in nature and hence cannot be disclosed to the applicant.

It was held that Muntakhab recognizes succession rights and when it determines those rights such determination is based on the enquiry. The declaration under the Muntakhab holds well not only against the rival parties but also against entire world. Therefore, it is a public document and can be disclosed by the PIO to the applicant.

[83]High Court of Andhra Pradesh at Hydarabad, *The Public Information Officer/Joint Secretary to Chief Commissioner Of land, Administration, Nampally, Hyderabad and another, v. A.P. Information Commissioner*, Writ petition No. 16717/2008 (Decision of 4 December 2008).

### 6.3.2 Shri Subhash Chandra Agarwal v. Supreme Court of India[84]

The appellant sought the copy of the resolution (dated 7 May 2007) passed by all the judges of the Supreme Court which required every judge to make a declaration of the assets in the form of real estate hold by them or their spouses or any person dependent on them to the Chief Justice of India. The appellant also asked for the information on any such declaration made by any judge. He also asked such information about judges of the High Court.

The CPIO of the Supreme Court gave the copy of the resolution, but declined the request of information on such declaration stating that such information is not with the Registry of the Supreme Court. Concerning the information about the judges of the High Court, the PIO stated that the appellant has adopted the short-cut to get information and has put the burden on the Supreme Court of India to provide such information at its expense. The matter finally came before the Chief Election Commission. The argument related to information about the judges of the High Court was not pressed. Therefore, the CIC dealt with the part of only Supreme Court.

The two questions which were to be decided by the CIC were (1) whether under the Sec. 2 point (h)[85] of the RTI Act, the Chief Justice of Indian and the Supreme Court of India are two distinct heads; (2) whether the information sought is protected by virtue of Sec. 8.1 point (e) or Sec. 8.1 point (j).

Regarding the first question, the CIC tried to define the term "institution" and examined the provision of the Constitution of India establishing the Supreme Court and Sec. 2 point (h) of the RTI Act. The CIC held that as per the above collection of material, the Supreme Court and the Chief Justice of India are not two distinct heads and therefore, the information with the Chief Justice of India must be with the registry of the Supreme Court. The CIC held that the fact that the rules framed by the Chief Justice of India or Chief Justice of High Courts for the Supreme Court and their respective High Courts respectively for carrying out provisions of the RTI Act are not to laid down before the Parliament or State legislature respectively shows that there is a great onus put on the Judiciary to implement the RTI Act in letter and spirit. Therefore, as a representative of Supreme Court, the CPIO must have all the information regarding the Supreme Court, it does not matter by whom it is being hold.

Concerning the second question, the CIC held that the appellant did not ask the details of the declaration of the assets. He just wanted the information that whether any declaration has been made by the judges. Such information does not attract the exemption provided under the Sec. 8.1 point (e) or Sec. 8.1 point (j).Therefore, CIC directed the CPIO to furnish such information.

[84]Central Information Commission, *Shri Subhash Chandra Agarwal v. Supreme Court of India*, Appeal No. CIC/WB/A/2008/00426 (Decision of 6 January 2009).

[85]Sec. 2 point (h) RTI Act: "..'public authority' means any authority or body or institution of self-government established or constituted."

## 6.4 Impediment of Investigation

In the case of *Bhagat Singh v. Chief Information Commissioner,*[86] the petitioner was facing a criminal charge of dowry filed against him by his wife. The wife alleged that she spent her income to give a dowry of Rs. 1,000,000. Consequently, the petitioner filed Tax Evasion Petition (TEP) in Income Tax Department. The proceedings were initiated. The petitioner asked the department the status of hearings but to no avail. Finally, he filed an RTI application to ask the status of the proceedings, sources of income of his wife and the action taken by the department on the petition. The application was rejected as this information is exempted because it is personal in nature, disclosure of such information will not serve any purpose, and the disclosure may impede the investigation. CIC ruled that the information sought results from a public action therefore, needs to be disclosed once the process of inquiry is complete. The petitioner challenged the order of CIC in Delhi High Court. He argued that the disclosure of information would not in any way hamper the investigation proceedings and the information is sought to protect himself in the criminal case.

The court ruled that the right to free speech includes the right to receive information. Further, the right to information was recognized as inherent right within the fundamental right of speech in *State of U.P. v. Raj Narain.*[87] The object of this Act is to promote transparency and arrest corruption. Disclosure of information under the Sec. 3[88] is the rule and the exemptions provided under Sec. 8 are the exception rule. Such exceptions have to be construed strictly, so that the very right of information under this Act is not shadowed by them.

The court ruled that the decisions of the CIC and the authorities blow do not justify that the disclosure of the information would hamper the investigation. The CIC ruled that information could be disclosed once the process of investigation and recovery is complete. The process of recovery takes a good amount of time and withholding information during that period is illogical. Moreover, the information is sought by the petitioner to defend himself in a criminal case. The court directed the department to release the information based on above said arguments and reasons.

---

[86]High Court of Delhi, *Bhagat Singh v. Chief Information Commissioner and Others*, Writ petition (C) No. 3114/2007, (2008) Indlaw DEL 385 (Decision of 3 December 2007).

[87]Allahabad High Court, *State of Uttar Pradesh v. Raj Narain and Others*, (1975) 3 SCR 333 (Judgment of 24 January 1975).

[88]Sec. 3 RTI Act: "Right to Information-Subject to the provisions of this Act, all the citizens shall have the right to information."

## *6.5 Interpretation of the Term "Information"*

The case *Khanapuram Gandiah v. Administrative Officer*[89] arises from the civil suit between the petitioner and the second party. The petitioner filed for permanent injunction by second party into his property, which was refused. In other case between the parties, an interim injunction was issued against the petitioner. He appealed, but the appeal was dismissed by the order. Thereafter, the petitioner filed an application under the RTI Act seeking the reasons that why the judge did not consider some documents and what was the reasoning behind the dismissal of appeal. The matter finally came up to Supreme Court.

The main issue to be decided was that whether the judge is under a duty to provide reasons for his Judgments through RTI Act applications. The High court held that the judge was under no such obligation and he was protected under Judicial Protections Act, 1850.

The Supreme Court, in this case, interpreted Sec. 2 point (f)[90] which gives the definition of the term "information". According to the definition, information means which is already in existence and accessible to public authority so that he can make it public provided that it does not fall within any exceptions provided under the Act. It ruled that an applicant can ask for the copy of an order, circular, judgment etc., but he cannot ask reasons for such documents. If he wants to challenge the award by the judge, the appropriate remedy is to go for appeal.

Moreover, PIO cannot give something that does not exist. The reasons behind any such judgment or order do not exist in documents, which the PIO has access to. A Judge is not bound to give reasons other than the one mentioned in the judgment. Therefore, when any such reasons do not exist, an application for the information in this regard is not maintainable. In addition, finally, the judges need to be protected. The idea behind is not to protect dishonest judges but to protect the administration of justice and the independence of Judiciary which might get affected from such inquiries.

The response of the Indian Judiciary to the various cases related to the disclosure of the information can be summed by two recent cases; they are: *Union of India v. Namit Sharma*[91] and *T.S.R. Subramanian and others v. Union of India and others*.[92] In the latter case, the Supreme Court held that democracy requires an

---

[89]Supreme Court of India, *Khanapuram Gandaiah v Administrative Officer and Others,* (2010) 2 SCC 1 (Judgment of 4 January 2010).

[90]Sec. 2 point (f) RTI Act: "[. . .] 'information' means any material in any form, including records, documents, memos, e-mails, opinions, advices, press releases, circulars, orders, logbooks, contracts, reports, papers, samples, models, data material held in any electronic form and information relating to any private body which can be accessed by a public authority under any other law for the time being in force."

[91]Supreme Court of India, *Union of India v. Namit Sharma*, (2013) 10 SCC 359 (Decision of 3 September 2013).

[92]Supreme Court of India, *T.S.R. Subramanium and Others v. Union of India*, SCC 2013 732 (Decision of 31 October 2013).

informed citizenry and the RTI Act is one such tool to spread awareness, transparency, and accountability in the society. It is the duty of the public authorities to maintain such records. The Court said that the present day trend of the Ministers to give oral records to Civil Servants is not the good trend because such verbal orders cannot be maintained as records by the public authority. It ruled that the civil servants and the government have to understand that the civil servants are accountable to not only the government of the day but also to the people. Therefore, a clear division of responsibility should be maintained between the government and the civil servants. In the former case, the Supreme Court held that the courts have to always maintain the balance between the right to information and any other such right of the individual or the state. The right to information is not an absolute right. However, there should be increasing accountability and transparency in the society, but there are some areas where disclosure is not wanted because of the right to privacy of the individual, national security, larger interest of public, etc. It is the duty of the Courts and the Commissions to give information in maximum cases as possible, however, when the need arises, this right has to be superseded by the larger interest of public health, good and security.

## 7 Conclusion

Primarily, in India, the Right to Information Act, 2005, is applicable to the whole country, except the state of Jammu and Kashmir. The scope covers central, state and local governments, including bodies and NGOs owned, controlled and indirectly or directly substantially financed by them and the Executive, Judiciary and the Legislature.

Under this right, citizens can demand access to request information, obtain copies of documents, inspect documents, works or records, take certified samples of materials of work and obtain information in any form, including records, documents, memos, opinions and advices, press releases, circulars, orders and logbooks, contracts, reports, papers samples and models.

The Brazilian Law regarding the right of access to information regiments all forms of the government to guarantee this right. These include the Executive, the Legislature and the Judiciary, the federal, state and local governments and NGOs receiving funds, along with state owned enterprises.

Both laws also envisage a system of active transparency, detailing a list of provisions that must be provided for in the public domain, irrespective of whether that information is sought for. This system is used in conjunction with the passive transparency model to ensure that the right of access to information is duly satisfied.

Thus, a cursory glance would indicate that both the Indian and Brazilian Laws regarding this right are quite similar. Both cover a vast array of organizations, and the scope of the right itself is similarly broad. In practice, both behave similarly, having nearly identical scope in legislation. However, the difference is seen in the practical application of the two. It is a common grievance that this right is not exercised effectively in Brazil because of the secretive legacy of its ex-dictatorial government. It can be argued that the differentiation arises in the context of the implementation of the scope, and not the scope itself.

## References

Commonwealth Human Rights Initiative. (2004). Detailed analysis of the Indian Freedom of Information Act 2002 & Recommendations for Amendments 1.

Khan, Y., & Premji, A. (2012, October 12). A critique of the Right to Information Act. *Journal of Development*.

Naib, Sudhir. (2011). *The Right to Information Act 2005: A handbook*. New Delhi, India: Oxford University Press.

PricewaterhouseCoopers. (2009). Key issues and constraints in implementing the RTI.

Sathe, S. P. (2004). *Administrative law*. New Delhi, India: Lexis-Nexis/Butterworths.

United Nations Department of Economic and Social Affairs/Population Division (2013). World population prospects: The 2012 revision, key findings and advance table. New York.

Wade, H. W. R., & Forsyth, C. E. (2010). *Administrative law*. London: Oxford University Press.

## List of Cases

### *Supreme Court of India*

Supreme Court of India 30.10.1972, *Bennett Coleman v. Union of India*, (1972) 2 SCC 788.

Supreme Court of India 25.01.1978, *Maneka Gandhi v. Union of India*, (1978) AIR SC 59.

Supreme Court of India 20.03.1997, *Dinesh Trivedi and Others v. Union of India and Others*, (1997) 4 SCC 306.

Supreme Court of India 03.03.2003, *People's Union of Liberty and Another v. Union of India and Others*, (2004) 2 SCC 476.

Supreme Court of India 04.01.2010, *Khanapuram Gandaiah v. Administrative Officer and Others*, (2010) 2 SCC 1.

Supreme Court of India 03.09.2013, *Union of India v. Namit Sharma*, (2013) 10 SCC 359.

Supreme Court of India 31.10.2013, T.S.R. *Subramanium and Others v. Union of India and Others*, SCC 2013 732.

Supreme Court of India 16.12.2015, *Reserve Bank of India v. Jayantilal N. Mistry*, (2016) 3 SCC 525.

Supreme Court of India 04.02.2016, *Kerala Public Service Commission and Another v. State Information Commission and Another*, (2016) 3 SCC 417.

## Other Courts

Allahabad High Court 24.01.1975, *State of Uttar Pradesh v. Raj Narain and Others*, (1975) 3 SCR 333.

High Court of Delhi 03.12.2007, *Bhagat Singh v. Chief Information Commissioner and Others*, (2008) Indlaw DEL 385.

High Court of Andhra Pradesh at Hydarabad 04.12.2008, *The Public Information Officer/Joint Secretary to Chief Commissioner Of land, Administration, Nampally, Hyderabad and another, v. A.P. Information Commissioner*, Writ petition No. 16717/2008.

High Court of Delhi 11.07.2012, *Union of India v. Central Information Commission and Another.*, available at https://indiankanoon.org/doc/151302580/.

## Central Information Commission

Central Information Commission 06.01.2009, *Shri Subhash Chandra Agarwal v. Supreme Court of India*, Appeal No.CIC/WB/A/2008/00426.

Central Information Commission 24.03.2011, *Manoj Kumar Saini v. The Chief Commissioner, Income Tax*, Appeal No. CIC/Ls/A/2010/001044-Ds.

Central Information Commission 11.12.2012, R.K. Jain v. CPIO, Cabinet Secretariat, CIC/SM/A/2012/000776.

Central Information Commission 18.12.2012, *R. K. Jain v. CESTAT*, Appeal No. CIC/SS/A/2011/001982.

# Chapter 12
# Japanese Information Disclosure Law

**Narufumi Kadomatsu and Joel Rheuben**

## Contents




N. Kadomatsu (✉)
Kobe University, Kobe, Japan
e-mail: kado@kobe-u.ac.jp

J. Rheuben
Freshfields Bruckhaus Deringer LLP, London, UK





H.-J. Blanke, R. Perlingeiro (eds.), *The Right of Access to Public Information*,
DOI 10.1007/978-3-662-55554-5_12

# 1 Introduction

## *1.1 History of the Information Disclosure Law*

Access to official information at the national level in Japan is principally governed by the *Law concerning Disclosure of Information Held by Administrative Organs*,[1] commonly abbreviated as the "Information Disclosure Law". Whereas the Brazilian Law N° 12.527/2011 (herein, the "Brazilian Law") appears to be relatively comprehensive, and covers a number of aspects of information regulation, the Information Disclosure Law is only one of several key information laws in Japan. The two other key information laws are, first, the *Law on the Protection of Personal Information Held by Administrative Organs* (or the "Personal Information Protection Law"),[2] which governs the collection and use of personal information by administrative organs and access by individuals to information relevant to them, and, second, the *Public Records and Archive Management Law*,[3] which deals with the creation, storage and destruction of administrative documents. As discussed below, both laws are relevant to the type of information that can be accessed under the Information Disclosure Law. An additional information law, the *Specified Secrets Protection Law*,[4] was enacted in December 2013 after wide-spread controversy. The law could have significant implications for administrative discretion to refuse disclosure on national defense and safety grounds, as well as for the practical operation of the Information Disclosure Law, as discussed below.

The purpose of the Information Disclosure Law, as stated in its opening clause, is to "*[. . .] strive for greater disclosure of information held by administrative organs, thereby ensuring that the government fulfills its duty to explain its various operations to the people, and to contribute to the promotion of a fair and democratic administration [. . .]*". These lofty goals to some extent reflect the history of the law as the outcome of a "bottom-up" citizen-led movement for a freedom of information law. The birth of this movement is commonly traced to the prosecution

---

[1]Law No. 42 of 1999. The law has been translated by Katsuya Uga (Tokyo University) and David Moses Schultz (Uga & Schultz 2001; this is the version included in this publication), as well as by the Ministry of Justice. Both include in their translated titles "*Access to* Information Held by Administrative Organs". The use of the word "access" is debatable from a purely linguistic point of view, as the relevant Japanese word (*kôkai* – literally, "opening to the public") better translates as "disclosure". However, it is a more accurate reflection of the content of the law, as information is disclosed passively and on an ad hoc basis in response to applications for access by individuals, rather than proactively and systematically on the initiative of administrative organs. Nevertheless, the term "information disclosure" is preferred here. Note that the translation of the law included in this book is based on the Uga/Schultz translation, updated by the authors to reflect subsequent amendments.

[2]Law No. 58 of 2003 (not to be confused with the Law on the Protection of Personal Information (Law No. 57 of 2003), which applies only to private actors).

[3]Law No. 66 of 2009.

[4]Law No. 108 of 2013. Cf. Rheuben 2013a.

of the journalist Takichi Nishiyama, in 1974, for "inducing" a public servant to leak evidence of a government cover-up.[5] The potential threat to freedom of the press galvanized transparency advocates to push for legislative protection. In a round table discussion held the same year, academics for the first time called for national legislation on information disclosure.[6] Civil society groups such as the Japan Civil Liberties Union and the Japan Consumers Union also joined in these calls.

The tactic adopted by the latter in particular was to encourage local governments to implement information disclosure ordinances under their local rule-making powers.[7] By the time the national Information Disclosure Law was enacted in 1999, all prefectures and the majority of municipalities had enacted such ordinances. These ordinances had a significant influence on the drafting of the Information Disclosure Law.[8]

In the mid-1990s, two incidents brought information disclosure systems to public attention.[9] The first were the activities of "Citizens' Ombudsmen", voluntary local watchdog groups monitoring public administration, which focused upon items in local budgets allocated as "food expenditure". It was known that such budget items were often abused by local administrations for entertaining central government bureaucrats in order for local governments to maintain a "good relationship" with central ministries. Making use of information disclosure ordinances, the network of "ombudsman" groups exposed the systematic abuse of "food expenditure".

The "AIDS file scandal" within the Ministry of Health and Welfare was the other incident that focused public attention on the issue of information disclosure. In Japan, because of delays in measures to deal with HIV-contaminated non-heat-treated blood products, at least 1806 hemophilia patients were infected with HIV, and many of them have already died. The affected patient group demanded disclosure of documents related to the "Study Group for the Prevention of Onset and Treatment of HIV-Infected Persons" in the Ministry of Health and Welfare during initial stages of infection, but the ministry denied the existence of such documents. However, in January 1996, the newly appointed minister *Naoto Kan* (who later

---

[5]Tokyo District Court (Judgment of 31 January 1974), 306 Hanrei Times 9. For more details on the Case in English, see Kadomatsu 1999, p. 35; Repeta 2011, p. 45–47.

[6]See e.g., Horibe 1992, p. 37; Schultz 2001, p. 130.

[7]Japanese local governments (both at the prefectural and municipal level) possess general rule-making powers pursuant to Article 94 of the Japanese Constitution and Article 14 of the Local Autonomy Law (Law No. 67 of 1947) (please note that, although the official translation of Article 94 of the Constitution refers to rules enacted by local governments as "regulations", the term "ordinance" is used here in accordance with custom). Local governments have adopted information disclosure ordinances based on these general rule-making powers, rather than as delegated legislation. The first municipality to do so was tiny Kaneyama Town in Yamagata Prefecture, while the first prefecture was the significantly more populous Kanagawa Prefecture, both in 1982. See Repeta 2003.

[8]See Kadomatsu 1999, p. 39.

[9]For detail, see Kadomatsu 1999, p. 36–37.

became prime minister from 2010–2011) ordered a search for the documents. The documents were soon "discovered" in the ministry's offices and made open to the public. The document file proved to contain crucial pieces of information related to the responsibility of bureaucrats and doctors who took part in the decision-making process.

The direct impetus for the eventual adoption of the national law emerged from the political upheaval of the 1993 House of Representatives election that ended almost 40 years of single-party rule by the Liberal Democratic Party ("LDP"). The newly-formed coalition government under Prime Minister Morihiro Hosokawa agreed to implement information disclosure legislation as part of an overall "administrative reform" agenda.[10] This agenda continued even after the LDP's return to power the following year, although the law was not finally passed until May 1999, and did not come into force until nearly 2 years later, in April 2001.

In 2004 a "Research Council on the Operation of the Information Disclosure Law" was established to review the law, and delivered its report in 2005.[11] The report recommended, for example, a tightening of the exemptions to disclosure under the law and a greater use of online applications and disclosure. The report was largely ignored by the LDP government, prompting the opposition Democratic Party of Japan ("DPJ") to put forward a private member's bill (ultimately rejected) in 2005, to implement the Research Council's recommendations.

Upon taking power in 2009, the DPJ established a new "Administrative Transparency Study Team" (herein, the "Transparency Team"), with terms of reference largely restricted to the matters covered by the DPJ's own 2005 bill. Unsurprisingly, the Transparency Team's 2010 report endorsed much of that bill's contents, and a substantially similar amendment bill was submitted to the Diet in April 2011.[12] However, the need to respond to the devastation caused by the March 2011 tsunami and nuclear disaster, as well as the general legislative paralysis after the LDP's victory in the 2010 upper house election, meant that the bill never made it past the committee stage. Instead, the bill expired with the dissolution of the Diet before the 2012 election, since which the new LDP government has shown little commitment to improving transparency (as evidenced by the passage of the *Specified Secrets Protection Law*).[13]

---

[10]In this sense, the legislative move was linked with the administration's "New Public Management" policies, and especially deregulation efforts. Although information disclosure is by its nature neutral to the deregulation discussion, legislation was realized at a national level only after a linkage between the two issues was established. See Kadomatsu 1999, p. 38–39.

[11]Research Council on the Operation of the Information Disclosure Law 2005. The Research Council had been established pursuant to a supplementary clause in the law requiring a review of the law within four years of it coming into force. The clause was included at the insistence of opposition parties, which felt that the law did not go far enough towards ensuring accountability.

[12]On the Transparency Team's report and amendment bill more generally, see Rheuben 2013b.

[13]The now-opposition DPJ did re-submit its amendment bill to the Diet on the same date as the LDP submitted the Specified Secrets Protection Law; however, the former has not been passed.

## 1.2 Scope of Application

While the Brazilian Law applies to "the Union, States, Federal District and Municipalities", the scope of the Japanese Information Disclosure Law is limited to administrative documents held by national "Administrative Organs".[14] Documents held by the Diet (the national parliament) and the courts are not the subject of disclosure. (Rather, both houses of the Diet and the courts operate their own information disclosure systems respectively based on their internal rules.) The law does not apply to Japan's prefectures and municipalities, although, as noted above, almost all of such local governments have enacted their own information disclosure ordinances.[15] With regard to quasi-governmental organizations, a separate law[16] was enacted in 2001.[17]

While the head of each administrative organ to which the Information Disclosure Law applies is responsible for implementing the law, the Ministry of Internal Affairs and Communications is responsible for overseeing the administration of the law more generally, including collating annual statistics on usage of the law and promoting public education. The Ministry of Internal Affairs and Communications is also responsible for administering the Personal Information Protection Law, although, somewhat disjointedly, it is the Cabinet Office that has oversight for the Public Records and Archive Management Law.

The proposed amendments to the Information Disclosure Law would have similarly seen oversight shift to the Cabinet Office (although not for the Personal Information Protection Law). This reflects a general trend in recent years of diverting politically sensitive policy developments to either the Cabinet Office, directly responsible to the Cabinet, or to the Cabinet Secretariat, directly responsible to the Prime Minister, on the apparent assumption that both are best placed to drive reform. However, both agencies are in practice considerably under-resourced, and their nominal independence from the central bureaucracy is debatable, as most staff are short-term secondees from other ministries.[18]

It is to be hoped that any future moves for reform of the Information Disclosure Law will consider the creation of a well-resourced and genuinely independent body along the lines of the UK Information Commissioner's Office, responsible for

---

[14]See Article 2.1 of the Information Disclosure Law.

[15]All prefectural governments and 99.9% of municipal governments have enacted such ordinances as of 1 October 2014. See Ministry of Internal Affairs and Communications 2015.

[16]Law concerning Disclosure of Information Held by Incorporated Administrative Agencies, etc., (Law No. 140 of 2001).

[17]Article 2 of the Brazilian Law applies the content of the law "to the extent possible, to non-profit public entities that receive public resources". In Japan, neither national law nor local ordinances have such a provision. However, some local governments conclude contracts with corporations that receive subsidies, which provide that the corporations shall supply certain important information to the government. In that case, the information will be subject to information disclosure as documents held by the local government.

[18]Cf. Rheuben 2013b, p. 269–270.

information policy more generally. Similar bodies anticipated by the Brazilian Law may also offer a model for Japan in the future.[19]

## 2 The Scope of the Right of Access

### 2.1 *The Right of Access and the Concept of the "Right to Know"*

The Information Disclosure Law indirectly guarantees the right of access to administrative documents. Although the text of the law only stipulates the right to "request" disclosure,[20] the administrative organs are obliged to disclose the requested documents to the applicant, excluding "Non-Disclosure Information",[21] as described below.

In the history of the "bottom-up" citizen-led movement that gave impetus to Information Disclosure Law, the concept of the "right to know" played an important role. The concept, which is theoretically derived from Article 21 of the Japanese Constitution, i.e., the Freedom of Expression Clause.[22] Hata explains as follows:

> Freedom of expression is a freedom to express one's thoughts freely. In order to express his or her opinion on a particular problem, a person must have ample information related to it. For it is not until he/she has enough information that he/she could form an informed opinion. From such a point of view, scholars in the mid-1960s began to insist that Article 21 para 1 guarantees the right to know as the premise for freedom of expression.[23]

This view, which stresses the importance of taking the recipient side of the communication flow into consideration, gained consensus among scholars as a constitutional principle. As early as in 1969, the Supreme Court mentioned the concept in the context of freedom of the mass media in the *Hakata* Railway Station Film Case.

> In our democratic society, as is pointed out by the appellants, news reports offer important materials for the people to make judgments on their participation in the government and make a contribution to the realization of their "right to know information". Therefore, it goes without saying that the freedom of reporting news together with that of expression of

[19] E.g., under Chapter II, Article 9 and Chapter VI, Article 41 of the Brazilian Law.

[20] See Article 3 of the Information Disclosure Law: "Any person, as provided for by this law, may request to the head of an administrative organ [...] the disclosure of administrative documents held by the administrative organ concerned."

[21] See Article 5 of the Information Disclosure Law.

[22] See Article 21.1 Japanese Constitution: "Freedom of assembly and association as well as speech, press and all other forms of expression are guaranteed." See Matsui 2011, p. 196–211 about the situation of freedom of expression in Japan.

[23] Hata & Nakagawa 1997, p. 129.

> thought is guaranteed under Article 21 of the Constitution providing the freedom of expression. And, for the purpose of supporting the news reported by the news media, the freedom of news-gathering activities as well as that of news reporting is to be sufficiently respected, in the light of the purport of Article 21 of the Constitution.[24]

In this case, the legality of the lower court's order to present a part of a news film for evidential use was in question. Although the court rejected the arguments of the broadcasting companies in the particular case, the *dicta* of the court was observed by a contemporary foreign observer as "much advanced when compared with the decisions on government secrecy by the highest courts in other leading democracies."[25] The "right to know" was also mentioned by the Supreme Court judgment in the above mentioned (see Sect. 1.1) *Nishiyama* Telegram case,[26] quoting the *Hakata* Railway Station Film judgment.

Limitations on the activities of the mass media were at issue in these two cases. These cases, as well as other cases that refer to the "right to know", do not explicitly speak of citizens' constitutional concrete rights against the state or mass media to obtain specific information. In addition, there is no unanimous view as to the legal grounds for the "right to know". Many scholars are of the opinion that it is founded upon Article 21 (Freedom of Expression), while some scholars find its basis in Article 13 (Liberty for pursuit of happiness) or in the general principle of democracy. In sum, the "right to know" has gained consensus as a principle, but has not been fully developed as a usable legal tool.[27] Nevertheless, the concept remained the impetus for the long-continuing movement toward the Information Disclosure Law.[28]

In the drafting stage of the Information Disclosure Law, there was a discussion as to whether to include the phrase "right to know" in the purpose provision[29] of the law. The government finally decided not to do so, claiming the concept allows too much room for interpretation. This decision became perhaps the most controversial aspect of the law, but it is open to discussion whether the inclusion would have made any practical difference.[30] The above-mentioned DPJ government bill would, incidentally, have included reference to the right in the law's purpose provision.[31]

---

[24]Japanese Supreme Court (Judgment of 26 November 1969), 23(11), *Keishû* 1490. http://www.courts.go.jp/app/hanrei_en/detail?id=33 (Accessed on 15 February 2017).

[25]Brown 1977, p. 117.

[26]Japanese Supreme Court (Judgment of 31 May 1978), 32(3) *Keishû* 457. An English translation can be found in Beer & Ito 1996, p. 543–547.

[27]Kadomatsu 1999, p. 35.

[28]Kadomatsu 2002, p. 459.

[29]It is a customary legislative technique in Japan to state the purposes of a statute in the first article. This "purpose provision" is understood to serve as a guideline for interpretation.

[30]Cf. Kadomatsu 1999, p. 39–40; Kadomatsu 2002, p. 458–460.

[31]See Rheuben 2013b, p. 276. It should also be noted that the right was mentioned in supplementary opinions of the two justices in Japanese Supreme Court decision of 15 January 2009, 63 (1) *Minshû* 46 (see Sect. 5.3). See Rheuben 2013b, p. 265.

It is in any event important to note that, despite the decision not to incorporate the concept of the "right to know" in the purpose provision, the Information Disclosure Law clearly stipulates the right of access in Article 3.

## 2.2 *Accountability or the "Duty to Explain"*

Instead of the "right to know", the Information Disclosure Law stipulates the government's "duty to explain" (*setsumei suru sekimu*) its activities to the people in the purpose provision. The inclusion of this phrase represented the first time that the concept of the "duty to explain", an equivalent concept to "accountability", was used in Japanese statute.[32] The law also establishes "accountability" as an issue for popular sovereignty. At least in this respect, the Government is understood to owe direct responsibility to the people, not indirectly via the Parliament.[33] However, it should also be noted that the right to request disclosure is guaranteed to "any person", not limited to Japanese nationals or to residents in Japan.[34]

## 2.3 *Object of Access*

In contrast to the Brazilian Law[35] (and despite the name of the law), the object of disclosure in the Information Disclosure Law is "administrative documents",[36] not "information". "Documents" naturally cover not only paper documents but also "electromagnetic records". However, documents must already exist to fall under the law: an applicant can only request existing documents *held* by the administration. When no documents have been created, or when the documents have already been discarded at the time of the disclosure request, the Information Disclosure Law has no effect. The law cannot control how administrative organs should *gather* or *process* information but only demands that the *product* of the information process,

[32]Today, three other laws (the Law concerning Disclosure of Information Held by Incorporated Administrative Agencies, etc., the Law on the Evaluation of Policies of Administrative Agencies (Law No. 86 of 2001) and the Public Records and Archive Management Law) also stipulate "accountability" in their purpose provisions. They can therefore be regarded as "accountability related legal schemes (ARLS)". Cf. Kadomatsu 2011, p. 6–7.

[33]Kadomatsu 1999, p. 41.

[34]See Article 3 of the Information Disclosure Law. The rationale for this is usually explained from a pragmatic point of view that it is practically impossible to limit the right holders. One could easily bypass any such limitation, as any non-right holder would be able to ask a right holder to request disclosure and to pass on documents received (Cf. Kadomatsu 1999, p. 42). However, there may also be theoretical explanations for this "any person" clause; cf. Kadomatsu 2011, p. 15–16.

[35]See Articles 4 and 7 of the Brazilian Law.

[36]See Article 2.2 of the Information Disclosure Law.

stored in a particular medium (documents), be disclosed. Put simply, the law is not a system that directly regulates information *flow*, but a system that makes rules about how the *stock* of information shall be treated.[37]

In this respect, it is noteworthy that the *Public Records and Archive Management Law*, enacted in 2009, emphasizes the importance of public documents as "an intellectual resource to be shared by the people in supporting the basis of sound democracy, in accordance with the principle of sovereignty of the people."[38] The law imposes upon administrative organs the duty to create documents for the enactment, amendment and abolition processes of laws and regulations, cabinet decisions or agreements etc., as written documents shall "enable a decision-making process to be reasonably traced or verified."[39] However, as this "duty to prepare documents" is limited to highly significant decisions such as the enactment of statutes, the Brazilian Law, which guarantees the right to obtain "information regarding activities carried out by entities and institutions, including activities regarding their policies, organization and services" appears to have a far wider scope.[40]

A judgment of the Supreme Court in 2014 considered the burden of proof for the existence of administrative documents in information disclosure suits.[41] This case involved secret financial documents concerning the reversion of *Okinawa* to Japan from the United States in 1972 (a matter related to the *Nishiyama* incident—see Sect. 1.1). In 2008, the plaintiffs filed an information disclosure request to the Minister of Foreign Affairs and the Minister of Finance. The ministers refused the requests because they did not hold the documents sought. At first instance, the Tokyo District Court revoked the administrative dispositions and ordered the ministers to disclose them.[42] According to the Court's judgment, as a general rule it is the plaintiff (the applicant) who bears the burden of proving a document's existence. However, where the plaintiff succeeds in proving that the documents were held by the administrative organ for organizational use at a certain point in the past, it can be presumed that those documents are still being held. In this case, the ministries needed to argue and prove the documents were lost by disposal or transfer. The Court found that the documents existed in 1971 and that the ministries did not search sufficiently to establish the existence or disposal of the documents. Therefore, it presumed their continued existence and ordered disclosure.

On appeal from the government, the Tokyo High Court reversed the judgment and approved the legality of the administrative disposition because of the non-existence of the documents.[43] It retained the burden of proof rule applied in

---

[37]Kadomatsu 2002, p. 457 et seq.

[38]See Article 1 of the Public Records and Archive Management Law.

[39]See Article 4 of the Public Records and Archive Management Law.

[40]See Article 7, item 5 of the Brazilian Law.

[41]Japanese Supreme Court (Judgment of 14 July 2014), 2242 *Hanrei Jihô* 51.

[42]Tokyo District Court (Judgment of 9 April 2010), 2076 *Hanrei Jihô* 19.

[43]Tokyo High Court (Judgment of 29 September 2011), 2142 *Hanrei Jihô* 3.

the first instance decision. However, the Court argued that the Ministry of Foreign Affairs had a strong intention to conceal the documents from the public so that one may assume that the documents were stored in an irregular way and discarded covertly. Hence, there is a reasonable doubt that those documents are still being held.

On appeal from the plaintiff, the Supreme Court affirmed the judgment of the High Court. The Court went further and varied the burden of proof rule adopted by the District Court. It held that, even where the plaintiff succeeds in proving that an administrative organ at a certain point obtained documents in the past, one cannot generally presume that the documents exist at the time of the disclosure request. Courts must instead consider the individual circumstances surrounding the document. With regard to diplomatic documents in particular, one must take note that those documents might sometimes be stored in an irregular way.

There is an obvious and probably universal incentive for administrative organs to seek to conceal documents of a highly sensitive political nature, and which may lead to such documents being stored or disposed of in an irregular manner. In this context, Article 5 of the Brazilian Law, which gives the interested party the right to request the opening of an inquiry to determine the disappearance of the documentation, is quite interesting.

## 3 Limitations on the Right of Access

### *3.1 Indifferent to the Purpose of the Request*

As mentioned above, Article 5 of the Information Disclosure Law stipulates a duty to disclose requested documents, unless the documents contain information mentioned in any of the six items in the article (non-disclosure information). In addition, when it is possible to easily divide and exclude any portion of a document in which non-disclosure information is recorded, the head of an administrative organ must disclose the remaining portion.[44]

The law is *indifferent to the purpose* of the disclosure request or the motive of the applicant.[45] The basic idea is that the administrative documents, when requested, shall be disclosed so long as the disclosure causes no harm, regardless of whether the disclosure may serve any kind of public interest.[46] Hence, it is also legitimate to

[44]See Article 6 of the Information Disclosure Law.

[45]See Sect. 4.1.

[46]Only in case of exceptional disclosure of non-disclosure information(information which is found necessary to be disclosed in order to protect a person's life, health, livelihood, or property" (Article 5, item 1 point (a), proviso to item 2, see Sect. 3.3.2) and in the case of Article 7 (discretionary disclosure, see Sect. 3.1) will there be a balancing between the public interest and the relevant harm.

request information disclosure for commercial purposes. However, confronted with a massive amount of such requests and administrative costs caused by them, some local governments amended their ordinances to collect disclosure application or processing fees (see below Sect. 4.2) for applications for commercial purposes while requests for non-commercial purposes remain free of charge. In addition, in extreme situations when a request is found to have been made out of an intention to obstruct business, the request may be regarded as an abuse of right, which can be a reason for non-disclosure under the Information Disclosure Law as well us under local ordinances.

## 3.2 No Provision on Designation and Classification of Secrets

As opposed to the Brazilian Law, the Information Disclosure Law does not have a provision concerning classification of secrets. This is because the law does not aim to provide a comprehensive scheme of information regulation in itself, but is only one of several important information laws (see Sect. 1.1). Aside from Article 96.2 of the Self Defense Forces Law,[47] and Article 2 of the Secrets Protection Law based on the Japan and U.S. Mutual Defense Assistance Agreement,[48] there was no statutory basis for the designation of documents as secret by administrative organs until relatively recently. The designation was in principle done based only on administrative internal rules. The new Specified Secrets Protection Law has expanded categories of information subject to secrecy designation and the list of organs empowered to designate information.[49]

## 3.3 Non-Disclosure Information

Six categories of non-disclosure information are enumerated in Article 5 of the Information Disclosure Law, namely personal information (item 1), corporate information (item 2), national security information (item 3), public safety information (item 4), information concerning deliberations, inquiries, or consultations (item 5), and information that concerns governmental affairs or business that, by the nature of said affairs or business, would risk causing a hindrance to its proper performance if made public (item 6). Express secret information categories in the Brazilian Law, such as information that could cause financial, economic or monetary instability[50] or information on scientific or technological research and

[47]Law No. 165 of 1954. However, the provision was inserted as late as in 2001.

[48]Law No. 166 of 1954.

[49]Repeta 2013.

[50]Chapter IV, Section II, Article 23 item 4 of the Brazilian Law.

development projects,[51] do not appear in Japanese Information Disclosure Law. On the other hand, the deliberative process information category (item 5) as such is not found in the Brazilian Law.

It should also be noted that those categories of non-disclosure information are not only *exempt* from disclosure. In principle, administrative organs have a duty *not* to disclose such information.[52] As an exception, it is stipulated in Article 7 of the Information Disclosure Law that the head of an administrative organ can disclose such information when there is a "particular public interest necessity". However, as each exemption category, as explained below, involves a balancing between the public interest and the interests protected by the category, it is quite rare for such discretionary disclosure to actually take place.[53] The DPJ government bill included a new provision by which the Prime Minister could recommend the use of Article 7 of the Information Disclosure Law by the head of an administrative organ in individual cases for encouraging greater use of this discretionary disclosure provision. The efficacy of this proposal may be debatable.[54]

### 3.3.1 Personal Information (Item 1)

*Personal identification type and privacy invasion type*: Article 5, item 1 (personal information) exempts "information concerning an individual" from disclosure. The category is further defined to mean, "where it is possible to identify a specific individual from a name, birth date or other description, etc. contained in the information concerned." This includes not only cases where a specific individual is identifiable by the information itself, but also cases "where through collation with other information" identification is possible (the so-called "mosaic approach").

This personal information exception is a common exemption in information disclosure laws of many countries, including the Brazilian Law. Broadly stated, regulations of this category can be divided into two types: (A) "personal identification type", such as the above definition in the Information Disclosure Law, and (B) "privacy invasion type", which limits this exemption category to personal information that affects privacy rights, such as under the FOIA in the U.S. The Information Disclosure Law, as well as many local ordinances that had been enacted before the law, chose type A because of the perceived "vagueness" of the

[51]Chapter IV, Section II, Article 23, item 6 of the Brazilian Law.

[52]Most of the categories of non-disclosure information in the Brazilian Law find their equivalents in the Information Disclosure Law, with the exception of Article 23, item 4 (elevated risk of financial, economic or monetary instability).

[53]Between business year (i.e., April until March 2001) (being the first year of operation of the Information Disclosure Law) and business year 2014, Article 7 was used only 34 times. Between 2002 and 2009, it was used only twice (Ministry of Internal Affairs and Communications 2017, Cf. Rheuben 2013b, p. 269).

[54]See Fujiwara 2012, p. 63.

definition of "privacy". However, there are some local ordinances for which type B was chosen, and still now use this type.[55]

Concerning this distinction, Sec. I of the Brazilian Law defines "personal information" for the purposes of the personal information exemption in that law as, "information related to the identified or identifiable natural person", and so appears to adopt type A.[56] However, in Article 31 of the Brazilian Law concerning treatment of personal information, the law limits personal information to that which relates "to intimacy, private life, honor and image". It therefore remains to be seen how far the Brazilian courts will extend the personal information exemption.

It should be noted that "information concerning an individual" in item 1 of the Information Disclosure Law does not include information "concerning the business of an individual who carries on said business". Such information falls within the framework of item 2 (corporate information).

Even in cases when identification of a specific person is impossible, information concerning an individual such as medical records is exempt from disclosure when there is a "risk that an individual's rights and interests will be harmed".

*Exceptions:* The Information Disclosure Law stipulates 3 exceptions by which documents must be disclosed even though they contain "information concerning an individual", namely public domain information (Article 5.1 point (a) of the Information Disclosure Law), public official information (Article 5.1 point (c) of the Information Disclosure Law), and public interest information (Article 5.1 point (b) of the Information Disclosure Law).

The first exception is "Information that is made public, or information that is scheduled to be made public, as provided for by law or by custom" (so-called "public domain information").[57] For example, the names of members of advisory councils are often disclosed for the reason that they are customarily made public. A further exception applies to "information that concerns the performance of [...] duties" of a public official.[58] In this case, the portion of the information that concerns the position of an official and the substance of the performance of their duties are to be disclosed, even in the case when such a disclosure would lead to identification of the official. The text of this exception implies that the name of the official itself may not be disclosed; however, it is now an established practice[59] among national administrative organs to disclose the name in principle.[60] It is

[55]For example, the Osaka prefectural ordinance enumerates categories of personal information (personal belief, religion, physical features, etc.) and further limits them by the requirement that "it is deemed justifiable that people generally prefer that this information not be known by others."

[56]See Article 4, item 4 of the Brazilian Law.

[57]See Article 5.1 point (a) of the Information Disclosure Law.

[58]See Article 5.1 point (c) of the Information Disclosure Law. "Public official" here includes not only national public employees but also local public employees and employees of incorporated administrative agencies, etc.

[59]Ministry of Internal Affairs and Communications 2005.

[60]The DPJ government bill proposed to entrench this practice in statutory form.

understood that names of officials are information that belongs in the public domain (under the previous exception). In addition, disclosure of career summaries of executive officials is now a common practice.[61]

The final exception stipulates that, "information recognized as necessary to be made public in order to protect a person's life, health, livelihood, or property" is exempted from the above "personal information". In judging whether this obligatory disclosure for public interests shall take place, it is necessary to carry out an adequate balancing between the public interests attained by the disclosure and the disadvantages to privacy and other interests.[62] In an opinion of the Information Disclosure and Personal Information Protection Review Board (hereafter, the "Review Board"; see below Sect. 5.2), information about the detailed medical process of a certain patient in a case report on adverse effects of a particular drug was deemed to belong to this exception.[63] Although a specific individual could not be identified by the disclosure, there was a risk "that an individual's rights and interests would be harmed" by the disclosure of the medical process. However, the public interest in disclosing information on the adverse effects was held to prevail to guarantee the safety of use of the drug.[64]

### 3.3.2 Corporate Information (Item 2)

Item 2 (corporate information) stipulates the two cases when information concerning a corporation[65] or other entity will be exempt from disclosure: (a) when there is a risk that disclosure of the information may harm "the rights, competitive standing, or other legitimate interests" of the corporation etc.; and (b) where the information was offered voluntarily at the request of an administrative organ on the condition that it not be made public. This requirement can only be met when the imposition of such a condition is "in light of the nature of the information and the circumstances [. . .] considered to be reasonable" (Article 5.2 point (b) of the Information Disclosure Law).

In contrast with personal information, corporate information is not regarded as non-disclosure information in principle, but only when either of the above

---

[61]Ministry of Internal Affairs and Communications 2007.

[62]A similar balancing of public interests and privacy seems to be required under Article 31 para 3, item 5 of the Brazilian Law.

[63]Opinion of the Information Disclosure and Personal Information Protection Review Board of 12 April 2002.

[64]Interestingly, the applicant was the patient herself in this case. Before the enactment of the Personal Information Protection Law, it was not unusual for an individual to request the disclosure of information that concerned his- or herself using the Information Disclosure Law. In most cases, such requests were rejected. See Kadomatsu 2002, p. 446–450; Schultz 2001, p. 156.

[65]As mentioned above, information "concerning the business of an individual who carries on said business" belongs to this category, and not item 1, notwithstanding that they are not, strictly speaking, legal persons.

requirements is met. Similar to item 1, obligatory disclosure in the public interest must be made when disclosure is deemed necessary "in order to protect a person's life, health, livelihood, or property" (Article 5.2 of the Information Disclosure Law).

An opinion of the Review Board applied this provision to a disclosure request of documents held by the Ministry of Health, Labor and Welfare submitted from a certain medical company concerning a drug that had caused hepatitis C.[66] The documents included names of private medical institutions to which the medicine was supplied. The Review Board acknowledged that, while disclosure of such information would harm "competitive standing, or other legitimate interests" and therefore met the above requirement (a), the necessity of disclosure for the protection of "a person's life, [and] health" was deemed more significant because disclosure may motivate possible patients to undertake a hepatitis examination.

A Judgment of the Supreme Court in 2011[67] dealt with disclosure of a periodic report with regard to energy consumption and other indicators of energy use in factories. According to Article 15 of the Law on the Rational Use of Energy,[68] designated businesses are obliged to submit such reports to the Minister of Economy, Trade and Industry each business year. Following a request for disclosure of the reports (1055 reports in total), the head of the ministry consulted the relevant businesses in accordance with Article 13.1 of the Information Disclosure Law (see Sect. 4.3). For those reports where the businesses opposed disclosure (171 reports), the head of the ministry made a non-disclosure decision, and the applicant subsequently filed a judicial appeal. The first and second instance decisions affirmed the applicant's claim and ordered disclosure of the reports. The Supreme Court reversed and affirmed the non-disclosure decision. According to the Court, disclosure of the periodic reports of a business may give competing businesses an improved competitive position. It may also give customers of the business a better position in price bargaining. Hence disclosure may harm "the rights, competitive standing, or other legitimate interests" of the business (Article 5.2 point a).

The above requirement (b) was one of the most disputed provisions in the legislative history of the Information Disclosure Law, partly because of the then-prevalent criticism against a prominent feature of Japanese administrative style, namely its heavy dependence on informal activities or non-binding "administrative guidance".[69] The DPJ government bill aimed to delete this provision.[70]

---

[66]Opinion of the Information Disclosure and Personal Information Protection Review Board of 20 February 2004.

[67]Japanese Supreme Court (Judgment of 14 October 2011), 2159 *Hanrei Jihô* 53.

[68]Law No. 49 of 22 June 1979.

[69]See Kadomatsu 1999, p. 44–45.

[70]Rheuben 2013b, p. 266.

### 3.3.3 National Security Information (Item 3) and Public Safety Information (Item 4)

Item 3 (national security information) excludes certain information from disclosure when the head of an administrative organ "with reasonable grounds deems [such disclosure] to pose a risk of harm to the security of the State, a risk of damage to trustful relations with another country or an international organization, or a risk of causing a disadvantage in negotiations with another country or an international organization."

In contrast with items 1 and 2, "the head of an administrative organ" appears in the definition, which is intended to grant discretion to the organs to make a judgment on whether the conditions are met. The same scheme is used in item 4 (public safety information), under which information will not be disclosed where disclosure is found by the head of the administrative organ to hinder "prevention, suppression or investigation of crimes, the maintenance of public prosecutions, the execution of sentencing, and other public security and public order maintenance matters" (Article 5.4 of the Information Disclosure Law).

In the Supreme Court Judgment in the above-mentioned *Nishiyama* case, the Court confirmed that "secrets" protected under the National Public Employee Law are "substantive facts not known to the public that are worthy of protection as secrets [. . .] and that their determination is subject to judicial review".[71] The Court held that it is not sufficient that the concerned administrative organs regard or designate certain facts to be secret. The position taken by the Court is commonly called "substantive secret theory", as opposed to "formal secret theory". It may be open to argument whether the discretion provisions in items 3 and 4 come into conflict with substantive secret theory.

The DPJ government bill would have replaced "reasonable grounds" with "sufficient grounds", thereby diminishing (although not removing entirely) agency discretion. The intention of the proposal was to increase the possibility of higher judicial scrutiny, although it is doubtful whether such a result will be attained by a change of wording alone.[72] Factors such as the burden of proof in judicial challenges, requiring applicants to show that non-disclosure of a document—to which neither they nor the court have access—was unreasonable, no doubt acts as a larger barrier than the standard itself. Conversely, the above-mentioned Specified Secrets Protection Law has moved the situation in the opposite direction, insofar as the law expands the statutory basis for secrecy designation by administrative organs, and allows the heads of the organs (who are also responsible for disclosure decisions under the Information Disclosure Law) to declare that information is secret by reason of its potential effect on national defense or diplomacy. This raises the fear that agency interpretation would come closer to "formal secret theory", not only in

[71]Japanese Supreme Court (Judgment of 31 May 1978), 32(3) *Keishû* 457. An English translation can be found in Beer & Ito 1996, p. 543–547.

[72]Rheuben 2013b, p. 266.

the National Public Employee Law but also in the Information Disclosure Law, because organs would ordinarily be bound by such secrecy designations.[73]

### 3.3.4 Deliberative Process Information (Item 5)

Item 5 exempts information about "deliberations, examinations, or consultations" within national government organs or between national and local governmental organs or incorporated administrative agencies, etc., from disclosure, when the disclosure has a risk of: first, unjustly harming the frank exchange of opinions or the neutrality of decision making; second, unjustly causing confusion among the public; or third, unjustly bringing advantage or disadvantage to specific individuals. The word "unjustly" is added to prevent the abuse of the item.

It is noteworthy that some prefectural ordinances include a category of "collegial organ information" as non-disclosure information. In those provisions, it is stipulated that when such collegial organs classify certain information that was discussed in their meetings as non-disclosable, such information will automatically be exempt from disclosure. However, the Information Disclosure Law did not include such a category, and handled the problem within the general framework of deliberative process information.

The DPJ government bill would have deleted the second category (unjustly causing confusion among the public) from this exemption. The rationale was the vagueness of the provision and the contention that it reminds one of the Confucian notions of "making people follow the ruler but not understand the reason."[74]

### 3.3.5 The Nature of Governmental Affairs or Business Matters (Item 6)

Item 6 is difficult to summarize concisely. It relates to information, disclosure of which, "by the nature of said affairs or business, would risk, such as in the following mentioned risks, causing a hindrance to the proper performance of said affairs or business." To avoid the abuse of such a broad and vague category, the item enumerates, although not restrictively, typical categories of activities that must be hampered by the disclosure for the exemption to apply. Namely, when the disclosure has the risk of (1) making difficult fact-finding along with facilitating illegal or unfair acts, etc., in relation to audits, inspections, supervision, and testing; (2) unfairly harming the property interests or the position as a party of the State or incorporated agencies etc. in relation to contracts, negotiations, or administrative appeals or litigation; (3) unjustly obstructing the impartial and efficient execution of research studies; (4) hindering the impartial and smooth maintenance of personnel

[73]Cf. Rheuben 2013c.

[74]Miyake 2012, p. 68–69.

matters; or (5) harming legitimate interests arising from the management of the enterprises run by a local government or an incorporated administrative agency, etc.

### 3.4 Partial Disclosure

As mentioned above, Article 6 of the Information Disclosure Law stipulates a duty of partial disclosure.[75] When it is possible to easily divide and exclude a portion of the document in which the non-disclosure information is recorded, the administrative organ must disclose the remaining portion, with the exception of cases when no meaningful information is recorded in the latter. This clause aims to encourage the disclosure of information to the greatest extent possible, so long as there is no harm. However, the practical application differs depending upon how one defines a "unit of information".

Let us suppose a situation where an official of an agency had business lunch with her private sector associate, paid for out of the "social expense budget" of the agency. An administrative document records the date of the business lunch, the name of the restaurant, the amount of expenditure, and the name of the associate. Let us also suppose that the name of the associate is non-disclosure information according to item 1 (personal information). When there is a disclosure request for the document, can the agency regard the set of records concerning the business lunch as "one unit of information" and totally reject the request? Or should the agency divide the information and disclose the date, the name of the restaurant, and the amount of expenditure?

In some similar cases, concerning not the Information Disclosure Law but local government ordinances, the Supreme Court took the former position. The Court held that, when there is "independent and integral information" in the requested document, the agency may, but need not, further divide the information and disclose part of it only.[76] This position of the Supreme Court is criticized by scholars.[77] The DPJ government bill would have amended the article so that this contested interpretation would not be possible.[78]

[75]The Brazilian Law has an equivalent proviso in its Article 7 para 2.

[76]Japanese Supreme Court (Judgment of 27 March 2001), 55(2) *Minshû* 530; Japanese Supreme Court (Judgment of 28 February 2002), 56(2) *Minshû* 467. Some other judgments, however, do not appear to follow this interpretation. See Japanese Supreme Court (Judgment of 11 November 2003), 1847 *Hanrei Jihô* 21; Japanese Supreme Court (Judgment of 17 April 2007), 1971 *Hanrei Jihô* 109. In the latter decision, JusticeTokiyasu Fujita severely criticizes the "independent and integral information" theory in his supplementary opinion.

[77]See Uga 2014, p. 114–118.

[78]However, it is debatable whether the text in the bill can really achieve its intent. See Fujiwara 2012, p. 61–62.

### 3.5 "Glomar" Response (Article 8)[79]

When confirmation or denial of the existence of requested documents practically means revealing the substance of the non-disclosed information, the head of the administrative organ may refuse the request for disclosure without making clear the existence or non-existence of the documents.[80] A typically featured example is a request for "documents concerning the clinical history of a specific person". This provision is based on the so-called "Glomar" response in the United States.[81]

Two Judgments of the Tokyo District Court and Tokyo High Court, respectively, both revoked a non-disclosure decision based on this provision.[82] In these cases, a disclosure request was made for documents concerning dinner parties held by the Japanese Embassy in the U.S. when a specific Diet member visited the country. The Minister of Foreign Affairs rejected the request, not making clear whether such documents existed or not. The minister contended that, given some parties might be a part of diplomatic activities, information on which may be protected by items 3 or 6, and given that parties may involve secret meetings, information about the existence or non-existence of the parties should not be revealed. In these cases, however, the courts did not admit this line of argument as the disclosure of existence of "documents concerning dinner parties" does not necessary reveal whether such secret meetings actually occurred.

## 4 Procedure for Application

### 4.1 Paper and Electric Applications

In contrast with the position under the Brazilian Law, which allows applications for disclosure of information to be made by "any legitimate means"[83]—or indeed in the UK, where applications may even be made by way of social media such as Twitter[84]—the Information Disclosure Law sets down a relatively narrow

[79]The Brazilian law seems to have no equivalent provision.

[80]See Article 8 of the Information Disclosure Law.

[81]The term "Glomar response" originates from a response of the U.S. Central Intelligence Agency to the information disclosure request by a journalist with regard to the agency's covert project using "the Glomar Explorer", a large salvage vessel built by the agency. The CIA rejected the request because the existence or nonexistence of the requested records was itself a classified fact exempt from disclosure. See https://www.justice.gov/oip/blog/foia-update-oip-guidance-privacy-glomarization.

[82]Tokyo District Court (Judgment of 20 September 2007), 1995 *Hanrei Jihô* 78; Tokyo High Court (Judgment of 29 May 2008). Unreported – see http://www.courts.go.jp/app/files/hanrei_jp/097/037097_hanrei.pdf (Accessed on 15 February 2017).

[83]Chapter III, Section I, Article 10 of the Brazilian Law.

[84]See the Information Commissioner's Office website: http://www.ico.org.uk/for_organisations/freedom_of_information/guide/receiving_a_request (Accessed on 15 February 2017).

application procedure, requiring all applications to be "in writing".[85] In principle, this requirement is not limited to paper applications. A ministerial order issued by the Minister of Internal Affairs and Communications in 2004 provides that disclosure applications may be made electronically.[86]

In practice, however, few administrative agencies have embraced electronic applications.[87] A small number of agencies received 7069 electronic applications in 2015, out of 111,415 applications received by all agencies.[88] Several other major agencies (including the Ministry of Internal Affairs and Communications itself) previously allowed electronic applications via a one-stop government online application website,[89] but appear to have stopped this service in 2010. None of these agencies received any online applications in 2015.[90]

Consequently, in practice most disclosure applications are made either in person at the relevant agency's dedicated information disclosure counter, or by post. In-person applications may also be popular because of the advantages for inexperienced applicants of consulting agency staff. Some 29% of applications in 2015 were in-person.[91] Many administrative agencies provide multiple counters at government offices around the country so as not to disadvantage applicants outside of Tokyo. Nevertheless, surprisingly, the Transparency Team did not touch on the merits of increasing online accessibility.

"On-paper" applications are made by way of a pro forma application form, which is essentially the same for each agency. The Information Disclosure Law requires that applications include the applicant's name and address,[92] precluding the possibility of anonymous applications. The application forms themselves generally also require further contact details.

The provision of such details is principally for contact purposes, reflecting the essentially on-paper nature of the application process, and not for gathering

[85]See Article 4.1 of the Information Disclosure Law.

[86]Ministerial Ordinance on Applicable Procedures, etc., under the Law in relation to the Disclosure of Information Held by Administrative Agencies pursuant to Article 3 of the Execution of the Law in Relation to the Use of Information Technology in Administrative Procedures, etc. (Ministry of Internal Affairs Ministerial Ordinance No. 39 of 2004). Article 3 of the Law in Relation to the Use of Information Technology in Administrative Procedures, etc. (Law No. 151 of 2002) authorizes the Minister of Internal Affairs to issue ministerial ordinances designating any application required by law to be made "in writing" as capable of being carried out electronically.

[87]Cf. Chapter III, Section I, Article 10 para 2 of the Brazilian Law, which requires relevant entities and institutions to facilitate online applications.

[88]Specifically, the National Personnel Authority (4827 applications), the Ministry of Land, Infrastructure, Transport and Tourism (1510), the Ministry of Health Labor and Welfare (552), the Imperial Household Agency (83), the Cabinet Legislation Bureau (81), the Board of Audit of Japan (15), and the Japan Meteorological Agency (1). See Ministry of Internal Affairs and Communications 2017, p. 25.

[89]http://www.e-gov.go.jp/shinsei/index.html (Accessed on 15 February 2017).

[90]Ministry of Internal Affairs and Communications 2017, p. 25.

[91]Ministry of Internal Affairs and Communications 2017, p. 25.

[92]See Article 4.1 (1) of the Information Disclosure Law.

information about the applicant. Nevertheless, in 2002 the National Defense Agency (as it then was) caused a scandal when it was revealed that staff had collated and internally distributed lists of applicants that included personal information not relevant to the Information Disclosure Law, such as occupation and known political sympathies.[93] The Defense Agency was roundly criticized,[94] leading to an internal investigation, which concluded that the practice breached existing privacy laws.[95] The current Personal Information Protection Law similarly provides that administrative organs must not retain personal information beyond the scope necessary to perform their functions,[96] and must not use personal information outside of the purpose for which it was retained.[97]

Applications for disclosure must also include the names of the documents sought, or otherwise sufficient details to allow the documents sought to be identified.[98] To assist with identification, the Public Records and Archive Management Law requires each agency to maintain registers of documents held by the agency.[99] A searchable database combining these registers is available online.[100] Heads of administrative organs are also required to provide applicants with any available information that would assist them in making their application.[101] Where no information about the documents sought is available, or applicants are unaware as to whether the documents exist, they may instead specify the content of the documents (e.g., "all documents pertaining to [. . .]").[102]

Neither the Information Disclosure Law nor the pro forma application form require applicants to disclose their reasons for seeking disclosure or their intended use of the information, although the Information Disclosure Law does not go as far as the Brazilian Law[103] in prohibiting administrative organs from requesting such information. Indeed, in practice many local governments request applicants to voluntarily provide such information for statistical purposes.[104] However, as noted above (see Sect. 3.1), reasons for seeking disclosure cannot be considered in deciding whether to provide disclosure.

---

[93]National Defense Agency 2002.

[94]See, e.g., Repeta 2002.

[95]National Defense Agency 2002.

[96]Article 3 of the Personal Information Protection Law.

[97]Article 8 of the Personal Information Protection Law.

[98]See Article 4.1 (2) of the Information Disclosure Law. Cf. Chapter III, Section I, Article 10 para 1 of the Brazilian Law.

[99]See Article 7 of the Public Records and Archive Management Law.

[100]http://files.e-gov.go.jp/servlet/Fsearch (Accessed on 15 February 2017).

[101]See Article 22 of the Information Disclosure Law.

[102]Ministry of Internal Affairs and Communications, Administrative Management Bureau (Ed.) 2001, p. 33–34.

[103]See Chap. III, Section I, Article 10 para 3 of the Brazilian Law.

[104]Uga 2014, p. 57.

## 4.2 Application Fee

All on-paper applications, whether in person or by post, must be accompanied by a flat JPY 300 (approx. USD 3) application fee.[105] For the most part fees must be paid by way of government revenue stamps, which must first be purchased from a government office, post office or one of Japan's ubiquitous convenience stores, further underlining the user un-friendliness of the on-paper system. The Implementation Regulations under the Information Disclosure Law make provision for a reduced application fee of JPY 200 (USD 2) for applications made electronically.[106] However, the potential reduction in revenue appears if anything to have been a disincentive to electronic applications, as again few administrative agencies offer online payment options.

In 2010 report, the Transparency Team proposed that application fees should be abolished in principle.[107] Under the DPJ government bill, application fees would no longer apply, except for applications made by corporations or for commercial purposes. A number of agencies were opposed to the in-principle removal of application fees because it could encourage a deluge of meritless requests.[108] However, given that application fees are currently the equivalent of only a few US dollars, it is unlikely that they were ever a significant deterrent to applications.

## 4.3 Time Limit

After receiving an application for disclosure, the head of an administrative organ must provide its decision within 30 calendar days,[109] unless this is impractical. Administrative agencies may unilaterally extend the time limit for a decision by up to an additional 30 calendar days,[110] or, where a large volume of documents has

[105]See Article 16.1 of the Information Disclosure Law and Article 13.1 of the Information Disclosure Implementation Regulations. Cf. Chapter III, Section I, Article 12 of the Brazilian Law, which does not appear to anticipate payment of an application fee.

[106]See Article 13.1 of the Information Disclosure Implementation Regulations. (The "Implementation Regulations" here refers to the cabinet order enacted under delegation pursuant to the Information Disclosure Law, and which sets out the various items necessary for the implementation of that law.).

[107]Administrative Transparency Study Team 2010, p. 8–9.

[108]Miki 2010, p. 10.

[109]See Article 10.1 of the Information Disclosure Law. The "clock" starts running from the date that a satisfactorily completed application form is received. Upon receiving an application form the agency must immediately review the application for defects, and notify the applicant of any found, providing a reasonable period of time to remedy (Article 4.2 of the Information Disclosure Regulations in combination with Article 7 of the Administrative Procedures Law). This period of time is not counted towards the agency's processing period.

[110]See Article 10.2 of the Information Disclosure Law.

been requested and collating them would affect the agency's ability to carry out their functions, must render their decision in respect of as many documents as possible within the allotted time frame, and the remainder "within a reasonable period".[111] In each case, the agency must notify the applicant in writing, and provide reasons why the decision cannot be rendered in full within the 30-day time limit.

In practice, most decisions are made within the 30-day period. In 2015, 90.4% of all decisions were made within the initial 30 days, without any extension of time.[112] Where the extended 60-day period was exceeded because of large volume requests, 48.6% of final decisions were completed in less than 90 days, 81.7% within 6 months, and 94.5% within 1 year.[113]

In light of these periods, however, it is arguably ambitious for the Brazilian Law to anticipate immediate disclosure,[114] or even disclosure within an extended 20 or 30-day period.[115] Even in Japan, there are some significant slippages: 146 responses to requests carried out in 2015 had taken more than 1 year.[116]

A common reason for delay in responding to disclosure applications is the need to consult with third parties affected by the potential disclosure of a document. The Information Disclosure Law allows administrative bodies to consult with third parties (again, in writing) on a voluntary basis to confirm whether either of the privacy or confidentiality exemptions to disclosure applies (for example, when it is unclear to an agency whether given information in respect of a private company constitutes commercially sensitive information).[117] Consultation with third parties is mandatory where it is apparent that a privacy exemption applies, but where the disclosure is deemed "necessary to be made public in order to protect a person's life, health, livelihood, or property."[118] The same applies in the case of public interest discretionary disclosure.[119]

Where, following consultation, the head of an administrative organ intends to disclose private information notwithstanding a written objection from the affected third party, the head of the organ must immediately inform the third party and wait a period of 2 weeks before proceeding with disclosure, within which time the third party may mount an appeal.[120] Three such appeals were made by affected third parties in 2014.[121] Although the Brazilian Law sets some limited exceptions to the

[111]See Article 11 of the Information Disclosure Law.

[112]Ministry of Internal Affairs and Communications 2017, p. 28.

[113]Ministry of Internal Affairs and Communications 2017, p. 29.

[114]Chapter III, Section I, Article 11 of the Brazilian Law.

[115]Chapter III, Section I, Article 11 para 1 and 2 of the Brazilian Law.

[116]Ministry of Internal Affairs and Communications 2017, p. 29.

[117]See Article 13.1 of the Information Disclosure Law.

[118]See Article 13.2, Article 5.1 point (b), and the provision contained in Article 5 item 2 of the Information Disclosure Law.

[119]See Article 13.2 and Article 7 of the Information Disclosure Law.

[120]See Article 13.3 of the Information Disclosure Law.

[121]Ministry of Internal Affairs and Communications 2017, p. 42.

general restriction on disclosing personal information,[122] there are no apparent obligations to consult with affected third parties, or rights of third parties to challenge a decision to disclose.

## 4.4 Notification of Decision

Once a decision to disclose or not to disclose a document has been made, it must be notified to the applicant in writing.[123] Where the decision is against disclosure (including where the document does not exist or has been destroyed), the head of an administrative organ must provide the applicant with reasons,[124] and inform the applicant about their right to appeal the decision, either by way of internal review,[125] or judicial review.[126]

Where the decision is in favor of partial or full disclosure, the written notification will identify all accessible documents pertinent to the request, and invite the applicant to indicate to which documents the applicant wishes to receive access, as well as the manner in which the applicant wishes to receive it. Applicants will ordinarily have the choice of inspecting original documents in person at the relevant offices, or receiving paper or electronic copies.[127] As only a small number of administrative organs provide online application facilities, copies of documents are similarly provided principally in hard copy or "physical" form, including by way of CD-ROM for electronic copies.

Disclosure decisions also notify the applicant of all fees payable for the documents disclosed (separate from the initial application fee). Unlike, for example, the UK or Australia, fees are calculated based on providing or reproducing the relevant documents, rather than on a time-cost basis for processing the request. Therefore, whereas in the former jurisdictions fees can quickly become quite expensive where documents have taken several days to locate and review, in Japan a relatively low flat rate applies, according to the size and format of the document disclosed. In-person disclosures, for example, are charged at JPY 100 (USD 1) per 100 pages viewed, while on-paper and digital copies are charged at JPY 10 (USD 10c) per page.[128] The first JPY 300 (or JPY 200, in the case of electronic applications) worth of documents are covered by the initial application fee and so are free.[129]

[122]Chapter III, Section V, Article 31 para 3 of the Brazilian Law.

[123]See Article 9 of the Information Disclosure Law.

[124]See Article 8 of the Administrative Procedure Law.

[125]See Article 57.1 of the Administrative Appeals Law.

[126]See Article 46.1 of the Administrative Case Litigation Law.

[127]See Article 14 of the Information Disclosure Law.

[128]See Article 16.1 of the Information Disclosure Law & Schedule to Information Disclosure Implementation Regulations.

[129]See Article 13.2 of the Information Disclosure Implementation Regulations.

The determination of fees essentially involves a trade-off between accessibility for applicants on the one hand, and the possibility to recoup costs and ensure proper resource allocation on the other. Japanese policymakers have ultimately sided with keeping fees low enough to avoid discouraging applications.[130] The Brazilian Law, which also requires fees to be calculated based on reproduction costs only (albeit in a more open-ended manner), appears to reflect similar considerations.[131]

Notwithstanding that fees are already relatively low, the Information Disclosure Law makes provision for reductions of fees in certain circumstances.[132] Unlike the Brazilian Law, which allows total exemption from fees for applicants in economic difficulties,[133] the Information Disclosure Law allows a reduction of up to JPY 2000 (USD 20) per application.[134] Reductions in fees are explicitly available for applicants in economic difficulties, but are arguably also available for applications by public interest organizations.[135] Perhaps unsurprisingly, administrative organs received only 38 applications for reductions in fees in 2015, of which 23 were granted.[136] Nevertheless, the Transparency Team proposed that the initial application fee should be abolished and disclosure fees lowered.[137]

Applicants must respond to a disclosure decision, together with payment of the requisite fee (again by way of revenue stamp for on-paper responses) within 30 calendar days, unless there are "justifiable reasons" for failing to respond within a timely manner.[138] After this, the head of an administrative organ can put disclosure into effect, whether by sending copies of the relevant documents by way of return, or by allowing in-person disclosure on a date designated by the applicant.

## 4.5 *Access and Administrative Procedure*

Decisions under the Information Disclosure Law, as with most other administrative decisions, are governed by the Administrative Procedure Law.[139] Like the Information Disclosure Law, the Administrative Procedure Law was one of the major

[130]Article 16.2 of the Information Disclosure Law requires fees to be as "accessible as possible". This provision was added to the Information Disclosure Law in the course of the Diet debates over the law. The Diet also passed a subsequent separate resolution to this effect. See Ministry of Internal Affairs and Communications, Administrative Management Bureau 2001, p. 148–149.

[131]Chapter III, Section I, Article 12 of the Brazilian Law.

[132]See Article 16.3 of the Information Disclosure Law.

[133]Chapter III, Section I, Article 12 of the Brazilian Law.

[134]Article 14.1 of the Information Disclosure Implementation Regulations.

[135]Uga 2014, p. 154.

[136]Ministry of Internal Affairs and Communications 2017, p. 42.

[137]Administrative Transparency Study Team 2010, p. 8–9.

[138]See Article 14.3 of the Information Disclosure Law.

[139]Law No. 88 of 1993. Chapter 2 of the law applies to decisions in relation to applications, which includes disclosure applications under the Information Disclosure Law.

administrative law reforms of the 1990s, although one that had been in contemplation for considerably longer.[140] It aims to improve the fairness and transparency of decision-making by setting out in broad terms appropriate procedures to be followed by administrative organs in respect of specific types of decisions (although many provisions of the law are hortatory only, requiring organs to "make efforts" to comply).

To some degree, both the Information Disclosure Law and Administrative Procedure Law overlap. For example, as noted above, the Information Disclosure Law requires administrative organs to consult with third parties where they intend to disclose those parties' private information.[141] However, the Administrative Procedure Law also arguably requires this, under which organs must "endeavor" to seek comment from affected third parties whose interests must be considered in granting approvals.[142]

In other respects, the Administrative Procedure Law is complementary. For example, while the Information Disclosure Law merely requires administrative organs to give written notice of a decision not to disclose documents,[143] the Administrative Procedure Law is the source of the additional obligation to provide reasons for non-disclosure.[144] The Transparency Team noted that in providing reasons for non-disclosure decisions in practice, administrative organs too often merely avert to the relevant disclosure exemption under Article 5 (for example, "national security") without setting out the relationship between the exemption and the document sought.[145] It recommended the Information Disclosure Law to be amended to require the provision of detailed reasons.[146] The DPJ government bill did include a new provision mirroring the reasons requirement under the Administrative Procedure Law, but this was still not explicit as to the level of detail required, other than that reasons should be "as specific as possible".[147] From this perspective, the provision of the Brazilian Law allowing applicants to obtain the "full content" of a non-disclosure decision is encouraging.[148]

Another important, although limited, way in which the Administrative Procedure Law complements the Information Disclosure Law is in respect of proactive disclosure. The Information Disclosure Law currently applies a passive model of

[140] As far back as the early 1950s: see Uga 2016, p. 32–39.

[141] Under Article 13.2 of the Information Disclosure Law.

[142] See Article 10 of the Administrative Procedure Law.

[143] See Article 9.2 of the Information Disclosure Law.

[144] See Article 8 of the Administrative Procedure Law.

[145] Administrative Transparency Study Team 2010, p. 7.

[146] Administrative Transparency Study Team 2010, p. 7.

[147] Note, however, that the Supreme Court has held in respect of reasons given under a local government information disclosure ordinance that reasons must make clear the relationship between the relevant exemption and the non-disclosure decision: Japanese Supreme Court (Judgment of 10 December 1992), 1453 *Hanrei Jihô* 116.

[148] Chapter III, Section I, Article 14 of the Brazilian Law.

disclosure insofar as it relies on applicants to request documents to access them.[149] Unlike the Brazilian Law, which requires the dissemination of certain fundamental information,[150] there are no obligations under the Information Disclosure Law to proactively make public types of documents commonly requested by applicants (although, as noted above, the Public Records and Archive Management Law does require the publication of document registers).[151] However, the Administrative Procedure Law does require the publication of certain information, including internal guidelines and standards upon which administrative organs make decisions,[152] and feedback received from interested parties when conducting public consultations.[153]

The DPJ government bill inserted an entire new chapter into the Information Disclosure Law that mandated the proactive disclosure of certain types of information not unlike those enumerated under the Brazilian Law (in relation to organizational structure, budgeting, etc.). The new chapter also required administrative organs to consider proactive disclosure of documents that have previously been requested by two or more separate applicants and are likely to be requested again in the future.

# 5 Judicial Protection

## *5.1 Overview*

A decision to disclose or not to disclose a document according to the Information Disclosure Law or local disclosure ordinances is regarded as an "administrative disposition",[154] therefore allowing the applicant to file an administrative litigation

---

[149]Cf. Kadomatsu 2002, p. 463.

[150]See Chapter II, Article 8 of the Brazilian Law.

[151]See Article 7 of the Public Records and Archive Management Law.

[152]Articles 5 and 12.1 of the Administrative Procedure Law.

[153]See Article 43.1 of the Administrative Procedure Law.

[154]Japanese administrative litigation centers around the concept of "administrative disposition"*(gyôsei shobun)*, which is derived from the traditional German law concept of "*Verwaltungsakt*" (administrative act), the exercise of a public authority that directly forms or establishes the scope of an individual's legal rights or duties. Whereas the concept of "administrative act" *(gyôsei kôi)* is used only as an academic concept, statute exclusively uses the term "administrative disposition". The Administrative Case Litigation Law (Law No. 39 of 1962) anticipates revocation suits, an ex-post and negative remedy against an administrative disposition already rendered, as the most typical form of administrative suit (for the classical features of administrative suits in Japan and the 2004 amendments to the Administrative Case Litigation Law, see Kadomatsu 2009, p. 149–152). The classification of administrative decisions concerning administrative information disclosure as "administrative dispositions" was not so self-evident in early stages of practice. A judgment of the Yokohama District Court (Yokohama District Court (Judgment of 25 July 1984), 1132 *Hanrei Jihô* 113) found a revocation suit filed by an applicant

(revocation litigation) under the Administrative Case Litigation Law against total or partial non-disclosure decision, or an affected third party against a disclosure decision.[155] The applicant can also file an application for internal review by the relevant agency in accordance with the Administrative Appeals Law.[156] He is not required to use the internal review system in advance before resorting to litigation. The use of the former, however, would usually be beneficial to the applicant for the reasons explained below.[157]

In the period between 2001 and 2015, there were 1045.1 applications for internal agency review and 18.2 administrative suits filed annually on average.[158]

## 5.2 *Information Disclosure and the Personal Information Protection Review Board*

When an application for internal review against a disclosure or non-disclosure decision is made by an applicant or by a third party (see below), the head of an administrative organ responsible for the review must ask for an advisory opinion of the Review Board.[159] The Review Board is established under the Cabinet Office with 15 members, appointed by the Prime Minister with the consent of both Houses of the Diet. As the name of the Review Board suggests, it is responsible for

against a non-disclosure decision under the Kanagawa Prefecture Information Disclosure Ordinance non-justiciable, stating that the requested public document did not affect the applicant's concrete rights or interests. On appeal, however, the Tokyo High Court reversed the judgment (Tokyo High Court (Judgment of 20 December 1984), 1137 *Hanrei Jihô* 26). It stated that the ordinance fictitiously regards any person who has an interest in the prefectural administration generally to have interest in having access to prefectural public documents, hence giving them an individual and concrete right to request access to public documents. Since this High Court judgment, the issue has rarely been disputed.

[155]Under Article 12 of the Administrative Case Litigation Law, applicants may only bring administrative suits in the defendant's local court (invariably Tokyo, in the case of national government organs), or in the district court with jurisdiction over the area of the seat of the high court with appellate jurisdiction for the applicant's local court. This complicated formula means, for example, that applicants in Okinawa may only bring suits in either the Tokyo or Fukuoka District Courts, and not in the central Naha District Court in Okinawa. The DPJ government bill would have expanded jurisdiction to the applicant's local court, as is already the case with some other specialized administrative laws.

[156]Law No. 160 of 1962. For an overview of the administrative appeal system, see Okamura et al. 2014, p. 2–19. Amendments to the law were enacted in June 2014 (Law No. 68 of 2014), and put into effect in 2016.

[157]Under the Brazilian Law, appeal to the Office of the Comptroller General against the refusal of disclosure appears to only be possible after having been assessed by superior authorities (Article 16 para 1 of the Brazilian Law).

[158]Ministry of Internal Affairs and Communications 2017, p. 5 and 8.

[159]Article 18 of the Information Disclosure Law.

considering appeals not only under the Information Disclosure Law, but also under the Personal Information Protection Law.

When the Review Board finds it necessary, it may examine the concerned documents *in camera*. The Review Board can also order the head of an administrative organ to classify the content of any relevant documents, according to the formula designated by the Review Board (similar to a "Vaughn Index" in the United States). Following examination, the Review Board may issue an opinion affirming, rejecting or altering—for example, recommending greater or lesser partial disclosure—the agency's original decision. The opinion is informed to the complainant and made open to the public.

Although the Review Board *de jure* only issues an "advisory" opinion, its opinions have been in fact highly respected by administrative bodies. Only in limited cases have these bodies not followed the opinion of the Review Board.[160]

## *5.3 In Camera Procedure*

As mentioned above, an *in camera* examination procedure is adopted in the inspection process of the Review Board. However, this is not the case in the litigation process. This is one of the reasons why it is usually beneficial for the applicant to file an administrative internal appeal before going to court.

The absence of *in camera* procedure is often regarded as one of the defects of the present Information Disclosure Law. The legislature in 1999 was concerned that such a procedure might be incompatible with (A) the constitutional principle of open justice,[161] and (B) a basic principle of civil procedure that evidence in litigation should be limited to evidence that the parties have been given the opportunity to inspect and challenge. However, many academics,[162] as well as two concurring opinions of a Supreme Court decision in 2009,[163] are today of the

[160]Between 2001 and 2013, there were only 14 cases (out of 6337) in which administrative organs did not follow the opinion of the Review Board. It may be noteworthy that the Information Disclosure Law does not have any provision allowing the punishment of administrative officials in the case of non-compliance, equivalent to Article 32 or 33 of the Brazilian Law. In extreme cases, however, non-compliance might result in the liability of the national government under to the State Redress Law (Law No. 125 of 1947).

[161]Article 82 of the Japanese Constitution reads as follows:

(1) Trials shall be conducted and judgment declared publicly.
(2) Where a court unanimously determines publicity to be dangerous to public order or morals, a trial may be conducted privately, but trials of political offenses, offenses involving the press or cases wherein the rights of people as guaranteed in Chapter III of this Constitution are in question shall always be conducted publicly.

[162]Uga 2014, p. 180–181; Murakami 2011, p.497–499; Fujiwara 2012, p. 64; Cf. Rheuben 2013b, p. 272–273.

[163]Concurring opinions of Justice Izumi and Justice Miyagawa in Japanese Supreme Court decision of 15 January 2009, 63(1) *Minshû* 46. The latter also points out that the fact that *in*

view that the introduction of the procedure would not violate the Constitution and that provision for a system of *in camera* review is a matter subject to legislative discretion.

The DPJ government bill proposed the introduction of an *in camera* procedure into judicial challenges under the Information Disclosure Law. Unlike in the inspection process conducted by the Review Board, the consent of the defendant (i.e., administrative bodies) would be necessary for the use of such a procedure. However, refusal of consent would be possible only in the case when the submission of the document to the court will hamper significant interests of the state such as national defense, diplomatic relations, or public safety.

### *5.4 Third Party Protection*

As mentioned above, the Information Disclosure Law has provisions to protect third parties whose information is recorded in administrative documents concerned with the disclosure request. The administrative agencies either voluntarily or mandatorily consult with the third party in such cases.

When the head of an administrative organ intends to disclose the documents notwithstanding the objection of the third party, the third party can also file an administrative suit or an application for internal review against the disclosure decision.[164] Article 13.3 of the Information Disclosure Law stipulates that, where third party consultation occurs, the agency should allot at least 2 weeks between the day of the disclosure decision and the day that disclosure will be implemented. The rationale for this provision is to ensure the possibility of filing the litigation or the appeal before the disclosure will be actually implemented.

## 6 Summary: Main Differences Between the Brazilian Law and the Japanese Law

By way of conclusion of this chapter, we concisely summarize the main differences between the Brazilian Law[165] and the Japanese Information Disclosure law.

*camera* inspection is possible in the case of inspection by the Review Board but not in the litigation process "may be inconsistent with the purpose of the information disclosure system, in which the judiciary is authorized to make a final decision".

[164]The Brazilian Law does not have express provisions concerning the standing of third parties.

[165]Because the authors' knowledge about the Brazilian Law is limited to its text, there is a considerable and unavoidable risk of misunderstanding.

### 6.1 Scope of Application

- The Japanese Information Disclosure Law is only one of several key information laws in Japan, which governs access to official documents at the national level. The law shares the role with other key information law such as the Personal Information Protection Law, the Public Records and Archive Management Law, and the Specified Secrets Protection Law. The Brazilian Law, however, appears to be relatively comprehensive, and covers a number of aspects of information regulation (see Sect. 1.1).
- While the Brazilian law applies to "the Union, States, Federal District and Municipalities", the scope of the Japanese Information Disclosure Law is limited to administrative documents held by national "Administrative Organs". Documents held by the national parliament and the courts are not the subject of disclosure. The law does not apply to prefectures and municipalities (see Sect. 1.2).

### 6.2 Object of Access

- In contrast to the Brazilian Law, the object of disclosure in the Japanese Information Disclosure Law is "administrative documents", not "information". However, the "documents" in the Japanese law cover not only paper documents but also "electromagnetic records" (Article 2.2 of the Information Disclosure Law) (see Sect. 2.3).
- While the Brazilian Law guarantees the right to obtain "information regarding activities carried out by entities and institutions, including activities regarding their policies, organization and services" (Article 7.5 of the Brazilian Law), the target of the Japanese Information Disclosure Law is limited to existing documents. The law does not regulate the duties of administrative organs to create documents. The Japanese Public Records and Archive Management Law stipulates such duties, but is limited to documents concerning highly significant decisions such as the enactment of statutes (see Sect. 2.3).

### 6.3 Non-Disclosure Information

- As opposed to the Brazilian Law (Sec. IV), the Japanese Information Disclosure Law does not have a provision concerning classification of secrets (see Sect. 3.2).
- Express secret information categories in the Brazilian Law, such as information that could cause financial, economic or monetary instability or information on scientific or technological research and development projects (Article 23, item

4 of the Brazilian Law), do not appear in the Japanese Information Disclosure Law. On the other hand, the deliberative process information category (Article 5, item 5 of the Information Disclosure Law) as such is not found in the Brazilian Law.

- Personal Information is in principle exempt from information disclosure in both Brazilian and Japanese law. Concerning the definition of "personal information", the Japanese Information Disclosure Law adopts "personal identification-type" information as opposed to "privacy invasion-type" information (Article 5, item 1 of the Information Disclosure Law). In this respect, the position of the Brazilian Law is not clear (see Sect. 3.3.1).

## 6.4 *Procedure for Application*

- While the Brazilian Law allows applications for disclosure of information to be made by "any legitimate means", the Japanese Information Disclosure Law sets down a relatively narrow application procedure, requiring all applications to be "in writing". In principle, this requirement is not limited to paper applications. A ministerial order issued by the Minister of Internal Affairs and Communications in 2004 provides that disclosure applications may be made electronically.
- The Japanese Information Disclosure Law does not require applicants to disclose their reasons for seeking disclosure or their intended use of the information, although the Japanese Law does not go as far as the Brazilian Law in its Article 10.3 in prohibiting administrative organs from requesting such information. Indeed, in practice many local governments request applicants to voluntarily provide such information for statistical purposes. However, reasons for seeking disclosure cannot be considered in deciding whether to provide disclosure (see Sects. 3.1 and 4.2).
- The Japanese Information Disclosure Law imposes a flat JPY 300 (approx. USD 3) application fee for all on-paper applications and JPY 200 (approx. USD 2) for online applications (Article 16.1 of the Information Disclosure Law, and Article 13 of the Information Disclosure Implementation Regulations). Separate from the initial application fee, when the requested documents are disclosed, a "disclosure implementation fee" is also imposed (Article 16.1 of the Information Disclosure Law and Schedule to the Information Disclosure Implementation Regulations). The Brazilian Law stipulates that "the service of search and supply of information is free", but that reproduction of the information may be charged to cover the cost of services and materials (Article 12 of the Brazilian Law). Both the Japanese Law and Brazilian Law make provision for reductions of fees in certain circumstances. Total exemption may also be possible in the latter (see Sects. 4.2 and 4.4).
- The Japanese Information Disclosure Law requires the head of an administrative organ to provide his or her decision within 30 days after receiving an application for disclosure. The administrative organ may unilaterally extend the time limit

up to an additional 30 days (Article 10 of the Information Disclosure Law). It is arguably ambitious for the Brazilian Law to anticipate immediate disclosure, or even disclosure within an extended 20 or 30 day period (Article 11 of the Brazilian Law) (see Sect. 4.3).

- The Japanese Information Disclosure Law does not have any equivalent provision to Article 32 or 33 of the Brazilian Law, allowing the punishment of administrative officials in the case of non-compliance. In extreme cases, however, non-compliance might result in the liability of the national government under to the State Redress Law (see Sect. 5.2, footnote 160).

**Acknowledgement** This work was supported by JSPS KAKENHI Grant Numbers JP15H03290, JP16H03681. The authors would like to thank Mr. Yukinobu Hori (Kobe University) for his editing work.

## References

Administrative Transparency Study Team. (2010). *Gyôsei Tômei-ka Kentô Chiimu [Report of the Administrative Transparency Study Team]*. Administrative Transparency Study Team, the Cabinet Office.

Beer, L. W., & Ito, H. (1996). *The Constitutional Case Law of Japan, 1970 through 1990*. Seattle, WA: University of Washington Press.

Brown, R. G. (1977). Government secrecy and the "People's Right to Know" in Japan: Implications of the NISHIYAMA case. *Law in Japan, 10*, 112.

Fujiwara, S. (2012). Jôhô Kôkai Hô Kaisei Hôan [The Information Disclosure Law Amendment Bill]. *Hôritsu Jihô, 84*(1), 59–64.

Hata, H., & Nakagawa, G. (1997). *Constitutional law of Japan*. The Hague, the Netherlands: Kluwer Law International.

Horibe, M. (1992). Making "Freedom of Information" laws in Japan. *Hitotsubashi Journal of Law and Politics, 20*, 33–45.

Kadomatsu, N. (1999). The new administrative Information Disclosure Law in Japan. *Zeitschrift für Japanisches Recht/Journal of Japanese Law, 8*, 34–52.

Kadomatsu, N. (2002). The right to be informed-the obligation for providing information: The case of Japanese Information Disclosure Law. *Hôsei Kenkyû, 69*(2), 441–464. (http://hdl.handle.net/2324/2300).

Kadomatsu, N. (2009). Judicial governance through resolution of legal disputes? — A Japanese perspective. *National Taiwan University Law Review, 4*(2), 141–162.

Kadomatsu, N. (2011). Accountability of administration in Japan after the mid-1990s. *Zeitschrift für Japanisches Recht/Journal of Japanese Law, 31*, 5–20.

Matsui, S. (2011). *The Constitution of Japan. A contextual analysis*. Oxford and Portland, OR: Hart.

Miki, Y. (2010). Jôhô Kôkai Hô Kaisei no Hôkôsei [On the direction of the amendment to the Information Disclosure Law]. *Jôhô Kôkai Digest, 21*.

Ministry of Internal Affairs and Communications, Administrative Management Bureau. (2001). *Shôkai Jôhô Kôkai Hô [Information Disclosure Law in detail]*. Tokyo: Ministry of Finance Printers.

Ministry of Internal Affairs and Communications. (2005). Kaku Gyôseikikan ni okeru Kômuin no Shimei no Toriatsukai ni tsuite [On the treatment of names of officials in each administrative agency], The agreement in liaison committee among ministries on information disclosure).

Retrieved September 22, 2016, from http://www.soumu.go.jp/main_sosiki/gyoukan/kanri/jyohokokai/pdf/110624_01.pdf

Ministry of Internal Affairs and Communications, Director-General of the Administrative Management Bureau. (2007). Kuni no Gyôseikikan ni okeru Kanbukômuin no Ryakureki no Kôhyô no Arikata ni tsuite [On disclosure of career summaries of executive officials of national administrative agencies]. Retrieved September 22, 2016, from http://www.soumu.go.jp/main_sosiki/gyoukan/kanri/070522_1.html

Ministry of Internal Affairs and Communications. (2015). Chihô Kôkyodantai ni okeru Jôhô Kôkai Jôrei no Seitei Jôkyô [Results of survey on the enactment of information disclosure ordinances]. Retrieved September 13, 2017, from http://www.soumu.go.jp/main content/000350962.pdf

Ministry of Internal Affairs and Communications. (2017). Heisei 27-nendo ni okeru Jouhou Koukai Hou no Shikou ni tsuite [On the implementation of the information disclosure law for administrative agencies in business year 2015]. Retrieved September 13, 2017, from http://www.soumu.go.jp/main_content/000473486.pdf

Miyake, H. (2012). Gyôsei Tômeika Kentô Chiimu ni okeru Jôhô Kôkai Hô Kaisei no Ronten Seiri [A summation of arguments on amendment of the Information Disclosure Law within the Transparency Team]. *Hôritsu Jihô, 84*(1), 65–71.

Murakami, H. (2011). *Jôkai Gyôsei Jôhô Kanren Sampô [Commentary on the three laws related to administrative information]*. Tokyo: Kobundo.

National Defense Agency. (2002). *Kaibaku Santou Kaisa Kaiji Seikyuusha Risuto Jian nado ni kakawaru Chousa Houkokusho [Investigation report into the incident involving a list of dis closure applicants by a Lieutentant Commander]*. Retrieved September 22, 2016, from http://www.mod.go.jp/j/approach/hyouka/chousa/list/chosa41.html

Okamura, S., & DBJEC (copyright 2014). Administrative complaints. In Z. Kitagawa (Ed.), *Doing business in Japan* (para 11.02).

Repeta, L. (2002, June 15). Defense Agency deals democracy a blow. *The Japan Times*.

Repeta, L. (2003). *The birth of the Freedom of Information Act in Japan: Kanagawa 1982* (National Security Archive Working Paper 03.03).

Repeta, L. (2011). Citizens: The founders of Japan's freedom of information movement. *Meiji Law Journal, 18*, 39–68.

Repeta, L. (2013). A New State Secrecy Law for Japan? *The Asia-Pacific Journal*, 11. Retrieved September 22, 2016, from http://www.japanfocus.org/-Lawrence-Repeta/4011

Research Council on the Operation of the Information Disclosure Law (2005). *Jôhô Kôkai Hô no Seido Un'ei ni kan suru Kentô Kai no Hôkoku [Report of the Research Council on the Operation of the Information Disclosure Law]*. Japanese Ministry of Internal Affairs and Communications.

Rheuben, J. (2013a). New law creates a less transparent Japan. *East Asia Forum*. Retrieved September 22, 2016, from http://www.eastasiaforum.org/2013/12/11/new-law-creates-a-less-transparent-japan/

Rheuben, J. (2013b). Enhancing the right to know in Japan: Translation of and commentary on proposed amendments to the Information Disclosure Law. *Zeitschrift für Japanisches Recht/Journal of Japanese Law, 17*, 261–293.

Rheuben, J. (2013c). The potential impact of Japan's New State Secrecy Bill. *Freedominfo.org*. Retrieved September 22, 2016, from http://www.freedominfo.org/2013/11/the-potential-impact-of-japans-new-state-secrecy-bill/

Schultz, D. M. (2001). Japan's Information Disclosure Law: Why a law full of loopholes is better than no law at all. *Law in Japan: An Annual, 27*, 128–169.

Uga, K., & Schultz, D. M. (2001). Translation of Japan's Information Disclosure Law. *Law in Japan: An Annual, 27*, 170–183.

Uga, K. (2016). *Gyôsei Tetsudzuki Sampô no Kaisetsu [Commentary on the 3 laws concerning administrative procedure]*. Tokyo: Gakuyou Shobou.

Uga, K. (2014). *Shin Jôhô Kôkai Hô no Chikujô Kaisetsu [New annotated information Disclosure Law]*. Tokyo: Yûhikaku.

# List of Cases

An incomplete collection of Japanese court judgments (for both the Supreme Court and lower courts). can be accessed at http://www.courts.go.jp/. Reported Supreme Court judgments (i.e. those published in the *Minshû* or *Keishû* reporting series) from around 1992 onwards have in large part been translated into English and can be searched via http://www.courts.go.jp/app/hanrei_en/search

## *Japanese Supreme Court*

Japanese Supreme Court 26.11.1969, 1969 (Shi) 68, 23(11) *Keishû* 1490.
Japanese Supreme Court 31.05.1978, 1976 (a) 1581, 32(3) *Keishû* 457.
Japanese Supreme Court 10.12.1992, 1992 (Gyo-Tsu) 48, 1453 *Hanrei Jihô* 116.
Japanese Supreme Court 27.03.2001, 1996 (Gyo-Tsu) 211, 55(2) *Minshû* 530.
Japanese Supreme Court 28.02.2002, 1997 (Gyo-Tsu) 137, 56(2) *Minshû* 467.
Japanese Supreme Court 11.11.2003, 1998 (Gyo-Tsu) 167, 1847 *Hanrei Jihô* 21.
Japanese Supreme Court 17.04.2007, 2006 (Gyo_Hi) 50, 1971 *Hanrei Jihô* 109.
Japanese Supreme Court 15.01.2009, 2008(Kyo)44, 63(1) *Minshû* 46.
Japanese Supreme Court 14.10.2011, 2008 (Gyo-Hi) 67, 2159 *Hanrei Jihô* 53.
Japanese Supreme Court 14.07.2014, 2012 (Gyo-Hi) 33, 2242 *Hanrei Jihô* 51.

## *High Courts*

Tokyo High Court 20.12.1984, 1984 (Gyo-Ko) 46, 1137 *Hanrei Jihô* 26.
Tokyo High Court 29.05.2008, 2007 (Gyo-Ko) 345. Unreported-see http://www.courts.go.jp/app/files/hanrei_jp/097/037097_hanrei.pdf (Accessed on 9 May 2017).
Tokyo High Court 29.09.2011, 2010 (Gyo-Ko) 18, 2142 *Hanrei Jihô* 3.

## *District Courts*

Tokyo District Court 31.01.1974, 1972 (Toku-Wa) 477, 306 *Hanrei Times* 91.
Yokohama District Court 25.07.1984, 1983 (Gyo-U) 26, 1132 *Hanrei Jihô* 113.
Tokyo District Court 09.04.2010, 2009 (Gyo-U) 120, 2076 *Hanrei Jihô* 19.

# Chapter 13
# The First Step in the Long March: The Legislation and Practice of Open Government Information in China

**Ming'an Jiang and Daoming Tan**

**Contents**



## 1 Introduction

In the Spring and Autumn Period of the ancient China, Zi Chan and Shu Xiang, two politicians in the state of Zheng, once debated an issue: whether a law should be let the people know.[1] Zi Chan released the criminal law to the public, but was strongly criticized by Shu Xiang, who believed that if the people knew the contents of that

---

The authors thank to Bu Chao, Ph. D. candidate of PKU Law School, for his generous help in the preparations of this paper.

[1]Zuo Qiuming, The Tso Chuan: the Sixth Year of Zhao Gong.

M. Jiang (✉)
Peking University, Beijing, China
e-mail: jma@pku.edu.cn

D. Tan
Chinese Academy of Social Sciences, Beijing, China



H.-J. Blanke, R. Perlingeiro (eds.), *The Right of Access to Public Information*,
DOI 10.1007/978-3-662-55554-5_13

law, they would not show respect to the officials anymore. However, although this kind of tradition of disclosing laws has not wholly disappeared in the following over 2000 years, the legislation and practice of Open Government Information (OGI) in today's China has little or nothing to do with this traditional legal legacy. In fact, it was mainly driven by the economic reform and opening up policies beginning with the year of 1978.[2]

Since the 1980s, China has gradually abandoned the model of planned economy and embraced the free-market policies. In this context, two incentives have been created by the governments at all levels in China to construct transparent governance. The first is on economic purposes. With increasing transnational corporations rushing to China and the township enterprises growing in full bloom, a large amount of demands was generated to push the governments at all levels more open and transparent to the world, as well as its domestic market. This driving force was further reinforced after China successfully joined the World Trade Organization (WTO) in 2001, because it is one of the obligations of international law for the members of WTO to enhance the governments' transparency.[3] The second is the need of fighting against corruption. Rapid economic growth and rampant corruptions always go together, especially in such a country without effective legal institutions like China. Just as sunshine is the best antiseptics, it is of great necessity for the governments at all levels in China to establish the system of OGI, which has already become a sign of a modern society.

Similar to the economic reform starting from the household contract responsibility system in the countryside, the legislation on OGI was also adopted with a bottom-up approach, which was relatively cautious and pragmatic for China at that time. The lineage of the OGI work in China can be traced to the "open village affairs" (*cunwu gongkai*) at the village level in the early 1980s.[4] In 1987, the Chinese Communist Party (CCP) launched a national campaign called "Two Disclosures and One Monitoring" (*liang gongkai, yi jiandu*).[5] This campaign included provisions to disclose administrative rules, procedures and results and to accept public monitoring at every level of government. Since then, OGI practices have gradually spread among villages, townships, and cities.[6] In January 2003, the Rules on Open Government Information of Guangzhou Municipality took effect. In 2004, following the Guangzhou's lead, the governments of Shanghai, Beijing, Shenzhen, Hangzhou, Chongqing, Chengdu, and Wuhan all promulgated their own rules on OGI. Based on such experiments at the lower governmental level, a nationwide legislation was put on the agenda of the State of Council in 2003. On 17 January 2007, the State Council of China approved the Regulations of the

---

[2]Liu Wenjing 2011, p. 987.

[3]Clarke 2003, p. 97.

[4]Zhou Liangjin, 2007 p. 710.

[5]Piotrowski, Zhang, Lin & Yu 2009, p. 129–135.

[6]Chen Zhifu 2007, p. 21.

People's Republic of China on Open Government Information (the OGI Regulations), taking effect on 1 May 2008.

The OGI Regulations established a uniform procedure for administration of OGI for localities and administrative agencies to enhance transparencies of governments, make government information helpful to the economic development and protect the people's right to know. While clearly far from perfect, the Regulations nonetheless stand as a striking mark for further steps on the OGI work in China. There is a conspicuous example to show this point. On 12 May 2008, just a few days after the enforcement of the OGI Regulations, Wenchuan County of Sichuan province, the western part of China, suffered a deadly earthquake with 8.0 magnitude, killing nearly 80,000 people.[7] This sudden disaster caused a massive upset to the lives of millions of people, but it did not cause social panic, for the significant reason that there was a timely and full disclosure of information to the public. The governments responded quickly and effectively, and the media reported full, timely, transparent and comprehensive information, in complete contrast to the Tangshan earthquake in 1976 where there was a news blackout. More importantly, the central government released the death toll caused by this earthquake for the first time, which was considered one of state secrets before.

In the following sections, we introduce the principles and main contents included in the OGI Regulations, as well as main deficiencies need to be perfected in the near future. Our interests not only focus on the legislations Chinese governments have made in this area, but also try to find out whether they are fully put into practice, with which we point out the big gap between the texts and the reality. The last part briefly looks into the future for the legislations of OGI in China.

## 2 General Principles

### *2.1 Principles in the OGI Regulations*

There are heated debates on which principles should be included in China's legislation, before the adoption of OGI Regulations and even after that. Some scholars believe that it is only one fundamental principle necessary and sufficient to be included in it. That is: disclosure is principle and non-disclosure exceptional. Other scholars once drew up their own proposals of OGI legislation, putting forward the following six principles: civil rights, openness, balance of interests, free of charge, free use and remedies.[8] However, literally, there are another six principles in total provided by the first Chapter of the OGI Regulations, covering three aspects from which the central government considers the most important.

[7] Yong Chen & Booth 2011, p. 196, 199.

[8] Zhou Hanhua 2002, p. 89.

First, from the perspective of civil rights, OGI should adhere to the three principles of justice, fairness, and convenience to the people (Article 5 of the OGI Regulations). It means, the actions of OGI should be guaranteed being equal to all of the Chinese people. On the one hand, any citizen, legal person and other organization can equally obtain the government information which is disclosed on the governments' own initiatives, without any additional costs. On the other hand, all of them can file requests based on the special needs of such matters as their own production, livelihood and scientific and technological research. Moreover, it is strictly prohibited not to give equal treatment to the citizens in terms of their ethnic groups, race, sex, occupation, property status or religious belief, and to the legal persons or other organizations in terms of the nature of businesses (state-owned enterprises, foreign-capital or private ones). In addition, when performing its functions on OGI work, the government should also provide easily accessible means such as government websites and government gazettes that make it more convenient for the public to be informed.

Second, the next two principles of promptness and accuracy, concerning the quality of government information. According to Article 6 of the OGI Regulations, government information should be disclosed promptly and accurately, which means that any delay of disclosure, issuing the false or incomplete information would not be allowed. These two principles aim to safeguard the government's credibility, and enhance the role the OGI played in serving the social and economic developments.

The third aspect focuses on safeguarding public interest. It requires that the government information disclosed may not endanger state security, public security, economic security and social stability (Article 8 of the OGI Regulations). Administrative agencies may not disclose government information that involves state secrets, commercial secrets or individual privacy (Article 14.4 of the OGI Regulations). Obviously, this principle that is safeguarding public interest, puts some limitations to the scope of OGI to protect some important public interests the legislators think might otherwise be in danger.

To be sure, as part of basic administrative laws, OGI legislation should also follow the fundamental principles of legality and reasonableness in the fields of China's administrative law, in particular of administrative openness and due process of laws.[9] However, these fundamental principles in China's administrative laws are not specific to OGI, but the requirements for all administrative acts.

## 2.2 Disclosure Is Principle and Non-disclosure Exceptional

The main controversy among the principles of OGI Regulations is whether the principle of "Disclosure is principle and non-disclosure exceptional" has been included in it. As the denomination implies, this principle requires that the

[9]Jiang Ming'an 2011, p. 77.

governments at all levels should disclose government information as much as possible, keeping the secrecy only under the specific situations explicitly listed in the laws. Many scholars pointed out that it shall be the most important and essential principle for China's OGI legislations. They believe that without the directions of this core principle the governments may refuse to release any government information at will by making use of vagueness of the terms in OGI Regulations. Considering this, as the first official legislation on OGI in China, the Rules on Open Government Information of Guangzhou Municipality formally and explicitly established the principle that "virtually all government information should be disclosed and that non-disclosure would be the exception".[10] However, "Disclosure is principle and non-disclosure exceptional" is not expressly provided in the OGI Regulations. This is mainly because of the legal status of the Regulations. In fact, the OGI Regulations are only provisions adopted by the State of Council, which is the highest administrative agency, not laws approved by the National People's Congress (NPC) as the supreme state power organ. It means that they shall not contradict with the Law of People's Republic of China on Safeguarding State Secrets (LSSS) and other related laws.

## 3 Main Contents

### *3.1 The Organs of OGI and Definition of "Government Information"*

As the term "Open Government" suggests, the organs of OGI are those responsible for the OGI work. To begin, administrative agencies are the most important organs of OGI, referring specifically to those with independent legal person status, performing the functions in their own names and assuming the obligations independently. They shall have the responsibility to disclose the government information stored within their own scope of functions and duties. On the contrary, those like the internal institutions, the temporarily coordinated institutions, the working bodies cannot be recognized as qualified organs of OGI, having no obligations of disclosure, even if they indeed obtain some government information. Second, although the organizations like Meteorological Bureau and Securities Regulatory Commission are not administrative agencies, they are also considered as the organs of OGI, because these organizations are authorized by laws or regulations to exercise the functions of managing public affairs. Third, public enterprises and institutions that are closely related to the people's interests like education, medical care, water supply and environmental protection shall also disclose information that is made or obtained in the course of providing public services. However, as OGI Regulations have been approved by the State of Council which is the highest

[10] Horsley 2006, p. 5.

executive body of China, they do not have a binding effect on the legislative branch (the congresses at all levels), the judicial branch (the courts and procuratorates at all levels), as well as party organizations, which up to date have no such obligations disclosing their documents to the public. It would be preferable to incorporate the legislative and judicial branch as the subjects of OGI when China's law of OGI is enacted in near future.

Furthermore, the OGI Regulations prescribe the special offices for OGI work. The General Office of the State Council shall be the national department in charge of OGI work, and the general offices of local governments at the county level and above or other departments in charge of OGI work designated by the local governments at the county level and above shall be responsible for promoting, guiding, coordinating and supervising OGI work within their respective administrative areas. These offices should undertake specific OGI matters, maintain and update government information, organize the compilation of OGI guides and annual reports, and conduct examination for secrecy for the administrative agency to which the special office belongs (Article 4 of the OGI Regulations). The establishment of special offices for OGI in fact made government information disclosure more convenient and smoother, as well as more standardized and, thus, more easily supervised.

"Government information" in the OGI Regulations refers to information made or obtained by administrative agencies in the course of exercising their responsibilities and recorded and stored in a given form (Article 2 of the OGI Regulations). According to this definition, government information can be characterized by the following aspects. Firstly, government information is formed by the governments in the course of exercising responsibilities. Consequently, the information unrelated to exercising the responsibilities cannot be considered as government information. This mainly points to the information concerning administrative agency's internal affairs, such as internal personnel and financial information. Secondly, government information is made or obtained by the governments, including the first hand materials made by their own and the second hand sources obtained from some third parties. Nonetheless, no matter the first hand or the second hand information, according to the basic requirement of "who holds, who discloses", the government who holds the information shall release it to prevent it from delaying, rejecting to disclosure or even shirking its legal obligations. Third, government information should be expressed by a given, tangible form. It can be paper documents, as well as digital and electronic formats, but cannot be those without definite forms like oral messages or even rumors. It should also be pointed out that the governments just provide the information available without the obligations to classify, categorize, count or compare it. Then an issue occurs: do the documents in the investigation process belong to government information? Although these documents are in preparation for coming up with the conclusions, it might be more meaningful to disclose them to the public if necessary, because in many instances, releasing the entire decision-making process is worth more than simply opening the findings.

## 3.2 The Scope of Disclosure and Its Limitations

Based on its importance and whether it concerns public interests or not, government information is divided into two categories by the OGI Regulations, with some information disclosed proactively and the other by requests. Article 9 of the OGI Regulations explicitly regulates the information should be disclosed on governments' own initiatives if it satisfies any one of the following basic criteria: (1) Information that involves the vital interests of citizens, legal persons or other organizations; (2) Information that needs to be extensively known or participated in by the general public; (3) Information that shows structure, function and working procedure of the government and other matters relating to it; and (4) Other information that should be disclosed on the government's own initiative according to laws, regulations and relevant state provisions. Besides the general provisions, in view of the various functions they perform, the governments at different levels have been assigned different responsibilities in the Articles 10 to 12 of the OGI Regulations respectively. For example, as for measures against sudden public events, the governments at the county level and above and their departments focus mainly on emergency plans for early warning information and counter measures, while the governments at the level of cities divided into districts and the county level should disclose information on the management, usage and distribution of social donations in funds and in kind for emergency and disaster relief etc., and the governments at the township level should be responsible for releasing the information on the distribution of social donations in funds and in kind for emergency and disaster relief, etc.

As for the information can be opened by requests, Article 13 of the OGI Regulations prescribe extensively that in addition to government information disclosed by the governments' own initiative, citizens, legal persons or other organizations may, based on the special needs of such matters as their own production, livelihood and scientific and technological research (the so-called "three special needs"), also file requests to the governments at all levels to obtain relevant government information. Does it mean that the requests would be rejected by administrative agencies, if the government information required by the applicants is considered unrelated to the three special needs mentioned above? Certainly, the governments tend to adopt a rigid explanation on this part. In fact, many governments at all levels in China refuse to disclose government information by frequently invoking this clause. However, they misinterpret purposely the legal implications of this regulation. Three special needs are just enumerated as part of many reasons in Article 13 of the OGI Regulations, and are impossible to exhaust all of the special needs the applicants based on. In addition to these three needs, the requesters may and shall have other various reasons to ask for the disclosure of government information. As the concept of "special needs" is too ambiguous to be defined clearly, the courts at all levels should interpret it in a broad way so as to limit the discretion possessed by administrative agencies, promoting the governments in accordance with the law and building transparent governments in China.

On the other side, the OGI Regulations impose several limitations to the scope of OGI as well. There is a general principle in Article 8, prohibiting the disclosure of government information from endangering state security, public security, economic security, and social stability. Furthermore, Article 14 stresses that administrative agencies may not disclose government information that involves state secrets, commercial secrets or individual privacy. It is obvious that Article 8 is much stricter than Article 14 of the OGI Regulations, leaving enormous discretion for the governments to determine what the “state security, public security, economic security and social stability” are, in particular during those days when maintaining social stability was put on the top agenda.

Leaving this issue aside, Article 14 of the OGI Regulations has its own implications. To begin, the mechanisms should be established and perfected by administrative agencies to examine the government information to be disclosed in accordance with the provisions of the Law on Safeguarding State Secrets and other laws, regulations and relevant state provisions. Secondly, the information concerning state secrets and commercial secrets or individual privacy is treated differently. On the one hand, the information is absolutely prohibited from being released to the public, when it is examined as one of state secrets. According to Article 9 of the LSSS amended in 2010, state secrets include 7 items that are expansive: (1) major policy decisions on state affairs; (2) matters of national defense and the activities of the armed forces; (3) diplomatic activities and matters of foreign affairs; (4) secrets in the areas of national economic and social development; (5) secrets concerning science and technology; (6) secrets concerning activities for safeguarding state security and the investigation of criminal offenses; (7) any other secrets determined by the State Administration for the Protection of State Secrets. On the other hand, for the information concerning commercial secrets or individual privacy, it can be disclosed with the consent of the rightholders or if the governments believe that non-disclosure might cause a major impact on the public interest. In this case, the governments should carefully weigh private interests with public interest, in accordance with the principle of balance of interests. If the disclosure infringes the justified and lawful rights and interests, the rightholders and potentially influenced parties can ask the courts to declaim these administrative acts illegal, thus seeking the corresponding compensation.

## 3.3 *Methods of and Procedures for Disclosure*

There are different requirements of open procedures between the information on governments’ own initiative and by requests. For the government information to be disclosed on administrative agencies’ own initiative, the OGI Regulations require it follows the principle of convenience to the people. First, the governments should compile and publish OGI guides and catalogues of OGI, and update them in a timely manner (Article 19.1 of the OGI Regulations). Among them, OGI guides should include such contents as the types of government information, the system of cataloguing, the methods for obtaining information and the name, office address, office hours, contact telephone number, fax number and e-mail address of the office for OGI work (Article 19.2 of the OGI Regulations). The OGI catalogues should include such contents as an index, the name of the information, a summary of the information contents and the date of creation of the information (Article 19.3 of the OGI Regulations). Second, in the means of access to information, the government information should be released by various ways of government gazettes, government websites, press conferences, as well as through newspapers and other publications, radio, television and other methods that make it easily accessible for the public (Article 15 of the OGI Regulations). Also, the governments at all levels should set up government information reading places in the state archives and public libraries and install appropriate facilities and equipment to make it convenient for citizens, legal persons and other organizations to obtain government information (Article 16.1 of the OGI Regulations). Besides, the governments may set up, as needed, places and facilities such as public reading rooms, materials request stations, information bulletin boards, and electronic information screens to disclose government information (Article 16.2 of the OGI Regulations). Third, in the respect of the authorities, generally speaking, administrative agencies shall be responsible for disclosing government information that they have made, and those agencies that store the information obtained from the people have the responsibilities to release it (Article 17 of the OGI Regulations). In addition, to keep its effectiveness and qualities, government information to be released proactively should be disclosed within 20 business days from the date the information is formed or changed (Article 18 of the OGI Regulations). Certainly, this period can be changed if other laws or regulations have different provisions on it.

For the information requested by the people, the OGI Regulations also provide the requirements for the requesters, as well as the governments. As far as the requesters are concerned, they should file requests in written form, including digital and electronic forms, except in oral form for those who truly have difficulties doing that (Article 20.1 of the OGI Regulations). Moreover, the requests should include the following contents: (1) the name of the individual or organization making the request, the request and the method of contact; (2) a description of the government information requested to be disclosed; and (3) requirements to the format in which the requested government information is to be supplied (Article 20.2 of the OGI Regulations). If having evidence that the information related to them provided by the administrative agencies is inaccurate, the requesters also have the right to demand corrections (Article 25.2 of the OGI Regulations).

As for the governments, they should strictly follow the procedures the OGI Regulations prescribe. After receiving the requests, the governments should reply on-the-spot to the extent possible (Article 24.1 of the OGI Regulations). If an on-the-spot is impossible, administrative agencies should provide a reply within 15 business days from receiving a request, within no more than 30 business days when extended (Article 24.2 of the OGI Regulations). Nevertheless, administrative agencies should examine the information on whether it includes contents such as state secrets, commercial secrets or individual privacy before replying to the requesters. If the requested government information contains some contents that should not be disclosed, but that can be handled through differentiation, the governments should provide that information content that may be disclosed (Article 22 of the OGI Regulations). If the information involves commercial secrets or individual privacy the disclosure of which might infringe upon the lawful interest of a third party, an administrative agency should write to the third party to seek its opinion (Article 23 of the OGI Regulations). If the third party does not agree to have the information disclosed, the information may not be disclosed. However, if the administrative agency believes that non-disclosure might have a major influence on the public interest, it should disclosure it and notify the third party in writing of the content they have decided to disclose and the reasons therefor (Article 23 of the OGI Regulations). The last issue is about fees. Article 27 of the OGI Regulations emphasizes, administrative agencies may not collect any fees except the cost-based fees for searching, photocopying, postage and the like. Furthermore, the relevant fee may be reduced or exempted for a citizen with truly economic difficulties, and a necessary assistance should be provided for the citizens having trouble reading or obstacles to hearing and seeing (Article 28 of the OGI Regulations). However, it should be pointed out that legal persons or other organizations cannot get such kinds of treatments.

## 3.4 *Supervision and Safeguards*

The OGI Regulations adopted several measures to guarantee the access to information for the people. Primarily, governments at all levels should publish their annual reports on open government information work before 31 March each year (Article 31 of the OGI Regulations). The annual report should include the following contents: (1) Information on disclosing government information on the administrative agency's own initiative; (2) Information disclosing government information public upon requests and of requests that are denied; (3) Information on fee collection and fee reductions and exemptions concerning OGI; (4) Information on applications for administrative reconsideration and filing of administrative lawsuits in respect of OGI; (5) The main problems existing in OGI work and the information on improvements thereof; and (6) Other items that need to be reported (Article 32 of the OGI Regulations).

Second, the departments in charge of OGI work and the supervision agencies shall be responsible for supervising and inspecting the implementation of OGI (Article 30 of the OGI Regulations). If an administrative agency violates the provisions of the OGI Regulations and has engaged in any one of the behaviors listed in Article 35 of the OGI Regulations, the supervision agency or the administrative agency at the next higher level shall order the administrative agency to correct the situation. If the circumstances are serious, administrative penalties shall be imposed in accordance with the law on person(s) directly in charge of the administrative agency, as well as other persons who are directly responsible (Article 35 of the OGI

Regulations). If any one of the following behaviors constitutes a crime, criminal responsibility shall be pursed in accordance with the law: (1) Failure to fulfill, in accordance with the law, OGI obligations; (2) Failure to timely update the contents of government information which has been disclosed, the guide to OGI and the catalogue of OGI; (3) Collecting fees in violation of provisions; (4) Providing government information as a paid service through other organizations or individuals; (5) Disclosing government information which should not be disclosed; and (6) Other actions that violate the provisions of these Regulations.

Just as "no remedies, no rights" said, judicial review is the last but the most important measure to safeguard the implementation of the OGI Regulations. If citizens, legal persons or other organizations believe a specific administrative action of an administrative agency in its OGI work has infringed their lawful rights and interests, they may, in accordance with the law, apply for administrative reconsideration or file an administrative lawsuit (Article 33.2 of the OGI Regulations). This is the one provision in the OGI Regulations concerning lawsuits of OGI, so it is necessary to further come up with the detailed instructions. Not surprisingly, on 29 July 2011, the Chinese Supreme People's Court promulgated a judicial interpretation on OGI litigation. This judicial interpretation provides a clear legal guidance on accepting an OGI lawsuit, which agency should be the defendant, the relevant burden of proof, and what kind of judgment should be issued under different circumstances. In addition, as one kind of administrative litigations, the lawsuit on OGI should also follow the provisions in the Administrative Litigation Law of People's Republic of China (ALL) enacted in 1989 and amended for the first time over 20 years. According to the new version of ALL taking effects on 1 May 2015, OGI cases can be heard by the summary procedure instead of the previous ordinary one, which would speed up the trail process and improve the efficiencies on OGI litigations.

## 4 Several Deficiencies

### *4.1 Lack of Clear Constitutional Basis*

On the year of 1999 and 2004, the principles of "Rule of law" and "The State respects and preserves human rights" were enshrined in the 1982 Constitution respectively. This is really a big leap for China's constitutional development. Under this context, China speeded up the steps toward constructing transparent governments, adopting the OGI Regulations in 2007. However, the freedom of information or the right to know is still not one of citizen's fundamental rights respected and preserved in current Constitution. Simply put, there is no clear constitutional basis for OGI legislations and practices in China. Although in theory it can be derived from the freedom of expression in the Article 35 of the 1982 Constitution, there has not been such kind of constitutional interpretations in practice until now, for the Standing Committee of the NPC (NPCSC), the only institution responsible for constitutional interpretations, is slack to perform this function. For this reason, the purposes of the OGI Regulations are more supervising the governments and servicing the economic growth, than defending the freedom of information or right to know as one of the most important human rights. This indeed makes a big difference.

## 4.2 *Limitations by the Laws*

As the OGI Regulations are just administrative regulations subject to the laws, it faces substantial obstacles and challenges arising from the provisions of various laws, which are eventually weakening the effectiveness of OGI in practice. To begin, when conflicting to the Law on Safeguarding State Secrets (LSSS), the provisions of OGI Regulations shall be given way to those of that law. In contrast to OGI legislations, the main principle in LSSS is that "the secrecy is principle while non-secrecy is exceptional". In addition, the definition of state secrets in LSSS is so broad and uncertain that even the matters like "secrets in the areas of national economic and social development" can be state secrets, leaving much room of discretion to the state secret-guarding departments.[11] Consequently, it is relatively easy for some governments to reject the release of government information because it falls within the scope of state secrets. Even worse, such decisions cannot be challenged and reviewed through the judicial process.

Second, the scope of OGI can be limited substantially by Archives Law of the People's Republic of China (AL). This law emphasizes the management and protection of archives, imposing too many restrictions on disclosing and making use of archives. Most of historic information of the governments, such as matters on the reorganization of state-owned enterprises, veterans resettlement and the documents in the Cultural Revolution period, was stored in the archives and could not be opened to the public till three decades passed. Therefore, how to disclosure government historic information is another tough issue to be resolved in the future.

Third, the requirements in OGI Regulations might contravene with some provisions of the Civil Servant Law of the People's Republic of China (CSL). According to Article 12 of the CSL, civil servants must maintain confidentiality with state and workplace secrets. However, there are no detailed legal interpretations on the concept of "workplace secrets", which is near to establish another new kind of secrets except of state secrets, and prevailing over the provisions of OGI Regulations in its application. For this reason, it is necessary to clarify the contents of "workplace secrets" should not beyond the scope of "commercial secrets" and "privacy" regulated in OGI Regulations.

---

[11] Shen Fujun 2009, p. 50.

### 4.3 Constraints from the Administrative Litigation Law

There are also many defects on the respect of judicial safeguards. According to Article 33.2 of the OGI Regulations, citizens, legal persons or other organizations who believe that a specific administrative action of an administrative agency in its OGI work has infringed their lawful rights and interests, they may, in accordance with the law, file an administrative litigation. Firstly, the plaintiffs should have the burden of proof that the administrative actions do infringe their own lawful rights and interests. Thus, it is critical to define what the lawful rights and interests included in it. Unfortunately, the provisions concerning the scope of accepting cases in the Administrative Litigation Law (ALL) adopted a restrictive approach, only limited to personal and property rights. In this case, other kinds of rights, such as the freedom of expressions or the freedom of information, cannot be accepted as the basis of the claim. Secondly, although the amended ALL does not differentiate the specific administrative actions from abstract administrative actions any more, it does not mean, the judicial branch can now directly review the legality of the abstract ones. The judicial review is not only confined to regulatory documents, but also this kind of judicial review should be supplementary, not independent of specific disputes. In addition, the system of state compensation in China is far from perfect, and it only compensates direct losses to the plaintiff's lawful interests and rights, but not indirect damages which illegal administrative actions on OGI tend to cause.

Finally, although the judicial interpretation on OGI litigation has been promulgated by the Supreme Court of China, it deals little with disclosure procedure, and therefore does not influence the broad discretion administrative agencies enjoy in pertinent administrative procedure. Moreover, even if judicial interpretation can make up for some of the procedural deficiencies the OGI Regulations have, and provide more effective provisions for courts to follow across the nation, it will not be compulsory in administrative procedures, because administrative agencies are not bound to the judicial interpretations of the Supreme Court of China, unless their decisions are sued to courts.

## 5 Some Aspects in Practice

One aspect in practice concerns a long-term, deep-rooted tradition of keeping secret in China's political culture, which still plays a substantial influence on today's political realm. For governments and officials, disclosing government information might be criticized by the citizens and mass media, and even blamed by its higher ones, while keeping it secret could not fail under any circumstances. As rational bodies, the governments at all levels do not have sufficient incentives to release the government information from their hands as soon as possible. For example, few government agencies at any level have actively complied with the OGI requirements to publish information disclosure annual reports before 31 March every year. Figures in *The Prosecutor Daily* show as of midnight on 31 March 2009, 9 of the State Council's 27 ministries, 13 of its 16 directly subordinate organizations, 5 of its 6 administrative agencies, 11 of its 14 directly subordinate institutions, and 15 of 19 national administrations did not release their annual OGI report on schedule.[12] These results indicate that the Regulations still have a long way to go towards consistent nationwide implementation.

Another aspect focuses on the role the judicial branch plays in OGI. As the last line to safeguard the implementation of OGI Regulations, judicial review faces many barriers arising from the whole judicial system. The courts at all levels frequently have to follow the instructions and directions from the officials of the administrative agencies and the leaders of Committee of Political and Legislative Affairs of CCP (CPLA). Consequently, the lawsuits on OGI are more susceptible to improper interventions from the administrative officials and party leaders, so that the plaintiffs believing his legitimate rights and interests are infringed have relatively fewer chances to win a lawsuit. In short, judicial independence cannot be ensured and guaranteed in current political environment of China. However, since 2012, the new Chinese central government has pushed forward a series of major reforms to strengthen rule of law, one of which are judicial reform. To protect the autonomy of judicial branch, the names of leaders and officials who intervene in individual judicial cases should be written down, and be accountable for their actions. This is a very Chinese characteristic measure and it is too early to say whether it would improve judicial review to OGI or not.

However, it is inspiring to see that, with the great progress of rule of law and particularly the rapid development of network in the past few years, the citizens in China increasingly require more governments that are transparent and press the governments to become more open to the world, as well as to its people. Many non-governmental organizations (NGO) in civil society, including academic institutions in some universities, also make great efforts to enhance the awareness of OGI among the ordinary citizens, and more importantly, put forward further improving the mechanism of the OGI work in China. For example, the Center for Public Participation Studies and Supports (CPPSS) of the Law School of Peking University has begun to issue "China Administrative Transparency Annual Watch" since 2009, providing fully observations and meaningful evaluations on the constructions of transparency governments in China, which played an important role in promoting and supervising the OGI work of governments at all levels of China.[13] We can say that millions of ordinary persons in China are the main driving forces to make OGI legislation and practice better than before.

---

[12]Zhi Yan 2009.

[13]See Center for Public Participation Studies and Supports 2011.

## 6 The Future of OGI in China

The 2007 OGI Regulations are extraordinarily prominent for Chinese governments and its people, for they represent a qualitative break with the past and are the first nationwide attempt to create transparency of governments. Because it has taken an irreversible road towards rule of law and protection of human rights, we can predict that China would enact its first law of OGI Law in the next decade or so. However, it should be noted that it is just the first step in the long march for OGI. It is almost impossible for China to fully realize the well protection of freedom of information and construct transparent governments in one night. Besides further improving legislations on OGI, China still needs a long time to improve its legal system and ensure the independence of the judicial branch, as well as form a political culture of openness across the society.

## References

Administrative Litigation Law of the People's Republic of China. (中华人民共和国行政诉讼法) (adopted by the National People's Congress, enacted on 4 April 1989; amended on 1 November 2014). Retrieved February 15, 2017, from http://www.lawtime.cn/faguizt/131.html.

Archives Law of the People's Republic of China. (中华人民共和国档案法) (adopted by Standing Committee of National People's Congress, 5 September 1987, effective 1 January 1988, revised 5 July 199). Retrieved February 15, 2017, from http://www.npc.gov.cn/englishnpc/Law/2007-12/12/content_1383932.htm.

Center for Public Participation Studies and Supports (CPPSS). (2011). *China Administrative Transparency Annual Watch: 2009* (中国行政透明度报告:2009). Beijing: Law Press.

Clarke, D. C. (2003). China's legal system and the WTO: Prospects for compliance. *Washington University Global Studies Law Review, 2*, 97–118.

Chen, Y., & Booth, D. C. (2011). *The Wenchuan Earthquake of 2008: Anatomy of a disaster*. Beijing: Science Press of Beijing and Springer.

Chen, Z. (2007). Several issues with the Chinese access to government information regulations (中国政府信息公开规定的若干问题). *Journal of Chinese Public Administration, 11*, 21–23.

Civil Servant Law of the People's Republic of China. (中华人民共和国公务员法) (adopted by the Standing Committee of National People's Congress, 27 April 2005, effective 1 January 2006). Retrieved February 15, 2017, from http://www.npc.gov.cn/englishnpc/Law/2007-12/13/content_1384101.htm.

Horsley, J. P. (2006). Introduction on Open Government Information Implementation. *Government Information Quarterly, 23*(1), 5–10.

Jiang, M. (2011). *Administrative Law and Administrative Litigation Law* (行政法与行政诉讼法), Beijing: Peking University Press.

Liu, W. (2011). Approaching democracy through transparency: A comparative law study on Chinese Open Government Information. *American University International Law Review, 26*(4), 983–1007.

Piotrowski, S. J., Zhang, Y., Lin, W., & Yu, W. (2009). Key issues for implementation of Chinese Open Government Information Regulations. *Public Administration Review, 69*(s1), 129–135.

Provisions of the Supreme People's Court on Several Issues Concerning the Trial of Administrative Cases About Open Government Information. (最高人民法院关于审理政府信息公开行政案件若干问题的规定) (promulgated by the Supreme People's Court, July 2011, effective

11 August 2011) (China). Retrieved February 15, 2017, from http://www.lawinfochina.com/Display.aspx?lib=law&ID=8897.

Regulations of the People's Republic of China on Open Government Information. (中华人民共和国政府信息公开条例) (adopted by the State Council on 5 April 2007; Effective 1 May 2008) (China). Retrieved February 15, 2017, from http://www.law.yale.edu/documents/pdf/Intellectual_Life/Ch_OGI_Regualtions_Eng_Final_051607.pdf (Translated by The China Law Center, Yale Law School).

Shen, F. (2009). Establishing the system of safeguarding secrecy in accordance with OGI system: From the perspective of amending LSSS. *Law Journal, 2009*(9), 50.

The Law of the People's Republic of China on Safeguarding State Secrets (中华人民共和国保守国家秘密法) (promulgated by Standing Committee of National People's Congress, 5 September 1988, effective 1 May 1989, revised 9 April 2010, effective 1 October 2010). Retrieved February 15, 2017, from http://www.lawinfochina.com/display.aspx?lib=law&id=1191.&CGid = (Translated by lawfochina.com).

The Rules on Open Government Information of Guangzhou Municipality (广州市政府信息公开规定) (Decree No. 8 of the Guangzhou Municipal People's Government, dated 6 November 2002, effective 1 January 2003) (China). http://www.freedominfo.org/documents/provisions.pdf (Trans. J. P. Horsley, The China Law Center, Yale Law School).

Zhi, Y. (2009). Open government information: How many governmental departments have not handed in their 'paper' yet (信息公开:还有多少部门到期未"交卷"). *The Prosecutor Daily*. Retrieved February 15, 2017, from http://unn.people.com.cn/GB/14748/9092952.html

Zhou, H. (2002). Some considerations on drawing a proposal of OGI regulations (起草《政府信息公开条例》(专家建议稿)的基本考虑). *Law Studies, 2002*(06), 89–91.

Zhou, L. (2007). Background and implication of the Chinese access to government ordinance (中国信息公开立法的背景和含义). *Law and Society, 7*, 710–711.

Zuo, Q. *The Tso Chuan: The Sixth year of Zhao Gong* [《左传·昭公六年》].

# Chapter 14
# Legal Situation of China in the Area of Access to Information

**Weibing Xiao**

**Contents**



## 1 Introduction

China adopted a model of Freedom of Information (FOI) legislation emphasizing proactive disclosure[1]—FOI Regulations—on 17 January 2007, and brought it into effect on 1 May 2008. This legislation is an administrative regulation, which was passed by the State Council and cannot override a law and the Constitution. China's FOI is not a strange and intriguing phenomenon generally held by many FOI

[1]Xiao 2010, p. 346.

W. Xiao (✉)
Shanghai University of Political Science and Law, Shanghai, China
e-mail: foichina@yahoo.com

 
H.-J. Blanke, R. Perlingeiro (eds.), *The Right of Access to Public Information*,
DOI 10.1007/978-3-662-55554-5_14

observers. It is actually an outcome of improved information flow resulting from social, political, legal and economic factors, forming part of a much longer process of increased transparency in the Chinese information environment. This improved information flow has constituted an enabling environment for the adoption of FOI legislation in China.[2] It is necessary to provide an overview of China's FOI legislation and assess its five years' implementation. This paper has five sections. The first section illustrates the access right in China. The second section explains FOI exemptions, which limit the scope of access. The third section introduces requesting procedures and access fees. The fourth section discusses the relationship between FOI legislation and other administrative laws in China. The final section overviews the judicial protection of the access right in China.

## 2 The Access Right in China

China's FOI legislation allows Chinese citizens to apply for government information.[3] However, it only has an implied access right subject to a potential need test and a limited scope of access.

### *2.1 An Implied Access Right*

While the FOI Regulations allow access to government information, they do not explicitly confer an access right. Before the passage of the Regulations, there were disputes about their ability to do so.[4] The access right was not specially mentioned under the Constitution as it is only regarded as an adjunct of the right to supervise and freedom of expression.[5] Consequently, there was a consensus that the FOI Regulations were an inappropriate legal document to confer this political right, signaling that it can only be protected indirectly by the Regulations. Indirect protection constrained Chinese citizens' capacity to access general government information, as there was much debate on whether the access right falls outside the scope of administrative lawsuits.[6] Only after the Chinese Supreme Court had issued an explanation on the Chinese FOI legislation, this debate has disappeared because it states that the court can accept a lawsuit regarding the access right.[7] This

[2]Xiao 2012, p. 8.

[3]Article 13 of the Chinese Freedom of InformationRegulations (FOI).

[4]Zhou 2005, p. 57.

[5]Zhou 2003, p. 16.

[6]Xiao 2012, p. 113.

[7]Article 1 of the Chinese Supreme Court's Explanation on Several Questions Related to the Trial of Freedom of Information Lawsuits (2011).

explanation strengthens the clause under the FOI Regulations that permit citizens to bring an FOI lawsuit to court.[8]

## 2.2 A Potential Need Test

The use of the access right is subject to a potential need test. International best practice dictates anyone should be able to exercise the access right, whether they have any ground or legal interest or not.[9] China's FOI Regulations do not meet this aspect of best practice. The Regulations enable citizens, legal persons or other organizations to request information held by government agencies in accordance with their needs in business, daily life, research or other special needs.[10] In terms of the concern that government agencies are likely to refuse access requests with the excuse that the information sought does not meet requesters' special needs, the State Council clarifies that government agencies may refuse access requests if information sought is irrelevant with requesters' special needs.[11] In practice, there is an agreement that the need test should be only applied to a small number of frequent requesters who have an abusive use of FOI legislation. The burden of proof rests on these requesters to prove whether their applications meet with their special needs or not. The access right is therefore restricted by this retreat.

## 2.3 A Limited Scope of Access

The Chinese FOI legislation allows Chinese citizens to apply for government information. However, the scope of access is restricted by limited bodies and subject matter covered by the Chinese FOI legislation. First, the legislation only covers government agencies at all levels. Chinese courts, congresses, procuratorates and party organs are not subject to this legislation. Thus, any application that aims at information generated or acquired by these bodies will be refused. Furthermore, the information that is generated or obtained by police offices in the course of performing criminal enforcement or prosecution functions is not regarded as a category of government information. It is argued that only information regarding public administration falls into the definition of government information under the Chinese FOI legislation.[12]

[8]Article 33 FOI.

[9]The Open Society Justice Initiative 2006.

[10]Article 13 FOI.

[11]Article 14 of the Chinese State Council General Office's Several Suggestions on the Implementation of the Freedom of Information Regulations (2008).

[12]Wu 2009, p. 39.

Second, not all information held by government falls into the scope of access. The information must meet three conditions: generated or acquired by government agencies, aimed at exercising power and performing functions, and recorded in certain forms.[13] An access request seeking information that does not meet any of these conditions will be refused with a reason of "non government information", especially the second condition, which has been used frequently to refuse information requests. This condition indicates that any information sought should be related to government responsibilities of economic and social management and public service.[14] Furthermore, there is an argument that only government information that has been generated or obtained after the passage of the FOI Regulations can be applied for. It is said that the legal principle of non-retroactivity or ex post facto does not require disclosure of the information generated or obtained before the effective date of the FOI Regulations.[15] In this regard, the non-retroactivity principle has been arguably misunderstood. It should be applied to the time when a request is submitted, not when the information is generated or obtained.[16]

## 3 FOI Exemptions in China's FOI Legislation

FOI exemptions in the Chinese FOI legislation are inconsistent with international standards. Generally, a harm test and a public interest test do not apply to all exemptions. Broad and vague FOI exemptions have increased the difficulties of compliance. Furthermore, various administrative grounds have been created to refuse access requests during implementation of the Chinese FOI legislation.

---

[13]Chen 2007, p. 21.

[14]Gang Li, the founder of the China Public Interest Litigation website, asked for information from the Shanghai government about tuition fees paid to the Shanghai National Accounting Institute for several senior figures' Executive Master of Business Administration training courses. The government replied that the information sought fell outside the category of government information, as it bore no relation to government responsibilities of economic and social management and public service. See Li 2008.

[15]Youjian Huang and his colleagues applied for a survey report on the restructure of a water supply company, but their request was rejected. The reason of refusal is the information sought was generated before the effective date of the Chinese FOI legislation. Jiang & Li 2009, p. 18. On 10 June 2008, Zihong Li and other villagers sent a request to a township government for information concerning the operation of a public coal company, but the government only replied in oral form. The requesters then filed a lawsuit in court. During the trial, the government's defense was that the information sought was created before the FOI Regulations took effect, so that the Regulations did not apply. Qin 2008, p. 14.

[16]Li 2008, p. 6.

### 3.1 Overview

International standards for exemption clauses indicate that a majority of exemptions should be harm-based.[17] A harm test and a public interest test should apply to all exemptions.[18] Discretionary exemptions should be allowed to assist government agencies in releasing more information.[19] The Chinese FOI legislation does not meet with all these international standards, as illustrated in the following way.

First, the avoidance of class-based exemptions is not the case in China. It is argued that any FOI law should avoid sweeping 'class exemptions',[20] which exclude 'entire classes of information from access'.[21] Under China's FOI Regulations, state secrets, trade secrets, and privacy are all class-based exemptions.[22]

Second, government agencies are prevented compulsorily from disclosing any exemption under the FOI Regulations. Discretionary rather than mandatory exemptions should be provided under FOI legislation,[23] as the former leaves the way open for government agencies to exercise their right in favor of disclosure, even though the information sought falls within an exemption provision.[24]

Third, although China's FOI Regulations include a harm test that features prominently in many FOI laws around the world and is advocated by FOI campaigners,[25] they envisage only a low degree of harm for exemptions concerning state security, public security, economic security or social stability. They contain the verb harm without any adverb, such as significantly or substantially, to describe the degree of injury. No harm test applies to an exemption concerning state secrets, trade secrets or privacy under the Regulations, which means these exemptions are 'class-based'.[26] Once the information sought falls into any of these categories, it is excluded from disclosure.

Fourth, China's FOI Regulations allow a special public interest test applied only to a few exemptions, rather than a general one that requires the consideration of public interest in every case.[27] FOI laws generally require that any exemption must

---

[17]Frankel 2001.

[18]'Article 19' 1999; Mclsaac 2001.

[19]Hart 2007.

[20]Iyer 2000.

[21]Frankel 2001.

[22]Article 14 FOI.

[23]Hart 2007.

[24]McDonagh 1998, p. 84.

[25]'Article 19' 1999.

[26]McDonagh 1998, p. 84.

[27]Mclsaac classifies a public interest test into two categories: a general and special test. See Mclsaac 2001.

be balanced against disclosure in the public interest.[28] This allows information to be released when 'public benefit in knowing the information outweighs any harm that may be caused from disclosure'.[29] In China, a public interest test is only applied specifically to exemptions of trade secrets and privacy.[30] The Chinese FOI legislation also requires government agencies to proactively disclose the government information that needs to be extensively known or participated in by the public. However, this test has been used rarely in practice. One major ground behind this rare use is the difficulty of defining public interest.

## 3.2 Exemptions

Whilst exemptions are a standard element of FOI legislation, exemptions under China's FOI Regulations remain less liberal than is ideal, in at least the following two aspects. First, the scope of exemptions under the FOI Regulations is inconsistent with best practice,[31] though the Regulations ostensibly set out very limited exemptions—the main exemption clause only prevents government agencies from disclosing information concerning state secrets, trade secrets and privacy.[32] Other exemptions are generally stated in Article 8 FOI, which exempts information that may prejudice state security, public security, economic security or social stability. Much government information will remain hidden under this general exemption.[33]

Second, exemptions and exclusions under FOI legislation should be clearly and narrowly defined[34] to 'exclude material which does not harm legitimate interests'.[35] This is not the case in China. Exemptions and exclusions are not clearly and narrowly defined under the FOI Regulations, which prevent government agencies from disclosing any information that may be injurious to state security, public security, economic security or social stability.[36] The definition of these securities is left to government agencies, and so can easily be used to refuse access requests. A possibility of disturbing anonymous reviewers' life after release of their names was accepted as a factor causing social instability.[37]

[28] A special public interest test is found in FOI legislation of Australia, Ireland, Canada and the United Kingdom. A general public interest test is found in FOI legislation of New Zealand, India and South Africa.

[29] Banisar 2005.

[30] Article 14 FOI.

[31] 'Article 19' 1999.

[32] Article 14 FOI.

[33] Geoffrey & Qin 2007, p. 6.

[34] 'Article 19' 1999.

[35] 'Article 19' 1999.

[36] Article 8 FOI.

[37] The Huangpu District People's Court of Shanghai (The First Instance), *Zhou v Shanghai Municipal Human Resources and Social Security Bureau* (Judgment of 11 May 2010), 31.

Meanwhile, state secrets, trade secrets and privacy are not well defined under the FOI Regulations and other laws. A broad scope for the state secret exemption will impede implementation of the FOI Regulations. The longstanding culture of secrecy, although beginning to change, has impeded efforts to narrow the scope of state secrets. China lacks privacy law. The definition of privacy has not yet addressed comprehensively in Chinese law, which in turn may negatively affect the operation of the FOI Regulations. In practice, government agencies have held a broad view, regarding all information related to individuals as privacy. Although trade secrets are defined in Article 10 of the Anti-trust Law,[38] this definition has been broadly explained in practice to cover any information related to companies.[39] This is because the FOI Regulations lay equal protection on trade secret with a technological nature and other commercially-valuable information.

### *3.3 Administrative Grounds*

Various administrative grounds have been used more frequently than exemptions to refuse access requests. Some of them can be found in other jurisdictions, but others are with Chinese characteristics. This can be explained by the following six points. First, repeated request has been considered as an administrative ground to refuse access requests.[40] This ground is not set out in the Chinese FOI legislation. However, it is regarded as an administrative ground for government agencies to exercise their discretion whether to respond in the central government's document or not.[41]

Second, non-existence of the information sought is used frequently as another administrative ground to answer access requests. Such a reply has been generally found in response to a request for the information that is oral,[42] missing[43] or needs compiling.[44]

[38]Trade secrets refers to any technology information or business operation information which is unknown to the public, can bring about economic benefits to the obligee, has practical utility and about which the obligee has adopted secret-keeping measures. Article 10 of the Chinese Anti-trust Law.

[39]The Pudong District People's Court of Shanghai (The First Instance), *Fan v Shanghai Pudong District Planning and Land Resources Bureau* (Judgment of 14 November 2011), 239.

[40]Article 13 of the Chinese State Council General Office's Several Suggestions on the Implementation of the Freedom of Information Regulations (2008).

[41]Article 13 of the Chinese State Council General Office's Several Suggestions on the Implementation of the Freedom of Information Regulations (2008).

[42]The Pudong District People's Court of Shanghai (The First Instance), *Cai v Shanghai Pudong District Construction and Transportation Commission* (Judgment of 11 January 2013), 306.

[43]The No. 2 Intermediate People's Court of Shanghai (The Second Instance), *Zheng v Shanghai Municipal Housing Administration Bureau* (Judgment of 6 May 2011), 97.

[44]The Pudong District People's Court of Shanghai (The First Instance), *Cai v Shanghai Pudong District Construction and Transportation Commission* (Judgment of 22 September 2008) 137.

Third, inappropriate agency to answer requests is regarded as an administrative reason to reply to access requests filed to a wrong agency.[45] There is a general rule that government agencies generating the information sought should be the one responsible for answering requests.[46] Thus, government agencies that obtain, rather than generate the information sought are not liable to answer requests.

Fourth, non-government information is an administrative ground with Chinese characteristic which has been used to reject requests for the information generated or obtained by party organs,[47] courts and procuratorates[48] as all these institutions are not subject to the Chinese FOI legislation. Internal documents,[49] deliberative process information[50] and information regarding governmental civil affairs[51] are considered as another category of non-government information. This is because they are not generated or acquired by government agencies during the process of exercising power or performing functions. Thus, it does not meet with one condition deriving from the definition of government information in the FOI Regulations.

Fifth, non-FOI request, another administrative ground with Chinese characteristic, has been applied to refuse vague requests,[52] and requests regarding citizens'

---

[45]The Putuo District People's Court of Shanghai (The First Instance), *Liu v Shanghai Municipal Housing Administration Bureau* (Judgment of 5 June 2012), 17;The Pudong District People's Court of Shanghai (The First Instance), *Chen v Shanghai Pudong District Planning and Land Resources Bureau* (Judgment of 16 March 2012), 83.

[46]Article 17 FOI.

[47]The Pudong District People's Court of Shanghai (The First Instance), *Cao v Shanghai Pudong District Audit Bureau* (Judgment of 16 April 2012), 101; The Pudong District People's Court of Shanghai (The First Instance), *Cao v Shanghai Pudong District Audit Bureau* (Judgment of 12 March 2012), 47; The Huangpu District People's Court of Shanghai (The First Instance), *Cao v Shanghai Huangpu District Audit Bureau* (Judgment of 13 February 2012), 33.

[48]The No. 2 Intermediate People's Court of Shanghai (The Second Instance), *Du v Shanghai Municipal Public Security Bureau* (Judgment of 6 May 2011), 86.

[49]The Huangpu District People's Court of Shanghai (The First Instance), *Wang v Shanghai Huangpu District Audit Bureau* (Judgment of 19 June 2012), 184; The No. 2 Intermediate People's Court of Shanghai (The Second Instance), *Chen v Shanghai Municipal Landscaping Administration Bureau* (Judgment of 16 March 2012), 93.

[50]The Huangpu District People's Court of Shanghai (The First Instance), *Dai v Shanghai Municipal Development and Reform Commission* (Judgment of 3 November 2011), 3; The No. 2 Intermediate People's Court of Shanghai (The Second Instance), *Wei v Shanghai Jing'an District Government* (Judgment of 15 March 2010), 13.

[51]The Pudong District People's Court of Shanghai (The First Instance), *Yang v Shanghai Pudong District Sanlin Township Government* (Judgment of 9 November 2011), 240; The No. 2 Intermediate People's Court of Shanghai (The Second Instance), *Chen v Shanghai Huangpu District Landscaping Administration Bureau* (Judgment of 11 January 2012), 345; The People's High Court of Shanghai (The Second Instance), *Ji v Shanghai Yangpu District Government* (Judgment of 26 January 2011), 1.

[52]The No. 2 Intermediate People's Court of Shanghai (The Second Instance), *Wu v Shanghai Municipal Government* (Judgment of 11 August 2011), 4; The Pudong District People's Court of Shanghai (The First Instance), *Zhan v Shanghai Pudong District Planning and Land Resources Bureau* (Judgment of 6 January 2012), 301.

inquiries[53] and complaining letters.[54] Such a reply has also been applied to a request for government information already transferred to and stored in archives.[55]

Sixth, irrelevance of special needs is the last administrative ground which has been found in China specifically and has been used to refuse access requests submitted by a few requesters who has an abusive use of FOI legislation. In terms of the concern that government agencies are likely to refuse access requests with the excuse that the information requested does not meet requesters' special needs,[56] the State Council clarifies that government agencies may refuse access requests if information sought is unrelated to requesters' special needs.[57]

# 4 Requesting Procedures and Access Fees

The Chinese FOI legislation sets out clear and relatively simple procedures for filing and answering access requests. However, on many occasions, government agencies are not required to assist requesters when their requests are vague or unduly broad. Access fees are limited to reproduction and delivery costs, meeting with international best practice that only allows the adoption of a cost-based approach.[58]

## *4.1 Requesting Procedures*

The Chinese FOI legislation sets out clear and relatively simple requesting procedures, as illustrated in the following way. First, requests can be submitted by any means of communication. In the event that it is truly difficult for a requester to submit a request in written form, the requester may do so orally with the assistance

[53]The Huangpu District People's Court of Shanghai (The First Instance), *Zheng v Shanghai Municipal Housing Administration Bureau* (Judgment of 22 February 2012), 58.

[54]The Huangpu District People's Court of Shanghai (The First Instance), *Zheng v Shanghai Municipal Housing Administration Bureau* (Judgment of 18 April 2012), 112; The No. 2 Intermediate People's Court of Shanghai (The Second Instance), *Zhao v Shanghai Jing'an District Government* (Judgment of 17 November 2011), 17.

[55]The No. 2 Intermediate People's Court of Shanghai (The Second Instance), *Wei v Shanghai Jing'an District Government* (Judgment of 18 January 2010), 2; The Huangpu District People's Court of Shanghai (The First Instance), *Zhao v Shanghai Huangpu District Planning and Land Resources Bureau* (Judgment of 22 June 2009), 133.

[56]Horsley 2007.

[57]Article 13 of the Chinese State Council General Office's Several Suggestions on the Implementation of the Freedom of Information Regulations (2008).

[58]Volman 2004, p. 95.

of an FOI officer.[59] Second, requesters are required to provide the details necessary for identifying and delivering the information, including an address for delivery, a description of the government information sought and the format for the requested government information to be supplied.[60] Third, after receiving an information request, government agencies should reply to the request as soon as possible. The time limit for answering a request is 15 business days from receiving a request. This time limit can be extended another 15 business days with the requirement of informing the requester.[61]

Fourth, government agencies are required to answer requests respectively in accordance with different circumstances.[62] Government agencies are liable to inform the requester of the methods and channels for obtaining the requested government information falling within the scope of disclosure. If the requested government information does not fall into the scope of disclosure, government agencies are obliged to inform the requester that such information cannot be disclosed, together with an explanation of the reasons. Moreover, government agencies have a duty to inform the requester if the requested government information is not generated by them. However, they are encouraged to refer the requester to another agency, rather than to directly transfer the request to an appropriate agency. If the information requested is vague, government agencies should inform the requester to amend and supplement the request, rather than reject the request directly.

Fifth, the Chinese FOI legislation sets out a severability requirement that obliges government agencies to provide the requester with the information that may be disclosed.[63] The third-party consultation is also required if the requested information involves trade secrets or individual privacy.[64] Government agencies are obliged to comply with requesters' preferences regarding how they access information.[65] If it is impossible to meet with the requester's preferences, government agencies may provide the information using other appropriate methods, such as making arrangements for the requesters to read the relevant documents and providing photocopies.

While the Chinese FOI legislation has set out clear and relatively simple requesting procedures, it has not required government agencies to provide more assistance to requesters in the process of filing requests. Government agencies are not required to assist requesters when their requests are vague or unduly broad. Furthermore, they are not obliged to assist requesters in identifying the appropriate agency liable for answering requests.

---

[59] Article 20 FOI.

[60] Article 20 FOI.

[61] Article 24 FOI.

[62] Article 21 FOI.

[63] Article 22 FOI.

[64] Article 23 FOI.

[65] Article 26 FOI.

## 4.2 *Access Fees*

Access fees are limited to reproduction and delivery costs, decreasing financial burden of requesters. There are no fees charged for filing requests. The cost for requesting information is limited to the cost of searching, photocopying, postage and the like.[66] The Chinese FOI legislation prohibits government agencies to provide government information as a compensated service through any organizations or individuals, indicating that charges for reuse or commercial exploitation of information are not allowed.[67] It also provides for fee waivers for impecunious requesters. If a requester truly has economic difficulties, the relevant fee may be reduced or exempted after an application for such reduction or exemption is submitted by the requester and approved by a responsible government agency. To set the standards for access fees, the National Development and Reform Commission and the Ministry of Finance jointly issued a notice to clarify the cost-based approach. To reduce the cost of the use of FOI legislation, the notice prohibits government agencies from collecting any fees arising from the handling of the information sought falling into a category of proactive disclosure.[68] While this prohibition reduces financial burden of requesters, it has created some difficulties for requesters to access the information sought directly. Because of cost consideration, government agencies are reluctant to provide requesters the information sought directly. They have chosen to provide a web address directing requesters to obtain the information sought, creating some problems for the applicants who have difficulties in using the Internet or have no Internet access.

# 5 FOI Legislation and Other Administrative Laws in China

While China has not yet adopted a general administrative procedure law, a series of administrative laws, which deal with access to information, have been adopted from the 1980s. The Chinese FOI legislation cannot trump restrictions on information disclosure in other laws to the extent of any conflict. To solve the conflicts between the Chinese FOI legislation and other administrative laws, two fundamental principles have been applied in practice. They are higher-level law preferred than lower-level law and special law preferred than general law.

---

[66]Article 27 FOI.

[67]Article 27 FOI.

[68]Article 1 of the Chinese National Development and Reform Commission and the Ministry of Finance's Joint Notice on Standards for Access Fees and Related Issues (2008).

## 5.1 Higher-Level Law Preferred to Lower-Level Law

The principle of higher-level law preferred than lower-level law stresses that when lower-level law conflicts with higher-level law, government agencies should give priority to higher-level law.[69] According to the Legislation Law, the Constitution enjoys the highest level of legal authority. A law is at the second level of legal authority. Regulations are at the third level.[70] The Chinese FOI legislation is an administrative regulation, which was adopted by the State Council. It cannot override a law, such as the Archives Law.

The Archives Law also deals with information access. In practice, government agencies have archived some information immediately after receiving access requests to preclude disclosure. This practice occurred in Shanghai.[71] This is because the Archives Law sets a higher standard that requires the requester to show lawful identifications before using archives and a longer period for access to archived information, generally 30 years.[72] Considering this, the Shanghai government adopted its own FOI legislation that prescribes that government agencies, when transferring government information to state archives, must inform state archives whether the government information transferred falls within the scope of proactive disclosure, reactive disclosure or non-disclosure or not.[73]

However, another problem occurs. Access to proactively-disclosed type of government information from state archives has no differences than that from government agencies. This is because the Chinese FOI legislation requires government agencies to set up government information reading places in state archives.[74] Thus, all proactively-disclosed types of government information coming from government agencies have been stored in these reading places in an open manner. However, requesters have difficulties in accessing reactively-disclosed types of government information from state archives, as they are required to show letters of introduction issued by government agencies transferred the requested information.[75] Such letters of introduction are hard for requesters to obtain because only government employees working in the agencies transferring the sought information are qualified for acquiring these letters. It should be noted that requesters are not required to provide any letter of introduction when they request such reactively-disclosed types of information stored in government agencies. This conflict will remain until the revision of the Archives Law.

China has experienced a gradual administrative law reform since the early 1980s. During the last 30 years, a series of administrative laws dealing with

[69] Article 78, 79 and 80 of the Chinese Legislation Law (2000).

[70] Article 78, 79 and 80 of the Chinese Legislation Law (2000).

[71] Cheng 2008, p. 17.

[72] Article 19 of the Chinese Archives Law (1987).

[73] Article 35 of the Shanghai Freedom of Information Rules (2008).

[74] Article 16 FOI.

[75] Article 22.2 of the Rules for the Implementation of Chinese Archives Law (1990).

administrative procedures were adopted prior to the introduction of a general administrative procedure law. All these administrative laws have provided a firm basis for the consideration of administrative procedure law that is still in progress. At moment, rare administrative laws allow public access to information, only obliging government agencies to provide a full account of decisions to any person who may be aggrieved by an administrative action, for example Administrative Penalty Law.[76] One exception is Administrative Permission Law, which allows the public to access governmental decisions on approving administrative permission and its records of supervision and inspection subject to state secrets, business secrets and personal privacy.[77] Administrative Permission Law has a higher level of legal authority than FOI Regulations, strengthening public access to information regarding administrative permission.

## 5.2 *Special Law Preferred to General Law*

The principle of special law preferred than general law indicates that when special law conflicts with general law, government agencies should give priority to special law.[78] A few administrative laws deal with access to specific government information, differing from the Chinese FOI legislation that deals with all kind of government information. If the information requested falls into a category of specific government information, the replied agency is obliged to refer the requester to apply for such information in accordance with the procedures set out in a special law.

China's Letters and Visits Regulations are a type of special law that deals with letter-writers or visitors' suggestions and complaints to government agencies. According to these Regulations, letter-writers or visitors can file requests for information related to the handling of their suggestions or complaints.[79] In practice, if letter-writers and visitors request such information, the agencies receiving such requests will reject their requests and inform them of applying for such information in accordance with Letters and Visits Regulations. Similarly, there are special rules that regulate access to house ownership register information. Government agencies receiving requests for such information generally refuse these requests and then ask them to request it in accordance with special procedures under other relevant laws.[80] Furthermore, there exist special rules dealing with access information related to administrative reconsideration, a kind of internal review.[81] If a

[76]Article 31 of the Chinese Administrative Penalty Law (1996).

[77]Article 40 and Article 61 of the Chinese Administrative Permission Law (2003).

[78]Article 83 of the Chinese Legislation Law (2000).

[79]Article 9.1 of the Chinese Letters and Visits Regulations (2005).

[80]Such as Shanghai Interim Rules on Access to House Ownership Register Information (1998).

[81]Article 23.2 of the Chinese Administrative Reconsideration Law (1999).

government agency receives a request for such information, it will ask the requester to apply for such information in accordance with the special rules, rather than FOI legislation.

## 6 Judicial Protection of the Access Right in China

The Chinese FOI legislation authorizes the requester to file an administrative lawsuit to court.[82] The number of administrative lawsuits has increased in the last 5 years. Shanghai serves as an example to substantiate this argument. The number of 2012's lawsuits is 583, more than twice as many as that in 2008, which is only 258.[83] Whilst Chinese courts have supported most of government FOI refusals, they have actually played a positive role in bolstering requesters' lawsuits regarding administrative grounds and proactively-disclosed information.

### *6.1 Positive Protection*

To a certain degree, Chinese courts have played a positive role in protecting the access right, as explained in the following way. First, Chinese courts have bolstered compliance with proactive disclosure requirements under the FOI Regulations. In the Xu case, the court adjudged the Bureau's refusal regarding a request seeking some proactively-disclosed information illegal.[84] An official questioned 'why the agency has not disclosed the information until the masses take it to court'.[85] This was not the only lawsuit regarding proactively-disclosed information upheld by courts. In the Zhou case,[86] the government did not answer Zhou's request for a building dismantlement license and other necessary legal documents, which are obliged to be disclosed proactively until he initiated court action. In the Xie case,[87]

[82]Article 33 FOI.

[83]See Shanghai FOI Annual Report 2008; Shanghai FOI Annual Report 2012.

[84]Jianguo Xu, a Beijing lawyer, filed a request dated 1 May 2008 to the Huangzhou District Bureau of Transport for some proactively disclosed information concerning this Bureau's structure, function and working procedures. The Bureau did not answer Xu's request. Xu thus brought the Bureau to court on 2 June. His action won support from the court. See Tian 2008, p. 10.

[85]Chu 2008, p. 13.

[86]On 4 May 2008, Zhou, the head of a relocated household, filed a request to the Rugao Construction Bureau of Jiangsu Province for a building dismantlement license and other necessary legal documents, which were in the category of proactively disclosed information set out in the FOI Regulations. The government did not answer his request until he took it to court. See Chen et al. 2008.

[87]Xie, a farmer, applied to the Xuchang Development and Reform Commission for policy documents regarding subsidies for breeding pigs on 16 June 2008. Xie took the Commission to

the government did not release the proactively-disclosed public policy regarding subsidies for breeding pigs to Xie until the court actively mediated in the dispute. All these lawsuits are related to government non-compliance with proactive disclosure requirements. In the end, courts will likely play a more positive role in ensuring compliance with these proactive disclosure requirements.

Second, Chinese courts have supported requesters' lawsuits related to FOI refusals based on administrative grounds. In the Zhang case,[88] Shanghai Huangpu District Construction Commission replied to the requester that the requested conference memo was not existed. However, at the trial, it provided a copy of conference memo to court. The court finally adjudged that the ground of non-existence of the information sought was misused. Another example is Wu v Shanghai Municipal Housing Administration Bureau,[89] the court adjudged that Shanghai Municipal Housing Administration Bureau should search the information sought carefully before the making of the reply of non-existence. Furthermore, the court has judged in the Zhan case that the ground of inappropriate agency to answer cannot be abused and misused.[90] It is obvious that the agency receiving the request has a duty to answer if the information sought is generated by it.

Third, Chinese courts have played a positive role in protecting the access right if an FOI reply violates procedural requirements set out in the Chinese FOI legislation. If a government agency only makes a partial reply,[91] delayed reply,[92] mute refusal,[93] or rushed reply without an accurate understanding of the information sought,[94] the court will generally require the agency to make a new FOI decision. If a government agency makes a reply without consulting the third party involved in the requested information, the court will adjudge that such a reply is illegal, as

---

court for its mute refusal. The court supported Xie's action, and held that the Commission had the duty to disclose the policy documents sought. The Commission finally gave these documents to Xie after the court actively mediated in this dispute. See He & Pu 2008, p. 6.

[88]The Huangpu District People's Court of Shanghai (The First Instance), *Zhang v Shanghai Huangpu District Construction Commission* (Judgment of 27 February 2009), 278.

[89]The Huangpu District People's Court of Shanghai (The First Instance), *Wu v Shanghai Municipal Housing Administration Bureau* (Judgment of 20 December 2010), 149.

[90]The Pudong District People's Court of Shanghai (The First Instance), *Zhan v Shanghai Pudong District Planning and Land Resource Bureau* (Judgment of 18 January 2012), 267.

[91]The Huangpu District People's Court of Shanghai (The First Instance), *Ding v Shanghai Huangpu District Construction Bureau* (Judgment of 19 January 2009), 288.

[92]The Huangpu District People's Court of Shanghai (The First Instance), *Wu v Shanghai Municipal Human Resources and Social Security Bureau* (Judgment of 20 December 2010), 260; The Huangpu District People's Court of Shanghai (The First Instance), *Wu v Shanghai Municipal Human Resources and Social Security Bureau* (Judgment of 20 December 2010), 261.

[93]The Songjiang District People's Court of Shanghai (The First Instance), *Yang et al. v Shanghai Songjiang District X Bureau* (Judgment of 25 June 2010), 14.

[94]The Huangpu District People's Court of Shanghai (The First Instance), *Zheng v Shanghai Municipal Housing Administration Bureau* (Judgment of 21 July 2011), 167.

shown in Zheng v Shanghai Municipal Housing Administration Bureau.[95] For a vague and unduly broad request, if the government makes an FOI decision without asking the requester to amend his or her request, the court will normally adjudge such a decision illegal.[96] It should be noted that no FOI decisions strictly follow the procedural requirements in the FOI Regulations.

Fourth, even for some FOI exemptions, Chinese courts are capable of improving government compliance. An example is Zhan v Shanghai Pudong District Planning and Land Resources Bureau[97]; the court judged that the information requested did not fall into a category of trade secrets as it lacked a commercial value. Also in the case of Wu v Shanghai Hongkou District Taxation Bureau,[98] the court considered that a wrong rejection was made as the requested contact details were not a category of trade secrets. This is because contact details are necessary for business and it should be publicly available. Moreover, in the case of Zhou v Shanghai Municipal Human Resources and Social Security Bureau,[99] the court held that the FOI refusal was based on a wrong reason as the release of some anonymous reviewers' names could not cause social instability.

## *6.2 Negative Protection*

Chinese courts have showed deference to government FOI decisions, thus adopting a conservative attitude toward FOI lawsuits. They have upheld most FOI decisions made by government agencies via various procedural and substantive constraints, restricting the capacity of requesters to apply for government information. This has caused concerns over Chinese courts' weak position in rectifying government non-compliance with access requests.[100]

First, Chinese courts interpreted a reviewable administrative action strictly at the beginning of implementing of the Chinese FOI legislation. Chinese courts are skeptical about whether the access right is actionable, as common understanding holds that a citizen can only sue for an infringement of personal or property rights pursuant to the Administrative Litigation Law.[101] The infringement of an access

[95]The Huangpu District People's Court of Shanghai (The First Instance), *Zheng v Shanghai Municipal Housing Administration Bureau* (Judgment of 29 March 2011), 53.

[96]The Huangpu District People's Court of Shanghai (The First Instance), *Zheng v Shanghai Municipal Housing Administration Bureau* (Judgment of 21 July 2011), 167.

[97]The Pudong District People's Court of Shanghai (The First Instance), *Zhan v Shanghai Pudong District Planning and Land Resources Bureau* (Judgment of 18 January 2012), 268.

[98]The Hongkou District People's Court of Shanghai (The First Instance), *Wu v Shanghai Hongkou District Taxation Bureau* (Judgment of 21 June 2011), 33.

[99]The Huangpu District People's Court of Shanghai (The First Instance), *Zhou v Shanghai Municipal Human Resources and Social Security Bureau* (Judgment of 11 May 2010), 31.

[100]Horsley 2007; Hubbard 2008.

[101]Li 2007, p. 6.

right, which is irrelevant to any infringement of personal or property rights, is thus considered not to belong to the category of cases that courts must accept.[102] Furthermore, it has been recognized that political rights, such as the access right, are excluded from the scope of a lawsuit.[103] All these skeptics have influenced the decisions of Chinese courts. Yet, the doubt about whether the access right is actionable should not persist, as the FOI Regulations permit citizens to bring an FOI lawsuit to court.[104] This stipulation does not conflict with the Administrative Litigation Law, which vests power in courts to accept an administrative lawsuit that may be brought pursuant to the provisions of relevant regulations.[105] This dispute has disappeared only after the Supreme Court issued an explanation on the Chinese FOI legislation.

Second, Chinese courts have conservatively interpreted a concrete administrative action, an administrative activity that aims at specified events or individuals and can only be carried out once.[106] They hold that an FOI refusal has no real impact on the complainant's right and duty, and so it falls outside the scope of administrative cases.[107] This is because the Supreme Court excludes review of the exercise of a concrete administrative action that has no real impact on a citizen's right or duty,[108] thus impeding courts' ability to accept an FOI lawsuit because they hold that an FOI refusal, a concrete administrative action, does not infringe on a requester's right, or impose a duty.[109]

Third, Chinese courts have rejected an FOI legal action because the information sought falls outside the scope of administrative lawsuits. The *Youjian Huang and other colleagues' request* was refused by the government.[110] The court did not accept the subsequent lawsuit on the ground that the information sought related to an enterprise's restructure, and not fall within the scope of administrative law-

[102]Li 2007, p. 6.

[103]Yin & Ding 2007, p. 41.

[104]Article 33 FOI.

[105]Article 11 of the Chinese Administrative Litigation Law (1989).

[106]Article 3 of the Chinese Administrative Litigation Law (1989).

[107]Jiang & Li 2009, p. 12.

[108]Article 1 of the Chinese Supreme Court's Explanation on Several Questions Related to the Implementation of the Administrative Litigation Law (1989).

[109]Jinsong Hao lodged a request to the Shaanxi Forestry Department for information on an investigation concerning the disclosure of controversial pictures of a rare wild South China tiger. The Department replied that it would disclose the information after the investigation was completed. Hao was dissatisfied with this reply, and took legal action against the Department, which the court rejected as it held that the FOI reply did not have any real impact on his rights and duties. The Lianhu District People's Court of Xi'an, *Hao v The Shaanxi Forestry Department* (Judgment of 30 June 2008), 1.

[110]On 4 May 2008, Youjian Huang and his colleagues applied for a survey report on the restructure of a water supply company. The government refused their request. The court did not accept their legal action. Zhao 2008, p. 8.

suits.[111] In this case, the court did not reject the case from the quality of being actionable, but rejected it from the category of the information sought, an enterprise's restructure, which is not reviewable.

Fourth, Chinese courts have used the purpose requirement under the FOI Regulations to reject FOI legal actions, especially contentious ones. The rationale is that the requester's purpose must be examined to control the abusive use of access rights.[112] Yulai Yuan filed a lawsuit to the Hefei Intermediary Court after his request for a letter sent by the Anhui government for instructions about laws and policies was refused.[113] The court rejected this application because the information sought lacked relation to the requester's special needs.

Fifth, Chinese courts have rejected an administrative lawsuit on the ground that the requester has no legal interest in the information sought. This rejection may have misunderstood the requirement under the Supreme Court's explanation, which states that only individuals who have legal interest with administrative actions are entitled to file an administrative lawsuit.[114] This sets a limit on the qualification of a plaintiff. However, the legal interest limit should be understood between the requester and the request, rather than the requester and the information sought.[115] Arguably, any government information is of interest to citizens from either a broad or a narrow standard. However, the legal interest limit presents an opportunity for courts to support a narrow standard, in particular when they process contentious cases.

## 7 Conclusion

The 2007's adoption of FOI legislation was a significant breakthrough in China, providing an opportunity for Chinese citizens to access government information. However, it has lots of room to improve. It is necessary to upgrade FOI Regulations into FOI law. In the future FOI law, the access right should be protected explicitly and the purpose requirement for exercising the access right should be deleted. More importantly, it should clarify all FOI exemptions and apply a harm test and a public interest test into most FOI exemptions. It should also limit its use of administrative

[111]The Supreme Court circulated Several Issues Related to the Trial of Civil Dispute Cases Related to Restructuring of Enterprises Provisions in 2003. Article 3 stipulates that courts shall not accept civil actions regarding disputes occurring in the course of administrative adjustment or transfer of an enterprise's state-owned assets by a competent government department. This Article became the basis for the court rejectingthe FOI lawsuit lodged by Huang and others. Wang & Yu 2008, p. 10.

[112]Yin 2007, p. 52.

[113]Qin 2008.

[114]Article 12 of the Chinese Supreme Court's Explanation on Several Questions Related to Implementation of the Administrative Litigation Law (1989).

[115]Li 2008, p. 6.

grounds for refusing access requests. Such a more liberal version of FOI legislation can assist Chinese government agencies and courts to follow better. Apart from that, it is necessary to improve Chinese government agencies and courts' willingness towards public access. This requires the Chinese central government to issue a series of best practice manuals to encourage more transparency, and the Chinese Supreme Court to issue an explanation of trying FOI disputes. In the future, more research is needed to assess the implementation of FOI legislation in China from the perspectives of the role played by Chinese government agencies and courts.

## References

'Article 19' – Global Campaign for free expression. (1999). Right to know: Principles on Freedom of Information Legislation. *Article 19*. Retrieved July 1, 2007, from http://www.article19.org/pdfs/standards/righttoknow.pdf

Banisar, D. (2005). Effective open government: Improving public access to government information. *OECD*. Retrieved August 11, 2007, from http://www.olis.oecd.org/olis/2005doc.nsf/0/cb40b8eb18975d01c1256fd300582d2d/$FILE/JT00181243.PDF

Chen, F. (2007). Several issues in relation to FOI regulations (Pt 1). *China Public Administration, 11*, 21–23.

Chen, H., et al. (2008). The first FOI lawsuit in Nantong City was finalized. *The Rugao Government*. Retrieved October 20, 2008, from http://www.rugao.gov.cn/html/2008/08/20080818094116-1.htm

Cheng, J. (2008). FOI regulations and public libraries. *Information and Documentation Services, 4*, 16–18.

Chu, C. (2008, October 11). The Hubei Government issued a bulletin on the Government's first failure in relation to FOI lawsuits. *The Beijing News*, A13.

Frankel, M. (2001). Freedom of Information: Some international characteristics. *The Campaign of Freedom of Information*. Retrieved November 13, 2006, from http://www.cfoi.org.uk/pdf/amsterdam.pdf

Geoffrey, F., & Qin, J. (2007, April 25). China moves to boost transparency, but much is kept hidden. *Wall Street Journal*, A6.

Hart, T. (2007). Freedom of Information/access to government information checklist: Minimum requirements for a Freedom of Information Act (FOIA) and its implementation. *EU-China Information Society Project*, 2005–2009.

He, Z., & Pu, J. (2008, August 28). The first FOI lawsuit in Henan Province reached out of court settlement. *Workers' Daily*, 6.

Horsley, J. (2007). China adopts first nationwide open government information regulations. *Freedom of Information Organization*. Retrieved May 12, 2007, from http://www.freedominfo.org/features/20070509.htm

Hubbard, P. (2008). China's regulations on open government information: Challenges of nationwide policy implementation. *Open Government: A Journal on Freedom of Information*. Retrieved July 22, 2009, from http://www.opengovjournal.org/article/viewArticle/265

Iyer, V. (2000). Freedom of Information: Principles for legislation. *UNPAN*. Retrieved July 13, 2007, from http://unpan1.un.org/intradoc/groups/public/documents/APCITY/UNPAN002177.pdf

Jiang, B., & Li, G. (2009). Discussion of issues related to FOI lawsuits. *Political Science and Law, 3*, 12–26.

Li, G. (2007, May 31). Acceptance issues related to FOI lawsuits. *People's Court Daily*, 6.

Li, G. (2008). The legal action against the Shanghai Government for refusing to disclose information on tuition fees paid for civil servants' Executive Master of Business Administration training courses. *Public Interest Litigation*. Retrieved October 10, 2008, from http://www.pil.org.cn/article_view.asp?uid=964

McDonagh, M. (1998). *Freedom of Information in Ireland*. Dublin, Ireland: Round Hall Sweet & Maxwell.

McIsaac, B. (2001). The nature and structure of exempting provisions and the use of the concept of a public interest override. *Access to Information Review Task Force in Canada*. Retrieved April 15, 2008, from http://www.atirtf-geai.gc.ca/paper-nature1-e.html

Qin, X. (2008). An FOI lawsuit was tried with the Anhui Government being sued. *Caijing*. Retrieved October 10, 2008, from http://www.caijing.com.cn/2008-10-09/110018705.html

The Open Society Justice Initiative. (2006). Transparency & silence: A survey of access to information laws and practices in 14 countries. *Open Society Institute & Soros Foundations Network*. Retrieved November 12, 2006, from http://www.soros.org/resources/articles_publications/publications/transparency_20060928/transparency_20060928.pdf

Tian, D. (2008, October 10). The government lost its FOI lawsuit for the first time, *People's Daily*, 10.

Volman, Y. (2004). Exploitation of public sector information in the context of the *eEurope* action plan. In G. Aichholzer & H. Burkert (Eds.), *Public sector information in the digital age: Between markets, public management and citizens' rights* (p. 95). Cheltenham, England: Edward Elgar.

Wang, W., & Yu, J. (2008, May 8). Are government agencies getting used to FOI? *People's Daily*, 10.

Wu, J. (2009). Issues related to FOI lawsuits. *E-Government, 4*, 39–42.

Xiao, W. (2010). China's limited push model of FOI legislation. *Government Information Quarterly, 27*, 346–351.

Xiao, W. (2012). *Freedom of Information reform in China: Information flow analysis*. London: Routledge.

Yin, Y. (2007). New thoughts on trying FOI cases. *Shanghai Journal of Law, 5*, 51–52.

Yin, Y., & Ding, Y. (2007). On legal issues of FOI lawsuits. *Shanghai Journal of Law,* (1), 40–40.

Zhao, W. (2008, May 6). Reflecting on the first lawsuit after FOI regulations took effect. *Legal Daily*, 8.

Zhou, H. (2003). *Academic draft of FOI regulations*. Beijing: China Legal Publishing House.

Zhou, Y. (2005). Analysis of FOI law-making activities in China. *Journal of Jinan University, 6*, 54–61.

## *List of Cases*

The Hongkou District People's Court of Shanghai (The First Instance) 21.06.2011, *Wu v Shanghai Hongkou District Taxation Bureau*, 33.

The Huangpu District People's Court of Shanghai (The First Instance) 13.02.2012, *Cao v Shanghai Huangpu District Audit Bureau*, 33.

The Huangpu District People's Court of Shanghai (The First Instance) 03.11.2011, *Dai v Shanghai Municipal Development and Reform Commission*, 3.

The Huangpu District People's Court of Shanghai (The First Instance) 19.01.2009, *Ding v Shanghai Huangpu District Construction Bureau*, 288.

The Huangpu District People's Court of Shanghai (The First Instance) 19.06.2012, *Wang v Shanghai Huangpu District Audit Bureau*, 184.

The Huangpu District People's Court of Shanghai (The First Instance) 20.12.2010, *Wu v Shanghai Municipal Housing Administration Bureau*, 149.

The Pudong District People's Court of Shanghai (The First Instance) 06.01.2012, *Zhan v Shanghai Pudong District Planning and Land Resources Bureau*, 301.
The Putuo District People's Court of Shanghai (The First Instance) 05.06.2012, *Liu v Shanghai Municipal Housing Administration Bureau*, 17.
The Songjiang District People's Court of Shanghai (The First Instance) 25.06.2010, *Yang et al. v Shanghai Songjiang District X Bureau*, 14.

# Part III
# Some Aspects of National Laws on Access to Public Information in Latin America

# Chapter 15
# Access to Government Information under Brazilian Law N° 12.527 of 18 November 2011

**Ana Paula de Barcellos**

## Contents



## 1 Introduction

The general subject of access to government information may be approached from two different angles. The first is to discuss the rights of all individuals to access their own personal information held by the State, involving questions such as the right to privacy, to exercise control of one's own personal information and, potentially, protection against discrimination.[1] The second concerns the right of all citizens to have ongoing access to government information about official actions and decisions of general interest, with a focus on civic activism, democratic participation and citizen oversight of the public authorities. This study focuses on this second aspect of information access.

[1]The Constitution of the Federative Republic of Brazil (1988) expressly established the rights of individuals to access their own personal information held by government agencies, except to the extent necessary to protect the security of society and the State (Article 5, items 14 and 33 in conjunction with item 72 ("habeas data"). A translation of that Constitution is available at: http://english.tse.jus.br/arquivos/federal-constitution (Accessed on 8.1.2017).

A.P. de Barcellos (✉)
Rio de Janeiro State University, Rio de Janeiro, Brazil
e-mail: anapauladebarcellos@gmail.com

 
H.-J. Blanke, R. Perlingeiro (eds.), *The Right of Access to Public Information*,
DOI 10.1007/978-3-662-55554-5_15

In keeping with the international movement that has led many countries to adopt specific laws on access to government information, Brazil enacted Law N° 12.527 of 18 November 2011 in an effort to increase transparency, democratic citizen participation and the fight against corruption.[2] It was not the first Brazilian law to address the subject. The 1988 Constitution had already guaranteed citizens the right of access to government information and imposed obligations of transparency and accountability on public agencies.[3] Law No. 8.429 of June 1992 established the principle that any civil servant who fails to render accounts when required to do so commits an offense of administrative misconduct punishable by a number of penalties, including imprisonment. The Complementary Law No. 101 of 4 May 2000 added that accounts should be rendered on electronic media, as well, to promote transparency (Campos 1990).

Despite the above-cited laws and subsequent efforts, Brazil is still having difficulties combating corruption and achieving transparency in governmental acts, as has been pointed out by certain national and international NGOs, including Amarribo Brazil and International Transparency.[4] Thus, it is only natural to wonder whether it will do any good to adopt yet another statute, such as Law N° 12.527? The answer is yes.

It is true that the mere articulation of rights and objectives in legislation does not, in and of itself, automatically produce effects in the real world. The process of transforming reality is complex and involves many factors, some of which can be controlled by law while others are almost totally immune to its effects. One of the factors that lies within the control of the law and that can help push reality in the direction indicated by the law is the question of *How? How* will the statutory objective formulated in general terms be specifically implemented in daily life? What acts or omissions will it require or prohibit? Law N° 12.527 has the praiseworthy preoccupation with building a solution to the question of *How?* The objective of this chapter is to ascertain the extent to which the statute's basic principles provide important building blocks to resolve the question of *how* and, in the final analysis, to achieve the law's general objectives.

## 2 The Basic Principles of Law N° 12.527 of 18 November 2011

Article 3 of the Law N° 12.527 defines three main bases for implementing the right of access to government information. Firstly, the introductory sentence indicates that the described procedures are intended to safeguard the fundamental right of

[2]Banisar 2002, p. 3–4; Mendel 2009, p. 7–14.

[3]Articles 5.14 and 5.33, 37.22 and 37.3, 49.9, 84.11 and 84.24, 74.1 and 74.2, and 216.2 of the 1988 Constitution of the Federative Republic of Brazil.

[4]See www.amarribo.org.br and www.transparency.org (Accessed on 3 November 2016).

information access established by the Constitution, with the proviso that those principles should be interpreted according to the clear guidelines created by the legislators themselves. Secondly, it states that the procedures are to be implemented in compliance with the constitutional principles of public administration, which it incorporates by reference. Strictly speaking, the reference to the Constitution was superfluous because its provisions are always applicable, but it shows that the intention of the legislators was to elaborate on the constitutional provisions and to specify their practical implications and applicability. Thirdly, Article 3 ends with a list of its own guidelines:

> Article 3 The procedures set forth in this law are intended to safeguard the fundamental right of information access and must be carried out in compliance with basic principles of public administration as well as the following guidelines:
>
> I – public disclosure is the general rule, with nondisclosure as the exception;
>
> II – disclosure of information of public interest unasked;
>
> III – means of communication made available by information technology;
>
> IV – fostering a culture of transparency in public administration;
>
> V – development of citizen oversight of public authorities.

The five guidelines listed above logically fall into three groups: (1) items IV and V define general objectives for the system; (2) items I and II add greater specificity to the general formulation of the right of information access, and (3) item III formulates an option for the means used to disseminate the information.

## 2.1 Article 3, Items 4 and 5 of Law N° 12.527 of 18 November 2011: Culture of Transparency and Citizen Oversight. General Objectives of the System

According to items IV and V listed in Article 3 of the above-cited statute, the procedures contained in the law are intended to foster, respectively, the development of a culture of transparency in public administration and citizen oversight of public authorities. Yet, what exactly is meant by the expressions "culture of transparency" and "citizen oversight"?

The idea of *transparency* in state action follows directly from the axiom of equality as a characteristic of the ideal republic where everyone is equal; no one is born with special privileges to dominate others, so that the leaders are delegated agents of the people acting in the name and on behalf of society. Thus, it is only natural to require civil servants to render accounts for their actions to ensure that all government actions are transparent, i.e., disclosed and justified to the public so that citizens can supervise and review the resulting actions and decisions.

Transparency requires government agencies not only to disclose their actions and decisions, as will be discussed in greater detail below, but also to explain the underlying reasons, like a judicial opinion explaining the grounds for a court judgment. It is true that certain actions require a more analytical statement of reasons than others.[5] No elaborate explanations are necessary when reporting the compensation of a civil servant who only receives the standard salary of his pay scale, for example; on the other hand, if his income exceeds the upper limit in a certain month, then transparency requires specifying not only the total amount but also justifying the individual wage components that make up the total. Decisions that are more complex will naturally involve more analytical statements of reasons.

The legislators' ambitious intention to foster the *development of a culture* of transparency in public administration reflects the accurate perception that the problems of non-transparency are extensive and will not be solved quickly or automatically just by enacting a new law. A culture of transparency also involves a transformation of the modes of interaction between individuals and civil servants: individuals must become citizens who are responsible members of society rather than mere welfare recipients with no political responsibilities or connection with the exercise of power, while civil servants must become true servants of the people, rather than adversaries.

Although a cultural transformation involves much more complex processes than those that can usually be controlled by law, the importance of legal changes should not be underestimated in this context. The requirement under Article 3 para 2 of the Law N° 12.527, for example, which imposes a duty of "(pro-)active disclosure" (i.e., unsolicited) rather than merely "passive disclosure" (i.e., in response to a request), may make a significant contribution to building the new culture.

A culture of transparency in public administration is valuable in and of itself in a democracy. Requiring justifications for government acts and public disclosure of both the acts and justifications can already go a long way towards preventing various forms of administrative abuse and mismanagement. Transparency is especially important, however, because it creates a favorable environment for the development of citizen oversight of the government. At this point, it would be useful to take a closer look at the relationship between transparency, access to government information and citizen oversight.

Citizen oversight comes in at least two different forms: pure citizen oversight and judicially enforced oversight. Public demonstrations, protests and the specific outcome of each election are examples of pure citizen oversight. Through such initiatives, various social groups demonstrate their interest in certain government actions or their discontent with a certain public policy, to influence, or even guide, the actions of administrative authorities.[6]

---

[5]This does not apply to regulatory acts, especially not those of the Legislature, which are not subject to Brazilian Law N° 12.527 of 18 November 2011. The question of providing public justifications for legislative acts deserves a study of its own.

[6]Mileski 2006, p. 95–98.

Judicially enforced oversight differs in that it is aimed at influencing the actions of administrative authorities accused not only of inefficiency but also of statutory offenses. Brazilian law has established public bodies like the Public Prosecutors Office and the Federal Audit Court that are in charge of reviewing the legality of government acts.[7] Moreover, NGOs and private associations can, under certain circumstances, petition for judicial review of government acts, and even an individual citizen can challenge government decisions if certain prerequisites are met, even if the citizen's individual rights are not directly affected by the decision in question.

In Brazil, judicially enforced oversight seems to be gaining in importance as individuals become increasingly frustrated with the ineffectiveness of pure citizen oversight. Despite the demonstrations on Brazilian city streets in recent years, there is a general lack of interest in politics and growing apathy when it comes to citizen oversight.[8]

Of the various explanations that have been proposed for the origins of this crisis of pure citizen oversight, the following three are especially relevant to our topic. Firstly, the disinterest in citizen oversight is fueled by a lack of information about public issues. This is a crucial point because no form of control is possible without information about the object of control. How can people agree or disagree with policies and priorities that they do not even know about? The information shortage is exacerbated by the fact that modern states produce an enormous number of actions and decision every day, making it practically impossible for an individual to keep up with the flow of information. The situation is even more complex in countries like Brazil with federal systems involving different coexisting levels of government.

Secondly, the crisis of citizen oversight is explained by the growing time shortage in contemporary societies, especially in urban environments. Keeping abreast of political issues and commenting on them requires time and effort that will necessarily be taken away from other personal activities. Most people, especially in developing countries, live on the outskirts of large cities so that enormous amounts of their "free" time are consumed by commuting, leaving them with little time and energy to spend on citizen oversight.

Finally, researchers have identified a third cause of disinterest: the individual's perception that their participation will have no practical effects and make no contribution to improving their life. The vicious circle is obvious: the less citizen oversight is practiced, the less the government's actions and decisions can be

[7]The Public Prosecutor's Office is an institution established by the constitution (Article 127 of the Brazilian Constitution). It is composed of independent civil servants whose mission, to put it simply, is to defend the legal-constitutional order. That mission is generally carried out by adjudicating legal claims filed against government authorities, civil servants or private individuals. The Federal Audit Courts are auxiliary agencies of the Legislative branch, likewise established by the Brazilian Constitution (Article 70 and others), with the mission of auditing the use of public resources.

[8]See Hardin 2006.

influenced by the individual's opinion.[9] Further, as citizens become less able to make a difference, they progressively lose interest in political participation.

There seems to be a relationship between the crisis of pure citizen oversight, particularly in developing countries, and the growth of judicially enforced oversight. Fortunately, however, the crisis in citizen oversight is partially compensated by NGOs and public agencies assigned the mission of monitoring government action: unlike ordinary citizens, who may have difficulty acquiring the relevant information, such NGOs and agencies have the necessary time and resources, including qualified employees, to devote to monitoring. Another point worth noting is that the growth of judicially enforced oversight may be a reaction to the void left behind by the crisis in citizen oversight, as the uncontrolled exercise of power can easily get out of hand.

Nevertheless, while there is no denying the fundamental importance of judicially enforced supervision, it is no substitute for routine citizen oversight, just as taking antibiotics cannot replace a balanced diet and regular sleep. Citizen oversight and judicially enforced supervision have different purposes. Judicially enforced supervision functions (or should function) to combat abuse and to prevent criminal offenses and violations of the law. Yet, such oversight is incomplete. Pure citizen oversight is still necessary because the government can always make decisions and implement policies that, although lawful *per se*, may not coincide with the interests or meet the needs of the majority. Although the borderline between law and policy may be a bit hazy in certainly areas, it certainly exists: pure citizen oversight and judicially enforced oversight cover different areas although there is some overlap.

Moreover, the solutions provided by judicial review are generally limited to a specific individual: e.g., a claimant may obtain funding for a medication that is not generally offered by the public health system while many others keep dying from a lack of medical care from the same system. Simply put, individual legal actions may solve the specific problems of the claimant but they are unlikely to change public policies. Even with class actions, the enforcement of a judgment intended to have a general impact is generally a slow and difficult process, unless the respondent agency has a political interest in enforcing it.[10]

Finally, it is not just that judicial supervision lacks the means to replace citizen oversight: in fact, it should not even try to do so. The Judiciary must not be allowed to usurp the role of the people in supervising and guiding public policy, even if all the court benches were occupied exclusively by the most honest, capable and wisest of sages and philosophers among the nation's men and women. The axiom of universal equality and the resulting system of democracy are incompatible with such an aristocratic conception of government action.

After this brief note on judicially enforced oversight, we shall now return to the question of disinterest in pure citizen oversight, which, as we have seen, has three causes. Besides the first one (the shortage of information on government acts),

[9]Bugarin et al. 2003, p. 12–14.

[10]Gauri & Brinks 2008, p. 1–37.

citizen oversight has two other causes that are difficult or impossible to control by law: it is beyond the power of the legal system to create free time in people's lives or to convince them of the benefits of keeping informed of their elected representatives' actions on a regular basis. Yet, the law can and must exercise some control over the accessibility of information about government actions, which is what makes this subject so relevant to creating the *culture* mentioned in Law N° 12.527.

As we have seen, difficulty in obtaining information discourages citizen oversight by requiring individuals to spend an enormous amount of time and effort to find the relevant data. In addition, effective oversight may be impossible if the available information is inaccurate or incomprehensible. If, on the other hand, such information is easy for the public to access and understand, the cost of keeping informed and exerting some type of citizen oversight would be significantly reduced. With that in mind, Law N° 12.527 aims at creating a culture of transparency to foster citizen oversight.

## 2.2 Intensification of Disclosure Obligations Through Article 3, Items 1 and 2 of Law N° 12.527 of 18 November 2011

The 1988 Brazilian Constitution expressly consecrates public disclosure as a duty of public administrative authorities and as the main tool for achieving transparency. In keeping with those constitutional principles, items I and II of Article 3 are intended to intensify disclosure obligations by deriving the following two logical corollaries: I) public disclosure of government actions is required as a general rule, so that non-disclosure on the grounds of secrecy is an exception that must be accompanied by appropriate justifications; II) disclosure should be (pro-)active rather than "passive", meaning that administrative authority must routinely and spontaneously disseminate information of public interest without waiting to be asked. Both of these notions will now be discussed in detail.

By stating that disclosure is the general rule and secrecy the exception, Article 3.1 adds little to the existing constitutional provisions, according to which public disclosure is a general duty and non-disclosure of government actions and decisions is permissible only when necessary for the "defense of privacy" or in the case of "information whose secrecy is essential to the security of society and of the State".[11] Yet, a mere general reference to the security of society and of the State does not suffice to justify non-disclosure. Public authorities cannot opt for secrecy at their freely exercised discretion but must provide a public statement of the reasons why the information must be kept secret. Such public statements are not

[11]Articles 5, items 33 and 60, Article 37 (introductory paragraph) and para 3, item 2, as well as Article 93, item 9 of the Brazilian Constitution.

an option of the civil servant but an obligation, the breach of which is subject to judicial review.[12]

An interesting public debate arose in early 2008 concerning the use of government credit cards by Brazilian politicians, especially by the President of the Republic. Much of the information about the use of such credit cards was considered confidential (and, in fact, still is) because of national security. In February 2008, a federal senator petitioned the Brazilian Federal Supreme Court for a writ of mandamus against the Brazilian President, alleging that he had refused to disclose information on government spending with such cards. The Reporting Judge Celso de Mello required proof of the President's refusal to disclose the information to be added to the case file. About a month later, the senator withdrew his petition and the Brazilian Federal Supreme Court never tried the case.[13]

Likewise in February 2008, the Popular Socialist Party (PPS) filed a lawsuit with the Brazilian Federal Supreme Court on the grounds of violation of a constitutional fundamental right, alleging that the 1967 law authorizing the non-disclosure of expenditures considered confidential (such as those involving government credit cards) was incompatible with the 1988 Constitution, which established the general principle that official information should be accessible to the public.[14] The plaintiff argued that secrecy, though permissible in certain cases, should be exceptional and must be justified on specific grounds through a statement of reasons.

The reporting judge Ricardo Lewandowski denied the motion *in limine* because, notwithstanding the general principle of accessibility of official information, non-disclosure was permitted by the Constitution and that the decision regarding secrecy had not been arbitrary because the subject matter was regulated by a set of laws, including provisions published after the 1967 law. The question is pending judgment by a plenary session of the Court.

[12]The exceptional nature of non-disclosure on the grounds of secrecy had already been pointed out by the Brazilian Superior Court of Justice as follows: "1. The general rule in a republican state is total transparency in access to government documents, with secrecy being the exception, as may be concluded directly from the wording of the Constitution (introductory paragraph and Sole paragraph of Article 1, Article 5, item 33, and introductory paragraph and para 3, item 2 of Article 37, as well as Article 216 para 2, and Article 3 para 1 of Law N° 12.527. 2. The compensation paid for parliamentary activities should be public in nature, and there are no reasons of security or privacy that generally justify non-disclosure on the grounds of secrecy." (Federal Supreme Court of Brazil [Supremo Tribunal Federal], *Writ of Mandamus*, 28.178/DF (Judgment of 7 October 2015); and "Disclosure and the right to information cannot be restricted on the basis of discretionary decisions except when justified, in exceptional cases, for the defense of honor, image and privacy of third parties or when the measure is essential to the protection of the public interest" (Federal Supreme Court of Brazil, *Appeal in Writ of Mandamus,* 23036/RJ(Judgment of 28 March 2006).

[13]Federal Supreme Court of Brazil, *Writ of Mandamus*, 27.141/DF (Judgment of 10 March 2008).

[14]Federal Supreme Court of Brazil, *Claim based on violation of a fundmental constitutional principle*, 129-3/DF (Judgment of 18 February 2008). The provision in question is Article 86 of Decree-Law No. 200 of 25 February 1967.

Regarding privacy as grounds for non-disclosure, the Federal Supreme Court has already issued relevant rulings, *e.g.*, that the disclosure on official websites of civil servants' terms of employment, including their salaries, is not a violation of privacy because there is no conceivable reason why such information should be kept secret. The consensus among legal scholars is that narrower legal protection should be provided for the privacy of public servants than for others, particularly in light of the fact that a number of laws require disclosure of public records.[15]

The second corollary of disclosure, formulated by Article 3 para 2 of the Law N° 12.527, is that civil servants have a duty of proactively ongoing disclosure of information of public interest. The objective of that Law is to relieve the individual of the burden and efforts necessary to find out about government acts and decisions. The goal is to create an active, rather than passive attitude among government officials. It should also be borne in mind that such disclosure is directly related to statutory reporting obligations, which involve an active rather than passive attitude.

Put simply: it is a duty of the government to act spontaneously and take measures to disclose its acts and decisions and communicate them to citizens unasked, even in the absence of a specific formal request. Naturally, the government's actions are incapable of ensuring that citizens actually learn of such acts if they simply have no interest in them, but they should be provided with every possible opportunity to do so if they wish. For that reason, the methods of communication and reporting may vary according to the type of government act and the parties involved, and the relationship between the two (the acts and the parties). Certainly, this idea is nothing new.

For example, to inform individuals that they are required to participate in judicial or administrative proceedings, the legal system requires serving a writ of summons in such a way as to guarantee actual receipt by the intended recipient.[16] Administrative acts and decisions affecting individual rights must also be communicated according to a specific procedure.[17] Statutes are assumed to become public knowledge upon publication in the Official Gazette,[18] although a *vacatio legis* of certain duration may be provided to ensure that persons directly or indirectly concerned have sufficient time to learn of the new law.

What is essential is that the procedures used by the State to publicize its acts and decisions be capable of informing the parties concerned as best as possible. This

---

[15]Federal Supreme Court of Brazil, *Revocation of Writ of Mandamus*, 3902/SP (Judgment of 9 June 2011): "Apparent conflict with constitutional provisions. Right to government-held information, including the pay statements of government entities and agencies. Principle of administrative transparency. The court did not recognize any violation of the civil servant's rights of privacy, safety or protection of the personal sphere."

[16]Articles 238 et seqq. of the Law No. 13.105 of 16 March 2015 (Code of Civil Procedure) (Novo Código de Processo Civil do Brasil), concerning various forms of summons. In the administrative sphere, Article 3 of the Law No. 9.784 of 29 January 1999 addresses the topic on the federal level.

[17]Article 28 of the Law No. 9.784.

[18]Article 3 of the Law N° 12.376 of 30 December 2010 (Introductory Act to the rules of Brazilian Law).

means that a mere formality is not sufficient. Quite the contrary, the State should use means which, at least presumably (i.e., based on general practical experience) effectively provide individuals with access to information about government actions and decisions. Legislators have counted on electronic communications media as the most effective—perhaps in the middle term—of publicizing such information. We will return to this topic later.

It is interesting to note that in other fields where public disclosure is required by law, such as the capital market and consumer relations, the same logic applies: the means of communication used to meet the disclosure requirements must be actually (or at least presumably) capable of providing the parties concerned with the relevant information. It is required by law that important information addressed to consumers be published in widely-read newspapers[19] and the regulatory agency (here, the Securities Exchange Commission) also requires making information available on websites and mailing the appropriate information to certain investors (such as unit-holders in investment funds). Similarly, the Consumer Defense Code imposes similar duties with two important adjectives: the information to be provided must be *clear* and *sufficient*.[20] The laws applicable to publicly held companies add the requirement that the information must be *relevant*.

As in the realms of consumer relations and capital markets, the information that the government should provide to individuals—the ultimate beneficiaries of the duty of disclosure—should be relevant and understandable. Intelligibility means that the information must be worded and presented in such a way that is understandable—or at least as understandable as possible—to the intended recipients. The duties of disclosure and reporting are not satisfied if the information is rendered incomprehensible by technical jargon, complex and chaotic formatting, or failure to provide the context necessary for the understanding of a specific government act or decision.

Relevance, in turn, relates to the content of the information: out of a vast universe of existing data, only information of practical importance to the target audience is considered relevant. Finding out the concrete results of municipal healthcare spending in a specific year—*e.g.*, how many cases where handled and what type, what equipment and medicine were purchased, how much growth was observed in the system, how many new professionals were hired through competitions, etc., all this is certainly relevant information for residents of the Municipality. The same cannot be said of the reference number assigned to every such expense. This point requires further reflection.

The law refers to "information of public interest." However, exactly what kind of information interests the public? The answer, provided by the law itself, is that, as a general rule, each government act or decision is of public interest so that the corresponding information should be made public. It appears obvious, however, that different types of public interest may justify different forms of disclosure, to

[19]Article 157 of the Law N° 6.404 of 15 December 1976 (Stock Corporation Act).

[20]Article 6 of the Law N° 8.078 of 11 September 1990 (Consumer Defense Act).

ensure that the interests are properly served and to provide relevant information in each case. At least two different major public interests come to mind in this context: the interest in citizen oversight and the interest of the individual beneficiaries of the government services. Let us start with the first.

As mentioned above, citizen oversight involves activities performed by citizens to monitor and react to government actions. Such reactions may involve protests, public demonstrations and electoral choices. In parallel with citizen oversight, there are institutional supervisory bodies, also mentioned above. Abstract spending statistics and the reference codes of the expenses may be useful to such entities but are largely irrelevant for citizen oversight. From the citizen's point of view, abstract figures may produce an emotional impact but not improve understanding. After all, what does it mean to invest "x" million on health? Is that a little? A lot? What are the needs to be satisfied? What does "x" million represent in terms of services? It would obviously be far more helpful to give an objective and tangible description of the planned services and the expected outcome.[21] In fact, the Constitution expressly mentions government plans, evaluation of achievement of the proposed objectives and implementation of government programs,[22] and the statutes regulating the subject provide for monitoring "compliance with the work program in monetary terms and in terms of *execution of the projects and provision of services*".[23]

Information of public interest for citizen oversight should be considered to include: (i) the investments to be made in various public policies (*inputs*) and, most importantly (ii) the services to be provided to the population in the context of such policies (*outputs*), on the local level, and (iii) the expected results (*outcomes*) of such services.[24] The description of the services to be provided and of the expected outcome should be as objective, concrete and measurable as possible. For example, the information that the federal government invested "x" million reals in basic education in year "y", considered in isolation, is of little interest and relevance to the public if taken out of context. The information is not relevant unless accompanied by a description of the public services resulting the investment (*e.g.*, a competition to hire "x" teachers who be put in charge of special tutoring in the schools of Brazilian States "X, Y and Z") and the final expected outcome (*e.g.*, an improvement of 1 point in the students' annual grade-point average).

This point is not very complex. Government actions use certain means—services, projects, etc.—to achieve specific ends. Thus, it is not until the population is informed of the services that are planned by the government entity in a certain region that citizens can verify, on an ongoing basis and in the immediate vicinity of their community, whether the services are actually provided in accordance with the

[21] Pederiva 1998, p. 17.

[22] Cf., e.g., Article 74, item 1 and Article 84, item 6 of the Brazilian Constitution.

[23] Article 75 of the Law N° 4.320 of 17 March 1964 (General provisions of the Financial Act on the Federal, State and Municipal Levels, and the Federal District).

[24] Norton & Elson 2002, p. 30.

entity's original objective and concrete description. Simply put, such information makes it possible for citizen oversight to be carried out under better conditions and at substantially less expense.[25] For example, if the planned service consists in providing catch-up lessons in Portuguese and math in public schools, the local population of each neighborhood will be able to check whether its school actually provides that service and whether it is sufficient. If, on the other hand, the only available information is that "x" million reals will be invested in basic education, citizen oversight will be substantially more difficult.

It should also be noted that information about the expected outcome of public policies would make it possible, over time, to perform more in-depth verification of whether the means selected by the public authority are suited to the desired ends. Simply put, it will be possible to assess whether the means employed are actually capable of producing the intended outcome. It is true that such an evaluation will be no simple matter in many cases, as the results of a government action may be influenced by countless factors. In any case, to perform such an evaluation—as complex as it may be—it is first necessary to establish a concrete and objective definition of the desired results, i.e., the goals to be achieved.[26] An example will help illustrate this question.

Imagine that the following services are planned by a certain municipal government in the sector of basic education: building and fitting out "x" public libraries in specified regions, an advertising campaign to stimulate reading among children and teenagers, a "y%" increase in the salaries of primary school teachers and, in all the municipal schools, tutoring for students with grade-point averages below certain standards. Imagine, too, that the expected outcome after 3 years of such activities is a "z%" improvement in the students' grades in Portuguese and mathematics.

The sample description in the preceding paragraph covers both the planned services and the expected outcome, allowing local citizens to make sure that the services are actually provided: whether libraries are actually built and fitted out in their neighborhood, whether the advertising campaign was carried out in their neighborhood, whether the salaries are in fact increased by the planned amount, and whether the tutoring is or is not provided in the public schools attended by their children. Further, 3 years later, once the national test scores have been published, it will be possible to check whether the students' performance improved and, if so, by how much. Thus, it will be possible to evaluate whether the desired outcome was achieved.

In addition to citizen oversight, which is practiced only by individuals concerned with civic activism, there is a more public interest in obtaining information about government acts, namely the interest of citizens who make use of government services. The 1988 Constitution assigns a number of powers to the government in

[25]Freitas 2001, p. 13.

[26]In this particular respect, despite their limitations, statistics would be especially useful. The Brazilian Constitution authorizes the Federal Government to maintain such services (Article 21, item 15).

general—on the Federal, State, and Municipal levels, as well as the Federal District—to provide various services, either directly or by delegation, many of which are related to the advancement and protection of fundamental rights. Such services include various forms of public education, healthcare services, pension benefits, legal aid for low-income clients, and dispute-resolution services, among others.

Thus, besides the general interest in citizen oversight, pregnant citizens have a specific interest in knowing how to make doctor's appointments in the prenatal phase and in which hospitals they may give birth. The parents and guardians of school-age children need information about enrollment, classes, tutoring and extracurricular activities in the local public schools, as well as information about pediatric services in the neighborhood healthcare centers. Adults who were deprived of formal education in their youth may also have an interest in being informed of educational services offered by the government for their age bracket. The jobless need information about how to obtain government aid for the unemployed and guidance concerning professional placement, and accident victims need information about government aid for accident victims.

The relevant information for the public interest citizen oversight differs from the specific information relevant to the citizens making use of public services, although both types complement one another and should be provided by the government. The two different interests and the different manners in which they are served are connected in very important ways. Firstly, many of the specific services are indispensable for the individual's exercise of civic rights and therefore lead to the formation of general citizen oversight. The case of education is emblematic: what actual possibilities does an illiterate citizen have to examine information about government acts and monitor them in general? The importance of education for the exercise of civic rights cannot be overemphasized.

Secondly, once individuals obtain access to suitable information about a specific service of interest—as potential beneficiaries—they are more likely to spend time and energy on citizen oversight to improve the quality of that service. As explained above, one of the frequently mentioned causes of social indifference to citizen oversight is that it requires individuals to invest a good deal of time and energy, which detracts from other necessary or desired activities, and produces few direct benefits. If individuals are directly interested in a certain government service they may be encouraged to re-evaluate the cost-benefit ratio in such a way as to favor the exercise of citizen oversight.

To summarize this section, the different characteristics of the two public interests identified above have an impact on the type of information to be disclosed and the manner of disclosure to be adopted by the public authorities. In terms of the type of information, citizen oversight is generally interested in any information about the government acts. The right to disclosure is the general rule and non-disclosure on the grounds of secrecy is the exception, requiring specific justifications. In the case of (potential) beneficiaries of government services, on the other hand, the interest consists in obtaining specific information on how to benefit from the service: e.g., which types of services are available, where and when, which documents and formalities are required, the time needed to obtain the desired service, etc. Such questions should be the focus of the information to be provided in this case. It is intuitively obvious that the information to be provided for this second public interest should be presented locally, preferably on the neighborhood level, as that is where such services are generally provided.

Another important effect concerns the choice of communication media as a function of the target audience. As mentioned above, public disclosure does not just mean that the information is not secret: it should be brought to the targeted population in such a way as to be received and understood, at least in theory. NGOs devoted to the monitoring of government agencies, for example, may have access to information through a wide range of media (newspapers, magazines, internet, etc.) but the same cannot be said of the general populace in Brazil. This point will be discussed in the following section.

## 2.3 Article 3, Item 3 of Law N° 12.527 of 18 November 2011. Means of Access to Information and Technology. E-Government

Finally, the last guideline listed in Article 3 para 3 of the Law N° 12.527 concerns the technical means by which access to information and public disclosure can be achieved. The laws of Brazil—in keeping with the global trend—indicate that the solution will necessarily include means of communication made possible by information technology, a term generally associated with electronic or digital equipment and, more specifically, with the internet(and any future technological developments). The relevant statutory provision reads as follows:

> Article 3. The procedures provided for by this Law are intended to guarantee the fundamental right of access to information and shall be carried out in compliance with the basic principles of public administration and the following guidelines:
>
> [...]
>
> III – utilization of means of communication made possible through information technology;

There is, in fact, a worldwide trend, among both governments and private organizations, to use electronic means, particularly the internet, to store data, disclose information and interact with the public (Bimber 2003). Many countries have endeavored to organize a system in which interactions with citizens are focused on internet (*e-government*) and Brazil is no exception: various public services in the country, for example, are already available only electronically, such as the filing of tax returns, school enrollment in various municipalities, appeals to the Judiciary, etc. This choice by Brazilian legislators, which seems inexorable in light of technological advancements and international trends, is in line with certain studies suggesting that the internet could have a positive impact on relations between citizens and the public authorities by increasing participation.[27]

There is no question that the internet provides means unprecedented in human history, with storage capacities and search engines that make it possible to locate specific information with incredible speed out of an enormous universe of available data. In addition, the online publication of information allows innumerable people to access it simultaneously, according to their personal interests, without having to travel long distances, greatly reducing the amount of time and money required. All these capabilities, however, are accompanied by a number of challenges worthy of attention, especially in developing nations such as Brazil.[28]

Primarily, there is the challenge of physical access to a device with an internet connection.[29] For citizens who lack effective internet access, making it the preferred (and eventually the only) means of information about government actions is of little benefit in exercising the right to information or training in the culture of citizen oversight. Only around 57% of Brazilians currently have internet access but the percentage is growing from year to year.[30] Part of the challenge is therefore to provide universal physical access to the internet, with a quality of transmission making it possible to take advantage of the resources available on the websites, which generally requires broadband internet access. There are various ways of promoting universal internet access,[31] which does not necessarily require every individual to have a computer and internet connection at home. Such access may be obtained through public or private collective systems, such as internet cafés.[32]

The challenge involves not only physical access but also digital education, to make citizens computer-literate, understand the basics of how the internet works and know how to search the desired information online. If an individual is not trained to take advantage of the available potential of the internet, physical access will be of little benefit. This is a considerable challenge in Brazil, especially in light of the high levels of functional illiteracy[33] and the growing population of the elderly, many of whom have had no prior experience with information technology and need special training. It goes without saying that digital education has become essential today not only for the exercise of civic rights but also to achieve complete personal development and the necessary skills and qualifications for the job market,

[27]Yang & Lan 2010, p. 441.

[28]Nascimento 2013, p. 15.

[29]In May 2011, the UN's Special Rapporteur for the promotion and protection of the rights of freedom of speech and opinion, Frank La Rue, published a report wherein he affirmed that right to internet access is a human right. The declaration raised some controversay and is still under debate.

[30]See, for example, the statistical forecast in www.statista.com/statistics/292757/brazil-internet-user-penetration (Accessed on 8 November 2016).

[31]The Decree signed by President Lula created the project: Connected Citizens – Computers for All.

[32]Lemos & Martini 2009, p. 31.

[33]National Education Research and Studies Institution Anísio Teixeira 2012.

which are the three objectives related to the right to education under Article 205 of the Brazilian Constitution.

A second challenge is to improve the quality of the electronic systems in which the government information is stored. By "quality", I mainly mean that the system must have a sufficiently comprehensive collection of accurate, up-to-date and clearly presented information. Another indicator of quality concerns the search engines and their capacities to retrieve information properly. It takes years to implement public policies and put them into effect, so that people who want to monitor the progress made require access to ongoing information over a sufficient period (e.g., not just the data of the current month).

Moreover, from the perspective of the citizens using the system, there is no point in converting the internet into the principal means of information access if only outdated information about the relevant services is available online: to find out about a certain type of treatment under the Brazil's unified healthcare system (SUS), for example, facts dating from 3 year ago are of little use. Besides being up-to-date, the information should also be available broken down by location and subject so that individuals can view information in which they are specifically interested and that is meaningful in their own social context and reality. This point is relevant for citizen oversight, as well as citizens who use the system in general. A citizen specifically interested in education for the disabled, for example, may have difficulty finding the relevant facts if all the information about general education is lumped together. Similarly, citizen oversight of local healthcare services cannot be exercised effectively unless the information can be searched by location.

Although such questions are technical in nature, it is easy to see that the legislators' efforts will be in vain if citizens cannot use the electronic system because the search engine does not work properly or the available information is not broken down properly. The importance of the practical details of implementation must not be underrated. Enacting a new law, no matter how important it may be, is just the starting point, not the final destination.

## 3 Closing Considerations

The Law N° 12.527, brings Brazil into line with an international movement leading countries to adopt specific laws governing access to governmental information, in an effort to fight corruption and to increase transparency and democratic citizen participation.

Although public access to information concerning governmental activities has been expressly required since the 1988 Constitution, the new law may contribute to developing a culture of transparency and citizen oversight, especially by imposing a duty on the authorities to disclose relevant information "proactively", i.e., without waiting to be asked. This makes public disclosure an active rather than a purely "reactive" duty, so that citizens no longer bear the full burden of searching for information about governmental actions.

Yet, certain questions remain unanswered. First, considering the enormous volumes of information generated by countries in today's world, it is of fundamental importance to decide which information should be disclosed to avoid overwhelming the public with irrelevancies. That decision, and the choice of the practical procedures of disclosure, should at least consider two major public interests: the general interest of citizen oversight of governmental actions and the interests of citizens who are beneficiaries of public services.

Brazilian Law N° 12.527 also specifies that communication systems enabled by information technology should be used in disseminating information. Electronic systems and, more generally, the internet have made it possible to develop the so-called *e-government*, with great potential for bringing citizens and their closer government closer together. Yet this, too, raises certain issues that must be confronted. Increased physical access to internet and expansion of digital education are key challenges in a country where functional illiteracy and socioeconomic inequalities remain grave problems. Secondly, the goal of improved access to governmental information in Brazilian society can be made or broken by the quality of the electronic system in which the public information is stored and the available search tools.

## References


Banisar, D. (2002). *Freedom of Information and access to government records around the world.* Freedominfo.org survey.

Bimber, B. (2003). *Information and American Democracy: Technology in the evolution of political power*. Cambridge, England: Cambridge University Press.

Bugarin, M. S., Vieira, L. M., & Garcia, L. M. (2003). *Controle dos gastos públicos no Brasil: instituições oficiais, controle social e um mecanismo para ampliar o envolvimento da sociedade*. Rio de Janeiro, Brazil: Konrad-Adenauer-Stiftung.

Campos, A. M. (1990). Accountability: quando poderemos traduzi-la para o português? *Revista de Administração Pública, 24*, 30–50.

Freitas, J. (2001). O controle social do orçamento público. *Revista Interesse Público, 11*, 13–26.

Gauri, V., & Brinks, D. (2008). Introduction: The elements of legalization and the triangular shape of social and economic rights. In V. Gauri & D. Brinks (Eds.), *Courting social justice. Judicial enforcement of social and economic rights in the developing world* (pp. 1–37). New York: Cambridge University Press.

Hardin, R. (2006). Ignorant democracy. *Critical Review, 18*, 1–3.

LaRue, F. (2011). *Report of the Special Rapporteur on the promotion and protection of the right to freedom of opinion and expression. A/HRC/17/27.* Retrieved March 12, 2016, from http://bit.ly/QD35W5

Lemos, R., & Martini, P. (2009). *LAN Houses: A new wave of digital inclusion in Brazil. Publius Project*. Retrieved March 12, 2016, from http://bit.ly/283TVWp

Mendel, T. (2009). *Liberdade de informação: um estudo comparado*. Brasília: UNESCO.

Mileski, H. (2006). Controle social: um aliado do controle oficial. *Revista Interesse Público, 36*, 85–98.

Nascimento, B. (2013). *O Direito Humano de Acesso à Internet: fundamentos, conteúdo e exigibilidade*. Kindle e-book.

Norton, A., & Elson, D. (2002). *What's behind the budget? Politics, rights and accountability in the budget process*. London: ODI.

Pederiva, J. H. (1998). Accountability, Constituição e Contabilidade. *Revista de Informação Legislativa.*, *35*(40), 17–39.

Yang, L., & Lan, G. (2010). Internet's impact on expert–citizen interactions in public policymaking – A meta analysis. *Government Information Quarterly*, *27*, 431–441.

## List of Cases

Superior Court of Justice of Brazil (Superior Tribunal de Justiça) 28.03.2006., *Recurso em Mandado de Segurança,* 23036/RJ, http://bit.ly/1sqNtYR (Accessed on 2 June 2016).

Superior Court of Justice of Brazil (Superior Tribunal de Justiça) 10.03.2008., *Mandado de Segurança*, 27.141/DF, http://bit.ly/1Vzjj1e. (Accessed on 2 June 2016).

Superior Court of Justice of Brazil (Superior Tribunal de Justiça) 18.02.2008., *Arguição de descumprimento de preceito fundamental,* 129-3/DF, http://bit.ly/1r3RH7z (Accessed on 2 June 2016).

Superior Court of Justice of Brazil (Superior Tribunal de Justiça) 09.06.2011., *Suspensão de Segurança*, 3902/SP, http://bit.ly/1P8tFOR (Accessed on 2 June 2016).

Superior Court of Justice of Brazil (Superior Tribunal de Justiça) 07.10.2015., *Mandado de Segurança*, 28.178/DF, http://bit.ly/1X0H96X (Accessed on 2 June 2016).

# Chapter 16
# Access to Information and Its Disclosure

**Cristiana Maria Pinto e Silva Fortini and Mariana Magalhães Avelar**

**Contents**



## 1 Introduction

Brazilian Law N° 12.527 of 18 November 2011 on Access to Information (LAI) establishes fundamental rules to ensure citizens find information on government websites (active transparency) and can request information not previously made available by the government (passive transparency). The Brazilian FOI law applies to all public entities that are members of the direct administration of the Executive, Legislative, Judiciary and Autonomous Bodies, as well as public companies, joint stock companies and other entities of indirect public administration.

This paper purposes to shine some light on the access to information and its disclosure in Brazil,[1] especially after the approval of the Freedom of Information Law N° 12.527 (FOI) and its regulation by the Decree N° 7.724 of 16 May 2012.

Mainly, the FOI makes effective fundamental rights guaranteed by the Brazilian Constitution (Constituição da República Federativa do Brasil de 1988), specifically

[1]For a better understanding of the legal system of Brazil, see: http://1.usa.gov/1Qc1WCD (Accessed on 15 February 2017).

C.M.P.e.S. Fortini (✉) • M.M. Avelar
Federal University of Minas Gerais, Belo Horizonte, Brazil
e-mail: cristianafortini@carvalhopereirarossi.adv.br; mmagalhaesavelar@gmail.com

 
H.-J. Blanke, R. Perlingeiro (eds.), *The Right of Access to Public Information*,
DOI 10.1007/978-3-662-55554-5_16

by Article 5, item 33,[2] Article 37 para 3, item 2[3] and Article 216 para 2.[4] The Brazilian Constitution guarantees access not only to personal information but also to information of collective or general interest. The Brazilian Constitution makes it clear that access to information is a basic right and not only a measure of corporate governance.[5]

Before Brazilian Law N° 12.527 was declared, the access to information right was partially regulated by the following laws: Brazilian Law No. 8.159 of 8 January 1991 (Public Archive Law, partially revoked), Brazilian Law No. 9.507 of 12 November 1997 (Habeas Data Law), Brazilian Law No. 101 of 4 May 2000 (Fiscal Responsibility Act), Brazilian Decree No. 4.553 of 27 December 2002 (Non-disclosure Hypotheses, revoked) and Brazilian Law No. 11.111 of 5 May 2005 (Non-disclosure Hypotheses, revoked).

Lastly, the Brazilian Law N° 12.528 of 18 November 2011[6] was promulgated in the same historic context as the Brazilian FOI Law and this created the National Truth Commission, whose main goal was to investigate facts and circumstances of human rights violations and crimes which occurred between 09/18/1946 and 10/05/1988, including the military dictatorship period (1964–1985).

In this fragmentary context, Brazilian FOI Law and Brazilian Law N° 12.528 were milestones for the transparency movement.

The FOI Law especially regulated the extent of the right to information and the sanctions for its violation. It also sets duties for passive and active transparency.

This study will investigate the access to information and its disclosure as stated in the (FOI) Law N° 12.527, Chapter II, and its regulation by the Decree N° 7.724.

---

[2]Article 5, item 33 of the Brazilian Constitution (Constituição da República Federativa do Brasil de 1988) states: "[. . .] all persons have the right to receive from public agencies information in their private interest or of collective or general interest; such information shall be furnished within the period established by law, under penalty of liability, except for information whose secrecy is essential to the security of society and of the National Government".

[3]Article 37 para 3, item 2 of the Brazilian Constitution, provides that "The direct or indirect public administration of any of the Branches of the Union, States, Federal District and Counties, shall obey the principles of legality, impersonality, morality, publicity and efficiency, as well as the following: The law shall regulate the forms of user participation in direct and indirect public administration, specifically regulating: [. . .] II – user access to administrative registries and information about governmental acts, observing the provisions of Article 5, items X and XXXIII".

[4]Article 216 of the Brazilian Constitution, provides that "Brazilian cultural heritage includes material and immaterial goods, taken either individually or as a whole, that refer to the identity, action and memory of the various groups that form Brazilian society, including: I. forms of expression; II. modes of creating, making and living; III. scientific, artistic and technological creations; IV. works, objects, documents, buildings and other spaces intended for artistic-cultural manifestations; V. urban complexes and sites with historical, landscape, artistic, archeological, paleontological, ecological and scientific value." Article 216 para 2, provides that "It is the responsibility of public administration, as provided by law, to maintain governmental documents and take measures to make them available for consultation by those that need to do so."

[5]Mendel 2009, p. 3.

[6]Ghione 2012.

Furthermore, it will analyze if Brazilian legislation complies with international conventions and treaties and if it respects the access to information good practices. For this last scope, a method proposed by Robert Gregory Michener, who analyzes FOI Laws according to the following six basic principles, will be used.

1. A *broad scope* that reflects the principle of maximum openness. Access should be the rule and secrecy the exception. A broad scope provides clear definitions and regiments to the law in and for as many public entities and branches of government as possible. Optimally, it provides for a strong central authority to promote implementation and compliance and to resolve appeals and complaints.
2. *Simple procedures* that safeguard and facilitate information requests and responses. They should also include clear obligations for officials to keep the applicant informed of the ongoing status of a request, and provide strict time limits and minimum costs for requesters. Delays in fulfilling requests should be limited and justified.
3. *Requirements to proactively publish* a wide assortment of public information are critical. Proactive publication increases the accessibility of information and may diminish the need for formal requests. Government should publicly acknowledge reserved information and report disclosure activity to the legislature on an ongoing basis.
4. A list of *unambiguous and limited exceptions* exempts harmful or justifiably sensitive information from disclosure, such as some issues of national security. The exemptions of other laws should be validated by the access to information law's list of exceptions. Reserve periods ought to be limited.
5. *A simple and fair appeals system* that resolves complaints and appeals within clear timeframes, providing several channels for appeal.
6. *Fair sanctions and protections* that apply to officials who knowingly fail to comply with the law, err in compliance, or report illegal acts.[7]

## 2 Access to Information and Democracy: A Culture of Access, the Duty of Transparency and the Availability of Information

The intimate relationship between the access to information and democracy is clear, especially when you consider that popular participation can only be effective to the extent that one allows access to data and information concerning the reality of that which one desires to influence.

In a study sponsored by the organization Article 19, called The Public's Right to Know: Principles on Freedom of Information Legislation, already stated that:

[7]Michener 2010, p. 10–11.

> Information is the oxygen of democracy. If people do not know what is happening in their society; if the actions of those who rule them are hidden, then they cannot take a meaningful part in the affairs of that society. But information is not just a necessity for people, it is an essential part of good government. Bad government needs secrecy to survive. It allows inefficiency, wastefulness and corruption to thrive. As Amartya Sen the Nobel Prize-winning economist has observed there has not been a substantial famine in a country with a democratic form of government and a relatively free press. Information allows people to scrutinize the actions of a government and is the basis for proper, informed debate of those actions.[8]

In the case of Brazil, there is the fact that the democratic environment that the 1988 Constitution sought to establish promotes a reevaluation of the understanding of the State and its relationship to civil society to overcome a supposed dichotomy by which they are labeled as antagonistic spheres and not penetrable, subject to distinct juridical organizations.

On the one hand, one can no longer allege the existence of opposing legal frameworks regulating public action and private action in isolation given that one recognizes the possibility and perhaps the need of the State to use institutes and standards initially forged for private activity—the example being the employment relationship stated in the Consolidated Laws, the practice of outsourcing, among others, in which one can also observe the penetration of such "public" standards moving to action oblivious to the State's space.[9]

It is evident that one cannot ignore the existence of one's own principles when educating a public agent in his behavior in the exercise of his administrative functions. However, in awareness of these principles, it is clear that the administrator can use management mechanisms that, without clashing with that principled framework, can contribute to the administrative action.

From another angle, the State's actions have to consider, for deepening the democratization process, the duty of submitting public officials and State bodies to the control of the population, favoring in principle the greatest legitimate conduct.

Thus, more than accountability in the accounting and financial senses by those who are exercising a portion of power—the prerogatives conferred by law, such as instruments of concretion of the public interest—the densification of the democratic regime imposes a growing and varied knowledge of the different actions perpetrated by public officials, propitiating social control of its actions.

---

[8]Mendel 1999.

[9]Among the many examples of standards of matiz publicistica that focus on the role of private agents, one can cite Article 10 of the Federal Law N° 9.637 of 15 May 1998 (Law of Social Organizations), which provides that "when the seriousness of the facts or the public interest demand, having founded evidence of misappropriation of assets or public origin resources, those responsible for oversight offer representation to the Prosecutor, the Attorney General of the Union or the entity's Attorney to request from the competent court the decree of the unavailability of the entity's assets and the seizure of the assets of its leaders, as well as public agents or third parties that may have been enriched illicitly or caused damage to public property."

In this sense, Clemerson Merlin Cleve Franzoni and Julia Franzoni have also taught:

> The process of constitutional concretization, therefore, considering the recognition of the complexity of society and the necessary coexistence of a plurality of interests in the translation and the composition of the meaning of the Constitution, should be informed by the regulatory parameters of the text; inscribing the opening requirements, participation and equality in its everyday practice.
>
> The aspects of the *renovation* manifest themselves in the opening of an "other" constitutional moment that presupposes epistemic comprehension of the role of the Constitution, claiming policies of control and citizen participation in public institutions. The Constitution can now be understood in a context where significance is open to the complex and plural network composition of meaning, leading to the intertwining of the premises of theoretical reason with the demands of practical reasoning. In this case, the constitutional concretization requires justification from the external point of view of law and, at the same time, the extracted legitimacy of the internal point of view of the legal system. For these reasons, the State and the institutions begin to be perceived as "sites of control" – there are tests to overcome, submitted to the mechanisms of the rationalization of conduct and parameters of justification and legitimation.
>
> It is in this context of requalification of the institutional legitimacy that democratic premises incorporated in the Constitution are arranged with the fundamental rights and allow a *normative construction* that increases the transparency to a condition of possibility of the plural state, republican and open to requirements of rational control of decisions. Reference is made here to the normative construction authorizing the transit of the constitutionalism guaranteed for the *emancipatory constitutionalism* which has, as a backdrop, the recognition of the constitutional subject as author of the change processes.[10]

It is true that democracy presupposes not only knowledge of the public machine and its acts, reports, programs, projects, among many other pieces of information, but the possibility to intensify the direct participation in decisions that trigger them.

Obviously, direct citizen presence in every state act, even in the scenario of public administration, is not possible or will not be possible in its plenitude. However, being concerned with the creation of increasing channels of dialogues allowing the exchange between state and society to discuss more central themes, in particular the development of public policy, is not only possible but a true duty and an unequivocal manifestation of the democratic regime.

A relevant lesson about the mechanisms of popular participation is given by Perez (2009, p. 139):

> Many of the institutes of popular participation in Public Administration assume a deliberative character or have binding force, that is to say, stem from the organization of processes of formation of administrative acts, with the participation of society at the time of decision making.
>
> In such cases, the citizen takes part, directly or through representatives, in the act of deciding and, as it is necessary to recognize, shares the constitutional powers attributed to the Public Administration.

[10]Clève & Franzoni 2013.

> It is worth noting that, by so acting, the citizen does not alter the constitutional division of powers. The decision is still made by the Administration with no part of the constitutional division of powers and state functions being usurped. There is, rather, an open organization of the process of the construction of the administrative decision, enabling the citizen, in return, to exercise the powers that he himself has constitutionally delegated to the Administration.

Nevertheless, even for the densification of democracy and the verification of the appropriateness of the behavior performed—especially after overcoming the *premise* of simple support in the law of literalness for the justification of public practices—the citizen's knowledge of the State's actions is essential.

This is all because democracy requires the availability of information as a tool for its existence. Absent knowledge, absent evaluation, absent criticism and present the secret, the door is opened to practices that allow the regime to be more antagonistic.

Given the importance of ensuring access to information, for the concretization of democracy and to define the core of the right of access to information, Brazilian Law N° 12.527 established a series of obligations to agencies and government entities, with a view to protect qualitative and quantitative levels for the minimum availability of information.

In this scenario, it is impossible to study the right of access to information apart from national guidelines provided in Article 3 of the Law N° 12.527 which must guide the procedures to ensure the fundamental right of access to information, namely (1) the duty of publicizing as a general rule except in exceptional cases of confidentiality, (2) the duty of active and passive transparency, (3) the broad use of various media made available by information technology in the dissemination of information, (4) encourage the development of culture transparency in public administration and, finally, (5) the development of social control of public administration.

These guidelines show the core of the right of access to information and at the same time, are interpretative beacons of the content of access legislation and the ideal of open government. That is, they provide the first step in the study of the extension of the right of access. In this last point, one can highlight the work of Stiglitz, which states that the ideal of open government in an implementation context of a culture of transparency is an end in and of itself, and could be an instrument for other important objectives to the Democratic State of Law.[11]

[11]Greater openness, as I have argued, can be justified on instrumental grounds, as a means to an end, such as reducing the likelihood of the abuse of power. Greater openness is an essential part of good governance, but I also believe that greater openness has an intrinsic value. Citizens have a basic right to know. I have tried to express this basic right in a number of different ways: the public has paid for the information; for government officials to appropriate the information that they have access to for private gain, if only for the nonmonetary return of good newspaper coverage, is as much theft as stealing any other public property. While we all recognize the necessity of collective action and the consequences of collective actions for individual freedoms, we have a basic right to know how the powers that have been surrendered to the collective are being used. This seems to me to be a basic part of the implicit contract between the governed and those they have selected to

This present study focuses on the study of the obligation of having transparency, in the templates of Article 6.1 LAI that establishes the transparent management of information as a duty of the public authority of the agencies and entities, which should also ensure open access to such information and its disclosure.

It should be noted, preliminarily, that the obligation of transparency has broad spectrum incidences, considering that the Federal Law N° 12.527 subjects not only the organs and entities of the direct and indirect management pursuant to Article 1, but also applies, as appropriate, to private non-profit entities that receive funds directly from the budget or through social grants, management or partnership agreements, contracts, agreement adjustments or other similar instruments for carrying out public interest actions.

The Brazilian Law on Access to Information does not regulate the cases in which its provisions apply to non-profit organizations, but merely says, in the Sole paragraph of Article 2 that the publicity to which these entities are submitted refers to the share of public funds received and their destination, without prejudice to the checks and balances to which they are legally obligated. This omission creates considerable legal uncertainty in relation to the limits of applicability of Federal Law N° 12.527 to the above entities. It should be noted that such uncertainty was partially mitigated at the federal level, with the Decree edition N° 7.724, that regulate the situation of the non-profit entities in its Articles 63 and 64.[12]

---

temporarily govern them. The less directly accountable a government agency is to the public, the more important it is that its actions be open and transparent. By the same token, the more independent and less directly politically accountable a government agency is, the greater the presumption for openness. Openness is one of the most important checks on the abuse of public fiduciary responsibilities. While such openness may not guarantee that wise decisions will always be made, it would be a major step forward in the ongoing evolution of democratic processes, a true empowerment of individuals to participate meaningfully in the decisions concerning the collective actions that have such profound effects on their lives and livelihoods.

The challenge is to create a truly transparent and open government. The incentives for secrecy are great, and so too are the opportunities for evading the intent of any disclosure regulations. If formal meetings have to be open, then all decisions can be made in informal meetings. If written material is subject to disclosure, then officials will have an incentive to ensure that little is written down, and what is written down will be for the public record. Given these limitations of legalistic approaches, the emphasis must be on creating a culture of openness, where the presumption is that the public should know about and participate in all collective decisions (Stiglitz 2002, p. 42).

[12]The referred to provisions delimit the information that should be published by private entities, as well as the procedure for the transfer of information relating to agreements, contracts, terms of partnerships, arrangements or other similar instruments. Article 63 of the Brazilian Decree N° 7.724 of 16 May 2012, provides that "The private non-profit organizations that receive public funds to carry out public interest actions should publicize the following information: I – copy of the updated bylaws of the entity II – an updated list of names of entity leaders; III – a full copy of the agreements, contracts, terms of partnerships, arrangements or similar instruments made with the Federal Executive branch, respective addendums, and final reports of accountability, in the form of legislation applicable. §1 The information contained in the introductory paragraph will be posted on the website of the private entity and on the general public access bulletin board in its headquarters. §2 The disclosure on the website referred to in §1 may be waived by decision of the public body or entity, by express justification of the entity, in the case of private non-profit

With this preliminary consideration already made, it should be noted that Article 6 LAI establishes for those who are passive subjects to the liabilities of the law both the duty for active transparency and passive transparency concerning access to information.

The duty of active transparency is stated in Article 8 LAI and consists of the obligation of public bodies and entities to promote the dissemination of information of collective or general interest produced by them or in their custody, regardless of the request. Such disclosure should take place to ensure timely and permanent access to information of public interest with respect to transparency concerns and enable anyone—whether they exercise any public and official function of control or not—to access public information. The active transparency should have a dual function: it contributes, on the one hand, to greater effectiveness of the fundamental right of access to information, and on the other, helps to reduce the amount of repetitive claims to obtain certain information, avoiding useless reproduction of disclosure efforts by the Public Administration. Brazilian law at this point is in tune with the best practices of access to information, in particular with those established by the Principles on Freedom of Information Legislation, created by the organization Article 19, in particular with its Principle 2,[13] which explains that freedom of information implies not only that public bodies accede to requests for information but also that they publish and widely disseminate documents of significant public interest, subject only to reasonable limits based on resources and capacity. Which information should not be published will depend on the public body's concern. The law should not establish both the general obligation to publish and key categories of information that must be published.[14]

Joaquim José Gomes Canotilho, commenting on the Portuguese Constitution, gives a relevant lesson about the essential content of this duty, which is fully applicable to the Brazilian legal system:

---

organizations that do not have the means to carry it out. §3 the information referred to in the introductory paragraph must be published from the moment the agreement, contract, partnership agreement, adjustment or like instrument is concluded and will be updated regularly and available no later than one hundred and eighty days after delivery of the final accountability"? (does not work here) and Article 64, "Requests for information relating to agreements, contracts, terms of partnerships, arrangements or similar instruments provided for in Article 63 should be submitted directly to the agencies and entities responsible for the transfer of funds".

[13]Mendel 1999, p. 8.

[14]The aforementioned Article 2 also establishes the minimum amount of information on the list that must be put at the disposition of the citizens, such as: [1] operational information about how the public body functions, including costs, objectives, audited accounts, standards, achievements and so on, particularly where the body provides direct services to the public; [2] information on any requests, complaints or other direct actions which members of the public may take in relation to the public body; [3] guidance on processes by which members of the public may provide input into major policy or legislative proposals; [4] the types of information which the entity holds and the form in which this information is held; and [5] the content of any decision or policy affecting the public, along with reasons for the decision and background material of importance in framing the decision. See Mendel 1999.

> Note that the Constitution doesn't make the freedom of access to administrative documents dependent on the existence of a personal interest. With the exception of cases of nominative documents or confidential documents for security reasons or justice, the idea of administrative democracy points not only to a right of access to the archives and public records for the defense of individual rights, but also a right to know what goes on under the political-bureaucratic sphere, allowing citizens access to files, reports, studies, statistics, directives, instructions, circulars and notes. [. . .] The right of open access to information today should be conceived not only as the right to information by citizens, but also as the right to open communication between authorities and citizens. Open communication will imply, among other things, the duty of the administration to actively provide information.[15]

Article 8 LAI presents guidelines about the duty of active transparency that must be observed by the public administration at the federal, state and municipal levels.

Article 8.1 LAI, in particular, presents a list of information that must be disclosed proactively and involve data on the entity itself—such as their skills, organizational structure, address, phone numbers, among others—expense reports and fund transfers, information on bids and contracts made by the agencies and ultimately answers to the society's most frequently asked questions. The information listed in the provision consists of the minimum content to be made available in an active way. The organizations and entities spontaneously make decisions about the expansion of the types of information to be disseminated.

Within the scope of the Federal Public Administration and other entities controlled directly or indirectly by the Union, the duty of active transparency is regulated by Chapter III of Federal Decree N° 7.724. It is interesting to note that this Decree expands the kinds of information that must be disclosed proactively when, for example, it demands the disclosure of "programs, projects, actions, works and activities with the indication of the unit responsible, the main goals and results, if any, indicators of results and the impact" (Article 7 para 3, item 2 of the Federal Decree N° 7.724). This initiative is commendable especially because it places the duty of transparency on those who control public policies.

For the active dissemination of information to occur widely, Article 8 para 2 of the Access Act states that public entities and authorities should "make use of all legitimate means and tools available with the mandatory dissemination at official sites of the World Wide Web (Internet)". The dissemination of information via the Internet receives prominent position in the Brazilian Law N° 12.527 establishing minimum operating standards and accessibility of such sites, to be detailed by regulation, as provided in Article 8 para 3. As an additional step to the full implementation of the provision of information via the Internet, it would be desirable if the Brazilian Law on Access to Information could foresee guidelines for the articulation of the exercise of the right to information with governmental inclusion of digital policies, in particular the guarantee of public access to the internet, as well as training citizens and public managers to use such an important tool well. These thoughts are supported by the report that deals with the promotion and protection of the right to freedom of opinion and expression of the Council of

[15]Canotilho 2002, p. 510–511.

the UN Human Rights dated 16 May 2011 (Report of the Special Rapporteur on the promotion and protection of the right to freedom of opinion and expression). Otherwise, see:

> Given that the Internet has become an indispensable tool for realizing a range of human rights, combating inequality, accelerating development and human progress, ensuring universal access to the Internet should be a priority for all States.
>
> Each State should thus develop a concrete and effective policy, in consultation with individuals from all sections of society, including the private sector and relevant Government ministries, to make the Internet widely available, accessible and affordable to all segments of the population.
>
> At the international level, the Special Rapporteur reiterates his call on States, in particular developed States, to honour their commitment, expressed inter alia in the Millennium Development Goals, to facilitate technology transfer to developing States, and to integrate effective programmes to facilitate universal Internet access in their development and assistance policies.
>
> *Where the infrastructure for Internet access is present, the Special Rapporteur encourages States to support initiatives to ensure that online information can be accessed in a meaningful way by all sectors of the population, including persons with disabilities and persons belonging to linguistic minorities.*
>
> States should include Internet literacy skills in school curricula, and support similar learning modules outside of schools. In addition to basic skills training, modules should clarify the benefits of accessing information online, and of responsibly contributing information. Training can also help individuals learn how to protect themselves against harmful content and explain the potential consequences of revealing private information on the Internet.[16]

However, the duty of passive transparency, regulated by Article 10 and others of Brazilian Law N° 12.527, is by its nature an eminent guarantor and requires the holder of information to answer the request for information when requested and must proceed expeditiously and justifiably, including cases in which there is a possible restriction of access in accordance with Article 6 para 3 of the Brazilian Law N° 12.527. The trend is that the more efficient the actions of active transparency, the lower the demand for requested information.

However, there are and there will be situations in which the requested information was not previously offered by the agency or entity. Regardless of what the reason for the absence of the active availability of information, the interested party may address the agency or entity, addressing their request that their claim be upheld.

It is also important to point out that, to ensure access to public information upon request, Article 9, item of Law N° 12.527 requires the creation of a service of integrated information to the citizens (SIC), to be installed in a place with appropriate conditions to attend to and guide the public regarding the access to information, docketing documents and requests for access to information, as well as

[16] LaRue 2011, para 85–87.

reporting on the processing of documents in their respective units. In addition, an alternative for the routing of access requests through official websites of agencies and government entities on the Internet should be made possible. At the federal level, the e-sic (electronic service of integrated information) was implanted. It must contain the registration of the request for access number in a specific electronic system and the delivery of the protocol number, which will contain the date of submission of the application pursuant to Article 9 para 2 of the Federal Decree N° 7.724.

At this point, the Access Act brought significant advances by inducing the centralization of response services to citizens. The internal organization of the public administration is too complex in the eyes of the citizen, who does not profoundly know its structure.

An interesting experience took place in the city of Belo Horizonte, whose Executive Branch regulated the right of access to information with the publication of Decree No. 14.906 of 15 May 2012. This city maximized the possibilities of access to information when they enabled citizens to be serviced through various communication channels. There are two portals of access to information available to the citizens, namely the portal "Access to Information",[17] and the portal "Transparency Cup 2014".[18] Besides the possibility of access via the Internet, there are communication channels available via a telephone exchange or even in person at the citizen's center—BH Resolve. The personal attendance brings together in one place the possibility to access a variety of information of social interest, in particular regarding municipal services. The Ombudsman of the Municipality is also installed in this location, and it can be accessed by telephone or through an internet portal.[19]

Another important way to ensure access to information according to the Brazilian Law on Access to Information is holding hearings or public consultations, encouraging public participation and conducting other forms of dissemination.

It is noteworthy that for the public hearing to be an instrument of the consensual action of public administration, able to give rise to transparency and public participation, it is necessary to conduct it in accordance with due process and effectively listening to those interested. In this sense, Lucia Valle Figueiredo has masterfully concluded:

> The purpose of the public hearing, following the worldwide guideline, is transparency, loyalty and fair play in administrative behavior. It is taken into consideration that, if the Constitution prescribes a participative action, as Gordillo states, even without constitutional or legal requirements, major projects or major decisions to be made must be preceded by a public hearing.

[17] Available at the address www.pbh.gov.br/acessoainformação. Accessed on 15 February 2017.

[18] Available at www.pbh.gov.br/transparênciacopa2014 (Accessed on 15 February 2017).

[19] See www.pbh.gov.br/faleconosco (Accessed on 15 February 2017).

> However, the public hearing cannot be a mere formality, but must truly be the means by which decisions will be made after giving those interested the opportunity to actually be heard (audire).
>
> And certainly, if the law imposes a public hearing and there is none or it is not done properly that invalidates the procedure.
>
> The public hearing, if properly executed, will bring legitimacy and efficiency to administrative decisions.
>
> Moreover, when is it mandatory, as in various Brazilian laws, it is part of a process – and, as such, is to be applied in its entirety with due process and all the principles inherent therein. Specifically where there is an omission in a specific law if we have before us a process within the federal sphere, we must apply Law No. 9.784 of 29 January 1999, which regulates the administrative procedure in the Federal Public Administration. This law expressly mandates public hearings.[20]

To ensure compliance with the duty of transparency, the Brazilian Law N° 12.527 establishes disciplinary measures to penalize the denial of access to information when such negative is not properly grounded (Article 7 para 4 LAI). Likewise, Article 7 para 4 and 5 LAI ensure an applicable procedure to situations of requested information being lost—with the possibility of formal inquiry to determine the cause of the document's disappearance—thus avoiding the willful concealment of information or negligence by those responsible for the safekeeping of that information.

It must be noted that the establishment of the legislative framework of the transparency obligation, especially in its active facet, does not imply the immediate disappearance of the difficulties of public bodies and entities in disclosing information. Mendel says, especially about the difficulties in the proactive disclosure of information:

> The scope of this obligation depends to some extent on resource limitations. However, the amount of information covered should increase over time, particularly as new technologies make it easier to publish and disseminate information. The Joint Declaration has special mandates which specifically call for progressive increases in the scope of pro active disclosure: "Systems should be put in place to increase, over time, the amount of information subject to such routine disclosure." The longer term goal should be to make information available proactively, so as to minimize the need for individuals to have to resort to requests to access it.[21]

Some actions to overcome the difficulties of the realization of the Brazilian Law commands have already been adopted by the Union, notably by the Comptroller General of the Union (CGU), which plays an innovative role in the implementation of the Brazilian law concerning the access to information by promoting better integration between agencies and public entities and encouraging cooperation among federal entities.

[20]Figueiredo 2003.

[21]Mendel 2008, p. 33. See Portal Brasil 2013.

In particular, as a way to assist states and municipalities in complying with their obligations to guarantee access to information, as well as promoting a culture of transparency and open government, the Comptroller General, in February 2013, amplified the scope of the "Transparent Brazil" program, which will offer technical and guidance material, skills training, both in-person and virtually, as well as making the Electronic System source code of the Citizens Information Services (e-SIC) available to those interested. Another recent initiative of the CGU is the disclosure of documents on the implementation of government programs and audit reports on municipalities, made by the Surveillance Programme of the aforementioned entity in 2003, on its website.

Having established the outline of active and passive transparency and the form of dissemination of information, we move to the analysis of the content of the right of access to information in the Brazilian legal system.

## 3 The Right of Access to Information in Brazilian Law N° 12.527 of 18 November 2011

In the Brazilian legal system, the right of access to information has a constitutional matrix and includes the right to receive information of particular, collective or general interest from public agencies and entities according to the terms of regulatory law, as stated in Article 5, item 33 of the Brazilian Constitution.

According to the meaning of the statement made by UNESCO, a connotation, either more restrictive or amplified, can be attributed to the right of access to information (as in Brazilian law) and is intrinsically linked to other rights and principles, such as the freedom of expression. See below:

> Freedom of information may be interpreted narrowly to the right to access information held by public bodies or, more broadly, including the access to and circulation of information held by other actors. It is intrinsically linked to the basic human right of freedom of expression. Freedom of information is, therefore, also fundamentally connected to the freedom of press, representing a crucial element that enables the media to strengthen democratization, good governance and human development through its roles as: a "watch-dog over the abuse of power" (promoting accountability and transparency), the civic forum for political debate (facilitating informed electoral choices), and the agenda-setter for policymakers (strengthening government responsiveness to social problems)". In turn, the complete realization of the right to know cannot take place without the free, independent, plural, ethical and professional press.[22]

Brazilian Law N° 12.527 was enacted, therefore, to regulate the right of access to the information as outlined in item 33 of Article 5, item 2 of para 3 of Article 37 and para 2 of Article 216 of the Brazilian Constitution and in those terms, ensures the autonomous right of access to information (not only to documents), but also establishes procedural guidelines for the availability of information. As a guarantee

[22]United Nations 2011.

to ensure the broad right to information, this guideline of the Brazilian Law N° 12.527 is consistent with international good practices regarding the access to information. This conclusion is reinforced by comparative law studies done by Toby Mendel, who states that:

> Establishing the right to access information held by public bodies is the fundamental reason for adopting the right to information law, and most legislation does this pretty clearly. In some cases, such as the laws of Mexico and Jamaica, this is set out as a free-standing right, subject to the regime of exceptions. In other cases, for example in Thailand and the United Kingdom, the right is cast in more procedural terms, providing that anyone may make a request for information and, subject to certain conditions – procedural and substantive – have the information communicated to him or her. It is not clear whether this makes much difference in practice, although a more rights-based approach may prove important over time.
>
> Some laws – for example Those of South Africa and Jamaica – provide for the right of access to documents or records while most others provide for the right of access to information. A few, like Uganda, provide for the right of access to both. There are problems with restricting the right of access to documents, since most applicants will not have a specific document in mind when submitting their information requests. There have been problems in some cases with officials applying an unduly rigid understanding of the right to documents to reject, instead of responding in substance to, requests. At the same team, when an applicant can specify a particular document, he or she should, obviously, be given access to it. In this respect, the Ugandan approach may have some advantages.[23]

To understand the right of access, one must have in mind the meaning of the term "information". The definition of the term is determined by the LAI, which in its Article 4 defines as "information" all data, processed or not, which can be used for the production and transmission of knowledge, contained in any medium or format.

Owing to the broad definition of "information", the right of access pertains to an innumerable amount of situations, illustrated by Article 7 LAI. The aforementioned device establishes, in an exemplary list, a series of rights covered by the access to information and which spans the gamut from forecasts of instrumental character, such as receiving guidance for the attainment of the access to information, to autonomous access rights, such as receiving various types of public information, such as those related to the management of public assets, the realization, implementation and results of public policies, among many others.

As a way to synthesize the non-exhaustive list of information subject to disclosure, the following summary table was created:

| Legal Provision | Information to which the right of access is guaranteed by the LAI |
|---|---|
| Article 7, item 1 | Guidance on the procedures for access, as well as the location where the desired information can be found or obtained. |
| Article 7, item 2 | Information contained in records or documents produced or accumulated by agencies or entities, collected or not, in the public archives. |

(continued)

[23] Mendel 2009, p. 141.

| Legal Provision | Information to which the right of access is guaranteed by the LAI |
|---|---|
| Article 7, item 3 | Information produced or guarded by an actual individual or a private agency arising from any bond with their entities, even if the connection has already ceased. |
| Article 7, item 5 | Information about activities carried out by agencies and entities, including those relating to their policies, organizations and services. |
| Article 7, item 6 | Information pertaining to the administration of public property, using public resources, procurement and administrative contracts. |
| Article 7, item 7 | Information related to (a) the implementation, monitoring and results of programs, projects and actions of public entities and agencies, as well as proposed targets and proposed indicators; (b) the results of inspections, audits, and the accountability for the care of accounts under the control of internal and external agencies including accountability for prior years. |

This device also includes the right to receive primary, honest, authentic, and updated information, concepts that are defined in part by Article 4 LAI. In legal terms, authentic means "information that can be known and used by individuals, authorized equipment or systems," while genuine means "information that has not been modified regarding its origin, transit and destination." Finally, primary means "information collected at the source, with as much detail as possible and without modifications."

The law, by giving such qualifications, ultimately regulates how information will be made available, repudiating the disclosure of documents or data that do not meet the requirements of origin, integrity, authenticity and timeliness. It does not mean that the administration can use such claims to evade the provision of information, but rather, it must excel in its efforts to protect the quality of the information to be disclosed.

The theme of the right of access to information, its dissemination and in particular the duty to guarantee its quality has recently faced the judgment of the Court Injunction No. 16.903-DF by the Ministers of the First Session of the Superior Court of Justice.[24] This is a class action brought by a journalist, together with a major newspaper, which aimed to combat the act of authority that denied them the provision of public information provided by Article 5, items and 33 and Article 37 para 3, item 2, and Article 220 of the Brazilian Constitution. They sought information on the distribution of advertising money among federal entities, according to the category of advertising (a), media type (b), the vehicle of communication (c) and, finally, the contracted advertising agencies (d). In its reasoning the controlling authority—The State Secretary of the Chief Minister of Social Communication of the Presidency—has claimed, in summary, the impossibility of the disclosure of such information filed justifies the rejection, arguing that "the amounts allocated to each vehicle of communication are not available in order to preserve the negotiation strategy of the media promoted annually by SECOM with these

[24]Federal Supreme Court of Brazil (Supremo Tribunal Federal), *Mandado de Segurança*, 16903/DF (Judgment of 14 November 2012).

vehicles. That is to say it was alleged to be in the interests of the public to maintain the confidentiality of such information". In the course of processing the injunction, the Law regarding Access to Information was enacted. This ended up modifying the strategies of both the defense and the Union, an interested party in the case.

The Union, in particular, presented a new petition which argued that, with the enactment of Law N° 12.527, this injunction would not be the appropriate means to satisfy the claims of the plaintiffs, because (a) the request for information is no longer made directly to the Minister of State; and (b) the interposition of administrative appeals with suspensive effect is optional. It was alleged at that time that (a) the money spent by the agencies and entities on the vehicles of communication through their advertising agencies were not forwarded to SECOM, (b) it has only the information passed on by the Institute for the Monitoring of Advertising—IAP and that c) the data collected by the IAP is not a reliable source of information that can be understood as characterizing expenditures actually made with each reporting vehicle. Thus, the claim of the plaintiffs could not be met because Article 7, item 4 of the Law N° 12.527 only guarantees the attainment of the following types of information: primary, complete, authentic and updated information.

Security was unanimously granted, recognizing the right of access to the information requested. It is helpful to analyze in greater depth the fundamentals of this judgment, as it certainly sheds light on the application of the Access Act.

The rapporteur, Minister Arnaldo Esteves Lima, centered his vote on the deconstruction of the reasons bandied about by the controlling authority, concluding that the concretion of the public interest in the case analyzed takes place prior to the release of information to society, according to the dictates of the Constitution and ordinary legislation, and not the denial of access to information requested. In reading the theory of compelling reasons, the rapporteur states that:

> In this case, the reasons cited as determinants of unavailability by means of communication and the amounts spent on advertising, which get separated entirely from our legal and constitutional order, should not exist because they violate fundamental precepts, sufficient in and of themselves, of direct and immediate applicability, such as stated in para 1 of Article 5 of the Federal Constitution.[25]

The rapporteur also concluded that the disclosure of spending on advertising, according to the manner in which it was requested, did not fit in any of the constitutional hypotheses of secrecy and that, in that case, "the observance of the principle of advertising by the public administration falls within their social order and meets the common good."[26]

We also highlight the content of the vote of the Minister Herman Benjamin, completely in line with the principles of the access law. While stressing the importance of the matter, said Minister argued that:

---

[25]Federal Supreme Court of Brazil, *Mandado de Segurança*, 16903/DF (Judgment of 14 November 2012). p. 9.

[26]Federal Supreme Court of Brazil, *Mandado de Segurança*, 16903/DF (Judgment of 14 November 2012). p. 9.

> The matter is relevant, since the subject has novelty, especially after the advent of a new legal framework concerning public access to government information. It's obvious that Article 37, introductory paragraph, of the Federal Constitution had already entered the principle of publicity as one of the founding stones of the action of the Public Administration and the State, in a broad sense. However, with the law regarding access to public information in effect, Federal Law N° 12.527, I believe that there is a direct application of the need to provide the desired information. [. . .] In fact, from the reading of the transcripts it can be inferred that the new law requires broad access to the information requested. This is because – for the record – they are not labeled as confidential or do not even involve the privacy of individuals and their rights. In my opinion, the denial to provide the requested data was not properly justified, since it is not possible to seal the access to public information through the motivation indicated in relation to contract negotiations or even to administrative entanglements.[27]

The Minister Mauro Campbell, on the other hand, emphasized that the vagueness of some requested information and documents should not be, by themselves, obstacles to access. He claims that "[despite the] imprecision of these reports concerning the expenses incurred by means of communication, there is no reason to maintain the confidentiality of such information, especially because there is no legal requirement that such data be created in the form of a certificate, or even with accuracy, but only made available to interested parties."[28]

## 4 Concerning the Limitations on the Right of Access to Information

As already discussed above, the study of the principles of the legislation about the access to information points to the need to give maximum publicity to public information. This finding does not imply, however, any guarantee of unrestricted access to information. Some limitations on the exercise of that right are set out in the Constitution. More than that, the Constitution, when it ensures access to information, says that such access will occur in terms of regulatory law, which obviously links those subjected to the law to the legislative limitations on the right of access to information.

Obviously, the limitations on the right of access to information have exceptional character. In this sense, Article 7 para 2 LAI provides that "when full access to information is unauthorized because a part of it is confidential, access to the non-confidential part via certificate, extract or copy, with the confidential part redacted, is guaranteed".

Stiglitz makes a relevant summary of the hypotheses of the exceptions to the duty of disclosure of information. See below:

---

[27] Federal Supreme Court of Brazil, *Mandado de Segurança*, 16903/DF (Judgment of 14 November 2012). p. 20.

[28] Federal Supreme Court of Brazil, *Mandado de Segurança*, 16903/DF (Judgment of 14 November 2012). p. 12.

> Several exceptions to the disclosure of information exist (for more details see Stiglitz 1999). First, the most important and convincing exception involves privacy matters concerning individuals and organizations. In exercising its duties the government gathers enormous amounts of information on individuals, such as income and health statistics, but few, if any, of the issues discussed here fall within the privacy exception. Second, a closely related exception concerns certain information that an informed party would never disclose to the government if he or she knew that it would subsequently be made public. The importance of the confidentiality of doctor-patient and lawyer-client relationships has long been recognized, and a limited number of interactions within the public sector should fall within the confidentiality exception. Third, the importance of secrecy in times of war is indisputable. When a nation's survival is at stake, it must do everything in its power to increase its chance of winning. The success of a military attack may well depend on surprise. The problem is that national security exceptions have been extended to issues where national security is clearly not an issue.[29]

The last kind of limitation mentioned by Stiglitz in the above quote shows equivalence in the Brazilian legal system and refers to the exceptional hypotheses of secrecy when certain information is temporarily submitted to the public access restriction because of its indispensability to the security of society and State pursuant to Article 4, item 3 LAI. The Access Act, in fact, determines the protection of confidential and personal information, considering its availability, authenticity, integrity and possible restriction of access. A typical example of this kind of restriction on the right of access is the provision in Article 7 para 1 LAI that the right of access does not include information relating to research projects and scientific and technological development whose secrecy is vital to the security of society and the State.

Although the study of sensitive information is not the object of this work, it is necessary to acknowledge brief considerations about the content of Article 22 LAI. According to that article, the provisions of the Federal Law N° 12.527 do not exclude other legal hypotheses of secrecy and judicial confidentiality or the hypotheses of industrial secrets arising from the direct exploitation of economic activity by the State or by individuals or private entities that have any connection to the public authorities. The ideal draft would exhaustively list the hypotheses of secrets contained in other laws, validating them to bring greater uniformity to the law and further guarantee a higher level of legal certainty for the activities that involve the dissemination of information and the eventual restriction of access to the information.

Another limitation of access originates from the systematic protection of personal information in accordance with Article 6, item 3 LAI. Such protection derives from the very fundamentality of the human being in our legal framework and aims to safeguard their sphere of intimacy. The issue of protection of personal information is potentially problematic in some extreme situations, such as the case of nominal disclosure of the salaries of administrative agents.

[29]Stiglitz 2002, p. 36; Michener 2010, p. 10–11.

Regarding the nominal disclosure of the remuneration and allowances of administrative agents, we have already stated our position in an article written in co-authorship with Raquel Ferreira Bastos. At that time, we wrote:

> We believe that, despite the classification of the remuneration of public agents as information of public interest, there should be more caution in the way such data is disclosed. The nominal disclosure, despite the potential of damaging the content of fundamental rights and of personality, is not, in any way, proportional to the purpose it intends to achieve.
>
> It is not in doubt that the nominal disclosure is not essential to the control of the amounts paid as compensation to public officials. You can replace the name – the first form of identification of any person in their social environment – with other data that does not expose their privacy or endanger their personal and family security; for example their functional number or registration.
>
> The publication of names only facilitates the control of the destination of public funds by citizens in a surreal "witch hunt" scenario in which they are considered detectives searching for specified targets.
>
> The incongruity between the means of disclosure of public spending and the ends protected by the legal framework – in this case, those established by the principles of advertising and the right of access to information – ultimately disrespects the principle of proportionality regarding the need for the recipients of the standard to adopt the least restrictive mandate [. . .].
>
> Besides the always inevitable discussion when the real framework of proportionality as a principle or as a rule is evident, especially taking into account the reading of Virgilio Afonso da Silva on the widespread theory of Robert Alexy, the fact is that the issue calls for consideration under the optics of the subdivision of the aforementioned standard in its vectors of suitability, necessity and proportionality in the strict sense.
>
> That is to say it is crucial, either as a principle or rule, to subject nominal disclosure to the test of proportionality.
>
> Does the nominal disclosure achieve or promote the desired result? Considering that the desired result is to appropriate the data collectivity that may be of interest without navigating the challenging issue of the social legitimacy of the knowledge of information that has to do with information with some personal trait, it might even be possible to conclude that the indication of the names appropriate.
>
> But if we move forward and think about the situation from the standpoint of necessity, it alters understanding. This is because the desired result, whether or not the society knows how much is paid to each public servant, makes possible an increment of control concerning illegal activity, such as the perception above the ceiling, and is achieved with less cost to the public official. That is, the goal can be achieved by some other act that limits less and affects less the fundamental right.
>
> Thus, the individualized disclosure, without, however, providing the name, achieves the scope. Therefore, if there is no need, there is no proportionality, making even further consideration unnecessary to confronting the proportionality in a limited sense. But, even if one interpreter was convinced that the individualized disclosure, done in another way, so as to not nominally indicate the recipient of the portion of the remuneration, would not achieve the same results, would not have the same intensity, all that would be left would be to continue the examination of whether the conduct was proportional in its strictest sense.

> And yet, there does not seem to be enough reason, enough motive to promote such disclosure. That is to say, the right to information does not seem to legitimize the insignificance of the intimacy that is constitutionally guaranteed. It is critical to consider that the right to information cannot transform any public agent into an object of information, removing their protective shell assured by the Constitution.
>
> For this reason, in our opinion, the interpretation given to date by the Supreme Court is not in line with our legal system. This is because if one wants to seek proportionality in any constitutional provision, the fact is that proportionality is allocated in the very essence of the Constitution as a bulwark of fundamental rights (. . .).[30]

Finally, it is important to put an end to the equivocal information that the Federal Law N° 12.527 establishes the nominal disclosure of this kind of information. There is no rule to this effect in the stated law and, as said, even if eventually it was envisaged, one would need to question its constitutionality.[31]

It turns out that despite the non-existence of any determination in the Law on Access to Information regarding the nominal disclosure of the salaries of servers, as there are more appropriate and proportionate ways to disclose such information, the Supreme Court has considered the possibility of such nominal disclosure, under the argument that the obligation of transparency should prevail in these cases:

> Constitutional. Publication of the name of its servers and the corresponding amount of remuneration on the electronic site maintained by the municipality of São Paulo. Legitimacy. 1. The publication is legitimate, including on electronic sites maintained by the public authorities of the names of its servers and the value of their corresponding salaries and financial benefits. 2. Extraordinary Appeal acknowledged and granted.[32]

Another limitation concerning the proportionality of the request for access to information is usually relegated to oblivion by the doctrine. About this limitation, it was previously stated on another occasion:

> It should also be noted that the Federal Law N° 12.527 does not allow the formulation of requests for "custom" information. Explanation: our experience in front of the Comptroller General of the Municipality of Belo Horizonte has provided us with the opportunity to get to know about the applications in that Law through which one "demands" that the information be addressed to him in a specific format. The citizen demands data according to particular models. However, this duty does not exist. Existing information, if able to be provided given the limits, will be provided in the form that it exists. This does not mean that there is no need to provide it in clear, direct and objective language. What is repudiated is any request that overloads the reporting entity, claiming an individualized product.
>
> Thus, the transparency campaigns have a domestic and external focus. With regards to the external recipient, the campaigns need to educate citizens about the scope and limits of the Federal Law N° 12.527, including explaining that the aforementioned law does not, itself, have the duty to deviate from specific or insurmountable procedures. Thus, if a special law says that 30 days should be expected in order to obtain a reply to a formulated request pertaining to the acceptance or rejection of a certificate or a welfare benefit, the Law on

[30]Fortini, Avelar & Ferreira 2013, p. 1032–1041.

[31]Fortini, Avelar & Ferreira 2013, p. 1032–1041.

[32]Federal Supreme Court of Brazil, Agravo no Recurso Extraordinário 652.777 (Judgment of 23 April 2015).

Access to Information does not override this command and does not diminish the stated time needed.[33]

Expressly adopting this guideline, Article 13 of Decree N° 7.724, established that requests for access to generic, disproportionate or unreasonable information, or requests that require additional analyzes, interpretation or consolidation of data and information, services of production or processing of data other than what falls under the purview of the entity will not be attended to. In the case of the latter situation, the Decree states that the agency or entity shall, if known, indicate the location where the information can be found and the interpretation, consolidation or data processing performed.[34]

Having analyzed the main provisions concerning the access to information and its availability, we move to the difficulty of implementation of this right in the Brazilian legal system.

## 5 Difficulties in Implementing the Right of Access and the Dissemination of Information

At another time, the nature of the challenges that would arise with the entry into force of the Access to Information Act, namely the cultural, operational and organizational challenges, was outlined. Largely, these are obstacles to the access itself and the dissemination of public information.[35]

The cultural difficulties are those arising from the historic consecration of secrecy within the public administration. The still young Brazilian democracy was recovering from authoritarian practices rooted in the way of thinking and acting of public officials. The abandonment of this mentality is essential for regular access and dissemination of public information.

It has already been stated that:

> [. . .] the difficulty of implementing the culture of transparency within the public administration. The holders of public information will be out of their comfort zone when exposing their actions – including any possible errors – to the eyes of citizens and control agencies. It will be necessary to abolish the patrimonial perspective that identifies public information as property of public officials, and overcome the historical understanding that the citizen is unable to understand the fundamentals, the purposes and the contours of state action. Also, it will be important to raise awareness that offering information is not a favor graciously granted to citizens, but a duty to be carried out with professionalism.[36]

It is critical to work to raise the awareness of public officials to the highly technical content of certain information classified as confidential. Overcoming the

---

[33]Fortini, Avelar & Ferreira 2013, p. 1032–1041.

[34]Fortini, Avelar & Ferreira 2013, p. 1044.

[35]Fortini, Avelar & Ferreira 2013, p. 1041 et seq.

[36]Fortini, Avelar & Ferreira 2013, p. 1041.

culture of secrecy—with the effective provision of information—is an important step to decrease the gap between citizens and Public Administration.

The Administration, in general, has positional privilege in relation to production, storage and access to public information, as much of this information is gestated in its organizational structure and manipulated by its agents. Thus, *a priori*, it is natural that citizens are at a disadvantage regarding access to public information. What cannot happen is the abuse of this disadvantage, the asymmetric *status quo* that makes it difficult or even impossible to control these agents.[37]

Another relevant cultural challenge is the abandonment of the anti-ecological "paper culture", with the consequent promotion of the registration of information in a systematic, digital and shared manner. Digital information that is publicly available is accessible in various forms and locations, with the preservation of its essential characteristics, as opposed to information restricted to physical methods or even in inaccessible digital files.

Moving to the organizational challenges, it is possible to list difficulties concerning the structuring of technical, financial and human resources of the Public Administration facing the duty to provide information. The implementation of the access law along with the disclosure of information demands, within its terms, the restructuring of responsible and competent areas for receiving and tracking information requests.

The issue becomes more serious when considering a specific situation in some areas and, in particular, in the case of small municipalities. The desire to maximally extend the fundamental right of access to information is frequently hindered in the absence of human, technical and financial resources, among many other needs of small entities. The provision that exempts municipalities with a population of up to 10,000 inhabitants from the mandatory disclosure of the information of collective or general interest produced by or guarded by them on the Internet is commendable. Nevertheless, it is a well-known fact that there are numerous other locations with populations of more than ten thousand that do not have the technical or financial capacity to attend to the dictates of the Federal Law N° 12.527. Overcoming these difficulties can only occur through technical cooperation and the allocation of sufficient funds to meet the costs of implementing the Access Act. At this point the cooperation of States and, in particular, of the Union may be the only way to enable the effectiveness of the right of access throughout the country. As highlighted above, the collaboration of the Comptroller General has proved extremely relevant and necessary in this area.

The operational challenges, in turn, are related to the pressing need to use electronic resources and information technology to enable the processing of information in accordance with Article 4 para 5 LAI. So, it has already been stated that[38]:

[37]Fortini, Avelar & Ferreira 2013, p. 1031.

[38]Fortini, Avelar & Ferreira 2013, p. 1045.

> The satisfactory use of these technologies requires staff trained to operate them, which does not always occur. Regarding this point, the National Institute of Information Technology (ITI) may play a relevant role in supporting the entities by encouraging the development of actions that promote the availability and the certification of public information in order to preserve its integrity and authenticity.
>
> Finally, considering that the right of access to information includes the right to primary, genuine, authentic and updated information, it is necessary to prepare the agencies, organizations and entities to implement access according to these terms. In this way, we have adapted the list below, which was presented in a CGU report, with the operational measures necessary to give effect to the provisions of the Federal Law N° 12.527:
>
> 1) The universalization of electronic document management and monitoring processes, with interfaces that allow direct access to concerned citizens;
>
> 2) The creation, expansion, consolidation and availability of databases (including management systems enabling internal trace 'decision-making'), with a minimum of barriers to the access by ordinary citizens, such as passwords and other inhibitory requirements, queries or requests;
>
> 3) The scanning of documents produced by the agencies and management entities of the administration;
>
> 4) The expansion of proactive transparency through well-designed, user-friendly websites to interested citizens, which will help to relieve excess demand for information and data;
>
> 5) The definition of budgets that effectively enable the new environment of access to public information outlined above.[39]

Added to these difficulties is the lack of regulation of the Access to Information Act within many Brazilian states and municipalities. The absence of rules of law and the lack of the establishment of procedures and organizational requirements for its application in accordance with the reality of each location implies a severe reduction in the application of the provisions of the Access Act. The form of the dissemination of information, in particular, is severely damaged.

The analysis of the effectiveness of the Brazilian Law on Access to Information and the impact of stated difficulties is partially demonstrated in a diagnosis undertaken by the Union's General Office.[40]

After 3 years of the validity of that Law, the "Transparent Brazil Scale" was created to assess the transparency of actions in the states and cities (see Fig. 16.1).

According to the results obtained by the CGU, 63% of municipalities obtained a score of zero; 22.6% were graded between 1 and 2; 4.7% received a score between 3 and 4; 4.3% received score between 5 and 6; 4.1% were graded between 7 and 8; and only 1.4% received a score of 10.

When one talks about the access to information in a country where the culture of secrecy has prevailed for many years, a hard road is to be expected, with many

[39]Diagnostic Research into the Values, Knowledge and Culture of Access to Public Information in the Executive Branch of the Federal Republic of Brazil.

[40]Portal Planalto 2015.

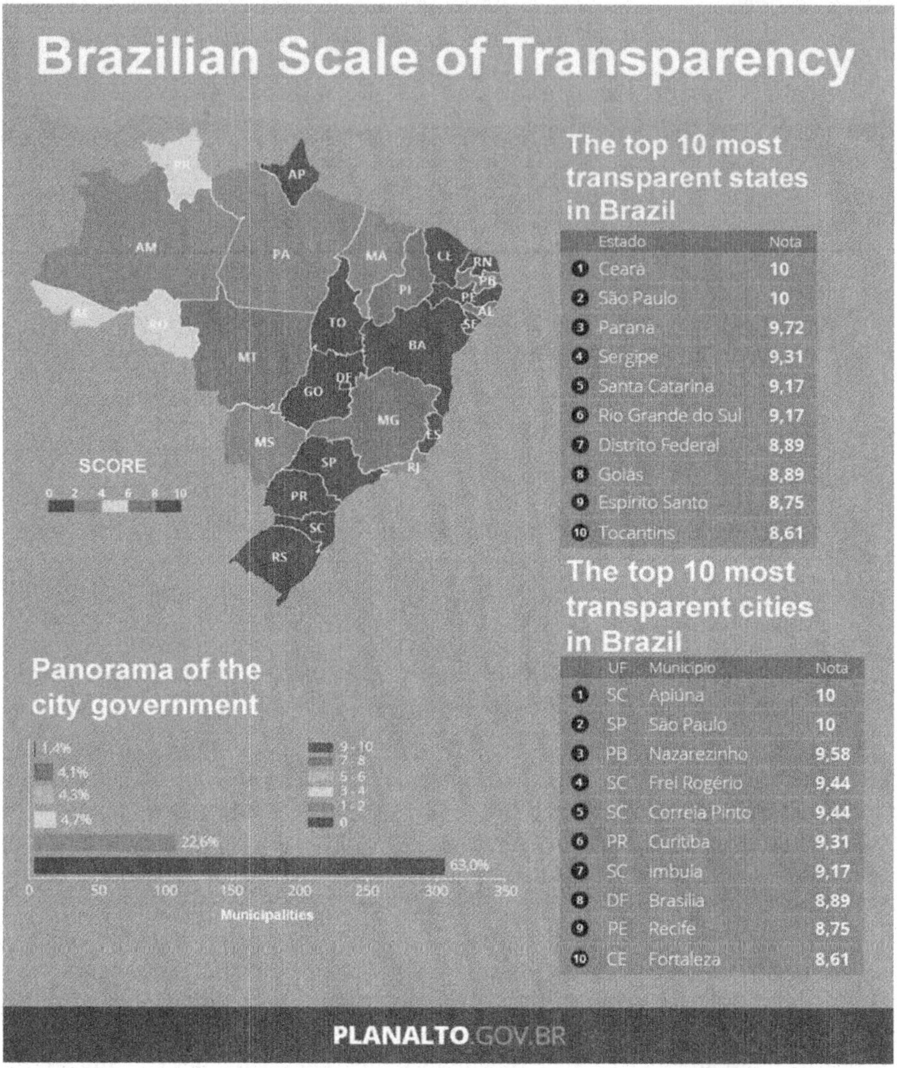


**Fig. 16.1** According to information provided by the CGU, the scale is constructed from the methodology by which the passive transparency of actions of the 26 states, the Federal District, as well as capitals and municipalities with more than 50,000 inhabitants, was analyzed. To those entities that were evaluated, a score from 0 to 10 points was given; the result of which is derived from the sum of two criteria with different weights: the regulation of the Access Act (25%) and the performance of the Citizens Information Service (CIS) (75%). In addition, the score is composed of the response from the entities to the CGU, which requested information about health, education, social assistance and access to information (Source: http://bit.ly/23gxr0t. Accessed on 15 February 2017)

challenges to be overcome, as demonstrated by the collated data above. This finding does not, however, impede the visualization of the remarkable progress already seen in the actions of transparency and access to information.

In a similar sense, the evaluation report of the Access to Information Act prepared by Gregory Michener, Luiz Fernando Marrey Moncado and Rafael Velasco points out the next steps for advancement of the realization of the right of access, highlighting in particular:

> Law N° 12.527/11 represents a significant achievement in the legislative history of the country. However, the task of changing the culture of secrecy that prevailed for decades will not be instantaneous. It is not enough to introduce a Freedom of Information Law for public transparency to become a reality. There must also be both political and administrative commitments and the broader use of the law by civil society. This study should suggest that grounds for conducting further research and evaluation on transparency are very fertile. This study adhered to one of many possible research designs and there is a need for more research to be undertaken in order to understand the workings of the FOI law in other regions, especially outside the major metropolitan centers. Likewise, ample space exists for conducting specific assessments by sector in areas such as health, education, public safety, and urban mobility, among others. Finally, the transparency of some agencies has not been scrutinized in sufficient detail. Such entities include state and local prosecutors, entities of the indirect public administration and also private and non-profit entities receiving state funds.[41]

# 6 Closing Considerations

The Brazilian Access to Information Act is written in a global context of the recognition of the fundamentality of the right of access to information, which has a constitutional matrix in the Brazilian legal system.

Despite the undeniable challenges for the realization of the right of access to information in Brazil, one can already feel some effects of the application of the Federal Law N° 12.527, after more than 3 years since the beginning of its enactment.

In the initial measurement of that Law results, The Comptroller General of the Union (CGU) released the Balance in the Federal Executive Branch, which logs the access requests made between 16 May 2012 and 21 December 2012. In this period, 55,214 requests for access to information were recorded, of which the majority were executed in a positive manner, meaning that the information requested by the citizen was delivered. The agencies and entities responded to these requests, on average, in 11.16 days, almost half the maximum prescribed in the Federal Law N° 12.527.

Still, in measuring the implementation of the Federal Law N° 12.527 in the federal government from its inception until 2015, the Comptroller General of the Union (CGU) reached the following results:

[41]Michener et al. 2014.

> The Comptroller General of the Union (CGU) recorded at the end of 2015, 334,463 requests for access to information to the Federal Executive Branch. The number refers to the requests made since May 2012, when the Brazilian Access to Information Act came into force. Just last year, 102,423 applications were received, which was a historic record.
>
> Of the total requests made, 331,747 (99.19%) were answered. Of these, 240,903 (72.61%) were completely fulfilled, while 31,999 were denied because they dealt with personal data or confidential information, or were generic or incomprehensible demands, among other reasons. Of the 58,845 remaining requests, 21.5% had the requested access partially granted and 78.5% could not be fulfilled due to the fact that they were not a matter for the legal competence of the entity, because the information did not exist or it was repeated question.[42]

Despite the constitutional provision, one should not downplay the importance of the Access Act in the Brazilian legal system, given that the legislation of access performs the significant function of regulating the details of the constitutional rights.

In detailing the content of the right of access to information and limiting the form of access and disclosure, the Law fulfills an extremely important purpose when it improves the *modus operandi* of Public Administration to definitively break the non-transparent practices of the past and make public agencies closer to the citizens.

We have already concluded elsewhere that:

> The dialogical and rational democracy does not necessarily involve only the attainment of the tools capable of promoting itself. It is important to ensure the real possibility of using them, which depends on the education of the citizens and the training of the population after the years of the dictatorial period.
>
> Democratic maturity demands time and practice and so it is necessary to move on to the search for everyday progress in close cooperation with the citizen. Because of that the discussions occur locally.[43]

## References


Canotilho, J. J. (2002). *Direito constitucional e teoria da constituição*. Coimbra, Portugal: Almedina.

Clève, C. M., & Franzoni, J. Á. (2013). Administração Pública e a nova Lei de Acesso à Informação. *Interesse Público — IP*, 15(79). Retrieved September 2, 2013, from http://bit.ly/261KBni

Figueiredo, L. V. (2003). Instrumentos da Administração Consensual: A Audiência Pública e sua finalidade. *Interesse Público – IP, 18*(5.) Retrieved July 1, 2013, from http://bit.ly/1UE726Q.

Fortini, C. (2011). A experiência belohorizontina do orçamento participativo como ferramenta para o desenvolvimento local. *Revista da Procuradoria-Geral do Município de Belo Horizonte, 7*, 120–124.


[42]The Access to Information Act: Federal Executive Branch. See Transparência Pública 2016.

[43]Fortini 2011, p. 120.

Fortini, C., Avelar, M. M., & Ferreira, R. B. (2013). Comentários à Lei de Acesso à Informação: Contexto, desafios e polêmicas. In F. de Azevedo Marques Neto et al. (Eds.), *Direito e Administração Pública: Estudos em Homenagem a Maria Sylvia Zanella di Pietro* (pp. 1032–1041). São Paulo, Brazil: Atlas.

Ghione, L. (2012). *Addressing past violence: The new Brazilian truth commission*. Costa Rica: University for Peace. Retrieved June 15, 2016, from http://bit.ly/1UgjaAI

LaRue, F. (2011). *Report of the Special Rapporteur on the promotion and protection of the right to freedom of opinion and expression. A/HRC/17/27*. Retrieved March 12, 2016, from http://bit.ly/QD35W5

Mendel, T. (1999). *The public's right to know. Principles on Freedom of Information Legislation*. London: Article 19. Retrieved June 14, 2016, from http://bit.ly/1knelAp

Mendel, T. (2008). *Freedom of Information: A comparative legal survey*. Retrieved June 14, 2016, from http://bit.ly/1tudmqY

Mendel, T. (2009). *El derecho a la Información en América Latina-Comparación Jurídica*. Ecuador: UNESCO. Retrieved January 2, 2016, from http://bit.ly/1MVf6BA

Michener, G. (2010). *The surrender of secrecy: Explaining the emergence of strong access to information laws in Latin America*. Austin, TX: The University of Texas at Austin. Retrieved October 15, 2012, from http://bit.ly/1OpzfBP.

Michener, G., Moncau, L. F. M., & Velasco, R. (2014). *The Brazilian state and transparency*. FGV. Retrieved January 15, 2016, from http://bit.ly/28KN9oJ

Perez, M. A. (2009). *A Administração Pública Democrática: Institutos de Participação Popular na Administração Pública*. Belo Horizonte, Brazil: Editora Fórum.

Portal Brasil (2013). *Lei de acesso à informação chega aos estados e pequenos municípios*. Retrieved June 15, 2016, from http://bit.ly/1XtYDsP

Portal Planalto. (2015). *CGU lança índice para medir transparência de cidades e estados. Escala Brasil Transparente*. Retrieved January 20, 2016, from http://bit.ly/23gxr0t

Stiglitz, J. (2002). Transparency in government. In World Bank Institute (Ed.), *The right to tell: The role of mass media in economic development* (pp. 27–44). Washington, DC: The World Bank.

Transparência Pública. (2016). *Governo Federal fecha 2015 com 334 mil pedidos de acesso à informação*. Retrieved June 15, 2016, from http://bit.ly/1SmhUtu

United Nations. (2011). Freedom information: The right to know. *World Press Freedom Day 2010*. UNESCO. Retrieved June 16, 2016, from http://bit.ly/1PyvJQh

## List of Cases

Federal Supreme Court of Brazil (Supremo Tribunal Federal) 23.04.2015., *Agravo no Recurso Extraordinário*, 652.777/SP, http://bit.ly/1R1BN6l (Accessed on 15 June 2016).

Federal Supreme Court of Brazil (Supremo Tribunal Federal) 14.11.2012., *Mandado de Segurança*, 16903/DF, http://bit.ly/1UAvmu9 (Accessed on 15 June 2016).

Federal Supreme Court of Brazil (Supremo Tribunal Federal) 10.07.2012., *Suspensão Liminar* 623, http://bit.ly/1UAuaah (Accessed on 15 June 2016).

# Chapter 17
# Restrictions on Access to Information

Germana de Oliveira Moraes and Álisson José Maia Melo

## Contents



## 1 Introduction

The legal treatment of the restrictions on access to information, according to the articles of the Brazilian Law Nº 12.527/2011, is analyzed in this chapter. Although this study concerns positive law, it does a critical analysis over the options adopted by the Legislative Power, as well as it proceeds to the interpretation of the provisions given by the Brazilian Constitution.

The restrictions on access to information are organized in a single chapter of the Brazilian Law Nº 12.527/2011 and regulated in Articles 21 to 31. Brazilian Law Nº 12.527/2011 aims to unify the modalities of restrictions in a single legal document, also because Article 46 revokes Brazilian Law Nº 11.111/2005, that regulated Article 5, item 33, final sentence of the Brazilian Constitution, and Articles 22 to 24 of the Brazilian Law Nº 8.159/1991, that made provisions about the national policy on public files, avoiding that sparse laws complicated even further the systematic comprehension of the exceptions on access to information. However,


G. de Oliveira Moraes (✉) • Á.J.M. Melo
Programa de Pós-Graduação em Direito, Federal University of Ceará, Fortaleza, Brazil
e-mail: germanadeoliveiramoraes@gmail.com





H.-J. Blanke, R. Perlingeiro (eds.), *The Right of Access to Public Information*,
DOI 10.1007/978-3-662-55554-5_17

Article 22 of the Law Nº 12.527/2011 states in contrary sense, by giving a rule of openness in the exceptions on access system, not excluding hypotheses of confidentiality, of secrecy of justice and of industrial secrets.

Nonetheless, with the publication of the Law Nº 12.527/2011, it is believed that the Executive and Legislative Powers will make efforts to avoid the creation of other exceptions outside that Law.

As they configure an exceptional right,[1] the rules of confidentiality must be interpreted strictly, because the right to access to information, qualified as a fundamental right (Article 5, item 33 sentence 1 of the Brazilian Constitution), becomes the rule,[2] and exceptions to this right, even constitutional ones, must be as minimum as possible[3] to ensure the normative force of the Constitution. In principle, the general rule is the publicity of information and documents produced by the State (under the principle of publicity of the Public Administration, established by Article 37 of the Brazilian Constitution) or obtained by the State from the regular execution of its public activity,[4] an idea synthesized in the principle of maximum openness[5] or maximum disclosure.[6]

This study is divided in four sections: after this introduction (Sect. 1), the foundations to restrictions on access to public information authorized by law (Sect. 2), the treatment procedures of confidential information, as well as any exceptions to confidentiality prescribed by Law Nº 12.527/2011 (Chap. 4, Section V) (Sect. 3) and, in separate, the exception concerning the information necessary to the protection of fundamental rights (Sect. 4) are analyzed.

## 2 Authorized Foundations to Restrictions on Access to Information

Although the Federative Republic of Brazil qualifies itself as a legal democratic State (Article 1 of the Brazilian Constitution), it must be observed that even in the democratic model, in which wide access to information substantiates adequate control and the exercise of the political power of the people, it is necessary and acceptable that restrictions on access to public information may exist.[7] Despite of

---

[1]Mota Junior 2012, p. 21.

[2]Bulos 2012, p. 198.

[3]See Inter-American Court of Human Rights, *Gomes Lund and Others (Guerrilha do Araguaia) v. Brazil* (Judgment of 24 November 2010), Series C, No. 219, para 229. http://www.corteidh.or.cr/docs/casos/articulos/seriec_219_ing.pdf (Accessed on 12 January 2017).

[4]Alves 2012, p. 130.

[5]Michener 2011, p. 7.

[6]Article 19 1999, p. 3; Mendel 2008, p. 30.

[7]See Inter-American Court of Human Rights, *Gomes Lund and Others (Guerrilha do Araguaia) v. Brazil* (Judgment of 24 November 2010), Series C, No. 219, para 229. http://www.corteidh.or.cr/docs/casos/articulos/seriec_219_ing.pdf (Accessed on 12 January 2017).

being the government of the visible power,[8] it must be recognized that, under a realistic perspective, even democracy demands a minimal need for secrecy, in accordance to the notion of "secret not private" (in the objective sense). On the one hand, the majority rule cannot overcome citizens' individual freedoms, especially those that concern the domestic field of life, privacy.[9] On the other hand, it is understandable that a majority of the citizens can understand and decide that in very specific matters the people's representative in Executive Power, objectively, must keep reservation, by a mandatory protection in the name and in the own interest of the society.[10]

Thus, it is possible to share the authorized foundations to restrictions on access to information according to the interest involved, not only by didactic means, but also for legal purposes, because it is possible that, in the analysis of the kinds of interest involved, the interpretation of the restrictions and of its exceptions may vary. A dual division can be made, between the restrictions that are justified as a requirement of public interest and those that aim to protect fundamental individual rights.[11]

## 2.1 Restrictions by Reason of Public Interest

Restrictions as a requirement of public interest have its specific constitutional foundation in the final part of Article 5, item 33 of the Brazilian Constitution, by mentioning the information "on whose confidentiality is essential to the security of society and of the State". The highest constitutional foundation, which justifies that exception, is the sovereignty of the Republic (Article 1, item 1 of the Brazilian Constitution) in all its forms of externalization (international, internal, political, military and economic), whose power emanates from the people (Article 1, Sole paragraph of the Brazilian Constitution).

Moreover, the Brazilian Constitution does not solve the debate of the specific cases in which there is an authorized restriction on access to public information, without mentioning the need for a law to detail them. Nonetheless, through Brazilian Law Nº 12.527/2011, the Legislative Power decided to specify the situations that are essential to the security of the society and of the State, meeting the recommendations of the Organization of the American States (OAS) in its

[8]Cademartori & Cademartori 2011b, p. 336.

[9]Cademartori & Cademartori 2011b, p. 339.

[10]Cademartori & Cademartori 2011b, p. 339.

[11]See Inter-American Court of Human Rights, *Gomes Lund and Others (Guerrilha do Araguaia) v. Brazil* (Judgment of 24 November 2010), Series C, No. 219, para 229. http://www.corteidh.or.cr/docs/casos/articulos/seriec_219_ing.pdf (Accessed on 12 January 2017). The Court decided that restrictions must respond to an objective displayed in Article 13.2 of the American Convention, "the respect for the rights and reputation of others" or "the protection of national security, public order, or public health, or morals".

resolutions.[12] Article 23 of Law Nº 12.527/2011 enlists the legal hypotheses of restriction, categorized according to the possible harmful results of disclosure, in line with Article 41, point (b) of the Model Inter-American Law on Access to Information.[13] This is, therefore, a solution that, despite an attempt at making a finalistic determination ("harmful results"), maintains some margin of discretion for an evaluative assessment by administrators competent to confer confidentiality (listed in Article 27 of Law Nº 11.527/2011), who must undertake a serious consideration of all interests in conflict to achieve a legitimate decision.[14] Discretionarity, however, may confer to authorities an overbroad margin of decision.[15] Although the legal hypotheses always state the likely existence of risk, commitment or injury, the fundamental right to access information must always counterbalance them. The legislator could have made the option, notwithstanding the adoption of discretionary finalistic clauses, to establish an illustrative list of specific types of documents and information whose access could be forbidden when its disclosure gave way to any of those harmful consequences, providing a more objective control on restrictions and some guidance for non-prescribed situations through analogy.

Article 23, item 1 of Law Nº 12.527/2011 ("jeopardize national defense, sovereignty, or the integrity of national territory") aims at both the international sovereignty, foreground, and for the internal integrity of state power. In addition, Article 23, item 2 of that Law ("damage or jeopardize negotiations or the country's international relations, or even secret information provided by other states or international organizations") concerns specifically of the sovereignty of the State in the international field, which has been object of criticism, because it encourages a culture of confidentiality by favoring the rules of the less transparent State or international organization.[16]

Article 23, item 3 of the Brazilian Law Nº 12.527/2011 ("jeopardize the life, safety or health of the population") protects the internal sovereignty of the Republic to prevent the release of documents and information that could cause social insecurity. On the other hand, that justification cannot be argued to hide administrative failures or to avoid public exposure of State authorities in the exercise of their functions, keeping the confidentiality by reasons of political expedience[17] in

[12]See the following Resolutions of the General Assembly of the Organization of American States: AG/RES. 2057 (2004); AG/RES. 2121 (2005); AG/RES. 2252 (2006); AG/RES. 2288 (2007); AG/RES. 2418 (2008); AG/RES. 2514 (2009). http://www.oas.org/ (Accessed on 12 January 2017).

[13]See Organization of American States. General Assembly. Model Inter-American Law on Access to Information (2010). *AG/RES. 2607*. Appendix. XL-O/10. Washington D.C.: OAS. http://www.oas.org/ (Accessed on 12 January 2017).

[14]Mendel 2008, p. 34.

[15]Cademartori & Cademartori 2011a, p. 11.256.

[16]Mendel 2008, p. 150.

[17]Tourinho 2009, p. 74.

opposition to the constitutional requirement of an honest government,[18] grounded in the principle of morality in Public Administration (Article 37 of the Brazilian Constitution). The use of confidentiality by public authorities to hide information that compromise them legally and politically must be avoided[19]; that is why Article 44 of Law Nº 12.527/2011, by modifying Brazilian Law Nº 8.112/1990—which disciplines the legal regime of federal public service—adds an article stating that no servant shall be liable for notifying superior authorities about information related to the possible commitment of a crime or an administrative impropriety.

Article 23, item 4 of the Brazilian Law Nº 12.527/2011 ("expose the Nation to elevated risk of financial, economic or monetary instability"), in turn, focuses on national sovereignty in the economic order and the national financial system, raised to the rank of a constitutional principle (Article 170, item 1 of the Brazilian Constitution). The goal, in this case, is to avoid the economic insecurity of the country.

While the first four items of restriction refer to questions mainly about national sovereignty, the last four concern strategic issues, although they are also based in the security of the State and society. Thus, there are restrictions on access to information related to military questions (Article 23, item 5), to scientific and technological development, especially those involving patents (Article 23, item 6, sentence 1), to institutions and high national and international authorities (Article 23, item 7), and to activities of intelligence and ongoing investigations (Article 23, item 8).

In relation to Article 23, item 6, final sentence, the text calls for a "national strategic interest", interpretation of which may induce a vast relativization of situations. The second sentence of the provision must be read together with Article 7, item 3 of the Brazilian Law Nº 12.527/2011 to safeguard information about public policies during its planning and implementation stages, whose disclosure may harm the effectiveness of the desired results. Risks in situations like these usually involve prejudice for the formulation or development of a public policy, frustration of the success by premature disclosure, or sabotage of deliberative process or reduction of the effectiveness of control procedures.[20]

The restrictions mentioned by Brazilian Law Nº 12.527/2011 are mainly concerned with the sovereignty and strategic policies, and cover mainly the Federal Public Administration.[21] Despite this fact, in some provisions a symmetric interpretation can be made for the other federated entities, for instance in Article 23, items 3 and 8 sentence 2 of the Law Nº 12.527/2011,[22] regarding health (a common competence among federative entities, according to Article 23, item 2 of the Brazilian Constitution) and security (relatively to States and Federal District with their respective police forces). Moreover, the exception in Article 23, item 6 of the Law Nº 12.527/2011, on strategic decision-making processes within public policies

[18]Levy 2009, p. 1.

[19]Michener 2011, p. 9; Article 19 1999, p. 8.

[20]Mendel 2008, p. 150.

[21]Tourinho 2009, p. 73.

[22]Tourinho, 2009, p. 74.

of national interest, could be applicable to other federative entities, because it can also involve equivalent interests in state and municipal interests, but demanding respective laws do that the symmetric exception can be created.

Regarding Article 23, item 8 sentence 2 of the Law Nº 12.527/2011, the provision given under Article 20 of the Criminal Process Code, Brazilian Legislative Decree Nº 3.689/1941, has originally established the confidentiality of police investigations: "Article 20. The authority must ensure in the investigation the confidentiality necessary to the elucidation of the fact or demanded by the interest of the society." Differently from cases of instrumental restriction, here there is a public interest that it be avoided, by leaking information, the person or persons investigated can destroy physical evidences or vitiate its origin.

## 2.2 *Restrictions by Reason of Private Interest*

In the context of restrictions by reasons of private interest, the focus of the Law is to prevent that information concerning natural or legal persons to whom the Public Administration had access, within the respective fields of protection of rights, may be subject to unjustified disclosure. The situations have its main constitutional foundation based upon the fundamental right that states that "the privacy, private life, honor and image of persons are inviolable" (Article 5, item 10 of the Brazilian Constitution). Article 31 of Law Nº 12.527/2011 has special concern with the protection of privacy, private life, honor and image of persons, by restricting access to personal information for a maximum period of a century, regardless of classification of confidentiality.

The mentioning of personal information may lead to doubts when dealing with information of public interest. In this respect, soon after the edition of Law Nº 12.527/2011, administrative and judicial discussions arouse about the possibility of disclosing the value of salaries of civil servants, the control bodies as Audit Courts and the National Council of Justice decided for the prevalence of public transparency.[23] In the paradigmatic Security Suspension 3.902/SP, the Supreme Federal Court[24] understood that the "gross salary, position and functions" occupied by public agents and their respective bodies of occupation must be object of disclosure, because these are information of "collective and general interest" that "pertains to public agents while public agents themselves; [...] state agents acting 'as such'", and forbade that disclosure of "the home address, the CPF [natural person register] and the CI [ID number]" of such persons are made. The decisions are correct, by analogy to rules regarding private institutions that receive public resources, that must inform how much the State pays to citizen with institutional ties (as input);

---

[23] Alves 2012, p. 131.

[24] Supreme Federal Court (Supremo Tribunal Federal), *Second regulatory appeal in mandamus suspension 3,902 São Paulo* (Judgment of 9 June 2011).

what cannot be disclosed, on the other hand, is what is done (either by the servant himself or by payroll deductions) with this valor (as output).

Brazilian Law Nº 12.527/2011 could have stipulated an alternative period, running from the date of the death of the person to whom information pertains, as did the Model Inter-American Law on Access to Information,[25] allowing for publicity of the information with the expiration of said term.

Article 31 para 1 of that Law highlights in its final sentence that, beyond the restriction on access regardless of classification, wide access to the information must be given to the person to whom it refers. To forbid access to such information by the own person can, in the terms of Article 32 para 1 of Law Nº 12.527/2011, trigger a disciplinary process to identify the occurrence of military transgression or administrative offense. Against that prohibition, as well as against the refusal to rectify information in State owned database, natural, as well as legal persons can make use of the *habeas data*, provided by Article 5, item 72 of the Brazilian Constitution, in the terms of Article 38 of Law Nº 12.527/2011, notwithstanding the possibility of an ordinary lawsuit to be pursued in secrecy of justice.

The Brazilian Supreme Federal Court[26] upheld an extraordinary appeal in *habeas data* to ensure a taxpayer access to his personal information in tax payments control systems belonging to the Federal Revenue of Brazil, arguing that the "tax information related to the taxpayer, if confidential, no matter what level of confidentiality, should be protected from society at large, according to the law or the constitution, but not from whom it concerns, by virtue of the consecration of the right to information."

Another modality of restriction by private interest, derived from Article 31 of the Law Nº 12.527/2011, involves private communications to which Public Administration incidentally have access, even those obtained from judicial authorization for criminal investigation (regulated by Brazilian Law Nº 9.296/1996). These must be given the same treatment dispensed to personal information. This protection accrues from the fundamental right provided in Article 5, item 12 of the Brazilian Constitution, according to which "the secrecy of correspondence and of telegraphic, data and telephone communications is inviolable [. . .]", and must be subject to equal interpretation.

Finally, it also makes for an exception on access to information by reasons of private interest those related to industrial secrets. The industrial secret can be construed as the scope of the company's privacy, and should be subject to similar restrictions on access. Moreover, Article 22 sentence 2 of Law Nº 12.527/2011 states that the "provisions in this Law does not exclude [. . .] the hypotheses of industrial secrets derived from the direct exploration of economic activity by the

[25]See Organization of American States. General Assembly. Model Inter-American Law on Access to Information (2010). *AG/RES. 2607*. Appendix. XL-O/10. Washington D.C.: OAS. http://www.oas.org/ (Accessed on 12 January 2017).

[26]Supreme Federal Court (Supremo Tribunal Federal), *Extraordinary appeal 673,707 Minas Gerais* (Judgment of 17 June 2015).

State or by natural person or private entity that have any bond with the public power". Unfortunately, the Federal Legislative Power made an option to exclude from the Law the specific rules of this modality of restriction on access.

In this context, information related to the companies' business, either of public or private nature, to which the State must have access, especially because the exercise of police power (for instance, in the exercise of taxation activity or patents register), whose disclosure may harm the exercise of the activity economic, cannot be divulged.

Regarding the exploration of economic activity, there must be made an interpretation that the restriction must be the case preferably when the economic activity operates through a competitive system; i.e., in the case of activities under natural or legal monopoly, as typically occurs in cases of public services strict sense or of activities heavily controlled by the State, disclosure must be progressively pursued, as long as it does not entail other cases of restriction on access to information.

In this sense, Law Nº 12.527/2011 reflects,[27] but goes beyond the protection conferred before by Articles 20 and 21 of the Civil Code, Brazilian Law Nº 10.406/2002, the former conditioning restriction on access to an application from the person to whom information (writings, words or images) refers, or from its spouse, descendants or ascendants, as legitimate parts (Article 20 para 1), and the latter determining the inviolability of private life. Thus, there was a partial revocation of Article 20.

## 2.3 *Instrumental Restrictions*

Brazilian Law Nº 12.527/2011 also did not consolidate in its text legislation that regulates instrumental restrictions, especially in what refers to the secrecy of justice. According to Article 22 sentence 1, "The provision in this Law does not exclude other legal hypotheses of confidentiality and of secrecy of justice [. . .]". The secrecy of justice has its foundation in Article 93, item 9 of the Brazilian Constitution.

This restriction is instrumental, as it does not protect an interest itself, but rather safeguards other interest protected by such restriction. Regulated by Article 189 of the Civil Process Code, Brazilian Law Nº 13.105/2015, the secrecy of justice in civil process has four justifying hypotheses: when the public or social interests requires, or when dealing with typical family lawsuits, when the lawsuit deals with data protected by the constitutional right to intimacy, and when arbitration is involved. The separation of the hypotheses made by Civil Process Code is similar to the division made by Brazilian Law Nº 12.527/2011: secrecy of justice aims to both protect the public interest and guard privacy, and Article 189 indicates the

---

[27] Mota Junior 2012, p. 25.

matters subject to immediate restriction, and the working mechanism of the restriction in its two paragraphs.

Article 201.6 of the Criminal Process Code, in turn, confers to the judge the competence to determine the secrecy of justice for the preservation of privacy, private life, honor and image of the offended.

Thus, in criminal process, the secrecy of justice aims to safeguard, in particular, the private interests of the offended related to the constitutional protection (privacy, private life, honor and image). By protecting public interest associated with ongoing investigations, Article 1 of the Brazilian Law Nº 9.296/1996, by regulating the interception of telephonic communications for criminal investigation or procedural criminal instruction, which always require judicial order in the terms of Article 5, item 12 of the Brazilian Constitution, for instance, establishes that the process must be carried out "under secrecy of justice".

However, it is not only in judicial process that restrictions can occur. Similarly, administrative processes can have equally restricted access. As states Article 3, item 2 of the Brazilian Law Nº 9.784/1999, which regulates the administrative process in Federal Public Administration, the citizen has the right to access administrative processes in which it plays the role of interested party. It is an instrumental restriction for protection of private interest. A hypothesis of instrumental confidentiality in public administration for protection of public interest can be extracted from Article 150 of the Brazilian Law Nº 8.112/1990, which provides for the investigative commission of the administrative disciplinary process: "Article 150. The Commission must exercise its activities with independence and impartiality, ensuring the necessary confidentiality to the elucidation of the fact or demanded by the interest of the administration". It aims to safeguard, thus, the good conduction of the investigation. Finally, in a broad sense, the interpretation *e contrario* of Article 7.3 of Law Nº 12.527/2011 can be recalled: whilst the administrative process does not reach a decision, the access to information contained in its records is restricted.[28]

In this sense, the Brazilian Superior Court of Justice[29] denied access to information to federal public servants involved in an administrative investigative process of alleged commission of improper conduct, still in progress, including those regarding to the identity of the whistleblower. The court understood it to be expendable the observance of the adversarial and legal defense principles in investigative inquiries, of an inquisitorial character, and, based on Article 7.3 and Article 23, item 8 of Law Nº 12.527/2011, as well as the Comptroller General of Brazil Ordinance 335/2006, which regulates this law, to exist an instrumental restriction in this case to ensure the effectiveness of the procedure.

[28]Fregapani & Botelho 2012, p. 18.

[29]Superior Court of Justice (Superior Tribunal de Justiça), *Writ of mandamus 19,243-DF* (Judgment of 11 September 2013).

# 3 Treatment of Confidential Information and Exceptions to Confidentiality

Once analyzed the situations in which the restriction on access to information is legitimate, the study of the structural rules that relate to the attribution of confidential nature and to the treatment of confidential information can be made, as well as on the exceptions to the demand of confidentiality.

## *3.1 Classification of Information Confidentiality and Its Revision*

As for to the classification and attribution of confidentiality status to information, Brazilian Law Nº 12.527/2011 is not adequately systemized, establishing part of the relevant rules in Article 24 and partially in Articles 27 and 28. Thus, an analysis synthesizing the two texts is in order. Attribution of confidentiality respects exclusively to restrictions on access to information by reasons of public interest, because, as seen, restrictions grounded on private interest are free from classification.

Article 24 of Law Nº 12.527/2011 establishes three confidentiality levels: "Information held by public entities or institutions, considering their content and indispensability to the safety of society or the state, may be classified as top-secret, secret or restricted." Law Nº 12.527/2011 fulminated the later type of classification as "confidential", provided by Brazilian Decree Nº 4.553/2002, but revoked by Decree Nº 7.845/2012. The existence of distinct levels corresponds to the hierarchical criterion inside of the Executive Power, with attribution of restrict competences for the classification of confidentiality to reduce the access to given information, including internally to the Public Administration itself. According to Article 27 of Law Nº 12.527/2011, the top-secret classification can only be conferred by the highest federal authorities (item 1); the label "secret", also by the indirect Public Administration representatives (item 2); and the classification "restricted", by all authorities exerting functions of direction, command or leadership (item 3).

Brazilian Decree Nº 7.845/2012, which regulates the mentioned provision, establishes more security procedures of information control according to confidentiality status. Indeed, in the terms of its Article 27, information classified as top-secret must be personally dealt with or, when compatible cryptography resources require the use of electronic means.

Comparatively, to information classified as secret or restricted, according to Article 26 of Decree Nº 7.845/2012, the mandatory requirement of "personally" made acts by the authorized public agent was not provided.

The single practical effect provided by Brazilian Law Nº 12.527/2011 consists only in the determination of the maximum time for restriction on access. According to Article 24.1, items 1 to 3, the maximum periods of restriction are of 25 years for top-secret information, 15 years for secret information, and 5 years to restricted information.

The attribution of periods, *per se*, is praiseworthy, because of the history of eternal confidentiality of top-secret information in the country.[30] The choice made by the Legislative Power is censurable, though, considering that the attribution of a 25 years period goes against item 43 of the Model Inter-American Law on Access to Information, which stipulated a maximum period of 12 years, extendable by another equal period.[31] However, it shows an important improvement in the transparency culture because it drastically reduces the confidentiality period of documents, in comparison to previous laws. It should be noted that maximum periods are established, so the authority competent to attribute the confidential status may establish lower periods.

In the final provisions, Article 35.1 of Law Nº 12.527/2011 institutes the Joint Commission for Information Revaluation, which will decide on extending the confidentiality period of top-secret information, always by predetermined periods, as long as the original reasons for the restriction are maintained, observing the limit of 25 years (item 3). Article 35.2 of Law Nº 12.527/2011, then, indicates that "The period referred in subparagraph III is limited to a single renewal". However, Article 35.1, item 3 mentions more than one "period", allowing for the interpretation that the Commission could renew the "the deadline stipulated in Article 24.1", i.e., the maximum period of 25 years, extending confidentiality by 50 years.[32] That is an unfortunate interpretation, that must be repelled at any costs, firstly because the item itself demands compliance of the maximum period, secondly because maximum period renewals must be provided by Article 24 (setting an immoral legislative strategy), and thirdly, because the fundamental right to access to information prevails. Thus, a better interpretation is the one that establishes that the Joint Commission will have the faculty to renew the "predetermined period" of the extension a single time; simply put, the Commission could extend by up two times the period of confidentiality, only if comprised in the total maximum limit of 25 years of Article 24.1.

However, Brazilian Decree Nº 7.724/2012, which generally regulates Law Nº 12.527/2011, by enlisting the attributions of the Joint Commission for Information Revaluation, states in Article 47, item 4 the same period extension, expressly mentioning the maximum limit of 50 years.

Regulation, in this point, seems to extrapolate legal and constitutional limits established in the Brazilian legal system, providing for an interpretation to the legal provision contrary to the principle of maximum disclosure. Nonetheless, Article 52, item 1 of the Brazilian Decree Nº 7.724/2012 provides that absolute majority

---

[30] Cademartori & Cademartori 2011a, p. 11.262–11.263.

[31] See Organization of American States. General Assembly. Model Inter-American Law on Access to Information (2010). *AG/RES. 2607*. Appendix. XL-O/10. Washington D.C.: OAS. http://www.oas.org/ (Accessed on 12 January 2017).

[32] Mota Junior 2012, p. 24.

must give the extension decision; moreover, it is a decision that escapes the sphere of competence of the authority that initially conferred confidentiality. If victorious the thesis of the extension of the period to a maximum of 25 years—to authorize that top-secret information sustain confidentiality by half a century—it is worth noting that period limitations create a presumption of temporal loss of potential injury to the public interest, which is why the decision of the Joint Commission for Information Revaluation must be especially justified.[33]

Still in relation to the periods, it runs from the date of the release of the information, being applicable, therefore, to all documents and information currently in existence. Thus, to those documents whose period has already extrapolated the new legislation, the rule of Article 24.4 of the Brazilian Law Nº 12.527/2011 applies: “The expiration of classification having been reached or the event that determines its expiration having occurred, the information shall automatically be available for public access.”

Exceptionally, Article 24.2 of the Brazilian Law Nº 12.527/2011 assigns specific secrecy, in the degree of restricted to information that can put in risk the security of the President and Vice-President of the Republic and their families. Thus, only in this situation, the degree of restricted could be maintained for a maximum of 8 years, corresponding to two mandates. In fact, this must not be understood as an exception to Article 24.1, item 1, given that the President’s mandate in Brazil has a maximum of 4 years. However, it is a restriction on access to information conditioned to the occurrence of determined fact, whose incidence may occur twice in a row.

Regarding classification attributions, Article 27.1 of the Brazilian Law Nº 12.527/2011 allows the delegation of the attribution to confer secret and top-secret labels to “to a public agent by the responsible authority, including on mission abroad, when sub-delegation is forbidden” and Article 27 para 2 conditions the attribution of the top-secret label to orders from Armed Forces Commanders and Chiefs of Diplomatic or Consular Missions to ratification, respectively, of the Ministers of Defense and of Foreign Affairs.

In respect to the decision on confidentiality classification, Article 28 of the Brazilian Law Nº 12.527/2011 states that it must be formalized, i.e., instrumentalized by a written administrative act, indicating as its basic elements the subject, the grounds for classification, the indication of the secrecy period and the identification of the classifying authority.

The subject (Article 28, item 1) must be as explicit as possible, to allow for individualization of information and to collate the matter with the grounds for restriction on access to information, without anticipating the information content to disenable the confidentiality. As for the justification of the attributed classification (Article 28, item 2), the mere indication by the authority of which item from Article 23 of the Law Nº 12.527/2011 the information fits the situation is not

[33]Mendel 2008, p. 36.

enough, for he must include the reasons that leads him to this conclusion,[34] as well as the concrete indications of expected risks, impairments or injuries from disclosure. Therefore, the authority has the burden of indicating the protected public interest.[35] The procedure provided by Article 24.5 of the Law Nº 12.527/2011 ("the least restrictive criterion possible shall be used"), introduces the three-part test for exceptions,[36] equivalent to the weighing underlying the proportionality principle,[37] which considers (1) the existence of a legitimate objective, backed by Law, to the proposed restriction to the right to information, (2) the real injury or a realistic estimative of the injury to the legitimate objective that drives the disclosure, and (3) the harm in disclosure, which should be greater than the public interest in access to information. Through this procedure, it may be decided, firstly, between restriction and disclosure of information; secondly, the confidentiality status according to the classification and the competence of the authority; and, thirdly, the identification of the adequate period (Article 28, item 3). With relation to the period, Article 24.3 of the Law Nº 12.527/2011 allows that the authority establishes the occurrence of a given event as final term, but observing the maximum expiration of classification. The identification of the classifying authority (Article 28, item 4) allows the verification of the required competence for the attribution of determined confidentiality status.

Article 31 of the Brazilian Decree Nº 7.724/2012 establishes a specific rule for deciding upon the classification of document confidentiality. According to this rule, the formalization must be made by an Information Classification Term (ICT), which must contain, among other relevant information, the indexation code of the document (item 1). This indexation code of documents is regulated by Decree Nº 7.845/2012, in which it is named Indexation Code of Document that contains Classified Information (ICDCI). After determining that all information or document classified must have this code (Article 50), it establishes that the ICDCI is composed by two parts (Article 50 Sole paragraph): one for the Unique Protocol Number (UPN) relative to document management (Article 51 of Decree Nº 7.845/2012), and the other relative to the conferred confidentiality, which contemplates six elements: (a) the confidentiality status by the initials (T, S or R); (b) the category of information with two digits; (c) the production date of information; (d) the probable declassification date; (e) indication of reclassification (Y or N); and (f) the indication of the extension date, when occurred.

Also according to Brazilian Decree Nº 7.845/2012, until the implementation of the ICDCI, on 1 June 2013, the indexation code of the document consisted only of the UPN (Article 54) and, once implemented, the ICDCI must be conferred to all classified documents, including the previous to Brazilian Law Nº 12.527/2011 (Article 55).

---

[34]Tourinho 2009, p. 75.

[35]Cademartori & Cademartori 2011a, p. 11.255.

[36]Mendel 2008, p. 30, 35; Article 19 1999, p. 7.

[37]Tourinho 2009, p. 71.

**Table 17.1** Categories of information framework

| Categories | Numeric code |
|---|---|
| Agriculture, Extraction and Fisheries | 01 |
| Science, Information and Communication | 02 |
| Trade, Services and Tourism | 03 |
| Culture, Leisure and Sport | 04 |
| Defense and Security | 05 |
| Economy and Finance | 06 |
| Education | 07 |
| Government and Politics | 08 |
| Housing, Sanitation and Urban Planning | 09 |
| Industry | 10 |
| Justice and Legislation | 11 |
| Environment | 12 |
| Individual, Family and Society | 13 |
| International relations | 14 |
| Health | 15 |
| Labor | 16 |

Source: Brazilian Decree Nº 7.845/2012

The categories in which the information can be framed, present in the ICT and in the ICDCI, as shown in Annex II of the Brazilian Decree Nº 7.845/2012

The categories in which the information can be framed, present in the ICT and in the ICDCI, are provided in Annex II of the Brazilian Decree Nº 7.845/2012, whose contents are shown in Table 17.1.

By indicating the category in the classificatory decision (ICT), Brazilian Decree Nº 7.724/2012 determines the statement of the item in full, and not the reproduction of the number that will be in the CIDIC, which is also part of the decision.

Once the decision is made, the administrative act receives the same confidentiality status of the information (Article 28 Sole paragraph of the Brazilian Law Nº 12.527/2011). This is not a good rule, because it prevents that citizens become aware of it and to take the appropriate follow-up actions on the information classified as confidential. When the same confidentiality status is maintained, the more strengthened it becomes the recommendation for an explicit decision of the content and the reasons for the confidentiality status. As a form of compensation for the restriction on access to the administrative decision, Article 30 of the Brazilian Law Nº 12.527/2011 proposes full disclosure of a more succinct report on the confidential information, in all public bodies and entities, informing the lists of information that have been declassified in the last 12 months (item 1) and a list of documents classified at every security classification, with identification for future reference (item 2), and a statistical report containing the amount of information requests received, replied to and refused, as well as generic information about the applicants (item 3). Concerning the identification of classified documents in each confidentiality status (Article 30, item 2), Article 45, item 2, points (a) to (d) of the Brazilian Decree Nº 7.724/2012 explains that the list must contain, for each classified document, its indexation code, the category of the information, the legal provision that motivates the classification, the production and classification dates and the classification period.

In the case of the decision (ICT) that classifies information has top-secret label, Brazilian Law Nº 12.527/2011 states that the authority must automatically send it to the Joint Commission for Information Revaluation to analysis and deliberation (Article 27.3), which must review the classification *ex officio* (Article 35.1, item 2) and may "request from the authority classifying information as top-secret or secret" (Article 35.1, item 1).

Apart from classifications, Article 29 of the Brazilian Law Nº 12.527/2011 also establishes rules related to the revaluation of information classification, which may be made only by the classification authority or its hierarchical superior, whose outcome can only result in the information declassification or the reduction of the period, but it can never allow the extension of the period, because it belongs to the exclusive attribution of the Joint Commission for Information Revaluation (Article 35.1, item 3). Articles 35 to 38 of the Brazilian Decree Nº 7.724/2012 establish specific rules for classification revaluation. Regarding the need for a new instance to realize the three-part test provided by Article 24.5 of the Brazilian Law Nº 12.527/2011, Article 35 Sole paragraph determines that it must be considered by the revaluation authority the maximum period of restriction, the maximum period of 4 years to revision *ex officio* of ultra-secret and secret information, the permanence of the reasons, the possibility of damages or risks and the peculiarity of the information produced abroad.

Furthermore, in the case of dismissal of the revaluation done upon request (and not *ex officio*), Article 37 of the Brazilian Decree Nº 7.724/2012 also establishes the right of appeal to the requester, within a ten-day period, to the maximum authority of the body or entity (respective Minister of State, Armed Forces Commander or head of the body or entity), who must manifest his position in 30 days and, from the dismissal of this appeal, a new appeal to the Joint Commission for Information Revaluation is suitable, within an equal ten-day period, running from the notification of the decision.

Once the information or the document that holds it is declassified, it will lose its ICDCI, keeping only its UPN, in the terms of Article 51.1 of the Brazilian Decree Nº 7.845/2012.

Article 39 of the Brazilian Law Nº 12.527/2011 establishes, as transitory determination, the obligation of an *ex officio* revaluation, by all public bodies and entities, of information classified as secret or ultra-secret, to be done in the period of 2 years from the validity of the Law. The revaluation in Article 39 must proceed accordingly to the same general guidelines of revaluation in Article 29 of the Law Nº 12.527/2011, i.e., it can only be done for declassification of information as confidential, or for maintenance or reduction of the period of confidentiality conferred before.

Article 34 of the Brazilian Decree Nº 7.724/2012, in addition, authorizes the creation in federal bodies and entities of a Permanent Commission for Classified Documents Evaluation (PCCDE), of eminently opinionated and advisory nature in questions relating to classification, declassification, final destination and elaboration of the annual report, already analyzed.

Under the Joint Commission for Information Revaluation, according to Article 35.1, item 2 of the Brazilian Law Nº 12.527/2011, the revision could be done under two modalities: *ex officio* or upon request of interested person. In the first case, Article 35.3 establishes that "Review by right of office mentioned in subparagraph II of para 1 shall occur, at the most, every (four) years, after the reassessment stipulated in Article 39, when dealing with top-secret and secret documents." The absence of deliberation on the review by the Joint Commission of Information Reassessment within the deadlines stipulated by Article 35.3 shall result in the automatic declassification of the information (Article 35.4). In relation to the second case, the Joint Commission for Information Revaluation cannot demand from the interested the determining reasons for the revision request, applying by analogy Article 10.3 of the Law Nº 12.527/2011. The deliberation of the Commission to review classification must be made by absolute majority (Article 52, item 1 of Decree Nº 7.724/2012).

### *3.2 Protection and Control of Confidential Information*

The definition of the exceptional hypotheses of restriction on access to information and the establishment of the classification of information in confidentiality statutes are not enough. It is essential that procedural rules of treatment of confidential information are provided internally to ensure the protection of the legitimate objective that confidentiality aims to safeguard. Indeed, Article 25 of the Brazilian Law Nº 12.527/2011 establishes the State duty to control the access and the disclosure of confidential information, which must be restricted to authorized public agents and to persons who need to know them and are duly credentialed, as well as the repercussion of the confidentiality duty for those who access information, notwithstanding specific regulations.

These are procedural rules to the safety of the confidentiality, differing therefore of the instrumental hypotheses of restriction on access to information. Further, the provision's text, as well as the guarantee of the right to access to information (Article 5 of Law Nº 12.527/2011), the control of access and disclosure of confidential information, once identified through the process of weighing the involved interests and regularly registered, also comes to be a duty of the State.

Doubt might arise about the exceptions related to private interest that affect privacy, private life, honor and image of citizens, as the restriction on access, in the terms of Article 31.1, item 1 of Law Nº 12.527/2011, is independent of confidentiality classification. Thus, it is recommended that public bodies and entities establish uniform rules that guide the public servants and other agents of the State about the recognition of individual information protected by confidentiality to avoid injuries to private interests without violation of the right to access to information. In this respect, Law Nº 12.527/2011 did not ease the liability of the public or military agent that "disseminating, allowing for the dissemination, accessing or allowing for the improper access to secret or personal information", which configures an illicit conduct (Article 32, item 4) that can subject the violator to punishments, from suspension (Article 32.1, item 2) up to dismissal for the sake of public service, independently of its prosecution as typified conduct of administrative impropriety (Article 32.2).

Indeed, Article 26 of Law Nº 12.527/2011 seeks to obligate public authorities, as well as other natural or legal persons who are responsible for the treatment of confidential information that promotes an internal education policy about procedures of security, control and protection of confidential information.

Specifically for the Union, Article 37 of Law Nº 12.527/2011 institutes, as a final determination of that Law, the Safety and Credentialing Core (SCC) that aims to work in the federal administration the security of confidential information.

The legal provisions cited in this section were specifically regulated in separate, namely, in Brazilian Decree Nº 7.845/2012, applicable to Federal Executive Power. The mentioned regulation is, in its substance, didactically divided into three parts. In the first part, it regulates the SCC (Article 3), besides disciplining its attributions, and creates the Credentialing and Safety Management Committee (Article 4), to which it is assigned the competence to propose guidelines and to define parameters of security credentialing (Article 5), contradicting Article 37, item 1 of Law Nº 12.527/2011, and define the competences of the Institutional Security Office of the Presidency of the Republic (Article 6), of the named register bodies levels 1 and 2 (Articles 7 and 8, respectively) and of what the Decree calls the control post (Article 9). It also disciplines the procedures of habilitation and credentialing (Articles 10 to 16).

In the second part, Decree Nº 7.845/2012 states specifically about the treatment of confidential information, stipulating, in its general provisions, similarly to Article 26 of Law Nº 12.527/2011, that federal bodies and entities, as well as natural or legal persons which have ties with them, must take steps so that their subordinates know the norms of treatment of confidential information and observe them (Article 17), and that the access to confidential information will be restrict to accredited or legally authorized persons, unless, exceptionally, to third parties not accredited nor authorized, that must sign a Confidentiality Maintenance Commitment Statement (CMCS) (Article 18). It brings also various procedural specific rules about the elaboration of Controlled Document (Articles 21 to 22), marking of the information classified (Articles 23 to 25), and conditions of quality and security in shipping, processing and communication (Articles 26 to 32), in the reproduction (Articles 33 and 34), in the preservation and safekeeping (Articles 35 to 37), in the utilization of systems of information (Articles 38 to 41) and in relation to areas, installations and materials (Articles 42 to 47). Special emphasis is put on the celebration of confidential contracts, "whose object contains information classified in any confidentiality degree, or whose execution involves information classified" (Article 38), establishing the need for a signature by the CMCS, in the format established in Annex I, and the provision of mandatory clauses in these contracts which warrant a security of the information.

The last part states over the Indexation Code of Document that contains Classified Information (ICDCI) (Articles 50 to 55), already analyzed in Sect. 3.1.

### 3.3 *Exceptions to Confidentiality*

For exceptions to exceptions, by its own nature, in classic interpretation rules, the same rule of exceptional norms applies; i.e., its interpretation must be strict. However, giving that it is a constitutional interpretation that deals with fundamental freedom rights (to access to information), the inverse methodology must be adopted. Thus, exceptions to restrictions on access to information must be interpreted as widely as possible.

Apparently, Brazilian Law Nº 12.527/2011 did not establish specific cases of exception to confidentiality conferred by reasons of public interest. It is presumed that the exceptional hypotheses must be considered only in the procedure of weighing (three-part test) realized by the authority competent to confer confidentiality in a three-part test (Article 24.5), or during the revaluation (Article 29) or revision by the Joint Commission for Information Revaluation (Article 35.1, item 2). Nonetheless, Article 21 of Law Nº 12.527/2011 opens a generic exception to the cases of information necessary to the judicial or administrative protection of fundamental rights, carefully examined below (see Sect. 4). Moreover, other exceptions to restrictions can be conferred by sparse laws, according to the power of political bargaining of specific interested groups, for instance, in matters of environmental right in Law Nº 10.650/2003,[38] or consumer's defense, of essential public services, as well as in relation to the public spending, involving issues of financial and budgetary law and of administrative bidding and contract law.

Indeed, the Brazilian Superior Court of Justice[39] has already manifested for the access to citizens who submit a complaint against a public servant for the alleged commission of administrative misconduct acts, to the process of investigation classified as restricted (Article 23, item 8 and Article 24.1, item 3 of the Law Nº 12.527/2011), because he is considered an interested party in the administrative proceeding, pursuant to Article 9 of the Brazilian Law Nº 9.784/1999. However, unrestricted access is not allowed, so as to safeguard the strategic information of intelligence activity, the same for the reproduction or the disclosure of information (duty of confidentiality).

In what concerns to the restrictions by private interest, Article 31.1, item 2 and Articles 31.2 to 31.4 of the Brazilian Law Nº 12.527/2011 establishes specific exceptional rules. That Law provides two genera of exceptions to confidentiality

---

[38] Barros 2003, p. 76.

[39] Superior Court of Justice (Superior Tribunal de Justiça), *Writ of mandamus 20,196-DF* (Judgment of 8 October 2014).

of personal information: one in the case of express consent of the person to whom the information refers, and the other in the occurrence of situations specified in Law. Express consent must be supplied by unequivocal document, duly signed and notarized, in which the person to whom the information refers authorizes that a particular person has access, or by a document that authorizes the public disclosure of the personal information contained in public bodies. According to the Model Inter-American Law on Access to Information, it can also be included in the notion of consent the situations in which "it was clear when the information was provided that it [...] was subject to disclosure."[40] The access authorization can also be conferred by instrumental means: to the defense of the interests of the person in administrative or judicial process, the access of information contained in the case records cannot be denied to properly constituted attorneys; or, in the same sense, third parties with explicit powers to access information conferred by proxy (Article 60.1, item 1 of the Brazilian Decree Nº 7.724/2012).

In cases in which access to particular information is consented individually, people who were franchised the information become liable for the proper use of it, according to Article 31.2 of the Law Nº 12.527/2011. As for lawyers, the use is strictly allowed in the defense of the person's interests in administrative or judicial proceedings; in other cases, it must be observed the conditions and purposes of consent and conferred power. In any case, according to Article 61 of the Decree Nº 7.724/2012, access to personal information by third parties could be conditioned to the signature of a statement of responsibility.

Regarding the existence of legal exceptions, although the exceptional situations are not limited to the cases prescribed in Article 31.3 of Law Nº 12.527/2011, this lists the cases in which consent is considered not to be required, divided in five items. Item 1 ("for medical prevention and diagnosis, when the person is physically or legally incapacitated, and for the single and exclusive purpose of medical treatment") tries to safeguard the life and health of the person, through the disclosure of information that can be helpful to adequate medical diagnosis and treatment. In this case, it is necessary that the utility of the information in relation to the purpose of the disclosure is checked; i.e., it must involve personal information related to the health and physical condition of the person (medical tests contained in personnel files of public bodies and entities). Law Nº 12.527/2011 requires that the person must be neither in full physical conditions to request referred information nor in legal conditions to confer the express consent. Moreover, the publicity of the information must be restricted to those responsible for conducting medical treatment.

Item 2 alludes to "carrying out of statistical or scientific research of noticeable public or general interest, as stipulated by law, the identification of the person to which the information refers being prohibited". That is an unfortunately open

[40]See Organization of American States. General Assembly. Model Inter-American Law on Access to Information (2010). *AG/RES. 2607*. Appendix. XL-O/10. Washington D.C.: OAS. http://www.oas.org/ (Accessed on 12 January 2017).

clause, because it does not mention which statistics and researches are meant, nor does it say to which laws the provision refers. State should disclose, in general character by Law, which statistics or scientific researches shall utilize information contained in public database. In the same sense, Article 31.3, item 5 also allows for a wide margin of discretionarity in the weighing of involved values, authorizing the disclosure of personal information before "overriding general public interest". The authority responsible for that disclosure must adopt at least the same necessary procedures to classify the confidentiality of information, especially the weighing within the three-part test (Article 24.5 of Law Nº 12.527/2011), notwithstanding the hearing of the person to whom information pertains.

Article 31.3, item 3 ("for compliance with judicial decision") is an instrumental exception, i.e., although it must be inevitably complied with, it has to protect another exceptional interest, as would be the cases, for instance, in access to information necessary to investigations and investigative proceedings of irregularities (Article 31.4), or for the defense of human rights (Article 31.3, item 4). The provision of this item protects the separation of powers. Based on this provision, it is also admissible the possibility of exemption of consent for compliance with an order from the Parliamentary Inquiry Committee, which, according to Article 58.3 of the Brazilian Constitution, has "the same investigative powers as judicial authorities".[41]

In relation to Article 31.3, item 4 ("for the defense of human rights"), by its specificity and its correlation with Article 21 of the Brazilian Law Nº 12.527/2011, it will be analyzed in detail below (see Sect. 4). It is worth noting that the Brazilian Law is shier than the Model Inter-American Law on Access to Information (point 45), which establishes the application of the exceptions "in cases of serious violations of human rights or crimes against humanity."[42]

As mentioned, Article 31.4 of the Brazilian Law Nº 12.527/2011 also withdraws confidentiality of personal information in the case of a determination of irregularities in which the holder of information is involved. In this case, it means that privacy protection cannot be invoked to shelter legal violations and crimes.[43] The same provision also includes in this legal exception the situation of "jeopardizing the retrieval of highly relevant historical facts", as a sign of prevalence of the collective public right to the historical truth. As Article 31.4 has a distinct formulation of Article 31.3, it covers unconventional situations, in which consent is not required. Thus, one should interpret such provision in the sense that access to such information could only be granted by judicial decision (Article 31.3, item 3) as result of a process in which the interested public authority outlines the need for information regarding the realization of one of the purposes provided in

[41]Levy 2009, p. 12.

[42]See Organization of American States. General Assembly. Model Inter-American Law on Access to Information (2010). *AG/RES. 2607*. Appendix. XL-O/10. Washington D.C.: OAS. http://www.oas.org/en/sla/dil/docs/access_to_information_Text_edited_DDI.pdf (Accessed on 2 May 2017).

[43]Levy 2009, p. 14.

Law Nº 12.527/2011, as well as to assess the "high relevance" of the historical facts considering also the periods of confidentiality classification prescribed in the Law, as an objective way to ensure the historical character of the information.

Article 59 of the Brazilian Decree Nº 7.724/2012, on the other hand, states specific provisions to the use of personal information for purposes of recovering historical facts of high relevance, but unfortunately left all the processing of this special case within the Federal Executive Power.

In the case of third parties, according to Article 60.1, item 3 of the Brazilian Decree Nº 7.724/2012, they must demonstrate interest. Generally, the exceptions to confidential information inside the legal cases, regardless of classification, demand proof of a legitimate interest in the information, as established by the Inter-American Court of Human Rights.[44]

Article 31.4 of Law Nº 12.527/2011 states that the allegation of it being a personal information, subject, in theory, to confidentiality, cannot be invoked *per se* to invalidate or impede its utilization in those situations, thus denoting instances outside the essential core of protection of the fundamental right to privacy, private life, honor and image (Article 5, item 10 of the Brazilian Constitution), determined by the Legislative Power.

## 4 The Necessary Information for the Judicial or Administrative Protection of Fundamental Rights

The goal of judicial or administrative protection of fundamental rights is inserted as a general exception to the confidentiality of information under protection of the State. Article 21 of the Brazilian Law Nº 12.527/2011 confirms that by forbidding the denial of access to that information. Article 21 Sole paragraph disciplines a specific rule on prohibition of restrictions on access to information derived from acts committed by public agents in the exercise of their functions who violate human rights. Regarding the use of personal information to that purpose, Article 31.3, item 4 of Law Nº 12.527/2011 also exempts the need for consent to the "defense of human rights".

Despite the distinction between human rights and fundamental rights, based on the positivity in the Constitution criterion, in which the first would be broader than the latter, it is correct to state that, in the Brazilian legal context, there is almost no differentiated treatment between them, as Article 5.2 of the Brazilian Constitution establishes an openness clause of fundamental rights, by providing that "The rights and guarantees expressed in this constitution do not exclude others deriving from

[44]Inter-American Court of Human Rights, *Claude Reyes et al. v. Chile* (Judgment of 19 September 2006), Series C, No. 151, para 77. http://www.corteidh.or.cr/docs/casos/articulos/seriec_151_ing.pdf (Accessed on 12 January 2017).

the regime and from the principles adopted by it, or from the international treaties in which the Federative Republic of Brazil is a party."

Alluding to human rights can affect the administrative or judicial levels in which access to information is pursued. For instance, the Inter-American System on Human Rights can be included, composed by the Inter-American Commission on Human Rights, with an administrative nature, and the Inter-American Court of Human Rights, with judicial nature, both based in the Pact of San Jose, Costa Rica (American Convention on Human Rights). Similarly, in the United Nations System on Human Rights related to the competence of the International Criminal Court.

The Inter-American Court of Human Rights decided that access to information related to violations of human rights is a right of the victims and their families, from which derives the right to the truth about the events and the liabilities of the state bodies.[45]

In terms of applicability of the cited provisions, with respect to information of public nature about violations of human rights committed by public agents, they must be immediately made public and must not be subject to restriction. That is a real "stony clause" within the regime of restrictions on access to information. The public authority that confers confidentiality, destroys or subtracts documents and information related to possible violations of human rights, practices an illicit conduct (Article 32, items 5 and 7 of Law Nº 12.527/2011) and is subject to the consequences of the Law—the application of medium or grave military transgression or administrative offense with the minimum penalty of suspension, notwithstanding the administrative impropriety lawsuit (Article 32.2).

On the other hand, depending on the situation, the identification of the violation of fundamental human rights can become complicated. There is no precise line of separation between a situation of violation of rights and a situation of mere restriction of information that may be necessary for the protection of fundamental rights. Depending on the circumstances of the case, the agent's intention and the inexcusability of the mistake must be evaluated in administrative or judicial proceedings. In other cases, despite the silence of the Law on it, the jurisdictional and administrative authorities, national and international, must submit the request to access to documents or information to the body or entity that holds it. In principle, those authorities must clarify the utility of this information for fundamental or human rights' protection. In the case of personal information for human rights' protection, whose disclosure is independent of consent from the person to whom the document or information refers (Article 31.3, item 4), for judicial authorities a simples order would be sufficient, because it would be framed in the exception of the Article 31.3, item 3). In the case of third parties, according to Decree Nº 7.724/2012, the request must be accompanied by the "outline on the need for the required

[45]Inter-American Court of Human Rights, *Barrios Altos v. Peru* (Judgment of 14 March 2001), Series C, No. 75, para 48. http://www.corteidh.or.cr/docs/casos/articulos/seriec_75_ing.pdf (Accessed on 12 January 2017).

access to information for the defense of human rights" (Article 60 Sole paragraph, item 4).

Doubts about what kinds of information and in relation to which fundamental rights it would be possible to franchise access may arise. That is so because fundamental rights, according to the theory underpinning the principle structure of these rights, have a radiant efficacy; put simply, the need for protection of fundamental rights is present to a greater or lesser extent in all situations. Nonetheless, it is necessary that objective conditions should be established to an assessment of the situations that undoubtedly seeks to protect fundamental human rights. In this context, the requests of those international bodies, whose attributions are immediately linked to the protection of human rights, must be complied with. In the same sense, lawsuits in the form of the constitutional writs, in the terms of Article 5, items 68 to 73 of the Brazilian Constitution (*habeas corpus*, *habeas data*, writ of mandamus, writ of injunction and people's legal action), the public civil suit (Article 129, item 3 of the Brazilian Constitution) in charge of Public Prosecution and, in Supreme Federal Court—giving that other abstract constitutional review suits are against laws—by the claim of non-compliance with a fundamental precept (Article 102.1 of the Brazilian Constitution) and the claim against an administrative act or judicial decision that contradicts the Court's decision (Article 102, item 1, point (a) of the Brazilian Constitution) can be made.

For other cases, namely within administrative proceedings, and in requests to access information by the interested persons themselves, before the filing of a lawsuit, a cautious weighing of the fundamental right that one seeks to protect against the utility of the information to be disclosed to that desideratum must be made. According to Article 42 Sole paragraph of the Brazilian Decree Nº 7.724/2012, "The applicant must give reasons which substantiate the existence of a nexus between the required information and the right intended to protect."

The refusal to disclose information allegedly necessary for judicial or administrative protection of fundamental rights, after the evaluation procedure of adequacy between the necessary information and the fundamental right that one seeks to protect, can, because it is a clear legal right, with the possibility of immediate documental evidence, be attacked by the writ of mandamus, while *habeas data* serves only to personal information. Article 19.1 of Law Nº 12.527/2011, originally submitted to the President of the Republic's sanction, established that bodies and entities must refer to the Public Prosecution the denied applications of access to information based on essentiality for the protection of fundamental rights, as well as the reasons of the denial. However, this provision was vetoed for alleged violation of the separation of powers,[46] giving margin only to lawsuits, notwithstanding the competences of the Public Prosecution regarding the occurrence of administrative impropriety of the practiced conduct (Article 32.1 and Article 32.2 of the Law Nº 12.527/2011).

[46]See Presidency of the Federative Republic of Brazil, *Message 523/2011*. http://www.planalto.gov.br/ccivil_03/_ato2011-2014/2011/Msg/VEP-523.htm. Accessed on 12 January 2017.

## References

Alves, M. S. D. (2012). Do sigilo ao acesso: análise tópica da mudança de cultura. *Revista do Tribunal de Contas do Estado de Minas Gerais*, 30, Edição Especial (Transparência e Controle Social), 120–134.

Article 19. (1999). *O direito do público a estar informado*: *princípios sobre a legislação de liberdade de informação*. London: Article 19.

Barros, L. V. (2003). A proteção legal do acesso a informações sobre atividades causadoras de impactos ambientais. *Boletim científico da Escola Superior do Ministério Público da União, 3* (10), 73–84.

Bulos, U. L. (2012). *Constituição federal anotada*. São Paulo, Brazil: Saraiva.

Cademartori, D. M. L., & Cademartori, S. U. (2011a). O direito fundamental de acesso no ordenamento jurídico brasileiro. In Conselho Nacional de Pesquisa e Pós-Graduação em Direito (Ed.), *Anais do XX Congresso Nacional do CONPEDI* (pp. 11.251–11.277). Florianópolis, Brazil: Fundação Boiteux.

Cademartori, S. U., & Cademartori, D. M. L. (2011b). O poder do segredo e os segredos do poder: uma análise histórico-conceitual dos limites e possibilidades de convivência entre o segredo e a democracia. *Novos estudos jurídicos, 16*(3), 329–344.

Fregapani, G. A. F., & Botelho, A. C. M. P. (2012). A lei de acesso à informação e sua regulamentação no âmbito do TCU. *Revista consulex: ciência jurídica em foco, 16*(376), 16–18.

Levy, J. L. (2009). Das restrições ao pedido de informações a órgão público. *Rede: Revista Eletrônica de Direito do Estado, 5*(17.) Retrieved January 12, 2017, from http://bit.ly/2c0BEAC.

Mendel, T. (2008). *Freedom of information: A comparative legal survey*. Paris: UNESCO.

Michener, G. (2011). Liberdade de informação: uma síntese dos dilemas de conformidade e suas possíveis soluções. In Article 19 (Ed.), *Leis de acesso à informação*: *dilemas da implementação* (pp. 7–23). London: Article 19.

Mota Junior, J. F. (2012). A nova lei de acesso à informação e o fomento à gestão democrática da educação. *Reflexão, ações e educação: revista de ciências sociais e humanas, 1*(1), 12–29.

Organization of American States. General Assembly. (2010). Model Inter-American Law on Access to Information. AG/RES. 2607. Appendix. XL-O/10. Washington, DC: OAS. Retrieved January 12, 2017, from http://www.oas.org/

Presidency of the Federative Republic of Brazil. (2011). Message n° 523/2011. Retrieved January 12, 2017, from http://bit.ly/2c2Owqv

Tourinho, R. (2009). Do direito à informação e a prerrogativa pública do sigilo: análise crítica do Projeto de Lei n° 5.228/09. *Interesse público, 9*(57), 59–76.

## List of Cases

### *Inter-American Court of Human Rights*

Inter-American Court of Human Rights 14.03.2001, *Barrios Altos v. Peru*, Series C, No. 75.

Inter-American Court of Human Rights 19.06.2006, *Claude Reyes, et al. v. Chile*, Series C, No. 151.

Inter-American Court of Human Rights 24.11.2010, *Gomes Lund and Others (Guerrilha do Araguaia v. Brazil)*, Series C, No. 219.

## *Brazilian Courts*

Supreme Federal Court (Supremo Tribunal Federal) 09.06.2011, Second regulatory appeal in mandamus suspension 3,902 São Paulo.
Superior Court of Justice (Superior Tribunal de Justiça) 11.09.2013, Writ of mandamus 19,243-DF.
Superior Court of Justice 08.10.2014, Writ of mandamus 20,196-DF.
Supreme Federal Court 17.06.2015, Extraordinary appeal 673,707 Minas.

# Chapter 18
# Procedural and Remedial Aspects of Access to Information

**Pedro Aberastury, Alexandre Arruda, Rosnell V. Carrasco Baptista, and Rogelio Robles**

## Contents



P. Aberastury (✉)
University of Buenos Aires, Buenos Aires, Argentina
e-mail: pedro@aberastury.com

A. Arruda
Fluminense Federal University, Rio de Janeiro, Brazil

R.V. Carrasco Baptista
Andrés Bello Catholic University, Caracas, Venezuela

R. Robles
National Autonomous University of Mexico, Mexico City, Mexico

 
H.-J. Blanke, R. Perlingeiro (eds.), *The Right of Access to Public Information*,
DOI 10.1007/978-3-662-55554-5_18

## 1 Introduction

The right of access to information has its origin in the right of freedom of speech, insofar as the latter includes the power to express ideas and opinions freely in a State based on the rule of law.[1] In some Latin American constitutional systems, the right to access to information is expressly codified, for example in Article 5, items 14 and 33 and, related to the knowledge of personal information and the correction of personal data in official files, in the procedural guarantee of Article 5, item 72 (*habeas data*) of the Brazilian Constitution, further in Article 20 subparagraph (B), item 3 of the Mexican Constitution or in Articles 28 and 143 of the Venezuelan Constitution. Yet even constitutions, which do not expressly mention that right, may incorporate it through adherence to international conventions. In Argentina, for example, the right to access to information is now considered equivalent to a constitutionally guaranteed fundamental right thanks to the country's adherence to human rights conventions pursuant to Article 75.22 of the Constitution as amended in 1994,[2] and it has repeatedly been interpreted as such in Argentinian Supreme Court judgments. Moreover, the Supreme Court has held that the rulings of the Inter-American Court of Human Rights and the reports of the Inter-American Commission on Human Rights are *binding*,[3] an innovative interpretation in international public law that is gradually being accepted in Latin American legal systems.

Indeed, protection of the right to information is taking on great importance in international law, as recognized in Article 19 of the Universal Declaration of Human Rights of 10 December 1948: "Everyone has the right to freedom of opinion and expression; this right includes freedom to hold opinions without interference

[1]López-Ayllon 2002, p. 472.

[2]Article 75.22 of the Argentinian Constitution reads as follows: "To approve or reject treaties concluded with other nations and international organizations, and concordats with the Holy See. Treaties and concordats have a higher hierarchy than laws. *The American Declaration of the Rights and Duties of Man; the Universal Declaration of Human Rights; the American Convention on Human Rights; the International Pact on Economic, Social and Cultural Rights; the International Pact on Civil and Political Rights and its empowering Protocol; the Convention on the Prevention and Punishment of Genocide; the International Convention on the Elimination of all Forms of Racial Discrimination; the Convention on the Elimination of all Forms of Discrimination against Woman; the Convention against Torture and other Cruel, Inhuman or Degrading Treatments or Punishments; the Convention on the Rights of the Child; in the full force of their provisions, they have constitutional hierarchy, do no repeal any section of the First Part of this Constitution and are to be understood as complementing the rights and guarantees recognized herein.* They shall only be denounced, in such event, by the National Executive Power after the approval of two-thirds of all the members of each House. In order to attain constitutional hierarchy, the other treaties and conventions on human rights shall require the vote of two-thirds of all the members of each House, after their approval by Congress." (emphasis added)

[3]National Supreme Court of Justice, Argentina (Corte Suprema de Justicia de La Nación Argentina), CIPPEC c/ EN – M° Desarrollo Social – dto. 1172/03 s/amparo, Ley 16.986, Fallos C. 830. XLVI, 2014 (Judgment of 26 March 2014) para 32.

and to seek, receive and impart information and ideas through any media and regardless of frontiers."[4]

If this article affirms that the right of access to information is a fundamental right, it is because the case-law of the I/A Court H. R. considers it so, which has now made it possible to extend the right to effective judicial protection to cover the right to information. Regarding this procedural right, Article 1 of the recently issued Argentinian Law 27275/2016 on *Derecho de Acceso a la Información* ("Right of Access to Public Information")[5] has set out the following principle: "*Control*: compliance with the statutory freedom-of-information provisions shall be subject to constant review. Decisions which deny requests for access to information, or the authority's failure to respond to such requests, or to respond in an ambiguous or inaccurate manner, may be appealed to the competent body."[6]

The right of access to information in the contemporary world has attained the status of a fundamental right[7] that may be affirmed to exist even in legal systems in which it is not expressly enshrined, as the aim of a democratic State is the defense of rights and freedoms of the individual,[8] including free access to information, which is a fundamental element of all democratic governance. In that article the term "fundamental right" is used to mean a right that is essentially inviolable, so that it can be "set up as a general barrier against infringements on the essence of fundamental rights,"[9] as it was established in Article 19.2. of the German Basic Law.[10] It should also be noted that Article 25 of the American Convention has already used this term and the Inter-American Court of Human Rights (I/A Court H. R.) has quoted it on repeated occasions. In the case "Cinco Pensionistas vs. Perú" *(Five Pensioners v Peru)* of 28 February 2003, in the concurring opinion of Judge Cançado Trindade, he stated that "cultural diversity has never hindered the formation of a universal core of non-derogable fundamental rights, enshrined in a lot of Human Rights Treaties."[11]

---

[4]In the Latin American System, it was embodied, mainly, in Article 19.2 the International Covenant on Civil and Political Rights and in Article 13 of the American Convention on Human Rights, granting a wider protection to the right to information because it was understood as making up of the freedom of thought and speech. To protect these rights, it is necessary that the freedom of looping up, receiving and Spreading information and ideas of all types, without considering borders, either orally, in writing or printed or artistic, or by any other procedure of their choice.

[5]Cf. Boletín Oficial de la República Argentina, available at: https://www.boletinoficial.gob.ar/#!DetalleNorma/151503/null.

[6]Cf. Article 1 (principle 10) of Law 27275/2016.

[7]Vallefín 2009, p. 24 et seqq.

[8]"Limit the State and provide with security to the individual against it were two characteristics of that organization". Bidart Campos 1996, p. 320.

[9]Casal 2010, p. 281.

[10]The term fundamental right is used for the first time in the German Constitution of *Paulskirche*, of 1848/9, in which it was understood as an element of the established constitutional system, of the corresponding National State, with independence of religious tenets or of natural law. Sommermann, in Casal 2010, p. xxv.

[11]Spielmann & Drzemczewski 2014.

In conclusion, we can state that the right to information, as it has been incorporated expressly from Human Rights Treaties, has a meaning of universality which allows it to be considered as a fundamental right which promotes the individual's development and, therefore, the State and the international community to which it belongs, have to provide protection even in the case in which it is not expressly established.

In this way, even in cases in which it is not expressly established in a specific legal system, it can be guaranteed, by providing adequate procedural tools, to be recognized in all its wide range, that is to say, to seek, request and receive information from the State so we will analyze, from this starting point, the systems and scope of protection.

## 2 Access to Information

### 2.1 *Regulations Which Enable Access*

Our comparative view of information access in Latin America will be limited to an analysis to the existing rules and regulations in Argentina, Brazil, Mexico and Venezuela.

For example, it is worth mentioning that the Argentinian legislator has recently enacted Law 27275/2016 regulating the right to information (Sect. 1).[12] It should be noted that, according to the Argentinian Constitutional System, the Federal Congress has jurisdiction in all those issues that have been delegated by the Provinces and, in the case of Law 27275/2016, the scope of application is in relation to the organs that make up the National State. Therefore, the Provinces keep the power to enact it.[13] Previously, on the level of Argentinian Federal Administration, the governing law was Decree 1172/2003, Annex VII, which applied only to centralized and local bodies of the National Public Administration, but not to the rest of the powers of the State. It also coexisted with other substantive regulations enacted by the Federal Congress, such as Law 25831/2004, on the right to public environmental information,[14] the Personal Data Protection Law (Argentinian Law 25326/

[12]Article 1.1 of Law 27275/2016 reads as follows: "The purpose of this law is to ensure the effective exercise of the right of access to official information, to promote citizen participation and the transparency of public information [...]". The different principles that regulate it, making it clear that it is not necessary to request motivation to have access to the requested information. It is applicable to all the national state level and an Agency of Access to Public Information will be established as a self-sufficient entity for the control of the implementation of the Law (Article 19 of Law 27275/2016).

[13]See Article 36 of Law 27275/2016: "Adhesion. The provinces and the Autonomous City of Buenos Aires are called upon to adhere to the dispositions of the present law."

[14]Together with Argentinian Law 25675/2002 on national environmental policy and Argentinian Law 26331/2007 on environmental protection of native woods.

2000), which regulates access of existing data in databases and the Administrative Procedures Law 19549/1972[15] as its Regulatory Decree establishes right to access to administrative proceedings.[16]

To these provisions, other special regulations are added which refer to the possibility of obtaining information in the corresponding area such as the Broadcasting Law 26522/2009, in which Sec. 3 establishes the access to public information as an objective of audiovisual communication, the Acts referred to regulatory bodies for public services which set forth the duty to publish information obtained from the companies subject to its regulation (Argentinian Law 24065/1992 and 24076/1992) and the Consumer Protection Law, which states that the consumer has to have clear and free information (Argentinian Law 24240/1993), among others.[17]

Brazil, Law N°12.527 of 18 November 2011, constitutes an important framework in the realization of the fundamental right stated in Article 5, item 33 of the Federal Constitution, which guarantees the right "to receive, from the public agencies, information of private interest to such persons, or of collective or general interest, [...] except for the information whose secrecy is essential to the security of society and of the State." The Brazilian Constitution also guarantees access to public information.[18]

Hence, national legislation is applicable to both the Federal State and municipalities, their agencies and, in some cases, to the individuals who have a special link with the Administration.

The case of Mexico, whose system, in our opinion, is advanced thanks to the enactment on 11 June 2002 of the Federal Law for Transparency and Access to Public Government Information, which innovated by protecting the right to information, by regulating how to obtain information held by any federal authority and by creating the Federal Institute of Access to Public Information. This Institute is in charge of ruling on the denials of requests of access to information and of protecting personal data held by agencies, entities and even on the occasion of the publication on 5 July 2010 of the Federal Law on the Protection of Personal Data held by Private Parties, i.e., personal data which is collected by private individuals, it has become the Federal Institute of Access to Information and Data Protection.

---

[15]This regulation can be consulted in http://servicios.infoleg.gob.ar/infolegInternet/anexos/20000-24999/22363/texact.htm (Accessed on 6.1.2017).

[16]These regulations will lose effects one year after the publication of Law 27275/2016 in the Argentinian Boletín del Estado (Article 38.2 of Law 27275/2016).

[17]It is worth highlighting the Argentinian Public Ethics Law (Argentinian Law 25188/1999), which sets forth the need to give publicity to the affidavits of public officials, recently modified by Law 26857/2013 and, more recently, Law 26856/2013, of publicity of judicial sentences stating that they are of public type, of free accessibility and will be able to be consulted by all interested people, free of charge through the Internet, according to the procedure which the regulation sets forth. Also "any other norm regulating the publicness of acts of government on the right of access to official information" will lose effects one year after the publication of Law 27275/2016 in the Argentinian Boletín del Estado (Article 38.2 of Law 27275/2016).

[18]Article 5, item 14, Article 37 para 3, item 2, and Article 216 para 2 of the Brazilian Constitution.

Notwithstanding the foregoing, the above-mentioned Institute has been renamed since the publication of the General Law on Transparency and Access to Public Information of 4 May 2015, to become the National Institute on Transparency, Access to Information and Personal Data Protection (*Instituto Nacional de Transparencia, Acceso a la Información y Protección de Datos Personales*—INAI). Because of this, the Institute broadens its revision powers at a national level, obliging any authority, entity, body and agency of the Executive, Legislative and Judiciary Power, autonomous agencies, political parties, trusts and public funds, as well as any private individual, moral person or Trade Union which receives and exercises public resources or perform acts of authority at the federal level, of federative and municipal entities.

Venezuela has not enacted a Transparency Law or a Law on Access to Public Information, but it has been dealt with in the Decree 5890 of 31 July 2008, which expressly states, in Sec. 158, that every person has the right to have access to administrative files and records. The only limitations imposed on this right are the ones established in the Constitution and Law mentioned before, that is to say, "acceptable limits within a democratic society" which the constitution itself states in a restrictive way, referred to: (1) in the areas of internal and external security, (2) criminal investigation, and (3) private life. However, case-law of the Venezuelan Constitutional Court, between the protection of the right to privacy and the right to information, even in the cases which are referred to a situation derived from the civil service or public proceedings, has preferred personal protection.[19] Further, despite what is provided in Article 143 of the Constitution, which grants citizens the right to information of the status on proceedings in which they are directly interested, case-law has not shown a broad approach, on the contrary, it has developed a restrictive criterion.[20]

Within this context, there is a gradually extension of rights to private individuals to demand from the State information on its acts, as a participatory exercise of the citizen in its control because, traditionally, its concealment or restraint has been a way of exercising its power, to the detriment of ethical and moral principles which have to safeguard its actions, thus favoring corruption.

## 2.2 Types of Legal Claims

Although authors refer to the right to information and the right to access to information, we consider that the right to information is the right dealt with

[19]Constitutional Section of the Supreme Court of Justice of the Bolivarian Republic of Venezuela, *Ruth Carriles Méndez and others*, Sentence N° 1050/00 (Judgment of 23 August 2000).

[20]Constitutional Section of the Supreme Court of Justice of the Bolivarian Republic of Venezuela, *INSACA Case*, Sentence N° 332 (Judgment of 14 March 2001).

generally and the right to access to information is *the legal claim which regulates the request to obtain information.*

Considering the right to access of information as a procedural claim, we can distinguish the existence of a general right to information from that regulation which provides for specific situations, which allows to distinguish institutions which pursue the same topics, the acquisition of information, but with a different purpose, that is to say, the protection of rights of the individual being necessary the existence of personal grievance as far as the type of information which they wish to obtain, because it can produce a personal injury to the individual or cannot allow to exercise the corresponding right.

Therefore, we will analyze access to information as a procedural framework of application of requests anticipating that, in our opinion, within the right to information, we can find that it involves not only the right to know the acts of the Administration but also a series of claims which are exercised when the right of a private individual is in crisis. These claims can be classified, depending on their objects, so, to seek greater clarification, we will briefly examine the so-called right to access and access to data of the individual himself, which are in a data base, to distinguish it from the right to access to general information.

## 2.3 Access to Administrative Proceedings

The access to administrative proceedings has been a first advance, by the interested party. That has been the consequence of the application to administrative procedure of the right of due process.[21]

The right to access to proceedings is connected with the necessary publicity given to acts of government inasmuch as it enables the full enjoyment of rights of the governed individuals on the general principle that the Administration decides whether the proceedings before it should be made public or whether, on the contrary, the impediment to the right of access to the file is justified by an exception.[22] Furthermore, "the concept of governed individual must not be limited to that one who has been accepted as interested party in an administrative file as the

[21]Cf. Argentinian Law 19549/1972, of national administrative procedures as Sec. 38 of its Regulatory Decree 1759/1972, which read as follows: "The interested party, its representative or legal counsel will be able to access to administrative proceedings during the whole procedure, except those files, proceedings, reports or expert opinion which, on request from a competent body and previous advice of the corresponding legal service, if they were considered confidential or secret through reasoned decision of the corresponding assistant secretary of the ministry or of the head of the corresponding decentralized entity [...}."

[22]Referring to the Spanish administrative law, it has been stated that "The Administrative procedure" keeps debating, as, between publicity and secret, with a clear advantage for the latter, which, in its favour, plays the wish of administrators to ascertain freedom of movements which, in another case, they would lack" García de Enterría and Fernández 1983, T.II, p. 406.

knowledge of the Administration's activity cannot be restricted – on the grounds of legal standing – to a specific type of subjects or to the ones who hold a particular legal status."[23]

Nevertheless, it cannot be overlooked that the right to access to the proceedings, in procedural administrative law, is regulated to be exercised by the interested party, including the third party concerned within this category, and as long as a legitimate interest or subjective right is invoked as it is a procedure of defense of the governed individual before administrative authorities; its restriction to be imposed will have to be well-founded.

Therefore, we can differentiate the right to access to a file because it has as objective the exercise of the right of due process for whom is or can be a party to an administrative proceeding, whereas the right to information can be exercised by any person, to obtain information about any data which is in the Administration without having to invoke a right which has been affected personally.

## 2.4 Personal Data Protection (Habeas Data)

The Acts on personal data protection[24] can also be distinguished because the affected party has legal standing as he seeks to know his personal data kept in records, files, registers, data banks, or other technical media of data processing, either public or private intended to provide reports, as well as access to information which is recorded about them to guarantee the right to honor and personal privacy. In case that the data kept about the person is incorrect or affects him, its correction or deletion can be requested, through the specific action.

The writ of *habeas data* differs from the right to general information in as much as the object of protection is, especially, the individual's privacy and, thus, it constitutes a limitation to access to information on the part of third parties. In addition, it allows making effective an array of rights referred to individuals' data, either natural persons or legal entities and its purpose to be able to obtain, in case of false or distorted data, its rectification, update and cancellation.[25]

The legal claim has as its only purpose the elimination, rectification, confidentiality or update of data, when that piece of information or the purpose considered for its collection is false or discriminatory. That is to say that, even when a personal detail is exact or correct, if it has been collected with a purpose and then it is used with another, or has been captured without the consent of the owner of personal data, or with an illegal or socially reprehensible purpose, has to be suppressed as it affects the sphere of privacy of the individual, irrespective of its discriminatory potential. In the same way, all personal information that is collected has to be

[23]Aberastury and Cilurzo 1998, p. 60.

[24]In Argentina: Article of the National Constitution and Habeas Data Law (Law No. 25326/2000).

[25]Aberastury and Gottschau 2001, p. 31.

notified to the subject concerned, and has to be the result of the use of legal means, either by the subject's consent or by legal authorization,[26] but for the exceptions provided by law.

## 2.5 Legal Standing

Having distinguished the actions which, generally speaking, are set forth in legislations and which entail specific procedural actions of protection, provided in the corresponding Acts, we will deal with access to information on the part of an individual which does not invoke a personal concrete grievance, which are the requirements of the procedural claim which protects the right to access to information.

The general principle is that legal standing has to be broad so any person with the purpose of obtaining information that is in the state Administration or public authorities can assume it.

According to this, the right to access to information does not require invoking any legal standing on the requested information and persons who do not belong to the State required to give access to information can even exercise it. That is this way because, in this case, information allows the knowledge to all people about the State's activity to enforce the principle of transparency and be able to control corruption; it does not pursue, in principle, a personal interest but a general interest whereas the right to access to proceedings, as well as the writ of *habeas data*, pursue a personal and concrete interest of the applicant.

In this way, the rules connected with this issue state the lack of need to substantiate the applicant's standing, in case information is required to the State, as it is not a requirement to prove certain interest or reason to obtain information, as it results from the mentioned rules from Argentina, Brazil and Mexico.[27]

In all of them, it is enough to identify information and that the petition is not hindered, so it is enough that the request to access is made by any legitimate means, being a duty of public agencies to proceed with it accordingly. Thus, the Argentinian Law establishes that it is neither necessary to prove any subjective right or legitimate interest, nor to substantiate the request because it is assumed that all information produced or obtained by all the state bodies included in the statute is public.[28]

---

[26] Altmark and Molina Quiroga 1996, p. 1565.

[27] Sacristan and Ratti Mendaña 2012, p. 884 et seq.

[28] Cf. Article 4 of the Argentinian Law 27275/2016.

Recent Brazilian legislation states, following these guidelines, the absence of need of a specific standing, so that it can be requested for any interested person, national or foreigner, who identifies himself previously and specifies the desired information. That is guaranteed as it prohibits the required government agency to demand the reasons why the person requests information, as well as unreasonable requests regarding the petitioner's identification to allow a broader exercise of this fundamental right.

The Brazilian Decree N°7.724/2012,[29] which regulates the mentioned Law N° 12.527/2011 in the scope of the Executive Power, sets forth that the request should have the petitioner's name, his ID number, the specification, in a clear manner, of the requested information and the petitioner's physical or electronic address.

The request of access to information can be made by any means and it is a duty of the government bodies and public entities to make the request viable through the official web pages on the Internet. As a way of making the request and access easy, the Internet websites, which belong to government bodies and public entities, have to provide search engines that allow access to information, in an objective, transparent and clear manner and in a language that is easy to understand. Besides, the government bodies and Brazilian public entities have the duty to disclose in their websites the collective or general interest information produced by them or in their power.

The Union Audit Office, central organ of the Brazilian Federal Executive Power, responsible for internal control and correction, considers that a request is not reasonable when it is against the State public interest regarding public security, promptness and efficiency of the civil service. Examples of unreasonable requests are those that can be considered disrespectful and obsessive, which blatantly reveal the intention to overload the agency's capacity, with the objective of adversely affecting its operations.[30]

Subsequently, in the understanding that the request implies a disproportionate financial and administrative expenditure, reducing the body's operational capacity and creating an impairment of the other fundamental rights in the specific case, the request will have to be denied. The Audit Office understands that the Law's objective is to guarantee citizens access to information and not to create a situation of institutional halting, in which a body stops complying with its specific competence to search documents which, many times, can take long periods to be finished.

---

[29] Sec. 12 of the Brazilian Decree N° 7724 of 16 May 2012. Available at: http://www.planalto.gov.br/ccivil_03/_ato2011-2014/2012/decreto/d7724.htm (Accessed on 14 March 2016).

[30] Union Audit Office, Administrative Process n° 09200.000284/2015-47 (31 July 2015). It was about a petition made by a citizen to the Ministry of Foreign Affairs with the purpose of obtaining the whole content of diplomatic telegrams elaborated or received by the Ministry between the months of May and June of 2015, as well as the indication of how many would receive the classification of ultra secret, secret or reserved. The Audit Office understood that although the request was not unreasonable or generic, it had a disproportionate character, because it would include over 20,000 files, or around 50 different investigations would be needed, with its selection and digital recording of documents.

This is called active transparency and consists of the spontaneous disclosure of society's general interest information, irrespective of the request. This duty includes the communication of all the registers connected with wire transfers or transfers of funds, expenditure records, information related to tender offer procedures and contracts, sworn statements of public officials to observe their asset growth, among others.[31]

Publicity given to acts of government can be referenced in the so-called *e-government:* it is sought that as much information as possible which is searched on the Internet about government measures, is found on the web, without requiring the person's identification, who is surfing the Internet, to be able to have access to it for we find ourselves before a parallel of situations when information about a more precise question is requested before a specific body.

In this respect, it is useful to highlight that recent Argentinian legislation, Law 26856/2013, has established the publication of judicial rulings by the National Supreme Court of Justice and Courts of Appeal which make up the Judiciary Power of the Nation having to publish all the conventions of judges and their resolutions entirely once they have been notified to all the parties, through a judiciary Journal in digital format which is accessible to the public, free of charge, through the Internet webpage of the National Supreme Court of Justice, safeguarding the right to privacy, dignity and honor of individuals, especially workers' rights, as well as teenagers and children's rights.

Therefore, in our view, it would not even be appropriate to ask for the petitioner's identification because the right to access to information does not require essential formalities and, in this way, it complies with the objective of making government acts more transparent at the federal level, by getting to know the documents that they have. As for legal standing, we find that in some systems all branches of government are included, such is the case of Argentina, Mexico and Brazil, and the discussion is focused on whether it reaches businesses and corporations in which the State has a stake and/or state concessionaires and license holders, as well as those entities which have been granted public funds.[32]

It is worth noticing that in Brazil, in a case in which the Bank of Brazil[33] was involved, regarding a petition made by an ex-employee who requested access to the

[31]The Argentinian Law 27275/2016 establishes in its Article 29 an interjurisdictional body, the Federal Council for Transparency (*Consejo Federal para la Transparencia*), which will have as objective technical cooperation and an agreement on policies on transparency and access to public information.

[32]Cf. National Supreme Court of Justice, Argentina (Corte Suprema de Justicia de La Nación Argentina) which obliges a company, whose shares are in power of the State to deliver information on a contract signed with a private individual. National Supreme Court of Justice, Argentina (Corte Suprema de Justicia de la Nación Argentina), *Giustiniani, Rubén Héctor v/ YPF S.A. on legal protection proceedings for default (amparo por mora),* -CSJN-10/11/2.015 (Judgment of 10 November 2015). The Argentinian Law 27275/2016, in its Article 7 makes an extensive application of who is obliged to provide information ("obliged subjects").

[33]Recourse 99901.000091/2012-39 (*Banco do Brasil S.A.*). Available at: http://www.acessoainformacao.gov.br/precedentes/BB/99901000091201239.pdf, and p. 74 et seq. in: http://

whole information, public or not, with reference to the act which led to his dismissal and in which that access was denied on the grounds that the petition was outside the scope of the Access to Information Law and that there was no regulation from the National Securities and Exchange Commission—the agency that regulates the disclosure of information on the part of the private corporation which takes part in the negotiation—which compels the bank to disclose the requested information, the recourse was received by the Minister of the Union Audit Office, stating that the disclosure requirement is already provided in the Access to Information Law and that the rules and regulations of the National Securities and Exchange Commission were not applicable to the case because the bank did not prove that it was acting with a private interest. Further, on the contrary, the Union Court of Audit,[34] when evaluating the dispute between the Passarelli-Gel Consortium against Petrobras, which intended access to costs spreadsheets of modernization work of President Getúlio Vargas Refinery, in Parana, based on the Access to Information Law, the Union Court of Audit stated that the Access to Information Law has mechanisms which have as objective to keep adequate reservations on information considered strategic because it can influence on their business or market interests.

The Argentinian National Supreme Court of Justice has stated that information is the oxygen of democracy and that it promotes transparency and accountability so the request against any type of public entity is appropriate.[35]

The general principle, in relation to legal standing, will be that it can be applied to private organizations as long as they are linked to the public realm, such is the case of private legal entities which receive funds, subsidies or input coming from the public sector, or which have been granted the supply of a public service or the management of public property (Article 7 of Law 27275/2016 on its scope of application).

---

www.acessoainformacao.gov.br/assuntos/recursos/recursos-julgados-a-cmri/decisoes/2012-1/18.pdf (Accessed on 15 May 2017).

[34]Brazilian Court of Audit, C 009.831/2010-0 (Judgment of 20 March 2013).

[35]Civil Rights Association cl EN – PAMI – (Decree No.1172/03), *Amparo* Law 16986 of 4 December 2012 (The *writ of amparo* is a remedy for the protection of constitutional rights). There, it was stated: "(14) Whereas in the same sense, it is worth mentioning that Information has been described "democracy's oxygen", whose importance can be seen at different levels. Fundamentally, democracy consists of the ability of individuals to participate effectively in the decision-making processes that affect them. This participation depends on the information which is available." In addition, it is worth remembering that "In view of the above [...] the importance of the existence of a clear, complete and consistent legal system is implied, which sets forth the guidelines of the right to access to information so that measures which guarantee its exercise are taken. Access to information promotes accountability and transparency within the State and allows having a solid and well-informed public debate. In this way, an appropriate legal system of access to information allows people to play an active role in the government, necessary condition for keeping a healthy democracy" (see point 9, "Relationship between the right to access to information in the power of the State and the right to political participation", stated in Article 23 of the American Convention on Human Rights CIDH, paragraphs 138 and 140 of the Special Study [. . .])."

Conversely, it appears that private individuals, in principle, are not obliged to provide information produced by them, unless a Law explicitly determines this; such is the case of a company that has a data bank to issue reports.

## 2.6 *The Cost of Information*

Information to be provided has to be free of charge. That is because it is considered that it is a duty of the State to provide it as the right to information constitutes a way of control and cooperation of the private individual with the State.

In the Argentinian case, Article 6 of Argentinian Law 27275/2016 incorporates the principle of gratuity as long as its reproduction is not required.[36] Article 3 of Law 25831/2004 states that access to environmental information will be free and gratuitous for every private individual or legal entity, with the exception of those expenses linked to the resources used for the delivery of the requested information.

In the Mexican case, the General Law states in Sections 17, 41 and 134 that the cost of reproduction will be charged to private individuals, and when the delivery does not imply over twenty simple sheets of paper it will be free of charge, or, considering the socio-economic circumstances of the petitioner, he could be exempted from paying its reproduction and delivery. Further, if there is lack of response from the obliged party, within the prescribed time, and in case access is admissible, the costs of reproduction, as well as delivery will be imposed on the obliged party. Similarly, the Brazilian Law N° 12.527 transfers the cost of reproduction to the petitioner, with the restriction that the material will be delivered within 10 days after the payment has been made. In Brazil, the service of search of information is free, except in the case there is a need to have a physical reproduction of the documents by the body or public entity. In this case, only the necessary amount for the reimbursement of the cost of services and materials used will be charged. However, even in this latter case, if it is proved that the person cannot afford the expenses of reproduction of information, it will be solved in accordance with the Brazilian Law 7115 of 29 August 1983.[37]

The principle of freedom from costs is based on the principles that govern administrative procedure as charging the request of information with a fee means hindering or preventing its exercise. However, every rule has its exception and, in some legal systems, it is expressly provided not to put a burden on the public purse regarding the expenses that are necessary to obtain and deliver information.

Accordingly, a distinction must be made regarding the cost of material used to provide information (e.g., photocopies) and the cost of man-hours which have to be spent to meet the request. We consider that labor cost cannot be charged to the private individual because all the inhabitants through tax payment pay the civil

---

[36]See also Article 1 principle 9 of Law 27275/2016.

[37]http://www.planalto.gov.br/ccivil_03/LEIS/L7115.htm (Accessed on 30 March 2016).

servant's salary and if it were attempted to charge the petitioner for this cost, there would be unequal treatment and therefore, it will affect the principle of equality in relation to public burdens.[38]

## 2.7 *Restriction on Access to Information*

The International Covenant on Civil and Political Rights in its Article 19 and the American Convention on Human Rights, (Article 13) set limits on information collection, although the American Convention is more restrictive in setting such limits as Article 13.3, prohibits restrictions by "indirect methods or means [...] tending to impede the communication and circulation of ideas and opinions."[39] A rule of this type is neither found in the European Convention nor in the Covenant. To this, it is worth adding that, according to Article 29 of the American Convention, the right protected in it cannot be interpreted in a more restrictive way.

So it has been stated that "If the Convention itself sets forth that its regulations do not have a restrictive effect on other international instruments, restrictions imposed on those other instruments but not in the Convention, cannot be brought to limit the exercise of the rights and freedoms that it acknowledges."[40] Article 13.2 of the Convention states that "The exercise of the right provided for in the foregoing paragraph shall not be subject to prior censorship but shall be subject to subsequent imposition of liability, which shall be expressly established by law to the extent necessary to ensure: a). respect for the rights or reputations of others; or b). the protection of national security, public order, or public health or morals."

Indeed, in the first place, prohibition on censorship is established, but the Law has to ensure respect and protection of rights and the protection of national security, public order or public health or morals.

Although these latter concepts are indeterminate, they can be determined based on the control of proportionality which can be exercised over them. It is sought that the right to information is not considered an absolute one and that this exercise is not conditional on arbitrariness by the State powers.

Exceptions to the duty to provide information refer to, in the first place, e.g., the classification of it as reserved, secret or confidential on the grounds of security, defense or foreign policy[41]; in the case, information which is not affected by these

---

[38] Aberastury and Cilurzo 1998, p. 39.

[39] Cf. I/A Court H. R., *Case of Claude Reyes, et al. v. Chile* (Judgment of 19 September 2006), Series C No. 151.

[40] García Ramírez and Gonza 2007, p. 22.

[41] Cf. the exhaustive list of "exceptions" in Article 8 of Law 28275/2016; previously: Sec. 17 of the Decree 1172/2003.

exceptions must be provided.[42] Further, when by an explicit law, information is considered reserved, as in the case of information in financial entities or tax information, as it is considered sensitive data of the private individual or that if affects the right to privacy.

The total or partial denial to access to information will have to be on reasonable grounds, that is to say, must be adequately reasoned and, in case of administrative authority, comply with the requirements of reasonableness of an act performed by a governmental authority stated by the laws of the corresponding jurisdictions. Although the characterization of this type of information depends on the discretionary power of the Administration, in accordance with a previous Law that empowers it,[43] this does not mean that the denial to provide information cannot be controlled judicially and, in that case, the Judge will have to decide according to a criterion of reasonableness whether he has to release the information or not, which is explicitly stated in the Argentinian, Mexican and Venezuelan systems. To do this, it will be necessary for the Administration to allow the judge to have access to the documentation whose delivery has been denied. Besides, it has to be added that law must regulate the judicial control of the denial on the part of the Administration. The rules, which impose the duty of confidentiality or secret, are numerous, such as the secret of financial transactions or information collected by tax revenues entities, as well as the regulations that impose the duty of secret on the grounds of State security.

Consequently, the denial of the right of access to information must be done by an express act performed by a governmental authority and as long as it is an act that displays the Administration's discretion, it is required that this act is duly reasoned and substantiated unless there is implied rejection or administrative silence and the private individual will have the right to appeal because of the omission of issuing an express act restricting or denying the request.

In the case of *Claude Reyes*,[44] the I/A Court H. R. stated that "(88) The right of access to information under the State control admits restrictions. This Court has already ruled, in other cases, about the restriction that can be imposed on the exercise of the right of freedom of thought and expression"[45] as long as these restrictions are stated by Law as a means of ensuring that it is not left to the discretion of public authorities, apart from the fact that these restrictions adjust to the Convention's restrictions and are compatible with a democratic society. Thus,

[42] Cf. Article 1 principle 12 of Law 28275/2016: "[. . .] the limits on the right of access to official information must be exceptional, established in advance as stipulated in this law, and formulated clearly and precisely [...]".

[43] Cf. also Sec. 29 of the German Law of administrative procedure regarding "inspection of records by participants"; cf. Aberastury & Blanke 2012.

[44] I/A Court H. R., *Case of Claude-Reyes, et al. v. Chile* (Judgment of 19 September 2006), Series C No. 151.

[45] Cf. I/A Court H. R., *Palamara Iribarne Case (Judgment of 22 November 2005)*, para 85; *Case of Ricardo Canese* (Judgment of 31 August 2004), para 96; *Case of Herrera Ulloa* (Judgment of 2 July 2004), para 121 and 123; Advisory Opinion OC-5/85, para 46.

in paragraph 91, it finishes stating that "That is to say, the restriction has to be proportional to the interest that justifies and has to be conducive to reach the achievement of that legitimate objective, interfering as least as possible in the effective exercise of this right."[46]

Another aspect to consider is the prohibition of censorship but this prohibition, which protects freedom of expression and is set up in Article 13 of the Convention, does not mean that it is exempted from a subsequent reproach. A paradigmatic case is the decision reached by the I/A Court H. R. in the case "The Last Temptation of Christ. Olmedo Bustos and Others v. Chile."[47]

In the Separate Opinion of Antônio Augusto Cançado Trindade it was said: "The case "The Last Temptation of Christ", which the Inter-American Court comes to decide in the present Sentence on the substance, is truly a landmark case, not only because of being the first case on freedom of thought and expression solved by the Court, in the first work session which takes place in the twenty-first century, but also—and above all—because of having an impact on an issue which is common to so many Latin American and Caribbean countries, and that reaches the legal foundations of the Law of International Responsibility of the State and the very origin of that responsibility."

## 2.8 *Deadlines for Provision of Information*

Generally, in the countries where the right to information has been regulated, delivery times are brief.

The Argentinian Law 27275/2016 sets forth the duty to provide information within 15 days which can be extended for 15 days more.[48] The Argentinian Law

[46]Cf. I/A Court H. R., *Palamara Iribarne Case (Judgment of 22 November 2005)*, para 85; *Case of Ricardo Canese* (Judgment of 31 August 2004), para 96; *Case of Herrera Ulloa* (Judgment of 2 July 2004), para 121 and 123; Advisory Opinion OC-5/85, para 46.

[47]I/A Court H. R., *Case of The Last Temptation of Christ. Olmedo Bustos and Others v. Chile* (Judgment of 5 February 2001). There it was held: "(64) With regard to the content of the right to freedom of thought and expression, those who are protected by the Convention not only have the right and the freedom to express their own thoughts, but also the right and freedom to seek, receive and impart information and ideas of all kinds. Consequently, freedom of expression has an individual and a social dimension: It requires, on the one hand, that no one be arbitrarily limited or impeded in expressing his own thoughts. In that sense, it is a right that belongs to each individual. Its second aspect, on the other hand, implies a collective right to receive any information whatsoever and to have access to the thoughts expressed by others [. . .] 66 [. . .] For the ordinary citizen, the knowledge of other people's opinions and information is as important as the right to impart their own. 67. The Court considers that both dimensions are of equal importance and should be guaranteed simultaneously in order to give total effect to the right to freedom of thought and expression in the terms of Article 13 of the Convention [...] 68. As the cornerstone of a democratic society, freedom of expression is an essential condition for society to be sufficiently informed."

[48]Article 11 of the Argentinian Law 27275/2016.

No. 25831/2004 states a deadline of 30 days to provide environmental information (Article 8).[49]

The Brazilian Law N° 12.527 sets forth a time limit of 20 days to inform the date, place and manner of obtaining information or the reasons why access has been denied (Article 11 para 1). If the answer is negative, it has to be informed within the same time limit by grounded decision informing about the procedural remedies to appeal it (Article 11 para 4).

In case of denial of access to information classified as confidential, the reasons for denial will have to be grounded indicating its substratum, its legal basis, and the classification code of the confidential document. Further, it will have to be made clear to the applicant, the possibility of filing a request for declassification of the information.

Similarly, the General Mexican Law states in Article 132 that the "response to the request shall be notified to the person concerned in the shortest possible time, not exceeding twenty days, counting from the day following the submission of the request." And, exceptionally, this "term may be extended for ten more days, provided there are reasonable grounds, which must be approved by the Transparency Committee, by issuing a decision to be notified to the applicant before its expiration". In all these cases, the possibility of extending the time limit is given but as an exceptional instance.

Finally, it is worth mentioning that EU Directive 2003/4/CE established a time limit of a month or two months according to the volume and complexity of the information (Article 3.2 points a and b).

## 3 Legal Protection of the Right to Information

### *3.1 Procedural Remedies*

It has been claimed that the statement to enshrine a right is totally insufficient if there is not a guarantee that allows its recognition or defense. More precisely, the

[49]As an example of what we have stated, we can refer to the different Acts in force in the Argentinian provincial system. In relation to this, Law No. 12475 of the Province of Buenos Aires can be mentioned, which stipulates that after 30 business days without the Authority having issued an answer, the request will be considered rejected. Law No. 104 of the Autonomous City of Buenos Aires, Law No. 8,803 of the Province of Cordoba, Law No. 3764 from Chubut, Decree No. 1169/2005 of the Province of Entre Rios, Law No. 4444 from Jujuy and Law No. 653 of Tierra del Fuego state a time limit no longer than ten (10) days for the delivery of the information requested. Law No. 6,753, from Santiago del Estero, sets forth a deadline of 20 days. Law No. 6,437, of the Province of Chaco and Decree No. 0692 of the Province of Santa Fe grant a deadline no longer than fifteen (15) business days and Law No. 4,184 of the Province of Misiones, 15 or 30 days according to the fact that the information is before the enforcement authority or a Third Party. Finally, Decree No. 1574/02 of the Province of Salta establishes a time limit no longer than thirty (30) business days.

guarantees are the legal weapons which are given to the private individual to make individual rights effective, which constitute together civil and political freedom.[50] The lack or restriction of legal actions which the private individual can start, when talking about the State, or the restrictions of the judge's powers so as to be able to provide for compliance of his decisions are two aspects which restrict the guarantees and the right protected by them. The right to effective judicial protection, which is realized as long as a quick and effective access to justice is regulated, that is to say, to the extent that there is an impartial and independent judge who can intervene towards the resolution of the case.

As for the American Convention of Human Rights, the right to effective judicial protection finds grounds, mainly, in Articles 8.1 and 25.1, being considered a "substantive" right, which has to be exercised and dealt with effectively. It is worth mentioning that the Commission has comprised, within the rights enshrined in the Convention, the right to a fair, quick and due process, which gives the possibility but never the guarantee of a favorable result.[51]

Access to justice, when it has to do with suing the State, is governed, currently, by the principles which arise from the Convention and the enforcement by State agents or officials of a Law which is manifestly in violation of the Convention, results in the State's international liability[52] as the principles of administrative procedure have to protect access to justice in such a way that formal impediments which hinder it, do not arise.

The Inter-American Convention on Human Rights has claimed that "the principle of effective judicial protection can be translated into the guarantee of free access to courts for the defense of rights and interests against public power, even when ordinary legality has not recognized a remedy or concrete action. This principle implies, logically, a set of elementary guarantees on the filing of judicial processes. However, it can happen that uncertainty or lack of clarity to enshrine these admissibility requirements can constitute a violation of that fundamental right."[53]

Moreover, the Inter-American Convention on Human Rights has stated, on various occasions, that every State Party to the Convention "has to take all measures so that what is established in the Convention is effectively enforced within its domestic legal system, as Article 2 of the Convention states.[54] The duty included in this provision of the Convention recognizes a customary law which prescribes that,

---

[50]Sanchez Viamonte 1957, p. 137.

[51]I/A Court H. R. Commission Report N° 39/96, Case 11,673, of 15 October 1996.

[52]Inter American Court of Human Rights Advisory Opinion OC -14/94 of 9 December, 1994, Court I.D.H. (SER.A) N° 14.

[53]Cfr. para 57 and 58 in re: Inter American Commission of Human Rights, 1999/09/29, Report 105/99, Case 10.194: Palacios, Narciso v. Argentina; cfr Botassi 2000.

[54]Cfr. Case "The Last Temptation of Christ" (Olmedo Bustos and others) v. Chile. Merits, Reparations and Costs, Sentence of 5 February 2001. Series C Number 73, paragraph. 87; Case La Cantuta v. Peru. Merits, Reparations and Costs, Sentence of 29 November 2006, Series C Number 162. (171); and Case Zambrano Vélez and others, Reparations and Costs, Sentence of 4 July 2007 para 79.

when a State has entered an international agreement, it has to introduce in its domestic law all the necessary changes to ensure the enforcement of the international obligations assumed.[55]

The Organization of American States (OAS) has stressed the importance of access to public information and the need of its protection. Indeed, through the Resolution of 3 June 2006, the OAS General Assembly "urged States to respect and make others respect access to public information to all people and to encourage the adoption of legislative provisions or of another type which are necessary to ensure their recognition and effective application."

In the aforementioned case of *Claude Reyes, et al. v. Chile*, the I/A Court H.R. stated: "137. When State-held information is refused, the State must guarantee that there is a simple, prompt and effective recourse that permits determining whether there has been a violation of the right of the person requesting information and, if applicable, that the corresponding body is ordered to disclose the information. In this context, the recourse must be simple and prompt, bearing in mind that, in this regard, promptness in the disclosure of the information is essential. According to the provisions of Articles 2 and 25(2) point (b) of the Convention, if the State Party to the Convention does not have a judicial recourse to protect the right effectively, it must establish one."

Books of authority have interpreted that an act or an omission can have positive or negative facts,[56] and comprise administrative facts and all those conducts, which have the ability to affect private individuals' rights including administrative silence.[57] In consequence, if there is a lack of an express remedy for protection, other procedural remedies can be used to obtain its recognition and, to be effective, they will have to be restricted proceedings to decide a legal issue.

Regarding this, regarding Argentina, Brazil and Mexico, the need of a reasoned decision in case of a denial of the request to access to information is stated and different procedural remedies are regulated, which will be examined below but administrative silence or implied rejection of the request also plays a role to resort to law or court proceedings for protection.

## 3.2 Procedural Remedies in Argentina

The Argentinian Law 27275/2016 has established the Agency of Access to Public Information as a governmental entity which is permitted to act independently and which will work with a functional autonomy in the scope of the national Executive

[55]Cfr. Case Garrido and Baigorria v. Argentina. Reparations and Costs. Sentence of 27 August 1998. Series C No. 39, par. 68; Case La Cantuta, par. 170; and *Case Zambrano Vélez, et al.*, Sentence of 4 July 2007 para 55.

[56]Bidart Campos 1968, p. 227.

[57]Lazzarini 1987, p. 157; Sagües 1979, p. 73; Rivas 1990, p. 119.

Power (Articles 19 et seqq.). Further, in each of the other branches of government and constitutional bodies an agency with similar jurisdiction has to be created (Article 28).

In Brazil and Mexico, a body with sufficient jurisdiction to review the denial to provide the requested information has been set up irrespective of its judicial review. The delay or denial of access to the right to information is reviewed in the administrative field through official channels, enabling the exhaustion of administrative remedies so that later, this denial can be reviewed by an independent court of justice.

The Argentinian Law 27275/2016 requires a reasoned decision to deny a request for information and in case it has not been satisfied or if the answer to the request has been ambiguous, partial or inaccurate, it will be considered as an unjustified denial to provide the information. That Law prescribes that, in the light of this refusal, there is a legal recourse to a court of justice directly through a legal action, i.e., the "writ of amparo" which is a prompt and summary proceeding regarding the protection of constitutional rights, to challenge the denial.[58] A complaint can also be filed with the Agency of Access to Public Information (*Consejo Federal para la Transparencia*).[59]

Case-law has considered the legal action stipulated in Article 43 of the national Constitution and Law No. 16986/1966 admissible as the relevant legal action (*amparo*) is regulated there. This action, which is admissible "against any act or omission of public authorities or individuals which currently or imminently may damage, limit, modify or threaten rights, with open arbitrariness or illegality", was created by judicial decision in the case "Siri"[60] and in the case "Kot",[61] and

[58] It can be said that in the Case "AGN v/ SIGEN", held by the Chamber II of the National Court of Appeal on Federal Contentious Administrative matters on 12 April 2011, a legal proceeding for the protection of constitutional rights (*amparo* action), was substantiated for the delay of the negative decision from SIGEN (*Sindicatura General de Empresas Publicas* – General Auditing Office for Public Enterprises) to deliver a documentation which was referred to 2009 and requested in March 2010. In the Case Morales, Gerardo Rubén and other v. National State – Ministry of Economy, National Court of Appeal on Federal Contentious Administrative matters, Chamber V of 18 October 2007, where it was recognized legislators' legal standing, applying what was prescribed in Decree 1172/2003, admitting the *amparo* action for delay submitted to obtain information related to wrongdoings allegedly committed in the proceedings of payment requests of a debt claimed by the National State (Greco affair).

[59] Article 14 of Law 27275/2016 states on "complaint procedures": "Rulings on access to official information may be appealed directly to the courts of first instance in the federal administrative law section, without prejudice to option of filing an administrative compliant with the Agency of Access to Official Information or the corresponding body, depending on the party that has standing to be sued. [. . .]". Regarding the "complaint for violation" the Argentinian legislators have established the following: "In the case justifying denial of a request for information under Article 13 of the present law or any other violation of the present law, the applicant may, within forty (40) working days after the expiry of the time limit for the response [. . .] under the present law, file a complaint with the Agency of Access to Public Information or, at the applicant's option, with the organization to which the request was originally made." (Article 15 of Law 27275/2016).

[60] National Supreme Court of Justice, Cases 239:459.

[61] National Supreme Court of Justice of Argentina, Arguments Cases 241:291.

incorporated legislatively in Article 1 of Law No. 16.986, against the Administration and in Article 321 of the Code of Civil and Commercial Procedure regarding the act of private individuals[62] with similar drafting in relation to the cases of admissibility, where fast summary proceedings have been prescribed.

In addition to this, the *habeas data* action has been used to have information provided regarding the fate of missing people or in relation to children born in captivity, events which happened during the dictatorship that ended in 1983, according to the right to know the truth, which was incorporated by our national Supreme Court of Justice.[63] Besides, it has recognized the use of the regular process, if there is a lack of an express rule, which regulates the issue for the other branches of government (legislature and judiciary).

Hence, we can infer that the remedy of "amparo", stated in Article 43 of the Argentinian Constitution, is the most suitable action to challenge the denial of information as it is a fast summary proceeding and as such, it meets the conditions—fast and effective route—provided in Article 25 of the Convention ("simple and prompt recourse") irrespective of the existence of other procedural remedies which are found in the procedural rules which meet the requirements of promptness and effectiveness.[64]

## 3.3 Procedural Remedies in Brazil

In Brazil, with the enactment of the Access to Information Law, the denial to its access is protected, as the Administration has to inform the petitioner, in the same time limit of answer, the reasons for the denial with the duly legal ground. In that case, there are four appellate instances, being the last instance the Joint Committee of Revaluation of Information, a body made up of ten ministers of State which has as the objective to review classification, extension and recourses on the requests of declassification of information in appeals which are secret and top secret, and decide against decisions of the third instance of the Union Audit Office regarding

---

[62] Aberastury & Gottschau 2001.

[63] The claim of the plaintiff – aimed at having access to data recorded in State, military or civil files, from which it could be found out what the fate of his brother who was missing during painful circumstances which occurred in the country – must not be appreciated within the specific legal framework of an informative legal protection proceeding – *habeas data*–, but within the legal protection proceeding (amparo) in general (from Judges Belluscio and López's Opinion). National Supreme Court of Justice, Argentina (Corte Suprema de Justicia de la Nación Argentina), case of *Urteaga, Facundo R. v Joint Staff of the Armed Forces* (Judgment of 15 October 1998).

[64] Cf. regarding the use of the legal protection proceedings for delay (*amparo por mora*) cf. the Case *Giustiniani, Rubén Héctor v YPF. S.A.*, which compelled the defendant to provide information about an oil contract, signed by the defendant, by making reference to case-law of the I/A Court H.R; National Supreme Court of Justice, Argentina (Corte Suprema de Justicia de la Nación Argentina),*Giustiniani, Rubén Héctor v/ YPF S.A.* on legal protection proceedings for default *(amparo por mora),* 10/11/2.015 (Judgment of 10 November 2015).

the requests of access to information. It is not necessary; however, the exhaustion of administrative procedures to recourse to the legal route because it is a unique jurisdiction, according to what Article 5, item 35 of the Brazilian Constitution[65] prescribes.

The full Federal Supreme Tribunal, in sentence *Suspensão de Segurança SS 3902 AgR-segundo/SP*, confirmed the President's decision about the fact that several sentences from domestic courts do not allow the disclosure of information of public officials including their remuneration on the official electronic site. In the understanding that the information had collective or general interest and, therefore, disclosure had to prevail over the protection of privacy of these agents for the only reason of having chosen a state career in a Republican State. In the scope of the Legislative Power, Judiciary Power and of the Prosecution Authorities, the proceedings of revision of a negative decision ruled in an appeal to a higher authority stated in Article 15 of Law N°12.527/2011 on Access to Information, will have to be ruled by the regulation adopted by each of these organs. Nevertheless, there is a duty to inform by the Judiciary Power and the Prosecution Authorities about negative decisions to the National Justice Council and to the National Prosecution Authorities Council, respectively.

Finally, the alternative rules prescribed by Law No. 9784/99 are applied. They regulate the administrative procedure in the Federal Public Administration, the appellate procedure included in the Access to Information Law. Nonetheless, the legal action brought for the protection of a constitutional right has been considered applicable (*mandato de segurança*).

### 3.4 Procedural Remedies in Mexico

We must stress that Mexico has regulated the right to information at the beginning through the Federal Law on Transparency and Access to Governmental Public Information at a federal level (2002), and now with the General Law on Transparency and Access to Public Information (2016)[66] at a nationwide level, setting forth with this, the basis that both federal and local legislation have to follow in this area. In this way, the procedures stipulated before the bodies that act as guarantors, which are autonomous, specialized, independent, unbiased and collegiate, with legal personality and their own budgets, with full technical and management autonomy, responsible for guaranteeing, within their jurisdiction, the exercise of the rights to access to information and personal data protection. Their formation will be in an

[65]"[...] the law shall not exclude any injury or threat to a right from the consideration of the Judicial Power".

[66]Argentinian Law 27275 was modified by decree 746/2017 and regulated by decree 206/2017. http://servicios.infoleg.gob.ar/infolegInternet/anexos/265000-269999/265949/texact.htm.

odd number and their members will be called Commissioners, whose duration in office will not be longer than 7 years and will be done in a phased manner.

In case of classification; declaration of non-existence; declaration of incompetence by the legally bound reporting party; delivery of incomplete information; delivery of information which does not correspond with what it has been requested; lack of response to a request for access to information within the time limit stated in the Law; notification, delivery or making information available in a different modality or format from the one requested; delivery or making information available in an incomprehensible or non-accessible format for the petitioner; cost and delivery times of information; lack of processing of the request; the denial to allow the direct information enquiry; lack, deficiency or insufficiency of the legal grounds and/or legal motivation in the response, and the orientation to a specific procedure, the petitioner will be able to seek judicial review before the corresponding guarantor body, within the time limit of 15 days.[67] This legal action will have to solve in a time limit which will not be longer than 40 days, as from its admission and will be able to be extended only once and up to a period of 20 days to dismiss or suspend the complaint, or to confirm, revoke or modify the response to the legally bound reporting party. In addition to this, in plenary session, the Federal Institute of Transparency, Access to Information and Personal Data Protection (Sect. 2.1), approved by the majority of its Commissioners, of its own motion or on guarantors bodies' request, that it will be able to exercise the power to deal with appeals for review which are pending of resolution because its interest and importance merit so.

Because they are resolutions to appeals for review from the guarantors bodies of federal entities, private individuals will be able to choose to resort through a disagreement appeal before the Federal Institute of Transparency, Access to Information and Personal Data Protection, or before the Judiciary Power of the Federation. The disagreement appeal will have to be filed within 15 days after having known of the resolution or the deadline for its resolution has expired, and will be solved in a time limit that will not exceed 30 days. This deadline can be extended only once and up to the same period.

Against the appeal for review or disagreement appeal's resolution the so-called "constitutional complaint", stipulated in Articles 103 and 107 of the Mexican Constitution. To make this judicial remedy applicable it is necessary to exhaust the legal procedure through the aforementioned appeal for review, although recent case-law has moderated this "principle of finality" in the cases in which the authority to whom the information is requested does not reply. To do this, the violation of the right to petition must be alleged and not the violation of the right to access to information because, in this case, as the appeal for review is regulated, it has to be exhausted previously within the legal proceedings brought for the protection of constitutional rights (*amparo*).

[67] According to Sec. 126 of the General Law on Transparency and Access to Public Information, the time limits of all notices stated in this Law, shall run from the day after they have been served, and when the deadlines are stipulated in days, they shall be considered business days.

Therefore, once the appeal for review has been resolved by the guarantor bodies, it will be appropriate to file before the judicial courts the indirect legal proceedings enshrined in Sec. 107 of the Mexican Protection Law derived from law resolutions ("Amparo Law"), based on what is set forth in point II of that regulation, and against that, the appeal for review before a court, prescribed in Sec. 81 of the aforementioned Law, which can be filed before the Circuit Collegiate Courts or before the National Supreme Court of Justice, depending on the case.

## 4 Conclusions

The right to information and, more precisely, the right to access to public information constitutes a scope of freedom which the citizen can and must exercise and its restriction has to be done reasonably so as not to affect the right of other persons and/or their scope of confidentiality.

Within this context, the right to access to public information is the general rule and its restriction is the exception. As for its restriction, it can only be set forth by substantive and formal Law and as long as the principle of confidentiality is respected.

The I/A Court H.R. has considered as a violation to fundamental rights the impossibility of access to justice[68] as the private individual not only has the right to an effective recourse but also because the public authorities have to issue the necessary measures to make effective the rights in accordance with the guarantees set forth in the American Convention of Human Rights.[69] Hence, it is a duty of the States Parties to adopt all the internal law provisions to implement the rights and freedoms established by the Convention, i.e., Articles 1 and 2 of the Convention which have to be interpreted pursuant to Articles 8.1 and 8.25. These guarantees have been interpreted by extending them to all the rights protected by the Convention, following the precedent *Baena*,[70] of the case-law of the I/A Court H.R.[71]

The criterion which was established in the aforementioned case "Baena Ricardo and others v. Panamá", regarding the fact that the set of minimum guarantees stated in 8.2 of the Convention is applicable to the commands mentioned in para 1 of the same Article, reveals the wide scope of due process, not only in criminal matters but

[68]See Separate Opinion of Judge Antonio Cançado Trindade in the Dismissed Congress Workers' Case of *Aguado Alfaro and others v Peru* (Judgment of 24 November 2006), Preliminary Objections, Merits, Reparations and Costs, Series C Number. 158, paragraph 11 and subsequent ones. Quote from Case of *Goiburú and Others v Paraguay* (Judgment of 22 September 2006).

[69]Series on Treaties, Organization of American States (OAS) Number 36,1144, Series on Treaties United Nations Organization (UN), 123 entry in force on 18 July 1978, re printed in Basic Documents Concerning Human Rights in the Inter-American System, OAS/Ser.L.V/II.82 doc.6. rev.1 p. 25 (1992).

[70]Sentence of 2 February 2001 Series C 72.

[71]Aberastury and Gottschau 2001, p. 90.

also in all other areas."[72] The same is pointed out in the case *Ivcher Bronstein v. Peru*, paragraphs 103 and 104, as well as in the case "Almonacid Arellano"[73] where the Court has observed: "The Court is conscious that judges and internal courts are subject to the rule of law and, because of that, they are obliged to apply the enforceable regulations in the national legal system. However, when the State has ratified an international treaty such as the American Convention, its judges, as parts of the State framework, are also subjected to it, which obliges them to ensure that the Convention's effects are not diminished by applying national legislation which is contrary to the object and purpose of the Convention and that such action lacks legal effects from the very beginning. Simply put, the Judiciary Power has to consider not only the treaty, but also the interpretation that the I/A Court H.R. has made of it, as it is the ultimate interpreter of the American Convention."

Finally, being the right to information a fundamental right, the States Parties have to receive those actions which are of the type of summary proceedings to protect a right promptly and effectively. For this purpose, the Judiciary Power, even through case-law, has to consider the rapid adoption of interim measures designed to remedy any alleged infringement of the fundamental right to access to information admissible. In Brazilian Law, as well as Argentinian and Mexican case-law, it has to be noted that judges have followed these rules and there is no opposing view regarding the fact that the right to information is a fundamental right.

## References

Aberastury, P., & Blanke, H.-J. (Eds.). (2012). *Tendencias Actuales del Procedimiento Administrativo en Latinoamérica y Europa*. Buenos Aires, Argentina: Eudeba.

Aberastury, P., & Cilurzo, M. R. (1998). *Curso de procedimiento administrativo*. Buenos Aires, Argentina: Abeledo Perrot.

Aberastury, P., & Gottschau, E. P. (2001). *Derecho a la Recopilación de Datos*, en Poder Político y Libertad de Expresión. Buenos Aires, Argentina: Sociedad Científica Argentina–Instituto de Ciencia Política y Constitucional: Abeledo Perrot.

Altmark, D. R., & Molina Quiroga, E. (1996). Hábeas data. *Revista La Ley*, 1996-A-1565.

Bidart Campos, G. (1968). *Régimen Legal y Jurisprudencial del Amparo*. Buenos Aires, Argentina: Ediar.

Bidart Campos, G. (1996). *Tratado Elemental de Derecho constitucional Argentino*. Buenos Aires, Argentina: Ediar.

Botassi, C. (2000). Comentario al caso Palacios, Narciso c/Argentina. *Revista La Ley, del 11/12/2000.*

Casal, J. M. (2010). *Los Derechos Fundamentales y sus Restricciones*. Venezuela: Legis.

García de Enterría, E., & Fernández, T. R. (1983). *Curso de Derecho Administrativo*. Madrid, Spain: Civitas.

García Ramírez, S., & Gonza, A. (2007). *La libertad de expresión en la Jurisprudencia de la Corte Interamericana de Derechos Humanos*. México: Corte Interamericana de Derechos Humanos.

[72]Sentence of 2 February 2001 Series C 72.

[73]*Almonacid Arellano and others v Chile*, Judgment of 26 September 2006.

Lazzarini, J. L. (1987). *El juicio de Amparo*. Buenos Aires, Argentina: La Ley.
López-Ayllon, S. (2002). Derechos fundamentales y acceso a la información pública: los desafíos de una legislación necesaria. In M. Carbonell (Ed.), *Derechos Fundamentales y Estado, Memoria del VII Congreso Iberoamericano del Derecho Constitucional*. México: ed. Instituto de Investigaciones Jurídicas, UNAM.
Rivas, A. A. (1990). *El amparo*. Buenos Aires, Argentina: Ediciones La Rocca.
Sacristan, E. B., & Ratti Mendaña, F. S. (2012). Procedimiento Administrativo y Acceso a la Información. In H. Pozo Gowland, D. Halperin, O. Aguilar Valdez, F. J. Lima, & A. Canosa (Eds.), *Procedimiento Administrativo*. La Ley.: Buenos Aires, Argentina.
Sagües, N. P. (1979). *Ley de Amparo* (Law of "Amparo" – Legal protection proceedings). Buenos Aires, Argentina: Astrea.
Sanchez Viamonte, C. (1957). *El Constitucionalismo. Sus problemas (El orden jurídico positivo. Supremacía, defensa y vigencia de la Constitución)*. Buenos Aires, Argentina: Ed. Bibliográfica Argentina.
Spielmann, D., &Drzemczewski, A. (2014). *Concurring opinion of Judge A.A. Cançado Trindade in the case of the five pensioners versus Peru (Reparations, Judgment of 28.02.2003)*. Leiden, the Netherlands: Brill.
Vallefin, C. A. (2009). *El Acceso a la información pública (Access to public information)*. Buenos Aires, Argentina: Ad Hoc.

## List of Cases

## *Inter-American Court on Human Rights*

I/A Court H. R. 19.09.2006, *Case of Claude-Reyes, et al. v. Chile*, Series C No. 151.
I/A Court H. R. 28.02.2003, *Case of Five Pensioners v Peru*.
I/A Court H. R. 05.02.2001, *Case of The Last Temptation of Christ. Olmedo Bustos and Others v Chile*.

## *Argentinian Courts*

### National Supreme Court of Justice (CSJN)

Argentinian National Supreme Court of Justice 10.11.2015, *Giustiniani, Rubén Héctor v YPF S.A. on legal protection proceedings for default (amparo por mora)*, -CSJN-10/11/2.015.
Argentinian National Supreme Court of Justice 04.12.2012, *Civil Rights Association v EN–PAMI – (Decree 1172/03) on "amparo" Law 16986*, (legal proceedings for protection of rights).

### National Court of Appeal on Federal Contentious Administrative matters

Chamber II 12.04.2011, *AGN v SIGEN*.
Chamber V 18.10.2007, *Morales, Gerardo Rubén and other v National State–Ministry of Economy*.

## *Brazilian Courts*

### Federal Supreme Court of Brazil

Federal Supreme Court of Brazil 09.06.2011, *Suspensão de Segurança SS 3902.*

### Supreme Court of Justice, Constitutional Chamber

Supreme Court of Justice, Constitutional Chamber 23.08.2000, *Ruth Carriles Méndez and others*, sentence N° 1050/00.

Supreme Court of Justice, Constitutional Chamber 14.03.2001, *INSACA*, sentence N° 332.

# Chapter 19
# The Imposition of Sanctions Concerning Access to Information

**Carla Huerta**

**Contents**



## 1 Liability and the Imposition of Sanctions

Sanctions in the area of access to information are related to liability issues, but have not been addressed by international jurisprudence because the imposition of sanctions corresponds to national authorities under the terms established in the laws in force. Nevertheless, the non-existence of a special law or specific regulation on the imposition of sanctions or liability concerning access to information does not justify inaction or pose an impediment for the State to protect this right.

The need to regulate on liability is an issue that both the Inter-American Court of Human Rights and the European Court of Human Rights hold as important. Although in principle, more stress is placed on the States' obligation to adopt regulatory measures that ensure the recognition and effective implementation of the right of access to public information.[1]

As Asdrubal Aguiar noted in his study on freedom of expression, the issue of the so-called "further liability" or "Blackstone Doctrine" has just begun to be addressed by the Inter-American Court in terms of its content and scope, with the exception of

[1]For instance, Report 60/03 of the Inter-American Commission on Human Rights refers to the obligation of providing adequate access to public information, as well as an effective legal remedy, but no mention is made to a liability and sanctions regime.

C. Huerta (✉)
National Autonomous University of Mexico, Mexico City, Mexico
e-mail: chuerta@unam.mx



H.-J. Blanke, R. Perlingeiro (eds.), *The Right of Access to Public Information*,
DOI 10.1007/978-3-662-55554-5_19

the right of correction and reply (also known as the right of reply) that helps those affected by inexact or damaging information issued to their detriment.[2]

Although the right to information is considered a fundamental right in the countries analyzed below and is regulated in their constitutions, this right is enforced in the administrative sphere.[3] Therefore, this right is generally made effective first through ordinary administrative processes although claims can also be made before a competent court. In the case of non-compliance with the resolutions issued, each country regulates the administrative liability procedures, but only the specific measures set forth in special laws on access to information will be analyzed here.

In the international sphere, the right of access to information is linked to freedom of expression. For instance, Article 19 of the 1948 UN Universal Declaration of Human Rights establishes that "[e]veryone has the right to freedom of opinion and expression; this right includes freedom to hold opinions without interference and to seek, receive and impart information and ideas through any media and regardless of frontiers."[4] The fundamental aspect of this Declaration lies in establishing the bases for the right to information along two aspects: investigating, which means performing the actions needed to identify and locate the information; and effectively receiving the information requested.

It falls to national States to guarantee this right, not only by providing the means to give access to information, but also mainly by establishing the liability of public officials and sanctions in the event of non-compliance. Therefore, in general terms, more precise development on the imposition of sanctions in cases of violations to the right of access to information is not found in decisions of an international nature.

Article 13 of the 1969 American Convention on Human Rights (Pact of San José) focuses on the freedom of thought and expression, the above-mentioned bases of the right to information.[5] The Inter-American Court of Human Rights has noted that the right to seek and receive information is substantiated during the administrative phase through a procedure carried out by the corresponding authority. Therefore, any response to a request for access to information must be duly reasoned and legally justified. The separate opinion of Judge Sergio García Ramírez points out that the obligation of its being reasoned and legally justified according to the principle of legality is a procedural guarantee that is not exclusive to court proceedings, but it also constitutes an obligation for administrative authorities.[6]

---

[2]Aguiar 2012, p. 89.

[3]Cf. Huerta 2015, p. 149–183.

[4]http://www.un.org/es/documents/udhr/ (Accessed on 26 October 2016).

[5]This Article states that: "2. The exercise of the right provided for in the foregoing paragraph shall not be subject to prior censorship but shall be subject to subsequent imposition of liability, which shall be expressly established by law to the extent necessary [...]", https://www.oas.org/dil/treaties_B-32_American_Convention_on_Human_Rights.htm (Accessed on 26 October 2016).

[6]Judgment and Separate Opinion of Judge Sergio García Ramírez regarding the judgment delivered by the Inter-American Court of Human Rights, *Claude Reyes, et al. v. Chile* (Judgment of 19 September 2006), available at http://www.corteidh.or.cr/docs/casos/articulos/seriec_151_ing.pdf (Accessed on 26 October 2016).

## 2 The Constitutional Framework of Liabilities

The right to information in Brazil is a fundamental right set forth in Article 5 of the Brazilian Constitution. In terms of the principle of equality before the law, it guarantees Brazilians and foreign residents in the country the right of access to information as provided in Sec. 33. This Section states that all persons have the right to receive from the public agencies information of their private interest, or of collective or general interest; this information must be provided within the periods established by law, under penalty of liability, except for information whose secrecy is essential to the security of the society and of the State.

The Brazilian Constitution (1988) recognizes a general right to information like the freedom to inform and be informed in Article 5, item 14, which guarantees access to information to everyone for professional activity. Article 5, item 33 is more specific on the right of access to public information while Article 5, item 72 guarantees the mechanism of *habeas data* to assure knowledge of personal information about the petitioner and to correct data.

The Mexican Constitution only stated after the amendment made to the first paragraph of Article 6 in 1977 that "[f]reedom of information shall be guaranteed by the State".[7] Thus, the Mexican State became the guarantor of freedom of information in the positive sense as an obligation to allow access to public information and to provide the requested information, as well as in the negative sense as an obligation to safeguard information that for various reasons the State is compelled to protect. The law that lays down the principles, general bases and procedures to guarantee the right of access to information is called the General Law on Transparency and Access to Public Information (General Freedom of Information Act).[8]

The addition of a second paragraph to Article 6 of the Constitution in 2007 was made to specify the form and scope of the exercise of the right of access to information, as well as the obligation of federal and state administrative bodies to allow access to information within the scope of their respective powers. These provisions were modified in 2013 to expressly state that everyone has the fundamental right to "free access to plural and timely information, and to seek, receive and impart information and ideas of any kind by any means of expression."[9]

---

[7]Decree published in the Mexican Federal Official Gazette (DOF) of 6 December 1977.

[8]The Mexican Federal Law on Transparency and Access to Governmental Public Information, published in the DOF on 11 June 2002 (Federal Freedom of Information Act), the last reform to which was published in the DOF on 14 July 2014, was replaced by a new law, the General Law on Transparency and Access to Public Information, published in the DOF on 4 May 2015, which came into force on the day after its publication. However, this law was not repealed until the new Federal Law entered into force on 10 May 2016, after its publication in the DOF on 9 May 2016. This law was last reformed on January 27, 2017.

[9]Decrees published in the DOF on 20 July 2007, and 11 June 2013, respectively. The amendment of 13 November 2007 incorporates the right of reply.

Regarding the sanctioning system, Sec. 7 of this Article, which was added in 2007, establishes that "the non-compliance with provisions concerning the access to public information shall be sanctioned in the conditions defined by the laws." While this article was later substantially reformed,[10] the mandate to legislate and the obligation to sanction any behavior that goes against access to information has not been modified, but specifically strengthened in the law.

In Argentina, the right of access to information is not a fundamental right expressly set forth in the Constitution, but it can be guaranteed as it is regulated in Human Rights Treaties. However, Articles 41 on environmental information, 42 on users and consumers and 43 third paragraph on *habeas data*—that operates as a subtype of an *amparo*—regulated by Law No. 25.326 called "Of personal data protection" along with that provided in Article 75.22 of the Constitution provide specific regulation regarding the right of access to information.[11] Meanwhile, Article 38 of the Constitution guarantees political parties access to public information and the dissemination of their ideas, but no express mention is made of a sanction and liability system for non-compliance with the obligation to give access to information.[12]

Before the recently enacted Law 27275/2016 published in the Official Bulletin and already in force, there was no specific law regulating the right of access to public information, although under Decree No. 1172/2003, Annex VII,[13] the National Executive Branch had expressly recognized the right of access to information for centralized and decentralized agencies under national administration. The aim of that law is to regulate the mechanisms that ensure citizens equal access to state information and subsequent participation in decisions on public affairs in the cases compatible with this regulation.

Regulatory framework on access to information at the federal level also includes Law No. 25831 on the right to public environmental information, Law No. 25326 on personal data protection that regulates access to information contained in databases and Law No. 19549 on administrative procedures in so far as its regulatory decree establishes the right of review of administrative acts, as well as Law No. 24240 on consumer protection that regulates the obligation to provide information.

Neither the new law nor the abovementioned laws on access to information regulate any specific sanctions or actions for authorities' non-compliance with their

[10]The latest reforms to this precept were published in the DOF on 7 February 2014, and 29 January 2016.

[11]Sagüés 2006, p. 104–106.

[12]In Argentina, the right to information was established through the Supreme Court of Justice of the Nation case-law based on freedom of expression as a right to seek information. Some of the precedents that gave rise to the establishment of this right include: CSJN, "Vago c/La Urraca", "La Ley" 1992-B-367, consid. 5°, and CSJN, Ponzetti de Balbín, *Fallos*, 306; 1892, consid. 7° as a social right to information. It has evolved considerably since then.

[13]Published in the Official Gazette on 4 December 2003.

obligations in matters of access to information, nor a specific action.[14] Therefore, as Aberastury points out, the only recourse is an *amparo*.[15] Article 9 of Law No. 25831 establishes that obstruction, misrepresentation, concealment, lack of response within the established period or an unjustified refusal to provide the requested information and any act or omission that, without just cause, affects the regular exercise of the protected right gives way to direct judicial action with summary character before the competent courts.

Venezuela does not have a law on access to information either. Therefore, the exercise of this right is set forth in the terms of the Constitution of the Bolivarian Republic of Venezuela under the articles that provide for "access to information". Article 28 establishes access to personal information that consists of public and private records, legally known as *habeas data*, but this right is exercised "[. . .] with such exceptions that may be established by law", a law that has yet to be issued. This provision also provides for the right to know "what use is being made of the same and the purpose thereof, and to petition the competent court for the updating, correction or destruction of any records that are erroneous or unlawfully affect the petitioner's right. Access to documents of any nature containing information of interest to communities or groups of persons is also warranted. The foregoing is without prejudice to the confidentiality of sources from which information is received by journalists, or secrecy in other professions as may be determined by law."[16]

Regarding the possibility of imposing a sanction to the authority that limits the right to information, only Article 58 on freedom of expression states that "Communications are free and plural, and involve the duties and responsibilities indicated by law. Everyone has the right to timely, truthful and impartial information, without censorship, in accordance with the principles of this Constitution, as well as the right to reply and correction when they are directly affected by inaccurate or offensive information" (Article 58 of the Constitution of the Bolivarian Republic of Venezuela). The right of minors to receive adequate information for their overall development was also included. However, it cannot be said that there is a special system to sanction behavior that goes against the right of access to information.

Article 143 of the Venezuelan Constitution establishes the limitations to the right of access to public information as being within "the limits acceptable in a democratic society in matters relating to internal and external security, criminal investigation and the intimacy of private life," but the law that should regulate these situations has not yet been issued. Finally, the Central Bank is subject to issuing

[14]Nevertheless, Article 1 of the Argentinian Law 27275/2016 has provided among other principles also the rule of "liability": "[. . .] the breach of the obligations which this law imposes will give rise to liability and applicable penalties." Moreover, Article 21 point (q) of this Law enshrines as one of the competences of the Agency for Access to Public Information: "To apply the relevant administrative sanctions to the competent authorities in the case of infringements of the rules of this law."

[15]Aberastury 2014, p. 705–722.

[16]Article 28 of the Constitution of the Bolivarian Republic of Venezuela.

reports that result in public accountability, but Article 319 of the Constitution, which provides for this obligation, currently lacks effectiveness.

## 3 The System Applicable in Brazil

Brazil's new Law on Access to Information was drafted according to recognized international standards for the right of access to information. It incorporates new concepts that expand the common understanding of the principle of disclosure and includes the principle of maximum transparency. It should be noted, however, that the sanctions provided in Law N° 12.527 of 18 November 2011 (Law on Access to Information) are not new to the Brazilian legal system as two other legal instruments already established sanctions in the event of failing to comply with the obligation to inform in their various aspects.

Item 72 of Article 5 of the Brazilian Constitution establishes the right of "habeas data", a constitutional remedy aimed at protecting the intimate sphere of persons; it is a procedural instrument that ensures knowledge of the information to be provided to the petitioner, which is found in government agency or public records or databases (point a), as well as allowing the correction of data (point b). Item 77 of Article 5 of the Brazilian Constitution states that " [...] habeas data proceedings [...]are free of charge". It should be noted that the Brazilian Constitution explicitly states in Article 5 para 1 that "rules defining fundamental rights and guarantees apply immediately".

Law N°12.527/2011 currently in force and regulated by Decree N°7.724 of 16 May 2012 applies to the entire Brazilian Federation. It also implements Article 5, item 33 and Article 37 para 2, item 2 (user access to administrative registries and information about governmental acts)and para 2 of Article 216 (responsibility of public administration to maintain governmental documents and take measures to make them available for consultation) of the Federal Constitution to guarantee full access to information. Article 37 para 3, item 1 establishes that "complaints relating to providing public services in general, assuring maintenance of services for attending users [...]" must be regulated by law and Article 216.2 states that the public administration is responsible for processing government documentation and authorizations to access said information for consultation to as many as may request it under the terms of the law.

Law N° 12.527 regulates the sanction system for liability in matters of access to information. As set forth in Article 32, the system of liability for authorities, whether public agents or military personnel, considers the following illicit behaviors:

I – to refuse to deliver the requested information under the terms of the law, to deliberately delay its delivery or deliver it incorrectly, incompletely or inaccurately[17];
II – to give undue use to, as well as remove, destroy, damage, misrepresent, alter or conceal information, either totally or partially, under its care or of which it has access or knowledge because of the exercise of the functions of the position, job or public service;
III – to act in bad faith or willful intent in examining the requirements for access to information;
IV – to disclose or allow the disclosure of or to access or allow undue access to confidential or personal information;
V – to impose confidentiality on the information to obtain personal gain or that of third parties, or hide an illegal act the authority or another has committed;
VI – to conceal confidential information from the examination of a higher competent authority for his own benefit or that of another, or to the detriment of third parties; and
VII – To destroy or remove, by any means, documents concerning possible human rights violations committed by State agents.

It also establishes that once the principles of the right to be heard, of defense and of due legal process have been met, the above-mentioned behaviors are under consideration to be regulated by the disciplinary measures of the Armed Forces, in the case of moderate or serious transgressions, according to the criteria established in the corresponding laws, as long as these misbehaviors are not typified as a crime or a criminal offense. Under Law No. 8.112 of 11 December 1990, and its reforms regulating the legal system for civil public servants, these behaviors can also be considered administrative offenses that must be sanctioned with, at least, suspension and not a warning as stipulated in the liability law because the information act is the special law that applies in these cases.

On the other hand, this same precept establishes that in view of the behaviors described as causing liability, military personnel or public agents can be sanctioned by temporary administrative suspension, as provided in Laws No. 1.079 of 10 April 1950, and No. 8.429 of 2 June 1992.

Article 33 stipulates that the sanctions applicable to an individual or private entity that holds information from any kind of relation with public authorities when what is set forth in this law is not observed. These sanctions are:

I – a warning;
II – a fine;
III – termination of relations with the public authority;
IV – temporary suspension from participating in public bids and impediments for entering into a contract with the public administration for a period of no longer than 2 years; and
V – a declaration of ineligibility for participation in public bids or entering into a contract with the public administration, until the authority that imposed the sanction files for the reinstatement of the entity.

The sanctions set forth in Sec. 1, 3 and 4 can be applied along with those contained in Sec. 2, as long as the interested party is guaranteed the right to defense during the corresponding proceedings within a period of 10 days. Meanwhile, the

[17]This behavior was a matter of interpretation for the Superior Court of Justice. Before the law entered into force, it was considered an act of misconduct associated with the obligation of accountability.

reinstatement referred to in Sec. 5 shall only be authorized when the interested party has compensated the agency or entity for the resulting damages and the period of the sanction applied under Sec. 4 has elapsed. This provision also establishes that the sanction provided in Sec. 5 falls within the exclusive competence of the highest authority of the public agency or entity as the one responsible for guaranteeing the right to defense of the interested party in the corresponding proceedings, within a period of 10 days as of the start of said proceedings.

According to Article 34 of this law, in cases of bad faith or willful intent, while the liability of officials is being determined, public bodies and entities shall directly answer for the damages caused by non-authorized disclosure or inappropriate use of confidential or personal information and guarantee the corresponding right of appeal. It also indicates that the provisions in this article can likewise be applied to an individual or private entity that has access to confidential or personal information through any kind of relation with public bodies or entities and give undue use to this information.

The contribution of Law N° 12.527/11 to the access to information system lies in specifically regulating the behaviors the infringement of which pose liability and the administrative sanctions for non-compliance with the duty of information. These sanctions can be applied not only to public servants, but also to individuals with a contractual relation with the public administration. The sanction that applies to public servants is suspension, first, though compounded by the public institution's financial responsibility to compensate for the damages while the official's liability is being determined.

In general terms, it can be observed that the judicial interpretation of the laws in force before the enactment of Law N° 12.157/11 shows greater concern in guaranteeing the appropriate information than it does toward the disciplinary authority of its violation. This, however, does not imply the absence of a system of sanctions as the joint application of Law No. 8.429/1992 or Law of Administrative Misconduct, which defines and sanctions behaviors associated with the obligation of providing information, must be observed.

Only two of the behaviors set forth in Article 33 hold any similarity with that set forth in Law No. 8.112, which regulates the legal system for federal government officials. These are provided in Sec. 5 of Article 116, which establishes the official's obligation to promptly attend:

a) the general public by providing the required information, except in the case of confidential information;
b) the issuance of the certificates needed for defense or for the clarification of situations of personal interest.

Administrative sanctions, however, are not specifically linked to violations of these rights. Nonetheless, according to Article 129 of the Law No. 8.112, it is possible to conclude that the initial disciplinary sanction for non-compliance of an official duty, as stated in Article 116, is a warning, except in the case of recidivism.

The disciplinary sanctions set forth in Article 127 of this law are warning, suspension, dismissal, loss of retirement pension or its availability, the removal from office and the dismissal from the commissioned office. Article 128 establishes that the application of sanctions must consider the nature and seriousness of the crime committed, the damage it causes to public service, extenuating circumstances, as well as the precedents of the public officials. It is also stated that the legal act of the imposition of the sanction must indicate the legal grounds and the cause of the disciplinary action.[18]

Regarding warnings, Article 129 of the Law No. 8.112 states that a warning should be given in writing in cases of constant violation of the prohibitions established in Article 117, Sections I to VIII and XIX, as well as in the case of any non-compliance with official duties stipulated by law, regulations or internal provisions that does not justify a more severe sanction.[19]

Meanwhile, Article 130 of the Law No. 8.112 states that an up to 90-day suspension proceeds in the case of recidivism in the sanctioned offenses and for other prohibitions that are not sanctioned with dismissal. On the other hand, a public servant who without just cause refuses to undergo the medical examination ordered by the competent authority shall be sanctioned with a 15-day suspension, which may be terminated when the requested medical examination is performed. In cases in which there is still a possibility of continuing in service, the penalty of suspension can be commuted for a fine on the basis of 50% per day of expiration or remuneration, to allow the public servant who needs to stay in service to do so.

As to the cancelation of registrations, Article 131 of the Law No. 8.112 establishes that warnings and suspensions are to be canceled after a period of 3 and 5 years of effective exercise, respectively, as long as the public servant does not commit a new disciplinary offense during this period. It also states that the cancelation will not have retroactive effects.

According to Article 132 of the Law No. 8.112, dismissal proceeds in cases of crimes against public administration, abandoning the position, frequent non-attendance, administrative misbehavior, public unruliness and scandalous behavior while in office, serious insubordination while on duty, physical damage caused while on duty to a public servant or an individual with the exception of legitimate self-defense or defense of a third party, misuse of public funds, *revealing secrets* obtained in the performance of duties, harm to public coffers and waste of national assets, corruption, illegal accumulation of offices, jobs or public offices and non-compliance with Sections 9 to 16 of Article 117.

In turn, Article 11 of the law that regulates administrative behavior (the Law of Administrative Misconduct) also regulates conducts associated with the duty of information, as well as the confidentiality of administrative information. This precept states that any action or omission that violates the obligations of honesty, impartiality, legality and loyalty to the institutions is an act of misconduct that goes against the principles of public administration, and specifically to carry out an act for a purpose prohibited by law or regulation or anything not pertaining to its

[18]This was added by Law No. 9527 of 10/12/97. That Law was consulted on 21 March 2016 at http://planalto.gov.br/ccivil_03/leis/l8112compilado.htm (Accessed on 26 October 2016).

[19]Added by Law No. 9527 of 10 December 97.

faculties; to delay or unduly cease doing any official act; to *reveal information* or circumstance that is known through the exercise of his or her functions and that should be kept confidential; to refuse disclosure of public records; to thwart the legality of a public bid; to refrain from rendering accounts when obligated to do so, as well as to disclose the content of a political or economic measure that could affect the price of basic products, a commodity or service or allow it to be known to third parties before official disclosure.

The corresponding sanctions are set forth in general terms in Article 12.3 of the Law No. 8.112. However, a judge must evaluate the magnitude of the damages to determine the sanction. Sec. 3 of this article establishes that regardless of the criminal, civil and administrative sanctions provided in specific legislation, the person responsible for the act of misconduct shall be subject to sanctions that can be imposed individually or collectively, depending on the seriousness of the act.[20] Under Article 11, sanctions can consist of compensation for damages, and if necessary, loss of public office, suspension of political rights from 3 to 5 years, a fine of up to 100 times the amount of the agent's salary and the prohibition of entering into a contract with the State or receiving tax or credit benefits or incentives either directly or indirectly for a period of up to 3 years even if the legal person is a major stockholder. However, it is stipulated that in determining the sanctions provided in this law, the judge must consider the extent of the damages, as well as the pecuniary gains obtained by the agent.

As a general conclusion, it can be said that despite the fact that the new law on access to information has yet to be the object of Supreme Court of Justice rulings, it does not seem to influence the habeas data system, at least in principle. What is more, until another legal instrument for obtaining information is not established, it should be understood that the proceeding remedy is still the habeas data, which is a legal writ corresponding to the right of access to information.

Within the scope of administrative sanctions, the sanctions stipulated in Law No. 8.112/90 can be perceived as more serious than those in Law N° 12.157/11, which only regulates the sanctions applicable to individuals who work with in the public administration. The sanctions applicable to authorities depend on that provided in the system for federal public officials, the first option of which is a warning. It should be noted, however, that the Law of Administrative Misconduct provides for more severe sanctions.[21] The question that must be made, therefore, is whether these administrative sanctions are accumulative.

[20]Provision modified by Law No. 12.120, of 2009. Law consulted on 21 May 2012, at http://planalto.gov.br/ccivil_03/leis/l8429compilado.htm (Accessed on 26 October 2016).

[21]This Supreme Court of Justice precedent affirms the possibility of being sanctioned administratively under the Law of Misconduct. Injunction 16418/DF (Rel. Min. Herman Benjamin) established that the administrative offense for the disclosure of an act or circumstance known in the exercise of their duties is an act of dishonesty, subject to the sanctions set forth in Law No. 8.429/1992, which unlike Law N° 12.157/11 and the Law on the status of federal public servants (Law No. 8.112/1990), are more rigorous as they include the punishment of dismissal and loss of retirement pension. Brazilian Superior Court of Justice, Case No. MS 16707/DF (Judgment of 8 February 2012).

The answer to this question is found in the decision on administrative disciplinary proceedings that has indicated the possibility of convicting a public servant according to the Administrative Disciplinary Procedure, which is subsumed in that of Administrative Misconduct. It maintains that the axiomatic condemnation of administrative misconduct is not new to the system because it was already set forth in Article 37 of the Federal Constitution when actions go against the principles of legality, morality, publicity and efficiency. It also stresses that the Article 12 *caput*, of the administrative misconduct law, establishes that the official, "regardless of the criminal, civil and administrative sanctions provisions of specific legislation, is responsible for the act of misconduct subject to the following sanctions, which can be applied individually or collectively, according to the severity of the act." This indicates that the law has not yet developed a sole subsystem for the fight against misconduct, as several subsystems are compatible and coordinated with others.[22]

## 4 The Imposition of Sanctions in Mexico

In general terms, it can be said that the right to information is actually manifested as a "right of access to information" implemented through administrative proceedings. Therefore, it differs from other fundamental rights, as it cannot be regarded like that of freedom, equality or right to provision (*s.s.*) even if it is established as a right to obtain something. Because of the way it is exercised, this right is similar to the right of action through administrative remedies, which by the Mexican General Law is verified in two stages: presenting a request before the authority, and when appropriate, reconsideration when the petitioner obtains a negative response. This last stage is where the fundamental right emerges as it makes it possible to file a remedy of review to prevent a violation to the right of access to information.

The National Institute of Transparency, Access to Information and Personal Data Protection (Instituto Nacional de Transparencia, Acceso a la Información y Protección de Datos Personales, INAI) is an autonomous national body in charge of overseeing compliance to the right of access to information and transparency and of personal data protection in the possession of entities bound by the obligation.[23] This institute has the power to impose enforcement measures and sanctions set forth in the General Law on Transparency and Access to Public Information to ensure compliance with its decisions. What is more, one of the objectives of this law is

[22]Brazilian Superior Court of Justice, Case No. MS 16418/DF (Judgment of 8 August 2012) S1 – First Section.

[23]Reform published in the DOF on 7 February 2014.

to establish mechanisms to guarantee compliance and the effective application the corresponding enforcement measures and sanctions.[24]

The 2014 constitutional reform was carried out to strengthen the powers of the national guarantor agency for the right of access to information and personal data protection and to create a coordination system between the states and the Federation to procure the same standards of transparency and access to information nationwide. Therefore, autonomy was granted to both national and state guarantor agencies of access to information[25] and the scope of entities bound by this obligation was extended to include all authorities—in any area of government (federal, state or municipal) and the three branches of power (executive, legislative and judiciary), autonomous bodies, public trusts and funds, political parties and individuals or corporations that receive and make use of public funds or carry out acts of authority.[26]

The scope of application of this general rule covers all national territory, and is to be enforced concurrently on both federal and state levels. The object of this law is not to allocate responsibilities among the different levels of government, but to set the general bases for federal and local laws on transparency and access to information. Therefore, it should operate as the national reference parameter to ensure consistency in the exercise of this fundamental right.

The INAI does not provide information; its role is that of an oversight body that establishes and reviews the criteria of classification, declassification and custody of undisclosed and confidential information. Its rulings are binding and must be conformed to under punishment of liability. The INAI now has power of coercion; this is a new faculty because the Federal Information Act that regulated the matter did not include provisions regarding enforcement measures that make it possible to ensure due compliance by the Institute itself. The General Law on Transparency and Access to Public Information sets forth measures that include public reprimands and fines.

The new sanction system model is the result of a combination of systems as guarantor agencies of the right of access to information and internal oversight agencies (órgano interno de control, OIC) are empowered to sanction behavior that violates the General Law. The reasons that led legislators to award guarantor agencies the authority to impose sanctions and make them responsible for establishing disciplinary proceedings, as the main objective of these agencies is to ensure access to information and promote the exercise of this right, are rooted in the expansion of the number of entities bound by this obligation as these not only include public servants, but also entities from private or social sectors. Therefore, the ordinary punitive model for the imposition of sanctions by the Ministry of

[24]Article 2, item 9 of the Mexican General Law on Transparency and Access to Information.

[25]The authority of state agencies arises from a correspondence made based on the text of the constitutional reform to Article 6, as well as on the dictates for state legislators contained in Article 116.2, item 8 of the Mexican Constitution.

[26]Article 6.4 subparagraph (A), item 1 of the Mexican Constitution.

Public Administration and the OICs was modified because the Federal Law on the Administrative Liability of Public Servants (LFRASP)[27] did not apply to trusts from private funds, political parties or labor unions. This Law states that any liability arising from non-compliance with the federal law must be sanctioned under the terms of the LFRASP.

For federal matters, the sanction system is provided in the 2016 Federal Information Act. Its Article 188 establishes that when the INAI determines that a public servant may have incurred in liability, the OIC of the agency or body responsible must be made known to start the corresponding liability proceedings, when necessary. Articles 174 to 185 of the Federal Information Act regulate the enforcement measures while Articles 186 to 206 set the sanctions, differentiating the types of offenders and the corresponding sanction proceedings. As the Federal Law on Transparency and Access to Public Government Information replicates the provisions of the General Law, the latter is only mentioned when a new or additional element is regulated.

Under the terms of the transitory articles, the new system for the imposition of sanctions provided in the Federal Information Act should be implemented, but the necessary provisions, now called "general guidelines", have yet to be issued. Therefore, the new powers regarding enforcement measures aimed at ensuring due compliance with the rulings issued by the guarantor agencies, such as the means to force the public servant or union members, political parties, or individual or corporation to deliver the information identified as public information and to do so within the established periods, must be exercised under the terms of the Federal Law.

The General Law on Transparency and Access to Public Information differentiates enforcement measures and sanctions. It falls to the guarantor agencies to impose the enforcement measures that ensure compliance with its rulings, now called "determinations" on the party responsible. The enforcement measures set forth in Article 201 are public reprimands and fines that shall be imposed by the guarantor agencies and applied within a maximum period of 15 days as of the date on which notification of the enforcement measure is received. These measures can be imposed by the agencies themselves or with the support of the competent authority according to that established in Article 203. The federal and local laws to be issued were charged with regulating criteria to determine the enforcement measure according to the seriousness of the offense and, when necessary, the financial conditions and recidivism of the offender. The federal law only addresses the issue of the seriousness of the offense in Article 175, and refers the issue of regulating the powers to rate the seriousness of the offense to the general guidelines to be issued. Moreover, there are other measures provided in other laws on the matter that may be also imposed as stated in Article 205.

[27]This law regulates those bound by administrative responsibility in public service, obligations in public service and the liabilities and corresponding sanctions in public service. Published in the DOF on 13 March 2002, last reform published in the DOF on 18 December 2015.

Furthermore, the non-compliance of those bound by the obligation must be made public on guarantor agency websites on the obligations of transparency and considered in the assessments that are carried out. The federal law, for instance, specifically mentions the "national platform". If the non-compliance involves the alleged commission of a crime or one of the behaviors stipulated in Article 206 of the Federal Information Act, the guarantor agency must report the act before the competent authority.

If, despite the enforcement measures provided, the "determination" issued is not adhered to, it may require compliance from the superior authority for it to order the offender to comply within a period of 5 days. If the non-compliance persists, enforcement measures may also apply to the respective superior authority. Once the period has elapsed without fulfilling these measures, the corresponding sanctions shall be determined according to that set forth in Article 202.

Regarding the sanctions, the laws to be enacted must at least include the causes provided in the following sections of Article 206.[28] Acts of non-compliance with the obligations as established in the General Freedom of Information Act are:

Non-response to requests for information within the regulated periods;

I. Acting with negligence, willful intent or bad faith in the substantiation of access to information requests or by "not conveying information on the obligations of transparency";
II. Failure to adhere to the deadlines for providing the requested service;
III. Using, removing, disclosing, concealing, modifying, mutilating, destroying or render useless, either totally or partially, the information in the keeping of the agencies bound by the obligation and of their public servants or to which they have access to or knowledge of through their job, position or commission without justified cause, based on their corresponding powers;
IV. Delivering incomprehensible, incomplete information in a non-user-friendly format, a delivery method different to that requested beforehand by the petitioner in his or her request for access to information, by responding without due reason and justification;
V. Not updating the information on the obligations of transparency within the stipulated periods;
VI. Declaring with willful intent or negligence the unavailability of the information when the entity bound by the obligation must produce it as part the exercise of its authority, powers or functions;
VII. Declaring the non-existence of the information when it can be found either totally or partially in it records;
VIII. Not documenting with willful intent or negligence the exercise of its authorities, powers, functions or acts of authority, as stipulated in the applicable provisions;
IX. Carrying out acts to intimidate those requesting information or obstructing the exercise of their right;
X. Intentionally denying information that is not considered classified or confidential;
XI. Rating information as classified with willful intent or negligence without its fulfilling the specifications regulated by the General Law on Transparency and Access to

[28]These are the same causes provided in Article 186 of the Federal Law on Transparency and Access to Governmental Public Information (2002).

Public Information. In this case, the imposition of a sanction proceeds when the guarantor agency has previously emitted a definite ruling on the issue;

XII. Not declassifying undisclosed information when the reasons for its non-disclosure no longer exist or the term has expired. When the guarantor agency determines that it is in the public interest for this classification to continue or not, an extension is requested from the Transparency Committee;

XIII. Not abiding by the requirements established in this Law or those issued by guarantor agencies, and

XIV. Not adhering to guarantor agency rulings in the exercise of their functions.

According to that set forth in Article 207 of the General Freedom of Information Act, the guarantor agencies are responsible for the imposition of sanctions and, when necessary, for informing the competent authority so the latter can impose or carry out the sanction.

As in the case of enforcement measures, federal and local legislators are charged with regulating the types of sanctions, proceedings and terms for their execution. Likewise, they must establish the criteria for classifying the sanctions based on the seriousness of the offense, as well as the financial conditions of the offender and recidivism, when necessary. It also expressly states that the administrative liability is separate from other types of liabilities, such as civil, criminal or any other that may result from the same acts, as stated in Article 208. Both the INAI and the guarantor agencies have the power to report any act or omission that violates the General Freedom of Information Act to the competent authorities and present evidence.

In the case of public servants, Article 210 establishes the obligation of the INAI or guarantor agency to send a file with all the evidence that supports the alleged administrative liability, along with the corresponding report, to the competent authority. According to Article 188 of the Federal Law, the OIC or the competent court of administrative justice must notify the INAI of the termination of the proceedings, as well as the execution of the sanction that may have proceeded.

Moreover, Articles 211 and 212 specifically regulate which institutions and procedure proceeds when the offenders are not public servants. As according to the law the INAI and the state guarantor agencies are the authorities empowered to examine and decide sanction proceedings, these bodies can also carry out the actions leading to the imposition and execution of sanctions. In the event of cases or situations not regulated by this law, sanction proceedings must additionally abide by that provided in the corresponding laws on administrative proceedings of the legal system as stipulated in Article 213.

In the case of non-compliance by political parties, the National Electoral Institute or local public electoral agencies must also be informed, without prejudice to the sanctions established for political parties in the applicable laws. For public trusts or funds, labor unions or individuals or corporations that receive and make use of public resources or perform acts of authority, the notification must be given OIC of the corresponding agency bound by the obligation when these are public servants.

Entities bound by this obligation that are not public servants are regulated by Article 214 of the General Freedom of Information Act, which states that offenses to the General Law will be sanctioned by:

I. A single warning so that the entity bound by the obligation complies immediately under the terms provided in this law, specifically the provisions set forth in Article 206, Sections 1, 3, 5, 6 and 10. If once the warning has been given, the obligation is not complied with, a fine of 150 to 250 days general minimum wage in force in the corresponding geographical area can be imposed;
II. A fine of 250 to 800 days general minimum wage in force in the corresponding geographical area in the cases provided for in Article 206, Sections II and IV, of this law, and
III. A fine of 800 to 1500 days general minimum wage in force in the corresponding geographical area, in the cases provided in Article 206, Sections VII, VIII, IX, XI, XII, XIII, XIV and XV, of this Law.

Moreover, an additional fine of up to 50 days general minimum wage in force in the corresponding geographical area per day to whoever continues to commit the above offenses.[29]

Article 215 states that in the event the non-compliance of the resolutions issued by guarantor bodies involves the alleged commission of a crime, the corresponding guarantor agency must report the acts before the competent authority.

Article 216 does not establish a sanction, but an obligation for individuals or corporations that receive and make use of public funds or exercise acts of authority to provide information that allows the corresponding entity bound by the obligation to fulfill its obligations of transparency and to attend the corresponding requests of access to information.

The innovative part of the Federal Law is that its Articles 193 to 201 establish the general rules for sanction proceedings for violations to this law and to the General Law on Transparency and Access to Public Information. Moreover, in the event of cases or situations not regulated by this law the Federal Law of Administrative Proceedings[30] would be applied.

In conclusion, it can be said that because the national authority has the power to impose sanctions to ensure compliance with the provisions on access to information, it is essential to have laws that regulate the sanction system, whether in general terms through provisions of administrative liability or specifically in special laws on information. However, this is not enough, as can be noticed in what has been explained regarding the case of Mexico, as the current situation has not reached the expected results after so many reforms. The lack of certainty in terms of the applicability of the provisions on access to information leads to legal uncertainty.

In addition to overregulation and redundancy, a problem that has been heightened in the new information act, the new General Law has produced a model that is far from being clear, adding also new concepts and procedures. Access to

[29]Instead of using the concept of "days of minimum wage", the Federal Law employs that of "unit of measure and updating" to quantify fines.

[30]Published in the DOF on 4 August 1994.

information is a topic that is already complicated for experts. Instead of making it easier for citizens to understand so they can exercise their right, poor legal drafting and deficient legislative technique provide an inaccessible, obscure and repetitive legal framework that only produces citizens' indifference and thus makes it irrelevant. This, along with a sanction system that has yet to be implemented and that rather than guaranteeing the right to access to information will produce a bureaucratic overload because of lack of organization and professionalism in documenting and recording public information, compromises the effectiveness of the right of access to information.

## References

Aberastury, P. (2014). La tutela del acceso a la información. *Revista de Derecho Administrativo, 93*, 705–722.

Afonso da Silva, J. (2006). *Constituciones Iberoamericanas–Brasil*. México: Instituto de investigaciones Jurídicas, UNAM.

Aguiar, A. (2012). *Memoria, verdad y justicia. Derechos transversales de la democracia*. Caracas, Venezuela: Editorial Jurídica Venezolana.

Basterra, M. (2009). El derecho al acceso a la información pública. *Derecho Comparado de la Información, 13*, 3–64.

Huerta, C. (2015). El carácter administrativo del derecho a la información. *Boletín Mexicano de Derecho Comparado, 141*, 149–183.

Mendel, T. (2008). *Libertad de Información, Comparación Jurídica*. Paris: UNESCO.

Pérez, E., & Makowiak, J. (2003). *El derecho de acceso a la información en Europa y América Latina: Un enfoque constitucional*. Quito, Ecuador: Ediciones Legales.

Sagüés, N. (2006). *Constituciones Iberoamericanas – Argentina*. México: Instituto de investigaciones Jurídicas, UNAM.

Serau Junior, M. (2009). O direito de acesso à informação pública no ordenamento jurídico brasileiro. *Derecho Comparado de la Información, 13*, 187–219.

## List of Cases

Argentinian Supreme Court of Justice of the Nation (Suprema Corte de Justicia de la Nación) 11.12.1984, *Ponzetti de Balbín, Fallos, 306: 1892*.

Argentinian Supreme Court of Justice of the Nation (Suprema Corte de Justicia de la Nación) 01.01.1991, *Vago c/La Urraca, La Ley*, Fallos 1992-B-367.

Inter-American Court of Human Rights 19.09.2006, *Claude Reyes, et al. v. Chile*, Series C No. 151.

Brazilian Superior Court of Justice (Superior Tribunal de Justiça) 08.02.2012, Case No. MS 16707/DF.

Brazilian Superior Court of Justice (Superior Tribunal de Justiça) 08.08.2012, Case No. MS 16418/DF, S1 – First Section.

# Appendix 1 Websites Containing Regional Conventions on the Protection of Human Rights

**African Charter on Human and Peoples' Rights (1987/1998)**
http://www.achpr.org/instruments/achpr/
**American Convention on Human Rights (1969/1978)**
http://www.oas.org/dil/treaties_B-32_American_Convention_on_Human_Rights.htm
**European Convention on Human Rights (1950/1953)**
http://www.echr.coe.int/Documents/Convention_ENG.pdf
**Council of Europe Convention on Access to Official Documents (2007/not yet entered into force)**
http://www.coe.int/en/web/conventions/full-list/-/conventions/treaty/205



H.-J. Blanke, R. Perlingeiro (eds.), *The Right of Access to Public Information*,
DOI 10.1007/978-3-662-55554-5

# Appendix 2 Argentina: National Freedom-of-Information and Transparency Legislation (Extracts)

## 1. Constitution of the Argentine Nation (1853)[1]

**Article 38**
Political parties are basic institutions of the democratic system. This Constitution guarantees the free establishment and exercise of their activities, as well as their democratic organization and performance, representation of minority groups, competition for those standing as candidates for elective public positions, access to public information and communication of their ideas.

**Article 42**
As regards consumption, consumers and users of goods and services have the right to the protection of their health, safety, and economic interests; to adequate and ruthful information; to freedom of choice and equitable and reliable treatment [...]

**Article 43**
Any person shall file a prompt and summary proceeding regarding constitutional guarantees, provided there is no other legal remedy, against any act or omission of the public authorities or individuals which currently or imminently may damage, limit, modify or threaten rights and guarantees recognized by this Constitution, treaties or laws, with open arbitrariness or illegality. In such case, the judge may declare that the act or omission is based on an unconstitutional rule [...].

Any person shall file this action to obtain information on the data about himself and their purpose, registered in public records or data bases, or in private ones intended to supply information; and in case of false data or discrimination, this action may be filed to request the suppression, rectification, confidentiality or

[1]Constitution of 1 May 1853, most recently amended by the Act of 22 August 1994, Boletin Oficial de la República Argentina of 10 January 1995 (*Official Gazette of the Republic of Argentina*).

 
H.-J. Blanke, R. Perlingeiro (eds.), *The Right of Access to Public Information*,
DOI 10.1007/978-3-662-55554-5

updating of said data. The secret nature of the sources of journalistic information shall not be impaired [. . .]

## 2. Right of Access to Information (Law 27275)[2]

**Article 1 [Purpose]**

This Law has the purpose to guarantee the effective exercise of the right to access public information, promote public participation and transparency in public management. This Law is substantiated in the following principles:

*Publicity presumption*: All information held by the State is presumed to be public, except for the exceptions provided by this Law.
*Transparency and maximum disclosure* [. . .]
*Absence of formal requirements* [. . .]
*Maximum access* [. . .]
*Unfettered access* [. . .]
*Dissociation* (*'anonymisation' of data*) [...]
*No discrimination* [. . .]
*Maximum need to act urgently* [. . .]
*Gratuity* [. . .]
*Control*: Compliance with the statutory freedom-of-information provisions shall be subject to constant review. Applicants may appeal to the competent body if an authority rules against an information access request, fails to respond to the request, or responds in an ambiguous or inaccurate manner.
*Liability*: The breach of the obligations which this Law imposes will give rise to liability and applicable penalties.
*Limited scope of exceptions* [. . .]
*In dubio pro petitor*: In case of doubt, the interpretation of the provisions of this Law or of any regulation on the right of access to information must always favour the greatest effectiveness and scope of the right to information.
*Facilitation* [. . .]
*Good faith* [. . .]

**Article 2 [Right of access to public information]**

The right of access to public information comprises the possibility to freely search, access, request, receive, copy, analyze, reprocess, re-use and redistribute the information which is under the custody of the obliged subjects listed in Article 7° of the present law, with the only limitations and exceptions which this Law states.

It is presumed to be public all information generated, obtained, transformed, controlled or under custody of the obliged subjects which are under the scope of this Law.

[2]Boletín Oficial de la República Argentina of 28 September 2016 (*Official Gazette of the Republic of Argentina*). Translation by Daniela Sota Valdivia and Hermann-Josef Blanke.

**Article 3 [Definitions]**

a) Public information: all kind of data contained in documents in any kind of format which the obliged subjects, listed in Article 7° in the present law, have generated, obtained, transformed, controlled or hold in custody;
b) Document: every record which has been generated, which is controlled or held in custody by the obliged subjects listed in Article 7° of the present law, regardless of its form, method of storage, origin, date of creation or official character.

**Article 4 [Active legitimation]**

Every natural or legal person, public or private, has the right to request and receive public information. It is not allowed to require the applicant to state to motivation for the request, to attest a subjective right or legitimate interest, or to be assisted by a legal adviser.

**Article 5 [Information delivery]**

The information must be provided in the conditions which it has at the moment when the request is made. It is not the obliged subject's duty to process or classify it.

The State has the obligation to deliver the information in digital-open formats. In exceptional cases in which it is impossible its accomplishment or it would mean an excessive public effort, this provision is not applicable. On the applicability of the exceptions will decide the *Agencia de Acceso a la Información Pública* (Agency of access to public information).

**Article 6 [Gratuity]**

The access to public information is free of charge as long as its reproduction is not required. The costs of reproduction are in charge of the applicant.

**Article 7 [Scope of application]**

The obliged subjects to provide public information are:

a) The national public administration, which consists of the central administration and the decentralized authorities, the last ones comprise social security institutions;
b) The legislative branch and the administrative bodies which are under its scope;
c) The Nation's judicial branch;

[...]

**Article 8 [Exceptions]**

The obliged subjects can only be exempted from providing the information in the following cases:

a) Information expressly classified as reserved, confidential or secret, due to defense or foreign policy reasons;

b) Information which could threaten the appropriate operation of the financial or banking systems;
c) Trade, commercial, financial, scientific, technical or technological secrets which disclosure could harm the level of competitiveness or diminish the interests of the obliged subject;
d) Information obtained in a confidential character which jeopardizes the rights or legitimate interests of a third party;
e) Information under the control of the *Unidad de Información Financiera* (Unit of Financial Information), in charge of the analysis, processing and transmission of information intended to prevent and investigate the legitimation of assets of illicit origin;
f) Information drawn up by the obliged subjects devoted to regulate or supervise financial institutions or information prepared by third parties to be applied by themselves and which refer to situation analysis, its operational system evaluation or its functioning condition;
g) Information elaborated by legal advisers or national public administration's lawyers which publicity could reveal the defense's strategy or the processing of a judicial cause or disclose the techniques or investigation procedures of a crime or other irregularities or when the information deprives a person's full enjoyment of the guarantee of a due process;
h) Information protected by professional secrecy (in the meaning of: trade secrets and commercial or financial information);
i) Information which contains personal data and cannot be provided by applying procedures to make them anonymous, unless the unlawfulness conditions stated in the Law 25.326 of protection of personal data and its amendments are applicable;
j) Information which could endanger human life or security of a human being;
k) Information of judicial character which disclosure is banned by other laws or by compromises made by the Argentinian Republic in international treaties;
l) Information obtained in investigations conducted by the obliged subjects which have a confidential character and which disclosure could dash the success of an investigation;
m) Information corresponding to a stock corporation subject to the public offering regime.

The exceptions contained in this article will not be applicable in cases of severe violations of human rights, genocide, war crimes or crimes against humanity.

**Article 9 [Information request]**
The request for information must be submitted to the obliged subject which possesses it or which is presumed to have it in its possession. The obliged subject will forward the request to the subject in charge of access to public information in the stipulated terms stated in Article 30 of the present law. The request can be made by written or electronic means and without formalities except for the identity of the applicant, the clear identification of the requested information

and the contact data of the applicant, with the aim of forwarding the requested information or announcing that it is available.

**Article 11 [Terms]**
All public information request which has been made in line with the terms of this Law must be fulfilled in a term no longer than fifteen (15) working days. The term can be exceptionally prorogued for other fifteen (15) working days if reasonable grounds exist which make it difficult to gather the required information.

In this case, the obliged subject must clearly communicate the reasons of the extension in a reasoned document before the due date.

The applicant is allowed to require, under reasoned arguments, the reduction of the term to answer and satisfy his request.

**Article 12 [Partial Information]**
The obliged subjects must provide the complete requested information. When a document partially contains information which access is restricted in the terms of Article 8 of this Law, this information must be crossed out and the remaining requested information must be provided.

**Article 13 [Denial]**
Only in a reasoned decision the requested subject is allowed to refuse to give access to the required information if it is verified that the information does not exist and that it is not legally obliged to produce or that it is contained in the exceptions listed in Article 8 of the present law. The absence of substantiation will determine the nullity of the act of denial and will force the delivery of the required information.

The denial of the information must be determined by the highest authority of the Agency or required entity.

The silence of the obliged subject, after the legal terms established in Article 11 of this Law have expired, as well as the ambiguity, inaccuracy or the incomplete delivery of the information, will be considered as an unjustified denial to provide the information.

The denial, in all cases, will will open up the possibility to lodge the complaint procedures set out in Article 14 of the present law.

**Article 14 [Complaint procedures]**
Rulings on access to official information may be appealed directly to the courts of first instance in the federal administrative law section, without prejudice to option of filing an administrative compliant with the Agency of Access to Public Information or the corresponding body, depending on the party which has standing to be sued [. . .]

[...]

In any of these two situations, the administrative procedures exhaustion could be demanded.

[. . .]

The complaint promoted through a legal action will be processed under an *amparo* proceeding and must be filed within forty (40) working days since the denial resolution of the request was notified or since the term to respond to it has expired, or, from the verification of any other breach to the provisions of this Law [. . .]

[...]

**Article 15 [Claim of breach]**
In the case justifying denial of a request for information under Article 13 of the present law or any other violation of the present law, the applicant may, within forty (40) working days after the expiry of the time limit for the response [...] under the present law, file a complaint with the Agency of Access to Official Information or, at the applicant's option, with the organization to which the request was originally made.

[...]

**Article 19 [Agency of Access to Public Information] (*Agencia de Acceso a la Información Pública*)**
The *Agencia de Acceso a la Información Pública* (Agency of Access to Public Information) is hereby established as an autarchic entity which will work under functional autonomy within the national executive power. The *Agencia de Acceso a la Información Pública* must ensure compliance with the principles and procedures which have been established in the present law, guarantee the effective exercise of the right to access public information and promote measures of active transparency.

[...]

**Article 29 [Federal Council for Transparency] (*Consejo Federal para la Transparencia*)**
The *Consejo Federal para la Transparencia* (Federal Council for Transparency) is hereby established as an inter-jurisdictional agency with permanent character, which will have as a purpose the technical cooperation and the concertation of the policies in the area of transparency and access to public information.

[...]

# Appendix 3 Brazil: National Freedom-of-Information and Transparency Legislation (Partially in the Form of Extracts)

## 1. Constitution of 1988[3]

**Article 5**
All persons are equal before the law, without any distinction whatsoever, Brazilians and foreigners residing in the country being ensured of inviolability of the right to life, to liberty, to equality, to security and to property, on the following terms:

[...]

XXXIII – all persons have the right to receive, from the public agencies, information of private interest to such persons, or of collective or general interest, which shall be provided within the period established by law, subject to liability, except for the information whose secrecy is essential to the security of society and of the State;

[...]

**Article 37**
The governmental entities and entities owned by the Government in any of the powers of the Union, the states, the Federal District and the Municipalities shall obey the principles of lawfulness, impersonality, morality, publicity, and efficiency, and also the following:

[...]

[3]Constitution of the Federal Republic of Brazil of 5 October 1988 (Constituição da República Federativa do Brasil), published in *Diário Oficial da União* 191-A, 5 October 1988, and most recently updated by the Constitutional Amendment 91, of 18 February 2016, published in *Diário Oficial da União* of 19 February 2016.



H.-J. Blanke, R. Perlingeiro (eds.), *The Right of Access to Public Information*,
DOI 10.1007/978-3-662-55554-5

Paragraph 3. The law shall regulate the forms of participation of users in governmental entities and in entities owned by the Government, especially as regards:

[...]

II – the access of users to administrative records and to information about Government initiatives, with due regard for Article 5, items X and XXXIII;

[...]

**Article 216**
The Brazilian cultural heritage consists of the assets of a material and immaterial nature, taken individually or as a whole, which bear reference to the identity, action and memory of the various groups that form the Brazilian society, therein included:

[...]

Paragraph 2. It is incumbent upon the Government, in accordance with the law, to manage the keeping of the governmental documents and to make them available for consultation to whomever may need to do so.

## 2. Law N° 12.527 on Access to Information[4]

### Chapter 1
### General Provisions

**Article 1**
This Law establishes the procedures to be followed by the Union, States, Federal District and Municipalities, with the purpose of guaranteeing access to information as stipulated in subparagraph XXXIII of Article 5, in subparagraph II of §3 of Article 37 and in §2 of Article 216 of the Federal Constitution.

Sole paragraph. This Law is applicable to:

I – Public entities integrated in the direct administration of Executive, Legislative (including Court of Accounts) and the Judicial powers, and of the Public Prosecutor's Office;

II – Quasi-governmental organization, public foundations, public enterprises, mixed capital corporations and remaining entities directly or indirectly controlled by the Union, States, Federal District and Municipalities.

[4]Law N° 12.527 of 18 November 2011 on Access to Information (Lei que regula o acesso a informações), published in *Diário Oficial da União*,of 18 November 2011. Translation by William Stein.

**Article 2**

The provisions of this Law are applicable, to the extent possible, to non-profit public entities that receive public resources, to undertake actions of public interest, directly from the budget or by means of social aid, management contract, partnership agreement, conventions, adjustments or other similar instruments.

Sole paragraph. The publicity requirement to which the entities cited by the main paragraph of Article 2 refer to the share of public resources received and their destination, without prejudice to the reporting requirement established by law.

**Article 3**

The procedures established in this Law are intended to assure the fundamental right of access to information and must be executed in conformity with the basic principles of public administration and the following guidelines:

I – observance of a general rule of publicity with secrecy being an exception;

II – dissemination of information of public interest, independent of requests;

III – use of communication means made feasible by information technology;

IV – promotion of the development of a culture of transparency in public administration;

V – development of social control of public administration.

**Article 4**

For the purposes of this Law, the following definitions shall apply:

I – information: data, processed or not, that can be used to produce and convey knowledge, contained on any medium or support and in any format;

II – document: unit of recorded information, regardless of the medium or format;

III – secret information: information that is temporarily subject to public access restrictions due to its indispensability for the security of society;

IV – personal information: information related to the identified or identifiable natural person;

V – information processing: set of actions related to the production, receipt, classification, utilization, access, reproduction, transport, transmission, distribution, archiving, storage, deletion, evaluation, intended use or control of the information;

VI – availability: characteristic of information that can be known and used by authorized individuals, devices or systems;

VII – authenticity: characteristic of information that has been produced, issued, received or modified by a certain individual, device or system;

VIII – integrity: characteristic of information that has not been modified, including with respect to its origin, movement and destination;

IX – primariness: characteristic of information collected at the source, in the greatest possible detail, without modifications.

**Article 5**
It is the duty of the state to guarantee the right to access information, which will be conceded by means of objective and speedy procedures, in a transparent and clear manner, and in easily understandable language.

**Chapter II**
**Access to Information and its Dissemination**

[...]

**Article 7**
The access to information that this Law addresses contemplates, among others, the right to obtain:

[...]

§ 1 The access to information stipulated by the main paragraph of Article 7 does not contemplate information referring to research projects and scientific or technological development whose secrecy is indispensable to the safety of society and the state.

§ 2 When full access to information is not authorized because it is partially secret, access to the non-secret portion is guaranteed by means of a certificate, extract or copy with the secret information redacted.

§ 3 The right to access documents, or the information they contain, based upon which administrative decisions were made and the administrative act will be guaranteed with the publication of the corresponding decision act.

§ 4 Refusal of access to information subject of a request addressed to the entities and institutions referred to in Article I, if not properly justified, will subject the responsible party to disciplinary measures established in Article 32 of this Law.

§ 5 After having been informed of the misplacement of the information requested, the interested party may request that the competent authority order the immediate opening of an inquiry to determine the disappearance of the requested documentation.

[...]

**Article 8**
It is the duty of public entities and institutions to promote, apart from applications within the scope of their responsibilities, the dissemination of information of collective or general interest produced or held by such bodies in an easily accessible location.

§ 1 The dissemination of the information stipulated by the main paragraph of Article 8 should include at a minimum:

I – record of the responsibilities and structure, addresses and telephones of the respective units and schedules of office hours;

II – records of any relocation or transfer of financial resources;

III – records of expenses;

IV – information regarding a bidding process, including the respective notices and results, and all the contracts signed;

V – general data for monitoring programs, actions, projects and works undertaken by entities and institutions; and

VI – answers to society's most frequently asked questions.

§ 2 To fulfil the stipulations of the main paragraph of Article 8, public entities and institutions shall use all legitimate means and tools available, with mandatory dissemination at official sites of the world wide web (Internet).

[...]

**Chapter III**
**Procedure to Access Information**

**Section I**
**Information Access Request**

**Article 10**
Any interested party may present a request to access information to the entities and institutions referred to in Article 1 of this Law, by any legitimate means, and such request shall contain the identification of the applicant and the specifications of the information requested.

§ 1 In order to access information of public interest, the identification of the applicant shall not contain demands that make it impossible for the request to be granted.

§ 2 The entities and institutions of public power shall offer an alternative route for access requests through their official Internet sites.

§ 3 Any demands regarding the motives of the request for public interest information are banned.

**Article 11**
The public entity or institution shall authorize or grant immediate access to the information available.

§ 1 When it is impossible to grant immediate access, in the manner stipulated in the main paragraph of Article 11, the entity or institution that receives the request shall, within 20 (twenty) days:

I – indicate the date, place and manner in which the applicant may consult the information, reproduce it or obtain a certified copy;

II – indicate the factual or legal reasons for total or partial refusal of the intended access; or

III – communicate that it does not possess the information, indicate, if it has the knowledge, the entity or institution that holds the information, or forward the request to that entity or institution, while notifying the interested party of the referral of the request for information.

[...]

§ 4 When access is not authorized due to the fact that the information is completely or partially secret, the applicant shall be informed of the possibility of appeal, deadlines and requirements for petition; in addition, the competent authority for its assessment shall be indicated.

[...]

**Article 14**
It is the right of the applicant to obtain the full content of the decision to refuse access, through certificate or copy.

**Section II**
**Resources**

**Article 15**
In case of denial of access to the information or denial to the reasons for the refusal, the interested party may lodge an appeal within 10 (ten) days of being informed of the decision.

Sole paragraph. The appeal shall be addressed to the authority hierarchically above the one that registered the disputed decision, this authority is required to reply within 5 (five) days.

**Article 16**
If access to information has been denied by entities or institutions of the Federal Executive, the applicant may appeal to the Office of the Comptroller General, which will deliberate within 5 (five) days if:

I – access to information classified as non-secret is denied;

II – the decision to deny access to information totally or partially classified as secret does not implicate the authority that classified it or the authority hierarchically superior to which an access or declassification request may be addressed;

III – the procedures for classifying secret information stipulated by this Law have not been observed: and

IV – deadlines or other procedures stipulated by this Law have not been complied with.

[...]

§ 3 If the Office of the Comptroller General denies access to the information, an appeal to the Joint Commission of Information Reassessment, referred to in Article 35, may be lodged.

[...]

**Article 18**
The review proceedings of denials of access given in the appeal stipulated in Article 15, as well as the proceedings to review the classification of secret documents shall have their own regulations established by the Legislature and the Judiciary and by the Public Prosecutor's Office, within their respective scopes, always guaranteeing the applicant the right to be informed of the progress of the request.

**Article 20**
Law No. 9.784, of January 29, 1999, applies as a subsidiary and to the extent possible to the proceedings that this Chapter addresses.

**Chapter IV**
**Restrictions on Access to Information**

**Section I**
**General Provisions**

**Article 21**
Access to information required for the judicial and administrative protection of fundamental rights may not be denied.

Sole paragraph. Information or documents that address conduct that implicate the violation of human rights carried out by public agents or ordered by public authorities may not be subject to restricted access.

**Article 22**
What is stipulated by this Law does not exclude the other legal possibilities of secrecy, investigative secrecy, and industrial secrecy resulting from the direct exploration of economic activity by the state or person or private institution that may have any relationship to public power.

**Section II**
**Classification of Information as to Degree and Expiration of Secrecy**

**Article 23**
It is considered indispensable to the safety of society or the state and, therefore, susceptible to classification, information whose dissemination or unrestricted access may:

I – jeopardize national defence, sovereignty, or the integrity of national territory;

II – damage or jeopardize negotiations or the country's international relations, or even secret information provided by other states or international organizations;

III – jeopardize the life, safety or health of the population;

IV – expose the Nation to elevated risk of financial, economic or monetary instability;

V – harm or jeopardize the strategic operations or plans of the Armed Forces;

VI – harm or jeopardize scientific or technological research and development projects, as well as systems, assets, installations or areas of national strategic interest;

VII – jeopardize the safety of institutions or of high national or foreign authorities and the family members thereof;

VIII – compromise intelligence activities, as well as ongoing investigations or inspections related to the prevention or suppression of crime.

**Article 24**
Information held by public entities or institutions, considering their content and indispensability to the safety of society or the state, may be classified as top-secret, secret or restricted.

§ 1 The maximum deadlines for restricting access to information, according to the classification stipulated by the main paragraph of Article 24, come into force at the date of its production and are the following:

I – top-secret: 25 (twenty five) years;

II – secret: 15 (fifteen) years; and

III – restricted: 5 (five) years.

§ 2 Information that might jeopardize the safety of the President of the Republic, the Vice-President and the spouses and children thereof shall be classified as restricted and remain secret until the end of the current term of office or of the final term of office in case of reelection.

§ 3 Alternatively to the deadlines stipulated by §1, the occurrence of a given event may be established as expiration of the access restriction, as long as it occurs before the period of time of the maximum expiration of classification.

§ 4 The expiration of classification having been reached or the event that determines its expiration having occurred, the information shall automatically be available for public access.

§ 5 To classify information at a determined security classification, the public interest of the information shall be considered and the least restrictive criterion possible shall be used, bearing in mind:

I – the seriousness of the risk or damage to the safety of society and the state; and

II – the maximum duration of the classification under the security classification or the event that will determine when the classification is lifted.

[...]

**Section V**
**Personal Information**

**Article 31**
The treatment of personal information shall be carried out in a transparent manner and respecting intimacy, private life, honor and public image, as well as individual freedom and guarantees.

§ 1 The personal information, referred to in this article, relating to intimacy, private life, honor and image:

I – shall have access to it restricted, regardless of the secrecy classification and for a maximum period of 100 (one hundred) years from the date of its production, to legally authorized public agents and the persons it refers to;

II – may be disseminated and accessed through an authorization obtained by means of legal provision or express consent of the person to whom the information refers.

§ 2 Whoever obtains access to the information addressed in this article shall be held accountable for its improper use.

§ 3 The consent mentioned in subparagraph II of §1 shall not be required when the information is necessary for:

I – medical prevention and diagnosis, when the person is physically or legally incapacitated, and for the single and exclusive purpose of medical treatment;

II – the carrying out of statistical or scientific research of noticeable public or general interest, as stipulated by law, the identification of the person to which the information refers being prohibited;

III – compliance with a judicial decision;

IV – for the defence of human rights; or

V – the protection of an overriding general public interest.

§ 4 Restricted access to information related to private life, honor and public image of the person may not be for with the purpose of jeopardizing the determination of irregularities in which the holder of information is involved, as well as actions related to jeopardize the retrieval of highly relevant historical facts.

[...]

### Chapter V
### Responsibilities

#### Article 32

The following constitute illicit conducts that elicits responsibility of the public or military agent:

I – refusing to provide the information requested under the terms of this Law, deliberately delaying the conveyance of the information or intentionally providing incorrect, incomplete or imprecise information;

II – improper use, subtraction, destruction, rendering useless, damaging, altering or concealing, totally or partially, information under the agent's responsibility, access or knowledge as a result of the duties of the post, job or public office;

III – acting with wrongful intent or bad faith when analyzing requests to access information;

IV – disseminating, allowing for the dissemination, accessing or allowing for the improper access to secret or personal information;

V – imposing secrecy on information for personal gain or for gain of a third party, or to conceal illegal actions carried out by the agent or a third party;

VI – concealing secret information from review of the competent higher authority to benefit such agent or a third party, or to the detriment of others; and

VII – destroying or subtracting, by any means, documents regarding possible human rights violations on the part of state agents.

[...]

## 2. Decree N° 7.724, of 16 May 2012[5]

### Chapter I
### General Provisions

#### Article 1

This Decree regulates, within the sphere of the Federal Executive Branch, the procedures to guarantee information access and to classify information subject to restricted access, in accordance with the levels and durations of secrecy stipulated by the provisions of Law No. 12.527, of November 18, 2011, which

[5]Decree No. 7.724, of 16 May 2012 (Decreto que regulamenta a Law No. 12.527 of 18 November 2011 on Access to Information), published in *Diário Oficial da União* of 16 May 2012, updated by the Decree N° 8.4087 of 24 February 2015, published in Diário Oficial da União of 25 February 2015, and the Decree N° 8.777 of 11 May 2016, published in Diário Oficial da União of 12 May 2016. Translation by William Stein.

provides for access to the information referred to in subparagraph XXXIII of the main paragraph of Article 5, in subparagraph II of §3 of Article 37 and in §2 of Article 216 of the Constitution.

**Article 2**

The organs and entities of the Federal Executive Branch shall ensure natural and juridical persons the right of access to information to be supplied through objective and prompt procedures, transparently, clearly and in easily understandable language, in accordance with the principles of public administration and the guidelines under Law No. 12.527 of 2011.

**Article 3**

For the purposes of this Decree, the following definitions shall apply:

I – information - data, processed or not, that can be used to produce and convey knowledge, contained on any medium or support and in any format;

II – processed data - data that undergoes any operation or treatment through electronic processing or automated means using information technology;

III – document – unit of recorded information, regardless of the medium or format;

IV – secret information - information that is temporarily subject to public access restrictions due to its indispensability for the security of society and of the state or information in any of the other situations in which secrecy is required by law;

V – personal information - information related to the identified or identifiable natural person that deals with privacy, private life, honor or image;

VI – information processing – set of actions related to the production, receipt, classification, utilization, access, reproduction, transport, transmission, distribution, archiving, storage, deletion, evaluation, intended use or control of the information;

VII – availability - characteristic of information that can be known and used by authorized individuals, devices or systems;

VIII – authenticity - characteristic of information that has been produced, issued, received or modified by a certain individual, device or system;

IX – integrity - characteristic of information that has not been modified, including with respect to its origin, movement and destination;

X – primacy - characteristic of information collected at the source, in the greatest possible detail, without modifications;

XI – up-to-date information - information that brings together the latest data about the subject, according to its nature, within the time periods specified in the applicable regulations or at the intervals established in the computer systems that organize such information; and

XII – preparatory document - formal document used as a basis for making a decision or an administrative act, such as expert opinions and technical notes.

**Article 4**

Information shall be searched and supplied free of charge, except for collecting an amount equal to the cost of the services and materials used, such as document reproduction, digital media and postage.

Sole paragraph. Any persons whose economic situation does not permit reimbursing the costs of services and materials used without jeopardizing their own subsistence or that of their family shall be exempt from such charges, subject to declaring their situation in accordance with Law No. 7.115 of August 29 1983.

## Chapter II
## Scope

**Article 5**

All government entities of direct administration, quasi-governmental organizations, mixed capital corporations, public or semi-public companies and other entities controlled directly or indirectly by the Federal Government are subject to the provisions of this Decree.

§1 – The disclosure of information of public companies, mixed capital corporations and other entities controlled by the Federal Government that operate under a competitive system governed by the provisions of Article 173 of the Constitution, shall be subject to the applicable regulations of the Securities Commission [Comissão de Valores Mobiliários], in order to ensure the competitiveness and corporate governance thereof and to safeguard the interests of any minority shareholders.

§2 – Information about the business activities of individuals or legal entities governed by private law that is collected by Central Bank of Brazil, through regulatory agencies or other entities in the exercise of control, regulation and supervision of economic activities shall not be subject to the provisions of this Decree if the disclosure thereof would create a competitive advantage for other economic actors.

**Article 6**

Access to the information regulated by this Decree shall not apply:

I – to the cases of secrecy prescribed by law, such as fiscal and banking secrecy, operations and services of capital markets, trade, professional and industrial secrecy, or judicial secrecy; and

II – to information referring to scientific or technological research and development projects the secrecy of which is indispensable to ensure the safety of society and of the state, in accordance with §1 of Article 7 of Law No. 12.527 of 2011.

## Chapter III
## Active Transparency

### Article 7

It is the duty of all institutions and entities without being asked to disclose on their websites, information of collective or general interest produced or kept by said institutions and entities, in accordance with the provisions of Articles 7 and 8 of Law No. 12.527 of 2011.

§1 – The institutions and entities shall implement in their websites a specific section for the disclosure of the information referred to in the main paragraph of Article 7.

§2 – The following items shall be made available on the websites of the institutions and entities, in accordance with the standard established by the Presidential Public Relations Office:

I – **banner** on the homepage, providing access to the specific section referred to in §1; and

II – identity bar of the Federal Government, containing a link to the federal website *Portal Brasil* and to the main website about Law No. 12.527 of 2011.

§3 –The specific section referred to in §1 shall disclose information about:

I – the organizational structure, areas of responsibility, applicable legislation, main posts and post holders, address and telephone numbers of the units, hours open to the public;

II – programs, projects, actions, work and activities, with an indication of the unit in charge, the main objectives and results and any indicators of the results and impact;

III – movements or transfers of financial resources;

IV – detailed financial and budget execution;

V – past and present invitations for bids, with the announcements, attachments and results, besides the contracts signed and guarantees of payment issued;

VI – remuneration and benefits received by the holder of the public office, post, rank, public function or employee, including assistance, cost allowances, director's fees and any other pecuniary advantages, as well as retirement income and pensions of those who were actively employed, individually, in compliance with the regulations of the Ministry of Planning, Budgeting and Management;

VII – Answers to society's most frequently asked questions; (*As worded by Decree no. 8.408 of 2015*)

VIII – Monitoring authority's contact person, designated in accordance with art. 40 of Law No. 12.527 of 2011, and the telephone number and e-mail address of the Citizen's Information Service; and (*As worded by of Decree no. 8.408 of 2015*)

IX – Programs financed by the FAT (Workers' Assistance Fund). (*Included by Decree no. 8.408 of 2015*)

§4 – Information that is already available on other government websites may be supplied by using a website redirection tool.

§5 – The provisions of §1 of Article 5 shall apply in the case of public companies, mixed capital corporations and other entities controlled by the Federal Government that operate under a competitive system, subject to the provisions of Article 173 of the Constitution.

§6 – The Central Bank of Brazil shall periodically disclose information about the credit operations practiced by financial institutions, including the minimum, maximum and average interest rates and the corresponding bank rates.

§7 – The disclosure of the information stipulated in §3 shall be without prejudice to the other cases in which the publication and disclosure of information are required by law.

§ 8° Joint act by the Ministers of State of the Federal Office of the Comptroller-General, Planning, Budgeting and Labor and Employment Management, which will decide on the publication of the programs mentioned in §3 (IX), which shall be carried out in accordance with the provisions of Chapter VII: (*Included by Decree No. 8.408 of 2015*)

I – in a individual manner; (*Included by Decree No. 8.408 of 2015*)

II – by means of consolidated information available on the website of the Ministry of Labor and Employment; and (*Included by Decree no. 8.408 of 2015*)

III – by making available database variables to perform comparisons for the purposes of study and research, in compliance with the provisions of art. 13. (*Included by Decree no. 8.408 of 2015*)

**Article 8**

The websites of the institutions and entities shall, in accordance with the regulation of the Ministry of Planning, Budgeting and Management meet, among others, the following requirements:

I – contain an information access request form;

II – contain a content search tool that enables access to information objectively, transparently, clearly and in easily understandable language;

III – make it possible to record reports in various electronic formats, including open and non-proprietary formats, such as spreadsheets and text, so as to facilitate the analysis of information;

IV – enable automated access by external systems in open, structured, machine-readable formats;

V – provide detailed disclosure of the formats used for information structuring;

VI – ensure the authenticity and integrity of the accessible information;

VII – instruct the applicant on how to communicate with the institution by e-mail or telephone; and

VIII – ensure that the contents are accessible to persons with disabilities.

## Chapter IV
## Passive Transparency

### Section I
### Citizen Information Service

#### Article 9

The institutions and entities shall create a Citizen Information Service (CIS) with the objective of:

I – providing the public with support and guidance for information access;

II – providing information about the processing of documents in the units; and

III – receiving and registering information access requests.

Sole paragraph. It is the responsibility of the CIS:

I – to receive access requests and, whenever possible, to supply the information immediately;

II – to register the access request in a specific electronic system and issue a reference number, which shall contain the date of submission of the request; and

III – to forward the received and registered requests to the unit in charge of supplying the information, where appropriate.

#### Article 10

The CIS shall be established in a specified physical unit that is easily accessible and open to the public.

§1 – Local units that do not have a CIS shall offer a service of receipt and registration of information access requests.

§2 – If the local unit does not have the information, the request shall be routed to the CIS of the central institution, which shall give the applicant the reference number and date of receipt of the request, which shall mark the commencement of the time limit for response.

## Section II
## Information Access Requests

### Article 11
Any natural or juridical person may formulate an information access request.

§1 – The request will be presented on a standard form, made available in both electronic format and hardcopy on the website and in the CIS of the institutions and entities.

§2 – The time limit for response will commence on the date of submission of the request to the CIS.

§3 – The institutions and entities are entitled to receive information access requests by any other legitimate means, such as by telephone, e-mail or postal correspondence, as long as the requirements of Article 12 are met.

§4 – In the case referred to in §3, the applicant will be sent a communication containing the reference number and date of receipt of the request by the CIS, which opens the time limit for response.

### Article 12
The information access request shall contain:

I – the applicant's name;

II – the number of [the applicant's] current identity document;

III – a clear and precise specification of the requested information; and

IV – the applicant's postal or e-mail address for receipt of communications or of the requested information.

### Article 13
Information access requests of the following kinds shall not be processed:

I – generic requests;

II – disproportionate or unreasonable requests; or

III – requests that require additional work of analysis, interpretation or consolidation of data and information, or that require a data production or processing service outside the scope of authority of the institution.

Sole paragraph. In the case of subparagraph III of the main paragraph of Article 13, the institutions or shall indicate, if it knows, the location of the information that the applicant can use for interpretation, consolidation or data processing.

### Article 14
It is prohibited to impose requirements related to the motives of the information access request.

## Section III
## Access to Information Procedure

### Article 15

Once a request is received, and if the information is available, access will be granted immediately.

§1 – If immediate access is impossible, the institution shall, within 20 days:

I – send the information to the specified postal or e-mail address;

II – indicate the date, place and manner in which the applicant may consult the information, reproduce or obtain a certified copy;

III – communicate that it does not possess the information or know of its existence;

IV – indicate, if it knows, the institution that holds or is responsible for the information; or

V – indicate the reasons for full or partial denial of access.

§2 – In cases in which the access request requires handling a large number of documents, or in which moving the document might interfere with its proper processing, the measure stipulated in subparagraph II §1 will be adopted.

§3 – Whenever handling might jeopardize the integrity of the information or document, the institution shall specify the date, place and manner in which the applicant may consult said information or provide a certified copy thereof.

§4 – If it is impossible to obtain a copy of the type referred to in §3, the applicant is entitled to ask for a reproduction to be made by other means that do not jeopardize the integrity of the original document, under the supervision of the public service provider at the applicant's own expense.

### Article 16

The time limit for responding to the request may be extended by ten days subject to sending the applicant a statement of justification before the expiration of the initial 20-day time limit.

### Article 17

If the information is available to the public in printed, electronic or other universally accessible form, the institution shall provide the applicant with guidance as to the place and manner in which to consult, obtain or reproduce the information.

Sole paragraph. In the case referred to in the main paragraph of Article 17, the institution is released from the obligation to supply the information directly, unless the applicant declares that he or she does not have the means to consult, obtain or reproduce the information.

**Article 18**
When supplying the information involves the reproduction of documents, the institution, within the time limit for response to the request, shall provide the applicant with the Federal Payment Form [*Guia de Recolhimento da Unión* (GRU)] or an equivalent document in order to pay for the costs of the services and materials used.

Sole paragraph. The reproduction of documents shall occur within ten days after the date of proof of payment by the applicant or the submission of the declaration of poverty signed by the applicant, in accordance with Law No. 7.115 of 1983, except in justified cases in which given the volume or condition of the documents reproduction requires more time.

**Article 19**
In the event of denial of the information access request, the applicant will be sent, within the time limit for response, a communication containing:

I – the reasons for denying access and the underlying legal basis;

II – the possibility of appeal, to which authority appeal shall be made, and within what time limit; and

III – the possibility of presenting a request to declassify the information, where applicable, with an indication of the classifying authority that will evaluate the request.

§1 – The statement of reasons for denying access to classified information shall indicate the legal basis for the classification, the authority that classified it and the index code of the classified document.

§2 – The institutions and entities shall provide a standard form for filing the appeal and the declassification request.

**Article 20**
Access to the preparatory document or information in such document used as the grounds for the decision or administrative act will be ensured through a publication of the act or decision.

Sole paragraph. The Ministry of Finance and the Central Bank of Brazil shall classify documents on which they base their economic policy decisions, such as fiscal, tax, monetary and regulatory policies.

## Section IV
## Appeals

**Article 21**
If access to information is denied or the reasons for denial of access are not supplied, the applicant may submit an appeal within ten days after the date of notice of the decision to the authority hierarchically superior to the authority that

made the decision, which shall evaluate the appeal within five days after the submission of the appeal.

Sole paragraph. If the appeal referred to in the main paragraph of Article 21 above is denied, the applicant may submit another appeal within ten days after notice of the decision to the institution's or 's highest authority, which shall express its opinion within five days after receipt of the appeal.

**Article 22**
If the information access request goes unanswered, the applicant may submit a complaint within ten days to the monitoring authority referred to in Article 40 of Law No. 12.527 of 2011, which shall express its opinion within five days after receipt of the complaint.

§1 – The time limit for submitting a complaint shall commence thirty days after the submission of the request.

§2 – The highest authority of the institution may designate another authority directly subordinate to the highest authority to be in charge of receipt and evaluation of the complaint.

**Article 23**
In case of denial of the appeal referred to in sole paragraph of Article 21 or dismissal of the complaint referred to in Article 22, the applicant may submit an appeal within ten days after notice of the decision to the Federal Comptroller-General's Office, which shall express its opinion within five days after receipt of the appeal.

§1 – The Federal Comptroller-General's Office may order the organ or to provide explanations.

§2 – If the appeal is denied, the Federal Comptroller-General's Office shall set a time limit for the institution to comply with the decision.

**Article 24**
In the event of denial of access to information or failure to explain the reasons for the denial of access referred to in the main paragraph of Article 21, if the appeal is denied by the Federal Comptroller-General's Office the applicant may submit an appeal, within ten days after notice of the decision, to the Joint Committee of Information Re-evaluation in accordance with the procedures stipulated in Chapter VI.

## Chapter V
## Information Classified under a Security Classification

### Section I
### Classification of Information According to the Level and Period of Secrecy

**Article 25**
Information may be classified if it is considered indispensable to the security of society or the state and disclosure or unrestricted access might:

I – jeopardize national defence, sovereignty, or the integrity of national territory;

II – damage or jeopardize the Nation's negotiations or internal relations;

III – damage or jeopardize secret information supplied by other states or international organizations;

IV – jeopardize the life, safety or health of the population;

V – expose the Nation to elevated risk of financial, economic or monetary instability;

VI – harm or jeopardize the strategic operations or plans of the Armed Forces;

VII – harm or jeopardize scientific or technological research and development projects, as well as systems, assets, installations or areas of national strategic interest, in compliance with the provisions of subparagraph II of the main paragraph of Article 6;

VIII – jeopardize the safety of institutions or of high national or foreign authorities and the family members thereof; or

IX – compromise intelligence activities, as well as ongoing investigations or inspections related to the prevention or suppression of crime.

**Article 26**
Information held by public entities or institutions, considering their content and indispensability to the safety of society or the state, may be classified as top-secret, secret or reserved.

**Article 27**
When classifying information by security classification, consideration shall be made of the public's interest in knowing the information and to apply the least restrictive criteria possible, considering:

I – the seriousness of the risk or damage to the safety of society and the state; and

II – the maximum expirations of the classifications under the security classification or the event that will determine when the classification is lifted.

**Article 28**
The maximum expirations of classifications are as follows:

I – top secret: twenty-five years;

II – secret: fifteen years; and

III – restricted: five years.

Sole paragraph. It may be stipulated that the restriction of access will be lifted when a certain event occurs, without prejudice to the maximum expirations of classification.

**Article 29**
Information that might jeopardize the safety of the President of the Republic, the Vice-President and the spouses and children thereof shall be classified as restricted and remain secret until the end of the current term of office or of the final term of office in case of reelection.

**Article 30**
The classification of information falls within the authority of:

I – at the top secret level, the following authorities:

a) the President of the Republic;

b) the Vice-President of the Republic;

c) the Ministers of State and authorities with the same prerogatives;

d) the Navy, Army and Air Force Commanders; and

e) Heads of permanent Diplomatic and Consular missions abroad;

II – at the secret level, the authorities mentioned in subparagraph I of the main paragraph of Article 30, and the heads of quasi-governmental organizations, foundations, public companies and mixed capital corporations; and

III at the restricted level, the authorities mentioned in subparagraphs I and II of the main paragraph of Article 30 and those that exercise the managerial, command or supervisory duties of the DAS [Senior Management and Consulting Group], of DAS level 101.5 or higher, and the equivalents thereof.

§1 – It is prohibited to delegate the authority to classify as top secret or secret.

§2 – The head of the institution may delegate the authority to classify as restricted to a public servant who exercises managerial, command or supervisory duties.

§3 – It is prohibited to sub-delegate the authority referred to in §2.

§4 – The public servants referred to in §2 shall give notice of the act of classification to the delegating authority within 90 days thereafter.

§5 – The classification of information as top secret by the authorities referred to in items "d" and "e" of subparagraph I of the main paragraph of Article 30 is subject to ratification by the Minister of State within thirty days thereafter.

§6 – Pending such ratification, the classification referred to in §5 is considered valid for all legal effects and purposes.

## Section II
## Information Classification Procedures

### Article 31

The decision that classifies information under any security classification shall be formalized in the Information Classification Document [*Termo de Classificação de Informação* or TCI], in accordance with the model in the Annex, and shall contain the following:

I – the index code of the document;

II – the degree of secrecy;

III – the category in which the information is classified;

IV – the type of document;

V – date of production of the document;

VI – indication of the statutory provision on which the classification is based;

VII – the reasons for the classification, in accordance with the criteria stipulated by Article 27;

VIII – indication of the expiration of secrecy, in years, months or days, or of the event that determines when the classification will be lifted, without prejudice to the time limits stipulated in Article 28;

IX – date of the classification; and

X – identification of the authority that classified the information.

§1 – The TCI will be appended to the information in question.

§2 – The information stipulated by subparagraph VII of the main paragraph of Article 31 shall be kept at the same security classification as the classified information.

§3 – The ratification of the classification referred to in §5 of Article 30 shall be recorded in the TCI.

### Article 32

The authority or other civil servant who classifies information as top secret or secret shall forward a copy of the TCI to Joint Committee of Information Re-evaluation within thirty days after the decision of classification or ratification.

**Article 33**
In the case of a document that contains classified information of various levels of secrecy, the document shall be treated as belonging to the highest of those levels of secrecy, and access to the unclassified parts shall be granted by means of a certified copy, extract or ordinary copy, with the secret parts blacked out.

**Article 34**
The institutions and entities may form a Standing Committee of Secret Document Evaluation [Comissão Permanente de Evaluação de Documentos Sigilosos – CPADS], with the following responsibilities:

I – to express an opinion on the information produced within its scope of action for the purposes of classification under a given security classification;

II – to advise the classifying authority or hierarchically superior authority on declassification, reclassification or re-evaluation of classified information of a given security classification;

III – to suggest what should ultimately be done with the declassified information, indicating which documents should be kept permanently in accordance with the provisions of Law No. 8.159 of January 8, 1991; and

IV – to assist with preparing the annual list, to be published online, of declassified information and documents classified under each security classification.

**Section III**
**Declassification and Re-evaluation of the Information Classified under a Security Classification**

**Article 35**
The classification of information shall be re-evaluated by the classifying authority or an authority hierarchically superior thereto, either by request or *ex offício*, for the purposes of declassification or reduction of the expiration of secrecy.

Sole paragraph. For compliance with the provisions of the main paragraph of Article 35, in addition to the provisions of Article 27, shall take the following factors into account:

I – the maximum expiration of restriction of information access stipulated in Article 28;

II – the maximum time interval of four years for *ex officio* review of information classified as top secret or secret, stipulated in subparagraph I of the main paragraph of Article 47;

III – the continued relevance of the initial reasons for clarification;

IV – the possibilities of harm or risks that would result from disclosure or unrestricted access to the information; and

V – the special nature of information produced by authorities or civil servants abroad.

**Article 36**
The request for declassification or re-evaluation of the classification may be submitted to the institutions and entities irrespective of whether a prior information access request was made.

Sole paragraph. The request referred to in the main paragraph of Article 36 shall be addressed to the classifying authority, which shall decide on the request within thirty days thereafter.

**Article 37**
If the request for declassification or re-evaluation is denied by the classifying authority, the applicant may submit an appeal within ten days after the notice of denial, to Minister of State or to an authority with the same prerogatives, which shall decide on the appeal within thirty days thereafter.

§1 – In cases in which the classifying authority [that denied the request] is subordinated to a quasi-governmental organization, foundation, public company or mixed capital corporation, the appeal shall be submitted to the head of the relevant entity.

§2 – In the case of the Armed Forces, the appeal shall be submitted first to the relevant Commander and, in case of denial, to the State Defense Minister.

§3 – In the case of information produced by authorities or civil servants abroad, the request for declassification and re-evaluation shall be evaluated by the hierarchically superior authority located in Brazilian territory.

§4 – If the appeal referred to in the main paragraph of Article 37 and §§1 to 3 is denied, the applicant may submit an appeal to the Joint Committee of Information Re-evaluation within ten days after notice of the decision.

Article 38 – The decision of declassification, reclassification or reduction of the duration of secrecy of classified information shall be recorded on the relevant document's front cover, if any, and in the appropriate field in the TCI.

**Section IV**
**General Provisions**

**Article 39**
Information classified as top secret or secret shall be strictly safeguarded pursuant to Law No. 8.159 of 1991 in accordance with the access restriction procedures so long as the classification remains in effect.

**Article 40**
Information that was classified as a document to be permanently archived and is subsequently declassified will be sent to the National Archives and to the

permanent archives of the public organ, public entity or public institution for purposes of organization, safekeeping and access.

**Article 41**
Information about behavior involving human rights violations committed by civil servants or by order of public authorities must not be classified under any security classification whatsoever and access thereto shall not be denied.

**Article 42**
Access shall not be denied to information necessary for judicial or administrative protection of basic rights.

Sole paragraph. The applicant shall provide reasons demonstrating that the requested information is relevant to the right that the applicant claims to defend.

**Article 43**
Access, disclosure and processing of information classified under any security classification shall be restricted to persons who need to know such information and who are accredited in accordance with the regulations established by the Security and Accreditation Center [Núcleo de Segurança e Credenciamento] instituted within the framework of the Institutional Security Bureau [Gabinete de Segurança Institucional] under the authority of the President of the Republic, without prejudice to the powers granted to public servants by Law.

**Article 44**
The authorities of the Federal Executive Branch shall take such measures as are necessary to ensure that the staff members in their employ are familiar with the regulations and comply with the security procedures and measures for the treatment of information classified under a given security classification.

Sole paragraph. Any individual or private entity who processes classified information, by reason of any relationship with the public authorities shall take such measures as are necessary to ensure that its employees, agents or representatives comply with the information security measures and procedures.

**Article 45**
The highest authority of each institution shall publish on its website, by 1 June of each year:

I – a list of the information declassified within the past twelve months;

II – a list of the information classified under each security classification, which shall contain:

a) the index code of the relevant document;

b) the category in which the information is classified;

c) a citation of the statutory provision on which the classification is based; and

d) the production date, classification date and expiration of the classification;

III – statistical report including the number of information access requests received, the number of requests granted and requests denied; and

IV – aggregated statistical information on the applicants.

Sole paragraph. The institutions and entities shall store the information referred to in the main paragraph of Article 45 on a physical medium for public inspection on their premises.

## Chapter VI
## On the Joint Committee for the Re-evaluation of Classified Information

### Article 46

A Joint Committee of Information Re-evaluation, instituted in accordance with §1 of Article 35 of Law No. 12.527 of 2011, shall be composed of the heads of the following institutions:

I – Chief of Staff of the President of the Republic, who shall act as chairperson;

II – Ministry of Justice;

III – Ministry of Foreign Relations;

IV – Ministry of Defense;

V – Ministry of Finance;

VI – Ministry of Planning, Budgeting and Management;

VII – Presidential Human Rights Office;

VIII – Presidential Bureau of Institutional Security;

IX – Federal Attorney-General's Office;

X – Federal Comptroller – General's Office.

Sole paragraph. Each member shall designate a deputy to be appointed by the Committee Chairperson.

### Article 47

It is the responsibility of the Joint Committee of Information Re-evaluation:

I – to review, *ex officio* or on request, the classification of information as top secret or secret, or the re-evaluation thereof at least once every four years;

II – require from the authority that classifies the information as top secret or secret an explanation or the content, in whole or in part, if the information in the TCI [Information Review Document] is insufficient for a review of the classification;

III – to rule on appeals filed against decisions pronounced:

a) Federal Office of the Comptroller-General, on the appellate level, [concerning a?] request to access information or open the database, or the reasons to deny access to information or to open the database; or (*As worded by of Decree No. 8.777 of 2016*)

b) by the Minister of State or authority with the same prerogatives, on the appellate level, concerning a request for declassification or re-evaluation of classified information;

IV – to extend for one time only, and for a certain period not to exceed twenty-five years, the time limit of secrecy of classified information as top secret, while access to such information or disclosure thereof might cause an external threat to national sovereignty, to the integrity of the national territory or a grave risk to the Nation's international relations, provided that the total period of the classification does not exceed fifty years under any circumstances; and

V – to establish general regulatory guidelines in order to make up for any gaps in the application of the Law No. 12.527 of 2011.

Sole paragraph. The failure to hold the *ex officio* review within the time limit stipulated in subparagraph I of main paragraph of Article 47 shall result in automatic declassification of the information.

**Article 48**
The Joint Committee of Information Re-evaluation shall meet, ordinarily, once a month, and extraordinarily, whenever convened by its Chairperson.

Sole paragraph. Meetings shall be held with at least six members present.

**Article 49**
Requests for extension of the period of classification of information as top secret referred to in subparagraph IV of the main paragraph of Article 47, shall be forwarded to the Joint Committee of Information Re-evaluation at least one year before the expiration date of restricted access.

Sole paragraph. The request for extension of the time limit of secrecy of information classified as top secret shall be evaluated, on a non-postponable basis, within three successive meetings after the date of notice [of said request], and all other item to be put to vote shall be deferred until the Committee has deliberated on said request.

**Article 50**
The Joint Committee of Information Re-evaluation shall evaluate the appeals referred to in subparagraph III of the main paragraph of Article 47, on a non-postponable basis, within three successive ordinary meetings after the date of notice of the relevant appeal.

**Article 51**
The *ex officio* review of information classified as top secret or secret shall be evaluated within three meetings after the date of the automatic declassification thereof.

**Article 52**
The resolutions of the Joint Committee of Information Re-evaluation shall be adopted:

I – by an absolute majority, in the case of resolutions involving the responsibilities referred to in subparagraphs I and IV of the main paragraph of Article 47; and

II – by a simple majority of votes in all other cases.

Sole paragraph. The Chief of Staff of the President of the Republic shall have, in addition to an ordinary vote, the deciding vote in case of a tie.

**Article 53**
The Chief of Staff of the President of the Republic shall exercise the duties of Executive Secretary of the Joint Committee of Information Re-evaluation, whose responsibilities shall be defined by said Committee's internal rules of procedure.

**Article 54**
The internal rules of procedure regulating the organization and operation of the Joint Committee of Information Re-evaluation shall be adopted by said Committee by an absolute majority of votes.

Sole paragraph. The internal rules of procedure shall be published in the gazette "*Diario Oficial da União*" within ninety days after the Committee is established.

## Chapter VII
## Personal Information

**Article 55**
Information held by institutions and entities that is related to a data subject's privacy, private life, honor or image:

I – shall be accessible solely to legally authorized public servants and to the data subject, regardless of the security classification, for a period not to exceed one hundred years after the date of production of said information; and

II – may be disclosed or accessible to third parties authorized by law or by the data subject's express consent.

Sole paragraph. If the data subject is dead or absent, the rights referred to in this Article shall be enjoyed by the data subject's spouse or companion, descendants or ascendants, in accordance with the provisions of the sole paragraph of Article 20 of Law No. 10.406 of January 10, 2002, and Law No. 9.278, of May 10, 1996.

**Article 56**

Personal information shall be processed transparently and with respect for the information related to the data subject's privacy, private life, honor and image, liberties and guaranteed rights.

**Article 57**

The consent referred to in subparagraph II of the main paragraph of Article 55 shall not be required whenever access to the personal information is necessary for:

I – medical diagnosis and prevention, if the person is physically or legally incapable, for the exclusive purpose of medical treatment;

II – scientific research and statistics of obvious public or general interest as defined by Law, the identification of the data subject being prohibited;

III – compliance with a judicial decision;

IV –defense of a third party's human rights; or

V – the protection of an overriding general public interest.

**Article 58**

Access to personal information dealt with in Article 55 cannot be invoked:

I – with the intent to interfere with an audit conducted by the Public Authority to detect irregularities of the data subject or of which the data subject has an interest; or

II – whenever the non-classified information is contained in sets of documents necessary for the recovery of highly relevant historical facts.

**Article 59**

The head of the institution may, *ex officio* or on request, recognize, subject to substantiation, that the status referred to in subparagraph II of the main paragraph of Article 58 is applicable to documents that the head of the institution has produced or collected and of which the head of the institution is the custodian.

§1 – To substantiate the decision to declare the status referred to in the main paragraph of Article 59, the institution may ask universities, research institutes or other entities with well-known experience in historical research to issue an opinion on the matter.

§2 – The decision to declare the status referred to in the main paragraph of Article 59 shall be preceded by publishing an extract from the information at least thirty days in advance, with a summary description of the subject matter, origin and period of the set of documents to be considered accessible without restriction.

§3 – After a decision to declare the status referred to in §2, the documents shall be considered accessible to the public without restriction.

§4 – In the case of documents of great historic value intended to be permanently archived, it shall be the prerogative of the head of the National Archives or to the authority in charge of archiving of the public entity or institution that receives said documents to decide, after receipt, whether to declare the aforementioned status in accordance with the procedure stipulated by this Article.

**Article 60**
Access to personal information shall be requested according to the procedures stipulated in Chapter IV and shall be conditioned upon proof of the applicant's identity.

Sole paragraph. Requests for access to personal information by third parties shall be accompanied by:

I – proof of the express consent referred to in subparagraph II of the main paragraph of Article 55, through a power of attorney;

II – proof of conformity with the circumstances contemplated by Article 58;

III – demonstration of the interest in recovering highly relevant historical facts, in accordance with the procedures stipulated in Article 59; or

IV – demonstration of the need to access the requested information in order to defend human rights or safeguard the overriding interests of the general public.

**Article 61**
Access to personal information by third parties shall be conditioned upon signing a declaration of assumption of responsibility concerning the obligations to be assumed by the applicant, which shall regulate the purpose and intended use underlying the third party's authorization.

§1 – The utilization of personal information by third parties is restricted to the purpose and intended use underlying the access authorization, and any other manner of use is prohibited.

§2 – Any person who obtains access to the personal information of third parties shall be held responsible, in the manner prescribed by Law, for the misuse of said information.

**Article 62**
To the extent relevant, Law No. 9.507 of November 12, 1997 shall apply in relation to information about a natural or juridical person contained in a register or database of governmental or public institutions or entities.

**Chapter VIII**
**Non-Profit Private Entities**

**Article 63**
Non-profit private entities that receive public resources to carry out actions of public interest shall publicly disclose the following information:

I – a copy of the entity's updated articles of association;

II –an updated list of the names of the entity's managers; and

III – a complete copy of the conventions, contracts, partnership agreements, settlement agreements, covenants or similar instruments entered into with the Federal Executive Branch, with the corresponding addenda and final statement of accounts, in the manner prescribed by the applicable legislation.

§1 – The information referred to in the main paragraph of Article 63 shall be disclosed on the private entity's website and on a bulletin board accessible to the general public in the entity's head office.

§2 – Subject to providing express justifications, non-profit private entities that cannot afford the website disclosure referred to in §1 may be released from that obligation by decision of the relevant public entity or organ.

§3 – The information referred to in the main paragraph of Article 63 shall be published from the date of signature of the relevant conventions, contracts, partnership agreements, settlement agreements, covenants or similar instruments and shall be periodically updated and remain accessible for one hundred and eighty days after the submission of the final statement of accounts.

**Article 64**

The requests for information related to the conventions, contracts, partnership agreements, settlement agreements, covenants or similar instruments referred to in Article 63 shall be presented directly to the institutions and entities responsible for the disbursement of funds.

## Chapter IX
## Responsibilities

**Article 65**

Any member of the military or civil service guilty of the following forms of misconduct is subject to prosecution:

I – refusing to supply requested information in accordance with this Decree, deliberately delaying the supply thereof or intentionally supplying incorrect, incomplete or inaccurate information;

II – misusing, subtracting from, destroying, rendering unusable, disfiguring, altering or concealing, in whole or in part, information that is in the agent's or military personnel's custody, to which the agent or member of the military has access or of which the agent or member of the military is aware by reason of the exercise of the duties of the public function, post or job;

III – acting with malicious intent or in bad faith when analyzing the access to information access requests;

IV – disclosing, permitting the disclosure, accessing or permitting unauthorized access to information classified under a security classification or to personal information;

V – imposing secrecy on information to obtain personal gain or gain for a third party or for the purposes of concealing an illegal act committed by oneself or by another;

VI – to conceal information classified under a security classification from scrutiny by a competent higher authority for one's own or another's benefit, or to the detriment of third parties; and

VII – to destroy or subtract from, by any means, documents concerning possible human rights violations by agents of the state.

§1 – With due consideration for the principles of adversary proceedings, the right to a fair hearing and due process of law, the conduct described in the main paragraph of Article 65 will be considered:

I – for the purposes of the disciplinary regulations of the Armed Forces, moderate to severe military misconduct, depending on the criteria established therein, unless defined by law as crimes or criminal offences; or

II – for the purposes of provisions of Law No. 8.112 of December 11, 1990, administrative infractions, punishable at least by suspension, in accordance with the criteria established in said Law.

§2 – Member of the military or civil services engaging in misconduct referred to in the main paragraph of Article 65 may also be liable for abuse of office *[improbidade administrativo]*, in accordance with the provisions of Laws no. 1.079 of April, 10 1950, and no. 8.429 of June 2, 1992.

**Article 66**

A private entity or individual who possesses information by virtue of any relationship with the Public Authority and engages in misconduct referred to in Article 65 shall be subject to the following punishments:

I – a warning;

II – a fine;

III – termination of the relationship with the Public Authority;

IV – temporary suspension of the right to participate in calls for bids and disqualification from contracting with public authorities for a period not to exceed two years; and

V – declaration of ineligibility to bid or contract with the public authorities until reinstated by the authority that applied the penalty.

§1 – The fine may be applied concurrently with the other punishments under subparagraphs I, III and IV of the main paragraph of Article 66.

§2 – The fine under subparagraph II of the main paragraph of Article 66 shall be applicable without prejudice to compensation for damages and shall be:

I – no less than BRL 1,000.00 (one thousand Reais) and no more than BRL 200,000.00 (two hundred thousand Reais), in the case of an individual; or

II – no less than BRL 5,000.00 (five thousand Reais) and no more than BRL 600,000.00 (six hundred thousand Reais), in the case of a private entity.

§3 – The reinstatement mentioned in subparagraph V of the main paragraph of Article 66 shall be authorized only after the private entity or individual has compensated the institution for any resulting losses and the period of punishment referred to in subparagraph IV of the main paragraph of Article 66 has lapsed.

§4 – Only the highest authority of the public entity or institution shall have the authority to apply the punishment referred to in subparagraph V of the main paragraph of Article 66.

§5 – The time limit for submission of a defense in the cases mentioned in this Article is ten days after receipt of notice of the act.

## Chapter X
## Monitoring of Enforcement of the Law

### Section I
### Monitoring Authority

#### Article 67

The head of each institution shall designate a directly subordinate authority to exercise the following duties:

I – to ensure compliance with the laws concerning access to information, efficiently and in keeping with the objectives of Law No. 12.527 of 2011;

II – to evaluate and monitor the implementation of the provisions of this Decree and present an annual compliance report to the head of each institution, which shall be forwarded to the Federal Comptroller-General's Office;

III – to recommend measures to improve the regulations and procedures necessary for the implementation of this Decree;

IV – to provide the units with guidance concerning compliance with this Decree; and

V – to express his opinion on complaints filed against the competent authority's omission, in accordance with the provisions of Article 22.

## Section II
## Responsibilities Related to Monitoring

### Article 68

It is the responsibility of the Federal Comptroller-General's Office, with due consideration for the areas of responsibility of the other institutions and entities and specific provisions of this Decree:

I – to design the standard form to be made available as a hardcopy or electronically on the website and in the Citizen Information Services of the institutions and entities, in accordance with §1 of Article 11;

II – to promote a national campaign of to encourage a culture of transparency in public administration and to raise awareness of the fundamental right of access to information;

III – to promote the training of public servants and, to the extent relevant, of non-profit private entities with respect to the development of practices related to transparency in public administration;

IV – to monitor the implementation of Law No. 12.527 of 2011, concentrating and consolidating the publication of the statistics referred to in Article 45;

V – to prepare an annual report with information related to implementation of Law No. 12.527 of 2011, to be forwarded to the National Congress;

VI – to monitor the enforcement of this Decree, especially compliance with the time limits and procedures; and

VII – to define, together with the Chief of Staff of the President of the Republic, any supplementary guidelines and procedures necessary for the implementation of Law No. 12.527 of 2011.

### Article 69

It is the responsibility of the Federal Comptroller-General's Office and the Ministry of Planning, Budgeting and Management, with due consideration for the responsibilities of the other institutions and entities and the specific provisions of this Decree, to act jointly in order to:

I – establish procedures, rules and standards of public disclosure of information, specifying maximum time between updates; and

II – to describe the procedures necessary for searching, structuring and supplying information in the Citizen Information Service.

### Article 70

It is the responsibility of the Institutional Security Bureau under the authority of the President of the Republic, with due consideration for the areas of responsibility of the other institutions and entities and specific provisions of this Decree:

I – to establish rules of indexing related to the classification of information;

II – to issue supplementary [regulatory] acts and establish security accreditation procedures for public or private institutions and entities for the processing of classified information; and

III – to promote, by means of the Security and Accreditation Center, security accreditation procedures for public or private institutions and entities for the processing of classified information.

## Chapter XI
## Transitional and Final Provisions

### Article 71

The institutions and entities shall adapt their information management policies by bringing about the necessary adjustments to the processes of registration, processing, handling and archiving of documents and information.

### Article 72

Institutions and entities shall re-evaluate information classified as top secret and secret at least every two years, counting from the date Law No. 12.527 of 2011 comes into effect.

§1 – Any restriction of access to information by reason of the re-evaluation referred to in the main paragraph of Article 72 shall comply with the time limits and conditions stipulated in this Decree.

§2 – Within the time period for re-evaluation stipulated in the main paragraph of Article 72, the classification of information shall be maintained, in accordance with time limits and provisions of the prior legislation.

§3 – Any information classified as top secret or secret that is not re-evaluated by the appointed time stipulated in the main paragraph of Article 72 shall automatically be considered declassified.

### Article 73

The annual publication referred to in Article 45 shall commence in June 2013.

### Article 74

The treatment of classified information resulting from international regulatory acts, agreements or treaties shall comply with the rules and recommendations of said instruments.

### Article 75

The Law No. 9.784 of January 29, 1999 shall apply in a subsidiary capacity to the procedures stipulated by this Decree.

### Article 76

This Decree shall enter into force on 16th of May 2012.

# Appendix 4 China: National Freedom-of-Information and Transparency Legislation (Extracts)

## 1. Regulations of the People's Republic of China on Open Government Information[6]

**Article 1**

In order to ensure that citizens, legal persons and other organizations obtain government information in accordance with the law, enhance transparency of the work of government, promote administration in accordance with the law, and bring into full play the role of government information in serving the people's production and livelihood and their economic and social activities, these Regulations are hereby formulated.

**Article 4**

The people's government at all levels and the departments of the people's governments at the county level and above should establish and perfect systems for open government information work for their respective administrative agencies and designate an office (hereafter referred to as the "office for open government information work") to be responsible for the daily work of open government information for their respective administrative agencies.

The specific functions of the office for open government information work are:

1) To undertake specific open government information matters for that administrative agency;
2) To maintain and update government information disclosed by that administrative agency;

[6]Adopted by the State Council on 17 January 2007; effective since 1 May 2008. Translated and published by the China Law Center, Yale Law School, https://www.law.yale.edu/system/files/documents/pdf/Intellectual_Life/CL-OGI-Regs-English.pdf (Accessed on 23 August 2016).



H.-J. Blanke, R. Perlingeiro (eds.), *The Right of Access to Public Information*,
DOI 10.1007/978-3-662-55554-5

3) To organize for that administrative agency the compilation of an open government information guide, open government information catalogue and annual reports on open government information work;
4) To conduct examinations for secrecy of government information to be disclosed; and
5) To carry out other responsibilities related to open government information stipulated by that administrative agency.

**Article 6**
Administrative agencies should disclose government information promptly and accurately. When administrative agencies discover false or incomplete information that affects or might affect social stability and disturbs the social management order, they should release, within their scope of responsibility, accurate government information to clarify the situation.

**Article 8**
The government information disclosed by administrative organs may not endanger state security, public security, economic security and social stability.

**Article 9**
Administrative agencies should disclose on their own initiative government information that satisfies any one of the following basic criteria:

1) Information that involves the vital interests of citizens, legal persons or other organizations;
2) Information that needs to be extensively known or participated in by the general public;
3) Information that shows the structure, function and working procedures of and other matters relating to the administrative agency; and
4) Other information that should be disclosed on the administrative agency's own initiative according to laws, regulations and relevant state provisions.

**Article 10**
People's governments at the county level and above and their departments should determine the concrete content of the government information to be disclosed on their own initiative within their scope of responsibility in accordance with the provisions of Article 9 of these Regulations, and emphasize disclosure of the following government information:

1) Administrative regulations, rules, and regulatory documents;
2) Plans for national economic and social development, plans for specific projects, plans for regional development and related policies;
3) Statistical information on national economic and social development;
4) Reports on financial budgets and final accounts;
5) Items subject to an administrative fee and the legal basis and standards therefor;

6) Catalogues of the government's centralized procurement projects, their standards and their implementation;
7) Matters subject to administrative licensing and their legal bases, conditions, quantities, procedures and deadlines and catalogues of all the materials that need to be submitted when applying for the administrative licensing, and the handling thereof;
8) Information on the approval and implementation of major construction projects;
9) Policies and measures on such matters as poverty assistance, education, medical care, social security and job creation and their actual implementation;
10) Emergency plans for, early warning information concerning, and counter measures against sudden public events;
11) Information on the supervision and inspection of environmental protection, public health, safe production, food and drugs, and product quality.

**Article 11**

The government information to be emphasized for disclosure by the people's governments at the level of cities divided into districts and the county level people's governments and their departments should also include the following contents:

1) Important and major matters in urban and rural construction and management;
2) Information on the construction of social and public interest institutions;
3) Information on land requisition or land appropriation, household demolition and resettlement, and the distribution and use of compensation or subsidy funds relating thereto; and
4) Information on the management, usage and distribution of social donations in funds and in kind for emergency and disaster relief, special care for families of martyrs and military service personnel, and assistance to poverty stricken and low income families.

**Article 12**

People's governments at the township (town) level should determine the concrete content of the government information to be disclosed on their own initiative within their scope of responsibility in accordance with the provisions of Article 9 of these Regulations, and emphasize disclosure of the following government information:

1) Information on the implementation of rural work policies of the state;
2) Information on fiscal income and expenses and the management and use of various specialized funds;
3) Overall township (town) land use plans and information on the verification of land to be used by farmers for their primary residences;
4) Information on land requisition or land appropriation, household demolition and resettlement, and the distribution and use of compensation or subsidy funds therefor;

5) Information on township (town) credits and debts, fund raising and labor levies;
6) Information on the distribution of social donations in funds and in kind for emergency and disaster relief, special care for families of martyrs and military service personnel, and assistance to poverty stricken and low income families;
7) Information on contracting, leasing and auctioning of township and town collectively owned enterprises and other township and town economic entities; and
8) Information on implementation of the family planning policy.

**Article 13**

In addition to government information disclosed by administrative agencies on their own initiative provided for in Articles 9, 10, 11 and 12, citizens, legal persons or other organizations may, based on the special needs of such matters as their own production, livelihood and scientific and technological research, also file requests departments of the State Council, local people's governments at all levels and departments under local people's governments at the county level and above to obtain relevant government information.

**Article 14**

Administrative agencies should establish and perfect mechanisms to examine for secrecy the government information to be released, and clarify the examination procedures and responsibilities.

Prior to disclosing government information, administrative agencies should examine the government information to be disclosed in accordance with the provisions of the Law of the People's Republic of China on Safeguarding State Secrets and other laws, regulations and relevant state provisions.

When an administrative agency is unable to determine if certain government information may be disclosed, it should submit the matter for determination to relevant departments in charge or departments for safeguarding secrecy at the same level as theadministrative agency.

Administrative agencies may not disclose government information that involves state secrets, commercial secrets or individual privacy. However, government information involving commercial secrets or individual privacy may be disclosed by administrative agencies with the consent of the rightholder(s) or if administrative agencies believe that non-disclosure might give rise to a major impact on the public interest.

**Article 16**

The people's governments at all levels should set up government information reading places in the state archives and public libraries and install appropriate facilities and equipment to make it convenient for citizens, legal persons and other organizations to obtain government information.

Administrative agencies may set up, as needed, places and facilities such as public reading rooms, materials request stations, information bulletin boards, and electronic information screens to disclose government information.

Administrative agencies should provide the state archives and public libraries with government information disclosed on their own initiative in a timely manner.

**Article 17**
Administrative agencies shall be responsible for disclosing government information that they have made. Administrative agencies that store government information obtained from citizens, legal persons or other organizations shall be responsible for disclosing it. If laws or regulations have different provisions on the scope of authorization to disclose government information, those provisions shall be followed.

**Article 20**
Citizens, legal persons or other organizations should file requests with government agencies to obtain government information in accordance with Article 13 of these Regulations in written form (including digital and electronic forms). In the event that it is truly difficult for a requester to submit a request in written form, the requester may do so orally and the administrative agency accepting the request shall fill out the request for open government information on the requester's behalf.

Requests for open government information should include the following contents:

1) The name of the individual or organization making the request and the method of contact;
2) A description of the government information requested to be disclosed; and
3) Requirements as to the format in which the requested government information is to be supplied.

**Article 21**
Administrative agencies shall reply to requests for open government information respectively in accordance with the following circumstances:

1) If the requested government information falls within the scope of disclosure, the requester should be informed of the methods and channels for obtaining that government information;
2) If the requested government information does not fall into the scope of disclosure, the requester should be informed that such information cannot be disclosed, together with an explanation of the reasons;
3) If, in accordance with the law, the requested government information should not be disclosed by that administrative agency or the requested government information does not exist, the requester should be informed of the situation and, if the agency that has the obligation to disclose that government

information can be determined, the requester should be informed of the name of that administrative agency and the method to contact it;
4) If the content of the requested government information is not clear, the requester should be notified to amend and supplement the request.

**Article 22**
If the requested government information contains some contents thatshould not be disclosed but that can be handled through differentiation, the administrative agency should provide the requester with that information content that may be disclosed.

**Article 23**
If an administrative agency believes that the requested government information involves commercial secrets or individual privacy the disclosure of which might infringe upon the lawful rights and interests of a third party, it should write to the third party to seek its opinion. If the third party does not agree to have the information disclosed, the information may not be disclosed. However, if the administrative agency believes that non-disclosure might have a major influence on the public interest, it should disclose the information and notify the third party in writing of the content of the government information they have decided to disclose and the reasons therefor.

**Article 24**
After receiving requests for open government information, administrative agencies should reply to the requests on-the-spot to the extent possible.

If an on-the-spot reply is not possible, administrative agencies should provide a reply within 15 business days from receiving a request. If an extension of the time limit for replying to a request is needed, the agreement of the responsible person in charge of the office for open government information work should be obtained and the requester notified. The maximum extension of the time limit for replying to a request may not exceed 15 business days.

If the requested government information involves the rights and interests of a third party, the time needed by administrative agencies to seek the opinion of the third party shall not be counted against the time limit provided in Paragraph 2 of this Article.

**Article 26**
When providing government information on request, administrative agencies shall provide the information in the format requested by the requesters. If it is impossible to provide the information in the format requested by the requesters, administrative agencies may provide the information through making arrangements for the requesters to read the relevant documents, providing photocopies or using other appropriate methods.

### Article 27

When disclosing government information on request, administrative agencies may not collect any fees except they may collect cost-based fees for the cost of searching, photocopying, postage and the like. Administrative agencies may not provide government information as a compensated service through any organizations or individuals.

### Article 33

If citizens, legal persons or other organizations believe an administrative agency has failed to fulfill, in accordance with the law, its obligations in respect of open government information, they may report it to the higher level administrative agency, the supervision agency or the department in charge of open government information. The agency that receives the report should investigate and handle it.

# Appendix 5 France: National Freedom-of-Information and Transparency Legislation (Extracts)

## 1. Act on Various Measures for Improved Relations Between the Civil Service and the Public and on Various Arrangements of Administrative, Social and Fiscal Nature (Law 78-17 of January 6, 1978)[7]

### Title 1
### Freedom of Access to Administrative Documents and Re-Use of Public Information

### Part I
### Freedom of Access to Administrative Documents

#### Article 1
(Ordinance No. 2009-483 of 29 April 2009, Article 2)

Parts 1, 3, and 4 of this Title specify and guarantee the right of everyone to information as far as the freedom of access to administrative documents is concerned.

For the purposes of Parts 1, 3, and 4 of this Title, "administrative documents" shall mean any documents originating from or received by the State, territorial authorities, or from public or private-law organisations managing a public service, as part of their public service mission, regardless of their date, repository, format or medium. Such documents include files, reports, studies, records,

[7]Last amended by *Law 525 of May 17, 2011;* consolidated text as of 19 May 2011. Published in *Journal Officiel de la République française* of 18 May 2011, p. 8537 (originally published in the *Journal officiel de la République française* of 18 July 1978, p. 2851). Act partially codified by Ordinance No. 2015-1341 of 23 October 2015, *Journal officiel de la République française* of 25 October 2015, p. 19872.



H.-J. Blanke, R. Perlingeiro (eds.), *The Right of Access to Public Information*,
DOI 10.1007/978-3-662-55554-5

minutes, statistics, orders, instructions, ministerial circulars, memoranda or replies, correspondence, recommendations, forecasts and decisions.

Proceedings and documents originating from or received by the parliamentary assemblies are governed by Act No. 25-1100 of 17 November 1958 on the functioning of the parliamentary assemblies.

**Article 2**
(Ordinance No. 2009-483 of 29 April 2009, Article 3)

Subject to the provisions of Article 6, the authorities referred to in Article 1 shall be bound to hand over administrative documents in their possession to all persons applying for production of them in accordance with the conditions provided for in this Part.

The right to delivery shall apply to completed documents only. It shall not apply to documents that are instrumental in an administrative decision until the latter has been taken. Such a right cannot be exercised once the circulation of the documents is public.

The depositing in the Public Record Office (public archives) of administrative documents that may be handed over under this Part shall not be considered as an obstacle to the right to delivery of such documents at any time.

If a public service referred to in Article 1 is asked to communicate an administrative document that is not in its possession but in the possession of another public service referred to in the same Article, it shall transfer the request to the latter and advise the person involved.

If a public service referred to in Article 1, or the Committee of Access to Administrative Documents, is asked to communicate an administrative document that may be governed by several access regimes referred to in Articles 20 and 21 of this Act, it shall proprio motu examine the requests under all such regimes, except under that set out under Article L. 213-3 of the heritage code.

The appealed public service shall not be bound to allow requests that appear unreasonable either because of their number or because of their repetitive or systematic nature.

**Article 3**
(Ordinance No. 2005-650 of 6 June 2005, Articles 2 and 3 JORF 7 June 2005)

Subject to the provisions of Act No. 78-17 of 6 January 1978 on Data processing and individual liberties regarding personal data contained in files, everyone shall have the right to know information contained in an administrative document whose submissions are set up against him/her.

On his/her request, his/her observations regarding the aforementioned submissions must be written down as an annex to the document concerned.

The use of an administrative document in disregard of the above provisions is forbidden.

**Article 4**
(Ordinance No. 2005-650 of 6 June 2005, Articles 2, 3 and 6 JORF 7 June 2005)

Access to administrative documents may be given, according to the requesting person's preference within the limits of what is technically possible to the public service:

a) by way of on-the-spot, free-of-charge consultation, unless the preservation of the document makes it impossible to do so,
b) provided that reproduction does not adversely affect the preservation of the document, by the supplying of a copy on a medium identical to or compatible with the one used by the public service and at the requesting person's own expense, without such expense exceeding the reproduction cost, under such conditions as provided for by decree,
c) by electronic mail, without charge, if the document is available in electronic format.

**Article 6**
(Act No. 2011-525 of 17 May 2011, Article 50)

I. Shall not be handed over:

1. Council of State and administrative court opinions, documents of the Court of auditors referred to in Article L. 141-10 of the code of financial courts and documents of the regional audit chambers referred to in Article L. 241-6 of that code, documents drafted or held by the Competition authority in the performance of its powers of investigation and decision, documents used to develop the accreditation reports of health institutions according to Article L. 6113-6 of the public health code, documents used in the accreditation of health staff according to Article L. 1414-3-3 of the public health code, health institution audit reports referred to in Article 40 of Act No. 2000-1257 of 23 December 2000, the Social Security Financing Act for 2001, and any documents prepared in the performance of a service contract performed for one or several specific persons;

2. any other administrative documents whose consultation or delivery would be harmful to:

- the secrecy of the proceedings of the Government and responsible authorities within the executive power;
- the national defence secrecy;
- the conduct of France's foreign policy;
- the State's security, public safety and security of individuals;
- the currency and public credit;
- the proper conduct of proceedings begun before jurisdictions or of operations preliminary to such proceedings, unless authorisation is given by the authority concerned;
- actions, by the proper services, to detect tax and customs offences;
- or, subject to Article L. 124-4 of the environmental code, to other secrets protected by the law.

II. Can only be handed over to the person involved, administrative documents:

- whose delivery would be harmful to privacy, to the secrecy of personal files, to medical secrecy or to trade and manufacturing secret;
- passing remarks or value judgement on a natural person, referred to by his/her name or easily identifiable;
- showing the behaviour of a person, the disclosure of which could harm the latter.

Information of medical nature shall be handed over to the person involved, directly or through a doctor designated for that purpose by the person involved, in accordance with his/her choice under the conditions provided for by the provisions of the Article L.1111-7 of the code of public health.

III. When the requested document includes information that may not be handed over under this Article, but that may be concealed or severed from it, the document shall be handed over to the requesting person once that information has been concealed or severed.

Any administrative documents that may not be handed over within the meaning of this Part shall become accessible at the end of the periods and under the conditions set out in Articles L. 213-1 and L. 213-2 of the heritage code. Prior to the end of these periods and notwithstanding the provisions of this Article, access to these documents may be authorised under the conditions set out in Article L. 213-3 of that code.

**Article 7**
(Ordinance No. 2009-483 of 29 April 2009, Article 5)

All ministerial orders, instructions, circulars, memoranda and replies containing an interpretation of positive law or a description of administrative procedures shall be published.

The public services referred to in Article 1 may also publish any other administrative documents elaborated or held by them.

However, subject to contrary legal provisions, any administrative documents that include information falling within the scope of Article 6 or, without prejudice to Article 13, personal data, may only be made public if such information has been concealed or the individuals named therein cannot be identified.

A decree enacted by the Council of State after recommendation by the Committee of Access to Administrative Documents referred to in Part III shall establish the implementing provisions of the first paragraph of this Article.

**Article 8**
(Ordinance No. 2005-650 of 6 June 2005, Articles 2 and 3 JORF 7 June 2005)

Unless provision is made for an implicit decision of denial or a tacit agreement, any individual decision taken on behalf of the State, of a territorial authority, of a public corporation or any organisation, be it of a private nature when in charge of managing a public service, can be binding on the person concerned only if the latter has received prior notification.

**Article 9**
(Ordinance No. 2005-650 of 6 June 2005, Articles 2, 3 and 9 JORF 7 June 2005)

The handing over of administrative documents is subject to copyright.

## Part II
## Re-Use of Public Information

**Article 10**
(Ordinance No. 2009-483 of 29 April 2009, Article 6)

The information stored in documents elaborated by or in possession of the public services mentioned in Article 1, whatever the format may be, may be used by any person who would wish it and for other reasons than those of the public service mission for the needs of which the documents have been elaborated or are held. The limits and conditions of this re-use shall be governed by this Part, even if said information was obtained under the freedom of access to administrative documents governed by Part I.

Information shall not be considered public for the purpose of this Part if it is contained in documents:

a) access to which is not guaranteed under Part I or any other legal provisions, except if the information has been circulated in the public domain, or
b) elaborated or held by the public services referred to in Article 1 as part of an industrial or commercial public service mission, or
c) in respect of which third parties hold intellectual property rights.

The exchange of public information among the authorities referred to in Article 1, for the purpose of their public service mission, shall not be deemed re-use in the sense of this Part.

**Article 11**
(Ordinance No. 2009-483 of 29 April 2009, Article 6)

By way of derogation from this Part, the conditions under which the information may be re-used may be determined by the public services referred to in paragraphs a and b of this Article when they are included in documents elaborated or held by:

a) teaching and research establishments and institutions, or
b) cultural establishments, organizations or services.

**Article 12**
(Ordinance No. 2005-650 of 6 June 2005, Article 10 JORF 7 June 2005)

Unless the public service agrees, the re-use of public information is subject to the condition that this information not be altered, its meaning not be transformed, and the sources and the date of the last update of this information be mentioned.

**Article 13**
(Ordinance No. 2009-483 of 29 April 2009, Article 7)

Public information that includes personal data may be re-used if the person involved has consented to its re-use, if the authority holding the information can depersonalise it, or, if the information cannot be depersonalised, if legal or regulatory provisions allow for this re-use.

The re-use of public information that includes personal data is subject to the provisions of Act No. 78-17 of 6 January 1978 Data processing and individual liberties.

**Article 14**
(Created by Ordinance No. 2005-650 of 6 June 2005, Article 10 JORF 7 June 2005)

The re-use of public information may not be granted exclusively to any third party, except if such an exclusive right is necessary for the fulfilment of a public service mission.

The validity of the reason for granting such an exclusive right shall be reviewed periodically, at least every three years.

**Article 15**
(Ordinance No. 2009-483 of 29 April 2009, Article 8)

The re-use of public information may give rise to the payment of fees.

In establishing such fees, the public service that elaborated or holds the documents containing public information that may be re-used shall take into account the cost of providing such information, including, if necessary, the cost of depersonalising it.

The public service may also take into account the cost of collecting and elaborating the information and include in the fee basis a reasonable return on its investment, including, if necessary, a fee for intellectual property rights. In such cases, the public service must ensure that the fees are set in a non-discriminatory manner and that their total proceeds, as assessed over an appropriate accounting period for investment amortisation, shall not exceed the total sum of the cost of collecting, elaborating and providing information and the remuneration set out under this paragraph.

If the public service that elaborated or holds the documents containing public information uses this information in commercial activities, it may not charge other operators more for its re-use than it charges itself, or impose less favourable conditions to such operators than it applies to itself.

**Article 16**
(Created by Ordinance No. 2005-650 of 6 June 2005, Article 10 JORF 7 June 2005)

When the re-use of public information is subject to payment of a fee, a licence shall be issued.

The licence shall set out the conditions of re-use of the public information. Such conditions may only limit the re-use for reasons of general interest and in a proportionate manner. They may not have the object or the effect of limiting competition.

The public services that elaborate or hold documents containing public information that may be re-used under the conditions set out in this Article shall make standard licences available ahead of time to any persons interested in re-using this information, where appropriate by electronic means.

The conditions under which a licence may be offered to applicants shall be specified by regulations.

**Article 17**
(Created by Ordinance No. 2005-650 of 6 June 2005, Article 10 JORF 7 June 2005)

The public services that elaborate or hold public information shall give users access to a directory of the main documents in which such information is presented.

The public services that elaborate or hold public information shall provide any person who requests them with the conditions for the re-use of such information, as well as with the base used for calculating any fees.

**Article 18**
(Created by Ordinance No. 2005-650 of 6 June 2005, Article 10 JORF 7 June 2005)

Any person re-using public information in violation of the provisions referred to in the second and third paragraphs of this Article shall be punished with a fine imposed by the Committee mentioned in Part III.

The maximum amount of such a fine shall be equal to that set out in Article 131-13 of the penal code in respect of category 5 offences, if public information is re-used for non-commercial purposes in breach of Article 12, of the conditions of re-use set out under a licence issued for that purpose, or in breach of the licensing requirement.

If public information is re-used for commercial purposes in breach of Article 12, of the conditions of re-use set out under a licence issued for that purpose, or in breach of the licensing requirement, the amount of the fine shall be determined by the seriousness of the breach and the advantages derived from such breach.

For the purposes of the third paragraph, the amount of the fine imposed in sanction of a first breach may not exceed 150,000 euros. In the event of a repeated breach in the five years following the date upon which the previous sanction became final, it may not exceed 300,000 euros or, in the case of a company, 5% of the revenue excluding taxes of the previous year ended, up to 300,000 euros.

The Committee mentioned in Part III may, instead of or in addition to the fine, ban the perpetrator from re-using the public information for up to two years. This period may be extended to five years in the event of a repeated breach within five years of the first breach.

The Committee may also order publication of the sanction at the expense of the perpetrator, as decreed by the Council of State.

Such fines shall be recovered as sums due to the government other than taxes and outside the realm of activity.

**Article 19**
(Created by Ordinance No. 2005-650 of 6 June 2005, Article 10 JORF 7 June 2005)

Rules for the application of this Part shall be decreed by the Council of State.

## Part III
## Committee of Access to Administrative Documents

**Article 20**
(Ordinance No. 2009-483 of 29 April 2009, Article 9)

The Committee of Access to Administrative Documents is an independent administrative authority.

It is responsible for ensuring freedom of access to administrative documents and public archives, and the implementation of Part II on the re-use of public information in accordance with the provisions of this Title and Book II, Title I of the heritage code.

It shall issue opinions on receipt of a request by an individual denied access to an administrative document under Part I, denied consultation or communication of public archive documents, with the exception of the documents referred to in of Article L. 211-4, paragraph c of the heritage code and the instruments and documents elaborated or held by parliamentary assemblies, or having been issued an adverse finding related to the re-use of public information.

The Commission's opinion must be sought prior to any legal action.

**Article 21**
(Ordinance No. 2010-462 of 6 May 2010, Article 1)

The Commission is also competent to hear cases related to:

A. The access to administrative documents and the re-use of public information under the following provisions:

    1. Article 2449 of the civil code;
    2. Article 79 of the local civil code of Alsace-Moselle;
    3. Articles L. 2121-26, L. 3121-17, L. 4132-16, L. 5211-46, L. 5421-5, L. 5621-9 and L. 5721-6 of the general local authorities code;
    4. Articles L. 28, L. 68 and LO 179 of the electoral code, as well as that code's provisions on the proxy vote register;
    5. Provisions of the rural and maritime fishing code on the electoral lists of regional chambers of agriculture;
    6. Provisions of the forestry code on the electoral lists of regional centres of forest ownership;
    7. Articles L. 121-5, L. 123-1 to L. 123-19, L. 213-13 and L. 332-29 of the town planning code;
    8. Parts III and IV of Title II of Book I of the environmental code;
    9. Articles L. 225-3, L. 225-5 and L. 330-2 to L. 330-5 of the highway code;
    10. Provisions of the roadway code on public enquiries regarding the commissioning, opening, straightening, setting of the width and decommissioning of local roads;
    11. Paragraphs a and b of Article L. 104 and Articles L. 106, L. 111 and L. 135 B of the tax procedure code;
    12. Article L. 107 A of the tax procedure code;
    13. Article L. 421-4 of the social work and family code;
    14. Articles L. 1111-7 and L. 1131-1 of the public health code;
    15. Article L. 161-37 of the social security code;
    16. Article 10 of Act No. 2000-321 of 12 April 2000 on the rights of citizens in their relations with public services;
    17. Article 17 of the Act of 31 December 1913 on historic monuments;
    18. Provisions related to the land register conservation;
    19. Article 5 of the Act of 1 July 1901 on the contract of association;
    20. Article 12 of the Act of 1 May 1889, amended by the Act of 20 May 1898, on producer and consumer cooperatives;
    21. Provisions related to the session minutes of the children publication commission.

B. The access to information held by operators of basic nuclear installations and individuals responsible for the transportation of radioactive materials under the conditions set out in Article 19 of Act No. 2006-686 of 13 June 2006 on nuclear transparency and safety.
C. The re-use of public information falling under Title II, Part III of the Act of 1 June 1924 implementing French civil legislation in the departments of the Bas-Rhin, the Haut-Rhin and the Moselle.

**Article 22**

(Created by Ordinance No. 2005-650 of 6 June 2005, Article 10 JORF 7 June 2005)

Upon receiving a request by a public service referred to in Article 1, the Commission may, after an *inter partes* procedure, impose such sanctions as set out in Article 18 upon the perpetrator of breaches under Part II.

**Article 23**

(Act No. 2011-334 of 29 March 2011, Article 1)

The Commission is composed of eleven members:

a) A member of the Council of State, whose grade is at least equal to that of councillor, who shall preside the Commission, a judge of the Court of Cassation, and a judge of the Court of Auditors, either active or honorary; to be appointed respectively by the vice-president of the Council of State, the first president of the Court of Cassation and the first president of the Court of Auditors;
b) A member of parliament and a senator, to be appointed respectively by the president of the National Assembly and the President of the Senate;
c) A member of an elected regional body, appointed by the President of the Senate;
d) A professor of higher education, either active or honorary, proposed by the President of the Commission;
e) An archive expert, proposed by the General Director of Heritage;
f) A personal data protection expert, proposed by the President of the National Commission for Data Protection and Liberties;
g) A competition and price expert, proposed by the President of the Competition authority;
h) A public distribution of information expert.

A substitute for each member shall be appointed under the same conditions.

The Commission members shall be appointed by decree of the Prime Minister. Except for those members referred to in paragraphs b and c, who shall serve for the entire term of office under which they were appointed, their term shall be of three years, renewable once.

The Commission shall also include, in an advisory capacity, the Human rights defender or his/her representative.

A Government commissioner, appointed by the Prime Minister, shall serve with the Commission and attend its deliberations, except when the Commission must make decisions under Articles 18 and 22.

In case of a tied vote, the President of the Commission shall have a casting vote.

The functioning of the Commission shall be determined by decree of the Council of State. Among others, this decree shall set out the cases and conditions in which the Commission may deliberate in restricted formation.

# Appendix 6 Germany: National Freedom-of-Information and Transparency Legislation (Extracts)

## 1. Basic Law[8]

### Article 5 [Freedom of expression]

(1) Every person shall have the right freely to express and disseminate his opinions in speech, writing and pictures, and to inform himself without hindrance from generally accessible sources. Freedom of the press and freedom of reporting by means of broadcasts and films shall be guaranteed. There shall be no censorship.
(2) These rights shall find their limits in the provisions of general laws, in provisions for the protection of young persons, and in the right to personal honour.

### Article 19 [Restriction of basic rights – Legal remedies]

(1) Insofar as, under this Basic Law, a basic right may be restricted by or pursuant to a law, such law must apply generally and not merely to a single case. In addition, the law must specify the basic right affected and the Article in which it appears.
(2) In no case may the essence of a basic right be affected.
(3) The basic rights shall also apply to domestic legal entities to the extent that the nature of such rights permits.
(4) Should any person's rights be violated by public authority, he may have recourse to the courts. If no other jurisdiction has been established, recourse shall be to the ordinary courts. The second sentence of paragraph (2) of Article 10 shall not be affected by this paragraph.

[8]Basic Law of the Federal Republic of Germany of 23 May 1949, most recently amended by Article 1 of the Act of 23 December 2014, Federal Law Gazette, part I, p. 2438 (*Bundesgesetzblatt – BGBl.*).



H.-J. Blanke, R. Perlingeiro (eds.), *The Right of Access to Public Information*,
DOI 10.1007/978-3-662-55554-5

**Article 20 [Constitutional principles]**

(1) The Federal Republic of Germany is a democratic and social federal state.
(2) All state authority is derived from the people. It shall be exercised by the people through elections and other votes and through specific legislative, executive and judicial bodies.
(3) The legislature shall be bound by the constitutional order, the executive and the judiciary by law and justice.

[...]

## 2. Federal Act Governing Access to Information held by the Federal Government (Freedom of Information Act)[9]

**Section 1 [Underlying principles]**

(1) Everyone is entitled to official information from the authorities of the Federal Government in accordance with the provisions of this Act. This Act shall apply to other Federal bodies and institutions insofar as they discharge administrative tasks under public law. For the purposes of these provisions, a natural or legal person shall be treated as equivalent to an authority where an authority avails itself of such a person in discharging its duties under public law.
(2) The authority may furnish information, grant access to files or provide information in any other manner. Where an applicant requests a certain form of access to information, the information may only be provided by other means for good cause. In particular, substantially higher administrative expenditure shall constitute good cause.
(3) Provisions in other legislation on access to official information shall take precedence, with the exception of Section 29 of the Administrative Procedure Act (VwVfG) and Section 25 of Book Ten of the Social Code.

**Section 2 [Definitions]**
For the purposes of this Act,

1. official information shall be defined as every record serving official purposes, irrespective of the mode of storage. This shall not include drafts and notes which are not intended to form part of a file;
2. a third person shall be defined as anyone on whom personal data or other information are held.

[9]Last amended by Art. 2.6 of the Law of August 7, 2013 (BGBl. I S. 3154); http://www.gesetze-im-internet.de/englisch_ifg/.

**Section 3 [Protection of special public interests]**
The entitlement to access to information shall not apply

1. where disclosure of the information may have detrimental effects on
    a) international relations,
    b) military and other security-critical interests of the Federal Armed Forces,
    c) internal or external security interests,
    d) monitoring or supervisory tasks of the financial, competition and regulatory authorities,
    e) matters of external financial control,
    f) measures to prevent illicit foreign trade,
    g) the course of current judicial proceedings, a person's entitlement to a fair trial or the pursuit of investigations into criminal, administrative or disciplinary offences,
2. where disclosure of the information may endanger public security,
3. where and for as long as
    a) the necessary confidentiality of international negotiations or
    b) consultations between authorities are compromised,
4. where the information is subject to an obligation to observe secrecy or confidentiality by virtue of a statutory regulation or the general administrative regulation on the material and organisational protection of classified information, or where the information is subject to professional or special official secrecy,
5. with regard to information obtained on a temporary basis from another public body which is not intended to form part of the authority's own files,
6. where disclosure of the information would be capable of compromising fiscal interests of the Federal Government in trade and commerce or economic interests of the social insurance institutions,
7. in the case of information obtained or transferred in confidence, where the third party's interest in confidential treatment still applies at the time of the application for access to the information,
8. with regard to the intelligence services and the authorities and other public bodies of the Federal Government, where these perform duties pursuant to Section 10 No. 3 of the Security Clearance Check Act (SÜG).

**Section 5 [Protection of personal data]**

(1) Access to personal data may only be granted where the applicant's interest in obtaining the information outweighs the third party's interests warranting exclusion of access to the information or where the third party has provided his or her consent. Special types of personal data within the meaning of Section 3 (9) of the Federal Data Protection Act (BDSG) may only be transferred subject to the express consent of the third party concerned.

(2) The applicant's interest in accessing information shall not predominate in the case of information from records relating to the third party's service or official capacity or a mandate held by the third party or in the case of information which is subject to professional or official secrecy.
(3) The applicant's interest in accessing information shall generally outweigh the third party's interests warranting exclusion of access to the information where the information is limited to the third party's name, title, university degree, designation of profession and function, official address and official telecommunications number and the third party has submitted a statement in proceedings in the capacity of a consultant or expert or in a comparable capacity.
(4) Names, titles, university degrees, designations of professions and functions, official addresses and official telecommunications numbers of desk officers shall not be excluded from the scope of access to information where they are an expression and consequence of official activities and no exceptional circumstances apply.

**Section 6 [Protection of intellectual property and business or trade secrets]**
No entitlement to access to information shall apply where such access compromises the protection of intellectual property. Access to business or trade secrets may only be granted subject to the data subject's consent.

**Section 7 [Application and procedure]**

(1) The authority which is authorised to dispose of the requested information decides on the application for access to information. In the case of Section 1 (1), sentence 3 the application is to be filed with the authority which avails itself of the natural or legal person under private law in discharging its duties under public law. Pertinent reasons must be stated for applications concerning third parties within the meaning of Section 5 (1) and (2) or Section 6. In the case of uniform applications from more than 50 persons, Sections 17 to 19 of the Administrative Procedure Act shall apply mutatis mutandis.
(2) Where an entitlement to partial access to information applies, the appurtenant application is to be granted to the extent to which information can be accessed without revealing information which is subject to confidentiality or without unreasonable administrative expenditure. The same shall apply where the applicant agrees to information concerning the interests of third parties being blanked out.
(3) Information may be furnished verbally, in writing or in electronic form. The authority is not obliged to verify that the contents of the information are correct.

(4) When examining official information, the applicant may take notes or arrange to have photocopies and print-outs produced. Section 6, sentence 1 shall remain unaffected.
(5) The information is to be made accessible to the applicant forthwith, with due regard to his or her interests. Access to the information should be provided within one month. Section 8 shall remain unaffected.

**Section 8 [Procedure when third parties are involved]**

(1) The authority shall grant a third party whose interests are affected by the application for access to information opportunity to submit a written statement within one month when there are indications that the said third party may have an interest warranting exclusion of access to the information.
(2) The decision pursuant to Section 7 (1), sentence 1 shall be provided in writing and shall also be notified to the third party. The information may only be accessed when the decision is final and absolute in relation to the third party or if immediate enforcement has been ordered and a period of two weeks has elapsed since notifying the third party of the order. Section 9 (4) shall apply mutatis mutandis.

**Section 9 [Rejection of the application – Legal remedies]**

(1) Notification of a ruling rejecting the application in part or in its entirety is to be provided within the period stipulated in Section 7.5 sentence 2.
(2) In cases in which the authority rejects the application in part or in its entirety, it is to provide notification as to whether and when partial or full access to the information is likely to be possible at a later juncture.
(3) The application may be rejected where the applicant is already in possession of the requested information or can reasonably be expected to obtain the information from generally accessible sources.
(4) It is permissible to challenge the decision to reject the application by lodging an administrative appeal or bringing an action to compel performance of the requested administrative act. Administrative appeal proceedings pursuant to the provisions of Part 8 of the Code of Administrative Court Procedure (VwGO) are also to be carried out when the decision has been reached by a supreme federal authority.

**Section 10 [Fees and expenses]**

(1) Fees and expenses shall be charged for official acts pursuant to this Act. This shall not apply to the furnishing of basic items of information.
(2) With due regard to the administrative expenditure involved, the fees shall be calculated such as to ensure that access to information pursuant to Section 1 can be claimed effectively.

(3) The Federal Ministry of the Interior is authorised to assess the facts and circumstances determining the commensurate fee and to fix the scales of fees for official acts pursuant to this Act by means of statutory instruments, without the approval of the Bundesrat. Section 15 (2) of the Administrative Costs Act (VwKG) shall not be applicable.

**Section 11 [Obligations to publish information]**

(1) The authorities should keep directories identifying the available information resources and the purposes of the collected information.
(2) Organisational and filing plans without any reference to personal data shall be made generally accessible in accordance with the provisions of this Act.
(3) The authorities should make the plans and directories stated in subsections 1 and 2 and other appropriate information generally accessible in electronic form.

**Section 12 [Federal Commissioner for freedom of information]**

(1) Anyone considering their right to access to information pursuant to this Act to have been violated may appeal to the Federal Commissioner for Freedom of Information.
(2) The function of Federal Commissioner for Freedom of Information shall be performed by the Federal Commissioner for Data Protection.
(3) [...]

## 3. Administrative Procedure Act[10]

**Section 17 [Representatives in the case of identical submissions]**

(1) In the case of applications and petitions submitted in an administrative proceeding signed by more than fifty persons, or presented in the form of duplicated and identical texts (identical submissions), the person deemed to be representing the other signatories shall be that signatory who is identified by his name, profession and address as being their representative unless he is named by them as authorised representative [Bevollmächtigter]. Only a natural person may be a representative [Vertreter].
(2) The authority may disregard identical submissions which do not contain the information referred to in paragraph 1, first sentence clearly visible on each page containing a signature or which do not comply with the requirements of paragraph 1, second sentence. [...]

[...]

[10] http://www.iuscomp.org/gla/statutes/VwVfG.htm.

**Section 18 [Representatives for participants with the same interests]**
(1) If more than fifty people are involved as participants in administrative proceedings with the same interests and are unrepresented, the authorities may require them within a reasonable period to appoint a joint representative where otherwise the regular execution of administrative proceedings would be impaired. If these persons do not comply within the period set, the authority may ex officio appoint a joint representative. Only a natural person may be a representative.

[...]

**Section 25 [Advice and information]**
(1) The authority shall cause statements or applications to be made or corrected when it is clear that these were not submitted or were incorrectly submitted only due to error or ignorance. [...]

[...]

**Section 28 [Hearing of participants]**
(1) Before an administrative act affecting the rights of a participant may be executed, the latter must be given the opportunity of commenting on the facts relevant to the decision.

[...]

**Section 29 [Inspection of documents by participants]**
(1) The authority shall allow participants to inspect the documents connected with the proceedings where knowledge of their contents is necessary in order to assert or defend their legal interests. Until administrative proceedings have been concluded, the foregoing sentence shall not apply to draft decisions and work directly connected with their preparation. Where participants are represented as provided under Sections 17 and 18, only the representatives shall be entitled to inspect documents.

[...]

**Section 39 [Grounds for an administrative act]**
(1) A written or electronic administrative act, as well as an administrative act confirmed in writing or electronically, shall be accompanied by a statement of grounds. This statement of grounds must contain the chief material and legal grounds led the authority to take its decision. The grounds given in connection with discretionary decisions should also contain the points of view which the authority considered while exercising its powers of discretion.

[...]

## 4. Code of Administrative Court Procedure[11]

### Section 99

(1) Authorities shall be obliged to submit certificates or files, to transmit electronic documents and provide information. If the knowledge of the content of these certificates, files, electronic documents or this information would prove disadvantageous to the interests of the Federation or of a *Land*, or if the events must be kept strictly secret in accordance with a statute or due to their essence, the competent supreme supervisory authority may refuse the submission of certificates or files, the transmission of the electronic documents and the provision of information.

(2) On request by a party concerned, the Higher Administrative Court shall find by order without an oral hearing whether the refusal to submit certificates or files, to transmit the electronic documents or to provide information is lawful. If a supreme federal authority refuses the submission, transmission or information on grounds that the interests of the Federation would be impaired were the content of the certificates or files, of the electronic documents and the information to become known, the Federal Administrative Court shall decide; the same shall apply if the Federal Administrative Court has jurisdiction for the main case in accordance with Section 50. [...] The supreme supervisory authority shall submit the certificates or files refused in accordance with subsection 1, second sentence on request by this panel of judges, transmit the electronic documents or provide the refused information. [...] If these cannot be complied with, or if the competent supervisory authority claims that special reasons of confidentiality or classification of information oppose the submission of the certificates or files or the transmission of the electronic documents to the court, the submission or transmission shall be effected in accordance with the fifth sentence by the certificates, files or electronic documents being made available to the court on premises designated by the supreme supervisory authority. Section 100 shall not apply to the files and electronic documents submitted in accordance with the fifth sentence, and to the special reasons claimed in accordance with the eighth sentence. [...]

### Section 100

(1) Those concerned can inspect the court files and the files submitted to the court.

[...]

[11] http://www.gesetze-im-internet.de/englisch_vwgo/index.html.

## 5. Security Clearance Check Act[12]

### Section 4 [Classified information]

[...]

(2) Classified information shall be considered

1. TOP SECRET, if knowledge of it by unauthorised persons could pose a threat to the existence or vital interests of the Federal Republic of Germany or one of its states,
2. SECRET, if knowledge by unauthorised persons could pose a threat to the security of the Federal Republic of Germany or one of its states, or could cause severe damage to its interests,
3. CONFIDENTIAL, if knowledge by unauthorised persons could be damaging to the interests of the Federal Republic of Germany or one of its states,
4. RESTRICTED, if knowledge by unauthorised persons could be disadvantageous to the interests of the Federal Republic of Germany or one of its states.

## 6. General Administrative Regulation for the Protection of Classified Information[13] (Allgemeine Verwaltungsvorschrift des Bundesministeriums des Innern zum materiellen und organisatorischen Schutz von Verschlusssachen [VS-Anweisung – VSA)

### Section 3 [Level of classification]

According to the level of protection required information shall be in accordance with Section 4 paragraph 2 of the Security Clearance Check Act classified as follows:

1. TOP SECRET, if knowledge of it by unauthorised persons could pose a threat to the existence or vital interests of the Federal Republic of Germany or one of its states,
2. SECRET, if knowledge by unauthorised persons could pose a threat to the security of the Federal Republic of Germany or one of its states, or could cause severe damage to its interests,
3. CONFIDENTIAL, if knowledge by unauthorised persons could be damaging to the interests of the Federal Republic of Germany or one of its states,
4. RESTRICTED, if knowledge by unauthorised persons could be disadvantageous to the interests of the Federal Republic of Germany or one of its states.

[12] https://bmwi-sicherheitsforum.de/ghb/suche/ergebnis/374,0,0,1,0.html (No. 41 of the list).

[13] Translation by Robert Böttner.

**Section 8 [Classification, limited duration]**

(1) The originating authority determines the necessity and the level of classification. [...]

[...]

## 7. Federal Data Protection Act[14]

**Section 3 [Further definitions]**

(1) "Personal data" means any information concerning the personal or material circumstances of an identified or identifiable individual (the data subject).

[...]

(9) 'Special categories of personal data' means information on a person's racial or ethnic origin, political opinions, religious or philosophical convictions, union membership, health or sex life.

## 8. Federal Environmental Information Act[15]

**(Umweltinformationsgesetz – UIG)**

**Section 1 [Purpose and scope]**

[...]

(2) This Act shall apply to authorities of the Federation and Federal legal persons under public law which are required to provide information.

**Section 2 [Definitions]**

(1) Authorities required to provide information are

1. the government and other public administrative bodies. Consultative bodies are considered part of the authority that appoints their members.. Authorities not required to provide information are
   a) the highest Federal authorities, when acting in the framework of the legislative process or issuing statutory instruments, and
   b) Federal courts insofar as they do not discharge public administration tasks;

[14]http://www.gesetze-im-internet.de/englisch_bdsg/englisch_bdsg.html

[15]Translation by Robert Böttner.

2. natural or legal persons under private law insofar as they discharge public tasks or provide public services in the context of the environment, in particular environmental public services of general interest, and are subject to control by the Federation or a legal person under public law under the Federation's supervision.

[...]

**Section 3 [Right of access to environmental information]**

(1) In accordance with the provisions of this Act, everyone shall be entitled to free access to environmental information from the authorities required to provide information as stipulated by Section 2 paragraph 1 without having to set forth any legal interest. [...]

[...]

**Section 4 [Application and procedure]**

(1) Upon application, authorities required to provide information shall make environmental information accessible.

[...]

(3) If the application is filed with an authority required to provide information that does not dispose of the environmental information, said authority shall, if aware that the information is held by another authority, forward the application to the authority in possession of the requested information and shall inform the applicant.. Instead of forwarding the application the authority can indicate to the applicant any other authority required to provide information if it is aware that the latter is in possession of the requested information.

**Section 8 [Protection of public interests]**

[...]

(2) If an application

1. is evidently improper,

[...]

it shall be rejected unless public interest in disclosure prevails.

## 9. Consumer Information Act[16]

### (Verbraucherinformationsgesetz – VIG)

### Section 2 [Right of access to information]

(1) In accordance with this Act, everyone shall have free access to all data concerning

1. inadmissible deviations, ascertained by the competent authorities under federal or state law, from requirements
   a) of the Food and Feed Code and the Product Safety Act,
   b) of statutory regulations based on these laws,
   c) directly applicable legal acts of the European Community or the European Union within the scope of the aforementioned Acts as well as measures and decisions that have been adopted in connection with the deviations mentioned in letters a through c,
2. dangers and risks of a produce or consumer product for the health and security of the consumers,
3. the composition of produces and consumer products, their quality, the physical, chemical and biological properties including their interactions with and effects on the human body, taking into account the intended use or foreseeable misapplication,
4. the labelling, the origin, the use, the production and the treatment of produces or consumer products,
5. admissible deviations from the legal actions mentioned in No. 1 of this paragraph regarding the properties or actions mentioned in No. 3 and No. 4,
6. the raw materials and the procedures used to extract these raw materials,
7. surveillance measures or other actions and measures for the protection of the consumers taken by the authorities, including the analyses of these actions and measures, as well as statistics on infringements of legal acts mentioned in Section 39 paragraph 1 sentence 1 of the Food and Feed Code and Section 26 paragraph 1 sentence 1 of the Product Safety Act, insofar as these infringements concern a produce or a consumer product, (information), that is available with an authority within the meaning of paragraph 2, irrespective of the mode of storage. [...]

### Section 4 [Application]

(1) Information is provided upon application. [...]
[...]
(4) An improper application shall be rejected. [...]

[16]Translation by Robert Böttner.

## 10. Book Ten of the Social Code[17]

### (Zehntes Buch Sozialgesetzbuch – SGB X)

**Section 25 [Access to files by a party concerned]**

(1) The authority shall grant the party concerned access to files of the procedure, insofar as knowledge of these files is essential for the enforcement or the protection of the party's legal interests. Until the conclusion of the administrative procedure, sentence 1 does not apply to drafts of decisions or directly preparative works.

[...]

## 11. Crafts Code[18]

### (Gesetz zur Ordnung des Handwerks – Handwerksordung)

**Section 6**

(1) The Chamber of Crafts keeps a register of the owners of craft businesses in their district that are subject to prior authorisation in accordance with Annex D Title I of this Act, indicating also the craft or crafts exercised (*Handwerksrolle*).

[...]

(3) Upon request, public authorities shall have access to data of the *Handwerksrolle*, insofar as knowledge of the factual or legal situation of the owner of a business that is subject to prior authorisation (Section 1 paragraph 1) is necessary for the performance of their tasks.

## 12. Freedom of Information Act Berlin[19]

**Section 3 [Right to information]**

(1) Under this Act every person shall have the right, with regard to the public bodies mentioned in Section 2, at its own choice, to access or to receive information about the contents of the files held by the public body. The rights under sentence 1 may also be asserted by legal persons.

[...]

[17]Translation by Robert Böttner.

[18]Translation by Robert Böttner.

[19]http://www.datenschutz-berlin.de/content/informationsfreiheit/berlin/berliner-informationsfreiheitsgesetz, please click on the link „Engl. Fassung" for the English version.

**Section 13 [Application, procedure of access to and information from files]**

(1) [...] If a request is submitted in writing to an inappropriate public body, the latter is obliged to immediately forward the request to the competent authority and inform the applicant accordingly.

[...]

## 13. Law on the Access to Files and Information Brandenburg[20]

**(Akteneinsichts- und Informationszugangsgesetz Brandenburg – AIG)**

**Section 4 [Protection of predominant public interests]**
The application for access to files is to be rejected, if

[...]

(2) The application for access to files shall be rejected,

1. insofar as the content of the files refers to the decision-making process within one or between authorities or administrative bodies or to a process that, in accordance with Section 36 paragraph 2 of the Municipalities Code of the State of Brandenburg, is or has been deliberated or decided on in a non-public meeting,
2. if premature disclosure of the files' content could jeopardise the success of the imminent measure of the authority,
3. if it refers to the transmission of unfinished documents or drafts of decisions as well as immediately preparative works or
4. if the proper performance of tasks of the public authority would be severely jeopardised, unless the interest in disclosure prevails over the opposing public interest in the individual case.

**Section 6 [Procedure]**
[...] If an application is filed with an incompetent authority, this authority has to forward the application without delay to the competent authority and inform the applicant thereof. [...]

[20]Translation by Robert Böttner.

## 14. Freedom of Information Act Bremen[21]

**(Bremer Informationsfreiheitsgesetz)**

**Section 3 [Protection of special public interests]**
The entitlement to access to information shall not apply,

[...]

7. in the case of information obtained or transferred in confidence, where the third party's interest in confidential treatment still applies at the time of the application for access to the information,
8. with regard to the Office for the Protection of the Constitution of the *Land* and other public bodies of the *Land*, where they perform duties pursuant to Section 10 No. 3 of the Security Clearance Check Act (SÜG),

[...]

**Section 11 [Obligations to publish information]**

(1) The authorities should keep directories identifying the available information resources and the purposes of the collected information.

(2) Organisational and filing plans without any reference to personal data shall be made generally accessible in accordance with the provisions of this Act.

(3) Every public authority shall in particular publish all administrative rules of public interest that have been adopted or amended after entry into force of this Act. There shall be no publication if an application for access to information would be rejected in accordance with this Act.

(4) The authorities should make the plans, directories and administrative rules mentioned in paragraphs 1, 2 and 3 as well as other information, excluding personal data and professional and trade secrets, generally accessible in electronic form and forward the information to the electronic registry mentioned in paragraph 5. [...]

[...]

(5) The Free Hanseatic City of Bremen establishes a central electronic registry for information in order to facilitate the finding of said information. [...]

(6) Details are established by the Senate by statutory regulation.

[21]Translation by Robert Böttner.

## 15. Transparency Act Hamburg[22]

### Section 2 [Definitions]

[...]

(8) Duty to publish is the duty to actively add information to the information register in accordance with this Act.

[...]

### Section 3 [Scope of application]

(1) The duty to publish concerns, subject to Sections 4 through 7 and 9:

1. Front page and petitions of Senate decisions,
2. Communications of the Senate to the Hamburg State Parliament,
3. Decisions adopted in public session, together with associated protocols and annexes,
4. Contracts pertaining to services of general interest,
5. Household, establishment, management, organization, business distribution and filing plans,
6. Comprehensive directives, technical instructions and administrative regulations,
7. Official statistics and activity reports,
8. expert opinions and studies, as far as they were commissioned by public authorities, incorporated in the public authority's decision, or serve its preparation,
9. Spatial data (geodata),
10. Results of measurements, observations and other surveys of harmful environmental effects, environmental hazards, and of the state of the environment that are performed by an authority outside of its regular control activities in particular cases,
11. The tree registry,
12. Public plans, particularly land use plans and landscape plans,
13. the main provisions of granted building permits and preliminary building permits,
14. Allocations of subsidies and benefits,
15. The key corporate data of municipal participations, including a presentation of annual salaries and fringe benefits at the top-management level,

[22]Translation by Tranparency International (http://www.transparenzgesetz.de/fileadmin/user_upload/materialien/Transparency_Act_of_the_Free_and_Hanseatic_City_of_Hamburg.pdf) and Svenja Solka.

(2) The authorities obliged to provide information shall also publish, subject to Sections 4 to 7 and 9:

1. Contracts whose publication is in the public's interest, provided economic interests of the Free and Hanseatic City of Hamburg are not considerably impaired,
2. operational instructions, and any other information of public interest comparable to that referred to in para. 1 and in this paragraph.

[...]

**Section 4 [Protection of personal data]**

(1) Personal data are to be disguised when published in the information register. This does not apply to

1. contracts according to Section 3.1 No. 4 and according to Section 3.2 No. 1 with regard to the name of the contracting party,
2. expert opinions and studies according to Section 3.1 No. 8 with regard to the name of the authors,
3. geodata according to Section 3.1 No. 9, as far as its publishing is allowed pursuant to the current data protection provisions,
4. the main provisions of granted building permits and preliminary building permits according to Section 3.1 No. 13 with regard to the description of the land parcel number and
5. personal data in connection with allocations of subsidies and benefits according to Section 3.1 No. 14, as far as it concerns recipients of individual grants; personal data in the purpose are not to be published.

The further limitations of the duty to provide information set forth in Section 9 shall be applied.

(2) Name, title, academic degree, professional and functional designations, business address and phone number of the agent are not subject to the duty to publish; these data are made available upon application, as far as they are expression and result of public activity, no exemptions are fulfilled and they do not contradict legitimate security concerns.

(3) Upon application access to personal data is to be granted, if

1. it is allowed by legal provision,
2. it is crucial to avoid considerable disadvantages for the general public interest or dangers to life, health, personal freedom or other serious impairments of individual rights,
3. the person affected has consented to the transmission, or
4. if there is a legitimate interest in the information and it is not opposed by outweighing protected interests.

(4) Personal data of applicants, employees (civil servants and employees) and former employees of departments being responsible to provide information are excluded from the duty to provide information. Para. 2 and Section 3.1 No. 15 remain unaffected.
(5) In case personal data is to be released upon application, the person affected shall be informed about the release, if this does not cause an unreasonable expense. If access can affect interests worthy of protection, the authority obliged to grant access shall give the person concerned the opportunity to comment in advance.

**Section 5 [Exemptions from the duty to inform]**
There is no duty to provide information according to this Act

1. for courts, prosecuting and law enforcement authorities, as far as they were involved as organs of the administration of justice or in judicial independence under special legal provisions, as well as for disciplinary authorities and public procurement bodies,
2. for the Court of Auditors, as far as it acted in judicial independence; this does not apply to its reports,
3. for the State Office for the Protection of the Constitution, for information connected to the performance of tasks of the working group Scientology at the Authority for Internal Affairs and Sports, as well as for authorities and other public bodies of the Free and Hanseatic City of Hamburg, as far as they carry out duties in terms of Section 10 No. 3 of the Hamburg Security Clearance Check Act of 25 May 1999 (HmbGVBl., p. 82), as last amended on 17 February 2009 (HmbGVBl., p. 29, 32), in the respective current version,
4. for processes of tax assessment and tax collection as well as internal audits,
5. for forecasts, assessments, recommendations or instructions in connection with the judicial or extrajudicial assertion of or defence against claims,
6. for public broadcasting institutions with respect to journalistic-editorial information,
7. for basic research or application-oriented research; Section 3.1 No. 8 remains unaffected.

**Section 6 [Protection of public interests]**

(1) The immediate decision-making process of the Senate, drafts, preparatory notes and preparatory comments are excluded from the duty to provide information.
(2) From the duty to provide information should also be excluded

1. drafts of decisions as well as work and resolutions for their immediate preparation, as far as and as long as the information's early announcement would foil the success of the decisions or forthcoming measures. Statistics, compilations of data, geodata, regular results of the collection of evidence, information, expert opinions or statements of third parties do not serve the immediate decision-making according to sentence 1,
2. protocols and documents of consultations which are protected by specific legal confidentiality rules, as well as documents which are protected by the instruction regarding classified information for the authorities of the Free and Hanseatic City of Hamburg.

(3) The same applies to other information as far as and as long as

1. its publication would not just insignificantly endanger international relations, the relations to the federal or a state government, national defence, or internal security,
2. its publication would impair court proceedings, preliminary proceedings, administrative offence proceedings or disciplinary proceedings.

**Section 7 [Trade and business secrets]**

(1) Trade and business secrets are all facts, circumstances and processes referring to an enterprise which are not evident, but accessible only to a restricted circle of persons and whose owner has a legitimate interest in non-dissemination. A legitimate interest exists if the disclosure of a fact is likely to promote the competitive position of a competitor or to curtail the competitive position of the owner's company or if it is capable of causing economic harm to the bearer of the secrets. This does not apply to trade and business secrets in terms of Section 35.4 of the First Book of the Social Code of 11 December 1975 (BGBl. I p. 3015), as last amended on April 12, 2012 (BGBl. I p. 579, 599), in the respective current version.

(2) Information and contract elements which contain trade or business secrets are only subject to the duty to provide information as far as the interest in information outweighs the interest in confidentiality.

(3) When submitting information to authorities, trade and business secrets are to be marked and presented separately. The interest in confidentiality is to be stated. At the time of publication or granting of information upon application the information's confidential parts are to be disguised or separated. This can also be implemented by photocopies of the non-confidential parts. The extent of the parts separated or disguised is to be noted with reference to the existence of a trade or business secret.

(4) If access to trade and business secrets shall be granted upon application, the authority obliged to grant access has to give the person concerned the opportunity to comment in advance.

**Section 8 [Separation rule]**

The authorities shall take appropriate action in organizational terms so that information which is subject to Sections 4 to 7 can be separated without disproportionate effort.

**Section 10 [Arrangement of the duty to provide information]**

(1) Information in terms of Section 3.1 is to be published in its full text in electronic form in the information register immediately after the technical conditions according to Section 18.2 are met. [...]

[...]

(4) Access to the information register is free and anonymous. Access is provided through public communication nets. Access to the information register is sufficiently granted in public premises.

**Section 18 [Transitional provisions, entry into force]**

[...]

(2) The technical conditions for the implementation of this Act shall be established within two years after it has entered into force. [...]

[...]

## 16. Freedom of Information Act Mecklenburg-Vorpommern[23]

**Section 1 [Principles of free access to information]**

[...]

(2) Any natural or legal person under private law is entitled to access to information of which the authorities dispose. [...]

**Section 10 [Application]**

(1) Access to information is granted upon application. [...]

[. . .]

(3) [...] If the requested information is not or only partially available at the authority where the application is filed, the authority has to, with regard to the missing information, indicate the competent authority to the applicant without further delay if the authority is aware of it.

[...]

[23] Translation by Robert Böttner.

## 17. Freedom of Information Act North Rhine-Westphalia[24]

**Section 4 [Right to information]**
(1) In accordance with this Act, any natural person is entitled to access to official information of which the authorities mentioned in Section 2 dispose.

[...]

**Section 5 [Procedure]**
(1) Access to official information of public authorities is granted upon application. [...]

[...]

(3) If access to information is dependent on the authorisation of a party concerned, the authorisation is considered as not granted if it is not presented to the public authority within one month after the application.

[...]

**Section 9 [Protection of personal data]**
[...]

(2) [...] If access to information can interfere with interests worth being protected of the party concerned, the public authority has to give to the party concerned the opportunity to comment in advance.

[...]

**Section 12 [Obligations to publish information]**
Organisational and filing plans have to be made generally accessible in accordance with this Act. [...]

## 18. Freedom of Information Act Rheinland-Pfalz[25]

**(Landesgesetz über die Freiheit des Zugangs zu Informationen – Landesinformationsfreiheitsgesetz)**

**Section 4 [Right to information]**
(1) In accordance with this Act, any natural or legal person under private law is entitled to access to information the authorities mentioned in Section 2 dispose of. [...]

[...]

[24] Translation by Robert Böttner.

[25] Translation by Robert Böttner.

**Section 9 [Protection of public interests]**

(1) The application for access to information has to be rejected insofar and as long as

[...]

7. in the case of information obtained or transferred in confidence the third party's interest in confidential treatment still applies at the time of the application for access to the information.

(2) There is no right to access to information towards the constitution protection authority of the state.

**Section 12 [Protection of personal data]**

The application for access to information has to be rejected, insofar as knowledge of the public information would disclose personal data of third parties, unless,

1. the third party has given its consent,
2. the disclosure is permitted by law.

[...]

**Section 14 [Obligations to publish information]**

The authorities shall keep directories identifying the available information resources and the purposes of the collected information. Organisational plans without any reference to personal data shall be made generally accessible in accordance with the provisions of this Act. If possible, they shall be published electronically.

## 19. Access to Information Act Schleswig-Holstein[26]

### (Informationszugangsgesetz für das Land Schleswig-Holstein, IZG-SH)

**Section 3 [Right of access to information]**

Any natural or legal person is entitled to free access to information of which an authority required to provide information disposes. [...]

**Section 4 [Application]**

(1) Information is made accessible upon application by the authority required to provide information.

[...]

[26]Translation by Robert Böttner.

(3) If the application is filed with an authority required to provide information that does not dispose of the requested information, said authority forwards the application as early as possible to the authority in possession of the requested information and informs the applicant thereof. Instead of forwarding the application the authority can indicate to the applicant any other authority required to provide information that is in possession of the requested information.

**Section 8 [Support of access to environmental information]**
(1) The authorities required to provide information facilitate the access to environmental information of which they dispose, namely by indicating respondents or information centres, by publication of directories of available environmental information, by setting up publicly accessible information networks and data bases as well as by publication of information on the competences of the authorities. [...]

[...]

**Section 9 [Protection of public interests]**

(1) If disclosure of information had detrimental effects on

1. the international relations, the defence or important interests of public safety,
2. the relations to the federation or another *Land*,
3. the confidentiality of consultations of authorities required to provide information,
4. the conduction of an on-going court procedure, the right of a person to a fair trial or the conduction of criminal, administrative offence or disciplinary investigations or
5. the state of the environment and its components within the meaning of Section 2 paragraph 2 No. 1 or protected assets within the meaning of Section 2 paragraph 2 No. 6, the application is to be rejected, unless the public interest in disclosure prevails. [...]

[...]

**Section 10 [Protection of private interests]**
If knowledge of the information

1. would disclose personal data whose confidentiality is protected by legal provision,
2. would infringe intellectual property rights, in particular copyrights,
3. would give access to professional or trade secrets or information subject to fiscal or statistical secrecy or
4. would affect the interests of a person who, without being legally obliged, has voluntarily provided the authority with the requested information, the application is to be rejected, unless the parties concerned have given their consent and the public interest in disclosure prevails. [...]

**Section 11 [Information of the public]**
(1) The authorities required to provide information inform the public actively, systematically and to an adequate extent on the state of the environment. To this end, they disseminate environmental information that are of importance for their tasks and of which they dispose, or provide links to web pages where the information can be obtained.

[...]

## 20. Act on Access to Information Saxony-Anhalt[27]

**(Informationszugangsgesetz Sachsen-Anhalt)**

**Section 3 [Protection of special public interests]**

(1) The entitlement to access to information shall not apply

[...]

7. in the case of information obtained or transferred in confidence, where the third party's interest in confidential treatment still applies at the time of the application for access to the information,
8. with regard to the Office for the Protection of the Constitution and other authorities mentioned in Section 1 paragraph 1 sentence 1 of this Act, where these perform sensitive duties pursuant to Section 2 paragraph 1 No. 3 and paragraph 2 of the Security Clearance Check and Classification Act (GVBl. LSA p. 12, 14),

[...]

[...]

**Section 11 [Obligations to publish information]**

(1) The authorities mentioned in Section 1 paragraph 1 sentence 1 shall keep directories identifying the available information collections and purposes.
(2) Organisational and filing plans without any reference to personal data have to be made generally accessible in accordance with the provisions of this Act.
(3) The authorities mentioned in Section 1 paragraph 1 sentence 1 shall make the plans and directories stated in paragraphs 1 and 2 and other appropriate information generally accessible in electronic form.

[27]Translation by Robert Böttner.

## 21. Freedom of Information Act Saarland[28]

**Section 1 [Application]**
Under this Act and by application of Sections 1 through 9 and 11 of the Freedom of Information Act of 5 September 2005 (BGBl. I p. 2722), as amended, any person is entitled to access to public information against authorities of the state, of the municipalities and the local authority associations. [...]

**Section 2 [Protection of special public interests]**
There is no right of access to information against the Office for the Protection of the Constitution of the *Land* or against authorities and other public bodies within the whole or parts of the *Land* where these perform duties under Section 2 paragraph 1 No. 3 of the Saarland Security Clearance Check Act of 4 April 2001 (Official Gazette p. 1182) as amended by the Act of 15 February 2006 (Official Gazette p. 474, 530), in the respective current version.

## 22. Freedom of Information Act Thuringia[29]

**Section 3 [Definitions]**
Within the meaning of this Act is

[...]

2. third person: any natural or legal person about whom information, in particular personal data, is available.

**Section 6 [Procedure]**
[...]

(4) Insofar as a third person within the meaning of Section 3 No. 2 is concerned, the public authority provides him/her with an opportunity to present his/her written comments within one month, unless an interest worthy of protection of the third person can be excluded. In the case of Section 9 paragraph 1 sentence 2 the consent is deemed refused if it is not given within one month upon request by the public authority. [...]

**Section 7 [Protection of special public interests]**
[...]

(2) The application for access to information shall be rejected,

[...]

[28]Translation by Robert Böttner.

[29]Translation by Robert Böttner.

2. if

in the case of information obtained or transferred in confidence the third party's interest in confidential treatment still applies at the time of the application for access to the information,

[...]

**Section 9 [Protection of private interests]**

(1) [...]

Specifically protected data within the meaning of Section 4 paragraph 5 of the Thuringian Data Protection Act (ThürDSG) of 13 January 2012 (Official Gazette p. 27), as amended, may only be made accessible if the party concerned has expressly given his/her consent.

**Section 11 [Obligations to publish information]**

(1) The authorities shall keep directories identifying the available information collections and purposes. Organisational and filing plans without any reference to personal data have to be made generally accessible in accordance with the provisions of this Act. If possible, the plans and directories have to be made accessible in electronic form.
(2) Regardless of an application under Section 5 paragraph 1, information can also be made accessible via Internet or any other publicly accessible means. The authorities shall publish in particular administrative rules of public interest as well as other suitable information. [...]
(3) Information of a state authority under paragraph 2 have to be included in a publicly accessible central information register that is set up by the state government in accordance with technical and organisational capacities. Details with regard to the operation and use of the register shall be established by statutory regulation of the state government. [...]

## 23. Data Protection Act Thuringia[30]

**Section 4 [Admissibility of data processing and use]**

[...]

(5) The processing and use of personal data revealing racial and ethnic origin, political opinions, religious or philosophical beliefs or trade-union membership and data concerning health or sex life (specifically protected data) is admissible only if [...]

[30]Translation by Robert Böttner.

# Appendix 7 India: National Freedom-of-Information and Transparency Legislation (Extracts)

## 1. Constitution of India (1950)[31]

### Article 19

(1) All citizens shall have the right —

(a) to freedom of speech and expression;
(b) to assemble peaceably and without arms;
(c) to form associations or unions [or co-operative societies];
(d) to move freely throughout the territory of India;
(e) to reside and settle in any part of the territory of India; [and]
(f) to practise any profession, or to carry on any occupation, trade or business.

(2) Nothing in sub-clause (a) of clause (1) shall affect the operation of any existing law, or prevent the State from making any law, in so far as such law imposes reasonable restrictions on the exercise of the right conferred by the said sub-clause in the interests of [the sovereignty and integrity of India,] the security of the State, friendly relations with foreign States, public order, decency or morality, or in relation to contempt of court, defamation or incitement to an offence.]

[...]

[31]Constitution of India of 26 January 1950 as last amended by the Act of 31 Juli 2015.



H.-J. Blanke, R. Perlingeiro (eds.), *The Right of Access to Public Information*,
DOI 10.1007/978-3-662-55554-5

## 2. Right to Information Act (2005)[32]

### Chapter I
### Preliminary

**Section 2**
In this Act, unless the context otherwise requires,—

[...]

(f) "information" means any material in any form, including records, documents, memos, e-mails, opinions, advices, press releases, circulars, orders, logbooks, contracts, reports, papers, samples, models, data material held in any electronic form and information relating to any private body which can be accessed by a public authority under any other law for the time being in force;

[...]

(h) "public authority" means any authority or body or institution of self- government established or constituted—

(a) by or under the Constitution;
(b) by any other law made by Parliament;
(c) by any other law made by State Legislature;
(d) by notification issued or order made by the appropriate Government,

(i) "record" includes—

(a) any document, manuscript and file;
(b) any microfilm, microfiche and facsimile copy of a document;
(c) any reproduction of image or images embodied in such microfilm (whether enlarged or not); and
(d) any other material produced by a computer or any other device;

(j) "right to information" means the right to information accessible under this Act which is held by or under the control of any public authority and includes the right to—

(i) inspection of work, documents, records;
(ii) taking notes, extracts or certified copies of documents or records;
(iii) taking certified samples of material;
(iv) obtaining information in the form of diskettes, floppies, tapes, video cassettes or in any other electronic mode or through printouts where such information is stored in a computer or in any other device;

[...]

[32]The Gazette of India – Extraordinary, 21 June 2005, No. 25, p. 1 et seqq.

## Chapter II
## Right to Information and Obligations of Public Authorities

### Section 3

Subject to the provisions of this Act, all citizens shall have the right to information.

### Section 4

(1) Every public authority shall—

a) maintain all its records duly catalogued and indexed in a manner and the form which facilitates the right to information under this Act and ensure that all records that are appropriate to be computerised are, within a reasonable time and subject to availability of resources, computerised and connected through a network all over the country on different systems so that access to such records is facilitated;
b) publish within one hundred and twenty days from the enactment of this Act,—

(i) the particulars of its organisation, functions and duties;
(ii) the powers and duties of its officers and employees;
(iii) the procedure followed in the decision making process, including channels of supervision and accountability;
(iv) the norms set by it for the discharge of its functions;
(v) the rules, regulations, instructions, manuals and records, held by it or under its control or used by its employees for discharging its functions;
(vi) a statement of the categories of documents that are held by it or under its control;
(vii) the particulars of any arrangement that exists for consultation with, or representation F584by, the members of the public in relation to the formulation of its policy or implementation thereof;
(viii) a statement of the boards, councils, committees and other bodies consisting of two or more persons constituted as its part or for the purpose of its advice, and as to whether meetings of those boards, councils, committees and other bodies are open to the public, or the minutes of such meetings are accessible for public;
(ix) a directory of its officers and employees;
(x) the monthly remuneration received by each of its officers and employees, including the system of compensation as provided in its regulations;
(xi) the budget allocated to each of its agency, indicating the particulars of all plans, proposed expenditures and reports on disbursements made;

(xii) the manner of execution of programmes, including the amounts allocated and the details of beneficiaries of such programmes;
(xiii) particulars of recipients of concessions, permits or authorisations granted by it;
(xiv) details in respect of the information, available to or held by it, reduced in an electronic form;
(xv) the particulars of facilities available to citizens for obtaining information, including the working hours of a library or reading room, if maintained for public use;
(xvi) the names, designations and other particulars of the Public Information Officers;
(xvii) such other information as may be prescribed; and thereafter update these publications every year;

c) publish all relevant facts while formulating important policies or announcing the decisions which affect public;
d) provide reasons for its administrative or quasi-judicial decisions to affected persons.

(2) It shall be a constant endeavour of every public authority to take steps in accordance with the requirements of clause (b) of subsection (1) to provide as much information *suo motu* to the public at regular intervals through various means of communications, including Internet, so that the public have minimum resort to the use of this Act to obtain information.
(3) For the purposes of subsection (1), every information shall be disseminated widely and in such form and manner which is easily accessible to the public.
(4) All materials shall be disseminated taking into consideration the cost effectiveness, local language and the most effective method of communication in that local area and the information should be easily accessible, to the extent possible in electronic format with the Central Public Information Officer or State Public Information Officer, as the case may be, available free or at such cost of the medium or the print cost price as may be prescribed.

[...]

**Section 5**

(1) Every public authority shall, within one hundred days of the enactment of this Act, designate as many officers as the Central Public Information Officers or State Public Information Officers, as the case may be, in all administrative units or offices under it as may be necessary to provide information to persons requesting for the information under this Act.

[...]

(4) The Central Public Information Officer or State Public Information Officer, as the case may be, may seek the assistance of any other officer as he or she considers it necessary for the proper discharge of his or her duties.
(5) Any officer, whose assistance has been sought under subsection (4), shall render all assistance to the Central Public Information Officer or State Public Information Officer, as the case may be, seeking his or her assistance and for the purposes of any contravention of the provisions of this Act, such other officer shall be treated as a Central Public Information Officer or State Public Information Officer, as the case may be.

## Section 6

(1) A person, who desires to obtain any information under this Act, shall make a request in writing or through electronic means in English or Hindi or in the official language of the area in which the application is being made, accompanying such fee as may be prescribed, to—

  (a) the Central Public Information Officer or State Public Information Officer, as the case may be, of the concerned public authority;
  (b) the Central Assistant Public Information Officer or State Assistant Public Information Officer, as the case may be, specifying the particulars of the information sought by him or her:

  Provided that where such request cannot be made in writing, the Central Public Information Officer or State Public Information Officer, as the case may be, shall render all reasonable assistance to the person making the request orally to reduce the same in writing.

(2) An applicant making request for information shall not be required to give any reason for requesting the information or any other personal details except those that may be necessary for contacting him.
(3) Where an application is made to a public authority requesting for an information,—

  (i) which is held by another public authority; or
  (ii) the subject matter of which is more closely connected with the functions of another public authority, the public authority, to which such application is made, shall transfer the application or such part of it as may be appropriate to that other public authority and inform the applicant immediately about such transfer:

  Provided that the transfer of an application pursuant to this subsection shall be made as soon as practicable but in no case later than five days from the date of receipt of the application.

## Section 7

(1) Subject to the proviso to subsection (2) of Section 5 or the proviso to subsection (3) of Section 6, the Central Public Information Officer or State Public Information Officer, as the case may be, on receipt of a request under Section 6 shall, as expeditiously as possible, and in any case within thirty days of the receipt of the request, either provide the information on payment of such fee as may be prescribed or reject the request for any of the reasons specified in Sections 8 and 9:

Provided that where the information sought for concerns the life or liberty of a person, the same shall be provided within forty-eight hours of the receipt of the request.

[...]

(3) Where a decision is taken to provide the information on payment of any further fee representing the cost of providing the information, the Central Public Information Officer or State Public Information Officer, as the case may be, shall send an intimation to the person making the request, giving—

(a) the details of further fees representing the cost of providing the information as determined by him, together with the calculations made to arrive at the amount in accordance with fee prescribed under subsection (1), requesting him to deposit that fees, and the period intervening between the despatch of the said intimation and payment of fees shall be excluded for the purpose of calculating the period of thirty days referred to in that subsection;

(b) information concerning his or her right with respect to review the decision as to the amount of fees charged or the form of access provided, including the particulars of the appellate authority, time limit, process and any other forms.

(4) Where access to the record or a part thereof is required to be provided under this Act and the person to whom access is to be provided is sensorily disabled, the Central Public Information Officer or State Public Information Officer, as the case may be, shall provide assistance to enable access to the information, including providing such assistance as may be appropriate for the inspection.

(5) Where access to information is to be provided in the printed or in any electronic format, the applicant shall, subject to the provisions of subsection (6), pay such fee as may be prescribed:

Provided that the fee prescribed under subsection (1) of Section 6 and sub-sections (1) and (5) of Section 7 shall be reasonable and no such fee shall be charged from the persons who are of below poverty line as may be determined by the appropriate Government.

(6) Notwithstanding anything contained in subsection (5), the person making request for the information shall be provided the information free of charge where a public authority fails to comply with the time limits specified in subsection (1).

(7) Before taking any decision under subsection (1), the Central Public Information Officer or State Public Information Officer, as the case may be, shall take into consideration the representation made by a third party under Section 11. (8) Where a request has been rejected under subsection (1), the Central Public Information Officer or State Public Information Officer, as the case may be, shall communicate to the person making the request,—

(i) the reasons for such rejection;
(ii) the period within which an appeal against such rejection may be preferred; and
(iii) the particulars of the appellate authority.

(8) Where a request has been rejected under subsection (1), the Central Public Information Officer or State Public Information Officer, as the case may be, shall communicate to the person making the request,—

(i) the reasons for such rejection;
(ii) the period within which an appeal against such rejection may be preferred; and
(iii) the particulars of the appellate authority.

(9) An information shall ordinarily be provided in the form in which it is sought unless it would disproportionately divert the resources of the public authority or would be detrimental to the safety or preservation of the record in question.

**Section 8**

(1) Notwithstanding anything contained in this Act, there shall be no obligation to give any citizen,—

(a) information, disclosure of which would prejudicially affect the sovereignty and integrity of India, the security, strategic, scientific or economic interests of the State, relation with foreign State or lead to incitement of an offence;
(b) information which has been expressly forbidden to be published by any court of law or tribunal or the disclosure of which may constitute contempt of court;
(c) information, the disclosure of which would cause a breach of privilege of Parliament or the State Legislature;

(d) information including commercial confidence, trade secrets or intellectual property, the disclosure of which would harm the competitive position of a third party, unless the competent authority is satisfied that larger public interest warrants the disclosure of such information;
(e) information available to a person in his fiduciary relationship, unless the competent authority is satisfied that the larger public interest warrants the disclosure of such information;
(f) information received in confidence from foreign Government;
(g) information, the disclosure of which would endanger the life or physical safety of any person or identify the source of information or assistance given in confidence for law enforcement or security purposes;
(h) information which would impede the process of investigation or apprehension or prosecution of offenders;
(i) cabinet papers including records of deliberations of the Council of Ministers, Secretaries and other officers:

Provided that the decisions of Council of Ministers, the reasons thereof, and the material on the basis of which the decisions were taken shall be made public after the decision has been taken, and the matter is complete, or over:

Provided further that those matters which come under the exemptions specified in this section shall not be disclosed;
(j) information which relates to personal information the disclosure of which has no relationship to any public activity or interest, or which would cause unwarranted invasion of the privacy of the individual unless the Central Public Information Officer or the State Public Information Officer or the appellate authority, as the case may be, is satisfied that the larger public interest justifies the disclosure of such information:

Provided that the information which cannot be denied to the Parliament or a State Legislature shall not be denied to any person.

(2) Notwithstanding anything in the Official Secrets Act, 1923 nor any of the exemptions permissible in accordance with subsection (1), a public authority may allow access to information, if public interest in disclosure outweighs the harm to the protected interests.
(3) Subject to the provisions of clauses (a), (c) and (i) of subsection (1), any information relating to any occurrence, event or matter which has taken place, occurred or happened twenty years before the date on which any request is made under secton 6 shall be provided to any person making a request under that section:

Provided that where any question arises as to the date from which the said period of twenty years has to be computed, the decision of the Central Government shall be final, subject to the usual appeals provided for in this Act.

**Section 9**

Without prejudice to the provisions of Section 8, a Central Public Information Officer or a State Public Information Officer, as the case may be, may reject a request for information where such a request for providing access would involve an infringement of copyright subsisting in a person other than the State.

**Section 11**

(1) Where a Central Public Information Officer or a State Public Information Officer, as the case may be, intends to disclose any information or record, or part thereof on a request made under this Act, which relates to or has been supplied by a third party and has been treated as confidential by that third party, the Central Public Information Officer or State Public Information Officer, as the case may be, shall, within five days from the receipt of the request, give a written notice to such third party of the request and of the fact that the Central Public Information Officer or State Public Information Officer, as the case may be, intends to disclose the information or record, or part thereof, and invite the third party to make a submission in writing or orally, regarding whether the information should be disclosed, and such submission of the third party shall be kept in view while taking a decision about disclosure of information:

Provided that except in the case of trade or commercial secrets protected by law, disclosure may be allowed if the public interest in disclosure outweighs in importance any possible harm or injury to the interests of such third party.

(2) Where a notice is served by the Central Public Information Officer or State Public Information Officer, as the case may be, under subsection (1) to a third party in respect of any information or record or part thereof, the third party shall, within ten days from the date of receipt of such notice, be given the opportunity to make representation against the proposed disclosure.

(3) Notwithstanding anything contained in Section 7, the Central Public Information Officer or State Public Information Officer, as the case may be, shall, within forty days after receipt of the request under Section 6, if the third party has been given an opportunity to make representation under subsection (2), make a decision as to whether or not to disclose the information or record or part thereof and give in writing the notice of his decision to the third party.

(4) A notice given under subsection (3) shall include a statement that the third party to whom the notice is given is entitled to prefer an appeal under Section 19 against the decision.

[...]

## Chapter V
## Powers and Functions of the Information Commissions, Appeal and Penalties

### Section 19

(1) Any person who, does not receive a decision within the time specified in subsection (1) or clause (a) of subsection (3) of Section 7, or is aggrieved by a decision of the Central Public Information Officer or State Public Information Officer, as the case may be, may within thirty days from the expiry of such period or from the receipt of such a decision prefer an appeal to such officer who is senior in rank to the Central Public Information Officer or State Public Information Officer as the case may be, in each public authority:

Provided that such officer may admit the appeal after the expiry of the period of thirty days if he or she is satisfied that the appellant was prevented by sufficient cause from filing the appeal in time.

(2) Where an appeal is preferred against an order made by a Central Public Information Officer or a State Public Information Officer, as the case may be, under Section 11 to disclose third party information, the appeal by the concerned third party shall be made within thirty days from the date of the order.

(3) A second appeal against the decision under subsection (1) shall lie within ninety days from the date on which the decision should have been made or was actually received, with the Central Information Commission or the State Information Commission:

Provided that the Central Information Commission or the State Information Commission, as the case may be, may admit the appeal after the expiry of the period of ninety days if it is satisfied that the appellant was prevented by sufficient cause from filing the appeal in time.

(4) If the decision of the Central Public Information Officer or State Public Information Officer, as the case may be, against which an appeal is preferred relates to information of a third party, the Central Information Commission or State Information Commission, as the case may be, shall give a reasonable opportunity of being heard to that third party.

(5) In any appeal proceedings, the onus to prove that a denial of a request was justified shall be on the Central Public Information Officer or State Public Information Officer, as the case may be, who denied the request.

(6) An appeal under subsection (1) or subsection (2) shall be disposed of within thirty days of the receipt of the appeal or within such extended period not exceeding a total of forty-five days from the date of filing thereof, as the case may be, for reasons to be recorded in writing.

(7) The decision of the Central Information Commission or State Information Commission, as the case may be, shall be binding.

(8) In its decision, the Central Information Commission or State Information Commission, as the case may be, has the power to—

(a) require the public authority to take any such steps as may be necessary to secure compliance with the provisions of this Act, including—

(i) by providing access to information, if so requested, in a particular form;
(ii) by appointing a Central Public Information Officer or State Public Information Officer, as the case may be;
(iii) by publishing certain information or categories of information;
(iv) by making necessary changes to its practices in relation to the maintenance, management and destruction of records;
(v) by enhancing the provision of training on the right to information for its officials;
(vi) by providing it with an annual report in compliance with clause (b) of subsection (1) of Section 4;

(b) require the public authority to compensate the complainant for any loss or other detriment suffered;
(c) impose any of the penalties provided under this Act;
(d) reject the application.

(9) The Central Information Commission or State Information Commission, as the case may be, shall give notice of its decision, including any right of appeal, to the complainant and the public authority.
(10) The Central Information Commission or State Information Commission, as the case may be, shall decide the appeal in accordance with such procedure as may be prescribed.

**Section 20**

(1) Where the Central Information Commission or the State Information Commission, as the case may be, at the time of deciding any complaint or appeal is of the opinion that the Central Public Information Officer or the State Public Information Officer, as the case may be, has, without any reasonable cause, refused to receive an application for information or has not furnished information within the time specified under subsection (1) of Section 7 or malafidely denied the request for information or knowingly given incorrect, incomplete or misleading information or destroyed information which was the subject of the request or obstructed in any manner in furnishing the information, it shall impose a penalty of two hundred and fifty rupees each day till application is received or information is furnished, so however, the total amount of such penalty shall not exceed twenty-five thousand rupees:

Provided that the Central Public Information Officer or the State Public Information Officer, as the case may be, shall be given a reasonable opportunity of being heard before any penalty is imposed on him:
Provided further that the burden of proving that he acted reasonably and diligently shall be on the Central Public Information Officer or the State Public Information Officer, as the case may be.

(2) Where the Central Information Commission or the State Information Commission, as the case may be, at the time of deciding any complaint or appeal is of the opinion that the Central Public Information Officer or the State Public Information Officer, as the case may be, has, without any reasonable cause and persistently, failed to receive an application for information or has not furnished information within the time specified under subsection (1) of Section 7 or malafidely denied the request for information or knowingly given incorrect, incomplete or misleading information or destroyed information which was the subject of the request or obstructed in any manner in furnishing the information, it shall recommend for disciplinary action against the Central Public Information Officer or the State Public Information Officer, as the case may be, under the service rules applicable to him.

# Appendix 8 Italy: National Freedom-of-Information and Transparency Legislation (Extracts)

## 1. Law No. 241 (7 August 1990) - New Rules regarding Administrative Procedure and the Right of Access to Administrative Documents[33]

### Chapter I
### Principles

#### Section 1 [General principles underpinning administrative action]

1. Administrative action shall pursue the objectives established by law and shall be founded on criteria of economy of action, effectiveness, impartiality, publicity and transparency, in accordance with the modes of action provided for both by the present Law and by the other provisions governing individual procedures, as well as by the principles underpinning the Community's legal order.

[...]

### Chapter V
### Access to Administrative Documents

#### Section 22 [Definitions and principles regarding access]

1. For the purposes of the present chapter:

   a) "right of access" shall mean the right of interested parties to inspect and take copies of administrative documents:

[33]Published in the Official Gazette of 18 August 1990, n. 192. See for the full translation of Law No. 241 in Italian Journal of Public Law, 2010, volume 2 2010, at http://www.ijpl.eu (translation by Catharine de Rienzo). Accessed on 15 February 2017.



H.-J. Blanke, R. Perlingeiro (eds.), *The Right of Access to Public Information*,
DOI 10.1007/978-3-662-55554-5

b) "interested parties" shall mean all private parties (including those having interests that are public or diffuse) who have a direct, concrete and currently existing interest corresponding to a legally protected situation that is linked to the document to which access is requested;
c) "parties with conflicting interests" shall mean all those parties who have been identified or are easily identifiable on the basis of the nature of the document requested and whose right to privacy would be compromised by exercise of the access right;
d) "administrative document" shall mean every graphic, film-based, electromagnetic or other kind whatsoever of representation of the content of instruments, including internal instruments and those not relating to a specific procedure, that are held by a public authority and concern activities of public interest, independently of whether the substantive law governing them is public law or private law; and
e) "public authority" shall mean all natural or juristic persons governed by public law and natural or juristic persons governed by private law, in the limited context of those of their public-interest activities that are governed by national or community law.

2. In consideration of its important public-interest objectives, access to administrative documents shall constitute a general principle underpinning administrative action, with the aim of guaranteeing its impartiality and transparency and fostering participation.
3. All administrative documents shall be accessible, with the exception of those referred to under Section 24, subsections (1), (2), (3), (5) and (6).
4. Information in the possession of a public authority that is not in the form of an administrative document shall not be accessible, save as provided for by Legislative Decree No. 196, dated 30 June 2003, governing access to personal data by the person to whom the data refer.
5. The acquisition of administrative documents by public parties that does not fall within the scope of Section 43(2) of the Law consolidating the provisions in Laws and Regulations governing administrative documentation, referred to in Decree No. 445 of the President of the Republic, dated 28 December 2000, shall be guided by the principle of loyal institutional co-operation.
6. The right of access shall be exercisable for as long as the public authority has the duty to hold the administrative documents to which access is being requested.

**Section 23 [Scope of the access right's application]**

1. The right of access referred to in Section 22 shall be exercised *vis à vis* authorities, independent or special agencies, public bodies and public service providers. The right of access *vis à vis* independent regulatory authorities shall be exercised within the framework of their respective internal rules, in accordance with the provisions of Section 24.

### Section 24 [Access right exceptions]

1. The right of access shall not apply:

   a) in relation to documents having State-secret status pursuant to Law No. 801, dated 24th October 1977, as subsequently amended, and in the cases of secrecy or disclosure prohibition expressly provided for by law, by the Government Regulation referred to under subsection (6) or by public authorities pursuant to subsection (2) of the present section;
   b) in taxation procedures, in relation to which the specific rules governing them shall remain unaffected;
   c) with regard to public administrative action that is directed towards the issue of measures having a normative, general administrative, planning or programming function, in relation to which the specific rules governing their framing shall not be affected; or
   d) in selection procedures, in relation to administrative documents containing information of a psychometric nature regarding third parties.

2. Individual public authorities shall identify those categories of document created by them or, in any case, at their disposal, that shall be withdrawn from access pursuant to subsection (1).
3. Access applications made with the aim of generally monitoring the work of public authorities shall not be admissible.
4. Access to administrative documents may not be denied in cases where it is sufficient to have recourse to the power to postpone.
5. Documents containing information connected to the interests referred to in subsection (1) shall be deemed secret solely within the limited scope of such connection. To such end and where appropriate, public authorities shall also establish, in relation to every category of document, the timeframe during which such documents shall be withdrawn from access.
6. The Government may, by way of a Regulation adopted pursuant to Section 17 (2) of Law No. 400 dated 23 August 1988, provide for cases in which administrative documents may be withdrawn from access:

   a) when, outside the circumstances governed by Section 12 of Law No. 801 dated 24 October 1977, their disclosure may cause a specific and identified injury to security and national defence, to the exercise of national sovereignty or to the continuing and proper conduct of international relations, with particular reference to the circumstances provided for by treaties and their related implementing legislation;
   b) when access may prejudice the processes of framing, deciding or implementing monetary and currency policy;
   c) when the documents concern the structures, resources, equipment, staff and actions strictly instrumental to the safeguarding of public order, to the prevention and suppression of crime (with particular reference to methods of investigation, the identity of information sources and the

security of the property and persons involved) or to judicial police activities and the conduct of investigations;

d) when the documents concern the private life or privacy of natural persons, legal persons, groups, enterprises or associations, with particular reference to their concrete epistolary, health-related, professional, financial, industrial or commercial interests, even if the related data have been supplied to the public authority by those very persons to whom they refer; or

e) when the documents regard the on-going activity of national collective labour bargaining or internal documents linked to execution of the related mandate.

7. Applicants must nevertheless be guaranteed access to those administrative documents the knowledge of which is necessary for protecting or asserting their legal interests. In the case of documents containing sensitive or judicial data, access shall be permitted to the extent that it is strictly indispensable and according to the conditions provided for by Section 60 of Legislative Decree No. 196 dated 30 June 2003, in the case of data capable of revealing state of health or sex life.

**Section 25 [Ways of exercising the access right and appeals]**

1. The right of access shall be exercised by examining and taking a copy of administrative documents, in the ways and subject to the limitations indicated by the present Law. The examination of documents shall be free of charge. Without prejudice to the provisions currently in force governing tax-stamps, as well as document search and identification fees, the issue of copies shall be subject only to reimbursement of the reproduction costs.
2. Requests for access to documents must contain a statement of reasons. They must be addressed to the public authority that created the document or holds it permanently.
3. Access may be denied, postponed or restricted in the cases and to the extent established by Section 24. The reasons for such denial, postponement or restriction must be stated.
4. Upon expiry of thirty days from the date of a request without result, the request shall be deemed refused. In cases of either expressly or tacitly denied access or postponement of the same pursuant to Section 24(4), the requesting party shall have the right to appeal to the regional administrative court pursuant to subsection (5) or, within the same timeframe and in relation to the instruments of municipal, provincial or regional authorities, to ask the Ombudsman with competence in that territorial jurisdiction, where appointed, for the said decision to be reconsidered. Should such figure not have been established, competence shall lie with the Ombudsman with competence for the immediately higher territorial jurisdiction. As regards the instruments of the State's central and decentralised administrative

branches, such request shall be forwarded to the Commission for Access referred to in Section 27, as well as to the authority objecting to access. The Ombudsman or the Commission for Access shall make his/her or its finding within thirty days of the application's presentation. Once such timeframe has expired fruitlessly, the appeal shall be deemed refused. If the Ombudsman or the Commission for Access deems the denial or the postponement to be unlawful, they shall inform the requesting party of such fact and shall communicate it to the authority holding the document. If the latter does not issue a measure confirming and stating the reasons for its decision within thirty days of receipt of the communication from the Ombudsman or the Commission, access shall be permitted. Should the person requesting access have applied to the Ombudsman or the Commission, the timeframe referred to in subsection (5) shall run from the date of the requesting party's receipt of the communication of the outcome of his/her application to the Ombudsman or to the Commission itself. If access is denied or postponed for reasons concerning personal data referring to third parties, the Commission shall make provision, after prior consultation with the *Garante* for the Protection of Personal Data, who shall state his conclusions within ten days of the request, and whose opinion shall be deemed given should such period expire without result. Should a procedure referred to in Section III of Chapter I of Title I of Part III of Legislative Decree No. 196 dated 30 June 2003 or in Sections 154, 157, 158, 159 or 160 of the same Legislative Decree No. 196 of 2003, relating to the public processing of personal data by a public authority, involve access to administrative documents, the *Garante* for the Protection of Personal Data shall ask the Commission for Access to Administrative Documents for its mandatory but non-binding opinion. The request for an opinion shall suspend the timeframe for the *Garante's* finding until the opinion has been acquired but for no more than fifteen days in any event. Upon expiry of such timeframe without result, the *Garante* shall take his/her own decision.

5. Disputes relating to access to administrative documents are regulated by the Code of Administrative Process.

[...]

### Section 28 [Amendment of Section 15 of the Consolidation Law referred to in Decree No. 3 of the President of the Republic dated 10 January 1957, regarding Civil Service Secrecy]

1. Section 15 of the Consolidation Law containing provisions governing the Staff Regulations for state civil servants, adopted through Decree No. 3 of the President of the Republic, dated 10 January 1957, shall be substituted by the following:

*"Section 15 (civil service secrecy). – 1. Employees must preserve civil service secrecy. They must not transmit information regarding administrative measures or activities, whether ongoing or completed, or news that has come to their knowledge by virtue of*

*their duties, to persons who are not entitled to it except in the circumstances and in the ways provided for by the rules governing the right of access. Employees responsible for an office shall, within their individual fields of competence, issue copies of and extracts from instruments and documents ex officio in those cases that are not prohibited by the office's internal rules".*

## 2. Legislative Decree No. 33 dated 14 March 2013

Reorganization of the Rules concerning the Obligations of Publicity, Transparency and Dissemination of Information by Public Authorities[34]

**Section 1 [General principle of transparency]**

1. Transparency is meant as total accessibility of information about the organization and activities of public administration, in order to encourage widespread forms of control over the pursuit of institutional functions and the use of public resources.
2. Transparency, in compliance with the provisions of state secrecy, the secrecy, statistical confidentiality and personal data protection, contribute to implementing the principle of democracy and the constitutional principles of equality, impartiality, proper conduct, accountability, effectiveness and efficiency in the use of public resources, integrity and loyalty in service to the nation. It is a condition of guarantee of individual and collective freedoms and the civil, political and social, integrates the right to good administration and contribute to the creation of an open administration, to serve the citizens.
3. The provisions of this Decree and any implementing rules adopted under Article 48, supplement the identification of the essential level of benefits provided by general government for the sake of transparency, prevention, dealing with corruption and maladministration, in the meaning of Article 117, second paragraph, letter m) of the Constitution and also constitute exercise of statistical and computer information for coordination of data of state, regional and local administration, according to Article 117, second paragraph, letter r), of the Constitution.

**Section 2 [Object]**

1. The provisions of this Decree shall identify the requirements on transparency concerning the organization and activities of public administrations and modalities for its implementation.
2. For the purposes of this Decree, publication means the publication, in compliance with the specifications and technical regulations referred to in Annex A, in the institutional sites of public administrations of documents,

[34]Published in the Official Gazette of 5 April 2013, n. 80.

information and data about the organization and the public administration activities, which corresponds to the right of everyone to access the sites directly and immediately, with no authentication and identification.

**Section 3 [Publicity and right to know]**

1. All documents, information and data subject to mandatory publication under current legislation are public and everyone has the right to know them, is free to enjoy them, and to use them and re-use them in accordance with Article 7.

**Section 4 [Limits to transparency]**

1. The publication obligations of the various personal data different from sensitive data and judicial data, referred to in Article 4, paragraph 1, letters d) and e) of the Legislative Decree of June 30, 2003, n. 196, involve the possibility of a spread of same data via institutional websites, as well as their treatment under modes that allow the indexing and traceability through the motors for web search and their re-use under Article 7 in accordance with the principles on processing of personal data.
2. Publication in institutional sites, in implementation of this Decree, of data relating to holders of political bodies and offices or of position of direct collaboration, as well as of holders of administrative agencies is aimed at the realization of public transparency, which integrates an aim of public interest in compliance with the rules on protection of personal data.
3. Public authorities may arrange for the publication in their institutional websites of information and documents that they have no obligation to publish under this Decree or on the basis of specific law provisions, subject to the limits and conditions expressly provided by law, and proceeding to previous anonymisation of personal data that may be present.
4. In cases where the law or regulations provide for the publication of records or documents, public authorities shall not make intelligible such personal data which are irrelevant or, if sensitive or judicial, are not essential for the specific transparency purposes related to the publication.
5. Information concerning the conduct of the performance of any person assigned to a public function and its assessment shall be made available by the pertaining administration. Such information is on the contrary not ostensible, except when required by law, in as far as information concerning the nature of illness and personal or family impediments that cause absence from work is concerned, as well as for what concerns the single components of the evaluation or information concerning the employment relationship and which are suitable for disclosing out any of the information specified in Article 4, paragraph 1, letter d) of Legislative Decree No. 196 of 2003.
6. The limits to the dissemination and the access of information referred to in Article 24, paragraphs 1 and 6 of the Law of 7 August 1990, n. 241, as amended, of all the data referred to in Article 9 of Legislative Decree of

6 September 1989, No. 322, remain unchanged, as well as those referred to in European legislation on statistical secrecy protection and of those that are expressly qualified as confidential by the national and European regulations on statistics, as well as those relating to the dissemination of data disclosing health and sex life.

[. . .]

### Section 5 [Public access to data and documents][35]

1. The obligation established under the legislation in force for the public administration to publish documents, information, or data implies the right for everyone to request such documents, information or data in case of failure to publish them.
2. In order to promote widespread forms of control over the pursuit of official duties and the use of public resources and to encourage participation in public debate, everyone has the right of access to data and documents held by public authorities, other than those to be published in accordance with this Decree, within the limits for the protection of legally relevant public and private interests.

[. . .]

---

[35]The Decree 97/2016 which replaces the Decree 33/2013 entered into force on 8 June 2016 (date of publication in the Gazzetta Ufficiale). However, Article 5.2 of Decree 33/2013 remained applicable during six months after the entry into force of Decree 97/2016. Former text:

Section 5 [Public access (*Accesso civico*)]

1. The obligation established under the legislation in force for the public administration to publish documents, information, or data implies the right for everyone to request such documents, information or data in case of failure to publish them

2. The request for public access is not subject to any limitation as far as the subjective legitimacy of the applicant is concerned, does not need to be motivated, is free and must be submitted to the Responsible for transparency within the administration which is under the obligation of publication referred to in paragraph 1, who shall decide over the request.

3. The administration, within thirty days, shall proceed to the publication of the document, of the information or of the requested data in the web site and, at the same time, transmit it to the applicant or communicate about the publication by indicating the hyperlink to the request. If the document, information or data requested have already been published in compliance with current legislation, the administration shall notify the applicant its hyperlink.

4. In cases of delay or lack of response the applicant may appeal to the holder of the replacement power referred to in Article 2, paragraph 9-bis of the Law of 7 August 1990. 241, as amended, that, verified the existence of the obligation of publication, under the terms of paragraph 9-ter of the same article, shall provide for it according to paragraph 3.

5. The protection of the right to public access shall be governed by the provisions of the Legislative Decree of July 2, 2010, No. 104, as amended by this Decree.

6. A request of public access involves, by the Responsible for Transparency, the reporting obligation mentioned in Article 43, paragraph 5.

# Appendix 9 Japan: National Freedom-of-Information and Transparency Legislation (Extracts)

## 1. Constitution of Japan (3 November 1946)

**Article 21**

(1) Freedom of assembly and association as well as speech, press and all other forms of expression are guaranteed.
(2) No censorship shall be maintained, nor shall the secrecy of any means of communication be violated.

**Article 82**

(1) Trials shall be conducted and judgment declared publicly.
(2) Where a court unanimously determines publicity to be dangerous to public order or morals, a trial may be conducted privately, but trials of political offenses, offenses involving the press or cases wherein the rights of people as guaranteed in Chapter III of this Constitution are in question shall always be conducted publicly.

**Article 94**

Local public entities shall have the right to manage their property, affairs and administration and to enact their own regulations within law.



H.-J. Blanke, R. Perlingeiro (eds.), *The Right of Access to Public Information*,
DOI 10.1007/978-3-662-55554-5

## 2. Act on Access to Information held by Administrative Organs (Law No. 42 of 14 May 1999)[36]

### Chapter 1
### General Provisions

#### Article 1 [Purpose]

In accordance with the principle that sovereignty resides in the people, and by providing for the right to request the disclosure of administrative documents, etc., the purpose of this Law is to strive for greater disclosure of information held by administrative organs thereby ensuring that the government fulfills its duty to explain its various operations to the people, and to contribute to the promotion of a fair and democratic administration that is subject to the people's accurate understanding and criticism.

#### Article 2 [Definitions]

1. For the purposes of this Law "administrative organ" refers to the following organs.
   (1) Organs within the Cabinet (excluding the Cabinet Office) or organs under the jurisdiction of the Cabinet that were established pursuant to law.
   (2) The Cabinet Office, the Imperial House-hold Agency and organs established as provided for in Article 49, paragraph 1 and 2 of the Cabinet Office Establishment Law (Law No. 89 of 1999). (Provided that the organs is one in which an organ designated by the Cabinet Order referred to in the item (4) is established, the organ designated by the Cabinet Order is excluded.)
   (3) Organs established as provided for in Article 3, paragraph 2 of the National Government Organization Law (Law No. 120 of 1948). (Provided that the organ is one in which an organ designated by the Cabinet Order referred to in the item (5) is established, the organ designated by the Cabinet Order is excluded.)
   (4) Organs under Article 39 and 55 of the Cabinet Office Establishment Law and under Article 16, paragraph 2 of the Imperial House-hold Agency Law (Law No.70 of 1947), and extraordinary organs under Articles 40 and 56 (including the case applied mutatis mutandis in Article 18, paragraph 1 of the Imperial House-hold Agency Law), that are designated by Cabinet Order.

[36]This translation is based on a translation by Prof. Katsuya Uga (The University of Tokyo) and David Moses Schultz, which appeared in *Law in Japan: An Annual*, 27, p. 170-183. It has been partly amended by the authors to reflect changes in the law up to the beginning of 2017. An alternative translation of the law can be found on the Japanese Government's Translation of Japanese Laws database (see: http://www.japaneselawtranslation.go.jp/) (Accessed on 15 February 2017. Reflects amendments up to 2004).

(5) Facilities and other organs under Article 8-2 of the National Government Organization Law, and extraordinary organs under Article 8-3 of the same law, that are designated by Cabinet Order.
(6) The Board of Audit

2. For the purposes of this Law "administrative document" means a document, drawing, and electromagnetic record (Meaning a record created in a form that cannot be recognized through one's sense of perception such as in an electronic form or magnetic form. Hereinafter the same.), that, having been prepared or obtained by an employee of an administrative organ in the course of his or her duties, is held by the administrative organ concerned for organizational use by its employees. However, the following are excluded:

   (1) Items published for the purpose of selling to many and unspecified persons, such as official gazettes, white papers, newspapers, magazines, and books.
   (2) Specified Historical Public Records and Archives, etc., as provided for by Article 2 paragraph 7 of the Public Records and Archives Management Law(Law No. 66 of 2009)
   (3) Items that are, pursuant to the provisions of a Cabinet Order, specially administered as either historical or cultural materials, or as materials for academic research in the National Archives or other organs designated by a Cabinet Order (excluding items provided for in the previous item).

## Chapter 2
## Disclosure of Administrative Documents

### Article 3 [The right to request disclosure]

Any person, as provided for by this Law, may request to the head of an administrative organ (Provided that the organ is designated by the Cabinet Order of the preceding Article, paragraph 1, item (4) and (5), the person designated for each organ by Cabinet Order. Hereinafter the same.) the disclosure of administrative documents held by the administrative organ concerned.

### Article 4 [The procedure for requesting disclosure]

1. A request for disclosure as provided for by the preceding Article (Hereinafter referred to as a "Disclosure Request.") shall be submitted to the head of an administrative organ as a document in writing(Hereinafter referred to as a "Disclosure Application.") in which are entered the following items.

   (1) The Requester's full name or title, along with a permanent address or place of residence, as well as the full name of a representative in the case of a corporation or other group.
   (2) The titles of administrative documents or other particulars that will suffice to specify the administrative documents relevant to the Disclosure Request.

2. When the head of an administrative organ concludes that there is a deficiency in the form of the Disclosure Application, he or she may, fixing a suitable period of time, ask the person making the Disclosure Request (Hereinafter referred to as "the Requester.") to revise the request. In this case, the head of the administrative organ shall endeavor to put at the Requester's disposal information that will be helpful in the revision.

**Article 5 [The obligation to disclose administrative documents]**
When there is a Disclosure Request, excluding cases in which any of the information mentioned in each of the following item s (Hereinafter referred to as "Non-Disclosure Information.") is recorded in the administrative documents concerned with the Disclosure Request, the head of an administrative organ shall disclose said administrative documents to the Requester.

(1) Information concerning an individual (Excluding information concerning the business of an individual who carries on said business.), where it is possible to identify a specific individual from a name, birth date or other description, etc., contained in the information concerned (Including instances where through collation with other information it is possible to identify a specific individual.), or when it is not possible to identify a specific individual, but by making the information public there is a risk that an individual's rights and interests will be harmed. However, the following are excluded:

(a) Information that is made public, or information that is scheduled to be made public, as provided for by law or by custom.
(b) Information recognized as necessary to be made public in order to protect a person's life, health, livelihood, or property.
(c) In the case that the said individual is a public official, etc. (National public employees as described in Article 2, Section 1 of the National Public Service Law [Law No. 120 of 1947], executives and employees of the Executive Corporations as described in Article 2, paragraph 4 of the Law Concerning the General Rules of the Incorporated Administrative Agencies [Law No.103 of 1999] excluded; executives and employees of the incorporated administrative agencies, etc. as described in Article 2, paragraph 1 of the Law Concerning Access to Information held by Incorporated Administrative Agencies [Law No.140 of 2001. Hereinafter referred to as the "the Incorporated Administrative Agencies, etc., Information Disclosure Law"]; local public service personnel as described in Article 2 of the Local Public Service Personnel Law [Law No. 261 of 1950]; and executives and employees of the local incorporated administrative agencies as described in Article 2, paragraph 1 of the Local Incorporated Administrative Agency Law [Law No.118 of 2003] [Hereinafter the same.]), when the said information is information

that concerns the performance of his or her duties, from within the said information that portion which concerns the said public officer, etc. and the substance of the said performance of duties.

(2) Information concerning a corporation or other entity (Excluding the State, the incorporated administrative agencies, etc., local public entities and the local incorporated administrative agencies. Hereinafter referred to as a "Corporation, etc."), or information concerning the business of an individual who carries on said business, as set forth below. Excluding, however, information recognized as necessary to be made public in order to protect a person's life, health, livelihood, or property.

  (a) Where there is a risk that, by making such information public, the rights, competitive standing, or other legitimate interests of the Corporation, etc., or the said individual will be harmed.
  (b) Where upon the request of an administrative organ it was offered voluntarily on the condition that it not be made public, and where it could be considered reasonable to attach said condition, in light of the nature of the information and the circumstances, etc. at the time, such as when the Corporation, etc., or the individual do not ordinarily make the information public.

(3) Information that, if made public, the head of an administrative organ with reasonable grounds deems to pose a risk of harm to the security of the State, a risk of damage to trustful relations with another country or an international organization, or a risk of causing a disadvantage in negotiations with another country or an international organization.
(4) Information that, if made public, the head of an administrative organ with reasonable grounds deems to pose a risk of causing a hindrance to the prevention, suppression or investigation of crimes, the maintenance of public prosecutions, the execution of sentencing, and other public security and public order maintenance matters.
(5) Information concerning deliberations, inquiries, or consultations internal to or between either organs of the State, the incorporated administrative agencies, etc., local public entities or the local incorporated administrative agencies that, if made public, would risk unjustly harming the frank exchange of opinions or the neutrality of decision making, risk unjustly causing confusion among the people, or risk unjustly bringing advantage or disadvantage to specific individuals.
(6) Information that concerns the affairs or business conducted by an organ of the State, an incorporated administrative agency, etc., a local public entity or a local incorporated administrative agency that, if made public, by the nature of said affairs or business, would risk, such as the following mentioned risks, causing a hindrance to the proper performance of said affairs or business.

  (a) In relation to affairs concerned with audits, inspections, supervision, and testing, the risk of making difficult the grasping of accurate facts, along with the risk of facilitating illegal or unfair acts or making difficult the discovery of those acts.

(b) In relation to affairs concerned with contracts, negotiations, or administrative appeals, or litigation, the risk of unfairly harming the property interests or the position as a party of the State, an incorporated administrative agency, etc., a local party or a local incorporated administrative agency.

(c) In relation to affairs concerned with research studies, the risk that their impartial and efficient execution will be unjustly obstructed.

(d) In relation to affairs concerned with personnel management, the risk that the impartial and smooth maintenance of personnel matters will be hindered.

(e) In relation to the business of an enterprise managed by a local public entity, an incorporated administrative agency, etc., or a local incorporated administrative agency, the risk that legitimate interests arising from the management of the enterprise will be harmed.

**Article 6 [Partial disclosure]**

1. In the case that Non-Disclosure Information is recorded in a part of an administrative document concerned with a Disclosure Request, when it is possible to easily divide and exclude the portion in which the Non-Disclosure Information is recorded, the head of the administrative organ shall disclose to the Requester the portion other than the excluded portion. However, this shall not apply when it is deemed that meaningful information is not recorded in the portion other than the excluded portion.
2. In the case that the information of item (1) of the preceding Article (Limited to that which makes possible the identification of a specific individual.) is recorded in an administrative document concerned with a Disclosure Request, and if by excluding from said information the portion of the description, etc., that makes possible the identification of a specific individual, such as a name or birth date, there is considered to be no risk of harm to an individual's rights and interests even though it is made public, then the portion other than the excluded portion shall be regarded as not being included in the information of the said item, and the preceding paragraph shall apply.

**Article 7 [Discretionary disclosure for public interest reasons]**

Even in the case that Non-Disclosure Information is recorded in administrative documents concerned with a Disclosure Request, when it is deemed that there is a particular public interest necessity, the head of an administrative organ may disclose the administrative documents to the Requester.

**Article 8 [Information concerning the existence of administrative documents]**
When Non-Disclosure Information will be released by merely answering whether or not administrative documents concerned with a Disclosure Request exist or do not exist, the head of an administrative organ, without making clear the existence or non-existence of the documents, may refuse the Disclosure Request.

**Article 9 [Measures concerning disclosure requests]**

1. When disclosing all or a part of the administrative documents concerned with a Disclosure Request, the head of the administrative organ shall make a decision to that effect, and notify the Requester to that effect in writing as well as of matters determined by Cabinet Order relating to the implementation of disclosure.
2. When not disclosing any of the administrative documents concerned with a Disclosure Request (Including when refusing the Disclosure Request in accordance with the preceding Article, as well as when administrative documents concerned with the request are not held.), the head of the administrative organ shall make a decision to the effect of non-disclosure and notify the Requester to that effect in writing.

**Article 10 [Time limit for disclosure decisions]**

1. The preceding Article's decisions (Hereinafter referred to as "Disclosure Decisions, etc.") shall be made within thirty days after the day of the Disclosure Request. However, in the case that a revision is requested as provided for in Article 4, paragraph 2, the number of days required for the revision shall not be included within this time limit.
2. Notwithstanding the preceding paragraph, when there are justifiable grounds such as difficulties arising from the conduct of business, the head of the administrative organ may extend the time limit provided for in the same paragraph for up to thirty days. In this case, the head of the administrative organ shall without delay notify the Requester in writing of the extension period along with the reason for the extension.

**Article 11 [Exception to the time limit for disclosure decisions]**
In the case that there is a considerably large amount of administrative documents concerned with the Disclosure Request, and there is a risk that by making Disclosure Decisions, etc., for all of them within sixty days of the Disclosure Request the performance of duties will be considerably hindered, notwithstanding the preceding Article, it shall be sufficient if the head of the administrative organ makes Disclosure Decisions, etc., for a reasonable portion of the administrative documents concerned with the Disclosure Request within the said period of time, and if Disclosure Decisions, etc., are made for the remaining

administrative documents within a reasonable period of time. In this case, the head of the administrative organ shall within the period of time provided for in the first paragraph of the same Article notify the Requester in writing of the following items:

(1) The application of this article and the reason for its application.
(2) The time limit for making Disclosure Decisions, etc., for the remaining administrative documents.

[. . .]

**Article 13 [Granting third persons an opportunity to submit a written opinion]**

1. When information regarding a person other than the State, an incorporated administrative agency, etc., a local public entity, a local incorporated administrative agency or the Requester (Hereinafter in this article, Article 19, paragraph 2, and Article 20, paragraph 1, referred to as a "Third Person.") is recorded in the administrative documents concerned with a Disclosure Request, the head of the administrative organ, when undertaking Disclosure Decisions, etc.., may communicate to the Third Person concerned with the information a representation of the administrative documents concerned with the Disclosure Request and other items determined by Cabinet Order, and may provide the opportunity to submit a written opinion.
2. In the event that either of the following subparagraphs apply, before making a Decision to Disclose, the head of the administrative organ shall communicate in writing to the Third Person concerned with the information a representation of the documents concerned with the Disclosure Request and other items determined by Cabinet Order, and shall provide the opportunity to submit a written opinion. However, this shall not apply in the case that the Third Person's whereabouts are unknown.

   (1) Where, in the case that the intention is to disclose administrative documents in which information relating to a Third Person is recorded, it is deemed that said information will fall within the information provided for in Article 5, item (1)(b), or within the proviso contained in item (2) of the same article.
   (2) When administrative documents within which information concerning a Third Person is recorded are to be disclosed under Article 7.

3. In the case that the third party who was provided an opportunity to submit a written opinion as provided for by the preceding two paragraphs submits a written opinion indicating opposition to disclosure of the administrative documents concerned, the head of the administrative organ, when making a decision to disclose, shall place at least two weeks between the day of the Decision to Disclose and the day that disclosure will be implemented. In this case, upon making the Decision to Disclose the head of the administrative

organ shall immediately notify in writing the Third Person who submitted the written opinion (In Article 19 referred to as an "opposition written opinion.") to the effect that the Decision to Disclose was made, the reason, and the date of implementation of disclosure.

**Article 14 [Implementation of disclosure]**

1. The disclosure of administrative documents shall take place by inspection or by the provision of copies for documents or drawings, and for electromagnetic records by methods determined by Cabinet Order that take into consideration their classification and the state of development, etc., of information technology. However, when disclosure of an administrative document is to take place by the inspection method, if the head of the administrative organ considers that there is a risk that difficulties in the preservation of the administrative document will arise, or for other justifiable reasons, a copy of the document may be provided for inspection.
2. The person who will obtain disclosure of administrative documents based upon a Decision to Disclose, as provided for by Cabinet Order, shall request the desired method of implementation of disclosure and other items determined by Cabinet Order to the head of the administrative organ who made the Decision to Disclose.
3. The request as provided for by the preceding paragraph shall be made within thirty days after the notification provided for in Article 9, paragraph 1. However, this shall not apply when there is a justifiable reason for being unable to make the request within this time limit.
4. The person who has obtained disclosure of administrative documents based upon a Decision to Disclose, within thirty days after first obtaining disclosure, may request to the head of the administrative organ to the effect of again obtaining disclosure. In this case the provison in the preceding paragraph shall apply mutatis mutandis.

**Article 16 [Fees]**

1. The person who makes a Disclosure Request, and the person who obtains the disclosure of administrative documents, as provided for by Cabinet Order, shall pay respectively a fee for the Disclosure Request and a fee for the implementation of disclosure of an amount determined by Cabinet Order and within the limits of actual expenses.
2. In determining the amount of the fee of the preceding paragraph consideration shall be given to see that it is as affordable an amount as possible.
3. When it is deemed that there is economic hardship or other special reasons, as provided for by Cabinet Order, the head of an administrative organ may reduce or exempt the fee of paragraph 1.

[...]

## Chapter 3
## Applications for Review

### Section 1
### References

#### Article 18 [Exceptions to the application of provisions regarding review procedures by reviewers]

1. The provisions of Article 9, Article 17, Article 24, Chapter 2, Section 3 and Section 4, and Article 50, paragraph 2 of the Administrative Appeal Law (Law No. 68 of 2014) do not apply in respect of applications for review of omissions regarding Disclosure Decisions, etc., or Disclosure Requests.
2. With respect to the application of the provisions of Chapter 2 of the Administrative Appeal Law in respect of applications for review of omissions regarding Disclosure Decisions, etc., or Disclosure Requests, the reference in Article 11, paragraph 2 of that law to "the person designated by the provision of Article 9, paragraph 1 (hereinafter referred to as a "Reviewer")" shall be read as "the administrative organ against which an application for review was made (Including an administrative organ to which a request was transferred in accordance with the provision of Article 14. Hereinafter referred to as "the Review Agency".) in accordance with the provision of Article 4 (Including Cabinet Orders based on the provision of Article 20, paragraph 2 of the Law on Access to Information held by Administrative Organs (Law No. 42 of May 14, 1999.)", the reference in Article 13, paragraph 1 and paragraph 2 of that law to "Reviewer" shall be read as "the Review Agency", the reference in Article 25, paragraph 7 of that law to "in such case, or in the case that the Reviewer submits a written opinion that there should be a stay in accordance with Article 40" shall be read as "in such case", the reference in Article 44 of that law to "the Administrative Appeal Review Board, etc." shall be read as "the Information Disclosure and Personal Information Protection Review Board (When the head of the Review Agency is head of the Board of Audit, a review board separately provided for by law. The same applies for Article 50, paragraph 1, item 4.), and to "where [...] received (or, in the case that in accordance with the provision of paragraph 1 of the previous article no reference is required other than in the case that item 2 or item 3 of that paragraph applies), where the Reviewer has submitted a written opinion, or, in the case that item 2 or item 3 of that paragraph applies, where the review provided for in item 2 or item 3 of that paragraph has occurred)" shall be read as "where [...] received", and the reference in Article 50, paragraph 1, item 4 of that law to "the Reviewer's written opinion, or the Administrative Appeal Review Board, etc., or the Council, etc." shall be read as "the Information Disclosure and Personal Information Protection Review Board".

[...]

## Chapter 4
## Supplementary Provisions

### Article 22 [The provision on information to persons who intend to request disclosure]

1. So that it is possible for persons who intend to request disclosure easily as well as accurately, the heads of administrative organs shall provide information helpful in specifying the administrative documents held by the administrative organs and take other appropriate steps that take into account the convenience of the persons intending to request disclosure, other than the measures prescribed in Article 7, paragraph 2 of the Public Records and Archives Management Law.
2. In order to secure the smooth application of this Law, the Minister of Internal Affairs and Communications shall provide for general inquiry offices.

[...]

### Additional Provisions

1. This Law shall come into effect on a date to be provided for by Cabinet Order, but not more than two years from the date of promulgation. However, the provisions of the part of Article 23, paragraph 1, concerning receiving of the consent of both Houses, Article 40 through Article 42, and the following paragraph, shall come into effect from the date of promulgation.
2. Approximately four years after this Law comes into effect, the government shall examine the state of enforcement of this Law along with the manner of jurisdiction for information disclosure lawsuits, and shall take necessary measures based upon those results.

# Appendix 10 Mexico: National Freedom-of-Information and Transparency Legislation (Extracts)

## 1. Political Constitution of the United Mexican States[37]

**Article 6**

Expression of ideas shall not be subject to judicial or administrative inquiry, except for those cases when such expression of ideas goes against the moral, privacy or the rights of third parties, causes perpetration of a felony, or disturbs the public order. The right of reply shall be exercised according to law. The State shall guarantee the right to information.

Every person shall be entitled to free access to plural and timely information, as well as to search for, receive and distribute information and ideas of any kind, through any means of expression.

The State shall guarantee access to information and communication technology, access to the services of radio broadcast, telecommunications and broadband Internet. To that end, the State shall establish effective competition conditions for the provision of such services.

To accomplish the provisions of this article, the following points shall be observed:

A. In order to exercise the right of access to information, the Federation and the federal entities, according to their respective powers, shall act in accordance to the following basis and principles:

[37]Political Constitution of the Mexican United States of 5.2.1857 (as published in the Official Gazette of the Federation of 5 February 1917), most recently amended in 2017 and published in the Official Gazette of the Federation of 24 February 2017 (*Diario Oficial de la Federación – DOF*).



H.-J. Blanke, R. Perlingeiro (eds.), *The Right of Access to Public Information*,
DOI 10.1007/978-3-662-55554-5

I. All information in custody of any authority, entity or organ of the Executive, Legislative and Judicial Powers, autonomous organisms, political parties, public funds or any person or group, such as unions, entitled with public funds or that can exercise authority at the federal, state or municipal level is public. This information may only be reserved temporarily due to public interest or national security, following the law provisions for this. The principle of maximum disclosure shall prevail when interpreting this right. The obligated subjects (obligors) must record every activity which derives from their authority, competence or function, the law will specifically establish the assumptions under the declaration of inexistence of information shall proceed.

II. Information regarding private life and personal data shall be protected according to law and with the exceptions established therein.

III. Every person shall have free access to public information, his/her personal data and in the case to the rectification of his/her personal data, without the necessity to argue interest or justification.

IV. The mechanisms to access information and expedite review procedures shall be established. These procedures must be formalized before specialized and impartial autonomous agencies established by this Constitution.

V. Government agencies (obligors) shall record and keep their documents in updated administrative files, and shall disclose through electronic media, the complete and updated information about the use of public resources and their management indexes so that the information allows accountability procedures in regard to the fulfillment of their objectives and the results of their performance.

VI. The law shall establish procedures for governmental agencies (obligors) to disclose information concerning the use of public resources paid to individuals or companies.

VII. Failure to comply with these dispositions in regard to the access to public information shall be penalized according to the law.

VIII. The Federation shall establish an autonomous, specialized, impartial and collegiate agency. It must have a legal personality; own assets; full technical, managerial and decision power over its budget and internal organization; and shall be responsible for guaranteeing the fulfillment of the right of access to public information and the protection of personal data held by public agencies (obligated subjects), according to the terms established by law.

The autonomous transparency agency established in this fraction will be governed by the transparency and access to public information law, as well as the law for the protection on personal data held by obligated subjects, in the terms established by the general law issued by the Congress to set the basic principles, basis and procedures for the exercise of the information rights.

This agency will be governed by the principles of certainty, legality, independence, impartiality, efficiency, objectiveness, professionalism, transparency and maximum publicity.

The autonomous transparency agency has competence to receive inquiries related to the right of access to public information and the protection of personal data from any authority, entity, organism or agency which belongs to any of the Executive, Legislative or Judicial Powers, as well as any autonomous agency, political parties public trusts and public funds, or any other person, group, union or organization which receives or use public resources or which exercise authority at the federal domain with exception of those issues which correspond to the jurisdiction of the Federal Supreme Court, in which case the a committee of three Supreme Court Justices would decide the issue. The autonomous transparency agency has, also the competence to receive the inquiries from individuals in regard to the resolutions issued by the local autonomous specialized transparency which ruled the inexistence, reserve, and confidentiality of information or which refuses to disclose information according to the terms established by law.

The National Transparency Agency [organismo garante], ex oficio or by substantiated petition of the local agency from the federal entities may receive or analyze the inquiries that due to its importance or transcendence are in the interest of the National Transparency Agency.

The law will determine the information that shall be considered as reserved or confidential.

The resolutions of the National Transparency Agency are mandatory, definitive and indisputable for the obligated subjects (obligors). Only in the cases that the resolutions may be considered to attempt to public security according to the law in the matter, the Legal Councilor of the Federal Government may present a review inquiry to the Supreme Court.

The National Transparency Agency [organismo garante] shall be constituted by seven commissioners. To appoint them, the Senate, previous extensive consultation to social actors and by proposal of the different parliamentary groups, will appoint the commissioner with the vote of two-thirds of the Senators present in the session according to the vacancy which must be covered and following the procedure established by law.

The President may oppose the appointment within ten business days. If the President does not oppose the appointment within the given days, then the person appointed by the Senate will assume the commissioner office.

Given the case that the President opposes the appointment, the Senate will present a new proposal to occupy the vacancy according to the previous paragraph. However, to approve the proposal the vote of three-fifths of the Senators present is required. If this second appointment were objected, the Senate, according to the procedures in the previous paragraph, with the approval of three-fifths of the Senators present would appoint definitively the commissioner that will occupy the vacancy.

The commissioner office will be held during seven years, and the commissioners shall fulfill the requirements provided in the fractions I, II, IV, V and VI of the article 95 of this Constitution. The commissioners shall not hold other office; have an additional employment, or other commission with exception of the non-profit chairs or offices related to charities and academic or scientific institutions. The commissioners can only be removed from office according to the terms in the Fourth Title of this Constitution and they will be subject to political trial.

The conformation of the National Transparency Agency shall promote gender equality. The Commissioner President shall be selected by a peer process, through the secret vote of the commissioners.

The Commissioner President will remain in office for three years, with the possibility of being reelected to other three years. The commissioner president must render an annual report before the Senate in the date and terms described by the law.

The National Transparency Agency [organo garante] shall have an Advisory Board, formed with ten council members who shall be elected by the vote of two thirds of the present Senators. The law will establish the procedures to present the proposals to the Senate. Each year, the two council members with longer tenure will be replaced, unless they were proposed and ratified for a second term in office.

The law will establish the emergency measures and procedures which the Agency could implement to guarantee the fulfillment of its decisions.

Every authority and public servant is compelled to help the National Transparency Agency and its Commissioners for the adequate performance of the Agency. The National Transparency Agency will coordinate its actions with the Superior Comptroller Office, the entity specialized in archives and files, the organ in charge of gathering and process of statistical and geographical data, as well as, with the local agencies in the federal entities in order to strengthen the accountability within the Mexican State.

B. In matters of broadcasting and telecommunications:

I. The State shall guarantee the integration to the information and knowledge society of its population through a policy of universal digital inclusion crafted with annual and sexennial goals.

II. Telecommunications are deemed as public services of general interest and, therefore, the State shall guarantee that they are offered under competitive conditions, with quality, plurality, universal coverage, interconnection, convergence, continuity, free access, and free from arbitrary interferences.

III. Broadcasting is deemed as public services of general interest and, therefore, the State shall guarantee that it be offered with quality and under competitive conditions, to deliver the benefits of culture to the population, preserving plurality and veracity of the information so broadcasted, as well as the promotion of national identity values, contributing to the goals established in Article 3 of this Constitution.

IV. The broadcasting of publicity or propaganda presented as information coming from news or reports is hereby prohibited; the conditions to be met by the content and the contracting of the service for its broadcasting to the public shall be established, including those relative to the liability of concessionaires with regard to the information broadcasted for thirds parties, without prejudice to the freedom of speech and broadcasting.

V. A statute shall establish a decentralized agency with technical, operative, decision-making and management autonomy, which shall provide non-profit broadcasting to secure access to the population at large in each and every one of the Federation's jurisdictions, to media contents that promote: national integration; educational, cultural and civic training; gender equality; supply of impartial, timely and truthful information about national and international news, allowing for the broadcasting of independent productions, as well as the expression of diverse and pluralistic opinions which strengthen societal democratic life.

The agency shall have a citizens' council to secure independence and an impartial and objective editorial policy. The council shall have nine members to be elected, after ample public consultation, with a two-thirds vote by the Senate or, during recess, by the Permanent Committee. Council members shall serve in staggered terms. Each year, the two most senior members shall be replaced unless ratified for a second term by the Senate.

The Senate or, during recess, the Permanent Committee, shall appoint the President of the agency, upon the proposal of the Federal Executive, with a two-thirds vote. The President shall stay in office for five years, and may be re-appointed for only one additional term. The President may only be removed with a two-thirds vote by the Senate.

The President of the agency shall present and annual report of activities to the Executive and Legislative branches, and he will appear before both chambers of Congress in accordance with the law.

VI. A statute shall establish telecommunications consumers' and audience's rights, as well as the remedies for their protection.

## 2. Mexican General Law of Transparency and Access to Public Information (2015)[38]

**Article 201**
Guarantor Agencies, within the scope of their powers, may impose on the Public Servant responsible to comply with the resolution, or members of trade unions, political parties or the individual or company responsible, the following enforcement measures to ensure compliance with its determinations:

I. Public admonition, or
II. Fine of one hundred fifty to five hundred times the general minimum wage in force in the geographical area concerned.

The Federal Act and those of the States shall establish the criteria to qualify the enforcement measures, according to the seriousness of the offense and, where appropriate, the economic conditions of the offender and recidivism.

Failure of the regulated entities will be posted on the websites of transparency obligations of Guarantor Agencies and considered in the assessments made thereof.

In case the non-compliance of the determinations of Guarantor Agencies involves the alleged commission of a crime or of the conducts outlined in Article 206 of this Act, the respective Guarantor Agency shall report the facts to the competent authority.

The enforcement measures of an economic character may not be paid with public funds.

**Article 202**
If, despite the implementation of enforcement measures provided for in the previous article, the determination is not complied with, such compliance will be requested to the immediate superior so that within five days he instructs its compliance without delay. Should the non-compliance continue, the enforcement measures specified in the preceding Article shall apply on the immediate superior.

Once the term has elapsed, without having been complied, the appropriate penalties will be determined.

**Article 203**
The enforcement measures referred to in this Chapter shall be imposed by the Guarantor Agencies and executed by themselves or with the support of the competent authority in accordance with procedures established by the respective laws.

[38]Mexican General Law on Transparency and Access to Public Information, published in the Official Gazette of the Federation (DOF) of 4 May 2015.

Fines set by the Institute and the Guarantor Agencies will become effective before the Tax Administration Service or the Secretariats of Finance of the Federal States, as appropriate, through the procedures prescribed by law.

**Article 204**
The Federal Act and those of the States should establish mechanisms and terms for otification and execution to the Guarantor Agencies of the enforcement measures to be applied within a maximum period of fifteen days after the enforcement measure is notified.

**Article 205**
In addition to the enforcement measures provided for in this Chapter, the laws on the matter may establish any others deemed necessary.

**Article 206**
The Federal Act and those of the States will set forth as penalty causes for breach of its obligations under the terms of this Act, at least the following:

I. The lack of response to requests for information within the time specified in the applicable regulations;
II. Acting with negligence, willful misconduct or bad faith in the substantiation of requests regarding access to information or by not disseminating information concerning the transparency obligations under this Act;
III. Not meeting the deadlines under this Act;
IV. Using, removing, disclosing, hiding, altering, mutilating, destroying or rendering useless, totally or partially, without legitimate cause, according to a relevant authority, the information in the custody of the regulated entities and their Public Servants or to which they have access or knowledge by reason of their employment, office or commission;
V. Delivering incomprehensible, incomplete information, in an inaccessible format or a mode of shipment or delivery different from the one requested by the user in his request for access to information, responding without proper grounds as established by this Act;
VI. Not updating the information corresponding to the transparency obligations within the terms set forth in this Act;
VII. Intentionally or negligently declaring the lack of information when the regulated entity should generate it, derived from the exercise of its powers, duties or functions;
VIII. Declaring the lack of information when it wholly or partly exists in its archives;
IX. Not documenting with intent or negligence, the exercise of its powers, duties, functions or acts of authority in accordance with applicable regulations;
X. Performing acts to intimidate those seeking information or inhibit the exercise of the right;
XI. Intentionally denying information not classified as secret or confidential;

XII. Classifying as confidential, intentionally or negligently, the information without it meeting the characteristics indicated in this Act. The penalty shall apply when there is a prior ruling by the Guarantor Agency, which is final;
XIII. Not declassifying information as secret when the reasons which gave rise thereto no longer exist or have expired, when the Guarantor Agency determines that there is a cause of public concern that persists or no extension is requested by the Transparency Committee;
XIV. Not meeting the requirements laid down in this Act, issued by the Guarantor Agencies, or
XV. Not complying with the resolutions issued by the Guarantor Agencies in the exercise of their functions.

The Federal Act and those of the States shall establish the criteria to qualify the penalties, according to the seriousness of the offense and, where appropriate, the economic conditions of the offender and recidivism. Likewise, they shall include the type of penalties, procedures and terms for implementation.

The penalties of an economic character may not be paid with public funds.

**Article 207**
The behaviors referred to in the previous article shall be sanctioned by the Guarantor Agencies, as appropriate and, where appropriate, in accordance with their competence will notify the competent authority to impose or execute the relevant penalty.

**Article 208**
Responsibilities resulting from the administrative procedures associated with the violation of the provisions of section 206 of this Act are independent from any civil, criminal or other type which may arise from the same facts.

These responsibilities shall be determined independently, through the procedures provided in applicable laws and the penalties, if any, imposed by the competent authorities, will also be executed independently.

To this end, the Institute or the Guarantor Agencies may report to the competent authorities any act or omission in violation of this Act and provide the evidence they consider relevant, in terms of applicable law.

**Article 210**
In those cases where the alleged offender has the quality of Public Servant, the Institute or the Guarantor Agency must submit to the competent authority together with the corresponding report, a record in which all the elements which sustain the alleged administrative responsibility are contained.

The authority hearing the case shall report the conclusion of the proceedings and, where appropriate, the execution of the penalty to the Institute or the Guarantor Agency, as appropriate.

**Article 211**
In the case of suspected offenders from regulated entities which do not have the quality of Public Servant, the Institute or the Guarantor Agencies of the States, will be the authorities empowered to know and address the penalty procedure under this Act; and shall carry out the actions leading to the imposition and execution of the penalties.

**Article 212**
The procedure referred to in the preceding article will begin with the notification made by the Institute or the Guarantor Agencies of the States to the alleged offender, on the facts and allegations which led to the initiation of the procedure and will grant them a term of fifteen days submit the evidence and state in writing what they deem appropriate. Otherwise, the Institute or the relevant Guarantor Agency will immediately resolve with the elements of evidence available thereto.

The Institute or the corresponding Guarantor Agency, will admit the evidence it deems appropriate and will proceed address it; and once having a conclusion, whatever it might be, it shall notify the alleged offender of the right they have to, if deemed necessary, submit their claims within five days of notification.

Once the evidence and other items of evidence have been analyzed, the Institute or the corresponding Guarantor Agency, shall provide the final judgment, within thirty days of the date on which the infringement procedure started. Such decision shall be notified to the alleged offender and, within the ten days of the notification, the corresponding resolution will be published.

When there is good cause by non-delegable decision adopted by the Plenum of the Institute or the relevant Guarantor Agency, it may extend once only and up to a period equal to the same resolution period.

**Article 213**
The respective standards of the Institute and of the Guarantor Agencies of the States, shall detail all circumstances required on the form, terms and time frames referred to in the penalty procedure provided in this Act, including the submittal of evidence and allegations, hearings, the closing order and enforcement of sanctions. In any case, it will be supplementary to this penalty procedure anything provided for in the laws on administrative procedure of the legal order concerned.

**Article 214**
Violations of the provisions of this Act by regulated entities who do not have the quality of Public Servant shall be punished with:

I. The warning, on one occasion, for the regulated entity to fulfill its responsibility immediately, under the terms provided in this Act, in the cases provided for in sections I, III, V, VI and X of Article 206 of this Act.

II. If once the warning is made, the obligation is not forthwith met, under the terms provided in this Act, regarding the cases mentioned in this section, a fine of one hundred fifty to two hundred and fifty days of general minimum wage in force in the geographical area in question shall apply; Fine of two hundred fifty to eight hundred days of minimum wage in force in the geographical area in question, in the cases provided for in sections II and IV of Article 206 of this Act, and
III. Fine of eight hundred to one thousand five hundred days of minimum wage in force in the geographical area in question, in the cases provided for in sections VII, VIII, IX, XI, XII, XIII, XIV and XV of Article 206 of this Act.

An additional fine of up to fifty days of general minimum wage in force in the geographical area concerned, per day, to whom persists in the infringements referred to in the preceding paragraphs shall apply.

**Article 215**
In case the non-compliance of the determinations of Guarantor Agencies involves the alleged commission of a crime, the respective Guarantor Agency shall report the facts to the competent authority.

**Article 216**
The individuals or companies that receive and use public funds or carry out acts of authority must provide the information required to allow the regulated entities as appropriate, to meet their obligations of transparency and to meet the corresponding requests of access.

## 3. Mexican Federal Law on Transparency and Access to Public Information (2016)[39]

**Article 175**
To qualify the enforcement measures established in the present chapter, the Institute must consider:

I. The severity of the offense committed by the obliged individual, which will be determined by elements such as the damage caused; the indications of intention; the duration of the non-compliance with the decisions of the Institute and the harm to its execution of powers;
II. The economic situation of the offender and
III. The recidivism.

[39]Mexican Federal Law on Transparency and Access to Public Information, published in the Law Gazette of the Federation (DOF) of 9 March 2016, most recently amended in 2017 and published in DOF of 27 January 2017.

The Institute, by means of general guidelines, will establish the obligations of the areas in charge of qualifying the severity of the non-compliance with its decisions and the notification and execution of the enforcement measures which they apply and implement, according to the elements developed in this Chapter.

**Article 188**

In the cases in which the alleged offender is a civil servant, the Institute must forward to the Body of Internal Control of the competent authority the necessary documentation with all the elements which support the alleged administrative responsibility.

The competent Body of Internal Control or the Administrative Tribunal having jurisdiction to hear the case, must inform the Institute that the proceeding be terminated and if applicable, about the execution of the sanction.

**Article 206**

Regardless of the character of the alleged offenders, the competences of the Institute to acquaint, investigate, forward documentation and where appropriate, punish, will expire in a term of five years starting on the day following the day on which the infractions were committed or if they are of a continuing nature from the time when they ceased.

# Appendix 11 Portugal: National Freedom-of-Information and Transparency Legislation (Extracts)

## 1. Constitution of the Portuguese Republic of 2 April 1976[40]

### Article 20 [Access to law and effective judicial protection]

1. Everyone is guaranteed access to the law and the courts in order to defend those of his rights and interests that are protected by law, and justice may not be denied to anyone due to lack of sufficient financial means.
2. Subject to the terms of the law, everyone has the right to legal information and advice, to legal counsel and to be accompanied by a lawyer before any authority.
3. The law shall define and ensure adequate protection of the secrecy of legal proceedings.
4. Everyone has the right to secure a decision in any suit in which he is intervening, within a reasonable time limit and by means of fair process.
5. For the purpose of defending the personal rights, freedoms and guarantees and in such a way as to secure effective and timely judicial protection against threats thereto or breaches thereof, the law shall ensure citizens judicial proceedings that are characterised by their swiftness and by the attachment of priority to them.

### Article 26 [Other personal rights]

1. Everyone is accorded the rights to personal identity, to the development of personality, to civil capacity, to citizenship, to a good name and reputation, to their image, to speak out, to protect the privacy of their personal and family life, and to legal protection against any form of discrimination.

[40]According to the last amendment made by LC (Constitutional Law) 1/2005, of 12 August - *Diário da República*, n° 155, I SÉRIE-A,12 August 2005, p.4642-4686.



H.-J. Blanke, R. Perlingeiro (eds.), *The Right of Access to Public Information*,
DOI 10.1007/978-3-662-55554-5

2. The law shall lay down effective guarantees against the improper procurement and misuse of information concerning persons and families and its procurement or use contrary to human dignity.
3. The law shall guarantee the personal dignity and genetic identity of the human person, particularly in the creation, development and use of technologies and in scientific experimentation.
4. Deprivation of citizenship and restrictions on civil capacity may only occur in the cases and under the terms that are provided for by law, and may not be based on political motives.

### Article 35 [Use of information technology]

1. Every citizen has the right of access to all computerised data that concern him, which he may require to be corrected and updated, and the right to be informed of the purpose for which they are intended, as laid down by law.
2. The law shall define the concept of personal data, together with the terms and conditions applicable to its automatised treatment and its linkage, transmission and use, and shall guarantee its protection, particularly by means of an independent administrative entity.
3. Information technology may not be used to treat data concerning philosophical or political convictions, party or trade union affiliations, religious faith, private life or ethnic origins, save with the express consent of the data subject, or with an authorisation provided for by law and with guarantees of non-discrimination, or for the purpose of processing statistical data that are not individually identifiable.
4. Third-party access to personal data is prohibited, save in exceptional cases provided for by law.
5. The allocation of a single national number to any citizen is prohibited.
6. Everyone is guaranteed free access to public-use information technology networks. The law shall define the regime governing cross-border data flows, and the appropriate means for protecting both personal data and other data whose safeguarding is justified in the national interest.
7. Personal data contained in manual files enjoy the same protection as that provided for in the previous paragraphs, as laid down by law.

### Article 37 [Freedom of expression and information]

1. Everyone has the right to freely express and divulge his thoughts in words, images or by any other means, as well as the right to inform others, inform himself and be informed without hindrance or discrimination.
2. Exercise of these rights may not be hindered or limited by any type or form of censorship.

3. Infractions committed in the exercise of these rights are subject to the general principles of the criminal law or the law governing administrative offences, and the competence to consider them shall pertain to the courts of law or an independent administrative entity respectively, as laid down by law.
4. Every natural and legal person shall be equally and effectively ensured the right of reply and to make corrections, as well as the right to compensation for damages suffered.

**Article 268 [Citizens' rights and guarantees]**

1. Citizens have the right to be informed by the Administration, whenever they so request, as to the progress of the procedures and cases in which they are directly interested, together with the right to be made aware of the definitive decisions that are taken in relation to them.
2. Without prejudice to the law governing matters concerning internal and external security, criminal investigation and personal privacy, citizens also have the right of access to administrative files and records.
3. Administrative acts are subject to notification of the interested parties in the form laid down by law, and when they affect rights or interests that are protected by law, must be based on express and accessible grounds.
4. Citizens are guaranteed effective jurisdictional oversight of those of their rights and interests that are protected by law, particularly including the recognition of the said rights and interests, the impugnation of any administrative act that harms their rights and interests, regardless of its form, the issue of positive decisions requiring the practice of administrative acts that are required by law, and the adoption of adequate provisional remedies.
5. Citizens also have the right to challenge administrative norms which have external force and harm those of their rights or interests that are protected by law.
6. For the purposes of paragraphs (1) and (2) the law shall lay down a maximum time limit for responses by the Administration.

## 2. Act on Access to and the Re-use of Administrative Documents (Law No. 46 of August 24, 2007)[41]

**Article 1 [Open administration]**
Access to and the re-use of administrative documents shall be ensured in accordance with the principles of publicity, transparency, equality, justice, and impartiality.

**Article 2 [Object]**

1. The present Law shall regulate access to administrative documents, without prejudice to the provisions of legislation governing access to environment-related information.
2. The present Law shall also regulate the re-use of documents concerning activities undertaken by the bodies referred to by Article 4, thereby transposing Directive No. 2003/98/EC of the European Parliament and of the Council of 17 November 2003, on the re-use of public sector information, into Portuguese law.
3. The present Law shall govern access to nominative documents, particularly when they include health-related data, by the person to whom the information refers, by a third party authorised by the person to whom the information refers, or by anyone who demonstrates a direct, personal and legitimate interest.
4. The rules governing the exercise of a citizen's right to be informed by the Public Administration about the situation and progress of files in which he is directly interested, and to know any definitive resolutions that have been taken in relation thereto, shall be set out in specific legislation.
5. Access to documents kept by notaries public or in official registries, to civil and criminal identification documents, and to documents deposited in historical archives shall be governed by specific legislation.

**Article 3 [Definitions]**

1. For the purposes of the present Law the following terms shall mean:

   a) "Administrative document": any information medium in written, visual, aural, electronic or other material form, which is in the possession, or is held on behalf, of the bodies and entities referred to by the following Article;

[41]Regulates access to and the re-use of administrative documents, revokes Law No. 65/93 of 26 August 1993, as amended by Law No. 8/95 of 29 March 1995 and Law No. 94/99 of 16 July 1999, and transposes Directive No. 2003/98/EC of the European Parliament and of the Council of 17 November 2003, on the re-use of public sector information, into Portuguese law - *Diário da República*, n° 163, I SÉRIE-A, 24 August 2007, p.5680-5687.

b) "Nominative document": an administrative document which contains an assessment or value judgement, or information covered by the reservation on the intimacy of private life, about an identified or identifiable natural person.

2. For the purposes of the present Law the following shall not be deemed administrative documents:

a) Personal notes, sketches, notations, and other records of a similar nature;
b) Documents which are drawn up as a result of administrative activities, particularly those concerning meetings of the Council of Ministers and Secretaries of State, and the preparation thereof.

**Article 4 [Scope]**

1. The present Law shall apply to the following bodies and entities:

a) Bodies which belong to the State and the autonomous regions and form part of the Public Administration;
b) Other bodies which belong to the State and the autonomous regions, to the extent to which they perform materially administrative functions;
c) Bodies which belong to public institutes and public associations and foundations;
d) Bodies which belong to state-owned companies:
e) Bodies which belong to local authorities and to their associations and federations;
f) Bodies which belong to regional, inter-municipal and municipal companies;
g) Other bodies which engage in administrative functions or exercise public authority.

2. The provisions of the present Law shall also apply to documents held or drawn up by any body which possesses legal personality and has been created to fulfil needs of general interest that do not possess an industrial or commercial nature in a specific manner, and to which any of the following circumstances applies:

a) The majority of the funding for the body's activities is provided by any of the entities referred to by the previous paragraph or the present paragraph;
b) The body's management is subject to a control by any of the entities referred to by the previous paragraph or the present paragraph;
c) More than half the members of the body's management or supervisory boards are appointed by any of the entities referred to by the previous paragraph or the present paragraph.

**Article 5 [Right of access]**

Everyone shall possess the right of access to administrative documents without the need to state any interest, to include the rights of consultation, reproduction, and information as to the administrative documents' existence and content.

**Article 6 [Restrictions on the right of access]**

1. Documents which contain information, knowledge of which is deemed capable of endangering or damaging the internal and external security of the State, shall be subject to prohibited access or access with authorisation, for such time as is strictly necessary, by means of their classification as such in accordance with specific legislation.
2. Access to documents concerning the confidentiality of legal proceedings shall be governed by specific legislation.
3. Access to administrative documents which are preparatory to a decision or which are included in incomplete files may be delayed until the decision in question is taken, the file is archived, or one year has passed since they were drawn up.
4. Access to inquiries and investigations shall occur after the time period for any disciplinary proceedings has passed.
5. Third parties shall only possess the right of access to nominative documents if they are in possession of written authorisation from the person to whom the data refer, or if they demonstrate a direct, personal and legitimate interest which is sufficiently important under the principle of proportionality.
6. Third parties shall only possess the right of access to administrative documents which contain commercial or industrial secrets or the internal life of a company, if they are in possession of written authorisation from the company in question, or if they demonstrate a direct, personal and legitimate interest which is sufficiently important under the principle of proportionality.
7. Administrative documents which are subject to restricted access shall be the object of partial communication whenever it is possible to expunge the information concerning the reserved matter.

**Article 15 [Right of complaint]**

1. Applicants may complain to CADA about a lack of response, denial of an application, or any other decision which restricts access to administrative documents.
2. A complaint shall interrupt the time period for judicial submission of a request for a court order to provide information, consult files, or issue certificates, and shall be made within the said time period, to which the provisions governing the submission to a court of procedural items shall apply mutatis mutandis.

3. In the event that the complaint is not summarily dismissed, CADA shall invite the body to which the application was made to respond to the complaint within ten days.
4. In both the case of a complaint and that of the consultation provided for by Article 14 (1) e, CADA shall have forty days in which to draw up the applicable situation assessment report and send it with its due conclusions to all the interested parties.
5. Once it has received the report referred to by the previous paragraph, the body to which the application was made shall communicate its duly justified final decision to the applicant within ten days, failing which there shall be deemed to be an absence of decision.
6. An interested party may impugn either the decision or the absence of decision referred to by the previous paragraph before the administrative courts, whereupon the rules governing the process of requesting a court order referred to by paragraph (2) above shall apply.

**Article 33 [Administrative offences]**

1. The following natural persons and bodies corporate shall be deemed to have committed an administrative offence punishable with a fine:

   a) Those who or which re-use public sector documents without the authorisation of the competent body;
   b) Those who or which re-use public sector documents without complying with the conditions governing re-use laid down by Article 20(1);
   c) Those who or which re-use public sector documents without having paid the amount set by Article 20(2) and (3).

2. The infractions provided for by subparagraphs a) and c) of the previous paragraph shall be punishable by the following fines:

   a) In the case of a natural person, a minimum of € 300.00 and a maximum of € 3,500.00;
   b) In the case of a body corporate, a minimum of € 2,500.00 and a maximum of € 25,000.00.

3. The infraction provided for by paragraph (1)b above shall be punishable by the following fines:

   a) In the case of a natural person, a minimum of € 150.00 and a maximum of € 1,750.00;
   b) In the case of a body corporate, a minimum of € 1,250.00 and a maximum of € 12,500.00.

**Article 38 [Judicial impugnation]**

1. An impugnation of a final decision made by CADA shall take the form of a claim, which shall be submitted within ten days of notification of the decision.
2. In the event of such an impugnation, CADA may modify or revoke its decision, whereupon it shall notify the impugner of its new final decision.
3. In the event that it maintains its existing decision, within ten days CADA shall forward the claim to the Public Prosecutors' Office at the Lisbon Administrative and Fiscal Court.

**Article 39 [Course of judicial proceedings]**
With the assistance of a specialist or representative from CADA, the Public Prosecutors' Office shall complete the case file and present it to the Judge.

1. If the defence, the Public Prosecutors' Office and CADA do not oppose it, the Judge may decide the case in question in accordance with the present Law by issuing a simple court order.
2. If a hearing takes place, the applicable formalities shall be reduced to the indispensable minimum, evidence shall not be tape-recorded, and no more than three witnesses shall be heard in relation to each alleged administrative offence.
3. The Judge shall always possess the power to award compensation to whomsoever he deems entitled thereto.
4. The Judge's final decision shall be subject to appeal directly to the Supreme Administrative Court, which shall rule thereon ex officio.

## 3. Act on the Protection of Personal Data (Law No. 67/98 of 26 October 1998)[42]

**Article 3 [Definitions]**
For the purposes of this Act:

(a) "personal data" shall mean any information of any type, irrespective of the type of medium involved, including sound and image, relating to an identified or identifiable natural person ("data subject"); an identifiable person is one who can be identified, directly or indirectly, in particular by reference to

[42]Act on the Protection of Personal Data (transposing into the Portuguese legal system Directive 95/46/EC of the European Parliament and of the Council of 24 October 1995 on the protection of individuals with regard to the processing of personal data and on the free movement of such data). -*Diário da República*, n° 247, I SÉRIE-A, 26 October 1998, p.5536-5546.

an indication number or to one or more factors specific to his physical, physiological, mental, economic, cultural or social identity;

(b) "processing of personal data" ("processing") shall mean any operation or set of operations which is performed upon personal data, whether wholly or partly by automatic means, such as collection, recording, organisation, storage, adaptation or alteration, retrieval, consultation, use, disclosure by transmission, dissemination or otherwise making available, alignment or combination, blocking, erasure or destruction;

(c) "personal data filing system" ("filing system") shall mean any structured set of personal data which are accessible according to specific criteria, whether centralised, decentralised or dispersed on a functional or geographical basis;

(d) "controller" shall mean the natural or legal person, public authority, agency or any other body which alone or jointly with others determines the purposes and means of the processing of personal data; where the purposes and means of processing are determined by laws or regulations, the controller shall be designated in the Act establishing the organisation and functioning or in the statutes of the legal or statutory body competent to process the personal data concerned;

(e) "processor" shall mean a natural or legal person, public authority, agency or any other body which processes personal data on behalf of the controller;

(f) "third party" shall mean any natural or legal person, public authority, agency or any other body other than the data subject, the controller, the processor and the persons who, under the direct authority of the controller or the processor, are authorised to process the data;

(g) "recipient" shall mean a natural or legal person, public authority, agency or any other body to whom data are disclosed, whether a third party or not; however, authorities which may receive data in the framework of a law shall not be regarded as recipients;

(h) "the data subject's consent" shall mean any freely given specific and informed indication of his wishes by which the data subject signifies his agreement to personal data relating to him being processed;

(i) "combination of data" shall mean a form of processing which consists of the possibility of correlating data in a filing system with data in a filing system or systems kept by another or other controllers or kept by the same controller for other purposes.

### Article 5 [Data quality]

1. Personal data must be:

   (a) processed lawfully and with respect for the principle of good faith;
   (b) collected for specified, explicit and legitimate purposes and not further processed in a way incompatible with those purposes;
   (c) adequate, relevant and not excessive in relation to the purposes for which they are collected and/or further processed;

(d) accurate and, where necessary, kept up to date; adequate measures must be taken to ensure that data which are inaccurate or incomplete, having regard to the purposes for which they were collected or for which they are further processed, are erased or rectified;
(e) kept in a form which permits identification of their subjects for no longer than is necessary for the purposes for which they were collected or for which they are further processed.

2. The storing of data for historical, statistical or scientific purposes for longer periods than in (e) above may be authorised by the CNPD at the request of the controller in the case of a legitimate interest.
3. It shall be for the controller to ensure that the above numbers are complied with.

**Article 6 [Criteria for making data processing legitimate]**
Personal data may be processed only if the data subject has unambiguously given his consent or if processing is necessary:

(a) for the performance of a contract or contracts to which the data subject is party or in order to take steps at the request of the data subject prior to entering into a contract or a declaration of his will to negotiate;
(b) for compliance with a legal obligation to which the controller is subject;
(c) in order to protect the vital interests of the data subject if the latter if physically or legally incapable of giving his consent;
(d) for the performance of a task carried out in the public interest or in the exercise of official authority vested in the controller or in a third party to whom the data are disclosed;
(e) for pursuing the legitimate interests of the controller or the third party to whom the data are disclosed, except where such interests should be overridden by the interests for fundamental rights, freedoms and guarantees of the data subject.

**Article 7 [The processing of sensitive data]**

1. The processing of personal data revealing philosophical or political beliefs, political party or trade union membership, religion, privacy and racial or ethnic origin, and the processing of data concerning health or sex life, including genetic data, shall be prohibited.
2. The processing of the data referred to in the previous number shall be permitted by a legal provision or by the authorisation of the CNPD when, on important public interest grounds, such processing is essential for exercising the legal or statutory rights of the controller or when the data subject has given his explicit consent for such processing, in both cases with guarantees of non-discrimination and with the security measures provided for in Article 15.

3. The processing of the data referred to in 1 shall also be permitted when one of the following conditions applies:
   (a) when it is necessary to protect the vital interests of the data subject or of another person where the data subject is physically or legally incapable of giving his consent;
   (b) when it is carried out with the data subject's consent in the course of its legitimate activities by a foundation, association or non-profit seeking body with a political, philosophical, religious or trade union aim and on condition that the processing relates solely to the members of the body or to persons who have regular contact with it in connection with its purposes and that the data are not disclosed to a third party without the consent of the data subjects;
   (c) when it relates to data which are manifestly made public by the data subject, provided his consent for their processing can be clearly inferred from his declarations;
   (d) when it is necessary for the establishment, exercise or defence of legal claims and is exclusively carried out for that purpose.
4. The processing of data relating to health and sex life, including genetic data, shall be permitted if it is necessary for the purposes of preventive medicine, medical diagnosis, the provision of care or treatment or the management of health-care services, provided those data are processed by a health professional bound by professional secrecy or by another person also subject to an equivalent obligation of secrecy and are notified to the CNPD under Article 27, and where suitable safeguards are provided.

**Article 8 [Suspicion of illegal activities, criminal and administrative offences]**

1. Central registers relating to persons suspected of illegal activities, criminal and administrative offences and decisions applying penalties, security measures, fines and additional penalties may only be created and kept by public services vested with that specific responsibility by virtue of the law establishing their organisation and functioning, subject to observance of procedural and data protection rules provided for in a legal order, with the prior opinion of the CNPD.
2. The processing of personal data relating to persons suspected of illegal activities, criminal and administrative offences and decisions applying penalties, security measures, fines and additional penalties may be authorised by the CNPD, subject to observance of the rules for the protection of data and the security of information, when such processing is necessary for pursuing the legitimate purposes of the controller, provided the fundamental rights and freedoms of the data subject are not overriding.

3. The processing of personal data for the purposes of police investigations shall be restricted to the processing necessary to prevent a specific danger or to prosecute a particular offence and to exercise the responsibilities provided for in the respective implementing statutes or another legal provision or in the terms of an international agreement or convention to which Portugal is party.

**Article 9 [Combination of personal data]**

1. The combination of personal data not provided for in a legal provision shall be subject to the authorisation of the CNPD, requested by the controller or jointly by the corresponding controllers under Article 27.
2. The combination of personal data must be necessary for pursuing the legal or statutory purposes and legitimate interests of the controller, must not involve discrimination or a reduction in the fundamental rights and freedoms of the data subjects, and must be covered by adequate security measures and take account of the type of data subject to combination.

**Article 10 [Right to information]**

1. The controller or his representative shall provide a data subject from whom data relating to himself are collected with the following information, except where he already has it:

   a) the identity of the controller and of his representative, if any;
   b) the purposes of the processing;
   c) other information such as:

      The recipients or categories of recipients;
      Whether replies are obligatory or voluntary, as well as the possible consequences of failure to reply;
      The existence and conditions of the right of access and the right to rectify, provided they are necessary, taking account of the specific circumstances of collection of the data in order to guarantee the data subject that they will be processed fairly.

2. The documents supporting the collection of personal data shall contain the information set down in the previous number.
3. If the data are not collected from the data subject and except where he already has it, the controller or his representative must provide the data subject with the information set down in 1 at the time of undertaking the recording of data or, if a disclosure to third parties is envisaged, no later than the time the data are first disclosed.
4. If data are collected on open networks the data subject shall be informed, except where he is already aware of it, that personal data relating to him may be circulated on the network without security measures and may be at risk of being seen and used by unauthorised third parties.

5. The obligation to provide information may be waived by a legal provision or decision of the CNPD on the grounds of State security and criminal prevention or investigation and also in particular for processing for statistical purposes or for the purposes of historical or scientific research, when the provision of such information proves impossible or would involve a disproportionate effort or if recording or disclosure is expressly laid down by law.
6. The obligation to provide information under this Article shall not apply to the processing of data carried out solely for journalistic purposes or the purpose of artistic or literary expression.

**Article 11 [Right of access]**

1. The data subject has the right to obtain from the controller without constraint at reasonable intervals and without excessive delay or expense:
   a) Confirmation as to whether or not data relating to him are being processed and information as to the purposes of the processing, the categories of data concerned and the recipients or categories of recipients to whom the data are disclosed;
   b) Communication in an intelligible form of the data undergoing processing and of any available information as to their source;
   c) Knowledge of the logic involved in any automatic processing of data concerning him;
   d) The rectification, erasure or blocking of data the processing of which does not comply with the provisions of this Act, in particular because of the incomplete or inaccurate nature of the data;
   e) Notification to third parties to whom the data have been disclosed of any rectification, erasure or blocking carried out in compliance with (d), unless this proves impossible.
2. In the case of the processing of personal data relating to State security and criminal prevention or investigation, the right of access may be exercised by means of the CNPD or another independent authority in whom the law vests verification of compliance with legislation on the protection of personal data.
3. In the cases provided for in 6 above the right of access is exercised by means of the CNPD, securing the constitutional rules applicable, in particular those guaranteeing freedom of expression and information, freedom of the press and the professional independence and secrecy of journalists.
4. In the cases provided for in (2) and (3), if communication of the data might prejudice State security, criminal prevention or investigation and freedom of expression and information or the freedom of the press, the CNPD shall only inform the data subject of the measures taken.
5. The right of access to information relating to health data, including genetic data, is exercised by means of the doctor chosen by the data subject.

6. If the data are not used for taking measures or decisions regarding any particular individual, the law may restrict the right of access where there is clearly no risk of breaching the fundamental rights, freedoms and guarantees of the data subject, particularly the right to privacy, and when the data are used solely for purposes of scientific research or are kept in personal form for a period which does not exceed the period necessary for the sole purpose of creating statistics.

**Article 14 [Security of processing]**

1. The controller must implement appropriate technical and organisational measures to protect personal data against accidental or unlawful destruction or accidental loss, alteration, unauthorised disclosure or access, in particular where the processing involves the transmission of data over a network, and against all other unlawful forms of processing. Having regard to the state of the art and the cost of their implementation, such measures shall ensure a level of security appropriate to the risks represented by the processing and the nature of the data to be protected.
2. Where processing is carried out on his behalf the controller must choose a processor providing sufficient guarantees in respect of the technical security measures and organisational measures governing the processing to be carried out, and must ensure compliance with those measures.
3. The carrying out of processing by way of a processor must be governed by a contract or legal act binding the processor to the controller and stipulating in particular that the processor shall act only on instructions from the controller and that the obligations referred to in 1 shall also be incumbent on the processor.
4. Proof of the will to negotiate, the contract or the legal act relating to data protection and the requirements relating to the measures referred to in 1 shall be in writing in a supporting document legally certified as affording proof.

**Article 15 [Special security measures]**

1. The controllers of the data referred to in Article 7 (2) and Article 8 shall take appropriate measures to:

   a) prevent unauthorised persons from entering the premises used for processing such data (control of entry to the premises);
   b) prevent data media from being read, copied, altered or removed by unauthorised persons (control of data media);
   c) prevent unauthorised input and unauthorised obtaining of knowledge, alteration or elimination of personal data input (control of input);
   d) prevent automatic data processing systems from being used by unauthorised persons by means of data transmission premises (control of use);

e) guarantee that authorised persons may only access data covered by the authorisation (control of access);
f) guarantee the checking of the bodies to whom personal data may be transmitted by means of data transmission premises (control of transmission);
g) guarantee that it is possible to check a posteriori, in a period appropriate to the nature of the processing, the establishment in the regulations applicable to each sector of which personal data are input, when and by whom (control of input);
h) in transmitting personal data and in transporting the respective media, prevent unauthorised reading, copying, alteration or elimination of data (control of transport).

2. Taking account of the nature of the bodies responsible for processing and the type of premises in which it is carried out, the CNPD may waive the existence of certain security measures, subject to guaranteeing respect for the fundamental rights, freedoms and guarantees of the data subjects.
3. The systems must guarantee logical separation between data relating to health and sex life, including genetic data, and other personal data.
4. Where circulation over a network of the data referred to in Articles 7 and 8 may jeopardise the fundamental rights, freedoms and guarantees of their data subjects the CNPD may determine that transmission must be encoded.
5. Any person acting under the authority of the controller or the processor, including the processor himself, who has access to personal data must not process them except on instructions from the controller, unless he is required to do so by law. le 16

## Article 17 [Professional secrecy]

1. Controllers and persons who obtain knowledge of the personal data processed in carrying out their functions shall be bound by professional secrecy, even after their functions have ended.
2. Members of the CNPD shall be subject to the same obligation, even after their mandate has ended.
3. The provision in the previous numbers shall not exclude the duty to supply the obligatory information according to the law, except when it is contained in filing systems organised for statistical purposes.
4. Officers, agents or staff who act as consultants for the CNPD or its members shall be subject to the same obligation of professional secrecy.

**Article 18 [Principle]**
Without prejudice to the tax or customs decisions of the Community, personal data may move freely between Member States of the European Union.

1. Without prejudice to the following Article, the transfer to a State which is not a member of the European Union of personal data which are undergoing processing or intended for processing may only take place subject to compliance with this Act and provided the State to which they are transferred ensures an adequate level of protection.
2. The adequacy of the level of protection of a State which is not a member of the European Union shall be assessed in the light of all the circumstances surrounding a data transfer operation or set of data transfer operations; particular consideration shall be given to the nature of the data, the purpose and duration of the proposed processing operation or operations, the country of origin and country of final destination, the rules of law, both general and sectoral, in force in the State in question and the professional rules and security measures which are complied with in that country.
3. It is for the CNPD to decide whether a State which is not a member of the European Union ensures an adequate level of protection.
4. By means of the Ministry of Foreign Affairs the CNPD shall inform the European Commission of cases where it considers that a State does not ensure an adequate level of protection.
5. The transfer of personal data identical to those the European Commission has considered do not enjoy adequate protection in the State to which they are to be sent shall be prohibited.

**Article 20 [Derogations]**

1. A transfer of personal data to a State which does not ensure an adequate level of protection within the meaning of Article 19 (2) may be allowed by the CNPD if the data subject has given his consent unambiguously to the proposed transfer or if that transfer:

   a) is necessary for the performance of a contract between the data subject and the controller or the implementation of precontractual measures taken in response to the data subject's request;
   b) is necessary for the performance or conclusion of a contract concluded or to be concluded in the interests of the data subject between the controller and a third party; or
   c) is necessary or legally required on important public interest grounds, or for the establishment, exercise of defence of legal claims; or
   d) is necessary in order to protect the vital interests of the data subject; or
   e) is made from a register which according to laws or regulations is intended to provide information to the public and which is open to consultation either by the public in general or by any person who can demonstrate

legitimate interest, provided the conditions laid down in law for consultation are fulfilled in the particular case.

2. Without prejudice to paragraph 1 the CNPD may authorise a transfer or a set of transfers of personal data to a State which does not ensure an adequate level of protection within the meaning of Article 19 (2), provided the controller adduces adequate safeguards with respect to the protection of the privacy and fundamental rights and freedoms of individuals and with respect to their exercise, particularly by means of appropriate contractual clauses.
3. By means of the Ministry of Foreign Affairs the CNPD shall inform the European Commission and the competent authorities of the other Member States of the European Union of the authorisations it grants under 2.
4. The authorisations provided for in 2 shall be granted or derogated by the CNPD according to its own procedures and the decisions of the European Commission.
5. Whenever there are specimen contractual clauses approved by the European Commission according to its own procedures, because they provide the adequate guarantees referred to in 2, the CNPD shall authorise the transfer of personal data made under such clauses.
6. A transfer of personal data which is necessary for the protection of State security, defence, public safety and the prevention, investigation and prosecution of criminal offences shall be governed by special legal provisions or by the international conventions and agreements to which Portugal is party.

**Article 27 [Obligation to notify the CNPD]**

1. The controller or his representative, if any, must notify the CNPD before carrying out any wholly or partly automatic processing operation or set of such operations intended to serve a single purpose or several related purposes.
2. The CNPD may authorise the simplification of or exemption from notification for particular categories of processing which are unlikely, taking account of the data to be processed, to affect adversely the rights and freedoms of the data subjects and to take account of criteria of speed, economy and efficiency.
3. The authorisation, which must be published in the Diário da República, must specify the purposes of the processing, the data or category of data to be processed, the category or categories of data subjects, the recipients or categories of recipients to whom the data may be disclosed and the length of time the data are to be stored.
4. Processing whose sole purpose is the keeping of a register which according to laws or regulations is intended to provide information to the public and which is open to consultation by the public in general or by any person demonstrating a legitimate interest shall be exempted from notification.
5. The non-automatic processing of the personal data provided for in Article 7 (1) shall be subject to notification when they are processed under 3 (a) of that Article.

**Article 29 [Content of applications for opinions or authorisation and notification]**

Applications for opinions, authorisation and notifications submitted to the CNPD shall include the following information:

a) the name and address of the controller and of his representative, if any;
b) the purposes of the processing;
c) a description of the category or categories of data subjects and of the data or categories of personal data relating to them;
d) the recipients or categories of recipients to whom the data might be disclosed and in what circumstances;
e) the body entrusted with processing the information, if it is not the controller himself;
f) any combinations of personal data processing;
g) the length of time for keeping personal data;
h) the form and circumstances in which the data subjects may be informed of or may correct the personal data relating to them;
i) proposed transfers of data to third countries;
j) a general description enabling a preliminary assessment to be made of the adequacy of the measures taken under Articles 14 and 15 to ensure security of processing.

**Article 32 [Codes of conduct]**

1. The CNPD shall encourage the drawing up of codes of conduct intended to contribute to the proper implementation of the provisions in this Act, taking account of the specific features of the various sectors.
2. Trade associations and other bodies representing other categories of controllers which have drawn up draft codes of conduct shall be able to submit them to the opinion of the CNPD.
3. The CNPD may declare whether the drafts are in accordance with the laws and regulations in force in the area of personal data protection.

# Appendix 12 Russian Federation: National Freedom-of-Information and Transparency Legislation (Extracts)

## 1. Federal Act on Information, Informational Technologies and Protection of Information (Law No. 149-FZ of July 27, 2006)[43]

**Article 1 [Scope of the present Federal Act]**

1. The present Federal Act shall regulate the relationships arising at:
   1) execution of the right for search, obtaining, transfer, production and distribution of information;
   2) application of information technologies;
   3) provision of information protection.
2. The provisions of the present Federal Act shall not be applied to the relationships arising at legal protection of the results of intellectual activity and means of individualization equaled thereto, save the cases envisaged by the present Federal Law.

**Article 2 [Basic concepts used in the present Federal Act]**

1. The following basic concepts shall be used in the present Federal Act:

1) information – knowledge (messages, data) regardless of the form of presentation;
2) information technologies – processes, methods of search, collection, storage, processing, supply, distribution of information and methods of carrying out of these processes and methods;

[43] Russian Law Gazette, Russian Federal Law No. 149-FZ of July 27, 2006.



H.-J. Blanke, R. Perlingeiro (eds.), *The Right of Access to Public Information*,
DOI 10.1007/978-3-662-55554-5

3) information system – the aggregate of the information included in the data base and information technologies and technical devices ensuring processing thereof;
4) information-telecommunication network – technological system intended for transmission of information on the communication lines, access to which is provided by means of computer equipment;
5) possessor of information – person who created independently information or obtained, on the basis of a law or contract, a right to permit or restrict access to the information determined according to some signs;
6) access to information – possibility of obtaining of information and usage thereof;
7) confidentiality of information – a requirement not to transmit certain information to the third parties without consent of the possessor, which is obligatory for the person who got access thereto;
8) delivery of information – actions directed to obtaining of information by a certain range of persons or transmission thereof to a certain range of persons;
9) distribution of information – actions directed to obtaining of information by an indefinite range of persons or transmission thereof to an indefinite range of persons;
10) electronic message – information transmitted or obtained by the user of an information-telecommunication network;
11) documented information – information with requisites making it possible to determine this information and fixed on a material carrier by means of documenting, or the material carrier in the legally established cases;

    11.1) electronic document means documented information presented in electronic form, that is, in a form which is fit for human perception with the use of computers, as well as for transmittance via information telecommunication networks or for processing in information systems;

12) operator of information network – citizen or legal entity carrying out the activities on operation of the information system, including processing of the information included in the data base.
13) an "Internet" site is the totality of computer programmes and other information contained in an information system to which access is provided through the Internet (hereinafter referred to as the Internet) by way of using domain names and/or network addresses enabling to identify sites in the Internet;
14) a site page in the Internet network (hereinafter referred to as an Internet page) is a part of the Internet accessible on the basis of an indication consisting of the domain name and symbols defined by the owner of an Internet site;
15) the domain name is a designation made by symbols which is intended for addressing sites in the Internet for the purpose of providing access to the information placed in the Internet;

16) the network address is the identifier in a data communications network enabling to find the user terminal and other communication means forming part of an information system when rendering telematic communication services;
17) the owner of an Internet site is the person which independently or at the own discretion thereof defines a procedure for using the Internet site, in particular a procedure for inserting information on such site;
18) the hosting provider is the person engaged in rendering the services involved in providing the computational power for inserting information in an information system which is connected to the Internet on a permanent basis.
19) the comprehensive identification and identity verification system, this being the federal state information system in respect of which a procedure for its use shall be established by the Government of the Russian Federation and which shall provide, where it is established by the Government of the Russian Federation, an authorised access to the information contained in information systems.
20) searching system – information system searching information of certain content in "Internet" on user's request and providing to the user information on the index page of a site in "Internet" to have access to the requested information located on the sites in "Internet", belonging to other persons, excepting information systems used for the implementation of state and municipal functions, providing state and municipal services, as well as for other public authority established by federal laws.

**Article 3 [Principles of legal regulation of relationships in the sphere of information, information technologies and information protection]**
Legal regulation of relationships in the sphere of information, information technologies and information protection shall be based on the following principles:

1) freedom of search, obtaining, transmission, production and distribution of information by any legal method;
2) possibility for only federal acts to set restrictions on access to information;
3) openness of information on the activity of state authorities and local self-government bodies and free access thereto except for the cases established by federal acts;
4) equality of languages of the peoples of the Russian Federation in creation of information systems and operation thereof;
5) provision of security of the Russian Federation in creation of information systems and operation thereof and protection of the information included therein;
6) reliability of information and promptness of delivery thereof;

7) inviolability of private life, inadmissibility of collection, storage, usage and distribution of information on the private life of persons without their consent;
8) inadmissibility for normative legal acts to set any priorities of application of certain information technologies to others, unless obligatory application of certain information technologies for creation and operation of state information systems established by federal acts.

**Article 4 [Legislation of the Russian Federation on information, information technologies and information protection]**

1. Legislation of the Russian Federation on information, information technologies and information protection shall be based on the Constitution of the Russian Federation, international treaties of the Russian Federation and shall consist of the present Federal Act and other federal acts regulating relationships on information usage.
2. Legal regulation of relationships referring to organization and activity of the mass media shall be carried out in accordance with the legislation of the Russian Federation on the mass media.
3. The procedure of storage and usage of the documented information included within the archives funds shall be established by the legislation of the Russian Federation.

**Article 5 [Information as the object of legal relations]**

1. Information may be an object of public, civil and other regal relations. Information may be used freely by any person and transmitted by one person to another, unless restrictions to access to the information or other requirements to the procedure of delivery or distribution thereof established by federal acts.
2. Subject to the category of access to the information the latter shall be divided into generally accessible information and information where access restricted by federal acts (restricted access information).
3. Subject to the procedure of delivery or distribution the information shall be divided into:

    1) freely distributed information;
    2) information delivered as agreed with the persons taking part in the corresponding relationships;
    3) information which should be delivered or distributed in accordance with federal acts;
    4) information distribution of which shall be restricted or banned.

4. The legislation of the Russian Federation may establish types of information depending on the content of possessor thereof.

### Article 6 [Possessor of information]

1. The possessor of information may be represented by a citizen, a legal entity, the Russian Federation, a subject of the Russian Federation, or a municipal formation.
2. On behalf of the Russian Federation, subject of the Russian Federation, municipal formation, the legal competence of the possessor of information shall be ensured by the state authorities and local self-government bodies respectively within their competence established by the corresponding normative legal acts.
3. Unless otherwise provided by federal acts, the possessor of information shall have the right:

    1) to permit or restrict access to information, determine the procedure and terms of this access;
    2) use the information, as well as to distribute it at his own discretion;
    3) transmit information to other persons under contract or on other legally established grounds;
    4) protect his rights by legal methods in the case of illegal obtaining of information or illegal usage thereof by other persons;
    5) perform other actions with information or permit performance thereof.

4. When exercising his rights the possessor of information should:

    1) observe the rights and legal interests of other persons;
    2) take measures for information protection;
    3) restrict access to the information, if this responsibility is established by federal acts.

### Article 7 [Generally accessible information]

1. Generally accessible information should include well-known data and other information of non-restricted access.
2. Generally accessible information may be used by any persons at their discretion, with observance of the restrictions referring to distribution of this information established by the federal acts.
3. The possessor of the information, which became generally accessible by his decision shall have the right to require that the persons distributing this information should name themselves as the source of this information.
4. The information placed by the holders thereof in the Internet in the format enabling its automated processing without its preliminary alteration by a person for the purpose of its repeated use shall be deemed generally accessible information placed in the form of public data.
5. Information in the form of public data shall be placed in the Internet subject to the requirements of the legislation of the Russian Federation on state secret. Where the placement of information in the form of public data can lead to the

divulgence of data constituting state secret, the placement of the cited information in the form of public data must be terminated on demand of the body vested with the authority involved in the disposal of such data.

6. If the placement of information in the form of public data can entail a violation of the rights of holders of the information access to which is restricted in compliance with federal laws or a violation of the rights of the subjects of personal data, the placement of the cited information in the form of personal data must be terminated by a court decision. If information in the form of public data is placed in defiance of the requirements of Federal Law No. 152-FZ of July 27, 2006 on Personal Data, the placement of the information in the form of public data must be suspended or terminated on demand of the authorized body engaged in the protection of the rights of the subjects of personal data.

### Article 8 [Right to access to information]

1. Citizens (natural persons) and organizations (legal entities) (hereinafter referred to as organizations) shall have the right to search and obtain any information in any forms from any sources subject to observance of the requirements established by the present Federal Act and other federal acts.
2. Citizens (natural persons) shall have the right to obtain the information from state authorities, local self-government bodies, their official persons, if this influences directly their rights and liberties, in accordance with the procedure established by the legislation of the Russian Federation.
3. Organizations shall have the right to the information from state authorities, local self-government bodies, if it directly refers to the rights and responsibilities of this organization or is necessary because of interaction with these bodies at performance of the authorized activities by this organization.
4. The access may not be restricted to:

   1) normative legal acts influencing rights, liberties and responsibilities of man and citizen and setting the legal status of the organizations and powers of the state authorities;
   2) information on the state of the environment;
   3) information on the activity of state authorities and local self-government bodies, as well as on usage of the budget resources (except for the data representing state or official secrets);
   4) information accumulated in open funds of libraries, museums and archives, as well as in state, municipal and other information systems created or intended for delivery of this information to citizens (natural persons) and organizations;
   5) other information, if inadmissibility of restriction of access thereto is established by federal acts.

5. State authorities and local self-government bodies should provide access, in particular using the information telecommunication systems, including the

Internet, to information on their activity in the Russian and state language of the corresponding republic within the Russian Federation in accordance with the federal acts, acts of the subjects of the Russian federation and normative legal acts of local self-government bodies. The person wanting to get access to this information should not explain the necessity of obtaining thereof.

6. Decisions and actions (inaction) of state authorities and local self-government bodies, public associations, official persons breaching the right to access to information may be protested against to a superior authority or in court.
7. In the case of any losses incurred as a result of illegitimate refuse of access to information, unpunctual delivery thereof, delivery of deliberately unreliable information or non-corresponding to the content of the request, these losses shall be reimbursed in accordance with the civil legislation.
8. The following information shall be delivered free of charge:

   1) on the activity of state authorities and local self-government bodies placed by these bodies in information-telecommunication networks;
   2) concerning rights and responsibilities of the interested person established by the legislation of the Russian Federation;
   3) other information established by law.

Setting of payment for delivery of information on the activity of state authorities or local self-government bodies shall be possible only in the cases and on the terms established by federal acts.

### Article 9 [Restriction of access to information]

1. Restriction of access to information shall be established by federal acts or purposes of protection of the constitutional system, morality, health, rights and legal interests of other persons, provision of the defence of the country and security of the state.
2. Observance of confidentiality of information access to which is restricted by federal acts shall be obligatory.
3. Protection of information representing state secrets shall be provided in accordance with the legislation of the Russian Federation on the state secret.
4. Federal acts shall establish the terms of referring of information to the data representing commercial, official and other secret, obligatory character of confidentiality of this information and responsibility for disclosure thereof.
5. Information obtained by citizens (natural persons) while performing their professional duties or organizations while performing certain types of activities (professional secret) shall be protected, if these persons were entrusted with the responsibilities on observance of confidentiality of this information by federal acts.
6. Information representing a professional secret may be delivered by the third parties in accordance with the federal acts and (or) by court judgment.
7. The term of the performance of responsibilities for observance of confidentiality of information representing a professional secret may be restricted only

with a consent of the citizen (natural person) which delivered information about himself.

8. It shall be banned to require from the citizen (natural person) delivery of information about his private life, including information of personal or family secrecy and obtain this information apart from the will of the citizen (natural person), unless otherwise provided by the federal acts.
9. The procedure of access to personal data of citizens (natural persons) shall be established by the Federal Act on the personal data.

### Article 10 [Distribution of information and delivery of information]

1. In the Russian federation distribution of information shall be carried out freely, with observance of the requirements established by the legislation of the Russian Federation.
2. Information distributed without involving the mass media should include reliable data on possessor thereof or on another person distributing the information, in the form and volume sufficient for identification of this person. The owner of an Internet site is obliged to place on to his website information about his name, location and address, e-mail address for sending the application specified in Article 15.7 of the present Federal Law, and can provide the possibility to send this application by an electronic form on the "Internet" website.
3. If for distribution of information the means are used making it possible to determine recipients of information, including those of postal mailings and electronic messages, the person distributing the information should give the recipient of information a possibility of refusal thereof.
4. Delivery of information is ensured according to the procedure established by an agreement of persons taking part in the information exchange.
5. Cases and terms of obligatory distribution of information or delivery thereof, including delivery of obligatory copies of documents shall be established by federal acts.
6. Distribution of information directed to propaganda of war, stirring up hatred and hostility, as well as other information, which provides criminal or administrative responsibility shall be banned.

### Article 10.1 [The duties of an organizer of dissemination of information in the Internet]

1. Organizer of dissemination of information in the Internet is a person pursuing the activity of ensuring the operation of information systems and/or computer software which are intended and/or used to receive, transmit, deliver and/or process electronic messages of users of the Internet.
2. In the procedure established by the Government of the Russian Federation an organizer of dissemination of information in the Internet shall notify the federal executive governmental body carrying out the functions of control

and supervision in the field of mass media, mass communications, information technologies and telecom of the commencement of the activity specified in Part 1 of the present article.

3. The organizer of dissemination of information in the Internet shall store on the territory of the Russian Federation information about the facts of reception, transmission, delivery and/or processing of voice information, written text, images, sounds or other electronic messages of users of the Internet and information about these users for six months after the end of such actions and also provide said information to the empowered state bodies carrying out operative investigation activities or ensuring the security of the Russian Federation in the cases established by federal laws.
4. The organizer of dissemination of information in the Internet shall ensure the implementation of the requirements established by the federal executive governmental body in the field of telecom by agreement with the empowered state bodies carrying out operative investigation activities or ensuring the security of the Russian Federation as applicable to the equipment and software/hardware used by said organizer in the information systems operated by it so that these bodies implement measures in the cases established by federal laws for the purpose of fulfilling the tasks vested in them, and also shall take measures for preventing the disclosure of the organizational and tactical techniques used to implement these measures. The procedure for interaction of organizers of dissemination of information in the Internet with the empowered state bodies carrying out operative investigation activities or ensuring the security of the Russian Federation shall be established by the Government of the Russian Federation.
5. The duties envisaged by the present article shall not extend to the operators of state information systems, the operators of municipal information systems, the telecoms operators that provide communication services under a relevant licence, in as much as licensable activities are concerned and also they shall not extend to the citizens (natural persons) who pursue the activities specified in Part 1 of the present article for personal, family and household needs. For the purposes of applying the provisions of the present article the Government of the Russian Federation shall define a list of personal, family and household needs in the event of pursuance of the activities specified in Part 1 of the present article.
6. The composition of the information that is subject to storage under Part 3 of the present article, the place and the rules for the storage thereof, the procedure for the provision thereof to the empowered state bodies carrying out operative investigation activities or ensuring the security of the Russian Federation, and also the procedure for exercising control over the activities of organizers of dissemination of information in the Internet which are relating to the storage of such information and the federal executive governmental body empowered to exercise that control shall be defined by the Government of the Russian Federation.

**Article 10.2 [The details of dissemination of generally accessible information by a blogger]**

1. The owner of a website and/or a website page in the Internet on which generally accessible information is placed and to which access exceeds 3,000 users of the Internet per day (hereinafter referred to as "blogger") when said information is placed and used, for instance when said information is placed on the given website or website page by other users of the Internet shall ensure the observance of the legislation of the Russian Federation, for instance:

   1) shall not allow the website or website page in the Internet to be used for the purpose of committing the acts punishable under a criminal law, disclosing the information classified as state or another specifically law-protected secret, disseminating the materials containing public appeals for carrying out terrorist activities or publicly justifying terrorism, other extremist materials and also the materials propagating pornography, the cult of violence and cruelty and the materials containing obscene language;
   2) shall verify the reliability of placed generally accessible information before it is placed and shall immediately delete unreliable information that has been placed;
   3) shall not allow the dissemination of information about the private life of a citizen in breach of the civil legislation;
   4) shall observe the bans and restrictions envisaged by the legislation of the Russian Federation the referendum and the legislation of the Russian Federation on elections;
   5) shall observe the provisions of the legislation of the Russian Federation that regulate the procedure for disseminating mass information;
   6) shall observe the rights and lawful interests of citizens and organisations, for instance the honour, dignity and business reputation of citizens as well as the business reputation of organisations.

2. The following is hereby prohibited when information is placed on a website or website page in the Internet:

   1) the use of the website or website page in the Internet for the purpose of concealing or falsifying information of public significance, disseminating knowingly unreliable information under the disguise of reliable messages;
   2) the dissemination of information for the purpose of discrediting a citizen or some categories of citizens on the basis of sex, age, race or ethnicity, language, religion, trade, place of residence and work and also in connection with their political convictions.

3. The blogger is entitled to:

1) freely search, receive, transmit and disseminate information by any method in accordance with the legislation of the Russian Federation;
2) set out on his website or website page in the Internet his personal judgements and assessment with an indication of his name or pseudonym;
3) place or allow the placement on his website or website page in the Internet texts and/or other materials of other users of the Internet, unless the placement of such texts and/or other materials contravenes the legislation of the Russian Federation;
4) disseminate advertisements on an onerous basis in keeping with the civil legislation, Federal Law No. 38-FZ of March 13, 2006 on Advertisement on his website or website page in the Internet.

4. An abuse of the right of disseminating generally accessible information that has manifested itself as breach of the provisions of Parts 1, 2 and 3 of the present article shall entail criminal, administrative or another liability in accordance with the legislation of the Russian Federation.
5. On his website or website page in the Internet the blogger shall place his name and initials and an e-mail address for sending legal-significance messages to him.
6. On his website or website page in the Internet the blogger shall place immediately after receiving a court's decision that has become final and contains demand for its being published on the website or website page.
7. The owners of websites in the Internet who have registered as network editions in accordance with Law of the Russian Federation No. 2124-I of December 27, 1991 on Mass Media are not bloggers.
8. The federal executive governmental body carrying out the functions of control and supervision in the field of mass media, mass communications, information technologies and telecom shall keep a register of the websites and/or website pages in the Internet on which generally accessible information is placed and to which access exceeds 3,000 users of the Internet per day. For the purpose of ensuring the formation of the register of websites and/or website pages in the Internet the federal executive governmental body carrying out the functions of control and supervision in the field of mass media, mass communications, information technologies and telecom:

   1) shall organise the monitoring of websites and website pages in the Internet;
   2) shall endorse a methodology for assessing the number of users of a website or website page in the Internet per day;
   3) has the right of requesting from organizers of dissemination of information in the Internet, bloggers and other persons the information required for keeping such register. Within 10 days after receiving a request from the federal executive governmental body carrying out the functions of control and supervision in the field of mass media, mass communications, information technologies and telecom said persons shall provide the information so requested.

9. In the event of detection in information-telecommunication networks, for instance in the Internet, of a website or website page which contain generally accessible information and to which access exceeds 3,000 users of the Internet per day, including the consideration of relevant applications of citizens or organisations, the federal executive governmental body carrying out the functions of control and supervision in the field of mass media, mass communications, information technologies and telecom:
   1) shall include said website or website page in the Internet in the register of the websites and/or website pages in the Internet on which generally accessible information is placed and to which access exceeds 3,000 users of the Internet per day;
   2) shall identify the hosting provider or the other person which ensures the placement of the website or website page in the Internet;
   3) shall send to the hosting provider or the person mentioned in Item 2 of the present part a notice in electronic form in Russian and English concerning the need for provision of details allowing to identify the blogger;
   4) shall record the date and time of dispatch of the notice to the hosting provider or the person mentioned in Item 2 of the present part in the relevant information system.
10. Within three working days after receiving the notice mentioned in Item 3 of Part 9 of the present article the hosting provider or the person mentioned in Item 2 of Part 9 of the present article shall provide the information allowing to identify the blogger.
11. Having received the information specified in Item 3 of Part 9 of the present article, the federal executive governmental body carrying out the functions of control and supervision in the field of mass media, mass communications, information technologies and telecom shall send a notice to the blogger informing that his website or website page has been included in the register of the websites and/or website pages in the Internet on which generally accessible information is placed and to which access exceeds 3,000 users of the Internet per day, with reference to the provisions of the legislation of the Russian Federation applicable to said website or website page in the Internet.
12. If during three months access to the website or website page in the Internet is below 3,000 users of the Internet per day that website or that website page in the Internet shall be removed on the blogger's application from the register of the websites and/or website pages in the Internet on which generally accessible information is placed and to which access exceeds 3,000 users of the Internet per day, with a notice to this effect being sent to the blogger. The given website or website page in the Internet may be removed from that register when no application is filed by the blogger if access to the given website or website page in the Internet during six months is below 3,000 users of the Internet per day.

## Article 11 [Documenting of information]

1. The legislation of the Russian Federation or an agreement of the sides may establish requirements to documenting of information.
2. In the federal executive authorities documenting of information is carried out according to the procedure established by the Government of the Russian Federation. The rules of the office work and document turnover established by other state authorities, local self-government bodies within their competence should correspond to the requirements set by the Government of the Russian Federation in the part of office work and document turnover for federal executive authorities.
3. *Repealed by the Federal Law No 65-FZ from April 06, 2011*
4. For purposes of making civil-legal contracts or execution of other legal relations involving people exchanging electronic messages, the exchange of electronic messages each of which is signed by an electronic signature or another analogue of the sender' autograph shall be regarded as an exchange of documents, according to the procedure established by the federal acts.
5. The right of ownership and other property rights to material carriers containing documented information shall be established by the civil legislation.

## Article 11.1 [Exchange of information in the form of electronic documents in the exercise of powers of public authorities and local self-government]

1. The government bodies and bodies of local self-government as well as organizations exercising specific public authorities in accordance with federal laws are obligated within their powers to provide information in the form of electronic document signed by a reinforced qualified electronic signature and (or) the documents in hard copy, for the choice of citizens (individuals) and organizations, unless federal laws or other legal acts of the Russian Federation regulating the relations in the named field of activity, provides a different procedure.
2. The information required for government bodies and bodies of local self-government, organizations exercising specific public authorities in accordance with federal laws, to exercise their authorities, can be represented by citizens (natural persons) and organizations to the public authorities, government bodies and bodies of local self-government, organizations exercising specific public authorities in accordance with federal laws, can be provided in the form of electronic document signed by a electronic signature unless federal laws or other legal acts of the Russian Federation regulating the relations in the named field of activity, provides otherwise
3. The Government of the Russian Federation establishes the requirements for the electronic cooperation between the citizens (natural persons) and organizations and government bodies and bodies of local self-government, and organizations exercising specific public authorities in accordance with the Federal Law of April 6, 2011 No 63-FZ "On electronic signature".

**Article 12 [State regulation in the sphere of application of information technologies]**
State regulation in the sphere of application of information technologies shall provide:

1) regulation of relations connected with search, obtaining, transmission, production and distribution of information involving information technologies on the basis of principles established by the present Federal Act;
2) development of information systems of various purpose in order to supply citizens (natural persons), organizations, state authorities and local self-government bodies with information, as well as provision of interaction of these systems;
3) creation of conditions for efficient usage of information-telecommunication systems in the Russian Federation, including the Internet and other similar information-telecommunication systems.
4) ensuring children's information safety.

In accordance with their competence the state authorities, local self-government bodies shall:

1) take part in the development and implementation of target programmes of application of information technologies;
2) create information systems and provide access to the included information in Russian and the state language of the corresponding republic within the Russian Federation.

**Article 13 [Information systems]**

1. Information systems shall include:
    1) state information systems – federal information systems and regional information systems created on the basis of federal acts, acts of the subjects of the Russian Federation, legal acts of state authorities respectively;
    2) municipal information systems created on the basis of decisions of local self-government bodies;
    3) other information systems.
2. Unless otherwise established by federal acts, the operator of an information system shall be the owner of the technical devices used for processing of the information included in the data base, who legitimately uses these data base, or a person with whom the owner made a contract of operation of the information system. In the case and in the procedure established by federal laws, the information system operator shall provide the possibility of placing information on the Internet in the form of open data.

2.1. Technical means of information systems used by government bodies, bodiesof self-government, state and municipal unitary enterprises or state and local government agencies, should be placed in the territory of the Russian Federation.

3. The rights of the owner of information containing in the data bases of the information system shall be protected regardless of the copyright and other rights thereto.
4. The requirements to the state information systems established by the present Federal Act shall be applied to municipal information systems, unless otherwise provided by the legislation of the Russian Federation on local self-government.
5. Specifics of operation of state information systems and municipal information systems may be established in accordance with technical regulations, normative legal acts of state authorities, normative legal acts of local self-government bodies making decisions on creation of these information systems.
6. The procedure for creation and operation of information systems other than state or municipal information systems shall be determined by operations of these information systems in accordance with the requirements established by the present Federal Act or other federal acts.
7. The Government of Russian Federation establishes the procedure of monitoring of compliance with the requirements specified in part 2.1 of present article and part 6 of Article 14 of this Law.

**Article 14 [State information systems]**

1. State information systems shall be created for purposes of implementation of powers of state authorities and ensuring of information exchange between these authorities, as well as for other purposes established by federal acts.
2. The state informational systems shall be created and operated subject to the requirements provided by the legislation of the Russian Federation on the contractual system in the sphere of purchasing goods, works and services for government and municipal needs.
3. State information systems shall be created and operated on the basis of statistical and other documented information provided by citizens (natural persons), organizations, state authorities, local self-government bodies.
4. The lists of the types of information provided without fail shall be established by federal acts, terms of provision – by the Government of the Russian Federation or corresponding state authorities, unless otherwise provided by federal acts. If the generally accessible information provided for by the lists enforced in compliance with Article 14 of Federal Law No. 8-FZ of February 9, 2009 on Providing Access to information about the Activities of the State Bodies and Bodies of Local Self-Government is processed or it is planned to be processed in the state information systems, these systems shall provide the placement of such information on the Internet in the form of open data.

4.1. The Government of the Russian Federation shall specify the instances when an access through the use of the Internet to the information contained in the state information systems is provided exclusively to the information users that have passed authorization in the comprehensive system of identification and identity verification, as well as a procedure for using the comprehensive system of identification and identity verification.

5. Unless otherwise established by the decision on creation of the state information system, the functions of its operator shall be carried out by the customer who made a state contract for creation of this information system. The state information system shall be put in operation according to the procedure established by this customer.
6. The Government of the Russian Federation improves the requirements to the procedure of creating, developing, commissioning, operating and decommissioning of state informational systems, further storage of information contained in their database, including a list of the content and timing of the stages of the activities of creating, developing, commissioning, operating and decommissioning of state informational systems, further storage of information contained in their database.
7. Operation of state information systems without proper execution of the rights to usage of its components being objects of intellectual property shall not be permitted.
8. Technical means intended for processing of information included in state information systems, as well as software means and means of information protection should correspond to the requirements of the legislation of the Russian Federation on technical regulation.
9. Information included in state information systems, as well as the other data and documents available at the disposal of state bodies shall constitute state information resources. The information contained in state information systems shall be deemed official. The state bodies specified by the normative legal act which regulates the functioning of a state information system are obliged to ensure the reliability and relevance of the information contained in the given information system, access to the cited information in the cases and in the procedure provided for by law, as well as the protection of the cited information against unlawful access thereto, elimination, modification, blocking, copying, supply, dissemination and other wrongful actions.

**Article 15 [Usage of information-telecommunication networks]**
Usage of information-telecommunication networks on the territory of the Russian Federation shall be provided with observance of the requirements of the legislation of the Russian Federation in the sphere of communication, the present Federal Act and other normative legal acts of the Russian Federation.

Regulation of usage of information-telecommunication network access to which is not limited to a certain range of persons shall be carried out in the Russian federation with the account of the generally accepted international practice of the activity of self-regulated organizations in this sphere. The procedure of usage of other information-telecommunication network shall be determined by the owners of thereof with the account of the requirements established by the present Federal Act.

Usage of information-telecommunication networks on the territory of the Russian Federation in economic and other activities may not be the basis for establishing additional requirements or restrictions referring to regulation of the above-mentioned activity carried out without these networks, or for non-observance of the requirements established by the federal acts.

Federal Acts may provide obligatory identification of the personality, organizations using information-telecommunication networks in entrepreneurial activity. The recipient of an electronic message located on the territory of the Russian Federation shall have the right to make an inspection to establish the sender thereof, and in the cases established by federal acts or agreements of the sizes, should make this inspection.

Transfer of information by information-telecommunication networks shall not be limited, provided the legally established requirements to information distribution and protection of the objects of intellectual property are observed. Transfer of information may be restricted only according to the procedure and on the terms established by federal acts.

Specifics of connection of state information systems to information-telecommunication networks may be established by normative legal acts of the President of the Russian Federation or normative legal acts of the Government of the Russian Federation.

### Article 15.5 [The procedure for restricting access to the information processed in violation of the Russian legislation in the field of personal data]

1. In order to restrict access to information in the network "Internet", processed in violation of the Russian legislation in the field of personal data, created an automated information system "Register of violators of the rights of personal data subjects" (hereinafter - the register of violators).
2. The register of violators include:
    1) domain names and (or) page indexes of websites in the Internet, containing the information processed in violation of the Russian legislation in the field of personal data;
    2) network addresses, enabling the identification of sites in the network "Internet", containing the information processed in violation of the Russian legislation in the field of personal data;

3) an indication of the entered into force court act;
4) information about elimination of Russian legislation in the field of personal data violation;
5) the date when the data concerning the information resource was communicated to telecoms operators in order to restrict access to this resource.

3. Federal executive authority responsible for the control and supervision in the sphere of mass media, mass communications, information technologies and communication creates, forms and operates register of of violators in the procedure established by the Government of Russian Federation.
4. The federal executive body responsible for the control and supervision in the sphere of mass media, mass communications, information technologies and communications, in accordance with the criteria established by the Government of Russian Federation can involve the registry of violators operator - an organization registered on the territory of the Russian Federation to the forming and maintening of this register.
5. The basis for information specified in paragraph 2 of this Article inclusion to the register of violators is an entered into force court act.
6. The personal data subject is entitled to apply to the federal executive body responsible for the control and supervision in the sphere of mass media, mass communications, information technology and communications, with a statement to adopt measures to restrict access to information processed in violation of the Russian legislation in the field of personal data, on the basis of entered into force court act. The form of the mentioned statement is approved by the federal executive body responsible for the control and supervision in the sphere of mass media, mass communications, information technology and communications.
7. Within three working days of entered into force court act receipt the federal executive body responsible for the control and supervision in the sphere of mass media, mass communications, information technologies and communication, on the base of the court decision:

1) identifies the hosting provider or other person providing the information processing in the telecommunication network, including the Internet, in violation of the Russian legislation in the field of personal data;
2) gives the hosting provider or other person specified in paragraph 1 of this part a notification in an electronic form in Russian and English languages about the violation of the Russian legislaion in the field of personal data with the information on entered into force court act, the domain name and network address, enabling to identify a site in the Internet where the information is processed in violation of the Russian legislation in the field of personal data, as well as on the site page indexes in the Internet, enabling to identify such information, and with a demand to take measures to eliminate violations of the Russian legislation in the field personal data specified in the court act;

3) records the date and time when the notification was given to hosting provider or any other specified in paragraph 1 of this part of the person in the register of of violators.

8. Within one working day of the notification specified in paragraph 2 of Part 7 of this article was received, hosting provider, or otherwise person referred in paragraph 1 of Part 7 of this article, shall inform the owner of the information resource about it and about the need to take immediate measures to eliminate violations of the Russian legislation in the field of personal data specified in the notice, or to take measures to restrict access to information processed in violation of the Russian legislation in the field of personal data.
9. Within one working day of the notice about the need to eliminate violations of the Russian legislation in the field of personal data from the hosting provider or other persons specified in paragraph 1 of Part 7 of this article was received, the owner of an information resource is obliged to take measures to eliminate the violations specified in the notice. In case of the owner of an information resource refusal or inaction, the hosting provider or other persons specified in paragraph 1 of Part 7 of this article are obliged to restrict access to relevant information resource no later than in three working days of the notification referred to in paragraph 2 of Part 7 of this article was recieved.
10. In case of hosting provider, or other person specified in paragraph 1 of Part 7 of this article a and (or) the owner of the information resource failed to take the measures specified in paragraphs 8 and 9 of this article, the domain name of the site in the Internet, its network address, page site indexes in the Internet, enabling to identify the information processed in violation of the Russian legislation in the field of personal data, as well as other information on this site and the information are sent by the automated information system to telecoms operators to take measures to restrict access to this information resource, including including the network address, domain name, the index pages of a site in the Internet.
11. The federal executive body responsible for control and supervision in the sphere of mass media, mass communications, information technologies and communication, or registry of violators operator involve by it this body in accordance with part 4 of this article excludes from such register a domain name, an index of the site page in the Internet or the network address, enabling to identify a site in Internet, on the base on the request of the Internet site owner, hosting provider or telecoms operator no later than within three days from the day of the treatment after the measures to eliminate violations of the Russian legislation in the field of personal data was adopted or on the basis of an enforceable court decision on the abolition of the previously adopted judicial act.
12. The federal executive body authorized by the Government of the Russian Federation establishes the procedure for interaction between the register of violators operator and hosting provider registry and the procedure for obtaining access to the information contained in this register by telecoms operator.

**Article 16 [Protection of information]**

Protection of information shall represent making of legal, organizational and technical measures directed to:

1) protection of information against illegal access, elimination, modification, blocking, copying, supply, distribution and other illegitimate actions with reference thereto;
2) confidentiality of information of restricted access;
3) implementation of the right to access to information.

State regulation of the relations in the sphere of information protection shall be carried out by establishing the requirements on information protection and responsibility for breach of the legislation of the Russian Federation on information, information technologies and information protection.

Requirements to protection of generally accessible information may be established only to achieve the goals specified in clauses 1 and 3 of the present article.

In the cases provided by the legislation of the Russian Federation the possessor of information, operator of an information system should ensure:

1) prevention of unsanctioned access to information and (or) transfer thereof to the persons that do not have access thereto;
2) prompt revelation of facts of unsanctioned access to information;
3) prevention of a possibility of unfavourable consequences of infringement of the procedure of access to information;
4) prevention of influence on technical means of information processing resulting in functioning disorders;
5) a possibility of prompt restoration of information modified or eliminated as a result of unsanctioned access thereto;
6) permanent control over information protection.
7) the presence on the territory of the Russian Federation database of information used to collect, record, systematization, accumulation, storage, clarification (update, modification), extraction of the personal data of Russian citizens

The requirements to protection of the information included in state information systems shall be established by the federal executive authority for security and the federal executive authority for counteraction to technical intelligence services and technical protection of information within their competence. In the case of creation and operation of state information systems the methods and ways of information protection should correspond to the above-mentioned requirements.

Federal acts may set restrictions on usage of certain means of information protection and performance of certain types of activities in the sphere of information protection.

**Article 17 [Responsibility for legal offenses in the sphere of information – Information technologies and information protection]**

1. Violation of the requirements of the present Federal Act shall entail disciplinary, civil-legal, administrative or criminal responsibility in accordance with the legislation of the Russian Federation.
2. Persons, whose rights and legal interests were breached because of disclosure of information of restricted access or other illegitimate usage shall have the right to appeal to court to protect their rights according to the established procedure, as well as to sue for reimbursement of losses, compensation for moral damage, protection of dignity, honour and business reputation. The requirement of reimbursement of losses may not be satisfied if it is made by the person who did not take measures ensuring confidentiality of information or breached legally established requirement on information protection, if these taking of these measures and observance of these requirements were a responsibility of this person.
3. If distribution of certain information is restricted or banned by federal acts, civil-legal responsibility therefore shall be born by the person rendering the following services:
    1) transfer of information provided by another person subject to transfer thereof without changes and corrections;
    2) storage of information and provision of access thereto, provided this person could not know on the illegal character of distribution thereof.
4. A hosting provider, telecoms operator and the owner of a website in the Internet are not liable to a right-holder and a user for restrictions on access to information and/or restrictions on the dissemination thereof in accordance with the provisions of the present Federal Law.

## 2. Law on Providing Access to Information on the Activities of Government Bodies and Bodies of Local Self-Government[44]

### Chapter 1
### General provisions

**Article 1 [Basic definitions used in the present Federal Law]**
For the present Federal Law, the following basic definitions have been used:

[44]Russian Law Gazette, Russian Federal Law No. 8-FZ of February 9, 2009, Translation by Freedom of Information Foundation (http://old.svobodainfo.org).

1) Information on the activities of government bodies and bodies of local self-government – information (including documented), created by government bodies, their territorial bodies, bodies of local self-government or organizations subordinate to government bodies, bodies of local self-government (hereinafter referred to as the subordinate organizations), acting within their competence, or received by the above-specified bodies and organizations. Information on the activities of government bodies and bodies of local self-government also includes laws and other normative legal acts concerning information on the activities of bodies of local self-government – municipal legal acts defining structure, competence, formation and operating procedures of the above-specified bodies and organizations, and other information concerning their activity;
2) government bodies – government authorities of the Russian Federation, government authorities of subjects of the Russian Federation and other government bodies, formed according to the legislation of the Russian Federation and the legislation of subjects of the Russian Federation;
3) information user – the citizen (natural person), organization (legal entity), or public association, carrying out a search for information on the activities of government bodies and bodies of local self-government. Information users are also government bodies and bodies of local self-government, which are carrying out a search of the above-specified information in accordance with the present Federal Law;
4) request – application of the information user in oral or written form, including in the form of an electronic document, to the government body or body of local self-government or to an official of such a body, for granting information on the activity of this body;
5) the official website of a government body or body of local self-government (hereinafter referred to as the official website) – the website in the information-telecommunication network, the "Internet" (hereinafter referred to as the "Internet"), containing information on the activities of the government body or body of local self-government, the electronic address of which includes the domain name, the rights to which belong to the government body or body of local self-government.

**Article 2 [Scope of the present Federal Law]**

1. The scope of the present Federal Law extends to relations arising in connection with providing access for information users to information on the activities of government bodies and bodies of local self-government.
2. If federal constitutional laws, federal laws, and other normative legal acts of the Russian Federation adopted according to the above-specified laws stipulate distinctions in the granting of specific types of information on the activities of government bodies and bodies of local self-government, the provisions of the present Federal Law shall be applied, taking into account

the distinctions stipulated by such federal constitutional laws, federal laws and other normative legal acts of the Russian Federation.

3. If laws and other normative legal acts of subjects of the Russian Federation, adopted under the jurisdiction of subjects of the Russian Federation, stipulate distinctions in the granting of specific types of information on the activities of government bodies of subjects of the Russian Federation and bodies of local self-government, the provisions of the present Federal Law shall apply, taking into account the distinctions stipulated in such laws and other normative legal acts of subjects of the Russian Federation.
4. The scope of the present Federal Law extends to relations arising in connection with the granting, by government bodies and bodies of local self-government, of information on their activities, upon the request of an editorial board of a mass media entity, in areas which remain unregulated by the legislation of the Russian Federation on mass media.
5. The scope of the present Federal Law does not extend to:

   1) relations arising in connection with providing access to personal data, the processing of which is carried out by government bodies and bodies of local self-government;
   2) procedures for consideration by government bodies and bodies of local self-government of applications of citizens;
   3) procedures for granting by government bodies and bodies of local self-government to other government bodies and bodies of local self-government of information on their activity arising in connection with the carrying out, by the above-specified bodies, of their competence.

### Article 3 [Legal regulation of relations arising in connection with providing access to information on the activities of government bodies and bodies of local self-government]

1. Legal regulation of relations arising in connection with providing access to information on the activities of government bodies and bodies of local self-government is carried out according to the Constitution of the Russian Federation, federal constitutional laws, the present Federal Law, Federal Law dated December 22, 2008, N 262-FZ, “On providing access to information on the activity of courts in the Russian Federation” (hereinafter referred to as the Federal Law “On providing access to information on the activity of courts in the Russian Federation”), other federal laws, and other normative legal acts of the Russian Federation. Legal regulation of relations arising in connection with providing access to information on the activities of government bodies of subjects of the Russian Federation and bodies of local self-government is also carried out according to laws and other normative legal acts of subjects of the Russian Federation, and, with respect to bodies of local self-government, by municipal legal acts.

2. If an international treaty of the Russian Federation defines other rules than those stipulated in the present Federal Law, the rules of such international treaty shall apply.

**Article 4 [Basic principles of providing access to information on the activities of government bodies and bodies of local self-government]**
The basic principles of providing access to information on the activities of government bodies and bodies of local self-government are:

1) openness and accessibility of information on the activities of government bodies and bodies of local self-government, except for the cases stipulated by federal law;
2) reliability of information on the activities of government bodies and bodies of local self-government and timeliness of its granting;
3) freedom of search, receipt, transmission and dissemination of information on the activities of government bodies and bodies of local self-government by any legal means;
4) observance of rights of citizens to the inviolability of private life, to personal and family secrets, to protection of their honor and business reputation, and the right of organizations to the protection of their business reputation, in the granting of information on the activities of government bodies and bodies of local self-government.

**Article 5 [Information on the activities of government bodies and bodies of local self-government, access to which is restricted]**

1. Access to information on the activities of government bodies and bodies of local self-government is restricted in cases in which the above-specified information refers to data which, according to procedures defined by federal law, constitutes government or other secrets protected by law.
2. The list of the data referring to information to which access is restricted, as well as the procedure of referring the above-specified data to the status of information of restricted access, are defined by federal law.

**Article 6 [Methods of providing access to information on the activities of government bodies and bodies of local self-government]**
Access to information on the activities of government bodies and bodies of local self-government can be provided through the following methods:

1) promulgation (publication) in mass media by government bodies and bodies of local self-government of the information on their activities;
2) placement on the "Internet" by government bodies and bodies of local self-government of information on their activities;

3) placement in the premises occupied by the above-specified bodies, and in other places designated for these purposes by government bodies and bodies of local self-government of information on their activities;
4) familiarization of information users with information on activities of government bodies and bodies of local self-government in the premises occupied by the above-specified bodies, as well as through library and archival collections;
5) presence of citizens (natural persons), including representatives of organizations (legal entities), public associations, government bodies and bodies of local self-government, at meetings of collegium government bodies and collegium bodies of local self-government, as well as at meetings of collegium entities within government bodies and collegium entities within bodies of local self-government;
6) granting to information users, at their request, information on the activities of, government bodies and bodies of local self-government;
7) other methods, stipulated by laws and (or) other normative legal acts relating to access to information on activities of bodies of local self-government, as well as municipal legal acts.

**Article 7 [Form for granting information on the activities of government bodies and bodies of local self-government]**

1. Information on the activities of government bodies and bodies of local self-government can be granted in oral form and in the form of documented information, including in the form of the electronic document.
2. The form for granting information on the activities of government bodies and bodies of local self-government is defined by the present Federal Law, Federal Law "On providing access to information on the activity of courts in the Russian Federation", other federal laws and other normative legal acts of the Russian Federation. The form for granting information on the activities of government bodies of subjects of the Russian Federation and bodies of local self-government can also be defined by laws and other normative legal acts of subjects of the Russian Federation, and, with respect to information on the activities of bodies of local self-government, by municipal legal acts. If the form for granting information on the activities of government bodies and bodies of local self-government is not defined, the form can be determined according to the request of the information user. If it is impossible to grant the above-specified information in the requested form, the information is granted in the form in which it exists within the government body or the body of local self-government.

   2.1. Public information about the activities of government bodies and bodies of local self-government is provided by the government bodies and bodies of local self-government to the general public through its placement in the "Internet" in the form of open data.

3. Information on the activities of government bodies and bodies of local self-government in oral form is granted to information users during their visit. The above-specified information is also granted through the telephone support services of the government body or body of local self-government, or by telephone by officials authorized by the government body or body of local self-government for the granting thereof.
4. Information about activities of government bodies and bodies of local self-government can be transmitted over networks of the public communications. The Government of Russia determines the cases in which the access by means of the "Internet" to the information contained in state and municipal information systems provided only for users having passed the authorization in the unified system of identification and authentication.

**Article 8 [Rights of the information user]**
The information user has the right:

1) to receive reliable information on the activities of government bodies and bodies of local self-government;
2) to refuse receipt of information on the activities of government bodies and bodies of local self-government;
3) not to substantiate the necessity of receiving the requested information on the activities of government bodies and bodies of local self-government, provided access to this information is not restricted;
4) to appeal, in accordance with the defined procedure, acts and (or) actions (omissions) of government bodies and bodies of local self-government, or by their officials, that violate the right to access information on the activities of government bodies and bodies of local self-government and the defined procedure of realization of this right;
5) to demand, in accordance with the procedure defined by law, compensation for damage caused by violation of the right to access information on the activities of government bodies and bodies of local self-government.

## Chapter 2
## Organizing Access to Information on the Activities of Government Bodies and Bodies of Local Self-Government – Basic Requirements for Providing Access to this Information

**Article 9 [Organizing access to information on the activities of government bodies and bodies of local self-government]**

1. Access to information on the activities of government bodies and bodies of local self-government is provided according to the limits of the competence of government bodies and bodies of local self-government.

2. Government bodies and bodies of local self-government, for the purpose of organization of access to information on their activities, determine corresponding structural divisions or authorized officials. The rights and duties of the above-specified divisions and officials are defined by regulations of government bodies and (or) other normative legal acts, and by regulations of bodies of local self-government and (or) other municipal legal acts, governing the activities of corresponding government bodies and bodies of local self-government.
3. The organization of access to information on the activities of government bodies and bodies of local self-government is carried out, taking into account the requirements of the present Federal Law, in the procedure defined by government bodies and bodies of local self-government, according to the limits of their competence, and with respect to access to information on activity of courts in the Russian Federation – also taking into account the requirements of the Federal Law "On providing access to information on the activity of courts in the Russian Federation".

**Article 10 [Organization of access to information on the activities of government bodies and bodies of local self-government, placed on the "Internet"]**

1. Government bodies and bodies of local self-government place information on their activities on the "Internet", where they create official websites, stating e-mail addresses to which information users can forward requests and the requested information can be received. If a body of local self-government is not able to place information on its activity on the "Internet", the above-specified information can be placed on the official website of the subject of the Russian Federation within which the corresponding municipal entity is located. Information on the activities of bodies of local self-government of settlements in such a municipal district can be placed on the official website of that municipal district. Information on the activities of inner city areas local self-governments can be placed on the city district with inner-city division official website.
2. In order to ensure the right of an unlimited circle of persons to access the information specified in part 1 of the present article, "Internet" connection points are created at places accessible to information users (at the premises of government bodies and bodies of local self-government, government and municipal libraries, other places accessible to visitors).
3. In order to ensure the right of information users to access to information specified in part 1 of the present article, government bodies and bodies of local self-government take measures to protect such information according to the legislation of the Russian Federation.

4. Requirements for technological, programmatic, and linguistic means of ensuring the use of official websites of federal executive government bodies are defined by the federal executive government bodies, authorized by the Government of the Russian Federation. Requirements for technological, programmatic, and linguistic means of ensuring use of official websites of other government bodies, as well as websites of bodies of local self-government, are defined by the above-specified bodies according to the limits of their competence.
5. Requirements to technological, software, and linguistic tools needed to organize information placement by government bodies and bodies of local self-government in the "Internet" in the form of open data, and to enable of its usage are defined by the federal executive government body authorized by the Government of the Russian Federation.
6. The procedure of providing conditions of official websites of federal authorities, public authorities of subjects of the Russian Federation and and bodies of local self-government in the "Internet" accessibility for the visually impaired is defined by the federal executive government body, authorized by the Government of the Russian Federation.

**Article 11 [Basic requirements for providing access to information on the activities of government bodies and bodies of local self-government]**
The basic requirements for providing access to information on the activities of government bodies and bodies of local self-government are:

1) reliability of the granted information on the activities of government bodies and bodies of local self-government;
2) observance of time periods and procedures for granting information on the activities of government bodies and bodies of local self-government;
3) redaction from the granted information on the activities of government bodies and bodies of local self-government of the data pertaining to information of restricted access;
4) creation by government bodies and bodies of local self-government, according to the limits of their competence, of organizational, technical and other conditions necessary for the realization of the right to access information on the activities of government bodies and bodies of local self-government, as well as creation of governmental and municipal information systems for assisting information users;
5) accounting of expenditures related to providing access to information on the activities of government bodies and bodies of local self-government in the budgetary financing planning of the above-specified bodies.

## Chapter 3
## Granting of Information on the Activities of Government Bodies and Bodies of Local Self-Government

### Article 12 [Promulgation (publication) of information on the activities of government bodies and bodies of local self-government]

1. Promulgation (publication) of information on the activities of government bodies and bodies of local self-government in mass media is carried out according to the legislation of the Russian Federation on mass media, except for the cases provided by parts 2 and 3 of the present article.
2. If legislation of the Russian Federation for specific types of information on the activities of government bodies and bodies of local self-government, and, if legislation the subjects of the Russian Federation and municipal legal acts for specific types of information on the activities of government bodies of subjects of the Russian Federation and bodies of local self-government, stipulate requirements for publication of such information, then its publication is carried out taking into account such requirements.
3. Official publication of laws and other normative legal acts and municipal legal acts is carried out according to the procedure for official publication defined by the legislation of the Russian Federation, the legislation of subjects of the Russian Federation, and municipal legal acts.

### Article 13 [Information on the activities of government bodies and bodies of local self-government, placed on the "Internet"]

1. Information on the activities of government bodies and bodies of local self-government, placed by the above-specified bodies on the "Internet", depending on the field of activity of the government body or body of local self-government, contains:
    1) general information on the government body or body of local self-government, including:
        a) name and structure of the government body or body of local self-government, mailing address, e-mail address (if any), telephone numbers of support services of the government body or body of local self-government;
        b) data on competence of the government body or body of local self-government, tasks and functions of the structural divisions of the above-specified bodies, as well as the list of laws and other normative legal acts defining such competence, tasks and functions;
        c) list of territorial bodies and representatives of government bodies abroad (if any), data on their tasks and functions, as well as mailing addresses, e-mail addresses (if any), and telephone numbers of support services of the specified bodies and representatives;

d) list of subordinate organizations (if any), data on their tasks and functions, as well as mailing addresses, e-mail addresses (if any), and telephone numbers of support services of subordinate organizations;
e) data on heads of the government body, its structural divisions, territorial bodies and representatives abroad (if any); data on heads of the body of local self-government, and its structural divisions; and data on heads of subordinate organizations (surname, name, patronymic, as well as at other data thereon subject to consent of such persons);
f) lists of information systems, databanks, and registers maintained by the government body, body of local self-government, or subordinate organizations;
g) data on mass media institutions established by the government body or body of local self-government (if any);

2) information on the norm-creating activity of the government body or body of local self-government, including:

a) normative legal acts issued by the government body, municipal legal acts issued by the body of local self-government, including data on entering of amendments therein, their nullification, invalidation by the court, as well as data on government registration of normative legal acts and municipal legal acts if such registration is required by the legislation of the Russian Federation;
b) texts of drafts of legislative and other normative legal acts proposed to the State Duma of the Federal Assembly of the Russian Federation or to legislative (representative) bodies of government power within subjects of the Russian Federation, and texts of drafts of municipal legal acts proposed to representative bodies of municipal entities;
c) information on purchases of goods, works and services for government and municipal needs according to the legislation of the Russian Federation on the contract system in the purchasing of goods, works and services for government and municipal needs;
d) administrative regulations, standards of government and municipal services;
e) defined forms of applications, statements and other documents to be received by government bodies, their territorial bodies, and bodies of local self-government for consideration according to laws and other normative legal acts and municipal legal acts;
f) procedure for appeal of normative legal acts and other decisions adopted by the government body and its territorial bodies, and municipal legal acts;

3) the information on the participation of the government body or body of local self-government in target and other programs and international

collaboration, including official texts of corresponding international treaties of the Russian Federation, as well as on measures conducted by the government body or body of local self-government, including data on official visits and business trips of heads and official delegations of the government body or body of local self-government;

4) the information on the condition of protection of the population and territories from extreme situations and accepted measures of ensuring of their safety, on foreseeable and already-occurred extreme situations, on methods and ways of protection of the population against them, as well as other information which is subject to distribution by the government body or body of local self-government to citizens and organizations according to federal laws and laws of subjects of the Russian Federation;
5) information on the results of inspections conducted by the government body, its territorial bodies, bodies of local self-government, and subordinate organizations, acting within the limits of their competence, as well as information on the results of inspections conducted of the government body, its territorial bodies, body of local self-government, and subordinate organizations;
6) texts of official appearances and statements of heads and deputy heads of the government body, its territorial bodies, and body of local self-government;
7) statistical information on the activities of the government body or body of local self-government, including:

    a) statistical data and indicators characterizing the condition and dynamics of development of economic, social and other fields of vital activity, regulation of which is attributed to the competence of the government body or body of local self-government;
    b) data on use by the government body, its territorial bodies, bodies of local self-government, and subordinate organizations of allocated budgetary funds;
    c) data on privileges, grace periods, installment plans, and debt forgiveness for payments into budgets of the budgetary system of the Russian Federation granted to organizations and entrepreneurs;

8) the information on staffing of the government body or body of local self-government, including:

    a) procedure for hiring of citizens into government service or municipal service;
    b) data on vacant positions in government service available in the government body and its territorial bodies, and on vacant positions in municipal service available in the body of local self-government;
    c) qualifying requirements for candidates for vacant positions of government service and vacant positions of municipal service;

d) conditions and results of competitions related to filling vacant positions of government service and vacant positions of municipal service;
e) telephone numbers by which it is possible to receive information concerning the filling of vacant positions in the government body, its territorial bodies, and bodies of local self-government;
f) list of educational institutions subordinate to the government body or body of local self-government (if any), stating mailing addresses of such educational institutions, as well as telephone numbers by which it is possible to receive reference information about such educational institutions;

9) information on the activity of the government body or body of local self-government pertaining to applications of citizens (natural persons), organizations (legal entities), public associations, and government bodies and bodies of local self-government, including:

a) procedure and receiving hours for citizens (natural persons), including representatives of organizations (legal entities), public associations, government bodies, and bodies of local self-government, and procedure for consideration of their applications, with reference to legal acts regulating these procedures;
b) surname, name and patronymic of the division head or other official whose competence includes organization of reception for the persons specified in subparagraph "a" of the present part and provision for consideration of their applications, as well as the telephone number by which it is possible to receive reference information;
c) surveys of applications of persons specified in subparagraph "a" of the present part, as well as summarized information on the results of the consideration of such applications, and measures taken.

2. Government bodies and bodies of local self-government, along with the information specified in part 1 of the present Article and related to their activities, can place in the "Internet" other information on their activities taking into account requirements of the present Federal Law.

2.1. The information on staffing of the government body or body of local self-government specified in subparagraphs "b" – "e" of paragraph 8 of part 1 of the present article is placed also on the official website of state information system in the sphere of state service in the "Internet" in the procedure determined by Government of Russia. If a body of local self-government is not able to place information on staffing on the official website of state information system in the sphere of state service, the above-specified information can be placed on the official website of the subject of the Russian Federation within which the corresponding municipal entity is located.

3. The composition of public information posted by government bodies and bodies of local self-government in the "Internet" including information posted in the form of open data (except for the information specified in Article 7-1 of the 14 of this Federal Law) is determined by the relevant lists of information provided for in Article 14 of this Federal Law.
4. The procedure for information to be defined as public information posted by government bodies and bodies of local self-government in the "Internet" in the form of open data is determined by the Government of the Russian Federation with regard to the Russian Federation legislation on state secrets, the Russian Federation legislation on information, information technologies, and protection of information, and by the Russian Federation legislation on personal data.

**Article 14 [Lists of information on the activities of government bodies and bodies of local self-government, placed on the "Internet"]**

1. The list of information on the activities of federal government bodies and their subordinate federal government bodies, activity of which is managed by the President of the Russian Federation, must be approved by the President of the Russian Federation.
2. The list of information on activities of federal government bodies and their subordinate federal government bodies, activity of which is managed by the Government of the Russian Federation must be approved by the Government of the Russian Federation.
3. The lists of information on the activities of the Council of Federation of the Federal Assembly of the Russian Federation and the State Duma of the Federal Assembly of the Russian Federation are approved accordingly by the Council of Federation of the Federal Assembly of the Russian Federation and the State Duma of the Federal Assembly of the Russian Federation.
4. The list of information on the activities of courts in the Russian Federation and distinctions for placement of judicial acts are defined by the Federal Law "On providing of access to information on activity of courts in the Russian Federation".
5. The lists of information on the activities of the federal government bodies formed according to the legislation of the Russian Federation and not specified in parts 1-3 of the present article, are approved by these federal government bodies.
6. The lists of information on the activities of government bodies of subjects of the Russian Federation are approved according to the procedures determined by subjects of the Russian Federation.
7. The lists of information on the activities of the bodies of local self-government are approved according to the procedures determined by the bodies of local self-government.

7.1. The Government of the Russian Federation shall determine the composition of public information about the activities of government bodies of the Russian Federation and bodies of local self-government as well as the procedure for mandatory placement of such information, created by the said bodies or made available to them within exercise of powers in areas of competence of the Russian Federation and the powers of the Russian Federation in areas of joint jurisdiction of the Russian Federation and the subjects of the Russian Federation transferred for execution to government bodies of subjects of the Russian Federation or to bodies of local self-government, by the said bodies in the "Internet" in the form of open data.

8. Upon approval of the lists of information on the activities of government bodies and bodies of local self-government specified in parts 1-3, 5-7 of the present article, the following shall be defined: frequency of placement of information on the "Internet", except for information posted in the form of open data; time periods for its updating, providing timeliness of execution and protection by information users of their rights and legal interests, as well as other requirements for placement of the above-specified information.
9. Frequency of posting of publicly available information about the activities of government bodis and bodies of local self-government on the "Internet" in the form of open data, as well as terms for its updating to ensure timely implementation and protection of their rights and lawful interests by the users, as well as other requirements for the placement of this information in the form of open data, are determined in the way prescribed by the Government of the Russian Federation.

**Article 16 [Placing of information on the activities of government bodies and bodies of local self-government in the premises occupied by the above-specified bodies, and other places designated for these purposes]**

1. Government bodies and bodies of local self-government, in the premises occupied by the above-specified bodies, and other places designated for these purposes, place information boards and (or) other technical means of analogous function, for familiarizing information users with current information on the activities of the corresponding government body or body of local self-government.
2. The information specified in part 1 of the present article, should contain:
   1) the procedure of activity of the government body or body of local self-government, including procedure for receiving citizens (natural persons), including representatives of organizations (legal entities), public associations, government bodies and bodies of local self-government;
   2) conditions and procedure for receiving information from the government body or body of local self-government.

3. Government bodies and bodies of local self-government have the right to place other data necessary for day-to-day informing of information users in the premises occupied by the above-specified bodies, and other places designated for these purposes.

### Article 17 [Familiarization with information on the activities of government bodies and bodies of local self-government in the premises occupied by the above-specified bodies, as well as library and archival collections]

1. Upon the decision of the government body or the body of local self-government, by the procedure defined by them, the information user can be granted an opportunity to familiarize himself with information on their activities, in the premises occupied by the government body or body of local self-government.
2. A body of local self-government which is not able to place the information on its activities on the "Internet", provides information users with the opportunity to familiarize themselves with the above-specified information in the premises occupied by this body of local self-government.
3. Familiarization of information users with information on the activities of government bodies and bodies of local self-government which is located in library and archival collections, is carried out in the procedure defined by the legislation of the Russian Federation, the legislation of subjects of the Russian Federation, and municipal legal acts.

### Article 18 [Request for information on the activities of government bodies and bodies of local self-government]

1. The information user has the right to apply to government bodies and bodies of local self-government with a request both directly and through his or her representative, whose competence is formed according to the procedure defined by the legislation of the Russian Federation.
2. The request should specify the mailing address, telephone number and (or) fax number or e-mail address for forwarding the response to the request or clarification of the contents of the request, as well as the surname, name and patronymic of the citizen (natural person) or name of the organization (legal entity), public association, government body, or body of local self-government requesting information on the activities of government bodies and bodies of local self-government. Anonymous requests are not considered. The written request should also include the name of the government body or body of local self-government to which the request is forwarded, or surname and initials or position of the corresponding official.
3. In drafting the request, the official language of the Russian Federation must be used. In drafting a request to the government body or body of local self-government of a republic that is part of the Russian Federation, use of the official language of this republic is determined by the legislation of such

republic. Use, in drafting a request to the government body of a subject of the Russian Federation or a body of local self-government, of other languages of peoples of the Russian Federation is determined by the legislation of the subject of the Russian Federation.

4. In case of receipt by the government body or body of local self-government of a request drafted in a foreign language, this request can be considered according to the procedure defined by the corresponding body.
5. A written request is subject to registration within three days from the date of its receipt by the government body or body of local self-government. An oral request is subject to registration on the day of its receipt, stating the date and time of receipt.
6. The request is subject to consideration within thirty (30) days from the date of its registration unless otherwise stipulated in the legislation of the Russian Federation. If granting of the requested information is not possible within the specified term, the information user shall be notified, within seven days from the date of registration of the request, of the delay of response to his request, including the reason for the delay and the time period in which the requested information will be granted, which cannot be more than fifteen (15) days in excess of the period defined by the present Federal Law for a response to a request.
7. If the request does not concern the activity of the government body or body of local self-government to which it is forwarded, within seven days from the date of registration of the request it is forwarded to the government body or body of local self-government which is authorized to grant the requested information. The requesting information user shall be notified of the readdressing of the request within the same time period. If the government body or body of local self-government has no data on the availability of the requested information in another government body or body of local self-government, the information user shall also be notified of this within seven days from the date of registration of the request.
8. Government bodies and bodies of local self-government have the right to clarify the content of the request for the purpose of granting the information user necessary information on activities of the above-specified bodies.
9. The requirements of the present Federal Law for a written request and for a response thereto shall apply to a request received by the government body or body of local self-government via the "Internet", as well as to the response to such request.

### Article 19 [Procedure for granting information on the activities of government bodies and bodies of local self-government by request]

1. Information on the activities of government bodies and bodies of local self-government is granted by request in the form of response to the request, which contains the requested information or to which the requested information is attached, or which according to Article 20 of the present Federal Law

contains a justified refusal to grant the above-specified information. The response to the request should specify the name, mailing address of the government body or the body of local self-government, the official position of the signatory to the response, as well as identification information of the response to the request (registration number and date).

2. In responding to a request, the official language of the Russian Federation is used. In responding to a request received by the government body or body of local self-government of a republic that is part of the Russian Federation, the use of the official language of this republic is determined by the legislation of such republic. Use in response to a request received by the government body of the subject of the Russian Federation or a body of local self-government of other languages of peoples of the Russian Federation is determined by the legislation of the subject of the Russian Federation.
3. Upon request for information on the activities of government bodies or bodies of local self-government, which is published in mass media or placed on the "Internet", the government body or body of local self-government may, in response to the request, limit itself to stating the name, outgoing date and number of the issue of mass media in which the requested information is published, and (or) the electronic address of official website on which the required information has been placed.
4. If the requested information pertains to information of restricted access, the response to the request should specify the type, name, number and date of issue of the act, according to which access to this information is restricted. If part of the requested information relates to information of restricted access, and the remaining information is of public domain, the government body or body of local self-government is obliged to provide the required information, except for information of restricted access.
5. Response to the request is subject to obligatory registration by the government body or body of local self-government.

### Article 20 [Conditions excluding possibility of granting of information on the activities of government bodies and bodies of local self-government]

1. Information on activities of government bodies and bodies of local self-government is not granted in the following cases:

   1) the content of the request does not allow for determination of the requested information on the activities of government bodies and bodies of local self-government;
   2) the request does not specify mailing address, e-mail or fax number for forwarding a response to the request, nor telephone number by which it is possible to contact the information user who had sent the request;
   3) the requested information does not relate to the activities of the government body or the body of local self-government which received the request;

4) the requested information relates to information of restricted access;
5) the requested information was previously granted to the information user;
6) the request poses a question of legal assessment of acts taken by the government body or the body of local self-government, or poses a question of carrying out an analysis of activities of the government body, its territorial bodies, the body of local self-government or subordinate organizations, or poses a question of carrying out other analytical work which is not directly connected with protection of rights of the requesting information user.

2. The grounds excluding possibility of granting of information on the activities of courts in the Russian Federation are defined by the Federal Law "On providing of access to information on the activity of courts in the Russian Federation".
3. A government body or body of local self-government has the right not to grant information on its activities by request if this information was published in mass media or placed on the "Internet".

**Article 21 [Information on the activities of government bodies and bodies of local self-government given free of charge]**
The information user is granted free of charge the following information on activities of government bodies and bodies of local self-government which are:

1) transferred in oral form;
2) placed by the government body or body of local self-government on the "Internet", as well as in places designated for placement of information on the activities of government bodies and bodies of local self-government;
3) touching upon rights and duties of the concerned information user defined by the legislation of the Russian Federation;
4) other information, defined by law, on the activities of government bodies and bodies of local self-government, as well as other information, defined by municipal legal acts, on the activities of bodies of local self-government.

**Article 22 [Payment for granting of information on the activities of government bodies and bodies of local self-government]**

1. Payment for granting information on the activities of government bodies and bodies of local self-government is levied if in granting this information by request, the volume of the requested and received information exceeds the volume of information given free of charge, as defined by the Government of the Russian Federation. The payment collection procedure is defined by the Government of the Russian Federation.

2. Upon occurrence of the case provided in part 1 of the present article, the information user pays expenses for manufacturing of copies of the requested documents and (or) materials, as well as the expenses connected with their sending by mail.
3. Funds received as payment for granting information on the activities of government bodies and bodies of local self-government are subject to transfer to corresponding budgets of the budgetary system of the Russian Federation.
4. The government body or body of local self-government which has given information containing incorrect data is obliged to eliminate such discrepancies, free of charge, upon received a justified written statement from the information user.

## Chapter 4
## Liability for Violation of Procedure for Access to Information on the Activities of Government Bodies and Bodies of Local Self-Government

### Article 23 [Protection of the right to access to information on the activities of government bodies and bodies of local self-government]

1. Decisions and actions (omissions) of government bodies and bodies of local self-government, or by officials of these bodies, that violate the right to access information on the activities of government bodies and bodies of local self-government, can be appealed to a higher body or to higher official or in court.
2. If as a result of wrongful refusal in access to information on activities of government bodies and bodies of local self-government, or its untimely granting, or granting of intentionally misleading information or information not corresponding to the content of the request, the information user was caused damages, such damages are subject to compensation according to the civil legislation of the Russian Federation.

### Article 24 [Control and supervision over providing access to information on the activities of government bodies and bodies of local self-government]

1. Control over providing access to information on the activities of government bodies and bodies of local self-government is carried out by heads of government bodies and bodies of local self-government.
2. The procedure of carrying out control over providing access to information on the activities of government bodies and bodies of local self-government is defined by normative legal acts of government bodies and by municipal legal acts, respectively.
3. Supervision of execution of the present Federal Law by government bodies and bodies of local self-government, and their officials is carried out by bodies of the Prosecutor's Office of the Russian Federation in the procedure defined by the Federal Law "On the Office of the Prosecutor of the Russian Federation".

**Article 25 [Liability for violation of the right to access information on the activities of government bodies and bodies of local self-government]**
Officials of government bodies and bodies of local self-government and government and municipal employees, guilty of violation of the right access to information on the activities of government bodies and bodies of local self-government, bear disciplinary, administrative, civil and criminal liability according to the legislation of the Russian Federation.

# Appendix 13 Sweden: National Freedom-of-Information and Transparency Legislation (Extracts)

## 1. Freedom of the Press Act (1949)[45]

### Chapter 2
### On the Public Nature of Official Documents

**Article 1**
Every Swedish citizen shall be entitled to have free access to official documents, in order to encourage the free exchange of opinion and the availability of comprehensive information.

**Article 2**
The right of access to official documents may be restricted only if restriction is necessary having regard to

1. the security of the Realm or its relations with another state or an international organisation;
2. the central fiscal, monetary or currency policy of the Realm; 3. the inspection, control or other supervisory activities of a public authority; 4. the interest of preventing or prosecuting crime; 5. the economic interest of the public institutions; 6. the protection of the personal or economic circumstances of private subjects; 7. the preservation of animal or plant species.

Any restriction of the right of access to official documents shall be scrupulously specified in a provision of a special act of law, or, if this is deemed more appropriate in a particular case, in another act of law to which the special act

[45]Law of 5 April 1949 (1949:105), amended by Law of 30 June 2009, Swedish Code of Statutes – SFS 2009:400, last amended by Act 2014 (2014:1370).

 
H.-J. Blanke, R. Perlingeiro (eds.), *The Right of Access to Public Information*,
DOI 10.1007/978-3-662-55554-5

refers. With authority in such a provision, the Government may however issue more detailed provisions for its application in a statutory instrument.

The provisions of paragraph two notwithstanding, the Riksdag or the Government may be empowered, in a regulation under paragraph two, to permit the release of a particular document, having regard to the circumstances.

**Article 3**
Document is understood to mean any written or pictorial matter or recording which may be read, listened to, or otherwise comprehended only using technical aids. A document is official if it is held by a public authority, and if it can be deemed under Section 6 or 7 to have been received or drawn up by such an authority.

A recording under paragraph one is deemed to be held by a public authority, if it is available to the authority using technical aids, which the authority itself employs, for communication in such form that it may be read, listened to, or otherwise comprehended. A compilation of information taken from material recorded for automatic data processing is however regarded as being held by the authority only if the authority can make it available using routine means.

A compilation of information taken from material recorded for automatic data processing is not however regarded as being held by the authority if the compilation contains personal information and the authority is not authorised in law, or under a statutory instrument, to make the compilation available. Personal information is understood to mean any information which can be referred back directly or indirectly to a private person.

**Article 4**
A letter or other communication which is directed in person to an official at a public authority is deemed to be an official document if it refers to a case or other matter falling within the authority's purview, and if it is not intended for the addressee solely in his capacity as incumbent of another position.

**Article 5**
The Riksdag and any local government assembly vested with decision-making powers is equated with a public authority for the purposes of this Chapter.

**Article 6**
A document is deemed to have been received by a public authority when it has arrived at the authority or is in the hands of a competent official. A recording under Section 3, paragraph one, is instead deemed to have been received by the authority when it has been made available to the authority by another in the manner indicated in Section 3, paragraph two.

Competition documents, tenders and other such documents which it has been advertised shall be delivered under sealed cover are deemed not to have been received before the time appointed for their opening.

Measures taken solely as part of the technical processing or technical storage of a document which a public authority has made available shall not be construed to mean that the document has been received by that authority.

**Article 7**
A document is deemed to have been drawn up by a public authority when it has been dispatched. A document which has not been dispatched is deemed to have been drawn up when the matter to which it relates has been finally settled by the authority, or, if the document does not relate to a specific matter, when it has been finally checked and approved by the authority, or has otherwise received final form.

The provisions of paragraph one notwithstanding, a document of the nature referred to below is deemed to have been drawn up

1. in the case of a day book, ledger, and such register or other list as is kept on an ongoing basis, when the document has been made ready for notation or entry;
2. in the case of a court ruling and other decision which shall be pronounced or dispatched under relevant provisions of law, and records and other documents insofar as they relate to such a decision, when the decision has been pronounced or dispatched;
3. in the case of other records and comparable memoranda held by a public authority, when the document has been finally checked and approved by the authority or has otherwise received final form, but not the records of Riksdag committees, auditors of local authorities, official commissions of inquiry or local authorities where they relate to a matter dealt with solely in order to prepare the matter for decision.

**Article 8**
If a body which forms part of, or is associated with, a public authority or other similar organisation for the public administration has transferred a document to another body within the same organisation, or has produced a document for the purpose of transferring it in this manner, the document is not deemed thereby to have been received or drawn up, other than if the bodies concerned act as independent entities in relation one to the other.

**Article 9**
Neither shall a memorandum which has been prepared at a public authority, but which has not been dispatched, be deemed to be an official document at that authority after the time at which it would be deemed to have been drawn up under Section 7, unless it has been accepted for filing and registration. Memorandum is understood to mean any aide memoire or other note or record produced solely for the preparation or oral presentation of a matter, but not such part of it as contributes factual information to the matter.

Preliminary outlines or drafts of decisions or written communications of a public authority and other like documents which have not been dispatched are not deemed to be official documents unless they have been accepted for filing and registration.

**Article 10**

A document held by a public authority solely for the purpose of technical processing or technical storage on behalf of another is not deemed to be an official document held by that authority.

Is not considered being an official document a document that an authority keeps for the sole purpose of being able to recover information that has been lost in a system for automated processing of information of a public authority (backup).

**Article 11**

The following documents are not deemed to be official documents:

1. letters, telegrams, and other such documents delivered to or drawn up by a public authority solely for the purpose of forwarding a communication;
2. notices or other documents delivered to or drawn up by a public authority solely for the purpose of publication in a periodical published under the auspices of the authority;
3. printed matter, recordings of sound or pictures, or other documents forming part of a library or deposited by a private person in a public archive solely for the purpose of care and safe keeping, or for research and study purposes, and private letters, written matter or recordings otherwise transferred to a public authority solely for the purposes referred to above;
4. recordings of the contents of documents under point 3, if such recordings are held by a public authority, where the original document would not be deemed to be an official document.

The provisions of paragraph one, point 3, concerning documents forming part of a library do not apply to recordings held in databases to which a public authority has access under an agreement with another public authority, if the recording is an official document held by that authority.

**Article 12**

An official document to which the public has access shall be made available on request forthwith, or as soon as possible, at the place where it is held, and free of charge, to any person wishing to examine it, in such form that it can be read, listened to, or otherwise comprehended. A document may also be copied, reproduced, or used for sound transmission. If a document cannot be made available without disclosure of such part of it as constitutes classified material, the rest of the document shall be made available to the applicant in the form of a transcript or copy.

A public authority is under no obligation to make a document available at the place where it is held, if this presents serious difficulty. Nor is there any such obligation in respect of a recording under Section 3, paragraph one, if the applicant can have access to the recording at a public authority in the vicinity, without serious inconvenience.

**Article 13**
A person who wishes to examine an official document is also entitled to obtain a transcript or copy of the document, or such part thereof as may be released, in return for a fixed fee. A public authority is however under no obligation to release material recorded for automatic data processing in any form other than a printout except insofar as follows from an act of law. Nor is a public authority under any obligation to provide copies of maps, drawings, pictures, or recordings under Section 3, paragraph one, other than in the manner indicated above, if this would present difficulty and the document can be made available at the place where it is held.

Requests for transcripts or copies of official documents shall be dealt with promptly.

**Article 14**
A request to examine an official document is made to the public authority which holds the document.

The request is examined and approval granted by the authority indicated in paragraph one. Where special grounds so warrant, it may however be laid down in a provision under Section 2, paragraph two, that in applying this rule, examination and approval shall rest with another public authority. In the case of a document of central significance for the security of the Realm, it may also be laid down in a statutory instrument that only a particular authority shall be entitled to examine and approve questions relating to release. In the aforementioned cases, the request shall be referred to the competent authority forthwith.

No public authority is permitted to inquire into a person's identity on account of a request to examine an official document, or inquire into the purpose of his request, except insofar as such inquiry is necessary to enable the authority to judge whether there is any obstacle to release of the document.

**Article 15**
Should anyone other than the Riksdag or the Government reject a request to examine an official document, or release such a document with a proviso restricting the applicant's right to disclose its contents or otherwise dispose over it, the applicant may appeal against the decision. An appeal against a decision by a minister shall be lodged with the Government, and an appeal against a decision by another authority shall be lodged with a court of law.

The act referred to in Section 2 shall set out in greater detail how an appeal against a decision under paragraph one shall be lodged. Such an appeal shall always be examined promptly.

Special provisions apply to the right to appeal against decisions by authorities under the Riksdag.

**Article 16**
A note concerning obstacles to the release of an official document may be made only on a document covered by a provision under Section 2, paragraph two. Such a note shall refer to the relevant provision.

**Article 17**
It may be laid down in law that the Government, or a local government assembly vested with decision-making powers, may determine that official documents relating to the activities of a public authority which are to be taken over by a private body may be transferred into the safe keeping of that body, if it requires the documents for its work, without the documents ceasing thereby to be official. Such a body shall be equated with a public authority in respect of documents so transferred when applying Sections 12 to 16.

It may also be laid down in law that the Government may determine that official documents may be transferred to the Church of Sweden, or any part of its organisation, for safe keeping, without the documents ceasing thereby to be official. This applies to documents received or drawn up no later than 31 December 1999 by

1. public authorities which no longer exist and which performed tasks relating to the activities of the Church of Sweden; or
2. decision-making assemblies of the Church of Sweden.

In applying Sections 12 to 16, the Church of Sweden and any part of its organisation shall be equated with a public authority in respect of documents so transferred.

**Article 18**
Basic rules concerning the storage of official documents, weeding and other disposal of such documents are laid down in law.

## 2. Public Access to Information and Secrecy Act (2009)[46]

**Chapter 2**

**Section 2**
The Riksdag and decision-making local assemblies should be equated with public authorities for the application of this Law.

---

[46]Swedish Code of Statutes – SFS 2009:400, Law of 30 June 2009.

**Section 5**
A private body shall for the purposes of this Act equated with a public authority when it handles such official documents that it keeps under the Act (2015: 602) for delivery of official documents for storage. The same applies to the Swedish Church and its organizational parts when it concerns the handling of official documents held under the Act (1999: 288) on the handover of official documents to the Swedish Church or any of its organizational parts for storage, etc.

**Section 3**
The provisions of the Freedom of the Press Act concerning the right of access to official documents at public authorities shall also apply when it is pertinent to documents held by limited companies, partnerships, for-profit associations and foundations where a municipality or a county council exercise legal powers of control. Such companies, associations and foundations shall equate with public authorities for the application of this Law.

**Chapter 5**

**Section 1 [The scope of the obligation of registration]**
Official documents shall be registered as soon as they have been received or drawn up by an authority, unless other rules apply according to the second to fourth sections.

If an authority has, by another authority, electronic access to a recording for automated data processing that constitutes an official document, shall that document only be registered by the authority which made the recording available to the other authority.

Documents that are not covered by secrecy do not need to be registered if they are kept arranged so that it can be ascertained without difficulty whether they have been received or drawn up.

If it is clear that a public document is of little importance to the authority's activities there is no need to register this document nor to keep it in a arranged manner.

**Section 2**
When it concerns the documents registered according to Section 1, the register provides

1. the date the official documents have been received or drawn up
2. the registration number or other designation the document received at the registration
3. when appropriate, information about the sender or addressee of the document, and
4. briefly what the document is about

Data under paragraphs 3 or 4 shall be omitted or separated from the others data if it is needed in order to make the other parts of the register available to the public.

**Section 3 [Exemptions from the obligation of registration, etc.]**
If there are special reasons, the Government may provide that documents of a certain kind that are found in significant extent by an authority do not need to be registered under Section 1.

[...]

**Section 5 [Secrecy mark]**
If it likely that information contained in an official document may not be disclosed because of a secrecy provision, the authority may mark it by a special note (secrecy mark) put on the document or, if it is an electronic one, entered it into the document or in the data system where the electronic document is handled. The note shall provide for:

1. the applicable secrecy provision,
2. the date when the record was made, and
3. the authority which has made the note.

If, according to a Government's regulation, disclosure to an individual of information contained in an official document which is of great importance to national security only shall be examined by a particular authority, the secrecy marking has to be made as soon as possible. The note shall indicate which authority shall examine the access request.

**Chapter 6**

**Section 3**
If an employee of a public authority, according to the rules of procedure, or because of a special decision, is endorsed with the responsibility for the care of a document, it is he or she who in the first place shall examine if the document may be disclosed. In doubtful cases, the employee let the authority do the examination, if it can be done without undue delay.

The Authority shall examine whether the document shall be disclosed if

1. the employee refuses to disclose the document or disclose it with a reservation which restricts the right of a person to divulge its content or otherwise his/her right to dispose of the document, and
2. the individual requests an examination from the authority.

The individual should be informed of the possibility of requesting the examination by the authority and that a written decision is required in order to lodge an appeal against the decision.

**Section 4 [Release of information]**
An authority shall, on request of an individual, release information from an official document held by the authority, unless the information is confidential or the release would impede the work of the authority.

**Section 5**
§ 5 A public authority shall, at the request of another authority, release information it has to its disposal, unless information is confidential or the release would impede the work of the authority.

[...]

**Chapter 7**

**Section 2**
If an authority receives confidential data from another authority, secrecy applies to the data at the receiving authority only if secrecy is applicable according to a primary secrecy provision that is applicable by the receiving authority or because of a provision concerning the transfer of secrecy. The same applies if an authority has electronic access to a confidential data that is kept at another authority

**Section 3 [Competition between secrecy provisions]**
If several secrecy provisions are applicable to a data by an authority and the examination in an individual case results in that the information is not confidential under one or more provisions whereas it is confidential under one or more other provisions, the latter provisions shall prevail, unless otherwise provided in this Act.

**Chapter 8**

**Section 2 [Privacy within an authority]**
What is provided for about secrecy towards other authorities in Section 1 and what is provided for in other provisions of this Act about disclosure to other authorities and the transfer of secrecy between authorities, also applies between different branches within an authority when they are to be considered as independent of each other.

[...]

**Chapter 10**

**Section 1 [Consent]**
The rules stating that secrecy to protect an individual does not prevent that a data may be disclosed to another individual or to an authority if the individual consents to it, results from Chapter 12 and is applicable within the limits specified therein.

**Section 3 [Disclosure to the party]**
Secrecy does not prevent an individual or a public authority who is or which is party to a case or matter before a court or other authority and because of his/her/its party's position has the right of insight in the investigation, to access a document or other material related to the case or the matter. Such a document or such material may however not be disclosed to the party insofar as it, with regard to a public or a private interest, is of utmost importance that confidential data from the material is not disclosed. In such cases the authority shall in another manner provide the party with information about the content of the material in the extent necessary for the party to exercise he/her/its right, when it can be done without serious injury for the interest secrecy is meant to protect.

Secrecy never prevents a party to a case or a matter to access a court's decision or decision in the case or matter. Nor does secrecy entail any limitation in the right of the party, under the Code of Procedure, to have access to the circumstances that forms the basis for a court's decision in a case.

**Section 5 [Environmental information]**
If a confidential data constitutes such environmental information as referred to in Section 2 of the Act (2005: 181) about environmental information detained by certain organs, secrecy does not apply if it can be deemed that the information is of such significant importance from an environmental standpoint that the interest of making the information public has precedence over the interest secrecy is meant to protect.

Secrecy under Chapter 19-40 does not apply to information about emissions in the environment.

**Chapter 12**

**Section 1 [Secrecy in relation to the individual himself]**
Secrecy aimed at protecting an individual does not apply towards that individual, unless otherwise is provided in this Act.

**Section 2**
An individual may fully or partially waive secrecy aimed to protecting him or her secrecy, unless otherwise is provided in this Act.

**Chapter 14**

**Section 2**
The Penal Code contains provisions on the liability for anyone who violates the prohibition under this Act to disclose or make use of information or for anyone who violates a reservation that has been made on the basis of the law at the time of the disclosure.

Liability under Chapter 20, Section 3 of the Penal Code will however not follow if someone whose employment by an authority has ceased, discloses or uses data in contravention of Chapter 19, Sections 1 and 2. Act (2010: 1348).

**Chapter 21**

**Section 7 [Treatment in violation of the Personal Data Act]**
Secrecy applies on personal information if it can be deemed that disclosure can lead to a violation of the Data Protection Act (1998: 204).

**Chapter 25**

**Section 1**
Secrecy applies within the Health and Care sector for data concerning an individual's state of health or other personal circumstances, if it is not evident that information can be disclosed without causing harm to the individual or someone close to him/her. The same applies to other medical activities, such as forensic and psychiatric examination, insemination, fertilization outside the body, establishment of gender, abortion, sterilization, circumcision and measures against infectious diseases.

**Chapter 30**

**Section 1 [Supervision and investigation]**
Secrecy applies to the Competition Authority's activities consisting of supervision and investigation

1. for data concerning an individual's business or operations conditions, inventions or research results, if it can be deemed that the individual will suffer damage if the information is disclosed, and
2. for data concerning other financial or personal circumstances than those referred to in 1 for those who have entered into business relationship or similar relationship to the one who is subject to the activity of the authority.

# Appendix 14 United States of America: National Freedom-of-Information and Transparency Legislation (Extract)

## The Freedom of Information Act (1966/1967)[47]

### § 552 [Public information; agency rules, opinions, orders, records, and proceedings]

(a) Each agency shall make available to the public information as follows:

(1) Each agency shall separately state and currently publish in the Federal Register for the guidance of the public—

(A) descriptions of its central and field organization and the established places at which, the employees (and in the case of a uniformed service, the members) from whom, and the methods whereby, the public may obtain information, make submittals or requests, or obtain decisions;
(B) statements of the general course and method by which its functions are channeled and determined, including the nature and requirements of all formal and informal procedures available;
(C) rules of procedure, descriptions of forms available or the places at which forms may be obtained, and instructions as to the scope and contents of all papers, reports, or examinations;
(D) substantive rules of general applicability adopted as authorized by law, and statements of general policy or interpretations of general applicability formulated and adopted by the agency; and
(E) each amendment, revision, or repeal of the foregoing.

[. . .]

[47] 5 U.S.C. § 552, as amended by Public Law No. 110-175, 121 Stat. 2524, and Public Law No. 111-83, § 564, 123 Stat. 2142, 2184.



H.-J. Blanke, R. Perlingeiro (eds.), *The Right of Access to Public Information*,
DOI 10.1007/978-3-662-55554-5

(2) Each agency, in accordance with published rules, shall make available for public inspection and copying—

(A) final opinions, including concurring and dissenting opinions, as well as orders, made in the adjudication of cases;
(B) those statements of policy and interpretations which have been adopted by the agency and are not published in the Federal Register;
(C) administrative staff manuals and instructions to staff that affect a member of the public;
(D) copies of all records, regardless of form or format, which have been released to any person under paragraph (3) and which, because of the nature of their subject matter, the agency determines have become or are likely to become the subject of subsequent requests for substantially the same records; and
(E) a general index of the records referred to under subparagraph (D);

[...]

(3) (A) Except with respect to the records made available under paragraphs (1) and (2) of this subsection, and except as provided in subparagraph (E), each agency, upon any request for records which (i) reasonably describes such records and (ii) is made in accordance with published rules stating the time, place, fees (if any), and procedures to be followed, shall make the records promptly available to any person.
(B) In making any record available to a person under this paragraph, an agency shall provide the record in any form or format requested by the person if the record is readily reproducible by the agency in that form or format. [...]

[...]

(ii) Such agency regulations shall provide that—

(I) fees shall be limited to reasonable standard charges for document search, duplication, and review, when records are requested for commercial use;
(II) fees shall be limited to reasonable standard charges for document duplication when records are not sought for commercial use and the request is made by an educational or noncommercial scientific institution, whose purpose is scholarly or scientific research; or a representative of the news media; and
(III) for any request not described in (I) or (II), fees shall be limited to reasonable standard charges for document search and duplication.

[...]

(B) On complaint, the district court of the United States in the district in which the complainant resides, or has his principal place of business, or in which the agency records are situated, or in the District of Columbia, has jurisdiction to enjoin the agency from withholding agency records and to order the production of any agency records improperly withheld from the complainant. [...]

[...]

(6)(A) Each agency, upon any request for records made under paragraph (1), (2), or (3) of this subsection, shall—

(i) determine within 20 days (excepting Saturdays, Sundays, and legal public holidays) after the receipt of any such request whether to comply with such request and shall immediately notify the person making such request of such determination and the reasons therefor, and of the right of such person to appeal to the head of the agency any adverse determination; [...]

[...]

- (C) (i) Any person making a request to any agency for records under paragraph (1), (2), or (3) of this subsection shall be deemed to have exhausted his administrative remedies with respect to such request if the agency fails to comply with the applicable time limit provisions of this paragraph. [...]

[...]

(b) This section does not apply to matters that are—

(1)(A) specifically authorized under criteria established by an Executive order to be kept secret in the interest of national defense or foreign policy and (B) are in fact properly classified pursuant to such Executive order;
(2) related solely to the internal personnel rules and practices of an agency; [...]

[...]

(4) trade secrets and commercial or financial information obtained from a person and privileged or confidential;
(5) inter-agency or intra-agency memorandums or letters which would not be available by law to a party other than an agency in litigation with the agency;
(6) personnel and medical files and similar files the disclosure of which would constitute a clearly unwarranted invasion of personal privacy;
(7) records or information compiled for law enforcement purposes, but only to the extent that the production of such law enforcement records or information (A) could reasonably be expected to interfere with enforcement proceedings, (B) would deprive a person of a right to a fair trial or an impartial adjudication, (C) could reasonably be expected to constitute an unwarranted invasion of personal privacy, (D) could reasonably be expected to disclose the identity of a confidential source, including a State, local, or foreign agency or authority or

any private institution which furnished information on a confidential basis, and, in the case of a record or information compiled by a criminal law enforcement authority in the course of a criminal investigation or by an agency conducting a lawful national security intelligence investigation, information furnished by a confidential source, (E) would disclose techniques and procedures for law enforcement investigations or prosecutions, or would disclose guidelines for law enforcement investigations or prosecutions if such disclosure could reasonably be expected to risk circumvention of the law, or (F) could reasonably be expected to endanger the life or physical safety of any individual;

(8) contained in or related to examination, operating, or condition reports prepared by, on behalf of, or for the use of an agency responsible for the regulation or supervision of financial institutions; or

(9) geological and geophysical information and data, including maps, concerning wells.

[...]

# Index





H.-J. Blanke, R. Perlingeiro (eds.), *The Right of Access to Public Information*,
DOI 10.1007/978-3-662-55554-5

## S

CPSIA information can be obtained
at www.ICGtesting.com
Printed in the USA
LVOW13*1950210618
581517LV00011B/356/P

9 783662 555521